The E

C000300828

Dr. GARY Jones

The European Union
Economics and Policies

EIGHTH EDITION

Edited by

Ali M. El-Agraa

CAMBRIDGE
UNIVERSITY PRESS

CAMBRIDGE UNIVERSITY PRESS
Cambridge, New York, Melbourne, Madrid, Cape Town, Singapore, São Paulo

Cambridge University Press
The Edinburgh Building, Cambridge CB2 8RU, UK

www.cambridge.org
Information on this title: www.cambridge.org/9780521697279

First published under the Philip Allan imprint in 1980
Second edition published 1983
Third edition published 1990
Fourth edition published under the Harvester Wheatsheaf imprint in 1994
Fifth edition published under the Prentice Hall Europe imprint in 1998
Sixth edition published under the Financial Times Prentice Hall imprint in 2001
Seventh edition published 2004

Eighth edition published 2007

Printed in the United Kingdom at the University Press, Cambridge

A catalogue record for this publication is available from the British Library

ISBN 978-0-521-87443-4 hardback
ISBN 978-0-521-69727-9 paperback

To all those who believe in and actively support an ever closer unity for Europe.

———————————————————————

Lest it be forgotten, the European Union stands for the harmonized integration of some of the oldest countries in the world with very diverse cultures, languages and economic and political systems. The European Union is about unity within diversity.

Contents

Figures

Tables

Contributors

Brian Ardy is Reader in Economics and Head of the European Institute, the Business School at London South Bank University, UK.

Harvey W. Armstrong is Professor of Economic Geography, Department of Geography, University of Sheffield, UK.

Marius Brülhart is Professor of Economics, Départment d'économétrie et économie politique, École des HEC, University of Lausanne, Switzerland.

Kenneth Button is University Professor of Public Policy, School of Public Policy, George Mason University, USA, and is also director of both the University's Aerospace Research Center and the Center for Transportation, Policy, Operations and Logistics.

Damian Chalmers is Professor of European Law, London School of Economics and Political Science, University of London, UK.

Nigel Grimwade is Principal Lecturer in Economics and Head of Economics, the Business School at London South Bank University, UK.

Luke Haasbeek used to be a Junior Legal Adviser at the Directorate for Legal Affairs (International), the Ministry of Housing, Spatial Planning and the Environment, the Netherlands. She is now studying for her doctorate at the Law Department, College of Europe, Bruges, Belgium.

Juha Kilponen is Research Supervisor with the Research Department of the Bank of Finland.

Ulrich Koester is Professor at the Institute of Agricultural Economics, University of Kiel, Germany.

Jurian Langer is a solicitor with Stek Amsterdam where he practises economic law. He also lectures on European Law at the University of Amsterdam. In 2006, he defended his PhD on the Antitrust Economics of Tying and Building at the European University Institute in Florence, Italy.

Alan Marin is Senior Lecturer in Economics, London School of Economics and Political Science, University of London, UK.

Stephen Martin is Professor of Economics and Faculty Director of the Technology Transfer Initiative at the Krannert School of Management, Purdue University, USA, and is co-Managing Editor of the *International Journal of Industrial Organization*.

Alan Matthews is Jean Monnet Professor of European Agricultural Policy in the Department of Economics, Trinity College Dublin, Ireland.

David G. Mayes is Adviser to the Board of the Bank of Finland and Adjunct Professor in the National Centre for Research on Europe at the University of Canterbury, New Zealand. In 2006/7, he was Visiting Professor at the University of Auckland, New Zealand.

Wolf Sauter is with the Financial Markets Directorate, Ministry of Finance, the Netherlands, and was National Expert with the EU's Directorate General for Competition, Policy Adviser to the Independent Authority for Telecommunications and Posts (OPTA), The Hague, and Professor of Economic Law, Groningen University, the Netherlands.

Preface

Since the first edition of this book, *The Economics of the European Community*, in 1980, it has undergone many changes. This is not the place to go through all of them, but three warrant particular mention. First, new policy areas have been added, either because they were non-existent at the beginning or have become prominent since then. Second, new contributors have joined my team, some replacing those who, for one reason or another, could no longer be with me. Third, since the fifth edition in 1998, a new title has been adopted to reflect the changes that have taken place within the Community itself, as well as in the general nature and contents of the book, and for the sixth edition in 2001 the subtitle was amended.

In this eighth edition there are no new areas to cover and no need to change the name of the book, which I should stress is not just about economics. As far as new contributors are concerned, we have been joined by Jurian Langer, a practising solicitor, lecturer in EU law and active researcher in his field, who has co-authored chapter 13 on EU competition policy with Wolf Sauter. Also with us for the first time is Luke Haasbeek, a rising star who was a Junior Legal Advisor at the Ministry of Housing, Spatial Planning and the Environment in the Netherlands, and is now studying for her doctorate at the Law Department, College of Europe, Bruges, Belgium; she has co-authored chapter 4 on the legal dimension in EU integration with Damian Chalmers. New with us is Brian Ardy, who in addition to continuing his joint efforts with me on EU tax harmonization and the general budget (chapters 15 and 19 respectively), is also doing likewise on the Single European Market (replacing Iain Begg in chapter 7) and the Common Fisheries Policy (substituting for Ella

Ritchie in chapter 21). He has also contributed chapters 14 and, with me, 23 on industrial policy and the Lisbon Strategy, respectively (replacing Victoria Curzon Price), and social policies (replacing Doreen Collins and Robert Salais). I welcome the three of them and thank them for their excellent contributions.

It follows from the above that Professors Iain Begg, Victoria Curzon Price, Ella Ritchie and Robert Salais as well as Dr Doreen Collins have left us. Begg has found himself overstretched in his pure research capacity at the LSE, securing more projects than he can physically cope with. Ritchie has assumed the heavy responsibility of Pro-Vice-Chancellor for Teaching and Learning at the University of Newcastle. Dr Doreen Collins, who has been with me since the first edition, has found that she is unable to devote so much time to EU matters now that she has settled in New Zealand. Given the dramatic changes in EU industrial and social policies and Ardy's increasing commitment to these areas, both Professors Victoria Curzon Price (also a long-standing collaborator here and in other works) and Robert Salais have welcomed the relief. I am deeply grateful to them all for their excellent contributions over the years and bid them farewell.

Although there is no change in either the book's title or subtitle, the chapters have been rearranged in a more logical fashion and now come under seven parts. The first covers EU history, institutions, legal dimension and basic statistics (four chapters); hence sets the general background to the book. Part II deals with the theory and practice of EU market integration (also four chapters, including the Single European Market). Part III is devoted to EU monetary integration (three chapters). Part IV tackles the policy integration aspects of the Single European Market (six chapters). Part V is about the EU budget and structural policies (four chapters). Part VI is on EU external relations (two chapters). And the final part is on EU enlargement and the success and future of the EU (three chapters). I am particularly grateful to Brian Ardy for recommending the rearrangement, but must add that there will never be a perfect sequencing of all the chapters, given the nature of the book, the width of policies considered and the fact that every chapter can be read on its own – but see below for suggestions on how to use selected chapters for different purposes.

Simply updating the book when so much change is taking place is enough justification for a new edition. The book has been thoroughly updated, dealing with the EU of twenty-seven, to which Bulgaria and Romania have only just acceded. But this edition also includes major changes in the contents of some of the chapters, especially those devoted to EMU, and competition, industrial and social policies. We have also made innovations, using case studies wherever appropriate.

Again, let me thank all my contributors, not only for their excellent chapters but also for working with me under the very strict conditions (see the guide to users which follows), and bid farewell to departed members. Also, many thanks to all those who continue to use the book and send me comments on it, and to the many professional reviewers solicited by Cambridge University Press who read the seventh edition thoroughly before judging it and making recommendations for improvement. Last, but by no means least, I wish to express my deepest appreciation to Chris Harrison, Publishing Director for the Social Sciences with Cambridge University Press, for his encouragement, support and guidance and to all his production teams for their excellent work.

Ali M. El-Agraa
Fukuoka University, Japan
October 2006

A guide for users

The book is written in such a way that pure theory and measurement techniques are confined to separate chapters. This means that the policy chapters should be accessible to all readers. However, it also means that those who seek a rigorous, yet brief, background on international economic integration can find it handily in the same book. Moreover, as my contributors will no doubt attest, my editing style has been to ensure that the book reads as a complete whole, not as a collection of independent articles, each contributed for its own sake. This has been ensured through thorough editing and consultation with the contributors, cross-referencing, allowing repetition only where absolutely necessary, logical sequencing and a setting which begins with an introductory chapter and finishes with two on the success and future of the EU. In the process, I have tried my best not to distract from any contributor's own writing style. Therefore the reader has a unique product which offers a truly single entity, yet is authored by several acknowledged authorities in the various fields.

Those truly interested in the EU as a whole will of course have to read the entire book if they really want to understand it as a most successful scheme of international economic integration, with aspirations going beyond that. However, those who are simply interested in the EU itself without the global context can skip chapters 6, 9 and 10, since these are devoted to theoretical and measurement considerations which pertain to all schemes. Those interested in only the EU policy areas can drop chapters 2–6 and 9, although chapter 2 is important for a proper understanding. Those interested in only the EU economic policies can drop chapters 2–4 and 23 and, if not interested in the future of the EU, can also drop chapter 28. Those interested in only the EMU and the euro can confine themselves to chapters 7, 8 and 10–12, but are advised to read chapters 2 and 28 for a proper understanding; those interested in this area with emphasis on the UK will find my 2002 book *The Euro and Britain: Implications of Moving into EMU* more appropriate. Also various combinations of chapters can be made, depending on what the reader has in mind. For example, those interested in a very basic understanding of the EU can use chapters 2, 3, 5, 27 and 28.

Finally, the entire book is written with those who want to pursue further study in mind. Thus within every chapter the reader is referred to the most relevant research publications in the field and these are fully set out in the References at the end of the book. This means that there are no guides to further reading at the end of each chapter and certainly no guides to other texts, since it is not our task to supply them, especially when this book is a pioneer in its field and it covers more than one field of study; it is not confined to economics.

Abbreviations

AAMS	Association of African and Malagasy States
AAU	Arab–African Union
ACC	Arab Cooperation Council
ACM	Arab Common Market
ACP	African, Caribbean and Pacific countries party to the Lomé Convention (now the Contonou Agreement)
ADAPT	Community initiative concerning the adaptation of the workforce to industrial change
AEC	Arab Economic Council
AIM	advanced informatics in medicine
AL	Arab League
ALADI	Association for Latin American Integration
Altener	specific actions to promote greater penetration of renewable energy sources
AMU	Arab Maghreb Union
ANZCERTA	Australia and New Zealand Closer Economic Relations and Trade Agreement (also CER)
ARION	programme of study visits for decision-makers in education
ASEAN	Association of South-East Asian Nations
ASEM	Asia–Europe meeting
AU	African Union
BAP	biotechnology action programme
BATNEEC	best available technology not entailing excessive cost
BC-NET	Business Cooperation Network

BCR	Community Bureau of References
BENELUX	Belgium, the Netherlands and Luxembourg Economic Union
BEP	biomolecular engineering programme
BEST	Business Environment Simplification Task Force
BLEU	Belgium–Luxembourg Economic Union
BRAIN	basic research in adaptive intelligence and neurocomputing
BRIDGE	Biotechnological Research for Innovation, Development and Growth in Europe
BRITE/EURAM	basic research in industrial technologies for Europe/raw materials and advanced materials
BSE	bovine spongiform encephalopathy
BU	Benin Union
CAA	Civil Aviation Authority
CACM	Central American Common Market
CADDIA	cooperation in automation of data and documentation for imports/exports and agriculture
CAEU	Council for Arab Economic Unity
CAP	Common Agricultural Policy
CARICOM	Caribbean Community
CARIFTA	Caribbean Free Trade Association
CCP	Common Commercial Policy
CCT	Common Customs Tariff

CEAO	Communauté Économique de l'Afrique de l'Ouest	COSINE	Cooperation for open systems interconnection networking in Europe
CEC	Commission of the European Communities	COST	European cooperation on scientific and technical research
CEDB	component event data bank		
CEDEFOP	European Centre for Development of Vocational Training	CREST	Scientific and Technical Research Committee
CEEC	Countries of Central and Eastern Europe	CRS	computerized reservation system
CEEP	European Centre for Population Studies	CSCE	Conference on Security and Cooperation in Europe
CEN	European Committee for Standardization	CSF	Community support framework
CENELEC	European Committee for Electrotechnical Standardization	CSTID	Committee for Scientific and Technical Information and Documentation
CEP	common energy policy	CTP	Common Transport Policy
CEPGL	Economic Community of the Countries of the Great Lakes	CTS	conformance testing services
CER	closer economic relations	CU	customs union
CERN	European Organization for Nuclear Research	DAC	Development Assistance Committee (OECD)
CET	common external tariff	DDR	German Democratic Republic (now part of Germany)
CFP	Common Fisheries Policy		
CFSP	Common Foreign and Security Policy	DELTA	developing European learning through technological advance
CI	Community initiative		
CIS	Commonwealth of Independent States	DG IV	Directorate General Four
		DI	divergence indicator
CM	Common Market	DRIVE	dedicated road infrastructure for vehicle safety in Europe
CMEA	Council for Mutual Economic Assistance		
		DV	dummy variable
CN	combined nomenclature	EAC	East African Community
CODEST	Committee for the European Development of Science and Technology	EAGGF	European Agricultural Guidance and Guarantee Fund
COMECON	see CMEA	EBA	'Everything But Arms'
COMETT	Community programme in education and training for technology	EBRD	European Bank for Reconstruction and Development
CORDIS	Community research and development information - service	EC	European Community
		ECB	European Central Bank
		ECHO	European Community Humanitarian Office
COREPER	Committee of Permanent Representatives		
		ECIP	European Community Investment Partners
CORINE	Coordination of information on the environment in Europe	ECJ	European Court of Justice

ECLAIR	European collaborative linkage of agriculture and industry through research	EQS	Environmental quality standard
ECMT	European Conference of Ministers of Transport	Erasmus	European Community action scheme for the mobility of university students
ECOFIN	European Council of Ministers for Financial Affairs	ERDF	European Regional Development Fund
ECOSOC	Economic and Social Committee (also ESC)	ERM	exchange-rate mechanism
		ESA	European Space Agency
ECOWAS	Economic Community of West African States	ESCB	European System of Central Banks
ECPE	European Centre of Public Enterprises	ESF	European Social Fund
		ESI	electricity supply industry
ECSC	European Coal and Steel Community	ESPRIT	European strategic programme for research and development in information technology
ECU	European currency unit		
EDC	European Defence Community		
		ETUC	European Trade Union Confederation
EDF	European Development Fund		
		EU	European Union
EDIFACT	electronic data interchange for administration, commerce and transport	EUA	European Unit of Account
		Euratom	European Atomic Energy Commission
EEA	European Economic Area	Eureka	European Research Coordinating Agency
EEC	European Economic Community		
		EURES	European Employment Services
EEZ	Exclusive Economic Zone		
EFTA	European Free Trade Association	EUROCONTROL	European organization for the safety of air navigation
EGE	European Group on Ethics in Science and New Technologies		
		EURONET-DIANE	direct information access network for Europe
EIB	European Investment Bank	EUROSTAT	statistical office of the EC/EU
EIF	European Investment Fund		
EMCF	European Monetary Cooperation Fund	EVCA	European Venture Capital Association
EMF	European Monetary Fund	FADN	EEC farm accountancy data network
EMI	European Monetary Institute		
EMS	European Monetary System	FAO	Food and Agriculture Organization of the United Nations
EMU	European monetary union or economic and monetary union		
		FAST	forecasting and assessment in the field of science and technology
EP	European Parliament		
EPC	European political cooperation		
		FCO	Foreign and Commonwealth Office
EPOCH	European programme on climatology and natural hazards		
		FEER	Fundamental Equilibrium Exchange Rate

FEOGA	European Agricultural Guidance and Guarantee Fund	IDO	integrated development operation
FIFG	Financial Instrument for Fisheries Guidance	IEA	International Energy Agency (OECD)
FLAIR	food-linked agro-industrial research	IEM	internal energy market
		IGC	intergovernmental conference
FSAP	Financial Services Action Plan	IIT	intra-industry trade
FSU	Former Soviet Union	ILO	International Labour Organization
FTA	free trade area		
GATS	General Agreement on Trade in Services	IMF	International Monetary Fund (UN)
GATT	General Agreement on Tariffs and Trade (UN)	IMP	integrated Mediterranean programme
GCC	Gulf Cooperation Council	IMPACT	information market policy actions
GDP	gross domestic product		
GFCM	General Fisheries Council for the Mediterranean	INSIS	inter-institutional system of integrated services
GNI	gross national income	INTERREG	Community initiative concerning border areas
GNP	gross national product		
GSP	generalized system of preferences	IPR	intellectual property rights
		IRCC	International Radio Consultative Committee
HDTV	high-definition television		
HELIOS	action programme to promote social and economic integration and an independent way of life for disabled people	IRIS	network of demonstration projects on vocational training for women
		IRTE	integrated road transport environment
HS	Harmonized Commodity Description and Coding System	ISIS	integrated standards information system
		ISPA	instrument for structural policies for pre-accession
IAEA	International Atomic Energy Agency (UN)	ITA	information technology agreement
IATA	International Air Transport Association	ITER	international thermonuclear experimental reactor
IBRD	International Bank for Reconstruction and Development (World Bank) (UN)	JESSI	Joint European Submicron Silicon Initiative
		JET	Joint European Torus
ICES	International Council for the Exploration of the Seas	JHA	judicial and home affairs
		JOP	joint venture programme PHARE-TACIS
ICONE	comparative index of national and European standards	JOULE	joint opportunities for unconventional or long-term energy supply
IDA	International Development Association (UN)		
		JRC	Joint Research Centre
IDB	Inter-American Development Bank	KALEIDOSCOPE	programme to support artistic and cultural

	activities having a European dimension	NAFTA	North Atlantic Free Trade Agreement; New Zealand Australia Free Trade Area
LAFTA	Latin American Free Trade Area	NAIRU	non-accelerating inflation rate of unemployment
LDC	less-developed country		
LEDA	local employment development action programme	NATO	North Atlantic Treaty Organization
		NCB	National Central Bank
LIFE	Financial Instrument for the Environment	NCI	new Community instrument
M&A	mergers and acquisitions	NEAFC	North-East Atlantic Fisheries Commission
MAGP	multi-annual guidance programme		
		NET	Next European Torus
MARIE	mass transit rail initiative for Europe	NETT	network for environmental technology transfer
MAST	marine science and technology	NGO	non-governmental organization
MB	marginal benefit	NIC	newly industrializing country
MC	marginal cost	NIE	newly industrializing economy
MCA	monetary compensatory amount		
		NIEO	New International Economic Order
MEDIA	measures to encourage the development of the audio-visual industry	NIESR	National Institute of Economic and Social Research
MEP	Member of the European Parliament	NiGEM	National Institute Global Econometric Model
MERCUSOR	Southern Cone Common Market	NIS	Newly Independent States (of the former USSR)
MERM	multilateral exchange rate model	NMS	new member states
		NOHA	Network on Humanitarian Assistance
MFA	Multifibre Arrangement (arrangement regarding international trade in textiles)	NPCI	national programme of Community interest
		NPT	Treaty on Non-proliferation of Nuclear Weapons
MFN	most-favoured nation		
MFP	multi-annual framework programme	NTB	non-tariff barrier
		NTM	non-tariff measure
MFT	Multilateral free trade	NUTS	Nomenclature of Territorial Units for Statistics
MISEP	mutual information system on employment policies		
		OAPEC	Organization of Arab Petroleum Exporting Countries
MNE	multinational enterprise		
MONITOR	research programme on strategic analysis, forecasting and assessment in research and technology	OAU	Organization for African Unity
		OCTs	overseas countries and territories
MP	marginal productivity	ODA	overseas development aid
MRU	Mano River Union	OECD	Organization for Economic

	Cooperation and Development		concerning the most remote regions
OEEC	Organization for European Economic Cooperation	REIMEP	regular European interlaboratory measurements evaluation programme
OPEC	Organization of Petroleum Exporting Countries		
OSCE	Organization for Security and Cooperation in Europe	RENAVAL	programme to assist the conversion of shipbuilding areas
OSI	open systems interconnection	REPAs	regional economic partnership agreements
PAFTAD	Pacific Trade and Development Conference	RESIDER	programme to assist the conversion of steel areas
PBEC	Pacific Basin Economic Council	RIA	regional impact assessment
PECC	Pacific Economic Cooperation Conference	ROO	rules of origin
PEDIP	programme to modernize Portuguese industry	RTA	regional trade agreement
		RTD	research and technological development
PETRA	action programme for the vocational training of young people and their preparation for adult and working life	SACU	Southern African Customs Union
		SAP	social action programme
		SAST	strategic analysis in the field of science and technology
PHARE	programme of community aid for Central and Eastern European countries	SAVE	Specific Actions for Vigorous Energy Efficiency
PO	producer organization	SCENT	system for a customs enforcement network
POSEIDOM	programme of options specific to the remote and insular nature of the overseas departments	SCIENCE	plan to stimulate the international cooperation and interchange necessary for European researchers
PPP	polluter pays principle		
PTA	preferential trade area	SDR	special drawing rights
PTC	Pacific Telecommunications Conference	SEA	Single European Act
		SEDOC	inter-state notification of job vacancies
PTT	Posts, Telegraphs and Telecommunications	SEM	Single European Market
QMV	qualified majority voting	SEM 2000	sound and efficient management
RACE	research and development in advanced communication technologies for Europe	SFOR	multinational stabilization force
RARE	réseaux associés pour la recherche européenne	SLIM	simpler legislation for the internal market
R&TD	research and technological development	SMEs	small- and medium-sized enterprises
RCD	Regional Cooperation for Development	SPD	single programme documents
REGIS	Community initiative	SPEAR	support programme for a

	European assessment of research		exchange of information between national social
SPES	stimulation plan for economic science		security institutions
		TEU	Treaty on European Union
SPRINT	strategic programme for innovation and technology transfer	TRIPs	trade-related aspects of intellectual property rights
		TSEs	transmissible spongiform encephalopathies
SPS	WTO's agreement on the application of sanitary and phytosanitary measures	t/t	terms of trade
		TUC	Trades Union Congress
STABEX	system for the stabilization of ACP and OCT export earnings	TVA	taxe à la valeur ajoutée
		UDEAC	Union Douanière et Économique de l'Afrique Centrale
STAR	Community programme for the development of certain less-favoured regions of the Community by improving access to advanced telecommunications services	UEMOA	West African Economic and Monetary Union
		UES	uniform emission standards
		UN	United Nations
		UNCLOS	United Nations Conference on the Law of the Sea
STEP	science and technology for environmental protection	UNCTAD	United Nations Conference on Trade and Development
SVER	structural vector autoregression	UNECA	United Nations Economic Commission for Africa
SYNERGY	multinational programme to promote international cooperation in the energy sector	UNEP	United Nations Environment Programme
		UNESCO	United Nations Educational, Scientific and Cultural Organization
SYSMIN	special financing facility for ACP and OCT mining products	UNHCR	United Nations High Commissioner for Refugees
TAC	total allowable catch		
TACIS	Technical Aid to the Commonwealth of Independent States	UNICE	Union of Industries of the European Community
		UNIDO	United Nations Industrial Development Organization
TARIC	integrated Community tariff		
TBT	WTO's agreement on technical barriers to trade	UNRWA	United Nations Relief and Works Agency for Palestine Refugees in the Near East
TEDIS	trade electronic data interchange systems		
		URAA	Uruguay Round Agreement on Agriculture
TELEMAN	research and training programme on remote handling in nuclear hazardous and disordered environments	URBAN	Community initiative for urban areas
		UTR	unilateral tariff reduction
		VALOREN	Community programme for the development of certain less-favoured regions of the Community by exploiting endogenous energy potential
TEMPUS	trans-European cooperation scheme for higher education		
TENs	trans-European networks		
TESS	modernization of the		

VALUE	programme for the dissemination and utilization of research results	WFC	World Food Council (UN)
		WFP	World Food Programme (UN)
		WIPO	World Intellectual Property Organization (UN)
VAT	value added tax		
VER	voluntary export restraint	WTO	World Trade Organization
VSTF	very short-term financing facility	YES	'Youth for Europe' programme (youth exchange scheme)
WEU	Western European Union		

General introduction: the EU within the global context of regional integration

ALI EL-AGRAA

The European Union (EU) is the most prominent scheme of 'international economic integration' (hereafter, simply economic integration). The aim of this chapter is to provide a precise definition of the term economic integration, to describe the various schemes that have been adopted worldwide, hence to set the EU within their broader context, and to provide a general outline of this book.

1.1 What is economic integration?

Economic integration is one aspect of 'international economics' which has been growing in importance for over five decades. The term itself has quite a short history; indeed, Machlup (1977) was unable to find a single instance of its use prior to 1942. Since then the term has been used at various times to refer to practically any area of international economic relations. By 1950, however, the term had been given a specific definition by economists specializing in international trade to denote *a state of affairs or a process which involves the amalgamation of separate economies into larger free trading regions*. It is in this more limited sense that the term is used today. However, one should hasten to add that economists not familiar with this branch of international economics, not to mention the layperson, have for quite a while been using the term to mean simply increasing economic interdependence between nations, now glamorized as *globalization*.

More specifically, economic integration (also referred to as 'regional integration', 'regional trading agreements' (RTAs), 'preferential trading agreements' (PTAs) and trading blocs) is concerned with the discriminatory removal of all trade impediments between at least two participating nations and with the establishment of certain elements of cooperation and coordination between them. The latter depends entirely on the actual form that integration takes. Different forms of economic integration can be envisaged and many have actually been implemented (see table 1.1 for schematic presentation):

1. *Free trade areas* (FTAs or PTAs), where the member nations remove all trade impediments among themselves but retain their freedom to determine their own policies vis-à-vis the outside world (the non-participants). Recently, the trend has been to extend these treatments also to investment. Examples of FTAs are the European Free Trade Association (EFTA), the defunct Latin American Free Trade Area (LAFTA), and the North American Free Trade Agreement (NAFTA) which explicitly covers investment.

2. *Customs unions* (CUs), which are very similar to free trade areas except that member nations must conduct and pursue common external commercial relations – for instance, they must adopt common external tariffs (CETs) on imports from the non-participants as is the case in, inter alia, the EU (which is in this particular sense a CU, but, as we shall presently see, it is more than that), the Central American Common Market (CACM) and the Caribbean Community and Common Market (CARICOM).

3. *Common markets* (CMs), which are CUs that also allow for free factor mobility across national members' frontiers, i.e. capital, labour, technology and enterprises should move unhindered between the participating countries. An example of this is the EU, but again it is more complex.

Table 1.1 Schematic presentation of economic integration schemes

Scheme	Free intra-scheme trade	Common commercial policy (CCP)	Free factor mobility	Common monetary and fiscal policy	One government
Free trade area (FTA)	Yes	No	No	No	No
Customs union (CU)	Yes	Yes	No	No	No
Common market (CM)	Yes	Yes	Yes	No	No
Economic union (EcU)	Yes	Yes	Yes	Yes	No
Political union (PU)	Yes	Yes	Yes	Yes	Yes

4. *Complete economic unions*, simply economic unions (EcUs), which are CMs that ask for complete unification of monetary and fiscal policies, i.e. the participants must introduce a central authority to exercise control over these matters so that member nations effectively become regions of the same nation. The thirteen EU nations which have adopted the single currency, the euro (called the eurozone), are close to becoming one.

5. *Complete political unions* (PUs), where the participating countries become literally one nation, i.e. the central authority needed in EcUs should be paralleled by a common parliament and other necessary institutions needed to guarantee the sovereignty of one state. An example of this is the unification of the two Germanys in 1990.

However, one should hasten to add that political integration need not be, and in the majority of cases will never be, part of this list. Nevertheless, it can of course be introduced as a form of unity and for no economic reason whatsoever, as was the case with the two Germanys and as is the case with the pursuit of the unification of the Korean Peninsula, although one should naturally be interested in its economic consequences (see below). More generally, one should indeed stress that each of these forms of economic integration can be introduced in its own right; hence they should not be confused with *stages* in a *process* which eventually leads to either complete economic or political union, although many schemes evolved in stages.

It should also be noted that there may be *sectoral* integration, as distinct from general across-the-board integration, in particular areas of the economy, as was the case with the European Coal and Steel Community (ECSC, see chapters 2 and 16), created in 1951 and valid for fifty years, but sectoral integration is a form of cooperation not only because it is inconsistent with the accepted definition of economic integration but also because it may contravene the rules of the General Agreement on Tariffs and Trade (GATT), which, on 1 January 1995, became the World Trade Organization (WTO) – see below. Sectoral integration may also occur within any of the mentioned schemes, as is the case with the EU's Common Agricultural Policy (CAP, see chapter 20), but then it is nothing more than a 'policy'.

One should further point out that it has been claimed that economic integration can be *negative* or *positive*. The term negative integration was coined by Tinbergen (1954) to refer to the simple act of the removal of impediments on trade between the participating nations or to the elimination of any restrictions on the process of trade liberalization. The term positive integration relates to the modification of existing instruments and institutions and, more importantly, to the creation of new ones so as to enable the market of the integrated area to function properly and effectively and also to promote other broader policy aims of the scheme. Hence, at the risk of oversimplification, according to this classification, it can be stated that sectoral integration and free trade areas are forms of economic integration which require only negative integration, while the remaining types require positive integration, since, as a minimum, they need the positive act of adopting common relations. However, in reality this distinction is oversimplistic not only because practically all existing types of economic integration have found it essential to introduce some elements of positive integration, but also because theoretical considerations clearly indicate that no scheme of economic integration is viable without certain elements of positive integration; for example, even the ECSC deemed it necessary to establish new institutions to tackle its specified tasks – see below and chapter 2.

1.2 Economic integration and WTO rules

Article XXIV of WTO (see appendix to this chapter), GATT's successor, allows the formation of economic integration schemes (WTO calls them RTAs) on the understanding that, although free trade areas, customs unions, etc. are discriminatory associations, they may not pursue policies which increase the level of their discrimination beyond that which existed prior to their formation, and that tariffs and other trade restrictions (with some exceptions) are removed on *substantially* (increasingly interpreted to mean at least 90 per cent of intra-members' trade) all the trade among the participants. Hence, once allowance was made for the proviso regarding the external trade relations of the economic integration scheme (the CET level, or the common level of discrimination against extra-area trade, in a customs union, and the average tariff or trade discrimination level in a free trade area), it seemed to the drafters of Article XXIV that economic integration did not contradict the basic principles of WTO – trade *liberalization* on a most-favoured-nation (MFN) basis (the lowest tariff applicable to one member must be extended to all members), *non-discrimination*, *transparency* of instruments used to restrict trade (now called *tariffication*) and the promotion of *growth and stability* of the world economy – or more generally the principles of *non-discrimination*, *transparency* and *reciprocity*.

There are more serious arguments suggesting that Article XXIV is in direct contradiction to the

spirit of WTO – see chapter 6 and, inter alia, Dam (1970). However, Wolf (1983, p. 156) argues that if nations decide to treat one another as if they are part of a single economy, nothing can be done to prevent them, and that economic integration schemes, particularly the EU at the time of its formation in 1957, have a strong impulse towards liberalization; in the case of the EU at the time mentioned, the setting of the CETs happened to coincide with GATT's Kennedy Round of tariff reductions. However, recent experience, especially in the case of the EU, has proved otherwise since there has been a proliferation of non-tariff barriers, which is why the 'single market' programme (chapter 8) was introduced in 1992, but the point about WTO not being able to deter countries from pursuing economic integration has general validity: WTO has no means for enforcing its rules; it has no coercion powers.

Of course, these considerations are more complicated than is suggested here, particularly since there are those who would argue that nothing could be more discriminatory than for a group of nations to remove all tariffs and other trade impediments (import quotas and the so-called non-tariff trade barriers, NTBs) on their mutual trade while *at the same time* maintaining the initial levels against outsiders. Indeed, it would be difficult to find 'clubs' which extend equal privileges to non-subscribers, although the Asia Pacific Economic Cooperation (APEC) forum aspires to 'open regionalism', one interpretation of which is the extending of the removals of restrictions on trade and investment to all countries, not just the members. This point lies behind the concern with whether economic integration hinders or enhances the prospects for the free multilateral regime that the WTO is supposed to promote (see El-Agraa, 1999, for the arguments for and against). Moreover, as we shall see in chapter 6, economic integration schemes may lead to resource reallocation effects which are economically undesirable. However, to deny nations the right to form such associations, particularly when the main driving force may be political rather than economic, would have been a major setback for the world community. Hence, all that needs to be stated here is that as much as Article XXIV raises serious problems regarding how it fits in with the general spirit of WTO, and many proposals have been put forward for its reform, its adoption also reflects deep understanding of the future development of the world economy.

1.3 The global experience

Although this book is concerned with the EU, it is important to view the EU within the context of the global experience of economic integration. This section provides a brief summary of this experience – see El-Agraa (1997) for a full and detailed coverage and Crawford and Fiorentino (2006) for the latest update.

Since the end of the Second World War various forms of economic integration have been proposed and numerous schemes have actually been implemented. Even though some of those introduced were later discontinued or completely reformulated, the number adopted during the decade commencing 1957 was so great as to prompt Haberler in 1964 to describe that period as the 'age of integration'. Since 1964, however, there has been such a proliferation of integration schemes that Haberler's description may be more apt for the post-1964 era: by January 2005, 312 RTAs (84 per cent being FTAs) were notified to WTO, 196 of them since 1995.

The EU is the most significant and influential of these arrangements. There are three reasons for this significance:

1. The EU comprises (see table 1.2 for a tabulation of integration arrangements in Europe) Austria, Belgium, Bulgaria, Cyprus, the Czech Republic, Denmark, Estonia, Finland, France, Germany, Greece, Hungary, Ireland, Italy, Latvia, Lithuania, Luxembourg, Malta, the Netherlands, Poland, Portugal, Romania, Slovakia, Slovenia, Spain, Sweden and the UK. Croatia entered into EU membership negotiations in 2004 and Turkey did likewise in October 2005. Also, Macedonia has applied for membership and Iceland is seriously considering doing so. Hence the EU is set to include practically the whole of Europe (see also EEA below) and may go beyond the geographical area if Turkey succeeds in becoming a member in 2015.

2. From a voluntary viewpoint, it is the oldest such scheme.

3. Most vitally, the EU is the only scheme seeking the most involved and demanding type of economic integration. This is because the EU is almost a complete economic union since twelve of the fifteen pre-2004 members have the same currency (the euro) and they will be joined by all the twelve new members when they have met the necessary criteria, and has a common central bank (the European Central Bank) in charge of the euro and inflation control. Also, it has a number of common policies, elements of common foreign, security and defence policies and may even have a Constitution in the not so distant future.

The influence is simply due to the relative global weight of the EU (see the tables in chapter 5, especially 5.1 and 5.2 for data). With a population of about 481 million, the EU is comparable to NAFTA (see below), comprising Canada, Mexico and the United States, with 425 million, and likewise with gross national product measured in terms of *purchasing power parity* (PPP).

The EU was founded by six (although Germany was then not yet united) of these nations (Belgium, France, West Germany, Italy, Luxembourg and the Netherlands, usually referred to as the *Original Six*, simply the Six hereafter) by two treaties, signed in Rome on the same day in 1957, creating the *European Economic Community* (EEC) and the *European Atomic Energy Community* (Euratom). However, the Six had then been members of the *European Coal and Steel Community* (ECSC) which was established by the Treaty of Paris in 1951 and which was valid for fifty years. Thus, in 1957 the Six belonged to three communities, but in 1965 it was deemed sensible to merge the three entities into one and to call it the *European Communities* (EC). Denmark, Ireland and the UK joined in 1973; Greece became a full member in January 1981; Portugal and Spain joined in 1986; East Germany united with West Germany in 1990; Austria, Finland and Sweden joined in 1995; and of the remaining twelve Central and Eastern European

Table 1.2 Economic integration in Europe

Scheme Founded Aim	EU 1957 CM/EcU	When to join EU? CM/EcU	EFTA 1960 FTA	EEA 1992 FTA
Austria	✓			✓
Belgium	✓			✓
Bulgaria	✓			✓
Cyprus	✓			✓
Czech Rep.	✓			✓
Denmark	✓			✓
Estonia	✓			✓
Finland	✓			✓
France	✓			✓
Germany	✓			✓
Greece	✓			✓
Hungary	✓			✓
Ireland	✓			✓
Italy	✓			✓
Latvia	✓			✓
Lithuania	✓			✓
Luxembourg	✓			✓
Malta	✓			✓
Netherlands	✓			✓
Poland	✓			✓
Portugal	✓			✓
Romania	✓			✓
Slovak Rep.	✓			✓
Slovenia	✓			✓
Spain	✓			✓
Sweden	✓			✓
UK	✓			✓
Croatia		2007		
Turkey		2015?		
Iceland			✓	✓
Norway			✓	✓
Switzerland			✓	
(Liechtenstein)			✓	✓

Countries (CEECs), ten joined in 2004 and Bulgaria and Romania in 2007.

Note that a change in regime brought Croatia closer to joining. Moreover, after thirty-six years of temporizing, it was agreed at the 2002 Copenhagen EU summit that Turkey was a recognized candidate, but the EU wanted to see big improvements in Turkey's political and human rights behaviour, including the rights of Kurds and other minorities, and the constitutional role of the army in political

life, which might require changes in its constitution. The EU also wanted the country to resolve territorial squabbles with Greece in the Aegean Sea and to help end the division of Cyprus, where a Turkish-backed regime has occupied the north of the island since 1974. However, one should add that these conditions are not new since they are consistent with those in *Agenda 2000*, the EU's official document on enlargement (CEC, 1997b). Turkey has since made great progress and was given the go-ahead to start membership negotiations on 3 October 2005, but France has decided that membership will be conditional on a successful French referendum.

Note also that most of the CEECs, had already signed *Agreements of Association* with the EU and the twelve also signed accession treaties on 16 April 2003. Furthermore, the EU, Iceland, Liechtenstein and Norway belong to the *European Economic Area* (EEA), a scheme introduced in 1992 which provides Iceland and Norway with virtual membership of the EU, but without having a say in EU decisions; indeed the EEA is seen as a stepping-stone to full EU membership. Thus, if all goes according to plan, the EU is set to comprise the whole of Europe, since Switzerland has not withdrawn the application it lodged several years ago.

Although the EEC Treaty relates simply to the formation of a customs union and provides the basis for a common market in terms of free factor mobility, many of the originators of the EEC saw it as a phase in a process culminating in complete economic and political union. Thus the *Treaty on European Union* (the Maastricht Treaty, later ratified and extended by the *Treaty of Amsterdam* – see chapter 2), which transformed the EC into the EU in 1994 and which provides the EU with, inter alia, a single central bank, a single currency (presently for only thirteen members), and common foreign and defence policies, would be regarded in some quarters as a positive step towards the attainment of the founding fathers' desired ideal.

EFTA is the other major scheme of economic integration in Europe. To understand its membership one has to know something about its history (detailed in chapter 2). In the mid-1950s, when an EEC of the Six plus the UK was being contemplated, the UK was unprepared to commit itself to some of the economic and political aims envisaged for that community. For example, the adoption of a common agricultural policy and the eventual political unity of Western Europe were seen as aims which were in direct conflict with the UK's powerful position in the world and its interests in the Commonwealth, particularly with regard to 'Commonwealth preference', preceded by 'Imperial preference', which granted special access to the markets of the Commonwealth. Hence the UK favoured the idea of a Western Europe which adopted free trade in industrial products only, thus securing for itself the advantages offered by the Commonwealth as well as opening up Western Europe as a free market for its industrial goods. In short, the UK sought to achieve the best of both worlds for itself, which is, of course, quite understandable. However, it is equally understandable that such an arrangement was not acceptable to those seriously contemplating the formation of the EEC, especially France which stood to lose in an arrangement excluding a common policy for agriculture (see chapter 20). As a result the UK approached those Western European nations which had similar interests with the purpose of forming an alternative scheme of economic integration to counteract any possible damage due to the formation of the EEC. The outcome was EFTA, which was established in 1960 by the Stockholm Convention, with the object of creating a free market for industrial products only; there were some agreements on non-manufactures but these were relatively unimportant.

The membership of EFTA consisted of Austria, Denmark, Norway, Portugal, Sweden, Switzerland (and Liechtenstein) and the UK. Finland became an associate member in 1961, and Iceland joined in 1970 as a full member. But, as already stated, Denmark and the UK (together with Ireland) joined the EC in 1973; Portugal (together with Spain) joined in 1986; and Austria, Finland and Sweden joined the EU in 1995. This left EFTA with a membership consisting mainly of a few relatively smaller Western European nations – see table 1.2.

Until recently, economic integration schemes in Europe were not confined to the EU and EFTA. Indeed, before the dramatic events of 1989–90, the socialist planned economies of Eastern Europe had their own arrangement which operated under the CMEA, or COMECON as it was generally known in the West. The CMEA was formed in 1949 by Bulgaria, Czechoslovakia, the German Democratic Republic, Hungary, Poland, Romania and the USSR; they were later joined by three non-European countries: Mongolia (1962), Cuba (1972) and Vietnam (1978). In its earlier days, before the death of Stalin, the activities of the CMEA were confined to the collation of the plans of the member states, the development of a uniform system of reporting statistical data and the recording of foreign trade statistics. However, during the 1970s a series of measures was adopted by the CMEA to implement their 'Comprehensive Programme of Socialist Integration', hence indicating that the organization was moving towards a form of integration based principally on methods of plan coordination and joint planning activity, rather than on market levers (Smith, 1977). Finally, attention should be drawn to the fact that the CMEA comprised a group of relatively small countries and one 'superpower' and that the long-term aim of the association was to achieve a highly organized and integrated bloc, without any agreement ever having been made on how or when that was to be accomplished.

The dramatic changes that have taken place in Eastern Europe and the former USSR have inevitably led to the demise of the CMEA. This, together with the fact that the CMEA did not really achieve much in the nature of economic integration – indeed some analysts have argued that the entire organization was simply an instrument for the USSR to dictate its wishes to the rest – are the reasons why El-Agraa's (1997) book does not contain a chapter on the CMEA; the interested reader will find a chapter in El-Agraa (1988b). However, one should hasten to add that soon after the demise of the USSR, twelve of the fifteen former Soviet Republics formed the Commonwealth of Independent States (CIS) to bring them closer together in a relationship originally intended, but to no avail, to match that of the EU nations. The countries are Armenia, Azerbaijan, Belarus, Georgia, Kazakhstan, Kyrgyzstan, Moldova, Russia, Tajikistan, Turkmenistan, Ukraine and Uzbekistan, the missing three being Estonia, Latvia and Lithuania which, as already mentioned, joined the EU in 2004.

Before leaving Europe it should be mentioned that there are also the Central European Free Trade Agreement (CEFTA), in force since 1993, the Baltic Free Trade Area (BFTA), in force since 1994, and the Nordic Community. The CEFTA comprises Bulgaria, the Czech Republic, Hungary, Poland, Romania, the Slovak Republic and Slovenia, so it was established between the then transition countries, now all members of the EU. The Nordic Community consists of the five Nordic countries: Denmark, Finland, Iceland, Norway and Sweden. However, in spite of claims to the contrary (Sundelius and Wiklund, 1979), the Nordic scheme is one of cooperation rather than economic integration since its members belong to either the EU or EFTA, and, as we have seen, the EU and EFTA are closely linked through the EEA.

Africa has numerous schemes of economic integration, with practically all the African countries belonging to more than one scheme (table 1.3), and if one ignored the above stated emphasis on the voluntary nature of economic integration, then Africa could claim to have the oldest two schemes in the world: the *Southern African Customs Union* (SACU, 1910, in which South Africa ruled supreme and in which all members except for Botswana run a Rand-based common monetary area), and the *East African Community* (EAC, established by the British for their own colonial administrative ease in 1919).

In West Africa, the *Union Économique et Monétaire Ouest-Africaine* (UEMOA) and *Mano River Union* (MRU) co-exist with the *Economic Community of West African States* (ECOWAS), with all members belonging to ECOWAS. In Central Africa, the *Economic Community of Central African States* (ECCAS), the *Communauté Économique et Monétaire des États de l'Afrique Centrale* (CEMAC) and the *Economic Community of the Countries of the Great Lakes* (CEPGL) all co-exist. In Eastern Africa, there is the *Common Market for Eastern and Southern Africa* (COMESA), with the *Intergovernmental Authority on Development* (IGAD) and EAC as smaller inner groups. In Southern Africa, there are the *Southern African Development Community* (SADC) and SACU. Northern Africa used to be the only sub-region with a single scheme, the *Arab Maghreb Union* (UMA), but the recent creation of the *Community of Sahel-Saharan States* (CENSAD) has brought it in line with the rest of Africa.

UMA, created in 1989, aimed for a CU before the end of 1995 and a CM by 2000, but has yet to achieve a mere FTA. CENSAD, established in April 1999, has no clear objectives, not even with regard to a trade liberalization strategy, but since its members belong to other blocs, the aims of these are pertinent. ECOWAS was launched in 1975 with the aim of creating an economic and monetary

Table 1.3 Economic integration in Africa

Scheme[a]	A	B	C	D	E	F	G	H	I	J	K	L	M	N	AEC	AU
Algeria	✓														✓	✓
Angola									✓				✓		✓	✓
Benin			✓	✓											✓	✓
Botswana													✓	✓	✓	✓
Burkina Faso			✓	✓											✓	✓
Burundi						✓	✓		✓						✓	✓
Cameroon					✓	✓									✓	✓
Cape Verde			✓												✓	✓
Central African Rep.		✓			✓	✓									✓	✓
Chad		✓			✓	✓									✓	✓
Comoros									✓			✓			✓	✓
Congo					✓	✓									✓	✓
Congo Dem. Rep.							✓		✓			✓			✓	✓
Côte d'Ivoire			✓	✓											✓	✓
Djibouti		✓							✓		✓				✓	✓
Egypt		✓							✓						✓	✓
Equatorial Guinea					✓	✓									✓	✓
Eritrea									✓		✓				✓	✓
Ethiopia									✓		✓				✓	✓
Gabon					✓	✓									✓	✓
Gambia			✓												✓	✓
Ghana			✓							-					✓	✓
Guinea Bissau			✓	✓											✓	✓
Guinea Conakry			✓					✓							✓	✓
Kenya									✓	✓	✓				✓	✓
Lesotho, Kingdom of													✓	✓	✓	✓
Liberia			✓					✓							✓	✓
Libya	✓	✓													✓	✓
Madagascar									✓			✓			✓	✓
Malawi									✓				✓		✓	✓
Mali			✓	✓											✓	✓
Mauritania	✓														✓	✓
Mauritius									✓				✓		✓	✓
Morocco	✓	✓													✓	
Mozambique													✓		✓	✓
Namibia													✓	✓	✓	✓
Niger			✓	✓											✓	✓
Nigeria			✓	✓											✓	✓
Réunion												✓			✓	
Rwanda						✓	✓		✓						✓	✓
Saharawi Arab D. R.															✓	✓
São Tomé and Príncipe						✓									✓	✓
Senegal			✓	✓	✓										✓	✓
Seychelles									✓			✓	✓		✓	✓
Sierra Leone			✓					✓							✓	✓
Somalia		✓									✓				✓	✓
South Africa													✓	✓	✓	✓

Table 1.3 (continued)

Scheme[a]	A	B	C	D	E	F	G	H	I	J	K	L	M	N	AEC	AU
Sudan									✓		✓			✓	✓	✓
Swaziland									✓				✓	✓	✓	✓
Tanzania										✓			✓		✓	✓
Togo			✓	✓											✓	✓
Tunisia	✓	✓													✓	✓
Uganda									✓	✓					✓	✓
Zambia		✓							✓				✓		✓	✓
Zimbabwe									✓				✓		✓	✓

[a] A is UMA, B is CENSAD, C is ECOWAS, D is UEMOA, E is CEMAC, F is ECCAS, G is CEPGL, H is MRU, I is COMESA, J is EAC, K is IGAD, L is IOC, M is SADC and N is SACU.

union, but its revised treaty envisaged a mere CU by 2000, later delayed to 1 January 2003, and some members do not even apply a FTA. UEMOA, created in 1994 by the francophone members of ECOWAS, is now a CU, introducing its common external tariffs (CETs) in January 2000, but applying them to the rest of ECOWAS as well, and some member nations are still not even FTAs! MRU, established in 1973, is a CU with a certain degree of cooperation in the industrial sector. ECCAS has been dormant for almost a decade, but has recently been resuscitated. CEPGL was created in 1976, but is virtually inactive due to the conflicts within the bloc. Most activity in this part of Africa is confined to CEMAC, which has a common currency and has taken steps towards a CU. COMESA, established in 1993, launched a FTA in October 2000 comprising nine of its member states. Note that of the member nations of the EAC (first *truly* established in 1967), Kenya and Uganda are also members of COMESA, while Tanzania also belongs to SADC, having earlier withdrawn from COMESA. EAC and COMESA, in their May 1997 *Memorandum of Understanding*, agreed to become a CU. SADC aims to achieve a FTA within the next five years. Note that IGAD (formed in 1996 to replace the equivalent Association on Drought and Development of 1986) and the *Indian Ocean Commission* (IOC, set up in 1982 with vague aims and ambitions, except for concentration on some functional cooperation areas such as fisheries and tourism) have agreed to adopt the aims of COMESA.

Hence a unique characteristic of economic integration in Africa is the multiplicity and overlapping of its schemes, both made more complicated by the co-existence of inter-governmental cooperation organizations. For example, in the West alone, in 1984 there was a total of thirty-three schemes and inter-governmental cooperation organizations, and by the late 1980s, about 130 inter-governmental, multi-sectoral economic organizations existed simultaneously with all the above-mentioned economic integration schemes (Adedeji, 2002, p. 6). That is why the United Nations Economic Commission for Africa (UNECA) recommended in 1984 that there should be some rationalization in the economic cooperation attempts in West Africa. Therefore, some would claim that the creation, by all the African nations except Morocco, of the *African Economic Community* (AEC) in 1991, and the *African Union* (AU) in 2001 by the Constitutive Act, are the appropriate response; the AU replaced the *Organization for African Unity* (OAU). However, that response would be incorrect, since the AEC not only officially endorses all the existing African economic integration schemes, but also encourages the creation of new ones while remaining silent on how they can all co-exist (El-Agraa, 2003). When this uniqueness is combined with the proliferation of schemes, one cannot disagree with Robson (1997) when he declares that, regarding economic integration, '*Reculer pour mieux sauter* is not a dictum that seems to carry much weight . . . On the contrary, if a certain level of integration

Table 1.4 Economic integration in the Americas

Scheme	NAFTA	CACM	LAIA	CARICOM	AP	MERCUSOR
Founded	1993	1961	1960/80	1973	1969	1991
Aim	FTA	FTA	FTA	CU/CM	FTA	FTA
Canada	✓					
Mexico	✓		✓			
USA	✓					
Belize		✓		✓		
Costa Rica		✓				
El Salvador		✓				
Guatemala		✓				
Honduras		✓				
Nicaragua		✓				
Panama		✓				
Antigua and Barbuda				✓		
Bahamas				✓		
Barbados				✓		
Dominica				✓		
Grenada				✓		
Jamaica				✓		
Montserrat				✓		
St Kitts and Nevis				✓		
St Lucia				✓		
St Vincent and Grenadines				✓		
Trinidad and Tobago				✓		
Argentina			✓			✓
Bolivia			✓		✓	
Brazil			✓			✓
Chile			✓		✓	
Colombia			✓		✓	
Ecuador			✓		✓	
Guyana			✓			
Paraguay			✓			✓
Peru			✓			
Uruguay			✓		✓	✓
Venezuela			✓		✓	✓

cannot be made to work, the reaction of policy makers has typically been to embark on something more elaborate, more advanced and more demanding in terms of administrative requirements and political commitment.'

Economic integration in Latin America has been too volatile to describe in simple terms, since the post-1985 experience has been very different from that in the 1960s and 1970s. At the risk of misleading, one can state that there are four schemes of economic integration in this region – see table 1.4. Under the 1960 Treaty of Montevideo, the *Latin American Free Trade Association* (LAFTA) was formed between Mexico and all the countries of South America except for Guyana and Surinam. LAFTA came to an end in the late 1970s but was promptly succeeded by the *Association for Latin American Integration* (*Associación Latinoamericana de Integración*, ALADI or LAIA) in 1980. The Managua Treaty of 1960 established the *Central American Common Market* (CACM) between Costa Rica, El Salvador, Guatemala, Honduras and Nicaragua. In 1969 the *Andean Pact* (AP) was established under the Cartagena Agreement between Bolivia, Chile, Colombia, Ecuador, Peru and Venezuela; the AP forms a closer link between some of the least developed nations of LAFTA, now LAIA.

Since the debt crisis in the 1980s, economic integration in Latin America has taken a new turn, with Mexico joining Canada and the US (see below) and Argentina, Brazil, Paraguay and Uruguay, the more developed nations of LAIA, creating MERCOSUR (*Mercado Comùn del Sur*) by signing the Treaty of Asunción in 1991. MERCOSUR became a customs union on 1 January 1995 and aimed to become a common market by 1995, but this has yet to happen. Bolivia and Chile became associate members in mid-1995, a move which Brazil sees as merely a first step towards the creation of a *South American Free Trade Area* (SAFTA), a counterweight to the efforts in the north (see below); indeed, by 2005 the number of associates increased to six by including Colombia, Ecuador, Peru and Venezuela, and on 4 July 2006 Venezuela joined and will become a full member in 2010. In June 1999 MERCOSUR reached agreement with the EU to start negotiations in November 1999 on an arrangement for free trade and investment between them, which is yet to be concluded. Also, on 29 April 2006, Cuba, Bolivia and Venezuela signed an agreement creating the *Bolivarian Alternative for the Americas* (ALBA) to thwart the US plans for a *Free Trade Area of the Americas* (FTAA; see below).

There is one scheme of economic integration in the Caribbean. In 1973 the *Caribbean Community* (CARICOM) was formed between Antigua, Barbados, Belize, Dominica, Grenada, Guyana, Jamaica, Montserrat, St Kitts–Nevis–Anguilla, St Lucia, St Vincent, and Trinidad and Tobago. CARICOM replaced the *Caribbean Free Trade Association* (CARIFTA) which was established in 1968.

In 1988 Canada and the United States established the *Canada–US Free Trade Agreement* (CUSFTA or CUFTA), and, together with Mexico, they formed the *North American Free Trade Agreement* (NAFTA) in 1993 which started to operate from 1 January 1994. NAFTA also covers investment, hence is in line with the present trend for FTAs (see above). The enlargement of NAFTA to include the rest of the western hemisphere was suggested by George Bush (senior) while he was US president. He hoped to construct the FTAA, to be concluded by 1 January 2005, but due to a strong movement against increased poverty, led by Argentina, Bolivia, Brazil and Venezuela, this did not happen. Chile has been negotiating membership of NAFTA. It should be added that a *Central American Free Trade Agreement* (CAFTA), between the United States, five Central American nations (Costa Rica, El Salvador, Guatemala, Honduras and Nicaragua) and the Dominican Republic was to take effect on 1 January 2006, but due to various inconsistencies in the process of legal reforms in these countries, bar the United States, this did not happen.

Until recently, Asia did not figure prominently in the league of economic integration schemes, but this was not surprising given the existence of such large (if only in terms of population) countries as China and India. Nevertheless, there was the *Regional Cooperation for Development* (RCD), a very limited arrangement for sectoral integration between Iran, Pakistan and Turkey. There were also the *Association of Southeast Asia* (ASA), which was a collaborative effort between Malaysia, the Philippines and Thailand; and *Maphilindo*, which followed soon after ASA, joining together Indonesia, the Philippines and Thailand. Moreover, the *Association for South-East Asian Nations* (ASEAN) comprises ten nations: Brunei, Cambodia, Indonesia, Laos, Malaysia, Myanmar, the Philippines, Singapore, Thailand and Vietnam. ASEAN was founded in 1967 by five of these countries. Brunei joined in 1984, Vietnam in July 1995, Laos and Myanmar in July 1997 and Cambodia in December 1998. After almost a decade of inactivity, ASEAN 'was galvanized into renewed vigour in 1976 by the security problems which the reunification of Vietnam seemed to present to its membership' (Arndt and Garnaut, 1979). The drive for the establishment of ASEAN and for its vigorous reactivation in 1976 was both political and strategic. However, right from the start, economic cooperation was one of the most important aims of ASEAN; indeed most of the vigorous activities of the group since 1976 have been predominantly in the economic field, and the admission of Vietnam in 1995 is a clear manifestation of this. Moreover, at the fourth ASEAN summit, held in Singapore in January 1992, ASEAN initiated the *ASEAN Free Trade Area* (AFTA), which laid out a comprehensive programme for intra-member tariff reductions, to be implemented in phases by 2008. This deadline was later advanced to 2003 and then to 2002. In the meantime, the programme of tariff reductions has been broadened and accelerated, and a host of 'AFTA Plus' activities initiated, including efforts to eliminate NTBs and to harmonize customs nomenclatures, valuation and procedures, and develop common product certification standards. In addition, ASEAN later signed framework agreements for intra-regional liberalization of trade in services and for regional IPR cooperation, and on 23 August 2006 its trade ministers agreed on an EU-style association by 2015 instead of 2020. On 4 November 2002, ASEAN and China signed a PTA, covering both trade and investment, to be completed by 2010 by the original six members and by 2015 by the remaining four. Moreover, an ASEAN+3 PTA was agreed with China, Japan and South Korea in 2003, but is yet to be finalized, with an *East Asian Community* in mind.

On 8 December 1985, the South Asian Association for Regional Cooperation (SAARC) was established by Bangladesh, Bhutan, India, the Maldives, Nepal, Pakistan and Sri Lanka. Its aim is to accelerate the process of economic and social development of the members, but within the wider context of working together in a 'spirit of friendship, trust and understanding'. In November 2005, at the thirteenth summit, held in Dhaka, Bangladesh, SAARC agreed to admit Afghanistan as a member from the next summit meeting; to grant China and Japan observer status; and to firmly commit to the realization of a South Asian Economic Union as well as a FTA (SAFTA).

In 1965 Australia and New Zealand entered into a free trade arrangement called the *New Zealand Australia Free Trade Area*. This was replaced in 1983 by the more important *Australia New Zealand Closer Economic Relations and Trade Agreement* (CER, for short): not only have major trade barriers been removed, but significant effects on the New Zealand economy have been experienced as a result.

A scheme for the Pacific Basin integration–cum-cooperation was being hotly discussed during the 1980s. In the late 1980s I argued (El-Agraa, 1988a, 1988b) that 'given the diversity of countries within the Pacific region, it would seem highly unlikely that a very involved scheme of integration would evolve over the next decade or so'. This was in spite of the fact that there already existed:

1. the *Pacific Economic Cooperation Conference* (PECC) which is a tripartite structured organization with representatives from governments, business and academic circles and with the secretariat work being handled between general meetings by the country next hosting a meeting;
2. the *Pacific Trade and Development Centre* (PAFTAD) which is an academically oriented organization;
3. the *Pacific Basin Economic Council* (PBEC) which is a private-sector business organization for regional cooperation; and
4. the *Pacific Telecommunications Conference* (PTC) which is a specialized organization for regional cooperation in this particular field.

The reason for the pessimism was that the:

region under consideration covers the whole of North America and Southeast Asia, with Pacific South America, the People's Republic of China and the USSR all claiming interest since they are all on the Pacific. Even if one were to exclude this latter group, there still remains the cultural diversity of such countries as Australia, Canada, Japan, New Zealand and the USA, plus the diversity that already exists within ASEAN. It would seem that unless the group of participants is severely limited, Pacific Basin *cooperation* would be the logical outcome (El-Agraa, 1988a, p. 8).

However, in an attempt to provide a rational basis for resolving Japan's trade frictions, I may appear to have contradicted myself:

it may be concluded that . . . Pacific Basin cooperation-cum-integration is the only genuine solution to the problems of Japan and the USA (as well as the other nations in this area). Given what is stated above about the nature of the nations of the Pacific Basin, that would be a broad generalisation: what is needed is a very strong relationship between Japan and the USA within a much looser association with the rest of SE Asia. Hence, what is being advocated is a form of involved economic integration between Japan and the USA (and Canada, if the present negotiations for a free trade area of Canada and the USA lead to that outcome), within the broad context of 'Pacific Basin Cooperation', or, more likely, within a free trade area with the most advanced nations of SE Asia: Australia, New Zealand, South Korea, the nations of ASEAN, etc. (El-Agraa, 1988b, pp. 203–4).

I added that the proposed scheme should not be a protectionist one. Members of such a scheme should promote cooperation with the rest of the world through their membership of GATT (now WTO) and should coordinate their policies with regard to overseas development assistance, both financially and in terms of the transfer of technology, for the benefit not only of the poorer nations of SE Asia, but also for the whole developing world.

Thus the *Asia Pacific Economic Cooperation* (APEC) forum can arguably be considered as the appropriate response to my suggestion. It was established in 1989 by ASEAN plus Australia, Canada, Japan, New Zealand, South Korea and the USA. These were joined by China, Hong Kong and Taiwan in 1991. In 1993 President Clinton galvanized it into its present form and increased its membership to eighteen nations by adding Chile, Mexico and Papua New Guinea. In Bogor, Indonesia, in 1994 APEC declared its intention to create a free trade and investment area by the year 2010 embracing its advanced members, with the rest to follow suit ten years later. APEC tried to chart the route for realizing this vision in Osaka,

Japan, in November 1995, and came up with the interesting resolution that each member nation should unilaterally declare its own measures for freeing trade and investment, with agriculture completely left out of the reckoning; China immediately obliged by declaring that it would do this for a vast number of products, an act conditional on WTO membership which China was negotiating at the time. In November 1998, Peru, Russia and Vietnam joined the APEC forum, increasing its total membership to twenty-one nations – see table 1.5. Furthermore, in its 2004 meeting in Bangkok, Thailand, it outlined its priorities to be the promotion of trade and investment liberalization, the enhancement of human security, and using the organization to help people and societies benefit from globalization. Officially speaking, APEC aims to further enhance economic growth and prosperity in as well as strengthen the Asia-Pacific region. It claims to be the only inter-governmental grouping in the world that operates on the basis of non-binding commitments, open dialogue and equal respect for the views of all participants. It has no treaty obligations and reaches decisions by consensus and commitments entered into voluntarily, hence WTO consistent.

There are several schemes in the Middle East, but some of them extend beyond the geographical area traditionally designated as such. This is natural since there are nations with Middle Eastern characteristics in parts of Africa. The *Arab League* (AL) clearly demonstrates this reality since it comprises twenty-two nations, extending from the Persian Gulf in the east to Mauritania and Morocco in the west. Hence the geographical area covered by the scheme includes the whole of North Africa, a large part of the Middle East, plus Djibouti and Somalia. The purpose of the AL is to strengthen the close ties linking Arab states, to coordinate their policies and activities and to direct them to their common benefit and to mediate in disputes between them. These are vague terms of reference, which remain so even when other schemes are mentioned. For example, the *Arab Economic Council*, whose membership consists of all Arab Ministers of Economic Affairs, was entrusted with suggesting ways for

Table 1.5 Economic integration in Asia–Pacific and the Middle East

Scheme	CER	ASEAN	ACM	GCC	AFTA	APEC	EAEC
Founded	1983	1967	1964	1981	1991	1989	1990
Aim	FTA	FTA	CU	CU	FTA	FTA	FTA
Australia	✓					✓	
Brunei		✓			✓	✓	✓
Cambodia		✓			✓		
Chile						✓	
China						✓	✓
Hong Kong						✓	✓
Indonesia		✓			✓	✓	✓
Japan						✓	✓
Laos		✓			✓		✓
Malaysia		✓			✓	✓	✓
Myanmar		✓			✓		✓
New Zealand	✓					✓	
Papua NG						✓	
Philippines		✓			✓	✓	✓
Singapore		✓			✓	✓	✓
South Korea						✓	✓
Taiwan						✓	✓
Thailand		✓			✓	✓	✓
Vietnam		✓			✓	✓	✓
Bahrain				✓			
Egypt			✓				
Iran Islamic Rep.							
Iraq			✓				
Jordan			✓				
Kuwait				✓			
Libya			✓				
Oman				✓			
Qatar				✓			
Saudi Arabia				✓			
Syrian Arab Rep.			✓				
UAE				✓			
Yemen Rep.			✓				
Canada						✓	
Mauritania							
Mexico						✓	
Pakistan					✓		
Peru						✓	
Russian Federation						✓	
Turkey					✓		
USA						✓	

economic development, cooperation, organization and coordination. The *Council for Arab Economic Unity* (CAEU), which was formed in 1957, had the aim of establishing an integrated economy of all AL states. Moreover, in 1964 the *Arab Common Market* was formed by Egypt, Iraq, Jordan and Syria, but in practice never got off the ground. The exception seems to be the *Gulf*

Cooperation Council (GCC), established on 25 May 1981 between Bahrain, Kuwait, Oman, Qatar, Saudi Arabia and the United Arab Emirates. The GCC is keen to stress that long-lasting and deep religious and cultural ties link its members, and strong kin relationships prevail amongst its citizens. The GCC claims to have concrete objectives as an economic and political policy-coordinating forum and has growing cooperation on, inter alia, customs duties, intellectual property protection, standard setting and intra-area investment, and has practical details for establishing an effective CU. This was set for January 2003, but has yet to happen. It has set 2010 for introducing a single currency. In short, the GCC wants to bring together the Gulf states and to prepare the ground for them to join forces in the economic, political and military spheres.

The latest schemes of economic integration in the Middle East have already been mentioned, but only in passing in the context of Africa. The ACC was founded on 16 February 1989 by Egypt, Iraq, Jordan and the Arab Yemen Republic with the aim of boosting Arab solidarity and acting as 'yet another link in the chain of Arab efforts towards integration'. Moreover, on 18 February 1989 the AMU was formed by Algeria, Libya, Mauritania, Morocco and Tunisia. The AMU aims to create an organization similar to the EU.

All these schemes are connected by an increasing number of PTAs between them. This had resulted in an intricate web of interrelationships. Considering the EU alone, since it is the main protagonist of PTAs, and adding the seventy-eight APC nations of the ACP–EU (Cuba became the seventy-ninth member in 2000, but has not participated in the agreements) as well as those of the EEA, one can imagine why the term spaghetti bowl has been used to describe this web surrounding the EU.

Moreover, there are two schemes of sectoral economic integration which are not based on geographical proximity. The first is the *Organization for Petroleum Exporting Countries* (OPEC), founded in 1960 with a truly international membership; its aim was to protect the main interest of its member nations, petroleum, by setting production quotas, and hence determining prices. The second is the *Organization for Arab Petroleum Exporting Countries* (OAPEC), established in January 1968 by Kuwait, Libya and Saudi Arabia, joined in May 1970 by Algeria, and the four Arab Gulf Emirates (Abu Dhabi, Bahrain, Dubai and Qatar); in March 1972 Iraq and Syria became members and Egypt followed them in 1973; Tunisia joined in 1982, but withdrew in 1986 (OAPEC was temporarily liquidated in June 1971). There are also the *Organization for Economic Cooperation and Development* (OECD) and the *World Trade Organization* (WTO). However, all these are *organizations* for intergovernmental cooperation rather than for economic integration. Therefore, except where appropriate, nothing more shall be said about them.

1.4 The EU

Since this book is devoted to the EU, it is important to establish the nature of the EU within the context of the different types of economic integration discussed at the beginning of this chapter – readers interested in the other schemes will find a full discussion of them in El-Agraa (1997) and Crawford and Fiorentino (2006).

Article 2 of the treaty establishing the EEC, now incorporated, with appropriate adjustments due to developments since 1957, in the Amsterdam Treaty, pronounces that:

The Community shall have as its task, by establishing a common market and an economic and monetary union and by implementing common policies or activities referred to in Articles 3 and 4, to promote throughout the Community a harmonious, balanced and sustainable development of economic activities, a high level of employment and of social protection, equality between men and women, sustainable and non-inflationary growth, a high degree of competitiveness and convergence of economic performance, a high level of protection and improvement of the quality of the environment, the raising of the standard of living and quality of life, and economic and social cohesion and solidarity among Member States (Amsterdam Treaty, Article 2, Part One, Principles, p. 39).

Article 3 then states that:

1. For the purposes set out in Article 2, the activities of the Community shall include, as

provided in this Treaty and in accordance with the timetable set out therein:

(a) The prohibition, as between Member States, of customs duties and of quantitative restrictions on the import and export of goods, and of all other measures having equivalent effect;

(b) a common commercial policy;

(c) an internal market characterised by the abolition, as between Member States, of obstacles to the freedom of movement for goods, persons, services and capital;

(d) measures concerning the entry and movement of persons as provided for in *Title IV*;

(e) a common policy in the sphere of agriculture and fisheries;

(f) a common policy in the sphere of transport;

(g) a system ensuring that competition in the internal market is not distorted;

(h) the approximation of the laws of Member States to the extent required for proper functioning of the common market;

(i) the promotion of coordination between employment policies of the Member States with a view to enhancing their effectiveness by developing a coordinated strategy for employment;

(j) a policy in the social sphere comprising a European Social Fund;

(k) the strengthening of economic and social cohesion;

(l) a policy in the sphere of the environment;

(m) the strengthening of the competitiveness of Community industry;

(n) the promotion of research and technological development;

(o) encouragement for the establishment and development of trans-European networks;

(p) a contribution to the attainment of a high level of health protection;

(q) a contribution to education and training of quality and to the flowering of the cultures of the Member States;

(r) a policy in the sphere of development cooperation;

(s) the association of overseas countries and territories in order to increase trade and promote jointly economic and social development;

(t) a contribution to the strengthening of consumer protection;

(u) measures in the spheres of energy, civil protection and tourism.

2. In all the activities referred to in this Article, the Community shall aim to eliminate inequalities, and to promote equality, between men and women (Amsterdam Treaty, Article 3, Part One, Principles, pp. 39–40).

Article 3 A and B elaborate on the adoption of an economic policy based on the close coordination of those of the member nations and set out the conditions of European monetary unification (EMU, see chapters 9 and 10) and the principle of 'subsidiarity' (see chapters 2 and 3). It can, therefore, be categorically stated that the EU is at present certainly much more than a common market, although in some respects it falls a bit short of being a complete economic union and in others goes beyond it. Moreover, despite recent upsets regarding an EU constitution, at least some members would like to go even further, edging closer to a political union (see chapters 2 and 28).

1.5 The possible gains from economic integration

We shall see in chapters 2 and 10 that the driving force behind the formation of the EU, the earliest and most influential of all existing integration schemes (see above), was the political unity of Europe with the aim of realizing eternal peace in the continent. Some analysts would also argue that the recent attempts by the EU for more intensive economic integration can be cast in the same vein, especially since they are accompanied by one currency, the euro, and by common foreign and defence policies. At the same time, during the late 1950s and early 1960s economic integration among developing nations was perceived as the only viable way for them to make some real economic progress; indeed that was the rationale behind the United Nations' encouragement and support of such efforts. More recently, frustrations with the WTO's slowness in reaching agreement, due to its many participants and their variable interests, have led some to the conclusion that economic integration would result in a quicker pace for negotiations since, by definition, it would reduce the number of parties involved. There are also practical considerations and countries may feel that economic integration would provide security of markets among the participants. However, no matter what the motives for economic integration may be, it is still necessary to analyse the economic implications of such geographically discriminatory associations; that is one of the reasons why I have included political unification as one of the possible schemes.

At the customs union (CU) and free trade area (FTA) levels, the possible sources of economic gain from economic integration can be attributed to:

1. enhanced efficiency in production made possible by increased specialization in accordance with the law of comparative advantage, due to the liberalized market of the participating nations;

2. increased production levels due to better exploitation of economies of scale made possible by the increased size of the market;

3. an improved international bargaining position, made possible by the larger size, leading to better terms of trade (cheaper imports from the outside world and higher prices for exports to them);

4. enforced changes in efficiency brought about by intensified competition between firms;

5. changes affecting both the amount and quality of the factors of production due to technological advances, themselves encouraged by (4).

If the level of economic integration is to go beyond the free trade area and customs union levels, then further sources of economic gain also become possible:

6. factor mobility across the borders of the member nations will materialize only if there is a net economic incentive for them, thus leading to higher national incomes;

7. the coordination of monetary and fiscal policies may result in cost reductions since the pooling of efforts may enable the achievement of economies of scale; and

8. the unification of efforts to achieve better employment levels, lower inflation rates, balanced trade, higher rates of economic growth and better income distribution may make it cheaper to attain these targets.

It should be apparent that some of these possible gains relate to static resource reallocation effects while the rest relate to long-term or dynamic effects. It should also be emphasized that these are *possible* economic gains, i.e. there is no guarantee that they can ever be achieved; everything would depend on the nature of the particular scheme and the type of competitive behaviour prevailing prior to integration. Indeed, it is quite feasible that in the absence of 'appropriate' competitive behaviour, economic integration may worsen the situation. Thus the possible attainment of these benefits must be considered with great caution.

However, in the case of the EU, one should always keep in mind that the 'founding fathers' had the formation of a United States of Western (hopefully all) Europe as the ultimate goal and that economic integration became the immediate objective so as to facilitate the attainment of political unity via the back door (see chapter 2). Those who fail to appreciate this by stressing that today the concern is confined to only economic integration will always be at a loss to understand new developments in the EU – see chapter 6.

1.6 Areas of enquiry

The necessary areas of enquiry, emphasizing the economic and social aspects, are quite apparent now that we have established the nature of the EU. It is necessary to analyse the effects and consequences of the removal of trade impediments between the participating nations and to make an equivalent study of the establishment of the common external relations; these CU aspects are tackled in chapters 6 and 9. It is also vital to discuss the single market and the role of competition and industrial policies and the presence of multinational firms in making it operative; these are covered in, respectively, chapters 7, 13 and 14. Moreover, it is essential to analyse the special provisions for agriculture (chapter 20), fisheries (chapter 21), transport (chapter 16), EMU (chapters 10–12), tax harmonization and general budget (chapters 15 and 19), regional disparity (chapter 22), energy (chapter 17), social dimensions, especially employment and unemployment (chapter 23), factor mobility (chapter 8), environmental considerations (chapter 18) and external relations (chapters 24 and 25). The book also contains chapters on the history and institutions of the EU (chapters 2 and 3), the legal dimension in European integration (chapter 4), the basic statistics (chapter 5), enlargement (chapter 26), and the success and future of the EU (chapters 27 and 28).

These chapters come under seven coherent parts. Part I deals with the history, institutions, legal dimension and basic statistics of the EU; hence it offers, in four chapters, the vital general background to the EU. Part II, consisting of four chapters, is concerned with EU market integration in terms of both theory and practice; this covers pure theory, the single market, factor mobility and the measurement of the CU aspects of economic integration. Part III, comprising three chapters, is devoted to economic and monetary union (EMU), and hence considers the theoretical and operational aspects of EMU. Part IV deals with various areas which constitute policy integration as it relates to the single EU market and does this in six chapters on competition, industry, tax harmonization, transport, energy and the environment. Part V tackles budgetary and structural policies in five chapters on the EU budget, common agricultural and fisheries policies, and regional and social policy dimensions, emphasizing employment/ unemployment. Part VI deals with EU external affairs in two chapters on trade policy and relations with the developing countries. The final part, comprising three chapters, deals with enlargement and the success and future of the EU.

1.7 About this book

This book offers, more or less, a comprehensive but brief coverage of the theoretical issues: trade creation, trade diversion and the Cooper–Massell criticism; the domestic distortions argument; the terms of trade effects; and the economies of scale argument. It also offers a fresh look at the different attempts at the economic justification for customs union formation. A full chapter deals with the methodology and results of the measurements of the effects of EU formation on the member states and the outside world. These are discussed briefly since a comprehensive book on them is available – see El-Agraa (1989a and 1999). There is also a full treatment of all major policy considerations – see previous section.

Although chapters on EU political cooperation, distributional problems and political considerations may seem to be absent, these aspects have not been omitted: some elements of political cooperation are discussed in chapters 2, 27 and 28, while some of the most significant elements of the distribution problem are tackled in the chapters on the role of the EU budget and social and regional policies. This does not imply that these aspects are not worthy of separate chapters, as one could in fact argue that these are the most important issues facing the EU. The treatment given to them in this book is such that the significant aspects of these policies are tackled where they are particularly relevant. Moreover, with regard to some of these policies, the EU is not yet certain in which direction it is heading, and this in spite of the adoption and endorsement of the Maastricht and Amsterdam treaties, which specify certain details. The wider political considerations lie outside our scope. In short, the book is aimed at those who want to understand the EU in more or less its entirety, and those interested in learning about only some aspects of it will have to select the appropriate chapters and the sequence they should follow, although each chapter can be read in its own right; a Guide for users is provided in the preliminaries to the book (see p. xix).

Appendix 1.1: WTO's Article XXIV

Territorial application – frontier traffic – customs unions and free trade areas

1. The provisions of this Agreement shall apply to the metropolitan customs territories of the contracting parties and to any other customs territories in respect of which this Agreement has been accepted under Article XXVI or is being applied under Article XXXIII or pursuant to the Protocol of Provisional Application. Each such customs territory shall, exclusively for the purposes of the territorial application of this Agreement, be treated as though it were a contracting party; provided that the provisions of this paragraph shall not be construed to create any rights or obligations as between two or more customs territories in respect of which this Agreement has been accepted under Article XXVI or is being applied under Article XXXIII or pursuant to the Protocol of Provisional Application by a single contracting party.

2. For the purposes of this Agreement a customs territory shall be understood to mean any territory with respect to which separate tariffs or other regulations of commerce are maintained for a substantial part of the trade of such territory with other territories.

3. The provisions of this Agreement shall not be construed to prevent:
   (a) advantages accorded by any contracting party to adjacent countries in order to facilitate frontier traffic;
   (b) advantages accorded to the trade with the Free Territory of Trieste by countries contiguous to that territory, provided that such advantages are not in conflict with the Treaties of Peace arising out of the Second World War.

4. The conracting parties recognize the desirability of increasing freedom of trade by the development, through voluntary agreements, of closer integration between the economies of the countries parties to such agreements. They also recognize that the purpose of a customs union or of a free-trade area should be to facilitate trade between the constituent territories and not to raise barriers to the trade of other contracting parties with such territories.

5. Accordingly, the provisions of this Agreement shall not prevent, as between the territories of contracting parties, the formation of a customs union or of a free-trade area or the adoption of an interim agreement necessary for the formation of a customs union or of a free-trade area; provided that:

   (a) with respect to a customs union, or an interim agreement leading to the formation of a customs union, the duties and other regulations of commerce imposed at the institution of any such union or interim agreement in respect of trade with contracting parties not parties to such union or agreement shall not on the whole be higher or more restrictive than the general incidence of the duties and regulations of commerce applicable in the constituent territories prior to the formation of such union or the adoption of such interim agreement, as the case may be;
   (b) with respect to a free-trade area, or an interim agreement leading to the formation of a free-trade area, the duties and other regulations of commerce maintained in each of the constituent territories and applicable at the formation of such free-trade area or the adoption of such interim agreement to the trade of contracting parties not included in such area or not parties to such agreement shall not be higher or more restrictive than the corresponding duties and other regulations of commerce existing in the same constituent territories prior to the formation of the free-trade area, or interim agreement, as the case may be; and
   (c) any interim agreement referred to in sub-paragraphs (a) and (b) shall include a plan and schedule for the formation of such a customs union or of such a free-trade area within a reasonable length of time.

6. If, in fulfilling the requirements of sub-paragraph 5(a), a contracting party proposes to increase any rate of duty inconsistently with the provisions of Article II, the procedure set forth in Article XXVIII shall apply. In providing for compensatory adjustment, due account shall be taken of the compensation already afforded by the reductions brought about in the corresponding duty of the other constituents of the union.

7. (a) Any contracting party deciding to enter into a customs union or free-trade area, or an interim agreement leading to the formation of such a union or area, shall promptly notify the CONTRACTING PARTIES and shall make available to them such information regarding the proposed union or area as will enable them to make such reports and recommendations to contracting parties as they may deem appropriate.
   (b) If, after having studied the plan and schedule included in an interim agreement referred to in

paragraph 5 in consultation with the parties to that agreement and taking due account of the information made available in accordance with the provisions of sub-paragraph (a), the CONTRACTING PARTIES find that such agreement is not likely to result in the formation of a customs union or of a free-trade area within the period contemplated by the parties to the agreement or that such period is not a reasonable one, the CONTRACTING PARTIES shall make recommendations to the parties to the agreement. The parties shall not maintain or put into force, as the case may be, such agreement if they are not prepared to modify it in accordance with these recommendations.

(c) Any substantial change in the plan or schedule referred to in paragraph 5(c) shall be communicated to the CONTRACTING PARTIES, which may request the contracting parties concerned to consult with them if the change seems likely to jeopardize or delay unduly the formation of the customs union or of the free-trade area.

8. For the purposes of this Agreement:

(a) A customs union shall be understood to mean the substitution of a single customs territory for two or more customs territories, so that

(i) duties and other restrictive regulations of commerce (except, where necessary, those permitted under Articles XI, XII, XIII, XIV, XV and XX) are eliminated with respect to substantially all the trade between the constituent territories of the union or at least with respect to substantially all the trade in products originating in such territories, and,

(ii) subject to the provisions of paragraph 9, substantially the same duties and other regulations of commerce are applied by each of the members of the union to the trade territories not included in the union.

(b) A free-trade area shall be understood to mean a group of two or more customs territories in which the duties and other restrictive regulations of commerce (except, where necessary, those permitted under Articles XI, XII, XIII, XIV, XV and XX) are eliminated on substantially all the trade between the constituent territories in products originating in such territories.

9. The preferences referred to in paragraph 2 of Article I shall not be affected by the formation of a customs union or of a free-trade area but may be eliminated or adjusted by means of negotiations with contracting parties affected. This procedure of negotiations with affected contracting parties shall, in particular, apply to the elimination of preferences required to conform with the provisions of paragraph 8(a)(i) and paragraph 8(b).

10. The CONTRACTING PARTIES may by a two-thirds majority approve proposals which do not fully comply with the requirements of paragraphs 5 to 9 inclusive, provided that such proposals lead to the formation of a customs union or a free-trade area in the sense of this Article.

11. Taking into account the exceptional circumstances arising out of the establishment of India and Pakistan as independent States and recognizing the fact that they have long constituted an economic unit, the contracting parties agree that the provisions of this Agreement shall not prevent the two countries from entering into special arrangements with respect to the trade between them, pending the establishment of their mutual trade relations on a definitive basis.

12. Each contracting party shall take such reasonable measures as may be available to it to ensure observance of the provisions of this Agreement by the regional and local governments and authorities within its territory.

Part I

EU history, institutions, legal dimension and basic statistics

2 A history of European integration and evolution of the EU

3 EU institutions

4 The legal dimension in EU integration

5 The basic statistics

The aim of this part of the book is to provide the reader with a general background to the EU. Chapter 2 gives a short account of the history of European integration and development of the EU. Chapter 3 provides a mere description of the EU institutions and their functioning. Chapter 4 explores the legal dimension in EU integration. Chapter 5 offers a general statistical survey of the major economic indicators for the present twenty-seven member nations of the EU as well as for those involved in the imminent enlargement and, to enable comparison, also for the rest of those in the group of eight (G8): Canada, Japan, the Russian Federation and the United States.

2 A history of European integration and evolution of the EU

ALI EL-AGRAA

This book contains a full and detailed coverage of all the significant facets of the EU as well as the international contexts and constraints within which they operate, with specific chapters devoted to each. There is therefore a need for a chapter providing an overall perspective of the EU. Also, a proper appreciation of why the EU has been created and how it has evolved would not be possible without an understanding of the history of European unity. This is because in a world presently dominated by immediate considerations, recently bordering on the purely economic, the driving force behind European integration is often forgotten, and attempts to reform existing policies and to steer the EU in new directions seem to be frustrated. Thus the overall perspective must not only include this wider historical dimension, but history must also colour the entirety of its exposition. This chapter is therefore devoted to these considerations and comes in two main sections. The first provides a very brief history of European unity; brief since otherwise this book would become too long and those interested in a detailed and comprehensive coverage can always consult the voluminous literature on the subject, including, inter alia, Haas (1958), Palmer and Lambert (1968), Lipgens (1982) and, for modern aspects, Wallace (1990) and Gillingham (2003). The second offers a bird's-eye view of the evolution of the EU.

2.1 A short history of European unity

Most, if not all, actual steps taken to achieve economic and political unity in Europe originated after 1945. However, the idea of European unity is deeply rooted in European thinking. History shows that there have been a number of proposals and arrangements designed to create it. In the fourteenth century, the idea of a united Christendom inspired Pierre Dubois to propose a *European Confederation* to be ruled by a *European Council* of wise, expert and faithful men. In the seventeenth century, the duc de Sully desired to keep peace in Europe by means of a *European army*. In 1693, William Penn, the English Quaker, then the eponymous governor of Pennsylvania, wanted the creation of *An Imperial Dyet, Parliament or State of Europe* in his *Essay towards the Present and Future Peace of Europe*. In the nineteenth century, Pierre-Joseph Proudhon was strongly in favour of the formation of a *European Federation* and predicted that the twentieth century would witness an era of federations, forecasting disaster in the absence of such a development.

Immediately after the First World War, politicians began to give serious consideration to the concept of European unity. For example, in 1923 Count Coudenhove Kalergi, the Austrian founder-leader of the *Pan-European Movement*, called for the formation of a *United States of Europe*, his reason being the successful assertion of Swiss unity in 1848, the forging of the German Empire in 1871 and, most significantly, the independence of the United States in 1776. And on 5 September 1929, in a renowned speech, delivered to the *League of Nations Assembly* in Geneva, the French Foreign Minister, Aristide Briand, with the backing of his German counterpart, Gustav Stresemann, proposed the creation of a *European Union* within the framework of the League of Nations, and reiterated this later, when Prime Minister, by declaring that part of his political manifesto was the building of a *United States of Europe*.

The main reason for the pursuit of European unity was the achievement of lasting peace in

Europe. It was realized that there was no other means of putting an end to the continent's woeful history of conflict, bloodshed, suffering and destruction. However, economic reasons were also a contributing factor. These were influenced by the tradition of free trade and Adam Smith's argument, in his *An Inquiry into the Nature and Causes of the Wealth of Nations* (1776), that 'the division of labour is limited by the extent of the market', which the German philosopher Friedrich Naumann utilized to propose in 1915 that European nation states were no longer large enough to compete on their own in world markets; therefore, they had to unite in order to guarantee their survival.

Despite the fact that there was no shortage of plans for creating a united Europe, it was not until 1945 that a combination of new forces and an intensification of old ones prompted action. First, Europe had been at the centre of yet another devastating war, caused by the ambitions of nation states. Those who sought and some of those who still seek a united Europe have always had at the forefront of their minds the desire to prevent any further outbreak of war in Europe. It was believed that if the nations of Europe could be brought closer together, such war would become unthinkable. Second, the Second World War left Europe economically exhausted, and this led to the view that if Europe were to recover, it would require a concerted effort on the part of the European states. Third, the Second World War also soon revealed that for a long time Western Europe would have to face not only a powerful and politically alien USSR, but also a group of European nations firmly fixed within the Eastern European bloc. It was felt that an exhausted and divided Europe (since the war embraced co-belligerents) presented both a power vacuum and a temptation to the USSR to fill it. Fourth, the ending of the war soon revealed that the wartime allies were in fact divided, with the two major powers, the USA and USSR, confronting each other in a bid for world supremacy. Hence, it should come as no surprise to learn that members of the *European Movement*, who wanted to get away from intergovernmental cooperation by creating institutions leading to a *Federal Europe*, felt the need for a third

world force: 'the voice of Europe'. This force would represent the Western European viewpoint and could also act as a bridge between the Eastern and Western extremities.

2.1.1 Concrete unity efforts

The first concrete move for regional integration in Europe was made in 1947 with the establishment of the *Economic Commission for Europe* (ECE), which was set up in Geneva as a regional organization of the United Nations (UN). Its objective was to initiate and participate in concerted measures aimed at securing the economic restructuring of the *whole* of Europe. A year later, the *Brussels Treaty Organization* (BTO) was founded by the UK, France, Belgium, the Netherlands and Luxembourg. In recognition of the newer threat of the USSR, it was designed to create a system of mutual assistance in times of attack on Europe, but it simultaneously perpetuated the wartime alliance against Germany. The BTO took an Atlantic form in 1949 when the five nations, together with the USA and Canada as well as Denmark, Iceland, Italy (significantly, since it had been an Axis power), Norway and Portugal founded the *North Atlantic Treaty Organization* (NATO). The aim of NATO was, and continues to be, to provide military defence against attack on any of its members. Greece and Turkey joined NATO in 1952, West Germany became a member in 1955, and Spain was added in 1982, after the disappearance of General Franco from the political scene. After the collapse of communism in Eastern Europe, the Czech Republic, Hungary and Poland joined in 1997 and Bulgaria, Estonia, Latvia, Lithuania, Romania, Slovakia and Slovenia in 2004 to give NATO twenty-six members, and, vitally, NATO and Russia signed the *Act on Mutual Relations, Cooperation and Security*.

Also, in 1948 the *Organization for European Economic Cooperation* (OEEC) was formed and was followed a year later by the *Council of Europe*. These marked the beginning of the division of Western Europe into two camps, with, on the one hand, the UK and some of the countries that later formed the *European Free Trade Association* (EFTA), and, on the other, Belgium, France, West Germany, Italy, Luxembourg and the Netherlands, usually referred to as the Original Six (hereafter, simply the Six) who subsequently established the *European Economic Community* (EEC). The main reason for this division was that the UK was less committed to Europe as the main policy area than the Six. This was because, until the second half of the 1950s, the UK was still a world power which had been on the victorious side and a major participant in some of the fateful geo-political decision-making at the time, and it still had the Empire to dispose of. Therefore, British policy was bound to incorporate this wider dimension: relations with Europe had to compete with Empire (later, Commonwealth) ties and with the *special relationship* with the USA. In addition, the idea of a politically united Europe (as we have seen, in some quarters this meant a United States of Europe) was strongly held by the other countries, particularly by France and Benelux: Belgium, the Netherlands and Luxembourg agreed in 1944 to form a customs union (for a technical definition, see chapter 1, section 1.1), which did not become effective until 1948. But, despite the encouraging noises made by Winston Churchill, the British Prime Minister, both during the Second World War and after, this was not a concept that thrilled British hearts (see Young, 1998, for an excellent exposition of the British attitude towards European unification).

The different thinking between the UK and the Six about the political nature of European institutions was revealed in the discussions leading up to the establishment of the OEEC and the Council of Europe. The Second World War had left Europe devastated. The year 1947 was particularly bleak: bad harvests in the previous summer led to rising food prices; the severe winter of 1946–7 led to a fuel crisis; the continental countries were producing very little, and what was produced tended to be retained rather than exported, while imports were booming, hence foreign exchange reserves were running out. It was at this junction that the USA entered the scene to present the *Marshall Plan*. General George Marshall proposed that the USA make aid available to help the European economy find its feet and that European governments 'should get together' to decide how much assistance was needed. In short, the USA did not feel it appropriate that it should unilaterally

decide on the programme necessary to achieve this result. Although it seemed possible that this aid programme could be elaborated within the ECE framework, the USSR felt otherwise. Soviet reluctance was no doubt due to the fear that if its satellites participated, this would open the door to Western influence. Therefore, a conference was convened without the USSR, and the *Committee for European Economic Cooperation* (CEEC) was established.

The attitude of the USA was that the CEEC should not just provide it with a list of needs. The USA perceived that the aid it was to give should be linked with progress towards European unification. This is an extremely important point since it shows that right from the very beginning, the *European Movement* enjoyed the encouragement and support of the USA. Of course, the driving force behind the USA's insistence on European unity was its desire to establish a solid defence against any western advance by the USSR, i.e. the US did not insist on unity for unity's sake. Indeed, the USA also asked that its multinational companies should have free access to European markets. The CEEC led in turn to the creation of an aid agency: the OEEC. Here, the conflict between the UK and the Six, especially France, came to a head over the issue of *supranationalism*. France in particular (and it was supported by the USA) wanted to introduce a supranational element into the new organization. But what is supranationalism? It can mean a situation in which international administrative institutions exercise power over, for example, the economies of the member states; or in which ministerial bodies, when taking decisions (to be implemented by international organizations), work on a majority voting system rather than insisting on unanimity.

The French view was not shared by the British since they favoured a body which would be under the control of a ministerial council in which decisions should be taken on a unanimity basis. The French, on the other hand, preferred an arrangement in which an international secretariat would be presided over by a secretary-general who would be empowered to take policy initiatives on major issues. Significantly, the organization which emerged was substantially in line with the British wish for unanimity rule. This was undoubtedly a reflection of the UK's relatively powerful position in the world at the time and her close alliance with the USA.

In the light of subsequent events, it is also interesting to note that the USA encouraged the European nations to consider the creation of a customs union. Although this was of considerable interest to some continental countries, it did not appeal to the UK. In the end the OEEC convention merely recorded the intention to continue the study of this proposal. For a variety of reasons, one of which was the opposition of the UK, the matter was not pursued further.

The creation of the Council of Europe, with broad political and cultural objectives, including the notable contribution of protecting the individual through the *Convention for the Protection of Human Rights and Fundamental Freedoms* (its statute expresses a belief in a common political heritage based on accepted spiritual and moral values, political liberty, the rule of law and the maintenance of democratic forms of government), also highlighted the fundamental differences in approach between the countries which later founded the EEC, on the one hand, and the British and Scandinavians, on the other. The establishment of the Council of Europe was preceded by the *Congress of Europe* at The Hague in May 1948. This was a grand rally of 'Europeans' which was attended by leading European statesmen, including Winston Churchill. The Congress adopted a resolution which called for the giving up of some national sovereignty before the accomplishment of economic and political union in Europe. Subsequently, a proposal was put forward, with the support of the Belgian and French governments, calling for the creation of a *European Parliamentary Assembly* in which resolutions would be passed by majority vote. A *Committee of Ministers* was to prepare and implement these resolutions.

Needless to add, the UK was opposed to this form of supranationalism and in the end the British view largely prevailed. The Committee of Ministers, which was the executive organ of the Council of Europe, alone had power of decision and generally these were taken on the unanimity principle. The *Consultative Assembly* which came into existence was a forum (its critics called it a debating society), not a European legislative body. In short, the British and Scandinavian *functionalists* – those who believed that European unity, in so far as it was to be achieved, was to be attained by *intergovernmental cooperation* – triumphed over the *federalists* – those who sought unity by the radical method of creating European institutions to which national governments would surrender some of their sovereignty. The final disillusionment of the federalists was almost certainly marked by the resignation of Paul-Henri Spaak (see below, p. 30), a devoted European federalist, from the presidency of the Consultative Assembly in 1951.

The next step in the economic and political unification of Western Europe was taken without the British and Scandinavians. It was the creation in 1951 of the *European Coal and Steel Community* (ECSC) by the Six, and marked the parting of ways in post-war Western Europe. The immediate factor in these developments was the revival of the West German economy. The passage of time, the efforts of the German people and the aid made available by the USA through the Marshall Plan all contributed to this recovery. Indeed, the West German *economic miracle* was about to unfold.

It was recognized that the German economy would have to be allowed to regain its position in the world, and that the Allied control of coal and steel under the *International Ruhr Authority* could not last indefinitely. The fundamental question was how the German economy in the sectors of iron, coal and steel, which were the basic materials of any war effort, could be allowed to regain its former powerful position without endangering the future peace of Europe. The answer was a French plan, elaborated by Jean Monnet, a French businessman turned adviser (see box for his true place in European unity), but put forward by Robert Schuman, French Minister of Foreign Affairs, in May 1950. The *Schuman Plan* was essentially political in character. It was brilliant since it sought to end the historic rivalry of France and Germany by making a war between the two

Jean Monnet has a strong claim to be called the Father of Europe. Monnet deserves almost single-handed credit for creating in 1951 the first of Europe's epochal institutions for integration, the European Coal and Steel Community (ECSC) . . . As president from 1954 to 1975 of the Action Committee for the United States of Europe, a lobby for the integration cause, Monnet would be an inexhaustible front of unification and federation initiatives . . . the Frenchman's great achievements belong to the years immediately after World War II – when Europe was still recovering; the United States was supreme; power was held in relatively few hands; socialist, quasi-socialist, state corporatist, and organized capitalist systems were in vogue; and planning was de rigueur. They could not have taken place in any other setting.

Jean Monnet thought of himself as an institution builder and has often been so regarded by posterity, but his greatest gift . . . was in devising and circulating important ideas and putting words into action. He created, and to a considerable extent still shapes, the rhetoric of integration. To highlight this fact is not to denigrate Monnet's accomplishments but to underscore the inability of any other politician, technocrat, social scientist, or sloganeer to come up with comparable formulations: the big ideas that move the minds of men; concepts that can be organized, marshalled, and made to move in orderly fashion; terms that capture the realities that otherwise elude definition; and words that morph into policies, programs, and institutions when nurtured in bureaucratic hothouses. Monnet's idiomatic language has taken on a life of its own and captured the minds of many. Key analytical concepts – the big words used even today to describe the integration process in textbooks, in political discourse, and in public relations campaigns – are Monnet's words: terms that he and his associates coined or that other students of his work invented to give meaning to what he was doing. *Supernationalism*, *sectoral integration*, and *functionalism* are perhaps the most important examples of such interpretive concepts that still shape academic and professional research. Countless other terms have entered legal, administrative, and economic vocabularies, and out of them has oozed modern Eurospeak. The apparent inescapability of this linguistic legacy makes Monnet an avatar of integration, albeit less owing to his powers as a pure thinker than to his uncanny knack – in an age of science and technology, mass production, and instant communication – to harness the powerful and fertile minds of others to his goals and policies. One might well call him a modern prophet.

Jean Monnet was pre-eminently a man of his times, one whose unsurpassed knack for getting things done derived from experience gathered over a long and extraordinary career. Monnet was driven by a stirring and powerful *idée fixe*: that the economic modernization and very political survival of both France as a nation and Europe as a civilization depended upon the creation of a federal union. Monnet was a go-getter and a deal maker *extraordinaire*, a man educated not so much formally or academically as on the job and in war management. As a remarkably young senior administrator responsible for France's overseas supply during the Great War, he soon understood the meaning of global interdependence and learned how to use the power of the state to strengthen the national economy. While serving in Washington in the unusual capacity of a French citizen on the British Lend-Lease mission during World War II, Monnet concluded from the miracle of American armaments production that the future would belong economically to the big battalions. Massive state intervention, huge markets, and central control were the order of the day.

Jean Monnet had plenty of additional experience. He had been deputy director of economic affairs for the League of Nations. He had made (and lost) a fortune between the wars as a financier and roving policy entrepreneur operating internationally in the realms of central banking, public finance, and project development. He had connections with powerful friends and policy makers on Wall Street, along the Potomac, and throughout Europe who would prove invaluable after 1945. Monnet's contacts, knowledge, indefatigability, and practicality opened doors to the movers and shakers of his age.

But such political savvy would have counted for little without his intense commitment to European union. His determination to unite the continent deeply impressed the many brilliant and strong-willed individuals whose energies he channelled into the task of 'building Europe'. To them, quite simply, he was *l'Inspirateur* – The Inspiration (Gillingham, 2003, pp. 16–18).

nations not only unthinkable but also materially impossible. This was to be achieved in a manner which ultimately would have the result of bringing about that European federation which is indispensable to peace. The answer was not to nationalize or indeed to internationalize the ownership of the means of production in coal, iron and steel, but to create, by the removal of customs duties, import quota restrictions and similar impediments on trade and factors of production – a common market (for a technical definition, see chapter 1, section 1.1) in these products. Every participating nation in such a common market would have equal access to the products of these industries wherever they might be located, and, to reinforce this, discrimination on the grounds of nationality was to be forbidden.

The plan had a number of attractive features. First, it provided an excellent basis for solving the 'Saar problem': the handing back of the Saar region to West Germany was more likely to be acceptable to the French if Germany was firmly locked in such a coal and steel community. Second, the plan was extremely attractive to Germany since membership of the community was a passport to international respectability; it was the best way of speeding up the end of occupation and avoiding the imposition of dampers on the expansion of the German economy. Third, the plan was also attractive to the federalists who had found the OEEC fell far short of their aspirations for the Council of Europe (its unanimity rule and that no powers could be delegated to an independent commission or *Commissariat* were extremely frustrating for them), and, in any case, the prospects for the OEEC were not very good since by 1952 the four-year period of the Marshall Plan would be over, and the UK attitude was that thereafter the OEEC budget should be cut and some of its functions passed over to NATO.

As it turned out, the ECSC was much more to the federalists' taste since its executive body, the

High Authority, was given substantial direct powers which could be exercised without the prior approval of the *Council of Ministers* (the ECSC's second institution; it also had a *Parliamentary Assembly* and a *Court of Justice*).

The plan received favourable responses from the Six. The UK was invited to join but refused. Clement Attlee, British Prime Minister at the time, told the House of Commons: 'We on this side [of the House] are not prepared to accept that the most vital economic forces of this country should be handed over to an authority that is utterly undemocratic and is responsible to nobody.' However, the Six were not to be deterred, and in April 1951 the *Treaty of Paris*, valid for fifty years, was signed. The ECSC was born and it embarked on an experiment in limited economic integration, albeit a sectoral one, on 1 January 1952.

The next stage in the development of European unity was also concerned with Germany. When the Korean War broke out in 1950, the US, faced with the need to reduce its forces in Europe for deployment in Korea, put pressure on the Western European nations to do more to defend themselves against possible attack by the USSR. This raised the issue of a military contribution from West Germany, the implication being that Germany should be rearmed. However, this proposal was opposed by France, which was equally against Germany becoming a member of NATO. This was not a purely negative attitude. Indeed, René Pleven, French Prime Minister at the time, put forward a plan which envisaged that there would be no German army as such, but that there would be a *European army* to which each participating nation, including Germany, could contribute.

Britain was not against this idea but did not herself wish to be involved. The Six were positively enthusiastic and discussion began in 1951 with a view to creating a *European Defence Community* (EDC). It was envisaged that there would be a *Joint*

Defence Commission, a *Council of Ministers*, a *Parliamentary Assembly* and a *Court of Justice*. In other words, the institutions of the EDC were to parallel those created for the ECSC. The Six made rapid progress in the negotiations and the *EDC Treaty* was signed in May 1952.

Having gone so far, there were a number of reasons for further integrative efforts. First, the pooling of both defensive (NATO) and offensive capabilities (EDC) inevitably reduced the possibility of independent foreign policies. It was logical to follow integration in defence with measures which served to achieve political integration as well. Second, it was also desirable to establish a system whereby effective control could be exercised over the proposed European army. Third, there was also the Dutch desire that progress in the military field should be paralleled by more integration in the economic sphere as well. Therefore, the foreign ministers of the Six asked the ECSC Assembly, together with co-opted members from the Consultative Assembly of the Council of Europe, to study the possibilities of creating a *European Political Authority*.

In 1953, a draft of a *European Political Community* (EPC) was produced in which it was proposed that, after a period of transition, the political institutions of the ECSC and the proposed EDC be subsumed within a new framework. There would then be a *European Executive* responsible to a *European Parliament* (which would consist of a *People's Chamber* elected by direct universal suffrage, and a *Senate* elected by national parliaments), a *Council of Ministers* and a *European Court* to replace the parallel bodies created under the ECSC and EDC treaties.

This was a watershed in the history of the European movement. The Six had already successfully experimented in limited economic integration in the fields of iron, coal and steel; they had now signed a treaty to integrate defence; and they were about to proceed further by creating a community for the purposes of securing political unity. Moreover, the draft treaty proposed pushing economic integration still further by calling for the establishment of a general common market based on the free movement of commodities and factors of production.

However, on this occasion the success that had attended the Six in the case of iron, coal and steel was not to be repeated. Five national parliaments approved the EDC treaty, but successive French governments felt unable to guarantee success in asking the *French Assembly* to ratify. Finally, the Mendès-France government attempted to water down the treaty but failed to persuade the other five nations. The treaty as it stood was therefore submitted to the French Assembly, which refused to consider it, and in so doing killed the EPC too.

There were a number of reasons for the refusal of the French Assembly to consider the treaty. First, there was opposition to the supranational elements which it contained. Second, the French 'left' refused to consider the possibility of the rearmament of Germany. Third, the French 'right' refused to have the French army placed under foreign control. Fourth, British aloofness was also a contributing factor: one of the arguments employed by those who were opposed to the treaty was that France, fearing German domination, could not participate in the formation of a European army with Germany if the UK was not a member.

It is perhaps worth noting that the failure of the EDC was followed by a British initiative also aimed at dealing with the problem of rearming Germany in a way acceptable to the French. A series of agreements was reached in 1954 between the USA, the UK, Canada and the Six under which the BTO was modified and extended: Germany and Italy were brought in and a new intergovernmental organization was formed – the *Western European Union* (WEU). These agreements also related to the termination of the occupation of Germany and its admission into NATO. As a counterbalance to the German army, the UK agreed to maintain specified forces on the continent. In short, the gist of the agreements was to provide a European framework within which Germany could be rearmed and become a member of NATO, while also providing for British participation to relieve French fears that there would be no possible German predominance. It should be pointed out that the response of Eastern Europe to these agreements was a further hardening of the East/West division in the shape of the formation of the *Warsaw Pact* by the USSR and its Eastern European satellites.

2.1.2 Unity via the back door

The year 1954 was a bad year for European unity since those advocating the creation of supranational bodies had suffered a reverse and the establishment of the WEU, an organization cast more in the traditional intergovernmental mould, had thereafter held the centre of the stage. However, such was the strength of the European Movement that by 1955 new ideas were being put forward. The relaunching initiative came from the Benelux countries. They produced a memorandum calling for the establishment of a general common market and for specific action in the fields of energy and transport.

The basic idea behind the Benelux approach was that political unity in Europe was likely to prove difficult to achieve. It was the ultimate objective but it was one which could be realized in the longer run. In the short and medium terms the goal should be overall economic integration. Experience gained in working together would then pave the way for the achievement of political unity, i.e. *political unity should be introduced through the 'back door'*. The memorandum called for the creation of institutions which would enable the establishment of a *European Economic Community* (EEC).

These ideas were considered at the meeting of the Foreign Ministers of the Six at Messina, Italy, in June 1955. They met with a favourable response. The governments of the Six resolved that work should begin with a view to establishing a general common market and an atomic energy pool. Moreover, a committee should be formed which would not merely study the problems involved but should also prepare the texts of the treaties necessary in order to carry out the agreed objectives. An inter-governmental committee was therefore created and, significantly enough, Paul-Henri Spaak (see above, p. 26), by then Foreign Minister of Belgium, was made its president: what a triumph for members of the European Movement.

The Messina resolution recorded that since the UK was a member of the WEU and had been linked with the ECSC, through an *Agreement of Association* in 1954, it should be invited to participate in the work of the committee. The position of the other OEEC countries was not so clear. In fact, the question of whether they should be allowed to participate was left for a later decision by the Foreign Ministers of the Six.

The *Spaak Committee* held its first meeting in July 1955. British representatives were present, and then and subsequently played an active role in the committee's deliberations. However, as the discussions continued, differences between the Six and the UK became evident. The UK was in favour of a free trade area (for a technical definition, see chapter 1, section 1.1) arrangement, while the Six were agreed upon the formation of a customs union: the Messina resolution had explicitly called for this type of arrangement. Moreover, the UK felt that only a little extra machinery was needed to put the new arrangement into effect; the OEEC, perhaps somewhat strengthened, would suffice. This view was bound to anger the federalists who put emphasis on the creation of supranational institutions which should help achieve more than just economic integration. These differences culminated in the withdrawal of the UK representatives from the discussions in November 1955 (for a detailed exposition, see Young, 1998).

Meanwhile, the Spaak Committee forged ahead, although not without internal differences. For example, the French had apprehensions about the transition period allowed for the dismantling of the intra-member tariffs, escape clauses, the harmonization of social charges and the level of the common external tariffs (CETs); they wanted high CETs while the Benelux nations desired low ones.

The Spaak Committee reported in April 1956 and its conclusions were considered by the Foreign Ministers of the Six in Venice, Italy, in May of the same year. However, the attitudes amongst the Six were not uniform. On the one hand, the French naturally liked the idea of an atomic energy community, given that France was the only country of the Six to have atomic energy then, but were not keen on the proposition for a general common market, while, on the other, the remaining five had reverse preferences. Nevertheless, in the end the Six agreed that the drafting of two treaties, one to create a general common market and another to establish an atomic energy community, should begin. Treaties were subsequently signed in Rome on 25 March 1957. These were duly ratified by the national parliaments of the Six. The *EEC* and *Euratom* came into being on 1 January 1958. Thus, in 1958 the Six belonged to three separate entities: the ECSC, EEC and Euratom.

But what are the aims set out in these treaties? The overall guiding light is the achievement of an 'ever closer union' of Europe. The aims of the EEC are stated in Article 3 of its treaty and can be summarized as:

(a) The establishment of free trade between the member nations such that *all* impediments on intra-union trade are eliminated. The impediments included tariffs, import quota restrictions and export subsidies as well as all measures which had an equivalent or similar effect (now generally referred to as *non-tariff trade barriers* – NTBs). Moreover, that treaty called for the creation of genuine free trade and therefore specified rudiments of common competition and industrial policies.

(b) The creation of an intra-EEC free market for all factors of production by providing the necessary prerequisites for ensuring factor mobility. These included taxes on, and subsidies to, capital, labour and enterprise.

(c) The formation of common policies with regard to particular industries which the members deemed necessary to single out for special treatment: namely, agriculture (hence the *Common Agricultural Policy* – CAP) and transport (hence the *Common Transport Policy* – CTP).

(d) The application of procedures by which the economic policies of the member nations could be coordinated and disequilibria in their balances of payments remedied.

(e) The creation of a *European Social Fund* (ESF) to improve the possibilities of employment for workers and to contribute to the raising of their standard of living.

(f) The establishment of a *European Investment Bank* (EIB) to facilitate the economic expansion of the EEC by opening up fresh resources.

(g) The establishment of a common commercial policy vis-à-vis the outside world, i.e. the creation and management of the CETs, the adoption of a common stance in multinational and multilateral trade negotiations, the granting of a *Generalized System of Preferences* (GSP) treatment to imports of certain manufactured and semi-manufactured products coming from the least developed countries (LDCs) and the reaching of trade pacts with associated nations.

It should be noted that a period of transition of twelve years, divided into three four-year stages, was granted for the elimination of intra-EEC trade barriers and for the establishment of the CETs.

Euratom asked for (h) a common approach to atomic energy, although at the time only France had such capabilities. We have already seen that the ECSC created (i) a common market for, and equitable access to, iron, coal and steel. Thus the totality of all these aims (a–i) depicted the aspirations of the Six at the time.

2.2 The evolution of the EU

2.2.1 The EC

Each one of the three EC entities had its own institutions. These centred on a *Council of Ministers* (Council, hereafter) and a *Commission* (*High Authority* in the case of the ECSC, see above), backed by a *European Parliament* (*Assembly* in the case of the ECSC) and a *Court of Justice*. Although there were some differences of legal competences, it later became convenient to consider the three entities as branches of the same whole and, in this, the EEC became the dominant partner. When the *Merger Treaty* was passed in 1965, it seemed more logical to refer to the whole structure as the European Communities (EC), or European Community, whose main constitutional base was the Treaty of Rome creating the EEC.

By the 1970s, however, it was clear that the EC needed institutional strengthening. Having completed the early tasks laid down in the treaties (see chapter 27), further internal objectives had to be formulated and a way found to ensure that the EC could act more effectively on the international stage. The result was to bring national political leaders more closely into EC affairs by the introduction of summit meetings. These were formalized under the name of the *European Council* in 1974, but the first summit was held in 1969 (the end of the transition period), in The Hague, when the member states agreed that they were then so interdependent that they had no choice but to continue with the EC. That decision provided the necessary political will to reach agreement on the development of the CAP (see chapter 20), on budgetary changes (see chapter 19), on embarking on *economic and monetary union* (EMU, to be achieved in three stages, beginning in 1970 and completed in 1980 – see the Werner Report (CEC, 1970a) – and chapter 10) and, most importantly, on the need to work on enlargement. At that time, this meant settling the teasing question of relations with the UK, which, as we have seen, had vexed the EC from the very beginning.

Moreover, it was recognized that the EC needed institutional development to match its growing international stature. Its existing international responsibilities neither matched its economic weight nor allowed effective consideration of the political dimensions of its external economic relations. Individual members still conducted most of their external affairs themselves and could easily cut across EC interests, and this was apart from the issue of whether the EC should begin to move into the field of wider foreign affairs. Since the member states had very different interests, and often conflicting views on relations with the USA, with the USSR and on defence, it was clear that the EC was not ready to take over full competences. However, the Foreign Ministers were asked to study the means of achieving further political integration, on the assumption of enlargement, and to present a report. Consequently, the EC began, gingerly, to move into political cooperation with an emphasis on foreign affairs. This did not result in a common foreign policy, but it did mean

that efforts were to be exerted to identify common aims and it led to further institutional innovation alongside the institutions of the EC rather than as part of them, although the new and the old gradually came together.

A second landmark summit was held in 1972 (in Paris) and was attended by the three countries set to join in 1973: Denmark, Ireland and the UK. It devoted considerable attention to internal affairs and notably to the need to strengthen the social and regional aims of the EC as part of an ambitious programme designed to lead to EMU, thus to a full 'European Union'. It also saw a continuous need to act externally to maintain a constructive dialogue with the USA, Canada and Japan and for member states to make a concerted contribution to the *Conference on Security and Cooperation in Europe* (CSCE, which began in Helsinki, Finland, in July 1973 and issued its Final Act, or *Helsinki Accord*, in 1975, comprising the USSR and thirty-five European nations), which led to a 1990 Paris Charter on peaceful relations in Europe. Foreign Ministers were to meet more frequently to discuss this last issue. This meeting marked the realization that the heads of governments would have to meet more frequently than in the past. At first sight this seemed to strengthen the intergovernmental structure of the EC at the expense of the supranational element, but this was not really the case. Rather it showed that the future was a joint one, that the international climate was changing and often bleak, and that if the members dealt with their internal economic difficulties alone this could undermine the efforts of the EC to strengthen its economies. Informal discussion of general issues, whether economic or political, domestic or worldwide, was a necessary preliminary to action which often seemed stronger if it were to be EC-based. Through the summit meetings and the *Political Cooperation Procedure* (ECP) the subject matter coming to the EC steadily enlarged.

Indeed, 1969–72 can be described as a period of great activity. Apart from what has just been mentioned, in 1970 the Six reached a common position on the development of a *Common Fisheries Policy* (CFP, see chapter 21), although total agreement was not to be achieved until 1982. Also, at another Paris summit in 1973, agreement was reached on the development of new policies in relation to industry and science and research (see chapter 13). Moreover, the summit envisaged a more active role for the EC in the area of regional policy (see chapter 22) and decided that a *European Regional Development Fund* (ERDF) should be created to channel EC resources into the development of the backward EC regions; the UK demanded such a fund during the accession negotiations, expecting to get most of it since it was the only country to have a 'regional policy', but that proved otherwise (see chapters 19 and 22). Furthermore, later in the 1970s, the relationship between the EC and its ex-colonies was significantly reshaped in the form of the *Lomé Convention*, which became the EU-ACP agreements when the Caribbean and Pacific ex-colonies were later added (see chapter 25).

It was obvious from all these developments that the EC needed financial resources not only to pay for the day-to-day running of the EC but also to feed the various funds that were established: the ESF, ERDF and, most important of all, the *European Guidance and Guarantee Fund* (EAGGF; see chapter 20) to finance the CAP. In 1970, the EC took the important step of agreeing to introduce a system that would provide the EC, and specifically the EC general budget, with its 'own resources' (see chapter 19), thus relieving it of the uncertainty of annual decisions on national contributions for its finances as well as endorsing its political autonomy in this respect. Another step of great importance was the decision that the European Parliament (EP, discussed in chapter 3) should be elected directly by the people, not by national parliaments. In addition, the EC decided to grant the EP certain powers over the EC general budget, which proved to be a very significant development (chapter 19). Finally, but by no means least, was the development of the political cooperation mechanism. It is important not to forget that the dedicated members of the European movement had always hoped that the habit of cooperation in the economic field would spill over into the political arena, one aspect of which is foreign policy matters.

By the 1980s, it was clear that the political and economic environment in which the EC operated was changing fast. Tumultuous events in the former USSR and the countries of the *Warsaw Pact* threw the institutional arrangements of Western Europe into disarray and brought the need to reassess defence requirements, the role of NATO and the continuance of the US defence presence. The unresolved issue of whether the EC needed a foreign policy, or at least some halfway house towards one, was bound to be raised once more. Meanwhile, the economic base upon which the EC had been able to develop became much more uncertain. Recession, industrial change, higher unemployment, slower growth and worries about European competitiveness undermined previous confidence (see chapters 5, 12, 13 and 23).

The twin issues of constitutional development and institutional reform continued to exercise EC circles but little progress was possible and the EC seemed to be running out of steam. The deepening of the integrative process required action which governments found controversial, the new members – now including Greece (1981), Spain (1986) and Portugal (1986) – inevitably made for a less coherent group, while the recession hardened national attitudes towards the necessary compromise required for cooperative solutions. EC finances were constrained (the EC budget amounted to less that 1 per cent of EC GDP; see chapter 19) such that new policies could not be developed, and this in turn led to bitter arguments about the resources devoted to the CAP (which exhausted more than 75 per cent of the EC budget) and its inequitable impact, especially on the UK. Internal divisions were compounded by fears of a lack of dynamism in the EC economy, threatening a relative decline in world terms. Such worries suggested that a significant leap forward was required to ensure a real common market, to encourage new growth and at the same time to modernize EC institutions.

2.2.2 The single European market

As the debate progressed, a major division emerged between those who were primarily interested in the political ideal of political union and who wished to develop the EC institutions accordingly and those, more pragmatic in approach, who stressed the need for new policies. It was not until 1985 that the lines of agreement could be settled. These were brought together in the *Single European Act* (SEA) which became operative on 1 July 1987.

The SEA contained policy development which was based upon the intention of creating a true single market (usually referred to as the single European market – SEM – and '*internal market*', see chapter 8) by the end of 1992 (hence the popular term *EC92*), with free movement of goods, services, capital and labour (the so-called '*four freedoms*') rather than the patchy arrangements of the past. The SEA also introduced, or strengthened, other policy fields. These included: responsibilities towards the environment; the encouragement of further action to promote health and safety at work; the promotion of technological research and development (R&D); work to strengthen economic and social cohesion so that weaker member nations could participate fully in the freer market; and cooperation in economic and monetary policy. In addition, the SEA brought foreign policy cooperation within its purview and provided it with a more effective support than it had in the past, including its own secretariat, housed in the Council building in Brussels. Institutionally, it was agreed that the Council would take decisions on a qualified majority vote (QMV, see chapter 3) in relation to the internal market, research, cohesion and improved working conditions, and that in such cases the EP should share in decision-making (see chapter 3). These developments were followed later by agreement regarding the control of expenditure on the CAP, which, as we have seen, had been a source of heated argument for a number of years and, most importantly, a fundamental change in the EC general budget.

The single market provided a goal for the next few years and the EC became preoccupied with the necessary preparations (300 directives – see chapter 3 – had to be passed and then incorporated into national law for this purpose), giving evidence of its ability to work together as one unit. However, it also brought new complications. It raised the question of how much power should be held by the EC institutions, presented member

states with heavy internal programmes to complete the changes necessary for the single market, and exposed the very different economic conditions in member states which were bound to affect their fortunes in the single market. Meanwhile, the unification of Germany in 1990 fundamentally changed its position within the EC by giving it more political and economic weight, but at the same time it was required to expend considerable effort eastwards.

A further challenge at the time came from new bids for membership (so far there has been one withdrawal: the position of Greenland was renegotiated in 1984, but it remains associated and has a special agreement to regulate mutual fishing interests). The single market finally convinced the doubters in Western Europe that they should try to join. This was both a triumph and an embarrassment for the EC in that it was preoccupied with its own internal changes and a belief that it had not yet fully come to terms with the southern enlargement which had brought in Greece, Portugal and Spain. The reaction was mixed in that some member states wished to press on with enlargement as a priority, while others wished to complete the single market and tighten internal policies before opening the doors. A closer economic relationship was negotiated between the EC and the EFTA countries, except for Switzerland, to form the *European Economic Area* (EEA), on 2 May 1992, which was widely assumed to be a preliminary step towards membership since it extended all the privileges of the EC except in agriculture to these countries, but, understandably, without giving them voting rights. Austria, Finland, Sweden and Switzerland all formally applied between 1989 and 1992 and Norway followed them shortly afterwards; Switzerland's application remains on the table, which is odd, given its snub of the EEA. Hungary, Poland and Czechoslovakia signed association agreements and hoped that they might join in a few years' time. Turkey and Morocco applied in 1987, although the former application was laid aside and the latter rejected. Cyprus and Malta applied in 1990. Later, most states in Central and Eastern Europe expressed their desire to join and formal negotiations were opened in 1998 with those most likely to succeed: Cyprus, the Czech Republic, Estonia, Hungary, Poland and Slovenia. However, the instability in the Balkans and the war in Kosovo showed the need to hasten the process and, at Helsinki in December 1999, it was agreed to open accession talks with Bulgaria, Latvia, Lithuania, Malta, Romania and Slovakia. Moreover, after thirty-six years of temporizing, it was also agreed at the same summit that Turkey should be a recognized candidate, but negotiations were then not expected to start for a very long time, since the EU wanted to see big improvements in Turkey's political and human rights behaviour, including the rights of Kurds and other minorities and the constitutional role of the army in political life, which might require changes in her constitution (these are known as the *Copenhagen criteria*, introduced in June 1993 at the Copenhagen summit; see below). Therefore, there was then an active list of the thirteen candidates, which included Turkey, and a change in regime brought Croatia closer to joining this group (for the latest on this, see the section below on the Copenhagen 2002 summit).

It did not seem easy to generalize about the issues involved in admitting such a variety of countries for membership, but the brief history shows that integration was always meant to apply to all of Europe, although it would require a stretch of the imagination to claim that Turkey was in Europe. However, the EC already had a series of agreements with the applicants through which it provided aid and advice on development and reform; these are set out in *Agenda 2000* (CEC, 1997b) and are discussed in detail in chapters 19, 22 and 26. In particular, the EC was looking for economic reform, the development of democratic political institutions and the protection of minority and human rights as necessary preconditions for closer relationships before full membership (the Copenhagen criteria). Partnership and cooperation agreements with Russia and the newly independent states also existed, but these countries did not aspire to join.

Clearly, an organization with such a large and varied membership would be very different from the original EEC of the Six, and the application challenged received wisdom as to its nature. This

is one reason why pursuing the question of enlargement was made consequent upon the finalizing of the Maastricht Treaty (see below) and agreement upon new financial and budgetary arrangements for the existing member states (see chapter 19). Continuing issues about defence and the appropriate reaction to conditions in Central and Eastern Europe, the Gulf War and the collapse of Yugoslavia all suggested further considerations of foreign and defence capabilities were important.

2.2.3 The Treaty on European Union

It was therefore against a troubled background that the EC set up two *Inter-governmental Conferences* (IGCs; see chapter 3) to prepare the way for a meeting of the European Council in Maastricht in December 1991 which produced a new blueprint for the future. It aimed to integrate the EC further through setting out a timetable for full EMU, introducing institutional changes and developing political competences, the whole being brought together in the *Treaty on European Union* (popularly known as the Maastricht Treaty) in which the EC should form a part of a wider European Union. Since this treaty was later added to and adapted as the 1997 *Amsterdam Treaty*, we shall discuss its details in the next section.

It is not surprising that the Maastricht Treaty's ratification process, for which some have argued not a great deal of time was allowed, produced furious argument across Western Europe after Denmark, the first to begin the ratification process, rejected it in a referendum on 2 May 1992. Although each nation had its own peculiar worries, a general characteristic which the treaty made obvious was the width of the gap between political elites and the voters in modern society. Even though political leaders rapidly expressed contrition that they had failed to provide adequate explanations for their moves, they seemed less able to accept that there were strong doubts about many of the proposed new arrangements as being the best way forward, and that a period of calm reflection, with less frenetic development, might in the end serve the EC and its people better.

2.2.4 The Amsterdam Treaty

Maastricht left contentious problems for the Amsterdam conference to tackle. Although the hard core, comprising changes to the voting system in the Council and the size of the Commission, was not tackled (but the 2000 *Nice Treaty* does so – see below), the 1997 Amsterdam Treaty was useful in updating aims and policies, in clarifying the position regarding foreign and defence policies and justice and home affairs, and in strengthening the social side. The treaty itself modified the existing treaties, notably those on the EEC and the Union, and these, together with the *acquis communitaire* (legislation deriving from the treaties), can be considered as the constitution of the EU (see below). Supplementary treaties must be used when developments go beyond the existing ones. Past examples include changes in budget procedures, agreements to admit new members and the single market (see above). In addition, a unique arrangement was attached to the Maastricht Treaty in 1991: an agreement and a protocol were annexed because the UK could not accept changes in the social field endorsed by the other members. The EC, i.e. EEC, ECSC and Euratom, forms the most developed section (or, in current jargon, one of the three pillars of the EU, the other two being 'foreign and defence policies' and 'justice and home affairs') of the Union and its legislation takes precedence over national decisions in the appropriate field. A moment's reflection will show that this is a necessary precondition for the EC to work at all; it would otherwise be impossible to create a single economic unit, to establish the confidence needed between members or to handle external relations.

The Amsterdam Treaty gives the EU a more coherent structure and a modern statement of its aims and policies, and brings some necessary improvements in the working of the institutions. Naturally, it highlights the new aspects, but these are not necessarily more important than more long-standing policies: for example, publicity is given to provisions on foreign and defence policy, yet they remain far less developed than arrangements in the economic sphere. Despite being thought of as a tidying up of the Maastricht loose ends, the treaty is a substantial document, but naturally greatly overlaps with Maastricht. Thus it has three parts on substantive amendments to previous treaties, their simplification and modernization and their renumbering, ratification procedures and official language versions. In addition, there are an annexe, thirteen protocols, often dealing with very difficult issues, fifty-one declarations and eight declarations by individual member states.

The post-Amsterdam EU has broad objectives, but again these naturally overlap with those in the Maastricht Treaty. The classic aim, set out long ago, is to lay the foundations of, and subsequently develop, the 'ever closer union'. It promotes economic and social progress, an aim which includes the abolition of internal frontiers, better economic and social cohesion to assist the less-developed members to catch up with the EU average (facilitated by the creation in 1993 of a *Cohesion Fund*), and an EMU, complete with a single currency (see chapter 10). It wishes to assert an international identity through a common security and defence policy and new provisions designed to enhance this, and to draw closer to the WEU (see above), which has been dormant since it was launched in 1954, by turning it into the equivalent an EU defence force. Thus for the first time the EU is set to have a common defence policy with the implication that the WEU will eventually be responsible for implementing decisions of an inevitable political union. Appreciation for (or is it accommodation of?) NATO was reiterated by stating that the revival of the WEU is to be linked to NATO, thus ensuring a continued alliance with the USA and Canada for the defence of Europe. It has not only introduced a formal Union citizenship, but also taken steps to strengthen the commitment to democracy and individual rights, to promote equality and to combat discrimination. It has a procedure to be followed should a member state appear to breach human rights. The treaty has also established the EU as an area of free movement, security and justice and is attempting to establish clearer and more uniform rules in these fields. These goals should be complemented by those in the EEC treaty (see last part of section 2.1.2). Internally, the EU has general economic objectives relating to the single market (chapter 8), agriculture (chapter 20) and transport (chapter 15), the aim of economic and social cohesion and a new emphasis on policy-making in employment (chapters 5, 10, 11 and 23), social (chapter 23) and environmental matters (chapter 17). The need for enhanced competitiveness for EU industry (chapters 12 and 13), the promotion of R&D, the construction of trans-European infrastructure, the attainment of a high level of health protection, better education, training and cultural development all find their place (chapters 12, 13 and 23). Recognition is given to development policies (chapter 25), consumer protection (chapter 23) and to measures in energy policy (chapter 16) and tourism. There are, of course, a host of subsidiary and supporting objectives.

After many arguments, the concept of flexible integration has been brought out into the open. Articles 40, 43 and 44 (EU) allow some member states to establish closer cooperation between themselves with the aim of developing EU policies which not all members wish to pursue, subject to veto by dissenting members. This was fully endorsed in the 2000 Nice Treaty by stating that groups of eight or more member countries may pursue greater integration in certain areas. Such a move must be supported by a majority of members, must not harm the interests of others and must allow the non-participating members to be involved in the discussion of developments, but without voting on them. There are some important examples of policies which are less than fully inclusive, amongst them membership of the single currency, the Danish opt-outs from the free movement provisions (although Denmark accepts the *Schengen Principle* dictating them) and from decisions with defence implications, and the British and Irish non-acceptance of the abolition of border controls.

The Maastricht conference touched fears of the creation of a super state. In an attempt to counter this, the *subsidiarity principle* was agreed during the Edinburgh summit in December 1992 and the Amsterdam Treaty tried to clarify it further. Article 5 (EC) explains that, where the EU does not have exclusive competence, it may proceed only if the member states cannot pursue the action

themselves, or it is an objective better achieved by EU action. A protocol attached to the treaty has tried to clarify how this concept should be applied and, in particular, insists that the reasons for action must be stated, EU action must be simple and limited and a report given to EU institutions on what has been done. These provisions are meant as a check on an insidious growth of EU power, allowing it to slip in a direction which has never been agreed. This brake is supported by the right of member states to bring a case in the Court of Justice arguing that the EU is extending its powers unjustifiably.

One element in the debate about subsidiarity is doubt concerning the remoteness of decision-making in Brussels. There is a need to make the EU more responsive to the needs of the general public and more sensitive to the effects of the intrusiveness that EU legislation appears to bring. The 'democratic deficit' is an issue that has long been discussed and there are several ways of addressing it, of which greater powers to the EP is one (see the section below on the constitutional convention and chapter 3). Individuals have long had the right to petition the EP and this has been supported by the appointment of an *ombudsman*, chosen by the EP but independent of it.

One particular issue is the undermining of national parliaments, especially those that have an important legislative function and that have found it hard to find ways of exercising control over the EU. In practice, they have been limited to scrutiny of proposals which, once they are at an advanced stage, are very difficult to change. Some efforts have also been made, through scrutiny committees, to discuss general issues, thus helping to suggest policy positions for the future, while Denmark, in particular, has tried to define the parameters within which ministers may negotiate. A protocol of the Amsterdam Treaty tries to increase the influence of national parliaments. It requires that all Commission consultation papers be forwarded promptly, that proposed legislation should be made available in time for parliaments to consider it and that there should be a six-week gap between a legislative proposal being submitted to the EP and the date it is sent to the Council (see chapter 3). Of course, it is to a great extent up to national parliaments to keep abreast of events and to improve contacts with the EP. Associated with this was the general acceptance of the need to keep the public better informed and to provide access to EU documentation. A declaration attached to the treaty stresses the importance of transparency, access to documents and the fight against fraud, Article 255 (EC) giving citizens a right to access official documents. A further declaration accepts the importance of improving the quality of drafting in legislation. Over the years, efforts have been made, too, to help individuals question the EU. The right to petition the EP was buttressed by the establishment of the ombudsman (see above). A further change, directly affecting individuals, was to confer the citizenship of the EU on the nationals of member states. Although such changes are intended to encourage a greater openness in decision-making, their implementation will take time. Actual decision-making in the Council remains private.

Flexible policies and subsidiarity have been tackled together, although they deal with very different circumstances, because they both suggest that the EU is still uneasily balanced between the two opposing views on how to organize (Western) Europe which have been so eloquently expressed since the end of the Second World War. To some observers the Amsterdam Treaty is one more step towards a federal Europe, but to others it is a means of keeping a check upon this drive and retaining a degree of national governmental control. The final outcome remains uncertain.

2.2.5 Nice Treaty

Hammered out over four bitter days and nights on the French Riviera, the Nice Treaty of 11 December 2000 is both complex and insubstantial; one of its authors even called it 'lousy'. The treaty's main concern is with EU enlargement, especially with the institutional changes that would be needed to accommodate twelve to fifteen new members (see above). Since its provisions will not make sense until we have discussed the EU institutions, they will be dealt with in chapter 3. Here it suffices to state that the treaty both amends QMV and extends it to new areas, including trade in ser-

vices; asks the larger member nations to drop their second commissioner after 2005; limits the total number of commissioners to twenty after 2007; and proclaims the Charter of Rights, but without legal force.

One should add that the ratification of the treaty followed almost the same path as Maastricht's. The Irish, whose constitution demands a referendum on such issues, were the first to kick off the process and shocked everyone by rejecting it on 7 June 2001 by 54 per cent to 46 per cent. Although technically that meant the death of the treaty, the other member nations stubbornly went ahead with ratification, leading to a dramatic situation in 2002 when all but Ireland had ratified. However, in a second referendum on 20 October 2002, Ireland recorded an emphatic 'yes' (by 62.9 per cent against 37.1 per cent). This then set the tone for the Copenhagen summit of 12–13 December 2002 when it was agreed that: (a united) Cyprus, the Czech Republic, Estonia, Hungary, Latvia, Lithuania, Malta, Poland, the Slovak Republic and Slovenia could join the EU on 1 May 2004; Bulgaria and Romania could join in 2007, provided they met the necessary criteria, which they have done; and Turkey could open accession negotiations immediately after the December 2004 summit pending a favourable report by the Commission on its status on the Copenhagen criteria. Indeed, the ten countries signed accession treaties with the EU on 16 April 2003 at the Athens summit, ratified their accession treaties, nine through popular referendums, with Cyprus not needing one (see table 2.1 for details on the outcome of the referendums, a table which may seem unnecessary, but it indicates with more authority than any opinion polls the overwhelming support for membership), and became members on 1 January 2004, but, alas, not a united Cyprus. And in the Brussels 16/17 December 2004 summit, in the light of a positive report from the Commission, Turkey was given the go-ahead to start negotiations on 3 October 2005, which are expected to take ten years. It should be added, however, that the decision to grant Turkey the right to negotiate EU membership has since proved controversial: France has decided that it

Table 2.1 Results of the referendums on EU membership

Country	Date	Turnout (%)	Yes (%)	No (%)
Malta	8 March 2003	91.00	53.6	46.4
Slovenia	23 March 2003	99.97	89.61	10.39
Hungary	12 April 2003	99.44	83.76	16.24
Lithuania	10–11 May 2003	63.37	89.95	8.82
Slovakia	16–17 May 2003	52.15	92.46	6.20
Poland	7–8 June 2003	58.85	77.45	22.55
Czech Republic	13–14 June 2003	55.21	77.33	22.67
Estonia	14 September 2003	64.06	66.83	33.17
Latvia	20 September 2003	72.53	67.00	32.30

will hold a referendum on Turkey's membership and many have attributed France's referendum rejection of the Constitution to this issue; the present German Chancellor Angela Merkel is not keen on full membership, preferring a 'privileged partnership'; and there are many who are not happy with Turkey's claims to being 'European' in terms of both geography and character. Also, in June 2005, the 'Thessaloniki agenda' was reaffirmed, allowing the assessment of progress towards EU membership of the western Balkan countries: Albania, Bosnia and Herzegovina, Croatia, the former Yugoslav Republic of Macedonia and Serbia and Montenegro, including Kosovo. Finally, on 26 September 2006 the Commission offered a positive report on the progress made by Bulgaria and Romania, which led to endorsement by the member nations; they joined on 1 January 2007.

2.2.6 A Constitution for the EU?

It is vital to add that at the Nice summit meetings it was decided to 'engage in a broader and more detailed analysis of the future of the EU, with a view to making it more democratic, more transparent and more efficient'. The ensuing debate culminated at the 2001 Laeken summit when, on 12 December, it was decided to create a

convention for this purpose. On 28 February 2002, the *Convention for the Future of Europe* was set up under the chairmanship of ex-French President Valéry Giscard d'Estaing, with ex-Italian Prime Minister Giuliano Amato and ex-Belgian Prime Minister Jean-Luc Dehaene as vice-chairpersons, to discuss the matter further and then report to an IGC in mid-2003. The convention had 105 delegates, representing EU governments, parliaments and institutions, and was set two tasks:

(a) to propose a set of arrangements to enable the EU to work when it has twenty-five to thirty member nations; and

(b) to express the purpose of the EU, so that the citizens whom it is meant to serve will understand its relevance to their lives and, with luck, feel some enthusiasm for its activities.

Surprisingly, the Convention issued a draft constitution for the EU on 6 February 2003, with the contents being mainly about the consolidation of the various EU treaties, but they included proposals for the reform of existing EU institutions and on the future of the EU. A changed final draft was adopted on 20 June 2003 at the Thessaloniki summit, but although the December summit failed to endorse it, the Brussels June 2004 intergovernmental Conference did; hence it was set to become the EU Constitution if and when it was ratified by all the member nations. However, during the early months of 2005, both France (on 29 May) and the Netherlands (on 1 June) rejected it in national referendums (by, respectively, 55/45 per cent and 62/38 per cent); therefore it is technically dead. However, as we have just witnessed in the cases of the Maastricht and Nice Treaties, this cannot be taken as a foregone conclusion. Indeed, eighteen member nations, including Bulgaria and Romania, representing two-thirds of the twenty-seven member nations and 56.12 per cent of the EU population, have gone ahead and ratified the Constitution (see table 2.2). Moreover, on 26 January 2007, the Foreign Ministers of twenty[1] so-called 'friends of the Constitution' declared in Madrid that far from slashing the original treaty to make it more palatable to voters, it should be more ambitious, giving the EU a bigger role in social policy, fighting climate change and

Table 2.2 The state of play on the Constitutional Treaty

	Procedure	Ratification date
Austria	Parliamentary	25 May 2005
Belgium	Parliamentary	8 February 2006
Bulgaria	Parliamentary	With ratification of Accession Treaty on 21 December 2006
Cyprus	Parliamentary	30 June 2005
Czech Rep.	Referendum	Expected during 2007
Denmark	Binding referendum	Referendum postponed
Estonia	Parliamentary	9 May 2006
Finland	Parliamentary	5 December 2006
France	Referendum	Rejected on 29 May 2005
Germany	Parliamentary	27 May 2005
Greece	Parliamentary	19 April 2005
Hungary	Parliamentary	20 December 2004
Ireland	Parliamentary + binding referendum	Referendum postponed
Italy	Parliamentary	7 May 2005
Latvia	Parliamentary	2 June 2005
Lithuania	Parliamentary	2 June 2005
Luxembourg	Parliamentary + consultative referendum	25 October 2005
Malta	Parliamentary	6 July 2005
Netherlands	Parliamentary + consultative referendum	Rejected in referendum on 1 June 2005
Poland	Not yet decided	Not yet decided
Portugal	Referendum	Not yet decided
Romania	Parliamentary	With ratification of Accession Treaty on 20 December 2006
Slovakia	Parliamentary	11 May 2005
Slovenia	Parliamentary	1 February 2005
Spain	Parliamentary + consultative referendum	18 May 2005
Sweden	Parliamentary	Not yet decided
UK	Parliamentary + consultative referendum	Not yet decided

immigration, which attracted the new headline 'Use the pen not the scissors'. I shall therefore return for further consideration of the future of the EU in the final chapter (28). However, because at this stage its future has to be considered uncertain, it would not be justifiable here to offer more than a mere skeleton of the agreed Constitution:

(a) It sets out a single simplified EU treaty.
(b) It creates a post of president of the EU Council, serving up to five years instead of six-monthly rotation.
(c) It creates a post of EU Foreign Minister, who will head a newly created EU diplomatic service.

(d) It gives greater scope for defence cooperation among member states, including procurement.
(e) It gives new powers to the EP over legislation and the annual EU budget.
(f) It enables national parliaments to ensure EU law does not encroach on member states' rights.
(g) It abolishes the national veto in some areas, including immigration and asylum policy.
(h) It retains the national veto in tax, defence and foreign policy, and over financing the EU budget.
(i) It introduces a new 'double majority' voting system for the EU Council of Ministers, requiring at least fifteen member nations to make a

decision, comprising 65 per cent of the EU population.

(j) It introduces a mechanism for those member nations wishing to leave the EU.

(k) It increases the power of the 'eurogroup' (the countries that have adopted the euro) to decide own policies.

(l) It incorporates an EU Charter of Fundamental Rights, including the right to strike, with legal provision limiting its application in national courts.

(m) It reduces the size of the EU Commission starting in 2014, with commissioners sent from only two-thirds of member states on a rotation basis.

(n) It raises the minimum number of seats in the EP for small member states from four to six, and sets out a limit of ninety-six for the big members.

Since a number of these points concern institutional changes, it makes more sense to discuss them in chapter 3.

2.3 Conclusion

The adherents to the original ideal of European unity would stress that, from what has been stated in this chapter, one cannot escape the conclusion that although the EU has not yet reached the finishing line, it has gone a long way towards achieving the dream of its founding fathers: the creation of a United States of Europe. They would add that the long march is easily explicable in terms of the difficulties inherent in securing the necessary compromises needed for going forward while accommodating new members, and the tackling of unforeseen economic and political problems, from both within and without. They would concede that it would, of course, require a big leap from the present 'union' to a full state of Europe, but would insist that it did not really matter when, or even if, the EU realized that dream, especially when there are more ways than one of achieving a federation and some members do not share it, since what is important is that one should never forget that this vision has been the guiding light without which disaster might have struck at any time, and it remains so at least for France and Germany (see chapter 28). They would also add that it behoves all those who would like to think of the EU as, or dearly want to reduce it to, a mere trading bloc to think twice. However, several member nations – most definitely the UK, and some would claim many EU citizens (they have never been asked the question directly and straightforwardly) – do not share this view. They would insist that the EU has more or less reached the pinnacle of what they have aspired for it, and would add that even though the creation of a powerful united European economy with most of its members using the same currency is a historic achievement, nothing further should ensue, certainly not political unity.

I shall leave it there since my own position, if it is not yet apparent, should not matter; it is what you believe in the light of the facts and your own deep reflection as well as your personal vision that really matters. I shall, however, return to this issue in the final chapter on the future of European integration (chapter 28).

NOTE

1 The missing seven were the Foreign Ministers of the Czech Republic, Denmark, France, the Netherlands, Poland, Sweden and the UK.

3 EU institutions

ALI EL-AGRAA

The EU has a unique institutional structure, which is not surprising, given that it is neither a federal state nor a purely intergovernmental cooperative venture – vital facts often forgotten by critics comparing EU institutions to their equivalents in single states. EU member nations delegate sovereignty in specific areas to independent institutions, entrusting them with defending the interests of the EU as a whole as well as of both its member states and citizens. The *European Commission* (Commission, hereafter) upholds the interests of the whole EU. The *Council of the European Union* (Council, hereafter) upholds those of the governments of the member nations through their ministerial representatives. And the *European Parliament* (EP) upholds those of the EU citizens, who directly elect its members.

The Commission, Council and EP, known as the 'institutional triangle', are flanked by the *European Court of Justice* (ECJ) and the *Court of Auditors*, as well as by five other bodies: the *European Central Bank* (ECB), the *European Investment Bank* (EIB), the *European Economic and Social Committee* (EESC), the *Committee of the Regions* (CoR), and the *European Ombudsman*. Furthermore, there is the *European Data Protection Supervisor*, as well as nineteen agencies (four more are being prepared), created by specific legislation, for taking care of specialized concerns, which are basically of a technical, scientific or managerial nature.

This chapter provides a basic coverage of these institutions, but does so more adequately for the institutional triangle. This is due not only to the fact that the Commission, Council and EP between them initiate and finalize most new EU legislation, and thus constitute the core of the EU legislative process, but also because the others are dealt with in some detail in the chapters

where they are most relevant: for example, the ECB operations are fully covered in chapter 11, the EESC's in chapter 23, the EIB's in chapters 13 and 22 and the Ombudsman's in chapter 23. Moreover, due to the obvious nature of the European Data Protection Supervisor, it suffices to state here that the call for this goes back to Article 286 of the EC treaty, but it was the Council/EP regulation 45/2001 (of 18 December 2000) which enacted the protection of individuals with regard to the processing of personal data by the EU institutions and bodies and on the free circulation of such data, and that the appointment of the first five-year term supervisor, who has a deputy, was made in 2004, following a public call for candidates; the office has fifteen authorized permanent posts.

Before explaining these institutions, one should recall from chapter 2 that the EU also has the *European Council*, which is a summit meeting of heads of state or government and generally meets twice a year. As mentioned in that chapter, although the European Council was afforded official recognition in 1974 and given a formal status in the Maastricht Treaty, summit meetings were introduced during 1957–69, with the first formal one being held in 1969 in The Hague at the end of the twelve-year transition period for the EEC. No more needs to be mentioned on this since it is not an institution, except to add that it simply offers general guidelines and blueprints, providing impetus for the development and political guidance of the EU as a whole, which the Commission then studies carefully before it lodges a proposal for legislation with the Council and EP – see below. One should also add that occasionally special summit meetings are held under the title of *Intergovernmental Conferences* (IGCs), called to order for specific issues of major importance which require changes in existing treaties or the adoption of new ones.

3.1 The Commission

The EU treaties assign the Commission a wide range of tasks, but these can be narrowed down to four major roles. The Commission initiates EU policy by proposing new legislation to the Council and EP. It serves as the executive arm of the EU by administering and implementing EU policies. Jointly, with the ECJ, it acts as the guardian of the EU treaties by enforcing EU law. And it acts as the EU spokesperson and negotiator of international agreements, especially in relation to trade and cooperation, such as the Lomé Convention, which links the EU with seventy-eight African, Caribbean and Pacific nations (EU–ACP; see chapter 25). It may prove helpful to elaborate somewhat on some of these roles.

As the initiator of EU policies, the Commission formulates proposals in areas defined by the treaties. These areas cover a wide spectrum and particularly relate to agriculture, development cooperation, energy, the environment, industry, regional development, social policy, trade relations and transport. Due to the 'subsidiarity principle' (chapter 2), such proposals should be confined to those where action at the EU level would be more productive than at the national, regional or local level. However, once the Commission has lodged a proposal with the Council and EP, the three institutions collaborate together to ensure an agreed outcome for it. Note that the Council generally reaches its decision by qualified majority voting (QMV, see section 3.2), needing unanimity only when it rejects a proposal. Also, the Commission carefully scrutinizes amendments by the EP (section 3.3) before offering, where deemed appropriate, an amended proposal.

As the EU Executive, the Commission is involved in all the areas in which the EU is concerned. However, the role it plays assumes particular significance in certain fields. These include: 'competition policy', where it monitors cartels and mergers and disposes of or monitors discriminatory state aid (section 3.4 and chapter 12); agriculture, where it drafts regulations (chapter 20); and technical R&D, where it promotes and coordinates through EU framework programmes (chapter 13). The Commission is also entrusted with the management of the EU general budget, and for this purpose it is supervised by the Court of Auditors, whose annual reports are relied upon by the EP for granting the Commission the go-ahead for their implementation of the budget (chapter 19).

As the joint guardian of the EU treaties, the Commission has to see to it that EU legislation is properly implemented in the member nations. In doing so, it is hoped that it can maintain a climate of mutual confidence so that all concerned, be they the member nations, economic operators or private citizens, can carry out their obligations to the full. If any member state is in breach of EU legislation, say by failing to apply a EU directive (section 3.2.1), the Commission, as an impartial authority, should investigate, issue an objective ruling and notify the government concerned, subject to review by the ECJ, of the action needed to rectify such infringement of EU obligations. If the matter cannot be dealt with through the infringement procedure, the Commission then has to refer it to the ECJ, whose decision is binding. Likewise, with the supervision of the ECJ, the Commission monitors companies for their respect of EU competition rules.

Until 2004, the Commission consisted of twenty members, one of whom was the president and two were vice-presidents. Two commissioners came from each of the then five large member nations and one from each of the remaining ten, i.e. the number of commissioners was determined, very roughly, by population size (see table 5.1). However, the Nice Treaty required that the larger member nations should drop their second commissioner after 2005 and that the total number of commissioners should be limited to twenty after 2007, when the EU was expected to comprise at least twenty-seven members, but that a decision should not be reached until then. That decision has not yet been made, hence the present Commission, which assumed office on 22 November 2004, three weeks after intended (see

Table 3.1 The Commissions

Commission of	Period	Commission of	Period
Walter Hallstein I	1958–62	Jacques Delors I	1985–9
Walter Hallstein II	1962–7	Jacques Delors II	1989–93
Jean Rey	1967–70	Jacques Delors III	1993–5
Franco Maria Malfatti and	1970–2	Jacques Santer	1995–9
Sicco Mansholt	1972–3		
François-Xavier Ortoli	1973–7	Romano Prodi	1999–2004
Roy Jenkins	1977–81	José Manuel Barroso	2004–
Gaston Thorn	1981–5		

below), consists of twenty-seven members, one from each of the then twenty-five EU nations plus one for each from Bulgaria and Romania.

All commissioners are appointed for five years (four until 1994) and have renewable terms. They are chosen for their *competence and capacity to act independently in the interest of the EU itself*, not of their own nations. They have all been prominent politicians in their own countries, often having held ministerial positions: the incumbent President, José Manuel Barroso, who was not the first choice, was recruited while still Prime Minister of Portugal; his immediate predecessor, Romano Prodi, was Prime Minister of Italy during 1996–8 and has been again since May 2006; before him, Jacques Santer was Prime Minister of Luxembourg during 1984–95; and the noted Jacques Delors was the French Minister of Economy and Finance in 1981 (table 3.1 gives the full list of Commissions). That is because they need to be familiar with the political scene and able to meet senior politicians on equal terms, for without this stature and ability to understand political pressures they would lose the senses of touch and timing which are essential for effective functioning. Indeed, two of them have been so assertive that they have been accused of exceeding their duties: Hallstein for trying to give more

powers to the Commission to build it into a government for Europe, and Delors for attempting to impose his French socialist approach on the rest of the member nations (Gillingham 2003). One has to recall, however, that Hallstein was following in the footsteps of Monnet and the Benelux drive for bringing about the political unity of Europe through the back door at a time when seeking the support of the European populace for a 'united states of Europe' was out of the question: who in his/her right mind would have attempted to seek the endorsement of the average person when the war devastation was so fresh in people's minds? As to Delors, his record speaks for itself, but it is conceived that his misguided obsession with a 'socialist' Europe was shared by many EU organizations and citizens at the time.

The commissioners' appointment process begins within six months of the elections to the EP. This is to allow time for the necessary procedure taken by the EP to approve the Commission. This procedure commences with the appointment of the President, who is nominated by the member states and has to be approved by the EP. Once confirmed, the President, with the collaboration of the governments of the member states, nominates the remaining commissioners, twenty-four in the last case. The EP then gives its opinion on the entire college of twenty-five through an approval process – the EP has the power to dismiss the entire Commission, not individual commissioners (see below). Once the college is approved by the EP, the new Commission assumes its official responsibilities in the following January.

It is pertinent to add here that, following the exposure of ineptness and laxity of some parts of the Commission (box 3.1), the EP has taken the question of approval even more seriously and has subjected nominees to detailed scrutiny, including their suitability for their intended posts (box 3.2), the allocation of which is the prerogative of the President. Indeed, the EP succeeded in doing precisely that when Barroso nominated Rocco Buttiglione of Italy for the justice portfolio, which includes anti-discrimination policy, when Buttiglione had stated that homosexuality was a sin and women should stay at home and raise children (box 3.2).

Box 3.1 The need to reform the Commission

There have been many complaints regarding the functioning of the Commission, often resulting in the publication of reports recommending drastic change, but to no avail in terms of implementation. The Santer Commission (1995–9), however, initiated two such programmes: (i) 'Sound and Efficient Management'; and (ii) 'Modernization of Administration and Personnel Policy'. Among other things, the first was concerned with the improvement of financial management, together with the introduction of more effective planning and control. Simplifying internal procedures and reducing administrative costs were the objectives of the second. Neither was successful. Indeed, the Santer Commission suffered the unique humiliation of having to resign nine months prematurely in March 1999. The resignation had been instigated by the EP following a report by a Committee of Independent Experts which condemned the Commission and its President for not assuming responsibility for financial irregularities and other acts of misconduct within their services. Serious allegations were also made against Commissioner Édith Cresson of France regarding the appointment of her former dentist for a research job within the Commission. Cresson's stubborn refusal to resign and the belief of several commissioners that resignation was necessary, if only to clear their names, left Santer with no alternative but to announce the resignation of the entire Commission, even though the EP had not censured it, but the Santer Commission stayed in a caretaker capacity. When the Prodi Commission took over, Commissioner Neil Kinnock galvanized several initiatives started in the dying days of the Santer Commission.

Box 3.2 The EP forces a vital decision

After two days of arguing with members of the EP (MEPs) over his nomination of Rocco Buttiglione – a Catholic Italian conservative who believes that homosexuality is a sin and that women should stay at home to raise children – as Justice Commissioner, Barroso had to back down. One hour before the EP was to vote, he told MEPs that if the vote were to go ahead, on 27 October 2004, the outcome would 'not be positive'. Then, to loud cheers and clapping, he added that under 'these circumstances I have decided not to submit a new commission for your approval today'. He went on to say 'I need more time to look at this issue and to consult with the Council [of European leaders] and consult further with you, so we can have strong support for the new Commission. It is better to have more time to get it right.' Then, displaying some of the diplomatic skills for which he was chosen (he was not the first choice) to lead the new Commission, he uttered: 'Ladies and gentlemen, these last days have demonstrated that the European Union is an intensely political construction and that this Parliament, elected by popular vote across all of our member states, has indeed a vital role to play in the governance of Europe.' The crisis came to an end when the Italian Prime Minister, Silvio Berlusconi, did the unusual thing of replacing Buttiglione by Franco Frattini.

It has also been made clear that the commissioners must work under the political guidance of the President (Article 219 EC) while the present commissioners have had to agree to resign if asked to do so by the President. The procedures have enhanced the EP's powers considerably, since it can satisfy itself about the Commission's programme and intended initiatives before giving its approval.

While these moves are intended to ensure a more efficient Commission, the episode has brought a latent contradiction to the surface. The Commission was designed as the powerhouse of political momentum for the EU. Although, as we have seen, this function is to some extent now shared with the European Council and the EP, it has been less effective in administrative and managerial functions where its weaknesses have been exposed. This has led some critics to argue that reform should include a shift of responsibility

Table 3.2 EU Directorates General and services

Policies	External relations
Agriculture and rural development	Development
Competition	Enlargement
Economic and financial affairs	EuropeAid – Cooperation Office
Education and culture	External Relations
Employment, social affairs and equal opportunities	Human Aid Office – ECHO
Enterprise and industry	Trade
Environment	
Fisheries and marine affairs	**General services**
Health and consumer protection	Communication
Information society and media	Europe Anti-Fraud Office
Internal market and services	Eurostat
Joint research centre	Publications Office
Justice, freedom and security	Secretarial General
Regional policy	
Research	**Internal services**
Taxation and customs union	Budget
Transport and energy	Bureau of European Policy Advisers
	Informatics
	Infrastructures and Logistics – Brussels
	Infrastructures and Logistics – Luxembourg
	Internal Audit Service
	Interpretation
	Legal Service
	Personnel and Administration
	Translation

away from policy towards execution so that the Commission becomes more like a national civil service.

Each commissioner is responsible for a portfolio, which in many cases is a mixture of policy areas and administrative responsibilities, generally referred to as *Directorates General* (DGs). However, since there are thirty-six DGs (table 3.2), some commissioners have more than one portfolio. That does not mean that they are busier since the workload for each DG depends on its relative weight within the EU. The DGs used to be numbered in roman style (e.g. DG I, DG II), but the numbers have now been dropped, so table 3.2 gives the latest designations.

A *director general* is in charge of a DG; under him/her is a *director*, followed by *head of division*. Each commissioner has a private office or *cabinet*, the staff of which is selected by the commissioner and has traditionally come from the same member nation, for ease of communication (but

see next paragraph). When the commissioner is away, the head of his/her private office, the *chef de cabinet*, will act on his/her behalf at the weekly meetings, held on Wednesdays in Brussels, but in Strasbourg during the plenary sessions of the EP.

One should add that, over time, some directorates have acquired greater prestige than others; not surprisingly, those that deal with core EU policies are most prominent, and as the EU has developed so the possibility for conflict between directorates over policy matters has arisen. Agricultural, competition and regional and external trade policies, especially imports from the LDCs, are obvious examples. A new development brought in with the 1999 Commission is to have a senior commissioner responsible for an oversight of external affairs whether of an economic or political nature. The reform of the Commission has therefore begun. The personal cabinets of the commissioners are being opened to wider recruitment so that they are less obviously national enclaves attached to a particular commissioner; reform of financial controls and stronger management systems are being put into place and merit is to account for more, and nationality less, for promotion to senior posts. Personnel are to receive more training and be subject to tighter controls. These reforms are the remit of Neil Kinnock, an energetic Vice-President, who is trying to lift the Commission to modern standards of public administration, but, as expected, he has been meeting with strong resistance, as union control of internal staff matters has traditionally been very tight.

Once the Commission has reached a decision on a matter presented by the commissioner concerned, the decision becomes an integral part of its policy and will have the unconditional backing of the entire college even if simple majority voting led to its adoption. In a sense, the Commission follows the British practice of 'collective responsibility', i.e. it acts as a collegiate body accepting responsibility as a group, but in practice policy rests mainly with the responsible commissioner, perhaps in association with two or more colleagues.

In carrying out its responsibilities, the Commission seeks the opinions of national parliaments, administrations, and professional and trade union organizations. For the technical details of its legislative provisions or proposals, it consults the experts meeting in the committees and working groups that it organizes. In carrying out implementing measures, the Commission is assisted by committees of representatives of the member nations. Also, it works closely with the ESC and the Committee of the Regions since it has to consult them on many proposed legislative acts. The Commission also attends all the sessions of the EP, where it must clarify and justify its policies, and regularly replies to both written and oral questions posed by MEPs.

One should point out that, in some ways, both for interest groups and for the man or woman in the street who wishes to make the effort, the Commission is more accessible than national administrations. This is in part because the consultation processes, although clumsy, do bring a wide range of people in touch with EU affairs. The danger of this web of machinery and consultation is indecision and slowness of action. At the same time it puts a premium on the views of those who are effectively organized. Additionally, there is a well-established Commission policy of informing and educating the public in order to mobilize public opinion behind the integration process. Unfortunately, this policy often fails to reach its target, so that considerable unease remains and its relative success in establishing relations with bankers, organizational representatives, industrialists and other power groups has contributed to a widespread belief that the EU is an elitist institution far away from the ordinary citizen. Hence a new drive towards better information, and public access to it, was promised in the Maastricht Treaty and is continuing.

Finally, one should add that it is possible that the term Commission may be confusing. This is because it is used to refer to both the college of twenty-five commissioners and to the entire institution with approximately 25,000 staff, most of them in Brussels, but about 2,000 in Luxembourg, with representatives in every EU nation, as well as in delegations in almost all other countries. However, one should encounter no major difficulties since it is easy to judge from the context. Note that although the number of people working for the Commission may seem excessive, it is actually less than that employed by a medium-sized EU city council.

3.2 The Council

As mentioned in chapter 2, the three Councils of Ministers, one for each of the ECSC, EEC and Euratom, were merged in 1965. With the adoption of the Treaty on European Union (the Maastricht Treaty) in 1992, the name was changed in 1993 to the Council of the European Union (hereafter simply the Council; see above) to reflect the three pillars of the EU. Recall that the pillars are based on 'community' action in the case of the 'EC' and on 'intergovernmental cooperation' in the two cases of 'common foreign and security policy' (CFSP) and 'judicial and home affairs' (JHA). Hence, the field of Council activities covers all three pillars, but in this context the precise term for the third should be 'police and judicial cooperation in criminal matters'.

The Council consists of representatives of the governments of the member states, who are accountable to their national parliaments and citizens; hence it is the embodiment of national interests, but representatives of the Commission always attend its meetings. Note that, although the Commission has no voting rights, it plays an active role in helping to reach a decision, and that it is here that it can perform an important mediating function between national viewpoints and its own, which, as we have seen, is intended to represent the general EU interest. Who constitutes the Council would depend upon the matter under consideration: if the matter were about finance, it would be the Ministers of Finance of the member nations; if the matter concerned agriculture, it would be the Ministers of Agriculture; and so on. Thus, unlike the Commission, the Council is not made up of a fixed body of people. The Council is seated in Brussels and most of its meetings are held there except during April, June and October when they take place in Luxembourg.

Since membership of the Council varies according to the subject matter under review, this has led to problems for the member states. Because EU issues are handled by various ministers, briefed by their own civil servants, it becomes harder for any government to see its EU policy as a coherent whole. In turn, coordination within the government machine becomes important. For the EU too, the greater specialization of business creates difficulties, for it has become far harder to negotiate a package deal whereby a set of decisions can be agreed, and each member nation has gains to set off against its losses, although in the long run governments need to show the benefits they have won.

The presidency of the Council rotates, with each member nation holding it in turn for a period of six months, and the chairmanship of the many committees alters correspondingly. The President plays an active role as the organizer of the Council's work and as the chairperson of its meetings; as the promoter of legislative and political decisions; and as an arbiter between the member states in brokering compromises between them. It has become the practice for each member state to try to establish a particular style of working and to single out certain matters to which it wishes to give priority. Since any chairperson can influence business significantly, the President may occupy an important, albeit temporary, role. The President also fulfils some representational functions both towards other EC institutions, notably the EP, and in external negotiations where the presidents of the Council and Commission may act in association. However, discussions have taken place (section 3.10) for limiting the presidency to the larger nations, due to its international importance and the ability of the assuming nation to cope with the extra costs involved in preparing for and hosting the meetings. As stated in chapter 2, these led to agreement in the Constitutional Treaty for a full-time President. Naturally, the general secretariat assists the presidency.

The Council has six major responsibilities. It is the main EU legislative body, but in many areas it exercises this prerogative jointly with the EP through the 'co-decision procedure' (section 3.3). The Council coordinates the broad economic policies of the member states. It also concludes EU international agreements. Together with the EP, it has authority on the EU general budget. On the basis of general guidelines from the European Council, it takes the necessary decisions for framing and implementing the CFSP. And it coordinates the activities of the member nations as well as adopting measures in the area of JHA.

It may prove helpful to elaborate on three of these roles. With regard to its decision-making powers, generally speaking the Council only acts on a proposal from the Commission (see above) and in most cases acts jointly with the EP in the context of a co-decision, consultation or assent procedure (section 3.3). Under the co-decision procedure, the Council and EP originally shared legislation in the general areas, which included the completion of the internal market, the environment and consumer protection, but with the ratification of the Amsterdam Treaty, new areas were added in 1999, such as non-discrimination, free movement and residence and combating social exclusion. However, the Council plays a dominant role when it comes to the CFSP and JHA when they relate to essential components of national policy, since both the EP and the Commission have a more limited say in these areas. Also, although the Commission is entrusted with the enforcement of EU legislation, the Council may reserve the right for it to perform executive functions.

The Maastricht Treaty calls for an economic policy that closely coordinates those of the individual EU member nations. In order to achieve this task, each year the Council adopts draft guidelines for the economic policies of the member countries, which are then incorporated into the conclusions of the European Council. They are then converted into a Council recommendation and accompanied by a multilateral surveillance mechanism. This coordination is performed entirely in the context of EMU, where the Economic and Financial Affairs (ECOFIN) Council plays a leading role (chapters 10 and 11).

Finally, with regard to the joint responsibility of the Council and EP for the EU general budget, each year the Commission submits a preliminary draft budget to the Council for approval. Then two successive readings allow the EP to negotiate with the Council the modification of certain items of expenditure and to ensure that budgetary revenues are allocated appropriately. In the case of disagreement with the EP, the Council is entrusted with making the final decision on the so-called 'compulsory expenditures' (chapter 19), relating mainly to agriculture and financial commitments emanating from EU agreements with non-member nations. However, with regard to 'non-compulsory expenditures' and the final adoption of the whole budget, the EP has the final say.

Council decisions are taken by unanimous, simple or qualified majority voting (QMV), with QMV being the most common. When QMV is used, each member nation is endowed with a number of votes. The votes are weighted so that at least some of the smaller member nations must assent. For the EU of twelve, the total number of votes was seventy-six (France, Germany, Italy and the UK ten each; Spain eight; Belgium, Greece, the Netherlands and Portugal five each; Denmark and Ireland three each; and two for Luxembourg), with fifty-four votes needed for a decision. Thus the large countries could not impose their wishes on the rest; indeed, the weights favour the smaller

countries. For the EU of fifteen, it was agreed that sixty-two votes, out of a total of eighty-seven (France, Germany, Italy and the UK ten each; Spain eight; Belgium, Greece, the Netherlands and Portugal five each; Austria and Sweden four each; Denmark, Finland and Ireland three each; and two for Luxembourg), would be needed for a decision, but if twenty-six votes are recorded against a decision, 'reasonable time' should be allowed for further discussion. The UK suggested that it should be indefinite, but the others believe that it should be no more than three months.

This general picture remains basically true after the Nice Treaty and the accession of the twelve new members in 2004 and 2007, in spite of increased votes for the larger member nations (twenty-nine for each of France, Germany, Italy and the UK; twenty-seven for Poland and Spain; fourteen for Romania; thirteen for the Netherlands; twelve each for Belgium, the Czech Republic, Greece, Hungary and Portugal; ten each for Austria, Bulgaria and Sweden; seven each for Denmark, Finland, Ireland, Lithuania and Slovakia; four each for Cyprus, Estonia, Latvia, Luxembourg and Slovenia; and three for Malta). A decision requires a majority of member states and a minimum of 255 votes (73.9 per cent of the total of 355) and the blocking minority is ninety-one votes. The proviso is added that a member of Council can request verification on whether the member nations constituting the 255 votes represented at least 62 per cent of the total EU population; if not, the decision cannot be adopted. Thus a decision requires a triple majority.

As a final word on QMV, one should add that its proponents often claim that it is a device meant to ensure that the large countries cannot impose their wishes on the smaller member nations since the largest six countries need another sixty-two to secure the needed 232 votes. However, it can equally be claimed that it is a system which prevents majority opinion from being stymied by a few smaller nations, which is what could happen in the case of a decision requiring a simple majority of the EU nations, i.e. thirteen out of twenty-five: hence the intricate play with figures.

The Council is served by its own secretariat and is supported by an important body called the

Committee of Permanent Representatives (COREPER). The membership of COREPER comprises senior representatives from the member nations holding ambassadorial rank. This body prepares the work of the Council, except for agricultural matters, since these are entrusted to the *Special Committee on Agriculture*. The Council is also assisted by working groups, which consist of officials from the national administrations.

In 1966, it was agreed that it would be desirable for the Commission to contact national governments via COREPER before deciding on the form of an intended proposal. As a result of its links with both the Council and Commission, COREPER is involved in all major stages of EU policy-making. Many matters of policy are in fact agreed by COREPER and reach the Council only in a formal sense. While this is one way of keeping business down to manageable proportions, it has meant that the Council itself has become concerned only with the most important matters or those which may not be of great substance but which are nevertheless politically sensitive. This has encouraged domestic media to present Council meetings as national battles in which there has to be victory or defeat, and politicians too have become extremely adept at using publicity to rally support for their point of view. As a result, the effect has become the opposite of that originally intended when it was thought that the experience of working together would make it progressively easier to find an answer expressive of the general good, and for which majority voting would be a suitable tool. Instead, conflict of national interests is often a better description. The Council also encounters practical problems. The great press of business, the fact that ministers can only attend to Council business part-time, the highly sensitive nature of their activities and the larger number of members all contribute to a grave time-lag in reaching policy decisions, and the move towards QMV was one measure designed to overcome this difficulty.

The General Affairs, ECOFIN and Agriculture Councils meet once a month, whilst the others meet between twice and four times a year, the frequency depending on the number and urgency of the issues under consideration. Because the ministers of finance and foreign affairs also meet in other capacities, due to the nature of EU activities, their meetings have attracted the term 'Senior Council'.

3.2.1 Types of EU decision

It will become clear later that all EU institutions have a part to play in the decision-making process, depending on a modus vivendi existing between them to allow the process to operate. It is, however, at the Council that decisions are declared; hence this is the appropriate place to specify their nature. Formally, an 'action', by the EU results in: a *regulation*, a *directive*, a *decision*, a *common action/position*, a *recommendation*, or an *opinion* (Article 249 EC). Also, 'conclusions', 'declarations' and 'resolutions' can be adopted. A regulation is directly applicable and binding in its entirety in all the member states without the need for any national implementing legislation; hence it is automatic EU law. A directive binds the member states to the objectives to be achieved within a certain period of time while leaving the national authorities the choice of form and means to be used; thus directives have to be implemented by national legislation in accordance with the procedures of the individual member states and in this respect the UK has been the fastest, Italy the slowest. A decision, which is a more specific act and often administrative in nature, is binding in all its facets only for the party it is addressed to, whether it be all member states, an individual member state, an enterprise, an individual or individuals. Recommendations have no binding force, but they express detailed EU preferences on an issue, and opinions are not binding, nor do they have direct effect. The formal acts, notably recommendations and directives, are constantly adding to EU law (chapter 4). Note that the majority of decisions are directives and, as mentioned in chapter 2, the SEA required about 300 of them.

3.3 The European Parliament

Originally, the European Parliament (EP) was a consultative rather than a legislative body, since the Council (of Ministers) had to seek its opinion, but without obligation, before deciding on a

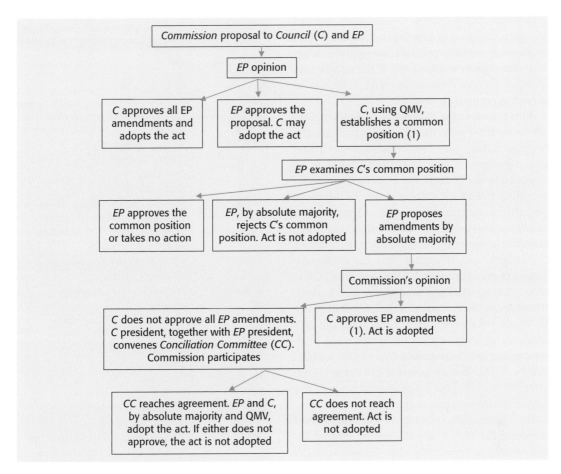

Figure 3.1 The co-decision procedure (Article 251)

Commission proposal. It did have the power to dismiss the entire Commission, but because it did not possess the right to appoint commissioners, many analysts did not attach much significance to this. However, as mentioned in chapter 2 and above, the EP acquired budgetary powers in 1970 and financial provisions powers in 1975. The SEA gave it more powers in 1986. And the Maastricht (1992) and Amsterdam (1997) treaties have turned the EP into a true legislative body as well as strengthening its role as the democratic overseer of the EU. Some elaboration on this is warranted.

The EP acts together with the Council in formulating and adopting certain legislation emanating from the Commission. Here, the most common path is through the *co-decision procedure*, which gives equal weight to both and results in

the adoption of joint acts (figure 3.1). In the case of disagreements between the two, *conciliation committees* would be convened to find a common ground. The co-decision procedure applies particularly in the case of: the management of the single market; freedom of movement of workers; technological research and development; the environment; consumer protection; education; culture; and public health.

Also, the EP's approval is needed in certain areas. These include accession by new member nations; association agreements with non-members, notably in the Mediterranean; the conclusion of international agreements; decisions affecting the right of residence for EU citizens; its own electoral procedures; and the task and powers of the ECB.

Moreover, although the Commission remains the main instigator of new legislation, the EP also provides significant political momentum, especially through its examination of the annual programme for the Commission and asking it to submit appropriate proposals.

With regard to the EU general budget (chapter 19), as we have seen, the EP and Council are the key players. Each year, the Commission has to prepare a *preliminary draft budget*, which has to be approved by the Council. Then two *readings* ensue, providing the EP with the occasion to negotiate with the Council the amendment of certain items of expenditure, although such amendments are generally subject to the financial constraints of the budget, and to ensure that the budgetary resources are appropriately allocated. Finally, it is the EP that has the right to adopt the final budget, which needs the signature of the president of the EP before it can come into force. Also, the EP's *committee on budgetary control* is entrusted with monitoring the implementation of the budget, and each year the EP grants a discharge to the Commission for the implementation of the budget for the previous year.

The cooperation procedure was established following the SEA. It was the testing ground for the co-decision procedure. The implementation and management of the internal market was one of the main areas, but this is now under the co-decision procedure. However, under the Maastricht Treaty, the cooperation procedure now includes: social policy; education and training; the environment; legislation for EMU and implementing measures for the EU structural funds, trans-European infrastructure networks, etc.

Thus the EP of today performs three important functions: together with the Council, it legislates; together with the Council, it shares authority on the EU general budget and its adoption of the budget is the end of the budgetary procedure; and it approves the nominations of commissioners, has the right to censure the Commission, forcing its resignation, and exercises political supervision over all the institutions.

The EP operates in three different places. It meets in Strasbourg, where it is seated, for its plenary sessions, which all members must attend. Its parlia-

Table 3.3 Committees of the European Parliament

Committee	On
AFCO	Constitutional affairs
AFET	Foreign affairs
AGRI	Agriculture and rural development
BUDG	Budgets
CONT	Budgetary control
CULT	Culture and education
DEVE	Development
DROI	Human rights
ECON	Economic and monetary affairs
EMPL	Employment and social affairs
ENVI	The environment, public health and consumer policy
EQUI	Collapse of the Equitable Life Assurance Society
FEMM	Women's rights and gender equality
ITRE	Industry, research and energy
JURI	Legal affairs
LIBE	Civil liberties, justice and home affairs
PECH	Fisheries
PETI	Petitions
REGI	Regional development
SEDE	Security and defence
TDIB	Alleged use of European countries by the CIA for the transport and illegal detention of prisoners

mentary committees (table 3.3) hold their meetings in Brussels and additional plenary sessions are held there too. Its secretariat is located in Luxembourg. This set-up has attracted harsh criticism not only for its inconvenience and money and time wasting, due to the travel and accommodation expenses involved, but more importantly for making it difficult for the EP to become a more coherent and effective organization. It is often claimed that the reasons for these locations are mainly historical going back to the creation of the ECSC, EEC and Euratom, but the history was no accident, given the prestige the EP extends to the countries where it is located and the economic value of the assets.

The EP is still in an evolutionary stage and cannot be expected to follow the path of national parliaments which, in any case, differ among themselves. Some have suggested (e.g. Gillingham 2003) that it should become a merely advisory body, just falling short of the powers of the British House of Lords, on the assumption that the EU is not a single state, but such a proposition would not be consistent with the very nature of the EU as a dynamic association still in the making (chapter 2). The EP operates in a different environment and its power struggles, so far, have been with the Council and Commission rather than with national parliaments.

The EP had its first elections by direct universal suffrage on 7 and 10 June 1979. Elections are based on a system of proportional representation and are held either on a regional basis (as, for example, Belgium, Italy and UK) or nationally. The EP elected in June 2004 had 732 members, but although EU treaties dictate that the number should not exceed 736 after that, when Bulgaria and Romania joined in 2007 no adjustment was made, with the total now being 785 (see last column of table 3.4). Using the figures in that column for comparison, Cyprus, Estonia, Germany, Luxembourg, Malta and Slovenia retain their numbers; France, Italy and the UK drop to seventy-two each, losing six apiece; Poland and Spain get fifty each, losing four each; Belgium, the Czech Republic, Greece, Hungary, the Netherlands and Portugal lose two each; and the remaining eight lose one apiece. Bulgaria and Romania get seventeen and thirty-three respectively.

MEPs are elected for a term of five years. Once elected, they are organized in political rather than national groups, although in some cases national identity remains very strong. Nineteen MEPs from at least five member nations are needed for a group and no member can belong to more than one group. Each group appoints its own chairperson, bureau and secretariat.

The preceding EP had a membership of 626 for the fifteen EU nations. Comparing the numbers with those in 2004 (i.e. before Bulgaria and Romania joined, hence the reference is to the figures in the last column of table 3.4), Germany had ninety-nine members; France, Italy and the UK eighty-seven each, down nine each; Spain sixty-four, down ten; the Netherlands thirty-one, down four; Belgium, Greece and Portugal twenty-five each, down one each; Sweden twenty-two, down three; Austria twenty-one, down three; Denmark

and Finland sixteen each, down two each; Ireland fifteen, down two; and Luxembourg six as before. The number of MEPs has therefore been reduced for thirteen countries, raised for Germany and kept the same for Luxembourg, bringing representation closer to their respective populations. These have been reinforced by the above changes in the present distribution of MEPs.

As table 3.4 shows, in terms of group distribution, the EP elected in 2004 and augmented by MEPs from the twelve new members consisted of: 276 from the group of European People's Party (Christian Democrats) and European Democrats (EPP-ED); 217 from the Party of European Socialists (PES); 105 from the Alliance of European Liberals and Democrats for Europe (ALDE); 42 from the group of Greens and European Free Alliance (G/EFA); 41 from the group of European United Left and Nordic Green Left (GUE/NGL); 30 from the Union for Europe of Nations (UEN); 29 from the group of Independence and Democracy (IND/DEM); and 44 are unattached (NI). Since the ideologies of the different factions in a group are not identical, one may wonder how such motley collections ever get anything useful done. The response would be that in reality they do agree on many issues, but of course the pace at which they do so is dictated by the time needed to reach consensus. Moreover, for the EP to be effective, it has proved necessary to have such large coalitions (Tsoukalis 2005).

3.4 The courts

3.4.1 The European Court of Justice

There are three reasons why the ECJ is needed. First, a body of legal experts is indispensable for ensuring that the EU institutions act in a constitutional manner, fulfilling the obligations laid out for them by the treaties. Second, a court is essential for seeing that the member states, firms and individual citizens observe the (increasing number of) EU rules. And a court at the EU level is vital for guiding national courts in their interpretation of EU law, hence for ensuring that EU legislation is uniformly applied (chapter 4).

Table 3.4 Members of the European Parliament elected in June 2004

	EPP-ED	PES	ALDE	G/EFA	GUE/NGL	UEN	IND/DEM	NI	Total
Austria	6	7	1	2				2	18
Belgium	6	7	6	2				3	24
Bulgaria	4	6	7					1	18
Cyprus	3		1		2				6
Czech Republic	14	2			6		1	1	24
Denmark	1	5	4	1	1	1	1		14
Estonia	1	3	2						6
Finland	4	3	5	1	1				14
France	17	31	11	6	3		3	7	78
Germany	49	23	7	13	7				99
Greece	11	8			4		1		24
Hungary	13	9	2						24
Ireland	5	1	1		1	4	1		13
Italy	24	15	12	2	7	9		9	78
Latvia	3		1	1		4			9
Lithuania	2	2	7			2			13
Luxembourg	3	1	1	1					6
Malta	2	3							5
Netherlands	7	7	5	4	2		2		27
Poland	15	10	4			10	7	8	54
Portugal	9	12			3				24
Romania	9	11	9					6	35
Slovakia	8	3						3	14
Slovenia	4	1	2						7
Spain	24	24	2	3	1				54
Sweden	5	5	3	1	2		3		19
United Kingdom	27	19	12	5	1		10	4	78
Total	276	217	105	42	41	30	29	44	784

Note: EPP-ED is a group of European People's Party (Christian Democrats) and European Democrats; PES is a Socialist group; ALDE is a group Alliance of Liberals and Democrats for Europe; G/EFA is a group of Greens and European Free Alliance; GEU/NGL is a group of European United Left and Nordic Green Left; UEN is the group of the Union for Europe of Nations; IND/DEM is the group of Independence and Democracy; and NI is the unattached.

The ECJ is seated in Luxembourg. It has twenty-seven judges and eight advocates general, appointed on the joint agreement of the member states for six-year renewable terms, with partial reappointment every three years. They are selected from lawyers in the member nations whose independence is beyond doubt; thus they come from the highest national judiciary. The treaties do not lay down any rules on the nationality of the judges, since this might compromise this independence, but in reality there is one judge from each of the member states.

The ECJ has a president, elected by and from the twenty-seven judges for a three-year term. The advocates general are responsible for (a) the preliminary investigation of a matter and (b) presenting publicly and impartially reasoned opinions on the cases brought before the ECJ to help the judges in reaching their decisions (more on this at the end of this section). Each judge has a cabinet to take care of administrative responsibilities and its members are recruited directly by the judge. A cabinet comprises three law clerks to the ECJ and two to the Court of First Instance – see below. The clerks help the judges draw up their reports and draft their rulings. The administrative service of the ECJ is led by the Registrar, who is also responsible for following the cases procedurally – see below.

In carrying out its responsibilities, the ECJ has a wide jurisdiction that it exercises in the context of various categories, the most common of which are: preliminary rulings, failure to fulfil obligations, annulment, failure to act and appeals. Preliminary rulings were introduced in the treaties to institutionalize cooperation between the ECJ and national courts, thus ensuring that the latter are also upholders of EU law. When the national courts receive cases involving EU law, they will ask the ECJ for the interpretation or validity of the law when in doubt, and sometimes they are obliged to consult the ECJ. The actions for failure to fulfil obligations endow the ECJ with the power to monitor the member nations for their carrying out of EU law. Such a process is commonly initiated by the Commission and sometimes by a member state, and if the offending party is proved guilty, it must rectify the situation with immediate effect. Proceedings for annulment arise when an applicant seeks for a regulation, directive or decision adopted by an institution. The ECJ has exclusive jurisdiction in any action lodged by a member state against the EP and/or Council (excluding those concerning state aid, dumping and implementing powers) or by one institution against another; the Court of First Instance (see below) has jurisdiction in all other cases, particularly those arising from individuals. Proceedings for failure to act apply where the EP, Council or Commission fails to take a decision when the treaties stipulate it should. Under such circumstances, member states and other EU institutions and, under certain conditions, individuals or their legal representatives can lodge a complaint with the ECJ requesting that the violation be officially recorded. Finally, appeals can be lodged only against judgment by the Court of First Instance (see below).

A few words on how business is handled by the ECJ may be in order. After cases are lodged with the registry, they are distributed among the judges. A specific judge and advocate general assume responsibility for each case. A judge, appointed as *juge rapporteur*, has to write a report for the hearing, providing a summary of the legal background to the case and the observations of the parties to the case submitted in the first written phase of the procedure. In the light of the reasoned opinion of the responsible advocate general, the *juge rapporteur* writes a draft ruling, which is then submitted to the other members of the ECJ for examination. Thus the procedure has both a written and an oral phase. The written one consists of the statements exchanged between the parties concerned and the report by the *juge rapporteur*. The oral one is the public hearing where the lawyers for the parties involved are invited to argue their case before the judges and advocates general, who have the right to question them. The advocate general then submits his/her conclusion, i.e. reasoned opinion, before the judges deliberate and deliver their judgment on the case.

The ECJ sits as a full court, a grand chamber of thirteen judges, or a chamber of three or five judges, depending on the nature, complexity or importance of the case. Chambers of five have three-year presidents; those of three, one-year presidents. The full court considers cases prescribed by its statues, such as the dismissal of a member of the Commission; a grand chamber deals with a request by a member state or institution and exceptionally important cases; and the other chambers deal with the rest. ECJ judgment is reached by majority decisions and is pronounced at public hearings. There is no expression of 'dissenting opinions' and all the judges partaking in the deliberations must sign the judgment.

3.4.2 The Court of First Instance

Because the ECJ had been too busy to reach quick decisions, essential for a smooth operation of the integration process, the SEA introduced a *Court of First Instance* in 1989 to deal with: (a) matters relating to the ECSC treaty, (b) the enforcement of competition rules, (c) disputes between the EU institutions, and, from June 1993, (d) actions brought by individuals against EU institutions and agencies, except in cases concerning trade protection. The court's rulings are subject to appeal to the ECJ on points of law only. In the past five years, however, even this court has become too busy, so the Nice Treaty, which became effective on 1 February 2003, allowed for the creation of 'judicial panels' in specific cases. And on 2 November 2004 the Council decided to establish the *European Union Civil Service Tribunal*, comprising seven judges, to deal with disputes involving the civil service, with its decisions subject to appeal to the Court of First Instance for only points of law, which in turn may, exceptionally, be reviewed by the ECJ. Given the demise of the ECSC and that competition enforcement is with the Commission, today the jurisdiction of the Court of First Instance is confined to direct actions brought by individuals and member states, except for those assigned to the 'judicial panels'.

The court has the same number of judges as the ECJ, and they are subject to precisely the same conditions. It elects it own President as well as the presidents of its chambers of three or five judges, all on three-year renewable terms, and can meet as a grand chamber in especially important cases. Although it has no advocates general, a judge may be nominated for the task in a limited number of cases. It appoints its own six-year term Registrar, but depends on the ECJ for its administrative needs.

3.4.3 The Court of Auditors

The *Court of Auditors* was established on 22 July 1975 by the Treaty of Brussels and became operative in October 1977 when the EC budgetary arrangements were revised. It joined the Commission, Council, EP and ECJ as a major institution on 1 November 1993, following the Maastricht Treaty. It was given further responsibilities in 1999, following the Amsterdam Treaty. It is located in Luxembourg.

The main function of the court is to ensure that the EU budget is properly implemented, i.e. it is entrusted with the external monitoring of EU revenues and expenditures. In exercising this function, it also tries to secure sound financial management and to enhance the effectiveness and transparency of the whole system. It has no legal enforcement powers, so it informs the European Anti-Fraud Office when it detects any irregularities.

To carry out these responsibilities, the court needs to be independent, and indeed it is. However, the court does communicate and collaborate with other institutions. It assists the EP and the Council, the joint budgetary authority, by presenting them each year with observations on the report for the previous year. These observations are taken seriously by the EP and influence its decision on the granting or otherwise of the implementation of the budget. It also submits to them statements of assurance regarding the proper use of EU revenues. Moreover, it gives its opinion on the adoption of financial regulations; it can submit observations on specific issues and respond with opinions to any request from any EU institution. Furthermore, in the reports issued by the court, based on its investigation of documents and where necessary of organizations managing revenues and expenditures on behalf of the EU, it draws the attention of both the Commission and the member nations to any outstanding problems.

The court consists of twenty-seven members, one from each member state, appointed by the Council, but consulting the EP, and it must decide by unanimous agreement. The appointees are chosen from those who have worked for auditing institutions in their member states or are specifically qualified for the job, and must meet the requirements of independence and full-time work. They have six-year renewable terms, they elect one of their number to be President for three years and they have the option of operating in chambers. The court has a staff of about 800, 250 of whom are qualified auditors, divided into 'audit groups' according to the nature of their work, and they prepare reports for the court to help it reach its decisions.

3.5 The Ombudsman

Following the Maastricht Treaty's call for the establishment of a European Ombudsman to deal with complaints raised by EU citizens, the post was created in July 1995. The appointment, which is for five renewable years, is the prerogative of each new EP; hence it coincides with the each EP's life. The office is located in Strasbourg where there is a secretariat whose principal administrator is appointed by the Ombudsman.

Being authorized to act independently as a full-time intermediary between EU citizens, including foreigners residing or having registered offices in the EU, and authorities (only the ECJ and Court of First Instance, in their judicial roles, do not come under the Office's jurisdiction), the Ombudsman uncovers malpractices in EU institutions and bodies and makes recommendations for their elimination. The Ombudsman can also investigate on his own initiative. His findings are referred to the EP to act on. The Ombudsman also presents an annual report on his/her activities to the EP.

Complaints to the Ombudsman must be submitted within two years of their being brought to the attention of the offending party, provided that the administrative procedures have already been undertaken and no legal proceedings have been initiated. When the Ombudsman has lodged his/her comments on an issue with the institution or body concerned, it can respond to them and it is also obliged to provide the Ombudsman with any solicited information or access to relevant files, except where there are justifiable confidentiality grounds. If a case of malpractice has been established, the Ombudsman notifies the institution or body involved and the latter must respond in three months with a detailed opinion. The Ombudsman then lodges a report with both the EP and the institution or body involved, and notifies the complainant of the outcome of the investigations.

3.6 The European Economic and Social Committee (EESC)

Two Economic and Social Committees (ESCs) were established in 1957 in the Rome treaties, one for each of the EEC and Euratom, following the lines of that for the ECSC of 1951. Thus in 1957 there were three such committees, but as mentioned in chapter 2 and above, these were merged into one in 1965 and are now referred to as the EESC.

The EESC is a forum for organized EU civil society. It comprises the various categories of economic and social activity such as employers, unions and the self-employed together with representatives from community and social organizations (in particular, producers, farmers, carriers, workers, dealers, craftsmen, professional occupations, consumers and the general interest). These are considered as three groups: group I, which consists of employers' representatives from both the private and public sectors; group II, the vast majority of whom come from national trade union organizations; and Group III, which is a miscellaneous group, including members from farmers' organizations, small and medium-sized enterprises (SMEs), various NGOs, etc.

The EESC plays an important role of a general consultative and informative nature. Its opinions are sought by the Commission, Council and EP (since the Amsterdam Treaty) on all matters under its jurisdiction, some mandatory. Since 1972 the EESC itself can also formulate its own opinions on issues it deems important. It also offers 'exploratory opinions' when approached by the Commission or EP to discuss and make suggestions on an issue which could lead to a Commission proposal.

The Maastricht Treaty endowed the EESC with a status akin to that of the other EU institutions, especially in terms of its procedural rules, budget, the reinforcement of its right of initiative and the management of its staff with the secretariat general. The committee saw a broadening in its field of action, notably in social matters, in 1997 as per the Amsterdam Treaty.

It has 331 members, appointed by the Council by lists forwarded by the governments of the member nations. Each member is appointed for four years and acts independently in a personal capacity in the interests of the whole EU. The national distribution of the 331 members is such that France, Germany, Italy and the UK have twenty-four members each; Poland and Spain have twenty-one each; Romania has fifteen; Austria, Belgium, Bulgaria, the Czech Republic, Greece, Hungary, the Netherlands, Portugal and

Sweden have twelve each; Denmark, Finland, Ireland, Lithuania and Slovakia have nine each; Estonia, Latvia and Slovenia have seven each; Cyprus and Luxembourg have six each; and Malta has five.

The Committee is housed in Brussels, but although most of its meetings and plenary sessions are held there, meetings are also scheduled in other locations. It has a plenary assembly, a bureau, the three groups just mentioned, six sections and a secretariat general, with a staff of 135. It elects its own thirty-seven-member bureau, president and two vice-presidents from the three groups in rotation, who hold office for two-year terms. The president acts as its external representative.

The six sections deal with the main activities of the EU: (i) agriculture, rural development and the environment; (ii) EMU and economic and social cohesion; (iii) employment, social affairs and citizenship; (iv) external relations; (v) the single market, production and consumption; and (vi) transport, energy, infrastructure and the information society.

In reaching its decision, the EESC follows a certain procedure. When the president receives a request for an opinion from the Council, Commission or EP, the bureau lodges it with the appropriate section. The section then sets up a study group, consisting of about twelve persons, and appoints a 'rapporteur' assisted by about four experts in the field. Based on the recommendations of the group, the section adopts its opinion on the basis of simple majority and this is then considered in the plenary session, which decides likewise before addressing it to the requesting institution. Usually about ten plenary sessions are held every year.

3.7 The Committee of the Regions (CoR)

The Committee of the Regions (CoR) was set up in 1994, following the Maastricht Treaty, in response to demands by several member nations that regional and local authorities should be directly involved in deliberations at the EU level. In many countries these authorities enjoy wide-ranging powers, either because of the federal structure of the country concerned or by virtue of legislative or constitutional measures adopted over the past few decades; hence they are in direct touch with the average EU citizen, whose involvement in EU affairs, as we have seen, has been a major issue. The treaty specifies that members of the CoR must hold a regional or local authority electoral mandate or be politically accountable to an elected assembly, but must act independently.

The CoR is an advisory body to the Council, Commission and EP and its main work entails advancing its own opinions on Commission proposals. Also, as is expected, it ensures that the subsidiarity principle is safeguarded. Moreover, the Council and Commission must consult it on any issue of direct relevance to local and regional authorities, and it can initiate its own opinions on matters of particular concern to itself and lodge them with either, or the EP.

The structure and procedures of the committee resemble those of the EESC in most respects. The exceptions are fourfold. First, for every one of the 331 members there is an alternate. Second, as just mentioned, the members are mainly politicians, either elected or exerting influence on local or regional authorities. Third, the members are assigned to six specialist commissions whose job is to prepare for the five annual plenary sessions (it also holds two extraordinary meetings, each in the member nation acting as president at the time), which decide its 'opinion': Commission for Territorial Cohesion Policy (COTER); Commission for Economic and Social Policy (ECOS); Commission for Sustainable Development (DEVE); Commission for Culture and Education (EDUC); Commission for Constitutional Affairs and European Governance (CONST); and Commission for External Relations (RELEX). Fourth, its bureau consists of the President, the first vice-president, twenty-seven other vice-presidents, one from each member state, twenty-seven other members and the leaders of its four political groups (PES, EPP, ALDE and ALE). The bureau has three seats for each of France, Germany, Italy, Poland, Spain and the UK; one each for Cyprus, Estonia, Latvia, Luxembourg, Malta and Slovenia; and one each for the remaining fifteen.

3.8 The European Central Bank (ECB)

The ECB was established on 1 June 1998 and is located in Frankfurt, but its foundations were laid through the European Monetary Institute (EMI), introduced on 1 January 1994, during the second stage of EMU (chapter 10). It is given total independence to carry out its mandate (chapter 11).

The ECB and the thirteen central banks of the euro nations are known as the *Eurosystem*, which distinguishes them from the *European System of Central Banks* (ESCB), since the latter includes the central banks of all twenty-seven EU nations. The ECB lies at the very heart of the Eurosystem (chapter 11) whose primary task is to ensure price stability in the eurozone; price stability has been defined to be an annual increase in the consumer price index of less than 2 per cent. To achieve this, a so-called two-pillar strategy is followed: (i) setting a target for the growth of money supply, defined in the broadest sense; and (ii) assessing future price trends and risks to price stability by examining trends in wages, exchange rates, long-term interest rates, various measures of economic activity and the like. It is also responsible for collecting all necessary statistical information, from both the national authorities and economic agents, e.g. financial institutions, and for following developments in the banking and financial sectors and promoting the exchange of information between the ESCB and banking authorities.

In executing its task, the ECB defines and implements the monetary policy of the eurozone; holds and manages the foreign exchange reserves of the eurozone and conducts foreign exchange operations; issues euro notes and coins; and promotes the smooth operation of the payment systems.

The head of the ECB is its *executive board*, which is responsible for the daily running of the bank, the implementation of its monetary policy and transmitting the necessary instructions to the national central banks. It comprises the president, vice-president and four other members, all six being appointed on the agreement of the heads of state or government of the nations in the eurozone. All six hold non-renewable eight-year terms.

The top decision-making body of the ECB is the *governing council*, which comprises the six members of the executive board and the thirteen governors of the eurozone banks. The president of the ECB acts as its chairperson. It meets twice a month, and during the first meeting it normally examines the economic conditions and the position of monetary policy and determines the key interest rate; in the second it concentrates on its other tasks (chapters 11 and 12).

There is also the *general council* consisting of the president and vice-president of the ECB as well as the governors of the national central banks of all twenty-seven EU nations. Its task is to contribute to the advisory and coordinating work of the bank and to assist with the future enlargement of the eurozone.

3.9 The European Investment Bank (EIB)

The EIB was set up in 1958 in Luxembourg, following the 1957 Treaty of Rome (EEC), to fund both private and public investment projects that enhance economic integration, and to update, promote the balanced development and economic and social cohesion of the EU nations (chapter 13). In global terms, the EIB meets the financial obligations of EU agreements on development aid and cooperation policies. Its capital is provided by the member states, each contributing according to its relative GNP standing within the league of EU nations, and it is empowered to make its own decisions on the projects to finance.

The bank has a *board of governors*, a *board of directors*, a *management committee* and an *audit committee*. The board of governors, consisting of ministers appointed by the member states, usually the Finance Ministers, defines the general guidelines for lending, approves the balance sheet and annual report, decides on the funding of projects outside the EU (see below) and further capital generation, and appoints the members of the other three boards. The board of directors, comprising twenty-eight members on five-year terms, one nominated by each member state and one by the Commission, and headed by the bank's president, has sole responsibility for decisions on loans,guarantees and borrowings, and ensures that the bank is run properly and in accordance with EU treaties. The board also has eighteen alternates, necessitating sharing between the member states, and can co-opt up to six non-voting experts (three members and three alternates) for their advice. Since 1 May 2004, it has been deciding by a majority of those eligible to vote, but who must constitute a minimum of 50 per cent of the subscribed capital. The management committee is the full-time executive and consists of the EIB president and eight vice-presidents, appointed for six-year renewable terms. The audit committee, comprising three members and three observers on three-year terms, not only oversees the proper management of the bank's operations and financial resources, but also cooperates with the Court of Auditors for the external auditing of the bank.

The bank is usually invited by the EP to participate in the committees concerned with the bank's operations. It also has an input in preparing the work of the Council – hence the bank's president may be asked to attend some meetings of the Council – and it cooperates with other institutions concerned with its activities.

The bank finances its activities by borrowing on the financial markets; thus it does not receive any EU budgetary contribution, and is run as a non-profit-making entity. It is, however, different from traditional banks since it does not offer current and savings accounts. It follows three criteria in deciding which investment projects it should fund. First, the investment must be instrumental in enticing other sources of funding; second, it must be in specified fields; third, it must be in the most disadvantaged regions. It has steadily grown in stature and is now ranked AAA, the highest credit rating on the capital markets, and this enables it to raise funds on the most competitive of terms. It is also a majority shareholder in the European Investment Fund (EIF), created in 1994 and located in Luxembourg, to assist with the financing of investments in SMEs. The bank deals directly with those promoting large-scale projects, worth at least 25 million euros, but cooperates with about 180 banks and specialist European financial intermediaries in the case of SMEs and local authorities.

The bank's activities promote EU integration in a wider sense. This is because about 10 per cent of its funding goes to projects in applicant countries (chapters 22 and 26), Mediterranean nations (chapter 22) and the ACP countries (chapter 25) as well as to some Asian and Latin American nations for ventures of common interest.

3.10 Institutional reform

Given that the EU Constitution is now on hold (chapter 2), most of what was stated here in the previous edition remains valid. Finding a satisfactory voting system for the Council, which allows decisions to be reached and at the same time effectively represents the forces at work in the EU, is one of the hardest problems. Reforming the Commission to become an efficient machine and clarifying its role comes close to that. The interrelationship between the EU institutions and national systems of government receives less publicity, but also requires attention. With the growth in importance of the EU and the loss of national power, the question must arise whether national parliaments can still perform a democratic role satisfactorily. It is clear that the EU has not been able to exert adequate control over the application of its policies within member states. The EU writ does not always run to achieving the uniform application of a regulation, an effective interpretation of a directive or even the proper use of EU funds. National parliaments have not shown much interest in controlling these matters on behalf of the EU, and it remains primarily up to the Commission to ensure the smooth running of policies on the ground. 'To do less, but do it better' remains a valid goal.

Substantive policy issues are looming (chapters 2 and 28). Political events in the world change quickly, so that the foreign policy role of the EU and its corresponding security and defence policy, including the complications in the NATO relationship, are sure to be tested – witness the Iraq war situation and the present Iran confrontation. Many practical difficulties must arise consequent upon the greater mobility of people, both internally and from the rest of the world, so it is indeed essential that the institutional structure is adequate. However, no matter how good reform may be in itself, the changes will not endure if they are not supported by public opinion – and this has shown itself to be somewhat uncertain about the developments of recent years. As mentioned in chapter 2, the Maastricht Treaty was greeted with widespread hostility and was nearly lost in referendums in Denmark and France; the same applied to the Nice Treaty when the initial Irish vote rejected it. Also, despite recent efforts by the Commission to counter public ignorance, Denmark and France have rejected the Constitution. Moreover, less has been done to improve awareness of the EP and Council. A major criticism of the latter remains its lack of openness and the failure of existing democratic institutions to control decisions taken. No obvious remedy exists. National parliaments have perhaps too often allowed decisions and developments to pass them by, displaying little, or only a desultory, interest in the work of the European institutions. At the same time the institutions themselves have been too absorbed in the excitement of creating a political first to remember that time is needed for the general public to come to terms with these changes. All in all, there is indeed a democratic deficit in the EU, but this is not to be solved simply by increasing the powers of the EP – which is often put forward as the solution. Understanding and support of the EU is not a question of reform of the institutions alone but of long years of hard grind and painstaking effort on everyone's part to ensure that the EU commands support.

The strange thing is that even if the Constitution had been ratified, not all these problems would have disappeared. Take, for example, the appointment of a full-time President of the Council who would champion the EU's internal agenda and represent it to the outside world. Those who supported it insisted that it made sense only if the Commission itself were also strengthened at the same time, with its president elected directly by the EP. Those who opposed it, including then Commission President Romano Prodi, however, believed that this solution had a number of drawbacks. It needed to ensure that rivalry between the presidents of the Commission and Council did not become a divisive factor; it needed to avoid any risk of creating a second administration; to ensure that reforms actually improved the quality of work in the Council and the various council configurations; and to settle satisfactorily the issue of the accountability of the presidents of the Council and General Affairs Council (speech delivered by Romano Prodi to the French National Assembly in Paris on 12 March 2003). Prodi urged a clarification of how competences should be shared by the two presidents and how long their terms of office should be; who the president of the European Council should be accountable to; how to avoid duplicating the administration; and how the work of the Council, and in particular the presidency of the General Affairs Council should, be organized. In short, there is still a long way to go.

4 The legal dimension in EU integration

DAMIAN CHALMERS AND LUKE HAASBEEK

In one sense, it should not be difficult to pinpoint the legal dimension to EU integration. As a political system, the EU has been constituted through a legal instrument, the Treaty on European Union (TEU); it has its own system of administration of justice; and its output has traditionally been measured in terms of the number of legally binding acts it has adopted (Majone, 1994; Wessels, 1997). Viewed through these lenses, the contribution of law to European integration seems considerable (on 'legalization' see Abbott et al., 2000). Few systems, either national or transnational, have given the judiciary such a pre-eminent role and the measure of EC (one of the three EU pillars – see chapters 2 and 3) legislative outputs alone can be gauged by estimates which suggested that more than a third of legislation adopted in France between 2000 and 2004 emanated from the EC[1] and that 30 per cent of all legislation in the Netherlands comprises provisions implementing EC directives[2] (on this see Mancini, 1998, p. 40).[3] Yet to stop there is to beg the question of how EU law acts upon and reconfigures the behaviour of the actors that invoke it and are subject to it. Instead of attempting the impossible task of trying to recount the contents of all this legislation, this chapter addresses this latter question, considering in particular how the use of law steers the integration process.

'Integration through law' pulls this process in three broad directions. The first direction is an actor-interest-based one. This considers the opportunity structures provided through the creation of specifically legal institutions (see chapter 3), in the form of the European Court of Justice (ECJ) and the Court of First Instance (CFI), and of specifically 'legal relations' between these and national courts, most notably in the form of the Article 234 EC reference procedure, but more gen-

erally in the authority conferred on the former's judgments by the latter. This leads not merely, in crude policy terms, to both national and EC courts becoming significant players and agenda setters, with the Article 234 EC reference procedure having to be considered as a relationship as influential in its own way as that of the Commission and Council (for a particularly important early analysis of this see Volcansek, 1986). It also leads to fresh opportunities for new types of actor, in the shape of litigants and lawyers, and for new forms of knowledge, in the form of EC law, at the expense of other actors and forms of knowledge.

Many EU legal scholars, by contrast, look not so much at the opportunities provided by EU law, but at its mapping functions: namely, how it shapes expectations and understandings of the integration process, which in turn influences how parties act within that process. They thus note how debates about the values and directions of the EU, its legitimacy and the patterns of inclusion and exclusion established by it, invariably involve first and foremost, debates about the contours of EU law (on an informative discussion about these two approaches, see Alter, Dehousse and Vanberg, 2002).

The third direction in which EU law pulls the integration process is in its communicative functions. The establishment of a series of networks by EU legal instruments creates a series of new interrelationships and modifies existing relations between parties across a variety of fields. Parties have to adapt to and communicate with each other through and within these legal relationships. This process not only generates new forms of power, practices, understandings and identities, but in so far as these relationships are generated in a 'transnational' manner, contributes to the emergence of a transnational society. It is in this that EU law is perhaps broadest in its embrace and most sweeping in its ambition.

4.1 Actor-interest-based approaches

The capacity to determine the content of a legal provision is a cherished prize within any communal arrangement, be it an international, national or sub-national one. For a legal provision will do a number of things. It will stabilize expectations as to what is required of parties and provide a benchmark by which each party judges the behaviour of the other. In addition, in so far as any legal provision must allow for the possibility that it will be obeyed out of a sense of duty, legal provisions can induce more wide-ranging assumptions over what constitutes appropriate behaviour. The ability to influence the content of norms occurs at a variety of points in their life cycle, be it in their formulation, enactment, application or enforcement. Within classic international treaty regimes, national governments, as both authors and addressees of the international treaty in question, preserve a monopoly over this capability through the device of auto-interpretation, namely their ability to interpret the substantive content of the norms to which they are subject (Gross, 1984). This has been only marginally disturbed through the increasing resort, since the Second World War, to judicial or quasi-judicial decision-making bodies in both regional human rights and regional and global trade treaties (Merrills, 1998). Access to such bodies is limited and they do not disturb the national governments' monopoly of violence over their territories as no sanctions are provided for in the event of non-compliance with these bodies' rulings. The central actors brought into play by these instruments, therefore, continue to be bureaucrats, be they national civil servants or the international organizations or secretariats set up by the treaties.

The legal arrangements of the TEU, particularly those of the EC pillar, stand in marked contrast to this. The public spheres surrounding most EC legislative and quasi-legislative procedures involve a wide variety of actors beside national govern-ments. Most explicitly, these procedures provide for the participation of a whole series of supranational institutions, depending upon the field in question. These can take the form of a wide array of bureaucratic interests, be they the Commission, the European Central Bank (ECB, see chapter 9), scientific committees or euro agencies; representative institutions in the form of the Economic and Social Committee (ESC) and the Committee of the Regions; and, finally, directly elected interests in the shape of the European Parliament (EP). Even in those areas, such as Common Foreign and Security Policy (CFSP), that are characterized by limited supranational institutional influence and national government vetoes, the requirement to carry out measures through the Union's institutional procedures generates structures and dialectics which constrain and shift preferences and curb unilateralism (Hill, 1997).

An even more potent feature of the EU than the pluralism surrounding its law-making is that national governments have lost their monopoly over the application and enforcement of law in the EC pillar and, since the Treaty of Amsterdam, over certain areas of EU law in the Justice and Home Affairs (JHA) pillar. This has had particularly disempowering consequences for national governments, as the legislative dynamics of the EU render unexpected interpretations or applications particularly difficult to remedy. Interpretations of the treaties themselves can only be rectified through the unanimous agreement of the national governments (Article 48 TEU). Pressures militate against even amendment of secondary legislation. Most EC legislative procedures require a national government to negotiate amendments with a number of actors, notably the Commission and the Parliament, both of which, depending upon the legislative procedure deployed, may be able to veto any proposed amendments. In addition, the voting thresholds within the Council of Ministers will, depending upon the area in question, require the national government to co-opt either all or a qualified majority of its fellow governments into agreeing to its amendments. Within even highly rationalist accounts, which place national governments at the centre of the EU integration, these features grant those actors responsible for the application and enforcement of EC law a considerable degree of autonomy and power (Alter, 1998b; Garrett and Tsebelis, 1999). This autonomy has allowed these actors to develop autonomous dynamics and agenda-setting powers of their own (Armstrong, 1998; Armstrong and Bulmer, 1998, pp. 263–9).

4.1.1 The European Court of Justice

The organization of the work of the European Court of Justice

The most salient of these actors is the ECJ. At the centre of the court sit twenty-seven judges, one from each member state (Article 221 EC). Judges do not need to have held prior national judicial office, but are to be chosen 'from persons whose independence is beyond doubt and who possess the qualifications required for appointment to the highest judicial offices in their respective countries or who are jurisconsults of recognised competence' (Article 223 EC). The EC Treaty also demands them to be completely independent of the government which selected them as well as from other interest groups. Judges are appointed for a renewable term of six years by the common accord of the national governments. To ensure continuity, judges shall be partially replaced every three years (Article 223(2) EC); twelve or thirteen judges shall be appointed or reappointed alternately (Article 9 Statute of the Court of Justice). The court works on the principle of collegiality. Drafted in the first place by a single judge, a *juge rapporteur*, and then negotiated between the different judges and their offices, a single judgment is given with no possibility for dissenting opinions. This, together with the relatively remote location of the court in a rather drab Luxembourg suburb and the similar social backgrounds of the judges, is credited with giving it a certain *esprit de corps* which contributes to its collective autonomy (Kenny, 1998).

The court is assisted in its work by eight advocates general. The conditions for office and length of term for these are the same as for judges of the court. There is a convention that one is taken from each of the five larger member states and the other three are rotated among the smaller member states. The duty of the advocate general is to present in open court 'with complete impartiality and independence . . . reasoned submissions on cases, which, in accordance with the Statute of the Court of Justice, require his involvement' (Article 222 EC). The opinions of the advocate general are in no way binding upon the court.

The workload of the court is considerable. Up until the end of 2004 it had given 6,465 judgments (ECJ, 2005, table 15, p. 182). Despite this, since the late 1970s, backlog has been a recurring feature of the caseload. This combination of workload and backlog has given rise to a number of problems. The most practical of these is obviously delay to individual litigants, which, in turn, provides incentives for national courts not to refer matters to the court, irrespective of the wider importance of the legal questions raised. The workload has also affected the quality of judgments, partly by placing the court under considerable time constraints. The large number of judgments also gives national legal communities little time to digest EC law. This both contributes to the unfamiliarity of many national lawyers with important areas of EC law and prevents quick feedback on judgments, with unforeseen or unfortunate results (Jacqué and Weiler, 1990).

The ECJ made attempts to address this, first, by expanding the chamber system. The ground rule is that cases before the court will be heard by a chamber consisting of three or five judges. Upon request of a member state or EC institution that is party to the proceedings, the court will sit in a Grand Chamber of thirteen judges. Only in cases that involve difficult or important points of EU law and other particular cases referred to in the statute of the court, will a full court hear the case. Yet the influence of the chamber system is illustrated by its enabling the court to decide 423 cases in 2004, as compared with an average of 133 cases per annum in the period 1979–81, with 370 of those decisions being made in 'normal' chambers and thirty-two in Grand Chamber (ECJ, 2004, table 4).

The second innovation was the establishment of a Court of First Instance (CFI) in 1988.[4] The CFI was essentially an 'administrative court' (Dehousse,

1998, p. 28) which had jurisdiction for all direct actions brought by individuals reviewing the action or inaction of the EC institutions. This jurisdiction has, however, been enlarged, amongst other reasons in order to repair the backlog of the ECJ, to include the competence to hear and determine at first instance all direct actions brought by both individuals and member states, which comprise actions for annulment, failure to act and damages against Community institutions, as well as actions based on an arbitration clause and actions concerning the civil service. Next to that, the Treaty of Nice conferred upon the CFI the competence to hear preliminary references in specific areas, to be appointed by the statute of the court. Also to reduce the court's backlog, judicial panels were to be created by the Council to ease the workload of the CFI by deciding areas that are less central to the development of EC law (Article 225a EC). The first of these panels was founded in 2004 and its competence relates to disputes between the EC institutions and their staff. It has to be noted that the Treaty establishing a Constitution for Europe aimed at the creation of specialized tribunals in more policy areas.

Like the ECJ, the CFI has twenty-seven judges whose terms of office are of the same length as those of the ECJ judges, and, as with the ECJ, it operates a chamber system. The required qualification of the judges is almost the same as that of ECJ judges. In 2004 the CFI gave 361 judgments (ECJ, 2005, table 7, p. 197).

Third, the ECJ has developed a system of docket control (Strasser, 1995; Barnard and Sharpston, 1997). Since the two *Foglia* cases in the early 1980s,[5] it has been clear that the ECJ itself would determine the scope of its jurisdiction. On the basis of this case law, the ECJ has refused to accept references where a dispute is not pending before a national court or where it considers there is no genuine dispute at hand and the questions referred are merely hypothetical in nature.[6] It will also refuse to answer references where the questions are not relevant to the resolution of the dispute pending before the national court,[7] where the questions are not formulated in a clear enough manner to enable the court to give a meaningful legal response,[8] or where it considers

insufficient information is provided about the factual and national legal context to the dispute. Yet such docket control has proved to be controversial on the grounds both that it might lead to a 'denial of justice' in individual cases and that, through its second-guessing of national courts, the ECJ is introducing unwarranted hierarchies between it and national courts (O'Keeffe, 1998). In any case, it led to the ECJ refusing to rule in fewer than thirty cases in the 1990s.

The largely internal developments had little long-term impact on the problem of backlog until the changes made by the Treaty of Nice and the arrival of ten new judges following the accession of the ten new member states. The number of cases pending before the court, as well as the length of proceedings, continually increased until a critical point was reached at the end of 2003. At that time, 974 cases were still pending before the court and the length of proceedings averaged, depending upon the procedure, between 24.7 and 28.7 months (ECJ, 2004, table 8). In 2004, the positive effects of the measures started to show: 'only' 840 cases were pending at the end of that year and the length of proceedings decreased to 20.2–23.5 months. The same positive trend cannot be observed in relation to the CFI: the extended competences of this court have led to a backlog of 1,174 cases pending at the end of 2004 (CFI, 2004, table 1).

This situation has caused a number of difficulties. The most obvious is that of *bottlenecking*. The delays incurred are in addition to those incurred before national courts. A reference not only affects the ability of parties to ensure a timely securing of their rights, it also provides opportunities for parties to abuse the litigation process through using threat of a reference to pressurize the other party into accepting claims they would otherwise not accept (Chalmers, 2000b). A second difficulty is that of *expertise*: the sheer breadth of subject matter upon which the ECJ is called to adjudicate requires it to pronounce on many areas (e.g. tax, competition, anti-dumping, intellectual property) in which it does not have a specialized knowledge. Finally, the structure of the reference system leads to the ECJ being used as a forum for '*outsider elites*'. The unwieldy nature of the process leads to relatively few litigants coming before the ECJ who are interested in simple monetary compensation. Instead, an ECJ judgment is an important vehicle through which national or EC law can be changed. Typically, groups will use such an avenue when they doubt they will be able to achieve their goals through administrative or legislative procedures, and where their policy goals are narrow enough to be met by a judgment (Alter, 2000). The consequence is that there is an asymmetry in the type of claims coming before the ECJ. The vast majority seek revision of the domestic settlement. The ECJ need only adjudicate in favour of a few to be seen as a revisionary, supranational institution unsympathetic to established domestic interests.

The problems threatened to be exacerbated by a number of developments. An expansion of workload is likely as a consequence of the expansion of the EC into new domains. Single market legislation, the development of a considerable corpus of intellectual property law in the late 1990s, and the emergence of EC law on asylum and migration of non-EU nationals will all increase the docket of the ECJ. In addition, ECJ decisions have created more, not less, work for the institution. A feature of the case law before national courts is its very narrow remit. Some 61 per cent of all reported litigation within the United Kingdom has been found to occur within five very narrow areas – taxation, sex discrimination, free movement of goods, free movement of persons and intellectual property (Chalmers, 2000b, pp. 179–80). This suggests not only that the judicial contribution to the EU is narrowly focused, but also that it is intensely focused with litigants seeking to challenge, explore, expand and qualify any new ruling by the ECJ. Also, the accession of ten new member states entering the Union in 2004 was a factor in this respect. Naturally, this has increased the workload of the ECJ. The enhanced number of judges that is a consequence of the accession has, however, also led to an increased capacity of the courts. This, in combination with some reforms made by the Treaty of Nice, such as extending the competences of the CFI and using the chamber system on as many occasions as possible, has led to a more efficient functioning of the courts.

The ethos behind these reforms was that the crisis in the EC judicial system can be managed through the EC judiciary maximizing output, and deciding more cases for discussion of these reforms (see Rasmussen, 2000; Meij, 2000; Craig, 2001; Johnston, 2001; Dashwood and Johnston, 2001; Weiler, 2001). Reforms that tried to limit the flow of references to the ECJ through creating a system of intermediary regional courts similar to the US Courts of Appeal (Jacqué and Weiler, 1990), or through the provision of guidelines that would enable national courts to refer less (CEC, 2000b),[9] were rejected, so if there is a perception that the ECJ is already deciding too many cases for the good of EC legal doctrine, then the Treaty of Nice simply contributes to a deterioration of the status quo. It remains to be seen whether these short-term developments will also offer a long-term progression in terms of the functioning of the courts, since the chamber system was already heavily utilized and the CFI has a considerable backlog of its own. It seems highly unlikely that resort to either of these devices alone will resolve the question of backlog. The reforms threaten, furthermore, to generate other problems. Increasing reliance upon chambers or the CFI will raise questions about the variable quality of judgments and the influence of individual judges. Questions of expertise and specialization are unaddressed. It could, however, be argued that the increased use of the chamber system will work in favour of the specialization of judges, since similar cases could be referred to the same chamber. The creation of more specialized tribunals, as intended by the Treaty establishing a Constitution for Europe, would certainly help to resolve this issue.

The jurisdiction of the European Court of Justice

The only parts of the TEU that the ECJ is now fully excluded from ruling upon are the opening Common Provisions and the Title on CFSP (Article 46 TEU). Since the Treaty of Amsterdam it is now possible for it to rule on the third pillar of the TEU – police and judicial cooperation. This possibility is substantially reduced by its having no jurisdiction to review the validity of police or law enforcement agency operations or the exercise of member state responsibilities with regard to the maintenance of law and order and the safeguarding of internal security (Article 35(5) TEU).

The ECJ has contributed to this wide remit by bestowing upon itself a unique authority to comment upon the quality of EC law. In its judgments of *Van Gend en Loos* and *Costa* in 1963 and 1964, it began its 'constitutionalizing' jurisprudence which bestowed attributes upon EC law that are not possessed by any other international legal order.[10] In these judgments, the ECJ distinguished the EC Treaty from other international treaties, which it characterized as compacts between sovereign states. By contrast, in the EC Treaty the member states had transferred sovereignty to a new legal order which acted for the benefit not just of national governments and individuals. The immediate practical effects of this were that the ECJ considered in *Van Gend en Loos* that EC law contained provisions which could be invoked directly in national law and that, in *Costa*, in the instance of conflicts between EC law and national law the national courts should give precedence to EC law.

These judgments and the subsequent line of case law also had important institutional implications for the ECJ. It gave it a capacity to adjudicate upon conflicts between national law and EC law and upon the effects of provisions of EC law in national courts. This capacity has not really been questioned by national courts. The ECJ has also interpreted this as granting it the exclusive capacity both to adjudicate upon the boundaries between EC and national competencies[11] and to declare EC acts illegal.[12] This has been challenged by national courts. Stated most aggressively by the Germans and the Danish Constitutional Courts,[13] a number of courts from other states, notably Belgium,[14] Spain,[15] France,[16] the United Kingdom[17] and Italy,[18] have asserted that the sovereignty of the EC has a limited material remit and cannot be extended beyond the powers, as they see it, conferred by the treaty. Secondly, EC law must not violate fundamental rights recognized in the national constitutions. Notwithstanding the development of EC law on fundamental rights, national courts will disregard EC law if they see it as violating national fundamental rights, and have guarded this power jealously. There has been well-noted resistance to intervention by EC law and the ECJ in Italy,[19] Germany,[20] Sweden[21] and Ireland[22] on this point. Such decisions suggest that there are

national constitutional sanctuaries which must not be violated by the ECJ if there is not to be national judicial resistance. Yet, for all this, they still allow a considerable de facto hegemony to the ECJ to delimit the boundaries of national and EC jurisdiction. So much so in fact, that, although the *Kompetenz-Kompetenz* debate attracted considerable academic attention (Arnull, 1990; Schilling, 1996; Weiler and Haltern, 1998; Eleftheriadis, 1998; Kumm, 1999), there is no example of a judgment of the ECJ being actively challenged in these jurisdictions in recent years.

The sweeping material jurisdiction of the ECJ is limited by the circumstances in which actions can be brought before it. There are four routes. The first is an appeal from the CFI. Appeals accounted for thirty-three judgments in 2004. Second, a variety of enforcement actions can be brought before the ECJ. These accounted for 182 of its judgments in 2004. They are enforcement actions against individual EC institutions. Within the EC pillar a distinction is made between acts which breach EC law and failures to act. The former can be brought by any member state, the European Parliament, the Commission and the Council (Article 230(2) EC). They can also be brought by the ECB and the Court of Auditors where the measure touches on their institutional prerogatives (Article 230(3) EC). The jurisdiction for failures to act is more sweeping, as actions can be brought by the member states or any other institution (Article 232 EC). In the case of policing and judicial cooperation under the third pillar, enforcement actions can only be brought against the Council, and only by member states or the Commission (Article 35(6) TEU). More common than enforcement actions against the EC institutions are enforcement actions against the member states. In theory, these can be brought by other member states or the Commission (Articles 227 and 226 EC respectively). However, only once in the history of the ECJ has an action been brought by one member state against another.[23] It is more usual for them to co-opt the Commission into action. That said, the central dynamic of enforcement actions brought by the Commission against member states is negotiation in the shadow of litigation. In 2004 the Commission commenced 1,946 proceedings but referred only 202 to the ECJ.[24] Since the Maastricht Treaty the possibility has existed for the Commission to bring member states back to the ECJ to be fined if they fail to comply with ECJ judgments. At first, the procedure proved unwieldy. The Commission did not instigate the proceedings until January 1997 when it brought a series of actions against Italy and Germany. These were settled and it was not until July 2000 that a periodic penalty payment was imposed on the first government – the Greek government.[25] More recently, Spain and France (twice) were also sanctioned by the court in an Article 228 procedure. In response to the judgment of the ECJ in *Commission v. France*,[26] the Commission changed its policy in relation to Article 228 EC in order to ensure strict compliance with EC law.[27] According to the judgment, periodic penalty payments and lump sum fines can be cumulatively imposed upon a member state. The Commission decided to make full use of this possibility and always to demand both sanctions in Article 228 proceedings against member states, the advantage of this being that the ECJ can sanction a member state for non-compliance, even if the situation violating EC law is remedied during the proceedings before the court. The communication also establishes new standards as to the level of the sanctions. The flat rate for the periodic penalty payment will be 600 euros per day, which will be multiplied by three coefficients, two of which reflect the seriousness and duration of the offence and one that relates to a differential fixed per country (varying from 0.36 for Malta to 25.40 for Germany). For the lump sum fines, the calculation will be founded on two elements: a minimum fine (different for each country) and a daily amount, calculated on the basis of a flat rate of 200 euros per day, multiplied by coefficients relating to the seriousness and duration of the infringement as well as the above mentioned coefficient set per country.

Third, member states, the Commission and the Council can ask the ECJ to rule on the EC's competence to sign an international agreement (Article 300(6) EC). In the 1980s and 1990s as well as in more recent years, perhaps one ruling every two years was given on average under this heading. Fourth, the Treaty of Amsterdam provides that the ECJ shall rule on disputes between member states about the interpretation and application of any measures adopted under police and judicial cooperation where the matter has not been resolved by the Council within six months of its being referred by one of its members (Article 35(7) TEU). The same provision also allows for disputes between the Commission and any member state about the interpretation or application of any of the conventions adopted under the pillar to be brought before the ECJ. No case has yet been brought under this heading.

Finally, questions of EC law can be referred by national courts to the ECJ. Prior to the Treaty of Amsterdam the position was relatively simple. National courts against whose decisions there is no judicial remedy were required to refer those matters of EC law that were necessary to enable them to decide the dispute before them (Article 234(3) EC). Other courts had a discretion whether to refer (Article 234(2) EC). The matter was blurred both formally and in practice. In formal terms, all national courts were obliged to refer a matter if they considered a piece of EC secondary legislation might be invalid.[28] Conversely, higher courts were not obliged to refer where a materially identical question of EC law had already been resolved by the ECJ (*acte éclairé*) or where the interpretation of the provision is so clear as to 'leave no scope for any reasonable doubt' (*acte clair*[29]). In a recent case, the ECJ clarified things by judging that the exceptions of the *acte clair* and the *acte éclairé* only affect questions relating to the interpretation of Community law and cannot be extended to questions concerning the validity of Community measures.[30] According to the court, such an extension could endanger the uniform application of Community law. On top of that, in the coherent Community system of judicial protection the ECJ is the sole institution entrusted to rule upon the validity of EU law. The ECJ expressly ruled that national courts against whose decision no judicial remedy under national law is available, are obliged to refer a preliminary question to the ECJ when the validity of EC measures is at stake. The matter is obscured in practice by there being no effective remedy against national courts of last resort that do not refer.

Undoubtedly facilitated by the ECJ's case law stating that some provisions of EC law generate rights that individuals may invoke in national courts, the preliminary reference procedure was the ECJ's principal source of work until 2003. In 2004 it still accounted for 215 out of the 603 cases decided by the ECJ, but direct actions (299 cases) constituted the principle source of work of the court. The matter was complicated by the Treaty of Amsterdam in two respects. Only national courts against whose decisions there is no judicial remedy in national matters may refer questions on the interpretation and application of the new title in the EC Treaty on Visas, Asylum, Immigration and Other Provisions Relating to the Free Movement of Persons (Article 68(1) EC). This Article is consistent with the foregoing in *requiring* national courts of last resort to refer a preliminary question to the ECJ. In addition, non-judicial bodies, namely the Council, the Commission or a member state, may refer questions on interpretation of this title or acts adopted under it to the ECJ. The reason for barring lower courts from referring was, allegedly, that it would lead to the ECJ being swamped with references on asylum and other immigration-related matters. The Treaty of Amsterdam also allowed member states to make a declaration stating whether they would allow national courts to refer questions to the ECJ about EC secondary legislation adopted under policing and judicial cooperation (Article 35(2) TEU). Those adopting this path had two options (Article 35(3) TEU). They could choose to allow the national courts against whose decisions there is no judicial remedy to refer (Article 35 (3) under 1 TEU) or, alternatively, allow all national courts a discretion of referral (Article 35 (3) under 2 TEU). Belgium, Germany, Spain, Italy, Luxembourg, the Netherlands, Austria and the Czech Republic adopted declarations that go further than indicated in the treaty text: they allow all national courts to refer questions to the ECJ, with the courts of last instance being obliged to do so. However, at the time this chapter was written, twelve member states – Denmark, the United Kingdom, Ireland and all member states that entered the EU on 1 May 2004 except the Czech Republic – had not yet adopted any declaration.

This causes a lacuna in the EU system of judicial protection, especially since the importance of the system of Article 35 TEU has been emphasized by the ECJ in its case law.[31] It is not clear whether those member states who have not given their courts the possibility to refer will be bound by judgments of the ECJ given in response to referrals from other jurisdictions. They may, however, submit statements or written observations in cases which arise under Article 35 (1) TEU (Article 35 (4) TEU).

Explaining the powers of the European Court of Justice

The institutional design and jurisdiction of the ECJ raises interesting questions about its role in the integration process and the motivations behind its establishment. The most complete research on the historical background to the development of the ECJ (Alter, 1998a; Alter, 2001, pp. 5–11) suggests that the member states intended three roles for it. The first of these was to prevent the other EC institutions from exceeding their powers. Second, the ECJ was to solve the 'incomplete contract problem' by being a forum for dispute resolution where EC laws were vague. Third, while responsibility for monitoring compliance lies with the Commission, the enforcement action mechanisms allowed the ECJ to 'mediate Commission charges and member state defences regarding alleged treaty breaches' (Alter, 1998a, p. 125). A similar pattern emerges with regard to the jurisdiction of the ECJ over policing and judicial cooperation, except that the Commission is deprived of its monitoring role: national governments take that responsibility upon themselves. Central to this paradigm was a perception amongst participants that the preliminary reference was not to be used as a mechanism for reviewing national laws but more as a vessel for advice over EU law. This was certainly the view of the EEC Treaty negotiators in 1957, and a not dissimilar view is apparent in the Treaty of Amsterdam negotiations, where the possibility of references from national courts is left to the national government's discretion.

Notwithstanding this, a variety of writers have argued that a number of mechanisms exist at the disposal of the national governments which severely curtail the autonomy of the ECJ (Garrett, 1992, 1995a; Garrett and Weingast, 1993; Garrett, Keleman and Schulz, 1998). These mechanisms include non-compliance with ECJ judgments; replacement of judges at the end of their term; and amendment of legislation to circumvent unfavourable judgments. Non-compliance with any unfavourable judgment would lead to a breakdown in the credibility of the rules underpinning the single market, which the authors argue is in the social and economic interests of the national governments to promote. In order to avoid non-compliance with ECJ judgments, the sanctioning system under Article 228 EC has been enhanced and made more stringent. As a strategic actor, however (so the argument goes), the ECJ is aware that it cannot diverge over a long period from the preferences of the central member states and a de facto principal–agent relationship emerges between it and the national governments.

Any hope that the ECJ could be caged by national governments was a foolish one. As Bzdera has observed, central judicial institutions almost invariably have centralizing rather than particularist tendencies, and are therefore rarely sensitive to locally specific concerns of constituent states (Bzdera, 1992, pp. 133–4). There is little evidence, moreover, that the ECJ systematically behaves in a strategic manner, free from the arguments and legal reasoning presented to it in each individual case. It has taken decisions, for example, that were clearly against the interests of virtually all the national governments, such as declaring the European Economic Area (EEA; see chapter 1) agreement void[32] and holding national governments to be liable to individuals for loss suffered as a result of their failure to comply with EC law.[33]

Such principal–agent accounts suffer from two further structural weaknesses. The first is why, as principals, the national governments should, in these terms, allow such an inefficient agent to endure. The ECJ's inefficiencies lie not just in its backlog. The wide array of matters upon which it is called to adjudicate ranges from constitutional theory through to environmental science, questions of economics, fiscal arrangements and accounting. The ECJ being a collection of generalists, its expertise is obviously found wanting in some of these specializations, the most commented upon being competition (e.g. Bishop, 1981, pp. 294–5; Korah, 2000, pp. 347–57). As an agent it is also inefficient in its inability to generate feelings of wider identification with and support for its behaviour. Studies have shown that while there is reasonable voter satisfaction with the behaviour of the ECJ, it was the least salient of the institutions and enjoyed low diffuse support (Gibson and Caldeira, 1995, 1998). This lack of any reservoir of goodwill renders it particularly vulnerable to attacks where it makes decisions deviating from short-term public opinion.

The second weakness of this account is that it gives an impression which differs so radically from that of the lawyers who work in the field. There is considerable consensus that the judgments of the ECJ follow highly idiosyncratic paths, which appear simultaneously bereft of any long-term strategic vision and highly individualistic. Differences among legal scholars are apt to congregate around the normative characterization of this. To some, it is positive evidence of the upholding of judicial autonomy and the rule of law (Arnull, 1996; Tridimas, 1996) or the upholding of important liberal ideals (Cappelletti, 1987). To others, it smacks of a lack of judicial objectivity (Hartley, 1996, 1999) or unattractive centralizing activism (European Research Group, 1997; Neill, 1996; Rasmussen, 1986, 1998). Yet the bedrock of all this debate is a shared agreement that the ECJ has behaved in such a highly autonomous manner that it is difficult to either explain or predict its case law on the basis of a relationship or series of relationships that it has with a group of other institutional actors.

4.1.2 The national courts

The constitutional case law of the ECJ has resulted in the emergence of three discrete doctrines which allow EC law to be invoked before national courts, and thereby bring them into play in the integration process.

The oldest is that of *direct effect*, which is based on the ECJ's ruling in *Van Gend en Loos*.[34] This allows a provision, which is sufficiently clear, precise and unconditional, to be invoked before a national court. It does not prescribe the remedy that must be applied if the provision is breached other than to stipulate that the remedy should be effective and should not be less favourable than those remedies applying to similar domestic claims.[35] Typically, there are two forms of direct effect. Vertical direct effect is where a provision may be invoked against state or public bodies. It is particularly important in fields of market liberalization where a trader is normally arguing that a law, regulation or administrative measure be disapplied. Horizontal direct effect, by contrast, allows individuals to invoke an EC provision against other private individuals. It is central to fields that rely upon associative obligations such as labour law, consumer law and environmental law where, in the vast majority of cases, it will be a private party that is being sued. Depending upon the wording of the provision, EC Treaty provisions, provisions of regulations and provisions of certain international agreements entered into by the EC can be vertically and horizontally directly effective (for more on this see Weatherill and Beaumont, 1999, pp. 392–413). Directives, by contrast, are only vertically directly effective; they cannot generate a cause of action against private parties.[36] Nevertheless, this limit on the direct effect of directives has been tempered by a number of things. First of all, it has become clear from the case law of the ECJ that the concepts of 'state' and 'public body', in relation to which provisions of directives can be vertically directly effective, must be broadly interpreted.[37] In addition, directives are allowed to be used as a defence against actions brought in national law by private parties.[38] As directives are the central instruments used in the fields of the single market, the environment, social policy and consumer protection, the fact that they do not have horizontal direct effect has diminished judicial protection in these fields. It has also given rise to inequalities where the capacity of parties performing identical functions to sue depended on the wholly extraneous circumstance of the status of the defendant, namely whether it was a private or public body.[39]

A second doctrine emerged, that of *indirect effect*. This requires national courts to interpret all national law so as to conform with EC law in so far as it is given discretion to do so under national law. A strong interpretive duty is thereby placed on national courts, which applies whether or not the national legislation was intended to implement EC law and whether or not the national precedes the EC provision in question.[40] The effect of this was to allow all binding EC law, including directives, to be invoked, albeit indirectly, in disputes between private parties. Nevertheless, the results were unsatisfactory. Apart from the uncertainty and instability this doctrine brings to national law (De Búrca, 1992), there are circumstances where it will not guarantee the judicial application of EC law. The doctrine is of little effect where either the national provision explicitly or implicitly contradicts the EC provision or there is no national provision to interpret. There is a further exception which prevents this doctrine being applied to directives where the effect would be to determine or aggravate criminal liability.[41]

The third doctrine that seeks to compensate for this is that of *state liability*.[42] Individuals can sue the state for compensation where an EC provision grants them individual rights and they have suffered loss as a consequence of the state's illegal conduct. While the doctrine provided strong incentives for national governments to implement and apply EC law, it met strong opposition from national administrations which, in the light of the inherent uncertainties in EC law, saw it as imposing open-ended, financially onerous duties upon them (United Kingdom Government, 1996, paras. 8–10). The doctrine was thus mitigated so that a breach of EC law by a member state, *simpliciter*, was insufficient to ground liability. It was necessary that the breach be sufficiently serious.[43] While the full doctrinal implications of this are still being probed, it appears there are three scenarios that justify liability. These are a failure to transpose a directive;[44] a failure to follow settled case law;[45] and a failure to follow EC law where there is no reasonable doubt about the application of the provision.[46]

While these doctrines still leave gaps where individuals will be unable to invoke EC provisions before national courts, their sweep is still considerable. The Registrar of the ECJ estimated therefore that it has, on its records, 30,000 instances of

EC law being considered by national courts (conversation with author, 9 July 1999). In this, the importance of national courts is threefold.

First, they act as gatekeepers to the preliminary reference procedure. Enabling EC law to be invoked in national courts transformed the preliminary reference procedure into the central source of jurisdiction for the ECJ. This is not simply a quantitative process. In qualitative terms, in all areas other than the institutional prerogatives of the EU institutions the most difficult and path-breaking questions upon which the ECJ has had to adjudicate have come via this procedure. This is, in itself, hardly surprising given the heterogeneity of courts and litigants who contribute to this procedure and the legal training and resources that these collectively can put into the formulation of questions of EC law.

Second, national courts have become important interlocutors of EC law. Only a small proportion of cases go to the ECJ. In the UK, for example, it is estimated that about one in six of the recorded judgments in which EC law is considered in any depth by the national court results in a reference to the ECJ (Chalmers, 2000b). A similar study in Spain found an even lower proportion of references, with 90.1 per cent of cases not referred (Rameu, 2002, pp. 23–4). Yet the disciplines of EC law have been generally accepted by national courts (Slaughter, Stone Sweet and Weiler, 1998). This entails a transformation of the national legal system, so that, in Weiler's words, national courts 'render Community law not as a counter-system to national law, but as part of the national legal order to which attaches "the habit of obedience" and the general respect, at least of public authority, to the "law"' (Weiler, 1994, p. 519). At its narrowest, the assertion that an EC provision can be invoked before a national court will involve the tailoring of surrounding national procedures and remedies. More far-reaching, however, is the fact that it often involves substantial administrative reorganization. This can take the form of the creation of new powers of judicial review not previously available to the courts, or the widening of those courts which are to have powers of judicial review. It can also mean that areas such as competition policy and environmental law, which

traditionally were not dealt with in a substantial way in the judicial arena, have increasingly to be decided by judges. Matters previously dealt with through the language of collective goods now have to be considered in terms of individual rights.

There is, however, another aspect to national courts' roles as interlocutors of EC law. They act, in many ways, as laboratories for the understanding of and experimentation in EC law. National courts provide arenas for the testing, debating and refining of EC norms. Furthermore, the preliminary reference procedure allows the experiences of one national court and the responses of it and the ECJ to be communicated across the Union (de la Mare, 1999). This results in national courts acting, in many areas of EC law, as important dynamos for the transformation not just of national law but also of EC law.

National courts have a final role as enforcers of EC law. In this, their involvement significantly enhanced the formal effectiveness of EC law in a number of ways. The institutional position of national courts within national constitutional settlements resolves the compliance problems that have traditionally bedevilled judgments of international judicial bodies. Failure to comply with the judgment of a national court is seen as a breakdown in the rule of law in all EU jurisdictions. Application of EC law by national courts also allows for a wider interpretation of EC norms than would be likely to be the case if they were merely subject to the auto-interpretation of national ministries. Enforcement of EC law through national courts brings other benefits. It decentralizes the system of enforcement, thereby reducing costs and barriers to enforcement. By enabling private parties, through litigation, to become involved in the process of enforcement, it also provides incentives for more effective enforcement by attaching the power of initiative, in the form of the grant of individual rights, to those whose property or interests are impaired.

That said, this system of decentralized judicial enforcement is not without its limits. By only allowing those who can show infringement of their individual rights to bring a matter before a national court, the constitutionalizing case law of the ECJ privileges private interests over collective goods, such as the protection of the environment, public health, social cohesion and prevention of regional disparities (Harlow, 1996). A feature of the latter is that their 'public' nature prevents any one individual being able to appropriate and thereby assert an individual interest in them. The result is that legislation protecting the latter has generally been less fully applied and been subject to more individual complaints about non-compliance by national governments than EC law asserting market or other private rights (CEC, 1996e).

In their capacity as gatekeepers, interlocutors and enforcers, national courts act as the fulcrum of the ECJ's power. This has prompted debate as to why they have been generally ready to accept EC law. Undoubtedly, such acceptance has been facilitated by the ECJ being sensitive to the arguments of higher national courts. Thus, it has responded to prompts from national courts that it develop a fundamental rights doctrine; not accord the EC unlimited powers; nor allow directives to impose duties on individuals by tailoring EC law accordingly (Chalmers, 1997a). Yet these, by their nature are high-profile and occasional. They cannot explain the structural conditions that might induce national courts more generally to apply EC law.

A variety of theories has emerged in this regard. There are, on the one hand, theories that cast national courts as strategic actors who apply EC law because it allows them to maximize their interests or preferences. It has been argued that acceptance of EC law was prompted by courts wishing to acquire or exercise powers of judicial review at the expense of other arms of government (Weiler, 1993; Burley and Mattli, 1993; Mattli and Slaughter, 1998); lower courts wishing not merely to acquire new powers of review, but also to escape existing judicial hierarchies (Alter, 1996, 1998b, 2001; Mattli and Slaughter, 1998); and courts wishing to exercise their own policy preferences at the expense of national legislatures (Golub, 1996a). While such analyses may have some force in some cases, they make highly contestable assumptions about the motivation for judicial decisions and disregard any impact that the surrounding legal con-

text or legal reasoning will exert upon the decision. They are unable to explain why national courts should behave in this manner when, traditionally, there has been resistance to the application of international legal norms (Benvenisti, 1993). Empirical studies therefore suggest little general support for any of these theses (Stone Sweet and Brunell, 1997). Other arguments rely more upon courts acting as socialized institutions. It is therefore argued that they are induced to accept EC law by the formal pull of legal language (Weiler, 1993) or because it fits with their perception of this being the appropriate judicial thing to do, either because this was being done by their peers or because EC law asserted rights-based discourses and notions of judicial autonomy (Chalmers, 1997a; Plötner, 1998; Rameu, 2002). Others have observed that its incorporation into national legal orders results in a transmutation of EC law, with it becoming tailored to the culture and context of these legal orders, with a corollary limiting its ability to bring about substantial change (Conant, 2002). These theories are more case-sensitive and bring questions of identity and context more to the fore. Yet, by relying on existing identities, they suffer from being unable to explain transformation other than to rationalize it, unconvincingly, as being some form of extension of existing processes.

The limitations of these respective accounts have led some authors to amalgamate them so that weight is given to all of the above factors (Slaughter, Stone Sweet and Weiler, 1998; Alter, 1998b, 2001, pp. 45–52). Such amalgamations probably give a more complete list of the motives that are likely to lead national courts to accept EC law. Yet, in their inability to explain how competing variables should be weighed against each other, the last paradigms hint at the difficulties in this area of providing a single explanation across such a wide field where individual courts will be subject to varying institutional, cultural and sectoral contexts.

4.1.3 Litigants and other players

Most actor-based theories of EC law acknowledge that national courts, while important, act only as intermediaries. The opportunity structures they provide lead to their being surrounded by networks of actors and interests. They serve not merely to inform these interests of EC law and resolve disputes between them. As reactive bodies which must respond to the arguments and interests that appear before them, they enjoy a dialectical relationship with actors. These articulate, refract and test their judgments as well as provide the legal disputes and legal arguments that constitute the raw material of litigation. Attention has focused on a variety of groups.

Materialist analyses argue that the growth of transnational exchange within the EU has generated a demand for a supranational organization in order to reduce transaction costs. Part of any such organization must include a system of legal rules and a system of dispute resolution. Such analyses therefore draw a causal link between the degree of intra-EC trade and the quantity of litigation of EC law (Stone Sweet and Caporaso, 1998; Stone Sweet and Brunell, 1998). They infer this from two features. On the one hand, the increase in preliminary references over the long term mirrors the increase in intra-EC trade. In addition, fewer references have come from those jurisdictions where intra-EC trade constitutes a lower proportion of national GDP. Such analyses see the transnational merchant as someone who is not only the central motor behind the development of EC litigation, but has used the opportunities created by the EC court structure to develop a governance regime outside the nation-state. Yet such actors have traditionally developed private legal regimes, such as the *lex mercatoria*, outside the court system altogether (Teubner, 1997). This transnationalization of exchange, combined with the restructuring and internationalization of the European legal profession, has led increasingly to large law firms and arbitrators acting as important additional generators of rules of the game for the single market (Dezalay, 1992; Trubek et al., 1994).

As a paradigm, materialist analyses treat as unproblematic the processes which lead parties to go to court and which they use in going to court. There has been criticism of analyses which focus predominantly on transnational exchange. It has been argued that the time it takes for new transnational alliances to emerge is so great that they arrive on the 'scene too late to play the game' (Conant, 2001). Instead, on the basis of a comparative analysis of references from France, Germany and the UK, Conant argues that the extent to which EC law is invoked will depend far more upon pre-existing domestic institutions. They will be affected, on the one hand, by the extent to which they are able to adjust to and 'fit' with substantive EC law. She argues that equally important are pre-existing patterns of civil litigation and the presence of resources or public institutions that facilitate access to the courts. The high number of referrals in the UK, by contrast to the other two, in areas such as social security, labour law (and one could add VAT) is thus influenced by a system of accessible, low-cost tribunals and public support in the form of Citizens' Advice Bureaux.

Other commentators have noticed a division within domestic structures between 'one-shotters' and 'repeat players' (Mattli and Slaughter, 1998, pp. 186–92). The former are litigants merely interested in winning the particular case in hand. Repeat players, by contrast, treat litigation as part of a two-level game (on this more generally within the EU see Anderson and Liefferink, 1997). EC law and courts are used as a counterweight by parties where they have been unable to attain their objectives through local law or in national administrative and legislative arenas. They take a more prospective view of law in which the gains they seek are modifications of the rules of the game. As a consequence, they are less inclined to settle out of court and more likely to engage in repeated litigation, 'forum-shopping' before a number of tribunals. In a limited number of instances, such actors come directly before the ECJ (Harding, 1992). This institution's restrictive standing requirements and the proximity of the national courts have meant that, more frequently, they come before the latter. Such actors can be commercial groups of actors, as was the case in the Sunday trading saga, where a series of DIY stores engaged in repeated litigation under EC law to bring about a change in the legislation in Britain on trading hours (Rawlings, 1993). They can also be non-governmental organizations which seek to further certain post-material values and may seek to do this either by litigating directly or by providing support for litigants in areas of strategic interest – the latter tactic was pursued by the Equal Opportunities Commission in the UK (Barnard, 1995; Alter and Vargas, 2000). Repeat actors not only influence some areas of EC law – notably free movement of goods, gender discrimination and some areas of environmental law – disproportionately more than others, although their effects ripple out across the Union, but their incidence is unevenly distributed across the different member states. Alter and Vargas have noted that a number of conditions normally have to materialize for such groups to take action (Alter and Vargas, 2000). As litigation is an avenue of last resort, there have to be strong patterns of institutional exclusion from other arenas for such groups. It would appear to be an advantage that such groups have a narrow mandate and constituency. More dispersed groups may not have the concentration of expertise, and internal conflicts of interest might arise that will prevent litigation and provide incentives to spend resources elsewhere. Furthermore, such groups will seek narrowly focused policy gains, the costs for which may be widely distributed and therefore not strongly opposed.

All interest-group theories acknowledge that interest groups cannot, alone, engineer EC legal change. They point, in particular, to the importance of sympathetic judiciaries (Mattli and Slaughter, 1998; Alter and Vargas, 2000). Yet there is another group of actors who are important to the development of EC law and that is the EC legal community. It was widely acknowledged that, certainly in the first thirty years, the capacity of the ECJ to establish EC law doctrine was dependent upon a community of lawyers and academics, specialists in EC law, who could provide new arguments for the fleshing out and development of EC law, analogize it to national legal systems and doctrines, and disseminate and advocate it amongst both lay and legal communities (Stein, 1981). This community was, certainly in each member state, relatively small and many of the high-profile writers had strong institutional links with either the Commission or the ECJ. It is also not unfair to suggest that most of the early writing was sympathetic both to the general idea of EC integration and to the process of integration being done

through legal instruments and judicial interpretation (Schepel and Wesseling, 1997). The unfolding of EC law over time and its expansion into new areas have destroyed this cohesion. New academics, with axes to grind and totems to smash, have emerged on the one hand (for a discussion of this see Shaw, 1999), and academics and professionals from other fields, reticent about the destabilizing effects of EC law on those fields, have begun to discuss EC law (e.g. Teubner, 1998). This is not leading to legal communities ceasing to have influence over the integration process. It is probably more accurate to suggest a recasting of this influence within which specialized legal communities, increasingly brought together by the function of the law in which they specialize rather than its designation, have a heightened influence over narrow areas of expertise (on trade marks see Chalmers, 1997b).

4.2 The structuring of EU integration through EU law

All actor-interest theories of EU law conceive of EU law in relatively passive terms. It is something used by particular actors to prosecute particular advantages. Its enabling qualities are confined to the creation of particular legal institutions, notably courts, which provide opportunity structures for additional actors. Yet law is not infinitely malleable. Even as an agent of national preferences the ECJ can only express these in terms of individual rights and win–lose (as opposed to mediated) scenarios and act on the basis of the limited information that parties, constrained by processes of standing and intervention, can put before it. The relationship is therefore a dialectic one, in which the very features of EU law that make it attractive for actors to be involved in its formulation and application also configure those and other actors' actions.

4.2.1 The symbolic effects of EU law

Giving legal value to certain arrangements carries with it certain symbolic effects (Dehousse and Weiler, 1990, p. 244). The formality of legal texts confers greater weight to commitments. Even instruments such as recommendations, which do not formally oblige parties to do anything, nevertheless indicate a description of good practice agreed by all the parties who have adopted the instrument. Yet it is nevertheless true that the degree of commitment, in symbolic terms at least, is often reflected in the prescriptive terms of the instrument used. The increasing commitment to integrate environmental concerns into other EC policies was therefore reflected in the manner in which it started as an undertaking in the Third Action Plan on the Environment in 1983 (see chapter 17); was made a treaty commitment (Article 130r(4) EC in 1986 by the SEA); was placed at the head of the Title on the Environment by the Maastricht Treaty in 1991 (Article 130r(2) EC); and was then placed as one of the principles of the treaty by the Treaty of Amsterdam in 1996 (Article 6 EC). While the commitment was not actively pursued in a general manner until the mid-1990s (Wilkinson, 1997), this intensification made it increasingly difficult for the principle to be contested at the policy-making level, with debate focusing far more on the modalities of operation.

Translating a matter into law also confers a recognition upon it, which gives it both a greater importance and greater priority. Dehousse and Weiler therefore mention how it was the legal nature of the Élysée Treaty between France and Germany in 1963 on military cooperation that caused controversy. For it suggested a prioritization of defence links between these states over commitments to other states, despite the agreement being relatively empty of substantial commitments (Dehousse and Weiler, 1990, pp. 244–5). More recently, the European citizenship provisions introduced into the EC Treaty by the TEU conferred few new rights upon individuals.[47] The provisions provoked such a backlash, however, that the member states felt, at the Edinburgh European Council in 1992, that to enable the second Danish referendum on Maastricht to be successful the provision had to be revised to indicate explicitly that it did not encroach upon national citizenship. In symbolic terms, the adoption of laws at an EU level has a tri-dimensional quality.

As EU law signifies law beyond the nation-state, it relativizes national law, irrespective of the form it takes. EU law, whether intended to supplant or supplement national measures, exposes the functional limits of nation-state legal structures and pluralizes legal authority within the territory of any state. Legal authority becomes something constructed from a variety of sources rather than simply the national constitution (MacCormick, 1993, 1999). The opposition between EU law and national law leads to further dichotomies. At its crassest, the justifications for EU law residing in the limitations of national law create a characterization within which the EU acts as a form of enlightened, cosmopolitan counterweight to the atavistic qualities of the nation-state (Fitzpatrick, 1997); some even urge this (e.g. Weiler, 1997a). Others have noted a tension within which EU law may justify itself by reason of arguments of rationalization, efficiency and integration, but the pluralization of its implementation creates new schisms and dislocations within the national legal system (Wilhelmsson, 1995; Schepel, 1997; Teubner, 1998).

Second, the 'Euro-centrism' of EU law lies also in its signifying an intensification of cooperation and integration between certain polities and societies to the exclusion of others. Numerous commentators have therefore pointed to its creating new insider/outsider pathologies (Geddes, 1995; Hervey, 1995; Ward, 1996, pp. 147–52). This dichotomy does not simply run along crude EU/non-EU lines. All legal instruments, in so far as they generate their own processes of bounding, will contain elements of integration/inclusion and elements of exclusion/disintegration. For any legislation will empower or disempower and impose duties or rights selectively (Shaw, 1996). As a text, it will, furthermore, translate roles, identities, etc. in a manner in which only facets are recognized, to the exclusion of other aspects.

The third symbolic quality of EU law derives from the interaction between it and the policy domain it governs. EU law enlarges understanding of a policy domain, not through creating that policy domain for the first time – be it environment, health and safety, etc. – but by giving it a European dimension. The policy domain can no longer be understood without taking account of this dimension. A new horizon is added which might include new networks, technologies, instruments or values (Barry, 1993). In this manner, EU law is a practical manifestation of the way in which 'Europe' transforms understandings and expectations of a particular field, irrespective of questions of fact, interests and preferences (Christiansen, 1997).

4.2.2 The stabilization of expectations about EU government

A feature of EU law is its normativity. This norma-tivity provides that EU law cannot be falsified by subsequent conduct. That is to say, where conduct deviates from the norm, it will be the conduct rather than the norm that will be considered deviant (i.e. illegal). This results in EU law being the central instrument through which expecta-tions are stabilized about the distribution, reach and modalities of power within the EU system of government. It is the legal instruments which detail what powers the EU enjoys and how it empowers and restricts those within its embrace.

At the very least, therefore, EU law sets out the rules of the game, and there is an expectation that they will be habitually obeyed. Rational choice institutionalists qualify this by claiming that while such rules may not affect parties' deep-seated preferences, they do, by forestalling certain options, determine the strategies adopted by the parties (e.g. Pollack, 1997; Tsebelis and Kreppel, 1998; Tsebelis and Garrett, 2000). Classically, therefore, legal constraints on national govern-ments' ability to curb the Commission's exercise of its powers may lead to their trying to secure influence within the Commission. Even within the parameters of this analysis, the influence of EU law is considerable.

It prevents certain outcomes being achieved, irrespective of the preferences of the parties. The decision of the ECJ in 1975 that the Community should enjoy exclusive competence in the field of external trade did not bring about a uniform com-mercial policy.[48] Yet it forestalled national govern-ment unilateralism, by requiring any autonomous measure to be first approved by either the Council or the Commission, with the consequence that any unilateral measure had to illustrate that it did not impinge excessively on other national or Community interests.

EU law also challenges existing asymmetries of power. In the case of the legislative influence of the EP, not only do legal provisions 'constitute' the Parliament through providing for its existence, but it is the legal peculiarities of the cooperation and co-decision procedures which enable the Parliament to act, in many circumstances, as a 'conditional agenda-setter' (Tsebelis, 1994; Scully, 1997; Tsebelis and Garrett, 1997). For they make it easier for the Council to accept parliamentary amendments (which with Commission agree-ment can be approved by qualified majority voting (QMV) in the Council) than to introduce its own (which require unanimity). The consequence of this is an increased propensity on the part of member states to accept Parliament's amend-ments. For the test is no longer whether this is an 'ideal' amendment, but, *faute de mieux*, becomes whether this is an improvement on the original proposal. In such circumstances, the legal proce-dures have resulted in the preferences of a player other than the national governments becoming important, and inevitably require that national governments realign their behaviour, and, to some degree, thereby adjust their preferences, if legislation contrary to their interests is not to be passed. The increased use of the co-decision pro-cedure, which confers a veto right upon the Parliament, has led to a greater incentive on the part of the member states to compromise. This is illustrated by practice, where informal meet-ings (trialogues) between representatives of the Council, the Commission and the Parliament have been instituted in order to facilitate compromise in the decision-making procedure.

Legal structures determine outcomes in another way. As outcomes have to be translated into legal structures, actors are able to use prior legal structures to pattern outcomes and negotia-tions. Most famously, the Commission exploited the *Cassis de Dijon* judgment to provide the basis for its New Approach to Harmonization which lay at the heart of the 1992 programme (Alter and Meunier-Aitsahalia, 1994). This judgment stated that Article 28 EC, on the provision on free movement of goods, required member states, in the absence of a compelling public interest, to grant market access to products lawfully marketed or manufactured in another member state.[49] Undoubtedly, it shifted Article 28 EC away from being an instrument that exclusively tackled discriminatory, protectionist measures to one that was essentially deregulatory in nature, which was concerned with sweeping away measures that had unnecessarily restrictive effects upon inter-state trade. Beyond that, the parameters of the judgment were inconclusive (Barents, 1982; Chalmers, 1993). The Commission argued, however, that the judgment entrenched the principle of mutual recognition, whereby a member state should accept that the regulatory requirements of the member state where the good (or service) was produced were, in principle, equivalent to its own ([1980] OJ C256/2). This alleviated the need for total harmonization of regulatory requirements by the Community. Instead, an approach based on mutual recognition transformed the role of the EC legislature into that of providing minimum guarantees. It would harmonize only those essential health and safety standards that were necessary to prevent member states claiming that trade infringed some essential public interest ([1985] OJ C136/1). This governance structure was conceived as placing limits on EC legislative output, preserving national regulatory traditions and increasing consumer choice. To be sure, it allowed different interests to be reconciled in a manner which had not previously been possible. It also structured future relations and provided the source of future tensions. These included doubts about the standardization bodies' capacity to develop standards quickly enough or in a sufficiently pluralist manner (Vos, 1998, pp. 281–308); and breakdowns in the mutual trust and national internal administrative organization required to bring about mutual recognition (CEC, 1999b, pp. 4–5).

While the autonomy given to actors by EU legal structures affords them the possibility of using these strategically, a feature of legal autonomy is that it always gives actors the possibility of complying with the law on no grounds other than simple legal obedience. Others have observed that

in so far as EU law allows, there exists the possibility of inculcating certain patterns of obedience and behaviour. In this manner, it is argued, EU law not only stabilizes patterns of behaviour, but also produces socializing effects which transform and adapt expectations and preferences (Armstrong and Bulmer, 1998; Armstrong, 1998; Shaw and Wiener, 1999). The general force of this argument is not undermined by such effects being difficult to prove or disprove in any one instance. It is also not necessarily incompatible with the argument that actors also use law strategically. In both instances, the law in question 'frames' the action in question. It influences the modalities of behaviour of the actor by simultaneously enabling and foreclosing certain courses of action. Thus, the legal structure of subsidiarity came to frame and emasculate debates about the intensity and breadth of EC law-making in the post-Maastricht era, so that protagonists on all sides couched their arguments in terms of that structure (Maher, 1995). The question of whether an actor responds strategically to this frame is both largely a matter of degree and one of ex post facto rationalization. The degree to which legal or other structures condition actions will vary according to the dynamics of the relations entered into at the time (Granovetter, 1985). No actor is ever completely conditioned by any one structure, but analysis of the level of conditioning will be assessed by reference to the extent of determined calculation on the part of that actor; that is to say to what extent the actor uses other recognizable structures in interactions with legal instruments (Callon, 1998). In the *Cassis de Dijon* example, therefore, the Commission was taken to be acting strategically because it used the judgment as the basis for a series of political structures which distributed governmental power. Nevertheless, a degree of framing was present as it perceived these in terms of an overarching principle, namely free movement of goods. It will be obvious from this that not only may EU law appear to socialize some actors more heavily than others, but a condition of law is that it allows for the possibility of strategic and socialized interaction with all actors. The degree to which particular players act strategically will therefore vary across context.

4.3 Law as the cipher for the legitimacy of the EU

One corollary to the normativity of law is that law always has the ability to acquire different meanings. A bald legal statement that 'theft is wrong' would transmutate, to prevent falsification, when confronted with the situation of the person who steals to survive, either by providing a justification or by modifying the definition of theft. This means that an invocation of law involves not merely its application to a particular situation but also an 'idealising moment of unconditionality that takes it beyond its immediate context' (Rehg, 1996, p. xiii). A legal interpretation is thus never just a description of the political settlement or social interaction it regulates, but also a prescriptive assertion of what it ought to be. Law is distinguished from morality or ethics in that it only governs social interaction and does not purport to regulate or judge behaviour that falls outside this interaction. Yet it is their shared features of normativity – namely that both prescribe norms which enjoy a priority over any subsequent conduct and which are never fully directly observable in that their meaning can never be derived from any single context – that allow government framed by law or enacted through legislation to describe itself as value-oriented (Chalmers, 2000b). It also leads to EU law being seen as the central cipher through which the values of the EU are to be understood. Most notably, therefore, debates about legitimacy and reform of the EU revolve around legal reform, as law is premised, perhaps falsely, as the enabling medium through which these questions can be gauged and re-established. A good example of this is the current debate on the legitimacy of further EU integration after the rejection by France and the Netherlands of the Treaty establishing a Constitution for Europe. In this debate, the values that are and should be characterizing European integration are thoroughly discussed, as is the shape future EU integration ought to be taking.

In this context legal integration, within the EC pillar of the TEU at least, has been seen as being characterized by a series of liberal attributes (Slaughter, 1995, pp. 510–14). These include the assurance of peaceful relations between member states; the assurance of some degree of civil and political rights, now brought together under the umbrella of 'European citizenship'; and the protection of transnational transactions and cross-boundary property rights. It also includes the emergence of transgovernmental communications, which not only involve ties between national administrations but collapse traditional foreign/domestic distinctions through the 'recognition of multiple actors exercising different types and modes of governmental authority' (Slaughter, 1995, p. 513) in increasingly pluralistic and heterarchical patterns (MacCormick, 1993, 1996, 1999).

The liberal paradigm draws a nexus between legal integration and achievement of these values (Reich, 1997). Within this understanding, the broader the reach of EC legal integration and the more intensely it is pursued, the greater the likelihood that these values will be achieved. These attributes provide the source for much of the criticism of EU law. Thus EC law is castigated for not going far enough to afford judicial protection to rights granted under EC law (Szyszczak, 1996); not extending market freedoms sufficiently widely (Arnull, 1991; Gormley, 1994); failing to extend its fundamental rights competence sufficiently broadly (Alston and Weiler, 1999); and not affording third-country nationals the same market rights as EU citizens (Hedemann-Robinson, 1996). Within the liberal paradigm, individual autonomy, protected through the grant of certain liberal rights, is to be complemented by the notion of public autonomy within which each individual agrees to limit his or her freedoms so as to ensure the freedom of others. The right to an equal distribution of liberties and constraints can only be given concrete shape, however, through the exercise of legislation in which all have the right to participate (Habermas, 1996, p. 125). It is possible, therefore, to argue that a similar line of liberal reasoning underpins those 'republican' theories which push for a broadening of participatory and dialogic opportunities for private parties in EC law-making and administration (Craig, 1997; Weiler, 1997b; Scott, 1998; Bellamy and Warleigh, 1998).[50]

The above suggests that all that is needed to remedy the 'legitimacy deficit' of the Union is for the reforms they recommend to be adopted. This legal vision of integration posits this deficit as simply residing in the Union not being sufficiently ideological.

This view has been criticized on the ground that there is an inevitable 'integration/disintegration' nexus to any liberal paradigm of law. Within this it is argued that, within the EU, any system of law inevitably generates new patterns not merely of inclusion but also of exclusion and alienation (Shaw, 1996). This is likely to be particularly the case with the liberal paradigm. By seeking to enhance the autonomy of the Imaginary Subject this rewards the attributes of the competitive and the efficient and those with the resources to translate their autonomy into substantive gains at the expense of those without these capacities.

Others have also observed that it is too simplistic to attribute a single set of values to an organization such as the EU, and that within any legal instrument a plurality of values is present (Joerges, 1996). Thus it has been argued that central structures within much of EC regulation are knowledge-based, with EC regulation acting to secure the primacy of certain forms of knowledge over other forms (Sand, 1998). It has been noted in the field of policing that the principal values are those of 'securitization', the central pathologies of which are surveillance and re-establishing or consolidating certain territorial patterns of control (Chalmers, 1998). Within this mêlée, EU law acts more as an arena for bringing to the fore and institutionalizing conflicts between values. In so far as particular values are recognized, conflicts become patterned, recurrent and routinized (e.g. trade versus the environment, freedom versus security, etc.). Within such an environment it becomes increasingly difficult to argue for the priority of particular values. Instead, legitimization becomes centred around the perfection of dispute-resolution processes that seek to rationalize or mediate between these interests or values. This might be through seeking to optimize a set of outcomes having regard to a set of pre-given preferences (Majone, 1998) or through exclusively processual means, such as requiring all decision-makers either to recognize (Shaw, 1999) or to enter into dialogue with and be accountable

to certain interests or identities (Joerges, 1996; Shapiro, 1996).

4.4 Actor-network theories

Like the two sides of a coin, structural accounts of EU law encounter the reverse objections to those made against actor-interest accounts. By failing to consider the contexts in which EU law is invoked, which actors invoke EU law and which frames are adopted by actors when considering EU law, they are criticized for treating EU law in too isolated a manner. Nuances are thus skated over and contingencies dismissed. Centrally, as they have no theory of agency, they struggle to explain how EU law is transformed over time or even adopted in the first place.

While both actor-interest and structural accounts present valuable insights into how EU law contributes to the integration process, it is the dichotomy that they draw that leads to the failings of each. More generally, they tend to centre upon the contribution of law to EU government and administration. A feature of law, however, is that it transcends the political system. On the one hand, it is through law that claims are made against or on the political system. Conversely, a feature of law is that it communicates a vision of governance to social, economic and cultural arenas outside the political system (within the EU context see Chalmers, 1999; Zürn and Wolf, 1999; Shaw and Wiener, 1999). EC environmental, labour and health and safety legislation all structure how the workplace is organized, and can be used as instruments in negotiations, for example between management and labour. EU law also serves to restructure expectations in these arenas. Thus, in its first significant review of the Single European Market in 1996 the Commission observed that a perennial complaint of traders was patchy transposition of EC directives and uneven enforcement of EC law (CEC, 1996f, p. 20). Nevertheless, after the enactment of the programme, while there were mixed views on whether restrictions on trade had been removed, 29 per cent of small and medium-sized enterprises (SMEs) and 7 per cent of large firms felt that the process, necessarily a legal one, had encouraged them to export (CEC, 1996f, pp. 12–13). A new structural review of the SEM will be carried out in the near future.

A paradigm that seeks to capture these features, as well as the mutually transformative qualities of agency and structure, is the actor-network theory. This conceives of EU law as being both implicated in and generating a series of networks (Ladeur, 1997). These are:

the process of co-operation itself which furnishes solutions to complex problems via joint problem definition and the drafting of a possible decision, which is then subject to ongoing evaluation on the basis of 'new' knowledge (that is new technology, new management forms, the definition of new social risks and so forth).

Networks do not merely consist in the identification of stable and pre-existing interests; rather they themselves generate new operating knowledge. (Ladeur, 1997, p. 46)

Such networks straddle any form of political/ economic or public/private delimitation. As the network defines the mode of participation of actors and the attributes through which others recognize them, it is the network that serves to reconfigure actors' identities. It will also be clear that at any one time any single actor will be participating in multiple networks. The model is not without its disadvantages. It is elusive on how networks emerge or terminate. In addition, while it emphasizes the interplay of relationships, as high levels of interdependence can stretch on indefinitely, it is obtuse about how networks bound themselves, so as to enable one network to start and another to stop. Yet it points to EU law contributing in a central manner to a transnational society through the putting in place of a series of interlocking, interdependent relationships which serve to reforge functions and identities around new axes.

In this, legal networks are differentiated from other networks by their relatively high levels of formalization and textual dependencies. A feature of any legislation is that it sets in place in a relatively immutable manner who may and may not participate in a network and the forms of relationship participants may enjoy with others. While such relationships are not so rigid that transformation cannot take place, this feature contributes to legal networks having a high

propensity for path dependency. The tracks down which the initial relationships are channelled cannot be changed. As time passes these routines become central to the constitution of the network, with the result that legal networks tend to be more stabilized and patterned than other forms. Through patterning and stabilization of transnational society, EU law performs another function, in that it allows this society to generate securities and routines which act as artefacts for participants to look to, in an otherwise unstable and fast-moving world.

The second feature of legal networks is that they revolve around the interpretation of a legal text. They are thus distinct from epistemic communities, which are centred around some form of prized, shared knowledge, and economic networks, which are centred around some form of material exchange. As actors configure their actions around the interpretation of this text, the text has the power to bring actors into mutually transformative relations not just with other actors but also with non-human objects (Callon, 1986; Latour, 1993). As others adapt their behaviour to the articulated qualities of these objects, EU law allows these to acquire a status and a power within the integration process.

For example, the qualities ascribed to Special Areas of Conservation (SAC) by the Habitats Directive (see chapter 17), namely their high conservation status, and the need for their status to be restored or for them to maintain that status has shaped a number of policies.[51] The establishment of both the specific guidelines on TENS and proposals for individual networks must take account of the needs of these areas.[52] They are eligible for specific finance under the funds earmarked for the environment[53] and grants under the Cohesion Fund will be influenced by whether a project contributes to a SAC.[54] The need for a development project to undergo an environment impact assessment will also depend upon whether it impairs a SAC.[55]

4.5 Conclusion

From all this it will be clear that it is better to conceive of EU law as bringing a variety of new dimensions to the integration process. How central does all this render EU law to the integration process? All the above perspectives agree upon the quintessentially formal nature of EU law. This formality establishes very clear limits for its contribution to governance. The only opportunities, values, behaviour and relationships that can be influenced by EU law are ones that respond to formal structures, typically those centred around economic transactions or political opportunities. There are plenty of forms of interaction that operate outside and that are largely unresponsive to these structures (Snyder, 1990a, 1999b) – be they economic networks, the dissemination of cultural images or various forms of communication. It is also dangerous to view those that do respond purely through the prism of the legal instruments (Chalmers, 1999). Such confining analysis can obscure the variety of other structures and tensions that impinge upon these actors. Notwithstanding this, the sheer intensity and breadth of EU law renders it an important point of organization within Europe. The formality of EU law contributes to this power by emphasizing the saliencies and certainties of EU law. In EU law one finds a vision both for integration within Europe – set out clearly in the primary texts – and for management of various policy sectors – explored in the secondary legislation. Even if actors choose not to respond to this vision – either positively or negatively – it inevitably forms a backdrop which casts a shadow over almost any form of participation in or resistance to transnational interaction.

NOTES

1 Conseil d'État, Rapport Public 2006, p. 19.
2 It had to be noted that other researchers found that only an average of 15 to 20 per cent of national legislation is influenced by EC directives (see, for example, studies in Denmark by Blom-Hansen and Christensen (2004), in Great Britain by Page (1998) and in the Netherlands by Bovens and Yesilkagit (2005)). These researches also indicate that the percentage of national legislation founded on directives differs greatly between different policy areas: agriculture and environment are areas in which much influence is felt from EC directives and areas like national defence and education are hardly affected.

Nevertheless, these researchers agree that EC legislation has an important impact on national legislation: directly effective regulations, several types of EC soft law and voluntary harmonization and cooperation between member states ensure that the EC has a wider influence on national legislation than the percentages above indicate (see Bovens and Yesilkagit, 2005).

3 The EC pillar is distinguished at various points throughout this chapter, as it involves a more intense form of 'legalization' in terms of the laws made and the actors implicated than the other two pillars.
4 Decision 88/591/EEC, *OJ L* (1988) 319/1.
5 Case 104/79 *Pasquale Foglia* v. *Mariella Novello* [1980] ECR 745 and Case 244/80 *Pasquale Foglia* v. *Mariella Novello* (No. 2) [1981] ECR 3045.
6 E.g. Case C-153/00 *Weduwe*, Judgment of 10 December 2002.
7. Case C-18/93 *Corsica Ferries Italia Srl* v. *Corpo dei Piloti del Porto di Genova* [1994] ECR I-1783.
8 Case C-88/99 *Roquette Frères SA* v. *Direction des Services Fiscaux du Pas-de-Calais* [2000] ECR I-10465.
9 A particularly important reiteration of this view is that of Advocate General Jacobs in Case C-338/95 *Wiener* v. *Hauptzollamt Emmerich* [1997] ECR I-6495.
10 Case 26/62 *Van Gend en Loos* v. Nederlandse *Administratie der Belastingen* [1963] ECR 1; Case 6/64 *Costa* v. *ENEL* [1964] ECR 585.
11 Opinion 1/91 on the Draft Agreement on a European Economic Area [1991] ECR I-6079.
12 Case 314/85 *Firma Fotofrost* v. *0HZA Lubeck Ost* [1987] ECR 4199.
13 *Brunner* v. *European Union Treaty* [1994] 1 CMLR 57; *Carlsen* v. *Rasmussen*, Judgment of the Danish Constitutional Court of 6 April 1998, available at www.um.dk/udenrigspolitik/europa/domeng.
14 CA, 3 February 1994, *École Européenne*, Case No. 12/94, B6.
15 *Re Treaty on European Union*, Judgment of 1 July 1992 of Spanish Constitutional Court [1994] 3 CMLR 101.
16 *Re Treaty on European Union*, Decision 92308 of the Constitutional Council, *Journal Officiel de la République Française* 1992, No. 5354.
17 *R* v. *MAFF ex parte First City Trading* [1997] 1 CMLR 250; *Marks and Spencer* v. *CCE* [1999] 1 CMLR 1152.
18 Granital Foro, it. 1984, I, 2064.
19 *Frontini* v. *Ministero delle Finanze* [1974] 2 CMLR 372.
20 The current German position is that the German Constitutional Court will not review individual EC acts for their compliance with fundamental

rights norms but reserves the right to do so if the general level of protection is not assured. *Bundesverfassungsgericht* 7 June 2000, *EuZW* 702.

21 The amendment to the Swedish Constitution, Chapter 10 Section 5, that paved the way for accession provides for the supremacy of EC law on condition that it complies with the European Convention on Human Rights, U. Bernitz, 'Sweden and the European Union: On Sweden's Implementation and Application of European Law' (2001) 38 *CMLRev* 903, 910–11.

22 *Attorney General* v. *X* [1992] 2 CMLR 277.

23 Case C-388/95 *Kingdom of Belgium* v. *Kingdom of Spain* [2000], ECR I-3123.

24 http://ec.europa.eu/community_law/eulaw/pdf/ XXII_rapport_annuel/annexe2_fr.pdf.

25 Case C-387/97 *Commission* v. *Greece* [2000] ECR I-5047.

26 Case C-304/02 *Commission* v. *France* [2005] ECR 0000.

27 Commission Communication, 14 December 2005.

28 Case 314/85 *Firma Fotofrost* v. *HZA Lubeck Ost* [1987] ECR 4199.

29 Case 283/81 *CILFIT* [1982] ECR 3414.

30 ECJ 8 September 2005, Case C-461/03 *Gaston Schul Douane-expediteur BV* v. *Minister van Landbouw, Natuur en Voedselkwaliteit* [2005] ECR I-10513.

31 See Case C-105/03 Criminal proceedings agains Maria Pupino (2005), ECR I-5285.

32 *Opinion 1/91 on the Draft Agreement on a European Economic Area [1991] ECR I-6079.*

33 Joined Cases C-6 and 9/90 and C-9/90 *Francovich and Others* v. *Italy* [1991] ECR I-5357.

34 Case 26/62 *Van Gend en Loos* v. *Nederlandse Administratie der Belastingen* [1963] ECR 1.

35 Case 45/76 *Comet* v. *Produktschap* [1976] ECR 2043.

36 Case 125/84 *Marshall* v. *Southampton and South-West AHA* [1986] ECR 723, confirmed by Case C-91/92 *Faccini Dori* v. *Recreb Srl* [1994] ECR I-3325. In the recent Case C-144/04 *Werner Mangold* v. *Rüdiger Helm*, it seems, however, that horizontal direct effect might be accorded to a non-discrimination clause from a directive. The exact impact of this case on the doctrine of horizontal direct effect remains unclear.

37 Case C-188/89 *A. Foster and others* v. *British Gas plc* [1990] ECR I-3313; Case 125/84 *Marshall* v. *Southampton and South-West AHA* [1986] ECR 723.

38 Case 194/94 *CIA Security International* v. *Signalson* [1996] ECR I-2201.

39 See the Opinion of Advocate General Jacobs in Case C-316/93 *Vaneetveld* v. *Le Foyer* [1994] ECR I-763.

40 Case C-106/89 *Marleasing* v. *La Comercial* [1990] ECR I-4135.

41 Case 80/86 Criminal proceedings against Kolpinghuis Nijmegen BV [1987], ECR 3969 and Joined Cases C-58, 75, 112, 119, 123, 135, 140–1, 154 and 157/95 *Gallotti* [1996] ECR I-4345.

42 Joined Cases C-6 and 9/90 *Francovich and Boniaci* v. *Italy* [1991] ECR I-5357.

43 Joined Cases C-46 and 49/93 *Brasserie du Pêcheur SA* v. *Germany* [1996] ECR I-1029.

44 Joined Cases C-178, 179, 188–190/94 *Dillenkofer* v. *Germany* [1996] ECR I-4845.

45 Case C-46/93 *Brasserie du Pêcheur* v. *Germany* [1996] ECR I-1029.

46 Case C-5/94 *R* v. *MAFF ex parte Lomas* [1996] ECR I-2553.

47 The scope and meaning of EU citizenship have been enlarged by more recent case law of the ECJ and the adoption of directive 2004/38 on the right of citizens of the Union and their family members to move and reside freely within the territory of the member states.

48 Opinion 1/75 *Local Cost Standard Opinion* [1975] ECR 1355.

49 Case 120/78 *Rewe* v. *Bundesmonopolverwaltung für Branntwein* [1979] ECR 649.

50 The Treaty establishing a Constitution for Europe contained a provision on the principle of participatory democracy (Article I-47), which enabled EU citizens and representative organizations to participate in a dialogue with the institutions and which provided for the possibility of public legislative initiative.

51 Directive 92/43/EC, [1992] *OJ* L 206/7, Articles 3 and 4(4).

52 Decision 1692/96/EC, [1996] *OJ* L 228/1, Article 6.

53 Regulation 1404/96/EC, [1996] *OJ* L 181/1, Article 2(1)(a) (LIFE).

54 E.g. Decision 93/707/EC on the grant of aid to the Closa rising bog in Ireland, [1993] *OJ*, L331/20; Decision 93/714/EC on the restoration of natural resources in natural parks in Spain, [1993] *OJ* L 331/83.

55 Directive 97/11/EC, [1997] *OJ* L 73/5, Annex III, 2(e).

5 The basic statistics

ALI EL-AGRAA

This chapter provides a brief summary of the basic statistics for the EU, its immediate candidates and the member nations of EFTA, since, except for Switzerland, they are all members of the European Economic Area (EEA), which is considered as a stepping-stone to full EU membership (see chapters 1 and 2 where it is also stated that Switzerland has a pending EU membership application). In order to preserve a general sense of perspective, similar information is given for Canada, Japan, the United States and the Russian Federation, since, together with the four largest EU nations, they comprise the group of eight (G8).

The main purpose of the chapter is to provide the latest information since the analysis of longer-term trends and the economic forces that determine them is one of the main tasks of the rest of this book. For example, the analysis of the composition and pattern of trade prior to the inception of the EU and subsequent to its formation is the aim of Part II of the book (EU market integration: theory and practice), especially chapters 8 and 9. Moreover, all the policy chapters are concerned with the analysis of particular areas of interest, such as the social policies, especially the problem of unemployment, the Common Agricultural Policy (CAP), the role of the EU general budget, competition and industrial policies, EU regional policy, etc., and these specialist chapters contain further detailed and pertinent information. In order to display the tables in a visually convenient way, they are provided at the end of the chapter.

5.1 Area and population concerns

Table 5.1a gives information on area, population and life expectancy at birth. Table 5.2 provides supporting data on various aspects of health. Table 5.3 offers data on the labour force and its distribution in terms of the broad categories of agriculture, industry and services, as well as on employment and unemployment. The data are self-explanatory but a few points warrant particular attention.

The EU of twenty-seven (EU27) has a larger population (about 490 million) than any country in the advanced Western world. This population exceeds that of the United States (about 294 million) by about two-thirds (56.6 per cent), is over 3.5 times that of the Russian Federation (about 144 million) and is just over 3.8 times that of Japan. It exceeds the combined population of the United States, Canada and Mexico, the member nations of the North American Free Trade Agreement (NAFTA), by about 60 million (Mexico has a population of about 104 million), and that of the United States and Japan, the world's two largest economies, by about 68 million.

The average annual rate of population growth during 1990–2004 was between −1.1 and 1.4 for the EU, the highest being recorded for Luxembourg, which is not surprising, given its administrative significance within the EU. It is 1 for Canada and 1.2 for the United States, both with high immigration rates. Thus Turkey, with 1.7, is the truly exceptional case within the sample.

Average life expectancy at birth in 2004 is 71–80 years for the EU (77–80 for EU15, i.e. without the twelve members joining in 2004 and 2007), and 77–82 for Canada, Japan and the United States. For the EU, it is 75–84 (79–83 for EU15) years for females and 66–78 (75–8 for EU15) for males and 80–5 for males and 75–8 for females for Canada, Japan and the United States. On the assumption that a difference of, say, a couple of years is of no major significance (there is hardly any need for a

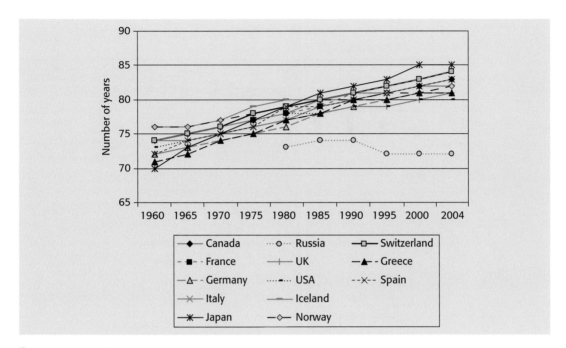

Figure 5.1 Female life expectancy at birth, 1960–2004

calculation of standard deviations here), one can assert that the advanced nations of the world have similar life expectancies. Indeed, ignoring Russia, this has been the case since 1960 as Figures 5.1–5.3, drawn from data in Table 5.1b, clearly reveal for females, males and both sexes. One can therefore throw out of the window all the claims for food affording the Japanese longer lives, for three reasons. First, they lagged behind the rest in the earlier years, i.e. they have not always been at the top. Second, in 2004 it is only Japanese women who are at the top, but by merely one year over their Swiss counterpart. Third, and vitally, Japanese life expectancy is highest in Okinawa where the main diet is pork! I should add that I make an exception using long-term data here simply because the issue is not discussed in this way elsewhere in the book.

One should note the high unemployment rates in the EU as a whole (over 8 per cent as against 5 per cent for the United States), which obscures the reality of Denmark (4.8 per cent) and the UK (4.7 per cent) having lower rates, but to attribute this to their staying out of the euro glosses over Ireland's even lower rate (4.3 per cent). Unemployment has become such an important

issue for the EU that it is now developing into a policy area of its own. Although this book does not contain a specific chapter on it, a large part of chapter 23 on EU social policies is devoted to it: unemployment is a major social concern. It is also touched on in various chapters, especially in chapters 10 and 11, since EMU impinges on it. Chapter 23 contains two tables and thirteen figures on this issue, which are easy to find there, so one can turn to them immediately without loss of continuity.

One should also note the dominance of the services sector in total employment. Services are mainly part of the tertiary sector, comprising such divergent items as banking, distribution, insurance, transport, catering and hotels, laundries and hairdressers, professional services of a more varied kind, publicly and privately provided, and so on. For the EU27, it is 32–64 per cent for men, but with the single exception of Portugal those under 50 per cent are the 2004 and 2007 new members, and 64–89 per cent (38–89 per cent for EU25) for women. This is significant, particularly since it has frequently been alleged that the size of this sector was the cause of the slow rate of growth of the UK economy a few decades ago; the United States,

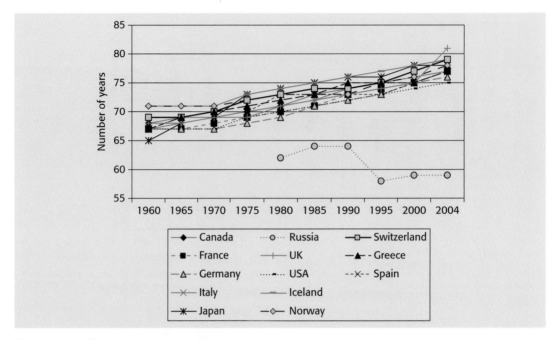

Figure 5.2 Male life expectancy at birth, 1960–2004

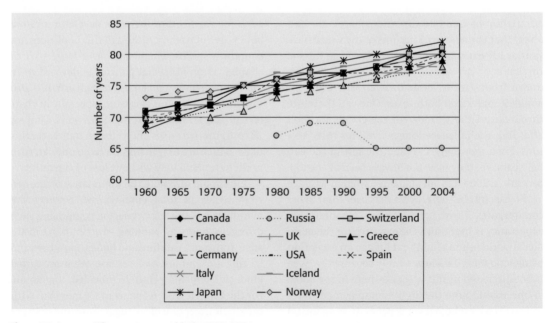

Figure 5.3 Average life expectancy at birth, 1960–2004

with its high growth rate, is on a par with the UK in this respect and the other advanced nations are not much different either (see next section). Also, the increasing size of this sector over time led to the doctrine of 'deindustrialization': as this sector grows in percentage terms, it automatically follows that the other sectors, especially industry, must decline in relative terms.

5.2 GNI per capita and GDP

Table 5.5 gives per capita GNI in 2004, using both exchange rate conversion and 'purchasing power parity' (PPP). The table also provides the ranking of nations in terms of both measures as well as the industry distribution of GDP. Table 5.6 provides the average annual rate of GDP growth for 1990–2000 and 2000–4.

One of the salient features is the disparity between the member nations of the EU in terms of per capita GNI: the rank ranges from 1 (Luxembourg, with $56,380) to 99 ($2,750) and 1 (again, Luxembourg, with $61,610) to 86 ($7,940) for the respective measures. Indeed, the dispersion of income levels among EU member states is much wider that between US states (see figure 19.1). However, for eleven of the EU15, the respective ranges are 1–19 ($30,370 for 19, France) and 1–20 ($29,460 for 20, again France); those excluded are Greece (42; 41, with $16,730 and $22,230), Italy (28 for both, with $26,280 and $28,020), Portugal (49; 43, with $14,220 and $19,240) and Spain (34; 33, with $21,530 and $24,750). Moreover, the twelve new members who joined in 2004 and 2007, rank, respectively, 52–99 ($12,050 for 52) and 45–86 ($20,830 for 45). For the EU, therefore, the ranges are between, respectively, $56,380 and $2,750 and $61,610 and $7,940. Of the EFTA countries, Norway and Switzerland are outperformed by only Luxembourg on both measures, and Iceland (7) is just behind Denmark (6, second to Luxembourg) on the first, and to Ireland (8, second to Luxembourg), but at 14, on the second. Note that one should not read too much into Luxembourg's number 1 ranking, given the dominance of high-ranking and well-paid EU officials there.

Of particular concern is the growth of GDP in the EU relative to that in the United States. As can be seen from table 5.6, of the EU15, only Ireland (7.5 per cent) and Luxembourg (5.9 per cent in 1997) performed better than the United States (3.5 per cent) during 1990–2000, and are joined by Greece (4.2 per cent) and Spain (3 per cent) during 2000–4, when the United States is at 2.5 per cent, with Finland and the UK not far behind (both at 2.3 per cent). Thus four of the twelve eurozone countries are doing fine relative to the United States, but the largest three economies are doing much worse (see chapter 11).

5.3 Demand

The structure of demand in 2004 is given in table 5.7. It is about the percentage distribution of GDP between household final consumption expenditure (private consumption), general government final consumption expenditure (public consumption), gross capital formation (investment expenditure), gross domestic savings and the export/import of goods and services. Tables 5.8 and 5.9 then provide detailed information on the government, export and import sectors, gross international reserves, official development assistance (ODA) and gross foreign direct investment (FDI) as percentages of GDP.

With regard to private consumption in the EU in 2004, except for Denmark (48 per cent), Ireland (45 per cent), the Netherlands (49 per cent) and Sweden (48 per cent), the others are on 50–70 per cent. The 10–28 per cent range for public consumption is much narrower. As to gross capital formation, the lowest percentages belong to Sweden (16 per cent), Germany (17 per cent), the United Kingdom (17 per cent) and Finland (19 per cent), with the rest in the 20–33 per cent range; the poorer new entrants naturally have the highest rates. The percentage on gross domestic savings shows less of a divergence between the lowest (15 per cent for Hungary, Lithuania, Portugal and the United Kingdom) and the highest (26 per cent for Slovenia). Exports of goods and services loom large in the case of Belgium (84 per cent) and Ireland (80 per cent), with the Czech Republic (72 per cent), Estonia (78 per cent) and Slovakia (77 per cent) not far behind; thirteen are on below 50 per cent, with Greece (21 per cent) and the UK (25 per cent) at the bottom end. Imports of goods and services behave in a roughly similar fashion, the exception being Latvia, with exports at 44 per cent and imports at 60 per cent. Norway, Switzerland and Canada fit into the general picture for the EU, but the United States is almost in a league of its own in terms of high private consumption coupled with low gross domestic savings, exports and imports. Japan has high gross domestic savings and capital formation and low export/import rates.

Table 5.8 shows the dissimilarity between the EU member nations with respect to both their total government expenditure and current revenue as percentages of the 2004 GDP (see chapter 19 for details and analysis). In terms of total expenditure, the range is between 25.9 per cent for Romania and 48.3 per cent for Malta. This is in stark contrast to Japan (15.3 per cent), Canada (18.3 per cent), Switzerland (19.1 per cent) and the United States (20.9 per cent).

Of particular interest for the EU is the overall budget balance since it is one of the five Maastricht criteria for EMU membership and a requirement of the Growth and Stability Pact (GSP; see chapter 11) which specifies 3 per cent of GDP as the maximum permitted. Of the eurozone twelve, only France fails on this count in 2004. Of the remainder, France is joined by the Czech Republic, Hungary, Poland and Slovakia, who have no option but to adopt the euro when ready, and by the 'opt-out' UK.

A frequently cited figure is the percentage of GDP spent on ODA extended to developing countries and multilateral agents, given in table 5.9, due to the developing countries' plea (through UNCTAD) that it should be 0.5 per cent (originally 1.0 per cent) of the major donor countries' GDP. As the table shows, only Norway (0.87 per cent), Denmark (0.85 per cent), Luxembourg (0.83 per cent), Sweden (0.78 per cent) and the Netherlands (0.73 per cent) would satisfy them, while Italy (0.15 per cent), the United States (0.17 per cent) and Japan (0.19 per cent) would appal them.

5.4 Price indices and real interest and exchange rates

Table 5.10 provides information on consumer and wholesale price indices as well as on the real interest and exchange rates. The first two items are under the control of the European Central Bank, which has a set inflation target (see chapter 11), and hence dictates the nominal interest rate for the eurozone nations. Of particular interest is the variation in the price indices, hence in the real interest rates, for the twelve, given a one-interest-rate policy for them all.

5.5 Direction of trade

Tables 5.11 and 5.12 are considered together since they give the percentages for the share of exports of the exporting country coming from the EU and their equivalents for imports going into the EU, i.e. they are especially about the extent of intra-EU trade. As the notes to the tables clearly indicate, these percentages are not strictly comparable, due to the changing number of EU nations; note, for example, the differences in the two columns for 2000, where the first relates to EU15, the second to EU25. For an analysis of the proper trends, the reader should consult chapter 9, and for a full analysis consult El-Agraa (1989a and 1999).

Table 5.11 shows that, in terms of exports, in 2005 Malta recorded the lowest percentage (51.6 per cent) and Luxembourg the highest (89.4 per cent). Malta, Greece, Finland, the UK, Sweden and Italy are in the 50–9 per cent range, France, Germany, Ireland, Lithuania, Slovenia and Austria in the 60–9 per cent range, the Czech Republic, Luxembourg and Slovakia in the 80 per cent plus range and the remaining twelve are in the 70–9 per cent range. With regard to imports, the lowest percentage is for the Netherlands (49.5 per cent), the only EU nation below 50 per cent, and the highest is for the Czech Republic (81.8 per cent), with twelve member nations in the 70–9 per cent range and only four in the 50–9 per cent zone. In both terms, the Czech Republic stands out with high percentages, but not far behind are Austria, Belgium, Denmark, Estonia, Latvia, Poland, Portugal, Slovakia and Slovenia. On the opposite side are Greece and the UK. Note that the EFTA nations are much closer to the EU core, while Canada, Japan and the United States are in the low part of 5.5–20.9 per cent zone.

5.6 Income/consumption distribution

Table 5.13 gives information on the distribution of income and consumption, but note that the survey years vary greatly: 1996 for the earliest and 2003 for the latest. The table shows that for all the countries under consideration the highest 10 per cent received about 21.3–29.9 per cent (Denmark, Slovakia, Slovenia, and Japan on about 21 per cent, the US being the highest) of income–consumption, while the lowest 10 per cent received about 1.9–4.8 per cent (Portugal, the UK, Turkey and United States, with the US the lowest on 1.9 per cent). The Gini index is in the 20–30 per cent region for ten EU nations, the 30–8 per cent region for fourteen (data being unavailable for Cyprus, Luxembourg and Malta) and about 44 per cent for Turkey and 41 per cent for the United States. Recalling that a Gini index of 0 represents perfect equality, it is interesting to note that the disparity is widest for Turkey, the Russian Federation and the United States.

5.7 The statistical tables

In all tables, *na* means not available. Unless otherwise stated, the sources for all the tables are the World Bank's *World Development Report* and *World Development Indicators*, Eurostat's *Basic Statistics of the EU*, *Statistical Review* and *Eurostat Yearbook*, and OECD publications for various years. The data are subject to technical explanations as well as to some critical qualifications; hence the reader is strongly advised to turn to the original sources for these.

Table 5.1a Area, population and life expectancy

	Area (000km²) 2005	Population (million) 2005	Average annual growth of population (%) 1965–80	1980–90	1990–2004	Life expectancy at birth Average 2004	Male 2004	Female 2004
EU countries								
Austria	84.0	8.2	0.3	0.2	0.4	79	76	82
Belgium	33.0	10.5	0.3	0.1	0.3	79	76	82
Bulgaria	111.0	7.8	0.4	−0.2	−0.8	72	69	76
Cyprus	9.3	0.8	na	na	1.0	79	77	82
Czech Republic	79.0	10.2	0.5	0.1	−0.1	76	73	79
Denmark	43.0	5.4	0.5	0.0	0.4	77	75	80
Estonia	45.0	1.4	0.8	0.6	−1.1	72	66	77
Finland	338.0	5.2	0.3	0.4	0.3	79	75	82
France	552.0	60.6	0.7	0.5	0.4	80	77	84
Germany	357.0	82.5	0.2	0.1	0.3	78	76	81
Greece	132.0	11.1	0.7	0.5	0.6	79	77	81
Hungary	93.0	10.1	0.4	−0.3	−0.2	73	69	77
Ireland	70.0	4.1	1.2	0.3	1.1	78	76	81
Italy	301.0	58.5	0.5	0.1	0.1	80	77	83
Latvia	65.0	2.3	0.4	0.5	−0.1	71	66	76
Lithuania	65.0	3.4	na	0.9	−0.5	72	66	78
Luxembourg	2.6	0.5	na	na	1.4	78	75	81
Malta	0.3	0.4	na	na	0.8	79	77	81
Netherlands	42.0	16.3	0.9	0.6	0.6	79	76	81
Poland	313.0	38.2	0.8	0.6	0.0	74	70	79
Portugal	92.0	10.5	0.4	0.7	0.4	77	74	81
Romania	238.0	21.7	na	0.4	−0.5	71	68	75
Slovakia	49.0	5.4	0.9	0.1	0.1	74	70	78
Slovenia	20.0	2.0	0.9	0.6	0.0	77	73	80
Spain	505.0	43.0	1.0	0.5	0.7	80	77	84
Sweden	450.0	9.0	0.5	0.4	0.4	80	78	83
United Kingdom	244.0	60.6	0.2	0.3	0.3	79	76	81
EU (27)	3333.2	489.7						
EU candidates								
Croatia	57.0	4.4	na	0.4	−0.5	75	72	79
Turkey	784.0	71.7	2.4	2.3	1.7	70	69	71
Iceland	103.0	0.3	na	na	1.0	80	79	82
Liechtenstein		0.03					79	82
Norway	324.0	4.6	0.6	0.4	0.6	80	78	82
Switzerland	41.0	7.4	0.5	0.6	0.7	81	79	84
Comparators								
Canada	9985.0	32.0	1.3	1.2	1.0	80	77	83
Japan	378.0	128.0	1.2	0.6	0.2	82	78	85
Russian Federation	17 098	144.0	0.6	0.6	−0.2	65	59	72
United States	9629.0	294.0	1.0	0.9	1.2	77	75	80

Table 5.1b Life expectancy at birth, selected countries

Year	1960	1965	1970	1975	1980	1985	1990	1995	2000	2004
Female										
Canada	74	75	76	77	78	80	81	81	82	83
France	74	75	76	77	78	79	81	82	83	84
Germany	72	73	74	75	76	78	79	80	81	81
Italy	72	73	75	76	77	79	80	81	82	83
Japan	70	73	75	77	79	81	82	83	85	85
Russia	na	na	na	na	73	74	74	72	72	72
UK	74	74	75	76	77	78	79	79	80	81
USA	73	74	75	77	78	78	79	79	80	80
Iceland	76	76	77	79	80	80	80	81	82	82
Norway	76	76	77	78	79	80	80	81	81	82
Switzerland	74	75	76	78	79	80	81	82	83	84
Greece	71	72	74	75	77	78	80	80	81	81
Spain	72	74	75	76	79	79	80	81	82	83
Male										
Canada	68	69	69	70	71	73	74	75	76	77
France	67	67	68	69	70	71	73	74	75	77
Germany	67	67	67	68	69	71	72	73	75	76
Italy	67	68	69	70	71	72	74	75	76	77
Japan	65	68	69	73	74	75	76	76	78	78
Russia	na	na	na	na	62	64	64	58	59	59
UK	68	68	69	69	71	72	73	74	75	81
USA	67	67	67	69	70	71	72	73	74	75
Iceland	71	71	71	73	74	75	76	77	78	79
Norway	71	71	71	72	73	73	73	75	76	78
Switzerland	69	69	70	72	73	74	74	75	77	79
Greece	67	69	70	71	72	73	75	75	75	77
Spain	67	69	70	70	73	73	73	73	75	77
Both										
Canada	71	72	72	73	75	76	77	78	79	80
France	70	71	72	73	74	75	77	78	79	80
Germany	70	70	70	71	73	74	75	76	78	78
Italy	70	70	72	73	74	75	77	78	79	80
Japan	68	70	72	75	76	78	79	80	81	82
Russia	na	na	na	na	67	69	69	65	65	65
UK	71	71	72	72	74	75	76	77	77	79
USA	70	70	71	73	74	75	75	76	77	77
Iceland	73	73	74	75	77	77	78	79	80	80
Norway	73	74	74	75	76	76	77	78	79	80
Switzerland	71	72	73	75	76	77	77	78	80	81
Greece	69	70	72	73	74	75	77	78	78	79
Spain	69	71	72	73	76	76	77	77	78	80

Source: the data for 1960–70 is kindly provided by Maurice Schiff of the World Bank; the rest comes from various issues of the World Bank, *World Development Indicators*.

Table 5.2 Health expendititure, mortality and fertility

	Total expenditure on health (% of GDP)		Total fertility rates	Infant mortality rate (per 1,000 live births)
	Total 2003	Public 2003	2004	2004
EU countries				
Austria	7.5	5.1	1.4	4.5
Belgium	9.4	6.3	1.6	4.3
Bulgaria	7.5	4.1	1.3	11.6
Cyprus	na	na	1.5	3.5
Czech Republic	7.5	6.8	1.2	3.7
Denmark	9.0	7.5	1.8	4.4
Estonia	5.3	4.1	1.4	6.3
Finland	7.4	5.7	1.8	3.3
France	10.1	7.7	1.9	3.9
Germany	11.1	8.7	1.4	4.1
Greece	9.9	5.1	1.3	3.9
Hungary	8.4	6.1	1.3	6.6
Ireland	7.3	5.8	2.0	4.9
Italy	8.4	6.3	1.3	4.1
Latvia	6.4	3.3	1.2	9.4
Lithuania	6.6	5.0	1.3	7.9
Luxembourg	6.1	5.2	1.7	3.9
Malta	na	na	1.4	5.9
Netherlands	9.8	6.1	1.7	4.1
Poland	6.5	4.5	1.2	6.8
Portugal	9.6	6.7	1.4	4.0
Romania	6.1	3.8	1.3	16.8
Slovakia	5.9	5.2	1.3	6.8
Slovenia	8.8	6.7	1.2	3.9
Spain	7.7	5.5	1.3	3.5
Sweden	9.4	8.0	1.8	3.1
United Kingdom	8.0	6.9	1.7	5.1
EU (27)			1.5	4.5
EU candidates				
Croatia	7.8	6.5	1.4	6.1
Turkey	7.6	5.4	2.2	21.5
EFTA countries				
Iceland	10.5	8.8	2.0	2.8
Liechtenstein	na	na	1.5	2.7
Norway	10.3	8.6	1.8	3.2
Switzerland	11.1	6.7	1.4	4.2
Comparators				
Canada	9.9	6.9	1.5	5.0
Japan	7.9	6.4	1.3	3.0
Russian Federation	5.6	3.3	1.3	17.0
United States	15.2	6.8	2.0	7.0

Table 5.3 Labour force, employment and unemployment rates, 2005

	Total labour force (million)	Employment rates[a]			Unemployment rates[b]		
		Total	% male	% female	Total	% male	% female
EU countries							
Austria	3.9	68.6	75.4	62.0	5.2	4.9	5.5
Belgium	4.5	61.1	68.3	53.8	8.4	7.6	9.5
Bulgaria	3.1	55.8	60.0	51.7	10.1	10.3	9.8
Cyprus	na	68.5	79.2	58.4	5.3	4.4	6.5
Czech Republic	5.2	64.8	73.3	56.3	7.9	6.5	9.8
Denmark	2.8	75.9	79.8	71.9	4.8	4.4	5.3
Estonia	0.7	64.4	67.0	62.1	7.9	8.8	7.1
Finland	2.6	68.4	70.3	66.5	8.4	8.2	8.6
France	26.9	63.1	68.8	57.6	9.5	8.7	10.5
Germany	40.8	65.4	71.2	59.6	9.5	8.9	10.5
Greece	5.1	60.1	74.2	46.1	9.8	6.1	15.3
Hungary	4.2	56.9	63.1	51.0	7.2	7.0	7.4
Ireland	2.0	67.6	76.9	58.3	4.3	4.6	4.0
Italy	24.0	57.6	69.9	45.3	7.7	6.2	10.1
Latvia	1.1	63.3	67.6	59.3	8.5	9.1	8.7
Lithuania	1.6	62.6	66.1	59.4	8.3	8.2	8.3
Luxembourg	na	63.6	73.3	53.7	4.5	3.5	5.9
Malta	na	53.9	73.8	33.7	7.3	6.6	8.8
Netherlands	8.6	73.2	79.9	66.4	4.7	4.4	5.1
Poland	17.3	52.8	58.9	46.8	17.7	16.6	19.1
Portugal	5.5	67.5	73.4	61.7	7.6	6.7	8.7
Romania	10.4	57.6	63.7	51.5	7.7	8.0	7.5
Slovakia	2.7	57.7	64.6	50.9	16.3	15.5	17.1
Slovenia	1.0	66.0	70.4	61.3	6.5	6.1	7.0
Spain	20.3	63.3	75.2	51.2	9.2	7.0	12.2
Sweden	4.7	72.5	74.4	70.4	7.8	7.9	7.7
United Kingdom	30.4	71.7	77.6	65.9	4.7	5.1	4.3
EU (27)		63.8	71.3	56.3	8.7	7.9	9.8
Eurozone (12)		63.5	71.8	55.2	8.6	7.4	10.0
EU candidates							
Croatia	2.0	55.0	61.7	48.6	13.6[c]	12.0[c]	15.6[c]
Turkey	26.5	46.0	68.2	23.8	10.3	10.4	10.2
EFTA countries							
Iceland	na	83.8	86.9	80.5	na	na	na
Liechtenstein	na	na	na	na	na	na	na
Norway	2.2	74.8	77.8	71.7	4.6	4.8	4.4
Switzerland	4.2	na	na	na	na	na	na
Comparators							
Canada	17.4	na	na	na	na	na	na
Japan	67.0	68.7	80.0[c]	57.4[c]	4.4	4.6[c]	4.2[c]
Russian Federation	73.1	na	na	na	na	na	na
United States	153.7	71.2	77.2[c]	65.4[c]	5.1	5.1[c]	5.1[c]

[a] Number of persons in employment aged 15–64 divided by the total population of that age group.
[b] Unemployed persons as a percentage of the total labour force.
[c] The figures are for 2004.

Table 5.4 Employment by basic economic sector, 2000–4*

	Agriculture		Industry		Services	
	Male[a]	Female[b]	Male[a]	Female[b]	Male[a]	Female[b]
EU countries						
Austria	5	6	43	13	51	81
Belgium	2	1	35	12	63	87
Bulgaria	12	8	37	29	51	64
Cyprus	na	na	na	na	na	na
Czech Republic	6	3	50	27	45	70
Denmark	5	2	34	12	61	86
Estonia	9	4	42	23	50	73
Finland	7	3	39	13	54	84
France[c]	2	1	35	13	63	86
Germany	3	2	44	17	53	81
Greece	15	18	30	11	56	71
Hungary	8	3	42	24	50	74
Ireland	10	2	39	13	51	85
Italy	6	4	40	20	55	76
Latvia	17	10	35	18	47	71
Lithuania	21	15	35	22	44	64
Luxembourg	na	na	na	na	na	na
Malta	na	na	na	na	na	na
Netherlands	4	2	29	9	64	87
Poland	19	18	38	17	43	65
Portugal	12	14	43	20	45	66
Romania	34	37	34	25	32	38
Slovakia	8	4	49	26	43	71
Slovenia	8	8	46	26	45	65
Spain	7	4	42	14	52	82
Sweden	3	1	35	10	62	89
United Kingdom	2	1	35	10	64	89
EU candidates						
Croatia	16	18	39	19	45	64
Turkey	24	59	26	13	49	28
EFTA countries						
Iceland	na	na	na	na	na	na
Norway	6	2	35	9	60	89
Switzerland	5	3	33	12	62	85
Comparators						
Canada	4	2	32	11	64	87
Japan	5	5	36	19	59	75
Russian Federation	12	8	39	23	48	70
United States	4	1	31	11	65	88

[a] Percentage of male employment; [b] percentage of female employment; [c] data is for 1998–2001.
* The figures may not add up to 100 due to workers not being classified by sector.

Table 5.5 Gross national income and gross national product, 2004

	Gross national income (GNI)			Per capita GNI			Structure of GDP (%)				
	($b)	Rank	PPP ($b)	($)	Rank	PPP ($)	Rank	A[a]	I[b]	M[c]	S[d]
EU countries											
Austria	263.9	21	260	32,280	15	31,800	10	2	31	20	67
Belgium	326.0	18	329	31,280	17	31,530	13	1	25	18	73
Bulgaria	21.3	73	99	2,750	99	7,940	86	11	31	19	58
Cyprus	13.6	86	18	13,633	54	18,360	na	na	na	na	na
Czech Republic	93.3	42	188	9,130	59	18,420	51	3	38	26	59
Denmark	220.2	26	172	40,750	6	31,770	11	2	25	16	73
Estonia	9.5	99	18	7,080	67	13,630	62	4	29	18	67
Finland	171.9	14	156	32,880	14	29,800	19	3	31	23	66
France[c]	1,888.4	6	1,779	30,370	19	29,460	20	3	22	14	76
Germany	2,532.3	3	2,324	30,690	18	28,170	27	1	29	23	70
Greece	185.0	27	246	16,730	42	22,230	41	7	23	12	70
Hungary	84.6	46	160	8,370	62	15,800	57	3	31	23	66
Ireland	139.6	34	134	34,310	12	32,930	8	3	41	31	56
Italy	1,513.1	7	1,613	26,280	28	28,020	28	3	28	20	70
Latvia	12.9	91	27	5,580	75	11,820	70	4	23	13	73
Lithuania	19.7	77	44	5,740	74	12,690	65	6	34	21	60
Luxembourg	25.6	67	28	56,380	1	61,610	1	na	na	na	na
Malta	4.8	127	8	12,050	52	18,590	na	na	na	na	na
Netherlands	523.1	15	511	32,130	16	31,360	15	2	26	15	72
Poland	232.9	25	486	6,100	72	12,730	64	3	33	20	64
Portugal	149.3	33	202	14,220	49	19,240	49	4	27	17	70
Romania	64.2	51	181	2,960	98	8,330	85	14	37	31	49
Slovakia	34.9	59	78	6,480	71	14,480	59	4	30	19	67
Slovenia	29.5	62	42	14,770	47	20,830	45	3	37	27	61
Spain	919.1	8	1,057	21,530	34	24,750	33	4	29	16	67
Sweden	322.3	19	269	35,840	10	29,880	17	2	29	21	69
United Kingdom	2,013.4	4	1,882	33,630	13	31,930	14	1	26	19[e]	73
EU (27)	13,813.4		12,311								
EU candidates											
Croatia	30.3	61	53	6,820	69	11,920	69	8	30	19	62
Turkey	269.0	20	554	3,750	89	7,720	90	13	22	14	65
EFTA countries											
Iceland	11.1	97	10	37,920	7	32,370	14				
Liechtenstein											
Norway	237.8	24	178	51,810	2	38,680	4	2	39	11	59
Switzerland	366.5	17	264	49,600	3	35,660	6	1	29	20	70
Comparators											
Canada	905.0	9	984	28,310	21	30,760	16	3	40		57
Japan	4,734.3	2	3,809	37,050	9	29,810	18	1	31	21	68
Russian Federation	488.5	16	1,392	3,400	94	9,680	79	5	33	na	60
United States	12,168.5	1	11,693	41,440	5	39,820	3	1	22	15	77

[a] Agriculture [b] Industry [c] Manufacturing [d] Services [e] The figure is for 2001.

Table 5.6 Average annual percentage growth of GDP and its components

	GDP		Agriculture		Industry		Manufacturing		Services	
	1990–2000	2000–2004	1990–2000	2000–2004	1990–2000	2000–2004	1990–2000	2000–2004	1990–2000	2000–2004
EU countries										
Austria	2.4	1.2	1.6	0.6	2.7	1.8	2.7	0.8	2.3	0.9
Belgium	2.1	1.4	2.8	1.3	1.7	0.3	2.8	0.3	1.9	1.8
Bulgaria	−1.8	4.8	3.0	1.8	−5.0	5.3	na	8.2	−5.2	4.9
Cyprus	2.3[a]	3.9[b]	4.1[a]	3.1[b]	13.8[a]	12.1[b]	na	na	22.0[a]	23.9[b]
Czech Republic	1.1	2.8	2.4	1.2	−0.2	4.1	3.8	6.0	1.7	2.0
Denmark	2.5	1.1	2.9	0.2	2.4	−0.8	2.1	0.1	2.5	1.7
Estonia	0.2	7.0	−3.4	−2.0	−3.3	10.5	5.9	11.6	3.1	5.9
Finland	2.6	2.3	1.8	−0.6	3.9	1.8	5.8	0.9	2.2	2.5
France	2.0	1.5	2.0	−0.6	1.0	1.0	na	na	2.4	1.6
Germany	1.8	0.6	−0.2	−0.1	−0.1	−0.1	−0.1	−0.4	2.9	1.3
Greece	2.2	4.2	0.5	−0.3	1.0	4.0	2.0	2.7	2.6	4.9
Hungary	1.6	4.0	−2.4	5.5	3.5	3.3	7.9	4.5	1.2	3.9
Ireland	7.5	5.1	na	na	na	na	na	na	na	na
Italy	1.6	0.8	1.6	−0.8	1.1	0.2	1.5	−0.9	1.7	1.2
Latvia	−1.6	7.4	−5.7	2.7	−8.7	8.6	−7.8	8.1	2.6	7.4
Lithuania	−2.7	7.5	−0.8	2.7	3.3	10.5	5.7	9.6	5.5	6.4
Luxembourg	5.9[a]	4.2[b]	0.8[a]	0.6[b]	14.7[a]	10.9[b]	na	na	na	na
Malta	4.9[a]	−0.5[b]	2.8[a]	2.5[b]	22.4[a]	19.4[b]	na	na	na	na
Netherlands	2.9	0.5	2.0	0.1	1.5	−0.6	2.3	−1.4	3.3	1.0
Poland	4.6	2.8	0.9	4.7	7.3	2.3	10.0	5.2	4.6	2.9
Portugal	2.7	0.3	0.0	0.9	3.0	−1.2	2.4	−0.1	2.2	1.3
Romania	−0.6	5.9	−1.9	8.9	−1.2	5.9	na	na	0.9	5.6
Slovakia	1.9	4.6	2.7	3.6	2.4	5.2	6.6	5.7	5.7	4.4
Slovenia	2.7	3.2	−0.5	−1.2	1.6	1.6	3.9	1.4	3.2	3.3
Spain	2.6	3.0	1.2	−0.4	2.1	2.8	na	1.0	2.8	3.1
Sweden	2.2	2.0	−0.7	2.5	4.2	3.1	8.5	na	1.8	1.4
United Kingdom	2.7	2.3	−0.2	1.2	1.5	−0.1	na	na	3.5	2.9
EU candidates										
Croatia	0.6	4.5	−3.0	0.2	−2.5	5.5	−3.3	3.5	2.2	5.2
Turkey	3.8	4.2	1.4	0.6	4.1	3.4	4.9	5.2	4.0	4.4
EFTA countries										
Iceland	4.9[a]	8.2[b]	9.5[a]	6.5[b]	19.6[a]	16.2[b]	na	na	na	na
Liechtenstein	na	na	na	na	na	na	na	na	na	na
Norway	4.0	1.6	2.6	0.4	3.8	−0.2	1.6	na	4.0	2.6
Switzerland	1.0	0.5	−2.0	na	0.4	na	1.2	na	1.2	na
Comparators										
Canada	3.1	2.6	1.1	−1.5	3.2	0.5	4.5	−0.6	3.0	3.5
Japan	1.3	0.9	−3.1	−2.2	−0.1	−0.1	0.8	0.7	2.2	0.6
Russian Federation	−4.7	6.1	−4.9	5.4	−7.1	6.2	na	na	−1.7	6.0
United States	3.5	2.5	3.7	−0.7	3.7	0.0	na	0.6	3.4	2.5

[a] The figure is for 1997.
[b] The figure is for 2004.

Table 5.7 Percentage distribution of GDP, 2004

	Household final consumption expenditure	General government final consumption expenditure	Gross capital formation	Exports of goods and services	Imports of goods and services	Gross savings
EU countries						
Austria	56	18	22	51	46	24
Belgium	54	23	20	84	81	24
Bulgaria	68	19	24	58	69	16
Cyprus	na	na	na	na	na	na
Czech Republic	50	23	28	72	72	22
Denmark	48	27	20	44	38	23
Estonia	58	19	31	78	86	19
Finland	53	22	19	37	32	24
France	56	24	20	26	26	19
Germany	59	19	17	38	33	21
Greece	66	17	26	21	30	18
Hungary	69	10	24	64	68	15
Ireland	45	15	25	80	65	23
Italy	60	19	20	27	26	19
Latvia	63	20	33	44	60	18
Lithuania	67	16	24	54	61	15
Luxembourg	na	na	na	na	na	na
Malta	na	na	na	na	na	na
Netherlands	49	25	21	65	60	23
Poland	64	18	20	39	41	19
Portugal	63	21	24	31	38	15
Slovakia	56	20	26	77	80	23
Slovenia	54	20	27	60	61	26
Spain	58	18	28	26	29	23
Sweden	48	28	16	46	38	24
United Kingdom	65	21	17	25	28	15
EU candidates						
Croatia	na	na	na	na	na	na
Turkey	70	15	25	37	47	18
EFTA countries	67	13	26	29	35	20
Iceland	na	na	na	na	na	na
Liechtenstein	na	na	na	na	na	na
Norway	45	22	19	44	30	33
Switzerland	61	12	20	44	37	29
Comparators						
Canada	56	20	20	38	34	23
Japan	57	18	24	12	10	27
Russian Federation	50	17	21	35	22	31
United States	71	16	18	10	14	13

Table 5.8 Central government finances (% of GDP), 2004

	Revenue	Expenditure	Cash surplus or deficit (−)	Net incurrence of liabilities		Total debt	Interest payments (% of revenue)
				Domestic	Foreign		
EU countries							
Austria	38.2	40.1	−1.9	2.2	na	65.3	7.9
Belgium	43.7	43.9	−0.3	−4.6	1.8	139.8	11.4
Bulgaria	38.2	35.3	1.6	0.9	−3.0	na	4.6
Cyprus	30.9	38.0	na	na	na	71.7	na
Czech Republic	32.4	36.1	−3.3	0.6	3.0	21.4	3.1
Denmark	36.5	35.2	1.8	−2.5	na	42.8	8.4
Estonia	28.0	26.7	0.9	0.0	−0.1	2.5	0.6
Finland	39.1	36.9	2.5	−0.6	−1.3	45.9	4.3
France	43.3	47.1	−3.5	2.0	1.6	70.7	5.9
Germany	28.6	31.3	−2.4	na	na	na	6.1
Greece	29.2	38.7	−1.1	na	na	na	17.7
Hungary	37.1	41.6	−6.2	0.3	5.4	58.2	10.9
Ireland	44.3	33.7	na	na	na	29.4	na
Italy	37.7	40.0	−2.3	na	na	na	13.8
Latvia	25.9	28.1	−1.0	0.4	1.7	13.8	2.4
Lithuania	28.1	28.8	−1.6	−0.3	0.6	23.6	3.4
Luxembourg	28.2	30.8	na	na	na	6.6	na
Malta	43.2	48.3	na	na	na	76.2	na
Netherlands	41.1	42.6	−1.7	0.9	3.3	54.3	5.5
Poland	35.0	39.3	−3.4	3.7	0.4	43.2	7.7
Portugal	37.8	41.9	−2.3	1.2	3.2	na	7.5
Romania	25.8	25.9	−2.0	0.4	1.7	na	8.4
Slovakia	35.2	36.8	−3.3	2.9	−0.2	46.5	7.0
Slovenia	40.7	41.2	−1.3	2.3	−0.8	na	3.6
Spain	26.0	29.7	0.6	0.1	na	na	6.6
Sweden	38.0	37.5	0.3	1.6	0.5	62.4	5.3
United Kingdom	36.6	39.9	−3.2	3.6	0.0	na	5.4
EU candidates							
Croatia	41.9	42.0	−4.0	2.0	2.0	na	5.0
Turkey[a]	17.9	21.0	−4.1	5.5	na	na	na
EFTA countries							
Iceland	35.6	34.5	na	na	na	36.8	na
Liechtenstein	na	na	na	na	na	na	na
Norway	49.3	37.2	11.8	2.3	6.9	37.7	2.1
Switzerland	19.4	19.1	0.6	−0.6	na	28.5	4.5
Comparators							
Canada	19.9	18.3	1.4	−1.0	0.3	48.7	7.9
Japan	20.6[b]	15.3[b]	na	1.5[b]	na	164.0	na
Russian Federation	27.3	21.9	5.4	−0.1	−1.3	41.4	4.0
United States	17.2	20.9	−3.8	0.1	3.0	38.1	11.0

[a] The figures are for 2000.
[b] The figure is for 1995.

Table 5.9 Merchandise exports/imports, current account, reserves, ODA and FDI, 2004

	Merchandise		Current account balance ($ billion)	Total gross reserves ($ billion)	Net official development assistance % of GNI	Foreign direct investment ($ billion)
	Exports ($ billion)	Imports ($ billion)				
EU countries						
Austria	117.4	117.8	0.8	12.2	0.23	4.0
Belgium	306.5[a]	285.5[a]	11.9[a]	14.0	0.41	118.8[a]
Bulgaria	9.9	14.4	−2.1	9.3	[c]	2.0
Cyprus	na	na	na	na	na	na
Czech Republic	68.7	69.5	−5.6	28.5	na	4.5
Denmark	76.8	68.2	5.9	40.0	0.85	−8.8
Estonia	6.0	8.7	−1.4	1.8	na	1.1
Finland	61.3	50.8	9.7	13.0	0.35	3.1
France	448.7	465.5	−8.4	77.4	0.41	24.5
Germany	912.3	716.9	103.8	97.2	0.28	−34.9
Greece	15.2	52.6	−13.2	2.7	0.23	1.4
Hungary	54.9	59.3	−8.8	16.0	na	4.6
Ireland	104.3	60.7	−1.4	2.9	0.39	11.0
Italy	349.2	351.0	−15.1	62.4	0.15	16.8
Latvia	4.0	7.0	−1.8	2.0	[c]	0.7
Lithuania	9.3	12.3	−1.7	3.6	na	0.7
Luxembourg	[b]	[b]	[b]	na	0.83	[b]
Malta	na	na	na	na	na	na
Netherlands	358.2	319.3	54.4	21.1	0.73	0.4
Poland	74.9	89.2	−10.4	36.8	[c]	12.6
Portugal	35.8	54.9	−13.2	11.7	0.63	0.8
Romania	23.5	32.7	−5.6	16.1	[c]	5.4
Slovakia	27.6	27.5	−0.3	14.9	[c]	1.1
Slovenia	15.8	17.2	−0.7	8.9	[c]	0.8
Spain	178.6	249.3	−55.4	19.8	0.24	16.6
Sweden	122.5	99.3	27.5	24.7	0.78	−0.6
United Kingdom	346.9	463.5	−42.5	49.7	0.36	72.6
EU candidates						
Croatia	8.0	16.6	−1.6	8.8	[c]	1.2
EFTA countries	63.1	97.5	−15.5	37.3	[c]	2.7
Iceland	na	na	na	na	na	na
Liechtenstein	na	na	na	na	na	na
Norway	81.8	48.1	34.5	44.3	0.87	0.5
Switzerland	118.5	111.6	60.3	74.6	0.41	
Comparators						
Canada	316.6	279.8	22.0	34.5	0.27	6.3
Japan	565.8	235.4	172.1	844.7	0.19	7.8
Russian Federation	183.5	96.3	60.0	126.3	[c]	12.5
United States	818.8	1525.5	−668.1	190.5	0.17	106.8

[a] Includes Luxembourg.
[b] Data included in Belgium's.
[c] A recipient, not a donor.

Table 5.10 Consumer/wholesale price indices and real interest/exchange rates

	Consumer price index		Wholesale price index		Real interest rate		Real exchange rate (2000=100)
	1990	2004	1990	2004	1990	2004	2004
EU countries							
Austria	2.0	1.9	0.7	1.6	na	na	105.6
Belgium	1.9	1.9	1.6	0.9	9.9	4.3	106.5
Bulgaria	75.1	5.1	60.7	3.8	−53.3	4.4	121.6
Cyprus	na	na	na	na	na	na	na
Czech Republic	5.6	2.1	5.8	1.4	−3.6	2.9	115.8
Denmark	2.2	2.1	1.3	0.9	10.1	5.4	109.5
Estonia	13.3	3.2	4.9	1.6	−86.6	2.5	na
Finland	1.6	1.3	1.0	−0.1	4.9	2.9	106.1
France	1.6	2.0	na	0.9	8.2	4.9	107.8
Germany	1.7	1.5	0.8	1.3	8.1	8.1	108.1
Greece	6.8	3.4	3.4	2.8	5.7	3.2	111.3
Hungary	15.9	6.2	12.7	1.9	2.5	7.9	131.4
Ireland	2.8	3.9	1.4	−0.9	12.1	−0.9	118.5
Italy	3.2	2.5	2.5	1.3	5.4	2.0	111.0
Latvia	17.0	3.2	6.9	3.3	21.3	0.3	na
Lithuania	16.7	0.2	12.9	−0.5	−51.8	2.4	na
Luxembourg	na	na	na	na	na	na	na
Malta	na	na	na	na	na	na	na
Netherlands	2.6	2.7	1.6	2.0	9.3	1.5	111.9
Poland	17.5	2.6	13.6	2.9	−0.4	4.5	99.8
Portugal	3.9	3.4	na	1.5	7.6	na	109.9
Romania	72.3	20.4	69.5	24.0	na	na	109.9
Slovakia	8.1	6.5	7.8	5.1	−11.0	4.3	97.4
Slovenia	9.7	6.3	7.5	4.9	374.3	5.5	na
Spain	3.4	3.2	2.2	1.7	8.1	−0.1	111.6
Sweden	1.7	1.8	2.2	1.0	7.3	3.2	100.7
United Kingdom	2.7	2.3	1.7	0.9	6.7	2.2	100.8
EU candidates							
Croatia	19.7	2.3	44.3	1.4	81.0	8.1	104.7
Turkey	na	na	na	na	na	na	na
EFTA countries							
Iceland	na	na	na	na	na	na	na
Liechtenstein	na	na	na	na	na	na	na
Norway	2.2	1.8	1.3	0.6	9.9	−0.8	106.0
Switzerland	1.3	0.7	−0.3	0.2	2.9	2.7	105.4
Comparators							
Canada	1.9	2.4	2.2	0.5	10.5	0.9	111.1
Japan	0.3	−0.5	−1.0	−1.1	4.4	4.0	81.1
Russian Federation	59.4	15.3	37.9	−13.3	na	−5.6	136.5
United States	2.6	2.3	1.4	2.3	5.9	1.7	92.6

Table 5.11 Exports to EU countries

	Percentage share of total exports of exporting country							
	1957[a]	1974[b]	1981[c]	1986[d]	1995[e]	2000[e]	2000[f]	2005[f]
EU countries[g]								
Austria	na	na	na	60.1	65.5	61.7	73.7	69.3
Belgium	46.1	69.9	70.0	72.9	76.5	75.0	76.6	76.4
Cyprus	na	na	na	na	na	na	58.1	71.7
Czech Republic	na	na	na	na	na	na	85.0	84.2
Denmark	31.2	43.1	46.7	46.8	66.7	67.2	70.4	70.5
Estonia	na	na	na	na	na	na	88.1	77.9
Finland	na	na	na	38.3	57.5	55.7	62.9	56.0
France	25.1	53.2	48.2	57.8	63.0	61.4	64.5	62.6
Germany	29.2	53.2	46.9	50.8	57.1	56.5	64.1	63.4
Greece	52.5	50.1	43.3	63.5	59.1	43.4	54.9	52.9
Hungary	na	na	na	na	na	na	81.3	76.3
Ireland	na	74.1	69.9	71.9	73.4	62.9	64.6	63.4
Italy	24.9	45.4	43.2	53.5	56.8	54.9	60.3	58.6
Latvia	na	na	na	na	na	na	80.7	76.4
Lithuania	na	na	na	na	na	na	74.6	65.3
Luxembourg	na	na	na	na	na	83.9	86.7	89.4
Malta	na	na	na	na	na	na	33.9	51.6
Netherlands	41.6	70.8	71.2	75.7	79.9	78.7	81.1	79.2
Poland	na	na	na	na	na	na	80.4	77.2
Portugal	22.2	48.2	53.7	68.0	80.1	79.4	81.5	79.8
Slovakia	na	na	na	na	na	na	88.6	85.4
Slovenia	na	na	na	na	na	na	71.2	66.4
Spain	29.8	47.4	43.0	60.9	67.2	69.4	72.8	71.8
Sweden	na	na	na	50.0	59.3	55.9	60.1	58.4
United Kingdom	14.6	33.4	41.3	47.9	59.8	56.9	59.1	56.9
EU (25)							67.5	66.7
EU candidates								
Turkey	na	na	47.3	44.0	51.3	na	na	na
EFTA countries[h]								
Iceland	na	na	52.2	na	62.7	67.2	68.6	74.6
Norway	na	83.5	65.1	64.9	77.9	76.5	77.7	80.7
Switzerland	na	na	60.9	54.9	62.1	56.8	61.3	61.8
Comparators								
Canada	9.3	12.6	10.7	6.8	5.9	4.1	4.7	5.5[i]
Japan	na	10.7	12.4	14.8	15.9	15.2	16.8	15.8[i]
Russian Federation	na	na	na	na	33.1	na	na	na
United States	15.3	21.9	22.4	24.5	21.2	20.0	21.5	20.9[i]

[a] Data is for EC6. [b] Data is for EC9. [c] Data is for EC10. [d] Data is for EC12. [e] Data is for EU15. [f] Data is for EU25.
[g] Data is not available for Bulgaria, Croatia and Romania. [h] Data is not available for Liechtenstein. [i] Data is for 2004.

Table 5.12 Imports from EU countries

	Percentage share of total imports of importing country							
	1957[a]	1974[b]	1981[c]	1986[d]	1995[e]	2000[e]	2000[f]	2005[f]
EU countries[g]								
Austria	na	na	na	66.9	75.9	68.5	79.6	78.7
Belgium	43.5[h]	66.1[h]	59.3[h]	69.9[h]	72.2[h]	69.3[h]	70.4	71.7
Cyprus	na	na	na	na	na	na	58.2	68.3
Czech Republic	na	na	na	na	na	na	75.0	81.8
Denmark	31.2	45.5	47.9	53.2	71.0	71.0	72.0	71.1
Estonia	na	na	na	na	na	na	70.4	75.9
Finland	na	na	na	43.1	65.0	61.9	66.9	65.8
France	21.4	47.6	48.2	64.4	68.5	64.7	67.0	66.7
Germany	23.5	48.1	48.2	54.2	58.6	55.4	62.7	64.0
Greece	40.8	43.3	50.1	58.3	68.8	58.8	62.8	55.6
Hungary	na	na	na	na	na	na	65.0	67.4
Ireland	na	68.3	74.7	73.0	63.9	61.3	63.3	66.3
Italy	21.4	42.4	40.7	55.4	60.5	56.3	59.7	57.2
Latvia	na	na	na	na	na	na	74.0	75.2
Lithuania	na	na	na	na	na	na	54.5	59.0
Luxembourg	i	i	i	i	i	82.9	83.9	72.6
Malta	na	na	na	na	na	na	60.5	74.9
Netherlands	41.1	57.4	52.4	61.0	63.2	51.3	53.1	49.5
Poland	na	na	na	na	na	na	68.6	74.7
Portugal	37.1	43.5	38.0	58.8	73.9	74.0	76.3	76.5
Slovakia	na	na	na	na	na	na	69.9	78.9
Slovenia	na	na	na	na	na	na	75.9	78.2
Spain	21.3	35.8	29.0	51.3	67.5	64.6	67.6	63.0
Sweden	na	na	na	57.2	68.6	64.1	68.2	70.4
United Kingdom	12.1	30.0	39.4	50.4	55.3	49.3	51.6	55.7
EU (25)							63.1	63.8
EU candidates[j]								
Turkey	na	na	33.8[k]	41.0	47.9	na	na	na
EFTA countries[l]								
Iceland	na	na	51.7[k]	na	58.3	56.3	60.6	61.6
Norway	na	na	70.8[j]	50.1	71.7	63.6	66.2	69.2
Switzerland	na	na	74.5[j]	73.0	79.7	71.3	76.0	80.4
Comparators								
Canada	4.2	6.9	8.0	11.3	11.0	10.0	10.6	11.8[m]
Japan	na	6.4	6.0	11.1	14.7	11.8	12.5	12.7[m]
Russian Federation	na	na	na	na	38.8	na	na	na
United States	11.7	9.0	16.0	20.5	17.8	18.1	18.6	19.1[m]

[a] Data is for EC6. [b] Data is for EC9. [c] Data is for EC10. [d] Data is for EC12. [e] Data is for EU15. [f] Data is for EU25.
[g] Data is unavailable for Bulgaria and Romania. [h] Data includes that for Luxembourg. [j] Data is unavailable for Croatia. [k] Data is for 1980. [l] Data is unavailable for Liechtenstein. [m] Data is for 2004.

Table 5.13 Distribution of income or consumption

			Percentage share of income or consumption						
	Survey year[a]	Gini index	Lowest 10%	Lowest 20%	Second 20%	Third 20%	Fourth 20%	Highest 20%	Highest 10%
EU countries									
Austria	2000	29.1	3.3	8.6	13.3	17.4	22.9	37.8	23.0
Belgium	2000	33.0	3.4	8.5	13.0	16.3	20.8	41.4	28.1
Bulgaria	2003	29.2	3.4	8.7	13.7	17.2	22.1	38.3	23.9
Cyprus	na	na	na	na	na	na	na	na	na
Czech Republic	1996	25.4	4.3	10.3	14.5	17.7	21.7	35.9	22.4
Denmark	1997	24.7	2.6	8.3	14.7	18.2	22.9	35.8	21.3
Estonia	2003	35.8	2.5	6.7	11.8	16.3	22.4	42.8	27.6
Finland	2000	26.9	4.0	9.6	14.1	17.5	22.1	36.7	22.6
France	1995	32.7	2.8	7.2	12.6	17.2	22.8	40.2	25.1
Germany	2000	28.3	3.2	8.5	13.7	17.8	23.1	36.9	22.1
Greece	2000	34.3	2.5	6.7	11.9	16.8	23.0	41.5	26.0
Hungary	2002	26.9	4.0	9.5	13.9	17.6	22.4	36.5	22.2
Ireland	2000	34.3	2.9	7.4	12.3	16.3	21.9	42.0	27.2
Italy	2000	36.0	2.3	6.5	12.0	16.8	22.8	42.0	26.8
Latvia	2003	37.7	2.5	6.6	11.2	15.5	22.0	44.7	29.1
Lithuania	2003	36.0	2.7	6.8	11.6	16.0	22.3	43.2	27.7
Luxembourg	na	na	na	na	na	na	na	na	na
Malta	na	na	na	na	na	na	na	na	na
Netherlands	1999	30.9	2.5	7.6	13.2	17.2	23.3	38.7	22.9
Poland	2002	34.5	3.1	7.5	11.9	16.1	22.2	42.2	27.0
Portugal	1997	38.5	2.0	5.8	11.0	15.5	21.9	45.9	29.8
Romania	2003	31.0	3.3	8.1	12.9	17.1	22.7	39.2	24.4
Slovakia	1996	25.8	3.1	8.8	14.9	18.7	22.8	34.8	20.9
Slovenia	1998–9	28.4	3.6	9.1	14.2	18.1	22.9	35.7	21.4
Spain	2000	34.7	2.6	7.0	12.1	16.4	22.5	42.0	26.6
Sweden	2000	25.0	3.6	9.1	14.0	17.6	22.7	36.6	22.2
United Kingdom	1999	36.0	2.1	6.1	11.4	16.0	22.5	44.0	28.5
EU candidates									
Croatia	2001	29.0	3.4	8.3	12.8	16.8	22.6	39.6	24.5
Turkey	2003	43.6	2.0	5.3	9.7	14.2	21.0	49.7	34.1
EFTA countries									
Iceland	na	na	na	na	na	na	na	na	na
Norway	na	na	na	na	na	na	na	na	na
Comparators	2000	25.8	3.9	9.6	14.0	17.2	22.0	37.2	23.4
Switzerland	2000	33.7	2.9	7.6	12.2	16.3	22.6	41.3	25.9
Comparators									
Canada	2000	32.6	2.6	7.2	12.7	17.2	23	39.9	24.8
Japan	1993	24.9	4.8	10.6	14.2	17.6	22.0	35.7	21.7
Russian Federation	2002	39.9	2.4	6.1	10.5	14.9	21.8	46.6	30.6
United States	2000	40.8	1.9	5.4	10.7	15.7	22.4	45.8	29.9

[a] Except for Estonia, Hungary, Latvia, Lithuania, Poland, all EU candidates and the Russian Federation, the figure refers to 'expenditure shares' by percentile of population, ranked by per capita 'expenditure'; for the rest 'income' in both cases.

Part II   EU market integration: theory and practice

Part II of this book is devoted to the discussion of the theoretical and practical aspects of EU market integration. Chapter 6 covers the theory of economic integration, providing an overall picture of the analysis of the economic implications of the creation of a single market on both the partner nations and the rest of the world. It is followed by a consideration of these aspects in terms of the EU 'single market' in chapter 7, with chapter 8 dealing entirely with the question of the free movement of capital, labour and enterprise within the EU. Chapter 9 then deals with the nature and problems of the measurement of the impact of the formation of the EU on trade, production and factor mobility.

The theoretical aspect of this part is basically concerned with three concepts: 'trade creation', 'trade diversion' and 'unilateral tariff reduction'. These can be illustrated quite simply as follows. In Table II.1 the cost of beef per kg is given in pence for the UK, France and New Zealand (NZ). With a 50 per cent non-discriminatory tariff rate the cheapest source of supply of beef for the UK consumer is the home producer. When the UK and France form a customs union, the cheapest source of supply becomes France. Hence the UK saves 10p per kg of beef, making a total saving of £1 million for ten million kg (obviously an arbitrarily chosen quantity). This is 'trade creation': *the replacement of expensive domestic production by cheaper imports from the partner.*

In Table II.2 the situation is different for butter as a result of a lower initial non-discriminatory tariff rate (25 per cent) by the UK. Before the customs union, New Zealand is the cheapest source of supply for the UK consumer. After the customs union, France becomes the cheapest source. There is a total loss to the UK of £1 million, since the tariff revenue is claimed by the government. This is 'trade diversion': *the*

Table II.1 Beef			
	UK	France	NZ
The cost per unit (p)	90	80	70
UK domestic price with a 50% tariff rate (p)	90	120	105
UK domestic price when the UK and France form a customs union (p)	90	80	105

Table II.2 Butter			
	UK	France	NZ
The cost per unit (p)	90	80	70
UK domestic price with a 25% tariff rate (p)	90	100	87.5
UK domestic price when the UK and France form a customs union (p)	90	80	87.5

Table II.3 Beef			
	UK	France	NZ
The cost per unit (p)	90	80	70
UK domestic price with a 50% tariff rate (p)	90	100	105
UK domestic price with a non-discriminatory tariff reduction of 80% (i.e. tariff rate becomes 10%) (p)	90	80	77

Table II.4 Butter			
	UK	France	NZ
The cost per unit (p)	90	80	70
UK domestic price with a 25% tariff rate (p)	90	100	87.5
UK domestic price with a non-discriminatory tariff reduction of 80% (i.e. tariff rate becomes 5%) (p)	90	80	73.5

replacement of cheaper initial imports from the outside world by expensive imports from the partner.

In Tables II.3 and II.4 there are two commodities: beef and butter. The cost of beef per kg is the same as in the previous example and so is the cost of butter per kg. Note that Table II.3 starts from the same position as Table II.1 and Table II.4 from the same position as Table II.2. Here the UK does not form a customs union with France; rather, it reduces its tariff rate by 80 per cent on a non-discriminatory basis, i.e. it adopts a policy of unilateral tariff reduction.

Total cost before the customs union = 90p × 10 million kg = £9 million.
Total cost after the customs union = 80p × 10 million kg = £8 million.
Total savings for the UK consumer = £1 million.

Total cost to the UK government before the customs union
    = 70p × 10 million kg = £7 million.
Total cost to the UK after the customs union = 80p × 10 million kg
    = £8 million.
Total loss to the UK government = £1 million.

Total cost to the UK before the tariff reduction = 90p × 10 million kg
    = £9 million.
Total cost to the UK after tariff reduction = 70p × 10 million kg = £7 million.
Total savings for the UK = £2 million.

Now consider Tables II.3 and II.4 in comparison with Tables II.1 and II.2. The total cost for Tables II.1 and II.2 before the customs union = £9 million + £7 million = £16 million.

Total cost to the UK before the tariff reduction = 70p × 10 million kg
    = £7 million.
Total cost to the UK after the tariff reduction = 70p × 10 million kg
    = £7 million.
Total savings for the UK = nil.

The total cost for Tables II.1 and II.2 after the customs union
    = £8 million + £8 million = £16 million.

The total cost for Tables II.3 and II.4 after the customs union
    = £7 million + £7 million = £14 million.

This gives a saving of £2 million in comparison with the customs union situation. Hence, a non-discriminatory tariff reduction is more economical for the UK than the formation of a customs union with France. Therefore, *unilateral tariff reduction is superior to customs union formation*.

This dangerously simple analysis (since a number of simplistic assumptions are implicit in the analysis and all the data is chosen to prove the point) has been the inspiration for a massive literature on customs union theory. Admittedly, some of the contributions are misguided in that they concentrate on a non-problem due to definitional misspecification, as explained in the following chapter.

Chapter 6 tackles the basic concepts of trade creation, trade diversion and unilateral tariff reduction, considers the implications of domestic distortions and scale economies for the basic analysis, and discusses the terms of trade effects. Chapter 7 discusses the measurement of the theoretical concepts discussed in chapter 6.

6

The theory of economic integration

ALI EL-AGRAA

In reality, some existing schemes of economic integration, especially the EU, were either proposed or formed for political reasons even though the arguments popularly put forward in their favour were expressed in terms of possible economic gains. However, no matter what the motives for economic integration are, it is still necessary to analyse the economic implications of such geographically discriminatory groupings.

For the sake of convenience, I repeat here, from chapter 1, that at the customs union (CU) and free trade area (FTA) level, the *possible* sources of economic gain can be attributed to:

1. enhanced efficiency in production made possible by increased specialization in accordance with the law of comparative advantage;
2. increased production level due to better exploitation of economies of scale made possible by the increased size of the market;
3. an improved international bargaining position, made possible by the larger size, leading to better terms of trade;
4. enforced changes in economic efficiency brought about by enhanced competition;
5. changes affecting both the amount and quality of the factors of production arising from technological advances.

If the level of economic integration is to proceed beyond the CU level to the economic union level, then further sources of gain become *possible* as a result of:

6. factor mobility across the borders of member nations;
7. the coordination of monetary and fiscal policies;
8. the goals of near full employment, higher rates of economic growth and better income distribution becoming unified targets.

I shall now discuss these considerations in some detail.

6.1 The customs union aspects

6.1.1 The basic concepts

Before the theory of second best was introduced, it used to be the accepted tradition that CU formation should be encouraged. The rationale for this was that since free trade maximized world welfare, and since CU formation was a move towards free trade, CUs increased welfare even though they did not maximize it. This rationale certainly lies behind the guidelines of the GATT–WTO Article XXIV (see chapter 1) which permits the formation of CUs and FTAs as the special exceptions to the rules against international discrimination.

Viner (1950), and arguably Byé (1950), challenged this proposition by stressing the point that CU formation is by no means equivalent to a move to free trade, since it amounts to free trade between the members and protection vis-à-vis the outside world. This combination of free trade and protectionism could result in trade creation and/or trade diversion. Trade creation (TC) is *the replacement of expensive domestic production by cheaper imports from a partner*, and trade diversion (TD) is *the replacement of cheaper initial imports from the outside world by more expensive imports from a partner*. Viner stressed the point that trade creation is beneficial since it does not affect the rest of the world, while trade diversion is harmful; it is the relative strength of these two effects that determines whether or not CU formation should be advocated. It is therefore

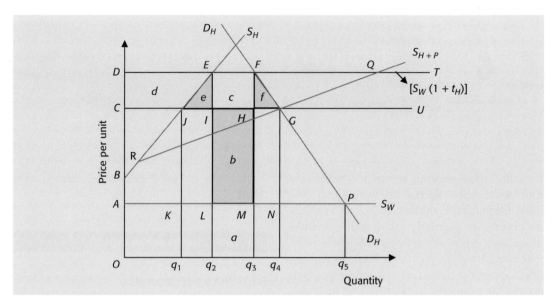

Figure 6.1 Trade creation and trade diversion

important to understand the implications of these concepts.

Assuming perfect competition in both the commodity and factor markets, automatic full employment of all resources, costless adjustment procedures, perfect factor mobility nationally but perfect immobility across national boundaries, prices determined by cost, three countries H (the home country), P (the potential CU partner) and W (the outside world), plus all the traditional assumptions employed in tariff theory, we can use a simple diagram to illustrate these two concepts.

In figure 6.1, I use partial equilibrium diagrams because it has been demonstrated that partial and general equilibrium analyses are, under certain circumstances, equivalent – see El-Agraa and Jones (1981). S_W is W's perfectly elastic tariff-free supply curve, for this commodity; S_H is H's supply curve, while S_{H+P} is the joint H and P tariff-free supply curve. With a non-discriminatory tariff (t) imposition by H of AD (= t_H), the effective supply curve facing H is $BREFQT$, i.e. its own supply curve up to E, then that of W inclusive of the tariff $[S_W(1+t_H)]$. The domestic price is therefore OD, which gives domestic production of Oq_2, domestic consumption of Oq_3 and imports of q_2q_3. H pays q_2LMq_3 (= a) for the imports while the domestic consumer pays

q_2EFq_3 ($a + b + c$), with the difference ($LEFM = b + c$) being the tariff revenue which accrues to the H government. This government revenue can be viewed as a transfer from the consumers to the government with the implication that, when the government spends it, the marginal valuation of that expenditure should be exactly equal to its valuation by the private consumers so that no distortions should occur.

If H and W form a CU, the free trade position will be restored so that Oq_5 will be consumed in H and this amount will be imported from W. Hence free trade is obviously the ideal situation. But if H and P form a CU, the tariff imposition will still apply to W while it is removed from P. The effective supply curve in this case is $BRGQT$. The union price falls to OC resulting in a fall in domestic production to Oq_1, an increase in consumption to Oq_4 and an increase in imports to q_1q_4. These imports now come from P.

The welfare implications of these changes can be examined by employing the concepts of consumers' and producers' surpluses. As a result of increased consumption, consumers' surplus rises by $CDFG$ (= $d + e + c + f$). Part of this (d) is a fall in producers' surplus due to the decline in domestic production and another part (c) is a portion of the tariff revenue now transferred back to the consumer subject to the same condition of equal marginal valuation. This leaves e and f as gains from CU formation. However, before we conclude whether or not these triangles represent net gains we need to consider the overall effects more carefully.

The fall in domestic production from Oq_2 to Oq_1 leads to increased imports of q_1q_2. These cost q_1JIq_2 to import from P while they originally cost q_1JEq_2 to produce domestically. (Note that these resources are assumed to be employed elsewhere in the economy without any adjustment costs or redundancies.) There is therefore a saving of e. The increase in consumption from Oq_3 to Oq_4 leads to new imports of q_3q_4 which cost q_3HGq_4 to import from P. These give a welfare satisfaction to the consumer equal to q_3FGq_4. There is therefore an increase in satisfaction of f. However, the *initial* imports of q_2q_3 cost the country a, but these imports now come from P costing $a + b$. Therefore these imports lead to a loss in government revenue of b (c being a retransfer). It follows that the triangle gains ($e + f$) have to be compared with the loss of tariff revenue (b) before a definite conclusion can be made regarding whether or not the net effect of CU formation has been one of gain or loss.

It should be apparent that q_2q_3 represents, in terms of our definition, trade diversion, and $q_1q_2 + q_3q_4$ represents trade creation, or alternatively that areas $e + f$ are trade creation (benefits) while area b is trade diversion (loss). (The reader should note that I am using Johnson's (1974) definition so as to avoid the unnecessary literature relating to a trade-diverting welfare-improving CU promoted by Gehrels (1956–7), Lipsey (1960) and Bhagwati (1971).) It is, then, obvious that trade creation is economically desirable while trade diversion is undesirable: hence Viner's conclusion that it is the relative strength of these two effects which should determine whether or not CU formation is beneficial or harmful.

The reader should note that if the initial price is that given by the intersection of D_H and S_H (due to a higher tariff rate), the CU would result in pure trade creation since the tariff rate is prohibitive. If the price is initially OC (due to a lower tariff rate), then CU formation would result in pure trade diversion. It should also be apparent that the size of the gains and losses depends on the price elasticities of S_H, S_{H+P} and D_H and on the divergence between S_W and S_{H+P}, i.e. cost differences.

6.1.2 The Cooper–Massell criticism

Viner's conclusion was challenged by Cooper and Massell (1965a). They suggested that the reduction in price from OD to OC should be considered in two stages: first, by reducing the tariff level indiscriminately (i.e. for both W and P) to AC which gives the same union price and production, consumption and import changes; second, by introducing the CU starting from the new price OC. The effect of these two steps is that the gains from the trade creation ($e + f$) still accrue while the losses from trade diversion (b) no longer apply since the new effective supply curve facing H is $BJGU$ which ensures that imports continue to come from W at the cost of a. In addition, the new imports due to trade creation ($q_1q_2 + q_3q_4$) now cost less, leading to a further gain of $KJIL$ plus $MHGN$. Cooper and Massell then conclude that *a policy of unilateral tariff reduction (UTR) is superior to customs union formation*. This criticism was challenged by Wonnacott and Wonnacott (1981), but their position was questioned by El-Agraa and Jones (2000a, b), although El-Agraa (2002a) demonstrates that it can be validated when WTO's Article XXIV rules are incorporated into the analysis; I shall return to these considerations in Section 6.1.7 since a different theoretical model is needed for these analyses.

6.1.3 Further contributions

Immediately following the Cooper–Massell criticism came two independent but somewhat similar contributions to the theory of CUs. The first development was by Cooper and Massell (1965b) themselves, the essence of which is that two countries acting together can do better than if each acts in isolation. The second was by Johnson (1965b) and was a private plus social costs and benefits analysis expressed in political economy terms. Both contributions utilize a 'public good' argument, with Cooper and Massell's expressed in practical terms and Johnson's in theoretical terms. However, since the Johnson approach is expressed in familiar terms this section is devoted to it, since space limitations do not permit a consideration of both. There is, however, another reason for doing so: most of the new developments mentioned later can be tackled within this framework.

Johnson's method is based on four major assumptions:

1. Governments use tariffs to achieve certain non-economic (political, etc.) objectives.
2. Actions taken by governments are aimed at offsetting differences between private and social costs. They are, therefore, rational efforts.
3. Government policy is a rational response to the demands of the electorate.
4. Countries have a preference for industrial production.

In addition to these assumptions, Johnson makes a distinction between private and public consumption goods, real income (utility enjoyed from both private and public consumption, where consumption is the sum of planned consumption expenditure and planned investment expenditure) and real product (defined as total production of privately appropriable goods and services).

These assumptions have important implications. First, competition among political parties will make the government adopt policies that will tend to maximize consumer satisfaction from both 'private' and 'collective' consumption goods. Satisfaction is obviously maximized when the *rate of satisfaction per unit of resources is the same in both types of consumption goods*. Second, 'collective preference' for industrial production implies that consumers are willing to expand industrial production (and industrial employment) beyond what it would be under free international trade.

Tariffs are the main source of financing this policy simply because GATT–WTO regulations rule out the use of export subsidies, and domestic political considerations make tariffs, rather than the more efficient production subsidies, the usual instruments of protection.

Protection will be carried to the point where the *value of the marginal utility derived from collective consumption of domestic and industrial activity is just* *equal to the marginal excess private cost of protected industrial production.*

The marginal excess cost of protected industrial production consists of two parts: the marginal production cost and the marginal private consumption cost. The marginal production cost is equal to the proportion by which domestic cost exceeds world market costs. In a very simple model this is equal to the tariff rate. The marginal private consumption cost is equal to the loss of consumer surplus due to the fall in consumption brought about by the tariff rate which is necessary to induce the marginal unit of domestic production. This depends on the tariff rate and the price elasticities of supply and demand.

In equilibrium, the proportional marginal excess private cost of protected production measures the marginal 'degree of preference' for industrial production. This is illustrated in figure 6.2 where S_W is the world supply curve at world market prices; D_H is the constant-utility demand curve (at free trade private utility level); S_H is the domestic supply curve; S_{H+u} is the marginal private cost curve of protected industrial production, including the excess private consumption cost (*FE* is the first component of marginal excess cost – determined by the excess marginal cost of domestic production in relation to the free trade situation due to the tariff imposition (*AB*) – and the area *GED* (= *IHJ*) is the second component which is the dead loss in consumer surplus due to the tariff imposition); the height of *vv* above S_W represents the marginal value of industrial production in collective consumption and *vv* represents preference for industrial production which is assumed to yield a diminishing marginal rate of satisfaction.

The maximization of *real* income is achieved at the intersection of *vv* with S_{H+u} requiring the use of tariff rate *AB/OA* to increase industrial production from Oq_1 to Oq_2 and involving the marginal degree of preference for industrial production *v*. Note that the higher the value of *v*, the higher the tariff rate, and that the degree of protection will tend to vary inversely with the ability to compete with foreign industrial producers. It is also important to note that, in equilibrium, the government is maximizing real income, not real product:

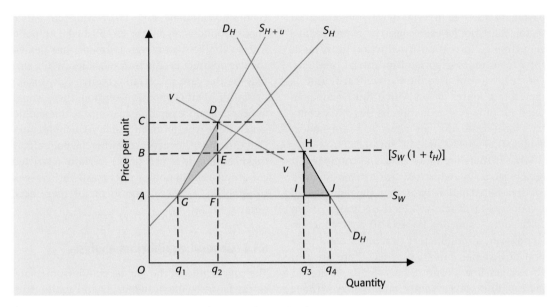

Figure 6.2 Marginal 'degree of preference' for industrial production

maximization of real income makes it necessary to sacrifice real product in order to gratify the preference for collective consumption of industrial production. It is also important to note that this analysis is not confined to net importing countries. It is equally applicable to net exporters, but lack of space prevents such elaboration – see El-Agraa (1984b) for a detailed explanation.

The above model helps to explain the significance of Johnson's assumptions. It does not, however, throw any light on the CU issue. To make the model useful for this purpose it is necessary to alter some of the assumptions. Let us assume that industrial production is not one aggregate but a variety of products in which countries have varying degrees of comparative advantage, that countries differ in their overall comparative advantage in industry as compared with non-industrial production, that no country has monopoly–monopsony power (conditions for optimum tariffs do not exist) and that no export subsidies are allowed (GATT–WTO).

The variety of industrial production allows countries to be both importers and exporters of industrial products. This, in combination with the 'preference for industrial production', will motivate each country to practise some degree of protection.

Given the third assumption, a country can gratify its preference for industrial production only by protecting the domestic producers of the commodities it imports (import-competing industries). Hence the condition for equilibrium remains the same: $vv = S_{H+u}$. The condition must now be reckoned differently, however: S_{H+u} is slightly different because, first, the protection of import-competing industries will reduce exports of both industrial and non-industrial products (for balance of payments purposes). Hence, in order to increase total industrial production by one unit, it will be necessary to increase protected industrial production by more than one unit so as to compensate for the induced loss of industrial exports. Second, the protection of import-competing industries reduces industrial exports by raising their production costs (because of perfect factor mobility). The stronger this effect, *ceteris paribus*, the higher the marginal excess cost of industrial production. This will be greater the larger the industrial sector compared with the non-industrial sector and the larger the protected industrial sector relative to the exporting industrial sector.

If the world consists of two countries, one must be a net exporter and the other necessarily a net importer of industrial products and the balance of payments is settled in terms of the non-industrial sector. Therefore for each country the prospective gain from reciprocal tariff reduction must lie in the expansion of exports of industrial products. The reduction of a country's own tariff rate is therefore a source of loss which can be compensated for only by a reduction of the other country's tariff rate (for an alternative, orthodox, explanation see El-Agraa, 1979b; 1979c).

What if there are more than two countries? If reciprocal tariff reductions are arrived at on a 'most-favoured nation' basis, then the reduction of a country's tariff rate will increase imports from *all* the other countries. If the tariff rate reduction is, however, discriminatory (starting from a position of non-discrimination), then there are two advantages: first, a country can offer its partner an increase in exports of industrial products without any loss of its own industrial production by diverting imports from third countries (trade diversion); second, when trade diversion is exhausted, any increase in partner industrial exports to this country is exactly equal to the reduction in industrial production in the same country (trade creation), thus eliminating the gain to third countries.

Therefore, discriminatory reciprocal tariff reduction costs each partner country less, in terms of the reduction in domestic industrial production (if any) incurred per unit increase in partner industrial production, than does non-discriminatory reciprocal tariff reduction. On the other hand, preferential tariff reduction imposes an additional cost on the tariff-reducing country: the excess of the costs of imports from the partner country over their cost in the world market.

The implications of this analysis are as follows:

1. Both trade creation and trade diversion yield a gain to the CU partners.
2. Trade diversion is preferable to trade creation for the preference-granting country since a sacrifice of domestic industrial production is not required.
3. Both trade creation and trade diversion may lead to increased efficiency due to economies of scale.

Johnson's contribution has not been popular because of the nature of his assumptions. His economic rationale for CUs, resting on public goods grounds, can only be established if for political or similar reasons governments are denied the use of direct production subsidies. While this may be the case in certain countries at certain periods in their economic evolution, there would appear to be no acceptable reason why this should generally be true. Johnson's analysis demonstrates that CUs and other acts of commercial policy 'may make economic sense under certain restricted conditions, but in no way does it establish or seek to establish a general argument for these acts' (Krauss, 1972).

6.1.4 General equilibrium analysis

The conclusions of the partial equilibrium analysis can easily be illustrated in general equilibrium terms. To simplify the analysis we shall assume that H is a 'small' country while P and W are 'large' countries, i.e. H faces constant t/t (t_p and t_w) throughout the analysis. Also, in order to avoid repetition, the analysis proceeds immediately to the Cooper–Massell proposition.

In figure 6.3, HH is the production possibility frontier for H. Initially, H is imposing a prohibitive non-discriminatory tariff which results in P_1 as both the production and consumption point, given that t_w is the most favourable t/t, i.e. W is the most efficient country in the production of clothing. The formation of the CU leads to free trade with the partner, P; hence production moves to P_2 where t_p is at a tangent to HH, and consumption to C_3 where CIC_5 is at a tangent to t_p. A unilateral tariff reduction (UTR) which results in P_2 as the production point results in consumption at C_4 on CIC_6 (if the tariff revenue is returned to the consumers as a lump sum) or at C_3 (if the tariff is retained by the government). Note that at C_4 trade is with W only.

Given standard analysis, it should be apparent that the situation of UTR and trade with W results in exports of AP_2 which are exchanged for imports of AC_4 of which C_3C_4 is the tariff revenue. In terms of Johnson's distinction between consumption and production gains and his method of calculating them (see El-Agraa, 1983b, chapters 4 and 10), these effects can be expressed in relation to food only. Given a Hicksian income compensation variation,

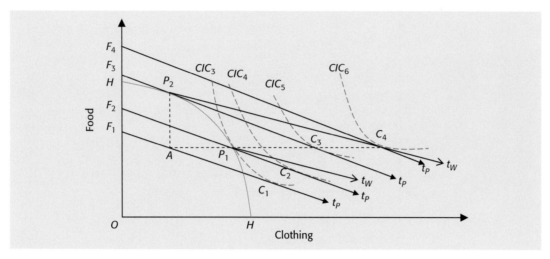

Figure 6.3 General equilibrium of the Cooper–Massell argument

it should be clear that: (i) F_1F_2 is the positive consumption effect; (ii) F_2F_3 is the production effect (positive due to curtailing production of the protected commodity); and (iii) F_3F_4 is the tariff revenue effect. Hence the difference between CU formation and a UTR (with the tariff revenue returned to the consumer) is the loss of tariff revenue F_3F_4 (C_4 compared with C_3). In other words, the consumption gain F_1F_2 is positive and applies in both cases but in the Cooper–Massell analysis the production effect comprises two parts: (i) a *pure* TC effect equal to F_2F_4; and (ii) a *pure* TD effect equal to F_3F_4. Hence F_2F_3 is the difference between these two effects and is, therefore, rightly termed the *net* TC effect.

Of course, the above analysis falls short of a general equilibrium one since the model does not endogenously determine the t/t (El-Agraa, 1983b, chapter 5). However, as suggested above, such analysis would require the use of offer curves for all three countries both with and without tariffs. Unfortunately such an analysis is still awaited – the attempt by Vanek (1965) to derive an 'excess offer curve' for the potential union partners leads to no more than a specification of various possibilities; and the contention of Wonnacott and Wonnacott (1981) to have provided an analysis incorporating a tariff by *W* is unsatisfactory since they assume that *W*'s offer curve is perfectly elastic – see chapter 4 of El-Agraa (1999) and section 6.1.7.

6.1.5 Dynamic effects

The so-called dynamic effects (Balassa, 1961) relate to the numerous means by which economic integration may influence the rate of growth of GNP of the participating nations. These ways include the following:

1. scale economies made possible by the increased size of the market for both firms and industries operating below optimum capacity prior to integration;

2. economies external to the firm and industry which may have a downward influence on both specific and general cost structures;

3. the polarization effect, by which is meant the cumulative decline either in relative or absolute terms of the economic situation of a particular participating nation, or of a specific region within it, due either to the benefits of trade creation becoming concentrated in one region or to the fact that an area may develop a tendency to attract factors of production;

4. the influence on the location and volume of real investment;

5. the effect on economic efficiency and the smoothness with which trade transactions are carried out due to enhanced competition and changes in uncertainty.

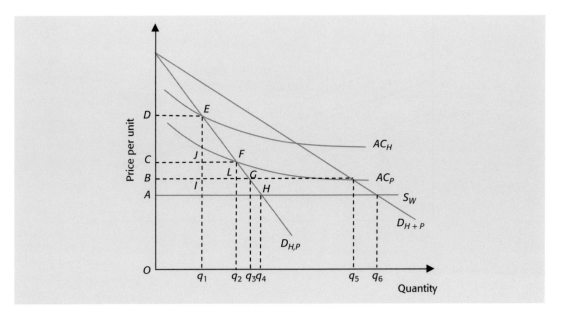

Figure 6.4 Internal economies of scale

Hence these dynamic effects include various and completely different phenomena. Apart from economies of scale, the possible gains are extremely long-term and cannot be tackled in orthodox economic terms: for example, intensified competition leading to the adoption of best business practices and to an American type of attitude, etc. (Scitovsky, 1958), seems to be a naïve socio-psychological abstraction that has no solid foundation with regard to either the aspirations of those countries contemplating economic integration or to its actually materializing.

Economies of scale can, however, be analysed in orthodox economic terms. In a highly simplistic model, like that depicted in figure 6.4 where scale economies are internal to the industry, their effects can easily be demonstrated – a mathematical discussion can be found in, inter alia, Choi and Yu (1984), but the reader must be warned that the assumptions made about the nature of the economies concerned are extremely limited, e.g. H and P are 'similar'. $D_{H,P}$ is the identical demand curve for this commodity in both H and P and D_{H+P} is their joint demand curve; S_W is the world supply curve; AC_P and AC_H are the average cost curves for this commodity in

P and H respectively. Note that the diagram is drawn in such a manner that W has constant average costs and is the most efficient supplier of this commodity. Hence free trade is the best policy resulting in price OA with consumption that is satisfied entirely by imports of Oq_4 in each of H and P giving a total of Oq_6.

If H and P impose tariffs, the only justification for this is that uncorrected distortions exist between the privately and socially valued costs in these countries – see Jones (1979) and El-Agraa and Jones (1981). The best tariff rates to impose are Corden's (1972a) 'made-to-measure' tariffs which can be defined as *those that encourage domestic production to a level that just satisfies domestic consumption without giving rise to monopoly profits*. These tariffs are equal to AD and AC for H and P respectively, resulting in Oq_1 and Oq_2 production in H and P respectively.

When H and P enter into a CU, P, being the cheaper producer, will produce the entire union output – Oq_5 – at a price OB. This gives rise to consumption in each of H and P of Oq_3 with gains of $BDEG$ and $BCFG$ for H and P respectively. Parts of these gains, $BDEI$ for H and $BCFL$ for P, are 'cost-reduction' effects. There is also a production gain

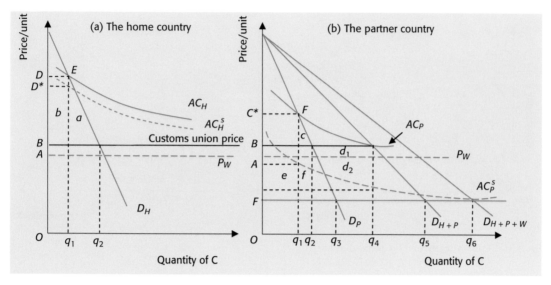

Figure 6.5 Social costs and economies of scale

for P and a production loss in H due to abandoning production altogether.

Whether or not CU formation can be justified in terms of the existence of economies of scale will depend on whether or not the net effect is a gain or a loss, since in this example P gains and H loses, as the loss from abandoning production in H must outweigh the consumption gain in order for the tariff to have been imposed in the first place. If the overall result is net gain, then the distribution of these gains becomes an important consideration. Alternatively, if economies of scale accrue to an integrated industry, then the locational distribution of the production units becomes an essential issue.

6.1.6 Domestic distortions

A substantial literature has tried to tackle the important question of whether or not the formation of a CU may be economically desirable when there are domestic distortions. Such distortions could be attributed to the presence of trade unions which negotiate wage rates in excess of the equilibrium rates or to governments introducing minimum wage legislation – both of which are widespread activities in most countries. It is usually assumed that the domestic distortion results in a

social average cost curve which lies below the private one. Hence, in figure 6.5, which is adapted from figure 6.4, I have incorporated $AC^s{}_H$ and $AC^s{}_P$ as the *social* curves in the context of economies of scale and a separate representation of countries H and P.

Note that $AC^s{}_H$ is drawn to be consistently above AP_W, while $AC^s{}_P$ is below it for higher levels of output. Before the formation of a CU, H may have been adopting a made-to-measure tariff to protect its industry, but the first best policy would have been one of free trade, as argued in the previous section. The formation of the CU will therefore lead to the same effects as in the previous section, with the exception that the cost-reduction effect (figure 6.5(a)) will be less by DD^* times Oq_1. For P, the effects will be as follows:

1. as before, a consumption gain of area c;
2. a cost-reduction effect of area e due to calculations relating to social rather than private costs;
3. gains from sales to H of areas d_1 and d_2, with d_1 being an income transfer from H to P, and d_2 the difference between domestic social costs in P and P_W – the world price;
4. the social benefits accruing from extra production made possible by the CU – area f – which is measured by the extra consumption multiplied

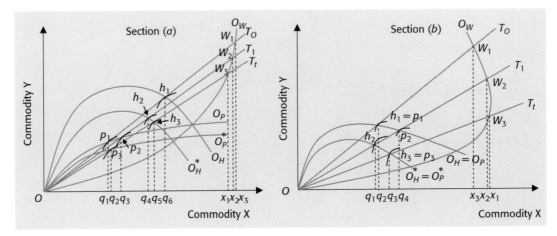

Figure 6.6 Customs unions and the terms of trade

by the difference between P_W and the domestic social costs.

However, this analysis does not lead to an economic rationale for the formation of CUs, since P could have used first best policy instruments to eliminate the divergence between private and social cost. This would have made AC^s_P the operative cost curve, and, assuming that D_{H+P+W} is the world demand curve, this would have led to a world price of OF and exports of q_3q_5 and q_5q_6 to H and W respectively, with obviously greater benefits than those offered by the CU. Hence the economic rationale for the CU will have to depend on factors that can explain why first best instruments could not have been employed in the first instance (Jones, 1980). In short, this is not an absolute argument for CU formation.

6.1.7 Terms of trade effects

So far the analysis has been conducted on the assumption that CU formation has no effect on the terms of trade (t/t). This implies that the countries concerned are too insignificant to have any appreciable influence on the international economy. Particularly in the context of the EU and groupings of a similar size, this is a very unrealistic assumption.

The analysis of the effects of CU formation on the t/t is not only extremely complicated but

is also unsatisfactory since a convincing model incorporating tariffs by all three areas of the world is still awaited – see Mundell (1964), Arndt (1968, 1969) and Wonnacott and Wonnacott (1981). To demonstrate this, let us consider Arndt's analysis, which is directly concerned with this issue, and the Wonnacotts' analysis, whose main concern is the Cooper–Massell criticism but which has some bearing on this matter.

In figure 6.6, O_H, O_P and O_W are the respective offer curves of H, P and W. In section (a) of the figure, H is assumed to be the most efficient producer of commodity Y, while in section (b), H and P are assumed to be equally efficient. Assuming that the free trade t/t are given by OT_0, H will export q_6h_1 of Y to W in exchange for Oq_6 imports of commodity X, while P will export q_1p_1 of Y in exchange for Oq_1 of commodity X, with the sum of H and P's exports being exactly equal to OX_3.

When H imposes an *ad valorem* tariff (percentage tariff), its tariff revenue-distributed curve is assumed to be displaced to O^*_H altering the t/t to OT_1. This leads to a contraction of H's trade with W and, at the same time, increases P's trade with W. In section (a) of the figure, it is assumed that the net effect of H and P's trade changes (contraction in H's exports and expansion in P's) will result in a contraction in world trade. It should be apparent that, from H's point of view, the competition of P in its exports market has reduced the appropriateness of the Cooper–Massell alternative of a (non-discriminatory) UTR.

Note, however, that H's welfare may still be increased in these unfavourable circumstances, provided that the move from h_1 to h_2 is accompanied by two conditions. It should be apparent that the larger the size of P relative to H and the more elastic the two countries' offer curves over the relevant ranges, the more likely it is that H will lose as a result of the tariff imposition. Moreover, given the various offer curves and H's tariff, H is more likely to sustain a loss in welfare the lower its own marginal propensity to spend on its export commodity, X. If, in terms of consumption, commodity Y is a 'Giffen' good in country H, h_2 will be inferior to h_1.

In this illustration, country H experiences a loss of welfare in case (a) but an increase in case (b), while country P experiences a welfare improvement in both cases. Hence, it is to H's advantage to persuade P to adopt restrictive trade practices. For example, let P impose an *ad valorem* tariff and, in order to simplify the analysis, assume that in section (b) H and P are identical in all respects such that their revenue-redistributed offer curves completely coincide. In both sections of the figure, the t/t will shift to OT_t, with h_3, p_3 and W_2 being the equilibrium trading points. In both cases, P's tariff improves H's welfare but P gains only in case (b), and is better off with unrestricted trade in case (a) in the presence of tariff imposition by H.

The situation depicted in figure 6.6 illustrates the fundamental problem that the interests, and hence the policies, of H and P may be incompatible. H stands to gain from restrictive trade practices in P, but the latter is better off without restrictions, provided H maintains its tariff. The dilemma in which H finds itself in trying to improve its t/t is brought about by its inadequate control of the market for its export commodity. Its optimum trade policies and their effects are functions not only of the demand elasticity in W, but also of supply conditions in P and of the latter's reaction to a given policy in H. H will attempt to influence policy-making in P. Given the fact that the latter may have considerable inducement to pursue independent policies, H may encounter formidable difficulties in this respect. It could

attempt to handle this problem in a relatively loose arrangement such as international commodity agreements, or in a tightly controlled and more restrictive set-up involving an international cartel. 'The difficulty is that neither alternative may provide effective control over the maverick who stands to gain from independent policies. In that case a [CU] with common tariff and sufficient incentives may work where other arrangements do not' (Arndt, 1968, p. 978).

Of course, the above analysis relates to potential partners who have similar economies and who trade with W, with no trading relationships between them. Hence, it could be argued that such countries are ruled out, by definition, from forming a CU. Such an argument would be misleading since this analysis is not concerned with the static concepts of TC and TD; the concern is entirely with t/t effects, and a joint trade policy aimed at achieving an advantage in this regard is perfectly within the realm of international economic integration.

One could ask about the nature of this conclusion in a model which depicts the potential CU partners in a different light. Here, Wonnacott and Wonnacott's (1981) analysis may be useful, even though the aim of their paper was to question the general validity of the Cooper–Massell criticism (see below), when the t/t remain unaltered as a result of CU formation. However, this is precisely why it is useful to explain the Wonnacotts' analysis at this juncture: it has some bearing on the t/t effects and it questions the Cooper–Massell criticism.

The main point of the Wonnacotts' paper was to contest the proposition that UTR is superior to the formation of a CU; hence the t/t argument was a side issue. They argued that this proposition does not hold generally if the following assumptions are rejected:

1. that the tariff imposed by a partner (P) can be ignored;
2. that W has no tariffs;
3. that transport is costless between members of the CU (P and H) and W.

Their approach was not based on t/t effects or economies of scale and, except for their rejection

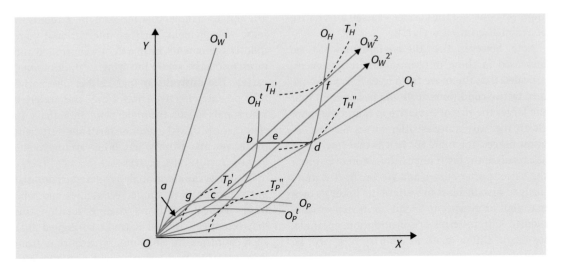

Figure 6.7 UTR versus customs unions

of these three assumptions, their argument is also set entirely in the context of the standard two-commodity, three-country framework of CU theory.

The basic framework of their analysis is set out in figure 6.7. 0_H and 0_P are the free trade offer curves of the potential partners while 0_H^t and 0_P^t are their initial tariff-inclusive offer curves. 0_W^1 and 0_W^2 are W's offer curves depending on whether the prospective partners wish to import commodity X (0_W^1) or to export it (0_W^2). The inclusion of both 0_H^t and 0_P^t meets the Wonnacotts' desire to reject assumption (1) while the gap between 0_W^1 and 0_W^2 may be interpreted as the rejection of (2) and/or (3) – see Wonnacott and Wonnacott (1981, pp. 708–9).

In addition to these offer curves, I have inserted in figure 6.7 various trade indifference curves for countries H and P (T_H . . . and T_P . . . respectively) and the pre-CU domestic t/t in H (0_t). $0_W^{2'}$ is drawn parallel to 0_W^2 from the point c where 0_P intersects 0_t.

The diagram is drawn to illustrate the case where a CU is formed between H and P with the CET set at the same rate as H's initial tariff on imports of X and where the domestic t/t in H remain unaltered so that trade with W continues after the formation of the CU. With its initial non-discriminatory tariff, H will trade along 0_W^2 with

both P (0a) and with W (ab). The formation of the CU means that H and P's trade is determined by where 0_P intersects 0_t (i.e. at c) and that H will trade with W along $c0_W^{2'}$ (drawn parallel to 00_W^2). The final outcome for H will depend on the choice of assumptions about what happens to the tariff revenue generated by the remaining external trade. If there is no redistribution of tariff revenue in H, then traders in that country will remain at point d. The tariff revenue generated by the external trade of the CU with W is then shown to be equal to ed (measured in units of commodity X) which represents a reduction of be compared with the pre-CU tariff revenue in H. Further, if procedures similar to those of the European Union were adopted, the revenue ed would be used as an 'own resource' (see chapter 19) to be spent or distributed for the benefit of both members of the CU, whereas the pre-union tariff (bd) would be kept by country H.

It can be seen that country P will benefit from the formation of the CU even if it receives none of this revenue, but that H will undoubtedly lose even if it keeps all the post-union tariff revenue. This is the case of pure TD (trade diversion) and, in the absence of additional income transfers from P, H clearly cannot be expected to join the CU even if it considers that this is the only alternative to its initial tariff policy. There is no rationale, however, for so restricting the choice of policy alternatives. UTR is unambiguously superior to the initial tariff policy for both H and P and, compared with the non-discriminatory free trade policies available to both countries (which take country H to T'_H at f and country P to T'_P at g), there is no possible system of income transfers from P to H which can make the formation of a CU Pareto-superior to free trade for both countries. It remains true, of course, that country P would gain more from membership of a CU with H than it could achieve by UTR but, provided that H pursues its optimal strategy, which is UTR, country P itself can do no better than follow suit so that the optimal outcome for both countries is multilateral free trade (MFT).

Of course, there is no a priori reason why the CU, if created, should set its CET at the level of country H's initial tariff. Indeed, it is instructive to consider the consequences of forming a CU with a lower CET. The implications of this can be seen by considering the effect of rotating 0_t anticlockwise towards 0^2_W. In this context, the moving 0_t line will show the post-union t/t in countries H and P. Clearly, the lowering of the CET will improve the domestic t/t for H compared with the original form of the CU and it will have a trade-creating effect as the external trade of the CU will increase more rapidly than the decline in intra-union trade. Compared with the original CU, H would gain and P would lose. Indeed, the lower the level of the CET, the more likely is H to gain from the formation of the CU *compared with the initial non-discriminatory tariff*. As long as the CET remains positive, however, H would be unambiguously worse off from membership of the CU than from UTR and, although P would gain from such a CU compared with any initial tariff policy it may adopt, it remains true that there is no conceivable set of income transfers associated with the formation of the CU which would make both H and P simultaneously better off than they would be if, after H's UTR, P also pursued the optimal unilateral action available – the move to free trade.

It is of course true that, if the CET is set to zero, so that the rotated 0_t coincides with $0^{2'}_W$, then the outcome is identical with that for the unilateral adoption of free trade for both countries. This,

however, merely illustrates how misleading it would be to describe such a policy as 'the formation of a CU'; a CU with a zero CET is indistinguishable from a free-trade policy by both countries and should surely be described solely in the latter terms.

One can extend and generalize this approach beyond what has been done here – see El-Agraa (1989b) and Berglas (1983). The important point, however, is what the analysis clearly demonstrates: the assumption that the t/t should remain constant for members of a CU, even if both countries are 'small', leaves a lot to be desired. But it should also be stressed that the Wonnacotts' analysis does not take into consideration the tariffs of H and P on trade with W, nor does it deal with a genuine three-country model since W is assumed to be very large: W has constant t/t.

Back to the Cooper–Massell criticism

Before finishing this section, it is important to address the question regarding what would happen to the Cooper–Massell criticism when WTO's Article XXIV is catered for within the context of the orthodox offer curve analysis. Such an analysis is fully set out in El-Agraa (2002a) so here is a brief taste of it.

The clearest way to demonstrate how the incorporation of the requirements of Article XXIV into the analysis would impact on the Cooper–Massell criticism is by adapting the very case which the Wonnacotts use to illustrate its validity. Here, W is 'very large' and has no tariffs or transportation costs and the potential CU partners H and P are 'very small'. Hence, in figure 6.8, W's offer curve (0_W) is a straight line: H and P being very small can trade with W without in any way influencing the prices of commodities X and Y. Before the formation of the CU, 0^t_H and 0^t_P are the respective H and P tariff-inclusive offer curves. H trades at A, exporting X in exchange for imports of Y while P trades at C, exporting Y in exchange for imports of X, the relevant distances along 0_W determining the volume of trade. When H and P form a CU with a prohibitive common external tariff (CET) – the Wonnacotts' assumption (1981, p. 707) – the respective offer curves for H and P become their tariff-ridden ones, i.e. their free-trade offer curves

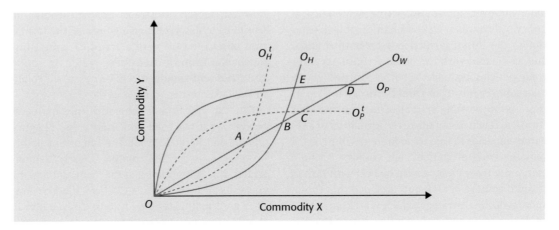

Figure 6.8 Vindicating the Cooper–Massell criticism when dominant W has no tariffs/transport costs

O_H and O_P, and the equilibrium trading point becomes E since W is excluded from trade by assumption.

The Wonnacotts stress that the move from A to E represents an improvement for H (they afford it better terms of trade) and that E is also superior for H in comparison with the position it can achieve by UTR (point B). However, not only is E inferior to C for P, but also P can reach a superior position (point D) by simply adopting UTR policy. Hence, the formation of the CU will depend on whether H can persuade P to join: H will have to compensate P for the loss of welfare, measured by the difference between E and D. This compensation cannot be met by H since, given standard assumptions, P's loss at E (vis-à-vis D) exceeds H's gain at E (vis-à-vis B). Hence, 'UTR dominates CU' and both H and P are better off adopting UTR. The Cooper–Massell criticism is therefore vindicated.

We have just seen that it is essential for the Wonnacotts to resort to their assumption of the CU needing a prohibitive CET in order to justify the only case they have that negates the Cooper–Massell criticism. Yet such an assumption is not only puzzling but is also in direct contradiction to WTO's Article XXIV which clearly specifies that the CET must not exceed the (weighted) average of the pre-CU tariffs – see section 1.2. If WTO rules were to be adhered to, at least one of the CU partners would continue to trade with W (and at an

expanded rate) since the CET must be lower for that country than its pre-CU tariff rate.

To put it differently, the analysis illustrated in figure 6.8 can be true only if the *non-discriminatory* tariffs imposed by H and P prohibited trade *between* them. This can be so only if W is both 'large' and the most efficient producer of the three countries while H and P are small, otherwise the Wonnacotts' reference to a country being 'dominant' has no theoretical meaning. However, such an interpretation does not dispose of the problem altogether since the formation of the CU need not result in a CET which is prohibitive of trade between H and P *and* W: as long as the CET is a (weighted) average of the initial tariffs, either H or P must end up with a lower tariff after the formation of the CU (unless their tariffs were initially equal, but as will be shown below the inferences are similar) and this *may* open up trade between the relevant CU partner and W.

Hence, figure 6.8 needs to be adapted to cater for Article XXIV requirements. Assuming that H's initial tariff is higher than P's, the CET will ensure a reduction in H's tariff; hence H must continue to trade with W after the formation of the CU. Moreover, the elimination of H and P's mutual tariffs may open up trade between them. Hence, in figure 6.9, H and P initially have the same (tariff-inclusive) offer curves for trade with all countries, but after the formation of the CU have in effect two offer curves each, one tariff-free for mutual

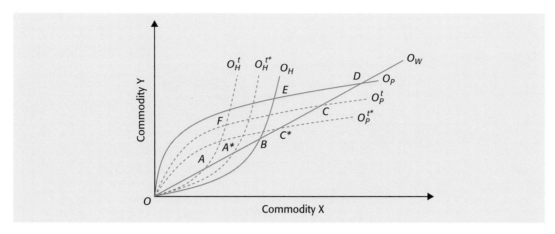

Figure 6.9 Dominant *W* has no tariffs/transport costs – non-discriminatory tariffs by *H/P* and a CET consistent with WTO rules: case I

trade, and another CET-inclusive for trade with *W*, with O_H and O_P defined as before. O_H^{t*} and O_P^{t*} are *H* and *P*'s respective offer curves when a CET consistent with WTO rules is adopted. Since after the formation of the CU *W* faces a lower *H* tariff, *H* and *W* will trade at A^* and since *H* and *P* have no mutual tariffs, *H* will want to trade with *P* at *E*: the vector *OE* (not drawn) indicates better terms of trade for *H* in comparison with vector OO_W. Note that both the movement from *A* to A^* and from A^* to *E* indicate welfare improvement for *H*.

Taking these considerations into account, it should be apparent that the Wonnacotts' analysis of this 'most general' case does not necessarily vindicate the Cooper–Massell criticism of UTR dominating a CU. One needs to evaluate not only *E* and *D* and *E* and *B* (an evaluation which leads to the conclusion that UTR dominates a CU since *H* cannot bribe *P* into joining the CU and still be better off – see the analysis illustrated by figure 6.8), but also AA^* (which is a gain for *H*) and CC^* (which is a loss for *P*). Since AA^* may be equal to, longer or shorter than CC^*, it follows that if AA^* is either equal to or shorter than CC^*, UTR must dominate a CU. However, if AA^* is longer than CC^*, the difference may enable *H* to bribe *P* into joining the CU and still become better off. Therefore, UTR need not dominate a CU.

This is a significant conclusion, given that this case is conceded by the Wonnacotts as vindicating the Cooper–Massell criticism. Surprisingly,

it turns out that a world trade rule-consistent, as opposed to a 'prohibitive', specification of the CET provides a clearer and more general case supporting a negation of the criticism. However, theoretical completeness necessitates that one should consider the alternative situation where the initial *H* tariff is lower than *P*'s before dwelling on this conclusion. Hence, in figure 6.10, after the formation of the CU, *H* would be interested in trading with *P* only (at *E*) since trade with *W* (at *A″*) would not be desirable: *A″* indicates a lower level of welfare relative to *A* while *E* indicates better terms of trade and a higher level of welfare. However, *P* will want to trade at *C″* since it gives a higher level of welfare relative to *C*, but will have no interest in trading with *H* since *OE* are worse terms of trade relative to OO_W. Therefore, it should be evident that since UTR takes *P* to *D* (giving a higher level of welfare relative to *C″*), P would have no interest in the CU. Whether *H* can bribe *P* to join the CU would depend on the relative lengths of *A″A* and *CC″*: more precisely, on *A″A* being shorter than *CC″* by a distance sufficient to make *BE* exceed *CD*. Hence, again, UTR need not dominate a CU, and therefore the conclusion reached here reinforces that arrived at in the previous case.

Note that in both cases, initially *H* would have been interested in trading with *P* rather than *W* since trade with *P* offers better terms of trade (*OF* relative to OO_W in both figures 6.9 and 6.10). However, *H*'s desires are frustrated simply because

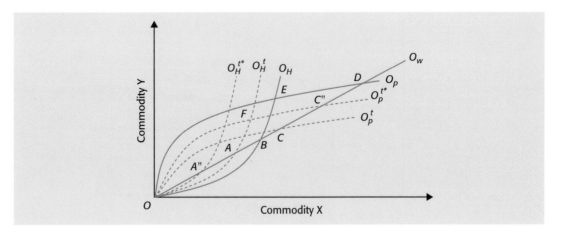

Figure 6.10 Dominant W has no tariffs/transport costs – non-discriminatory tariffs by H and P and a CET consistent with WTO rules: case II

P chooses to trade with W at better terms of trade for itself; once P chooses to trade with W, H has no alternative but to follow suit.

Analytical completeness requires a discussion of the two alternatives where the offer curves for H intersect O_W to the north-east of all the points where P's offer curves intersect it. However, it should be obvious that under such circumstances the same conclusions would be reached. Hence, UTR need not dominate CU formation.

A final question remains: would the assumption of equal initial H and P tariff rates nullify this generalization? The answer is in the negative and can be explained in the following way. If they were equal, the CET would also be equal to them. Hence, O_H^t and O_P^t will continue to be the respective H and P offer curves for trade with W. Therefore, in figure 6.8 trade with W would continue at the initial level: OA trade between H and W and OC trade between P and W. It follows that the evaluation of the CU formation versus UTR must lead to the same conclusion as that reached in the case illustrated by figure 6.8. However, there would be one significant difference: in the Wonnacotts' analysis, the conclusion reached from figure 6.8 rests entirely on the CET being prohibitive of trade between the CU partners and W, while in this (generalized) case trade between the CU partners and W would continue on the same basis and to the same extent as before the CU formation. The implication of this result is that the outright vin-

dication of the Cooper–Massell criticism would depend on assuming that the H and P tariffs were equal rather than on the CET being prohibitive. This implication is consistent not only with some of the literature on the subject, but also with practical notions: in the real world, the formation of CUs has never completely eliminated trade with the non-members, W – see, inter alia, El-Agraa (1999).

6.2 Customs unions versus free trade areas

The analysis so far has been conducted on the premise that differences between CUs and FTAs can be ignored. However, the ability of the member nations of FTAs to decide their own commercial policies vis-à-vis the outside world raises certain issues. Balassa (1961) pointed out that FTAs may result in deflection of trade, production and investment. Deflection of trade occurs when imports from W (the cheapest source of supply) come to the higher tariff partner via the member country with the lower tariff rate, assuming that transport and administrative costs do not outweigh the tariff differential. Deflection of production and investment occurs in commodities whose production requires a substantial quantity of raw materials imported from W – the tariff differential regarding these materials might distort the true comparative advantage in domestic materials, therefore resulting in resource allocations according to overall comparative disadvantage.

If deflection of trade does occur, then the FTA effectively becomes a CU with a CET equal to the lowest tariff rate which is obviously beneficial for the world – see Curzon Price (1974). However, most FTAs have been adopting 'rules of origin' so that only those commodities which originate in a member state are exempt from tariff imposition (see Shibata, 1967, for a different analysis). If deflection of production and investment does take place, we have the case of the so-called tariff factories; but the necessary conditions for this to occur are extremely limited – see El-Agraa in El-Agraa and Jones (1981, chapter 3) and El-Agraa (1984b, 1989a).

6.3 Economic unions

The analysis of CUs needs drastic extension when applied to economic unions. First, the introduction of free factor mobility may enhance efficiency through a more rational reallocation of resources but it may also result in depressed areas, therefore creating or aggravating regional problems and imbalances – see Mayes (1983) and Robson (1985). Second, fiscal harmonization may also improve efficiency by eliminating non-tariff barriers (NTBs) and distortions and by equalizing their effective protective rates – see chapter 15. Third, the coordination of monetary and fiscal policies which is implied by monetary integration may ease unnecessarily severe imbalances, hence resulting in the promotion of the right atmosphere for stability in the economies of the member nations.

These economic union elements must be tackled *simultaneously* with trade creation and diversion as well as economies of scale and market distortions. However, such interactions are too complicated to consider here: the interested reader should consult El-Agraa (1983a, 1983b, 1984a, 1989a). This section will be devoted to a brief discussion of factor mobility. Since monetary integration is probably the most crucial of commitments for a regional grouping and because it

is one of the immediate aspirations of the EU, chapter 10 is devoted to it.

With regard to *factor mobility*, it should be apparent that the removal (or harmonization) of all barriers to labour (L) and capital (K) will encourage both L and K to move. L will move to those areas where it can obtain the highest possible reward, i.e. 'net advantage'. This encouragement need not necessarily lead to an increase in actual mobility since there are socio-political factors which normally result in people remaining near their birthplace – social proximity is a dominant consideration, which is why the average person does not move (chapter 8). If the reward to K is not equalized, i.e. differences in marginal productivities (MPs) exist before the formation of an economic union, K will move until the MPs are equalized. This will result in benefits which can be clearly described in terms of figure 6.11, which depicts the production characteristics in H and P. M_H and M_P are the schedules which relate the K stocks to their MPs in H and P respectively, given the quantity of L in each country (assuming two factors of production only).

Prior to the formation of an economic union, the K stock (which is assumed to remain constant throughout the analysis) is $0q_2$ in H and $0q_1^*$ in P. Assuming that K is immobile internationally, all K stocks must be nationally owned and, ignoring taxation, profit per unit of K will be equal to its MP, given conditions of perfect competition. Hence the total profit in H is equal to $b+e$ and $i+k$ in P. Total output is, of course, the whole area below the M_P curve but within $0q_2$ in H and $0q_1^*$ in P, i.e. areas $a+b+c+d+e$ in H and $j+i+k$ in P. Therefore, L's share is $a+c+d$ in H and j in P.

Since the MP in P exceeds that in H, the removal of barriers to K mobility or the harmonization of such barriers will induce K to move away from H and into P. This is because nothing has happened to affect K in W. Such movement will continue until the MP of K is the same in both H and P. This results in q_1q_2 ($=q_1^*q_2^*$) of K moving from H to P. Hence the output of H falls to $a+b+d$ while its *national* product including the return of the profit earned on K in P ($= g + f$) increases by ($g − c$). In P, *domestic* product rises by ($f+g+h$) while *national* product (excluding the remittance of profits to H)

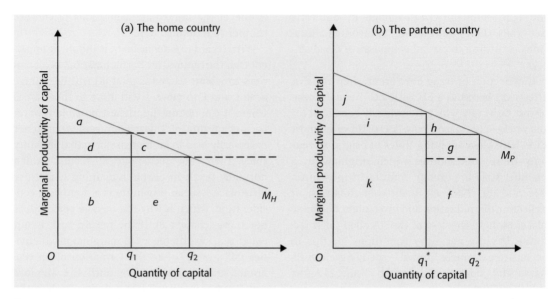

Figure 6.11 Capital mobility

increases by area h only. Both H and P experience a change in the relative share of L and K in national product, with K owners being favourably disposed in H and unfavourably disposed in P.

Of course, the analysis is too simplistic since, apart from the fact that K and L are never perfectly immobile at the international level and multinational corporations have their own ways of transferring K (see McManus, 1972; Buckley and Casson, 1976; Dunning, 1977), the analysis does not take into account the fact that K may actually move to areas with low wages after the formation of an economic union. Moreover, if K moves predominantly in only one direction, one country may become a depressed area; hence the 'social' costs and benefits of such an occurrence need to be taken into consideration, particularly if the economic union deems it important that the economies of both H and P should be balanced. Therefore, the above gains have to be discounted or supplemented by such costs and benefits.

6.4 Macroeconomics of integration

We have seen that trade creation and trade diversion are the two concepts most widely used in international economic integration. We have also seen that their economic implications for resource reallocation are usually tackled in terms of particular commodities under conditions of global full employment. However, the economic consequences for the outside world and their repercussions on the integrated area are usually left to intuition. Moreover, their implications for employment are usually ruled out by assumption.

In an effort to cater for these aspects, I have used a macroeconomic model (see chapters 6–8 of El-Agraa and Jones, 1981, and El-Agraa, 1989a); the model has been refined by Jones (1983). However, even the crude model indicates that the advantages of using a macro model are that it clearly demonstrates the once and for all nature of trade creation and trade diversion. It also shows the insignificance of their overall impact given realistic values of the relevant coefficients: marginal propensities to import, marginal propensities to consume, tariff rates, etc. The model also demonstrates that trade creation is beneficial for the partner gaining the new output and exports but is detrimental to the other partner and the outside world and that trade diversion is beneficial for the partner now exporting the commodity but is detrimental for the other partner and the outside world.

6.5 Economic integration in developing countries

It has been claimed that the body of economic integration theory as so far developed has no relevance for least-developed countries. This is because the theory suggests that there would be more scope for trade creation if the countries concerned were initially very competitive in production but potentially very complementary and that a CU would be more likely to be trade-creating if the partners conducted most of their foreign trade among themselves – see Lipsey (1960) and Meade (1980). These conditions are unlikely to be satisfied in the majority of the developing nations. Moreover, most of the effects of integration are initially bound to be trade-diverting, particularly since most of the least-developed countries seek to industrialize.

On the other hand, it was also realized that an important obstacle to the development of industry in these countries is the inadequate size of their individual markets – see Brown (1961), Hazlewood (1967, 1975) and Robson (1980, 1983, 1997). It is therefore necessary to increase the market size so as to encourage optimum plant installations: hence the need for economic integration. This would, however, result in industries clustering together in the relatively more advanced of these nations – those that have already commenced the process of industrialization.

I have demonstrated elsewhere (El-Agraa, 1979a) that there is essentially *no theoretical difference* between economic integration in the advanced world and the least-developed countries but that there is a major difference in terms of the *type* of economic integration that suits the particular *circumstances* of developing countries and that is politically feasible: the need for an equitable distribution of the gains from industrialization and the location of industries is an important issue (see above). This suggests that any type of economic integration that is being contemplated must incorporate as an essential element a common fiscal authority and some coordination of economic policies. But then one could equally well argue that *some degree* of these elements is necessary in *any* type of integration – see the Raisman Committee recommendations for the EAC (1961).

This raises the interesting question of what happens when economic integration takes place between advanced and poor nations, such as Mexico in NAFTA, but on this see section 6.7.

6.6 Economic integration among communist countries

The only example of economic integration among communist countries was the CMEA. However, there the economic system perpetuated a fundamental lack of interest by domestic producers in becoming integrated with both consumers and producers in other member countries. As Marer and Montias (1988) emphasize, the integration policies of member nations must focus on the mechanism of state-to-state relations rather than on domestic economic policies, which would make CMEA integration more attractive to producers and consumers alike. That is, integration must be planned by the state at the highest possible level and imposed on ministries, trusts and enterprises. It should also be stated that the CMEA operated different pricing mechanisms for intra- and extra-area trade. Moreover, the attitude of the former USSR was extremely important since the policies of the East European members of the CMEA were somewhat constrained by the policies adopted by the organization's most powerful member, for economic as well as political reasons. CMEA integration, therefore, had to be approached within an entirely different framework but this is not the appropriate place for discussing it, especially since the CMEA met its demise soon after the collapse of socialism in the former USSR and Eastern Europe.

6.7 New theoretical developments

There are many new developments in the analysis of economic integration, but they are mostly concerned with minute aspects, and hence do not amount to a body coherent enough to be briefly

explained and discussed within the general introductory nature of this chapter. I shall mention
only two. First, Schiff and Winters (1998) examine
regional integration as diplomacy. They do this by
modelling a scheme motivated by security concerns. Assuming that trade can help reduce frictions among antagonistic neighbouring nations
by raising trust between them, they show that: a
regional bloc is optimum or first-best under traditional static welfare terms; optimum CETs fall
over time; the CETs fall in the aftermath of deep
integration which includes such NTBs as harmonization and mutual recognition of standards,
investment codes and the like (see chapter 1); and
enlargement enhances the welfare of the members of the bloc, with optimum CETs likely to rise.
Their general conclusion is that the optimum
intervention under these circumstances is a subsidy on imports from the neighbour and the equivalent solution is for the neighbouring countries to
tax imports from the rest of the world, i.e. to form
a trading bloc, as well as to have domestic taxes.

The other is by Venables (2003), who examines
the distribution between the participants of the
benefits from integration. He finds that the outcome would depend on their 'comparative advantage', relative to both each other and the rest of
the world: countries with a comparative advantage between that of their partners and the rest of
the world fare better than those with an extreme
comparative advantage. This means that economic integration between poor (rich) countries
would lead to a divergence (convergence) in their
incomes. Venables concludes that the results suggest that developing countries are likely to be
better served by 'north-south' than by 'south-
south' agreements.

6.8 Conclusions

The conclusions reached here are consistent with
my 1979a, b and 1989a conclusions and with those
of Jones in El-Agraa and Jones (1981). They are as
follows.

First, the rationale for regional economic integration rests upon the existence of constraints on
the use of first-best policy instruments. Economic

analysis has had little to say about the nature of
these constraints, and presumably the evaluation
of any regional scheme of economic integration
should incorporate a consideration of the validity
of the view that such constraints do exist to justify the pursuit of second- rather than first-best
solutions.

Second, even when the existence of constraints
on superior policy instruments is acknowledged,
it is misleading to identify the results of regional
economic integration by comparing an arbitrarily
chosen common policy with an arbitrarily chosen
national policy. Of course, ignorance and inertia
provide sufficient reasons why existing policies
may be non-optimal; but it is clearly wrong to
attribute gains which would have been achieved
by appropriate unilateral action to a policy of
regional integration. Equally, although it is appropriate to use the optimal common policy as a
point of reference, it must be recognized that this
may overstate the gains to be achieved if, as seems
highly likely, constraints and inefficiencies in the
political processes by which policies are agreed
prove to be greater among a group of countries
than within any individual country.

Although the first two conclusions raise doubts
about the case for regional economic integration,
in principle at least, a strong general case for economic integration does exist. In unions where
economies of scale may be in part external to
national industries, the rationale for unions rests
essentially upon the recognition of the externalities and market imperfections which extend
beyond the boundaries of national states. In such
circumstances, unilateral national action will not
be optimal while integrated action offers the
scope for potential gain.

As with the solution to most problems of externalities and market imperfections, however, customs union theory frequently illustrates the
proposition that a major stumbling block to
obtaining the gains from joint optimal action lies
in agreeing an acceptable distribution of such
gains. Thus the fourth conclusion is that the
achievement of the potential gains from economic integration will be limited to countries
able and willing to cooperate to distribute the
gains from integration so that all partners may

benefit compared with the results achieved by independent action. It is easy to argue from this that regional economic integration may be more readily achieved than global solutions but, as the debate about monetary integration in the EU illustrates (see chapters 10 and 11), the chances of obtaining potential mutual gain may well founder in the presence of disparate views about the distribution of such gains and weak arrangements for redistribution.

7 The economics of the single market

BRIAN ARDY AND ALI EL-AGRAA

7.1 Introduction

Unlike many areas of EU policy-making, the single market is almost universally seen in a positive light, perhaps because it has been central to the development of the EU. The single market, more precisely the Single European Market (SEM),[1] is an important stepping-stone on the route from the customs union to a fully fledged economic union (see chapter 1), and many regard monetary union (EMU, see chapters 10–12) as the last stage and thus the final piece in the jigsaw of 'negative' integration. The SEM is defined in the Single European Act (SEA) as 'an area without internal frontiers in which the free movement of goods, persons, services and capital is ensured' (CEC, 1987c; Article 12). This means that borders should disappear within the EU: goods, services, capital and people should be able to move between countries as they move between regions within a country. This requires the removal of customs and passport controls at borders; the elimination of any national barriers to the sale of other EU countries' goods and services; and the ending of any national controls on the movement of capital. This is a very extensive agenda that has such wide implications that the subject of virtually every chapter of the book has been affected by its developments. This chapter, therefore, considers the development of the SEM, emphasizing its key characteristics and the continuing debates about how to measure its effects.

7.2 Why 'the single market'?

There were provisions for a single market in the 1957 EEC Treaty: Article 3 required not only the removal of all internal tariffs and quotas, but 'of all other measures having equivalent effect', and 'of obstacles to freedom of movement of persons, services and capital'. The procedure to eliminate these non-tariff barriers (NTBs) was harmonization or the approximation of laws (EEC Treaty, Article 100). After the successful early completion of the customs union (see chapters 2 and 27), internal factors and external events conspired against the completion of that single market. The EEC economy was under strain in the 1970s: the world recession associated with the oil price shocks of 1973 and 1979; rapid changes in technology; and the changing structure of the world economy associated with these changes and the emergence of significant new competitors – first Japan and then the newly industrializing countries of southeast Asia. With growth slow or negative and unemployment rising rapidly, national governments tried to protect their economies but with tariffs fixed by the GATT and the EEC Treaty commitments, only NTBs could be used; the 'New Protectionism'. Barriers went up within as well as outside the EU and these economic strains made countries much less willing to agree to integration initiatives in general and harmonization in particular.

The progress of harmonization was extremely slow for other reasons. It proved difficult to reach agreement on what were often complex technical issues, which were politically sensitive and often the subject of long-standing national legislation. For example, it was difficult to agree a definition for chocolate because in the UK significant amounts of non-cocoa fat could be added to the product, but in the rest of Europe this was not the case. So an agreed definition was seen as either undermining continental European standards or requiring UK manufacturers to change their recipes. The UK was able to hold up the process in this instance because harmonization required unanimous agreement in the Council of Ministers. Harmonization was also seen in some countries as over-regulation. The treaty also allowed national measures 'on grounds of public morality, public policy or public security; the protection of health and life of humans, animals or plants; the protection of national treasures possessing artistic, historic or archaeological value; or the protection of industrial and commercial property' (Article 36). This was exploited by some countries to restrict trade. As a result, between 1969 and 1985, the EC managed to adopt only 270 directives (Schreiber, 1991, p. 98). This was too slow to bring about any reduction in technical barriers, since new regulations were being introduced by member state governments at a faster rate.

Gradually attitudes towards the single market began to change. There was concern over the performance of the EC economies, because of slow growth and their falling share of world exports of hi-tech goods. Big business began to see the segmentation of the EC market into national markets as hampering their international competitiveness. They were unable to get the long production runs to keep costs down and to spread the costs of research and development. The Round Table of European Industrialists was particularly influential in lobbying national governments and the Commission. The limitations of nationalistic economic policies were being revealed by generally poor performance and failures, such as President Mitterrand's abortive attempt to expand the French economy from 1981 to 1983. The European Monetary System (see chapter 11) was seen as a successful example of what could be achieved by European cooperation. There was also support for further integration demonstrated by the European Parliament majority in favour of the Draft Treaty of European Union[2] in 1984. The awkward partner in the EC, the UK, was also prepared to cooperate on further integration for three reasons. First, in 1984 a more permanent solution to the UK's budgetary problems was agreed (see chapters 2 and 19). Second, the SEM was in tune with the free market orthodoxy of the time, particularly with the Thatcher government's philosophy. Third, Margaret (now Baroness) Thatcher believed that there were large potential gains for the UK from freer trade in services, especially financial services in the City of London.

The new Commission in 1984, presided over by Jacques Delors, was pushing at an open door when it chose the SEM as the priority for its period in office. Lord Cockfield, the Vice-President of the Delors Commission responsible for the SEM, drew up the Internal Market White Paper (CEC, 1985a) – at the time a novel approach for the Community – setting out an ambitious, but feasible strategy including a legislative programme designed to sweep away cross-border restrictions and to restore the momentum of economic integration. The necessary institutional changes were contained in the SEA (1987). The features of the strategy and legislation that characterize the SEM programme are as follows:

1. Minimum harmonization: new approach directives restricted harmonization to essential requirements: health, safety, and environmental and consumer protection. The general harmonization method, originating in too rigid an interpretation of the treaty was to be abandoned; in most cases, an 'approximation' of the parameters was sufficient to reduce differences in rates or technical specifications to an acceptable level (see chapter 16).
2. The deadline of 31 December 1992, combined with regular monitoring, was designed to speed progress (Article 12).
3. Qualified majority voting (QMV; see chapter 3) was to apply to most SEM measures, but not to fiscal (tax) provisions, the free movement of persons, or the rights of employed persons (Article 18).
4. Control of the emergence of new NTBs.
5. Mutual recognition, facilitated by the landmark judgment by the European Court of Justice in the *Cassis de Dijon* case (see chapter 4): goods which were 'lawfully' made and sold in one EU member nation should in principle be able to move freely and go on sale anywhere within the EU, and the same was true of potentially traded services such as banking or insurance.

6. European standards were to be developed but (except where they coincided with legal requirements) their absence should not be allowed to restrict trade. The detailed technical definition of these requirements should, where possible, be entrusted to European standards institutions.

To make the SEM for the EU like a national market required the removal of three types of barriers: physical, fiscal and technical.

Physical barriers were checks at borders for the control of the movement of persons for immigration purposes; customs borders were required due to differences in indirect taxes; animal and plant health was protected by inspections at borders; checks on lorries and drivers were ostensibly for safety reasons and to enforce national restrictions on foreign hauliers. Considerable expense was incurred in preparing the documentation needed and there were delays at borders, further increasing the cost of inter-EU transport.

Fiscal barriers were needed to check the goods crossing borders because differences in indirect taxes, VAT, and excise duties on alcohol, tobacco, etc. were dealt with by remitting these taxes on exports and imposing them on imports (see chapter 15).

Technical barriers cover an enormous range of measures that affect trade. The most pervasive of these are technical regulations and standards. *Regulations* are legal requirements which products must satisfy before they can be sold in a particular country; these cover health, safety and environmental requirements. Regulations are also important in relation to services (see below). *Standards* are not legally binding in themselves: they are technical requirements set by private standardization bodies like DIN in Germany, BSI in the UK and AFNOR in France. Although they are only voluntary, they often assume a quasi-legal status because they are used in technical regulations and in calls for tender in contracts. They are also important in marketing the product. The existence of different regulations and standards imposed additional costs on EU producers who had to make alterations to their products before they could sell them in another member states.

Another technical barrier related to *public procurement:* private sector purchases by governments. Governments frequently discriminated against bids from firms in other member states for a variety of reasons: strategic (e.g. weapons); support of employment; encouragement of emerging high-tech industries, to maintain employment; etc. However, such policies imposed costs on both the public authorities (who ended up paying more than they needed to) and on firms (because the market available for selling their goods was too limited). One consequence was too many producers, making it difficult to achieve an optimum scale in industries such as defence, electricity generating and telecommunications equipment.

Technical barriers were the main impediment to trade in *services*. For a range of services from plumbing to legal services the problems related to the recognition of qualifications[3] and the rights to establish businesses. For *financial services*, trade was limited by government regulatory measures. In banking, there were particular problems with establishing capital adequacy. Insurance could not be sold in most member states unless the insurer had a local permanent establishment. Capital movements were controlled by several member states which interfered with free trade in financial services.

What was remarkable about the SEM programme (IMP) was its broad aims and ambitions, and the development of a clear approach to achieving them. It embraced measures as diverse as animal health controls and licensing of banks; public procurement and standards for catalytic converters. It covered not just traditionally tradeable services such as banking, insurance and transport, but also the new areas of information, marketing and audio-visual services. With regard to transport, the agenda included the 'phasing out of all quantitative restrictions (quotas) on road haulage', and further liberalization of road, sea and air passenger services through the fostering of increased competition (see chapter 16). The aim for audio-visual services was to create a single EU-wide broadcasting area.

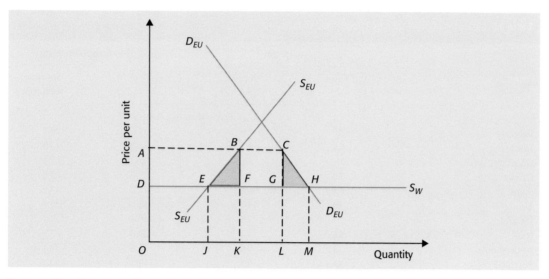

Figure 7.1 The effects of tariffs and non-tariff barriers

7.3 The economics of non-tariff barriers

Non-tariff barriers are any non-tariff government policy measure that intentionally or unintentionally alters the amount or the direction of trade. These are government not private measures. They are artificial not natural conditions: transport costs, language and cultural factors influence trade flows but are not NTBs. Natural conditions can, however, be exploited as NTBs, e.g. by requiring extensive documentation in the home language. Whether intentional or unintentional, it is the effect on trade that is important, not the declared purpose of the measure. It is notoriously difficult to establish intentions. A trade barrier implies a reduction of trade but the volume of trade or its direction could be altered by subsidies, which could lead to an excessive amount of trade.

The effects of NTBs are analogous to those of tariffs (see chapter 6). Figure 7.1, adapted from figure 6.1, is the basis for a partial equilibrium comparison of tariffs and NTBs. The world supply of this product to the EU, S_W, is assumed to be infinitely elastic at a price D and this would be the price in the absence of restrictions on trade. At this price, the EU demand (D_{EU}) would be OM, EU supply (S_{EU}) OJ and imports JM. If a tariff of AD was levied on imports, the EU price would rise to A, EU demand

would contract by LM to OL, EU supply would increase by JK to OK and imports would fall to KL. Thus the effects of the tariff are as follows:

1. Consumption is reduced and consumers are worse off. The consumers' loss is equal to the area ACHD,[4] made up of the higher price on their current consumption, an amount equal to the area ACGD, and the loss of the opportunity to buy LM at the lower price OD the area CHG.
2. Government tariff revenue is BCGF, so part of the consumer loss is transferred to the government.
3. Domestic producers' revenue increases from DEJO to ABKO; of this JEBK is the additional cost of production, so producers' surplus[5] increases by ABED.
4. The deadweight (net) loss associated with the tariff is relatively small, equal to the two dark triangles EBF and CGH; most of the additional cost to the consumer is extra tariff revenue for the government or producer surplus.[6]

If instead of a tariff there was an NTB of the same size, the effects on EU consumption, production, imports and producer surplus would be the same. There are, however, two important differences:

Table 7.1 Measures of protection by country and industry

	Tariff rate		Non-tariff barrier rate	
	Rate[1]	Standard deviation	Rate[1]	Standard deviation
	Protection by country			
Belgium	7.0	7.6	19.6	28.2
Denmark	7.1	4.1	18.2	27.0
Germany, West	7.4	6.0	22.3	27.4
Greece	7.0	8.6	25.5	25.8
Spain	6.8	4.8	13.9	22.1
France	7.4	14.3	18.4	26.1
Ireland	7.5	7.5	20.8	27.0
Italy	7.6	14.4	20.9	27.1
Netherlands	7.1	7.6	20.6	28.1
Portugal	7.1	3.4	19.1	20.2
	Protection by industry			
Food products	9.8	33.6	45.9	30.0
Textiles	11.7	24.5	69.8	38.2
Apparel	12.3	30.4	71.7	35.7
Footwear	13.3	44.5	33.8	41.9
Furniture	6.4	46.2	0.9	46.5
Industrial chemicals	10.2	23.5	9.1	30.1
Iron and steel	9.8	38.0	47.7	34.6
Machinery (electric)	8.6	28.3	14.3	33.3
Transport equipment	7.9	30.7	25.5	38.8
Professional and scientific equipment	6.5	23.6	2.7	30.3

Note:[1] Import weighted measure.

Source: Lee and Swagel (1997).

1. NTBs are cost-increasing rather than revenue-generating. NTBs protect the market by imposing additional costs on importers by, for example, requiring products to be modified to comply with different national regulations; this increases costs both directly and indirectly by reducing production runs. Complying with customs requirements involves administrative and other costs for importers, in addition to costs for the government of policing the measures. Thus the loss with an NTB could be equal to ACHD, which comprises the deadweight loss with tariff imposition, plus the area BCFG which is no longer government tariff revenue and the area ABFD which is no longer producer surplus; these represent the potential additional deadweight loss associated with NTBs.

2. Levels of NTB protection can be very high. Tariffs are relatively transparent: tariff rates are published and are subject to international negotiation. It is difficult to measure NTBs and thus levels of protection can be very high. Table 7.1 shows that NTBs in the EU were much higher than tariffs and their variation across industries considerably greater.

This means that the benefits from the elimination of NTBs are likely to be large for three reasons. First, the cost savings are large. Second, they apply to a larger proportion of output than with tariff reduction. And, third, they may impact more

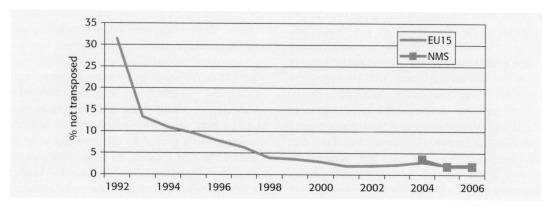

Figure 7.2 Average transposition deficit. *Source:* CEC (2006e, p. 11).

directly on economies of scale because production can be standardized. Indeed it is the OECD (2005b) that has suggested that the size of the benefits from the elimination of such barriers would be substantial.

7.4 An evolving programme

The White Paper (CEC, 1985a) contained 300 proposals for legislation. With QMV introduced by the SEA in 1987, due to the 1992 deadline and the enthusiasm of the member states for the project, by the deadline 95 per cent of the measures were in place. However, this was not the end of the process since additional legislation was needed: to close the remaining gaps in the SEM, e.g. finance, energy and services; to update and improve the existing legislative framework, to ensure it achieved its objectives; and to minimize the administrative burdens on business. Existing legislation needed to be transposed, directives (see chapter 3) needed to be incorporated into national legislation and this could take a considerable time. Continuing vigilance is needed to ensure the implementation of existing legislation; enforcement is the responsibility of national governments and there are sometimes problems with this enforcement. In addition to legislation, there is the enormous task of developing European standards, which is still far from complete.

By October 2005 there were 1,620 directives and 570 regulations (see chapter 3) related to the SEM

(CEC, 2006e, p. 11), which gives some idea of the increased coverage of the programme.[7] Despite this, the Commission continues to identify areas where further progress is needed (CEC, 2003i): the free movement of goods and services; network industries; reducing tax obstacles; public procurement; improving conditions for business, including simplifying the regulatory environment; enforcing the rules; and more and better information. While much of this sounds depressingly familiar, these concerns reflect the desire to improve still further the operation of the SEM and its further development, although there are some areas where progress has been depressingly slow, as in the case with the European Community Patent.

In order to enhance the SEM, the Commission has prioritized measures in a strategy which is part of the economic policy and Lisbon process (see chapter 14). Progress on the strategy is subject to periodic review of its implementation (CEC, 2005b). This is the process for new measures; for existing measures there is a scoreboard, which is updated twice yearly (CEC, 2006e). The purpose of this is to encourage member states to meet their obligations. This shows the transposition deficit, defined as the percentage of SEM measures that have passed the deadline for their operation, but which have not been incorporated into national legislation. For the EU15, the percentage fell rapidly after 1992, then more gradually, but since 2000 there has been little further progress (see figure 7.2).[8] The new member states (NMS), by contrast, have made rapid progress and all except for the Czech

Republic meet the target of having less than 1.5 per cent of outstanding measures not transposed. There are substantial differences between member states, with the worst performance in 2006 being in Luxembourg, Italy and Greece, with sixty-two measures still to transpose, a deficit of 3.8 per cent; the best performance is Denmark's with only eight measures outstanding, a deficit of 0.5 per cent.[9] This failure of transposition means that 9 per cent of operational directives have not been implemented in one or more member states. Twenty directives that should have been implemented over four years ago are still not incorporated into national law. There are also some problems with the enforcement of the legislation, but to some extent these reflect the dynamic and evolving nature of the SEM.

7.4.1 The services market

A major disappointment of the SEM has been the limited extent to which services markets have been integrated (Gros, 2006; OECD, 2005c), when services account for almost 70 per cent of output and employment in the EU (see tables 5.4 and 5.5). The EU has sought to open up the services market with two particular measures: a general services directive and the Financial Services Action Plan (considered below). The barriers to cross-border trade in non-financial services remain high: national regulatory regimes are very different and complex, so one cannot be confident that they would not be used to protect domestic companies. In sectors such as accountancy, retailing, wholesale trade and IT services, barriers remain high and the gains from their elimination could be significant. Trade in commercial services could rise by 30–60 per cent and the stock of foreign direct investment (FDI) by 20–35 per cent (Kok et al., 2004, p. 66); this could raise EU consumption by 0.6 per cent and employment by 600,000 (Copenhagen Economics, 2005a, p. 13).

These markets were to be opened up by new legislation on services (CEC, 2004k). This proposal sought to extend the principle of mutual recognition to services: a company able to operate a service in one member state should in principle be able to operate that service in any other member state. The directive proposed various measures to achieve these ends: freedom of establishment (easing of administrative requirements); freedom of movement (country of origin principle and rights of recipients to use services in other countries); and measures to establish consumer confidence in service provision. Coming as they did at a time of growing economic nationalism, these proposals proved so controversial as to be labelled the Frankenstein directive, in a pun on the name of Frits Bolkstein, the Internal Market Commissioner at the time. There were concerns over social dumping and that social standards (minimum wages and health and safety) would be undermined, because foreign service companies could use cheap foreign workers employed on lower standards. Particular concerns were raised over the regulation of private security and social care where the vetting of workers' suitability, e.g. for criminal convictions, could be undermined.

Although there were some problems with the directive, these criticisms were exaggerated. The Posted Workers Directive (Council of the EU, 1997c) requires employers to pay the minimum wages and satisfy the employment conditions, including health and safety, of the host country, although it would still have been possible to employ foreign workers at below normal wages for the service. Are standards that much lower in other countries? Wages are lower but whether standards are that much lower is questionable. A lot of the criticisms consist of special pleading by interest groups.

These objections have resulted in a significantly modified proposal for the services directive (CEC, 2006a). The modification includes a considerable number of exemptions from the directive: in addition to the original exemptions on financial services,[10] electronic communication networks and transport services,[11] are added healthcare and pharmaceutical services, audio-visual services whatever their means of transmission, gambling services, social services in the area of housing, childcare and support to families and persons in need. The other significant modification is that the principle of regulation by country of origin has been replaced by the freedom to provide services. The original proposal for mutual recognition was important because it would potentially have made cross-border service provision much more straight-forward, but this activity is likely to continue to have to meet two sets of regulations. Hence, provided requirements of non-discrimination, necessity[12] and proportionality are met, national authorities may regulate foreign services providers. There are some useful requirements on the authorization regime such as a single point of contact, charges and processing time. The impact of the directive will only become apparent later, but these modifications are likely to significantly reduce its impact by increasing the difficulty of establishing new service provision in another member state, so undermining its efficacy.

7.4.2 Financial services

The integration of financial markets is an essential component of the SEM which not only yields direct benefits but is essential for the SEM as a whole. The 'Costs of non-Europe' studies, carried out on behalf of the European Commission and summarized in the Cecchini Report (1988), attributed as much as a quarter of the potential gains for EC GDP from the SEM to the liberalization of financial services. The review of the SEM conducted in the mid-1990s (see the Monti Report, 1996) was markedly less optimistic about the benefits that would flow from it, largely because remaining regulatory and other barriers had inhibited the emergence of genuine pan-EU provision of services. This was especially the case for retail financial services (Schüler and Heinemann, 2002), but some barriers also remained in other areas and there was limited cross-border consolidation of the financial services industry. This led in 1999 to the Financial Services Action Plan (FSAP; CEC, 1999j) to restore the impetus towards integration, because the potential gains from greater capital market efficiency were being lost. More recent studies (Giannetti et al., 2002 and London Economics, 2002) maintain that there is still plenty of potential for the further integration of financial markets and that this will substantially enhance economic growth.

The key mechanisms through which financial integration translates into improved economic performance can be summarized as follows:

- Improvements in the 'x-efficiency' of financial intermediaries as competitive pressures oblige them to adopt new technologies, to pare operating costs and to restructure to more optimal sizes.
- A second competitive effect is that lower cost or more innovative provision (such as electronic trading) may lead to increases in retail demand for financial services in particular.
- Pooling of liquidity that deepens the supply of finance, an effect estimated to be capable of lowering the cost of capital by an average of forty basis points (London Economics, 2002).
- In macroeconomic terms, the gains from a truly integrated financial market are projected to be of the order of 0.5 per cent of GDP in the short term (European Financial Services Roundtable, 2003) to 1 per cent in the long term (London Economics, 2002). The latter increase in GDP should result in around 0.5 per cent more jobs. Not surprisingly, it is the member states with the least developed financial markets that stand to gain most from accelerated integration (Giannetti et al., 2002). In sum, the potential benefits from integration of financial markets are considerable.

The FSAP (CEC, 1999j) was designed to raise the efficiency of financial intermediation in the EU and especially to lower the costs of cross-border financing. It had four broad aims:

- completing a single wholesale market;
- developing open and secure markets for retail financial services;
- ensuring the continued stability of EU financial markets;
- eliminating tax obstacles to financial market integration.

The first legislative phase of the FSAP is now effectively complete and by the end of 2005, forty-one of the forty-two measures had been adopted (CEC, 2006c). There are still problems with transposition; only ten of the twenty-two had completed transposition in all member states by May 2006, despite the fact that all but three had passed their implementation deadline. The situation also varies considerably among member states: Poland,

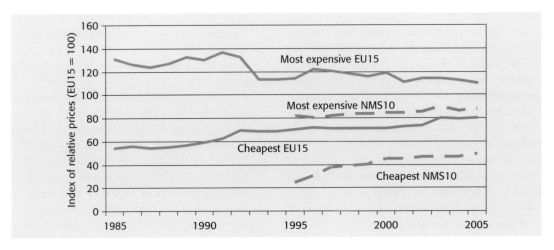

Figure 7.3 Price dispersion in the EU. *Source:* CEC (2006d).

Austria, Estonia and Denmark have transposed all the directives that are in force, while Luxembourg has still to transpose 30 per cent, and Portugal and Spain 20 per cent (CEC, 2006b). While this is far from satisfactory, it does represent substantial recent progress.

With the legislative programme still incomplete it is too early to judge whether the FSAP will be successful, but enforcement will be crucial. In this area, national regulators' trust of their foreign counterparts to protect consumers is limited, so vigilance is needed to ensure that barriers are eliminated. With the globalization of financial markets, the external competitiveness of EU financial institutions is essential. So cooperation on regulation needs to be international as well as European. Further legislation in this area is likely to be limited and financial services markets can be opened up by the use of other instruments such as competition policy (Casey, 2005). This is reflected in the White Paper (CEC, 2005c) where the emphasis is on improving implementation and enforcement and developing supervisory cooperation. Future legislation is likely to be limited to investment funds and retail financial services.

7.5 Assessment of the single market

The are two aspects to the assessment of the SEM. First is the assessment of the extent to which it

been achieved. Second is the measurement of its effects on economic performance. These are the subject of the next two sub-sections.

7.5.1 The extent of integration in the single market

There are a very wide range of potential measures of the extent of integration in the SEM but two stand out for their generality: price convergence and the extent of trade. The SEM makes trade easier between countries, which should make it harder to maintain price differences between national markets.[13] Arbitrage[14] and consumer cross-border trade should be much easier in the SEM. There was price convergence in the EU15 associated with the SEM period, most dramatically in the period leading up to 1993 (see figure 7.3). It has continued since 1992, but at a slower pace. The new member states (NMS10) show signs of price convergence both within their group and with the EU15.

The problem is of course one of causation: is the SEM the cause of price convergence? Price convergence of tradeable goods is the result of arbitrage, but price convergence of non-tradeable goods is the result of the Balassa–Samuelson effect. In poorer countries, the price of goods such as housing, and services such as restaurant meals, haircuts, etc., is cheaper. This is partly the result of lower demand relative to supply (resulting in

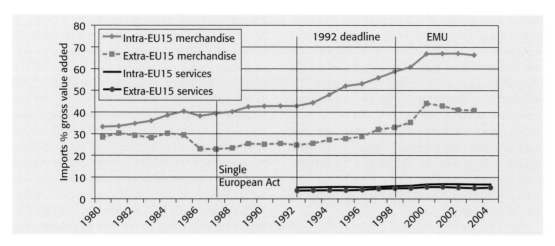

Figure 7.4 Intra- and extra-EU15 imports share of GVA. *Source:* WTO (2006); World Bank (2006a); own calculations.

lower land prices and rents) but also because lower wages mean lower costs of production. The development of these economies leads to increases in productivity, especially in the tradeable sector, so wages here can rise without affecting competitiveness. Wages in non-tradeable sectors also rise but without the accompanying increase in productivity, so prices rise.[15] Therefore the process of convergence in income levels will cause a reduction in price dispersion within the EU; so is price convergence the result of the SEM or income convergence? Indeed, is some of the income convergence the result of the SEM? In addition, the price convergence process may be very long-term as some recent evidence suggests (Mathä, 2006).

The SEM should cause price convergence by increasing the amount of trade in tradeable goods and by increasing the proportion of output that is tradeable, for example by encouraging cross-border public procurement contracts. Figure 7.4 shows imports as a percentage of gross value added (GVA), which is basically the value of output; both intra-EU15 and extra-EU15 imports are shown. For merchandise trade, i.e. trade in goods, imports are expressed as a percentage of the GVA of agriculture and industry. It can be seen that the share of intra-EU15 imports has been steadily climbing but there is no change in the general trend associated with either the introduction of the SEM programme in the mid-1980s or the 1992 deadline. Extra-EU imports stagnated in the 1980s, but showed steady growth in the 1990s. Both intra- and extra-EU15 imports stagnated in the period of slow growth that followed the end of the dotcom boom. Extra-EU15 imports were also affected by the weakness of the euro from 1999 to 2002. Merchandise imports have reached a very high level, so the potential for further growth in intra-EU trade seems fairly limited.[16]

The situation with trade in services is very different: both intra- and extra-EU imports are at low levels and show no major tendency to increase. This indicates a significant failure for the SEM, with services accounting for around 70 per cent of output and the integration of industry already at a high level;[17] significant benefits from the SEM require the integration of services markets, but the levels of trade suggest this has not been achieved. Trade is of course not the only indicator; the effects of integration could occur in the absence of trade if foreign service providers set up in other economies, but this does not seem to be happening (see section 7.4.1).

7.5.2 The single market and economic performance

The rationale for the SEM is that it reinforces the market opening principle of the common market by focusing not just on existing trade flows, but also on subjecting hitherto protected sectors to greater competition and the prospect of cross-border exchanges. In so doing, it establishes a number of channels for improved resource allocation and efficiency gains that, in turn, offer the promise of improved economic performance. The prospective economic gains can be summarized under five broad headings: four distinct sets of microeconomic benefits can be envisaged and there are also macroeconomic gains to be had. Achieving these benefits will incur some dislocations: unemployment can result from the changes needed to achieve overall benefits. The principal categories of benefit are:

- price reductions that provide benefits to consumers and businesses alike;
- increased competition that not only lessens producer power in imperfectly competitive markets, but also stimulates more rapid innovation and product development;
- opportunities to realize economies of scale by concentrating production, and of scope by broadening producers' markets and allowing sunk costs to be more broadly spread;
- a recasting and focusing of regulatory interventions, both to eliminate unnecessary duplication and to modernize processes;
- in aggregate, the prospective improvements in resource allocation make it possible for the output of the economy to be increased, provided always that factors of production are fully employed.

7.5.3 Empirical research on the single market: Commission studies

The Cecchini Report (1988) is a summary of Commission economic research (Emerson et al., 1988) to highlight the benefits of the SEM in the run-up to the 1992 deadline. The study estimated the total potential gain for the EC12 to be in the region of 200 billion ECUs, at 1988 prices. This would increase EC GDP by 4–6 per cent. The gains would come not only from the elimination of the costs of barriers to intra-EC trade, but also from the exploitation of economies of scale which were expected to lower costs by about 2 per cent of EC GDP. The medium-term impact of this on

employment was expected to be an increase of about two million jobs. These gains could be enhanced if the member state governments pursued macroeconomic policies that recognized the potential for faster economic growth: the total gains could reach 7 per cent of EC GDP and the increase in employment about five million jobs. The size of these gains is due to the combination of the elimination of barriers in an EU dominated by oligopolistic market structures, where there is 'a considerable degree of non-competitive segmentation of the market' (Emerson et al., 1988). Since the emphasis is on cost savings, the Cecchini Report stresses them as the 'cost of non-Europe'; the reduction of costs and the generation of benefits are two sides of the same coin.

It is important to emphasize the speculative nature of this exercise and the fact that it was undertaken by a Commission keen to underscore the benefits of the flagship policy. Instead of carrying out a microeconomic exercise to identify and assess the value of each NTB (see chapter 9), a Herculean task, the EU Commission opted for the novel approach of measuring the impact of economic integration by measuring departures from it. This inverted procedure involved specifying what an integrated economy might have looked like and comparing this with the actual economy.[18] In such an economy there would be little price dispersion and firms would operate on an EU-wide level. Thus, in setting out the potential impact, the Cecchini study looked at the extent of departures from the lowest prices and the extent to which economies of scale had not been exploited. Thus, this approach did not estimate the likely impact of economic integration; rather, it provided an estimate of the scope for gains (Mayes, 1997b). The sheer difficulty in calibrating the gains in an *ex ante* evaluation of this sort is demonstrated by the ranges of estimates that Emerson et al. (1988) felt obliged to report. Their estimates range from 70 billion ECUs (2.5 per cent of EC GDP) for 'a rather narrow conception of the benefits' of eliminating the remaining barriers to the single market, to about 125–190 billion ECUs (4.5–6.5 per cent of EC GDP) in the case of a more competitive and integrated market. Realizing these potential gains would take time – five or more years for the upper limits to be achieved – and policies at both the microeconomic and the macroeconomic level would have to ensure that the resources (basically labour) released by the savings in costs would be fully and effectively utilized elsewhere in the EC (Emerson et al., 1988).

These microeconomic estimates were fed into macro dynamic models to generate macroeconomic simulations (see chapter 9), with passive or active macroeconomic policies. In the case of passive macroeconomic policies, the major impact was expected in the medium term (five to six years), by the end of which a cumulative impact of 4.5 per cent increase in GDP and a 6 per cent reduction in the price level were expected. Active macroeconomic policies, it was argued, were appropriate, since inflation, the balance of payments and the government would improve; hence the medium-term macroeconomic stance could be more expansionary. This active strategy boosted GDP in the medium term by 7 per cent. Despite the many potential qualifications to these results, they were felt to be underestimates of the potential benefits of a fully integrated SEM (Emerson et al., 1988, pp. 6–7).

Compared with this very optimistic picture, the findings of the second major exercise conducted by the Commission in the mid-1990s have to be regarded as a disappointment. Enormous effort was put into this research which comprised some thirty-eight studies, plus a business survey (CEC, 1996f). The headline figure this time was that the SEM had raised EU GDP by just over 1 per cent by 1994 and had increased employment by about half a million.

Why was there such a difference, not only in the measured aggregate impact but also in the 'spin' put on it? The Commission (CEC, 1996f) identified three main problems. First, it argued that it was just too soon to observe the medium-term effects of the SEM. Not only were some measures not implemented until 1994 or 1995, but economic agents had also not yet had time to adjust. The Commission also argued that, at the macroeconomic level, there had been insufficient time for the effects of regulatory change to work through. A second 'defence' is one which bedevils many exercises in applied economics, namely that the data

that could be used was, at best, only up to 1994 and this only allowed a very short assessment from the time when the SEM measures – even if they had been fully implemented – were introduced. Third, in a context in which many other important influences are simultaneously affecting the economy, separating out the effects of a relatively small and incremental effect such as market integration is difficult. In fact, revisions to GDP data – quite reasonably made as national statisticians obtain further information about the output of the economy – can be as great as the effects in question. In addition, the impact of the SEM needs to be separated from cyclical effects, as well as from the impact of technological or structural change.

In spite of these difficulties (and it is worth recalling that the equally daunting methodological challenges of the 'Cecchini' estimates were rather glossed over), it is instructive how much the tone of the 1996 review differs from the optimism of the 1980s. Thus, in the working paper, the Commission report starts by stressing that it 'expected that the Review would not show very much change'.

Strong survey evidence is presented on the perceived benefits to business of the SEM, with respondents representing companies accounting for nearly half of all output and employment reporting a strong or significant impact of the SEM. Yet the more detailed responses have to do with the protection the SEM programme provides 'against the introduction of new barriers and the refragmentation of the market'. The report provides solid evidence about the detailed challenges and successes of the SEM, demonstrating that the SEM changes are a long haul, rather than the somewhat misleading impression of the 'costs of non-Europe' studies that suggested the provision of almost instant benefits. Obstacles such as the slow pace of adoption and transposition of measures are discussed and analysed, and shortcomings in the legislation itself are highlighted.

Additional insights are also provided into the economic processes required to achieve the desired outcomes. For example, the report notes that 'differences in market structure from country to country may deter new entry, even where this is legally feasible'. The impact of innovations and market-driven changes are also mentioned, and the fact that regulation has continually to adapt to these is salient: financial markets in particular have exhibited a capacity to evolve faster than their regulatory frameworks, and the incidence of environmental measures emerges as a phenomenon of growing significance. Another important factor mentioned as affecting the economic impact is the costs of compliance, which means that companies often incur heavy costs before they achieve benefits.

Ten years after the conclusion of the '1992' programme, the Commission, not surprisingly, was keen to celebrate the achievements of the SEM. It produced new estimates indicating that the SEM has raised EU GDP in 2002 by 1.8 per cent, or 164.5 billion euros, and increased employment by 1.46 per cent, which means that around 2.5 million extra jobs have been created (CEC, 2002q). This again indicates a significant but far from earth-shattering impact of the SEM, undermining the Commission's explanations for the low estimates in 1996. The idea that the SEM would transform EU economic performance has proved to be wide of the mark: there is no indication in the growth of output or productivity over this period that would support this contention (see chapter 14).

7.5.4 Other empirical studies of the single market

After the initial flurry of activity associated with the 1992 deadline (Pelkmans and Winters, 1988; Brenton and Winters, 1992; Sapir, 1996), independent empirical research on the SEM seemed to tail off. Of the few more recent studies, Allen et al. (1998) indicated significant benefits from the SEM via reductions in price-cost margins associated with a decrease in the market share of domestic producers in sensitive sectors. However, this study was written too soon after the 1992 deadline, so the time available to pick up its effects is limited. The econometric analysis was criticized for assuming that the SEM effect only related to the short post-1992 period and, strangely, that at least as far as market share is concerned the effect is similar for EU and non-EU producers (Flam, 1998; Sørensen, 1998). Bottasso and Sembenelli (2001)

confirm the Allen et al. (1998) finding of a decrease in the market share of domestic producers in sensitive sectors. They also find a positive shock to productivity in these sectors, but this is only transitory. The effect of reduced mark-ups/margins is confirmed by Siotis (2003), but here the 1992 effect is reinforced by the accession process for Spain. Finally, both the reduction in domestic market power and price-cost margins for industries with high NTBs prior to 1992 are found by Gullstrand and Johansson (2005). So the empirical evidence suggests pressure on margins and increased competition/falling home market share for a limited range of industries.

7.6 Conclusion

In political terms, the single market must be regarded as a success. Despite some foot-dragging in the implementation of key measures, the strategic aim of opening up markets has been consistently advanced and has retained wide political support. Although, in a sense, the internal market will never be fully completed, because there will always be barriers that give some advantage to indigenous producers, there can be little doubt that the EU has moved a long way since the White Paper was launched over twenty years ago. The scope of the SEM has also expanded significantly to encompass most production. Economic nationalism and protection remain potent forces and the development of the SEM continues to be a battle with these forces. The pace of regulation has slowed and the emphasis has gradually shifted to quality of regulation, implementation and enforcement.

Although much of the rhetoric surrounding the SEM has been about liberalization and deregulation, with the implication that it is principally concerned with *negative* integration (as explained in chapter 1), the reality is more complex. In a number of areas, the outcome has been more a recasting of the regulatory framework than its dismantling, and the resulting regulatory style is one that reflects European values.

In economic terms, the outcome of the SEM is much less clear-cut: ultimately its objective was to raise the performance of the EU economy by raising productivity growth. To paraphrase Robert Solow: you can see the single market programme everywhere but in the productivity statistics.[19] This analysis bears out Ziltener's (2004, p. 971) contention 'that we find no evidence for an integration-induced macroeconomic process with significant economic gains'. The interesting issue is why. It is possible to argue that the effect is confined to a relatively narrow range of industries, so that the overall effect is limited.[20] A response would be the view that the problem is an incomplete SEM and that what is required is further opening and pan-EU restructuring via mergers and takeovers. It is possible to identify areas of limited cross-border competition; the rarity of cross-border mergers and takeovers is an example of economic nationalism. An alternative view is that the internal market's impact may have been a transitory shock with little long-term impact on productivity growth. It is also important to note that the SEM is merely part of an increasingly globalized world market, generally subject to liberalization and deregulation; ultimately these developments may have more profound impacts on economic performance. Indeed, European companies' search for competitiveness in this market was at the heart of the SEM and in this sense it has been successful, enabling large companies to emerge, as well as to obtain subsidies for research and development.[21] The SEM remains central to the EU and despite its apparently limited economic impact it is a powerful attraction for potential members and a model for its many imitators.

NOTES

1 The official expression is the internal market but the single European market (SEM) will be used here.

2 An EP initiative which got no further, not to be confused with the Treaty *on* European Union, the Maastricht Treaty.

3 This was also a particular problem for labour mobility.

4 This is the reduction in consumer surplus, the difference between the maximum amount consumers are prepared to pay and the amount they actually have to pay (see chapter 6).

5 Producers' surplus is the excess of revenue over cost (see chapter 6).

6 Over time losses could be larger as a result of the inefficiency of protected producers.

7 Although it also relates to limitations in the original strategy, with additional legislation being required.

8 The number of new measures enacted into national legislation being offset by new measures being agreed.

9 Figures in this section are from CEU (2006e).

10 Subject to separate legislation, see below.

11 The exclusion of urban transport, taxis and ambulances, as well as port services, is made explicit.

12 For example, justified for reasons of public policy, public security, public health or the protection of the environment.

13 This effect should be further reinforced by the single currency.

14 The movement of products from low-price to high-price markets for profit.

15 Competitiveness is not affected because these goods/services are not traded.

16 It is possible for imports to exceed 100 per cent of GVA because exports can incorporate imported components.

17 As indicated by the high level of trade.

18 Normally the counterfactual would be the economy without economic integration.

19 The original was Robert Solow's (1987) remark: 'You can see the computer age everywhere but in the productivity statistics.'

20 This is particularly the case because of the limited impact of the single market in services (see section 7.3.1).

21 Which is at the heart of the EU's current flagship policy the Lisbon process (see chapter 14).

8

Factor mobility

DAVID MAYES AND JUHA KILPONEN

Although the freedom of mobility of labour and capital were objectives enshrined in the Treaty of Rome itself, only fairly limited progress had been made by the early 1980s in turning this into reality. Most countries had capital controls of one form or another and labour faced considerable constraints on movement through lack of recognition of qualifications and other problems over establishment and transfer of benefits. The slow progress stemmed from two sources. In the case of capital, member states were worried that having free movement would lead to destabilizing flows that would disturb the running of the domestic economy. The main fear was a capital outflow that would depreciate the currency, drive up the rate of inflation and require monetary and fiscal contraction to offset it. Labour controls, on the other hand, were more concerned with inflows. Employees in the domestic economy feared that an inflow from other countries would lose them their jobs – countries would export their unemployment. Much of this was dressed up as a need to have certain skills, standards and local knowledge for the protection of consumers. Much of the fear stemmed from ignorance of what others' qualifications meant and overcoming this required a long and tedious process of determination and negotiation.

The 1985 White Paper on completing the internal market and the 1986 Single European Act (SEA) signalled the determination to break through this complex of restrictions and move to a much more open market, with freedom of movement of capital and labour being two of four basic 'freedoms' set out as the objective of the market (the other two being freedom of movement of goods and of services). In the case of capital, this was to be achieved by 1 July 1990. This target was largely not met for the EC of nine, and Portugal

and Spain managed to participate in 1992 only for the ERM crisis of September 1992 (see chapter 11) to require some controls to be reintroduced by member states in the hope of stabilizing their exchange rates. The setback proved to be short-lived. The Maastricht Treaty, which came into force in 1993, had advanced progress further and capital markets have become even more open with the introduction of the euro at the beginning of 1999.

The legislative programme for the single market measures was intended to be complete by the end of 1992. While this was largely achieved, some of the labour mobility measures are still to have their full effect (see chapter 7). However, it has since become evident that these measures were by no means ambitious enough to achieve anything like a single capital market and this problem is still being tackled. This lack of completion of the single market by the legislative process was clarified by the White Paper on Growth, Employment and Competitiveness in 1993, which stressed labour market inadequacies and a need to improve the efficiency of product markets.

At the end of the millennium, attention turned to the various problems in the capital markets, including rigidities in capital movements across EU borders. Consequently, the European Commission undertook an important political initiative aimed at enhancing the development of the risk capital markets and, more generally, dealing with related problems in the financial markets, the rationale being that Europe had lost opportunities to create jobs and increase investment because its risk capital markets were underdeveloped, mainly due to the fragmentation of the regulation of the securities market (CEC, 1998d). Following the Lamfalussy Report (2001), a new Financial Services Action Plan is being implemented. This has been given special 'fast-track' procedures to try to drive it through more rapidly (despite some reservations by the European Parliament). When the plan is completed this may bring cross-border capital movement noticeably closer to that within individual nations, but many aspects, such as the Single European Payments Area, remain elusive and may require direct action by the authorities if they are to materialize: for example, provision of services by the ECB.

The Growth and Stability Pact (see chapter 12), agreed on 7 July 1997, created even more pressure for the liberalization and restructuring of the factor markets. In particular, it further strengthened the need for promoting labour mobility both within and across the European countries due to current inter-regional fiscal transfers being modest in comparison to those in most federal systems, such as the US.

Finally, in Lisbon in 2001, the EU heads of state and government agreed to a political commitment to a longer-term strategy aimed at making Europe the most dynamic and competitive knowledge-based economy in the world by 2010 (see chapter 14). The target is to achieve economic growth of 3 per cent per annum and to raise the employment rate to 70 per cent from around 2.5 per cent and 65 per cent respectively by 2010. This is a very challenging task and involves even further integration of product and factor markets within Europe. In particular, different aspects related to the accumulation of human capital, skills and technology transfer have assumed crucial importance for the EU member countries. The logic behind achieving 'free movement' of capital and labour, including human capital, is that it is crucial for the full exploitation of efficiency gains within the EU and for meeting the 2001 Lisbon summit's goals.

There are also some contradictions in these approaches. The logic behind the EU itself and the four freedoms is largely built on the neo-classical paradigm of perfect competition and its advantages. Yet the new development in the field with its associated knowledge-based economies is founded on notions based on new growth theory, increasing returns to scale and monopolistic competition. This means that earlier models of international factor mobility, basically static in character, are no longer useful for analysing international factor mobility since they consider the optimal allocation of given factors of production. In the new 'endogenous growth' literature, a country or region's factor endowments, hence its factor ratios, are allowed to change over time under conditions of balanced growth. Growth is endogenous in the sense that it depends on the amount of resources allocated to accumulating production factors, such as human capital. Consequently, factor mobility can have an important influence on growth and convergence of growth rates between the countries. In the earlier literature, per capita output grows in accordance with the exogenous growth rate of technology, with policies that affect savings only altering the level of per capita income. Hence, countries that have the same long-run growth rate in technology should have the same long-run growth rate in their per capita incomes, irrespective of their prevailing technology, size or level.

For new growth theories, the accumulation of knowledge, the generation of ideas, the development of human capital and the capacity to absorb new technologies are of the essence in explaining the forces underlying economic growth and determining the competitive position of individual countries. Thus, the long-term growth prospects of the EU countries importantly depend upon the flexibility and efficiency of the EU's own internal factor markets. Ongoing reallocation of production factors should transfer resources to those industries and sectors with comparative advantage and ability to achieve increasing returns to scale in the generation and application of new technology.

Moreover, according to the recent economic geography models, foreign direct investment is not simply determined by relative costs of production or national tax structures. Firms may be drawn to particular regions due to the possibility of obtaining 'agglomeration economies'. The idea is that growth can be faster if competitors, suppliers, customers and related services are all close together in dynamic interaction. Agglomeration effects can be compounded by the wider impact of inward investment. While this has certainly been beneficial for large multinational companies, the problem for economic development is that it leads to greater spatial polarization. Not surprisingly, regions do not want to be without such poles.

Globalization has turned physical capital into a much more mobile factor of production. Due to foreign investment, firms may own the export sector of another nation, and these foreign owners may repatriate most of their profits (Gill and Law, 1988). In such a case, the eventual problem from the point of view of economic development is the hierarchical and possibly exploitative character of transnational firms in a global economy: growth may be achieved, but only at the cost of international inequalities, combined with dependence on financial headquarters elsewhere. This may also apply to the eastern enlargement of the EU, if increasing flows of profit repatriation eventually outweigh the inward flows of foreign direct investment (FDI) to new member countries. It is thus not surprising to see that at the same time that the existing member states have been pulling down the barriers to the free movement of capital and labour, they have been cautious in both fields, increasing the protection of labour through the social chapter in the Maastricht Treaty, insisting on a transition period for the new member states (NMS) and seeking to limit the powers of company takeover.

Such cautiousness is certainly warranted in the classical models of production and trade, where labour supply and relative price effects dominate the economic outcomes of the opening of factor markets and where the goods under consideration are complete goods. However, in a recent paper, Grossman and Rossi-Hansberg (2006) argue that many complex industrial goods are nowadays a result of a multitude of tasks that are performed in separate locations. Because of dramatic developments in communication and information technologies, improved possibilities of relocating the tasks (they called it off-shoring) generate almost the same effects as technological progress does in a standard neoclassical model of production and trade. Their argument is that when some

of the tasks performed by a certain type of labour can be more effectively performed abroad, the firms that gain the most are the ones that use this type of labour intensively. The improved profitability of these firms gives them an incentive to grow relative to firms that rely most heavily on other types of labour. This enhances labour demand and some of this increase in labour demand may as well fall on local workers (and thus increases their wages), who perform tasks that cannot be moved abroad. Now, *if this productivity effect dominates the relative price, and labour supply affects off-shoring*, wages for low-skilled jobs will actually *rise* in the country where off-shoring takes place. Moreover, along with improved possibilities for off-shoring, high-skilled tasks can also boost the wages of domestic white-collar workers.

8.1 Single market

Although the single market programme should remove many of the remaining restrictions on factor movements, it is unlikely that capital, let alone labour, will be as mobile as it is within individual member countries. Factors reducing mobility include differences in tastes and customs, and variations in risk. Having a single currency is an important step in removing one source of risk and reducing transition costs.

The 1992 programme enables integration; it does not compel it. Thus, in the same way that the idealized total specialization of trade in economic theory is rarely realized, we would not expect total perfection in capital markets and nothing like it in labour markets where many other factors lead to continuing segmentation. To a considerable extent this is affected by the nature and treatment of the services in which labour is embodied, which have national diversity, in the same way as there is diversity in the demand for goods.

If factors and products can move between countries freely, then, neglecting any transport or transfer costs, the whole trading area can be treated as a single market with a uniform reward right across the area to each factor as well as uniform product prices. However, such a system is not only very far from a description of the reality of the EU after 1992, but is also indeterminate and does not tell us the extent to which the products rather than the factors move – a typical problem of under-identification (see Mayes, 1988). The imperfections of the real world, however, are actually an aid in this case as they increase the chances of being able to identify the determinants of the various movements.

There is a basic distinction between direct investment, which involves the setting up or acquisition of a 'subsidiary' in a foreign country, and portfolio investment, involving the purchase of shares and bonds or the making of other forms of loan to a company in a foreign country.[1] In the case of labour movement, individuals physically move from one country to another and then provide their labour services in the second country. Capital, on the other hand, in the sense usually considered, involves the transfer of claims through a financial transaction and not the transfer of capital goods themselves in the form of plant, machinery and vehicles. If existing physical capital is exported, then the financial transfer is lowered. If new physical capital is purchased from the home country, there is an additional export but the net inflow of physical capital is smaller. The net flow is largest when the new physical capital is all produced in the country where the new plant is set up.[2]

Some of the distinctions between types of capital movement may not be very important from the point of view of actual output and trade patterns. Portfolio investment resulting in control of the foreign enterprise may be largely indistinguishable from direct investment, for example. However, the major distinction normally lies in the type of investor. Direct investment is undertaken by firms on their own behalf (or by governments). Portfolio investment, on the other hand, is more usually undertaken by financial companies of one form or another, although cross-share holdings by commercial companies are common in some parts of the EU. Much of this latter investment may therefore not seem particularly relevant to the problem in hand, as it relates to a change in the ownership of existing assets, rather than the direct financing of the creation of new physical assets used for the production of goods and ser-

vices. However, this is mistaken from two points of view: direct investment may also be purely a change in ownership, this time involving control; second, we need to enquire what subsequent use the funds released to the seller were put to. The ability to exchange domestic debt for foreign equity can affect the range of options open to a firm. Moreover, even if the purpose of capital inflows into a country is to 'enable' the foreign government to run a deficit which cannot be financed fully by its private domestic sector, such lending may permit a higher level of investment in physical capital in that country than would otherwise be the case.

Clearly, the latter form of capital flow is of more than passing interest in a group of countries that are attempting some coordination of their economic actions. When exchange rates are fixed between member countries balance of payments surpluses/deficits on current account may open up rather wider than would otherwise be the case. In so far as these imbalances are not met by official movements (or reserves), they must be eliminated by countervailing capital movements, encouraged in the main by differences in covered[3] interest rates.[4] With freely floating exchange rates, the exchange rate can take rather more of the burden of adjustment between countries, and capital flows rather less. Coordination of fiscal or monetary policies between countries will also affect the ways in which capital flows have to balance the remaining transactions.[5] Now with the euro, there is no more concern about the private financial flows between the participating countries than there is about the flows between regions of the same member state. The burden of adjustment falls largely on the labour market (see chapters 10 and 12).

These considerations raise many issues which lie outside the scope of this chapter; but it must be borne in mind that capital transfers take place between countries for reasons that are not necessarily related to the essentially microeconomic decisions of the individual firm. To invert the argument, wider issues influence the values of the macroeconomic variables which affect firms' decisions over their overseas investment, and these wider issues themselves form part of the way in which the members of the EU choose to conduct the handling of economic policy, both jointly and independently. Since direct investment abroad and borrowing of foreign funds by enterprises in foreign countries may both involve not just the same size capital inflow but also the same increase in capital formation within the country, it is not possible to set aside either long-term or short-term portfolio investment as being irrelevant to the purpose in hand.

8.2 Capital movements

Exchange controls were eliminated in the UK in October 1979, but the reasons for that move had little to do with membership of the EU. At that stage, the remaining Community countries all had restrictions on capital flows, although these varied in their degree of tightness. After the start of the single market programme, these restrictions were steadily removed and there has been effective freedom of capital movements since the start of stage 2 of EMU. With the exception of the new members, freedom throughout the Community was in place by July 1990, the start of stage 1 of EMU. In most cases there was a distinction between controls applied to residents and those applied to non-residents, with the restrictions being lighter in the latter case. However, interestingly enough, such restrictions as did apply to non-residents usually applied equally to all such non-residents, regardless of whether they were residents of another EC country or of a third country. There is thus no counterpart to the preference system applied to trade through differential tariffs as far as capital movements are concerned, nor, it seems, was there any intention of taking the opportunity of introducing discrimination against third countries by making this freedom of movement only in respect of fellow members.[6] To a large extent this is a practical matter, because it is difficult to control some transactions when others do not have to be vetted. However, 'reciprocity' is an argument which has been used in other parts of the single market programme in order to obtain concessions for the EU in third-country markets. In one sense, therefore,

this simplifies the analysis, as one potential source of substitution and encouragement of capital flows does not in the main exist.

In general, the movement of financial capital among financial centres now entails only minimal intrinsic costs, due to the liberalization and development of information technology. Foreign direct investment and the (re-)establishment of productive capacity are neither costless nor prohibitively costly in terms of time and financial effort. The GATT and WTO rounds aimed at liberalization in world trade have also lowered customs duties (see chapter 24) and enhanced direct investments. Barriers to the trade of goods are nowadays based on dumping accusations and voluntary export restrictions rather than inefficient tariffs.

However, the restrictions that matter are not in the capital movements themselves but in how those funds can be used to purchase physical assets. Constraints, or indeed incentives, apply to inward investment, to mergers and acquisitions (M&A) and to the operation of multinational companies. Thus, freedom of capital movements is to some extent a myth if there are further constraints on how the funds can be used. Nevertheless, it is clear that restrictions are being progressively eliminated and it can only be hoped that this will also foster financial integration in Europe. Although it has been somewhat difficult to detect any direct growth benefits for financial integration as such, there is evidence that strengthening financial sectors has contributed to strong growth in the emerging Europe. Direct investments have played an important role as strengthening of financial sectors in these countries has at least in part been due to the entry of foreign banks.

The OECD (2000; also Nicoletti et al., 2000) has collected a useful indicator, which provides us with information on the current state of the regulations that may hinder capital flows between different European countries. It is based on restrictions on the rights of foreign citizens to own shares, discriminatory provision concerning international trade and competition policies, average tariffs, and regulatory barriers affecting trade and investment. According to this indicator, barriers to trade are now fairly low in all EU countries; in some cases even lower than in the US. There are, however, still quite large differences across countries; in particular, indicators are the highest in Greece, Portugal and France.

As in the case of trade flows, we would expect to observe a more rapid increase in direct investment abroad than in GDP itself. This duly occurred in the second half of the 1980s, but was not confined to the EU. However, the distribution of that investment by country of investor is unlikely to have been affected by any changes relative to the EU as such because liberalization has almost entirely been non-discriminatory. The influence of the EU on capital flows is as a result likely to be in changes in discrimination in the traded goods and services market. Increased trade flows are likely to involve changes in capital flows – to set up distribution networks and to establish local production as market penetration increases – although the direction of the change is still problematic, as we cannot tell a priori the extent to which trade and direct investment might be substitutes rather than complements.

Nevertheless, recent trends in capital movements in Europe give a clear message about the importance of capital flows in open economies. Gross flows of capital are of immense magnitude, many of the flows representing offsetting movements through which financial and other institutions achieve portfolio diversification and protection against exchange rate and other financial risks. FDI flows are naturally smaller, but since the second half of the 1990s they have continued to surge and have become substantially more important in the process of capital formation as well (table 8.1). This in part reflects the globalization process, which has entailed the rapid expansion of the number and coverage of multinational corporations in Europe. The overall scale of FDI began to increase strikingly during recent decades as countries began to locate portions of their manufacturing, sales and service enterprises in many other countries. For example, the sum of outward and inward FDI as a share of total 1997 investment exceeded 20 per cent for ten of the fourteen European countries. The corresponding figure was less than 10 per cent for all but the UK and the Netherlands in 1975.

Traditionally, the main net outward investors include Germany, Japan and the UK. The Netherlands, Switzerland and Sweden also rank high as net outward investors. One of the main reasons is that several multinational corporations reside in these countries which invest extensively abroad. On the other hand, other countries receive more foreign capital than they invest abroad. These include countries like Hungary and Poland, as well as Australia and Spain. Recently, however, the picture has changed. Ranking the EU member states according to the size of their respective cumulative inflows over 1992–2000, it appears that Germany has changed its position, since in 2000 it became a net recipient of EU FDI, while the Netherlands switched to a position of net recipient (table 8.1), but the figures for 2005 restore the German and Dutch positions.

8.3 On the determinants of direct investment

Investment flows between countries cannot really be treated in the same manner as investment within the economy because, although total investment can be explained through well-known relationships, the split between home and foreign expenditure, on an economy-wide basis, is not so clear. We are concerned in this case not just with what resources firms are prepared to put into capital for future production but where they are going to site them. Most consideration, therefore, has been devoted to the problem at the level of the firm itself, rather than through modelling the components of the capital account of the balance of payments. Even within the confines of aggregate explanation there has been a tendency to avoid modelling direct investment flows directly, and modelling them indirectly through the determination of the exchange rate as a sort of reduced-form approach (see Cuthbertson et al. (1980) for a discussion of this work.)

Such an approach may be appropriate for the explanation of portfolio investment, in particular, since much short-term portfolio investment is described as speculative in nature. It is much less useful for direct investment, because of the

Table 8.1 Direct investment flows of EU countries, 1987–2005 (ECU/euro million)

	1987			1993			1998			2000			2005		
	Intra	Extra	Total	Intra	Extra	Total	Intra	Extra	Total	Intra	Extra	Total	Intra	Extra	Total
Outward															
BLEU	1,655	545	2,200	2,675	1,333	4,008	16,778	6,035	22,813	1,58,640	78,329	2,36,969	69,488	52,726	1,22,214
Denmark	278	219	497	297	779	1,076	3,734	240	4,054	na	na	na	9,800	2,115	11,915
Germany	1,610	5,266	6,876	18,821	9,610	28,431	47,744	1,08,558	1,56,302	5,709	55,678	61,387	21,696	14,999	36,695
Greece	1	9	10	na	na	na	na	na	na	1,932	368	2,300	na	na	na
Spain	270	227	497	1,584	937	2,521	5,241	11,680	16,921	25,362	37,822	63,184	14,420	16,757	31,177
France	3,639	3,483	7,122	6,012	4,381	10,393	26,101	17,343	43,444	1,08,752	81,740	1,90,492	66,871	26,137	93,008
Irish Republic	65	86	151	na	na	na	1,126	2,363	3,489	-23	5,047	5,024	10,250	659	10,909
Italy	998	495	1,493	4,732	1,442	6,174	5,183	5,605	10,788	8,985	4,424	13,410	27,225	6,352	33,577
Netherlands	1,998	3,607	5,605	4,832	5,228	10,060	18,724	15,985	34,718	35,651	46,441	82,092	93,145	21,784	1,14,929
Portugal	8	6	2	84	7	91	1,491	2,129	3,620	3,705	5,122	8,827	1,620	-698	922
United Kingdom	1,730	16,728	18,458	7,866	11,700	19,566	16,940	91,777	1,08,716	2,04,378	48,694	2,53,072	23,314	59,370	82,684
Austria				na	na	na	1,329	1,036	2,452	3,068	3,162	6,230	2,816	5,244	8,060
Finland				1,190	13	1,203	15,411	1,245	16,656	12,849	13,233	26,082	4,817	-1322	3,495
Sweden				1,192	127	1,319	9,519	5,509	15,028	na	14,127	14,127	12,833	5,968	18,801
EU12/15	12,344	30,670	43,014	40,711	24,377	65,088	1,49,443	2,18,754	3,68,197	6,89,140	4,37,044	11,26,184	3,99,477	2,08,704	6,08,181
Inward															
BLEU	1,265	693	1,958	6,302	2,899	9,201	12,229	6,331	18,560	2,01,185	38,631	2,39,816	81,729	34,165	1,15,894
Denmark	2,127	151	24	843	582	1,425	1,053	4,640	5,747	na	na	na	5,657	4,888	10,545
Germany	250	215	465	1,048	-439	609	38,615	4,661	43,276	2,02,298	12,911	2,15,209	19,967	6,297	26,264
Greece	102	87	189	na	na	na	na	na	10	1,155	95	1,250	na	na	na
Spain	1,976	1,338	3,314	6,963	1,087	8,050	9,493	1,049	10,542	29,296	13,659	42,955	15,553	2,932	18,485
France	1,654	2,056	3,710	7,803	2,647	10,450	22,458	5,227	27,685	41,215	5,383	46,598	36,552	14,572	51,124
Irish Republic	160	327	487	na	na	na	4,647	3,271	7,919	40,936	-12,230	28,706	-19,956	-5,078	-25034
Italy	1,310	1,745	3,055	2,528	673	3,201	2,117	208	2,325	10,346	4,181	14,529	14,101	1,926	16,027
Netherlands	1,315	664	1,979	5,869	680	6,549	13,222	20,662	33,884	38,337	30,973	69,310	27,804	5,533	33,337
Portugal	230	97	327	1,062	232	1,294	1,112	1,588	2,700	6,934	268	7,202	2,952	-448	2,504
United Kingdom	4,085	5,619	9,704	2,037	10,609	12,646	16,863	46,146	63,010	85,965	42,825	1,28,790	1,03,166	25,124	1,28,290

Austria		na	na	4,342	−184	4,050	7,747	1,848	9,595	6,131	1,141		7,272
Finland		512	227	739	10,332	516	10,848	9,230	358	9,588	3,437	−278	3,159
Sweden		1,264	1,002	2,266	12,950	1,522	14,472	na	10,895	na	9,686	782	10,468
EU12/15	12,344	12,991	25,335	37,231	58,006	1,35,847	96,432	2,32,279	7,63,546	1,88,450	9,51,996	3,66,052	77,214	4,43,266

'Intra' refers to flows to or from other EU countries. 'Extra' refers to flows to or from the rest of the world. BLEU refers to Belgium–Luxembourg Economic Union.

Source: Adapted from Eurostat database for years 1993–2005. *European Union Direct Investment Yearbooks* (1984–93) for the year 1987.

degree of permanence embodied in the existence of physical capital held abroad and changes in the logic with which multinational firms organize their production.[7]

Nowadays a large proportion of trade is accounted for by large MNEs, and a significant proportion of global trade – estimates are between 30 per cent and 40 per cent – runs through the international production and distribution networks of MNEs as *intra-company trade*. The increase in intracompany trade reflects the motives of multinationals for diversifying risk and deepening economies of scope in the world market.

This internationalization strategy can be inspired by various motives such as market extension, efficiency-seeking, resource-seeking and strategic-asset-seeking. Whatever the motive of the investment, the transfer of resources and production capabilities, and therefore FDI, contributes to the industrial base of the host country. The increasing information content in nearly all products requires experts in various fields to participate in the design and development of almost every commodity. Consequently, many global companies seek to establish both production and research and development activities in different locations all over the world, providing them with either cost-effective production or an abundance of educated people and information infrastructure.

An illustrative example comes from the experience of Finland, a country that has recently been ranked as one of the most attractive targets for high-technology FDI. Due to intensive knowledge and technology investment in Finland many asset-seeking multinationals have acquired promising technology-based Finnish firms, for example in electrical engineering. In the IT sector, foreign companies have acquired innovative firms, which have advanced knowledge in some technology or business area. In knowledge-intensive sectors, asset-seeking FDI is motivated by tacit knowledge that comes in the form of know-how or competence and therefore cannot be separated from the person or organization containing it.

Another factor that may have affected the upsurge of FDI is related to changes in the production model of the multinational corporations. In the typical 'Fordist' production model, MNEs seek growth by expanding into new sectors and connected horizontal integration with diversification. Vertical integration, which was the characteristic of the Fordist production model, was a means of internalizing possible market risks in different phases of the value chain.

Globalization, however, has drastically changed the Fordist production model. In recent years, an increasing number of companies have chosen to narrow their segment of products and services and of the value chain, to concentrate on accumulating and developing core competencies. Such horizontal disintegration has become possible because companies can now balance their cash flow through differences in regional markets, which is again largely due to integration of the product and factor markets in Europe. For instance, Finnish companies have sold divisions for strategic purposes to release resources for the most promising niche markets. Recently the potential new owners have often been foreign firms. Foreign firms and small Finnish technology-oriented firms have also sought to forge strategic alliances to strengthen their competitive advantage and secure rapid internationalization. Traditionally, the behaviour of MNEs has been considered as only reflecting the variations in the costs of inputs in various locations and the structure of the markets they wish to serve.

Moreover, due to more open international competition and the complexity of the products, companies find it harder to achieve and maintain competitive advantage in several sectors or product and service segments at once. This has affected the factor flows across territorial boundaries, in particular FDI, and reinforced the development of a more concentrated economy.

This multinational structure of production, and pressures to expand it, also have consequences for trade. In the case of vertical FDI, where companies allocate different parts of their production chain to those countries where production costs are lower, FDI typically boosts international trade. In the case of horizontal FDI, a company places its production close to foreign markets. In this case, FDI acts as a substitute to trade, and provides strategic market access for the investor.

8.4 Capital movements in Europe

Most early empirical work on direct investment flows in the EU concentrated on inflows from the US, partly because of the quality of data available. Later on, attention turned towards Japan, whose direct investment increased dramatically in the second half of the 1980s. Japan replaced the US as an investment 'threat', with a heavier political overtone, as the US economy has always been fairly open to return investments and acquisitions. Indeed, the level of recent direct investment in the US has been so great that concern is being expressed, while Japan is a much more difficult economy to enter through either export or investment.

Traditionally, US investment in Europe had a strong element of taking over existing enterprises. Japanese investment, on the other hand, tended to be greenfield. Arrangements with existing European firms tended to be joint ventures without Japanese majority control. This generated worries about technology transfer, the greenfield sites often being assembly operations of established products, while the joint ventures were sometimes accused of being more effective in transferring technology to Japan. However, with the collapse of Japanese asset prices in the mid-1990s the pressure has changed. It has been outward investment by the EU in the US as well as an upsurge in intra-EU investment flows that has caught the headlines.

It is noticeable that most modelling of inward investment relates to flows into the EU from outside, not to the flows within the EU itself. Yet it is these internal flows that should be of prime interest in the case of the single market and the development of a knowledge-based society. The studies of external flows suggest that there are three basic mechanisms at work. First, investment tends to increase with sales to the EU, i.e. supporting trade rather than substituting for it (Scaperlanda and Balough, 1983). Barrell and Pain (1993) suggest, following Vernon (1966), that there is an initial level of exports that is required before it becomes worthwhile setting up dealer networks and other downstream services. Second, investment takes place to overcome trade barriers (Culem, 1988; Heitger and Stehn, 1990) or anti-dumping duties (Barrell and Pain, 1993). However, overseas investors with a choice of locations and flows are also affected by relative costs and relative barriers. Thus, when anti-dumping actions were at their height in the US in the mid-1980s, this acted as a spur to Japanese investment there. Finally, investment flows are crucially affected by the availability of funds in the investing country.

The UK has been the largest investor overseas in the EU and is the second largest in the world after the US.[8] Only the Netherlands among other EU countries has been a net direct capital exporter over the last ten years, although West Germany had substantial net exports between 1975 and 1990. More recently, there have been striking year-to-year variations as the data for 2000 shows, with strong outward investment by France and strong inward investment in Germany. Towards the end of the millennium large parts of EU outward FDI flows were accounted for by the UK, France, the Netherlands and Germany. In 2000 they made up 60 per cent of outward flows outside the EU (excluding the US) and 73 per cent of flows to the US. At the same time, these four countries accounted for 55 per cent of intra-EU flows.

More generally, in 2000 Europe participated in the strong worldwide FDI activity that was closely related to the reorganization of the telecommunications sector, and thus may not be indicative of the longer run. At the other end of the scale is the very low level of direct investment in Greece and Italy. Thus, despite any attractiveness which may have existed from surplus and cheaper labour in those countries, this factor advantage has been met by labour outflow rather than capital inflow. Italy similarly has a low level of direct investment abroad, although it is still sufficiently large to show net capital exports over the last four years.

Outward direct investment has been rising considerably faster than in the US, while inward investment has risen more slowly. Thus, while in 1981 and 1982 the US was a net capital importer, the EU was a substantial exporter. Much EU direct investment must therefore be 'directed' outside the EU rather than to other EU countries, as is clearly the case for the UK. Direct investment abroad, like domestic investment, has traditionally been affected by trade cycles.

It is also not realistic to treat the EU as a largely homogeneous unit from the point of view of direct investment. For example, direct investment flows between the UK and the Netherlands were far larger than relative economic size would suggest both before and after accession to the EU. This presumably reflects, among other things, the number of Anglo-Dutch multinational companies.

Other differences between EU countries can readily be observed. Although Germany is economically larger than France and the UK, while outward investment has reflected this, inward investment has followed a different pattern, with French investment tending to be the larger. However, in both cases UK investment has been larger than the reverse flow. Irish investment in the UK, which was negligible before accession to the EU, has picked up substantially since. This is perhaps more difficult to explain than geographical proximity might imply, as the easy movement of funds was possible prior to accession. The total picture is thus rather confused, but it suggests that there has been no dramatic switch in the nature of direct investment in the UK as a result of its accession to the EU. In more recent years there has been a similar debate about whether non-membership of the euro area is having much effect on the pattern of direct investment.

As noted earlier, between one-half and three-quarters of net investment abroad by the UK is composed of profits from overseas subsidiaries and associated companies which are not remitted to the UK. Net acquisition of overseas companies' share and loan capital is, partly by consequence, around one-sixth to one-third of the total, except for the two years 1970 and 1980 when it was about half. Unfortunately, these same figures are only available for EC countries for the period 1975–80, so we cannot make any contrast of the position 'before' and 'after' accession to the EU.[9]

It seems likely, therefore, that if we were to apply the same form of analysis as Scaperlanda and Balough (1983) to other flows of direct investment among the EU countries which involve the UK, we would not find any strong effect from changes in relative trade restrictions. Thus, while there may be some short-run effects, it does not appear likely that there are major changes in capital movements in the EU which involve the UK, as there have been in trade patterns, as shown in Mayes (1983), for example.

As mentioned earlier, figures on US direct investment are rather more detailed and hence we can get some idea of whether the US changed either the extent of its investment in the EC relative to other areas, after the expansion of the EU in 1973, or the pattern of it among the member countries.

Prior to accession, the UK had a much larger proportion of US direct investment (table 8.2) than its economic size alone would suggest. In the first few years after accession, although investment was still large in comparative terms, it was sufficiently lower to allow the UK's share of the existing stock of US investment in the EU to fall by nearly 4 per cent. However, since 1977 the share of investment has been running ahead of the stock share again: hence the stock share has more than recovered its previous loss. The shares of other EU countries in the total stock have also changed only slowly. This is partly because of the scale of the change in the flow (investment) required to make any substantial change in the capital stock over a short period. Nevertheless, Germany and France have seen a substantial change in share, the Netherlands being the main 'gainer'. Changes are nothing like as striking as for trade flows. Again, it must be remembered that this evidence is very limited in itself, but it contributes to the overall picture.

Now that the single market is well developed, one might have expected to see a change in behaviour. There has been no major diversion of US FDI to the EU. In fact, the share has remained remarkably stable. Expansion of the EC9 to EC12 and to EU15 shows relatively little impact, investment flowing to traditional destinations. Yet, the volumes have increased during the latter half of the 1990s. During the period of 1996–2000, the share of the US hovered between 53 per cent and 74 per cent of total FDI inflows to EU member countries. In the case of bilateral EU–US FDI, the latter half of the 1990s is characterized by substantial net outflows from the EU to the US in the manufacturing sector.

Table 8.2 US direct investment in the EU,[a] 1980–2005

	1980	1987	1995	2000	2005
Total stock ($ million)	215,375	326,253	699,015	1,316,247	2,069,983
Total stock to EU ($ million)	82,433	131,749	301,345	609,674	936,477
	Percentage of total stock to EU in individual countries				
UK	34.5	35.3	35.3	37.9	34.6
BLEU	8.4	6.5	8.2	7.5	10.5
Denmark	1.5	0.9	0.7	0.9	0.6
France	11.3	9.4	11.1	7.0	6.5
(West) Germany	18.7	19.1	14.7	9.1	9.2
Greece	0.4	0.1	0.2	0.1	0.2
Ireland	2.8	4.2	2.7	5.9	6.6
Italy	6.5	7.4	5.7	3.9	2.8
Netherlands	9.8	11.8	14.0	18.9	19.4
Portugal	0.3	0.4	0.5	0.4	0.3
Spain	3.2	3.3	3.6	3.5	4.6
Austria	0.6	0.5	0.9	0.5	0.9
Finland	0.2	0.3	0.3	0.2	0.3
Sweden	1.8	0.9	2.3	4.3	3.6
US investment in EC as a percentage of total US direct investment abroad	38.3	40.4	43.1	46.3	45.2

[a] Figures refer to EU15.

Source: US Department of Commerce, *Survey of Current Business*, Department of Industry, US Bureau of Economic Analysis.

More recently the European Commission has put together a database called AMDATA that provides a rather detailed list of M&A activity involving EU enterprises. For 2001 AMDATA records a total of 12,557 M&A involving EU enterprises. This represents a decrease of 25 per cent by comparison with 2000, yet there has been a marked increase in M&A activity in Europe since the early 1990s. On the one hand, there has been a strong upward trend in international operations since 1992. On the other hand, cross-border M&A inside the EC started to increase steadily only after 1996 (table 8.3). Looking at most recent data, the number of M&A fell temporarily in 2002, but increased again in 2003 and 2004. In 2004 there were 9,000 operations where EU companies were the target. While these recent numbers refer to EU25 and thus the enlarged EU, M&A takes still predominantly place in EU15.

It appears also that the evolution of M&A is linked to the evolution of the economy. The low economic growth rates and uncertainties surrounding the future development of the EU economies during 1992–3, 1996 and 2001 are reflected in the declines in M&A activity in those years. During 1998–2000 there was another boom in M&A, particularly in the financial and other services sector. Some transactions were extremely large, making the counting of transactions a very misleading indicator of activity. On the other hand, since ten new countries joined the EU in 2004, the investors from the US are increasingly attracted by Eastern Europe as a production location. The rapid growth of the Chinese economy has also been accompanied by increasing M&A activity, yet the absolute merger cases where Chinese firms act as bidder remains low.

Table 8.3 Mergers and acquisitions involving EU firms

Year	Total (no.)	National (%)	EC (%)	International (%)
1987	2,775	71.6	9.6	18.8
1988	4,242	65.9	13.5	20.6
1989	6,945	63.2	19.1	17.7
1990	7,003	60.7	21.5	17.8
1991	10,657	54.3	11.9	14.5
1992	10,074	58.1	11.6	14.2
1993	8,759	57.4	11.7	18.8
1994	9,050	58.7	12.9	20.5
1995	9,854	57.4	12.9	22.8
1996	8,975	54.8	12.6	26.0
1997	9,784	56.0	14.0	26.0
1998	11,300	53.5	14.1	28.4
1999	14,335	55.7	14.2	26.4
2000	16,750	54.7	15.2	25.4
2001	12,557	54.1	14.9	24.1
2002	9,000	59.0	16.0	20.0
2003	8,700	59.0	14.0	21.0
2004	9,000	57.0	14.0	24.0

Note: Figures do not necessarily add up to 100 per cent since in some cases the bidder is unknown. Figures for 1991–2001 are based on the recent revisions of the AMDATA, while those for 1987–90 are based on 1999 revisions.
Figures from 2002 onwards are based on EU25, while earlier figures are based on EU15.

Source: European Economy (CEC, 2001j, 2005k).

Intra-EU FDI flows have been expanding during the second half of the 1990s, confirming the importance of the deepening integration of the product and factor markets in Europe. In particular during 1999 and 2000, intra-EU FDI showed a significant increase in volume relative to GDP and trade. One of the reasons behind this upsurge was associated with the reorientation of the UK FDI flows in favour of EU member countries. This in turn was largely due to a few huge cross-border mergers, in particular the acquisition of Mannesmann by Vodafone Air Touch and successive ownership changes in two of the most important telecoms businesses (CEC, 2001j). Looking at the most recent data, total FDI flows into EU member countries increased substantially in 2005 over the previous year. There has also been a clear upsurge in intra-EU FDI flows. Much of this upsurge is explained by an increase in investments to the UK. This increase has largely been due to the merger of Shell Transport and Trading Company plc and the Royal Dutch Petroleum Company into Royal Dutch Shell. Country-by-country breakdown of FDI flows shows that the situation varies considerably across countries and time.

In summary, there has certainly been an increase in the cross-border movement of capital since the start of the 1992 programme. In particular towards the end of the millennium, there was a substantial increase in both intra- and extra-EU FDI flows. Intra-EU FDI transactions more than quadrupled during the last years of the millennium, reflecting, at least partially, the deepening of the single EU market. In 1999–2000, intra-EU FDI amounted on average to 80 per cent of total direct investment inflows into the EU. In the previous years, it remained around 50 per cent.[10]

8.5 Labour movements

Labour mobility is often assumed to be a substitute for capital mobility. However, this is rather misleading, given that labour migration is in many ways a much more complex process than international capital flows. Simply put, because the migration of labour necessarily requires the movement of a person or persons, such a move involves more than just the labour market and income considerations. Capital may be allocated internationally without requiring the movement of the capital owner. Moreover, there are many situations where the movements of capital and labour do not substitute but rather complement each other (Fischer, 1999). Such differences in behaviour are enormous from a practical and policy point of view.

On the one hand, total FDI statistics are sometimes affected by the behaviour of a single or very few large MNEs in a particular country. (For flows between any particular pair of countries, a single company can dominate the total effect.) Labour flows, on the other hand, are the result of the decisions of a large number of independent households (although actions by companies and communities can have a strong influence on these decisions). With some limited exceptions involving transient staff and actions in border areas, movement of labour simply involves a person shifting his residence from one country to another to take up a job in the second country. There is not the same range of possible variations as in the case of capital movements. There is also the considerable simplification that there is not the equivalent problem of the relation between the financial flows (or retained earnings) and the physical capital stock. The number of foreign nationals employed will be the sum of the net inflows, without any revaluation problems and only a relatively limited difficulty for 'retirements' (through age, naturalization, etc.).

On the other hand, early theories of migration argued that a major incentive to move is an income differential in real terms. However, it is not merely that the same job will be better paid in the second country; it may be that the person moving will be able to get a 'better' job in the second country (in the sense of a different job with higher pay). There are severe empirical problems in establishing what relative real incomes are, not just in the simple sense of purchasing power parities, but in trying to assess how much one can change one's tastes to adapt to the new country's customs and price patterns and what extra costs would be involved if, for example, the household had to be divided, and so on. This is difficult to measure, not just in precise terms for the outside observer, but even in rough terms for the individual involved.

This sort of uncertainty for the individual is typical of the large range of barriers that impede the movement of labour, in addition to the wide range of official barriers that inhibit movement. Ignorance of job opportunities abroad, living conditions, costs, ease of overcoming language difficulties, how to deal with regulations, etc., is reduced as more people move from one country to another and are able to exchange experiences. Firms can reduce the level of misinformation by recruiting directly in foreign countries.

Even if it were possible to sort out what the official barriers are and to establish the relative real costs, there would still be a multitude of factors which could not be quantified but could perhaps be given implicit values. These other factors involve differences in language, customs, problems of transferring assets (both physical and financial), disruptions to family life, changes in schooling, loss of friends, etc.

These considerations have led to the development of so-called microeconomic behavioural models of labour mobility or immobility. These theories argue, quite convincingly, that migration decisions are made in a complex environment, where the decisions are influenced by family or group considerations as well as by time and life-course events. In some of these approaches, location-specific information and the ability to make use of insider advantage play an important role in the decision to move (Fischer, 1999). Gaining knowledge about location-specific economic, social and cultural opportunities, building up a social network or getting involved in the activities of various interest groups all require a certain time of immobility. Thus immobility has a value, and in moving investment in gaining such insider advantage represents a sunk cost that needs to be covered by expected utility gains in the receiving region.

Of course, some of these factors could work in a favourable direction: it might be easier to find accommodation abroad and setting up a new household and finding new friends might be an attractive prospect. Moreover, the development of information technologies and the consequential reduction in communication and organizational costs across territorial borders help in solving at least some of the problems associated with insider advantage. Nevertheless, all this suggests that margins in labour rewards between countries may be considerable in practice, even if free movement of labour is theoretically permitted. It should thus be no surprise to find that many differences in labour rewards exist between the EC countries. However, it would also be a mistake to think that there are no barriers in practice to employment in other EU countries, as is clear from the next section.

8.6 Labour flows in the EU

The official position in the EU is straightforward. Freedom of movement of labour was part of the framework of the Treaty of Rome itself. However, the original six EU member nations had to start from a position of considerable restrictions of labour movement, and it was not until 1968 that work permits were abolished and preferences for home country workers no longer permitted. The single market programme involved a range of measures to try to eliminate those fiscal barriers, not just for the worker but for the accompanying family as well. Merely permitting geographic labour mobility does not in itself either facilitate or encourage it. It is quite possible to make mobility difficult through measures relating to taxes and benefits, which make a period of previous residence or contribution necessary for benefit.

Labour markets in the EU are in general characterized by relatively low levels of geographic mobility; EU citizens have about half the mobility rate of US citizens. According to Eurobarometer, 38 per cent of EU citizens changed residence, during the last ten years the majority of whom moved within the same town or village (68 per cent) and 36 per cent moved to another town in the same region. However, only 4.4 per cent moved across national borders into another member state. Furthermore, it has been estimated that annual migration between member states amounts to around 0.75 per cent of the resident population and perhaps only 0.4 per cent of resident EU nationals. In the US, these figures appear about six times larger. Moreover, occupational or professional reasons account for only a small proportion of the house moves; when people move it is mainly for family and housing reasons.

Of course, these relatively low labour mobility figures reflect cultural and institutional heterogeneity in Europe, but may also be due to a more systematic failure in the functioning of factor markets. In particular, it has been argued that real wage unresponsiveness to regional labour demand fluctuations and wage compression policies have hindered the functioning of internal labour markets.

The principal concern raised in Europe recently is that various barriers still exist and continue to keep labour mobility within the EU at a low level. Given the political commitment to enhance European competitiveness and growth in the global economy by establishing a 'knowledge-based economy', the EU has taken a look at the impediments on mobility of skills and labour.

The potential barriers to mobility in the EU can be roughly divided into man-made and natural barriers. Man-made barriers include inconsistent labour market institutions, problems in the portability of pensions and social security rights, and the lack of full mutual recognition of qualifications and experience. Natural barriers include a range of social, cultural and language barriers and also the ageing of the labour force. Given that the young tend to be more mobile than the old, demographic change will imply that there will be considerably fewer potential movers among the working-age population. Many empirical studies have found that, both in Europe and the US, moving declines sharply after the age of thirty to thirty-five.

The actual path of labour migration is, of course, heavily affected by the cyclical fluctuation of the economy. If an economy is growing and able to maintain 'full employment', it is likely to attract more labour from abroad for two reasons: first, because there are more job opportunities and, second, because there is less domestic opposition to immigration. In the period after the first oil crisis, when unemployment rose sharply and the EU economies moved into recession, there was much more resistance to the flow of labour between countries and encouragement for reversing the flow.

The clearest feature of the development of the permitted mobility of labour among EU countries was that restrictions were lifted on workers from other member countries rather than non-members. Nevertheless, only Belgium and Luxembourg have had a higher proportion of their foreign workers coming from within the EU than from outside it. The position has changed relatively little in recent years with the exception of Germany, where there has been a small rise, and Luxembourg, where there has been a small fall in the number of non-nationals in the workforce. Looking at it from the point of view of country of origin, in all cases except Ireland only a very small percentage of the labour force has moved to other countries. (Those who have moved and changed their nationality will be excluded, but that is unlikely to make more than a marginal difference to the total.) With the exception of Denmark and Italy, it appears that size and percentage of working population abroad have an inverse relation. Looking at the same figures from a different point of view, with the exception of Luxembourg it is the EU countries with the lowest incomes that had the highest outward mobility. Greece, Spain and Portugal alter the picture fairly considerably. They all had above average numbers of people working elsewhere in the EU even before they joined, particularly Portugal. Thus it might be expected that as restrictions were removed there would be some expansion in movement. However, despite high levels of unemployment, there are no obvious signs of this.

The picture is a little more complex for inward flows. Luxembourg stands out with around a third of the working population coming from foreign countries. France, Germany and Belgium form a second group with a little less than 10 per cent of their workforce from abroad; and the remaining countries have smaller proportions, down to negligible numbers in the case of Italy. Since Italy is a major exporter of labour to West Germany, France and Belgium, it is not surprising to find that it is a negligible importer, since these flows do not represent an exchange of *special* skills but a movement of workers with *some* skills towards countries with greater manufacturing employment opportunities.

Some special relationships are apparent which relate to previous history rather than the EC as a determinant of the pattern of flows: former colonies in the case of France and the UK and, to a lesser extent, in the case of Belgium and the Netherlands; and the relationship between the UK and Ireland. The West German policy of encouraging foreign workers is clear, with large numbers coming from Turkey and (the former) Yugoslavia. What is perhaps surprising is that despite the recruitment ban on countries outside the EU in 1973 the shares of member and non-member countries in the number of foreign nationals employed in West Germany remained at approximately the same levels after 1974, the share of non-members falling only as some of the countries joined the EC. The more recent data, provided in table 8.4, shows a fall in foreign labour in most countries by 1990 and stabilization thereafter. However, the switch is much larger for those from non-member states than for those from the other members.

At first glance it appears that labour, in proportionate terms, is rather less mobile than capital, particularly if one takes the UK as an example. The balance of labour and capital flows tends to be in opposite directions according to the development of the various economies. However, there are many specific factors overriding this general relation. The wealthier countries have attracted labour and invested overseas at the same time, thus helping to equilibrate the system from both directions. Yet there is little evidence inside the EU that there are large labour movements purely as a result of the existence of the EU. Some movement between

Table 8.4 Labour force by nationality in EU member states, 1990, 1995 and 2001 (% share of total labour force)

	National				Other EU				Non-EU			
	1990	1995	1997	2001	1990	1995	1997	2001	1990	1995	1997	2001
Belgium	94.6	92.2	92.2	–	5.2	5.4	5.8	–	0.2	2.5	2.0	–
Denmark	98.0	98.1	96.9	–	0.5	0.8	0.8	–	1.5	1.1	2.3	–
Germany	91.5	91.0	90.9	92.1	2.8	2.8	3.1	2.7	5.7	6.2	6.0	5.2
Greece	99.3	98.3	–	–	0.2	0.2	–	–	0.5	1.5	–	–
Spain	99.8	99.2	98.9	–	0.1	0.3	–	–	0.1	0.5	–	–
France	93.5	93.7	93.9	94.6	3.0	2.5	2.2	2.4	3.5	3.7	3.9	2.8
Ireland	97.4	97.0	96.6	96.4	2.1	2.4	–	2.8	0.5	0.6	–	0.8
Italy	98.7	99.6	100.0	–	0.4	0.1	–	–	0.9	0.4	–	–
Luxembourg	66.6	61.0	44.9	–	31.5	36.2	52.1	–	1.9	2.8	3.0	–
Netherlands	96.3	96.1	97.1	96.8	1.4	1.7	1.3	1.6	2.3	2.2	1.6	1.6
Portugal	99.4	99.6	98.2	98.3	0.1	0.2	–	0.5	0.5	0.2	–	1.2
UK	96.6	96.4	96.4	95.4	1.6	1.6	1.6	1.8	1.8	2.0	2.0	2.9
Austria	–	90.4	90.1	90.6	–	1.1	3.4	1.6	–	8.5	6.5	7.8
Finland	–	99.3	–	98.7	–	0.2	–	0.3	–	0.5	–	0.9
Sweden	–	95.9	94.8	95.9	–	2.0	2.4	2.1	–	2.1	2.8	2.0
EU[a]	95.2	95.3	–	–	2.0	1.7	–	–	2.8	2.9	–	–

[a] Last column refers to 2001 or to the closest available year.

Source: Adapted from OECD (1999a, p. 328), and own calculations. OECD©, 1999. Eurostat for 2001.

contiguous countries is to be expected, especially where they are small, and also movements from those countries with considerable differences in income, primarily Greece, Italy, Ireland, Portugal and, to a lesser extent, Spain. However, the major movements have been the inflow of workers from outside the EU, primarily into Germany and France. Thus, despite discrimination in favour of nationals of member countries, the relative benefits to employers (the ability to offer worse conditions, readier dismissal, lower benefits, etc.) and to employees (the size of the income gain and the improvement in living standards for their families) make flows from the lower-income countries more attractive to both parties.

Worries about the competitive exploitation of employees through reducing social protection (known colloquially as 'social dumping') have led the Community to develop the social dimension of the single market programme, expressed through the Charter of Fundamental Rights for Workers and the action programme for its implementation (see chapter 23). The measures are specifically designed to ensure a 'single market' for labour in the EC. This does not necessarily mean that labour will be more mobile or labour markets more flexible as a consequence. Indeed, the UK government has argued forcefully that these actions might make it more difficult to eliminate pockets of unemployment and hence harm some of those workers whom it is designed to protect. As a consequence, the UK did not initially sign the Social Charter nor accept the Social Chapter proposed by the Maastricht Treaty. In practice the 'social dimension' has led to relatively limited changes in labour market legislation and the Social Charter has not yet been fully adopted. Even the Working Time Directive, which caused a major debate, was ultimately watered down to the point where it did not change much existing behaviour (see chapter 23).

It should be no surprise that international mobility is limited when one sees the extent of reluctance to respond to economic stimuli for movement within countries. The existence of sharply different regional unemployment levels and regional wage differentials reveals this reluctance. In the UK the system of public sector housing is thought to aid labour rigidity. Possession of a council house in one district does not give any entitlement to one elsewhere. However, even for private sector house owners, negative equity and the very considerable transaction costs of sale and purchase act as a substantial restriction on mobility.

Idiosyncratic, region-specific shocks also importantly shape the flows of skills and labour and are related to the institutional aspects of the labour markets. Idiosyncratic employment fluctuations interact with the development of the aggregate economy and institutional differences across labour markets can steer the labour movements due to the adjustment of different sectors to idiosyncratic shocks. Decressin and Fatás (1995) suggest that economic shocks are increasingly less national and more regional in nature.

Yet regional and industrial data in the European countries reveals only moderate differences in wages across sectors for homogeneous labour. These moderate wage differentials more likely reflect the institutional rigidity of wages per se, rather than the efficient functioning of the factor markets. This is evident from the fact that regional unemployment rates are widely dispersed. Unemployment differentials across sectors are also fairly persistent in many European countries. European countries exhibit bigger variations across regional migration flows between the corresponding states in the US.

Decressin and Fatás (1995) note that in Europe region-specific shocks in the demand for labour are reflected in changes in regional participation rates, while unemployment rates react to a small extent during the first three years. Migration, in turn, plays a substantial role in the adjustment process only after three years. A large part of the changes in labour demand is met by people moving in and out of the labour force, instead of migrating or experiencing short unemployment spells. However, more recent evidence suggests that Europeans may be significantly more mobile than previously thought. Based on a panel of 166 regions for the period 1988–97, Tani (2002) shows that labour demand shocks trigger fairly similar responses in local labour markets across the EU and the US. According to his study, the absorber of a labour demand shock is net migration, accounting for around 50 per cent of the response in the first year and about 80 per cent during the next. In the US, the corresponding numbers are about 40 per cent and 50 per cent.

8.7 Capital and labour movements combined

Recent trends indicate that labour and capital are neither perfectly mobile nor perfectly immobile but rather adjust gradually to market conditions and economic policies. EU member countries do experience inter-regional movements of labour and capital that are of significant magnitude. Yet, these movements are far from instantaneous. Labour and capital are clearly linked across regions but there are still some obstacles to rapid adjustments of labour and capital stocks. At the same time, liberalized immigration policies, EU enlargement and other steps that promote integration of the factor markets of Western Europe with those of surrounding regions present a challenge to policymakers to maintain social cohesion and stable development across different regions in Europe.

As noted at the outset, factor movements cannot legitimately be examined without looking at the behaviour of the markets for internationally traded goods and services at the same time. Nor are the two factor markets independent. While the capital market has few of the characteristics of discrimination in favour of fellow members of the EU that form the basis of trading relationships between the countries, the decision over whether to invest abroad or at home is related to decisions over whether or not to export from the domestic market. Other things being equal, investment at home will generate more domestic employment and indeed it may encourage an inflow of labour from abroad. Investment abroad, on the other hand, will tend to encourage employment in that country and a transfer of labour abroad as well.

The final outcome will depend very much upon whether there is full employment. When there is a shortage of skilled employees, or indeed a shortage of unskilled employees, at wages consistent with successful international competition, investment abroad, especially where costs are lower, may be a preferable substitute for labour-saving investment at home.

Clearly, within the EU there is less incentive to invest abroad, where product prices are not subject to tariffs and hence no big gains in competitiveness can be made. Indeed, one would expect investment from non-members to increase because of the increased size of the internal market. Thus, capital flows could be expected to change in the opposite direction to trade flows, with both an investment-reducing equivalent of trade creation and an investment-increasing switch from third countries as an equivalent to trade diversion. Controls on labour movements have been removed in a manner that favours inflows from EU members rather than non-members.

Running across these considerations are two other factors. Labour can be expected to move from where rewards are lower to where they are substantially higher (to cover the costs of moving), as is evidenced by the outflow from Italy. Second, capital investment could be expected to move to areas where labour costs are much lower but this movement has been much less marked. Instead, capital movements have tended to follow sales opportunities and other locational advantages rather than just labour cost. In so far as labour and capital movements do not take place, factor price differentials will continue to persist, assuming they are not eliminated by trade flows, and the allocation of resources among the EU countries, and indeed between them and non-members, will be inefficient.

In recent years Krugman and Venables (1996) inter alia have argued that the pattern of location of industry will be rather different from that initially expected, as there are several factors that lead to increasing economies of scale and agglomeration, at least over a range above the position applying in the early 1990s. Proximity to the main markets, networks of suppliers, skilled labour, etc. may actually attract firms to the main centres of existing industry even though costs may be higher, thus encouraging labour and capital to move in the same direction and exacerbate rather than ease existing disparities.

This idea of the clustering of activity both in terms of location and in range of industrial activity has a long history, although it has more recently been popularized by Porter (1990). Porter offers not so much an explanation of why activity concentrates, as an encouragement to governments to reorient their policies to encourage the process so that they can reap a competitive advantage. The key to this comes from the exploitation of the immobile and less mobile factors of production such as land, physical and business infrastructure and services and, particularly in the case of the EU, highly skilled labour. The increasing returns occur because the process feeds on itself – endogenous growth.

EU structural policy has followed this line of argument (see chapters 22 and 23) using this policy as a means of helping disadvantaged regions compete through improving public and private infrastructure and human skills. Thus there have been counter-forces to those of increasing concentration in existing centres that market forces alone might have fostered.

This process of concentration has clearly been followed in practice in the EU but it is by no means the only force for development, as the Irish economy demonstrates. Here high-technology and IT-based industries have been able to flourish where their location was not very important, aided by favourable macroeconomic, wage-bargaining and other direct incentives. High-value, low-weight items, with a worldwide market are not so dependent on location but do require skilled labour. Similarly call centres, internet services and computer software can be located in any lower-cost region and their results transmitted electronically immediately. The 'new economy', widely talked about for the US, enables a society to change much more rapidly and hence grow faster without hitting traditional inflationary pressures from the labour market. While there are only limited signs that the 'new economy' has taken hold in the EU, except perhaps in Ireland and Finland (with the phenomenal development of Nokia), there is the potential for it to do so. If it does we can expect that there will be a further reason for labour to remain fairly immobile.

Until the downturn in the European economy, inefficiency would have been expected to take the form of insufficiently capital-sensitive investment, with a labour inflow being used to avoid restructuring. This would shift some more labour-intensive processes abroad to more labour-intensive EU members, or even outside the EU. Limits on labour mobility decrease this tendency but, with high levels of unemployment currently and for much of the foreseeable future in the EU, it seems unlikely that much further encouragement to move will take place. Indeed, the pressures are the other way round. There is a danger that protectionism will apply not just to goods but to factor movements as well. The difficulties over the new round of multilateral negotiations on reducing protection may be indicative of a gap between the liberalizing rhetoric and the more restrictive actions. In so far as the EU increased the ease of factor mobility, it may be able to maintain a competitive advantage over other countries which resort to this form of protection. It is not surprising, therefore, that third countries have been keen to operate inside the EU and are using just that freedom of capital movement to achieve it.

The experience with migration from Central and Eastern Europe after 1989 increased the caution over opening up the labour market more widely, and it was no surprise that most countries imposed a phase-in agreement for allowing unlimited migration from the new member states when they joined in 2004. This has been eased since, in part because those states that did permit migration, particularly the UK, seem to have benefited from an influx of skilled workers, and in part because the scale of flows has been fairly modest. It reinforces the suspicion that labour movement has been widely regarded as a key ingredient of the EU largely because it has not occurred on a substantial scale. Labour markets and capital markets once again complement and importantly interact with each other and factor endowments can no longer be taken as given. Regions that are open to factor flows have additional means of adjusting to external shocks and the changing economic and political environment. Factor flows,

however, are not instantaneous, but proceed at a rate that reflects economic incentives, intrinsic costs of adjustment, economic policy and institutional settings, as well as the reorganization of industrial production structures. In this sense, factor flows reflect a continuous process of adjustment towards equilibrium. What is crucial to the rate of integration in the internal market is whether differences in factor rewards persist across territorial boundaries of Europe. Even the Estonian and Finnish labour and capital investment markets that have been integrating rapidly still show major differences in wages between the two countries.

NOTES

1   It is the concept of control that distinguishes direct from portfolio investment. The technical definition adopted by the IMF (Balance of Payments Manual, fourth edition, 1977) is 'Direct Investment refers to investment that adds to, deducts from or acquires a lasting interest in an enterprise operating in an economy other than that of the investor, the investor's purpose being to have an effective voice in the management of the enterprise.' Clearly, this distinction can be made only by asking companies themselves about their overseas investment.

2   Other, more complicated arrangements exist which involve the effective transfer of capital between countries even if not recorded as such in the statistics on capital movements. 'Back-to-back' loans are a simple example whereby exchange controls can be evaded. In such a case, although the parent company can use only the domestic currency when investing in the foreign country, it can make the domestic funds available to a firm based in that same foreign country which wishes to undertake the same transaction but in the opposite direction – their funds are in their own currency while they wish to use the currency of the parent company's country.

3   'Covered' in the sense that the forward exchange rate premium or discount is taken into account in the computation of the difference in interest rates between countries.

4   This description of capital flows 'balancing' trade flows could equally be phrased as trade flows 'balancing' capital flows. They are two sides of the same coin. If there is a differential in rates of return, capital will be attracted into a country and this will raise the exchange rate, thereby tending to encourage

imports and lower exports, hence balancing the capital movement.

5 As was pointed out by Padoa-Schioppa et al. (1987), it is not possible to run a stable system with fixed exchange rates, free capital movements, free trade and independent fiscal policies. One or other of these must be constrained (the last in the case of an integrated single market).

6 There are, of course, differential restraints on the activities of financial institutions depending upon whether or not they are registered within the EU.

7 It is interesting to note that the pressure for the European single market came just as strongly from European multinationals as it did from political sources. Wisse Dekker, then head of Philips and the European Round Table of major companies, put forward a plan in January 1985 to achieve a single market in five years, i.e. by 1990, thus anticipating the White Paper.

8 On an annual basis, the UK was overtaken by Japan, but the UK's outstanding stock of foreign direct investment was still larger.

9 Unremitted profits by the UK as a percentage of total net outward investment in the EU alone and in all countries (in brackets) were 74 per cent (40 per cent) in 1975, 112 per cent (71 per cent) in 1979, 40 per cent (80 per cent) in 1982 and 122 per cent (55 per cent) in 1985 (*Business Monitor*).

10 However, not all is due to that programme. Research by Molle and Morsink (1991) shows that FDI does respond to exchange rate changes, while the dramatic fall in share prices in Japan has led to a substantial reduction in the pace of their investment throughout the world, including the EU. The pattern of this investment still strongly reflects the traditional pattern of ease of entry. It is by no means clear that entry by acquisition has become particularly harmonized, or indeed greatly eased, thus far.

9 Measuring the impact of economic integration

NIGEL GRIMWADE

9.1 Introduction

Chapter 6 discussed the theory of economic integration in an attempt to see how different forms of integration impacted on both the member states and rest of the world. We now need to turn to a consideration of the extent to which these theoretical expectations were borne out by the experience of integration in Europe. What were the effects of the formation and subsequent enlargement of the European Community/European Union on the allocation of resources? Was the net effect trade-creating or trade-diverting? By how much was the economic welfare of the member states increased as a result of integration? Also, how significant were the longer-run, dynamic effects, as opposed to the purely static, resource-reallocation effects? Did integration have any impact on the rate of economic growth in the countries involved? Finally, was the rest of the world harmed by the process of integration taking place in Europe or did it share in the gains?

The major problem that researchers face when seeking to find answers to these questions is the classic, counterfactual problem common to all areas of research of a similar kind. We simply do not know what would have happened to Europe or the rest of the world if European integration had not taken place. This means that we can never know for sure the precise impact of integration. We should, therefore, treat all attempts to estimate these effects with a high degree of caution. At best, they are 'estimated guesses' concerning their broad direction and magnitude. It is just as important to appreciate the limitations of studies carried out to measure these effects as to know the

results that were obtained. In this chapter, we begin with a brief review of the main kind of effects that it is important to consider. This is followed by a survey of the different types of studies carried out to estimate these effects. We finish with a discussion of the strengths and weaknesses of different approaches and an appraisal of the results obtained.

9.2 The effects of economic integration

Economic integration has a number of different effects on the countries participating and on the rest of the world, as follows.

9.2.1 Trade effects

A major concern of the orthodox theory of free trade areas (FTAs) and customs unions (CUs) is with the impact of integration on trade. The simple theory of FTAs and CUs distinguishes between two effects – trade creation and trade diversion. *Trade creation* is defined as the displacement of high-cost domestic production of a product in one member state by lower-cost imports from another member state. This improves the allocation of global resources and represents a step in the direction of free trade. *Trade diversion* is defined as the displacement of lower-cost imports of a product from a non-member state by higher-cost imports from a member state. This results from the discriminatory nature of the tariff. As it worsens the global allocation of resources, it represents a step towards protectionism.

However, it has long been recognized that economic integration may have other effects on trade. Where an FTA or CU results in a lower level of external tariffs or other restrictions compared with the situation before integration, the result may be *external trade creation*. The same may result if faster economic growth inside the area or union due to integration leads to the member states importing more from the rest of the world.

Another effect is that of *trade suppression*. This shows some similarities to trade diversion, but in other ways it is different. In this case, the production of a particular good in one of the member states disappears altogether following the formation of the union. Instead, production shifts to another member state where costs are lower. However, prior to the formation of the union, the latter imported the product from the rest of the world. The reason, of course, for this situation is that a high tariff in the former country before the formation of the union made it profitable to produce the good, but import nothing at all. In the latter country, however, the tariff was low, discouraging domestic production and resulting in the good being imported. As the resource reallocation effects are the same as with trade diversion, trade suppression may be regarded as a special form of trade diversion.

Finally, integration may result in *supply-side diversion*. This will take place when, due to a supply-side constraint (e.g. shortage of capacity), increased exports of a product to a member state following integration result in reduced exports of the product to a non-member state. However, such an effect is likely to be of a short-term nature only, as, given time, producers will expand their capacity to meet the greater demand for their product. This effect may, therefore, be regarded as being of trivial importance only.

As we have seen, these effects on trade can only be measured if we know for sure what the level of imports (or exports) would have been had integration not happened. As this cannot be known, we have to find a way of estimating what the level of imports (or exports) might have been. We shall see later that a variety of approaches have been used in studies of this kind to estimate the so-called *anti-monde*. Whatever method is used, several requirements must be satisfied. First, the *anti-monde* must be constructed for a time period that

is sufficiently long for the various integration effects to have taken place. Second, in doing so, a distinction must be made between different trading partners, in particular between those that are members of the union and those that are not. Finally, account must be taken of the effects of other influences on trade flows both before and after integration. For example, any tariff cuts made as a result of multilateral trading agreements entered into will have affected the actual level of trade flows. Changes in the real exchange rate will also be important, as these affect the prices of tradeable relative to non-tradeable goods.

9.2.2 Income effects

Trade effects are not of themselves very interesting. More important is the effect that changes in trade patterns have on *economic welfare*. In the orthodox theory, different trade effects have different impacts on economic welfare. From a *global* point of view, trade creation is welfare-enhancing, while trade diversion is welfare-decreasing. However, for *members of the union*, trade diversion will raise the real incomes of the exporting countries, while lowering the welfare of importing countries. The accurate estimation of these income effects, however, is difficult even for the members of the union alone. If the amount of trade creation is known, the welfare gain from tariff elimination can be estimated in the conventional manner by multiplying half the tariff reduction by the volume of extra trade generated. The loss of economic welfare from trade diversion can be measured by multiplying the volume of trade diverted by the difference between the world, free-trade price and the union price. For exports, the welfare gain is half the increase in price, following the adoption of the common external tariff, multiplied by the increase in the volume of exports following integration.

Although such a *partial equilibrium* approach is acceptable when estimating the gain from a tariff cut in a single sector, the procedure is less than satisfactory when considered across the whole economy. This is because it ignores the feedback effects of a tariff cut on a single product on other parts of the economy. These effects are better captured using a *general equilibrium* model that shows the interrelationships between different sectors of the economy. We discuss this further below. Another difficulty arises when measuring the impact of a tariff reduction on a product that is a differentiated good. In this case, imports and importables are not perfect substitutes. This means that the prices of importables fall by less than the price of imports after liberalization, resulting in a smaller welfare gain than where imports and importables are perfect substitutes. However, tariff liberalization in differentiated goods industries also tends to result in more intra-industry trade (IIT) – two-way trade in different varieties of the same product. This makes possible further gains to consumers from having a wider variety of goods to choose from. The gains from increased choice, however, are clearly more difficult to quantify than those resulting from lower prices.

IIT in differentiated goods is also more likely to yield dynamic welfare gain from decreasing average cost and increasing competition. Both inter- and intra-industry trade may have other positive long-run effects on output in the union/area. For example, output may be increased as a result of firms investing more both to take advantage of the wider market and to cope with increased competition. Increased competition may also spur firms to engage in more technological innovation. These dynamic gains are often more difficult to quantify, but must be included in any comprehensive estimate of the true welfare gain from integration. Most of the early studies of integration were concerned with the static welfare gain only, making no attempt to quantify the dynamic gains. This accounts for the small size of the gain that they estimated. More recently, however, trade economists have developed general equilibrium models that incorporate dynamic effects of this kind.

9.2.3 The balance of payments effect

Economic integration may also have an effect on the balance of payments of individual countries. This could be favourable (if exports increase by more than imports) or unfavourable (if imports

expand more than exports). At the time when the EC was set up, there was some concern that Italy would experience an adverse balance of payments effect because of a lower degree of industrial competitiveness. It is clear, however, that these concerns proved unwarranted, as the Italian economy thrived after the formation of the EC. Likewise, there was a concern when the UK joined the EC in 1973 that the effect on the balance of payments would be adverse. UK tariffs on industrial goods imported from the EC were slightly higher than on such goods when exported to the EC, so British imports from the EC could be expected to rise by more than British exports to the EC. Also, UK exports would suffer from the loss of tariff preferences in EFTA and the Commonwealth. Added to that, the need to make large net contributions to the EC budget was expected to have a harmful effect on the balance of payments.

An adverse balance of payments effect, however, need not be a matter of concern, providing the country is prepared to allow the real exchange rate to fall. This can happen either by lowering the nominal exchange rate or by reducing the country's price level below that of the rest of the world. Where the exchange rate is floating, the nominal rate may well fall anyhow if the balance of payments deteriorates, although this may not be the case if large inflows of capital from abroad create greater demand for the currency on foreign exchange markets. Reducing the price level may be more difficult to achieve, if prices are slow to fall in response to a tightening of monetary and fiscal policy. Both measures, however, will entail a resource cost for the country. Where the exchange rate bears the brunt of the adjustment, the cost is measured by the deterioration in the terms of trade necessitated by integration. Where, instead, adjustment is achieved by domestic inflation, the resource cost could be measured by the loss of output and employment in the short run that is necessitated by the fall in aggregate demand. In practice, both are likely to prove difficult to measure, as there is no way of distinguishing between those effects that are the result of integration and those which are due to extraneous factors. Nevertheless, these effects are potentially very important for individual countries, especially countries that are contemplating joining a regional trading bloc such as the EC.

9.2.4 Economic growth

In addition to the effects on income, economic integration can be expected to affect the rate of growth in GDP in individual countries. The relationship between trade liberalization and economic growth is a complex one. The explanation for how integration will affect growth depends on the model of growth that is used. In the *neoclassical theory of growth*, economic integration could bring about an increase in the growth rate through an increase in the rate of capital accumulation in the economy. Improvements in economic efficiency brought about by integration may induce more investment in the region. With a fixed capital-output ratio, the result will be a faster rise in output, which, in turn, will bring a further increase in savings and, hence, investment. However, as the stock of capital relative to labour is rising, the marginal productivity of capital will fall, reducing the incentive to invest more. Eventually, it will fall to a level where it is no longer profitable for firms to undertake any more new investment. As the rate of capital accumulation approaches zero, the growth rate declines, until it eventually returns to its former level. This is known in neo-classical growth theory as the 'steady state'. A number of EU countries experienced such a boost to their growth rates following entry (e.g. Spain after 1986). Such effects may take time to work their way through the economy, so that the boost to economic growth may be sustained for a considerable period of time.

In neo-classical growth theory, a permanent long-run boost to economic growth is not possible, as this would require ceaseless accumulation. The rate of capital accumulation would have to continue growing at the higher rate. However, in *new growth theory*, this is possible, because capital accumulation is treated as an endogenous variable in the growth process. Capital accumulation can refer to investment in physical capital, human capital or knowledge capital. Firms are motivated by the *private* rate of return on investment, which they perceive to diminish as the stock of capital

increases. However, the *public* rate of return from new investment, which determines the total amount of investment undertaken by firms as a whole, need not fall. In effect, a wedge is created between the private and public rates of return on investment.

One reason is that knowledge accumulation is itself an endogenous variable. As firms invest in knowledge capital, there occur technological spillovers to other firms, which offset any tendency towards diminishing returns. Integration may play a positive role in stimulating continuous accumulation of knowledge capital, making possible sustained GDP growth. By widening the market for new products, trade boosts the profitability of investment in R&D. At the same time, by lowering import barriers, trade stimulates competition. Although competition may reduce the profitability from investing in R&D, it forces domestic firms to step up the rate of their innovation in order not to lose market share to foreign rivals. Capital market integration may also stimulate greater investment in R&D by eliminating imperfections in capital markets and reducing the costs of borrowed funds.

9.3 Estimating the trade effects – different approaches

The starting point of any attempt to quantify the effects of economic integration must be the trade effects. This exercise may be carried out as an *ex ante* or as an *ex post* study. *Ex ante* studies are, generally, more problematic, as they are trying to find out in advance what the effects of integration might be. This is impossible to do, as we have no way of knowing how the future might turn out if integration did not take place. Estimating the income effect will also be more difficult, as the effects of tariff reductions on imports will have to be determined using historical estimates of the elastictity of demand for and supply of different goods. *Ex post* estimation is somewhat less hazardous, as we are looking back at what has taken place. There is still the difficulty of constructing a suitable *anti-monde*, but, as we shall see, techniques are available whereby economists can make a moderately intelligent guess at this. Not surprisingly, the greater number of studies conducted have been of the *ex post* variety. *Ex ante* studies are used where economists want to make predictions about the likely effects on integration, often the result of an individual country joining, or wanting to join, the EU or any economic integation scheme.

A number of different approaches have been used in the construction of the *anti-monde*. Broadly speaking, these fit into one of three broad categories:

(i)   **Residual models.** The commonest approach has been to use a residual model, in which hypothetical trade flows are imputed from existing trade flows, making plausible assumptions about demand-size variables such as GDP/GNP, consumption, economic growth and possibly some supply-side variables. The integration effect is then treated as being the difference between these imputed flows and actual trade flows. Some studies have used the trade flows of some third country as a normalizing factor.

(ii) **Econometric models**. An alternative approach is to use a formal econometric model that isolates the influence of different variables on trade, including economic integration, and then estimates the explanatory power of each. In this way, we can directly see how much of any increase (or decrease) in trade has been due to integration and how much to other factors. Such an approach has the advantage that all of the determinants of trade (including changes in relative prices, demand-side and supply-side factors, economic growth and multilateral trade liberalization) are taken into account rather than just some. The important question then becomes what type of model should be used for this purpose. Econometric models are especially useful when making *ex-ante* estimates of the effects of integration. Once the coefficients have been estimated for the different variables in the equation, these may be used to project trade flows, providing that plausible assumptions can be made about the values of the exogenous variables.

(iii) **Computable general equilibrium models (CGE).** More recently, economists have shown an interest in using general equilibrium models that are capable of being run on a computer to estimate the effects of integration. Such models have been widely used in estimating the probable impact of different multilateral trade liberalization scenarios on different countries and regions of the world. In this case, the models used are multi-country and multi-regional models, as well as being multi-sectoral. The advantage of such models is that they can estimate how the various effects of liberalization feed back into different sectors of the economy and how such effects are transmitted from different countries and regions to each other. The approach is to construct a model that sets out the conditions that are required for equilibrium to exist simultaneously in all sectors and all markets. Once constructed, the model can then be calibrated, usually for a single year as close as possible to the period under investigation. The model may then be used to simulate various policy scenarios, such as a reduction in tariffs and other trade costs. In the main, CGE models are used to make *ex ante* estimations of the likely effects of trade liberalization. However, they may be used to study the effects of integration, beginning from either an *ex ante* or an *ex post* premise.

9.3.1 Residual models

A number of different approaches have been used for the construction of the *anti-monde* in residual modelling.

(i) Simple extrapolation
The simplest approach of all is to assume that the value of imports coming from partner countries would have continued to grow at the same rate after integration as before, had integration not taken place. Then the difference between this figure and actual imports could be regarded as being the integration effect. Clearly, however, such an assumption is fatally flawed. There are no grounds for supposing that the growth in imports

that has taken place in previous years would have been repeated. The volume of imports in any given year is highly sensitive to the particular point reached in the business cycle, so that the pre- and post-integration periods would, at the very least, have to cover the full length of the cycle. However, these will be different for different countries. Changes in relative prices, including changes in the exchange rate, can also be expected to affect the growth of import volume. Any fall in the price of domestic goods relative to imports, including any fall brought about by a decline in the real exchange rate, might be expected to result in a slower growth in import volume. Structural changes within the country affecting both the composition of demand and output might also impact on the demand for imports, if some sectors or products have greater propensity to import than others. Finally, reductions in multilaterally negotiated tariffs either in the pre- or post-integration period could be expected to cause imports to grow at different rates in the two periods.

A slightly, more sophisticated approach is to extrapolate import *shares*. One possibility is to assume that the share of intra- and extra-area imports in total imports would have been unchanged had integration not taken place. However, such a procedure is subject to much the same objections as the linear approach discussed above. There is no reason to assume that these shares would have remained the same, as different factors can be expected to have affected these shares in the post- rather than in the pre-integration period. A further problem with this method is that it provides no way in which a distinction can be made between trade creation and trade diversion. An increase in the intra-area trade share (and decrease in the extra-area trade share) could be due to either imports from partner countries displacing high-cost domestic production or imports from partner countries displacing lower-cost imports from third countries.

The alternative is to extrapolate the share of imports to GNP/GDP or to the share of imports in apparent consumption, defined as domestic consumption less exports plus imports. Of these, apparent consumption is the preferred measure. One possibility is to assume that the share of

imports from domestic sources, partner sources and the rest of the world would have remained constant had integration not taken place. Then any decrease in the share of imports coming from domestic sources is evidence for gross trade creation. An increase in the share of imports coming from partner countries is evidence for net trade creation (gross trade creation less trade diversion) and any decrease in the share of imports coming from the rest of the world is evidence for trade diversion. In this way, the different effects of integration on trade can be identified and measured. The first study to use such an approach was Truman (1969). He found that, by 1968, the amount of new EEC trade created in manufactured goods was $9.2 billion (or 26 per cent of trade), while external trade creation (negative trade diversion) of $1.0 billion (or 7 per cent of trade) took place.

However, a more realistic approach is to allow for *changes* in the share of imports from different sources in apparent consumption over time. The simplest way of handling this is to assume that the change in the share of imports from different sources in apparent consumption in a suitable pre-integration period would have continued in the post-integration period. Such an approach was used by the EFTA Secretariat (1969, 1972) to estimate the trade effects of both the EC and EFTA. They estimated trade creation for EFTA at $2.3 billion and trade diversion at $1.1 billion respectively. In a later study, Truman (1975) allowed for increases in the share of imports in apparent consumption over time. This resulted in an estimate for trade creation of $2.5 billion (or 7 per cent of trade) and trade diversion of $0.5 billion (or 4 per cent of trade) for 1968.

One of the difficulties with this approach is that the trend extrapolated into the post-integration period is highly dependent on the years chosen for estimating the trend in the pre-integration period. A further difficulty concerns the assumptions made: namely, that import shares would have continued rising in the same way as they did in the pre-integration period had integration not taken place. This is simply not tenable, as many factors may have caused changes in the share of imports coming from different countries in the pre-integration period. Although the use of import shares makes it possible to incorporate economic growth, changes in import shares may still be affected by changes in relative prices, changes in real exchange rates and tariff reductions. Furthermore, the more disaggregated the data that is used (and disaggregation is desirable to capture the full effects of integration), the less tenable is the assumption of a linear trend in import shares. A further problem is that the GNP of the member states is itself affected by the process of integration. Using import shares will mean that these effects will not be fully captured in the estimation and, hence, the integration effect will be underestimated.

(ii) Changes in the income elasticity of demand for imports

An alternative solution to the problem of how to separate the trade creation and trade diversion effects was proposed by Balassa (1967, 1974). He suggested basing the *anti-monde* on the estimated *ex post* income elasticity of demand for imports in the pre-integration period. The income elasticity of import demand was defined as the average annual rate of change of imports divided by that of GNP, both being expressed at constant prices. A rise in the income elasticity of demand for intra-area imports following integration was then defined as gross trade creation. However, as this may have resulted from either imports displacing domestic production (trade creation proper) or imports from other member states displacing imports from the rest of the world (trade diversion), only a rise in the income elasticity of demand for imports from *all* sources taken together would constitute trade creation proper. A fall in the income elasticity of demand for extra-area imports would indicate that trade diversion had taken place. On the other hand, a rise in this ratio would be evidence for external trade creation. The *anti-monde* was determined in this way for seven separate commodity groups for the pre-integration period from 1953 to 1959. In his initial study (Balassa, 1967), the post-integration period was from 1959 to 1965, but in a later study this was extended to 1970 (Balassa, 1974). Balassa's results are summarized in table 9.1.

The results for *total imports* show that trade creation occurred in all product groups, except temperate-zone food, beverages and tobacco and other manufactures. Account must be taken of the fact that the income elasticity of demand for food was falling over time. If consumption or industrial production is used instead of GNP as the denominator, trade creation is found to have taken place. Other manufactured goods consisted of intermediate products and non-durable consumer goods. The absence of trade creation in this category may have been due to the rapid expansion of trade in the 1950s, which could not be replicated in subsequent years. The results for *extra-area imports* show trade diversion as occurring in temperate-zone food, beverages and tobacco, chemicals and other manufactured goods. Trade diversion in foodstuffs was undoubtedly due to the effects of the Common Agricultural Policy, which increased levels of external protection (see chapter 20). However, in several other categories (fuels, machinery and transport equipment), substantial external trade creation took place. In the case of fuels, this reflected the switch away from indigenous coal to imported oil during this period. In the case of machinery, the trend reflected, in part, the big increase in investment that took place following the establishment of the EC. Expressed in absolute terms, trade creation amounted to an estimated $11.3 billion (or 21 per cent of trade) and trade diversion at $0.3 billion (or 1 per cent).

Balassa's approach, however, is subject to many of the same objections as the import share approach discussed above. First, it cannot be assumed that income elasticities of import demand would have remained unchanged in the absence of integration. To do so is to disregard entirely the effects of price changes and changes in real exchange rates that took place in the two periods. Second, the results are highly dependent on the precise years chosen for the pre-integration period. If they do not represent equivalent years in the business cycle, the trend in the income elasticity of import demand will be a distorted one. Third, there is a further possibility that the trend in the pre-integration period could have been affected by special factors. Trade liberalization by the EC countries in their trade with non-EC countries in the 1950s may mean that

Table 9.1 Changes in *ex post* income elasticities of import demand in the EC

| Product group | *Ex post* income elasticity of import demand | | Difference |
	1953–9	1959–70	1959–70/1953–9
Total imports			
Non-tropical food, beverages, tobacco	1.7	1.5	−0.2
Raw materials	1.1	1.1	0
Fuels	1.6	2.0	+0.4
Chemicals	3.0	3.2	+0.2
Machinery	1.5	2.6	+1.1
Transport equipment	2.6	3.2	+0.6
Other manufactured goods	2.6	2.5	−0.1
Total of above	1.8	2.0	+0.2
Intra-area imports			
Non-tropical food, beverages, tobacco	2.5	2.5	0
Raw materials	1.9	1.8	−0.1
Fuels	1.1	1.6	+0.5
Chemicals	3.0	3.7	+0.7
Machinery	2.1	2.8	+0.7
Transport equipment	2.9	3.5	+0.6
Other manufactured goods	2.8	2.7	−0.1
Total of above	2.4	2.7	+0.3
Extra-area imports			
Non-tropical food, beverages, tobacco	1.4	1.0	−0.4
Raw materials	1.0	1.0	0
Fuels	1.8	2.1	+0.3
Chemicals	3.0	2.6	−0.4
Machinery	0.9	2.4	+1.5
Transport equipment	2.2	2.5	+0.3
Other manufactured goods	2.5	2.1	−0.4
Total of above	1.6	1.6	0

Source: Balassa (1974).

trade diversion after integration was overestimated. Equally, it may mean that the extent of trade creation after integration was underestimated. Finally, the method is unable to take into account any effects that the establishment of the EC may have had on economic growth and any possible pro-trade or anti-trade bias that they may have given rise to.

(iii) Normalizing trade shares

One way of getting round the problems involved in constructing the *anti-monde* from data drawn from the period before integration (that might be wholly uncomparable with the period after it) is to use data *for the same period* drawn from some third country. The third country or group of countries then acts as a 'normalizer' or control group. One possibility is to normalize changes in the imports/apparent consumption ratio for the EC for the post-integration period by using changes in the same ratio for some other country as the normalizer. Kreinin (1972) used the United States as the normalizing country, but made additional adjustments for differences in the rate of growth of incomes and prices. He estimated trade creation in manufactured goods and processed foods at $7.3 billion, compared with trade diversion at $2.4

billion. Using the United Kingdom as the normalizing country, trade creation was estimated to amount to $9.3 billion and trade diversion at $0.4 billion .

The choice of the normalizer is, clearly, of major importance. This must be a country that has experienced similar changes to the integrating countries but was not itself affected by the process of integration under investigation. Thus, for the purposes of measuring the effects of European integration, it should be a non-European country, as European countries that were not part of the EC would still have been affected by the integration process taking place in the EC. This, therefore, may be a good reason for not using the United Kingdom, since it belonged to EFTA. Other requirements for a good normalizer are that the country or group of countries should have growth and inflation rates similar to those of the EC over the period covered, as income and relative prices are known to be the major determinants of import demand. In a later study covering the two stages of integration in Western Europe involving both the EC and EFTA countries, Kreinin (1979b) used industrialized countries outside Europe, namely the United States, Canada and Japan, as the normalizer. He estimated the trade creation for the EC and EFTA countries from both stages of integration (1959/60 to 1977) at $20–31 billion and trade diversion at $5–8 billion. These results are summarized in table 9.2.

Row A shows Kreinin's own estimates for the two stages of integration. Row B shows the range of estimates of other studies for the first stage of integration (up to 1969/70). Row C shows the results of the adaptation of an earlier study by Kreinin (1973) for the period from 1970–1 to 1977.

Much earlier, Lamfalussy (1963) had suggested comparing changes in the share of trade of EC and EFTA members in the rest of the world as indicative of what would have happened had integration not taken place. In other words, changes in the share of EC and EFTA countries in non-European markets is taken as indicative of how they would have performed if integration had not taken place. There are obvious disadvantages to this approach. First, no account is taken of changes taking place in the importing country that might have altered

Table 9.2 Estimated annual effects of European integration on trade flows in manufactured products, $ billion

	Annual trade creation	Annual trade diversion
A. Two stages of integration combined (independent estimate)	20–31	5–8
B. First-stage integration:		
EEC	9–11	1–2
EFTA	2–4	1
EEC plus EFTA	11–15	2–3
C. Second-stage integration	11–17	2
D. Two stages added up	22–32	4–5

Source: Kreinin (1979b).

the share of imports coming from an individual partner country. Second, as with extrapolation based on the share of intra-area imports in total imports, the method cannot distinguish between trade creation and trade diversion without introducing information from other sources. Nevertheless, Williamson and Bottrill (1971) used this method in an early study of the effects of integration on trade flows in manufactures. They found that, in 1969, intra-EC trade was roughly 50 per cent greater than it would otherwise have been. By inserting estimates of trade creation and trade diversion from other studies, they estimated trade creation and trade diversion together at $12.4 billion.

9.3.2 Econometric models

Two types of econometric model have been used to estimate the effects of European integration as described under the following headings.

Gravity models

These were among the first type of models to be used in empirical work concerned with the effects of European integration. A gravity model is a model that seeks to explain trade flows between pairs of countries (bilateral trade flows) by variables drawn from both the importing and the exporting country. Such models were pioneered by Tinbergen (1962), but developed later by Linnemann (1966) and others. The major variables in a conventional gravity equation are the GNP/GDP of the two countries, their populations and the distance between them. Such an equation has the attraction that it incorporates both supply- and demand-side determinants of trade. While the GNP/GDP of the importing country will exert a positive influence on trade flows, the GNP/GDP of the exporting country will also do so. The *population* of the importing country can also be expected to increase the demand for imports. However, the population of the exporting country is, generally, considered as having a negative relationship with exports. This is because population is a proxy for size, and size results in greater self-sufficiency. Alternatively, *geographical size* may be added as an additional variable to capture the effect of physical area on the need to import natural resources. *Distance* exerts, of course, a negative effect on trade flows. Additional dummy variables may be added for countries that are *adjacent* to one another, for countries that share a *common language* or cultural affinity and to capture the effect on any *preferential trading agreement* existing between the two countries. Using logarithms, the regression equation might take a form such as the following:

$$\log X_{ij} = \log A + \beta \log Y_i + \beta \log Y_j + \mu \log H_i$$

$$+ \mu \log H_j + \gamma \log N_i + \gamma \log N_j + \alpha \log D_{ij}$$

$$+ \log \varepsilon_{ij}$$

where i and j stand for countries i and j, Y is GDP, H is geographical size, N is population, D is distance between the two countries and e is the error term. Such an equation is then estimated using ordinary least squares. Such models have been found to be capable of explaining a significant proportion of the bilateral trade flows taking place between countries in the world. Despite this, they have often been criticized for lacking

any robust theoretical basis. In particular, prices are excluded entirely from the model, it being assumed that markets adjust to equate demand and supply. It is possible, however, to modify the gravity equation to incorporate both prices and exchange rates. If this is done, Bergstrand (1985) has shown that gravity models are consistent with trade theory.

Verdoorn and Schwartz (1972) were among the first to use a gravity model to explain bilateral trade flows between countries in manufactured goods. They estimated trade creation at $10.1 billion ($10.4 billion including EFTA) in 1969 and trade diversion at $1.1 billion ($1.9 billion including EFTA). Aitken (1973) used a conventional gravity equation, with GNP and population in the importing and exporting countries, distance between commercial centres and dummy variables for adjacency and for trade among the partner countries of the EC and EFTA as the explanatory variables. The model was estimated annually for the period from 1951 to 1967. The equation for 1958 was used to represent the pre-integration situation. The study estimated trade creation in the EC as reaching $9.2 billion in 1967 or 1.4 per cent of trade. However, the method used only permitted the measurement of EC trade diversion against EFTA countries, which was estimated at $0.6 billion or 2 per cent of trade. In using 1958 trade flows as the normalizer, however, trade creation was overstated and trade diversion understated, as no allowance was made for a continuing upward trend in intra-trade that would have happened had integration not taken place.

Prewo (1974a, b) is another example of a study that used a gravity approach to estimate the trade effect. A special feature of this approach was the use of an input–output framework, which helped capture the effects of trade creation and trade diversion on intermediate products that other studies largely omitted. Using a share approach, he compared the actual level of intra- and extra-area imports of the EC for 1970 with the hypothetical level estimated using the gravity equation. The exercise was carried out for eleven product groups. He found that the formation of the EC has resulted in both internal and external trade creation in agriculture, fishing and forestry. This was explained in terms of increased demand for feeding stuffs required for expanded meat production and the need to import more forestry products that the EC lacked (see chapter 20). In processed food, beverages and tobacco, however, the expected trade diversion resulting from the CAP was recorded. Some trade diversion was found for minerals and metals, but external trade creation took place in fuels due to the switch from coal to oil. Trade creation was found for all six manufactured product groups, with trade diversion occurring only in the case of textiles, leather, shoes and clothing. Trade creation was greatest in chemicals, metal products, machinery and transport equipment.

More recently, Bayoumi and Eichengreen (1995) have drawn attention to weaknesses in some of these earlier studies. First, unless all the factors affecting trade between any pair of countries are controlled for, the dummy variable representing the integration effect picks up the effects of all of these factors. For example, if all countries in a particular region share the same language and there is no separate variable for common language, the effects of a common language will be attributed to membership of the same preferential trading agreement. A similar problem of misspecification arises with the incorporation of distance as a variable in the equation. Economic distance is not the same thing as geographical distance. Second, the gravity model omits third-country effects. It is not adequate to treat bilateral trade as affected only by economic conditions in the two countries. Third, problems arise when data for industrialized and developing countries are pooled, as the relationship between trade flows and economic conditions may be very different in the two sets of countries. To overcome these problems, Bayoumi and Eichengreen (1995) made use of a gravity equation estimated in differences rather than levels. This enables variables such as distance that do not change over time to be omitted. The same is true of other unobserved differences between different groups of countries that are constant over time. Third-country effects were captured by adding a variable for each country's real exchange rate vis-à-vis the United States which serves as a proxy for competitiveness. The model was estimated for twenty-one industrial countries over three separate periods from 1953 to 1992. With regard to the EEC and EFTA, they found that the formation of both had significant effects on European trade. In the first period, covering the formation of the EEC and EFTA, trade among the Six grew by an estimated 3.2 per cent per annum faster and among the Seven by an estimated 2.3 per cent per annum faster as a result of integration. However, in the case of the EEC, this was accompanied by some trade diversion, which was not the case for EFTA. Following both of the first two enlargements of the EEC, similar effects were apparent. After 1972, trade between the United Kingdom, Eire and Denmark increased significantly faster than predicted by the model, as a result of both trade creation and trade diversion. Following the accession of Greece in 1981 and Spain and Portugal in 1986, trade between the Nine and the newly acceding countries grew faster than predicted by the model, which, in the case of Spain and Portugal was due entirely to trade creation.

Frankel (1997) used a gravity model to estimate the explanatory power of all the conventional variables determining a comprehensive cross-section of data covering the period from 1965 to 1994. Ordinary least squares was used to estimate a gravity equation that included total bilateral exports and imports as the dependent variable and GNP, per capita GNP, distance, adjacency, language and membership of a regional trading arrangement as the independent variables. Five separate trading blocs were included in the equation. Bilateral trade flows from the United Nations trade matrix covering some sixty-three countries were included. An estimated 75 per cent of all bilateral trade flows were explained by the model. With regard to Europe, integration had a positive effect on trade flows between member states, although much depended on whether the EU15 or the EC12 was taken as the relevant trading bloc. For the EU, there was no statistically significant effect until after 1985, which is not surprising given that the EU did not come into being until the end of the period covered. By 1990, trade between members of the EU was found to be

35 per cent more than trade between two similar countries. The EC bloc effect was stronger, but not statistically significant until 1980. Again, however, membership of the EC was not complete until 1986, with the accession of Spain and Portugal. Frankel's results showed that, by 1992, bilateral trade between any two EC member states was 65 per cent higher than it would have been had the EC not existed. Both of the two enlargements in 1973 and 1985 were found to have contributed about one-half of the increase.

Gravity models have also been used to analyse the effects of increased integration between Western and Eastern Europe, following the collapse of communism and the break up of COMECON. Wang and Winters (1991) provided one of the first examples of such studies. They used a gravity model to estimate bilateral trade flows between some seventy-six countries over the period 1984–6, excluding the Central and East European countries (CEECs) and former Soviet Republic (FSR) countries. The reason for excluding the CEEC and FSR countries was to determine the relationship between bilateral trade flows and variables such as GDP, population and distance for 'normal' countries, defined as countries that are properly integrated into the world trading system, which the CEECs were not. Their equation predicted 70 per cent of all the observed bilateral trade flows, with the expected signs for the major variables. Next, data for GDP, population and distance for the CEEC countries was inserted into the equations to estimate the 'potential' trade flows for the base year 1985 if these countries were to become fully integrated. These *potential* trade flows were then compared with *actual* trade flows to determine how trade patterns could be affected if these countries were integrated with those of Western Europe. Their results predicted a big boost in trade between the two blocs, but decline in trade between the CEECs.

Baldwin (1994) also used a gravity model to estimate the effects of increased integration between the two halves of Europe. The model was estimated using trade flows between EC and EFTA countries and between these countries and the United States, Japan, Canada and Turkey for the period 1979 to 1988. Ordinary least squares was

then used to estimate the coefficients in an equation with all the standard variables, including a dummy variable for adjacency and membership of the European Economic Area (EEA) (see chapters 1 and 2). Using a random-effects estimator with a maximum likelihood correction for first-order autocorrelation, the equation was able to predict as much as 99 per cent of all bilateral trade flows. In a similar manner to Wang and Winters, data for GDP, population and distance for the base year 1989 was used to predict potential trade flows between the EFTA countries, EU member states, CEECs and FSR countries. The results showed a very large medium-term potential for export growth from Western to Eastern Europe, with Germany being the largest potential beneficiary. CEECs and FSR countries also enjoyed scope for increased exports to the EU and EFTA countries, although exports to other EECS and FSR countries could be expected to fall. The latter, however, was a case of reversed trade diversion, caused, in the past, by COMECON. In a second scenario, allowance was made for a rise in the per capita incomes of the CEECs and former Soviet Republics as they caught up with the levels of poorer West European countries. The result was a rise in the exports of the West European countries to Eastern Europe of 10–15 per cent per annum spread over several decades.

More recently, Rose (1999) used an augmented gravity model to evaluate the effects of European Monetary Union (EMU) on trade. In addition to the standard GDP, population and distance variables, the model included adjacency, common language, regional trading arrangements, common nationality and colonial relationship variables, as well as a variable for using the same currency and for volatility of bilateral exchange rates. The equation was estimated for 186 countries for five different years – 1970, 1975, 1980, 1985 and 1990. The model was found to explain 63 per cent of trade flows, with all the expected results. More importantly, exchange rate volatility (measured by the standard deviation of bilateral nominal exchanges in the preceding five years) was found to have a strong negative effect on trade and the effect of a common currency an even larger positive impact. Frankel (1997) also found that exchange rate volatility exerted a strong negative effect on worldwide bilateral trade flows. For the member states of the EC, he found that, if the level of exchange rate variability that prevailed in 1980 was eliminated, intra-EC trade would have been increased by 14.2 per cent.

Analytic models

As we have seen, a criticism of gravity models has been that they exclude relative prices and real exchange rates as determinants of trade flows. An alternative is, therefore, to construct a model that includes the full range of variables that are capable of explaining trade flows between countries. At a simple level, the main determinants of *total* imports in any year are the level of economic activity (with GNP or GDP or apparent consumption as the most suitable proxy) and the prices of domestic products relative to the price of imports. The relationship between GNP/GDP and imports is given by the income elasticity of demand for imports and between relative prices and imports by the price elasticity of demand for imports. However, in order to measure the impact of integration on imports, it is necessary to distinguish between *total*, *intra-area* and *extra-area* imports. Intra- and extra-imports will be determined by the relationship between the price of imports from partner countries and the price of imports in non-partner countries. This will depend on the elasticity of substitution of imports with respect to price changes between partner and non-partner countries. We may summarize these relationships as follows:

$$M_T = \alpha + \beta_1 GNP + \beta_2 Pd/Pw$$

$$M_I = \alpha + \beta_1 GNP + \beta_2 Pd/Pw - \beta_3 Pp/Pw$$

$$M_E = \alpha + \beta_1 GNP + \beta_2 Pd/Pw + \beta_3 Pp/Pw$$

M_T, M_I and M_E stand for total, intra-area and extra-area imports respectively, GNP for gross national product in the importing country, Pd/Pw for domestic prices relative to prices in the rest of the world and Pp/Pw for prices in partner countries and prices in the rest of the world. The coefficients measure income elasticity of import demand,

price elasticity of import demand and the elasticity of substitution of import demand with respect to partner and non-partner countries.

The integration effect may be assumed to work though changes in relative prices. Multilateral tariff reductions work through raising Pd/Pw and preferential tariff reductions through lowering Pp/Pw. However, this assumes that tariff changes are fully passed on to prices, which may not be the case where goods are differentiated and/or markets less than perfectly competitive. A further difficulty is that tariff changes may have an effect on imports other than through changes in relative prices. Balassa (1974) and others have drawn attention to the possible 'promotional effects' of integration, whereby integration stimulates imports through increased information flows, direct investment by firms in sales and distribution outlets, and a reduction of risk and uncertainty. For this reason, some models have preferred to include a separate variable for tariff changes.

Once the model is agreed, the next task is to estimate the coefficients in the equation for a suitable period of time, and then to use the completed equation to estimate what trade would have been had integration not taken place. Actual trade flows may, then, be compared with flows predicted by the model and the residual treated as the integration effect. In this case, the *anti-monde* is based on actual estimates of how income and relative prices have affected trade flows over the integration period. If the purpose is to make an *ex ante* prediction as to how integration will affect trade flows in the future, the coefficients in the equation may be used to compare the effects with and without integration. For this purpose, integration may be treated as a separate dummy variable taking the value of one or zero according to the simulation. Rather than estimating the model for the EC for a different period of time during which integration took place, an alternative is to estimate the equation for a comparable country or group of countries for the same period of time. Ideally, the estimation should be done at as disaggregated a level as possible, as individual countries and products do not behave in the same fashion.

Resnick and Truman (1974) used a regression model of the kind described above to measure the impact of European integration on trade in manufactured goods. Major variables in the model were real income, relative prices and a separate variable designed to capture the effects of greater pressure of demand. Coefficients were obtained by estimating the equations for EC trade for the period from 1953 to 1968. The model was then simulated to estimate the impact of integration by altering the 1968 values of the relative price variables for tariff changes in the EC and EFTA. Trade creation was estimated at $1.2 billion ($1.4 billion including EFTA) and trade diversion at $2.7 billion ($3.6 billion including EFTA). These figures were much lower than the estimates obtained by other studies, with trade diversion actually exceeding trade creation. Several reasons were given for this (see Balassa, 1974). First, Resnick and Truman used export price indices with respect to foreign products and the GNP deflator for domestic products to capture the relative price effect. However, as the GNP deflator included non-traded as well as traded goods, the estimated price elasticities of import demand may have been biased downwards and, hence, trade creation underestimated. This was borne out by separate tests for bias carried out by Resnick and Truman. The use of ordinary least squares in the trade creation equations was also criticized as imparting a downward estimate to the calculations. Finally, the use of price equations was criticized for failing to capture the so-called 'promotional effects' of integration discussed above.

In another example of an analytic model, Winters (1984, 1985) used a model based on the almost ideal demand system (AIDS) proposed by Deaton and Muellbauer (1980) to estimate the effects on the UK of accession to the EC. For each industry, the share of the market taken by individual supplier is denoted by S_{ik} where i denotes the ith supplier's share of the kth country's market for a particular industry. This is given by the following equation:

$$S_{ik} = \alpha + \sum \lambda_{ij} \ln p_{jk} \beta \ln Y_k / P_k$$

where p_{jk} is the price of the jth country supplier into the kth country market, Y_k is total nominal expenditure by k residents and P_k is a price index covering supplies from all sources. The attraction of this model is that it accounts for the allocation of consumer expenditure on manufactures among all suppliers, not just between domestic and foreign suppliers. The effects of tariff reductions on intra-area imports are incorporated into the model through the use of dummy variables. In this way, the effects of non-price factors can be included and possible data constraints regarding prices overcome.

CEPR/EU Commission (1997) used a similar approach to estimate the effects of the creation of the single European market (SEM; see chapter 7). They used three demand equations for fifteen three-digit sensitive goods sectors for four principal countries, namely, Germany, France, Italy and the UK. The equations estimated the share of nominal, sectoral expenditure accounted for by domestically produced goods, intra-EU imports and extra-EU imports. A separate dummy variable was included to capture the effect of the creation of the SEM, which was expected to affect trade flows not only through the *direct* effects of reductions in trade costs on demand, but also through the *indirect* effects of increased competition and reductions in price-cost margins. Separate price equations for each of the sectors covered were used to estimate these indirect, supply-side effects. The estimated impact of the SEM on price-cost margins was then used to simulate the impact of price reductions on trade flows applying the estimated demand equations. They found that the overall impact of the SEM programme was to cause a decrease in the domestic producers' share in the fifteen sectors covered of 4.2 per cent and a rise in the share of EU producers of 2.1 per cent and of the rest of the world of 2 per cent. A similar exercise was carried out for the manufacturing sectors as a whole in order to be able to examine the effects of the SEM on other manufacturing sectors. For manufacturing as a whole, the fall in the domestic producers' share was 2.3 per cent, with EU producers increasing their share by 0.5 per cent and the rest of the world by 1.8 per cent. In other words, the impact of the SEM was overwhelmingly one of both internal and external trade creation. These results are summarized in table 9.3.

Table 9.3 Estimated impact of the single market on market shares

| | Percentage change in market share | | | | | | | | |
| | Direct demand | | | Price competition | | | Overall impact | | |
	Home	EU	RoW	Home	EU	RoW	Home	EU	RoW
Glassware	−1.3	−0.1	+1.4	+0.7	−0.1	−0.5	−0.7	−0.2	+0.9
Ceramics	−4.2	+1.8	+2.4	−0.2	+0.3	−0.1	−4.4	+2.0	+2.4
Basic industrial chemicals	−4.3	+2.5	+1.8	+1.1	−0.7	−0.3	−3.3	+1.8	+1.5
Pharmaceuticals	−1.9	+0.4	+1.5	−0.1	+0.2	−0.1	−2.0	+0.5	+1.4
Boiler making, etc.	−5.3	+4.4	+0.9	+0.9	−0.9	+0.0	−4.4	+3.5	+0.9
Machine tools for metals	−2.0	−2.2	+4.2	−0.6	+0.2	+0.4	−2.6	−2.0	+4.6
Machine tools for foodstuffs	−7.4	+3.0	+4.4	+0.5	−0.4	−0.1	−6.9	+2.6	+4.3
Plant for mines	−1.7	+1.0	+0.7	+1.1	−0.6	−0.5	−0.6	+0.4	+0.2
Office machines	−7.8	+2.8	+5.0	+1.1	+0.1	−1.2	−6.7	+3.0	+3.8
Telecommunications equipment	−2.7	+1.7	+1.0	+1.0	−1.5	−0.5	−1.7	+0.2	+1.5
Electronic equipment	−15.7	+4.6	+11.1	+4.0	−2.2	−1.8	−11.7	+2.2	+9.5
Motor vehicles	−4.9	+3.7	+1.2	+0.3	−0.7	+0.3	−4.6	+3.0	+1.5
Aerospace equipment	−15.3	+14.6	+0.8	+7.0	−2.5	−4.4	−8.3	+12.0	−3.8
Brewing and malting	−6.3	+5.9	+0.4	+1.5	−1.4	−0.1	−4.8	+4.5	+0.3
Clothing	−2.9	−2.5	+5.4	+0.7	−0.5	−0.2	−2.1	−3.1	+5.2
Weighted average for 15 sensitive areas	−5.4	+3.0	+2.5	+1.2	−0.8	−0.4	−4.2	+2.1	+2.0
Rest of manufacturing	−0.4	−0.9	+1.3	−0.8	+0.4	+0.4	−1.2	−0.4	+1.7
Aggregate manufacturing	*−2.2*	*+0.5*	*+1.7*	*−0.1*	*+0.0*	*+0.1*	*−2.3*	*+0.5*	*+1.8*

Note: RoW = Rest of the World.
Source: European Commission/CEPR (1997).

9.3.3 Computable general equilibrium models

CGE modelling is a comparatively recent development in the empirical estimation of the effects of trade liberalization. Partly this is because the construction of a CGE model is a complex and time-consuming exercise. Partly, too, it is because the possibilities that such a model opens up have not been fully understood until now. Most applications of CGE modelling have been concerned with simulating the effects of various *multilateral* trade liberalization scenarios, such as the effects of cuts in tariffs and non-tariff barriers agreed through the GATT/WTO. However, CGE models have also been used to analyse the effects of *regional* trade liberalization, including the likely effects of further European integration. CEPR/EU Commission (1997) attempted to use a CGE model to simulate

the effects of the SEM programme. The model was a twelve-country model with 118 manufacturing industries. A particular attraction of the model was that it contained both a perfectly competitive, non-agricultural sector and an imperfectly competitive manufacturing sector, in which products are differentiated and produced under conditions of increasing returns to scale.

CGE modelling involves a two-stage approach. First, the model must be calibrated for a base year. This involves estimating the equations making up the model for a particular year using a data set containing values for all the variables in the model. However, not all parameters are estimated; of necessity, some are imposed using estimates taken from the literature. Second, the model is then subjected to a series of external shocks that simulate the effects of the liberalization process that is being analysed. This is then compared with what

Table 9.4 Changes in trade patterns in manufacturing resulting from the single market — an *ex ante* simulation by the EU Commission and CEPR

	Base shares (%)			Changes in shares (%)			% change in EU share
	Home	EU	Row	Home	EU	RoW	
France	76.75	16.05	7.19	−2.55	2.99	0.44	1.19
Germany	75.6	13.58	10.82	−2.28	2.83	−0.55	1.21
Italy	79.53	13.41	7.07	−2.15	2.5	−0.35	1.19
UK	74.19	14.48	11.32	−2.25	2.88	−0.63	1.2
Netherlands	62.63	25.7	11.67	−2.32	3.42	−1.1	1.13
Belgium-Luxembourg	58.34	31.21	10.45	−2.47	3.59	−1.11	1.11
Denmark	63.75	21.69	14.55	−1.85	3.05	−1.21	1.14
Ireland	71.53	20.34	8.13	−2.04	2.72	−0.68	1.13
Greece	73.29	18.47	8.24	−1.4	2.13	−0.73	1.12
Spain	77.55	16.45	6	−2.35	2.78	−0.43	1.17
Portugal	72.54	21.74	5.71	−1.6	2.29	−0.69	1.11

Note: RoW = Rest of the World.
Source: European Commission/CEPR (1997).

would have happened had no change taken place. In the case of the CEPR/EU Commission model, both *ex ante* and *ex post* simulations were undertaken. The *ex ante* exercise simulated the likely effects of the SEM on intra-EU trade costs by using sectoral estimates taken from an earlier study by Buigues, Ilzkovitz and Lebrun (1990). These estimates were imposed on the model for 1990 and the effects on the equilibrium were re-computed. The results showed the share of domestic producers in home consumption falling by just over 2 per cent in most member states, while the share of EU producers increased by roughly 3 per cent and the rest of the world declined by less than 1 per cent. Thus, about two-thirds of the effect of the SEM on intra-EU trade was trade creation and about one-third trade diversion. Table 9.4 summarizes the results of the *ex ante* simulation.

The *ex post* simulation involved performing the same exercise in reverse. The changes in trade costs needed to reproduce the equilibrium in import penetration that actually took place between 1988 and 1994 were estimated. It is assumed that during this period producers only had time to make limited adjustments to the changes taking place. In the long run, however, full adjustment is assumed to take place. Two simulations were then carried out, one in which price-cost margins were fixed (i.e. no competition effects were assumed) and one in which the full effects of the SEM were assumed to take place. By comparing the actual changes in trade shares with those resulting from the simulation, the SEM effect was determined. These showed that, for manufacturing as a whole, the share of domestic producers fell by roughly 1.5 per cent, whereas that of EU producers rose by 2 per cent and that of the rest of the world fell by roughly 0.5 per cent. However, this takes no account of the fall in extra-EU trade costs that the SEM brought. In a second simulation, the results of a fall in extra-EU trade costs were estimated. They are summarized in table 9.5.

9.3.4 Summary of the trade effects of integration

Table 9.6 summarizes the results obtained by different studies of the effects of the first and second stages of European integration on trade flows.

For the *first stage* of economic integration, trade creation for all goods was estimated at between $9.2 and $19.8 billion and trade diversion at between −$2.5 (i.e. external trade creation) and $0.5 billion. For manufactures only, trade creation

Table 9.5 Changes in trade patterns in manufactures resulting from the single market — an *ex post* simulation by the EU Commission

	Changes in shares: Base (%)			%Change in EU share	Changes in shares: competition effect (%)			%Change in EU share
	Home	EU	RoW		Home	EU	RoW	
France	−3.22	2.12	1.11	1.13	0.08	−0.04	−0.02	1.13
Germany	−2.78	1.63	1.14	1.12	0.04	−0.02	−0.03	1.12
Italy	−2.7	1.82	0.88	1.14	0.1	−0.07	−0.03	1.14
UK	−2.79	1.7	1.08	1.12	0.08	−0.05	−0.04	1.12
Netherlands	−2.8	1.78	1.02	1.07	0.19	−0.12	−0.06	1.07
Belgium-Luxembourg	−2.76	1.98	0.77	1.06	0.22	−0.16	−0.07	1.07
Denmark	−2.36	1.4	0.96	1.06	0.55	−0.34	−0.21	1.08
Ireland	−2.58	1.74	0.84	1.09	0.48	−0.34	−0.15	1.1
Greece	−1.46	0.92	0.54	1.05	0.61	−0.4	−0.21	1.07
Spain	−2.41	1.74	0.67	1.11	0.21	−0.16	−0.05	1.12
Portugal	−1.31	1.03	0.28	1.05	0.3	−0.24	−0.06	1.06

Note: RoW = Rest of the World.
Source: European Commission/CEPR (1997).

ranges from $1.2 to $18 billion, while trade diversion lies between −$3.1 and $2.7 billion. Subsequent enlargements of the EC have added to these effects. Estimates for the second stage of integration suggest that enlargement of the EC after 1973 resulted in further trade creation of $11–17 billion and trade diversion of $2 billion. For *both stages* of integration, Kreinin (1979b) has estimated the combined effects of EEC and EFTA for manufactures only as trade creation of $20 to $31 billion and trade diversion of $5 to $8 billion. To these gains should be added the gains from subsequent enlargements of the EC, including the admission of Greece in 1981, of Spain and Portugal in 1986, and finally of Sweden, Austria and Finland in 1995. No estimates have been made of the effects of these later enlargements. Finally, as we have seen above, the establishment of the SEM in 1992 appears to have resulted in further net trade creation.

9.4 The nature of European specialization

One important aspect of the trade effects is the evidence showing that trade creation mainly took the form of *intra-* rather than *inter*-industry spe-cialization. That is to say, individual member states have tended to increase their specialization in a narrow range of products within a given industry, rather than in the industry per se. Orthodox trade theory predicts that tariff liberalization will lead to countries specializing in those industries or activities in which they have a comparative cost advantage. This leads to industries being relocated in countries where relative costs are lowest. Although this will leave the member states as a whole better off, as resources are being used more efficiently than before, there may be considerable adjustment costs for particular groups of workers whose jobs disappear as a consequence and who must move to where new jobs are available and/or retrain. Where markets are imperfectly competitive, however, the effects of trade barriers disappearing may be for the number of varieties of a product to increase and for individual producers to specialize in particular varieties. This can be expected to result in fewer adjustment difficulties, as the geographical pattern of activity is not affected, only the nature of what is produced in each country.

Balassa (1974) used a representative ratio, showing trade imbalances for individual product

Table 9.6 A summary of the results of attempts to estimate trade creation and trade diversion in the EC, $ billion

Author/date of study	Period studied	Trade created		Trade diverted	
		All goods $ billion	Manufactures $ billion	All goods $ billion	Manufactures $ billion
Balassa, (1967)	1965	1.9		0.1	
Balassa, (1974a)	1970	11.3	11.4	0.3	0.1
Prewo (1974)	1970	19.8	18.0	−2.5	−3.1
Truman, (1969) (unadjusted)	1968		9.2		−1.0
Truman, (1975) (adjusted)	1968		2.5		0.5
Kreinin, (1972)	1970	7.3 (using UK as normalizer) 9.3 (using US as normalizer)		2.4 (using UK as normalizer) 0.4 (using US as normalizer)	
Kreinin, (1979)	1977		20–31 (EC plus EFTA)		5.8 (EC and EFTA)
Williamson and Bottrill, (1971)	1969		9.6		0
Verdoorn and Schwartz, (1972)	1969		10.1		1.1
Aitken (1973)	1973	9.2			
Resnick and Truman (1975)	1968		1.2		2.7

groups divided by the sum of exports and imports of products belonging to the group, to estimate the extent of intra-industry trade. The formula was as follows:

$$E_j = 1/n \sum |X_i - M_i| / (X_i + M_i)$$

where j stands for country j and i for product group i out of n industries and X and M for exports and imports respectively. A movement in the ratio towards unity was taken as evidence for inter-industry specialization and towards zero as evidence for intra-industry specialization. The ratios were calculated for ninety-one separate product groups at two-, three- and four-digit levels of aggregation and for bilateral trade flows in

manufactured goods between the six member states for the period 1958–70. Balassa's results are shown in table 9.7.

In all cases, the ratio was found to fall over the period covered, confirming that intra- rather than inter-industry specialization was taking place.

Balassa's results were confirmed by subsequent studies using different measures for the level of intra-industry trade. Grubel and Lloyd (1975) used a formula (GL index) in which the trade imbalance for an individual product group was deducted from total exports and imports before being divided by total exports and imports. The summary measure for all of a country's trade was as follows:

Table 9.7 Representative ratios of trade balances for ninety-one product groups for EEC member states, 1958–1970

	1958	1963	1970
Belgium	0.458	0.401	0.339
France	0.394	0.323	0.273
Germany	0.531	0.433	0.331
Italy	0.582	0.521	0.410
Netherlands	0.495	0.431	0.357

Source: Balassa (1974).

Table 9.8 Estimates of intra-industry trade for EC member states, 1970–1985

Country	1970	1978	1980	1983	1985
Belgium	0.800	0.835	0.841	0.875	0.867
Denmark	0.630	0.679	0.674	0.721	0.726
France	0.814	0.828	0.861	0.855	0.855
Germany	0.607	0.641	0.554	0.687	0.682
Ireland	0.444	0.600	0.685	0.723	0.703
Italy	0.617	0.614	0.696	0.662	0.695
Netherlands	0.741	0.759	0.779	0.776	0.763
UK	0.620	0.807	0.808	0.832	0.843

$$B_j = \sum (X_{ij} + M_{ij}) - \sum |X_{ij} - M_{ij}| /$$

$$\sum (X_{ij} + M_{ij}) \times 100$$

The summary measure had the further attraction that the individual intra-industry trade (IIT) ratio for each product group was weighted according to the importance of each product group in total trade. Their estimates showed that EC member states have among the highest levels of IIT of all OECD countries. The IIT ratios increased in all member states over the period from 1964 to 1974, with the single exception of the Netherlands. The highest levels of intra-industry trade were found for France, Belgium-Luxembourg and the Netherlands, with lower levels for Italy and West Germany.

Greenaway and Hine (1991) used the GL index to show that the level of intra-industry trade has continued to increase since 1970. Their results for the EC member states are summarized in table 9.8.

However, there is some evidence that, in the 1980s, the increase in intra-industry trade may have weakened in some countries (France, Germany and the Netherlands).

On the other hand, CEPII/EU Commission (1997) showed that, following the launch of the SEM, the importance of IIT has increased further. Using a Grubel–Lloyd index, they measured both vertical and horizontal IIT and inter-industry trade for bilateral trade flows in no fewer than 10,000 different products over the period from 1980 to 1994. The Grubel–Lloyd index showed

rising IIT during this period, but this mainly took the form of vertical rather than horizontal IIT. That is to say, countries specialized in product groups ranked according to quality differences, rather than products differentiated purely by branding and advertising. Table 9.9 summarizes their results.

Important country differences are apparent. France, Belgium-Luxembourg and Germany have high levels of horizontal IIT, while the UK, France and Germany have high levels of vertical IIT. By way of contrast, Greece, Portugal and Spain, all countries at a lower stage of development, have high levels of inter-industry trade, as does Denmark. Although Spain and Portugal enjoyed the largest rise in IIT over the period of the single market programme, it is apparent that the overall rise in IIT in the EC could not be attributed to this. IIT increased in all countries, except Ireland and Denmark.

9.5 Estimating the income effects

Most studies of the effects of integration have been concerned purely and simply with measuring the *trade* impact of integration. However, more important than the trade effect is the extent to which real *incomes* were raised or lowered by integration. Using a conventional approach to the measurement of the income effect, Balassa (1974) estimated the welfare gain from trade creation in manufactured goods at $0.7 billion in 1970, by multiplying increased trade in manufactures of

Table 9.9 Share of inter-industry and intra-industry trade in intra-EC trade 1987–1994, percentage change

Country	Shares in 1994 (%)			Variation 1987 to 1994 (%)		
	Inter-industry trade	Horizontal intra-industry trade	Vertical intra-industry trade	Inter-industry trade	Horizontal intra-industry trade	Vertical intra-industry trade
France	31.6	24.1	44.3	−6.4	2.8	3.6
Germany	32.6	20.5	46.9	−5.4	1.9	3.4
Belgium-Luxembourg	34.8	23.2	42.0	−3.8	1.6	2.2
United Kingdom	35.6	16.5	47.9	−7.0	−1.9	8.9
Netherlands	39.3	18.9	41.9	−4.8	−0.3	5.1
Spain	45.9	18.9	36.9	−12.0	8.7	3.3
Italy	46.9	16.2	36.9	−2.8	5.8	−3.1
Ireland	57.7	7.9	34.4	2.2	−0.9	−1.3
Denmark	60.0	8.1	60.0	1.1	−1.1	0.0
Portugal	68.6	7.5	23.9	−8.6	3.9	4.8
Greece	86.0	3.7	10.3	−0.2	0.8	−0.6
EC12	38.5	19.2	42.3	−5.1	2.0	3.1
EC without Spain and Portugal	37.4	19.5	43.1	−5.0	1.7	3.3

Source: European Commission/CEP II, 1997.

$11.4 by an average tariff of 12 per cent. Given negligible trade diversion, the welfare gain from trade creation was estimated at the equivalent of 0.15 per cent of GNP, a surprisingly small amount. With trade diversion in agriculture of $1.3 billion and an average external rate of protection of 47 per cent, the loss from trade diversion was estimated at $0.3 billion.

In fact, most studies of the welfare gain from tariff liberalization have found it to be quite small when expressed as a percentage of GDP/GNP. One reason for this is that trade typically accounts for a small proportion of total output, so that, when gains are expressed in relation to national output, they appear quite low. A further reason is that the tariff reduction that resulted from integration was small, as tariffs in several member states were already quite low by the time the EEC came into being. Another consideration is that most studies have been concerned purely and simply with the effects of *tariff* liberalization. No account is taken of the effects of the removal of *non-tariff* barriers, although most of this did not take place until the launching of the SEM programme in 1987. A more important consideration concerns the nature of the expansion of intra-European trade that took place following integration. As we have seen, this mainly took the form of *intra-industry specialization*. The gains from intra-industry specialization come more from increased choice as more varieties of the product become available than from lower costs and prices. Such gains are not readily captured by conventional methods of estimating the welfare effect.

Furthermore, the gains from intra-industry specialization accrue more in the long run. Where producers specialize in particular products or processes, average costs are often lowered as the scale of production can be increased. It will be the cost savings that come from increased plant specialization and longer production runs, rather than plant size, that will result from greater IIT. By expanding the number of varieties available, IIT will also increase the degree of competition facing individual producers, which may bring further benefits from the elimination of X-inefficiency (managerial slack). If producers are forced by this process to cut prices, consumers will enjoy a further increase in their real incomes. Such gains constitute the *dynamic* effects of integration.

Arguably, however, they may be the more important type of gains. One reason is that reductions in unit costs resulting from greater plant specialization and increased competition affect the full range of the output produced, not just the part that is traded. Another reason is that they are ongoing, not once-and-for-all effects, which continue being enjoyed for several years after the integration process is complete. The dynamic gains are not confined to industries in which intra-industry specialization takes place. They may also occur in industries where conventional *inter-industry specialization* occurs. Where an industry enjoys a relative cost advantage in a particular industry, increased specialization after integration will enable producers to expand the scale of their production and enjoy economies of plant size. These are different from the economies resulting from increased plant specialization and long production runs that result where intra-industry specialization is the outcome. Both forms of specialization are also likely to stimulate greater competition, which should lead to further efficiency gains as producers are forced to cut costs and rationalize their production operations.

Few of the early studies of the effects of integration tried to estimate these effects. Any attempt to do so confronts even bigger counterfactual problems than estimating the static effects alone. Balassa (1974) used estimates of the efficiency gains from increasing the scale of production in manufacturing to make a guess at the possible magnitude of the gain. According to a study by Walters (1963), a doubling of inputs in United States non-agricultural production led to a 130 per cent increase in output. Applying this to the amount of trade created by integration, Balassa estimated a gain in GNP for 1970 of slightly over 0.5 per cent, sufficient to add 0.1 per cent to the EC's actual growth rate. However, the gain might be greater if the cost reduction were applied to all intra-area trade in manufactures or to the entire manufacturing sector. One difficulty, however, with an exercise of this sort is knowing the extent to which producers in the individual member states were constrained before integration by the size of their domestic markets from operating at an optimum scale. Moreover, firms might have been able to achieve these scale economies through an expansion of their exports to the rest of the world without integration taking place. On the other hand, as Balassa argued, the fact that the elimination of tariffs between EC member states was irreversible reduced the risk for producers from investing in large-scale production methods.

One later attempt to estimate these effects of integration on manufacturing was a study by Owen (1983). He argued that, potentially, the gains from integration were quite large, because of the effects that integration had on both the scale of production and competition. As tariff barriers are lowered, Owen argued, firms are forced to rationalize their operations, closing small high-cost plants and concentrating production in large low-cost plants. Using detailed estimates of the efficiency gains in three branches of manufacturing industry – namely, washing machines and refrigerators, trucks and cars – Owen calculated the cost reductions resulting from intra-EC trade creation. The gains were put at 54 per cent for washing machines, 135 per cent for refrigerators, 53 per cent for cars and 4 per cent for trucks. Added to these gains from an increased scale of production were the cost savings from the elimination of high-cost marginal producers in importing countries. In total, the welfare gain to the original six EC members from these dynamic effects was estimated at 3–6 per cent of combined GNP. By way of contrast, the pure static welfare gains, amounted to only ⅔ per cent. However, Owen has been criticized for deducing a very large welfare gain from a comparatively narrowly focused study.

To the welfare gains from the first two stages of European integration must be added those resulting from the creation of the SEM. The most comprehensive attempt at estimating the potential to the EC from the realization of the SEM was a study carried out on behalf of the European Commission by a committee chaired by Paolo Cecchini. The Cecchini Report (1988) was, in fact, the popular version of a more definitive piece of technical work carried out by Emerson (1988). This sought to estimate the welfare gain from removing a wide range of non-tariff barriers by estimating

Table 9.10 Changes in GDP and welfare resulting from trade creation and trade diversion in the single market

Country	% change in GDP	Change in welfare as % of GDP	Change in welfare as % of manufacturing value added
France	2.0	2.27	8.72
Germany	2.2	2.47	2.22
Italy	1.9	2.22	7.33
UK	2.4	2.8	9.9
Netherlands	3.2	3.74	14.34
Belgium-Luxembourg	4.0	4.55	16.59
Denmark	2.0	2.36	11.68
Ireland	3.3	3.96	12.03
Greece	4.2	5.04	19.59
Spain	2.8	3.35	11.05
Portugal	8.6	10.02	27.49

Source: European Commission/CEPR (1997).

the costs to the EC of having these barriers. It included both the static welfare gains from trade creation as these barriers were removed *and* the longer-run dynamic gains that were expected to result from increased competition and the exploitation of economies of scale. These gains were estimated at ECU 70–190 billion or 2.5–6.5 per cent of EC GDP with the gain spread over a period of five years or more. In a separate macro-economic exercise, the effect of these cost savings on the whole economy were simulated, using different assumptions about the stance of macroeconomic policy. Assuming passive macroeconomic policies, an increase in real GDP of 4.5 per cent was predicted over a period of 5–6 years. With more active macroeconomic policies, an increase in real GDP of roughly 7 per cent was predicted.

However, Emerson's was essentially an *ex ante* study of the likely effects of the SEM. Subsequently, as part of the Single Market Review, the Commission has sought to estimate the actual effect of the SEM on EC GDP. As part of this study, the EU Commission/CEPR (1997) used the CGE model designed to calculate the effects of the SEM on trade to estimate the welfare gain from the SEM for the period 1991–4. If reductions in trade costs for extra- as well as for intra-EC trade are included, the gains range from 2 to 10 per cent of GDP. However, a later estimate (CEC, 2002q) indi-

cated trade gains of about 1.8 per cent of GDP (164.5 billion euros) and 1.46 per cent increase in employment (2.5 million extra jobs; see chapter 7, section 7.5.1). These are summarized in table 9.10.

9.6 Economic growth

Few of the early attempts to estimate the impact of integration had much to say about the effect of integration on growth. Balassa (1974) estimated that the formation of the EC added a further 1 per cent increase in GNP due to increased savings and investment. This was sufficient to raise the growth rate by 0.05 per cent. This occurred through higher incomes, leading to higher savings and higher investment. However, the exploitation of economies of scale and rationalization of production might be expected to lead to further new investment. Indeed, the share of fixed investment in GNP in the Six rose from 21 per cent in 1958 to 25 per cent in 1970. Suggesting that this share might have been about 1 per cent smaller than if integration had not taken place, Balassa estimated the rate of economic growth would be increased by a further 0.2 per cent as a result of integration.

Marques-Mendes (1986) proposed a simple balance of payments constrained growth model,

Table 9.11 The effects of economic integration on the growth rate of member states, 1961–72 and 1974–81

	1961–72		1974–81	
	Actual growth rate (%)	Growth rate due to EC	Actual growth rate (%)	Growth rate due to EC
Germany	4.39	−0.02	2.65	0.91
France	5.40	−2.71	2.66	1.57
Italy	4.97	1.04	2.74	0.42
Netherlands	5.17	2.94	1.99	0.53
Belgium-Luxembourg	4.56	2.45	2.03	0.71
UK	–	–	1.24	0.37
Ireland	–	–	3.84	0.31
Denmark	–	–	1.98	−0.64

Source: summarized from Marques-Mendes (1986).

based on the work of Thirlwall (1979, 1982) for analysing the effects of integration on growth. The model makes use of the concept of the foreign trade multiplier whereby an increase in export volume causes an increase in output, not only in the exporting country but also in trading partners through an increase in imports. Some of the increase in output in trading partners returns to the country that experiences the initial export expansion through increased imports by trading partners. The size of the foreign trade multiplier depends on the income elasticity of demand for imports in both countries. However, the extent to which output can grow is constrained by the need to achieve balance of payments equilibrium.

The model has the advantage that it can break down the integration impact on economic growth into a variety of different factors. In addition to increased exports, integration may affect a country's growth through a change in the trade balance and through any change in the terms of trade required to adjust for any change in the trade balance. Integration will have a negative effect on a country's growth if it leads to an increased propensity to import. Other negative effects will include the need to make net budget payments to the EC and/or to make net transfers to other member states under the CAP. Factor flows, such as net inward investment and/or labour remittances from abroad, will have a positive effect on the growth rate. Thus the model makes possible

the construction of a broader framework for analysing the effects of integration on GDP than reliance purely and simply on net trade creation effects. Using this framework, Marques-Mendes estimated the impact of integration on economic growth for the two phases of integration – 1961–72 and 1974–81. Table 9.11 summarizes the results he obtained.

For the first period of integration, despite the fact that France and, to a lesser extent, Germany experienced negative effects, integration appears to have had a sizeable positive effect on economic growth. For the second period all countries, except Denmark, enjoyed faster growth as a result of integration. Taking the figures as a whole, Marques Mendes found that the GDP of the EC was 2.2 per cent higher than it would have been had integration not taken place and, by 1981, 5.9 per cent higher.

With regard to the SEM, Baldwin (1989) showed how increased integration can result in a higher long-run growth rate in the member states. He argued that conventional estimates of the impact of the SEM (see Cecchini, 1988 and Emerson et al., 1988) underestimated the potential gain from integration because they were based on once-and-for-all gains only. He drew a distinction between two effects on economic growth – a *medium-term* acceleration as higher incomes boost savings and investment and a *long-term* effect as an increased rate of investment induces still further increases in investment in other parts of the economy. Taking the estimates of the Cecchini Report of an increase in EC GNP of between 2.5 and 6.5 per cent, Baldwin used the endogenous growth model first proposed by Romer (1986) to estimate the long-term effect on growth. His estimates showed that the SEM could add between 0.28 and 0.92 percentage points to the long-run rate of growth, resulting in much bigger gains than predicted by other studies.

One attempt to use econometric analysis to evaluate the effects of European integration on growth has identified strong long-run growth effects. Henrekson, Torstensson and Torstensson (1996) used a base regression, in which the average growth rate of real GDP per capita was a function of initial real per capita GDP, years of schooling, investment as a share of GDP, a dummy variable for EC or EFTA membership, and the real exchange rate to separate the effects of regional integration from those of trade policy in general. For the period from 1976 to 1985, they found that membership of the EC or EFTA had a positive and significant effect on growth, adding an estimated one percentage point to the growth rate. An interesting aspect of their work is the evidence they produced to show that technology transfer was the main mechanism through which growth was affected. This was obtained by conducting two additional regressions, one that controlled for the effects of macroeconomic policy on growth and the other for the effects of investment on growth. Not only did they find that integration had not led to higher investment ratios in the member states, but also that there was no evidence that the same level of investment in different countries produced different growth effects. As a result, they concluded that the effects of integration on growth were due entirely to the long-run effects of technology transfer, as predicted in endogenous growth models.

9.7 Conclusion

In this chapter, we have surveyed the various attempts made to measure the impact of European economic integration over the fifty years since the European Community came into being. The major problem with all of the studies undertaken is that we have no way of knowing what would have happened had integration not taken place. Methods for resolving the counterfactual problem have ranged from the simplistic to the sophisticated. At the simplistic end of the spectrum are the residual models that extrapolate pre-integration trends into the post-integration period, on the assumption that the post-integration period was no different from the period preceding. At the sophisticated end, economists seek to use models of import demand to estimate the impact of integration. Although the latter approach is preferable, it should be borne in mind that the results obtained are only as good as the model that is used. Partial equilibrium models seek to identify and isolate the impact of integration on trade flows, but are unable to capture the different ways in which effects in one sector or country feed back into other sectors or countries. Although CGE models overcome these problems by stipulating the conditions for equilibrium to exist simultaneously in markets, too much should never be claimed for the results obtained.

What is clear from the range of estimates available is that the net effect of integration on trade appears to have been positive. Most studies show that integration resulted in significant net internal trade creation in manufactures and many show external trade creation also resulting. Although the Common Agricultural Policy has resulted in net trade diversion in agricultural goods, this is much less than the trade creation occurring in manufactures. Economic welfare has, therefore, risen as a result of the establishment of both the EC and EFTA and from their subsequent enlargements. However, when trade effects are translated into income effects, the benefit to the citizens of the EC appears surprisingly small. One reason is that the effects are being measured in relation to the GNP/GDP of the member states, which appears small because trade is only one component of national income.

The effects are larger if account is taken of the gains from removing non-tariff barriers rather than tariffs alone. This is borne out by the studies carried out to estimate the gains from the completion of the internal market. Some further efficiency gains are also expected to have resulted from the adoption of the common currency. Furthermore, the gains appear much larger if account is taken of the dynamic, not just the static, effects. Attempts to measure these effects appear to show a sizeable gain to the EC, which is quantitatively more significant than the resource allocation effects. Cost savings from an enlarged scale of production affect the entire output of the firms producing the goods, not just the proportion of trade. Likewise, efficiency gains brought about as a result of increased competition affect a potentially much larger share of the output base than just the share that is traded. Integration also appears to result in firms restructuring their production to take advantage of the opportunities created by the larger market and in order to cope with the challenge posed by new competition.

However, integration does not affect just the level of national income; it has a positive effect on the rate at which income grows. At the very least, integration is likely to lead to faster growth in the medium term, as higher incomes lead to higher savings and investment and an enlarged capital stock. Recent developments in growth theory suggest that there might be more lasting effects, which enable all the member states participating in the integration process to grow at a permanently faster rate. Although the precise relationship between integration and growth has yet to be established, recent developments in growth theory suggest that the impact may be considerably greater than what has, in the past, been supposed. The modelling of these growth effects is clearly the major challenge for researchers of the future.

Part III   EU monetary integration

Part III covers all aspects of that far-reaching and most demanding element of integration, monetary unification, including the adoption of a single currency. The three chapters cover, respectively: the theoretical analysis of the gains and losses from economic and monetary union (EMU); the EU developments that have led to the present situation where twelve of the fifteen pre-2004 EU member nations are using the euro as their only currency and where all countries acceding after that are obliged to join them when deemed fit with Slovenia having done so on 1 January 2007; and the management of the euro by the European Central Bank and how the euro is operated.

10 The theory of monetary integration
ALI EL-AGRAA

Chapter 6 was devoted mainly to a theoretical analysis of the economic consequences of tariff removal, the establishment of the common external tariff (CET) and factor mobility, i.e. the 'common market' (CM) aspects (see chapter 1). However, it is now acknowledged that 'economic and monetary union' (EMU) is by far the most challenging commitment for any scheme of economic integration that adopts it. Therefore this and the two subsequent chapters deal in turn with: the theoretical analysis of EMU (this chapter); the current and planned development of EMU (chapter 11); and an appraisal of the operation of EMU (chapter 12). Between them, these chapters explain the reasons for the challenge as well as tracing EU endeavours in this respect.

10.1 Disentangling the concepts

One of the problems with EMU is that it is generally perceived as the acronym for European Monetary Union. This is understandable because the largest element of EMU (economic and monetary union) has been the setting up of the EU monetary union, with the establishment of a single currency, the euro, and the new central banking system to run it. The provisions of the treaty setting up EU EMU are heavily dominated by the monetary aspect and it is this which forms the heart of the present chapter.

However, in a unitary country or even a fairly weakly federal one, economic *and* monetary integration would involve having a countrywide fiscal policy as well as a single monetary policy. Arrangements vary as to how much of fiscal policy is handled at the country/federal level and how much at lower state/regional levels. But the norm is that the federal level imposes some limitations on what the states/regions can do even in very loose federations. The EU, however, has not attempted this level of integration. The centralized budget amounts to only around 1 per cent of EU GDP (see chapter 19) and at this level cannot constitute a real macroeconomic policy instrument. It is a structural budget whose form is largely set for periods of around five years. It is thus both too small and too inflexible to be used in any sense to manage the path of the EU economy in either real or nominal terms.

The EU adopts a different approach, which is to constrain the ability of the member states to run independent fiscal policies. There are three types of constraints. The first are laid down in the treaty, as part of the conditions for EMU membership – the so-called Maastricht criteria. These are considered in detail in the next chapter, but in the present context they can be regarded as constraints designed to impose prudence on fiscal policy so that no one country's debt can start to raise the interest rates/lower the credit ratings of the other EMU countries. The constraints relate to the ratio of debt to GDP as a measure of long-run sustainability and to the ratio of the government deficit to GDP in the short term.

The second set of constraints operationalize the membership requirements for the continuing behaviour of the member states inside EMU. These constraints are known as the Stability and Growth Pact (SGP) and are also dealt with in chapter 12. The coordination among the member states takes place through the framework of ECOFIN, assisted by the Commission, and includes the ability to impose financial penalties on member states that do not adhere to the prudent limits.

However, even though the SGP has the effect of coordinating fiscal policy to some extent through its constraints, the third aspect of policy among the member states is a more positive form of cooperation. This occurs through the annual setting of Broad Economic Policy Guidelines. Here, there is not only discussion among the member states to try to set a framework for policy consistent with the longer-term objectives of the EU, but also an informal dialogue between the fiscal and monetary authorities.

The ability to levy taxation is normally one of the key elements of economic independence, and the EU countries have only agreed fairly limited constraints on their individual behaviour. These relate to the nature of indirect taxation (VAT and specific duties; see chapter 15), which is largely a facet of the treatment of trade and the 'internal market' discussed in chapter 7. It is proving very difficult to get agreements on the nature of the taxation of income from capital and of company profits. Discussion of agreements on the levels of taxation of personal incomes is even further from practical realization, as the range between the highest and lowest is very large (chapter 15). It has, however, been possible to get agreement that reductions in the level of non-wage taxes on labour would assist the overall EU economic strategy.

Taken together, these measures represent rather soft and limited coordination, which affects the nature of the theoretical discussion on monetary integration. Fiscal policy in the EU is neither a single coordinated policy nor a set of uncoordinated national policies run for the individual benefit of each member state. Indeed the degree of automatic or discretionary coordination is difficult to estimate before the event. This makes the assessment of the impact of monetary integration a somewhat uncertain exercise.

10.2 What is monetary integration?

Monetary integration has two essential components: an exchange rate union and capital (K) market integration. An exchange rate union is established when member countries have what is in effect one currency. The actual existence of one currency is not necessary, however, because, if member countries have *permanently* and *irrevocably* fixed exchange rates among themselves with currencies *costlessly* exchangeable at par, the result is effectively the same. But having a single currency makes the aspect of permanence and irrevocability more plausible as there would be severe repercussions from exit, not least the need to produce new coins and notes. Giving the impression of permanence is a crucial ingredient for such fixed exchange rate regimes. Hence, those like 'currency boards', which permit the continuation of more than one currency, tend to back one currency with the other. This then offers full adoption of the backing currency as the likely way out of a crisis rather than a breaking of the union. In the same way, exchange-rate unions between more equal partners have tended to back the two currencies by a common medium, such as silver or gold. Again this offers a more rather than less unifying way forward.

Exchange rate integration requires convertibility: the *permanent* absence of all exchange controls for both current and K transactions, including interest and dividend payments (and the harmonization of relevant taxes and measures affecting the K market) within the union. It is, of course, absolutely necessary to have complete convertibility for trade transactions, otherwise an important requirement of customs union (CU) formation is threatened, namely the promotion of free trade amongst members, which is an integral part of an economic union – see chapter 1. That is why this aspect of monetary integration does not need any discussion; it applies even in the case of a free trade area (FTA). Convertibility for K transactions is related to free factor mobility (see chapter 8) and is therefore an important aspect of K market integration which is necessary in CMs, but not in simple CUs or FTAs. Nevertheless the pattern of both trade and production will be affected if there are controls on K transactions.

In practice, monetary integration should specifically include three elements if it is to qualify under this definition:

1. an explicit harmonization of monetary policies
2. a common pool of foreign exchange reserves
3. a single central bank or monetary authority.

There are important reasons for including these elements. Suppose union members decide either that one of their currencies will be a reference currency or that a new unit of account will be established. Also assume that each member country has its own foreign exchange reserves and conducts its own monetary and fiscal policies. If a member finds itself running out of reserves, it will want to engage in a monetary and fiscal contraction sufficient to restore the reserve position. Both these actions and the failure to undertake them could put pressure on the exchange rate. This will necessitate the fairly frequent meeting of the Finance Ministers or central bank governors, to consider whether or not to change the parity of the reference currency. If they do decide to change it, then all the member currencies will have to move with it (and with any consequent shifts compared to other currencies). Such a situation could create the sorts of difficulty that plagued the Bretton Woods system:

1. Each Finance Minister might fight for the rate of exchange that is most suitable for his/her country. Any such rate would be conceived relative to the others. If they also wanted to move, then this would become a rather involved set of contingent positions. This might make bargaining hard; agreement might become difficult to reach and the whole system might be subject to continuous strain.
2. Each meeting might be accompanied by speculation about its outcome. This might result in destabilizing speculative private K movements into or out of the union.
3. The difficulties created by (1) and (2) might result in the reference currency being permanently fixed relative to outside currencies, e.g. the US dollar.
4. However, the system does allow for the possibility of the reference currency floating relative to non-member currencies or floating within a band. If the reference currency does float, it might do so in response to conditions in its own market. However, this would only be the case if the union required the monetary authorities in the partner countries to vary their exchange rates so as to maintain constant parities relative to the reference currency. They would then have

to buy and sell the reserve currency so as to maintain or bring about the necessary exchange-rate alteration. Therefore, the monetary authorities of the reference currency would, in fact, be able to determine the exchange rate for the whole union (except in so far as the other members could also deal in third currencies).

5. Such a system does not guarantee the permanence of the parities between the union currencies that is required by the appropriate specification of monetary integration. There is the possibility that the delegates will not reach agreement, or that one of the partners might finally choose not to deflate to the extent necessary to maintain its rate at the required parity, or that a partner in surplus might choose neither to build up its reserves nor to inflate as required and so might allow its rate to rise above the agreed level.

In order to avoid such difficulties, it is necessary to include in monetary integration the three elements specified. The central bank (or monetary authority) would operate in the market so that the exchange parities are permanently maintained among the union currencies and, at the same time, it would allow the rate of the reference currency to fluctuate, or to alter intermittently, relative to the outside reserve currency. For instance, if the foreign exchange reserves in the common pool were running down, the common central bank could allow the reference currency, and with it all the partner currencies, to depreciate. This would have the advantage of economizing in the use of foreign exchange reserves, since not all partners would tend to be in deficit or surplus simultaneously (see below). Also surplus countries would automatically be helping deficit countries inside the exchange rate area: co-responsibility is of the essence.

However, without explicit policy coordination, a monetary union would not be effective. If each country conducted its own monetary policy, and could engage in as much domestic credit as it wished, surplus countries would be financing deficit nations without any incentives for the deficit countries to restore equilibrium. If one country ran a large deficit, the union exchange rate would depreciate, but this might put some partner countries into surplus. If wage rates were rising in the member countries at different rates, while productivity growth did not differ in such a way as to offset the effects on relative prices, those partners with the lower inflation rates would be permanently financing the other partners.

In short, monetary integration, as defined, requires the unification and joint management of monetary policy as well as of the union's external exchange-rate policy. This has two further consequences. First, the rate of increase of the money supply must be decided jointly. Beyond an agreed amount of credit expansion, allocated to the central bank of each member nation, a member state would have to finance any budget deficit in the union's K market at the ruling interest rate. A unified monetary policy would eliminate one of the main reasons for disparate price level movements in the members, and a major factor for the prevalence of intra-union payment imbalances prior to monetary union. Second, the balance of payments of the entire union with the outside world must be regulated at the union level. For this purpose the monetary authority must dispose of a common pool of exchange reserves, and the union exchange rates with other currencies must be regulated at the union level.

Monetary integration which explicitly included these three requirements would therefore enable the partners to do away with all these problems right from the start. Incidentally, this also suggests the advantages of having a single currency: with a single currency the members can all have a say in the setting of policy. With a reference currency, the tendency will always be for the country whose currency it is to dominate the decision-making, as the others will have to follow or leave the arrangement. A tighter arrangement is likely to give them explicit rights in decision-making, perhaps even including a veto.

10.3 The gains and losses

10.3.1 Gains from EMU

The gains from EMU membership could be purely economic, non-economic (e.g. political) or both. Some of the non-economic benefits are obvious; for example, it is difficult to imagine that a complete political union could become a reality without the establishment of a monetary union. However, because political, security and other issues lie beyond the scope of this chapter, the discussion will be confined to the economic benefits, which can be briefly summarized as follows:

1. As already mentioned, the common pool of foreign exchange reserves has the incidental advantage of economizing in their use, since it is unlikely that member nations will go into deficit *simultaneously*, so one country's surplus can offset another's deficit. Intra-union trade transactions will no longer be financed by foreign exchange, so the need for foreign exchange is reduced for any given trade pattern. Frankel and Rose (2002) argue that having EMU will in itself lead to an increase in intra-trade at the expense of trade with non-members. In the EU context, this will reduce the role of the US dollar or reduce EU dependence on the dollar.

2. In the case of the EU, the adoption of the common currency (the euro) may transform that currency into a major world medium able to compete with the US dollar or Japanese yen. The advantages of such a currency from seignorage are well established, but not huge. How long it would take the euro, if it were even possible, to supplant much of the role of the US dollar as an international vehicle currency is of course a moot point.

   One facet of having a second major currency to compete with the US dollar is that international market conditions can become more, or less, stable depending upon whether the two authorities decide to cooperate or permit major swings. Since, for a large currency bloc, foreign trade forms a small proportion of total transactions, wide swings in exchange rates can be accommodated with limited impact on the overall economy. These swings can have more striking effects on smaller countries, so large currency areas normally feel an obligation to consider the wider implications. Indeed, the group of seven (G7; now G8) was created in 1986 to establish a system of international coordination between the most advanced nations in the world for precisely such a reason.

3. Another source of gain could be a reduction in the cost of financial management (see below). Monetary integration should enable the overhead costs of financial transactions to be spread more widely. Also, some of the activities of the institutions dealing in foreign exchanges might be discontinued, leading to a saving in the use of resources. These gains are, however, thought to be a fraction of a percentage point of GDP (the EU Commission estimated them in 1990 at 0.2–0.5 per cent of EU GDP), but there is normally a clear interest rate gain for the smaller and previously high-inflation countries without any noticeable downside for the larger ones, if the area as a whole has credible institutions and policies.

4. There are also the classical advantages of having permanently fixed exchange rates (or one currency) among EMU members for free trade and factor movements. Stability of exchange rates enhances trade, through reduced price uncertainty (see below), encourages K to move to where it is most productively rewarded, and ensures that labour (L) will move to where the highest rewards prevail, *other things being equal*. Of course hedging can tackle the problem of exchange-rate fluctuations, but at a cost. Here again, however, the evidence suggests that hedging costs and penalties from uncertainty are relatively minor, except for smaller companies that tend not to hedge. The much greater advantage is that it seems to cement integration, encouraging greater trade and FDI than would be expected just from all the other economic variables; this is shown very clearly in the gravity model literature (see Mélitz, 2001).

5. The integration of the K market has a further advantage. If an EMU member is in deficit, it can borrow directly on the union market or raise its rate of interest to attract K inflow and therefore ease the situation. However, as mentioned above, the integration of economic policies within the union ensures that this help will occur automatically under the auspices of the common central bank. Fiscal transfers and continuing private sector transfers, as with retirement areas, can support indefinite deficits with no strain on the system.

6. When a monetary union establishes a central fiscal authority with its own budget, then, as already mentioned, the larger the size of this budget, the higher the scope for fiscal harmonization (CEC, 1977a and chapter 19). This has some advantages: regional deviations from internal balance can be financed from the centre and the centralization of social security payments, financed by contributions or taxes on a progressive basis, would have some stabilizing and compensating effects, modifying the harmful effects of EMU (see chapter 19).

Specific to the EU, there are also negative advantages in that EMU is helpful for maintaining the EU as it exists. For example, realizing the 'single market', i.e. making prices transparent (see below), would become more difficult to achieve and the common agricultural prices enshrined in the Common Agricultural Policy (CAP; see chapter 20) would become more complicated when members' exchange rates were flexible. These EMU benefits are clear and there are few economists who would question them; the only disagreement is about their extent (see above and chapter 7). However, there is no consensus with regard to the costs.

10.3.2 Losses from EMU

The losses from EMU have been elaborated in terms of the theory of optimum currency areas (OCAs), pioneered by Mundell (1961), with immediate contributions coming from McKinnon (1963) and Kenen (1969) and followed by, inter alia, Mundell (1973a, b) himself and, within the context of the UK and the euro, Buiter (2000) and Barrel (2002). The theory today is a body reflecting all the contributions to date, but given the broader nature of this text, this section is confined to a presentation of its main message; those interested in a comprehensive coverage should consult de Grauwe (2005).

Before presenting the bare OCA essentials, it may prove helpful to begin with later contributions by Fleming (1971) and Corden (1972a). Assume that the world consists of three countries: the home country (*H*), the potential partner country (*P*), and the rest of the world (*W*). Also assume that, in order to maintain both internal and external equilibrium (as defined in standard open-economy macroeconomics), *H* needs to devalue its currency relative to *W*, while *P* needs to revalue vis-à-vis *W*. Moreover, assume that *H* and *P* use fiscal and monetary policies for achieving internal equilibrium. If *H* and *P* were partners in EMU, they would devalue together (which is consistent with *H*'s policy requirements in isolation) or revalue together (which is consistent with *P*'s requirements in isolation), but they would not be able to alter the rate of exchange in a way that was consistent with both. Under such circumstances, the alteration in the exchange rate could leave *H* with an external deficit, forcing it to deflate its economy, increasing or creating unemployment, or it could leave it with a surplus, forcing it into accumulating foreign reserves or allowing its prices and wages to rise. If countries deprive themselves of rates of exchange (or trade impediments) as policy instruments, they impose on themselves losses that are essentially the losses emanating from *enforced departure from internal balance* (Corden, 1972a).

In short, the rationale for retaining flexibility in the rates of exchange rests on the assumption that governments aim to achieve both internal and external balance, and, as Tinbergen (1952) has shown, to achieve these *simultaneously* at least an equal number of instruments is needed. This can be explained in the following manner. Internal equilibrium is tackled via financial instruments, which have their greatest impact on the level of aggregate demand, and the exchange rate is used to achieve external equilibrium. Of course, financial instruments can be activated via both monetary and fiscal policies and may have a varied impact on both internal and external equilibrium. Given this understanding, the case for maintaining flexibility in exchange rates depends entirely on the presumption that the loss of one of the two policy instruments will conflict with the achievement of both internal and external equilibrium.

With this in mind, it is vital to follow the Corden–Fleming explanation of the enforced departure from internal equilibrium. Suppose a country is initially in internal equilibrium but has a deficit in its external account. If the country were free to vary its rate of exchange, the appropriate policy for it to adopt for achieving overall balance would be a combination of devaluation and expenditure reduction. When the rate of exchange is not available as a policy instrument, it is necessary to reduce expenditure by more than is required in the optimal situation, which results in extra unemployment. This *excess* unemployment, which can be valued in terms of output or some more direct measure of welfare, is the cost to that country of depriving itself of the exchange rate as a policy instrument. The extent of this loss is determined, *ceteris paribus*, by the marginal propensity to import and to consume exportables, or, more generally, by the marginal propensity to consume tradeables relative to non-tradeables (supply-side responses can, of course, mitigate any losses).

The expenditure reduction which is required for eliminating the initial external deficit will be smaller the higher the marginal propensity to import (see below). Moreover, the higher the marginal propensity to import, the less the effect of that reduction in expenditure on demand for domestically produced commodities. For both reasons, therefore, the higher the marginal propensity to import, the less domestic unemployment will result from abandoning the devaluation of the rate of exchange as a policy instrument. If the logic of this explanation is correct, it follows that as long as the marginal propensity to consume domestic goods is greater than zero, there will be some cost due to fixing the rate of exchange. A similar argument applies to a country which cannot use the exchange-rate instrument when it has a surplus in its external account and internal equilibrium: the required excess expenditure will have little effect on demand for domestically produced goods and will therefore exert little inflationary pressure if the country's marginal propensity to import is high.

This analysis is based on the assumption that there exists a trade-off between rates of change in costs and in levels of unemployment – the 'Phillips

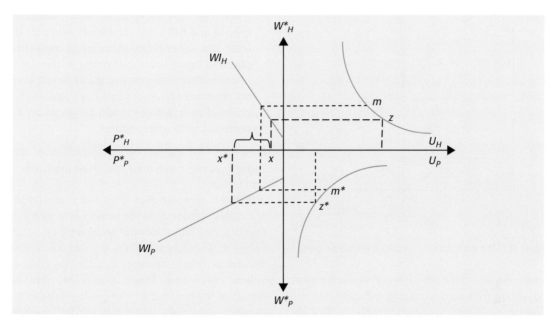

Figure 10.1 The Fleming–Corden analysis of monetary integration

curve'. Assuming that there is a Phillips (1958) curve relationship (a negative response of rates of change in money wages – W^* – and the level of unemployment – U), the Fleming–Corden analysis can be explained by using a simple diagram adapting one devised by de Grauwe (1975). Hence, in figure 10.1, the top half depicts the position of H while the lower half that of P. The upper and lower right-hand corners represent the two countries' Phillips curves, while the remaining quadrants show their inflation rates corresponding to the rates of change in wages – P^*. WI (which stands for *wage-rate change* and corresponding *inflation*) is determined by the share of L in total GNP, the rate of change in the productivity of L and the degree of competition in both the factor and the commodity markets, with perfect competition resulting in the WIs being straight lines. Note that the intersection of the WIs with the vertical axes will be determined by rates of change of L's share in GNP and its rate of productivity change. The diagram has been drawn on the presumption that the L productivity changes are positive.

The diagram is drawn in such a way that countries H and P differ in all respects: the positions of their Phillips curves, their preferred trade-offs

between W^* and P^*, and their rates of productivity growth. H has a lower rate of inflation (x), than P (x^*), equilibrium being at z and z^*. Hence, without EMU, P's currency should depreciate relative to H's; there is a minute chance that the two countries' inflation rates would coincide. Altering the exchange rates would then enable each country to maintain its preferred internal equilibrium: z and z^* for countries H and P, respectively.

When H and P enter EMU, their inflation rates cannot differ from each other, given a model without traded goods. Each country will therefore have to settle for a combination of U and P^* which is different from what it would have liked (m and m^*). The Fleming–Corden conclusion is thus vindicated.

However, this analysis rests entirely on the acceptance of the Phillips curve, which consensus today depicts as crude, at best. This is because many economists no longer believe that there is a fundamental trade-off between unemployment and inflation. If there is any relationship, it must be a short-term one such that the rate of unemployment is in the long term independent of the rate of inflation: there is a 'natural rate of unemployment' (NRU, generally referred to as NAIRU, defined as the 'non-accelerating inflation rate of

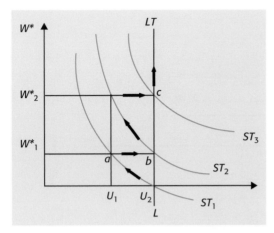

Figure 10.2 The expectations-augmented Phillips curve

unemployment', i.e. the rate of unemployment consistent with an unchanging inflation rate; see Stiglitz, 1997), which is determined by rigidities in the L market. Thus the simple version of the Phillips curve has been replaced by an expectations-augmented one along the lines suggested by Phelps (1968) and Friedman (1975), i.e. the Phillips curves become vertical in the long run. This is shown in figure 10.2, which depicts three Phillips curves for one of the two countries. Assume that unemployment is initially at point U_2, i.e. the rate of inflation is equal to zero, given the short-term Phillips curve indicated by ST_1. The expectations-augmented Phillips curve suggests that, if the government tries to lower unemployment by the use of monetary policy, the short-term effect will be to move to point a, with positive inflation and lower unemployment. However, in the long term, people will adjust their expectations, causing an upward shift of the Phillips curve to ST_2 which leads to equilibrium at point b. The initial level of unemployment is thus restored but with a higher rate of inflation. A repetition of this process gives the vertical long-term curve labelled LT.

If both H and P have vertical LT curves, figure 10.1 will have to be adjusted to give figure 10.3. The implications of this are:

1. EMU will have no long-term effects on either partner's rate of unemployment since this will be fixed at the appropriate NAIRU for each country – U_H, U_P.

2. If EMU is adopted to bring about balanced growth and NRU, this can be achieved only if, inter alia, other policy instruments are introduced to bring about uniformity in the two L markets. This is, however, only a necessary condition; other aspects of similarity in tastes and production structures would be necessary to make it a sufficient condition.

Therefore, this alternative interpretation of the Phillips curve invalidates the Fleming–Corden conclusion.

It should be noted that Allen and Kenen (1980) and Allen (1983) have demonstrated, using a sophisticated and elaborate model with financial assets, that, although monetary policy has severe drawbacks as an instrument for adjusting cyclical imbalances within EMU, it may be able to influence the demand for the goods produced by member countries in a differential manner within the short term, provided the markets of the member nations are not too closely integrated. Their model indicates that EMU, in this sense, can come about as a consequence of the substitutability between nations' commodities, especially their financial assets, and of country biases in the purchase of commodities and financial assets. The moral is that the EMU central bank can operate monetary policies in such a manner as to have differing impacts on the various partner countries and thus achieve real effects without compromising their internal and external equilibria. Moreover, once non-traded goods are incorporated into the model and/or K and L mobility is allowed for, it follows that the losses due to deviating from internal equilibrium vanish, a point which Corden (1972a, 1977) readily acknowledged. Finally, this model does not allow for the fact that EMU involves at least three countries, i.e. W has to be explicitly included in the model. Allen and Kenen (1980) tried to develop a model along these lines, but their model is not a straightforward extension of that depicted in figure 10.1.

To recap, it may be helpful to clarify some misconceptions and highlight others:

1. The fixity of exchange-rate parities within EMU does not mean that the different member currencies cannot vary in unison relative to

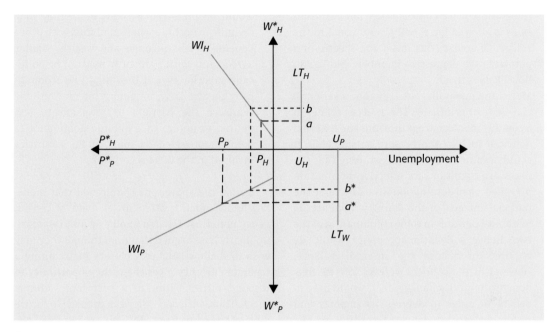

Figure 10.3 Monetary integration with expectations-augmented Phillips curves

extra-union currencies; the adoption of one currency by the union would clearly show that.

2. In a proper EMU, an extra deficit for one region (country) can come about only as a result of a revaluation of the union currency – the union as a whole has an external surplus vis-à-vis the outside world. Such an act would increase the foreign exchange earnings of the surplus region, therefore of the union as a whole, provided that the conditions for a successful revaluation existed. The integration of monetary policies through the common central bank will ensure that the extra burden on the first region is alleviated: the overall extra earnings will be used to help the region with the extra deficit. Such a situation may lead to surplus regions financing those in deficit indefinitely, but that is not likely.

3. One can perhaps think of the reservations in terms of Tinbergen's criterion of an equal number of policy instruments and objectives (see above). Although a country may lose an instrument individually, it is gaining other instruments from other aspects of EMU. The union as a whole does not lose the exchange rate route of adjustment (1 above). A voluntary EMU of depth is likely to offer a sufficient degree of 'political' union for unacceptably adverse effects on a particular country or part of it to be recognized and acted upon. When countries are in a voluntary union they will be prepared, within limits, to act in favour of other members, even when it is not in their immediate economic interest. Next time it may be they who would benefit from the voluntary assistance of others. Taking either a legalistic view of what actions union agreements lay down or a relatively short-run perspective of economic gains can be misleading. Ultimately, the alternative would be that the member would leave the union, which could also harm the other members and threaten the credibility of the union thereafter. Relevance to reality therefore requires taking a somewhat broader view of the policy problem.

4. Devaluation can work effectively only when there is 'money illusion', but are today's trade unionists so deluded?

5. In practice there would never be a separation between the exchange-rate union and K market

integration. Once convertibility for K transactions is allowed for, K will always come to the rescue. Of course, this raises the spectre of a permanently depressed member, but again how likely is that?

6. More fundamentally, but arguably, a very crucial element is missing. The analysis relates to a country in internal equilibrium and external deficit. If such a country were outside EMU, it could devalue its currency. Assuming that the necessary conditions for effective devaluation prevailed, then devaluation would increase the national income of the country, increase its price level or result in some combination of the two. Hence a deflationary policy would be required to restore the internal balance. However, if the country were to lose its freedom to alter its exchange rate, it would have to deflate in order to depress its imports and restore external balance. According to the above analysis, this alternative would entail unemployment in excess of that prevailing in the initial situation. The missing element in this argument can be found by specifying how devaluation actually works. Devaluation of a country's currency results in changes in relative price levels and is price inflationary for, at least, both exportables and importables. These relative price changes, given the necessary stability conditions, will depress imports and (perhaps) increase exports. The deflationary policy which is required (to accompany devaluation) in order to restore internal balance should therefore eliminate the *newly injected* inflation as well as the *extra* national income. Only if the 'inflationary' implications of devaluation are completely disregarded, can one reach the a priori conclusion that membership of EMU would necessitate extra sacrifice of employment in order to achieve the same target.

7. Even within a purely economic context, there will be a limit to how far the argument over the costs for a country from forgoing the ability to have its own exchange rate and monetary policy will go. The whole net benefit of the increased integration has to be taken into account. Hence, even if the rates of inflation and unemployment differed from those that would be preferred without EMU, they may dwindle to nothing when combined with other benefits to real incomes and wealth. Similar agreements with parts of W may not be politically superior even if they might be economically so. Similarly, monetary integration may reinforce the barriers to reversion to less desired examples of economic dominance (a point emphasized by some of the countries involved in the 2004 accession).

Against the above, one should add that monetary independence offers an element of contingency planning. Sweden explicitly and Denmark implicitly have argued that even though they may wish to shadow EMU very closely, maintaining a separate currency gives them the opportunity to respond rather better to a very large adverse shock. Thus, with care, they can manage to secure most of the gains from EMU and yet retain an element of flexibility.

10.3.3 Back to OCAs

OCA is generally presented in terms of national incomes and prices, relegating wages to the background. This is useful, since it provides a complementary picture to the above analysis, ensuring a better understanding, but of course inevitably leading to overlaps. Mundell (1961) attributed the loss to a shift in demand, due say to a change in consumer preferences, away from P, in favour of H. This is depicted (not by Mundell) in figure 10.4, where the vertical axis measures prices (P_H, P_p), the horizontal, the level of national economic activity (Y_H, Y_p), and D and S are, respectively, the aggregate national supply and demand curves. The two countries are initially in the equilibrium situations depicted by the solid S and D curves (D_H^1, S_H^1 for H and D_p^1, S_p^1 for P), with H at A^* (i.e. income Y_H^e) and P at A (income Y_p^e). The indicated shifts in demand (the dotted lines D_H^2 and D_p^2; follow the blank arrows) mean that H moves to the right while P moves to the left. Thus the equilibrium points move to B^* and B respectively, i.e. H experiences an increase in Y, hence in employment, while P experiences the opposite, i.e. an increase in unemployment. As mentioned

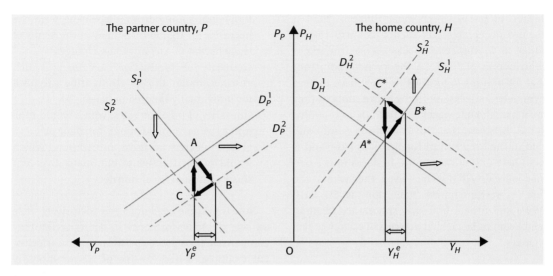

Figure 10.4 Shifts in EMU partners' aggregate supply and demand

above, it is the extent of these deviations from equilibrium Y_H^e and Y_P^e that constitute the costs of EMU for the two partners.

Given that the original income levels (Y_H^e; Y_P^e), hence of employment/unemployment, were the nations' desired ones, the question is then how to restore them. As above, there are two ways to do so. The first is that if *wages are flexible* in both countries, then the increased level of economic activity in H will push H's wages up, while the increased unemployment in P will depress P wages. The result will be an upward shift in S in H to S_H^2 (since S reflects costs, which have risen with increased wages) and a downward shift in P to S_P^2. The figure has been drawn in such a way that the new equilibrium positions (C^* and C) precisely restore the original Y levels (A^* and A) but of course increase H's price level and reduce P's. These price changes will stimulate demand in P and depress it in H and their change relative to each other in favour of P will result in reinforcing shifts in demand that take both countries back to their original curves (D_H^1, D_P^1), i.e. to points A^* and A.

The second is that if *labour (L) can move freely* between the two countries, then those losing jobs in P will migrate to H. The reduction (increase) in L in P (H) will enable both countries to maintain their initial wages; thus they can stay at B^* and B. Of course, this means different income levels from

the initial ones, but there is no disequilibrium due to the changes in L endowments.

What happens if wages are inflexible and L is immobile? Obviously, equilibrium in P will remain at C. In H, however, the increase in D will lead to increases in wages and shift the S curve upwards, resulting in higher prices there. Hence, H has to bear the full brunt of the adjustment, through higher prices, i.e. higher inflation. These increased prices will, again, make P products more competitive, leading to shifts in demand in their favour. The upshot is that, by being a member of EMU, H will have to accept higher inflation than it desired.

But how would the two countries fare outside EMU? If they followed a freely flexible exchange rate system, H would raise its interest rate, depressing demand, while P would do the opposite, enhancing demand. These policy changes lead to an appreciation of H's currency and a depreciation of P's, enhancing the competitiveness of P products in the H markets. The interest and exchange rate changes will thus enhance demand in P and depress it in H. The net effect of these policy changes is to shift the demand curves back to their original levels and restore equilibrium, i.e. go back to A^* and A.

This is the same conclusion reached above: as a member of EMU, a country will have to either persevere with more unemployment than it desired or put up with more inflation than it deemed acceptable, i.e. such a country cannot adjust to 'asymmetric' shocks. Hence, the major contribution of the OCA theory is to point out that for nations to form OCAs, they have to have 'symmetric' shocks, or, in the above context, they must have flexible wages and free labour mobility. Recall, however, that this conclusion is null and void in the long run in the previous case, and is valid here only if the change in demand is a permanent reality (if it is short-lived, then what is the fuss? – see de Grauwe, 2005); for the EU, Gros (1996) and others find that shocks are sectoral, hence cannot be tackled in terms of exchange rate changes.

10.3.4 OCA in a nutshell

The previous section considered explicitly only two prerequisites of OCA. Instead of doing likewise with others, here they are simply enumerated. This is because they have already been tackled.

The OCA message is very simple: two countries would benefit from having a single currency when the macroeconomic gains of lower transaction costs, elimination of exchange rate risks and enhanced price transparency outweigh the costs of adjusting to country-specific (asymmetric) shocks due to loss of control over their own interest and exchange rates. The theory sets out the conditions that would ensure this outcome:

1. price/wage flexibility, which would enable markets to clear fully, thus eliminating the need for the lost policy instruments;
2. labour/capital mobility, which would fully compensate for the adjustments that the lost policy instruments would achieve;
3. financial market integration, which would cater for inter-area payments imbalances and enhance long-term adjustment through wealth effects;
4. open economies, meaning members have high exports/income ratios and trade mainly with each other, thus would benefit from fixed exchange rates between them;
5. variety of goods and services, which would insulate against fluctuations in the demand for individual commodities, dispensing with the necessity for frequent changes in the terms of trade by way of exchange rate changes;
6. similarity of production structures, which ensures similar shocks, eliminating the need for individually tailored policies;
7. similarity of inflation rates, which would minimize the need for payment imbalances;
8. greater degree of fiscal integration, which would make it easier to eliminate divergent shocks through fiscal transfers.

Note that these need not apply inclusively since an acceptable performance in one criterion may compensate for a poorer performance on another. For example, a high degree of labour mobility would reduce the need for a high degree of wage flexibility. Also note, importantly, that these criteria say nothing about the gains from integration (above), but the next section does so.

Before we proceed, however, it should be added that when Mundell was receiving the Nobel Prize for economics in 1999, he was labelled a 'father' of Europe's EMU. How can this be when his analysis has been so sceptical? The answer is that in 1973 (1973a), he added a new dimension to his analysis: EMU provides an 'insurance mechanism' enabling members to manage asymmetric shocks better relative to having their own exchange rate uncertainty outside. Suppose members experience a temporary asymmetric shock. Inside EMU, consumers in the adversely affected country can borrow automatically from a member nation to mitigate their circumstances. In the absence of EMU, the existence of separate monies and uncertain exchange rates would deter the lenders; hence temporary shocks cannot be alleviated. Also, under uncertainty, movements in the exchanges themselves may be the cause of asymmetric shocks, rather than enabling members to cope with them. Theoretical considerations apart, in 2006 Mundell not only offered a positive assessment of the euro's performance (see box 10.1), but has added an interesting twist: 'Labour mobility is an important escape valve . . . but it isn't the end-all of the theory of optimum currency areas. Even if every European were completely immobile, rooted in one place, it wouldn't mean that Europe

Box 10.1 Mundell defends the euro

Mundell fiercely defends [the euro's] track record. 'In all aspects in which it was expected economically to make an improvement, it has performed spectacularly.'

He argues that every citizen in the euro area has a better currency than before, one that vies with the dollar in its prestige and stability. Every firm now has access to a capital market that is continental in scope. With the elimination of exchange rate uncertainty between members of the euro area, there aren't any more speculative capital movements within the euro area, and interest rates have become equalized. (Note that instead of double-digit interest rates for many of the countries, they are now at or below 5 per cent.) Every country in the euro area has a better monetary and fiscal policy mix than before. The possibility of a surprise inflation-cum-devaluation has been ruled out, and hedge funds can't make a dime between euro countries. And information and transaction costs have plummeted . . . clearing a path for a vast increase in the most beneficial type of intra-area trade and payments (Wallace, 2006).

should have 300 million currencies, one currency for each person' (Wallace, 2006).

10.4 A 'popular' cost approach

As mentioned, the OCA theory takes into account the pure economic costs and benefits of EMU and also examines the trade-offs between them. Here, a simple version, made popular in the context of the discussions concerning the euro as the single currency for the EU, is presented. It is known as the 'impossible trilogy' or 'inconsistent trinity' principle.

The principle states that only two out of the following three are mutually compatible:

1. completely free capital mobility
2. an independent monetary policy
3. a fixed exchange rate.

This is because, with full capital mobility, a nation's own interest rate is tied to the world interest rate, at least for a country too small to influence global financial markets. More precisely, any difference between the domestic and world interest rates must be matched by an expected rate of depreciation of the exchange rate. For example, if the interest rate is 6 per cent in the domestic market, but 4 per cent in the world market, the global market must expect the currency to depreciate by 2 per cent this year. This is known as the 'interest parity condition', which implies that integrated financial markets equalize expected asset returns; hence assets denominated in a currency expected to depreciate must offer an exactly compensating higher yield for the expected depreciation.

Under such circumstances, a country that wants to conduct an independent monetary policy, raising or lowering its interest rate to control its level of employment/unemployment, must allow its exchange rate to fluctuate in the market. Conversely, a country confronted with full capital mobility, which wants to fix its exchange rate, must set its domestic interest rate to be exactly equal to the rate in the country to which it pegs its currency. Since monetary policy is then determined abroad, the country has effectively lost its monetary independence.

The loss caused by EMU membership is as already indicated, but here its extent is determined by the combined Mundell–McKinnon–Kenen (respectively, 1961, 1963 and 1969) criteria, which render price adjustments through exchange rate changes less effective or less compelling:

(a) openness to mutual trade
(b) diverse economies
(c) mobility of factors of production, especially of labour.

Greater openness to mutual trade implies that most prices would be determined at the union level, which means that relative prices would be less susceptible to being influenced by changes in the exchange rate. An economy more diverse in terms of production would be less likely to suffer from country-specific shocks, reducing the need for the exchange rate as a policy tool. Greater factor mobility enables the economy to tackle *asymmetric shocks* via migration, hence reducing the need for adjustment through the exchange rate.

The EU nations score well on the first criterion since the ratio of their exports to their GDP is 20–70 per cent (combining both exports and imports for 2001 gives the EU 12.3 per cent, with Belgium 91.7 per cent and France, Germany, Italy and the UK around 30 per cent), while that for the USA and Japan is, respectively, 11 per cent (13.5) and 7 per cent (10.8). Note that the US is the preferred reference nation, but there is no evidence that it is an OCA (de Grauwe, 2005, and references cited there). They also score well in terms of the second criterion, even though they are not all as well endowed with oil or gas resources as the Netherlands and Britain. As to the third criterion, they score badly in comparison with the US since EU labour mobility is lower (see chapter 8) due to, inter alia, the Europeans' tendency to stick to their place of birth, not only nationally but also regionally. There is also a tendency for migration to be temporary and only involve part of a larger family (see chapter 8).

Although there is no definitive estimate of the costs due to the relative lack of labour mobility, it is generally thought to be considerable. However, it would have to be very large to offset the gains from EMU. In any case, much of the problem from lack of mobility is as relevant within the member states as between them and this applies to the US too. It therefore requires addressing through structural policy in each member state regardless of EMU, or regardless of membership of the EU itself for that matter. Tackling the problem has become more important since the late 1960s and will remain so in the face of faster rates of technical change in products and production methods; in part, it is a consequence of globalization, but that is not an aspect of economic integration.

Nonetheless, even on purely economic grounds alone, the longer-term perspective will not lend support to some of the more pessimistic assessments. Consider, for example, Krugman's (1990) model, which utilizes such a perspective when examining the costs and benefits of EMU. In figure 10.5, the costs are represented by line CC and the

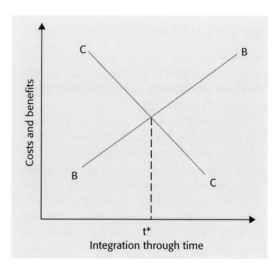

Figure 10.5 Krugman's (1990) cost-benefits of EMU

benefits by line BB and both are expressed in relation to GDP. The benefits from the single currency are shown to rise with integration, since, for example, intra-EU trade, which has been rising with integration over time (see above, Tables 5.11 and 5.12 and El-Agraa, 1999), will be conducted at lesser costs (Frankel and Rose, 2002), while the losses from ceding the exchange rate as a policy variable decline with time. In the economic jargon used above, changes in the exchange rate are needed to absorb asymmetric shocks but these will decline with time, becoming less asymmetric as integration proceeds and becomes more intensive. In short, as the member economies become more integrated, the use of the exchange rate instrument for variations against member nations' currencies would become undesirable. Thus, for countries seriously and permanently involved in EMU, sooner or later a time would arrive when the benefits will exceed the costs. All this is tantamount to stating that the OCA concept is non-operational, if not altogether irrelevant; indeed, a very long time ago, Corden (1972b) castigated it as one of 'feasibility', rather than 'optimality', and although Bayoumi and Eichengreen (1996) developed methods for identifying the suitability of various EU nations for EMU, their method only succeeds in ranking suitability rather than calculating actual costs/benefits, which would indicate where the line separating included from excluded countries should be (see Capie and Wood in El-Agraa, 2002b).

In many respects the key policy choice issue relates to uncertainty about the future. If a prospective member of EMU could be certain that the economies would grow more closely together, in the sense of becoming more economically similar, and that the chance of having a serious external shock that affects only one of them or both in opposite directions, then worries about a single monetary policy being inappropriate would be reduced, i.e. symmetry would be enhanced.

However, a priori, such developments can only be assessed; they cannot be known. Moreover, OCA analysis tends to ignore the fact that behaviour is likely to change after the event and assesses net EMU benefits on the basis of *ex ante* behaviour. Mayes and Suvanto (2002) take this even further and argue that in the case of Finland, for example, one of the factors swaying the authorities in favour of EMU membership is that it would force generally favourable changes in labour market behaviour. In other words, knowing that the exchange rate mechanism is not available to accommodate asymmetric shocks may actually cause people to change their behaviour so that the impact of the shocks is reduced to acceptable levels.

Furthermore, there is a tendency to ignore positive asymmetric shocks. In such cases the impact of the favourable shock will be magnified by EMU membership. Out of the union, such a shock would increase the demand for the currency as investors from other countries sought to join in the benefits. The surge in demand would probably push the domestic central bank into raising interest rates to head off any inflationary pressure, thereby also raising the exchange rate and reducing the expected rate of growth. Inside EMU, the capital inflow will have a much more limited impact on the exchange rate as it relates only to a part of the union. Similarly the response of monetary policy will be negligible. Knowing that there will be no offsetting policy changes will in turn help keep down inflationary pressures. Such an experience seems to have occurred with the favourable

technology shock or 'Nokia phenomenon' in Finland. The growth/inflation combination that occurred in the early EMU years was considerably more favourable than that which prevailed in earlier decades. Other factors such as the continuing impact of the collapse of the former Soviet Union and the banking crisis in the early 1990s may also have been influential but the evidence is at the very least suggestive.

10.5 A concluding remark

This chapter has gone to some lengths to emphasize three facets of EMU – the wider process of economic and monetary integration that has been dominating the integration process in Europe over the last decade and more. These are:

1. The rationale for current steps in EMU has to be seen in the light of both the longer term and the wider political context. Narrow short-run economic assessments can make the decisions that have been taken look illogical.

2. EMU is expected to change the behaviour and structure of the European economy. Assessment of the likely impact therefore has to include these structural changes. Many traditional models that have been used to assess the impact of integration either do not take this into account adequately or have sometimes been used in ways that ignore these essential structural components of the process of change.

3. While the focus on the monetary aspect of EMU is understandable in the context of the major institutional changes that have taken place since the Maastricht Treaty, it is the 'economic' E in EMU that is both the more complex issue and the key to the ultimate success of the enterprise.

Hence the next two chapters appraise both the development of EMU over the last thirty-five years, and the way in which it is currently operating and will develop as the accession countries join, in the light of these three observations.

The development of EU economic and monetary integration

DAVID MAYES AND ALI EL-AGRAA

The aim of achieving Economic and Monetary Union (EMU), although enshrined in the Maastricht Treaty, is not a new phenomenon for the EU – see chapters 2 and 27. This chapter provides a historical perspective by travelling the route taken by the EU in this direction. The actual route followed has been the combination of the objectives for increasing economic integration, paving the way for the political unity of Europe (section 2.1.2), and the more immediate economic needs and shocks along that path. While there is a danger, with the benefit of knowledge of the current outcome, of setting out the particular route that has been travelled as if that were the precise plan from the beginning, realizing the Benelux vision of political unity via the back door depended precisely on waiting for and then seizing the right opportunities when they arose. Nevertheless, the initial ideas, sketched out as early as 1970, bear striking similarities to what has eventually been accomplished.

11.1 The Werner Report

From 1967, the prevailing world order for exchange rates, established as part of the Bretton Woods agreement in 1944, began to fall apart. Until that point the system of having exchange rates that were 'fixed' but adjustable occasionally when the existing rate was shown to be unsustainable had worked rather well. Fixity permitted fluctuations within 1 per cent of a peg with the US dollar, which in turn was convertible for gold at $35 per ounce. Despite some initial repositioning after the war, the number of occasions on which pegs had been changed meant that the system had seemed credible. The contrast with problems after

the First World War, with hyperinflation in Germany and then the deflationary impact of trying to return to the gold standard, was striking. However, while the early problems lay with other countries trying to stabilize themselves with respect to the United States, the problem in the 1960s was that the US, hindered by the cost of the Vietnam war, was no longer able to act as the anchor for the international system.

Other countries therefore had to look elsewhere for stability. While the main initial thrust was towards a reform of the Bretton Woods system, the EC looked at the possibility of trying to create a locally stable system with the same sort of architecture for itself. In 1969, during The Hague summit (see chapters 2 and 27), the Six decided that the EC should progressively transform itself into an EMU, and set up a committee, led by Pierre Werner, then Prime Minister of Luxembourg, to consider the issues involved. The Werner Committee presented an interim report in June 1970 and a final report in October of the same year. The latter became generally known as the 'Werner Report', and was endorsed by the Council in February 1971.

According to the Council resolution, the EC would (*OJC*, 1971):

1 Constitute a zone where persons, goods, services and capital would move freely – but without distorting competition, or creating structural and regional imbalances . . .

2 Form a single monetary entity within the international monetary system, characterised by the total and irreversible convertibility of currencies; the elimination of fluctuation margins of exchange rates between the [members]; the irrevocable fixing of their parity relationships. These steps would be essential for the creation of a single currency, and they would involve a Community-level organisation of central banks;

3 Hold the powers and responsibilities in the economic and monetary field that would enable its institutions to ensure the administration of the economic union. To this end, the necessary economic policy decisions would be taken at Community level and the necessary powers would be attributed to community institutions.

The Community organisation of central banks would assist, in the framework of its own responsibilities, in achieving the objectives of stability and growth in the Community.

As progress was made in moving closer to the final objectives, Community instruments would be created whenever they seemed necessary to replace or complement the action of national instruments. All actions would be interdependent; in particular, the development of monetary unification would be backed by parallel progress in the convergence, and then the unification of economic policies.

The Council decided that EMU could be attained during that decade, if the plan had the permanent political support of the member governments. Implementation was envisaged in three stages, with the first beginning in 1971 and the third completed by 1980. The Council made quite clear how it envisaged the process leading to full EMU (emphasis added):

(a) The first phase should begin on January 1, 1971, and could technically be completed within three years. This phase would be used to make the Community instruments more operational and to mark the beginnings of the Community's individuality within the international monetary system;

(b) The first phase should not be considered as an objective in itself; it should be associated with the complete process of economic and monetary integration. *It should therefore be launched with the determination to arrive at the final goal*;

(c) In the first phase consultation procedures should be strengthened; the budgetary policies of the member states should accord with Community objectives; some taxes should be harmonised; monetary and credit policies should be coordinated; and integration of financial markets should be intensified.

The EMU launched by the EC in 1971 was thus consistent with the requirements for a full EMU discussed in the previous chapter. While the problems of integrating product markets may not have been clear then, the intention to have the free flow of capital and labour rather than just free trade and ordered payments is set out, foreshadowing later developments.

Although the 1971 venture did fail, after an earlier than expected successful negotiation of the first phase and making some progress during the second, the failure was not due to lack of commitment, determination or both. The Nixon shock, the first oil shock and the enlargement shock (the admission of three new members, each bringing with it its own unique problems) were the real culprits. The first step in coordinated monetary management had been that the EC countries would keep all their bilateral exchange rates within 2.25 per cent of each other. Their joint rates would therefore move quite closely together in a 'snake' round the US dollar, which was still treated as the numeraire of the system. (The Smithsonian Agreement that was in force at the time would have limited each currency's fluctuation with respect to the US dollar to 2.25 per cent. Thus without the 'snake' the EC currencies could have moved up to 4.5 per cent from each other. This would have been clearly more than is acceptable without renegotiating prices and hence would have violated the degree of stability required within the EC.) Not only were the lira, sterling and the French franc unable to hold their parity within the first year or so but the Smithsonian Agreement itself had collapsed into generalized floating by 1973.

11.2 The EMS

In some quarters, the European Monetary System (EMS) has been considered as the next EC attempt at EMU, but it was really little more than a mechanism devised to check the monetary upheavals of the 1970s by creating a 'zone of monetary stability'. The route to EMS was a fairly short one. The idea was floated not by the EC Commission but by the German Chancellor, Helmut Schmidt, and the French President, Valéry Giscard d'Estaing, and was discussed in the Council of Ministers in Copenhagen in April 1978. Roy Jenkins, the Commission President, had called for such a

Box 11.1 Provisions of the EMS (OJC, 1971)

1. In terms of exchange rate management, the ... (EMS) will be at least as strict as the 'snake'. In the initial stages of its operation and for a limited period of time, member countries currently not participating in the 'snake' may opt for somewhat wider margins around central rates. In principle, intervention will be in the currencies of participating countries. Changes in central rates will be subject to mutual consent. Non-member countries with particularly strong economic and financial ties with the Community may become associate members of the system. The European Currency Unit (ECU) will be at the centre of the system; in particular, it will be used as a means of settlement between EEC monetary authorities.

2. An initial supply of ECUs (for use among Community central banks) will be created against deposit of US dollars and gold on the one hand (e.g. 20% of the stock currently held by member central banks) and member currencies on the other hand in an amount of a comparable order of magnitude.

The use of ECUs created against member currencies will be subject to conditions varying with the amount and the maturity; due account will be given to the need for substantial short-term facilities (up to 1 year).

3. Participating countries will coordinate their exchange rates policies *vis-à-vis* third countries. To this end, they will intensify the consultations in the appropriate bodies and between central banks participating in the scheme. Ways to coordinate dollar interventions should be sought which avoid simultaneous reserve interventions. Central banks buying dollars will deposit a fraction (say 20%) and receive ECUs in return; likewise, central banks selling dollars will receive a fraction (say 20%) against ECUs.

4. Not later than two years after the start of the scheme, the existing arrangements and institutions will be consolidated in a European Monetary Fund.

5. A system of closer monetary cooperation will only be successful if participating countries pursue policies conducive to greater stability at home and abroad; this applies to deficit and surplus countries alike.

corrective initiative in a speech in Florence the previous October. By 5 December the Council had adopted the idea, in the form of a resolution 'on the establishment of the European Monetary System (EMS) and related matters', after a period of intensive discussion (Ludlow (1982) gives a full account of the negotiations involved).

The EMS, which started operating in March 1979, was introduced with the immediate support of six of the EC nations at the time. Ireland, Italy and the United Kingdom adopted a wait-and-see attitude; 'time for reflection' was needed by Ireland and Italy, which required a broader band of permitted fluctuation of ±6 per cent when they did enter, and a definite reservation was expressed by the United Kingdom. Later, Ireland and Italy joined the system, while the United Kingdom expressed a 'spirit of sympathetic cooperation'.

The main features of the EMS are given in the annex to the conclusions of the EC presidency (*Bulletin of the European Communities*, no. 6, 1978, pp. 20–1) set out in box 11.1.

In essence, the EMS is concerned with the creation of an EC currency zone within which there is discipline for managing exchange rates. This discipline is known as the 'exchange rate mechanism' (ERM), which asks a member nation to intervene to reverse a trend when 75 per cent of the allowed exchange rate variation of ±2.25 per cent is reached; this is similar to what happened within the preceding 'snake' arrangements. The crucial differences were, however, twofold. First was the creation of the European Currency Unit (ECU) as the centre of the system against which divergence of the exchange rate was to be measured. (The ECU followed on directly from the European Unit of Account as a basket of *all* the EC currencies, not just those participating in the

ERM. Weights in the basket, based on economic importance in the system, were revised every five years.[1] It was the means of settlement between the EC central banks.) Second, the EMS was to be supported by a European Monetary Fund (EMF), which (supposedly within two years) was to absorb the short-term financing arrangements operating within the snake, the short-term monetary support agreement which was managed by the European Monetary Cooperation Fund (EMCF), and the medium-term loan facilities for balance of payments assistance (*Bulletin of the European Communities*, no. 12, 1978). The EMF was to be backed by approximately 20 per cent of national gold and US dollar reserves and by a similar percentage in national currencies. The EMF was to issue ECUs to be used as new reserve assets, and an exchange-stabilization fund able to issue about US $50 billion was to be created.

It is clear from the above that the EMS asks neither for permanently and irrevocably fixed exchange rates between the member nations nor for complete capital convertibility. Moreover, it does not mention the creation of a common central bank to be put in charge of the member nations' foreign exchange reserves and to be vested with the appropriate powers. Hence the EMS was not EMU, although it could be seen as paving the way for one.

11.2.1 The success of the EMS

The survival of the EMS belied the early scepticism and there is little dispute that the EMS was something of a success. There was, however, a period from 1992 onwards when it looked as if the EMS might collapse altogether, just at the time that the final push to EMU was being agreed upon (see below). This success can be seen as embodied in three principal achievements.

First, despite occasional realignments and fluctuations of currencies within their pre-set bands, it seems that the EMS succeeded in its proximate objective of stabilizing exchange rates – not in the absolute sense but in bringing about more stability than would have been enjoyed without it. Moreover, up to 1992 this was done without provoking periodic speculative crises of the Bretton Woods system. This stability had two elements. Not only did the number of realignments in the central rates fall (with one minor exception there were none in the five years following 1987), but the variation of exchange rates between the ERM countries fell much faster than that of those outside even in the early period up to 1985 (Ungerer et al., 1986). Just having scope for realignments meant that, unlike the 'snake', a parity change did not entail a confidence-shaking exit from the system.

Second, the claim is made for the EMS that it provided a framework within which member countries were able to pursue counter-inflationary policies at a lesser cost in terms of unemployment and lost output than would have been possible otherwise. The basis of the claim is that the structure of the EMS began to attach a measure of 'reputation' to countries that managed to avoid inflation and hence depreciation of their exchange rate. This element of loss of reputation through 'failure' may have reduced the expectation of inflation and hence made counter-inflationary policy less 'costly'. However, estimates of the change in the 'sacrifice ratio' (ratio of the rise in unemployment to the fall in inflation in a period) do not indicate any improvements compared to countries outside the ERM (which were also successful in lowering inflation), although, as generally expected, sacrifice ratios observed did rise as inflation fell.

Third, while it is claimed that nominal exchange rate stability was secured, it is also argued that the operation of the EMS prevented drastic changes in *real* exchange rates (or 'competitiveness'). This is contrasted with the damaging experience in this respect of both the United Kingdom and the United States over the same period. However, in one sense it may merely have encouraged countries to put off necessary realignments, leading ultimately to the drastic changes and crisis in 1992/3 (see below and section 11.4).

Finally, while it was not an immediate objective of the EMS as such, the ECU became established as a significant currency of denomination of bond issues, which is testimony to the credibility of the EMS and the successful projection of its identity. In part, the use of the ECU in international bond issues may have reflected its role as a hedge by being a currency 'cocktail'. It also provided a means of getting round some of the currency restrictions in force, particularly in France and Italy. The high point for new ECU issues was 1991 and external issues never recovered after the 1992/3 crisis.

These achievements have not been without some qualifications. The 'divergence indicator' mechanism for triggering intervention before the limits of the band was reached did not withstand the test of time, for example.

The enforced changes to parities in and after September 1992 considerably reduced the credibility of the system and called into question the validity of the idea of approaching monetary union through increasingly fixed exchange rates while having no controls over capital flows. Although the widening of the bands to ±15 per cent in August 1993 appeared to remove much of the effective distinction between the ERM and freely floating exchange rates, the practice was a very considerable convergence and a system which took only limited advantage of the flexibility available.

11.3 The Delors Report and the Maastricht Treaty

As we have noted, by 1987 the EMS, and the ERM within it, appeared to have achieved considerable success in stabilizing exchange rates. This coincided with legislative progress towards EMU on other fronts. The EC summit held in Hanover on 27 and 28 June 1988 decided that, in adopting the Single European Act (see chapter 2), the EC member states had confirmed the objective of 'progressive realisation of economic and monetary union'. The heads of state agreed to discuss the means of achieving this in their meeting in Madrid in June of the following year, and to help them in their deliberations they entrusted to a committee chaired by Jacques Delors, then President of the EC Commission, and composed of the central bank governors and two other experts, the 'task of studying and proposing concrete stages leading towards this union'. The committee

reported just before the Madrid summit and its report is referred to as the Delors Report on EMU.

The committee was of the opinion that the creation of the EMU must be seen as a single process, but that this process should be in stages, which progressively led to the ultimate goal. Thus the decision to enter upon the first stage should commit a member state to the entire process. Emphasizing that the creation of the EMU would necessitate a common monetary policy and require a high degree of compatibility of economic policies and consistency in a number of other policy areas, particularly in the fiscal field, the report pointed out that the realization of the EMU would require new arrangements which could be established only on the basis of a change in the Treaty of Rome and consequent changes in national legislation.

According to the report, the first stage should be concerned with the initiation of the process of creating the EMU. During this stage there would be a greater convergence of economic performance through the strengthening of economic and monetary policy coordination within the existing institutional framework. The economic measures would be concerned with the completion of the internal market and the reduction of existing disparities through programmes of budgetary consolidation in the member states involved and more effective structural and regional policies. In the monetary field the emphasis would be on the removal of all obstacles to financial integration and on the intensification of cooperation and coordination of monetary policies. Realignment of exchange rates was seen to be possible, but efforts would be made by every member state to make the functioning of other adjustment mechanisms more effective. The committee was of the opinion that it would be important to include all EC currencies in the exchange rate mechanism of the EMS during this stage. The 1974 Council decision defining the mandate of central bank governors would be replaced by a new decision indicating that the committee itself should formulate opinions on the overall orientation of monetary and exchange rate policy.

In the second stage, which would commence only when the Treaty had been amended, the basic organs and structure of the EMU would be set up. The committee stressed that this stage should be seen as a transition period leading to the final stage; thus it should constitute a 'training process leading to collective decision-making', but the ultimate responsibility for policy decisions would remain with national authorities during this stage. The procedure established during the first stage would be further strengthened and extended on the basis of the amended Treaty, and policy guidelines would be adopted on a majority basis. Given this understanding, the EC would achieve the following:

1. establish 'a medium-term framework for key economic objectives aimed at achieving stable growth, with a follow-up procedure for monitoring performances and intervening when significant deviations occurred';
2. 'set precise, although not yet binding, rules relating to the size of annual budget deficits and their financing';
3. 'assume a more active role as a single entity in the discussions of questions arising in the economic and exchange rate field'.

In the monetary field, the most significant feature of this stage would be the establishment of the European System of Central Banks (ESCB) to absorb the previous institutional monetary arrangements. The ESCB would start the transition with a first stage in which the coordination of independent monetary policies would be carried out by the Committee of Central Bank Governors. It was envisaged that the formulation and implementation of a common monetary policy would take place in the final stage; during this stage exchange rate realignments would not be allowed, barring exceptional circumstances.

The report stresses that the second stage would require a number of actions, e.g.:

1. National monetary policy would be executed in accordance with the general monetary orientations set up for the EC as a whole.
2. A certain amount of foreign exchange reserves would be pooled and used to conduct interventions in accordance with the guidelines established by the ESCB.

3. The ESCB would have to regulate the monetary and banking system to achieve a minimum harmonization of provisions (such as reserve requirements or payment arrangements) necessary for the future conduct of a common monetary policy.

The final stage would begin with the irrevocable fixing of member states' exchange rates and the attribution to the EC institutions of the full monetary and economic consequences. It is envisaged that during this stage the national currencies will eventually be replaced by a single EC currency. In the economic field, the transition to this stage is seen to be marked by three developments:

1. EC structural and regional policies may have to be further strengthened.
2. EC macroeconomic and budgetary rules and procedures would have to become binding.
3. The EC role in the process of international policy cooperation would have to become fuller and more positive.

In the monetary field, the irrevocable fixing of exchange rates would come into effect and the transition to a single monetary policy and a single currency would be made. The ESCB would assume full responsibilities, especially in four specific areas:

1. The formulation and implementation of monetary policy.
2. Exchange-market intervention in third currencies.
3. The pooling and management of all foreign exchange reserves.
4. Technical and regulatory preparations necessary for the transition to a single EC currency.

As agreed, the report was the main item for discussion at the EC summit which opened in Madrid on 24 June 1989. In that meeting member nations decided to call a conference which would determine the route to be taken to EMU. This agreement was facilitated by a surprisingly conciliatory Margaret Thatcher, the British Prime Minister, on the opening day of the summit. Instead of insisting (as was expected) that the United Kingdom would join the exchange rate mechanism of the

EC 'when the time is ripe', she set out five conditions for joining:

1. a lower inflation rate in the United Kingdom, and in the EC as a whole;
2. abolition of all exchange controls (at the time and for two years after, Italy, France and Spain had them);
3. progress towards the single EC market;
4. liberalization of financial services;
5. Agreement on competition policy.

Since these were minor conditions relative to the demands for creating the EMU, all member nations endorsed the report and agreed on 1 July 1990 as the deadline for the commencement of the first stage.

The three-stage timetable for EMU did start on 1 July 1990 with the launching of the first phase of intensified economic cooperation during which all the member states were to submit their currencies to the EMS's ERM. The main target of this activity was the United Kingdom whose currency was not subject to the ERM discipline; the United Kingdom joined in 1991 (the decision was announced at the Madrid Summit of June 1989 while Margaret Thatcher was still in office), but withdrew from it in 1992, as did Italy.

The second stage is clarified in the Maastricht Treaty. It was to start in 1994. During this stage the EU was to create the *European Monetary Institute* (EMI) to prepare the way for a European Central Bank (ECB) which would start operating on 1 January 1997. Although this was upset by the 1992 turmoil in the EMS, the compromises reached at the Edinburgh summit of December 1992 (deemed necessary for creating the conditions which resulted in a successful second referendum on the treaty in Denmark and hence in ratification by the United Kingdom – see chapter 2) did not water down the treaty too much. Be that as it may, the treaty already allowed Denmark and the United Kingdom to opt out of the final stage when the EU currency rates would be permanently and irrevocably fixed and a single currency floated. However, in a separate protocol, all the then twelve EC nations declared that the drive to a single currency in the 1990s was 'irreversible'. Denmark, which supported the decision, was an exception because

its constitution demands the holding of a referendum on this issue. The rationale for the United Kingdom was its very specific problems (see El-Agraa, 2002b).

A single currency (the euro), to be managed by an independent ECB, was to be introduced as early as 1997 if seven of the then twelve EC nations passed the strict economic criteria required for its successful operation, and in 1999 at the very latest. These conditions were as follows:

1. *Price stability*. Membership required 'a price performance that is sustainable and an average rate of inflation, observed over a period of one year before the examination, that does not exceed by more than [1.5] percentage points that of, at most, the three best performing' EC member countries. Inflation 'shall be measured by means of the consumer price index on a comparable basis, taking into account differences in national definitions'.
2. *Interest rates*. Membership required that,
   observed over a period of one year before the examination, a Member State has had an average nominal long-term interest rate that does not exceed by more than two percentage points that of, at most, the three best performing Member States in terms of price stability. Interest rates shall be measured on the basis of long-term government bonds or comparable securities, taking into account differences in national definitions.
3. *Budget deficits*. Membership required that a member country 'has achieved a government budgetary position without a deficit that is excessive' (Article 109j). However, what is to be considered excessive is determined in Article 104c(6) which simply states that the Council shall decide after an overall assessment 'whether an excessive deficit exists'. The protocol sets the criterion for an excessive deficit as being 3 per cent of GDP. However, there are provisos if 'either the ratio has declined substantially and continuously and reached a level that comes close to the reference value; or . . . the excess over the reference value is only exceptional and temporary and the ratio remained close to the reference value'.
4. *Public debt*. Here the requirement in the protocol is that the ratio of government debt should

not exceed 60 per cent of GDP. But again there is an important proviso: 'unless the ratio is sufficiently diminishing and approaching the reference value at a satisfactory pace'. Whether such an excessive deficit exists is open to interpretation and is decided by the Council under qualified majority voting (see chapter 3). In helping the Council decide, the Commission is to look at the medium term and quite explicitly can have the opinion that there is an excessive deficit if there is risk, 'notwithstanding the fulfilment of the requirements under the criteria'.

5. *Currency stability*. Membership required that a member country

> has respected the normal fluctuation margin provided for by the exchange-rate mechanism of the [EMS] without severe tensions for at least two years before the examination. In particular, [it] shall not have devalued its currency's bilateral central rate against any other Member State's currency on its own initiative for the same period.

One is, of course, perfectly justified in asking about the theoretical rationale for these convergence criteria. The answer is simply that there is none; for example, the inflation criterion is not even based on NAIRUs (i.e. inflation could be convergent simply because the economy is out of internal equilibrium over the examination period) – see chapter 10 – and there is no way to evaluate whether or not a 60 per cent of GDP public debt is better or worse than, say, a 65 per cent of GDP rate. Normally the criterion used for assessing the debt position of a country in rating its debt is 'sustainability', which is subject to a wide range of considerations. One easy rationalization that could be applied is that 3 per cent of GDP happened to be the average level of public investment at that time, and the member nations deemed this percentage acceptable. Given this, it is often also accepted that investment – provided it has an equivalent financial rate of return – can be sustainably financed by a budget deficit. Calculating this at the steady state of equilibrium and a compound rate of interest of 5 per cent per annum results in a public borrowing of 60 per cent of GDP (see Buiter et al., 1993), which also happened to be the average at the time.

The important requirements for a stable system are that no member should be able to run their economy in a way that increases the cost for the others. Provided that the minimum standard set is high enough, then the euro area as a whole will get the finest credit ratings/lowest interest costs. Unless there is some means of differentiation, then the single exchange and interest rate for the EMU will reflect the aggregate behaviour. In a more developed federal system it becomes possible to have two sorts of public debt, such as in the US, for example. Then states have the ability to raise their own debt but subject to limits and very explicitly without a guarantee from the federal authorities. The US therefore shows noticeable spreads for local and state debt and some have indeed got into difficulty.

It is interesting to note that the timing of these convergence tests has been crucial. If they had occurred in 1992, only France and Luxembourg would have scored full marks, i.e. five points. The others would have scored as follows: Denmark and the United Kingdom four points each; Belgium, Germany and Ireland three points each; the Netherlands two points; Italy and Spain one point; Greece and Portugal no points. Hence, the EMU could not have been introduced since seven countries would have needed to score full marks for this purpose. The position at the end of 1996 was even worse since only Luxembourg qualified. Thus the third stage of EMU did not begin by the earlier date of 1997. What is extraordinary is the turnaround by the final qualifying date of 1998. Then only one country, Greece, was deemed not to qualify and even Greece was able to qualify at the first reassessment in 2000 (although it has been subsequently revealed that some of the statistics involved were knowingly inaccurate; therefore Greece did not meet all the criteria). However, one should hasten to add the proviso, regarding this test, that the text permitted the exercise of considerable discretion, reinforced by Article 6 of the protocol which states that the

Council shall, acting unanimously on a proposal from the Commission and after consulting the European Parliament, the EMI or the ECB as the case may be, and the Committee referred to in Article 109c, adopt appropriate provisions to lay down the details of the convergence criteria referred to in Article 109j of the Treaty, which shall then replace this Protocol.

The data on which the decision on 2 May 1998 was based – see table 11.1 – was deemed, in the opinion of the EU Commission, to indicate that eleven nations had passed the test. Of the remaining four, three (Denmark, the UK and Sweden) had already decided not to join in the first wave, and Greece was not in the running. The Commission's interpretation of the member states' performance was clearly 'flexible' (the EMI, which was also charged with issuing a convergence report, was of exactly the same opinion as the Commission (EMI, 1998)).

Fourteen member states had government deficits of 3 per cent of GDP or less in 1997: Belgium, Denmark, Germany, Spain, France, Ireland, Italy, Luxembourg, the Netherlands, Austria, Portugal, Finland, Sweden and the United Kingdom. Member states had achieved significant reductions in the level of government borrowing, in particular in 1997. This remarkable outcome was the result of national governments' determined efforts to tackle excessive deficits, combined with the effects of lower interest rates and stronger growth in the European economy.

In 1997 government debt was below the treaty reference value of 60 per cent of GDP in four member states – France, Luxembourg, Finland and the United Kingdom. According to the treaty, countries may exceed this value as long as the debt ratio is 'sufficiently diminishing and approaching the reference value at a satisfactory pace'. This was deemed to be the case in almost all member states with debt ratios above 60 per cent in 1997. Only in Germany, where the ratio was just above 60 per cent of GDP and the exceptional costs of unification continued to bear heavily, was there a small rise in 1997. All countries above the 60 per cent ratio were expected to see reductions in their debt levels. *The Commission concluded that the conditions were in place for the continuation of a sustained decline in debt ratio in future years* (CEC, 1998e, p. 33).

Thus, it should be clear that the EMU envisaged in the Delors Report and detailed and endorsed in the Maastricht Treaty is consistent with and satisfies all the requirements of a full economic and monetary union in the sense described in Chapter 10.

11.4 The transition to EMU

As the EU progressed towards EMU it was opening itself up to the possibility of severe strains through the EMS as exchange controls were removed as part of stage 1. The removal posed two problems for the EMS. First, a protection against speculation was lost. Second, because interest parity was no longer prevented, interest rates everywhere were tightly linked as the amount of expected depreciation was confined by the bands of permissible fluctuations of the currencies against one another. Because Germany was by far the largest economy in the EMS, this meant that interest rates, and hence monetary policy, everywhere in the system were dominated by Germany. Unless Germany in turn tempered its monetary policy by concern for the economic situation in other countries this could turn out to be an unacceptable state of affairs, as indeed proved to be the case in 1992–3.

These problems were realized and various solutions proposed. First, as regards the problem of speculation, the mechanisms of the EMS were improved by measures to accommodate automatic lending by a strong currency country to a weak currency country in the event of need; whereas previously this automaticity applied only when intervention was taking place at the edge of the band, since the deliberations of the EMS Finance Ministers in Nyborg in September 1987, it applied also to so-called intra-marginal intervention, i.e. foreign exchange operations taking place to support a currency before it has reached its limit. These new provisions were tested by a speculative run on the French franc in the autumn of 1987 and proved successful; the Bundesbank lent heavily to the Banque de France but the lending was rapidly repaid once the speculation subsided and confidence returned. The second problem, concerning excessive German dominance, was only resolved by moving on to full EMU. The Nyborg provisions called for much

Table 11.1 EU member states' performance with regard to the convergence criteria

	Inflation	Government budgetary position					Exchange rates	Long-term interest rates[d]
		Existence of an excessive deficit[b]	Deficit (per cent of GDP)[c]	Debt (per cent of GDP)	Change from previous year		ERM participation	
	HICP[a]						March	January
	1998		1997	1997	1996	1995	1998	1998
Reference Value	2.7[e]		3	60				7.8[f]
Austria	1.1	yes[g]	2.5	66.1	−3.4	0.3	3.8	yes	5.6
Belgium	1.4	yes[g]	2.1	122.2	−4.7	−4.3	−2.2	yes	5.7
Denmark	1.9	no	−0.7	65.1	−5.5	−2.7	−4.9	yes	6.2
Finland	1.3	no	0.9	55.8	−1.8	−0.4	−1.5	yes[h]	5.9
France	1.2	yes[g]	3.0	58.0	2.4	2.9	4.2	yes	5.5
Germany	1.4	yes[g]	2.7	61.3	0.8	2.4	7.8	yes	5.6
Greece	5.2	yes	4.0	108.7	−2.9	1.5	0.7	yes[i]	9.8[j]
Ireland	1.2	no	−0.9	66.3	−6.4	−9.6	−6.8	yes	6.2
Italy	1.8	yes[g]	2.7	121.6	−2.4	−0.2	−0.7	yes	6.7
Luxembourg	1.4	no	−1.7	6.7	0.1	0.7	0.2	yes[k]	5.6
Netherlands	1.8	no	1.4	72.1	−5.0	−1.9	1.2	yes[g]	5.5
Portugal	1.8	yes[g]	2.5	62.0	−3.0	−0.9	2.1	yes[g]	6.2
Spain	1.8	yes[g]	2.6	68.8	−1.3	4.6	2.9	yes[g]	6.3
Sweden	1.9	yes[g]	0.8	76.6	−0.1	−0.9	−1.4	no	6.5
United Kingdom	1.8	yes[g]	1.9	53.4	−1.3	0.8	3.5	no	7.0
EU(15)	1.6		2.4	72.1	−0.9	2.0	3.0		6.1

[a] Percentage change in arithmetic average of the latest twelve-monthly harmonized indices of consumer prices (HICP) relative to the arithmetic average of the twelve HICP of the previous period.

[b] Council decisions of 26.09.94, 10.07.95, 27.06.96 and 30.06.97.

[c] A negative sign for the government deficit indicates a surplus.

[d] Average maturity ten years; average of the last twelve months.

[e] Definition adopted in this report: simple arithmetic average of the inflation rates of the three best-performing member states in terms of price stability plus 1.5 percentage points.

[f] Definition adopted in this report: simple arithmetic average of the twelve-month average of interest rates of the three best-performing member states in terms of price stability plus two percentage points.

[g] Commission-recommended abrogation.

[h] Since March 1998.

[i] Average of the available data during the past twelve months.

[j] Since November 1996.

[k] Since October 1996.

Source: CEC (1998e), table 1.1, p. 34.

closer monetary cooperation, implying more continuous exchange of information, and interest rate movements within the EMS after that time displayed a high degree of synchronization. However, the cooperation called for also seemed to imply a degree of common decision-making going beyond simply following a German lead in a prompt and well-prepared way. Progress on this front is less evident. The anxiety of France on this score, however, led to important initiatives. First, France called upon Germany to discuss economic policy on a regular basis and an economic council was set up for this purpose. Second, it was on French initiatives that the EC was led to call for an investigation into the requirements of full monetary union, an investigation subsequently carried out by the Delors Committee, the recommendations of whose report were endorsed by all twelve nations of the EC in June 1989, leading to the Maastricht Treaty on European Union (see above).

The path which the EMS participants agreed to follow thus called for increasing intervention resources and other devices to combat the threat of speculation and for increased economic and monetary cooperation between member countries, eventually leading to the creation of the European Central Bank. But we should note that there were alternative short-run solutions. One way in which countries can recover a greater measure of independence from the dominant power is to enlarge the bands of exchange rate fluctuation, which is what they did in 1993; another would have been to compromise on the single market by retaining a measure of exchange control. Either device has obvious counter-speculative advantages too. If maintained over the long term, these alternative solutions would have been in effect a defeat for the higher aspirations of the EMS. The second mechanism was not used, but it is not difficult to think of circumstances in which it might have been, given the increasing popularity in the late 1990s of the idea of putting 'sand in the wheels' of international financial transactions in order to limit their volatility.

The forecast threat to the system duly occurred in September 1992. Uncertainty about the outcome of the French referendum on the Maastricht Treaty contributed to speculation against the weakest currencies in the ERM, sterling and the lira. Neither was able to resist the pressure despite substantial increases in interest rates. By the summer of 1993 not even the French franc could survive the pressure, and the bands had to be widened to ±15 per cent to allow it to devalue without realigning within the system.

Other currencies also came under pressure and were forced to devalue. There was considerable pressure on the French franc in September 1992 but it survived, aided by substantial intervention by the Bundesbank on its behalf. It is arguable that all the currencies which were devalued were in some sense overvalued in terms of their long-term sustainable values. (One interpretation of this is the fundamental equilibrium exchange rate, FEER, the rate at which the balance of payments is sustainable in the long run.) However, the problem was not merely one of great domestic inflation by the devaluing countries but of the special problems of the dominant German economy leading to a divergence from the domestic objectives of the other countries.[2] German interest rates were driven up by the need to finance unification over and above the willingness to raise taxes. With the tight linkage of EMS interest rates, other states also had to have rates that were high in real terms.

In the case of the United Kingdom it was clearly a relief that the constraints of the ERM could be broken. Interest rates had already been progressively cut to the point that sterling was close to its lower bound. A domestic recession was being exacerbated by the inability to use monetary policy to alleviate it. On exit, interest rates were lowered by four percentage points in virtually as many months. There was no immediate prospect of sterling re-entering the ERM and indeed its fall of over 15 per cent is no larger than that suggested by the FEER, and its subsequent rise as the economy recovered was predictable.

The EMS suffered considerably through being unable to organize an orderly realignment of exchange rates. The mechanisms existed but political pressures meant that the member states could not agree among themselves. Blame has been placed in a number of quarters – on the Bundesbank for not taking greater account of the impact of its policy on other countries and on the United Kingdom for not being sincere in trying to maintain parity within the bounds – but the basic weakness of the system remained: that trying to have narrow bands without exchange controls is really not sustainable when there are substantial shocks to the system. This was admitted in practice by widening the bands.

The EMS took a back seat after the devaluations of September 1992 and the widening of the band to ±15 per cent in August 1993. However, the system remained intact and slowly regained credibility. Despite three devaluations of the peseta and the escudo between November 1992 and March 1995, the participating currencies moved back into closer alignment. At the end of 1996 all bar the Irish punt were within the ±2.25 per cent band. Although sterling and the drachma remained outside the ERM and the Swedish krone did not join, Italy rejoined in November 1996 and Finland (October 1996) and Austria (January 1995) also became participants.

As we have noted, the EMS survived through to its replacement by the Eurosystem at the start of 1999 primarily because of the determination of EU governments to qualify for EMU under the Maastricht criteria. The restraints on fiscal policy from needing to keep deficits below 3 per cent of GDP and debt below 60 per cent (or make credible progress towards 60 per cent) simultaneously helped inflation to converge and the member states to get their business cycles in line. The steady development of the internal market has integrated them further.

In part the reason why stage 3 of EMU did not begin in 1997 was simply that the convergence period after the shocks of 1992–3 was just too short, particularly for countries like Sweden and especially Finland for which the shocks were greatest, but the evolution of the general economic cycles was not favourable. From then onwards, however, convergence was easier. Just as the adverse circumstances in the mid-1990s were bad luck, so the EU was extremely lucky that 1996–8 was a period of very considerable stability. Even the Asian crisis did not have a marked effect and decreased the chance of importing inflation from the rest of the world.

Once financial markets felt that fiscal convergence and EMU were likely, this expectation brought the required convergence in real interest rates. Had it not been possible for some of the countries that had experienced the greatest difficulty in converging to join then, it is likely that they would have experienced considerable pressures in the period immediately after the decision. The loss of credibility involved would then have made joining at a subsequent date much more expensive than it was for those who were successful earlier on.

The creation of the Eurosystem has established three groups of countries within the EU: those who are in the euro area, those who are outside but intend to join at some date in the reasonably near future and those who are outside but have no immediate plans. In one sense all member states that are outside the euro area except Denmark and the UK fall into this second group, as they are supposed to join as soon as they have met the convergence criteria – which are still the same as those applied originally under the Maastricht Treaty. Thus, rather than the more logical idea of converging to the performance of the existing euro area members, convergence is still required to that of the three best-performing members of the EU as a whole, which on some occasions have all been non-euro area members in the case of inflation. Denmark and the UK, have a derogation from this requirement to join, and are free to pursue their own independent monetary policies just as they could outside the ERM of the previous EMS. However, it appears that Sweden is at present a de facto member of the third group as well, since euro area membership was decisively rejected (by 14 percentage points) in a referendum on 14 September 2003 (see Mayes, 2004, and the other contributors to the same symposium in *Cooperation and Conflict* for a deeper discussion). The ten new member states that joined the EU in May 2004 and the two that joined in 2007 vary in their enthusiasm for how fast they wish to join the euro area, with Estonia, Lithuania and Slovenia indicating that they wish to join at the first opportunity. Latvia and then Cyprus and Malta have also opted for rapid entry, but others have set more cautious timetables.

The Eurosystem has created an extension of the ERM labelled ERM II, which countries that wish to adopt the euro should join during the convergence period. Thus the six countries mentioned above – Cyprus, Estonia, Latvia, Lithuania, Malta and Slovenia – joined, along with Slovakia which entered in November 2005. Denmark is also participating in ERM II voluntarily but operating in a tighter band. The rules are similar to those that faced the new members Austria, Finland and Sweden under the original ERM. Their currencies did not form part of the ECU basket and hence if their exchange rate moved with respect to the other members it did not affect the value of the ECU itself. Membership is notional for Estonia and Lithuania as they have currency boards based on the euro and their exchange rates with it are completely fixed.

A central value is agreed between the ECB and the member state for the exchange rate with the euro. The intention then appears to be for the rate to remain within the same 2.25 per cent range that prevailed within ERM. Realignments are possible and indeed have already happened for Greece (upwards). However, the terms are not precise. In its latest Convergence Report, the ECB (2006) explains its application of the treaty provisions as 'whether the country has participated in ERM II for a period of at least two years prior to the convergence examination without severe tensions, in particular without devaluing against the euro.' However, actual membership is not compelled for the full period: 'absence of "severe tensions" is generally assessed by (i) examining the degree of deviation of exchange rates from ERM II central rates against the euro; (ii) using indicators such as exchange rate volatility vis-à-vis the euro area and their development; and (iii) considering the role played by foreign exchange interventions' (p. 17).

ERM II is thus a rather one-sided affair, very much reminiscent of the early days of the original ERM. It is for the applicants to adjust to the behaviour of the euro area. Euro monetary policy is run without regard to their problems; it is the ECB that determines the parities. The ECB (and the Commission) will offer an opinion on whether convergence has occurred. In the case of Greece, the government was keen to go ahead with membership of the euro area as soon as possible. It was accepted for membership in June 2000 and joined the Eurosystem at the beginning of 2001. Even if all of the twelve new EU members were to join ERM II, the system would be highly unbalanced in favour of the Eurosystem in terms of relative economic size. In some ways dependency will actually afford strength to the system, as it makes stable alternatives substantially more costly for the applicants. Thus not only will they have a strong incentive to try to remain in the system and not follow policies that are likely to lead to downward realignments, but the existence of these incentives will be obvious to everybody else as well, thereby increasing the credibility of the commitment.

However, the new members have found ERM II a difficult proposition, as they are still undergoing a major process of structural change and have not in some cases achieved sustainably low inflation. It is therefore likely that, as with the original ERM, the weaker members will experience real exchange rate increases that will ultimately force them into realignments. Adopting a currency board based on the euro may offer greater credibility. Ironically, one element of convergence to the behaviour of the Eurosystem may be easier than for some of the existing ESCB members, as the applicants are in the main heavily integrated with the euro economy already, even though geography might have led one to expect closer links with third countries. Particularly in the case of the former Soviet bloc countries, the economic ties further east have been thoroughly broken. It is thus the problems of transition that are likely to present the greatest strains rather than worries about asymmetric shocks that have affected countries like the UK with substantial economic linkages outside the euro area.

Transition is likely to be slow in some cases, particularly for those countries that have not yet been accepted for membership of the EU, so ERM II is also likely to be a relatively long-lived arrangement. However, in many cases the new members will feel that they would rather complete the process of adjustment within EMU than outside. The credibility and hence much lower real interest rates offered by membership may very well be thought to outweigh the gains from exchange rate flexibility. Massive changes in their labour markets are known to be inevitable, so there may be a willingness to accept the pressures on non-monetary and non-fiscal routes to adjustment, a process that has presented considerable difficulties for many of the current EU members.

The combination of the single market and the absence of exchange controls clearly added to the risk from speculative pressures for the EMS. It is not surprising therefore that there was very strong pressure to move to stage 3 of EMU despite the costs of transition. This still applies and Lithuania and Slovenia asked to be evaluated in 2006. Slovenia succeeded and became the thirteenth member of the Eurosystem at the beginning of 2007, but Lithuania failed by the narrowest possible margin – its inflation rate was 0.1 per cent too high: 2.7 per cent compared to the average of the lowest three inflation countries of 1.1 per cent (and the area average of 2.3 per cent); it met all the other conditions. Attention was also drawn to its substantial current account balance of payments deficit (5.6 per cent of GDP). Since the three lowest inflation countries were Finland, Sweden and Poland, two of which are not in the euro area, there are strong grounds for contesting the economic sense of the process. (Estonia did not bother to apply, because although it met all the other criteria easily, it knew its inflation at the time would be clearly too high.)

11.5 The decision over membership of EMU

We address two questions in this section – the sensible strategy for the new member states in the face of the membership criteria, and the decision of Denmark, Sweden and the UK to stay out of the system – as they both reflect clearly on the economic logic of membership of a currency union for potential and existing members.

It might appear odd, prima facie, in purely economic terms that the UK, Sweden and Denmark have chosen to stay out of stage 3 of EMU, while other countries that seem less convergent on standard optimum currency area (OCA) criteria, such

as the Irish Republic, Finland and Greece have chosen to join. Setting aside the political issues, there are three simple economic reasons that help explain the decisions, but the case of the UK stands out for a further reason. The UK is larger in economic terms than the other five countries mentioned above taken together. It is the only EU member with a world-scale financial market, although Frankfurt has been improving its relative position. We therefore spend rather more time on the UK in the rest of this section.

The simple economic reasons are:

1. Life on the outside has been successful. It is very difficult in the case of Denmark, for example, to point to the extra costs from staying outside, but shadowing the euro very closely, except in terms of forgoing a seat at the table (both in the ECB and the euro group). With little right of veto, the impact of a single small country is rarely going to be decisive.

2. Some of the joining countries, particularly Finland (see Mayes and Suvanto, 2002) have put a much higher weight on the expectation that membership would change behaviour for the better. Furthermore, in the case of both Finland and the Irish Republic the expectation has been that membership would support their propensity for faster than average growth by offering lower real interest rates and dampening inflationary pressures through the threat of competition.

3. It is better to adjust first, making use of the extra flexibility available, and join second. This has been very much the view in Sweden, set out at length in the report of the Calmfors Commision that was appointed by the Swedish government to assess the costs and benefits of full EMU participation (Calmfors et al., 1997). This caution, particularly about being able to cushion the impact of shocks on employment and unemployment, remains in the more recent 'Committee on Stabilization Policy for Full Employment in the Event of Sweden Joining the Monetary Union' (Johansson et al., 2002). The committee concludes: 'Our view is that changes in the degree of nominal wage flexibility are likely to compensate only to a

minor extent for the loss of national monetary policy as an instrument of stabilization policy' (p. 3). Indeed they see that wages in Sweden might themselves be a source of shocks. This reaction reflects a general expectation that flexibility will not work. The same argument is applied to fluctuations in working hours. Because so much of the area of working hours is statutorily controlled, the committee (pp. 5–6) did not see this as being able to act as a shock absorber. If rules were changed they would apply to all sectors. The rigidities imposed on the labour market mean that it is necessary to look elsewhere for offsetting fluctuations in the system. This implies that much of the successful readjustment of the Swedish economy to the crisis at the beginning of the 1990s can be attributed to the operation of monetary policy and to the movement in the exchange rate.

One might wish to add two further reasons. The first is a much more pessimistic view of the secondary benefits that could accrue under a more complete EMU than in the partial or 'pseudo' union envisaged in the Corden–Fleming model (see chapter 10). This would be particularly true for countries that expect to be net payers rather than net recipients. The second is that, if a country feels that it is already more flexible than its potential partners, membership and a tendency towards common behaviour might actually be retrogressive and result in a structure that generates slower growth. Some of this flavour emerges from the discussion of the UK.

The new member states face a rather different balance of interests. In general their economic position and policies are less credible than those of the euro area members and hence they will get clear benefits from lower interest rates. Similarly the constraints that qualifying imposes on fiscal policy will provide helpful external pressures that domestic political conditions might otherwise find difficult. Most of the countries, Poland excepted, are also small, which limits their ability to build up an effective anchor for inflation on their own. They tend to meet many of the OCA criteria (see chapter 10), with the exception of real

convergence, and their trade pattern is strongly integrated with the EU. It is really only one main factor that inhibits their rushing to join stage 3 of EMU before something goes wrong. With the exception of Cyprus and Malta, they have low price levels, wages and output per head, and expect to grow faster than the existing euro area countries over at least the next twenty to thirty years (i.e. they expect an extended period of real convergence). This in turn will therefore mean that their rate of inflation is likely to exceed that of the current members. While this gives them a straightforward problem of meeting the convergence criteria – they would have to go through a period of unusually low inflation that looks sustainable – it also poses problems of whether it is better to adjust partly through the nominal exchange rate. The Czech Republic in particular regards it as beneficial to keep domestic inflation low by inflation targeting, which means that it will have comparable inflation to the euro area but some exchange rate appreciation. Countries that join early can only make such adjustments through the real exchange rate. If the process were smooth this might not matter but if it overshoots then adjustment through an independent exchange rate may well prove easier than having to rely entirely on fiscal policy to disinflate.

As noted earlier, it is largely an empirical question as to whether a country can achieve structural change rapidly without inflating. As noted above, Bulgaria, Cyprus, Estonia, Latvia, Lithuania and Malta have all successfully (thus far) already pegged their exchange rate and hence know how easy/difficult it is to adjust when they get asymmetric shocks that do not affect their partners.[3] The Baltic states have already had one such shock with the Russian crisis of 1998 and weathered it without the system collapsing. Other countries, including Poland and particularly Hungary, have experienced more difficulty, both in fiscal restraint and, in the Hungarian case, in maintaining a smooth exchange rate regime. The Czech Republic also encountered difficulties in the aftermath of the Asian crises as there was a general move of investors away from higher-risk countries.

The most common exposition of the problem is, however, to refer to the Balassa–Samuelson effect

(Björksten, 1999), which points out that prices of highly traded goods will tend to be at international levels round the world. Typically they will also show productivity growth relative to domestic services. Hence achieving balanced growth across the industrial spectrum will tend to involve non-traded goods and services rising in relative price. It may prove difficult for market forces to manage this without excess inflation in the price level as a whole. There have been a variety of estimates of the size of this effect but something of the order of 1 per cent a year or a little more seems to be widely accepted.

Taken together this will tend to mean that the states that are currently pegging to the euro will want to join early and will hope that at some stage they will meet the convergence criteria, as they have nothing to gain from being outside except leaving the peg, which would be a serious blow to credibility and have a cost for several years to come. Inflation-targeting countries on the other hand, along with countries that are managing the real exchange rate, as has been the case with Slovenia, are likely to want to wait longer until they are closer to real convergence. At that point nominal exchange rate movements are likely to be compatible with the convergence criteria.

11.5.1 The UK

The United Kingdom declined to participate in the operation of the EMS to begin with, out of a belief that the system would be operated in a rigid way that would threaten the UK, with its high 'propensity to inflate', with a decline in its competitiveness, especially vis-à-vis Germany. Opposition on different grounds was propounded by the incoming Conservative government headed by Margaret Thatcher, which wished to run an experiment in monetary policy in order to bring inflation down and reasoned, correctly, that if the instruments of monetary policy (principally interest rates) were to be directed at reducing the rate of growth of the money supply, they could not simultaneously be used to target the exchange rate. Technically, this dilemma could be avoided by maintaining a suitably strong set of exchange controls; such controls would allow a government some freedom to

maintain two different targets for monetary policy, but the Thatcher government was keen to remove these controls in any case and did so not long after taking office.

Events were to turn out somewhat paradoxically. The first phase of the Conservative government's monetary experiment was associated with a very marked *appreciation* of the exchange rate – so competitiveness would have been *better* preserved inside the EMS – and the deep recession that soon set in was attributed by many observers to this cause. In particular, the exchange rate would be steadier and competitiveness more assured, while inflation would be dragged towards the modest German level. This view gained momentum as official British policy towards the exchange rate as a target changed and as it became clear that monetary policy was no longer aimed in single-minded fashion solely at controlling the supply of money.

In September 1986, at the meetings of the IMF, the Chancellor of the Exchequer advertised the non-speculative realignment process of the EMS and not long afterwards followed this up with a policy of 'shadowing the EMS', keeping the sterling exchange rate closely in line with the Deutschmark. This policy initiative lasted for just over a year; by the end of February 1988, following a well-publicized exchange of views between the Chancellor and the Prime Minister, sterling was uncapped. Higher interest rates, invoked as a means of dampening monetary growth and in response to forecasts of inflation, caused the exchange rate to appreciate through its previous working ceiling. The incident underlined the inconsistency between an independent monetary policy and an exchange rate policy. Even when sterling ultimately went into the ERM in October 1990, it appeared to be with considerable reluctance.

Membership of the ERM only lasted until September 1992, when markets pushed sterling out of the system. It did not rejoin, even when a government with a more favourable attitude was elected in May 1997. The issue had been overtaken by whether the UK should join EMU. While a close shadowing of the euro, as has been followed by Denmark, could make sense in its own right to help acquire greater stability, the main reason for such a policy would be as part of the preconditions for membership of the Eurosystem. UK monetary policy was immediately focused on an explicit inflation target of 2.5 per cent a year in May 1997. Pursuit of this target with only narrow bands of 1 per cent either side almost inevitably means that UK monetary policy will vary from that of the ECB, with its medium-term target of inflation being less than but close to 2 per cent (see chapter 11).

The present UK government turned to a serious consideration of euro membership. It has decided that it would recommend the adoption of the euro in a referendum to the British people provided five tests, set by Chancellor Gordon Brown in October 1997, are met. The performance of the UK against these tests was evaluated during the summer of 2003 and gave a negative result, but the government said it would try again.

What are the five Brown economic tests? The first is about business cycles and economic structures being compatible 'so that we and others could live comfortably with euro interest rates on a permanent basis'. The second relates to whether there would be 'sufficient flexibility to deal with' any problems if they emerge. The third concerns whether the adoption of the euro would 'create better conditions for firms making long-term decisions to invest in Britain'. The fourth is about what the impact of euro adoption would be 'on the competitive position of the UK's financial services industry, particularly the City's wholesale markets'. The final sums up the other four since it is about whether the adoption of the euro would 'promote higher growth, stability and a lasting increase in jobs'.

However, when announcing these tests in October 1997, Brown added that the Treasury must decide that there is a 'clear and unambiguous' economic case for recommending British adoption of the euro. Since that would be unlikely in any circumstances, it would seem that this addition has been made to ensure that any decision on the matter would be based on purely political grounds.

It is now generally agreed that it is also vital to include an economic test, omitted by Brown, that would determine the economic performance of the UK for years to come: namely, the value at which sterling would enter the euro. Contrary to popular perception, this need not be the present market exchange rate. This raises the question of how much lower sterling should be relative to the euro at the appropriate time.

Since the decision on euro entry rests on the Treasury's own assessment of the performance of the British economy against its own tests, we do not advance our own. However, several such assessments have been published (see, inter alia, Barrell, 2002, and the various papers in the 2,000 pages that accompanied the Treasury assessment (UK Treasury, 2003)). While all agree that the British economy has been converging with the euro zone area, the overall assessment was firmly negative although leaving open the opportunity for reassessment. The problem is straightforward. There is no general public support for membership so it would be pointless to incur the embarrassment of a defeat, or follow Sweden into an extended period of non-membership following a referendum. The relative success of the UK economy inevitably influences the economic judgment over the appropriate timing of entry. A clear and unambiguous case can never be made, as the result depends on a comparison of two hypothetical futures that are unknowable by definition and cannot even be validated after the event. Moreover, even if the economic case can be established, it will ebb and flow as the performances of the EU and UK economies move relative to each other. The final decision is, therefore, bound to be a political rather than an economic one.

11.6 Conclusions

Only a few years before it occurred, conclusions on the prospects for EMU in the EU were cautious. In 1996 when the time for assessing whether stage 3 could start at the beginning of 1997 it was not even worth looking as only one country, the smallest, qualified under the Maastricht criteria. Only two years later the ECB was up and running and eleven member states had both qualified and decided upon membership. By 2002 the notes and coins of the euro currency were in circulation and the national currencies of member states, by then increased to twelve, had been withdrawn. There was a large element of luck in the specific timing but nevertheless one must conclude that the process to EMU has been a remarkable success. It is difficult to tell whether those framing the Maastricht Treaty a decade earlier really believed their efforts would turn out so well. Previous attempts had run into difficulty.

It will be some time before it is possible to estimate the degree of success of EMU in economic terms. In any case, any such assessment will always be highly contested, as it rests on comparison with a hypothetical alternative that did not occur. The years 1999 and 2000 were good years not just in the euro area but also more generally, although 2001 and 2002 saw a serious setback, which has continued in many of the euro area countries, with the overall economy only turning up clearly in 2006. Public support for EMU has risen and fallen with the general economic climate, irrelevant of whether EMU was actually causal. It is, however, difficult to gainsay the beneficial impact on those countries that previously faced problems of credibility in their macroeconomic policy. The enthusiasm of some of the new member states for moving on to membership of stage 3 of EMU as soon as possible after joining the EU, and the caution of some of the others, continue to illustrate the debate.

In this chapter we have deliberately concentrated on the 'M' in EMU, leaving the 'E' for the discussion in chapter 12 – not because it is less important but because the main developments have occurred more recently as the euro area became a reality. This emphasis on the monetary side is strongly reflected in the literature and may help explain some of the emphasis on the potential difficulties stemming from adverse asymmetric shocks within an EMU. The monetary side of EMU in Europe involves new institutions and a strong legal basis for a single monetary policy. The economic side, on the other hand, relies on relatively soft coordination among the member states through a series of 'processes' regulated by the Stability and Growth Pact (see chapter 12). As soon as the constraints of the SGP have started to bind, those affected have tended to complain and seek for ways round the restrictions. This has led to both popular scepticism and academic criticism because the terms of the pact are rather simplistic and pragmatic and not founded on clear economic principles.

The reality, however, has been a major turnaround in the macroeconomic behaviour of many of the EU economies, particularly those that were facing the greater inflationary and budgetary problems. This change has been perpetuated after the initial convergence conditions for membership of stage 3 were met and has resulted in a much more prudent fiscal basis for the EU. Conditions are not as good as they were in the period when the countries were seeking membership, but much better than in the previous period since the 1960s. As noted elsewhere (chapters 12 and 23), this process is by no means complete, given the challenges from ageing and the continuing problems of adjustment caused by increasing competition and the more rapid change in products and technology. It has, however, achieved a degree of success well beyond what many expected.

A key feature of this success is that assessments of the potential benefits of EMU based on pre-existing structures of behaviour have proved mistaken. The economies have become more symmetric. Thus, not only has the chance of adverse asymmetric shocks fallen, but also the automatic response of other countries (through the 'automatic stabilizers') has helped to offset some of the anticipated loss of flexibility from having a single monetary and exchange rate policy. Furthermore there is evidence that bargaining and other structures have themselves responded, irrespective of regulatory reform, to offer more flexibility and hence reduce the real impact of shocks.

Lastly, countries such as Finland and the Irish Republic have demonstrated that in EMU favourable asymmetric shocks are also amplified, resulting in faster growth and less inflation than would otherwise have been possible.

In the next chapter we look at the operation of EMU in more detail.

NOTES

1 These revisions ended in 1989 when Portugal and Spain were added and the same weight continued until the

ECU was replaced by the euro. Thus, when Austria, Finland and Sweden joined the EU in 1995, their currencies did not become components of the ECU, even though the first two later joined the ERM.

2 Cobham (1996) provides a helpful exposition of the different possible explanations of the crisis.

3 Other countries that are currently outside the EU but are hoping to join, such as Croatia and Albania, also experience constraints through substantial euro-ization. Bosnia-Herzegovina has a currency board backed by the euro and Montenegro and Kosovo use the euro and do not have their own currencies. Thus several of those wanting to adopt the euro at an early stage may also be those that are a long way off real convergence.

Economic and monetary union (EMU) has four broad ingredients: the euro and the single European monetary policy; the coordination of European macroeconomic policies through the *Stability and Growth Pact* (SGP), the Broad Economic Policy Guidelines (BEPG) and related processes; the completion of the internal market; and the operation of the structural funds and other cohesion measures. In this chapter we will look only at the first two, as the others are dealt with in chapters 11 and 22.

Although the euro did not come into existence until 1 January 1999 and then only in financial markets, most of the characteristics of stage 3 of EMU (chapter 11) were operating once the European Central Bank (ECB) opened in June 1998. The ECB, in the form of the European Monetary Institute (EMI), had been preparing for the day with all of the EU national central banks (NCBs) since 1994. The form of the coming single monetary policy was already known by 1998, both in framework and instruments. In the same way much of the framework for the operation of the economic coordination among the member states had been developed with the SGP of July 1997 and the BEPG that commenced in 1998. The generalized framework was incorporated in the Treaty of Amsterdam (October 1997). There was thus no great break in behaviour at the beginning of 1999, especially since the main qualification period under the convergence criteria had related to 1997. However, the SGP effectively broke down in 2003 and had to be revised in 2005 after a period of debate.

In what follows we begin by looking at the provisions for the single monetary policy, then consider those for policy coordination, before we explore how they have worked.

12.1 The Eurosystem and the euro

The institutional system behind the single monetary policy is quite complex because it has to deal with the fact that some EU members are not (yet) participants in stage 3 of EMU. The Treaty sets up the *European System of Central Banks* (ESCB), which is composed of all the national central banks and the ECB, which is sited in Frankfurt. The ECB and the participating NCBs form the *Eurosystem*, which is what is running the monetary side of the euro area. The term 'Eurosystem' has, however, only been coined by its members in order to make the set-up clearer. It does not occur in the treaty. The body responsible for the ECB and its decisions is the *Governing Council*, which is composed of the governors of the NCBs and the six members of the *Executive Board*, who provide the executive management of the ECB in Frankfurt. The Executive Board is composed of the *president* and *vice-president* and four other members, responsible for the various parts of the ECB, which are labelled Directorates General in the same manner as the Commission. If that were not enough, the ECB also has a *General Council*, which is composed of the president, vice-president and the governors of *all* the EU NCBs whether participating in the euro area or not. Thus the *General Council* has twenty-nine members, including Bulgaria and Romania (twenty-seven governors + two) but the *Governing Council* has nineteen members (thirteen governors + six) since Slovenia joined at the beginning of 2007, and it will increase in size as more member states join the euro area.[1] A representative from the Commission and from the Presidency may also attend but not vote.

The Eurosystem is relatively decentralized compared to the Federal Reserve System in the United States, although the names for the various institutions imply the opposite relative structures. The central institution in the US, the Board of Governors of the Federal Reserve System, which is the controlling body, having powers over the budgets of the twelve Federal Reserve Banks, does not have another label for its staff and administrative operations. The seven governors of the Federal Reserve Board hold a voting majority on the monetary policy-making body, the Federal Open Market Committee (FOMC), where only the president of the New York Fed and five of the presidents of the other Fed Banks, by rotation, can vote (although all are present at each meeting and can speak).[2]

The Eurosystem, on the other hand, operates through a network of committees, where each NCB and the ECB has a member.[3] The ECB normally provides the chairman and the secretariat. It is the Governing Council which takes the decisions but the Executive Board coordinates the work of the committees and prepares the agenda for the Governing Council. Many of these committees meet in two compositions, one for the Eurosystem and one for the whole ESCB, depending on the subject.

To complete the confusion over labels, the Eurosystem has a *Monetary Policy Committee*, but unlike the UK and many other central banks round the world, this is not the decision-making body on monetary policy. It organizes and discusses the main evidence and discussion papers to be put before the Governing Council on monetary matters.

There are, however, some key characteristics of this structure and other elements of the institutional set-up of the Eurosystem which have important implications for policy. As the Delors Committee (chapter 11), which designed the set-up for the Eurosystem, was composed almost entirely of central bank governors, it is not surprising that it is very well adjusted to the current views about the needs of monetary policy. First of all, although the treaty sets down the objective of monetary policy (maintaining price stability) – in general terms – the Eurosystem bank has a high degree of independence from political influence in exercising responsibility. Not only is the taking or seeking of advice explicitly prohibited, but the Governing Council members are protected in a number of ways in order to shield them from interest group pressures. First of all they have long terms of office – eight years in the case of the Executive Board, and not renewable – so that they are less likely to have any regard for their prospects for their next job while setting monetary policy. Secondly, the proceedings are secret so that people cannot find out how they voted. Each member is supposed to act purely in a personal capacity and solely with the aims of price stability at the euro area level in mind and without regard to national interests. No system can ensure this, but a well-designed one substantially increases the chance of this happening. More importantly it can reduce any belief that the members will act with national or other interests in mind. Thirdly, the Eurosystem is explicitly prohibited from 'monetizing' government deficits.

The point of trying to achieve this independence is simply 'credibility' – to try to maximize the belief that the Eurosystem will actually do just what it has been asked to do – namely maintain price stability. The stronger that belief can be, the less 'costly' monetary policy will be. If people do not believe that the ECB will be successful they will base their behaviour on that belief. Hence price and wage setters who believe that there will be increases in inflation substantially beyond what the ECB says it will deliver will set their prices with that higher outcome in mind. That means that the ECB then has to struggle against that belief, thereby entailing high interest rates. Thus, even though the ECB may intend exactly the same outcomes in both cases, it does not have to run such high interest rates to achieve them if it is 'credible'.

This credibility comes from sources other than independence. The structure of the governing council is strongly reminiscent of that of the Bundesbank. The Bundesbank was highly successful in maintaining low inflation. By having a similar structure (probably assisted by the Frankfurt location just a few kilometres down the road) the Eurosystem has been able to 'borrow' much of the Bundesbank's credibility.

12.1.1 The monetary policy of the Eurosystem

The Eurosystem is further assisted in the inherent credibility of its policy by having a single simple objective of price stability laid down by the treaty. If a central bank has multiple objectives then it will have difficulty explaining the balance between them, especially when they conflict. There was, for example, a short period of confusion at the outset over exchange-rate policy, as the Eurosystem is not responsible for the regime, only the execution. However, it rapidly became clear that since exchange-rate policy and the objective of monetary policy are inextricably linked, one of the two must have primacy, and ministers made it clear that it was price stability that was the driving force. The other common objectives for a central bank of maximizing employment and the rate of growth – in this case expressed as 'without prejudice to the objective of price stability, the ESCB shall support the general economic policies of the Community' – are clearly subservient.

However, for monetary policy to be credible it is necessary that the objective should be clear enough for people to act on and that the central bank's behaviour in trying to achieve that objective should be both observable and understandable as a feasible approach to success. Here the ECB had to define the objective since the Treaty's concept of price stability is far too vague to be workable. They opted for inflation over the medium term of less than 2 per cent. They also defined the inflation they were talking about as that in the harmonized index of consumer prices. After a swift clarification that this meant that zero inflation was the lower bound, the specification was widely criticized for being too inexact (compared with other central banks). Not only is the length of the medium term not spelt out but it is not clear how much and for how long prices can deviate from the target. Nor is there any indication of how fast inflation should be brought back to the target after a shock hits. In 2003 the target was reappraised and 'clarified' as being 'less than but close to 2 per cent'.

This means that a range of policy settings would be consistent with such a target. Policy is thus inherently not very predictable – something the Governing Council has sought to offset by trying to give clear signals about interest rate changes. Despite the inevitably diffused structure of decision-making with eighteen (now nineteen) independent decision-makers, the Eurosystem has come to offer a single explanation of how it regards the working of the economy and the appropriate response to it. One facet of the Eurosystem strategy that came in for criticism was what is known as the 'two-pillars' approach. Rather than adhering to any specific model or suite of models the Eurosystem announced that it would base its decisions on a wide range of indicators under two pillars. The first of these assigns a prominent role to money and has included a 'reference value' for the growth of broad money (M3). The second is a broadly based assessment of the outlook for price developments (section 3.7). In the 2003 reappraisal it was made clear that the monetary pillar was assigned a medium-term role and acted as a cross-check on the broad-based assessment that underpins policy decisions. While some controversy remains, this brings Eurosystem policy more into line with thinking in other central banks.

Assigning money such an important role by at least some of the members of the Governing Council was inevitable, given that this was the policy of the Bundesbank and some other successful predecessor NCBs. The particular reference value of 4.5 per cent growth (based on the sum of the expected medium-term inflation of around 1.5 per cent, the expected rate of growth of around 2 per cent and the drift in the velocity of circulation of around 1 per cent) has proved a problem, as it has been exceeded almost all of the time and a lot of effort has been spent explaining the discrepancies. Similarly the price assessment began as a narrative rather than a firmly based discussion of options and their possible outcomes. However, the process has developed steadily. The Eurosystem publishes its forecasts (broad macroeconomic projections) twice a year, with updating by ECB staff in the intervening quarters. Although these are 'staff' forecasts and do not necessarily represent the views of the Governing Council, they are increasingly being used as a basis for explaining policy.

The decentralized structure of the Eurosystem would make any closer 'ownership' of the forecasts by decision-makers impossible.

The Eurosystem is, of course, in good company. The Federal Reserve in the US has multiple objectives and offers no quantification at all for its target for the price level/inflation. It only publishes the staff forecasts by the Board of Governors with a lag.

Thus far policy has been generally successful, but since mid-2000 inflation has been stubbornly above 2 per cent (although at the time of writing the rapid decline in oil prices looks set to bring it down below that level). It is possible to blame the rapid rise in oil prices and some other shocks, but the deviation reached the stage where it had an effect on expectations (as calculated from French index-linked bonds). At that point the Governing Council reacted by raising interest rates ahead of a clearly revealed recovery in the economy. This helped enhance the Eurosystem's reputation as an inflation fighter but has been controversial in some political circles.

One concern, which does not seem to have proved relevant, was the fear that NCB governors and Executive Board members for that matter would, either explicitly or unconsciously, as a result of their backgrounds, tend to promote monetary policy decisions that supported the particular economic conditions in their country of origin rather than in the euro area as a whole. As a result, complex models of coalitions have been developed and there have been worries about whether those voting in favour are sufficiently representative of the euro area as a whole. The first reason why this is not relevant is that the Governing Council has not been voting on these issues. It has operated by consensus, in the sense that decisions are taken when the majority in favour is such that the minority withdraws its objection and does not feel the need to register dissent in some public manner.

The possible objection to that form of behaviour is not some form of country bias but that it might engender conservatism in policy-making. Since the records of the debates are not published, there is no way of finding out whether the particular structure has inhibited or delayed action. The simplest way of judging the issue is to look at the voting

records in the FOMC, where the results are published with a lag. Here it is immediately clear that deep divisions over what to do are relatively unusual. Most of the time there is not only no division at all, but also no proposal to change policy. When there are divisions the number of dissenters, even before the vote in the debate, tends to be quite small. The problem is thus predicated on a much more random and indeed contentious approach to policy-making than is actually the case.

There has been strong pressure for the Governing Council to be more open and publish minutes of its discussions, as this would inhibit the members from following obviously national interests. However, it is not at all clear what the impact would be. Publishing minutes or resolutions leads to more formal proceedings or taking positions for the sake of having them recorded if the US and Japanese experiences are anything to go by (Pollard, 2003). If the real discussion is pushed outside the meeting into informal sub-groups and consultations the result can be counter-productive and it will be even more difficult to sort out which opinions were responsible for which decisions.

12.2 The coordination of fiscal and other macroeconomic policies

Operating a single monetary policy for a diverse area has proved quite tricky. Policy which is well suited to some economies has been ill suited to others. It is important to be clear about the extent of the differences. Mayes and Virén (2000, 2002c) have shown that in some member states the exchange rate is at least twice as important as a determinant of inflation (as compared with interest rates). Similarly, the length of time it takes for the impact of policy on inflation to take its full effect also varies by a factor of two. Thus if the main problem lies in a region where policy has both a relatively small and a relatively slow effect, a policy based on the average experience of the euro area would not be very efficient.

The problem is further complicated because the main economic relationships involved, such as the Phillips curve, are non-linear and asymmetric. To spell this out a little: whereas a low unemployment/positive output gap has quite a strong upward pressure on inflation, high unemployment and a negative output gap has a considerably smaller downward impact for the same-sized difference. This means that simply adding up inflation rates and growth across the euro area and exploring aggregate relationships will be misleading. The analysis needs to be at the disaggregated level and then summed using the appropriate estimates of the effect in each region/member state.

However, once we look at fiscal and structural policy these differences become even more important because they have to offset the differential impact of monetary policy. The coordination of fiscal and other policies therefore needs not merely to permit different policy settings by each member state, subject to the constraints of prudence, but to expect it.

12.2.1 The coordination processes for macroeconomic policies

The structure of the 'economic' side of macroeconomic policy-making thus involves constraints from following policies that could harm the system as a whole – the Excessive Deficit Procedure (EDP) with the SGP and the system of enhanced policy learning or soft coordination under the Broad Economic Policy Guidelines. The annual Broad Economic Policy Guidelines form the framework that brings together three main elements:

*   the orientation of general fiscal policy (EDP, SGP and multilateral surveillance);
*   the European Employment Strategy (the Luxembourg process); and
*   the actions on structural reforms (the Cardiff process).

There is actually a fourth process – the Cologne process – which involves an informal exchange of views twice a year between, inter alia, the current, past and future presidents of ECOFIN, the Employment and Social Affairs Councils, the ECB, the Commission and the social partners. These processes are named after the location of the meeting places at which they were agreed.[4] The

coordination is somewhat broader than this as the annual reviews of the single market are also taken into account by the Economic Policy Committee (EPC): the committee of officials responsible for overseeing the Cardiff process. This is not to be confused with the Economic and Financial Committee (EFC), also composed of officials, which undertakes the preparation and offers advice for the decision-making Council of Economics and Finance Ministers (ECOFIN).

The general approach, spelt out in some detail in the Conclusions of the Lisbon Council in 2000 (see chapter 7), was to set 'a *new strategic goal* for the next decade: to become the most competitive and dynamic knowledge-based economy in the world, capable of sustainable economic growth with more and better jobs and greater social cohesion'. This involves aiming to change the structure of development of the EU so that it can achieve a rate of growth of 3 per cent a year (without inflationary pressure), which should be enough to bring down unemployment/increase employment to acceptable levels over the course of a decade. The key ingredients in this are continuing structural reform – overseen by the Cardiff process – a labour market strategy (Luxembourg) and the development of the appropriate fiscal incentives through a sound budgetary system within the member states. (It was amended at the end of 2002, at the Laeken Council, by the addition of a social policy strategy, which follows the same form of process as for the labour market.)

These processes do not compel, but by agreeing objectives, setting out how each member state intends to achieve the objectives, and evaluating progress, particularly through annual reports by the Commission, they act as considerable moral suasion. The meetings and the annual round of plans and evaluations enable the member states to learn from each other and encourage a search for best practice. These plans can be quite detailed. The annual National Action Plans under the Employment Strategy have, for example, covered over twenty guidelines grouped under four pillars: employability, entrepreneurship, adaptability and equal opportunities. Although the Commission produces assessments, much of the point of the arrangement is that it involves *multilateral surveillance*, so that each country is looking at the successes and failure of the others.

While there are obvious opportunities for window-dressing, this process, labelled 'the Open Method of Coordination', appears to have worked remarkably well. This does not, of course, mean that the objectives set out by the Lisbon Council will be achieved. Indeed since the EU economy experienced a downturn in the growth process in the first two years of the next decade there are obvious worries that there will be inadequate recovery thereafter to set the strategy back on track. It may nevertheless be the case that the practical ability to reform and introduce the flexibility required may be insufficient.

The key feature of the Open Method is that it does not compel specific actions but allows each member state and indeed the regions within them to respond to the challenges in the manner that best meets their local conditions, institutions and structures. Given that the whole structure of social welfare varies across the EU (Mayes et al., 2001, distinguish four different sorts of regime, for example), any given measure will have different outcomes in different member states. In a sense this is an example of the operation of the subsidiarity principle (section 2.2.4).

12.2.2 The Stability and Growth Pact and the Excessive Deficit Procedure

As was argued above, the SGP and the EDP have two features: a general orientation to ensure a policy that is sustainable over the longer term and a constraint on short-term actions – the excessive deficits – to ensure that the process is not derailed on the way. This general orientation is to achieve budgets that are 'in surplus or near balance'. This orientation will actually result in a continuing reduction in debt ratios. While this is necessary anyway for the member states exceeding the 60 per cent limit, it has been thought generally more desirable because of the expected strains on the system that are likely to occur with the ageing of the population. In any case it makes sense to have sufficient headroom to meet shocks. This headroom is required in two respects. First of all, given the structure of automatic stabilizers, each

member state needs to be far enough away from the 3 per cent deficit ratio limit for the normal sorts of adverse economic shock not to drive them over that limit. If that threatens to happen then the member state would need to take contractionary fiscal action when the economy is performing weakly.

This was precisely the problem that faced the German authorities in 2003. The combination of being too close to the limit and lower than expected growth forced them a little over the limit. Needing to raise taxes and restrain expenditure proved politically difficult. At the same time the French authorities also breached the terms of the Pact, although it is more arguable that this was deliberate rather than a result of incorrect forecasting. As a result ECOFIN agreed to suspend the pact rather than declare the two countries in breach of it, as recommended by the Commission. The Commission appealed this decision to the European Court of Justice, which ruled that ECOFIN could decide to take no action but that it could not suspend the process. This provoked an intensive debate on how to improve the pact in the light of the difficulties and a new agreement was reached in March 2005.

The extent to which a member state needs to be inside the 3 per cent boundary to avoid an undue risk of a breach and to maintain a stance that is sustainable in the long run depends on the extent of the automatic stabilizers and the distribution of expected shocks. Thus a country like Finland, which has fairly large stabilizers and seems prone to above-average shocks, would need to run a small surplus if it is to avoid hitting the 3 per cent boundary.

There is a danger (noted by von Hagen and Mundschenk, 2002) that having the 3 per cent deficit boundary will have a deflationary longer-term bias on the EU if member states compete too strongly to have very strong stabilizers. Sweden might be regarded as a case in point as its reaction to the pressures from membership has been to advocate the establishment of a substantial buffer fund (Johansson et al., 2002). These funds, if implemented, would be far larger than the Finnish buffer funds, which were put in place when Finland joined the euro area. However, Ricardian equivalence would suggest that simply repaying debt should have no influence on longer-term growth; it is simply having a higher tax burden today at the benefit of a lower burden in the future.

The pact can be viewed as having two parts: a preventative part that tries to discourage the member states from running imprudent and non-sustainable fiscal policies, and a corrective part that requires them to return to prudence as soon as possible if a mistake has been made. The 2005 agreement eased both sides of this, allowing more latitude for problems before declaring a breach (an excessive deficit) and hence permitting a less onerous return to compliance. This was not the full extent of the changes, as the member states also took the opportunity to improve the governance process of surveillance, tightening up the quality of statistics and accounting practices.

The general principles of the pact remain unchanged. Attempts to correct underlying problems with the pact such as the failure to take proper account of the economic cycle and to focus on the underlying problem of sustainable debt were discussed extensively in the debate on revision, but ultimately not adopted despite pressure from the Commission.

Views on how to evaluate these changes are divided. While the changes do not address the fundamental economic problems, they do represent a set of arrangements that are more likely to be adhered to. In practice the idea that a country could ever be harshly penalized was ambitious. The penalties were intended as a deterrent. If naming and shaming did not work then the pact was always likely to change if a significant number of countries were affected.

Various proposals were put forward for reforming the SGP and indeed the Commission itself advanced proposals (Buti et al., 2002; CEC, 2002a), which were then taken into account in considering the reform of the pact. These can be classified under three main headings but they all relate to means of easing the constraints somewhat without altering the overall principles. The first set of proposals relates to *symmetry*. Member state behaviour is constrained when deficits are in danger of becoming too large. There is no such restraint on surpluses. However, if we look at issues of macroeconomic management a switch from a 2 per cent surplus to balance can have just as much impact on aggregate demand as a switch from balance to a 2 per cent deficit. Hence countries which notch up major surpluses could destabilize the system somewhat simply by switching rapidly to a modest deficit well within the permissible limit. The Commission in particular suggested enhancing the ability to affect fiscal policy in 'good times' and this is reflected, albeit weakly, in the new provisions shown in box 12.1.

The second set of proposals sought to differentiate between member states according to whether they are well inside, near or above the 60 per cent limit for the debt ratio. Here the argument was simply that countries with no sustainability problem should be allowed more licence in the short run over deficits. This line of argument, of course, runs against that in the first group, as such licence could easily result in much bigger swings in fiscal policy that will affect the overall level of inflationary pressure in the euro area if we are talking about larger countries. Pisani-Ferry (2002) suggested that countries could choose to be in a Debt Stability Pact rather than the SGP if they keep their debt ratios below, say, 50 per cent.[5] This set of suggestions received only limited support in the revision of the pact.

The third group of suggestions relates to measurement issues.[6] In the traditional literature the concern is with 'cyclically adjusted' deficits. While measurement has indeed been improved, the idea of cyclical adjustment has not been followed. In the main this is because what is trend and what is cycle can only be established after the event, which is incompatible with the pre-emptive rather than corrective orientation of the pact.

There is a fourth set of suggestions that looked for a more market solution to the question of fiscal discipline. One of the big advantages of EMU has been that interest rates on sovereign debt in the previously more inflation-prone and more indebted parts of the euro area have converged on the lowest. Credit ratings have similarly increased. Although there is explicitly no agreement to bail out member states across the euro area, the market is behaving as if there were. Or at least it is behaving as if the EDP will restrain member states from running policies that will ever get them near

Box 12.1 Revisions to the Stability and Growth Pact agreed in March 2005

The revisions agreed by the Council on the recommendation of ECOFIN are quite detailed but can be summarized as follows:

(i)   The basic precepts are unchanged both in terms of the 60 per cent debt ratio and the 3 per cent deficit ratio and in terms of the sanctions to be applied if a member state is determined to have an excessive deficit and has undertaken insufficient measures to end it.

(ii) The adjustment processes required have been eased slightly, extending the time allowed by four months (to sixteen).

(iii) The criteria under which there can be exceptions to the 3 per cent rule for an excessive deficit have been softened. A decline in GDP or an extended period of low growth below potential are now admissible and 'all relevant factors' can be taken into account – although these are not specified in any detail.

(iv) The medium-term adjustment to a sustainable fiscal position has been eased slightly and the member states' structural balance* should be 'close to balance or in surplus' (CTBOIS) and now allows a lower limit of a 1 per cent deficit.

(v)   While member states are still required to reduce their structural deficits to reach CTBOIS by 0.5 per cent of GDP per year it is now admitted that they should do so faster in 'good times' and may do so more slowly in 'bad times' in the economic cycle.

(vi) Temporary divergences can be allowed for the costs of structural reforms aimed at improving the longer-term position.

(vii) If there are unforeseen events ECOFIN can issue changed deadlines and requirements.

(viii) Implicit liabilities such as those for the pension system from the ageing of the population should be taken into account.

In addition there is a set of requirements that should improve the governance and operation of the pact, which include: stronger peer pressure, better national fiscal rules and institutions – such as greater scrutiny by parliaments – improved forecasting, and better statistics and standards.

* Structural balance is defined as the cyclically adjusted deficit after removing the effect of temporary and one-off measures (as determined by the Commission).

default. This means that there is not so much pressure on marginal borrowing by those states that have debt or deficit ratio problems. The response of euro area interest rates as a whole to their difficulties will be muted. If, on the other hand, sovereign debt were specifically to be arranged in different tiers then there would be much more pressure on the marginal borrowers. The member states in a strong position would not be so adversely affected by their weaker colleagues and would get an interest rate reduction. The simplest way to introduce at least one tier might be for an EU guarantee to be offered for it. Since there are differences, even at present, the ECB could have an impact by not treating debt from all members identically and limiting the extent that it could hold debt from the lower-tier countries in its financing operations.

The difficulty with any such proposals is that they would involve an element of penalizing the countries with the less sustainable position compared to the current arrangements. Not surprisingly these proposals did not attract adequate support from the countries that would have been adversely affected and were not included in the revised pact. Furthermore, raising marginal interest rates makes the position of countries wanting to correct their budgetary balances even more difficult as their servicing costs rise. This could place a greater pro-cyclical pressure on the financial economy.

Mayes and Virén (2002a, b) show that there are considerable spillover benefits to the member states if they can become more coordinated. As a generality, the effectiveness of fiscal policy is doubled if countries move together rather than differently. However, the biggest gain is for the smaller countries, because fiscal policy is less effective in a more open economy. Without coordination the impact of fiscal policy in small countries is about half that in the larger. With coordination the effects become much more similar.[7]

A different and more fundamental concern for coordination is that the SGP relates to each member state individually. The normal concern for an EMU should be with the combined budgets of the member states. In that case the 3 per cent rule could be applied more leniently if some other states had much smaller deficits/larger surpluses. (The same could be applied to the structural requirement to be in surplus or near balance.) However, to run such a system, the sanctions would have to be much more effective and there would be the danger of a competition to be in the leniently treated group, which would tend to frustrate the overall criterion.

12.2.3 Policy coordination

The type of coordination described thus far differs from that normally discussed in the literature where much of the point is the coordination of monetary and fiscal policy. The argument is that there are some choices that can be made over how much to use fiscal policy rather than monetary policy to smooth fluctuations in the real economy or maintain price stability. The set-up within EMU rests upon a fairly simple economic model. The first side of it is that monetary policy cannot be used effectively to achieve longer-term real objectives, except in two senses:

- first, that having higher rates of inflation beyond levels near zero will tend to result in reductions in the overall rate of growth of the economy and indeed having falls in the price level may also be damaging; and,
- second, that inept policy that does not generate credibility will also impose a cost on society.

In general, taking these together the argument is in effect that the long-run Phillips curve is vertical and monetary policy per se will not have adverse effects on the longer-term level of unemployment (see chapter 10). Monetary policy can therefore be targeted appropriately at the stabilization of the price level rather than on objectives for the real economy. The scope for using monetary policy for smoothing real behaviour beyond that point is limited. As Thornton (2002) puts it, in general, the impact of monetary policy on inflation variation and output gap variation should be regarded as one of complements rather than trade-offs. A credible monetary policy aimed at restricting inflation to a fairly narrow range in a smooth manner should *ipso facto* also restrain the fluctuations in output round the sustainable path.

Similarly, in this simple paradigm fiscal policy can affect the rate of growth in terms of how funds are raised and spent. For example, one can view this in terms of incentives. Moreover, as discussed above, for fiscal policy to be consistent with price stability over the medium term it has to be sustainable (and believed to be such by markets). But discretionary fiscal policy, beyond the automatic stabilizers, is unlikely to be of much value, except to help exit the deflationary spiral, as Keynes identified in the 1930s (Feldstein, 2002, offers a clear exposition of this view). One of the main reasons for avoiding discretionary fiscal policy to address fluctuations in the economy is that policy operates with a lag, and there is a danger that by the time the problem is identified, the necessary measures are agreed by the legislature and implemented, and the impact occurs, it may destabilize what is then going on.

In these circumstances there is no need for much policy coordination between the monetary and fiscal authorities beyond transparency. The monetary authorities need to be able to make a reasonable assessment of the inflationary pressure likely to stem from fiscal policy, and the fiscal authorities need to know what to expect from monetary policy when setting their fiscal objectives. The potential conflict comes from the fact that, unlike fiscal policy, monetary policy can be changed quickly and substantially and indeed with fairly limited transaction costs. In the EU framework the coordination works because the monetary authorities are predictable. If they do react quickly it is to specific crisis signals like the shock of 11 September 2001. Given the time lag for fiscal changes, the fiscal authorities need to be confident that their monetary counterparts will not do anything in the intervening period that will render their policy stance inappropriate.

Pinning the ECB down to a single objective helps achieve this predictability. In the same way the rules of the SGP and macroeconomic coordination ensure that the ECB has plenty of warning about the way in which fiscal policy is likely to develop and hence is less likely to set inappropriate levels for interest rates. The EMU coordination will not work if the Eurosystem always believes that the fiscal authorities will always be too inflationary and/or if ECOFIN always believes that the Eurosystem will set interest rates that are too high. In these circumstances the problem will be self-fulfilling and monetary policy and fiscal policy will tend to push against each other. The resulting bias will be a cost. Fiscal policy needs to be credible to the monetary authority and vice versa. There is a danger of paying too much attention to the rhetoric in this regard. One of the strongest themes in the ECB *Monthly Bulletin* is the advocacy of fiscal prudence by the member states. It could be argued that if the ECB sees the need to make these remarks so frequently then there must be a problem. This does not follow. The problem only has to be in prospect. Exhortation can fulfil an important role in reinforcement.

The final part of the simple model which underlies the coordination mechanism is the belief that it is structural policies that will change the underlying rate of economic growth. Hence these form a key part of the continuing annual policy discussion. Once fiscal policy is largely automatic with respect to shocks, the surveillance mechanisms can focus on sustainability and on whether the size of budgetary swings that the automatic processes deliver are appropriate. If there were little concern for fine-tuning, then having more than the current six-monthly informal dialogue laid down by the Cologne process would seem unnecessary.

12.2.5 Asymmetry

Traditionally the focus on the *suitability and sustainability of EMU* has been on asymmetry in the sense of the differences between the member states, as discussed at the beginning of section 12.2. However, a different asymmetry is also present in the behaviour of the member states, namely asymmetry over the cycle (Mayes and Virén, 2002a).[8]

The total deficit is much more responsive in the downward than the upward phase. While responsiveness over the cycle as a whole is of the order of 0.2 to 0.3 (a 1 per cent increase in real GDP lowers the deficit ratio by 0.2–0.3 per cent) in the first year, it is five times as large in the downturn as the upturn. This bundles together all the influences – automatic stabilizers, discretionary policy changes, interest rate changes and any special factors. On unbundling, we can see that the automatic or cyclical part of the deficit behaves in a fairly symmetric manner. It is what governments choose to do with the structural part of the deficit which causes the asymmetry. What has happened is that governments increased the structural deficit in both downturns and upturns. Thus in good times governments tend to allow the system to ratchet up. The effect is split between revenues and expenditures but the asymmetry is more prominent on the revenue side. Tax rates are cut in upturns so that revenue to GDP ratios do not rise.

The SGP, EDP and the other components of macroeconomic coordination in EMU would have to lean against this tendency for asymmetric behaviour to reduce the pressures it generates. In practice the pressure is placed somewhat more on the downside: the area where governments have themselves responded more effectively in the past. Tackling this asymmetry and 'procyclicality in good times' was incorporated in general terms in the revised pact (box 12.1). Whether this will have much effect is debatable.

12.3 Completing EMU

It has to be said that the earlier discussion of coordination leaves a lot to the credibility of the process. Institutional credibility would be much greater if the degree of control over fiscal actions at the EU level were larger and there were some parallel institution to the ECB on the fiscal side. While this is not on the political agenda, its relevance would be much greater if one further plank, which characterizes most economic and monetary unions, were in place, namely a significant revenue-raising and spending capability at the EU level. This does not have to take the form of a larger budget per se (see chapter 19), as transfers from one region or member state to another in a form of fiscal federalism would also suffice. Currently stabilization takes place automatically within the member states. It only takes place between them to the extent that their agreed and automatic actions spill over from one to another because of their economic interdependence. The actual size of such a budget – around 2.5 to 7 per cent of Community GDP – to be highly effective (MacDougall Report, 1977; Mayes et al., 1992; chapter 19) is quite small compared to many existing federal states. It is, however, large compared to the structural funds and the current budgetary limit.

The enlargement of the EU has increased the need for fiscal federalism, although the current small economic size of the new members keeps the scale of any transfers needed down in the short term (see chapter 26). We are concerned here with cross-border fiscal flows to help balance out the effect of asymmetric shocks; dealing with income inequality is a problem of a very different order. Nevertheless, given the persistence of shocks, particularly with respect to their impact on the labour market, if fiscal flows do not ease the pressure then other changes will result to compensate. The most obvious would be an increase in migration. That is also not politically attractive at present (see chapter 8). It remains to be seen whether some greater integration on the macroeconomic side of EMU may not be preferred to increasing flexibility through cross-border migration. The relative attraction of stabilizing flows is that according to their definition they should be temporary. However, the shape of economic cycles does vary across the EU. Nevertheless, as economic and financial integration increases across the EU so self-insurance increases with diversification of income and wealth generation across the EU as a whole, helping to smooth the asymmetric shocks hitting any particular region without recourse to fiscal transfers (Mundell, 1973b and chapter 10).

12.3.1 Enlargement

It seems likely, however, that before EMU moves further towards 'completion', it will be expanded by the inclusion of new members. Adding Denmark and Sweden would make little difference to the structure of the eurozone or the issues that have been raised in this chapter. If the UK were to join, the position would be different, as the country is large enough to alter the balance of the single monetary policy. Also, since the UK is somewhat different both in its flexibility of response and its symmetry with the other member states, the consequences could be measurable. Whether it would affect the decision-making is a different matter. However, the bigger concern is the new members of the EU, several of whom have expressed a desire to move to eurozone membership as soon as possible. If that implies simply adhering to the present criteria, then it may be possible for some of these countries to join within quite a short number of years. With the exception of Slovenia, Cyprus and Malta, such membership is likely to take place with a level of income per head well below the average of the existing members, as convergence in these real terms is not one of the criteria. This could alter the character of the zone.

We have already noted that in the run-up to membership there was greater convergence of the member states than there has been in the period afterwards. This was because they had to run their monetary and fiscal policies individually to converge to quite a narrow band. Once inside the SGP, the EDP and the rest of the coordination under the BEPG apply, but the single monetary policy is no longer related to the inflation concerns of each country, just the total, so more inflation and indeed growth variation is possible and feasible. This experience is likely to be reflected even more strongly by the new members, as they are generally expected to 'catch up' quite rapidly with the existing members in real terms. This means that they will have faster rates of growth than the existing members, driven primarily by productivity. It has also been pointed out that this may have implications for inflation and monetary policy. While the price of tradeable goods and services may be reasonably similar across the EU, the same is not the case for non-tradeables. Large portions of non-tradeables are public and private services, where their principal input is labour. As productivity grows in the tradeable industries so wages are likely to rise with it. In turn, in a competitive economy, this is likely to result in wage increases in the non-tradeable sector. There it will not be so easy to find productivity growth to offset it and prices will tend to rise. Insofar as there are no offsets elsewhere, this will result in a rise in the general price level that is faster than in the rest of the euro area (see chapter 11).

This process, known as the Balassa–Samuelson effect, will probably not be substantial by the time the new members join the euro area: perhaps of the order of 1 per cent a year (Björksten, 1999). Given that the new members, taken together, will only contribute a fraction of the euro area GDP, this implies that the total effect on inflation would be of the order of 0.2 per cent a year. That may seem very small but with a medium-term target of inflation below 2 per cent it could represent an increase in the rate of interest. An increase would in any case be expected if the eurozone's growth prospects and hence rates of return increased. The actual impact is speculative and could vary from the disastrous to the trivial. It would be disastrous if some countries cannot cope with the increase in the real exchange rate that this relative inflation might imply. The problems of asymmetry that have worried some of the old members of the EU could be much larger for the new members, yet the drive for locking in credibility and buying lower interest rates by eurozone membership may be sufficient to play down the worries about sustainability at the time of joining. Too rapid an expansion of EMU could actually harm the prospects of the enterprise as a whole. It is therefore not surprising that the ECB has already blown relatively cold on some of the ideas implying early membership and has sought to toughen the interpretation of the convergence criteria.

NOTES

1 ECB (2001) is one of the most comprehensive and straightforward of the many available descriptions of the institutional arrangements; see also chapter 3.

2 The Eurosystem is also planning to move to a system where only some of the Governors have a vote (by rotation) when the number of member countries exceeds fifteen; see section 26.3.3 for an exposition. However, it will still be the case that the number of voting Governors will substantially exceed the number of Executive Board members.

3 Sometimes more than one.

4 See Hodson and Maher (2004) for a clear exposition of the processes and their role in policy-making. These various processes are brought together under the 'Helsinki process'.

5 Calmfors and Corsetti (2002) suggest allowing more deficit flexibility as the debt ratio falls below 60 per cent in a series of steps.

6 There were other proposals and concerns. For example, one concern was the unspecific nature of the requirement for the debt ratio to be diminishing and approaching the reference value 'at a satisfactory pace'. Some logical basis for defining 'satisfactory' would have been helpful.

7 These results are derived using the NIESR NiGEM model. They are higher than those achieved from SVAR models with a similar data set, so some caution in interpretation is merited. Mayes and Virén (2002b) use panel data for sixteen West European countries for the period 1960–2000 to estimate spillover equations and also obtain somewhat higher estimates of the benefit than traditionally estimated.

8 The study uses annual data for the period 1960–99 for the 2002 members of the EU excluding Luxembourg and treats them as a panel. The structural deficits are as defined by the Commission.

Part IV The single European market: policy integration

Part IV of the book covers areas which constitute the very foundations needed to facilitate a properly operating single European market. Hence it tackles in six chapters: competition rules; industrial policy; tax harmonization; transport policy; energy policy; and environmental policy. Industrial policy is included because variations in it would be tantamount to affording differing protection to national domestic industry. The absence of tax harmonization would have consequences equivalent to those of disparate industrial policies. Similar considerations apply to transport, energy and the environment. Of course, transport and energy are also dealt with as industries in their own right, as well as providers of social services, and the environment is treated in terms of tackling pollution and the consequent health benefits.

13 Competition policy[1]

WOLF SAUTER AND JURIAN LANGER

13.1 Introduction

The main purpose of competition policy is generally seen as protecting the market mechanism from breaking down. It does this by promoting competitive market structures and policing anti-competitive behaviour, thereby enhancing both the efficiency of the economy as a whole and consumer welfare in particular. In the EU this objective is pursued by means of enforcing prohibitions against (1) anti-competitive agreements between different companies, as well as against (2) anti-competitive behaviour by companies that are large enough – either individually or jointly – to harm competition, and (3) by vetting mergers between companies to verify whether these are likely to result in non-competitive market structures.

EU competition policy has three important characteristics that are not commonly found elsewhere. First, it not only aims to protect the competitive process as such, but also to promote and protect market integration between the EU member states. Second, apart from addressing private distortions of competition, it also curbs distortions of the market process by its member states. Both result from the third distinguishing feature of EU competition policy: it is implemented in a multi-level political system, that of the EU and its member states. In this context, it is worth noting that although until recently the application of the EU competition rules was highly centralized in the hands of the European Commission, due to its exemption monopoly for agreements infringing the cartel prohibition, this changed in May 2004. All these aspects are examined further below.

This chapter first discusses in greater detail the rationale for competition policy generally, and for EU competition policy in particular. Next, it sets out the basic instruments of the EU competition policy, its rules and procedures, and the manner in which they are implemented. Finally, three important developments in EU competition policy are addressed: the focus on public intervention, its shift to a more economic approach, and, most recently, towards decentralization.

13.2 The rationale for EU competition policy

The reasons for introducing competition rules have varied, both between different jurisdictions and over time. Although it is possible to draw up a long pedigree for competition law by pointing to Roman law, Magna Charta, common law or the statutes of medieval city-states, the first set of modern competition rules is contained in the US Sherman Act (1890). They were adopted as the result of political concern over the railroad, oil and financial 'trusts' emerging in the US at the end of the nineteenth century, an economic concentration of power that threatened to upset the popular consensus underpinning the economic as well as the political system of that country. In various European states from the early twentieth century onwards, national competition rules typically sought to balance the perceived benefits of economic collaboration between undertakings – cartels – against their acknowledged political and economic dangers (Gerber, 1998). Such competition policies often sought to provide protection against the socially and therefore politically undesirable results of 'unfair' competition, and aimed to ensure the survival of established undertakings by foreclosing markets from unregulated entry. In some cases, the legislation concerned enabled public authorities to impose the terms of existing private cartel agreements on entire economic sectors, as an alternative to state-designed market regulation, e.g. in the interest of price control. American ideas about competition policy were exported to both Germany and Japan after the Second World War, when the Allied occupation forces imposed new anti-monopoly legislation to curb the power of the financial–industrial combines that were widely seen as having powered the war effort of these two countries. For similar reasons, coal and steel being core essentials of the war industry of the time, anti-trust provisions were introduced into the 1951 Paris Treaty creating the European Coal and Steel Community (ECSC; see chapter 2), which consequently, unlike the EC Treaty, included the control of concentrations from the outset.

For the European Community beyond coal and steel, competition rules were introduced in the 1957 EEC Treaty, albeit for a different reason. In this case, the competition rules served primarily to ensure that restrictions on trade between member states – tariff and non-tariff barriers – that the member states' governments agreed to remove under this treaty would not be replaced by cartels between undertakings following national lines (Goyder, 2003). Hence, remarkably, competition rules addressed to undertakings were introduced into what at the time of its conclusion was otherwise still widely seen as an international treaty between independent states.

Initially, therefore, the EU competition rules essentially served to complement an inter-state trade policy of reducing trade barriers and promoting market integration. From this starting point, promoting market integration has developed into the overriding rationale of EU competition policy, alongside that of maintaining 'effective competition' (Bishop and Walker, 2002). This integration rationale has had a profound impact on the orientation of EU competition policy that has at times led it into conflict with the emerging economic consensus favouring efficiency considerations.

For example, the integration rationale tended to lead to a negative view of vertical agreements with territorial effects. This conflict is discernible in the groundbreaking ruling by the European Court of Justice (ECJ) *Consten & Grundig* of 1966. Consten was the exclusive distributor in France for Grundig, a German producer of televisions and radios. Consten agreed not to market products competing with those of Grundig. In exchange, Grundig granted to Consten an exclusive licence to use its trademark in France. Thereby, Consten was in practice shielded from exports from other countries and enjoyed absolute territorial protection. There may have been good economic reasons for Consten to require territorial protection to recover, for example, its investment in setting up a sales network and an after-sales service in France. However, the ECJ ruled that this contract infringed the cartel prohibition of the treaty as it had a market partitioning effect. Agreements that tend to restore the national divisions in trade between member states, so the court reasoned, frustrate the objective of the Community to abolish the barriers between states, and undertakings could therefore not be allowed to reconstruct such barriers. Although economic theory tells us that restrictions of intra-brand competition, i.e. between different suppliers of Grundig products, are unlikely to have harmful effects on competition so long as there is sufficient inter-brand competition, i.e. between suppliers of Grundig products and products from producers other than Grundig, the Court did not make this distinction in its ruling and considered the protection of both forms of competition equally important. The current competition rules on vertical restrictions recognize that vertical agreements generally produce efficiencies and should generally be treated more leniently. Under these rules, however, absolute territorial protection is still prohibited. The current rules only allow for active sales restrictions on distributors, limiting their active selling outside their own territories, while allowing them to react to unsolicited outside sales requests.

In spite of these varied origins, and while it is difficult to find an example where pure economic reasoning motivated the introduction of competition rules, the rationale of competition policy is increasingly defined in economic terms.

Evidently, the relevant economic theory has evolved over time as well (Motta, 2004).

The economic reasoning concerning the goals and limits of competition policy has been developed in particular in the US, where an early willingness of courts to entertain economic arguments was subsequently stimulated by the appointment of law and economics scholars to the bench and to influential regulatory positions. Over the past century, the resulting debate has had a profound impact on the way competition policy is applied both in the US and beyond. Originally, competition policy focused on the results of market structure and the behaviour of market participants associated with the 'Harvard School'. Increasingly, the so-called 'Chicago School' of anti-trust economics, focusing on efficiency, price effects, and the self-policing nature of the market (Posner, 1976), has become the new mainstream of industrial organization, and hence of much analysis underlying competition policy (Scherer and Ross, 1990). In addition, game theoretic approaches are increasingly used to deal with, for example, problems of collusion and joint dominance in oligopolistic markets (Phlips, 1995). EU competition policy has followed these trends to varying degrees, modified in particular by the intervening variable of its overriding integration objective (Mehta and Peeperkorn, 1999). A parallel development took place in the EU, especially due to the influence of the Freiburg School or Ordoliberalism (Gerber, 1998). The proponents of this school accepted the main ideas of classical liberalism, but they also extended the classical views by arguing that individual freedom should be protected not only against governmental interference but also against private economic power.

Today, the market mechanism is generally seen as the most efficient instrument to set prices and thereby allocate resources. To a large extent, however, the success of markets at doing this is determined by the degree of competition in the market involved. Economists have traditionally illustrated this argument by analysing 'ideal types' of the two theoretical extremes: contrasting, on the one hand, the maximum imaginable number of competitors in a given market, and, on the other hand, the least possible number. 'Perfect competition' in

fully contestable markets can be demonstrated to lead to Pareto-optimal, or maximal allocative efficiency: a situation in which the welfare of any single participant cannot be increased without another participant being disproportionately worse off. Conversely, monopoly markets can be demonstrated to lead to monopoly rents and net welfare losses, further aggravated by technical developments and efficiencies forgone, and with further losses caused by attempts to lock in monopoly advantage by political 'rent-seeking'. However, 'perfect competition', which presupposes homogeneous products and full transparency of prices and costs as well as the absence of market barriers, economies of scale and scope, and learning effects, is not a real-world phenomenon. Instead, market imperfections, or market failures, are likely to lead to restrictions of competition that produce sub-optimal results. Firms also have economic incentives to collude and to exclude competitors. Consequently, the role of competition policy is to substitute for competitive pressure by ensuring that restrictions on competition between undertakings that are harmful to the competitive process (rather than to individual competitors) are prevented or removed. Because pure market outcomes are likely to be theoretically sub-optimal in many cases, this leaves ample room for disagreement on what amounts to a restriction of competition that merits policy intervention. In the context of EU competition policy, the key concept in this regard is that of maintaining 'effective competition' or 'workable competition'.

In the *Metro* v. *Commission* case of 1977, the ECJ appealed to the concept of workable competition as the effective type of competition to realize the economic objectives of the EC Treaty. The court stated that:

[t]he requirement contained in Articles 3 and [81 of the EC Treaty] that competition shall not be distorted implies the existence on the market of workable competition, that is to say the degree of competition necessary to ensure the observance of the basic requirements and the attainment of the objectives of the Treaty, in particular the creation of a single market achieving conditions similar to

those of a domestic market. In accordance with this requirement, the nature and intensiveness of competition may vary to an extent dictated by the products and services in question and the economic structure of the relevant market . . . the requirements for the maintenance of workable competition may be reconciled with the safeguarding of objectives of a different nature and that to this end certain restrictions on competition are permissible.

Here again there is debate about whether effective competition concerns the process of competition as such, or the outcome that markets produce in terms of improving consumer welfare – generally equated with efficiency. In any event, it is by now well established that effective competition is seen in terms of preventing harm to competition as such, not to particular competitors (Bishop and Walker, 2002).

The *raison d'être* of EU competition policy was highlighted by Advocate General Jacobs in the *Oscar Bronner* v. *Mediaprint* case of 1998, when he reminded the court that 'the primary purpose . . . is to prevent distortion of competition – and in particular to safeguard the interests of consumers – rather than to protect the position of particular competitors'. Especially since the appointment of Mario Monti (an academic economist) as commissioner responsible for competition policy in 1999, the promotion of efficiency has been declared to be the core value under competition law. For example, in a speech in July 2001, he said that 'the goal of competition, in all its aspects, is to protect consumer welfare by maintaining a high degree of competition in the common market'. During his tenure, he has emphasized the importance of sound economic analysis. A number of reforms have taken place to reflect these objectives. As far as future developments are concerned, the present Commissioner, Neelie Kroes, has made it clear that economic reforms, and the contribution of competition policy towards these goals, are at the top of her agenda.

Whether there is effective competition has to be determined in relation to a specific 'relevant market' that is defined both in terms of the product concerned and geographically. Factors taken into account, such as the existence of market power, the number of competitors, relative market share and degree of concentration, demand and supply substitution, the existence of barriers to market entry and exit, and potential competition, affect both the evaluation of the degree of effective competition in the relevant market and market definition itself (CEC, 1997e).

13.3 General overview of the legal framework

Although EU competition policy is increasingly driven by economic considerations, its origins are found in European law, and it must evidently operate within the constraints of its legal framework. This legal framework consists of the substantive, procedural and institutional rules that govern EU competition policy (see chapters 3 and 4). It is important to understand that the framework only applies to 'undertakings' (Wils, 2000).

The notion of undertaking is defined in the *Höfner & Elser* v. *Macrotron* case of 1991 as 'every entity engaged in an economic activity, regardless of the legal status of the entity and the way in which it is financed'. The definition was refined in the *Commission* v. *Italy* case of 1998, where the court stated that 'any activity consisting in offering goods and services on a given market is an economic activity'. The notion of undertaking was further defined in two other cases. In the *Poucet & Pistre* v. *Cancava* case of 1993, the court held that an agency charged with managing a social security scheme was not an undertaking within the scope of competition as the scheme fulfilled an exclusively social function that is based on the principle of national solidarity and is entirely non-profit-making. Nor did the court consider a private organization entrusted by the public authorities with anti-pollution surveillance duties in an oil port to constitute an undertaking under the competition rules in the *Diego Cali & Figli* v. *Servizi Ecologici del Porto di Genova* case of 1997. More recently, in the *FENIN* case of 2006, concerning three Spanish ministries running the Spanish national health system which purchased medical goods from an association of undertakings marketing these goods, called FENIN, the court decided that where a public body purchases goods or services for social or other non-economic purposes it will not be engaged in economic activity, and consequently this will not be an undertaking for the purposes of the competition rules. For example, in the *Spanish Couriers* case of 1990, the Commission held that the Spanish post office constituted an undertaking within the meaning of competition law when providing special express services, even though it was part of the general administration of the Spanish state.

The legal basis of EU competition policy is found, first of all, in the EU Treaty itself (Articles 3, 10, 81–6 and 87–9). Second, it is found in implementing legislation adopted by the Council and Commission in the form of regulations and directives (see chapters 3 and 4), which develop in particular the wide-ranging powers of the Commission in this field, notably Council Regulation 1 of 2003 (reforming Council Regulation 17 of 1962), and Commission implementing Regulation 773 of 2004. Council Regulation 139 of 2004 (reforming Council Regulation 4064 of 1989) provides the framework for merger control by the Commission. In addition, an increasing number of notices and guidelines that are not formally binding provide essential information on the manner in which the Commission intends to apply EU competition policy. Examples are the Commission notice on the definition of the relevant market referred to above (CEC, 1997e); the Commission's guidelines on vertical restraints of 2000, the Commission notice on horizontal cooperation agreements of 2001; the Commission's guidelines on horizontal mergers of 2004; and, the notices that accompanied the modernization package in 2004 discussed later in this chapter. By issuing such guidance, both on how it interprets the binding rules of EU law and on how it intends to use the margin of discretion inherent in its policy powers, the Commission increases the predictability of its policy – and thereby facilitates the enforcement of EU competition law between private parties and at a national level.

The ultimate arbiter of the various rules, and on whether Commission policy remains within the bound of its powers, is the ECJ. The ECJ becomes involved either directly on a 'pre-judicial' reference by a national court, or in judicial review proceedings following a first appeal against Commission decisions to the EU Court of First Instance (CFI). In principle, the standards applied are those of administrative review of policy: i.e., they focus on formal competence to act, controlling respect for the rights of the defence and enforcing minimum standards of reasoned rationality. The ECJ and the CFI have nevertheless on a number of occasions led the way in demanding higher standards of economic argument, rather than more formal reasoning, from the Commission (Korah, 2004).

Particularly with regard to merger control, the Community courts have scrutinized the Commission's reasoning very closely. For example, the CFI concluded in the *Airtours* v. *Commission* case of 2002 that the decision to block the proposed merger, 'far from basing its prospective analysis on cogent evidence, is vitiated by a series of errors of assessment as to factors fundamental to any assessment of whether a collective dominant position might be created'. The judgment indicated that the court requires better economic evidence when reviewing the Commission's decisions. The CFI also addressed the burden of proof, arguing that it was the Commission which had to produce convincing economic evidence of the anti-competitive effects of the proposed merger. Another example in this context is the ruling by the ECJ in the *Tetra Laval* v. *Sidel* case of 2005. In its press release, the ECJ stressed that the 'fact that the Commission enjoys discretion in economic matters does not mean that the Community Courts must refrain from reviewing the Commission's interpretation of information of an economic nature, especially in the context of a prospective analysis'.

The European Commission is the institution that is responsible at EU level for the implementation of EU competition law and policy. It takes most formal decisions by simple majority, as a collegiate body. These decisions are prepared by the Directorate General for Competition, DG COMP (formerly known as DG IV), which reports to the commissioner responsible for competition policy; since November 2004 this has been Neelie Kroes.

Following the abolition of the system requiring notification of potentially anti-competitive agreements by the parties to these agreements, the Commission can be apprised of a competition problem by a complaint by an undertaking or member state, a leniency application by an undertaking trying to come clean, or can act on its own initiative ('*ex officio*') to investigate either specific cases or entire economic sectors ('sector inquiries'). It has considerable powers to require undertakings to collaborate in its investigations, backed up by fines, including the right to obtain evidence by unannounced inspections of company offices ('dawn raids'). In addition, the Commission can penalize all infringements of the competition rules with significant financial penalties, including fines of up to 10 per cent of the (global) group turnover of the companies involved, without any absolute upper limit. Fines of well over a hundred million euros have already been imposed in a number of cases.

For example, the Commission imposed in 2002 a total fine of 167.8 million euros on Japanese video games maker Nintendo and seven of its official distributors in Europe for colluding to prevent exports from low-priced countries to high-priced – another illustration of its focus on territorial restrictions with their effect on inter-state trade. In 2004, the Commission fined Microsoft more than 497 million euros for refusing to supply information necessary for interoperability and for bundling the Windows operating system with Windows Media Player. In 2005, the Commission adopted a decision fining AstraZeneca 60 million euros for having misused public procedures and regulations in a number of member states with a view to excluding generic firms and parallel traders from competing against one of Astra Zeneca's medicines. In the same year, the Commission imposed fines totalling €56 million on four Italian tobacco processors for colluding over a period of more than six years on the prices paid to tobacco growers and intermediaries and on the allocation of tobacco suppliers in Italy. In 2006, the Commission found that eight suppliers and six purchasers of road bitumen in the Netherlands participated in a cartel from 1994 to 2002 to fix prices in violation of Article 81. These fourteen companies have been fined a total of 266 million euros and one

of the participants was fined more than 100 million euros.

Because the treaty prohibitions on restrictions of competition (i.e. the cartel prohibition of Article 81(1) and the prohibition on abuse of dominant position) are directly effective, parties may choose to invoke these rules in procedures before national courts of all levels in the EU member states (Komninos, 2002).

The *Courage* case of 2001 is interesting here. Inntrepreneur Estates Ltd administrated the leased pubs of both Courage and Grand Metropolitan in the United Kingdom. The standard form of lease agreement contained the obligation that tenants must order their beer exclusively from Courage. Crehan, one of the tenants, failed to pay for supplied beer. When Courage started proceedings, Crehan claimed that the exclusive purchase obligation infringed the cartel prohibition of the EC Treaty. However, under English law, a claimant cannot rely on his own wrong. The CFI found that the English rule was not fully consistent with the long-established direct effect of the treaty prohibitions. Merely being party to an illegal agreement was not necessarily wrong, if the party was not responsible for the infringement of the cartel prohibition. The full application of the national rule made it too difficult for the plaintiff to enforce its rights to compensation under Community law, and hence the national rule should not be applied. This is particularly an issue where the claimant's bargaining position is too weak to choose the terms of the contract.

Finally, apart from the Commission, from 1 May 2004 all national competition authorities and national judges in the member states now have explicit powers (and the obligation) to apply the exemption provision of the cartel prohibition as provided for in Article 81(3) EC Treaty. Under the old Regulation 17 of 1962, parties could obtain such an individual exemption only from the Commission. Article 9(1) of Regulation 17 conferred 'sole power' on the Commission 'to declare Article [81(1)] inapplicable pursuant to Article [81(3)] of the Treaty'. After much debate and an extensive modernization exercise, Article 81(3) is now directly applicable. The direct applicability of the treaty rules on competition in general and Article 81(3) in particular may give rise to requests by national courts for the pre-judicial rulings on points of law by the ECJ that are an important mechanism to ensure the coherent application of EU competition law and policy. Depending on whether the modernization process may also lead to (more) private enforcement of the EU competition rules, it is expected that the role of the ECJ as supreme legal arbiter will increase as a result of modernization.

13.4 The substantive norms

There are three core substantive norms of EU competition law that are addressed to undertakings:

1. the prohibition of agreements and concerted practices between firms restricting competition;
2. the prohibition of abuse of (single firm or joint) dominance;
3. the obligation to submit mergers and acquisitions for prior clearance under the merger control rules.

In addition, there are specific competition rules that apply to aid by the member states, and to companies privileged in their relation to public authority.

13.4.1 The cartel prohibition

The prohibition of collusion restricting competition (cartels) is found in Article 81(1) EC. Prohibited cartel agreements cover, for example, price fixing, market sharing, tying and discrimination.

As far as collusive behaviour is concerned, for example, the ECJ has made clear in the *Sugar Cartel* case of 1975 that undertakings may not knowingly substitute the risk of competition for practical coordination between them that results in conditions of competition that do not correspond to normal market conditions of the market. In this case, the Commission found that various principal sugar-producing corporations had infringed the competition rules by colluding on the European market for sugar. The infringements ranged from concerted practices to unlawful economic pressure on other companies to restrict the export and import of sugar. The companies concerned tried to have the Commission's decision annulled by claiming that they had not coordinated their market conduct. The court explained that the requirement of independence does not deprive undertakings of the right to adapt themselves intelligently to the existing and anticipated conduct of their rivals, as long as there is no direct or indirect contact between the undertakings that influences the conduct on the market of an actual or potential competitor or discloses to such a competitor the course of conduct that they themselves have decided to adopt on the market.

By force of Article 81(2), infringement of the prohibition of Article 81(1) triggers the nullity of the restrictive clauses of the agreements involved, which can lead to civil law liability and hence to claims for damages under national law.

The ECJ addressed the scope nullity of an agreement that infringed Article 81 in the *Consten & Grundig* case and the *Société La Technique Minière* v. *Maschinenbau Ulm* case of 1966, where the court explained that Article 81(2) only applies to 'those parts of the agreement which are subject to the prohibition, or to the agreement as a whole if those parts do not appear to be severable from the agreement itself', and that 'any other contractual provisions which are not affected by the prohibition, and which therefore do not involve the application of the Treaty, fall outside Community law'.

The Commission can in addition penalize infringements by means of fines. Certain national systems in addition provide for penal sanctions. As explained above, Article 81(3), however, provides for the possibility of exemptions from the Article 81(1) prohibition. Under the old system of Council Regulation 17/62, such exemptions could only be awarded by the Commission, and only following mandatory notification of the agreements involved to the Commission. As a result of modernization, this highly centralized system was phased out in May 2004, when both the notification system and the exemption monopoly of the Commission were abolished. Under the new system, parties to agreements are required to assess for themselves whether their arrangement infringes the cartel prohibition and whether it may benefit from Article 81(3). In case of doubt or conflict, parties may invoke this article before a national court.

13.4.2 The prohibition on abuse of dominant position

The prohibition of abuses of dominant position (monopolies and oligopolies) in Article 82(EC) focuses on abusive anti-competitive behaviour associated with market power rather than on the securing of high market shares as such. Therefore, although it is not illegal to be dominant, provided dominance is achieved based on legitimate commercial advantage won in the market, there are evidently no exemptions for abuse of such dominance. Like the restrictions of competition covered by the cartel prohibition, possible abuses of dominance include unfair (e.g. excessive or predatory) pricing, discrimination and tying. Abuses are often qualified as either exploitative (of consumers and customers), exclusionary (foreclosing competition from the market), or discriminatory (between consumers, competitors, or downstream operations and competitors) in nature. However, unlike the cartel prohibition, which in principle applies to all undertakings, the prohibition of abuse of dominance is asymmetrical in nature: it only applies to those firms that can afford to behave – and price – independently of their competitors, suppliers and customers.

The definition of a dominant position was established in the famous *Hoffmann-La Roche* case of 1979. The court wrote the following: 'The dominant position thus referred to in [Article 82] relates to a position of economic strength enjoyed by an undertaking which enables it to prevent effective competition being maintained on the relevant market by affording it the power to behave to an appreciable extent independently of its competitors, its customers and ultimately of the consumers.'

The prohibition on abuse of dominance is intended to force such firms to behave as if they were subject to effective competition by abstaining from anti-competitive behaviour. In order to establish a breach of Article 82, first the relevant market must be established. The relevant market has a product and a geographic dimension. The product market consists of all products or services that are interchangeable or substitutable by the consumer, by reason of the products' characteristics, their prices and their intended use. The geographic market for the stated product is the area in which the conditions of competition are sufficiently homogeneous. Next, the existence of dominance in that relevant market should be established, and finally, the existence of an abuse must be shown, as well as an effect on trade between member states.

The legal test for abuse was also set out in the *Hoffmann-La Roche* case and later restated in the *Michelin* case. The court defined abuse as follows: 'In prohibiting any abuse of a dominant position on the market in so far as it may affect trade between member states, Article [82] covers practices which are likely to affect the structure of a market where, as a direct result of the presence of the undertaking in question, competition has been weakened and which, through recourse different from those governing normal competition in products or services based on trader's performance, have the effect of hindering the maintenance or development of the level of competition still existing on the market.'

13.4.3 Merger control

Unlike the prohibitions on cartels and abuse of dominance, which are normally enforced after the alleged infringement occurs (or *ex post*), EU merger control is based on a system of pre-notification (or *ex ante* control) that is elaborated in the Merger Control Regulation. This system is intended to provide legal certainty to firms before they implement their transaction, and to allow the Commission to vet all such transactions of a certain size (or Community dimension), based on a complex system of turnover thresholds. Merger control aims at preserving 'effective' or workable competition, based on an assessment of the structural characteristics of the relevant product and geographical markets. As elsewhere in EU competition policy, market definitions are essential here: if wide product and geographical market definitions are used, mergers are evidently less likely to be considered problematic than if narrower markets are concerned: size and the effects of size are relative to a specific factual context. In principle, mergers are considered useful to allow undertakings to realize potential efficiencies of scale and scope in contestable markets. Mergers cannot normally be executed until they have been formally approved. Such approval may be given subject to structural remedies (e.g. divestiture of assets such as brands and intellectual property rights, as well as production facilities), and frequently is. In addition, behavioural remedies such as non-discrimination obligations are sometimes considered (Jones and Gonzalez-Diaz, 1992). The latter type of remedy is, however, difficult to monitor and enforce effectively, and is generally avoided whenever possible.

The EU was long denied merger policy powers, because its member states preferred to vet themselves, or indeed promote the creation of national 'industrial champions', in particular in a wide and often ill-defined set of industries considered to be of strategic or political importance (see chapter 14). The failure of such mutually exclusive national strategies, the increasing desire of businesses to merge across national borders without engaging in multiple notifications subject to different rules, and the merger boom triggered by the 1985 internal market initiative, were all instrumental in finally convincing the member states to adopt the Merger Control Regulation in 1989 (Neven, Nutall and Seabright, 1993a). Since then, merger control has become widely acclaimed as a model for EU competition policy generally. The main reasons for this success are strict rules and deadlines that force the Commission to produce binding decisions within a limited timeframe, and undertakings to collaborate fully in the process of preparing these decisions. The scope of Community competence in this area – determined by the turnover thresholds in the regulation – remains politically sensitive: the member states are reluctant to agree to extend it further by lowering the relevant thresholds. In

1997, the Merger Control Regulation was nevertheless amended to lower the turnover thresholds above which it applies, bringing a larger number of mergers within its scope, and to apply to cooperative joint ventures (Council, 1997a). In the case of cooperative joint ventures, the Article 81(3) test was applied to decide whether they were likely to give rise to unacceptable anti-competitive economic effects, in particular in adjacent upstream or downstream markets where both parents remained present.

The reform of the Merger Control Regulation by Council Regulation 139 of 2004 has improved the system of referrals between the EU and national jurisdictions, and introduced a number of procedural changes. More importantly, the reform clarified the concept of dominance – i.e. the substantive test applied – as including collective dominance in tight oligopoly situations (Stroux, 2004). The regulation now applies a so-called SIEC test, meaning that a merger that 'significantly impedes effective competition' should be blocked or only be cleared after the acceptance of remedies.

The SIEC test is codified in Article 2(3) of the Merger Regulation. This provision reads as follows: 'a concentration which would significantly impede effective competition, in the common market or in a substantial part of it, in particular as a result of the creation or strengthening of a dominant position, shall be declared incompatible with the common market'.

13.4.4 Public undertakings

In addition to the rules that apply to undertakings in general, the EU Treaty includes specific provisions governing the application of competition rules for undertakings that are controlled, favoured or charged with executing key economic tasks by public authorities. Article 86(EC) provides rules concerning state-owned undertakings, undertakings that benefit from certain legal advantages assigned in an arbitrary manner or from legal monopoly rights and undertakings charged with tasks in the general economic interest, such as utilities (e.g. in the energy, transport and communications sectors). Article 86 contains three interrelated provisions. The prohibition in

Article 86(1) is addressed to member states, not to undertakings. It prohibits member states from enacting or maintaining in force any measures in relation to public undertakings and undertakings to which they have granted special or exclusive rights which are contrary to the rules of the treaty. Conversely, Article 86(2) is addressed to undertakings themselves. It states that, in principle, the competition rules apply to public undertakings charged with services in the general economic interest without limitation, unless this makes it impossible for such companies to carry out their duties.

For example, the *Höfner & Elser* v. *Macrotron* case of 1991 concerned the following facts. In Germany, a public agency called the *Bundesanstalt für Arbeit*, had the exclusive right of employment procurement, i.e. headhunting. The agency focused, however, primarily on the recruitment of non-key personnel, leaving executive recruitment activities untouched. Höfner and Elser were recruitment consultants. They contracted with Macrotron to find the latter a sales director. When Macrotron did not approve the candidate and refused to pay, Höfner and Elser started proceedings. In its defence, Macrotron claimed that the recruitment contract was void as it breached the agency's exclusive right of employment procurement. The German court dealing with the case turned to the ECJ to obtain a preliminary ruling. The ECJ explained that a member state is in breach of the prohibitions of Articles 86 juncto Article 82, if an undertaking with a certain legal advantage, merely by exercising the exclusive rights granted to it, cannot avoid abusing its dominant position. According to the court, there was an infringement in this case as the agency was manifestly incapable of satisfying the demand for executive recruitment prevailing on the market. Another example is the *Porto di Genova* case of 1991. In the port of Genova, Merci Commerciali held the exclusive right to load and unload ships. Although its services were not efficient, no other company was allowed to compete with Merci or to set up a similar service in the harbour. Enjoying its privileged position, subsequently, Merci demanded payments for services that had not been requested, charge disproportionate prices and refused to use modern technology, etc. One of

Merci's customers, Siderurgica, suffered losses due to this poor performance and started proceedings which resulted in a reference to the ECJ. The court clarified that a company like a port authority that is induced by national and municipal legislation to commit abuses may infringe Article 86 juncto Article 82.

Article 86(3) concerns the policing and legislative powers of the Commission. First, it provides that the Commission may address decisions to member states to ensure the observance of Article 86. Second, it gives the Commission power to issue directives to the member states to ensure the application of the Article. Exceptionally, it does not require permission from the European Parliament or the Council to adopt such rules. The importance of Article 86, long a dormant provision of the treaty, has increased markedly since 1988, when it was applied to the telecommunications sector. This is because 'natural monopoly' arguments that were long held to apply to public utilities have become contested, and public ownership is increasingly unpopular. Consequently, the application of the competition rules has worked in favour of the spread of independent private enterprise in sectors traditionally controlled by the state. The treaty itself, however, remains formally neutral concerning public and private ownership, by force of its Article 295.

13.4.5 State aid

Finally, in its Articles 87–9, the treaty contains rules on restrictions of effective competition that result from member states' authorities at any level favouring some companies over others by means of subsidies: i.e. state aid (Quigley and Collins, 2004; see also chapter 14). Illegal state aid covers subsidies in any form, including outright financial subsidies as well as tax advantages or exceptions, favourable loan terms, credit guarantees, the sale or lease of goods and real estate below market prices, and many other forms of discrimination by public authorities between undertakings. Some types of state aid are, however, acceptable. Hence, state aid is governed by a rule in Article 87(1) prohibiting aid that distorts competition, and two possible exceptions to this rule: first, aid that is by definition considered compatible with the internal market (see chapter 7), as listed in Article 87(2) (e.g. social aid to consumers and disaster relief); and, second, aid that the Commission may clear by decision, following mandatory notification, as listed in Article 87(3) (e.g. certain regional and sectoral aid). Commission findings of illegal aid can in theory be overruled by the Council, although in practice this rarely occurs. In this area, Commissioner Kroes announced in 2005 that more weight should be given to market failures. Only when market failures exist is there a potential for state aid to intervene. A comprehensive reform of the state aid rules is expected to be forthcoming in the coming years.

Although they are also applied by DG COMP, the state aid rules constitute a separate system under which the Commission is attributed powers that are considerably less significant than those it enjoys in relation to private undertakings, in particular because the Council was long unable to agree on any secondary implementing legislation for state aid. As will be discussed below, this has changed over recent years.

Whether directed at private undertakings or member states, the EU competition norms are triggered only if constraints on competition are both appreciable and have the effect of distorting trade between the member states (CEC, 1997f). This is consistent with the integration rationale of EU competition policy: unless they distort trade flows, restrictions of competition do not hamper integration, and consequently do not concern the EU. However, the integration rationale also means that certain types of territorial protection are prohibited that might not otherwise be particularly objectionable from an economic perspective, if they have the effect of reinforcing trade barriers along national lines. This still leaves EU competition policy a broad scope, which has often made it difficult to enforce effectively.

For example, in the *Distillers* case of 1978, the Commission condemned the export deterrent created by Distillers' dual pricing system for the UK and the rest of the EU. In the *Zanussi* case of 1979, the Commission objected to a system of after-sales guarantees that did not apply to washing machines used in a different member state from the one in which they had been bought. More recently, the Commission heavily fined Volkswagen in 1998 for setting up a system with its Italian dealers whereby end consumers in member states other than Italy were unable to order VW cars from Italian dealers.

13.5 Enforcement

The Commission's relatively limited human resources have long been dedicated largely to the enforcement of the prohibition of anti-competitive agreements contained in Article 81 (although, more recently, the relative weight of state aid policy has increased). This is the result of interrelated systemic, political and practical constraints.

Article 82 decisions remain relatively rare. This is in large part due to the high burden of proof the European courts have imposed on the Commission, given the inherently intrusive nature of this prohibition, which, based on their size, bars individual behaviour by companies that would otherwise be acceptable business practice. A clear indication of the difficulties involved is that over the period of almost forty years that the Commission has actively applied the competition rules, it has adopted only around forty decisions: evidently, it is likely that in reality significantly higher numbers of grave abuses of dominance occurred over this period. In December 2005, having accepted that the time was ripe to review the current law and practice on Article 82, the Commission published its 'Discussion Paper on the Application of Article 82 of the Treaty to Exclusionary Abuses'. The discussion paper is designed to promote a debate as to how EU markets are best protected from dominant companies' exclusionary conduct, i.e. conduct which risks weakening competition in a market by various means of foreclosure such as rebates, refusal to supply and tying. The paper suggests a framework for the continued rigorous enforcement of Article 82, building on the economic analysis carried out in recent cases, and setting out one possible methodology for the assessment of some of the most common abusive practices, i.e. rebates, predatory pricing, refusal to supply and tying.

Since 1989, however, effective EU merger control may also have played a role in preventing dominant positions from emerging in the first place. Due to political resistance, cases involving public authorities (including state aid) and public undertakings have also traditionally been difficult to pursue. The manner in which the system of Article 81 was implemented until the 2004 modernization effort, on the other hand, was clearly biased in favour of attracting cases to the Commission.

Article 81(1)(EC) prohibits agreements and parallel behaviour that restrict or distort competition within the common market. However, it is not always clear whether restrictions capable of affecting trade are involved, and in any event the benefits of such restrictions may be more significant than their negative effects (Odudu, 2006). In practice, there are therefore many agreements, which are at face value restrictive, that ought not to be prohibited, and are not. Because under Article 81(2)(EC) agreements that infringe the prohibition of Article 81(1)(EC) are automatically void, it was long held that undertakings require prior assurances that their prospective agreements are not caught by this prohibition. Under the key implementing Regulation 17/62 (Council, 1962), only the Commission could provide exemptions to the prohibition on policy grounds because notification to the Commission of the agreements involved was a precondition for obtaining an exemption. However, this resulted in a flood of thousands of notifications from the first day this system came into force. Due to the capacity constraints imposed on DG COMP (even today, about 400 'A-grade' Commission officials are responsible for dealing with the enforcement of the rules on merger control, cartel infringements and dominance abuse), a timely handling of all of these notifications eluded the Commission from the outset. Moreover, the effectiveness of this system was by no means self-evident in terms of measurable results: harmful cartels are rarely caught in this manner, as clearly illegal cartels are more likely to be carefully kept secrets. In over thirty-five years of the application of the notification system, the Commission adopted only

nine decisions prohibiting agreements based on notifications, without in addition a complaint having been lodged against them (CEC, 1999f).

Over time, the Commission developed a number of different ways of dealing with the problem of its anti-trust notification overload. These solutions shared the common feature of increasing reliance on instruments that allow the Commission to provide collective rather than individual clearances and exemptions, and to employ informal administrative solutions (so-called 'comfort' and 'discomfort' letters), rather than fully reasoned formal decisions that are subject to judicial appeal. Both the instruments defined by the treaty and those developed under secondary legislation or in administrative practice were categorized as based either on clearances or on exemptions.

Clearances concern cases in which the Commission considers that an agreement does not restrict competition or does not affect trade between the member states, and is therefore not caught by the prohibition of Article 81(1). They were rarely awarded on a formal basis: when addressed to individual undertakings, clearances were usually based on informal administrative letters instead (in fact, over 90 per cent of all notifications were closed informally, including informal clearances and informal exemptions). The most important instrument providing a collective negative clearance is the *de minimis* notice, concerning agreements of minor importance, i.e. with negligible effects on trade between the member states or on competition (CEC, 2001k). This concerns primarily agreements between small and medium-sized enterprises (SMEs), that do not affect goods and services representing more than 10 per cent of the relevant market, where the agreement is made between undertakings that are actual or potential competitors; or 15 per cent of the relevant market, where the agreement is made between undertakings that are not actual or potential competitors. In such cases, restrictions of competition between the undertakings involved are assumed sufficiently unlikely to result in uncompetitive markets to merit a contestable presumption of legality.

Aside from agreements covered by the *de minimis* notice, few agreements benefited from a negative clearance, largely because the Commission traditionally preferred to perform its antitrust analysis under Article 81(3)(EC) – as it appears to continue to be doing following modernization. This approach has been consistently criticized by advocates of a 'rule of reason' approach under Article 81(1) (Wesseling, 2005). Under Article 81(3), an agreement that is in principle prohibited under Article 81(1) may, if its effects are on balance considered beneficial to competition, obtain a waiver, or 'exemption' from this prohibition. Such waivers or exemptions were subject to structural and behavioural conditions, and were limited in time. They included the following categories:

- formal individual exemption decisions under Article 81(3)EC;
- informal individual exemptions by means of administrative 'comfort letters';
- general block exemptions covering certain types of agreements found across different sectors (concerning exclusive distribution, exclusive purchasing, franchising, specialization, technology transfer and R&D agreements);
- sector-specific block exemptions for agreements prevalent in particular sectors (e.g. air and sea transport, insurance, motor vehicle and beer distribution).

In order to be eligible for an exemption, agreements must make a contribution to production, distribution or technical or economic progress, and allow consumers a fair share of the resulting benefits (generally seen in terms of price and availability of new products). Moreover, the particular restraints of competition involved must be indispensable for achieving these benefits, and may not eliminate competition completely, for example by foreclosing market entry. In determining whether any competition remains, 'potential competitors', and hence barriers to entry, were taken into account.

Formal individual exemptions were relatively rare because the Commission was not required to respond to a notification within a specific deadline, and due to its limited resources it could not, in any event, in this way address the numerous agreements that might qualify. Alongside administrative 'comfort letters', block exemptions became the main solution to the problem of providing legal certainty to business, while reducing the overwhelming numbers of notifications for the Commission. The system of block exemptions as originally designed allowed large numbers of agreements to be cleared, based on 'white' lists of admissible restrictions and 'black' lists of strictly prohibited restrictions: if agreements contain only white-listed restrictions and no black-listed ones, they need not be notified. This had the disadvantage that businesses were forced to design their agreements to fit the template of an individual block exemption (as the benefits of several block exemptions cannot be applied to a single agreement), leading to a 'straitjacket effect' that was unlikely always to coincide with the optimal business case. Moreover, undertakings often sought to structure transactions so as to fall within the merger control regime, which provided the certainty of obtaining decisions within strict deadlines. This in turn added to the rapidly growing merger caseload, in effect shifting rather than resolving the notification problem. As is discussed below, more recent block exemptions no longer contain 'white lists', are less specific to certain types of agreement, focus on situations of 'market power', and are accompanied by interpretative notices that better enable undertakings to make their own assessment.

Its monopoly on exemptions from the prohibition on restrictive agreements set out in Article 81(1) gave the Commission sole control of key levers of competition policy. Although the direct effect of the EU competition prohibitions means that undertakings and individuals can invoke these norms in legal proceedings before national courts, the possibility that the Commission could still act to exempt the agreements involved tied the hands of the national authorities involved. The resulting centralization of EU competition law enforcement in the hands of the Commission had considerable benefits in terms of consistency and credibility, and was probably indispensable in order to allow a fully fledged EU competition policy to develop. With few exceptions (notably Germany), in the EU a true competition policy was long pursued only at Community level, and even there it was constructed step by step.

In recent years, however, this situation has changed fundamentally. All member states now accept, at least in principle, that state intervention and tolerance or promotion of private cartel arrangements cannot efficiently substitute for the market allocation of resources. Hence, in a process of 'spontaneous harmonization', most member states have adopted national competition rules based on the EU model, and have worked toward their increasingly effective enforcement. At the same time, it is clear that in order to advance the development of competition policy further, the Commission would have to focus on new problems such as those which arise in recently liberalized markets, in oligopolistic markets and in markets that extend beyond the EU. Likewise, to ensure proactive enforcement, it would have to focus more on complaints, and on (time-consuming) own-initiative action to pursue the gravest cartels and dominance abuses. Moreover the adoption of a 'leniency notice' (CEC, 2002l) led to a steep increase in the number of applications for a reduction of fines in cartel cases by undertakings 'coming clean' about cartel abuses in which they were involved, and providing the necessary evidence against their co-conspirators. Following up these cases in a timely and effective manner now requires increased resources. This means that many of the initial arguments to concentrate policy competence on the application of Article 81(3) at EU level in the hands of the Commission no longer hold, or at least no longer outweigh the negative effects of centralization, given the capacity constraints as sketched above. The above reasons gave a pressing impetus to decentralize and modernize the system of enforcement.

Even prior to modernization, the Commission started rationalizing its existing Article 81(3) practice by streamlining and consolidating its block exemptions, and by moving towards an approach that relies more on economic insights, in particular in the area of vertical restraints. Likewise at an earlier stage, following the momentum generated by the 1992 internal market programme (see chapter 7), the Commission had started focusing its competition policy more on public undertakings and state intervention. These three developments are each discussed below, in roughly chronological order.

13.6 The public turn

During the first three decades of its competition policy, the Commission focused on the basic task of enforcing the Article 81(EC) and Article 82(EC) prohibitions against private undertakings. This required it to elaborate implementing rules (the procedural regulations and group exemption regulations discussed above) and to develop its practice concerning a range of standard competition policy problems in this area. After consolidating this part of its competencies, the Commission started expanding the scope of its enforcement efforts to cover the politically more delicate areas of the public sector and state aid over the course of the 1980s and 1990s. This trend has been defined as the 'public turn' of EU competition law (Gerber, 1998).

In the first place, the Commission began more active enforcement of the competition rules against public undertakings, and undertakings that enjoy special and exclusive rights, such as legal monopolies, as well as licences or concessions limited in number and awarded on discretionary grounds. In doing so, it took to task not only the undertakings benefiting from such privileges, but also the member states responsible for awarding them. In some previously sheltered sectors, notably that of telecommunications, the Commission actually abolished such exclusive and special rights by means of competition law directives. In a number of other sectors concerned, such as posts, energy and transport, it relied more heavily on treaty infringement actions and sector-specific harmonization legislation adopted by the Council and the European Parliament, albeit inspired by the drive to create competitive conditions, and fuelled by (potential) competitors' complaints under the competition rules. Once statutory prerogatives are removed, the competition rules come to play a key role in ensuring the markets involved are contestable. This means that there are no longer any economic sectors that are completely immune from the competition rules, although significant differences in the degree to which they are subject to effective competition are likely to persist for some time.

The Commission's policy on state aid has matured, in particular following the completion of the internal market programme. This policy has included: targeting aid to public enterprises; the elaboration of the 'market investor test', which means aid is not acceptable unless private investors might have taken similar investment decisions; and enforcing the repayment of illegal aid (see chapter 14).

The market investor test has emerged from the case law. In the *Spain* v. *Commission* case of 1994, Advocate General Jacobs regarded aid as being granted whenever a state made available to an undertaking funds which in the normal course of events would not be provided by a private investor applying ordinary commercial criteria and disregarding considerations of a social, political or philanthropic nature. This approach has been favoured by the ECJ in the *SFEI* v. *La Poste* case of 1996, where it held that, in order to determine whether a state measure constitutes aid for the purposes of Article 87, it is necessary to establish whether the recipient receives an economic advantage which it would not have obtained under normal market conditions.

At the same time, the conviction that state control over the economy is inversely related to its performance is now widely shared by policymakers at national level. This realization has been reinforced by the move to Economic and Monetary Union (EMU), which imposes budgetary constraints that make member states reluctant to expose themselves to the significant potential liabilities represented by public investment that is not guided by efficiency considerations, and indeed by public ownership as such (Devroe, 1997; also chapters 11 and 12).

An indication of the fundamental change in the attitude of the member states is that the Council has at last started adopting secondary legislation implementing the state aid provisions of the treaty. Over the past decade, it has adopted both a regulation concerning the conditions under which horizontal state aid may be acceptable (Council, 1998) and a regulation concerning procedural rules for state aid (Council, 1999a) that also delegates new rule-making powers to the Commission. These implementation measures not only provide the Commission with improved enforcement instruments, but also increase the transparency of state aid policy, and therefore offer greater legal certainty to undertakings and national authorities.

The *Altmark* case of 2003 states the main principles for financing services of general economic interest. In that case, the court concluded that payments made by governments to companies providing essential services (e.g. public transportation) should not be classed as state aid as long as the following criteria are satisfied. First, the recipient must actually perform a public service obligation. Second, the parameters on the basis of which the compensation is calculated must be established in advance in an objective and transparent manner. Third, the compensation cannot exceed what is necessary to cover all or part of the costs incurred for supplying the public service. Fourth, where the undertaking that performs the public service obligation is not chosen on the basis of a public procurement procedure, the level of compensation needed must be determined on the basis of an analysis of the costs that a typical well-run undertaking in the same market would have incurred. In order to provide for greater legal certainty for financing such services, in 2005 the Commission adopted a package of measures, which ensure that companies can receive public support to cover all costs incurred, including a reasonable profit, in carrying out public service tasks as defined and entrusted to them by public authorities. Member states are able to grant compensation to small-scale public services, hospitals and social housing without notifying Commission. The measures take the form of a Commission decision, a Community framework for state aid in the form of public service compensation, and an amendment to the Commission directive on financial transparency.

Although the developments that constitute the 'public turn' of EU competition policy can certainly also be seen as a form of modernization and rationalization, they still remain distinct from the changes to its traditional core: antitrust enforcement (discussed below). In the utilities sectors, where traditional monopoly markets must be opened up to competitive entry, sector-specific competition rules enforced by independent sector regulators will continue to play an important role at least in the medium term, until competition becomes sufficiently effective for application of the general (or horizontal) competition rules to suffice. Meanwhile, the existence of such sector-specific national regulators helps to relieve the burden on the competition services of the Commission, and to spread an understanding of how the process of competition may be protected in often technically complex fields, such as telecommunications. A similar phasing out of the rules on state aid is, of course, not contemplated, as the need to distinguish legitimate public measures from illegal aid will persist as long as public authorities are tempted to interfere in markets. Moreover, unlike the antitrust provisions, the state aid rules are by definition not suited to decentralized application, and no such rules exist at national level. Therefore, they must be enforced in a centralized manner.

Hence, there is a clear case for the Commission services to focus on state aid, mergers and other cases with a significant Community interest due to the size, transnational nature and precedent value of the problems involved, while leaving the vast majority of competition cases to national competition authorities and, at least until effective competition in previously monopolized utility sectors takes off, to sector-specific regulators. A significant Community interest or dimension was arguably not involved in the bulk of competition cases currently examined under Article 81. Accordingly, Regulation 1 of 2003 empowered national authorities to deal with such cases. In addition, limiting the scope of the prohibitions to cases where economically significant effects are concerned would help to allow a clearer focus on more serious competition problems at both the national and EU levels. The developments in the area of vertical restraints and modernization indicate a clear policy trend in this direction.

13.7 Rationalization

Many commentators have criticized EU competition policy for its lack of economic analysis, in particular in relation to restraints on competition

under Article 81 (Hildebrand, 2002; Korah, 1998). In part, the Commission's approach, with its focus on formal and territorial restraints, was a logical consequence of the integration objective. The system of parallel block exemption regulations for similar types of agreement led to inconsistencies, and the practice of identifying exempted restrictions, rather than just those restrictions held to be illegal, led to the 'straitjacket' effects mentioned above. Moves towards consolidation and reform started in 1996, when the Commission adopted a single block exemption for technology transfer agreements, replacing previously separate regulations concerning patent and know-how licences. Since then EU competition policy has shifted away from an approach based on legal form towards one based on economic effects.

One of the reasons for this cultural change may have been the integration of economists at DG COMP. There is a large and increasing number of economists there: around 200 out of over 700 officials working at DG COMP have an economics or business background. About twenty of them have a PhD in economics, ten of whom are currently working in the Office of the Chief Economist. The Office of the Chief Economist was created in 2003 as a separate and independent division of DG COMP that mainly consists of economists (presently chaired by Professor Damian Neven). The Office's members are closely involved with the day-to-day work of case teams, getting involved early on in the investigation and giving economic guidance and methodological assistance.

The most important examples so far concern the Commission's approach to vertical and horizontal restraints. In 1999, it adopted a single block exemption regulation for vertical restraints, replacing the formerly separate legal instruments concerning exclusive distribution, exclusive purchasing and franchising agreements. In addition, the new block exemption covers selective distribution agreements, which were previously dealt with under individual decisions (CEC, 1999e). The block exemption for vertical restraints is accompanied by extensive guidelines that aim to enable undertakings to make their own assessment of the applicability of the relevant rules (CEC, 2000f). In

2000, the Commission adopted 'horizontal' block exemption regulations for specialization agreements and for research and development agreements (CEC, 2000g, 2000h), followed by a notice on horizontal cooperation agreements (CEC, 2001l). With regard to both vertical and horizontal agreements, the emphasis is now on undertakings with some significant measure of market power. Only the block exemption for vertical restraints regulation is discussed in more detail here.

Vertical agreements are entered into between undertakings operating at different levels of the production or distribution chain that relate to the purchasing, sale or resale of certain goods and services. The restraints involved in such agreements typically cover various forms of exclusivity, non-competition clauses and branding and pricing constraints that may foreclose market entry, reduce, in particular, intra-brand competition, and create obstacles to market integration. Especially for the latter reason, they have generally been frowned upon in EU competition law and a systematic policy based on the potential benefits of vertical agreements has been slow to develop. However, as the various specific block exemptions recognized, these potential benefits can be significant: vertical agreements can improve economic efficiency by reducing the transaction and distribution costs of the parties involved, and lead to an optimization of their respective sales and investment levels, in particular where there is effective competition between brands. Moreover, and most important from an integration perspective, vertical agreements offer particularly effective ways of opening up or entering new markets. The objective of the new block exemption is to secure these positive effects, turning away from the earlier focus of EU competition law on integration through protecting inter-brand competition (Peeperkorn, 1998).

In a first important move going beyond past practice, the block exemption for vertical restraints is no longer based on exemptions for specifically listed agreements: instead, there is a general exemption, subject only to a prohibition of a limited number of blacklisted clauses (such as resale price maintenance and most territorial constraints), leaving broader freedom for commercial contracts (Korah and Sullivan, 2002). As the efficiency-enhancing effects of vertical agreements are likely to outweigh the anti-competitive effects of restrictions they may contain, unless the undertakings involved enjoy market power, the block exemption creates a presumption of legality for vertical agreements concerning the sale of goods and services which are concluded by companies with less than 30 per cent of market share. Only cases involving undertakings that fall above this threshold require separate analysis regarding the applicability of Article (3). However, if cumulative effects occur in markets that are in large part covered by networks of agreements imposing similar vertical restraints, the Commission can decide the block exemption no longer applies, requiring individual notifications. In a move towards decentralization, national authorities are empowered to withdraw the benefits of the block exemption if vertical agreements have effects incompatible with Article 81(3)(EC) on a geographically distinct market within their jurisdiction. Guidelines will serve to inform undertakings of the way the block exemption is applied.

13.8 Modernization

For more than thirty-five years, following the Council's adoption of the key procedural Regulation 17 in 1962, the Commission was responsible for the administration of a highly centralized authorization system for exemptions to the cartel prohibition of Article 81(1). This system rested on the notification requirement and exemption monopoly introduced by Regulation 17. Over time, it has facilitated the uniform application of EU competition law, which in turn fostered a 'culture of competition' now shared with national competition authorities in all twenty-five member states, a majority of which obtained authority to apply both Community and national competition law even prior to modernization (Temple Lang, 1998). However, as described earlier in this chapter, this success came at significant cost to effective enforcement: mass notifications overburdened the Commission services, leading to administrative solutions that did not provide adequate legal certainty for undertakings, and which were used strategically to trump national courts and competition authorities in their own enforcement of the directly effective cartel prohibition (Wils, 2003).

Over time, many elements of the widespread criticism of this system have come to be shared by the Commission itself. In addition, it identified the impending further enlargement of the EU (see chapters 2, 19 and 26), the effects of economic restructuring following EMU, and the need to reallocate resources to respond adequately to the broadening geographic scope of various anticompetitive practices as the result of economic globalization, as reasons to adopt a programme of far-reaching modernization and reform of the manner in which Article 81 is applied. In its modernization White Paper of 1999 (CEC, 1999f), the Commission set three objectives for this exercise: ensuring effective supervision, simplifying administration and easing the constraints on undertakings while providing them with a sufficient degree of legal certainty (Wesseling, 2000). Subsequently, the Commission's proposals resulted in the adoption of the new Council regulation on the implementation of Articles 81 and 82, which came into force on 1 May 2004 (coinciding with enlargement).

The key element of modernization is that it replaces the mandatory notification and authorization system with a directly applicable legal exception system. This constitutes a shift from a system of *ex ante* control to a system of *ex post* supervision that relies more on direct effect, and hence on enforcement by national authorities and in private court actions by the undertakings concerned. Undertakings are now required to assess for themselves whether their contemplated agreements are likely to infringe the prohibition of Article 81(1), and, if they do, whether they remain within the scope of the legal exception of Article 81(3), because the restrictions involved are the minimum necessary to realize legitimate economic benefits shared with consumers, consistent with established EU competition policy practice. Of course, this assessment remains subject to challenge before national courts and by the competition authorities both at national and at Community level. The enforcement at national

level is facilitated by Commission guidance, both in the form of general notices and block exemptions, and by providing 'amicus curiae' input directly to national courts at their request. In its own handling of such cases, the Commission has announced that it will limit the scope of its review to undertakings with market power. Hence, as with the approach with regard to vertical restraints, market shares will come to play a key role.

Under the modernized system, all national competition authorities are not only to be empowered but also obligated to apply Articles 81 and 82 in cases where there is an appreciable effect on trade between the member states. This considerably reinforces decentralized application of EU competition law. To give guidance on the substance of competition law, the Commission has published notices explaining the 'effect on trade' concept and how Article 81(3) should be applied by undertakings, competition authorities and courts.

Because the national competition authorities have to keep the Commission informed of their intentions in such cases, and must submit substantive decisions to prior Commission scrutiny, while the Commission retains the right to take over cases where this is deemed in the Community interest, there will also be an increase in coordination at Community level. The ambition is that DG COMP will become the linchpin of a seamless network of closely cooperating competition authorities at national and EU level (Ehlermann, 2003). In order to facilitate coordination between national authorities and to ensure consistent application of competition rules by national courts, the Commission published notices regarding cooperation within the network of competition authorities in Europe, defining criteria and methods for effective case allocation in the network (Temple Lang, 2004).

The role of national authorities was at issue in the *Consorzio Industrie Fiammiferi* case of 2003. The Consorzio Industrie Fiammiferi (CIF) was an Italian consortium of domestic manufacturers of matches. The national law establishing and governing this body was scrutinized by the Italian competition authority. The CIF was established by royal decree in 1923, and enjoyed a commercial and fiscal monopoly that ended in 1994. According to an agreement that formed an integral part of the decree, the Italian state undertook to prohibit the distribution of matches that had been produced by non-CIF members. In return, CIF promised to ensure that its members paid the excise duty on matches. The Italian competition authority declared the national legislation to be contrary to Articles 3, 10 and 81 of the treaty as it required the CIF to engage in anticompetitive conduct. In response, CIF started proceedings, arguing that the competition authority was not competent to declare provisions of national law invalid or inapplicable. The Italian judge dealing with the case turned to the ECJ for a preliminary ruling. The CFI held that the duty to dis-apply national legislation that contravenes Community law applies not only to national courts but also to 'all organs of the state', including administrative authorities like the national competition authority.

The Commission has also adopted a notice facilitating the cooperation between the Commission and the courts of the EU member states (CEC, 2004c).

The role of the national courts was discussed in the *Masterfoods* v. *HB Ice Cream* case of 2000. HB Ice Cream Ltd, now called Van den Bergh, is the leading manufacturer of ice-cream products in Ireland. For some time, HB had supplied retailers in Ireland with freezer cabinets for no direct charge, provided that the cabinets were exclusively used for stocking and displaying HB ice-cream products. In 1989, Masterfoods, a subsidiary of Mars Inc., entered the Irish market. Some of the Irish retailers started to place Masterfoods products in their HB freezer cabinets. Of course, HB strongly objected to this practice by enforcing the exclusivity provision of its distribution agreements. In reaction, Masterfoods brought an action before the Irish High Court, claiming that the HB exclusivity clause infringed Articles 81 and 82. In May 1992, Masterfoods lost the case when the Irish High Court found for HB, and, in September 1992, Masterfoods appealed against this judgment to the Irish Supreme Court. Masterfoods also lodged a parallel complaint with the Commission, which, in 1998, found that the exclusivity clause did infringe the

Community rules on competition. HB appealed. As a result of the Commission's decision, the Irish Supreme Court, dealing with Masterfoods' appeal in Ireland, decided to stay proceedings and to refer questions to the ECJ. The ECJ held that where a national court is considering issues that are already subject to a Commission decision, the court may not reach a judgment which conflicts with the decision of the Commission, irrespective of the fact that the Commission decision in question had been appealed to the CFI. The court further stressed that it is for the national court to decide whether to stay proceedings pending final judgment in that action for annulment or in order to refer a question to the ECJ for a preliminary ruling. The Commission has codified the court's ruling in its notice on the cooperation between the Commission and the courts of the EU member states in the application of Articles 81 and 82(EC) (paras. 11–14).

However, because ending formal centralization gives rise to an increased need for coordination, it is by no means certain that the Commission's ambitions to refocus its own enforcement activities on intensified *ex post* control – including that against the gravest cartels – can be realized without additional resources. Whether sharing responsibility for competition law enforcement more broadly will create momentum in favour of providing the necessary means remains an open question. At a minimum, it will provide the Commission with increased flexibility in reordering its priorities.

13.9 Conclusion

Following its initial system-building efforts, EU competition policy became increasingly hampered by a mismatch between the scope of the Commission's powers and its capacity for effective enforcement. To some extent the Commission has been the victim of its own success at centralizing its competence in order to secure its key mission of promoting market integration. Nevertheless, its efforts have spawned the spontaneous harmonization of competition policy and an increasingly effective enforcement culture at national level which are now considered the key to modernization.

EU competition policy is in a process of rationalization and modernization that involves imposing increasingly stringent curbs on public intervention, and moving away from its former primary focus on the integration objective towards increasing reliance on economic logic and on enforcement at national level.

Although significant advances have already been made concerning previously privileged economic sectors, state aid and revising the block exemptions, the ongoing review of EU competition policy instruments is not complete: a review of policy on market power and dominance, including approaches to dominance and collusion in oligopolistic markets, remains to be worked out. The Commission will have to strengthen the proactive enforcement of its anti-cartel policy. The process of decentralizing the enforcement of the principles

established so far forms a precondition for such further modernization, which has only recently begun. Methods and principles for case allocation and cooperation within the fledgling network of European competition authorities have been recently defined and are 'tested' in practice. In a next round, the state aid machinery is likely to be reformed further. Priorities may have to be established in relation to a growing flow of cartels subject to leniency applications. Nevertheless, the outline of a fully fledged market power and effects-based 'second-generation' system of EU competition law is now clear.

NOTE

1 The authors would like to thank Johan van de Gronden for his valuable comments on an earlier draft of this chapter.

14 Industrial and competitiveness policy: the Lisbon Strategy

BRIAN ARDY

14.1 Introduction

This chapter is divided into four further sections: 14.2 defines industrial and competitiveness policy (ICP); 14.3 discusses its intellectual foundations and the elements of EU policy are analysed; 14.4 discusses the control of state aid; 14.5 discusses support for research and development; and in 14.6 the overarching policy seeking to improve competitiveness, the Lisbon Strategy, is examined.

14.2 What is industrial and competitiveness policy?

Industrial and competitiveness policy (ICP) can be defined as: acts and policies of the state designed to improve a country's economic performance. This definition of ICP potentially includes a very broad range of government policies that do not discriminate between economic activities, and therefore do not affect the inter-sectoral allocation of resources, which used to be defined as lying outside the boundary of industrial policy. However, this is a rather dated view, because the policies that the EU refers to as 'horizontal' policies (fiscal, competition, regional, social, labour and environmental policies, etc.) are increasingly seen as central to ICP. This is why competitiveness has been added to the title of this chapter. Thus, 'completing the internal market' has become central to EU ICP. An extreme version of this approach could define ICP as: 'designed not to specify and enforce particular *outcomes* but to alter market *processes* by attacking the rigidities which impede . . . the force of market selection' (Geroski and

Jacquemin, 1989, p. 298). The preference of these authors is for an industrial policy which provides 'a framework in which private sector flexibility is encouraged and adjustment to shocks is facilitated' (p. 305) and disapproval is expressed of industrial policy which 'might try to lead the private sector through a more or less explicit planning procedure' because it would take the form of 'picking winners', predicting the emergence of 'sunrise' sectors, and charting the rationalization of 'sunset' sectors. Today ICP would also be defined to include policies to provide industry with appropriate resources such as an educated and trained labour force, an appropriate research base and infrastructure. Thus ICP could be defined as acts and policies of government designed to improve economic performance by enhancing the effectiveness of market pressures and providing appropriate resources and infrastructure.

This discussion of definition reflects an evolution in the philosophy underlying government intervention in the economy in the last fifty years. Thus, from the 1940s to the 60s the prevailing orthodoxy was that government could and should correct market failures, and so microeconomic intervention in specific industrial sectors was normal. Thus in the 1970s the response to the oil crisis and structural change in the world economy was protection of companies and industries in difficulty and European industrial policies 'aimed to create European super-firms to compete with the US giants' (Geroski and Jacquemin, 1989, p. 299). The failures of these policies to raise EU industrial performance[1] meant that by the 1980s, the effectiveness of government action was increasingly questioned and respect for market forces increased. By the early 1990s the Commission's view of industrial policy was that 'it should promote adaptation to industrial change in an open and competitive market' (Bangermann, 1994). Now the Commission, along with mainstream academic opinion, treats firm and sector-specific policies with suspicion, but approves of 'horizontal' or general policies to support market activity in general. Accordingly, ICP in the EU has increasingly evolved in the horizontal direction with 'firm-specific' and 'sector-specific' industrial policy undertaken by member states constrained by EU rules on state aid.

Competition policy more generally would have had to be included in a discussion of industrial policy, since although it is general in intent, it is often specific in application. Thus competition decisions affect the internal structure of industries by controlling mergers, joint ventures and minority acquisitions, and by attempting to prevent cartels. Such decisions can support or discourage certain types of agreement between firms (for instance, collaborative R&D arrangements). Competition policy possesses considerable administrative discretion, and can even allow the establishment of a 'restructuring cartel' to ease the burden of adjustment in a declining sector. These aspects are, however, covered in chapter 13, but section 14.4 discusses the Commission's role in monitoring state aid to industry and the services sector, because state aid controls national industrial policy and hence is an important part of EU industrial policy.

Microeconomic industrial policy is often dualistic and contradictory; governments tend to simultaneously support 'sunrise' and 'sunset' industries, an apparently irrational approach, which can only be understood in its political context. The opportunity cost of specific industrial policy should also not be forgotten. Thus sums which are devoted to support A, B and C must come from somewhere, and will penalize all non-supported activities from D to Z. Governments avoid the evaluation of this hidden cost of industrial policy, and the public are certainly not aware of it.

Having considered the nature of ICP, what measures or *instruments* are used to implement it? The favoured instruments of traditional industrial policy are subsidies, tax breaks and protection from foreign competition. ICP today also uses regulation and deregulation,[2] the reorientation of public services (e.g. education reforms), subsidization of infrastructure and research. Over time ICP instruments have shifted from tariffs to non-tariff barriers (NTBs); to subsidies or tax breaks, with the tightening of trade rules in the GATT/WTO and internally within the EU. But the purpose remains the same: to encourage this or that economic activity. Most ICP measures either permit the local firms to raise their price, which means that they enjoy a hidden subsidy, or subsidies that directly reduce the cost or raise the quality of their inputs such as labour and research. Regulations can also be implicit or explicit instruments of industrial policy, since they can determine standards for a particular product/service. For this to be effective it is essential that the EU standard is adopted much more widely, as exemplified by the success of the GSM standard for mobile phones and the failure to establish such a standard for high definition TV.

The EU has a role in all these areas of industrial policy. It is the major actor in external trade policy (see chapters 2 and 24), and it has a shared but growing competence over regulatory policy, supervision of state aid, and limited but increasing subsidies in such areas as research, plus competition policy. This chapter concentrates on state aid, research and development and the attempt to raise economic performance more generally through the Lisbon Strategy.

14.3 Industrial and competitiveness policy: theory and evidence

International trade theorists have long asked why, as a matter of empirical observation, discriminatory protection (favouring some industries and penalizing others) is so prevalent. Most of the work on why governments practise *specific* industrial policy has therefore already been done by trade theorists. It just needs transposing to the slightly broader framework of industrial policy. The case for *general* industrial policy, however, is based simply on improving the competitive functioning of markets.

14.3.1 Market failure in general

The economic case for government action is based on market failure, generally associated with uncompetitive markets, externalities and informational or distributional problems. For example, the market may under-supply useful scientific and industrial knowledge because of the public-goods aspect of information. It is on this that public funding of R&D is based. This is the basis for horizontal industrial policy. With sector-specific industrial policy, however, the case for market failure is much harder to make, because the underlying assumption is that the government is better at allocating resources than the market, or at any rate can improve substantially upon it. This is increasingly questioned and has led to growing scepticism regarding selective industrial policy.

Several different types of market failure that arise under this heading are discussed below.

14.3.2 Infant industries

This is the oldest and most popular of the (economic) arguments for subsidization and/or protection. Even in its traditional formulation, it appeals to the notion of economies of scale. It asserts that an 'infant' industry operating below optimum size will never achieve the low costs associated with the large-scale production of established firms, because the latter possess a 'first mover advantage' that the newcomer simply cannot overcome. For this reason, it needs a start-up subsidy. Once it is up and running it will become competitive, in theory at least. In practice, many infants never grow up. The art is in selecting the right sector – in 'picking the winners'. This is not easy, even for entrepreneurs investing their own money. It is much harder for public officials investing other people's money. The process tends to become politicized, of which more below.

14.3.3 Strategic industrial policy

In the 1980s, trade theory turned to models of imperfect competition to explain phenomena such as intra-industry trade between developed countries (Krugman, 1979). From this exercise

there emerged not only an explanation for certain empirical observations in terms of oligopolistic rivalry, but also some policy prescriptions (Brander and Spencer, 1983). The policy prescriptions looked remarkably like the old infant-industry argument dressed up in modern clothes. What is perhaps new is the idea that comparative advantage is no longer a matter of traditional factor endowments, but can be *consciously shaped* by judicious industrial policy.

In a world where *technology* determines the competitiveness of firms and where location is no longer a question of hard geographic facts, but rather proximity to other firms in the same sector, economic activity can become (fairly) 'footloose'. Attracting specific sectors to particular locations therefore becomes a feasible, and potentially profitable, object of public policy. The market-failure reasons for why markets need a helping hand are the same as before: first-mover advantages, barriers to entry due to economies of scale, and perhaps lack of appropriate general infrastructure (high-speed communication networks, universities, publicly funded research laboratories, etc.). The problem, as always, lies in whether the response to the observed market failure is to be selective or general.

14.3.4 Industrial agglomerations

The idea that economies of scale are paramount, that geographic location is no longer an issue and that comparative advantage can be 'shaped', has led to some spectacular failures when, combining industrial with regional policy, governments have erected 'cathedrals in the desert' (such as huge steel and chemical complexes in Italy's Mezzogiorno). Clearly, something was missing from the recipe. Geography matters – but what kind? The failure of old-style regional policy to create viable industries in blighted areas, as well as the astonishing success of Silicon Valley, has led to a renewed interest in the economics of agglomeration (Fujita and Thisse, 1996). Agglomerations are also conducive to technological change. Information and ideas circulate informally within an agglomeration, speeding up the process of product development (Lucas, 1988). The emphasis on agglomeration has been reinforced by evidence that even for technology the spillovers are concentrated locally (Keller, 2002). The notion that people following the same skilled trade derive advantages from proximity to each other goes back to Alfred Marshall, who noted that they gained from lower factor prices and economies of scale (Marshall, 1920). A more modern version of this thesis is provided by Porter (1990).

The 'pull' factors which reduce costs for members of an agglomeration include: positive externalities based on mass production of specialized inputs (i.e. access to lower costs from efficient suppliers), access to specialized labour, specialized services, shared consumers, shared infrastructure (especially universities), and the flow of information (especially tacit information and informal gossip). This reflects the sheer efficiency of markets as coordinating agents (as compared with the corresponding inefficiency of hierarchical management as a method of coordination beyond a certain degree of complexity). An agglomeration reduces costs by allowing firms to contract out all but their core activities, but this is only efficient if the specialized suppliers can themselves operate on a large enough scale, thus offsetting market transaction costs. This is outsourcing which, to work well, requires many buyers and many service providers offering similar (but often subtly differentiated) specialized services. The spectacular benefits come when specialization and economies of scale, in turn, hit the service supply industry as well, spreading pecuniary externalities (Scitovsky, 1954) throughout the agglomeration and creating a Silicon Valley effect. At the extreme the company might become just a Coasian locus for a multitude of contracts (Coase, 1937).

One important implication for industrial policy is that while the agglomeration may be very large, most of the firms which compose it will be very small, at least relative to multinational corporations. In fact, the economies of agglomeration can be interpreted as being both substitutes for and complements of technical economies of scale. Thus an agglomeration of small specialized firms might compete head-on with a large vertically integrated corporation, each being equally efficient. On the other hand, a complementary structure would involve large firms capturing the available technical economies of scale, surrounded by a dense network of suppliers and subcontractors, all working to keep costs and prices down, and variety and innovation up.

This means that industrial policy can no longer simply target large firms and hope for the best. Support for small and medium-size enterprises (SMEs) is needed too. But we are far from understanding industrial agglomerations and even further from knowing how to create them. This is not an argument for an industrial policy based on market failure, but rather one based on mysterious market success, which we would dearly like to duplicate.

14.3.5 Research and development

The importance of technological change in explaining economic growth has long been recognized (Solow, 1957; Denison, 1974). In Solow's neoclassical growth model technology is exogenous, but with Romer's (1990) seminal contribution, models where technological change is endogenous have been developed. With innovation as a good, its production is driven by profit, but innovation has peculiar characteristics. Inventions are subject to increasing returns to scale, because there are large fixed costs in innovation which can be spread over the output produced. However, firms will only invest heavily in research and development (R&D) if they can appropriate for themselves the new knowledge they have created. Innovations are non-rival: once an i-Pod has been developed, its technology and design can relatively easily be copied. Under these circumstances firms have little incentive to innovate because other firms will use the expensively acquired knowledge – this is the free-rider problem.[3] This market failure (due to the public-goods nature of knowledge) suggests a policy which provides a patent system giving inventors a temporary and exclusive right to exploit the new knowledge they have created; provides public funding of basic research; and educates people so they can develop and implement ideas.

Public funding of R&D allows governments to be selective and to adopt a microeconomic industrial policy under the banner of a well-recognized general market failure in the area of knowledge creation. Governments can *indirectly* promote those industries which they wish to support by sponsoring R&D in selected areas. This is less risky than 'picking the winners' directly (by supporting investment in new production facilities, for instance), since the new knowledge thus created might spill over into other areas and be generally useful. For instance, the Apollo space programme is often credited with having developed the transistor, the grandfather of the silicon chip. But this is still a risk and there is the possibility of governmental failure: for example capture, i.e. researchers may end up influencing decisions so that it is their pet projects rather than those in the interests of society that are financed. In addition, there is a positive correlation between research expenditure and researchers' incomes (Goolsbee, 1998).

Technological loops, linkages, feedbacks and spillovers are at the heart of the argument. They help to translate scientific knowledge into commercially useful innovations, and vice versa. Industrial research by one firm takes known science, applies it to solving a particular problem, and in the course of this adds to general scientific knowledge, which can be exploited by other firms and perhaps find its way back to the universities. Thus the creation of new knowledge by one firm is assumed to generate positive externalities for other firms, in the form of both better and cheaper products, and new scientific (non-patented) information, as well as ensuring the firm's own longer-term survival through the development of patented information (Grossman and Helpman, 1991). The ability to assimilate existing technologies and generate new ones is by no means universal, but has to be cultivated. Countries in which technological research is carried out acquire a *comparative advantage in the form of human capital resource endowments that may persist for some time* (Ruttan, 1998). In turn, this human capital resource can be encouraged by government policy, especially as this seems to be crucial in determining growth (Temple Lang, 1999). It is also plausible that pure science will remain economically inert unless society possesses a steady supply of entrepreneurs operating through markets to convert it into something useful for everyday life. More generally the importance of the institutional setting to economic performance has been increasingly stressed (Gwartney et al., 2006).

The main question for policymakers is not so much whether R&D needs public support (there seems little doubt, even in the minds of many sceptical academics), but how and at what stage. The process of transforming general scientific knowledge into useful commercial applications can be viewed as a pipeline, running from academic institutions, with links to general industrial research laboratories, where much scientific knowledge is created but few innovations emerge, to the more focused development of prototype products or processes in an engineering laboratory, on to the testing of innovations on a small scale, and finally, after much trial and error, if successful, to their full-scale commercial development and marketing on a broad scale. New knowledge is created at each stage in the process. But which stage is the most deserving of public support? Generally speaking, the further away from 'the marketplace' and the more general the type of research, the more appropriate it is for public funding. In this way, one can avoid targeting public funds to particular firms which, as we have already seen, is a specially degenerate form of industrial policy. For this reason, the EU promotes 'pre-competitive' R&D, i.e. in principle it does not fund the development of prototypes or anything 'too close' to the market.

14.3.6 Entrepreneurship: small and medium-sized enterprises

The results of research have to be transformed into marketable innovation and this process emphasizes the role of entrepreneurs and SMEs. This dynamic approach to capitalism stems from the work of Joseph Schumpeter (1934) who emphasized capitalism as creative destruction, with innovations embodied in new firms, with the entrepreneur as the agent of change developing the commercial potential of the new idea. This new firm and its imitators would take over the market, displacing existing products, methods and jobs. The uncertainty of what the entrepreneur was attempting was emphasized by Knight (1921). This was important because the ability to innovate depends upon entrepreneurs' willingness to take these risks. The nature of this uncertainty is considered by Hayek (1945) who sees innovation as using tacit knowledge, i.e. making creative leaps without formal evidence. This suggests that the economic growth of a country will depend upon the supply of entrepreneurs and their ability to turn their ideas into new enterprises.

Entrepreneurs and SMEs seem to have become more important with changes in the world economy. From 1900 until 1970 economic conditions favoured concentration and the centralization of production (Chandler, 1990; Scherer and Ross, 1990) as technology and production were characterized by economies of scale and incremental innovation that could be undertaken by large firms. Since 1970 conditions have altered: technological change, outsourcing, globalization, deregulation and variety in demand have increased volatility and uncertainty encouraging lower concentration and decentralization (Audretsch et al., 2001). The evidence suggests that SMEs have become increasingly important but the extent of this change varies across countries (Loveman and Sengenberger, 1991; Acs et al., 1994). The link between entrepreneurship and SMEs and economic performance is confirmed by Audretsch and Thurik (2001) who find that increases in the relative share of economic activity accounted for by small firms and the self-employment rate are associated with higher rates of growth and a reduction of unemployment.

14.3.7 Attracting foreign direct investment

Many governments adopt policies to attract foreign direct investment (FDI). The reasons are obvious: to promote employment, help the balance of payments, increase the level of economic activity, benefit from new technologies, enhance exports, expand the tax base, etc. The problem with such policies, however, is that they discriminate between local and foreign investors. From an economic point of view, it is no more acceptable to give an artificial advantage to foreign investors over local investors, just because they are foreign, than it is to give local producers an artificial advantage over foreign producers, just because they are local. Discrimination on these grounds will simply produce wasteful distortions and ultimately too much FDI, as governments compete with each other to attract it. Discriminatory pro-FDI policies are quite different from structural reforms aimed at making a country more attractive to investors *in general*. Such policies do not distort the economy, but promote investment, growth and healthy institutional competition between countries.

14.3.8 An evaluation of ICP theory and evidence

If any general conclusion is to be drawn from this brief summary of the intellectual case for state intervention it is this: it should not target specific firms or sectors, but aim at improving the general functioning of markets. Another point is that it is not enough to demonstrate the existence of a market failure to justify government intervention. Government action is costly in its own right, and if selective it quickly becomes politicized. In fact, the direct and indirect costs of selective government action over time are probably far greater than the original market imperfection. Even general support for R&D can end up helping particular sectors. Once 'hooked' on industrial policy funds, sectors grow beyond their market-determined size and hence enjoy more political support than is their due. Industrial policies become 'path-dependent' and self-perpetuating. The whole process can be captured by rent seekers with increasing costs to consumers and taxpayers.

This is not to say that no ICP policy is the best policy, but to make a plea for very close scrutiny of what is advanced under this banner. Such policy will largely be horizontal, seeking to create the conditions for companies operating in competitive markets. It will also be very wide, taking into account the effects on companies of a swathe of government policies, from the environment to welfare.

14.4 The control of state aid

The 1957 EEC Treaty does not provide for a 'common industrial policy': this is no accident. Common policies were necessary in areas where government intervention at member-state level was so extensive that freeing markets could only produce a distorted outcome and policy competition. Where these loomed large, and the political will was present, the problem was elevated to Community level and a 'common' policy was born. In the case of industrial policies, the founding fathers deemed it sufficient to grant the Commission powers of supervision to ensure that state aid did not distort competition in the common market. Articles 87–9 (formerly Articles 92–4) set forth the general rules.[4]

Save as otherwise provided in this Treaty, any aid granted by a Member State or through State resources in any form whatsoever which distorts or threatens to distort competition by favouring certain undertakings or the production of certain goods shall, in so far as it affects trade between Member States, be incompatible with the common market.

Apart from the introductory caveat (see next paragraph), this is an extremely sweeping prohibition. It covers aid in 'any form whatsoever', targeted either at the individual firm ('favouring certain undertakings'), or at an entire sector ('the production of certain goods'), including services. Its purpose is to prevent member states' industrial policies from undermining the common market by favouring their national producers.

However, some industrial policies may be compatible with the common market. Article 87(3) lists aid to promote development of depressed or backward areas, aid for 'important projects of common European interest', aid for 'certain economic activities' or 'certain economic areas' (aid granted to shipyards is expressly mentioned), and 'such other categories of aid as may be specified by decisions of the Council'. These are known in Community-speak as 'horizontal' aids. In 1992 the Maastricht Treaty introduced a specific derogation for state aid to culture and heritage conservation (Article 87(3)(d)). In fact, Article 87(3) allows

the Commission considerable leeway in developing a policy with regard to state aid.

Article 88 empowers the Commission to 'keep under constant review all systems of aid' in member states and Article 89 allows the Commission to propose appropriate regulations to ensure the proper application of Articles 87 and 88. It was some time before the Commission developed these powers into a 'policy', since the role of *gendarme* was not an easy one to assume when the miscreants were member states. On the whole, however, the 1960s and early 1970s were good years and there was little excuse, or perceived need, for state intervention in industry. According to the Commission's *First Report on Competition Policy* (CEC, 1972) competition-distorting state aid was only significant in problem sectors such as shipbuilding, textiles and film production, and the Commission limited itself to exhortations to keep national aid within rather vague 'guidelines'. General aid schemes to promote investment were approved, and even dowries for industrial weddings in the French electronics industry (Machines Bull and CII) were passed without difficulty.

The late 1970s and early 1980s were much more turbulent. Two successive oil price increases plunged Europe into a prolonged recession, characterized by high rates of inflation and unemployment. Traditional macroeconomic policies were powerless to cope with this hitherto unprecedented combination. Firms continued to fail, unemployment to rise, and exchange rates gyrated. Many EC members resorted to the direct subsidization of loss-making firms. To begin with, the Commission did not appreciate the danger. It found that 'Member States, in an attempt to protect employment, were justified in boosting investment by granting firms financial benefits . . . it agreed to financial aid being granted to ensure the survival of firms which have run into difficulties, thereby avoiding redundancies' (CEC, 1976, para. 133). The list of sectors 'in difficulty' expanded to include automobiles, paper, machine tools, steel, synthetic fibres, clocks and watches, and chemicals. The number of subsidy schemes notified to the Commission rose from a handful in the early 1970s to well over one hundred by the end of the decade.

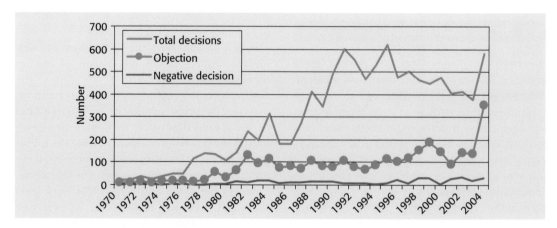

Figure 14.1 State aid decisions, 1970–2004. *Source:* CEC, *Annual Report Competition Policy*, various years.

Finally waking up to the danger, the Commission decided to take a less lenient view of subsidies to preserve employment (CEC, 1979a, paras. 173–4), putting more emphasis on the 'need to restore competitiveness' and to 'face up to worldwide competition'. The change in policy and circumstance emerges quite clearly from figure 14.1, which shows that while the total number of cases trebled from 1976 to 1978, the number of 'objections' hardly rose at all. This period of excessive leniency was succeeded by one (1979–86) when 'objections' rose substantially – evidence of a battle royal between the Commission and the member states. From 1987, not only did the economy pick up somewhat, but the member states had learned to avoid the inconvenience and embarrassment of going through the Commission's 'objection' process. The number of 'objections' steadied despite a rising number of cases, but the level of objections is related to the business cycle, rising again with the slowdown after 1999. The rise in the number of cases and objections in 2004 is associated with cases in the new member states.

The change from the Commission permitting, under supervision, the continuing subsidization by member states of 'sectors in difficulty' (coalmines, shipyards, textiles, etc.), to a more restrictive policy was associated with the development of the Internal Market Programme (see chapters 2 and 7). The creation of a genuine single market made it more important than ever that member states should not thwart the competitive

process by extensive use of state aid. The first step was to evaluate the extent of the problem with a general report on state aid every three years.

The level of state aid has been decreasing with changing attitudes towards it, the fiscal consolidation required for EMU, Commission policy and peer pressure. State aid as a percentage of GDP fell, from 3 per cent in the first half of the 1980s, to 0.9 per cent in 1993 and to 0.6 per cent in 2004 (CEC, 2006t). All countries have participated in this trend, the most spectacular declines being registered by Italy, Ireland and Belgium, with most of the reductions taking place in the 1980s. So by 2004 total aid in the EU15 varied between 1.1 per cent of GDP in Portugal and 0.2 per cent in the UK; in the ten 2004 new member states there is more variability, with aid at 0.4 per cent in the Czech Republic, Estonia and Latvia, and up to 3.1 per cent in Malta.

The breakdown of state aid by objective is changing over time. The Commission distinguishes between 'horizontal' aid programmes, regional aid and 'sectoral' aid programmes (mainly aimed at traditional sectors in difficulty, such as steel, coal, shipyards, automobiles, etc.). Sectoral aid is cyclical, rising in recessions and falling when the economy expands: in the 1980s and 1990s it fluctuated at around 40 to 60 per cent of total aid,[5] but since 1997 it has been on a downward trend, accounting for only 26 per cent in 2004.[6] This fall in total aid is the result of falling aid to sectors such as coal, steel and shipbuilding as countries have accepted the diminished size of these industries and changing attitudes towards state aid.

With the changing view of the government's role in ICP, the importance of horizontal programmes has increased, but within this category there have been changed priorities. Areas associated with competitiveness such as employment and training, R&D and SMEs plus the environment (another priority; see chapter 18) have become more important. Regional aid has declined (see chapter 22). The distinction between sectoral and horizontal is not as clear-cut as it might seem. The rescue and restructuring of East German industry after reunification, under the Treuhand, gave rise to a large number of firm-specific subsidies subjected to evaluation by DG Competition. These ad hoc aids to rescue companies in difficulty arose in other countries. These were recognized as damaging both to the single market and to the Commission's reputation for maintaining fair competition at Community level. In 1999 the Commission published a set of guidelines in an attempt to contain the problem (CEC, 1999i). *Rescue* aid must be given on a 'one time, last time' basis; it must be no more than a short-term holding operation and must take the form of transparent loans or loan guarantees. *Restructuring* aid must be justified by a detailed corporate plan to restore commercial viability. It is, however, very odd that the Commission should classify rescue and restructuring (R&R) aid as 'horizontal' (CEC, 2001i, paras. 389–93). It would be difficult to imagine anything *less* 'horizontal', or general, than emergency aid to bankrupt firms. It is difficult to believe that R&R aid is available on demand without any selectivity.

State aid for R&D has developed from the first Framework on State Aid for Research and Development in 1986.[7] This emphasized the Commission's generally favourable attitude to this type of aid, warned of the dangers of fruitless duplication of effort, pointed to the need for proper coordination by the Commission and required the notification of all R&D subsidies in excess of 20 million ECU.[8] A good part of the increase in the number of cases investigated by the Commission from 1987 onwards (see figure 14.1) was due to the adoption of this new framework. Other reasons include the increase in membership

and, according to the Commission, the growing efficiency with which it tracks such aid (CEC, 1987a, para. 174), but not an increase in the total volume of state aid, which has been declining. Because of the growing caseload, a regulation to grant group exemptions for certain categories of state aid deemed compatible with the Treaties was agreed (Council of the EU, 1998). The exempt categories are: horizontal aid (in particular, aid to SMEs, R&D, environmental protection, employment and training), regional aid and *de minimis* aid (aid so small as to have no discernible effect on competition). This follows current thinking in allowing general aid and, in particular, aid to SMEs and R&D, although R&R and ad hoc aid remains a problem.

The Maastricht Treaty added a title 'Industry' (Article 157), in which the Community was given a broad mandate to promote the competitiveness of European industry by improving its ability to adjust to structural change, encouraging SMEs, favouring cooperation between enterprises and increase the effectiveness of the Community's research and technological development (R&TD)[9] policies by promoting their dissemination. The Union has responded to the invitation contained in Article 157.2 to 'take any useful initiative to promote such coordination' in order to promote 'the competitiveness of the Community's industry', to develop the Lisbon Strategy (see section 14.6 below).

The European Commission has been gradually exerting its control over state aid, but most governments find it difficult to relinquish this instrument of policy. That this process has been particularly difficult for France, Italy and Spain is no surprise, given their tradition of state intervention and 'indicative' planning, but they have radically reduced the absolute level of public aid. That Germany should be in the same group is more surprising; this is partly the result of a more subtle tradition of interventionism and partly of the reunification process, which has forced Germany to become more interventionist. The Commission still has problems enforcing discipline on member states, but this is within the context of a declining overall level of state aid. There does seem to be a permanent improvement, associated with changing views on ICP. This is reflected in the growth of the EU's R&D programme and the Lisbon process to which the analysis now turns.

14.5 Research and technology policy

EU policy towards research and technological development (R&TD) is inspired by the idea that Europe fails to realize its full scientific and technological potential because its research efforts are dispersed, expensive and given to wasteful duplication. Much is made of the 'technology gap' which separates Europe from the United States and Japan. The answer, in the view of the Commission, is to create a 'European research area' by fostering long-term collaborative ventures between Community firms; between European firms and publicly funded research institutions; and between universities, at a European level. To this end, the EU uses two broad policy instruments: a dispensation from Article 81 for R&TD collaborative agreements between large firms, and direct subsidies to encourage such agreements.

14.5.1 Competition and trade aspects of research and technology policy

The EEC Treaty makes express provision for cooperative R&D within the private sector which 'contributes to improving the production or distribution of goods or to promoting technical or economic progress' (Article 81(3)). As early as 1968, the Commission established guidelines for the application of Article 81, which permitted agreements between firms (even large ones) for the exclusive purpose of developing joint R&D, provided the cooperation remained 'pre-competitive' (i.e. did not extend to actual production), and on condition that the results of the R&D were freely available to the members of the consortium, and preferably also to outsiders on a licensing basis (CEC, 1972, paras. 31–2). In 1984 the Commission extended this to a 'block exemption' for cooperative R&D schemes, which no longer had to be individually notified and could extend downstream to the joint exploitation including the marketing of the results. This represented a considerable shift in policy for which European industry had been

lobbying, on the grounds that it made little sense to pool R&D efforts if, once they were successful, competition between the members of the pool wiped out all the potential monopolistic rents: under such circumstances, firms would prefer not to pool R&D resources at all, but take the risk of going it alone. This dispensation from normal antitrust rules to permit long-term collaborative research agreements does not pre-judge the sectors which will avail themselves of the opportunity; therefore it is a truly *general* industrial policy. The Commission effectively gave up investigating R&TD state aid after it was the subject of a group exemption (Council of the EU, 1998).

In 1996 the Commission issued a new set of guidelines for state aid to R&TD (CEC, 1996f) to bring Community practice into line with new WTO obligations. In particular, the Commission highlighted the distinction between WTO-compatible support for R&D (squarely in the pre-competitive box) and illegal R&D support (aid for the commercial introduction of industrial innovations or the marketing of new products).

The subsidy arm of the R&D policy only goes as far as the 'pre-competitive' (i.e. pre-market) stage because it is selective to start with. It cannot go all the way to supporting the market-based stage of developing prototypes without laying itself open to accusations that it is 'picking the winners'. These two branches of Community policy (antitrust dispensation and direct subsidies) enable a third, non-Community instrument of joint industrial policy – the 'Eureka' initiative – to flourish under the benign dispensation of the European antitrust authorities, *and with financial support from member states*. Thus selective support for R&D at national level is permitted by the Commission as long as it involves agreements between firms from two or more member countries. As such, it promotes the 'ever-closer union among the peoples of Europe' which is the overriding political objective of the EU.

14.5.2 European subsidies to research and technological development

Despite the obvious advantages of pooling R&D efforts at a European level the EEC Treaty does not mention joint European R&D policy and it took many years to develop one. Member states were hesitant to relinquish their ability to subsidize 'sunrise' sectors and the experience of pooling research efforts in the nuclear field has not been happy (Guzzetti, 1995). However, the major concern over Europe's declining 'competitiveness' overcame member states' reluctance.

The origins of EU R&D policy lie in the problems of the European economy after the oil price increases of the 1970s; by contrast both the United States and Japan shook off the negative effects quickly. The EC response, organized by Viscount Davignon, was two-pronged: 'crisis cartels' in declining industries and support for 'sunrise' industries. He believed that there was a case for European high-technology firms to pool their R&D efforts, to avoid useless duplication and to benefit from trans-European synergies. Following Servan-Schreiber (1967), he and others were upset by the tendency of European firms to form technological alliances, if they did so at all, with American or Japanese partners, rather than with fellow Europeans.

Gradually a strategy emerged which involved linking universities, research institutes, the major European companies and some SMEs in an effort to narrow the 'technology gap' which had opened up between Europe and the United States in the area of electronics and information technology. A pilot programme was prepared and approved by the Council in 1981; Davignon's strategy of involving from the very start twelve major European firms, which then lobbied their respective governments to support the scheme, paid off (Peterson and Sharp, 1998). This led to the first multi-annual framework research programme, an important component of which was ESPRIT (European Programme for Research in Information Technology), which was enthusiastically supported by industry. It provided 750 million ECU of Community funding over the period 1984–8, matched ECU for ECU by private funding from the participating companies. Calls for research proposals produced over 900 projects, only 240 of which were finally approved, after consultation with the round-table representatives. This was followed by programmes in telecommunications research in

advanced communication technologies for Europe (RACE) and basic research in technologies for Europe raw materials and advanced materials (BRITE/EURAM), launched in 1985, and a host of other programmes followed.

The Single European Act (1987) for the first time provided a Treaty basis for 'research and technological development' (now Articles 163–73) with the new aim 'to strengthen the scientific and technological bases of Community industry and to encourage it to become more competitive at the international level'. This led to a multi-annual framework programme of research funding, and the Maastricht Treaty widened the policy to 'all the research activities deemed necessary by virtue of other Chapters of this Treaty' (Article 162). So research funding has been extended beyond the competitiveness of European industry to basic science and research connected with social objectives. This is significant, with research contributing to the entire range of Community objectives, such as regional and social cohesion, quality of life, the environment, etc.

Although it is difficult to make comparisons because of the shifting categorization of the research programme, some trends are clear. There was an expansion of the funds available for research, with expenditure accounting for an increasing share of GDP between the mid-1970s and the mid-1990s.[10] With increasing budgetary stringency since 1994 the share has stagnated, although under the new budgetary perspective research expenditure commitments are scheduled to increase from around 0.5 per cent of GDP in 2006 to 0.6 per cent in 2013 (European Parliament, Council and Commission, 2006, p. 10). The gradual rise in EU expenditure on R&D has been accompanied by shifts in priorities. The Framework Programme 1 (FP1) was dominated by energy, which accounted for 50 per cent of expenditure, but its importance has waned and in the proposals for FP7 (CEC, 2005f) energy is only scheduled to account for 4 per cent of expenditure. Information and communications technology (ICT) received another 25 per cent of expenditure under the FP1, which increased to 42 per cent of FP2. ICT remains the most important part of FP7 but its share of expenditure is to drop to 17 per cent. Industrial technologies, the third priority in the first four programmes, have been dropped. Life sciences (now health) have become more important and new priorities have emerged such as the environment and nanotechnology. The share of expenditure devoted to specific industrial priorities has declined and that on less directly targeted expenditure has grown; under the FP7 proposals nearly 40 per cent of expenditure is more generally targeted. This expenditure is on 'ideas' (individual peer-reviewed projects), 'people' (the development of the number and quality of researchers) and 'capacities' (the development of research infrastructure, encouraging research in SMEs, research clusters – a European Silicon Valley?). As would be expected, this changing distribution of research expenditure reflects changes in ideas about the priorities for research and how it should be fostered. In particular the gradual reduction in the role of industrially targeted research is the result of a growing emphasis on developing capacities rather than targeting the shift from old to new industrial policy. There is also some concern that what is happening here is the capture with ever larger sums of money of projects close to the heart of industry and the research community. Yet EU expenditure on R&D remains relatively modest: it has risen from 2.3 per cent of national government research expenditure in 1985 to 5.7 per cent in 2002 (CEC, 2004d, 2006d; OECD, 2005e).

Another objective is the creation of the 'European Research Area', or ERA, for the better coordination of European research efforts. The Commission's contribution to this effort is 'benchmarking of national research polices', and studying, comparing and evaluating individual member states' R&D policies, in an elusive search for 'best practices'. Ultimately the aim is to coordinate national research in order to prevent overlap, a favourite rationalist panacea to make limited research funds go further. It overlooks the paradoxical fact that independent, non-coordinated research scans a far broader area of the unknown and is more likely to stumble on solutions than so-called 'strategic' approaches. However, if spending more money on trying to make national R&D policies 'strategic' is difficult

to justify in terms of generating extra innovation, one can quite understand why the Commission should be making a bid to supervise and coordinate the R&D by member states.

14.5.3 Non-EU technological cooperation

European cooperation on R&D goes beyond the EU with the Eureka (European Research Coordinating Agency) programme. President Mitterrand of France launched the Eureka in 1985 in response to President Reagan's 'Star Wars' or Strategic Defence Initiative (SDI). This was scheduled to spend $26 billion on advanced electronic, nuclear and space technology, and threatened to siphon off the best European intellectual talent in these areas. Eureka began with the then twelve members of the European Community, plus the EFTA countries, Spain, Turkey and the European Commission, as an intergovernmental organization with a secretariat in Paris; today it has thirty-six members. In 2006 there were 700 projects running with a budget of 1.7 billion euros and 2,760 organizations involved (Eureka, 2006).

Its purpose is to promote, through public subsidies, any 'near market' R&D project involving firms in more than one member country. It possesses no central allocative function. Projects are generated in member states and circulated among members to see if other firms or governments might like to join. The Eureka secretariat simply keeps track of what is going on. It has no 'policy' as such and therefore fits the definition of a general or macroeconomic industrial policy (although individual projects are obviously the outcome of individual governments' different industrial policies). However, projects are organized in clusters (groups of projects in a strategically important area, e.g. ICT) and umbrellas (thematic networks specializing in a particular technology, e.g. laser and optical technology). In the early 1990s Eureka represented 'a total research effort only marginally smaller than the Framework programme' (Peterson and Sharpe, 1998, p. 90); this is no longer true today, partly because of the expansion of the EU research budget, but also because Eureka has become less important. After starting off with two *grands projets* which absorbed large amounts of public money (the ill-fated HDTV project and the more successful Joint European Submicron Silicon Initiative – JESSI), Eureka has settled down to sponsoring an ever-larger number of smaller research projects.[11] This larger portfolio increases the chances of 'stumbling on winners', and decreases the importance of R&D failures, increasing the overall prospects of success, but it no longer hits the headlines.

Eureka and the EU research effort are meant to be complementary, with the EU concentrating on 'pre-competitive' research, while Eureka sponsors 'near-market' development. The Commission retains its overarching supervisory function. The Commission, overwhelmed by the caseload all this had generated, made a strategic withdrawal in 1998 when it decided to sponsor a new Council regulation to grant group exemptions, inter alia, for R&D state aid (Council of the EU, 1998).

While there is clearly some overlap between Eureka and the EU FPs, there is also plenty of complementarity. At least theoretically, a project sponsored by the EU at the top end of the R&D pipeline could be taken up by a Eureka project at the lower end of the process. But one sees little or no mention of Eureka in the official Commission literature. In short, Mitterrand's Eureka has failed to become the spearhead for massive government-sponsored R&D projects.

14.5.4 Research and technology policy: an assessment

EU industrial policy has come a long way since the Commission first sponsored 'crisis cartels' in the 1970s. Thanks to the Commission's policies, the EU has shifted from selective support to 'sunset' sectors and 'sunrise' industries to a policy designed to raise the EU's competitiveness more generally. The Commission has been unfailingly critical of member states' ad hoc subsidies to individual firms and in order to claw back some illegal aid. It is correct in preferring 'horizontal' to 'sectoral' aid and its battle to contain selective state aid has been commendable.

The verdict on R&TD policy is less clear-cut. The EU has tried hard to avoid the trap of 'picking the winners' by supporting only 'pre-competitive' R&TD. The fundamental problem remains the difficulty of identifying potentially successful projects. Inevitably the process is politicized, with countries increasingly concerned with their share of the funding (Peterson and Sharp, 1998). In addition there is the general problem with EU projects of monitoring. In 2004 there were 118 completed audits on 7,696 contracts (European Court of Auditors, 2005, p. 169): a very low level considering there was 'a high incidence of errors at beneficiary level that affected the legality and regularity of transactions' (p. 179). There have been successes and failures – HDTV was a fiasco (European Court of Auditors, 1995, paras. 9.12–9.49) – but clearly support for telecommunications research has paid off, since the European global mobile telephone system (GSM) has proved to be a huge commercial success, and some of this success is perhaps attributable to the ESPRIT and BRITE programmes. The fact is that no one will ever know what the *anti-monde* (see chapter 9) would have looked like. The sums are huge, the opportunity costs are enormous, and the probability of a massive improvement on what markets would have achieved is small.

Looking to the future, it is clear that support for R&TD at European level (and perhaps also at member-state level) will become more and more involved with aims which have nothing to do with the competitiveness of European firms. Since the Maastricht Treaty, R&TD is supposed to serve any and all of the EU's many objectives. Is this to be welcomed or deplored? One suspects that the lack of focus will open the doors to plenty of nonsense.

One obvious problem with European research is the differential between European academic salaries and those of the US. At present, far too many young Europeans go to the US for their doctoral and postdoctoral research, never to return. Money spent at the top end of the R&TD pipeline, farthest away from the marketplace, is probably by far the most effective in the long run. The multi-annual framework programmes must also encourage links with firms from non-EU countries, with American, Japanese or *any* firms from any country. The technological community must be set free to seek partnerships wherever they happen to be the most fruitful. Discriminating between European and non-European firms

Table 14.1 Productivity and employment in the EU15 and the US, 2004

	GDP[1] per head	Employment rate	GDP[1] per worker	Hours worked	GDP[1] per hour
EU15	73.6	67.1	80.2	92.6	86.6
USA	100.0	72.0	100.0	100.0	100.0

Note:

1. GDP measured in purchasing power parities.

Source: CEC (2006d), OECD (2006e).

cannot possibly promote efficiency. The R&D policy of the EU must be given a clearer role distinct from that of member states' policies.

14.6 EU economic reform and competitiveness

The development of the EU's industrial and research policy could be characterized as moving from the particular, the support of specific initiatives, to the general, the improvement of the EU's competences. This change reflected changing views on the way to improve the performance of the economy. Today the conventional wisdom is that the improvement of individual aspects of economic policy is not enough and interaction between policies is crucial; so, for example, reform of labour policies works more effectively when product markets are reformed. This leads to the idea that the competitiveness of the economy requires a very broad range of policies, not intervention in particular industries. Since the late 1990s internal and external factors have led to economic reform in this general sense becoming one of the key items on the EU's policy agenda. Economic reform is seen to be urgently required if the EU is going to be able to meet the social and economic aspirations of its citizens and fulfil its global obligations.

14.6.1 Reasons for economic reform

There is a perception that the EU is 'confronted with a quantum shift from globalisation and the challenges of a new knowledge-driven economy' (European Council, 2000a). The Union must take radical steps to ensure that its economy and society are able to meet the new challenges and maintain/ improve its global competitiveness. EU productivity and employment are significantly below those of the US. In 2004 GDP per head was 73.6 per cent of the US level, partly due to the fact that 5 per cent fewer of the population aged 15–64 were employed and worked for 7.4 per cent fewer hours (table 14.1). Strong pressure was exerted by some member states (e.g. the UK and Spain) to move forward on the liberalization agenda to improve the environment for innovation and enterprise. The introduction of the euro in 1999 strengthened the argument for more flexibility in the labour, product and capital markets and introduced a new sense of urgency to reform.

Unemployment rates remain too high in many member states (see table 5.4), imposing unacceptable social costs and wasting valuable economic resources. Opinion poll data indicates that unemployment is the issue that worries EU citizens most and it is therefore politically imperative that the Union is seen to be taking steps to achieve full employment.

The EU's research and development performance urgently needs to be improved to keep up with new advances, especially in the information and communication technologies that are seen as the key to remaining competitive in the global marketplace. There is concern about the potential social consequences of the new communications revolution if some sections of the population find themselves excluded, either in terms of skills or access. In the interests of social cohesion and inclusiveness steps have be taken to widen access to new technologies.

Enlargement poses challenges of adjustment for both existing and new member states. Greater flexibility and a commitment to economic reform will help ensure that the potential dynamic gains of the creation of a single market of 480 million people are realized with the minimum of socioeconomic disruption.

14.6.2 The development of the Lisbon Agenda

The Treaty of Amsterdam (EU, 1997) introduced an employment title which provides the legal base for 'developing a coordinated strategy for employment and particularly for promoting a skilled, trained and adaptable workforce and labour markets responsive to economic change' (Article 125). These objectives are to be achieved by policy instruments such as joint annual reports, guidelines, exchanges of information and best practices and recommendations to member states rather than by adopting new EU legislation. This new approach was to become the model for the implementation of the economic reform agenda, the 'open method of coordination'.

An extraordinary European Council Meeting was held in November 1997 in Luxembourg (European Council, 1997), specifically to focus on the problem of the unacceptably high level of unemployment in the EU, which was seen to present a threat to the cohesion of society. In view of the urgency of the situation, it was decided to implement the new employment provisions of the Treaty of Amsterdam in advance of its ratification. This was possible because of the intergovernmental character of the approach (no legislation was required). Union-wide employment guidelines were to be agreed, setting specific targets and a common procedure adopted to monitor their achievement. The guidelines are implemented by being incorporated into national employment action plans drawn up by each member state and subject to a multilateral surveillance system.

Significantly, under the British Presidency of the EU,[12] the Cardiff European Council of June 1998 agreed that the Broad Economic Guidelines introduced under the EMU process should be developed as a key tool for economic recovery and self-sustaining, non-inflationary growth (European Council, 1998). This Council also highlighted the need for fresh initiatives to promote entrepreneurship and competitiveness, especially encouraging small businesses and innovation, improving the skills and flexibility of the labour market, and making the capital market more efficient.

The Cologne European Council of June 1999 (European Council, 1999b), the first European Council after the introduction of the euro in January 1999, gave a new impetus to the reform agenda and strengthened the commitment to macroeconomic dialogue. It gave approval of a European Employment Pact aimed at a sustainable reduction of unemployment by bringing together all the recent initiatives into a comprehensive policy strategy. It helped to shape the agenda for the planned Lisbon Council by arguing that 'the jobs of the future will be created by innovation and the information society'.

The Lisbon European Council in March 2000 (European Council, 2000a) brought together all the various initiatives adopted since the Amsterdam Council in a comprehensive policy strategy. There was a new strategic goal for the next decade: 'to become the most competitive and dynamic knowledge-based economy in the world, capable of sustainable economic growth with more and better jobs and greater social cohesion' (European Council, 2000a).

Achieving this goal requires an overall strategy aimed to:

- prepare the transition to a knowledge-based economy and society by better policies for the information society and R&D, as well as by stepping up the process of structural reform for competitiveness and innovation and by completing the internal market;
- modernize the European social model, investing in people and combating social exclusion;
- sustain the healthy economic outlook and favourable growth prospects by applying an appropriate macro-economic policy mix. (European Council, 2000a, I5.5).

To say that the Lisbon agenda is all-embracing is an understatement. It encompassed new technologies, particularly ICT; research and innovation; encouraging entrepreneurship and SMEs; a fully operational internal market, including services; liberalization of network industries; integrated financial markets; promotion of competition and reduction of state aid; coordination of macroeconomic policy; fiscal consolidation; reform of tax and benefit systems to improve employment; more and better jobs; modernizing the European social model; life-long learning; increasing physical and human capital; equal opportunities; working life balance; improved childcare provision; and promoting social inclusion. There are three reasons for the breadth of this agenda. The first is the belief that improving economic performance requires a wide range of interrelated measures. The second is that this is the result of a bargaining process to achieve unanimity where individual national leaders ensured that measures particularly important to them were included. And the third is that it is a reflection of the fact that there is considerable disagreement over how economic performance should be improved. One group of countries, led by the UK, believed that liberalization, particularly of the labour market, was essential, while others were keen to retain their high levels of protection of workers. There was therefore the need to include in the Strategy such elements as the European social model and better jobs. Thus the Lisbon Strategy contained twenty-eight main objectives, 120 objectives and 117 indicators. This wide and somewhat contradictory Strategy, differing attitudes (Boeri, 2005) and the reliance on the Open Method of Coordination (OMC) have undermined the effectiveness of the Lisbon process.

14.6.3 The Outcomes of the Lisbon Agenda

The Lisbon process operates under the OMC, with the Council agreeing guidelines that contain targets and recommendations, which are adopted at the discretion of member states. This process is intergovernmental because in most of these policy areas the EU has limited powers: the member states retain sovereignty. The policy operates via

reports[13] containing the policy, objectives and progress. Enforcement is by recommendation, peer pressure and benchmarking (seeing what is effective); there are no penalties or financial incentives to encourage compliance. This has not proved to be very effective because the political salience of failure to meet commitments is low (Ardy and Umbach, 2004) and so governments implement policies in line with their own priorities (Zeitlin and Pochet, 2005).

The results of the Lisbon process have been disappointing. There has been reform, tax burdens have been reduced, regulations eased and labour markets liberalized (Wanlin, 2006), but the changes have not been sufficiently widespread, comprehensive or deep (Gros, 2005). Even in areas within its remit, the EU has been unable to deliver, as shown by the failure to agree a really significant increase in the budget for R&D (section 14.5.2 above).

Although it is still too early to judge, the Lisbon process does not seem to have had much impact on the EU's economic performance. The familiar adverse comparison with the USA is confirmed by the figures in table 14.2. Economic growth in the EU15 measured by real GDP using purchasing power parity (PPP) exchange rates[14] was the same, at an average of 2.4 per cent, between 1976 and 1985 as it was between 1986 and 1995 despite the Single Market programme. The growth rate fell to 2.2 per cent between 1996 and 2004. Higher growth was achieved by the USA and a group of comparable OECD countries, comprising Australia, Canada, New Zealand and Switzerland (ACNZS), with their growth rates being higher during 1996–2004 after a dip in the 1986–95 period. Japan's growth rate was high until the early 1990s when economic problems led to a decade of very low growth, from which it is only now emerging.

Overall GDP growth depends not only on changes in productivity but also on changes in the inputs used: the amount of labour and capital. Employment has grown more slowly in the EU15 than in the USA and ACNZS, but not Japan. This is partly because of slower population growth but also participation in employment is lower as early retirement and similar measures have been used

Table 14.2 Growth of real purchasing power parity GDP[1]

	Annual % growth rate		
	1976–85	1986–95	1996–2004
Real PPP GDP			
EU15	2.4	2.4	2.2
Japan	3.7	3.1	1.0
USA	3.4	3.0	3.3
Australia, Canada, New Zealand and Switzerland	2.9	2.5	3.0
Real PPP per person employed			
EU15	2.3	1.3	1.1
Japan	2.8	2.2	1.3
USA	1.4	1.4	1.8
Australia, Canada, New Zealand and Switzerland	1.2	0.9	1.4
Real PPP GDP per hour worked			
EU15[2]	3.0	1.8	1.8
Japan	2.9	3.3	1.9
USA	1.3	1.3	2.4
Australia, Canada, New Zealand and Switzerland	1.7	1.0	1.6

Notes:
1. Real GDP measured in PPP US $2,000.
2. EU15, excluding Greece 1975–82, Portugal and Luxembourg 1975–85, and Austria 1975–85.

Source: World Bank (2006a), OECD (2006e), CEC (2006d), own calculations.

to limit the growth of unemployment. Calculating the growth of real PPP GDP per person in employment provides a macro measure of productivity, and produces a lower absolute difference in growth rates between the EU15 and the USA and ACNZS. But a more worrying picture emerges of slowing productivity growth in the EU15, contrasting with accelerating productivity growth for the USA and ACNZS. Not only was productivity growth slow but the EU15 was only achieving very limited employment growth: the overall employment rate[15] increased by 1.7 per cent during 1975–2004 compared to 9.2 per cent in the USA and 6.9 per cent in ACNZS (CEC, 2006d).

The amount of labour available for production is dependent not only on the number of workers but also on how many hours they work, and trends differ between countries: the average number of hours worked in the EU11[16] declined by 3.9 per cent during 1975–2004, but increased by 61.0 per cent in the USA. Taking account of these changes in hours of work by calculating GDP per hour worked changes the picture: the EU15 had faster growth of GDP per hour worked than the USA during 1976–95 but still lagged significantly during 1996–2004, yet had superior productivity growth to the ACNZS over the whole period.

To summarize, the EU15's GDP has grown relatively slowly since 1975. This is due to a combination of factors: a relatively slow growth of the labour force; limited growth of employment among the population of working age; a relative decline in hours of work; and recently slower growth in productivity per hour worked compared with the USA. These trends might be the result of different levels of capital, but gross fixed capital formation (GFCF)[17] as a percentage of GDP in the EU15[18] has been above that of the USA throughout the 1975–2004 period (CEC, 2006d). The EU15's productivity problem is well documented (Sapir et al., 2003b; Daveri, 2004; Denis et al., 2004, 2005) and it is seen to be associated with retaining significant production in low and medium technology industries, an ICT sector that is too small, and a failure to achieve the productivity benefits of ICT especially in service industries (Gordon, 2004; Inklaar et al., 2003).

14.6.4 Assessing the Lisbon process

Most of the objectives and the specific policy measures contained in the Lisbon Strategy are not new. What Lisbon achieved was to bring them together into a high-profile package which would demonstrate the Union's determination to embrace a radical and comprehensive reform agenda to meet challenges posed by globalization, the e-revolution and the demographic shift in Europe's population. One of the goals was to stimulate a wide public debate on the issues and to make people aware of the 'revolutions' taking place in the world at the turn of the millennium.

One of the achievements of the Lisbon process has been the extent to which so many of the key objectives have become very widely used in debates on public policy and have served as rallying calls, or 'slogans', to promote reform across a wide number of areas.

The political importance of the Lisbon agenda is recognized by the central role played by the European Council, and the summit meetings of the heads of state and government. The spring European Council (usually held in March) is devoted specifically to the Lisbon strategy and is based on the Commission's annual synthesis report on progress made in achieving the targets set. It is available on the Commission website and, together with the Presidency Conclusions agreed at the end of the meeting, provides an invaluable record of both the successes and shortcomings of the process so far and the priorities set for the future. This annual cycle of reports and meetings helps to maintain momentum but some political leaders have expressed frustration at the slowness to translate fine-sounding slogans into concrete reforms.

'Lisbon is about everything and thus nothing' (Kok, 2004, p. 16). The Lisbon Strategy encompasses so many things: investment, research, enterprise, social inclusion, environmental sustainability, etc. Because of this it is difficult to concentrate effort on what is vital, it is hard to assess progress, and there is the possibility of different objectives being contradictory.

The Lisbon commitment is rhetorical and was agreed at the height of the dotcom boom. The breadth of the policy reveals the difference in priorities between the member states. Thus member states are only committed to parts of the Lisbon agenda. The policy is not really owned by the particular governments or institutions which drive it forward. These problems have meant that there has been a failure to agree and implement measures. The policy lacks financial incentives to encourage compliance. The EU has made only limited progress on the core commitments.

The mid-term review of the policy (CEC, 2005g) recognized these problems and sought to address them by making the policy more effective, through more focus and setting it as the priority

in the new Barroso Commission's plans. There were to be three priorities for the policy concentrating on growth and jobs:

1. *Making Europe a more attractive place to invest and work:* completing the Single Market; and business-friendly regulation.
2. *Knowledge and innovation for growth:* raising expenditure on R&D to 3 per cent of GDP, to be pushed by a large increase in EU research expenditure; and encouragement to extend ICT usage for business and the population at large.
3. *Creating more and better jobs:* increase employment by making the labour force more adaptable through raising the level of education and skills.

There were concerns that this slimmer agenda downgraded the environmental and social aspects of the Lisbon agenda and these were re-emphasised by the Council agreement on the revised agenda (European Council, 2005a). The risk now is that the original weakness of a multiplicity of objectives will re-emerge. The OMC has had only limited success and by putting the Lisbon agenda at the top of its priorities the Commission will be in the dangerous position of being judged on the success of policies that are beyond its remit. The Commission is trying to make the policy a success by 'bending' other policies such as competition and structural policy to achieve the Lisbon objectives. The risk here is that these policies may not achieve either what Lisbon requires or the agreed objectives.

14.6.5 A radical view of the Lisbon agenda

Do we really want to be the world's most productive economy? Economists are increasingly questioning the link between material living standards and happiness. Becoming the world's most competitive economy might require long working hours and very rapid structural change in the economy. EU countries have consistently shown, in the choices they have made, over for example their welfare systems, that this is not what they really want. The US enjoys a higher level of GDP than the EU average, but in the US hours of work are longer, holidays are fewer, retirement is later and inequality is much greater. The EU has problems over unemployment among the young, early retirement and the sustainability of pensions systems, but to many the US model does not seem attractive.

Is it necessary? There is an implicit assumption that failure to be the best in the world implies declining living standards and general deterioration. Countries such as the UK failed to keep up with the growth of other countries for at least one hundred years whilst still enjoying rising living standards and retaining an important role in the world. There is a false analogy between the competitiveness of companies and the competitiveness of countries. If companies are not competitive they will become bankrupt and will cease to exist. If countries do not maintain their competitiveness relative to other countries, their relative living standards will decline. But they will not go bankrupt since they can still enjoy reasonable standards of living.

Do we really know how to raise overall economic performance? Countries succeed with very different economic institutions and policies. While there is general agreement that sound macroeconomic policies, the rule of law and good institutions are essential, there is little agreement beyond this. Indeed appropriate policies may vary between countries, so the policy choices are not clear-cut, otherwise governments would be likely to follow them anyway.

14.7 Conclusion

The development of ICP in the EU reflects changing economic circumstances and ideas about the appropriate role of government. But the one constant has been the desire of governments to improve economic performance first in narrow problem areas, but then more generally during the economic crises of the 1970s. The principal shift has been from intervention to encourage national champions or sunrise sectors, to more generally providing a suitable environment for the private sector to flourish. The understandable desire to help particular companies/industries in trouble remains, and so do some vestiges of interventionist industrial policy in the form of strategic sectors. With these developments the EU's role has changed and the EEC Treaty powers to control state aid have gradually evolved to become more effective. In addition to merely overseeing member states' ICP, the EU has gradually developed a role in ICP. At first this was in relation to R&D policy where the EU was viewed as a way of enhancing national policies; this has developed to become an important part of the Union's overall research effort. With the simultaneous processes of globalization and Europeanization, national power over economic policy has diminished, and concern has mounted over the performance of EU economies and the ability to sustain European standards in relation to employment, pensions and the environment. The response to this has been the development of a widening European economic policy agenda, encompassed in the Lisbon agenda and economic policy coordination.

Industrial policy has always suffered from the ability of interest groups to exploit policy so that their interests rather than the public good are served, and this problem remains. The developing EU ICP also suffers from two other major problems. The first is the difficulty of achieving a coherent policy when so many conflicting views have to be reconciled. The second is the difficulty of ensuring the policy is implemented when major elements remain national responsibilities. The first problem has led to the rather ramshackle edifice of the Lisbon Strategy, which tries to be all things to all people. Furthermore, it is difficult to achieve the consistency required of a policy which seeks to change long-term economic performance; it is no coincidence that the grandiose Lisbon goal was agreed at the height of the dotcom boom, and it is likely that if these goals were set today they would be considerably more modest. The second problem is one of delivery: the Barroso Commission has taken a risk by placing at the centre of their priorities a policy whose implementation is largely in the hands of the member states.

NOTES

1 As well as the failure of individual companies, illustrated vividly in 2005 by the final demise of Rover the

supposed national champion of the UK motor vehicle industry.

2 In its widest sense to include measures such as changes in labour market and social security legislation.

3 Innovation is still possible without patent protection because the innovator will enjoy benefits until the innovation is copied. There may also be first mover advantages.

4 Article numbers refer to the Consolidated Treaty (CEC, 2002o).

5 Total aid excluding agriculture, fisheries and railways.

6 This is a share of a declining total.

7 The adoption of this framework was related to President Mitterrand's 1985 launch of the Eureka research programme. This involved large research subsidies channelled towards national champions (a typical 'picking the winners' industrial policy), and the French government wanted to ensure that the Eureka programme would not be thwarted by the Commission.

8 Raised to 40 million ECU in 1996.

9 The inclusion of 'technological' reflected greater emphasis on the commercial application of research outcomes.

10 Except for the aberration in 1983–4.

11 See the Eureka website for information at www.eureka.be.

12 Economic reform was a UK priority.

13 Including, since 2005, national reports.

14 This is the most accurate assessment of the value of output over the long term.

15 The percentage of the population aged 16–65 in employment.

16 EU15, excluding Austria, Greece, Luxembourg and Portugal.

17 Investment in equipment and infrastructure but not in stocks.

18 GFCF in the ACNZS has been even higher.

15 Tax harmonization

BRIAN ARDY AND ALI EL-AGRAA

Tax harmonization has been a very thorny issue for the EU: witness the vehement argument in the 1980s when Margaret Thatcher, the British Prime Minister, flatly declared that tax harmonization was not EU business, only to be told by Helmut Kohl, the German Chancellor, and Jacques Delors, President of the Commission, that it was indispensable for EU integration. Such a bold statement cannot be treated lightly, since tax harmonization remains one of the few areas where new EU legislation requires unanimity: hence a single EU member nation can frustrate any new initiatives in this domain. The purpose of this chapter is to clarify what tax harmonization means and to consider to what extent it is necessary for the EU, before going on to assess the progress the EU has achieved.

15.1 Why is tax harmonization necessary?

Tax harmonization is the agreement and application of common rules for taxation across the EU. This involves three separate aspects: first, the object of taxation – what is to be taxed; second, the tax base – agreement on the calculation of what is to be taxed; third, harmonization of rates. Tax harmonization in the EU so far has been very limited, with an agreed base for VAT, and minimum rates for VAT, alcohol, cigarette and energy taxation, plus some agreements to limit unfavourable interaction between national tax systems.

The government plays a very important role in modern economies: in 2003 tax revenue accounted for 40.3 per cent of EU25 GDP.[1] Normally tax and government expenditure is primarily the responsibility of the highest tier of government, the federal or central government. As demonstrated in chapter 19, this is not the case in the EU, since the member states control most tax revenue and are responsible for most government expenditure. This makes the EU unusual because there is a large variation of taxes and government expenditure in a single market.

There are two basic types of taxation: direct and indirect. Direct taxes, such as income and corporation taxes, are levied on wages and salaries (income taxes), or on the profits of industrial or professional businesses (corporation taxes). Direct taxes are not intended to affect the price of commodities or professional services.[2] Indirect taxes are levied specifically on consumption and are, therefore, in a simplistic model, significant in determining the pricing of commodities.

Taxes can act as non-tariff barriers (NTBs) to international trade (see chapters 6 and 7) as well as affecting the international movement of factors of production (Bhagwati, 1969; Johnson, 1965a; and chapter 8). Therefore, to complete the Single European Market (SEM) and to realize the four freedoms (the free movement of goods, persons, services and capital) in the EU, some degree of tax harmonization is required.

The other reason for tax harmonization is that the ability of national tax systems to raise revenues, and the efficiency effects which they have, are affected by the tax regimes in the other member states of the single market. For example, the revenue from tobacco taxation will depend upon the rates of taxation in neighbouring countries. Thus there can be positive or negative spillovers/externalities between member states' tax systems. The movement of factors of production can be influenced by government tax and expenditure policies. The administrative and compliance costs for the government and taxpayers may be affected, and the ability of national governments to pursue redistributive policies is constrained. Tax harmonization in the EU is the alignment of tax bases, rules and rates to reduce the harmful interactions between different member states' tax systems.[3]

15.2 The principles of tax harmonization

Three criteria should inform tax harmonization: *jurisdiction*, *distortion* and *enforcement*.

Jurisdiction is the determination of who should receive the revenue from a particular tax. With EU taxation tightly controlled, member states are the jurisdiction for the overwhelming majority of tax revenue, but this sovereignty has to be pooled for the effective operation of national tax systems in a single market. Transparency is required, with clear definitions of tax bases and regulations. The operational independence of national tax systems should be possible within agreed rules; cooperation and information exchange should not be part of the day-to-day operation of the tax system. The clearest example of the jurisdictional principle applies to consumption taxes and the choice between the destination and origin principles (see section 15.3.1). Labour taxes are usually paid in the country of *residence*, which is normally the same as the *source* country where the income is earned. Income from capital is taxed at source as in the case of corporation tax, but income is also subject to residence-based tax. Where more than one tax jurisdiction is involved the interaction between national tax systems becomes important.

Distortion concerns the avoidance of tax-induced inefficiency in the operation of the internal market. Spillover/externalities can occur as a result of the operation of tax systems. The most common externality is tax competition, which will tend to lead to lower tax rates, because governments fear the loss of the tax base to countries with lower rates. This will reduce tax revenues overall and increase the marginal cost of public funds.[4] Tax competition encourages the taxation of less mobile tax bases and may cause lower provision of government services. Whether this is a problem is debatable; it can be argued that tax competition acts as a necessary discipline on government fiscal profligacy.

The extent of the problem of distortion depends upon the type and rate of tax. There are particular problems with excises on products such as alcohol and tobacco, with enormous differences in rates. Tax competition is not a significant problem with labour taxation because of the very low degree of international mobility in the EU[5] (Braunerhjelm et al., 2000, pp. 46–59). High-tax countries would also tend to offer a higher provision of public services, offsetting the higher taxes. The high mobility of capital, especially in a monetary union, means that capital will tend to move to where taxation is lowest. This process will continue until differences in the return on capital offset differences in taxation and returns on immovable factors, labour and land are accordingly depressed in high capital tax countries.

Enforcement is the ability to ensure that the agreed rules apply in practice. Large differences in excise taxes on cigarettes are difficult to enforce in the absence of borders. Taxes on labour are usually withheld by employers at source and so are relatively easy to enforce. Capital income taxation poses particular enforcement problems. If the tax is based on the source of the income, this requires separate national accounting for each member state, but this is not possible for multinational corporations, so unsatisfactory ad hoc arrangements are necessary. The location of profits can also be shifted by the manipulation of transfer prices[6] and other methods. Taxes based on residence also face problems associated with the need to allow for taxes paid elsewhere.

National tax independence within the EU necessitates a significant degree of tax coordination to ensure the effective operation of tax systems. The analysis now turns to the development of the EU's tax harmonization policies.

15.3 The EU's experience of tax harmonization

At the inception of the EEC in 1957, there were wide differences in tax levels and tax rates, a problem particularly acute in relation to consumption taxes. Four types of sales, or turnover, taxes operated in Western Europe (Dosser, 1973; Paxton, 1976): the *cumulative multi-stage cascade system* (West Germany, Luxembourg and the Netherlands) where the tax was levied on the gross value of the commodity at each and every stage of production without any rebate on taxes paid at earlier stages; *value added tax* (VAT), in France levied at each stage of production as a percentage of the value of sales less tax levied at earlier stages of production;[7] *mixed* systems (Belgium and Italy); and finally, *purchase tax* (UK), a single-stage tax charged at the wholesale stage by registered manufacturers or wholesalers, which meant that manufacturers could trade with each other without paying tax.

Although all these tax systems had a common treatment of trade with no tax paid on exports, and tax levied on imports at the point of entry, the cumulative systems involved distortions. Since the amount of tax in cumulative systems varied with the number of transactions in the supply chain, the precise amount of tax to be remitted on exports could not be calculated accurately, nor could the tax on imports; this meant that these taxes could be used as NTBs.[8]

A variety of excise duties taxed goods with inelastic demand, ranging from the classic five (tobacco products, hydrocarbon oils, beer, wine and spirits) to other products (including coffee, sugar, salt and matches). The means by which the governments collected revenue varied from government-controlled manufacturing, e.g. tobacco goods in France and Italy, to fiscal imposts based on value, weight, strength, quality, etc. (Dosser, 1973, p. 2).

The taxation of company profits was based on three different systems according to the treatment of dividends in relation to the personal tax system and these different systems still persist.

15.3.1 From the EEC Treaty (1958) to the internal market (1985)

In the EEC Treaty Articles 95–9, tax harmonization is solely concerned with indirect taxes. Harmonization was seen as vital for preventing indirect taxes from acting as NTBs on intra-EU trade. However, the Treaty only required the harmonization necessary to ensure the establish-ment and functioning of the internal market. The Treaty is rather vague about what it means by harmonization. This is the norm, however: the Treaty lays down the objective but further negotiations lead to detailed legislation. Given the technical nature of the issues, the whole development of tax harmonization during this period was influenced by the work of special committees, informal discussions, etc., in other words the procedure detailed in chapter 2.

In the area of indirect taxation, the major development was VAT, which the EU adopted as its turnover tax following the recommendations of the Neumark Committee in 1963, which was in turn based on the earlier Tinbergen (1953) study. Between 1967 and 1977, six directives were issued with the aim of achieving conformity relating to: the adoption of VAT as the EU sales tax; the use of VAT for the EU budget (see chapter 19); and the achievement of a harmonized VAT base.

Having chosen the tax and the tax base, the EEC had to decide on the tax jurisdiction; it had to opt for either the 'destination' or 'origin' principle. Taxation under the destination principle specifies that tax revenue would be attributable to the country of final purchase. For example, if the UK levies VAT at 8 per cent and France a similar tax at 16 per cent, a commodity exported from the UK to France would be exempt from the UK tax but would be subjected to the tax in France. Hence, France would collect the tax revenue and the UK's exports would compete on equal terms with French products in the French market. VAT under the origin principle would distribute taxation according to the value added in each country. Hence, a commodity exported by the UK to France would pay the UK tax (8 per cent) and in France additional tax would be levied to bring the overall tax on the commodity to 16 per cent. Under strict conditions equivalence would apply: tax revenue and its distribution would be the same under the destination and origin principles. These conditions are that the tax systems in both countries must be exactly the same in terms of base, rules and rates, and trade should be balanced. In this situation the tax collected from foreign countries on exports would be the same as the tax paid to foreign countries on imports. In the absence of these conditions, the destination and origin principles will lead to an uneven distribution of the tax burden between countries. The destination principle, however, is required for border tax adjustments, so it was argued that a borderless EU needed a shift to the origin principle (Shibata, 1967). In the absence of the equivalence conditions, both systems involve potential jurisdiction and distortion problems, so it is practical issues that will decide the choice of system (Bovenberg, 1994; Lockwood et al., 1994).

The EEC decided to keep the destination principle, which is consistent with undistorted intra-EU trade, provided that customs controls remain. This decision ensured that the EEC continued to have separate national markets divided by physical borders. A common base was agreed for VAT (Council of the EC, 1977) but there was no agreement on exemptions and rates, with significant variations among the member states.

Progress on the harmonization of excise duties was rather slow, and this can be attributed to the large differences in rates between member states and the different attitudes these represent. Thus northern Europe objected to lowering rates because of a loss of revenue and adverse effects on health, whereas southern Europeans objected to the implications for their lifestyle of raising rates. The greatest progress was achieved in tobacco, where a new harmonized tax system was adopted in January 1978. This system abolished duties on raw tobacco leaf and adopted a new tax at the manufacturing level, combined with a specific tax per cigarette and VAT. Prest (1979) argues that the overall effect of this was to push up the relative prices of the cheaper brands of cigarettes.

With respect to corporation tax, little was achieved; there is no agreement on the system, definition of profits or minimum rates, so member states still operate different systems. The only area of progress was on taxation of capital transactions where harmonization is necessary for free intra-EU capital flows, where the maximum rate of tax has been set at 1 per cent (Council of the EU, 1995b).

Nothing was attempted in the area of personal income taxation and only slight progress was achieved in social security payments, unemployment benefits, etc.; the only exception was in the area of equity in the taxation of migrant workers (see chapter 8).

There was, therefore, very limited progress on tax harmonization over this period and, with the exception of the use of VAT, member states continued to operate largely independent national tax systems. This was made possible by the retention of the fiscal frontiers, limited capital and labour mobility, and scarce intra-EU multinational company activity. However, all this was to change with the single market.

15.3.2 From the internal market to the single market

The aim of the Single European Act was to transform the EC into a single internal market by the end of 1992, i.e. create 'an area without internal frontiers in which the free movement of goods, persons, services and capital is ensured' (see chapters 2 and 7). The continuing existence of customs and immigration frontiers was the clearest symbol of divisions within the EU, permitting the continuation of protectionist measures.

The customs checks at frontiers limited the need for tax harmonization, by protecting the indirect taxes of one EU member state from tax bargains in others. Thus, customs controls guaranteed that governments could collect the VAT and excise duties on goods sold in their country. A frontier-free EU would potentially cause problems of jurisdiction, distortion and enforcement unless there was a greater degree of tax harmonization. Tax rates did not have to be equalized; the experience of the United States indicated that contiguous states can maintain differentials in sales taxes of up to about five percentage points without the tax leakage becoming significant.

In the 1985 Internal Market White Paper (CEC, 1985a), the Commission reached the conclusion that for the single market, tax harmonization was essential for the elimination of internal frontiers. Thus the White Paper made the following proposals for VAT:

1. Moving from the destination to the origin system of tax collection.

2. The introduction of an EC clearing mechanism, to ensure that revenues would continue to accrue to the EU member nation where consumption took place.
3. The narrowing of the differentials in national VAT rates so as to lessen the risks of fraud, tax evasion and distortions in competition.

With regard to excise duties, three reforms were deemed necessary:

1. An inter-linkage of the bonded warehouse system (created to defer the payment of duty, since goods in these warehouses do not have duties paid; excise duties are levied only once).
2. Upholding the destination principle.
3. An approximation of the national excise duty rates and regimes.

The ability to achieve this harmonization was, however, constrained by the fact that fiscal provisions remained subject to unanimity in decision-making. Agreement was reached on a transitional VAT regime in 1991 (Council of the European Communities, 1992a), and a VAT Information Exchange System (VEIS) was established to monitor VAT on trade in goods, and rate approximation with a minimum standard rate of 15 per cent and a minimum reduced rate of 5 per cent (Council of the European Communities, 1992a) was agreed.

The internal market with freedom of movement of capital meant that national differences in capital taxation would be more likely to affect international capital flows. Abandoning capital controls also meant that it would be more difficult to tax the income from capital via the personal tax system. The single market was also to lead to the development of pan-European multinational companies: the variations in corporation tax regimes could both create difficulties for the development of such corporations and distort their choice of locations for their activities. Despite these problems the harmonization of capital income taxation has made little progress, with a failure to finalize definitive proposals in relation to corporation tax, and an inability to agree on proposals for a withholding tax[9] on capital income.

15.4 Tax harmonization today

The extent to which member states have retained sovereignty over their tax systems is indicated by the very wide differences in total taxation and the structure of taxes between member states (table 15.1). The lion's share of taxes in all countries is collected by personal income tax and social security payments, and, as argued above, differences in these taxes can persist without distorting the single market or giving rise to problems from tax competition.[10] Corporation tax,[11] VAT and excises remain very differentiated despite the drive for harmonization, and the nature and effects of these differences are considered in this section.

15.4.1 Value added tax

There are three fundamental problems with VAT: first, the ageing definition of the tax base provided by the Sixth Directive; second, the widespread use of multiple rate VAT; third, the treatment of cross-border trade.

Under the Sixth Directive, exemptions from VAT include: activities such as healthcare, education, social services, cultural services, public broadcasting, postal services, immovable property, insurance, financial transactions and gambling; and organizations, public bodies, small business and farmers. Public bodies are exempt because it seems strange for the government to tax itself, but recent experience of privatization and contracting out has indicated that there is no clear division between public and private activities. The exemption of small business is the result of the high, largely fixed cost of operating VAT, which would function as regressive tax on small business.[12] The compliance costs of VAT are estimated to be 2 per cent of turnover for small businesses (turnover below 60,000 euros) but only 0.3 per cent for large companies (turnover greater than 1 million euros) – see Sandford et al. (1989). The problem with exemptions is that they can lead to distortions in prices, reduce the efficiency of tax collection and increase compliance and administration costs. A wider tax base with fewer exemptions is desirable, but very difficult to achieve

Table 15.1 EU25 tax structure, 2004

	Personal income tax	Corporation tax	Social contributions	VAT	Excises	Total tax revenue % of GDP
		% of tax revenue				
Belgium	12.8	3.2	14.1	7.0	2.5	45.2
Denmark	24.9	3.1	1.2	9.8	3.8	48.8
Germany	8.7	0.9	16.5	6.2	2.3	38.7
Greece	4.8	3.3	12.1	8.3	2.9	35.1
Spain	6.4	3.5	12.2	6.1	2.5	34.6
France	7.8	2.4	16.3	7.2	2.3	43.4
Ireland	7.4	3.6	4.6	7.4	3.4	30.2
Italy	10.4	2.2	12.3	5.9	2.3	40.6
Luxembourg	7.1	6.1	11.3	7.3	5.2	40.1
Netherlands	6.0	3.3	14.0	7.7	2.6	37.8
Austria	10.0	2.4	14.4	7.8	2.9	42.6
Portugal	5.5	2.9	11.3	8.1	3.3	34.5
Finland	13.5	3.6	11.9	8.7	4.0	44.3
Sweden	15.7	3.0	13.8	9.1	3.1	50.5
UK	10.3	2.8	6.6	7.0	3.4	36.0
EU15 average	**10.1**	**3.1**	**11.5**	**7.5**	**3.1**	**40.2**
Czech Republic	4.8	4.4	15.1	7.4	3.4	36.6
Estonia	6.7	1.8	11.1	8.2	3.7	32.6
Cyprus	3.6	3.8	7.8	9.3	4.5	34.1
Latvia	6.0	1.7	7.8	7.0	3.5	28.6
Lithuania	6.8	1.9	8.7	6.5	3.0	28.4
Hungary	6.7	2.1	13.5	9.0	3.4	39.1
Malta	7.2	4.2	6.9	7.7	3.0	35.1
Poland	4.0	2.0	13.4	7.2	4.2	32.9
Slovenia	5.9	2.0	14.7	8.9	3.5	39.7
Slovakia	3.3	2.8	12.2	8.0	3.1	30.3
NMS10	**5.5**	**2.7**	**11.2**	**7.9**	**3.6**	**33.7**
EU25	**8.3**	**2.9**	**13.2**	**7.7**	**3.3**	**37.6**

Source: CEC (2006k).

given the need for unanimity. A possible way forward would be to allow countries to use a VAT base that extends beyond the definition in the Sixth Directive.[13]

The EU is still a long way from achieving the approximation of VAT rates envisaged in the Internal Market White Paper. All countries respect the minimum standard rate of 15 per cent with a range from 15 per cent in Luxembourg and Cyprus to 25 per cent in Denmark and Sweden (see table 15.2). Lower rates vary between 0 and 10 per cent, with the majority of countries operating multiple-rate VAT.[14] As can be seen from the notes to table

15.2, a long list of exceptions considerably complicates the system.

The extent to which the variation in rates represents a problem with regard to cross-border shopping is arguable. Evidence suggests that its magnitude diminishes rapidly with distance, and differences in excises seem to be more important, accounting for two-thirds of the value of cross-border shopping (Bygrä et al., 1987; Fitzgerald et al., 1988). Similarly, Commission studies find that the abolition of border controls has not led to significant changes in cross-border shopping patterns, distortions of competition or changes in

Table 15.2 VAT in EU member states

	2006 VAT rates %		2004 VAT revenue%	
	Standard	Other	Total tax revenue	GDP
Single rate				
Denmark	25	–[a]	20.1	9.8
Solvakia	19	–[b]	26.4	8.0
Dual rate				
Czech Republic	19	5	20.2	7.4
Germany	16	7	16.0	6.2
Estonia	18	5	25.2	8.2
Latvia	18	5	24.5	6.5
Malta	18	5[c]	22.0	7.7
Netherlands	19	6	19.4	7.3
Austria	20	10	18.4	7.8
Slovenia	20	8.5	22.5	8.9
United Kingdom	17.5	0[c]	19.5	7.0
Multiple rate				
Belgium	21	6/12[d]	15.4	7.0
Greece	19	4.5/9	23.5	8.3
Spain	16	4/7	17.6	6.1
France	19.6	2.1/5.5	16.7	7.2
Ireland	21	0/12.5[c]	24.4	7.4
Italy	20	4/10	14.4	5.9
Cyprus	15	5/8[c]	27.2	9.3
Lithuania	18	5/9	22.9	6.5
Luxembourg	15	3/6/12	16.3	6.5
Hungary	20	5/15	23.0	9.0
Poland	22	3/7[e]	21.9	7.2
Portugal	21	5/12	22.9	8.1
Finland	22	8/17[d]	19.6	8.7
Sweden	25	6/12	18.1	9.1
Unweighted average EU15	**19.7**		**18.5**	**7.5**
Unweighted average NMS10	**18.7**		**23.6**	**7.9**
Unweighted average EU25	**19.4**		**20.6**	**7.5**
Minimum rates	*15.0*	*15.0*		
Bulgaria	20.0			
Romania	19.0			
Unweighted average EU27	**19.4**			

[a] Newspapers are taxed at 0 per cent.

[b] Scheduled passenger transport taxed at 0 per cent.

[c] Food and pharmaceutical products 0 per cent, plus books, magazines and newspapers in the UK.

[d] Newspapers and magazines are taxed at 0 per cent.

[e] Books and magazines are taxed at 0 per cent.

Source: CEC (2006f, pp. 2–7); CEC (2006k).

trade, due to differences in VAT rates (European Parliament, 2001b). So there does not seem to be any great need to further harmonize VAT rates to reduce distortions caused by cross-border shopping.

The existence of multiple rates is much more questionable. The major reason for special exemptions and reduced rates is to limit the regressive impact of VAT,[15] but the major beneficiaries of such exemptions are not the poor. The conclusion of a 1988 study, which has been supported by more modern evidence,[16] was that the distribution of the tax burden was not very different if products were zero-rated (UK), taxed at a reduced rate (Netherlands) or even at the same rate as other goods and services (Denmark) – see OECD (1988b). Thus, although expenditure on food is proportionally higher for poorer groups, the better-off spend more in absolute terms, thus the improvement in the progressivity of the tax system is minor. 'Differentiated VAT rates are an ineffective, ill targeted instrument for eliminating the impact of the tax on the poor' (Cnossen, 2002, p. 492).

Multiple rates are also not without cost since they increase the administrative complexity of the system and cause problems of compliance. One study suggested that UK firms found that having multiple rates rather than a single rate doubled compliance costs (Hemming and Kay, 1981). Imposing an additional VAT rate also reduces the compliance rate by 7 per cent (Agha and Houghton, 1996). This is not surprising when one realizes that the following factors need to be considered in applying the zero rate to food in the UK: 'place of consumption, timing of consumption, temperature, saltiness, number, volume, concentration, sugar content, use of fingers in consumption and alcoholic content' (Cnossen, 2002, p. 493). There is, therefore, no economic or social justification for the continued use of multiple rates.

The EU responded to the abolition of fiscal borders with a transitional regime of cross-border trade on a deferred payment or postponed accounting basis. Under this system exports are free of VAT but the exporter must inform the fiscal authorities in the country it is exporting to. Importers must declare imports and pay VAT at the local rate. A VAT Information Exchange System (VEIS) reinforces checks by requiring registered businesses to file quarterly reports of exports and imports. The Commission has in the past argued that the deferred payment system is bureaucratic, creates additional administrative burdens for companies and is subject to fraud. The European Parliament (2001b, p. 44) suggests that the identified 1,300 million euros of VAT fraud is merely 'the tip of the iceberg'. The Commission wanted to shift to the origin system (CEC, 1985a), but it has now accepted that this is politically too difficult and is seeking to improve the transitional regime (CEC, 2004e). This has become more urgent with the escalation of missing trader/carousel fraud. This occurs where fraudsters set up bogus companies to import high-value items (mobile phones and computer chips), which are VAT-free, then sell them on to other bogus companies charging VAT, but not paying it to the tax authorities. The goods are then exported and the VAT which has not been paid is reclaimed. The process can then start over again, hence the term carousel. When the tax authorities seek to claim the VAT, they are unable to trace the owners/officers of the companies involved. With organized crime involved, the losses are very high; 10 per cent VAT revenue (CEC, 2004e, p.5; *The Economist*, 2006). The suggestions for controlling this problem vary from tightening up the administrative arrangements to altering the VAT system by, for example, not charging VAT on business-to-business transactions or charging VAT on intra-EU trade. Such measures could be limited to certain items likely to be involved in carousel fraud. Such measures could weaken self-policing elements of the system and complicate and increase the costs of policing and compliance.

This analysis leads to the conclusion that VAT reform should extend the tax base and eliminate multiple rates. The problem of fraud may give the member states the incentive to finally achieve sufficient harmonization of rates to enable a move to the origin system to take place.

15.4.2 Excise duties

Excise duties are important for EU governments, being the fourth most important source of revenue (table 15.1). However, the importance of excises varies substantially between the member states, from 13.1 per cent of tax revenue in Cyprus to 5.4 per cent in France in 2003.[17] This reflects the very wide variations in rates, which have been subject to only very limited harmonization. This difference in rates encourages legal and illegal cross-border movement of dutiable goods.

The EU position on tobacco duties is a compromise between the southern and northern member states. The south favoured taxation based on the value of the product to protect their cheap home-grown tobacco. The north preferred specific taxes based on volume rather than value to discourage tobacco smoking. This led to wide differences in rates and in the total tax burden on cigarettes.[18] This has widened still further with low tax and low cigarette prices in the NMS (table 15.3). EU regulations (Council of the European Communities, 1992b, 1995a) have had to accommodate this wide variation. Thus the EU requires that the specific and *ad valorem* excises plus VAT must not be less than 57 per cent of the retail price. The total tax on a pack of twenty cigarettes varies between 0.38 euros in Latvia to 5.46 euros in the UK (table 15.3). With such a disparity of tax and consequent variation in prices, it is not surprising that high-tax countries such as the UK are suffering a substantial loss of revenue as a result of personal purchases overseas, and small- and large-scale smuggling. It is estimated that 25 per cent of the cigarettes smoked in the UK are smuggled (Public Accounts Committee, 2002). Tobacco smuggling is not simply a UK problem; it is indeed an EU-wide and global problem (Cnossen and Smart, 2005). As a result the rules have been tightened so that the total excise should not be less than 60 euros per thousand cigarettes (or 95 euros if the member state does not comply with the 57 per cent rule) (see Council of the EU, 2002a). This increase in specific taxation may, however, simply increase the volume of smuggling from outside the EU, with which it has been suggested the tobacco companies have cooperated (Public Accounts Committee, 2002). With internal harmonization of tobacco duties problematic and the threat of external smuggling, governments in high-tax countries are faced with a difficult choice between lower duties or revenue loss.

That excises on alcoholic drink should be based on a relative alcohol content was a rule established by a judgment of the European Court of Justice (1983) which was necessary to avoid taxation distorting trade between member states. Thus the most flagrant discrimination in favour of local producers has been eliminated (Cnossen, 1987), but national beverages are still protected by, for example, applying different excises to still and sparkling wine. Some convergence of rates has occurred as member states have moved towards the lowest rate: seven member states levy no excises on wine and in France it is only 3 euro cents a litre. Some high rates persist, with large differentials remaining: the excises on wine vary from 0 to 2.73 euros a litre and on spirits from 6.45 to 15.45 euros (table 15.4). Thus substantial smuggling still occurs; it is estimated that about a quarter of the spirits consumed in Denmark and Sweden are purchased outside the consumers' own member state (European Parliament, 2001b, p. 39). A directive on minimum rates was agreed in 1992 (Council of the EU, 1992c) but the minimum was very low and has not been revised since.

The differences in alcohol and tobacco taxation are causing significant problems of smuggling and revenue loss for the member states, and there is a strong case for EU action. Harmonization of rates is required, reducing rates in northern Europe, leading to some increase in consumption, and raising rates in the south, causing some inflation.[19] These largely transitional problems are a price worth paying to eliminate the difficulties caused by current large differences in rates.

With regard to the taxation of fuel, it is convenient to consider the taxation of private and commercial road users separately. Although there are large variations in the taxation of private road users (table 15.5), this does not raise tax harmonization problems. Taxes on car ownership are based on residence, which presumably is where the vehicle is used. Although the tax on unleaded gasoline varies between 0.32 euros in Greece to 0.79 euros in the UK, there is little possibility of cross-border shopping or smuggling.[20]

Differences in the excise duties on commercial diesel fuel can affect competition in road transport

Table 15.3 Cigarette taxation in EU member states, 2006

	% EU average price				€
	Specific	Ad valorem	VAT	Total	Total
Belgium	4.4	61.5	19.9	85.8	3.34
Denmark	54.8	18.2	26.7	99.7	2.89
Germany	55.5	38.0	20.7	114.2	3.46
Greece	3.3	48.4	14.4	66.1	2.58
Spain	5.3	41.2	10.0	56.5	2.15
France	9.7	93.2	26.3	129.2	4.97
Ireland	85.7	37.4	35.4	158.6	4.63
Italy	3.7	54.5	16.6	74.9	2.92
Luxembourg	9.1	43.6	12.1	64.8	2.41
Netherlands	43.2	24.3	18.9	86.4	2.59
Austria	15.6	42.8	16.6	75.1	2.69
Portugal	33.6	20.3	15.3	69.3	2.10
Finland	9.7	65.9	23.8	99.4	3.78
Sweden	13.8	54.1	27.6	95.6	3.55
UK	96.8	52.5	35.5	184.8	5.46
EU15 average[a]	29.6	46.4	21.3	97.4	3.30
Czech Republic	13	11.5	7.6	32.1	1.02
Estonia	11.3	10.5	6.1	27.9	0.89
Cyprus	13.5	41.2	12.1	66.7	2.40
Latvia	7	3	3.1	13.1	0.38
Lithuania	8.8	4.3	4.4	17.6	0.53
Hungary	17.6	15.2	9.4	42.3	1.34
Malta	10.9	59.6	17.7	88.3	3.31
Poland	12.3	15.0	8.7	36.0	1.19
Slovenia	8.9	25.5	10	44.3	1.6
Slovakia	18.2	13.3	9.2	40.8	1.27
NMS10 average[a]	12.2	19.9	8.8	40.9	1.39
EU25 average[a]	22.6	35.8	16.3	74.8	2.54
Bulgaria	4.9	19.2	6.7	30.8	2.31
Romania	5.8	9.5	6	21.4	2.37
EU27 average[a]	21.3	34.2	15.6	71.2	2.52

[a] arithmetical average.

Source: CEC (2006g, p. 7).

where goods in one country can be transported by lorries buying their fuel in another. The extent of such problems has been limited by a reasonable degree of similarity of rates; ten member states have rates between 3 and 4.55 euros per litre of normal diesel fuel (table 15.5). The UK is way out of line, with a rate of 8.69 euros per litre. Since the UK is such an exception the solution seems to lie in its own hands.[21]

This survey indicates that further reform of indirect taxes in the EU is desirable. The operation of VAT is complicated by multiple rates, which seem to have little merit. The transitional regime for the collection of VAT worked reasonably well but is now under pressure from growing fraud, and tackling this will either complicate the existing system or require more fundamental change to the origin system. Differences in excise rates are

Table 15.4 Alcohol taxation in EU member states, 2006 (per litre)

	Beer	Still wine Specific excise euro	Spirits	VAT %
Belgium	0.017	0.470	17.52	21.0
Denmark	0.068	0.823	20.101	25.0
Germany	0.008	0.000	13.030	16.0
Greece	0.011	0.000	10.900	19.0
Spain	0.009	0.000	8.303	16.0
France	0.026	0.034	14.50	19.6
Ireland	0.199	2.730	39.250	21.0
Italy	0.024	0.000	8.000	20.0
Luxembourg	0.008	0.000	10.412	12.0
Netherlands	0.055	0.590	15.040	19.0
Austria	0.020	0.000	10.000	20.0
Portugal	0.081	0.000	9.372	12.0
Finland	0.195	2.120	28.250	22.0
Sweden	0.158	2.372	53.865	25.0
United Kingdom	0.129	2.467	28.765	17.5
EU15 average[a]	**0.067**	**0.774**	**19.154**	**19.0**
Czech Republic	0.008	0.000	8.954	19.0
Estonia	0.037	0.665	9.715	18.0
Cyprus	0.049	0.000	6.107	15.0
Latvia	0.019	0.431	9.050	18.0
Lithuania	0.020	0.434	9.268	18.0
Hungary	0.020	0.000	8.801	20.0
Malta	0.007	0.000	23.288	18.0
Poland	0.018	0.347	11.611	22.0
Slovenia	0.069	0.000	6.951	20.0
Slovakia	0.013	0.000	7.284	19.0
NMS10 average[a]	**0.026**	**0.188**	**10.103**	**18.7**
EU25 average[a]	**0.051**	**0.539**	**15.533**	**18.9**
Bulgaria	0.008	0.000	5.624	20.0
Romania	0.007	0.000	4.654	19.0
EU27 average[a]	**0.048**	**0.499**	**14.764**	**18.9**
EU minima	**0.007**	**0.01**	**5.500**	**15.0**

[a] arithmetical average

Source: CEC (2006h).

a cause of substantial smuggling from both within and outside the EU. Further harmonization, with reductions, particularly in the highest rates, seems the only answer here.

15.4.3 Corporation tax

Corporation tax (CT) is a tax on company profits and thus on capital. Since capital is potentially mobile there are concerns that the movement of capital will undermine national corporation tax and governments' ability to finance the welfare state and public goods.[22] The received wisdom that tax competition would inevitably lead to a race to the bottom has, however, been questioned on both theoretical and empirical grounds. Not all capital is mobile and governments have consequently sought to tax immobile corporations

Table 15.5 Taxes on petrol and diesel fuel, 2006

	Unleaded petrol Excise duty (euros per litre)	Diesel fuel Excise duty (euros per litre)	Diesel and gasoline VAT %
Belgium	0.592	0.341	21.0
Denmark	0.508	0.404	25.0
Germany	0.670	0.470	16.0
Greece	0.316	0.245	19.0
Spain	0.396	0.294	16.0
France	0.589	0.417	19.6
Ireland	0.443	0.368	21.0
Italy	0.564	0.413	20.0
Luxembourg	0.442	0.278	15.0
Netherlands	0.668	0.365	19.0
Austria	0.417	0.297	20.0
Portugal	0.533	0.314	21.0
Finland	0.588	0.346	22.0
Sweden	0.366	0.394	25.0
United Kingdom	0.738	0.782	17.5
EU15 unweighted average	**0.522**	**0.382**	**19.8**
Czech Republic	0.400	0.336	19.0
Estonia	0.288	0.245	18.0
Cyprus	0.305	0.250	15.0
Latvia	0.276	0.236	18.0
Lithuania	0.287	0.245	18.0
Hungary	0.413	0.339	20.0
Malta	0.387	0.245	18.0
Poland	0.356	0.290	22.0
Slovenia	0.360	0.303	20.0
Slovakia	0.398	0.373	19.0
NMS10 unweighted average	**0.347**	**0.286**	**18.7**
EU25 unweighted average	**0.452**	**0.344**	**19.4**
Bulgaria	0.271	0.220	20.0
Romania	0.327	0.260	19.0
Agreed minima	**0.34**	**0.302**	

Source: CEC (2006j).

while reducing burdens on mobile capital. The widening of the corporation tax base and the lowering of rates can be seen as a move in this direction (Devereux et al., 2002). In addition, corporation tax is only one of the factors affecting choice of location, and to the extent that economies of scale can offer offsetting benefits, corporation tax can still be collected. These benefits could be agglomeration economies leading to a differential return on capital (Baldwin and Krugman, 2004) or natural resources. Alterna-

tively, the benefits could derive directly from the effects of government expenditure on productivity (Wooders et al., 2001). If this view is taken, then tax competition has the benefit that it encourages government expenditure which benefits the economy while constraining wasteful expenditure.[23]

Unfortunately this theoretical ambiguity cannot easily be resolved by empirical analysis. This is bedevilled by the complexity of corporation tax and the lack of aggregate measures of corporate profits. The complexity of the tax stems from the variation in the way in which profit is measured for tax purposes (depreciation of investment, treatment of research and development expenditure, etc.), the interaction with the personal tax system, the treatment of overseas earnings, etc. There are substantial differences between the statutory and effective rates within as well as between companies for different sectors and company sizes. There is little association between the actual and effective rates of the member states, and this is not the result of differences in tax bases (CEC, 2001g; Nicodème, 2001). This means that statutory corporation tax rates are poor indicators of the actual rate of tax on profits. One approach to this problem has been the attempt to estimate effective or implicit rates of tax which take into account the differences in tax legislation between countries (Devereux et al., 2002). However, these estimates are sensitive to assumptions which have to be made relating to tax policy, economic conditions and investor behaviour.

Given these problems, it is not surprising that the empirical evidence on globalization and corporate tax revenue is ambiguous. Some studies using OECD data actually suggested a positive relationship between the two (Garrett, 1995b; Swank, 1998). This result was reversed by a study using effective rates of corporation tax (Bretschger and Hettich, 2002). These studies rely on a single measure of the tax burden and this is questionable. There is agreement that rates of corporation tax have been reduced in the EU (Cnossen and Bovenberg, 1997; Gorter and Mooji, 2001) and more generally (Grubert, 2001); it does not follow that this is the result of tax competition. Rates may have been reduced and bases widened to improve the efficiency, equity and simplicity of the tax system. An alternative approach is to measure the yield of corporation tax (Stewart and Web, 2006) which finds little evidence of a secular downward trend in corporate tax revenue generally or in the EU.

This indicates that the harmonization of corporation tax rates is perhaps a less important issue for the EU than is sometimes supposed. Perhaps even more than with other taxes, the bewildering complexity of the different national systems is an issue. Corporation taxes vary in the extent to which the personal income tax liability on dividend income (distributed profits) makes allowance for them. There are two extreme systems: the classical and imputation systems. Under the classical system corporations pay tax on their profits but there is no allowance for this tax against personal taxation (PT). Under the imputation system the whole or part of the corporation tax can be used to offset PT liability on dividends. Another possibility is the subjecting of dividend income to a separate lower rate of PT. Enlargement has added yet another variant – only taxing dividends, not retained earnings. At present corporation tax systems in the EU run the whole gamut with four different systems in operation and a range of rates from 10 to 40 per cent (table 15.6). On top of the use of different systems, there are varying national rules for corporation tax, which when combined with the different treatment of wealth and capital gains makes the taxation of corporations extremely complex. Despite the large differences in nominal rates of corporation tax, the variability of the implicit rate is lower (table 15.6), indicating that higher rates are offset by other characteristics of the corporation tax system. The NMS generally have low corporation tax rates and for some this is reflected in very low implicit rates.

These variations in tax allowances for dividends when combined with PT lead to substantial differences within countries between the tax on distributed and retained profits; generally the tax on dividends is greater than the tax on retained profits. There are two views on the effect of this differential taxation: the 'traditional' and the 'new' (Sinn, 1991). The traditional view argues that dividends offer benefits, which can at least partially offset tax disadvantages. These advantages of distribution include the signalling to shareholders that the corporate performance is good and the limitation of management financial discretion and thus of potential misuse of retained profits.[24] The corporation would equalize the tax disadvantages with these non-tax advantages of distributing profits; thus tax discrimination distorts the choice between retaining and distributing profits. This distortion is effectively a

Table 15.6 EU25 corporation tax, 2006

	System	Main rate	Implicit rate[a]
Belgium	Special personal tax rate	33	18.5
Denmark	Special personal tax rate	28	21.4
Germany	Special personal tax rate	40	n.a.
Greece	Dividend exemption	32	20.1
Spain	Imputation	35	25.7
France	Imputation	33.3	24.1
Ireland	Classical	12.5	n.a.
Italy	Imputation	33	18.3
Luxembourg	Special personal tax rate	30	n.a.
Netherlands	Divdend exemption	29.6	20.2
Austria	Special personal tax rate	25	16.6
Portugal	Imputation	25	19.0
Finland	Imputation	26	19.2
Sweden	Special personal tax rate	28	19.5
UK	Imputation	30	14.9
EU15 unweighted average		**29.4**	**19.3**
Czech Republic	Classical	24	32.6
Estonia	Dividend tax	23[b]	8.3
Cyprus	Classical	10	–
Latvia	Exempt	15	7.2
Lithuania	Classical	15	5.7
Hungary	Classical	16	–
Malta	Imputation	35	–
Poland	Imputation	19	–
Slovenia	Classical	25	–
Slovakia	Classical	19	29.2
NMS10 unweighted average		**20.1**	**19.0**
EU25 unweighted average		**25.7**	**19.2**

[a] 2003.

[b] 23 per cent of gross dividend, no tax on retained profit, to be reduced to 20 per cent in 2009.

Source: CEC (2006k), Deloitte (2006).

decrease in the return on corporate investment, the overall level of which will be depressed. The new view suggests that there are no non-tax advantages to dividend distribution: the shareholders enjoy their return in the form of tax-efficient capital gains rather than dividends. The higher tax on dividends does not, therefore, involve any diminution in the level of investment. Empirical studies support the traditional rather than the new view (Cnossen, 2002, p. 523). Whichever view is correct, encouraging the retention of profits reduces the capital available for

new share issues to the detriment of new and fast-expanding firms, which will adversely affect the dynamism of the economy.

Corporate tax regimes not only favour profit retention but also the use of debt rather than equity for finance; this is reinforced by financial innovation blurring the distinction between equity and debt. Again this will tend to make it more difficult for new firms to raise capital, because of their limited credit history and asset bases for collateral. Devereux and Griffith (2001) calculate effective average CT rates on hypothetical investment projects using the rates and rules in current legislation, showing retained earnings have an effective CT rate on average 10 per cent higher than that on debt.

This analysis of the effects of CT suggests that the distortions caused can extend across EU borders. The bias in favour of retained earnings favours incumbent as opposed to new firms, limiting competition and reducing the dynamism of the single market. It also favours markets where shareholder involvement in the company is more direct, such as in Germany where banks typically have large holdings and where the need to satisfy shareholders with dividends is lower. The lower taxation of debt finance is to the advantage of member states with large firms that are creditworthy; where there are close links between banks and companies it can protect against foreign takeovers, because foreign firms do not have the same access to local bank finance. The favourable tax treatment of debt finance is reinforced by internationalization and liberalization of capital markets. With withholding tax on cross-border interest payments very low, a large part of internal interest income escapes taxation (Huizinga, 1994). Thus companies are encouraged to finance their activities with international debt affecting member states' tax bases.

The requirement that profits for corporation tax should be calculated separately for each member state creates problems for pan-European business. Tax losses in one member state cannot be offset against profits in another, and assets transferred between member states may be subject to capital gains tax. This discourages cross-border mergers and takeovers and constrains the operation of multinational companies within the EU. The administrative costs of complying with different corporation tax regimes can also be high.

The European Commission's (CEC, 2001g) Bolkestein Report scrutinized two approaches to these problems: first, piecemeal changes to legislation to correct particular distortions, e.g. improving double taxation conventions; second, general measures to establish a common tax base for EU activities. There are three possibilities for a common tax base: an EU corporation tax, common

base taxation (CBT) and home state taxation (HST). An EU-wide corporation tax would be difficult to agree, given the requirement for unanimity. CBT would harmonize rules for calculating taxable profits on cross-border operations (national rules would remain for domestic operations). HST means that multinational businesses would only be taxed in the member state in which their headquarters is located. With both systems, one set of consolidated accounts would be produced, and a formula using shares of sales, payroll and property would be used to apportion profit,[25] to which member states would apply their tax rates. The Commission is moving towards a CBT (CEC, 2006i).

A CBT is not without problems; it would tend to increase tax competition due to greater transparency, because differences in tax paid would depend solely upon rates. Distortions between states caused by national distortions, such as the favouring of debt over equity finance, are not dealt with: 'the elimination of in-state distortions is a prerequisite to the elimination of interstate distortions' (Cnossen, 2002, p. 531). Although one of the objectives is to make cross-border mergers easier, tax considerations will become a factor influencing such mergers. Formula apportionment of profit would lead to further distortions of the location of production. The problems are such that some commentators doubt whether CBT or CHT are worth the effort (Mintz, 2002). Whether such proposals would in any case carry sufficient support to be agreed is questionable.

Another problem is that of interest and dividend payments to foreign holders, who can avoid income taxation: a withholding tax was proposed to deal with this issue. This tax would have to be accepted to offset income tax liability in the member state of residence. In liberalized financial markets, an EU withholding tax would encourage an outflow of funds from the EU and the City of London in particular. So these proposals have been shelved and now there is reliance on the exchange of information on assets held by residents of other member states, so as to enforce residence-based taxation. This approach also suffers from the 'London' problem, so progress in this area is dependent upon cooperation with other countries, particularly Switzerland and the US.

15.5 Conclusion

It should not come as a surprise that tax harmonization continues to be a difficult issue for the EU: a sensitive area of national sovereignty that remains the prerogative of the member states collides with the need to avoid distortions to trade and investment in an increasingly integrated single market. It is clear from the foregoing that reform of member states' tax systems would benefit the domestic economy, as well as reduce cross-border distortions. The needs for these adjustments and for tax harmonization are principally in relation to taxes on consumption and on capital.[26]

Of the consumption taxes, VAT presents limited problems: the tax base of consumption is relatively immobile and consumers are not very sensitive to differences in rates. The tax is relatively cheap to collect and it is difficult to evade. The principal difficulties with VAT are associated with exemptions, multiple rates and their administrative costs. There is a good case, however, for making the tax base as wide as possible and for the abolition of multiple rates. The transitional regime on cross-border trade has worked satisfactorily but is now under increasing pressure from fraud; this calls into question the continued use of the destinations system of taxation.

Excise duties on cigarettes and alcohol do present substantial problems because of the enormous differences of rates that persist. This encourages a substantial illegal market, with suppliers ranging from small-scale smuggling to organized crime, operating in some cases with cooperation from multinational corporations. These problems can, probably, only be dealt with effectively by harmonization of rates. By contrast the taxation of motor vehicles and fuel presents few cross-border problems.

Taxation of capital presents difficulties because of the mobility of the tax base and the spread of corporate activities across states. This means that the taxation jurisdiction is somewhat arbitrary and the taxes levied will have considerable cross-border effects. Corporation tax is also notable for its complexity, which is not helped within the EU

by differences in its bases, rules and rates. The system at the moment distorts the choices of retaining and distributing profits and encourages financing by debt rather than equity. These distortions within member state also have cross-border effects on investment and business restructuring. The Commission's suggested common base taxation is not without problems.

Tax harmonization involves a trade-off between national sovereignty over tax and the difficulties caused by variations in rates and systems. The limited degree of tax convergence achieved so far indicates that tax competition cannot be relied on to achieve spontaneous harmonization. Tax competition moves rates to lower levels, but such a race to the bottom is not always undesirable: it may act as a restraining influence on taxation. Tax harmonization may, therefore, be regarded as a way of maintaining the level of taxation. There are some areas, however, where harmonization could achieve significant potential benefits (excise duties), but given the law of unintended consequences, which seems to hold sway in tax matters, a gradualist approach to harmonization is both practical and preferable.

NOTES

1 CEC (2006k). All other taxation statistics in this chapter are from this source unless otherwise indicated.
2 In competitive markets, taxes on labour will tend to be paid by workers as reductions in their real incomes.
3 Government expenditure can cause analogous effects to differences in taxes. These effects are dealt with by internal market legislation (chapter 7) and for industrial subsidies by competition policy (chapter 13).
4 Tax competition means that a higher rate of tax is needed to raise funds, increasing tax-induced inefficiency.
5 The main people affected will be very high-income earners, who would in any case be attracted by tax havens, which offer extremely low rates of tax.
6 This is the intra-company price for international trade which takes place within the company.
7 Thus the tax paid equals the rate of tax multiplied by the value added at that stage of production.
8 Such taxes also had variable effects on prices and encouraged the vertical integration of companies.

9 A withholding tax is a tax directly on interest payments before they are distributed to owners of the debt.

10 They may, however, have other economic effects, for example on the level of employment.

11 Including personal taxes on capital income and gains.

12 This is the reason for the exemption of farmers, although they receive flat rate compensation for tax on agricultural inputs.

13 Consistency of application should be improved by the 2005 implementing directive (Council of the EU, 2005d).

14 The NMS on average have marginally lower VAT rates than the EU15.

15 Some countries also use lower rates for labour-intensive services as an employment measure.

16 For example, Australian Society of CPAs (1998) estimated that only 15 per cent of the benefit of a zero rate on food in New Zealand would go to households with the lowest 20 per cent of income.

17 The difference in the excise taxes share of GDP is much narrower, from 5.2 per cent in Luxembourg to 2.3 per cent in Germany and Italy.

18 Ninety-five per cent of total tobacco consumption.

19 Although additional revenue could be used to lower other indirect taxes eliminating the inflationary effect.

20 There is the possibility of other distortions, e.g. the fact that taxation on diesel fuel is much lower than that on petrol in France gives manufacturers of diesel engine cars an advantage. French manufacturers have traditional strength in the manufacture of diesel cars.

21 Part of the justification for high vehicle taxes is to reduce emissions for environmental reasons. The Commission's proposal for a carbon tax was not approved but some member states have introduced carbon taxes (see chapter 18).

22 The problem of tax avoidance on interest by the use of accounts in another EU country has been dealt with by an agreement to exchange information on such accounts (Council of the EU, 2003a).

23 This of course could constrain government expenditure considered desirable by the population.

24 An advantage considerably enhanced by recent corporate scandals.

25 This is the system widely used in the US and Canada.

26 Since income taxes present few independent cross-border problems, they are not considered here.

16 Transport policy

KENNETH BUTTON

16.1 Introduction

Transport has exerted important influences in shaping the human geography of Europe. Military conquests in the past were largely along well-defined transport corridors and the growth of cities has mainly been at important junctions in transport networks. Technology advances and changes in political ambition, as well as new economic conditions and institutional developments, have altered the nature of these links but their fundamental importance remains. The role of transport as a lubricator of economic reconstruction was appreciated in the post-Second World War period. Institutions such as the European Conference of Ministers of Transport (ECMT) were set up under the Marshall Plan to assist in reconstructing transport infrastructure, while the European Coal and Steel Community (ECSC) devoted energies to improving the efficiency of the European rail transport system (Meade et al., 1962). It was even more transparent in the formation of the European Economic Community (EEC) whereby the explicit creation of a Common Transport Policy (CTP) was mandated (see chapters 1 and 2).

Transport is a major industry in its own right. It directly employs about 5 per cent of the European Union (EU – the term largely used throughout this chapter for simplicity although the title has changed over the years; see chapter 2) workforce, accounts for 7 per cent of total EU GDP and for about 30 per cent of final energy consumption. But this is perhaps not really the important point. The crucial thing about transport from an economic perspective is its role in facilitating trade and in allowing individuals, companies, regions and nation-states to exploit their various comparative advantages. Early debates concerning the merits of free trade tended to ignore the friction associated with moving goods to markets, and the analysis of migration patterns exhibited similar tendencies to assume transport costs to be negligible. Some economists, such as Von Thünen (1826), did take account of transport costs when trying to explain land use patterns, but such explicit consideration of space and the problems of traversing it was exceptional. The situation changed with the advent of new transport technologies in the mid-nineteenth century and as countries appreciated that manipulation of the transport system could influence their economic conditions. Manipulation of transport rates and the strategic design of infrastructure networks were used to protect domestic industries in ways akin to tariff and non-tariff trade barriers (NTBs; see chapters 6 and 7). Individual states sought to develop transport policies that were to their short-term benefit irrespective of their consequences for overall trade.

The contemporary upsurge of interest in supply chain management, just-in-time production and the like has led to a wider appreciation of the general need to enhance the efficiency of European transport if the region as a whole is to compete successfully in the global economy. The concern is that the effectiveness of transport logistics in the EU is at least comparable with that elsewhere to ensure that the labour, capital and natural resources of member states can be exploited in a fully efficient manner.

It was against this broad background that the EU initially sought to develop a transport policy, of which the CTP has been but one element, designed to reduce artificial friction. It has taken time for the CTP and other elements of policy to come together to represent anything like a coherent strategy. There have been shifts of emphasis since the signing of the EEC Treaty and frequent changes in the types of policy deemed appropriate to meet these moving objectives. This chapter provides details of the underlying issues that have been central to these efforts and charts out some of the paths that have been pursued to confront them. The process has not been smooth and has involved a number of discrete phases. To pre-empt the conclusions, it can be said that ultimately, and after many tribulations, the EU has emerged with a relatively coherent approach to transport that has removed many of the potential bottlenecks to economic integration that dogged the early development of the Union.

16.2 The European transport system

Problems with the creation of a transport policy began early. The EEC Treaty contained an entire chapter on transport, although apparently limiting itself to movement of freight by road, rail and inland waterways. Strictly the treaty said, 'The Council may, acting unanimously, decide whether, to what extent and by what procedure appropriate provisions may be laid down for sea and air transport.' It is thus not clear whether these modes were excluded only from the transport clauses or from the treaty as a whole, including its competition provisions. The Netherlands, having considerable maritime interests, was particularly concerned about retaining autonomy in these areas, and this concern contributed to the ambiguity.

While the treaty gave indications of what national obligations should be, it was not until 1961 that a memorandum appeared setting out clear objectives (CEC, 1961) and not until the following year that an Action Programme was published. The emphasis of these initiatives was to seek means to remove obstacles to trade posed by the institutional structures governing transport and to foster competition once a level playing field of harmonized fiscal, social and technical conditions had been established. That it has subsequently taken over forty years to make significant progress towards a CTP is in part due to the nature of European geography and the underlying transport market, although continued insistence on nation-states pursuing their individual agendas was also a causal factor.

Examination of a map of the EU provides information on some of the problems of devising a common transport policy. Even when the Community consisted of only six members, the economic space involved hardly represented a natural market. Ideally transport functions most effectively on a hub-and-spoke basis with large concentrations of population and economic activity located at corners and in the centre and with the various transport networks (roads, railways and the like) linking them. The central locations act as markets for transport services in their own right but also as interchange and consolidation points for traffic between the corner nodes. In many ways the US fits this model rather well but the EU never has. When there were six members, the bulk of economic activity was at the core, with limited growth at the periphery. The joining of such states as Ireland, Greece, Portugal, Finland and Sweden added to the problems of serving peripheral and often sparsely populated areas. The geographical separation of some states and the logical routing of traffic through non-member countries, together with the island nature of others, posed further problems.

Neither was the CTP initiated with a clean slate – member states had established transport networks and institutional structures that could not rapidly be changed even if a common set of principles could have been established. At the outset countries such as France and West Germany carried a significant amount of their freight traffic by rail (34 per cent and 27 per cent by tonne–kilometres respectively). Others, such as Italy and the Benelux nations, relied much more on road transport, the average length of domestic hauls being an important determining feature. The resultant differences were also not simply physical (including variations in railway gauges, vehicle weight limits and different electricity currents). They also reflected fundamental differences in the ways transport was viewed.

At a macro, political-economy level there were two broad views on the way transport should be treated. Following the continental philosophy, the objective was to meet wide social goals that require interventions in the market involving regulations, public ownership and direction. This approach particularly dominated much of twentieth-century transport policy thinking in continental Europe and has its genesis in the Code Napoléon with its focus on centralism. Its place has been taken in recent years by a wider acceptance of the Anglo-Saxon approach to transport policy. This treats the transport sector as little different to other economic activities. Transport provision and use should be efficient in its own right. Efficiency is normally best attained by making the maximum use of market forces. Of course, the extremes of the continental approach never existed and nowhere has the strict Anglo-Saxon philosophy been fully applied; it has been a matter of degree. Even in countries such as the UK that had in the past been seen as a bastion of the Anglo-Saxon ideology there existed extensive regimes of regulation and control and large parts of the transport system were in a state of local government ownership.

The periodic enlargements of the EU, together with broader shifts in the way that transport is viewed that transcended the narrow European situation, have resulted in a move away from the continental way of thinking to a more market-based approach to a CTP. The interventionist positions of Germany and France were initially set against the more liberal approach of the Netherlands. With the accession of the UK and Denmark in 1973 the more interventionist approach was now in the minority. Subsequent enlargements added to the impetus for less regulation of transport markets.

The situation can also be looked at from a more analytical perspective over time. This is in terms of the ways that efficiency is viewed. The approach until the 1970s was to treat efficiency in transport largely in terms of maximizing scale efficiency while limiting any deadweight losses associated with monopoly power. Most transport infrastructure was seen as enjoying economies of scale that could only be exploited by coordinated and, *ipso facto*, regulated and often subsidized, development. State ownership, the extreme of regulation, was also often adopted. Many aspects of operations were also seen as potentially open to monopoly exploitation and hence in need of oversight. This situation has changed since the late 1970s. From a pragmatic perspective, the high levels of subsidies enjoyed by many elements of the transport sector became politically unsustainable. Economists began to question whether the regulations deployed were actually achieving their stated aims. The regulations may, for example, have been captured by those that are intended to be the regulated or have been manipulated for the benefit of individuals responsible for administering the regime. Government failures, it was argued, were larger than the market failures they were trying to correct.

New elements also came into play in the 1970s, and especially concern about the wider environmental implications of transport. Attitudes towards the environmental intrusion associated with transport vary between member states as well as having changed more generally over time. To some extent this has been part of a wider effort within the Union to improve the overall environment (see chapter 18) and to fulfil larger, global commitments on such matters as reducing emissions of global warming gases (CEC, 1992b). Transport impacts the environment at the local level (noise, lead, carbon monoxide, and so on), at the regional level (e.g. nitrogen oxide emissions and maritime pollution) and at the global level (carbon dioxide). It is this diversity of implications and the trade-offs between them, as well as the absolute scale of some of the individual environmental intrusions, that make policy formulation difficult. Local effects have largely been left to the individual countries, but as the implications of regional and global environmental intrusions have become more widely appreciated so EU transport policy has become proactive in these areas. The main problem with these types of environmental issue is that their effects are often trans-boundary and thus give little incentive for individual action by governments.

16.3 The initial development of a CTP

As we have seen, the past forty years have produced important changes in the ways in which transport is viewed. There have always been periodic swings in transport policy but the period since the late 1970s provides a classic watershed (Button and Gillingwater, 1986) that has permeated EU thinking. The change has been a dramatic one that transcends national boundaries and modes. The liberalization of transport markets throughout the world and the extension of private sector ownership have also had the wider influence of providing important demonstration effects to other sectors that in turn have also been liberalized (Button and Keeler, 1993).

The early thinking regarding the CTP centred on harmonization so that a level playing field could ultimately be created on which competition would be equitable. The ECSC had initiated this approach in the early 1950s and it continued as EU interest moved away from primary products. The ECSC had removed some artificial tariff barriers relating to rail movements of primary products and the CTP initially attempted to expand this idea in the 1960s to cover the general carriage of goods and especially those moved on roads. Road transport was viewed rather differently to railways. It was perceived that the demand and supply features of road haulage markets could lead to excessive competition and supply uncertainties.

The early efforts involved such actions as seeking to initiate common operating practices (e.g. relating to driving hours and vehicle weights), common accounting procedures and standardized methods of charging. A forked tariff regime for trucking, with rates only allowed between officially determined maxima and minima, was aimed at meeting the dual problems of possible monopoly exploitation in some circumstances and of possible inadequate capacity due to excess competition in others. Maximum and minimum rates on international movements within the EU were stipulated and statutory charges established on this basis. Practically, there were problems in setting the cost-based rates, but besides that, questions must be raised concerning a policy that was aimed at simultaneously tackling monopoly and excess competition (Munby, 1962). Constraints on the number of international truck movements across borders were marginally reduced by the introduction of a small number of Community

quota licences – authorizing the free movement of holders over the entire EU road network (Button, 1984).

The 1973 enlargement of the Union to nine members stimulated a renewed interest in transport policy. The new members – the UK, Ireland and Denmark – tended to be more market-oriented in their transport policy objectives. Also, there was inevitable horse-trading across policy areas and with the enlargement arose the opportunity to review a whole range of policy areas. At about the same time, the Commission raised legal questions concerning the slowness of the Council of Ministers to move on creating a genuine CTP. It also followed a period of rapid growth in trade within the Union (see tables 5.11–5.12 and chapter 9), with a shift towards greater trade in manufactures. As a result infrastructure capacity issues were coming to the fore and the case for more flexible regulation of road freight transport was being argued (Button, 1990).

The outcome was not dramatic although new sectors entered the debates, most notably maritime transport, and wider objectives concerning environmental protection and energy policy played a role (table 16.1). Overall, the actions in this period were a gentle move towards liberalization by making the quota system permanent and expanding the number of licences, which increased international intra-EU road freight capacity. The option of using reference tariffs rather than forked tariffs was a reflection of the inherent problems with the latter. A major element of the measures involved transport infrastructure in terms of improving decision-making regarding its provision and with regard to consideration of the way that charges should be levied for its use. The importance of transport links outside of the EU, but part of a natural European network, also began to play a part in policy formulation, with the Union beginning to develop mechanisms for financing investment in such infrastructure.

The enlargements of the Union, as Greece and then Spain and Portugal joined, had little impact on the CTP. It still remained essentially piecemeal. The only significant change prior to major developments in the early 1990s was the gradual widening

Table 16.1 Summary of the policy of EC9

Emphasis on

- links between transport and regional, social, fiscal, industrial, environmental and energy affairs;
- intervention with transport within a Community-led framework;
- the joint movement forward on consistency of regulations and liberalization;
- the increasing importance attached to the coordination of infrastructure investment.

Policy

- Infrastructure coordination (important in the Action Programme, 1974–6):
  - new consultation procedure with a Transport Infrastructure Committee (1978);
  - Oort's study of infrastructure pricing (Oort and Maaskant, 1976);
- (contained in the Green Paper of 1979):
  - Creation of an infrastructure fund;
  - extension of interest in the infrastructure of non-members (e.g. Austria and Yugoslavia) where it affects links between members.

Liberalization

- reference tariff system (1978);
- permanent quota system (1976);
- common method for determining bilateral quotas (1980).

of the modes covered. There were, for example, moves to bring maritime and air transport policy in line with Union competition policy.

Efforts to develop a common policy on maritime transport represent one of the spheres in which there was a broadening out of EU transport policy (Brooks and Button, 1992) from the mid-1980s. Since 35 per cent of the international, non-intra EU trade of member states involves maritime transport (some 90 per cent of the Union's aggregate imports and outputs), it may seem surprising that it took so long for this mode to come within the CTP. The reason for this, as we have seen, was that the EEC Treaty required unanimous decisions regarding the extent to which sea transport was to be included in EU policy – although it was unclear whether this applied to EU policy as a whole or purely to the CTP.

The accession to membership in the 1970s and early 1980s of countries such as the UK and Greece with established shipping traditions brought maritime issues to the table, and then the Single European Act (SEA) of 1987 provided a catalyst for initiating a maritime policy (Erdmenger and Stasinopoulos, 1988). A series of measures were introduced aimed at bringing shipping within the Union's competition policy framework. This came at a time when major changes were beginning to permeate the way in which maritime services were provided. Technical shifts, such as the widespread adoption of containerization, had begun to influence the established cartel arrangements that had characterized scheduled maritime services. (These initial arrangements were 'conferences' that coordinated fares and sailings but later were more integrated 'consortia'.) The ability to discriminate in relation to price that these cartels enjoyed was beginning to be eroded as it became more difficult to isolate cargoes. Conferences had been permitted in most European countries since the late nineteenth century because they were seen as a way to offer scheduled services of less than a shipload at relatively stable rates to shippers. Action by the United Nations to limit the power of these cartels in the 1970s was largely aimed at protecting developing countries but was in conflict with the national policies of some EU members while others ratified it. The need for a more coordinated EU maritime policy emerged.

This view was reinforced in the 1980s as the size of the EU shipping sector declined significantly. The relative size of the sector had been falling for many years, but accelerated in the face of competition from Far East and Communist bloc fleets. Taxation and policies on such matters as wages and technical standards were adding to the problem by stimulating operators to 'flag out' and register in non-member states.

The 'First Package' in 1985 sought to improve the competitive structure of the European shipping industry and its ability to combat unfair competition from third countries (CEC, 1985c). It gave the Commission power to react to predatory behaviour by third-party shipowners which when initially applied (e.g. the Hyundai case) exerted a demonstration effect, especially on Eastern bloc shipowners. The measures also set out an interpretation of competition policy that allowed block exemptions for shipping cartels (shipping conferences), albeit with safeguards to ensure the exemption was not exploited (see chapter 13).

In 1986 a 'Second Package' – the Positive Measures Package – was initiated by the Commission and was aimed at addressing the decline in the competitiveness of the EU's fleets as well as covering safety and pollution issues. Greater coordination of fleets was seen as important and to stimulate this a common registry was proposed (CEC, 1991c). It has not, however, proved a success, and fleet sizes have continued to decline, bringing forth new ideas for capacity reduction from the EU Commission. Also, as part of the general effort to liberalize the European market and enhance the efficiency of the industry, agreement on cabotage (the provision of a domestic service within a country by a carrier from another nation) was reached, but with exceptions in some markets, e.g. the Greek islands.

Compared to shipping, ports policy can best be described as ad hoc (Chlomoudis and Pallis, 2002). Initial concerns in the early 1990s centred round modernizing European ports, and in particular ensuring that they could handle the large ships that were being introduced. Progress was relatively slow until 2000 when sea and inland ports were incorporated into the trans-European networks (TENs) initiative with the objective of integrating and prioritizing investment in transport infrastructure.

Air transport in general, since the initiatives of the US in the late 1970s that had liberalized its domestic passenger and freight markets and fostered an open skies policy for international aviation, was moving away from a tradition of strict regulation that had pertained since the pioneering days (Button et al., 1998). Until the early 1980s, however, it had also generally been thought that aviation policy was outside the jurisdiction of the EU Commission and a matter for national governments. This changed, following a number of legal decisions by the European Court of Justice (ECJ) (e.g. the Nouvelles Frontières and Ahmed Saeed cases) regarding the applicability of various aspects of EU competition rules to air transport.

The European bilateral system of air service agreements covering scheduled air transport between member states was, like those in other parts of the world, tightly regulated. Typical features of a bilateral agreement meant that: only one airline from each country was allowed to fly on a particular route with the capacity offered by each bilateral partner also often restricted; revenues were pooled; fares were approved by the regulatory bodies of the bilateral partners; and the designated airlines were substantially state-owned and enjoyed state aid. Domestic air markets were also highly controlled. The charter market, largely catering for holiday traffic from northern Europe to southern destinations, represented about 50 per cent of the revenue seat miles within the EU and was less strictly regulated, but the regulations were such that services seldom met the needs of business travellers.

A change in the policy climate began in 1979 when the Commission put forward general ideas for regulatory reform (CEC, 1984). The push for change came from the ECJ's verdict in the Nouvelles Frontières case concerning the cutting of airfares. This encouraged the Commission to adopt the view that its powers to attack fare-fixing activities were greater than the implementing regulation suggested. The Council subsequently decided that the best way to regain control was to agree to introduce deregulation, but of a kind, and at a pace, of its own choosing, hence the 1987 'First Package'.

The basic philosophy was that deregulation would take place in stages, with workable competition being the objective. A regulation was adopted that enabled the Commission to apply the antitrust rules directly to airline operations. Only interstate operations were covered; intrastate services and services to countries outside the EU were not at this stage affected. Certain technical agreements were left untouched. The Council also adopted a directive designed to provide airlines with greater pricing freedom. While airlines could collude, the hope was that they would increasingly act individually. The authorities of the states approved applications for airfare changes. Also the new arrangements did not constitute free competition since an element of regulation remained.

While conditions were laid down that reduced the national authorities' room for manoeuvre in rejecting changes in airfares, they could still reject them. However, if there was disagreement on a fare the disagreeing party lost the right of veto under arbitration.

The 1987 package also made a start on liberalizing access to the market. To this end the Council of Ministers adopted a decision in 1987 that provided for a deviation from the traditional air services agreement which set a 50/50 split. The capacity shares related to total traffic between the two countries. Member states were required to allow competition to change the shares up to 55/45 in the period to 30 September 1989 and thereafter to allow it to change to 60/40. Normally they could only take action if capacity shares threatened to move beyond such limits. Fifth-freedom traffic – the carriage of goods between two different countries, so long as the service begins or ends in the carrier's home country – was not included in these ratios but was additional. There was also a provision in which serious financial damage to an air carrier could constitute grounds for the Commission to modify the shift to the 60/40 limit.

The decision also required member states to accept multiple designations on a country-pair basis by another member. A member state was not obliged to accept the designation of more than one air carrier on a route by the other state (that is, a city-pair basis) unless certain conditions were satisfied. These conditions were to become less restrictive over time. The decision also made a limited attempt to open up the market to fifth-freedom competition.

The 1989 'Second Package' involved more deregulation. From the beginning of 1993 a system of double disapproval was accepted. Only if both civil aviation authorities refused to sanction a fare application could an airline be precluded from offering it to its passengers. From the same date the old system of setting limits to the division of traffic between the bilateral partners was to disappear totally in a phased manner. Member states also endorsed the vital principle that governments should not discriminate against airlines provided they meet safety criteria and address the problem of ownership rules. In the past, an airline had typically to be substantially owned by a European state before it could fly from that country, but the Council abolished this rule over a two-year period.

Air cargo services were liberalized so that a carrier operating from its home state to another member country could take cargo into a third member state or fly from one member state to another and then to its home state. Cabotage and operations between two freestanding states were not liberalized.

The most recent initiatives of the Union have involved the move to a 'single sky' over Europe and to the Union taking responsibility for the negotiation of external air traffic rights. The notion of a single sky is that air traffic control should be reorganized to reduce the excessive fragmentation of the current system, update the technology used and be operated under common EU rules. The aim was to achieve this by 2004 (CEC, 2001e) but there has been slippage. A ruling by the ECJ in 2001 was interpreted to imply that de facto the Commission has power over negotiating external air service agreements between members of the Union and certain third parties. Subsequent efforts to have a free market across the Atlantic to the US have proved difficult to negotiate, however. Ideologically, the EU sees a free market as allowing not only open access to transatlantic routes but also to ownership of airlines in the countries involved and the ability to conduct cabotage, while the US seeks simply to have open skies with regard to international air services.

16.4 The CTP and other aspects of policy from the 1990s

The creation of the Single European Market in 1992 (see chapters 2 and 17), and subsequent moves towards greater political integration, brought important changes to the CTP and related transport policies (Button, 1992). Broadly, the 1987 SEA stimulated a concerted effort to remove institutional barriers to the free trade in transport services. At about the same time, efforts at further political integration led to major new initiatives to provide an integrated European transport infrastructure – e.g. the TENs (CEC, 1989b). These strategic networks were aimed at facilitating higher levels of social and political integration at the national and regional levels. They also had purely economic objectives.

While there were moves to liberalize industries such as air transport from the late 1980s, the broad basis of the current phase of EU transport policy was established in the Commission's White Paper on *The Future Development of the Common Transport Policy* (CEC, 1992b). This set out as a guiding principle the need to balance an effective transport system for the EU with a commitment to the protection of the environment. The environmental theme was subsequently expanded (CEC, 1992a). This was to be set in the context of defending the needs and interests of individual citizens as consumers, transport users and people living and working in areas of transport activity.

Even if these effects were not present, questions arose at the time regarding the ability of regulators to serve the public interest with the information that they had to hand. The development of economic theories involving such concepts as contestable markets (where potential competition could be as effective as actual competition in blunting the power of monopoly suppliers), although subsequently the centre of intellectual and empirical debate, provided new ways of thinking about transport markets and were central to several EU initiatives. There was also a switch away from concern about problems of optimal scale and monopoly power that had been the intellectual justification for the state ownership and regulation of such industries as railways and air transport, to attempts at seeking to create conditions favourable to X-efficiency and dynamic efficiency. Technically, this largely, but not exclusively, involved a switch of emphasis from conventional consumer protection to a focus on reducing costs. In particular, there was mounting concern about the costs of regulated transport that had macroeconomic implications for inflation and also often led to the need for high levels of public subsidy. These undertakings were neither producing at the lowest possible costs for the technology they were using at the time nor moving forward to adopt lower-cost technologies.

One can also look at the situation in the much wider context of the past thirty years being a period of important economic change as the information age has gradually taken over. Improved new forms of communication of all types have come to the fore that affect both production and consumption activities. Transport is part of the supply side in that it involves the facilitation of personal and commercial interactions but it is also part of the demand side, being a major user of information services. Modern aviation services, for example, could not operate without this technology, and innovations in freight transport such as just-in-time management would hardly be possible on the scale on which they are now practised. As the structure of production has changed, not only in the EU but throughout the world, and as social changes have taken place, it would have been almost impossible for the institutional structure of a key industry such as transport to have been unaltered. In this sense EU policy in the 1990s must be seen as partly flowing with much stronger international tides of social and regulatory change.

The nature of the policy changes, however interpreted, has not been uniform in either time or space. Countries and regional groupings have differed in their approach. The US tended to lead the way as it deregulated its domestic transport markets between 1977 and 1982. Demonstration effects resulted in other countries following. The reforms in the US were, however, only partly copied elsewhere. There were different starting points but also later reformers benefited from the experiences of the first-time movers. Transport systems differ across countries. In the US, for instance, the average car is driven about 12,500 miles a year, whereas in Europe the figure is less than 9,000. Western Europe has only about 30 per cent of the freeway mileage of the US. Similarly, the demands placed on transport systems vary according to such things as the goods produced and the physical structure of the area. There are, however, common lessons to be learned, but they need to be taken in the context of the geography of the countries involved, the individual details of the reforms, their wider institutional context and their particular timing (Button, 1998). In some senses the EU benefited from the experiences of pre-1990s reforms when devising its current transport priorities and strategies.

Although terms such as multi-modalism abound in the official literature, and some initiatives have transcended the conventional bounds of modal-based actions, a useful and pragmatic way of treating these recent developments is by mode.

16.4.1 Road transport

Road transport is the dominant mode of both freight and passenger transport in the EU. The share of freight going by rail, for example, has fallen from 32 per cent of the EU total in 1970 to about 14 per cent today. Over the period, the total freight tonnage in Europe has increased 2.5 times and the share of this going by road has risen from 48 per cent to 74 per cent. However, as we have seen, the initial efforts to develop a common policy regarding road transport proved problematic. Technical matters were more easily solved than those of creating a common economic framework of supply, although even here issues concerning such matters as maximum weight limits for trucks have tended to be fudged. Economic controls lingered on as countries with less efficient road haulage industries sought to shelter themselves from the more competitive fleets from countries such as the UK and the Netherlands. There were also more legitimate efficiency concerns throughout the EU over the wider social costs of road transport, regarding both environmental matters and narrower questions of infrastructure utilization.

The single market initiative, also later influenced by the potential of new trade with the post-Communist states of Eastern and Central Europe (Button, 1993), has resulted in significant reforms to economic regulation in recent years. From the industrial perspective, road freight transport offers the flexibility that is required by modern, just-in-time production management, but from the social perspective it can be environmentally intrusive and, in the absence of appropriate infrastructure pricing, can contribute to excessive congestion costs.

Earlier measures had helped expand the supply of international permits in Europe, the EU quota complementing bilateral arrangements, and reference tariffs had introduced a basis for more efficient rate determination. The 1990s were concerned with building on this rather fragile foundation. In particular, as part of the 1992 single market initiative, a phased liberalization was initiated that both gradually removed restrictions on trucking movements across national boundaries and phased in cabotage that had hitherto not been permitted by member states.

The long-standing bilateral arrangements for international licensing led to high levels of economic inefficiency. This was not only because the system imposed an absolute constraint on the number of movements but also because cabotage was not permitted, and combinations of bilateral licences permitting trucks to make complex international movements were difficult to obtain – trucks had to travel long distances without cargo. The system also added to delays at borders as documents were checked. Besides leading to the gradual phasing out of bilateral controls and the phasing in of cabotage rights, the 1992 initiative also led to considerable reductions in cross-border documentation.

Passenger road transport policy has largely been left to individual member states, although in the late 1990s the Commission began to advocate the development of a 'citizens' network' and more rational road-charging policies (notably systems of congestion pricing). Perhaps the greatest progress has been made regarding social regulations on such matters as the adoption of catalytic converters in efforts to limit the environmental intrusion of motor vehicles. It has taken time to develop a common policy regarding public transport despite efforts in the 1970s to facilitate easier cross-border coach and bus operations.

16.4.2 Railways

Rail transport, while largely filling a niche market in many countries, is an important freight mode in much of continental Europe and provides important passenger services along several major corridors. At the local level, it serves as a key mode for commuter traffic in larger cities. Much of the important economic reform of European railways was undertaken in the early phase of integration by the ECSC, with actions on such matters as the removal of discriminatory freight rates. The recent phase has been concerned less with issues of economic regulation and with operations and more with widening access to networks and with technological developments, especially regarding the development of a high-speed rail network as part of the TENs initiative.

The earlier phase had initially sought to remove deliberate distortions to the market that favoured national carriers, but from the late 1960s and 1970s the emphasis shifted to the rationalization of the subsidized networks through more effective and transparent cost accountancy. However, the exact incidence of subsidies still often remained uncertain. The Union has also instigated measures aimed at allowing the trains of one member to use the track of another with charges based upon economic costs. The aim of EU Directive 91/440 (CEC, 1995a) was to develop truly European networks, but at the time of writing the open access rules explicitly do not apply to the new high-speed rail lines such as the French and Belgian Lignes à Grande Vitesse and the German Neubaustrecken networks. The implementation of the open access strategy has been slow and has had limited impact (CEC, 1998b).

The EU has traditionally found it difficult to devise practical and economically sound common pricing principles to apply to transport infrastructure despite the proposals of the Oort Report (Oort and Maaskant, 1976). With regard to railways, the gist of the overall proposals is for short-run marginal costs (which are to include environmental and congestion costs as well as wear on the infrastructure) to be recovered. Long-run elements of cost are only to be recovered in narrowly defined circumstances and in relation only to passenger services. This clearly has implications, especially on the freight side, if genuine full cost-based competition is to be permitted with other transport modes.

Rail transport has also received considerable support from the Commission as an integral part of making greater use of integrated, multi-modal transport systems. Such systems would largely rely upon rail (including piggy-back systems and kangaroo trains) or waterborne modes for trunk haulage, with road transport used as the feeder mode. This is seen as environmentally desirable and as contributing to containing rising levels of road traffic congestion in Europe.

The success of some of the French TGV services, and especially that between Paris and Lyon, where full cost recovery has been attained, has led to a significant interest in this mode. In 1990 the Commission set up a high-level working group to help push forward a common approach to high-speed railway development. A master plan for 2010 was produced. The EU's efforts to harmonize the development of high-speed rail have not been entirely successful and there are significant technical differences, for example between the French and German systems. Indeed, both countries actively market their technologies as superior (Viegas and Blum, 1993).

The difficulties that still remain with rail transport reflect technical variations in the infrastructure and working practices of individual states that are only slowly being coordinated. Some countries, such as the Netherlands, Sweden and the UK, have pursued the broad liberalization philosophy of the EU and gone beyond the minimal requirements of the CTP, but in others rigidities remain and the rail network still largely lacks the integration required for full economies of scope, density and market presence to be reaped.

16.4.3 Inland waterway transport

Inland waterway transport was already an issue in the early days of the EU. This is mainly because it is a primary concern of two founder member countries, the Netherlands and Germany, which in 1992 accounted for 73.1 per cent of EU traffic. France and Belgium also had some interest in this mode of transport. Progress in formulating a policy has tended to be slow, in part because of historical agreements covering navigation on the Rhine (e.g. the Mannheim Convention), but mainly because the major economic concern has been that of over-capacity. In 1998 over-capacity was estimated at between 20 and 40 per cent at the prevailing freight rates. Retraction of supply is almost always inevitably difficult to manage, both because few countries are willing to pursue a contraction policy in isolation and because of the resistance of barge owners and labour.

As in other areas of transport, the EU began by seeking technical standardization, and principles for social harmonization were set out by the Commission in 1975 and 1979 (CEC, 1975, 1979b), but economic concerns took over in the 1990s. In 1990 the EC initiated the adoption of a system of subsidies designed to stimulate the scrapping of vessels. Subsequent measures only permitted the introduction of new vessels into the inland fleet on a replacement basis. Labour subsidies operated in the Netherlands, Belgium and France (the rota system that provides minimum wages for bargemen) have also been cut back in stages. They were removed entirely in 2000.

These measures were coupled with an initiative in 1995 to coordinate investment in inland waterway infrastructure (the Trans-European Waterway Network), designed to encourage, for environmental reasons, the greater use of waterborne transport. More recently, in *European Transport Policy for 2010: Time to Decide* (CEC, 2001e), the Commission has put emphasis on its Marco Polo programme of integrating inland waterways transport with rail and maritime transport for the movement of bulk consignments within an intermodal chain.

16.4.4 Maritime transport

Much of the emphasis of the EU maritime policy from the late 1990s has been on the shipping market rather than on protecting the Union's fleet (Urrutia, 2006). In other words, it is user- rather than supplier-driven. In the 1990s the sector became increasingly concentrated as consortia grew in importance, mergers took place (e.g. P&O and Nedlloyd in 1997) and then the resultant large companies formed strategic alliances. (In 1999 all shipping companies, with the exception of two of the world's largest, were part of alliances.) An extension of the 1985 rules to cover consortia and other forms of market sharing was initiated in 1992 and subsequently extended as the nature of

maritime alliances has become more complex (CEC, 1995a).

The Commission also initiated a number of actions supporting this position. In 1994 it acted to ban the Transatlantic agreement reached the preceding year by the major shipping companies to gain tighter control over the loss-making North Atlantic routes. It did so on the grounds of capacity and rate manipulations and because it contained agreements over pre- and on-carriage over land. In the same year it also fined fourteen shipping companies that were members of the Far East Freight Conference for price fixing. The main point at issue was that these prices embodied multi-modal carriage and while shipping per se enjoyed a block exemption on price agreements, multi-modal services did not.

Ports also attracted the attention of the EU in the 1990s. Ports are major transport interchange points and in 1994 handled about 24 per cent of the world's tonne equivalent units. Advances in technology have led to important changes in the ways in which ports operate, and there has been a significant concentration on their activities as shipping companies have moved towards hub-and-spoke operations. The main EU ports have capacity utilization levels of well over 80 per cent and some are at or near their design capacity. Whether this is a function of a genuine capacity deficiency or reflects inappropriate port pricing charges that do not contain congestion cost elements is debatable. The Commission has produced further proposals for coordinating investment in port facilities (CEC, 1997d).

In 2001 the Commission launched an initiative to improve the quality of services offered by ports. This involves tightening access standards for pilotage, cargo handling, etc. and to make more transparent the rules of procedure at ports with the particular aim of bringing ports more fully into an integrated transport structure (CEC, 2001f). Some of the proposed rationalization measures that have been initiated at the national level, however, have met with strong resistance from labour unions.

The 2004 enlargement of the Union has meant a greater focus on the role of short-sea shipping that could allow bulk commodity movements from countries such as Poland to be kept away from congested roads and railways (CEC, 2003h). The notion of developing highways of the seas within a 'common maritime space' (CEC, 2006s) underlies much of the emerging philosophy with measures designed to allow more rapid and reliable coastal shipping around the geographical periphery of the Union.

16.4.5 Air transport policy

While liberalization of EU air transport may be considered one of the successes of the CTP, in the late 1980s the air market was still heavily regulated at the time of the Cockfield Report that heralded the single market. The final reform – the 'Third Package' – came in 1992 and was phased in from the following year. The programme aimed at a regulatory framework for the EU by 1997 similar to that for US domestic aviation (Button and Swann, 1992). The measures removed significant barriers to entry by setting common rules governing safety and financial requirements for new airlines. Since January 1993, EU airlines have been able to fly between member states without restriction and within member states (other than their own) subject to some controls on fares and capacity. National restrictions on ticket prices were removed; the only safeguards related to excessive falls or increases in fares.

From 1997, full cabotage has been permitted, and fares are generally unregulated. Additionally, foreign ownership among Union carriers is permitted, and these carriers have, for EU internal purposes, become European airlines. One result has been an increase in cross-share holdings and a rapidly expanding number of alliances among airlines within the Union. This change did not initially apply to extra-Union agreements where national bilateral arrangements still dominate the market. A ruling by the ECJ in November 2002, however, gives power to the Commission to undertake such negotiations. In 2003 the Council gave powers to the Commission to proceed with negotiations with the US to liberalize the transatlantic market. In 2007, the EU and the US agreed to open the transatlantic airline market, with some phasing-in arrangements for services involving London's Heathrow Airport.

Early analysis of reforms by the UK Civil Aviation Authority (1993) and the Commission indicated that the reforms of the 1990s produced, in terms of multiple airlines serving various market areas, greater competition on both EU domestic routes and international routes within the EU. The changes varied, but countries such as Greece and Portugal increased the number of competitive international services considerably. Many routes, however, either because multiple services are simply not technically sustainable or institutional impediments still limited market entry, remained monopolies in 1994.

More recently, the Commission, in examining the impact of the Third Package, reported important consumer benefits (CEC, 1996c). It found that the number of routes flown within the EU rose from 490 to 520 between 1993 and 1995; 30 per cent of Union routes are now served by two operators and 6 per cent by three operators or more; eighty new airlines have been created while only sixty have disappeared; fares have fallen on routes where there are at least three operators; and, overall, when allowance is made for charter operations, 90–5 per cent of passengers on intra-EU routes are travelling at reduced fares. One caveat is that there have been quite significant variations in the patterns of fares charged across routes.

There was little initial change in fares on routes that remain monopolies or duopolies. The number of fifth-freedom routes doubled to thirty between 1993 and 1996, although this type of operation remains a relatively small feature of the market, and seventh freedoms have been little used (seventh freedom is the right to carry passengers or cargo between two different countries without continuing the service to one's own country). Indeed, much of the new competition was on domestic routes where those routes operated by two or more carriers rose from 65 in January 1963 to 114 in January 1996, with the largest expansions being in France, Spain and Germany. The charter market continued to grow and in some countries accounted for more than 80 per cent of traffic.

Later analysis (BAE Systems, 2000) showed that while promotional fares fell between 1992 and

2000 (−15 per cent) there were rises in business (+45 per cent) and economy fares (+14 per cent) in nominal terms. There were regional differences in the patterns of fare changes, with business fares increasing relatively more for the northern European Economic Area (EEA; see chapters 1 and 2) routes (+6.5 per cent) than for southern routes where they fell (−2.1 per cent). The converse was true for both economy and promotional fares.

This was accompanied by an increase in the number of scheduled carriers within the EEA from 77 in 1992 to 140 in 2000. The conditions since September 2001 have led to volatility in the market that extends beyond the demise of Sabena and Swissair in 2002. In terms of the scheduled market, from September 2001 to May 2002 seventeen airlines withdrew and there were fourteen start-ups. In the French market the number of airlines fell from a peak of twenty-six in 1996 to twelve at the end of 2000 to six by mid-2002. There were also significant turnovers in Sweden and Greece. The traditional full-cost flag carriers have been forced to restructure their operations, as new low-cost carriers (such as Ryanair and easyJet) have taken over 15 per cent of the intra-European market.

16.5 The 2004 enlargement

The phased enlargement of the EU envisaged under the Treaties of Nice and Madrid has implications for transport. The 2004 enlargement affected the demands placed on the transport systems of the existing fifteen member states and those that acceded. Changes, however, have perhaps been less dramatic than some had supposed, in that trade had already expanded considerably between the accession states and EU15 over the preceding decade. The new members had also considerably reformed their economic structures – important for influencing what is transported and where – and their transport systems. Nevertheless, the difficulties to be overcome have not been trivial and challenges remain, especially since enlargement came as part of a wider set of developments:

- *Geographical.* Enlargement has had implications for the economics of the operation of long-haul

transport as well as necessitating investment in infrastructure. It has opened up new markets for trade and with them have come new demands for transport services internal to all members as well as between them. The scale effects and the ability to reap the benefits of comparative advantage have increased incomes and with this the demand for person movements. What the enlargement has not created is a 'natural' transport market. The spatial distribution of economic activities does not, for example, have the structure of the US market. In the latter, the overall physical market is essentially rectangular, with centres of population and economic activities at the corners and in the centre. This allows exploitation of efficiency benefits from long-haul carriage and hub-and-spoke structures. In the EU, economic activity is dichotomously distributed and enlargement has added to the central/peripheral nature of the Union.

- *Legal.* The Constitutional Convention sought to develop a longer-term basis for the EU (see chapters 2, 3 and 28). Issues concerning the nature of central legal responsibilities and the degree of local national autonomy inevitably arise and enlargements add to the challenges presented. One of the outcomes of the Constitutional Treaty would have been a more structured way of shaping the wider legal framework within which macroeconomic policies regarding transport could be formulated. It would also have influenced the external policies of the Union – important for transport in a world of global economies and global trade. The failure to ratify the Constitutional Treaty in France and Denmark – and no judgment is offered here on the actual details of the massive document (see chapters 2, 3 and 28) – leaves the situation in a sort of limbo with the enlarged Union functioning on an institutional basis designed for a smaller entity.

- *Economic.* In 2002 the Commission President raised the issue of the need for a common fiscal policy within the EU, or at least that part of it in the eurozone. Economists have long understood that a common currency requires a common fiscal policy as a concomitant (see chapters 10–12, 15 and 19). The persistently poor economic performance of some of the larger members of the eurozone over the past decade adds emphasis to this need. A common policy involves the centre having responsibility for fiscal transfers above that now controlled by Brussels. While the exact amount is debated, and depends on the extent to which the centre considers distribution as well as macroeconomic stabilization as part of its function, it may well be considerable. This would take away much national autonomy over major infrastructure works and influence short-term public expenditure patterns. The rejection of the Constitutional Treaty would inevitably make it more difficult to develop a Union-wide fiscal framework of any substance.

- *Security*. The attacks on US national edifices in 2001, and subsequent terrorist attacks in Spain, the UK and other EU countries, have led to an increased concern with transport security. Individual EU states have developed their own strategies, but umbrella Union-wide actions have also been of importance. In particular, the EU has been active in the wider global efforts to combat terrorism coordinated by the United Nations – for example, involving the International Civil Aviation Organization and the International Maritime Organization (CEC, 2004j). In addition the EU has as an entity entered into agreements with non-members, most notably the US, on specific areas of concern. All these measures add to the costs of transport and, given the uniformity of the requirements, add to the burden of the lower-income members: essentially they proportionately hit the new member states the hardest.

These are not trivial changes and new challenges. In most senses it is impossible to talk about any one in isolation from the others, or without considering the background and the current state of existing Union transport policy. The countries that gained membership in 2004 (Poland, the Czech Republic, Hungary, Slovakia, Lithuania, Latvia, Slovenia, Estonia, Cyprus and Malta) and 2007 (Bulgaria and Romania) also offer a variety of

different challenges from a transport perspective, with the latter two compounding the diversity.

The situation is also not one of combining two static blocks, but rather of bringing together two units that have started from different places and are moving forward at different speeds. The nature of the economies of the new members, and their relationships to the EU, has already changed considerably since 1989. European agreements have fostered trade and provided various aid. The EU15, and some member states unilaterally, had been involved in improving the communications systems within transition economies. The EU *Agenda 2000* (CEC, 1997b) identified key links in their transport networks – some 19,000 kilometres of road, 21,000 of rail, and 4,000 of inland waterway, forty airports, twenty seaports and fifty-eight inland ports. Potential new states experienced increases in the value of their euro trade between 1989 and 1999. Their industrial structures also changed gradually in the light of domestic reforms and exposure to international markets. Nevertheless, there are numerous ways in which their transport systems differ from much of EU15. The new member states (NMS) are largely distant from the core of the Union. Their remoteness means that railways, in cases such as Poland, become a potentially viable mode for long-distance freight transport. Indeed, the physical area of the enlarged EU offers the prospects of haul lengths comparable with those in the US where deregulated railways have at least been maintaining their market share. However, the rail networks that currently carry 40 per cent of freight by tonne–kilometre within the new member states are largely based on dated technologies and are only slowly being oriented to meeting transport demands for movements to/from the EU. Despite improvements, they remain excessively labour-intensive and often serve as job creators rather than transport suppliers.

Car ownership is considerably lower in the accession countries than in the existing EU. This is changing. While several of the national markets within EU15 are reaching maturity, markets are expanding rapidly in the NMS. This is putting strains on urban infrastructure and poses mounting environmental problems. Smaller states, and some regions within the larger ones, will find themselves subjected to significant transit traffic flows. This raises issues of infrastructure capacity and environmental degradation, but also matters of charging and pricing – a subject the EU itself has been singularly poor at addressing. The twelve newcomers also still suffer from poorly maintained transport networks largely for moving bulk raw materials to Russia. The road freight sector has begun to develop in response to the needs of modern just-in-time production and some countries are making use of the limited infrastructure links to the west.

Transition economies with maritime access and inland waterways make considerable use of them with about 40 per cent of tonnage moved by water. The island accession states inevitably do the same. Enlargement comes at a time of technical change in maritime transport with the increasing deployment of a post-panamax, and even a 'super post-panamax' fleet, exploiting scale economies and pressing for more hub-and-spoke operations and fleet rationalization.

The new EU countries are unlikely to generate a sufficient flow of resources in the short term to enhance their networks in line with demands resulting from EU membership. The EU has provided some resources to supplement those of the accession states – pre-accession sums of 520 million euros per annum (see chapters 19 and 22). But these are relatively small. Loan finance has been suggested and discussed in *European Transport Policy for 2010: Time to Decide* (CEC, 2001e). Essentially, the loans would be financed from user charges. A difficulty is that this is not the way most transport infrastructure is financed elsewhere in the EU. The majority of networks have been constructed from non-dedicated general taxation revenues and direct subsidies. Measures to make transport users more aware of their costs have been discussed, and limited efforts to introduce them made, but the situation is not one of a 'user pays' principle along the lines that seem to be suggested for the NMS.

Transport was hardly at the forefront of accession negotiations. Direct payments and agricultural subsidies inevitably dominated, the former due to the need to transfer resources to the NMS, the latter to satisfy the essentially Soviet style of agricultural policy sanctioned by both those giving and those taking, since the inception of the EEC in the late 1950s, and which politicians seem incapable either of confronting head-on or of finding an inventive path around (see chapters 20 and 26).

Enlargement has inevitably involved a transition period and transport is included within it. This may be seen as reflecting the time needed for the NMS to adjust their transport systems – if not completely, at least largely to the needs of an integrated Union-wide single market. In practice, this seems to be much less of a physical problem than one of psychology. There have already been major shifts in the way goods are transported in the NMS as new entrepreneurial talent has come into the trucking sector, in particular. There has also been some consolidation in rail networks, albeit not large by the scale of the likely cuts required.

Transitions inevitably pose problems. They are often used as an excuse for inertia and for extracting subsidies and grants to sustain stranded capital (infrastructure of no or little use in a new market environment). The EU has used transition mechanisms in the past to ease change – this was the initial justification for massive agricultural subsidies – but once in place they tend to take on permanency. But even if they are removed, the incumbent pre-reform actors have enjoyed a period in which to adjust their position and to capture the new institutional structure.

The EU's 2001 White Paper on transport policy offers a potpourri of ideas on what the future may look like for the larger new member countries and the transition economies in particular. The concern is very much to make use of the 'extensive, dense network and of significant know-how' in these countries to rebalance the transport modes in Europe: in other words, to maintain the modal share of the railways in the accession states and to have 35 per cent of freight moved on rail by 2010. Interim assessments (e.g. CEC, 2006s), however, indicate that progress is slower than had been hoped for. Congestion continues to be a major problem for many parts of the network and efforts to reduce it have still to produce significant results. This is despite the manifest and transparent results in places such as London and Stockholm that appropriate prices offer a remedy. Infrastructure remains deficient in many places and efforts to improve it have not been entirely successful. The money available from the Commission for the TENS 2004 revised programme of seventy-five projects, initially budgeted at 21 billion euros has, for example, been reduced to 7 billion euros. Equally, the goals for achieving environmentally cleaner transport have only been partially fulfilled. Much of the difficulty in these areas lies in the political unwillingness of the EU to consider applying the most elementary economic principles to what are largely economic problems.

16.6 Conclusions

Papers written in the early 1990s were extremely pessimistic about the prospects for any viable transport policy being initiated within the EU. That transport was important was seldom questioned, but prior attempts to do anything other than tinker with the prevailing, largely nationally driven, transport policies had proved disappointing. Early efforts in the 1960s to draw up what essentially amounted to a master plan or blueprint had failed. The problems of continued enlargement of the Union, coupled with fresh, often radical thinking on how transport as a sector should be treated, seemed to pose almost insurmountable problems for policy-makers in the 1970s and 1980s. These problems were not helped by mounting concerns over physical and institutional bottlenecks in the transport system of Europe that were manifestly an impediment to any radical shift towards a more rapid phase of economic integration.

At the time of writing the picture is somewhat different. Certainly many issues remain to be resolved (CEC, 2006s), such as the initiation of more rational pricing for most modes, but by and large transport inadequacies are no longer seen as a major threat to further economic and political integration within the EU. There is broad agreement that transparency and market-based systems afford an efficient way to meet the EU transport needs. While there has been much wasted time and effort, and significant economic, social and political costs are inevitably associated with this, the current phase of transport policy formulation can be seen as one of the important recent successes of the EU.

17 Energy policy and energy markets

STEPHEN MARTIN AND ALI EL-AGRAA

17.1 Introduction

Energy markets were present at the post-World War II start of the European integration process, the European Coal and Steel Community (ECSC). Since that time, energy markets have often held centre stage and sometimes faded into the background, but they have never left the scene entirely.

This chapter considers the EU role in energy policy, notes past attempts to create a common energy policy (CEP), assesses the factors behind their failure and examines why the Union has been able to influence national policies more successfully during the past few years. After discussing the situation in the different EU energy markets, current policy proposals and their context are reviewed. Finally, some of the difficulties the Commission faces in developing a credible CEP, and prospects for the future, are assessed.

That the EC attached great importance to the energy sector is demonstrated by the fact that two of the three treaties on which the EC is based are specifically concerned with energy: the 1951 Treaty of Paris creating the ECSC and the 1957 Treaty of Rome establishing Euratom were devoted to the coal and nuclear sectors, respectively. The details of these treaties (and their rationale) are covered in chapter 2, but their significance for energy policy is clear enough. The 1951 ECSC treaty reflected the dominance of coal in the energy balance of member states (as well as its role in the steel industry): by tackling coal, most EC energy supply and demand issues were addressed. The 1957 Euratom treaty sought to foster cooperation in the development of civil nuclear power, then perceived as the main source

of future energy requirements (Lucas, 1977). Both treaties, moreover, were in principle geared towards the creation of free and integrated markets in these sectors: the ECSC sought to abolish all barriers to trade between member states while controlling subsidies and cartel-like behaviour amongst producers; Euratom also paid lip-service to the idea of a common market in nuclear products.

A common market for other energy sectors was addressed in the EEC Rome Treaty. While the EEC was orientated towards more or less competitively structured sectors, it also applied to the more oligopolistic or monopolistic sectors such as oil, gas and electricity. Accordingly, in addition to being subject to the EEC Treaty's general provisions on opening up markets, these energy industries' special characteristics were covered by the Treaty's provisions on state enterprises and their conduct.

The gap between intentions expressed in the Treaties and the outcomes, however, has been a large one for energy – more so than for most other parts of the economy. The Commission's attempts to develop an energy policy of any sort, let alone one reflecting the ideals of the treaties, have proved to be of only limited success. Member state governments have been grudgingly willing to leave energy sectors to the marketplace during periods when energy markets seemed to be working well. When energy markets suffered disorienting shocks – all too often – member state governments intervened directly, or tried to do so. Throughout, the Commission has been true to its vocation, seeking to lay the foundations for a single EU energy market. The results have been mixed in terms of coping with episodic crises, and have impeded the development of an effective Community energy policy.

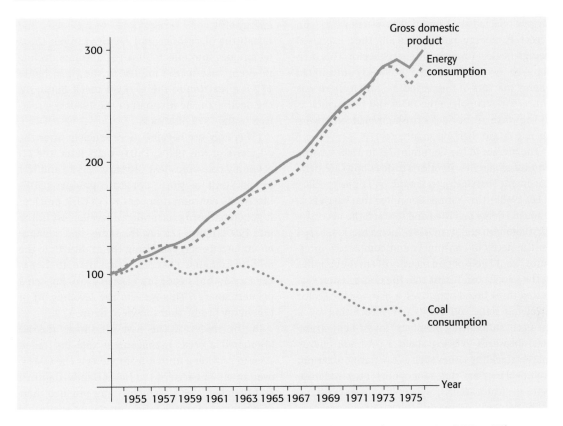

Figure 17.1 Indices of EC6 GDP, primary energy consumption and coal consumption, 1953–1979 (1953 = 100).
Source: CEC (1977b, table 1).

17.2 The golden years (mostly)

In the immediate aftermath of World War II, Europe faced shortages and rationing of food and fuel. The most pressing concern was to jump-start production. The idea that European coal would go into secular decline would have been inconceivable in the late 1940s. Yet that is what happened. European production took off in the 1950s, as shown in figure 17.1, and energy consumption went along with it. But the energy that was consumed was generated from crude oil, which was cheaper and cleaner than coal. Most of that crude oil came from the Middle East.

From the 1950s onwards, the Commission or its equivalents first sought to develop a policy for coal and then for energy more broadly (El-Agraa and Hu, 1984). On coal, the High Authority was unable to impose the spirit of the Paris Treaty on national industries. It was mainly involved in tackling the crises which beset the European coal industry from the mid-1950s onwards (Lindberg and Scheingold, 1970), crises triggered by the decline shown in figure 17.1.

In the sphere of energy generally, initial efforts were made as the negotiations for the EEC were progressing. The Messina conference recommended that the potential for coordinated energy policy be considered, but the Spaak Committee determined that this would not be necessary (Von Geusau, 1975).

Following the establishment of the new Communities, there was a renewed attempt to develop a CEP. The formation of an inter-executive Committee on energy in 1959 sought to develop a policy focusing on the creation of a common energy market. The main concerns of the Committee were with the effect of energy prices on industrial competitiveness and, to a lesser extent, with the security of energy supply (PEP, 1963). However, governments largely rejected the Committee's attempts to gain access to energy policy. Instead, they exercised benign neglect towards the energy sector. This inertia on energy policy reflected the largely untroubled energy markets of the period. Yet when there was concern over supply in the 1950s and 1960s (such as in the wake of the Suez crisis), governments were keen to retain their autonomy.

The merger of the Communities in 1965 saw the Commission renew its efforts to develop a CEP. In its document *First Guidelines towards an EC Energy Policy* (CEC, 1968b), the Commission noted that barriers to trade in energy persisted and stressed the necessity for a common energy market. Such a market, based on the needs of consumers and competitive pressures, would help obtain security of energy supplies at the lowest cost. To this end, the Commission suggested three broad objectives: a plan for the sector involving data collection and forecasting as a means of influencing members' investment strategies; measures to bring about a common energy market (tackling issues such as tax harmonization, technical barriers, state monopolies, etc.); and measures to ensure security of supply at lowest cost.

The proposals proved difficult to put into practice, partly because of the scale of objectives and contradictions between the substance of different goals, but mainly because of the resistance of member states. Even though the Council approved the strategy, it ignored most of the Commission's subsequent attempts to enact the proposals. The principal measures adopted in the wake of the Commission's proposals concerned oil stocks (following OECD initiatives) and some requirements for energy investment notification. These actions owed more to growing concern about security of supply than to the creation of a common energy market, and presaged a wider shift in Commission and member state perceptions of the priorities of energy policy.

17.3 Oil shocks and afterwards

The golden age of cheap oil and well-functioning energy markets came to an end with the oil shocks of 1973 and 1979. These shocks triggered downturns in worldwide economic activity.

Energy demand responds to price changes, but with a lag, reflecting the time needed to develop energy-efficient production techniques and install the physical capital required to put those techniques into effect. Thus the absolute decline in energy use in the mid-1970s shown in figure 17.2 is a reaction to the 1973 oil shock. Similarly, the decline in the first half of the 1980s is a reaction to the 1979 oil shock.

EU energy use became more efficient after the oil crises of the 1970s. Thirty years later, the EU economy consumes less primary energy and less oil per unit of gross domestic product (GDP). Electricity consumption per unit of GDP, much of it generated using natural gas, levelled off in the mid-1980s (figure 17.3). At the same time, reliance on imported energy fell from the mid-1970s to the mid-1980s (figure 17.4). Since that time, there has been a slow but steady increase in use of imported primary energy. This reflects the levelling-off of EU energy production shown in figure 17.2.

In the midst of the first oil shock, the EC attempted a crisis management role but failed even to provide a united front vis-à-vis the OAPEC over an oil embargo of the Netherlands (Daintith and Hancher, 1986). Member states pursued their own policies or worked through the International Energy Agency (IEA). Formed in 1974, the IEA overshadowed the EC both in breadth of membership (covering all the OECD countries except France) and in terms of its powers on oil sharing in a new crisis (Van der Linde and Lefeber, 1988).

Even so, the shock of oil price increases reinforced the reassessment of energy policies in member states and the Commission. The Commission attempted to develop a more strategic approach to the management of energy supply and demand. The 'New Strategy' (*Bulletin of the European Communities,* Supplement 4/1974), which was only agreed after much wrangling and dilution (a proposal for a European energy agency was abandoned after member state opposition – see Lucas, 1977), envisaged a number of targets to be met by 1985. These included the reduction of oil imports, the development of domestic energy capabilities (notably nuclear power) and the rational use of energy. The policy, while only indicative, mobilized resources for R&D and promotional programmes on energy, covering conventional and nuclear technologies, but also (albeit to a limited extent) renewables and energy-efficiency technologies. The new

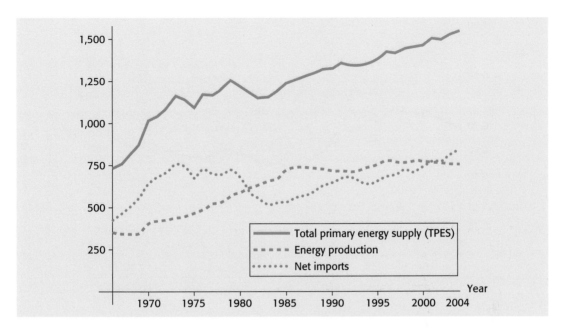

Figure 17.2 EU energy balances, 1966–2004 (millions of tonnes of oil equivalent). *Note:* TPES = energy production plus net imports minus stock increases. *Source:* OECD, *Energy Balances of OECD Countries*, various issues.

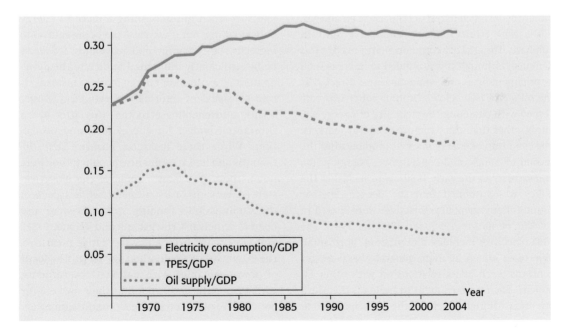

Figure 17.3 EU energy demand indicators, 1966–2004. *Notes:* TPES = total primary energy supply (millions of tonnes of oil equivalent); electricity consumption measured in kilowatt hours; oil supply measured in tonnes of oil equivalent; GDP measured in 1,000 1995 US dollars. *Source:* OECD, *Energy Balances of OECD Countries*, various issues.

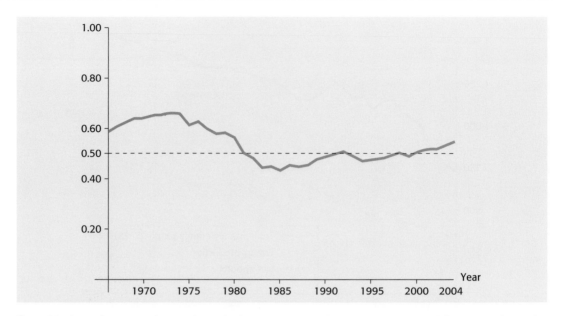

Figure 17.4 Share of net energy imports in total primary energy supply, 1966–2004. *Source:* OECD, *Energy Balances of OECD Countries*, various issues.

strategy also provided the basis for a handful of directives designed to restrict the use of oil and gas.

The New Strategy clearly entailed a shift in emphasis. The goal of a common energy market was demoted, although it was alluded to in areas such as pricing policies and some measures directed at the oil sector (see below). Overall, policy was concerned with changing the structure of energy balances rather than the structure of energy markets. The condition of energy markets (notably after the second oil shock) and concern over energy prices and security in the early 1980s were such that the policy was sustained into the decade. Further rounds of energy policy objectives were agreed in 1979 (to be met by 1990) and 1986 (for 1995). The 1995 objectives included a number of 'horizontal' objectives, aimed at more general energy policy concerns, such as its relationship with other EC policies. Each round sought to build on the previous one. Although in general the goals appeared to be on target, in some cases they reflected a degree of failure either across the EC or in certain member states, and subsequent rounds would then adopt a rather less ambitious agenda (CEC, 1984b; 1988d). The objectives approach later reappeared as part of EU energy strategy (CEC, 1996m).

By the mid-1980s, therefore, the Commission had succeeded in establishing a place in energy policymaking, but it was far from being central to member states' energy policy agendas, let alone being sufficiently influential to dictate the development of a common energy market. Instead, its role consisted of information gathering, target setting and enabling activities (the latter had a substantial budget for energy R&D and promotion). While these measures ensured that the Commission had an influence on policy, they were not without problems – some of the objectives showed few signs of achievement, while aspects of the Commission's funding strategies were also open to criticism (Cruickshank and Walker, 1981). Moreover, aside from a few legislative measures, the Commission's policy had few teeth. The locus of power remained with national governments, which generally chose to follow their own energy policies, resisting too strong a Commission role.

17.4 Demand and supply: the status quo

Table 17.1 gives a breakdown of EU primary energy sources for the year 2004. Oil remains the leading

Table 17.1 Composition of primary energy supply (millions of tonnes of oil equivalent), EU15, 2004

	Production	Imports	Exports	Net Supply	% TPES
Coal	91.05	140.49	9.75	223.12	14.44
Oil and oil products	135.44	846.85	329.24	604.22	39.09
Gas	185.58	252.91	60.51	376.16	24.34
Nuclear	237.22	–	–	237.22	15.35
Hydro	24.44	–	–	24.44	1.58
Geothermal and solar, etc.	11.02	–	–	11.02	0.07
Combustible, renewable, waste	65.68	1.59	0.40	66.84	4.32
Electricity		19.71	17.42	2.29	0.15
Heat	0.36	0	0	0.36	0.02
Total	750.79	1261.55	417.32	1545.67	100.00

Note: Net supply of oil and gas allows for stock and other changes.
Source: IEA (2006, p. II.35).

source of EU energy, and by far the largest part of that oil is imported (figure 17.4).

The trend in energy use shown in figure 17.2 is upward. This trend is expected to continue. Commission projections are that EU energy consumption in 2020 will be 22 per cent greater than EU energy consumption in 1990 (Council of the EU, 2001, p. 46). It is also expected that oil and gas will continue to supply the lion's share of EU energy needs (table 17.2). The share of natural gas is expected to rise (Kemp and Stephen, 2001).

The share of imported energy in overall EU energy use is expected to rise from the current near 50 per cent to 70 per cent (EU15; see table 17.2). The anticipated increasing share of oil imports reflects in part the decline in output of North Sea oil, which peaked in 1999. The rate of decline has been slowed by technological advance, but will continue.

17.5 Current energy policy agenda: single market, environment, security

In the course of the 1980s the agenda for energy policy began to change. Developments in energy markets, the attitudes of governments towards the energy industries and the overall position of the Commission in policymaking contributed to a turnaround in the concerns of EC energy policy. The new agenda rested on two broad objectives: the creation of a competition-oriented internal

Table 17.2 Projected oil and gas consumption, share of imported energy in EU energy consumption, 1998–2030

	Projected share of oil and gas in total EU energy consumption (%)		Projected import dependence (%)	
	EU	EU30	EU	EU30
1998	64	61	49	36
2010	66	63	54	42
2020	66	65	62	51
2030	67	66	71	60

Source: CEC (2001h, p. 67).

energy market and the pursuit of environmental protection (see chapters 13 and 18). Recent events have added to these a third objective, not always consistent with the other two: to promote security of energy supplies.

17.5.1 Internal energy market

A key factor in the changed regime was the shift in energy markets. Prices stabilized and faltered in the early 1980s and continued to weaken until the 1986 oil price collapse. The reasons for this were more fundamental than the rows within OPEC which precipitated the fall in prices. The price increases of the early 1980s had had the effect of boosting output in OPEC countries, as well as fostering exploration and production in the rest of world. Furthermore, many countries had sought to improve energy efficiency and diversify sources of energy (if not to the levels sought by the Commission). The economic recession of the 1980s also dampened demand. The combined effect of these factors was over-capacity in supply and minimal demand growth (see figure 17.2) which forced down prices. The effects were not confined to oil: gas and coal were in equally plentiful supply, while the consequences of past over-investment in electricity capacity also boosted the energy surplus.

The combined effect of these developments was to weaken the scarcity culture which had prevailed among suppliers, consumers, governments and the Commission. As prices fell and markets appeared well supplied, the concerns of policy focused less on energy supply per se and more on the price and the existence of obstacles to good market performance.

This change in market conditions made it difficult to sustain energy policies fostering conservation or diversification from high-price fuels. In some countries, governments abandoned traditional approaches to energy policy. The UK was the most notable example, making an explicit move to rely on market forces for determining supply and demand. A major plank of that policy was deregulation, with attempts to introduce competition to gas and power, and privatization, with the sale of oil interests and then the gas and electricity industries (Helm et al., 1989). Shifts in policy were under review in other parts of the EC (Helm and McGowan, 1989), although these were often conceived at a less ambitious level or pursued for rather different reasons.

The deregulatory thrust was not confined to the energy sector – indeed it was probably initially more widely spread in other areas of the economy. It was, for example, to the fore in the Commission's plans for the single European market (SEM; see chapters 2 and 7) as covered in the White Paper (CEC, 1985a). Partly as a reflection of past energy policy failures, the Commission did not include energy in the initial agenda for the SEM. However, areas where energy was affected

indirectly by more general SEM measures (such as indirect taxation and procurement policies) meant that the sector was not untouched by the proposals.

Indeed, there were already some signs of a different policy towards energy. The issue of price transparency was extended across the energy industries with attempts to agree a directive on the issue. While the moves failed, they indicated a greater interest in the issue by the Commission. The Commission was also taking a greater interest in energy subsidies (as in the case of Dutch support to its horticultural industry through the provision of cheap gas). Other indications of change included moves to tackle state oil monopolies and the types of support given to the coal industry in a number of member states.

The potential for more radical action was indicated by a number of moves taken by the Commission's Competition Directorate towards other 'utility' industries. It sought the introduction of more competitive arrangements in the civil aviation industry and was able to threaten the use of legal powers to this end. In the field of telecommunications, it sought to open access for equipment and service sales, using powers under Article 90 to do so (see chapter 14). These moves demonstrated not only a willingness to act but also a range of mechanisms which could be used in other sectors. The further the policy went in one industry the more likely it would be applied to others.

This changing agenda meant that the idea of an internal energy market (IEM) was once again an issue for the EC. While the 1995 goals were largely flavoured by energy security concerns, one of the 'horizontal' objectives was the creation of an IEM. As the prospect of an SEM became realizable with the '1992' campaign, the idea of extending it to energy took root, and in 1987 the Energy Commissioner, Nicolas Mosar, announced a study of the barriers to an IEM.

The Commission's thinking was revealed in *The Internal Energy Market* (CEC, 1988e), a review which set out the potential benefits of an IEM and the obstacles that faced it. The IEM would cut costs to consumers (particularly to energy-intensive industries), thereby making European industry as a whole more competitive; it would increase security of supply by improving integration of the energy industries; it would rationalize the structure of the energy industries and allow for greater complementarity among the different supply and demand profiles of member states. The benefits would stem from a mixture of cost-reducing competition and the achievement of scale economies in a number of industries. Taken together these would more than recover the 0.5 per cent of EC GDP which the Commission claimed was the 'cost of non-Europe' in the energy sector (although, as noted, energy was not part of the original SEM debate nor of the 'cost of non-Europe' exercise which assessed the benefits of the SEM – see Cecchini (1988), Emerson et al. (1988) and chapter 7).

According to the Commission, the obstacles to the IEM were to be found in the structures and practices of the energy industries. These ranged from different taxation and financial regimes to restrictive measures which protected energy industries in particular countries and conditions which prevented full coordination of supplies at the most efficient level (the latter applying to the gas and electricity industries). However, as the Commission admitted, the effects of particular practices were difficult to assess given the special nature of the energy industries. Indeed, in certain cases, the Commission appeared hesitant over the extent of the IEM. Nonetheless, the document demonstrated that the Commission was committed to implementing an IEM and would examine all barriers to its development. It has followed up that commitment with measures to implement the White Paper proposals (on taxation and procurement) and to apply EC law to the sector.

The historical choice for the organization of electricity and natural gas supply has been the vertically integrated, often publicly owned, regional monopolist, with the regional monopoly covering part or all of the member state concerned. Vertical integration was justified, if it was not simply regarded as the obvious choice, on the grounds that transmission was a natural monopoly (more on this below) and that, particularly in the case of electricity, the precise coordination between supply and demand required to make the system work made integration the only practical option.

The consensus behind the public firm/public utility model unravelled in the 1980s.[1] One contributing factor was the oil shocks of the early and late 1970s, which rendered invalid the projected increases in demand upon which energy-sector capacity plans had been based. Nuclear power also turned out to be more expensive than anticipated. Heightened public awareness of the environmental implications of nuclear and carbon-based power generation effectively internalized some costs that had hitherto been ignored or treated as external in energy-sector planning. In some EU member states, public firms had been directed to alter business behaviour in order to meet policy goals (hold down rates to fight inflation; maintain coal-fired generators to support the coal sector), with the effect of raising costs and, directly or indirectly, imposing burdens on the national budget. While the UK under Margaret Thatcher led the way (Newbery, 1999a, pp. 6–24), the Single European Act (SEA) of 1986 (see chapter 2) inevitably called the position of energy-sector member state monopolists into question. Further, the macroeconomic constraints adopted by the member states in connection with the introduction of the euro created incentives to balance energy-sector operating accounts and get them off government budgets.[2]

The supply-side structures of all industries are shaped by the technologies they employ. However, the impact of the laws of nature on the organization of the electricity industry is distinctive, and only slightly less so on the natural gas industry.

The electricity supply chain can be broken down into generation, transmission, distribution, and retailing (Jamasb and Pollitt, 2005, p. 12; Green, 2006, p. 2533). Transmission takes place over a grid. Electricity cannot be stored in a cost-effective way, and the electrons delivered to the grid by one generator are indistinguishable from those delivered by any other. The physical task of grid management is a daunting one (Green, 2001, p. 330):

Power flows from generators to consumers cannot be directed, but will be distributed along every line in the network, according to physical laws. If too much power attempts to pass along a given line, or through a particular transformer, that component of the network will fail. Following a failure in the network, the power flows will instantaneously redistribute themselves across the remaining circuits. If any of these are now over-loaded, they in turn will fail. Millions of consumers can be blacked out in seconds. To minimize the risk of this, the grid controllers must run the system in such a way that power flows will be within safe limits, not just given the present state of the network, but if any link in it suddenly fails. This implies leaving a margin of spare capacity on every part of the network.

To these physical challenges are added economic challenges. To achieve good economic performance, lower-cost generators should be used before higher-cost generators. The price received by generators should reflect the marginal cost of production, to give proper signals about the nature of maintenance and new capital investment needed for the future. At the same time, price must cover the average cost of suppliers efficient enough to stay in business over the long run. Further, the prices paid by final consumers should reflect the marginal cost of production, to give proper signals about the scarcity of electricity relative to other energy sources and about the overall cost of energy, and thereby to encourage efficient consumption of energy.

These considerations suggest that transmission should be treated as a natural monopoly. In markets of reasonable size – and this includes both the EU and most individual EU member states – electric power generation is not a natural monopoly. Technological progress has made it possible to organize distribution in ways that permit rivalry, if not perfect competition in the classroom sense. The critical element in the introduction of an element of rivalry to distribution is organization of access to the transmission grid, which is an essential facility standing between generation and distribution. Much the same role is played by the pipeline grid in the market for natural gas.

To promote competition where it was technically feasible and effective regulation where it was not feasible, the Commission issued draft directives for the completion of the internal market in electricity and gas in 1992.[3] The Commission sought (Argyris, 1993, p. 34):

to introduce competition in the generation of electricity, the possibility to construct transmission and distribution lines (and the right to hook these up to the network) and third-party access to the network. These three measures effectively eliminate the exclusive rights which currently exist in each of these areas.

The means by which these goals were to be accomplished included (Johnston, 1999):

- a transparent and non-discriminatory system for granting licences for generating stations;
- unbundling the management of and the accounting for production, transmission, and distribution activities of vertically integrated operators;
- third-party access to transmission and distribution facilities.

The question of access to transmission facilities proved to be a thorny one. The Commission first proposed a system of regulated third-party access, under which generators and retail distributors could use the grid to carry out contracts, subject to capacity constraints, at public and regulated rates. The idea of regulated third-party access was criticized by industry groups (Argyris, 1993, p. 39) and in the European Parliament (Hancher, 1997, p. 94). In later proposals, the Commission added the option of *negotiated* third-party access to transmission facilities, under which generators and retail distributors would work out contracts directly and the generator would negotiate the rate to be paid for use of the grid with the grid manager.

At the insistence of France, an insistence that was widely interpreted as reflecting a reluctance to expose Électricité de France to competition, the first Electricity Directive[4] included the Single Buyer model for managing grid access. The Single Buyer model mandated the use of the grid (Whitwill, 2000):

eligible consumers are free . . . to contract with independent (or foreign) suppliers but all energy is supplied through the Single Buyer, which in turn buys electricity from the contracted supplier at the agreed price (less any network access tariffs).

The Single Buyer model evoked considerable discussion. We will not review this discussion in any detail, since in the event the model was not adopted in its pure form by any member state. Most member states opted for regulated third-party access. Germany chose negotiated third-party access. Italy and Portugal chose a combination of regulated third-party access and the Single Buyer model.[5]

Article 19 of the Electricity Directive included a detailed specification of the pace of liberalization. It also included a reciprocity clause: member states could block access to their market of firms from other member states that had liberalized to a lesser degree (Pelkmans, 2001, p. 445, footnote omitted):

> The political background of this provision is the monopoly of Electricité de France (EdF), a fully integrated company, also fully state-owned . . . The reciprocity clause follows from the disparate progress in electricity liberalization among the member states: with a range of countries going faster than the EU calendar . . . the fear was that some countries, but in particular France, would stick to the minimum obligations, and otherwise exploit the many loopholes in the 1996 directives.

As things developed, the reciprocity clause did not have the desired effect of ensuring that market-opening went forward at a comparable rate across member states. EdF made acquisitions in eleven other EU member states, two of the EU candidate countries, and in South America (CEU, 2001c, p. 75), while the French market remained essentially closed to generators located in other member states.

The European Commission returned to the charge in 2003, with the second Electricity[6] and Gas[7] Directives, which seek (Jamasb and Pollitt, 2005, p. 17):

> to achieve, by July 2007 at the latest: (i) unbundling of transmission system operators (TSOs) and distribution system operators (DSOs) from the rest of the industry, (ii) free entry to generation, (iii) monitoring of supply competition, (iv) full market opening, (v) promotion of renewable sources, (vi) strengthening the role of the regulator, and (vii) a single European market.

The Commission's own assessment of progress toward the creation of internal electricity and gas markets is glum: as of November 2005 (CEC, 2005j, p. 2), 'electricity and gas markets remain[ed] national in scope'.[8]

For the Commission, factors contributing to the slow pace of market integration included the lacklustre pace at which member states transposed the directives into national law (CEC, 2005j, p. 4) and (for electricity in particular) constraints on interconnection capacity across member state boundaries (CEC, 2005j, p. 5). The Commission also noted a trend of mergers and increasing horizontal concentration of gas and electricity.[9]

On the one hand, consolidation is to be expected as market size increases and firms seek to take advantage of economies of large-scale operation. Indeed, this is one source of gains from market integration – lower average cost. But if concentration goes too far, more efficient surviving firms may refrain from vigorous competition (Green, 2006, p. 2540):

> The pattern is clear – Europe's larger electricity companies have been growing larger, acquiring footholds in new markets. These footholds could be used to compete aggressively across Europe, but the relatively limited number of really large companies, and the theory of multi-market contact, suggest a more worrying alternative, that the European electricity industry would become dominated by a few firms with little incentive to compete.

17.5.2 The environment

The Commission's interest in environmental issues is not new. The formal commitment of the EC to environmental policy dates from early 1972 when, in the wake of the Stockholm conference, the Council agreed a programme of action, while some measures on environmental problems predated even this initiative (Haigh, 1989). While the Commission's concerns on the environment are very wide-ranging (see chapter 18), covering issues such as chemical waste, water quality and noise pollution, the consequences of energy choices are a major part of the policy.

The importance of EC environmental policy for the energy sector has paralleled the ascent of the issue up the political agenda in an increasing number of member states, particularly as the Greens have become a political force. In those cases where governments have been obliged to introduce new controls on pollution, they have sought to have them accepted across the EC so as not to lose competitiveness. The best example was the acid-rain debate when the German government, forced to introduce major controls on domestic emissions from industrial and electricity plants, pressed for similar controls in all member states (Boehmer-Christiansen and Skea, 1990). These were agreed in 1988, setting targets for emission reduction into the next century.

The emergence of the environment has given the Commission a higher profile in energy matters and another, more robust, lever on energy policy (Owens and Hope, 1989). The importance of the issue to energy policy was demonstrated in the 1995 objectives where environmental concerns were identified as a major consideration in policy. The status of environmental issues overall was confirmed in the SEA where it was given its own provisions (allowing it to enforce decisions on a majority vote). The SEM proposals also identify the need for high standards of environmental protection in the EC and this has impacted on the internal energy market debate.

Integrating environment and energy has not been easy for the Commission; a document on the issue was apparently the focus for considerable dispute within the Commission because of the different perspectives of the Directorates for Energy and for the Environment (CEC, 1989c). However, the issue which has both brought the environment to the centre of Community energy policy-making and exposed the tensions between the two policies most starkly has been the greenhouse effect.

The Commission has sought to coordinate a common European response to the threat of global warming. In 1991 the member states, with the exception of the UK, agreed to stabilize emissions of CO_2 by the year 2000. In the following year it produced proposals for decreasing emissions of greenhouse gases, particularly CO_2 (CEC, 1992c). These comprised four elements: programmes to encourage the development of renewable energy sources (which have zero or very low carbon dioxide emissions) and of energy efficiency, a monitoring system and a carbon-energy tax to discourage the use of fossil fuels.

While much has been achieved by the Commission in incorporating conservation and renewables into a strategy for tackling global warming, the carbon tax has all but been abandoned. The proposed tax consists of two elements, one related to the energy used and the other to the carbon emitted by the fuel in question. The tax therefore penalizes coal use most strongly but not as much as if it were a pure carbon tax. Small renewable-based energy sources are not covered by the proposal. More importantly, large industrial consumers are also exempt from it, and the proposal will not be put into effect unless equivalent steps were undertaken by other industrialized countries (Pearson and Smith, 1991). Despite these conditions, which were included after considerable lobbying of the Commission, the proposal has drawn a good deal of criticism from industries and governments, and, although modifications have been made, the chances of an agreement in the Council appear slim. Subsequent attempts to use taxation as an instrument of environmental policy in the energy sector have also been opposed (Finon and Surrey, 1996).

Although the SEM and the environment have dominated energy policy, the Commission has pursued a variety of other energy policy objectives. It continues with its support for energy efficiency and renewables through research budgets and other measures designed to encourage their use (such as recommendations for preferential terms for renewable sources of supply). It has developed policies for supporting energy infrastructures primarily in less developed areas of the Community, although this goal has been broadened in the light of attempts to increase the integration of gas and electricity supply through the initiative on fostering 'trans-EC networks' (McGowan, 1993).

17.5.3 Security

The security situations regarding crude oil and natural gas supplies are different. The market for crude oil is a world market. Before 1973, it was a large-numbers oligopoly, the most important operators on the supply side being the eight 'Seven Sisters'.[10] The rise of OPEC, itself a large-numbers oligopoly, cut the vertically integrated majors loose from their crude supplies. The majors' distribution networks remained valuable

Table 17.3 World proven crude oil reserves, production by region, 2005

	Production		Proven reserves	
	1,000 b/d	% World total	Million barrels	% World total
Middle East	22,783.6	31.7	742,688	64.4
Latin America	10,206.5	14.2	118,364	10.3
Eastern Europe	11,098.1	15.5	93,660	8.1
Asia and Pacific	7,433.5	10.4	38,439	3.3
North America	6,480.0	9.0	26,071	2.3
Africa	8,856.7	12.3	117,774	10.2
Western Europe	4,904.4	6.8	16,967	1.5
Total world	71,762.9	100.0	1,153,962	
OPEC	30,673.3	42.7	904,255	78.4

Source: OPEC (2005, pp. 10 and 14).

assets, and oil provinces outside OPEC proved only too willing to hire the majors to develop their own oilfields. The majors thus integrated backwards, by ownership or contact, into production, and developed new oil supplies.

As the shares of output and proven reserves outside OPEC control rose, OPEC members learned the hard lesson that a business's most important asset is its customers. OPEC national oil companies integrated forwards into refining and distribution. The world oil market continues to be a large-numbers oligopoly, and the numbers are larger than they were in 1973.

Table 17.3 shows regional data on production and proven reserves of crude oil for the year 2005. Table 17.4 shows similar data for natural gas. The figures for proven reserves should be interpreted with caution, for at least three reasons. The first is that reported figures for proven reserves in the Middle East are widely believed to be understated. The second is that not all proven reserves are created equal: what one would really like, for each region, are not figures for total supply, but rather a kind of cumulative marginal cost curve: how much could be extracted at a cost less than x per barrel (per million BTUs, in the case of natural gas), how much at a price of $x + 1$ per barrel, and so on. The third, related to the second, is that the march of technological progress continually expands the amount of crude oil and natural gas that it is profitable to extract from known oil fields. Even if

no new fields are developed, proven reserves next year are not proven reserves today minus production during the year. Proven reserves next year are proven reserves today, minus production during the year, plus the additional deposits that it becomes profitable to produce from known oilfields as extraction technology improves.[11]

By luck of geology, most of the world's crude oil reserves are located in the Middle East. All evidence is that these deposits are much less costly to extract than oil deposits located elsewhere in the world.

Production of crude oil is much less geographically concentrated than are proven reserves. Middle Eastern producers, more generally OPEC member states, could easily supply most of the world's oil – at a lower price than they would like. By attempting to restrict their own output, OPEC member states (through their national oil companies) set two forces in motion.

First, OPEC as a group creates incentives for each individual OPEC member state, acting in its own immediate interest, to produce more than its OPEC quota output. Indeed, OPEC member states consistently produce more than they have agreed to produce. The interests of the various OPEC member states, not only those in the Middle East and those located elsewhere, but also those located in the Middle East taken as a group, are simply too diverse to expect most OPEC members to pay more than lip-service to agreed output levels.

Table 17.4 World proven natural gas reserves and marketed production, by region, 2005

	Production		Proven reserves	
	Million standard m^3	% World total	Billion standard m^3	% World total
Eastern Europe	821,430	29.0	57,678	32.0
North America	702,153	25.0	7,055	3.9
Asia and Pacific	368,200	13.0	14,825	8.2
Western Europe	292,240	10.3	5,931	3.3
Middle East	306,330	10.8	72,977	40.5
Latin America	174,800	6.2	7,490	4.2
Africa	171,735	6.1	14,283	7.9
Total world	2,836,888	100.0	180,238	100.0
OPEC	498,375	17.6	89,357	49.6

Source: OPEC (2005, pp. 12, 16).

Second, to the extent that OPEC succeeds in raising the price of crude oil, it makes it economic to exploit deposits which would otherwise remain in the ground for decades. This second effect works with long lags, and it is to those lags that OPEC owed the momentary market control it enjoyed in the 1970s. The effects of induced entry are also long-lasting. Given the high ratio of fixed to marginal cost in developing oil fields, and the fact that fixed investments are also largely sunk,[12] once higher-average-cost oilfields come on line they tend to produce as long as price remains above a level of marginal cost that is far lower than average cost.

Thus, from table 17.3, North America's share of world oil production in 2001 was 3.9 times its share of proven oil reserves. Western Europe's share of world oil production in 2001 was 4.5 times its share of proven oil reserves. It would be easy, and simplistic, to conclude that, at 2005 production rates, Western Europe will have completely exhausted its oil supplies in a little less than ten years and North America in eleven, at which point OPEC will have those regions over a barrel. Long before physical supplies are exhausted in the old oil provinces of North America and Western Europe – indeed, long before the world price of crude oil would make it profitable to exhaust those supplies – new oil provinces will come on line. Supplies from those provinces will be available in North America and Western Europe, not out of goodwill but because international trade based on comparative advantage is mutually beneficial.

Neither OPEC nor the core of Middle Eastern OPEC members were able to stop the rise in the price of crude oil to above $70 per barrel in the second week of August 2006, or its fall to under $54 per barrel in the second week of October 2006. Oil-producing states take such advantage as they can of fluctuations in the crude oil market, but they do not control those fluctuations.

The security issue with natural gas is not so much that EU member states import a substantial portion of their natural gas. The security issue is that a good deal of this natural gas is imported from the Russian Federation, a government whose understanding of the market mechanism must at present be held to differ from that of longer-established capitalist countries. The average share of natural gas imports through pipelines originating in the Russian Federation for the EU member states listed in table 17.5 is 37.2 per cent, and for some member states the figure is much higher.

The difficulties inherent in this relationship became clear in January 2006, when the Russian firm Gazprom reduced previously contracted deliveries of natural gas to Ukraine. Nominally, the motive was to impress on Ukraine the reasonableness of agreeing to pay prices closer to world

Table 17.5 Natural gas imports, by pipeline, of selected EU members states from the Russian Federation, 2006 (billion cubic metres)

Imports from Russian Federation		Total Imports
Austria	6.80	8.68
Belgium	0.30	18.92
Czech Republic	7.13	9.48
Finland	4.20	4.20
France	11.50	36.20
Germany	36.54	90.70
Greece	2.40	2.40
Hungary	8.32	10.82
Ireland	–	3.05
Italy	23.33	70.99
Latvia	1.75	1.75
Lithuania	2.93	2.93
Luxembourg	–	1.40
Netherlands	2.97	17.58
Poland	6.40	10.21
Portugal	–	2.62
Slovakia	6.40	6.40
Slovenia	0.56	1.10
Spain	–	11.59
Sweden	–	1.03
United Kingdom	–	14.65
Total	121.53	326.7

Source: British Petroleum (2006).

market levels. It was widely believed that Russian government displeasure over Ukraine's political shift toward the West also played a role in the interruption of natural gas supplies. Be that as it may, the bulk of EU natural gas imports from the Russian Federation passes through Ukraine, and the Russian action disrupted deliveries to major EU customers as well as to Ukraine.

The Commission has sought to develop a role in the traditionally difficult area of security of supply. It is largely for securing supplies that an increasingly important part of the Community's energy policy activities concern links with the rest of the world. These are focused on immediate neighbours to the north, east and south of the EU. The principal element of these links has been its efforts to draw Eastern Europe into secure energy links through the European Energy Charter (Council of the European Communities, 1989b). This was the initiative of the Dutch Prime Minister, Ruud Lubbers, who sought to use an agreement on energy, symbolically echoing the ECSC in ending the Cold War, and, more importantly, acting as a framework for closer energy links between the Community and the East. An agreement on a basic charter was reached at the end of 1991 and an Energy Charter Treaty signed at the end of 1994 (see Sodupe and Benito, 2001). The Energy Charter Treaty and the protocol on energy efficiency and related environmental aspects became effective on 16 April 1998, although France and Ireland did not ratify it until 1999.

Since that time, the EU has sought Russian adherence to the principles of the Energy Charter Treaty. In an October 2006 meeting with leaders of EU member states, Russian President Vladimir Putin once again declined to sign the Treaty.

Community and member state concern to diversify energy sources will no doubt continue. In the short run, pursuit of secure supplies may conflict with environmental concerns.[13]

Environment concerns are present in the June 2005 Green Paper, *Energy Efficiency or Doing More with Less* (CEC, 2005i), but the emphasis is clearly on demand-side measures to improve energy security. The measures suggested are sensible enough – structuring support for R&D to promote the development of energy-efficiency technologies, ensuring that state aid is not misused, and providing better information to consumers, among others. But the fundamental problem, which is recognized in the Green Paper (p. 13), is that energy prices do not include the external costs of patterns of energy use that are socially inefficient. The most direct way to address this fundamental problem, also recognized in the Green Paper (p. 16), is to use the tax system so that the prices individuals and firms see when they make consumption and investment decisions reflect full social costs. By and large, however, decisions in this area remain with the member states.

It is not surprising, therefore, that the March 2006 Green Paper, *A European Strategy for Sustainable, Competitive and Secure Energy* (CEC, 2006v) emphasizes (p. 4) the need for 'a common European response' to the energy situation. Here again, what is highlighted is security of supplies (De Vos, 2006). The measures mentioned by the Commission are at once strengths and weaknesses. Completing the internal electricity and gas markets, promoting interconnection, ensuring non-discriminatory grid access, and the like are all steps that will promote efficient energy use. They are also all measures that will increase competitive pressure on (possibly former) national champions, who can be expected to turn to their home governments for relief.

The Commission also notes the advantages of having the EU speak with one voice to its external energy suppliers (CEC, 2006v, p. 15):

The EU has an established pattern of relations with major international energy suppliers including OPEC and the Gulf Cooperation Council. *A new initiative is particularly opportune with regard to Russia*, the EU's most important energy supplier. The EU, as Russia's largest energy buyer, is an essential and equal partner in this relationship. The development of a common external energy policy should mark a step change in this energy partnership at both Community and national level. A true partnership would offer security and predictability for both sides, paving the way for the necessary long-term investments in new capacity. It would also mean fair and reciprocal access to markets and infrastructure including in particular third party access to pipelines. Work should start on an energy initiative based on these principles.

The Russian response to overtures along these lines at the October 2006 Finland meeting with EU leaders does not augur well for the establishment of such a 'true partnership'.

17.6 Conclusion

The European Union will increasingly rely on sources of primary energy located outside its borders. Efficient energy use, the development of alternative energy sources, and the geographic diversification of sources of supply can ensure long-run energy security. Strategic reserves are a way to insure against short-run disruptions of primary energy supplies.

Market integration is a process that brings short-run adjustment costs and promises long-run benefits. EU energy-sector integration will bring greater

efficiency and reduced costs for what is an essential input to virtually all EU economic activity. The long-run benefits of energy-sector integration are immense. Political pressures rooted in the short-run adjustment costs that come with market integration slow the process down. Commission proposals for energy integration date to 1992; full freedom of choice of supplier is coming into effect in 2007. The realization of the internal energy market will come after that. The internal EU energy market is not yet complete; that it will be completed is not in doubt.

NOTES

1 See Doyle and Siner (1999, pp. 1–3); Newbery (1999a, chapter 1); Johnston (1999).
2 It is also fair to note that the one-off injections of cash resulting from privatization were a welcome element to member state governments.
3 CEC (1991d), Argyris (1993, p. 34). The Transit Directive of 1990, Council Directive 90/547/EEC, 29 October 1990, sought to promote the construction of electricity and gas networks linking member state networks, a matter that remains on the front burner.
4 EC Directive 96/92 concerning common rules for the internal market in electricity. OJ L 27/20, 30 January 1997, adopted 19 December 1996, with effect from 19 February 1997 (and with delays for Belgium, Ireland, and Greece). The first Gas Directive was EC Directive 98/30 concerning common rules for the internal market in natural gas OJ L 207 21 July 1998, adopted 22 June 1998 and with effect from 10 August 1998.
5 On the Italian case, see Valbonesi (1998).
6 Directive 2003/54/EC of the European Parliament and of the Council of 26 June 2003 concerning common rules for the internal market in electricity and repealing Directive 96/92/EC OJ L 176, 15 July 2003, pp. 37–56.
7 Directive 2003/55/EC of 26 June 2003 concerning common rules for the internal market in natural gas and repealing Directive 98/30/EC.
8 See also European Commission press release IP/05/1421 of 15 November 2005, 'Energy: Member States must do more to open markets; competition inquiry identifies serious malfunctions.'
9 For details of gas and electricity mergers, see Codognet et al. (2002), Green (2006).
10 Five US-based firms (Exxon, Gulf, Texaco, Mobil, Socal), plus British Petroleum, Royal Dutch/Shell and

Compagnie Française des Petroles (later Total and later still TotalFinaElf).

11 Thus table 17.3 shows proven reserves outside OPEC control in 2005 of 249,707 million barrels. In 1970, world proven reserves were 548,452 million barrels, of which OPEC held 72.8 per cent; proven reserves outside OPEC control were 149,707 million barrels. Despite thirty-five years of consumption, OPEC and non-OPEC nations have substantially more proven reserves in 2005 than they acknowledged in 1970.

Similarly, in 1970 there were 28,739 billion standard cubic metres of proven gas reserves outside OPEC control, versus 90,437 in 2005.

12 Literally as well as financially.

13 It is worth noting that in responses to the energy situation at the national level, some member states are turning to coal as a primary energy source for electricity generation. Some of the planned coal-fired power stations will be carbon-free, many more will not.

18 Environmental policy

ALAN MARIN

18.1 Background

For a long time, it was not clear whether there was any legitimate basis at all for an EU policy on the environment. In the 1950s there was no influential generalized concern for the environment. Occasionally, a particularly harmful episode of pollution would give rise to remedial action to deal with the specific problem, but no more. For example, in the winter of 1952–3 there was an even denser than usual smog in London, leading to a dramatic increase in mortality among the elderly and bronchitic. As a result, new laws were introduced to allow the control of domestic coal fires. But the episode did not lead to a more widespread concern with air pollution generally. The same attitude was prevalent in other countries. Hence, the Treaty of Rome made no provision for any joint EU policy on controlling pollution, let alone more general environmental conservation. By the end of the 1960s, however, a new attitude had become widespread, leading to demands for new policies. Noticeable numbers of people in Western Europe had begun to express concern over the degradation of the environment.

Various groups had an effect on EU environmental policy, especially where they gave a stronger crusading force to the aspects of environmental concern which had most influence on policy. Some were the groups which stressed ecology and preservation. It is not simply that they have eventually succeeded in getting enough votes to have some Green Party members in the European Parliament, as well as representatives at national and lower levels; some national governments felt obliged to be seen to be responsive to public opinion on envi-ronmental issues, in order to try to keep the Greens from gaining enough seats to be a threat to government majorities. These governments, initially primarily the Germans and Dutch, have an extra incentive to support EU environmental policies (the Greens have since attracted enough votes to be part of a German governing coalition).

The areas which seem to be of general concern to the wider public (and where the Green movements have sometimes provided the impetus) are partly the preservation of natural amenity and wildlife, and, more importantly for EU policy, pollution. The change from 1957 is that pollution is seen to be a general, ongoing problem. Concern may still be heightened by particularly harmful and/or well-publicized cases, but it is now considered that action should not be limited to reacting to such cases but should be introduced to control harm before blatantly dangerous situations occur. Even uncertain but potential harm is to be controlled, according to the 'precautionary principle'. Perhaps the highest-profile example recently is the EU attempt to reduce emissions of greenhouse gases.

As a result of the changes in attitudes, in October 1972 the heads of government (prompted by a Commission report) called for an EU environmental programme, which led to the approval in November 1973 of the First Environmental Programme 1973–8.[1] This has been followed by subsequent programmes, the current one being the Sixth Environmental Action Programme. Under the title *Our Future Our Choice*, it was passed in July 2002 for a period of ten years.

The official basis for actions that were clearly not foreseen in the Treaty of Rome was twofold. First, a few of the types of pollution could result from the use of goods: for example, noise and exhaust emissions from vehicles, the packaging and labelling of solvents or the foaming and biodegradability of detergents. In these cases, joint EU standards could clearly be justified as part of product harmonization to prevent different national standards acting as non-tariff barriers to inter-state trade.[2] However, many of the directives concerned types of pollution and environmental standards that could not constitute a hindrance to inter-state trade on any reasonable criterion, such as the quality of bathing (i.e. swimming) water, the hunting of wild birds or some aspects of waste disposal.

The second basis claimed for EC environmental policies would justify joint policies even where trade is unaffected. Article 2 of the Treaty of Rome stated that 'The Community shall . . . promote throughout the Community a harmonious development of economic activities, a continuous and balanced expansion . . . an accelerated raising of the standard to living.' It was claimed that measures to protect the environment could be considered to further a balanced expansion and raised standard of living, given the importance now attached to the environment by public opinion and the extent to which people's sense of well-being was threatened by pollution and environmental degradation.

For some years there was doubt as to whether there really was a legal basis for issuing directives in this area. However, no court challenge was ever mounted to the Community's right to make decisions on the environment; and it is now beyond dispute. In 1986, Articles 174–6 were inserted by the Single European Act (SEA). (Consolidated Treaty numbering of Articles will be used in this chapter, unless specifically noted otherwise.) These Articles are explicitly devoted to the environment; see chapter 2 for more on this and other developments. Furthermore, according to Article 95, actions taken to further the 'completion of the internal market' are supposed to take as their basis a high level of environmental protection. In addition, allowance is made for individual member states to set higher environmental standards, provided that these do not constitute barriers to trade – though the acceptable boundaries can be contentious.[3]

Whatever the initial legality of EU directives on issues affecting the environment, there still remains the question of why the governments of the member states wanted *joint* policies at all on those aspects where individual national policies would not be a barrier to trade and where transfrontier flows of pollution were not a problem. (As already indicated, the small group which could lead to barriers could be dealt with under the procedures on product harmonization.) It is never possible to be completely sure what is in people's minds, but discussions at the time and subsequently suggest two primary motivations.

First, EU leaders often stressed that it was important that, if there were to be public support for the European ideal, the EU should be identified in the minds of the public with issues which concerned them. It should not be thought to be limited to 'boring' technical issues, whether product standard harmonization or the minutiae of calculating transport costs between Rotterdam and Duisburg. Joint EC policies on an issue which had recently become the focus of much media discussion and campaigning would help to convince the public that the Community was relevant to them and responsive to their worries.

Second, it was clear to governments in member states that they would have to respond to public pressures over pollution and environmental preservation. As already mentioned, this was especially true of the German and Dutch governments among the original Six, but the others were not immune. Many of the measures were likely to raise production costs. For example, firms would have to install new equipment rather than just pouring noxious waste into rivers or sewers, or would have to buy the more expensive low-sulphur fuels to limit emissions of sulphur dioxide. If some countries were to have tighter standards than others, then their firms would face 'unfair competition' from firms that had lower production costs just because they were located in countries that had laxer requirements on pollution abatement.[4] Uniform emission standards (referred to as UES in the literature) would prevent this threat to competitiveness, hence the desire of governments for joint EU environmental policies which would affect all member states equally.

18.2 Economic (or economists') assessment of environmental policies

In order to judge the appropriateness of EU environmental policies, it is necessary to have criteria. The criteria used elsewhere in this book are primarily (although not exclusively) those of standard neoclassical welfare economics.

For the policies examined in this chapter, equity – at least in terms of income distribution – has not been a major consideration.[5] However, it is worth noting that one difference between the approach of many environmentalists and that of many economists is related to the standard assumptions of welfare economics. Economists tend to judge policies and institutions by their effects on the welfare of individuals.[6] Environmentalists, however, often feel that some things are worthwhile even if no humans are affected. They place a value on the diversity of natural habitats and the continuation of species, even where there is no benefit to humans. By their training, many (although not all) economists are resistant to such a view.[7]

There have been few binding EU policies which deal with protection of species per se.[8] One exception was a 1979 directive on the conservation of wild birds, augmented by a 1992 directive on habitat protection and a 1999 directive on zoos, the purpose of which is to protect wild fauna and conserve biodiversity. The Habitat Directive is supposed to lead to a wider network of conservation sites, known as the Natura 2000 programme, but progress has been slow, with many member states minimizing their designation. Some have argued that the directives on water quality for rivers and estuaries containing fish or shellfish are not just to protect human health, but also to protect the fish per se. Another limited exception is the 1985 (amended 1997) directive requiring an environmental impact assessment before certain large development projects are undertaken. This exception is limited, both because the types of project requiring the assessment are largely left to national governments and because, once the assessment has been made, there is no requirement for any particular weighting to be given to adverse environmental effects in deciding whether the project should proceed. There are also EU directives concerning other endangered species (e.g. seals and whales), but, although motivated by environmental concerns (and repugnance at the methods of killing seal pups), these formally deal with trade in the products of the species – often as a result of international agreements.

18.2.1 Externalities

Most of the EU environmental policies have concerned pollution. For economists, pollution is a problem that cannot be solved by the market mechanism because it is an externality. Indeed, most textbooks on microeconomics use pollution as the classic example of an externality (see box 18.1).

There are two diagrams which are often used to analyse the problem of pollution and to indicate possible policy solutions. The first concentrates on the divergence between social and private costs, usually in the context of a competitive industry which causes pollution during the production of some good. In figure 18.1 the supply curve of the industry is, as always, equal to the sum of the marginal (private) costs (MPC) of the firms. Given the demand curve, Q_0 is produced and sold at a price of P_0. This is not optimal. If the pollution emitted during production is allowed for, the true sum of marginal social costs for the firms is given by MSC, and the optimal output is where P = MSC, i.e. at Q_1 and P_1.

Figure 18.1 has the advantage of stressing that part of the result of pollution is that the price to consumers is too low, and therefore consumption is too high. Conversely, any policy to achieve efficiency will involve a higher price and less output and consumption. It is therefore not surprising that both employers and trade unions in the industries affected are sometimes among those opposing particular EU policies to control pollution. Nor is it surprising that, in some countries of the EU, the importance attached to environmental policies declined in the second half of the 1970s and early 1980s, while the same was even true of Germany in the mid-1990s. The rise in unemployment led to more stress on the reduction in output that might result from pollution control measures: an example of the more general

Box 18.1 Externalities

One way of viewing externalities is that they occur when the actions taken by one economic agent (individual or firm) affect others, but where there is no feedback mechanism leading the agent to take correct account of the effects on others. It is not the existence of an effect on others that constitutes an externality, but the lack of incentive to take full account of it. Every economic action may affect others, but in a well-functioning system the price mechanism provides incentives to take account of the effects.

For example, when deciding whether to drive my car to the shops or walk, in reaching my decision I use my car only if the benefit is greater than the price I have to pay for the petrol. If the price equals the marginal cost (the usual criterion for Pareto optimality), then I will use my car only if the benefit is greater than the cost to society of the scarce resources used up in providing me with the petrol. Hence the price system provides me with the correct incentive to take account of the effects of my action (driving my car) on others (using up scarce resources, which are therefore not available to provide somebody else with that petrol). However, if the use of my car pollutes the air and causes annoyance, or more serious harm, to others, there is no incentive for me to allow for this. I could be said to be using up another scarce resource (quiet and clean air), but I do not have to pay for it. Hence, there will be times when I use my car even though the benefit to me is less than the true cost to society, i.e. the sum of the costs of which I take account (the petrol) plus those of which I do not (the pollution); the result is therefore not optimal. Thus another, exactly equivalent, way of expressing an externality is to define it as when the marginal private cost is not equal to the marginal social cost.

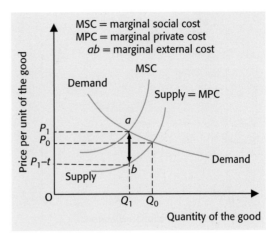

Figure 18.1 Social and private costs of pollution

goods (even allowing for the 'consumption' of 'bads' involved in pollution).[9]

As a means of analysing policies to control pollution, figure 18.1 has the disadvantage of neither explicitly showing what happens to pollution nor showing whether pollution can be reduced by means other than a drop in production of the final output of the industry. For these reasons, an alternative diagram is now often used, which draws attention to these aspects, although it has the disadvantage that the implications of figure 18.1 to which we have drawn attention are left implicit, and may therefore be inadvertently downplayed.

In figure 18.2, the pollution is measured explicitly. For convenience, we have drawn the diagram with the abscissa measuring pollution abatement from the level that would occur with no policy controls. Some authors use pollution emissions instead. This is equivalent to figure 18.2 working leftwards from the 100 per cent abatement (zero remaining pollution) point. The diagram shows the abatement of some particular form of pollution for some particular industry. The marginal benefits (MB) of pollution abatement are the avoidance of the external costs placed on others – health, loss of amenity, etc. The marginal costs (MC) of pollution abatement to the firms in the industry are the costs associated with various abatement techniques, such as the treatment plant for noxious effluents in our earlier example,

point that if displaced workers are not confident of finding alternative jobs easily, then employment becomes an aim in its own right and policies are not judged solely by the total consumption of

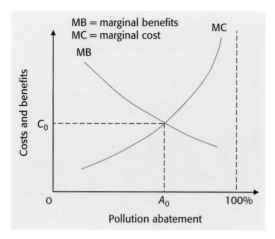

Figure 18.2 Costs and benefits of pollution abatement

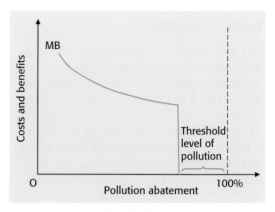

Figure 18.3 Pollution threshold

as well as the loss of profits if emissions are reduced by cutting back on the level of output of the final product sold. The approach in figure 18.2 draws explicit attention to the possibilities of using other resources (labour, capital) to reduce emissions (unlike figure 18.1 which is drawn on the assumption that the externalities associated with each level of output are fixed).

The shapes of the MB and MC curves in figure 18.2 follow from what is known for many types of pollution – some abatement is often easy but, when 95 per cent of potential emissions have already been removed, removal of the remaining 5 per cent is usually much more expensive. On the benefit side, the marginal curve is usually drawn downward-sloping, although the justification is less well founded and there may be some forms of pollution (especially affecting amenity) where the downward slope is not correct; for example, once a line of pylons has been put over a previously unspoiled mountain range, any further developments do less marginal harm. However, most of the EU pollution policies deal with worries about the effects of pollution on human health, and for this the downward MB curve is usually reasonable (as it is for the policies on sulphur dioxide and some car exhaust emissions where the motivation is also partly human, partly the effects on forests). In some cases it is suspected that there may be thresholds of pollution below which the body can cope, but above which harm may start. In these

cases, the MB curve may have the shape shown in figure 18.3.

Returning to the more general case of figure 18.2, one important implication of this way of analysing pollution is that there is an optimum level of pollution. Except in very special cases, it is not optimal to aim for the complete elimination of pollution.[10] Less than 100 per cent abatement is desirable. The optimum level, which maximizes welfare, is where the MC of further abatement just equals the MB, level A_0 in figure 18.2. This is an implication of the economists' approach which is uncongenial to some in the Green movement.

On the whole, EU policies have followed the economists' approach. In the early years of EU action there were some clashes. The United Kingdom, in particular, advocated its traditional policies, summed up in such expressions as 'best *practicable* means' of pollution control. The notion of 'practicable' involves a weighing up of costs and benefits – although this balancing seems to be implicit rather than explicit and to rely on the intuition of the relevant inspectorates. The UK feared that at times the other member states were proposing the approach of best *available* technology, i.e. pushing as far as technically feasible towards 100 per cent abatement, irrespective of costs. Ultimately, although some directives still mentioned that best available technology should be adopted, there was no time limit set for adoption, or else the phrase was qualified by saying that the adoption should be provided if it did 'not entail excessive cost' – which reduces it to practicable – or else some other let-out was included. It is actually doubtful that the other states were completely unconcerned with costs. In reality, the apparent disagreements seem to have been rather over how much abatement was desirable, with the other countries saying that the UK tended to overestimate the costs of abatement, to underestimate the benefits and urgency of reductions in pollution, and often to claim that more evidence was needed before action should be taken. One example is the UK position on sulphur dioxide, where for a long time the UK delayed reductions, partly because of claims that the evidence failed to show that UK emissions contributed significantly to forest damage elsewhere in West Europe.

The 'Environment' title inserted by the SEA specifically refers to the need to take account of 'the potential benefits and costs of action or lack of action' (Article 174(3)). From the other side, in an attempt to appear to bridge the gap, at least superficially, UK legislation has now adopted the principle of 'BATNEEC', which stands for 'best available technology not entailing excessive cost'. But the 'NEEC' implies that there has been no real change.

18.2.2 Control of pollution by regulations or taxes

If the problem is that of externality, the 'obvious' solution seems to be to 'internalize the externality'. It is often suggested that an implication of the economists' analysis is that polluters should pay a tax equal to the external costs imposed on others. In figure 18.2, if a tax equal to C_0 were levied for each unit of pollution emitted, firms would abate up to level A_0. At abatement levels less than A_0, it is less costly for them to abate than to pay a tax of C_0. From A_0 onwards, the marginal cost of further abatement is higher than the tax; hence it will be more profitable to continue to pollute and pay the tax. A tax will therefore achieve the optimum. The idea of controlling pollution by taxation rather than by quantitative regulations imposed on firms also seems to fit economists' predilection for relying on price (here the 'price' of using up clean air, etc.) rather

than on quantitative controls. The latter are supposed to require information rarely possessed by the central authorities.

In the early 1990s it became popular to argue that there is another advantage of taxes to control pollution. This argument is often called the 'double dividend' advantage. The first 'dividend' is the benefit from the reduction in pollution that is induced by the tax. The second 'dividend' is that the revenue from the pollution taxes can be used to reduce other taxes that are themselves distortionary from a welfare economics viewpoint, e.g. income tax (distorting the choice between working and leisure) or employers' taxes (distorting labour demand choices).[11] An alternative piece of jargon was that pollution taxes were thus 'win-win'.

A particularly strong version of the 'double dividend' was sometimes advocated: because of the second dividend, a pollution tax would be desirable even if it turned out there were no net benefits to reducing the pollution per se. For example, at the time of the proposed EU carbon tax discussed below, there was some residual scepticism over whether global warming would occur and, even if it did, whether the results would be harmful enough to justify the sacrifices required to have a noticeable effect on the warming. Some of the statements in favour of the carbon tax said that even if the doubts were eventually proved correct, the tax would still be worthwhile because of the second dividend from the use of the revenue. However, the double-dividend argument came under attack from other economists and the strong version is not now accepted (see box 18.2).

Despite the common view that analyses such as figure 18.2 show the desirability of controlling pollution by taxes, even if we abstract from the second 'dividend' of the use of the revenue,[12] and that all (respectable?) economists agree, there is a serious flaw in the argument.[13] To achieve the optimum level of pollution, a government needs to know the size of the correct tax, C_0. But to know C_0 requires knowing the marginal costs and benefits of abatement, and where the curves intersect. But this information is the same as is required to know, and directly to impose, A_0. Hence a government that can achieve optimality via taxes can achieve it via regulation as well.

Box 18.2 Doubts about the double dividend

The essence of the attack is that the idea of the double dividend inherently relies on a 'second-best' world' with existing distortions, in addition to the distortion of possibly uncorrected externalities. However, the existing distortions are likely to mean that there is too little paid work (too much leisure) because of taxes that impinge on labour supply and demand. Any imposition of a pollution tax will raise the price of some products (whose output or use involves the pollution), and thus further reduce the real return to working. This increased disincentive to employment will reduce welfare. It is quite possible to find situations where this latter effect could outweigh the second dividend of using the revenue to reduce distortionary taxes; thus pollution taxes would reduce welfare if there is no 'first dividend' and possibly reduce it even if there is a 'first dividend'. Another way of putting this is that, because of existing distortions, there is too little of most goods being produced, including too little of some goods which also cause pollution.

As often in 'second-best' analyses, all sorts of things could happen, depending on particular combinations of substitution/complementarity links. However, there is probably a consensus that in many of the cases investigated, both theoretically and empirically, the following results are typical:

1. If the question is whether a particular level of pollution emissions should be reached via quantitative regulations or taxes, the second dividend of using the tax revenue to reduce other distortionary taxes is a reason for pollution taxes rather than regulation.
2. When there are other distortionary taxes, the optimum level of pollution taxation is higher when the revenue is used to reduce those distortionary taxes than when the revenue is used in a lump-sum way.
3. Even if the revenue is used to reduce other taxes, the optimum level of a pollution tax is often lower in a second-best world of distortionary taxes than the level of the Pigovian tax (P = MSC, or MB = MC of abatement) that would result if there were no other distortions in the economy; but this optimal level is still often positive (i.e. some abatement is desirable) if there are benefits to the abatement.
4. The strong double-dividend argument is generally wrong, i.e. if there are no net benefits at all from 'pollution' abatement, then the second dividend does not give a valid reason to impose a 'pollution' tax.

Although it is easy to draw diagrams for hypothetical cases of unspecified pollutants and industries, to estimate reliable MB and MC curves quantitatively in real-life cases is much more difficult.[14] Very often the MB curves are little more than guesses. There is a two-stage problem:

1. working out the physical relationship between different levels of the pollutant and harm (the dose–response relationship);
2. putting a monetary valuation on the harm.

It is not just the economic problem of the latter stage – although that is often contentious enough – but that scientists usually have only sketchy and controversial evidence on the first stage, i.e. the way that the damage changes with different levels of the pollutant. The experts sometimes disagree over whether a substance is harmful at all, and often disagree over whether there is a safe threshold or whether even the minutest dose has some small chance of doing some harm to somebody: for example, whether there are any safe levels of lead absorption or nuclear radiation.

As a result, the target level of pollution – often called the 'standard' in the EU literature – is often at best a very rough guess. However, perhaps surprisingly, once it is accepted that the aim is not an optimal level of pollution, there is then a strong argument for achieving the fairly arbitrary standard by the use of taxes, rather than by simply telling all firms contributing to the pollution to abate by some particular percentage, or telling all firms that they can each emit only some particular amount of pollution. The reason is that typically some polluters have lower abatement costs than others. To minimize the costs of achieving any given arbitrary level of aggregate abatement, more of the abatement should be done by firms which can abate more cheaply. Normally, the abatement should be spread between firms in such a way that the *marginal* cost of abatement is equal for each firm. But the argument given above regarding how firms will react to a pollution tax shows that, in response to a given tax, each firm will abate up to the point where the tax equals its marginal cost of abatement. Since each firm faces the same tax, they will all end up where they have equal marginal costs of abatement. Hence taxes will minimize the cost of abatement.

Despite this cost-minimization argument, until recently pollution taxes have not been used very much in most EU countries, although recently their use has been increasing somewhat (Denmark is probably the EU country that uses them most).[15] Among the exceptions was the reduced tax in some countries on lead-free petrol compared with leaded petrol, during the period when both were available. In terms of figure 18.1, a tax differential of $t (= P_1 - (P_1 - t))$ was imposed on petrol containing lead.[16] In many of those cases where pollution charges are used in the EU they are part of a package of measures, not the sole instrument. For example, in the UK Climate Change Levy, firms which meet particular emissions reductions receive a discount of 80 per cent. However, the EU itself has tried taking pollution taxes more seriously. In 1989 the Council of Environmental Ministers requested the Commission to draft proposals on environmental taxation. Specific proposals by the Commission emerged with the debate on global warming, and the need to reduce emissions of carbon dioxide[17] (see box 18.3). Currently, EU directives merely 'encourage' member states to use environmental taxes.

Some interesting economic issues are raised by the account in box 18.3. One is the justification for the non-carbon part of the energy tax. The Commission mentioned the encouragement of energy efficiency. This is only justifiable if there are other externalities from using energy, which

> **Box 18.3** The EU energy tax: proposal and failure
>
> In 1991 the Commission proposed an energy tax in two parts: one related to the carbon content of fossil fuels and the other on all non-renewable energy. Thus, for example, nuclear power might be taxed at a rate which would be about half that levied on electricity from oil-burning power stations. The proposal also allowed for possible exemptions for some industries which are particularly energy-intensive, such as steel, in order to preserve international competitiveness – such exemptions could be removed if other competitor countries agreed to tax such industries in a similar way.
>
> The proposals aroused considerable opposition, especially from fuel producers and industrial groups. The result was that the Commission effectively agreed to make implementation contingent on the acceptance of carbon taxes in the major competitors, especially Japan and the United States. At the Earth Summit in Rio de Janeiro in June 1992, US opposition ensured that no binding international agreement was reached on controlling carbon dioxide emissions (at that time the US government claimed that lack of evidence on carbon dioxide emissions and global warming meant that the costs of controlling the emissions were unjustified – a position it later modified, then returned to under President Bush). As a result, the Commission did not push its energy tax proposal with much urgency, and the Council could not come to an agreement on it. Eventually, UK refusal to agree to directives which could be seen as giving the EU power over member states' taxation forced the abandonment of any EU-wide carbon tax, irrespective of its other merits. The Commission put forward new energy tax proposals in 1997, but no action was taken, and is unlikely to be taken given the new policies discussed in box 18.4.

are not fuel-specific and which cannot be taxed directly; but the case was not made. It is probable that the aim was really to avoid substitution by nuclear power, because of its own risks, but that it was considered politically more acceptable to achieve this as part of a new tax ostensibly aimed at global warming rather than as a control of nuclear power in its own right. The general economic issue is the interrelatedness of environmental impacts – as with any other aspect of resource allocation (e.g. the double dividend discussed above), affecting one input or output will have repercussions on others, and an overly partial analysis will miss these interconnections. The EU explicitly attempts to deal with such interrelatedness by its 1996 directive (96/61) on Integrated Pollution Prevention and Control, which is applicable to some heavily polluting installations.

18.2.3 Competitiveness and pollution policy

Another issue raised by the EU energy tax proposals is that of international competitiveness and distortion of trade, as exemplified both by the initial exemptions on energy-intensive industries and by the reluctance to impose carbon-content taxes unless competitor nations do the same. From an economic efficiency perspective, it is precisely the most energy-intensive industries that should either be induced to substitute other inputs for energy usage or else raise their prices and cut back production the most, as they are the heavy users of a resource which is now considered to have a high social cost. As seen in figure 18.1, the relative prices of their products should rise and their outputs should therefore fall. Furthermore, if there are any possibilities for a move away from energy use in production, then the cost-minimization argument implies that they should not be exempt from the tax, at least at the margin.[18]

The reluctance to impose any carbon-related tax unless other countries do so confuses a valid and an invalid argument. Since the benefits of any reduction in carbon dioxide emissions in the EU would accrue globally, it is reasonable to argue that the EU should not abate at all unless other countries do the same – it is a classic free-rider problem, since the pollution is a public 'bad' at the global level. This was the reason for the subsequent international Kyoto Agreement, and why some people have objected to the EU and other countries going ahead without US participation. However, if other countries were to agree to cut back their emissions, but decide to do so by means other than economic incentives, this should not affect the EU's decision on using taxes. For any cutback that the EU wishes to achieve, it will be better off if it achieves that cutback at the minimum cost – precisely the argument in favour of pollution taxes. As always in arguments over international trade, there is a conflict between the employment impacts of changes that alter the pattern of production, and the efficient allocation once employment has adjusted to the new pattern.[19]

The issue of competitiveness returns us to the underlying justification of having any *joint* EU policy at all. As already mentioned, a major (in my judgment, *the* major) reason was because otherwise some member states might suffer a loss of competitiveness vis-à-vis other member states with laxer controls on pollution. This was, and is, considered to be unfair, or distorted, competition.

Although the avoidance of 'unfair' competition (and subsequent loss of sales and employment) has always been a fundamental EU principle (e.g. Articles 87–8), standard economic analysis generally implies that this principle may be unnecessary. In the case of imposing uniformity of environmental standards, it may even reduce social welfare in the long run.

Left to themselves, different countries may well want different levels of environmental purity and exposure to pollutants. These choices could result from differences in culture, 'tastes' or income levels. For example, it might be expected that those with a higher level of income will demand (and be prepared to pay more for) higher levels of amenity and health.

Living standards fully defined will comprise both goods and services bought by individuals and also those provided publicly but not paid for by individual consumers. The latter include environmental quality. At any given level of national productivity and resources (i.e. a given production possibility frontier; see chapter 6), if more publicly provided goods are consumed then fewer privately purchased ones can be consumed, and vice versa. Conventional measures of net real wages and real personal incomes only account for privately purchased consumption possibilities. Thus if a country wishes to have a higher standard of environmental quality, the level of real wages (*as conventionally measured*) will have to be below that possible with lower environmental standards.

If a country raises its environmental standards, one path that could lead to the fall in real wages is that, at initial levels of wages, but with higher costs of meeting the more stringent pollution controls, firms will try to raise prices and thus become uncompetitive. They would then have to lay off workers.[20] As unemployment begins to rise, wage reductions will be needed to restore full employment. Wage cuts will enable firms to cut prices and to compete again. The final equilibrium will be one of full employment and capacity output. Although there will be lower real incomes than initially when defined only in terms of privately purchased goods, there should be higher living standards when these are viewed as including the enjoyment of environmental amenities and reduced pollution.

Since not all industries pollute equally, a country which wants less pollution will also need an industrial structure which comprises less production in industries which are heavily polluting per unit value of output, and more of its production in industries which emit less pollution. Again, a path by which the reallocation could occur would be the changes in relative prices of goods that result from the more heavily polluting industries being unprofitable at the initial prices (plus more stringent pollution controls), as well as the direct closing down of some of the now uncompetitive polluting firms. In order for those who were employed in the more heavily polluting industries to be deployed into other industries, their wages may have to fall, which should happen as a reaction to their temporary unemployment.

In the process just outlined, the interim period of 'unfair competition' is part of the market mechanism leading to the correct result. The problem is that if (as some believe) wages in EU countries are rigid downwards even in the face of protracted high unemployment, the unemployment may last a long time, together with its attendant social and economic troubles;[21] hence the pressure for common EU emission standards.

The analysis in this section applies both to the issue of unfair or distorted competition between EU states and to international competitiveness between the EU as a whole and the rest of the world. As indicated, the problems arise because the 'short run' during which wages would be too high, and thus unemployment also high, might last a long time. The long-run result of differing national environmental standards (where each country chooses the levels that reflect its own wishes) would eventually be higher social welfare, but it may take too long to be awaited passively. In Keynes' famous phrase, '*In the long run* we are all dead' (italics in the original).

18.2.4 Tradeable permits and the EU position on global warming

As stated in section 18.2.2, one advantage of taxes over regulations is that they minimize the aggregate cost of reaching any particular pollution reduction, even when governments are ignorant of firms' abatement cost functions. However, this same attribute can lead to what may be a major drawback. If the government does not know firms' marginal costs of abatement, it cannot be sure what aggregate level of abatement will be induced by any particular tax level. The tax it chooses may lead to more or to less abatement than it expects.

For some pollutants the failure to hit the standard exactly is not crucial – the target itself is only a rough guess. In other cases, however, this can be a major disadvantage. This is especially in cases (like figure 18.3) where there is thought to be a threshold of pollution above which serious effects become apparent. For example, no government is likely to use taxes to control radioactive emissions, because overshooting the target would be unacceptable.

There is an alternative instrument that does ensure that the target is met, and yet also minimizes the aggregate cost of abatement. This instrument is the use of tradeable emission 'permits' (or 'quotas'). The aggregate volume of permits equals the maximum pollution target, but the permits can be bought or sold by firms. Trading will establish a market price per permit.

Each firm will abate up to the point where its marginal cost of abatement equals the price of a permit. For example, if initially its emissions are at a level where its marginal cost (MC) of abatement is less than the price, it would be profitable to abate more and sell its surplus permits. Conversely, if its MC is above the price, it would be cheaper to buy permits and to abate less (pollute more). Since each firm sets its MC equal to the same (market) price of a permit, all will have equal MCs – which is the condition for minimizing the cost of abatement. (There may be other problems with permits: for example, if permits are initially 'grandfathered', i.e. handed out to firms, rather than being auctioned, there is no government revenue to provide a 'double dividend'.)

Although tradeable pollution permits have been widely used in the US, they have hardly figured in EU countries' national policies.[22] They have, however, become of practical importance in one EU pollution policy issue – global warming. In 1997, the Kyoto international agreement was reached on controlling emissions of 'greenhouse gases' (primarily, but not exclusively, carbon dioxide). The EU15 agreed that by 2008–12 its emissions would fall to 8 per cent below those in 1990. The EU15 is to be a 'bubble', i.e. the reduction applies to them as a whole, not to the fifteen individual countries. (The target equates to a 9.4 per cent reduction for EU25, as the new members have individual targets.) Within the total EU reduction, the Council agreed on an allocation in which the poorer member states (which emit less per capita) will actually be allowed to increase their emissions, in order not to inhibit their economic growth (see table 18.1).

One of the bitterly contested issues in the negotiations leading to the Kyoto Agreement was US insistence that internationally traded permits should be incorporated. Countries which emitted less than their targets would be allowed to sell their excess to other nations, which could then emit more than their targets. The EU was among those opposed to such trading, though eventually trading was conceded in order to obtain US participation in the agreement (the US later withdrew anyway, despite the concession).

Table 18.1 Greenhouse gas emission changes from 1990 to 2012

Country	%	Country	%
Austria	−13	Italy	−6.5
Belgium	−7.5	Luxembourg	−28
Denmark	−21	Netherlands	−6
Finland	0	Portugal	+27
France	0	Spain	+15
Germany	−21	Sweden	+4
Greece	+25	UK	−12.5
Ireland	+13		

Source: EU press document 9402/98 (Presse 205), C–98/205.

There were various reasons why the EU, and some others, opposed pollution trading. One was the fear that because the ex-Communist countries had suffered a large drop in their industrial production after 1990, they would automatically undershoot their targets. If they then sold their surplus allowances to others who thereby did not have to meet their own targets, the overall cutback would be less than would otherwise be achieved. Another basis of opposition was almost a moral one. It was considered wrong that the US should be able to use its wealth to buy permits, and thus continue to use energy profligately and not share in the 'pain' of controlling its energy use or of constraining its economic growth.[23]

The distrust of international trading continued. In May 1999 (to the disapproval of the US) the Commission proposed that at least half of the EU's target reduction of 8 per cent must be achieved by internal abatement. The accompanying press release by the Environment Commissioner included the statement, 'Everybody needs to contribute . . . We must reduce our carbon dependency.' However, the same Commission proposal also advocated serious consideration of emissions trading by firms *within* the EU. Some member states were already favourably inclined to the use of tradeable permits – US experience shows that they can achieve large savings in aggregate abatement costs.[24] A preliminary trading scheme started in 2005 with the full scheme to cover 2008–12 (see box 18.4).

Box 18.4 EU-wide pollution permit trading

In March 2000 the Commission issued a 'Green Paper on greenhouse gas emissions trading within the EU', eventually resulting in Directive 2003/87/EC (OJ L 275/32, 25.10.2003). The preliminary phase started in 2005; the full scheme will commence in 2008, coinciding with the starting date for implementing Kyoto commitments. The initial phase involves only carbon dioxide emissions (not all greenhouse gases) and firms in a specific set of industrial sectors, accounting for about 45 per cent of EU emissions.

The background is the EU's attempt to meet its Kyoto target for greenhouse gas reductions, combined with the allocation between member states (see table 18.1). Implicitly, one reason for the emissions trading scheme (ETS) was that the allocation between member states had not been based on the relative marginal costs of abatement. It was therefore likely that the overall EU reduction would not be the least cost pattern.

Allowing firms across the EU to trade emission allowances would remedy the defect. If production facilities end up trading emission allowances, rather than just limiting their emissions to their initial allowances, their actual emissions differ from their initial allowances. Correspondingly, if the trading is between facilities located in different member states, the states in which they are situated will be allowed to overshoot, or will be required to undershoot, their national targets.

The aggregate cost savings of an ETS have been estimated using econometric models. The savings vary according to the number of sectors to be covered and which 'greenhouse gases' are included. For carbon dioxide and the sectors included in the 2005 ETS, the Commission has estimated an annual saving of 1.3 billion euros, as compared to each member state implementing its own cut-back, with no trans-frontier trading. Of course, it will never be possible to validate or to disprove the accuracy of such quantitative estimates, as we will not experience the counter-factual state of the world with which to directly compare the actual outcome.

As discussed in this chapter, the desirability of decentralization to member states can clash with fears about unfair competition between firms in different countries. These fears similarly motivate uniformity in aspects of the ETS. For example, nations are required to allocate initial allowances between emitters according to harmonized 'Community provisions . . . to avoid distortions of competition'; in particular they may not allocate higher allowances to any producer than it is likely to need. The revenue from the sale of unused excess allowances would be equivalent to a subsidy, and hence 'distort' competition. Nevertheless, despite this attempt at harmonization, during the first year of the new scheme more permits were issued than required.

However, there are problems with a tradeable permits scheme for dealing with greenhouse gases. The costs of monitoring emissions and the transaction costs of trading mean that the permits scheme has to exclude the millions of sources emitting carbon dioxide through driving vehicles or heating buildings. This is in contrast to using taxation to induce the reduction of carbon dioxide. Because there is a unique relationship between the carbon content of fuels and the emission of carbon dioxide when they are burned, the tax could be levied on the production or sale of the fuel. It does not need to be levied on the emitters at the point of emission, and this cuts the transaction costs and monitoring to manageable levels even though the tax gives *all* emitters an incentive to reduce emissions. For this reason, tradeable permits are inferior to a carbon tax as a way of reducing carbon dioxide within the EU at the minimum aggregate cost.[25]

Another drawback with the EU Emissions Trading System is that mentioned above. Even in the full scheme in 2008–12, at least 90 per cent of the allowances will have to be allocated free of charge: i.e. at most 10 per cent can be auctioned. As compared with a carbon tax, there will therefore be almost no 'double dividend'.

18.3 Further implications for EU policies

Despite the cost-minimization argument discussed in section 18.2.2, as stated above, pollution taxes or tradeable emissions permits have been relatively rare in the EU. In the course of the discussion of the standard economic analysis of pollution control, we have already noted in passing a few of the other implications for EU policies. There are further important aspects of the policies which can also be usefully examined in the light of the theory outlined in section 18.2.

18.3.1 Polluter pays principle (PPP)

The EU has conformed with the OECD in accepting 'the polluter pays principle' (incorporated in Article 174(2) by the Maastricht Treaty). At first, many commentators mistakenly thought that PPP was an acceptance of the taxation approach ascribed to economists, in which polluters pay taxes on unabated pollution. However, this was incorrect. PPP was an agreement that governments should not subsidize firms for the costs imposed upon them by anti-pollution policies. PPP is also satisfied if the polluters bear the cost of achieving prescribed standards. PPP is thus a way of making firms 'internalize the externality'. If the standards they have to meet are correctly chosen, then, given the constraints placed on them, individual firms' own choices of abatement techniques and of output will be correct from a social standpoint.

It might also be noted that, from the point of view of the first-order conditions for achieving efficiency, a subsidy per unit abated would achieve the same result as a tax per unit emitted (though in the long run the size of the industry might differ because of the different profitability). The opportunity cost to the firm of continuing to pollute would include subsidy forgone. Thus the rationale for PPP is not to enforce efficiency, but rather fears of 'unfair competition', as discussed above.

Within the EU, although PPP (as well as the general limits to state aid in Articles 87 and 88 of the Treaty; see chapter 14) has meant that subsidies for pollution abatement are generally forbidden, this has been applied very strictly only for the higher running costs associated with operating equipment to reduce emissions. The rules have changed slightly over time.[26] The 2001 guidelines allow for temporary help with operating costs for energy saving and for some waste management schemes, where these exceed EU standards and could harm competitiveness. States may also help some firms' operating costs by granting them partial or full exemptions from environmental taxes, especially where this is necessary to avoid harming their competitiveness (the discussion earlier in this chapter on competitiveness is relevant here). Similarly, in 1998 when car emission limits were tightened, tax concessions on purchases of new cars were allowed, in order to expedite the purchase of new cars meeting the revised standard and the scrapping of older, more polluting, cars.

At times, the Commission has allowed some help with the initial investment costs of installing abatement equipment in order to adapt to new mandatory standards, but this is now only allowed for SMEs. However, help with investment costs is still allowed to encourage firms to go beyond mandatory standards, or if national standards are stricter than the EU's, also to foster energy saving or use of renewable energy. In the latter case the maximum limits are higher at 40 per cent of extra investment costs, as compared with 30 per cent for exceeding EU standards (10 per cent more in each case for SMEs or in assisted regions).

18.3.2 Thresholds and standards

As stated above, it is very difficult to get convincing evidence about the dose–response relationships of pollutants. The problems of obtaining evidence make the studies much closer to those of econometricians than those of laboratory-based science.[27] Where human health is concerned, it is simply unethical to conduct laboratory tests, for example taking very young babies and giving them feeds containing different levels of nitrates to observe the level which causes serious damage. Most EU policies are concerned with potential health effects. But even where only amenity is at stake, the number of possible interactions and natural variations in them still make it difficult to gather conclusive evidence. The arguments over the cause of forest die-back are a case in point. There are various possible pollutants which may interact in causing damage; damage may depend on soil and weather; and the route taken between emissions of sulphur dioxide and nitrogen oxides on the one hand and the precipitation of acid rain on the other is difficult to forecast.

One result of this is that it is important to try to obtain reliable data on a range of pollutants, over many years and at a sufficient number of locations, so as to enable statistical studies relating various aspects of health to pollution to be based on enough observations to be significant (in a statistical sense). One of the focuses of EU environmental policy has been to require the monitoring of pollutants. The earliest requirements were for smoke and sulphur dioxide (from 1975 onwards), water pollution (1977 onwards), and (from 1987) there has been an attempt to gather systematic data on damage to trees. The European Environment Agency, established by the EU in 1993, is similarly concerned with collecting and assessing data.

More fundamentally, the lack of definitive knowledge on the damage caused by different levels of pollution means that any standards are adopted largely by a political process disguised as a scientific one. Different groups put pressure on governments to be more or less lax, and the governments then take stands in the Council according to the balance of their feelings; often the position they have previously taken domestically is then taken with respect to EU policy. Each government will claim scientific backing for its stand, usually refusing to admit the uncertainty. Those pushing for the laxest standard will tend to claim that there is no conclusive evidence of harm, while not admitting that there is no conclusive evidence of lack of harm either: the UK position on sulphur dioxide mentioned above is one example. Others will mention the studies which suggest that there could well be serious damage caused by the current levels of pollution. As part of the process, there is the temptation to look for a threshold, as in figure 18.3, even where there are no strong grounds for expecting one. If a threshold did exist, it would often make sense to adopt it as the standard – the marginal cost curve would have to cut the marginal benefit curve to the left of the threshold to justify less abatement (higher pollution).

A large number of medical scientists are doubtful that overall thresholds exist for many pollutants. The levels of a pollutant, such as smoke, that may be harmless to a healthy person may be deleterious to somebody already vulnerable, such as a bronchitic old-age pensioner living in a damp flat. Thus, a threshold which would be applicable to all might well be at so low a level of pollution as to be useless for policy.

Once a standard has been decided upon, by whatever process of bargaining based on whatever motives and justifications, it is then too often treated as though the agreed standard were really a well-defined threshold.[28] On the one hand, governments may use the fact that an EU standard exists to try to allay public anxiety over the potential harm from some pollutant and to claim that because levels are below the accepted standard there is nothing at all to worry about – even if new evidence has since emerged to suggest that low levels are more harmful than was thought before. On the other hand, environmentalists and other pressure groups may use the breach of a standard as an indication that the health of the public is being seriously damaged and argue that pollution must be immediately reduced to the standard, whatever the cost.

In most cases, the EU has laid down that member states must notify the Commission if they cannot reach the agreed standard by the required date. The Commission then has to decide whether the failure can be condoned or not. At this stage, the pressures mentioned in the previous paragraph come into play again: is the standard just a rough guess at the level at which marginal costs equal marginal benefits, so that less abatement is justified if a particular country can plausibly claim that its costs are especially high, or is it a well-defined threshold of pollution above which completely unacceptable harm is caused? The decision is complicated by the worry that, if some member states are granted exemptions too readily, others will in future not comply because of fears of 'unfair competition' from those given exemptions.

18.3.3 Emission versus ambient standards

In figures 18.1–18.3 we followed most of the literature in simply linking pollution to damage. However, on examination it becomes apparent that there are various stages of pollution. There is the initial emission where the pollution is produced, such as the factory chimney or waste pipe outlet. The pollution may then flow through various media: for example, it may be carried by wind through air, then deposited on plants, then eaten by animals which are then slaughtered. During the processes, the pollution from any one source is augmented by pollution from other sources and simultaneously diluted by fresh air, water, etc., mixing with the carrying medium, and much of the substance may be deposited where it does no harm. The ultimate stage to be considered is where the pollution finally directly affects humans.

From the economist's anthropocentric viewpoint, the pollution that matters is that which affects human beings. Typically, therefore, we are concerned with the ambient levels of pollution, i.e. the concentration in the medium which affects health, such as micrograms per cubic metre of lead particles in the air or milligrams per litre of nitrates in drinking water.

In setting standards for pollution, a standard could be applied at any of the stages of the process. At the final stage, one could set standards of acceptable levels of absorption of pollution by people: for example, there was at one time a Commission proposal to set a maximum limit for the level of lead in people's blood. Obviously one would hardly fine or imprison people with more lead in their blood than the standard. Instead, the idea was that if tests showed that anybody was above the limit, then the government of their country should take agreed action to reduce their lead intake. In fact, governments do use monitoring of human exposure or absorption as a trigger for action, and occasionally set standards in this form, such as radiation exposure limits for workers. In the EU case, partly as a result of UK pressure, the directive on blood lead levels was watered down somewhat and became one for an EU-wide screening programme, primarily for information gathering and with a member state

required to take only such actions as the government itself thought were appropriate if too many people were above the specified values.[29]

The next stage back is the concentration in the medium that directly affects people. In the EU, standards defined for this stage are sometimes called 'exposure standards' or 'primary protection standards'. Another example of such standards, in addition to those for tap water or for air, would be the bacteria content of bathing water. Sometimes the standards are somewhat further back in the process, but still concern ambient levels. These are often called 'environmental quality standards' (EQS). The standards applying to water, in rivers or lakes, which could be taken for drinking, or those applying to water with shellfish, are examples. Standards may also be set at the initial emission stage. These are usually called 'emission standards'. A similar stage is when the pollution is caused by the use of products, such as car exhaust pollution or noise from lawnmowers. A somewhat similar stage is where the EU mandates labelling or other aspects of products to avoid *potential* danger from misuse: for example, the controls on the shipment of toxic waste.

As already stated, from an economist's viewpoint it would seem that, if standards are to be used at all, the relevant standard should be as far down the chain as is technically feasible – exposure standards, where possible, or at least EQS. The only cases for EU standards on emissions would be either where they were also product standards (to allow unhindered trade) or where there was some reason why even EQS were not feasible. Otherwise, it should be up to the relevant government inspectorate/agency to find the least-cost way of achieving the environmental quality or exposure standard. If pollution taxes (or tradeable permits) were not used, then the requirement for pollution abatement should be shared between the various sources of emissions in the most efficient way possible.[30] As explained earlier, the aim would be (subject to information/enforcement limitations) to require abatement by each polluter up to the point where the marginal cost of abatement was equal.

In the 1970s there was a heated controversy over whether the EC should define its policies by EQS or by UES, with the latter defined as maximum 'limit values' so that member states could have stricter emission limits if they wished. The contestants were the UK on the side of EQS and the other member states, plus the Commission, on the side of UES.[31]

The attachment of the Commission and other member states to UES was partly explicable in terms of one of the motivations for having a joint EC policy at all: the fear of 'unfair competition' if different countries had different emission standards for industrial effluents (see box 18.5).

Also, trans-frontier pollution was seen as a reason for having any joint EU policies at all. It was felt that the cooperation that should underlie the Community ought to lead to policies in a form that would help, not hinder, the solution of joint problems, including trans-frontier pollution. There is economic, not just political, justification for this view. The well-known 'Coase Theorem' (Coase, 1960), implies that optimum levels of pollution can be achieved by bargaining between the polluter (upstream country here) and the pollutee (downstream). If the polluter would otherwise have the right to pollute, then the pollutee will have to pay the polluter to abate. Since EU countries bargain over a wide range of issues, concessions by the pollutee country on other issues of interest to the polluter may enable an optimal level of pollution to be reached in circumstances where direct pecuniary payments would be unacceptable.

On the other side of the debate in box 18.5, the UK's views were close to the economists' approach outlined above. Since it is the damage to humans that is the problem, an EQS is more relevant than emissions per se. Emissions need only be limited to the extent that they lead to unacceptable damage.

On the question of unfair competition, although not stated in those terms, the UK government's argument was an application of the theory of comparative advantage, applied to polluting industries.

Despite the strong disagreements over UES or EQS, it could be argued that neither side was really consistent. The UK inspectorates, despite the type of statement in box 18.5, had often applied UES to

---

Box 18.5 The UK v. the rest: EQS v. UES

The dispute arose over a series of directives on water quality aimed at rivers and estuaries – there was a framework directive, finally passed in 1976, on the approach to 'dangerous substances discharged into the aquatic environment', followed by subsequent directives on specific pollutants/industries.

The Commission and other member states felt that without a UES it would be 'unfair competition' if different countries had different emission standards for a set of pollutants which were primarily industrial effluents. Countries such as the UK, which has a long coastline with relatively fast-flowing estuaries and rivers, would be able to achieve any given EQS with much higher emissions than their trade partners (rivals?).

In addition, countries which shared river systems (such as the Rhine) would find it difficult to allocate individual polluters' emission levels to achieve an EQS: upstream countries would have little incentive to impose severe cutbacks on their industries. The issue of trans-frontier pollution is of less importance for the UK, which is not only primarily an island (ignoring Northern Ireland and its border) but has the fortune to be mainly upwind of its nearest neighbours.

The UK's view was that it is the damage to humans that is relevant. Emissions need only be limited to the extent that they lead to unacceptable damage. In terms of a traditional British statement: 'There are no harmful substances, only harmful concentrations.' On the question of unfair competition, the UK government said that it was no more unfair that the UK should benefit from its coastline and estuaries than that Italy could benefit from its sunshine: it would be absurd to require the Italians to grow tomatoes in greenhouses just to stop them having an 'unfair' advantage over the Dutch.

In the end, a typical EU compromise was reached. Countries could choose *either* to accept UES in the form of limit values *or* to establish EQS, provided that they could show the Commission that the quality standard was being met. Only the UK chose the latter.

whole industries (in some cases only to new pollutants, but the EU also made a similar distinction). Conversely, other EU policies set EQS without any fuss from the member states: for example, the air quality standards for nitrogen dioxide, sulphur dioxide and particulates. It could also be argued that the dispute forced the UK to be much more rigorous about the EQS that were needed.

In view of the economic assessment of 'unfair competition' discussed in section 18.2.3, one could go even further than the UK argument that unfair competition considerations should not impose UES. In the absence of trans-frontier effects of pollution, there may not even be a case for an EU-level EQS. As noted, however, the strong dismissal of the 'unfair competition' criterion would completely undermine not only much of EU environmental policy (e.g. on drinking water standards, where typically there are virtually no trans-frontier effects), but many other EU policies as well.

18.3.4 Damage and designated areas

One last issue in EU environmental policy that we shall examine is also linked to the economic analysis. The stress on the costs and benefits of abatement implies that it is not merely the dumping itself of something into water, air or earth that matters, but the harm done relative to the benefits from the activity. The harm will depend on the potential use by people (directly or indirectly) of the medium. It therefore makes sense to vary the desired standard of pollution according to its use. Water used for drinking could well require stricter standards on nitrate concentration than water used only for boating. The EU has followed such a policy.

In some cases the use of the medium is obvious, in other cases less so. In the latter cases there may be some decentralization so that countries are allowed to designate particular areas for the application of particular standards. For example, the standards for bathing water apply to stretches of water where bathing is traditionally practised by large numbers of people. Similarly, member states can designate areas where water standards need to be set to protect shellfish.

Although the approach seems sensible, the application has not always been so. In particular, in so far as governments have discretion over the areas designated, they can use this as a way of avoiding the effective implementation of EU policies that they feel are unnecessary. This has indeed happened. In the case of standards for water supporting different sorts of freshwater fish, and for the shellfish case already mentioned, some member states simply did not designate any waters at all. Similarly, those readers who are familiar with English seaside resorts might be interested to know that the UK government originally used its discretion over how to assess where 'large numbers' traditionally bathed to exclude both Blackpool and Brighton. At that time the UK government was worried about public expenditure, and any improvement in water quality of beaches would require new sewerage works.[32]

An early example was a 1975 directive on the sulphur content of gas/diesel oil, which is a medium-grade oil used for heating commercial, light industrial and domestic buildings, as well as for diesel fuel for vehicles. The directive is interesting partly because it was a mixture of UES and EQS, although it is also concerned with product harmonization. It set two limits on the sulphur content of the oil: the higher sulphur type could be used only in areas designated by member states. The aim was that the oil with the higher sulphur content should only be used where there was no air pollution problem from sulphur dioxide. In the event, the UK government decided that the whole of the United Kingdom was to be designated for the use of the oil with the higher sulphur content *except for roads*. The road network would therefore be designated for the oil with the lower sulphur content – since diesel for vehicles was already low sulphur compared with other gas/diesel oil.[33]

18.4 Conclusions

In some ways the EU policies on the environment can be counted as a success story. Despite the argument that it may not be clear that common policies are required at all in many cases, nevertheless a set of policies has emerged. Furthermore, despite some of the problems mentioned above and despite the failure to move quickly on some other policies because of the conflicting interests of the member states, as compared with other common policies (such as transport or agriculture), progress has been fairly steady and not too divisive, acrimonious or blatantly inefficient.

Since the 1990s there has been a revival of public interest in the environment, even in those member states where interest waned in the decade after 1974. Those in favour of stronger environmental policies may well feel divided about EU actions. Those living in member states where Green pressures are strong will feel that they are held back, compared with what their governments could achieve (or be pressured into achieving) without the requirement to carry other member countries with them. There are limits as to how far member states can take advantage of the permission, in the Treaties and in some directives, for higher standards where these do not conflict with EU policies.[34]

Conversely, environmentalists living in those countries whose governments tend only to move on these issues when really compelled, can be grateful both for the more stringent standards set by EU policies and for the possibility that the Commission will enforce compliance.[35] In particular, following a European Agency Report in 1999 claiming that too many EU environmental decisions were not fully implemented by member states, the Commission has intensified its compliance efforts. For example, the first ever fine on a member state under Article 228, for not complying with an ECJ judgment, was on an environmental case. In July 2000 Greece was ordered to pay a daily fine for as long as it did not fulfil the directive on the safe disposal of waste.[36]

In the second half of 1992 it seemed as though EU environmental policy might be put into reverse. Following problems with ratification of the Maastricht Agreements, the UK (especially) stressed the notion of 'subsidiarity' that had been incorporated into the Treaty amendments (see chapter 2). To various extents, the other member states, and even the chastened Commission, also said that subsidiarity should be taken seriously,

and that EU policies should be scrutinized to see whether joint action was really necessary. As indicated at various points in this chapter, the justification of EU-level environmental policies is often debatable. It was possible, therefore, that the movement on subsidiarity might lead to the reconsideration of some existing EU environmental directives. Starting with a European Council meeting in 2000, there has also been an increased stress on reducing burdensome regulations.

However, neither subsidiarity nor deregulation has made a major difference as far as existing policies are concerned. It is difficult to judge whether new EU-level joint actions on the environment have been as readily adopted as previously, even where there is no strong reason for an EU policy rather than a national one. My own subjective judgment is that any diminution has been minimal or even non-existent.[37] Not only do the Articles on subsidiarity include transnational problems as a reason for joint actions, but they also include the correction of 'distorted competition'. As emphasized above, the standard interpretation of 'distorted competition' has always been a prime reason for EU-level environmental policy however misguided it may be from an economist's viewpoint.

NOTES

1 For earlier years, references to the *Official Journals* (OJ) for the environmental programmes and various directives can be found in the Economic and Social Committee (CEC 1987b), which contains a useful brief summary of early EU environmental directives, Haigh (1989), or Press and Taylor (1990). Many of the documents up to 1994 have been reprinted in the seven-volume *European Environmental Legislation* published by DGXI (updated edition, 1996 – CEC 1996k). Since 2003 the Commission has issued annual environmental policy reviews. At the time of writing, the most recent is COM (2006) 70, with an Annexe at SEC (2006) 218. Recent documents are also on the Europa website (http://europa.eu/), while European Environment Agency reports are at http://www.eea.europa.eu/. The *Sixth Environmental Programme* is in *OJ L* 242, 10 September 2002. The Commission's proposals and background are in COM (2001) 31.

2 Some of these directives predate the proposal for an EU environmental programme.

3 Kramer (2003) has a thorough discussion of the limits on member states' ability to set higher environmental standards, and of whether it still matters whether decisions are made using Article 95 (product harmonization under internal market) or Article 175 (environmental protection).

4 As in other applications of this notion of 'unfair competition', or 'distortion of competition' as it is often called in EU documents, it contains implicit assumptions about the fixity of wages, prices and exchange rates. These assumptions are often not realized and their validity may or may not be dubious. This point will be amplified in section 18.2.3 and will also be relevant to controversies discussed later in this chapter.

5 Although some of those opposed to action on the environment have alleged that concern about environmental issues is a middle-class luxury, which is not shared by the working class or the poorer members of society. Also see note 25 below on regressivity and pollution taxes. The agreement on sharing the burden of carbon dioxide reduction within the EU 'bubble' does make special provision for poorer EU member states (see section 18.2.4).

6 Formally, the arguments in the social welfare function are the individual welfares or utilities, even if the functional form (weighting of individual welfares) may reflect egalitarianism or some other values.

7 Theoretically, in formal treatments there would be no obstacle to putting concern for endangered species into somebody's utility function, even where the person does not know of the existence of some of the species. Conversely, environmentalists sometimes appeal to the possible future uses to man of endangered species of plants, which would be forgone if the species were destroyed before the discovery of their uses.

8 The EU environmental policies primarily comprise regulations and directives imposing implementation requirements on member states. Unlike some other policy areas (e.g. the CAP, regional policy; see chapters 20 and 22), there is little spending on the environment out of the EU's own budget. The only EU spending specifically on the environment (though funds in the Cohesion part of regional spending can be spent on the environment) is the LIFE programme. The priority in this programme is the protection of habitats and preservation of nature rather than simply control of pollution. However, compared to other EU spending, the amounts are trivial: the extension to the LIFE3 programme, covering 2005–6, has a budget of 317 million euros. In June 2006 the Council agreed on an expanded 'LIFE+' programme on the environment that will have a budget of 2.1 billion euros over 2007–13; 40 per cent of this will be on nature and biodiversity, as covered in previous LIFE programmes.

9 Another way of putting the same point is to say that the MPC curve in figure 18.1 is too high because the true opportunity cost of labour is below the wage rate. Hence the MSC, which should measure the cost of resources by the value of their alternative use, includes some components which make it lower than the MPC – see chapter 6. Note also that if the industry is not perfectly competitive, the output may be too low for the usual reasons, despite the externality – it depends on the balance between the strength of the externality (output too high) and the imperfection (output too low).

10 A possible exception is the case of pollutants which are cumulative (non-degradable) and highly toxic (see chapter 16 in Perman et al., 2003).

11 For example, in the UK, the expected revenue from the Climate Change Levy introduced in 2001 was explicitly used to finance a cut in employers' National Insurance contributions.

12 That is, even if the revenue is not used to reduce distortionary taxation elsewhere.

13 A more detailed discussion of this and other problems of using pollution taxes is in Marin (1979) or, in a US context, in Arnold (1994, chapter 11). Also see Kelman (1981) for a study of some other reasons for the hostility of non-economists to the idea of pollution taxes, and various articles by Frey, e.g. Weck-Hannemann and Frey (1997) or Frey and Stutzer (2006).

14 For a (rare) EU attempt at using a cost-benefit study, but to find the desirable *maximum* level of pollution concentrations, see COM (97) 500. A few others are listed at http://ec.europa.eu/environment/enveco/studies2.htm. It is unclear if any of these few have actually been used in the formulation of the limits in a directive, rather than in justifying decisions taken on other grounds.

15 A summary of EU countries' pollution charges can be found in OECD (2005a). It is not always straightforward to judge the extent of the use of pollution taxes. In particular, taxes imposed primarily for revenue raising purposes may have some anti-pollution side effects. For example, there are tables on proportions of tax revenue raised by environmental taxes. Greece shows up as the leading EU user in the 1990s.

However, this reflects its use of fuel and vehicle taxes as revenue raisers. These were not aimed at reducing pollution, and were not structured to encourage the use of less-polluting vehicles and fuels.

16 This case is suitable for figure 18.1, as once the leaded petrol has been put into the fuel tank, the motorist has no realistic options for varying the total emissions of lead for each gallon bought. The same applies to the carbon content tax discussed below.

17 The EU had already agreed to aim to stabilize CO_2 emissions at the 1990 level by the year 2000.

18 If we concentrate on the cost-minimization argument only, and (for the reasons already discussed) ignore overall optimality, imposing the pollution tax but giving lump-sum subsidies to these industries (to avoid a large rise in their average costs) might be acceptable.

19 The argument here and in the remainder of this section is made within a framework which assumes perfect competition inside countries. To what extent it still holds within the framework of the 'New Trade Theory' of oligopolistic competition is currently the subject of research.

20 Firms may also have to accept lower profits. Whether or not this happens depends on how internationally mobile capital is (see chapter 8). In the EU now, it may well be that profit rates cannot be forced down.

21 If the country is one of those EU member states not in EMU, the change in the aggregate real wage could be hastened by changes in nominal exchange rates, provided that money wages do not respond fully to the changes in the price of imports – the usual 'money illusion' condition for devaluations to have any real effects. However, the relative sectoral reallocations of resources cannot generally just be achieved by this route (the exception would be if all traded goods were uniformly more polluting than non-traded goods).

22 See OECD (2005a).

23 This objection parallels some of the early popular opposition to economists' advocacy of pollution taxes. Many felt it wrong that firms or wealthy consumers could continue to pollute if they were prepared to pay (see the Kelman and Frey references in note 13).

24 See, for example, Schmalensee et al. (1998) and Stavins (1998). EU reports estimate that the cost of reducing greenhouse gases by EU-wide trading will be 25–30 per cent less than it would have been without trading across member states' borders.

25 The issue of monitoring is discussed further in Marin (1979) and Arnold (1994). In its comments on and amendments to the Commission's proposals in September 2002, the European Parliament worried about the distortionary effects of the partial coverage of permit trading, but its amendments did not really deal with the issue.

It should also be noticed that although a full carbon tax avoids the problem with permits, i.e. of only requiring abatement from some emitters but not from all, energy taxes are also sometimes only applied to particular groups. For example, the UK Climate Change Levy is not applied to households and small businesses, probably because of the regressivity of a tax on household fuel use (poorer households spend a higher proportion of their income on heating). Of course regressivity could have been avoided had the revenue from the tax been used for income redistribution programmes rather than for reducing employment taxes.

26 The Commission's original position is briefly restated in CEC (1991a, para. 284), and given in greater detail in CEC (1987a, para. 159). Revised guidelines were published in OJ C 72, 10 March 94 and summarized in CEC (1996h). The current guidelines were published in OJ C 37, 3 February 2001.

27 The examples in this and the following paragraphs are taken from EU environmental policies.

28 Jordan (1999) shows in the context of water purity the way that, once a standard has been agreed, it can inhibit further adjustment.

29 The debates over this directive (77/312) illustrate not only the monitoring function of the EC mentioned above, but also the sensitivity to thresholds. Part of the objection to the original proposal was that it would suggest that the standard was a threshold which, if exceeded by anybody, would mean they were in danger.

30 Whether quantitative regulations or pollution taxes are used to apportion the necessary abatement between emitters, allowance should be made for the different contributions of emissions in different places to the pollution measured as environmental quality, e.g. because of prevailing wind or tide patterns. Tradeable pollution permits should similarly allow for differential contributions (which is one practical difficulty of using them for pollutants for which the location of emissions matters).

31 An excellent detailed account of the controversies is given in Guruswamy et al. (1983). As pointed out in this article, although the term 'environmental quality objective' originally meant something else, the EQS is now sometimes referred to as a 'quality objective'.

32 Later, in 1987, many more beaches were added to the list in response to threats from the Commission over infringement, strongly adverse comments from the Royal Commission on Environmental Pollution and the beginning of a changed attitude by the UK government to its poor reputation on environmental issues. However, even in 2001 the ECJ ruled against the UK for not remedying an earlier adverse decision over bathing water. The Commission alleges that most other member states also breach this directive, suggesting that the UK's scepticism over the scientific justification for the directive is more widely shared.

33 In 1992 the Council agreed on a new directive setting a uniform limit on the sulphur content of all gas/oils. More recently, diesel fuels for road transport have been included in the same directives as petrol.

34 See the reference in note 3. Weale et al. (2000) discuss differences in member states' national policies and their influence on EU decisions. For a discussion of how little environmental quality has converged across EU member states, despite a trend improvement overall, see Neumayer (2001).

35 A politically important example in the UK was the Commission's threat to prosecute over the failure to meet the standards for nitrates in water (other countries besides the UK were also threatened). In the absence of these threats, especially given UK official scepticism over the levels of the EQS actually laid down in the directive, there would have been an even greater lack of urgency over an issue which was so adverse for the privatization process. (In 1992 both the UK and Germany were found by the ECJ to be in breach of the directive, and subsequently other countries also. In 2002, according to the *Financial Times* (28 May 2002), the UK government, threatened by fines under Article 228, agreed to extend areas covered by the directive from 8 per cent to 80 per cent of England – the increase will still only be to 55 per cent according DEFRA (2002)).

36 Details of enforcement can be found in the series of annual surveys on the implementation and enforcement of Community environmental law, e.g. Seventh Annual Survey SEC (2006)1143.

37 Jeppesen (2002, chapter 3) comes to a similar conclusion, based on counting various types of decisions. Others may disagree: e.g. Golub (1996b) states that there was a fall in the number of Commission environmental proposals during the period 1992–5.

Part V   EU budget and structural policies

Part V of this book covers all EU policies which address certain structural aspects of the EU economy and society. The EU affords special treatment to those in the agricultural sector, fishing industry and depressed regions as well as dealing with EU-wide social problems, including unemployment, equal treatment of men and women, and migration. These areas are not only financed by the EU general budget, but also claim the bulk of its general budgetary resources. Thus, this part begins with the chapter on the general budget and follows on with chapters on each of the mentioned areas.

19

The general budget

BRIAN ARDY AND ALI EL-AGRAA

The general budget of the EU[1] (budget, hereafter) has always been an issue of high political salience. Member states are naturally concerned with their contributions to and receipts from it. Until 1988 the political significance of the budget was also heightened by inter-institutional rivalry within the EC. The right to approve the budget, one of the more significant powers of the European Parliament (EP), was used as a lever to force concessions from the Council (see chapter 3). This problem has been resolved by gradually increasing powers to the EP and its more direct involvement in budgetary planning.

The budget is also a window on the EU as a political and economic institution: an assessment of the nature of the EU can be made by comparing its budget with that of federal governments. The development of the budget parallels the development of the EU. The budget in the early years was very small and financed from national contributions. With the development of EU policies, in particular the Common Agricultural Policy (CAP; see chapter 20), expenditure rose and the growing maturity of the EU permitted the introduction of 'own resources' in 1970. There followed a period of continued growth of expenditure, principally on agriculture. The late 1970s and early 1980s were plagued by disagreements over the budget between the institutions and in relation to the British contribution. The resolution of this British problem was accompanied by measures to control agricultural expenditure, and was one of the factors that facilitated the development of the Internal Market Programme and the Single European Act (SEA; see chapters 2 and 7). The single market and the Mediterranean enlargement of the EU led in 1988 to the Delors I budgetary package. This resulted in a comprehensive

revision of the EU budgetary arrangements which expanded the budget: modified 'own resources'; expanded and concentrated structural expenditure; tightened control of agricultural expenditure; and modified the system of budgetary decision-making (European Council, 1988). Following agreement on the Treaty on European Union (TEU), the budget was further modified by the Edinburgh Agreement (European Council, 1992b), the Delors II package. This was accompanied by a radical CAP reform and further expanded budgetary resources to accommodate more expenditure on structural policies, internal policies (particularly research) and on external action, recognizing the impact of the changes in Central and Eastern Europe (CEE). The reduced dynamism in the EU in the second half of the 1990s is reflected in budgetary developments. Thus *Agenda 2000* (CEC, 1997b) proposed that CEE enlargement should be financed from existing budgetary resources with modest policy reform. Even these proposals were further watered down by the agreement in Berlin in 1999 (European Council, 1999b), which required further modification in Brussels in 2002 (European Council, 2002b). This only resolved the situation up to 2006; a further modest budgetary expansion and redistribution of budgetary finance was agreed in 2005 (European Council, 2005a).

This chapter commences with a short survey of the economic theory of the state (section 19.1), which examines why governments provide services and intervene in the economy. Section 19.2 considers fiscal federalism: the economic explanation of the assignment of policies between tiers of government. The application of fiscal federalism theory to the EU is examined in section 19.3. Consideration of the budgetary system of the EU begins in section 19.4, which covers the rules under which the budget operates and the procedure for the adoption of annual budgets. The revenue of the EU is the subject of section 19.5, which covers the requirements of tax systems, the EU sources of finance and how these compare with those of national federal states. The uses to which this finance is put, EU expenditure, is analysed in section 19.6. Then the problems facing the budget are examined: net contributions and equity in section 19.7; EMU in section 19.8; and enlargement in section 19.9.

19.1 The economic theory of the state

In his classic public finance text Richard Musgrave (1959) delineates the role of the state into three branches: allocation, distribution and stabilization. These days the regulatory role of the government would also be stressed (Bailey, 2002).

The government's role in allocation is the result of externalities, which are costs and benefits that arise in production but which do not directly affect either the producer or the consumer, i.e. they are suffered without compensation or enjoyed free of charge by third parties. Air pollution is an externality: when coal was the major source of energy, households and firms burnt coal without thinking of its effects on the atmosphere. In the UK it took government intervention in the form of Clean Air Acts, to encourage the burning of smokeless fuel to solve this problem of urban air pollution (see chapter 18). What is crucial about externalities is that in the absence of government intervention their costs/benefits are non-rival and non-excludable. Non-rivalry occurs where one person's benefit/cost from a service does not limit other peoples' enjoyment/suffering. Such non-rivalry implies that access should not be limited by price or other means. If it is not possible to prevent access to a service to individuals who have not paid, then the service is non-excludable: it is generally not possible to finance the service privately because it cannot be charged for – the free-rider problem. With public goods such as defence, all the benefits are non-rival and non-excludable, so governments finance them

from general taxation. The allocative role of government involves the provision or subsidization of services where externalities are significant.

The regulatory role of the state overlaps with that of allocation, by setting rules in markets to make them work in society's interests. So regulation encompasses competition policy (see chapter 13), the rules for natural monopolies (see chapter 17), the safety of products, financial services, etc. The reason for government regulation is either that there are problems with competition in the market or that there are informational problems. For example, with financial services there is a case for regulation because of systemic risk: the government has to ensure the viability of key financial institutions in a crisis, while avoiding moral hazard[2] in its underwriting of banks in difficulties. Financial services also need to be regulated because of information problems related to the complexity of the product, so consumers need to be protected from fraud and misrepresentation.

The distributive role of government recognizes the fact that markets are compatible with very unequal distributions of individual income levels (see table 5.13), which are unacceptable to modern societies. Redistribution occurs as a result of equity, insurance and special interest. Equity justifies the redistribution of income from rich to poor in accordance with society's views on fairness. Insurance is a payment to people with particular adverse circumstances: unemployment, sickness and retirement. The political power of special groups may also enable them to obtain redistribution in their favour, which is the case with farmers in the EU. Redistribution takes place via a progressive tax system,[3] a progressive benefit system and the provision of public services that are subsidized or free of charge. Central governments also redistribute income among regions. Part of this is explicit through grants and transfer mechanisms, but most occurs via the operation of national taxation, social security systems and the provision of government services (CEC, 1977a; Sala-i-Martin and Sachs, 1992). Governments provide insurance against unemployment and sickness and pensions for the elderly, even though this can be purchased privately. However, market provision is unlikely to cover all eventualities (e.g. long-term unemployment) and many individuals, particularly those at greatest risk, would be unable to pay the necessary premiums. Thus the government provides social insurance partly as an allocative measure because of gaps in the market, but largely for redistributive reasons.[4]

Government's stabilization role is the use of monetary and fiscal policy to try to achieve the objectives of full employment, price stability, economic growth and balance of payments equilibrium. Today there is much less confidence in government's ability to stabilize the economy than there was when Musgrave's book was published. Many governments have delegated authority over monetary policy to independent central banks, because it is believed that better decisions will result from technocratically driven decisions freed from short-term political considerations. Similarly, difficulties with the accurate timing and magnitude of discretionary fiscal policy have led governments to rely on automatic stabilization (see chapter 12).

Although these arguments provide a clear justification for state intervention in the economy, its extent is subject to discretion, with the size of the public expenditure and the extent of public services varying widely among nation-states. While part of this variation is due to differences in the level of development, much is the result of history, national values and institutions.

19.2 Fiscal federalism

Choices have to be made not only about the extent of the public sector but also the level of government at which the activity takes place. The traditional theory of fiscal federalism (Oates, 1999) examines the factors that will determine the choice of the level of government, which will undertake the various economic tasks of the state.[5] The theory assumes that each level of government cares exclusively about the welfare of its constituents. An efficient system of fiscal federalism would then balance the advantages and disadvantages of provision at various levels of government, and allocate competences accordingly.

The principal advantage of decentralization is that the lower the level of government the easier it is to assess the preferences of local residents, so the provision of services can be better tailored to their requirements. The existence of different sub-national units of government (regions) means levels of taxation and public services can be varied. Central government not only has informational problems, it also has a limited ability to differentiate policies across jurisdictions.[6] Democratic accountability is also best achieved with decentralized government where the connection between costs and public provision is most apparent. The correspondence between those who benefit from public expenditure and the taxpayers who fund it is most apparent with local provision (Oates, 1977).

Centralized public services may offer benefits provided the preferences of citizens in different jurisdictions are similar, i.e. everyone wants roughly the same thing. The policies of one region may have effects on other regions (spillovers) and central government can take account of these interactions. When there are economies of scale, i.e. where the cost per unit diminishes with the volume of the service produced, central government provision may be more efficient.[7] Centralization can be used to achieve uniformity in public provision, which may be regarded as important for equity reasons in health, or for equity and efficiency reasons in the case of education. There are also advantages of centralization in relation to taxation; generally, immobile tax bases should finance state/local government. Since mobility is potentially a problem with the major sources of taxation – personal income, corporate profits, social security and to an extent the taxation of consumption (see chapter 14) – state/local government financial autonomy is limited. Local variation in taxation is, however, possible provided differences in rates are not too great and where sub-national jurisdictions are large. The ability to finance public services will, therefore, vary across jurisdictions; the national government can reduce these inequalities to acceptable levels. Redistribution is difficult to achieve at the local level because the rich would tend to migrate to low-tax jurisdictions (the poor might migrate to high-benefit-level localities).

If the assumption of a benevolent government is relaxed then governments may also pursue their own ends, which will not always coincide with those of society. Governments have considerable discretion because parliamentary oversight is imperfect and elections infrequent. If this is the case, decentralization may be advantageous because it increases the options available to citizens (moving to a different jurisdiction), promoting competition between jurisdictions and providing an additional mechanism for achieving efficiency in the provision of public services. This argument is particularly strong in relation to the EU because of the strength of national democracy and concerns over the democratic deficit of the EU.

The Commission has examined the implications of fiscal federalism for the EU on three occasions, all related to the issue of economic and monetary union (EMU; see chapters 10–12, CEC, 1977a; Padoa-Schioppa et al., 1987; and CEC, 1993a). These reports mark a gradual retreat from a significant public finance role for the EU. In its last assessment, the Commission (CEC, 1993a) downgraded the importance of redistribution, emphasized decentralization and subsidiarity and suggested that a budget of 2 per cent of GDP was sufficient for EMU.

The large gap between public finances in the EU and existing federations is indicated by a comparison of EU and federal expenditure. Even in the leanest federation, Switzerland, the federal government expenditure amounts to 16.8 per cent of GDP compared with just 1.0 per cent in the EU (see table 19.1). The EU has significant responsibility in relation to only one area important to federal government expenditure: economic affairs (agricultural, industrial and regional policy, R&D); in the other important areas of defence, education, health and social security it has virtually no role (see table 19.2). Interest payments do not arise for the EU; since the EU cannot run deficits (see section 19.4) it does not have debt to service.

These comparisons indicate that the EU is currently very far from even a decentralized federation like Switzerland. Given the crucial differences between the EU and other federations, the latter are unlikely to provide an appropriate

Table 19.1 Expenditure at different levels of government in federal states (% of GDP), 2003

	Level of government			
	Federal	State	Local	Total
Australia	22.2	11.7	1.9	**35.8**
Canada	16.8	18.5	5.6	**40.9**
Germany	29.4	12.4	6.6	**48.3**
Switzerland[a]	16.8	12.2	7.7	**36.7**
US[a]	18.7	10.2	7.8	**36.7**
EU15[b]	1.0	34.2[c]	13.5[d]	**47.7**

Notes: [a] 2000, [b] 2001, [c] federal/central government, [d] state and local.

Sources: IMF (2004), OECD (2006d), Eurostat (2006e).

template. The next section considers the characteristics of the EU that will affect its economic role and what that role should be.

19.3 The EU and fiscal federalism

The EU is not a nation-state; it is made up of individual nation-states with their own institutions, history, culture and languages. Thus the evolving EU constitution is very different from that of national federal states and it is probable that the economic role and budget of the EU will remain distinct. One aspect of distinctness of the EU is the difference in income levels between EU member states, which are important for the provision of public services, especially social security. The non-economic differences between member states present problems for common policies in other areas such as defence/security and education.

The dispersion of income levels is much wider in the EU than in the US (figure 19.1), and this heterogeneity makes it unlikely and undesirable that the EU could have a significant distributional role. It is unlikely because redistribution would involve taxpayers in one country supplementing the income of citizens of another country. Besides the questionable political acceptability, the practical difficulties are immense: for example, how much should differences in income be reduced? The

Table 19.2 Federal government expenditure by main function (% of GDP), 2003

	Defence	Education	Health	Social security	Debt interest	Economic affairs	Other functions
Australia	1.4	2.1	3.2	7.6	1.1	1.4	6.8
Canada	1.0	0.4	0.5	7.8	1.6	1.0	4.6
Germany	1.1	0.1	5.7	16.1	1.7	2.0	2.8
US[a]	3.1	0.4	5.7	5.4	2.0	1.1	0.9
EU15	0.0	0.0	0.0	–	–	0.8	0.2

Note: [a] 2002.

Sources: IMF (2004), Eurostat (2006e).

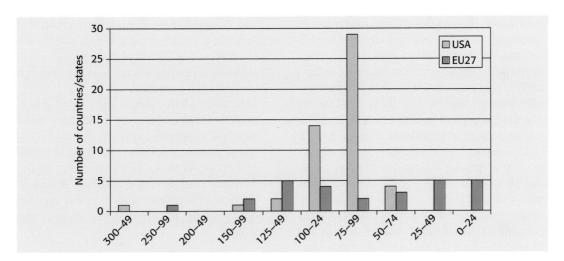

Figure 19.1 The distribution of GDP per capita in the EU and GSP per capita in the US, 2004. *Sources:* CEC (2006d), Bureau of Economic Analysis (2006), US Census Bureau (2006).

undesirability of EU redistribution is shown in an extreme form by the problems of East Germany: a powerful lesson in the economic problems of trying to impose a common redistributional policy on very different economies.

Where does this leave the EU's current redistributional role in the structural policies? The political stability of the EU in general, and EMU in particular, is dependent upon a reasonable degree of cohesion in the EU. While this probably does not require equality of income levels,[8] what is needed is that the poorer countries are at least converging on the rich. Convergence in income levels is not automatic (Ardy et al., 2002, pp. 46–50) and so some effective aid policy can be justified.[9]

There is no compelling externality or economies-of-scale argument for a significant EU involvement in health and education. With regard to defence a more compelling case can be made for a larger EU role. Defence is the classic public good, and with war in the EU increasingly unlikely, defence is against external threats to the EU as a whole, or is related to peace keeping/making beyond the EU. There is public support for the development of an EU defence policy (CEC, 2005d, p. 33). There are a number of obvious difficulties, such as the reluctance of governments to cede sovereignty over such a sensitive area, whether the public would be supportive of European armed forces, and the presence in the EU of neutral countries. Similarly, there are strong reasons for an important EU role in fighting organized crime and terrorism, where there is again public support (CEC, 2005e, p. 63).

Beyond these areas,[10] the EU economic role would seem to be confined to competences that are already part of its responsibilities, such as overseeing the single market, operating competition policy and regulation more generally, and also research and development policy where EU programmes are justified because there are potentially important economies of scale (Sapir et al., 2003b). External action is really part of foreign policy and related increasingly to defence. The current EU role in agricultural policy is more questionable; there seems little reason for the EU to be paying direct agricultural subsidies (see section 16.6 and chapter 20), so agricultural expenditure could shrink, with the EU role confined largely to regulation and trade policy. These arguments tend to suggest that there is a case for some limited expansion of the budget, if the EU were to acquire a significant defence role. It would, however, remain small – much smaller than that of existing federations. The conclusion must be that, at the present stage of development, a limited budget seems well suited to EU requirements. The EU has still to ensure that the operation of this limited budget is fair and efficient. These are the issues to which this chapter now turns.

19.4 Budget rules and procedure

There are five basic principles derived from the Treaties under which the budget operates:

1. *Annuality*, which means that the budget is only for the one year, so expenditure has to be made in that year. This prevents the build-up of long-term commitments, but has caused some problems because much EU expenditure is now on multi-annual programmes. The practical resolution of this problem has been the use of commitments for future years, which strictly do not have to be honoured, but which in practice usually are.

2. *Balance*, or equilibrium, which means that revenues must cover expenditure, and deficit financing is not possible. If expenditure is going to exceed revenue, additional resources have to be raised by supplementary or amending budgets in the current year. Surpluses at the end of the year are carried over to the next year as revenue.[11] The EU is not allowed to borrow to finance its own expenditure but can use its triple-A credit rating to borrow for loans.[12] Most of these loans take place via the European Investment Bank (EIB, see chapter 3), which is an independent EU development bank, borrowing on international capital markets and making loans for projects in the EU and beyond. These capital transactions are financially self-supporting and do not breach the principle of EU budgetary balance.

3. *Unity*: all expenditure is brought together in a single budget document.

4. *Universality*: all EU revenue and expenditure is to be included in the budget, and there are to be no self-cancelling items.

5. *Specification*: expenditure is allocated to particular objectives to ensure that it is used for the purposes the budgetary authority intended. There is some possibility for transfers between categories for the effective execution of the budget.

These rules indicate the extent to which member states wanted to limit EU competence in this sensitive area of government activity. So they ensure maximum control by member states and minimum discretion for the EU.

The budgetary procedure laid out in the 1971 Budget Treaty[13] contained the seeds of discord in decision-making. This Treaty granted the EP the responsibility for the final approval of the budget[14] (see chapter 3), a power the EP was determined to use. So in the early 1980s the annual budgetary cycle was one of frequent disputes between the institutions (Lindner, 2006, ch. 3). Two developments resolved this situation: first, the increase in powers of the EP which commenced with the Single European Act (SEA) in 1987; second, new budgetary procedures introduced with the 1988 Delors I package. This contained two innovations that continue to this day: a multi-annual financial perspective and an inter-institutional agreement on budgetary procedure.

The latest financial perspective covers the seven years 2007–13 (European Council, 2005b); it consists of agreed ceilings on broad categories of expenditure and for the budget overall. Each financial perspective is accompanied by an inter-institutional consensus under which the Commission, the Council and the EP commit themselves to respecting the agreed ceilings. Actual levels of expenditure are set by the annual budget, which must be within the limits set by the financial perspective. This budget has to be accepted through the procedure laid down in the Treaties: preliminary draft budget from the Commission, establishment of a draft budget by the Council, first reading by the Parliament, second reading by the Council and, finally, second reading by the Parliament and the adoption of the budget (see chapter 3). With the broad parameters of the financial perspective, and trialogue meetings of the three institutions throughout this procedure, the agreement of the annual budgets since 1998 has been straightforward. The decisions on the financial perspective are, however, far more hard fought.

19.5 EU budget revenue

Tax systems should be fair, efficient and transparent. Fairness can only be evaluated on the basis of consistent principles to decide tax liability.[15] There are two dimensions of fairness or equity – horizontal equity and vertical equity. Horizontal equity – the identical treatment of people in equivalent positions – implies that those with the same level of income and similar circumstances should pay the same amount of tax. Vertical equity requires the consistent treatment of people in different circumstances. In general, equity is taken to imply a progressive tax system. Depending upon how the EU raises its revenues this could apply to taxes on individuals or it could apply to member states.

Efficiency requires that the tax system should minimize harmful market distortions. Low collection and compliance costs are important additional aspects of tax efficiency. Transparency

Table 19.3 Tax revenue of different levels of government in federal states (% of GDP), 2003

	Level of government			
	Federal[a]	State	Local	Total
Australia	24.8	4.6	0.9	30.4
Canada	18.7	11.8	3.0	33.5
Germany	28.8	8.5	2.6	39.9
Switzerland[a]	17.0	6.8	4.7	28.5
US[a]	19.9	5.7	3.6	29.2
EU15	0.1[b]	32.6[c]	6.8[d]	39.4

Notes: [a] including social security contributions, 2001; [b] traditional own resources, agricultural and customs duties; [c] national current government; [d] state and local.

Sources: IMF (2004), OECD (2006a).

requires that the tax system should be simple to understand, so that taxpayers are aware of their tax liability and how this is determined. This requirement of transparency is essential for democratic accountability. This section will now consider development of the EU revenue system and how it matches up to these requirements, but first a comparison will be made between the EU revenue system and those of federal governments.

As tables 19.3 and 19.4 clearly demonstrate, the EU does not have a financing system like that of federal states. The amount of truly independent tax revenue is extremely low and taxation remains predominantly under the control of nation-states in the EU15. Federal governments typically raise a large part of their revenue from taxation of income directly through the personal income tax system or indirectly through the social security system (table 19.4). Corporation tax, VAT/general sales taxes and excises are other important sources of tax revenue for federal government. None of these revenue sources are available to the EU.

The EEC was initially financed like other international organizations by fixed national shares, but the EEC Treaty provided for the development of a system of 'own resources'. The significance of this was that the EEC would have financial autonomy, by acquiring financial resources distinct from those of the member states. This proved controversial and

Table 19.4 Tax systems: federal states and the EU (% of GDP), 2003

	Personal income tax	Corporation tax	Social security	VAT[a]	Excises	Total
Australia	11.7	5.1	0.0	4.1	2.7	**30.4**
Canada	6.2	1.9	3.9	2.1	0.7	**33.5**
Germany	3.9	0.4	15.7	2.7	2.8	**39.9**
Switzerland[a]	1.3	1.0	5.8	3.1	1.3	**28.5**
US[a]	8.0	1.3	7.2	0.7	0.0	**29.2**
EU15	–	–	–	–	–	**0.1[b]**

Notes: [a] 2001; [b] general sales taxes or VAT; traditional own resources.

Sources: IMF (2004), OECD (2006a).

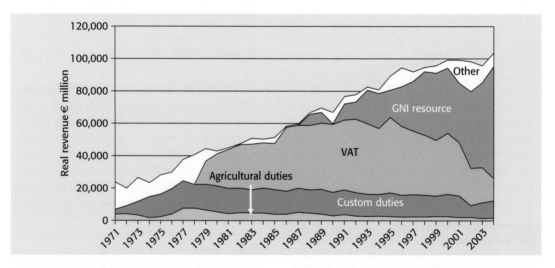

Figure 19.2 EU budgetary revenue resources, 1971–2004. *Source:* CEC (2004g, h), European Court of Auditors (2005).

it was not until April 1970, just before negotiations opened for the first enlargement, that agreement was reached. This provided for the EU to be financed by duties on agricultural imports and sugar production, revenue from the Common Customs Tariff (CCT) and VAT up to 1 per cent of the harmonized base (see chapter 15). The 'traditional own resources' (TOR), agricultural levies and customs duties are naturally EU revenue because they arise from EU policies: the Common Agricultural Policy (CAP) and Common Commercial Policy (CCP; see chapters 6 and 24). In a common market, it is difficult to assign these revenues to individual member states because goods imported through a member state where the duties are paid may then

be sold in another where the actual burden or incidence of the tax occurs.[16] As member states have not used the harmonized base, the VAT contribution has always rested on 'artificial' calculation (Begg and Grimwade, 1998, pp. 41–2), so it amounts to being just a particular way of calculating a national contribution.

The original own resources system had a number of problems as a system of finance for the EC. At first, revenue expanded as the call-up rate of VAT increased, but once the 1 per cent limit was reached, revenue grew comparatively slowly (figure 19.2). TOR revenue was constrained by falling agricultural imports as EC food self-sufficiency levels increased (see chapter 20), decreasing tariff rates,

Table 19.5 Sources of EU revenue, 2003 and 2004

	2003		2004	
	€ million	%	€ million	%
Traditional own resources	10,857.2	11.6	12,307.1	11.9
Agricultural duties	1,011.8	1.1	1,313.4	1.3
Sugar and isoglucose levies	383.2	0.4	401.6	0.4
Customs duties	9,462.1	10.1	10,592.1	10.2
VAT resources	21,260.1	22.7	13,912.1	13.4
GNI resources	51,235.2	54.8	68,982.0	66.6
Other revenue	9,836.1	10.5	8,458.7	8.2
Surplus from previous financial year	7,676.8	8.2	5,693.0	5.5
Miscellaneous revenue	2,159.3	2.3	2,765.7	2.7
Total	93,468.6	100.0	103,511.9	100.0

Source: European Court of Auditors (2005).

expanding EC membership and the extension of preferential trade agreements with third countries (see chapter 24). The VAT base also grew slowly because it excluded government expenditure and savings which tend to expand over time. It was regressive because these elements tend to increase as income levels increase. So the system was not equitable; contributions to the budget were not related to GNI per capita. The UK in particular seemed to be contributing more than its fair share, because of its high level of imports from outside the EU, and a relatively low level of government expenditure and savings.[17] Raising the VAT limit to 1.4 per cent in 1984[18] increased revenue but this was only a temporary solution, which did not address the problems of lack of buoyancy or of equity in contributions.

The own resources system was made more equitable and more buoyant by the introduction in 1988 of the fourth resource based on GNI. The base for own resources is now expressed as a percentage of EU GNI, currently 1.24 per cent. EU revenue now comes from the four own resources and miscellaneous revenue:

1. *Duties on agricultural imports and sugar production.* Agricultural duties are tariff revenue on imports of agricultural goods. Sugar levies are a tax on the production of sugar beyond quota limits and on the production of isoglucose.[19]

2. *Common Customs Tariff* (CCT). The revenue from EU taxes on non-agricultural imports. The importance of these TOR was diminished by the decision, taken in 1999, to increase the share of TOR retained by national governments to cover the cost of collection from 10 to 25 per cent (European Council, 1999a).

3. *VAT* revenue of 0.3 per cent of VAT on the harmonized base. To make VAT fairer the VAT base has since 1992 been capped at 50 per cent of GNI for member states whose per capita GDP is less than 90 per cent of the EU average.

4. *The GNI resource.* In the annual budget the revenue raised from TOR and VAT is subtracted from total EU expenditure and the difference is expressed as a percentage of EU15 GNI, with each member state contributing an amount equal to this percentage of its GNI.[20] With the revenue from other sources diminishing as a percentage of GNI, this resource is becoming the dominant source of EU revenues (figure 19.2 and table 19.5).

This system of finance has given the EU revenue which grows in line with GNI and which is reasonably fair because contributions are roughly proportional to GNI (figure 19.3).[21] The exceptions are Belgium and the Netherlands (the Rotterdam problem), Luxembourg (the obverse of the Rotterdam problem) and the UK (due to its

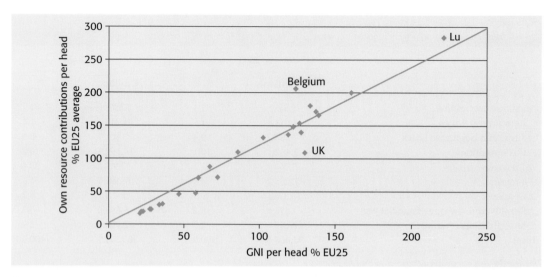

Figure 19.3 EU25 'own resource' contributions and GNI per head, 2004. *Sources:* European Court of Auditors (2005), CEC (2006d), own calculations.

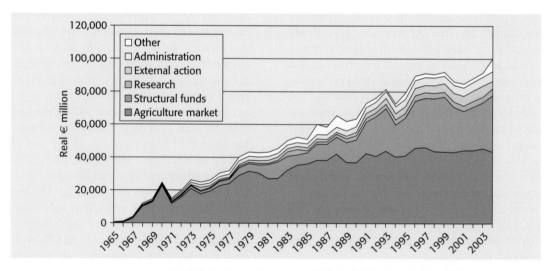

Figure 19.4 Real EU expenditure, 1965–2004. *Source:* CEC (2004g, h), European Court of Auditors (2005).

correction mechanism; see section 19.6). The increasing dependence on GNI-based contributions means that the EU has largely gone back to a system of national contributions.

19.6 EU budget expenditure

The development of budgetary expenditure follows the development of EU policies. For a long time the budget was dominated by agricultural expenditure, partly because other policies were underdeveloped but also because the CAP became expensive to operate. Up until the late 1980s, agricultural expenditure grew rapidly. Since then, however, real budgetary expenditure has been stabilized (figure 19.4). This was the result of production control measures (such as milk quotas) and limits being placed on agricultural expenditure, initially in 1984 but more effectively since 1988.

Table 19.6 EU expenditure, 2003 and 2004

	2003		2004	
	€ million	%	€ million	%
Common Agricultural Policy	44,379.2	49.0	43,579.4	43.5
CAP markets	39,699.6	43.8	37,861.6	37.8
Rural development	4,679.6	5.2	5,717.8	5.7
Structural operations	28,527.6	31.5	34,198.3	34.2
Internal policies	5,671.8	6.3	7,255.2	7.2
Research and development	3,279.6	3.6	4,174.7	4.2
External action	4,285.8	4.7	4,605.8	4.6
Administration	5,305.2	5.9	5,856.4	5.8
Reserves	147.9	0.2	181.9	0.2
Pre-accession aid	2,239.8	2.5	3,052.9	3.0
Compensation	0.0	0.0	1,409.5	1.4
Total	90,557.5	100.0	100,139.4	100.0
% EU GNI				

Source: European Court of Auditors (2004, 2005).

As enlargement increased the heterogeneity of the Community, it was felt necessary to introduce a greater redistributive element into the budget by expanding and concentrating expenditure on structural operations. Part of this additional expenditure was financed by an expansion of the revenue base of the budget, but the stabilization of agricultural expenditure freed resources for structural policies. Expenditure on research has increased as a result of concerns over EC competitiveness. The ending of the Cold War led to increased expenditure as the EU sought to bring stability to Central and Eastern Europe. This pre-accession expenditure remains significant despite the 2004–7 enlargements. Agriculture and structural expenditure continue, however, to dominate the budget (table 19.6).

19.6.1 CAP guarantee expenditure

Initially the CAP maintained high EC agricultural prices by import protection. As surpluses began to develop, support buying and dumping of surpluses on the world market led to increased agricultural expenditure. This form of the CAP, where the EU rapidly expanded its share of world agricultural trade on the basis of subsidized exports,

began to wane as a result of budgetary pressures in the 1980s and trade negotiations (the Uruguay Round of the GATT) in the 1990s (see chapter 20). The EU switched support for farmers to direct subsidies, with production restrained by lower prices and production controls. In 2004, 76.2 per cent of agricultural guarantee expenditure was on direct subsidies (ECA, 2005, p. 82). This change in the pattern of expenditure has substantially enhanced budgetary planning and control, because direct subsidies are much more stable and predictable than price support expenditure. It does, however, call into question the EU's role in agricultural policy. Price support in a single market requires EU finance because the EU price is maintained by support buying wherever this takes place. But there seems no good reason for the EU to finance direct subsidies to farmers; however, the EU should retain a regulatory role, to ensure fair competition between farmers from different countries.

There are substantial variations in CAP guarantee expenditure[22] among member states, which bear no relation to their GNP per head. In figure 19.5 the EU15 member states[23] are arranged in order of their GNI per head, with the highest to the right. CAP expenditure does not diminish as GNP

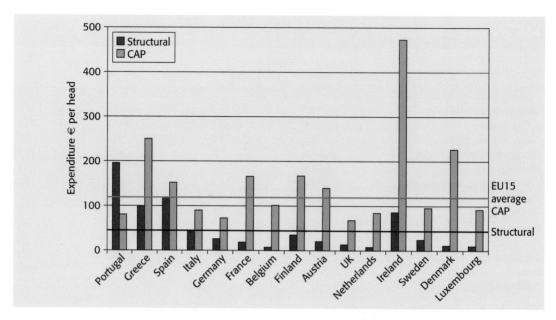

Figure 19.5 EU15 CAP and structural expenditure, 2003–4. *Sources:* European Court of Auditors (2004, 2005), CEC (2004g, h).

per capita increases. Ireland, Greece and Denmark receive substantial payments, although Greece is one of the poorest EU15 countries and Denmark and Ireland are among the richest. Countries receiving less than the average CAP expenditure are similarly diverse, ranging from the poorest, Portugal, to the richest, Luxembourg. With around half of the budget spent on agriculture it is difficult to achieve an equitable budget with such random distribution of CAP expenditure.

For farmers, landowners and industries associated with agriculture, EU support of prices and direct subsidies provide substantial benefits.[24] For taxpayers and consumers the CAP imposes substantial costs in two ways: first, by the taxation paid to finance the budgetary expenditure; and, second, by the additional expenditure on food due to EU prices exceeding world market prices. With the reformed CAP, and the high world prices of recent years, the gaps between EU and world prices have narrowed substantially. For most agricultural products, EU prices are near to world levels, so the additional costs to the consumer are minor. This is not the case for milk products, beef and sugar, but this consumption cost is relatively minor nowadays (Ardy, 2002a, pp. 96–7), so

measured CAP expenditure provides a reasonable approximation of national benefits from the CAP.

19.6.2 Structural policy expenditure

The structural funds – the European Social Fund (ESF), European Agricultural Guidance Fund (EAAGF), the European Regional Development Fund (ERDF) and the Cohesion Fund – were developed to try to achieve greater solidarity within the Union. They were justified, therefore, as a redistributive policy, to encourage political solidarity. Structural expenditure has also been useful as side payments to facilitate agreement between member states. The expansion of the structural funds and their concentration on poorer regions since 1988 was part of the bargain to achieve agreement on the Single European Act (SEA). This concentration of expenditure on poorer regions redistributes income to poorer countries.[25] The highest levels of expenditure in the EU15[26] are in the poorest member states: Portugal, Greece and Spain. Ireland's above-average expenditure receipts reflect its previous status as one of the EU's poorer states; levels of structural expenditure in Ireland are gradually being curtailed. All other member states have below-average structural expenditure per head. With structural spending aimed at regional rather than national redistribution, other objectives being pursued, and political factors affecting its distribution, its redistributive effect is somewhat uneven. With CAP and structural spending accounting for 80 per cent of EU expenditure it is their distribution which largely determines the distribution of expenditure among EU member states.

19.6.3 Internal policies

The largest element of internal policy expenditure is research and technological development (see chapter 14), which tries to enhance EU competitiveness. Also significant under this heading are education, vocational training, and trans-European networks (TENs). Education expenditure mainly finances grants for study in other EU countries. This expenditure should help forge a greater sense of EU identity and could have beneficial effects on the single market by encouraging labour mobility. Expenditure on TENs is very similar to ERDF expenditure, financing cross-border networks of roads, railways, energy and telecommunications grids. Such networks are important in fostering competition in the single market and, since they are cross-border, EU involvement is probably desirable to encourage their development.

19.6.4 External action

EU external expenditure is concentrated on three groups of countries:[27] the ACP countries, the Middle East and the southern Mediterranean (see chapter 25), and there is still some enlargement expenditure for the western Balkans. Pre-accession aid for the candidate and potential candidate countries[28] is a separate budget category to protect this expenditure if there is pressure on the budget and underlining the passage of relations with these countries from external to internal (see chapter 26). Russia and the former CIS countries have not been offered EU membership, but the development of a closer political and economic relationship and economic aid are an important part of this process.

Aid to the Mediterranean and the Middle East again tries to increase the stability of another volatile region close to the EU. Economic development in this area would also help to reduce the pressure for migration to the EU. Aid to the ACP reflects obligations and ties to former colonies. The EU channels aid both via the budget and by a separately financed European Development Fund (EDF), which is responsible for most of the EU aid to ACP countries. Expenditure under the EDF is decided separately from the budget by the Council and is financed by fixed national shares. There are concerns about the effectiveness of aid programmes (see chapter 25), as well as about individual elements of aid. For example, food aid accounts for around 20 per cent of budget expenditure on aid; this has sometimes been little more than an extension of the CAP facilitating the disposal of surpluses, with problematic consequences for recipient nations (Cathie, 2001).

Although there is public support for foreign aid, the EU role is not well understood, nor is it differentiated from national government aid programmes. The necessary scale of the operations, and the need to avoid wasteful duplication, justifies EU aid, but the continuance of national government programmes undermines the development of a clear role for the EU.

19.6.5 Administration

The least understood element of EU expenditure is that on administration. Constant references in the press to the Brussels bureaucracy, their gravy train lifestyle, and pictures of enormous edifices in Brussels and Strasbourg, suggest a vast and expensive bureaucracy. Thus paying for officials, meetings and buildings was the category selected by the public as the area on which expenditure is the largest item in the budget (CEC, 2005e, p. 90). This is a very distorted picture: the number of people employed by the European institutions is relatively small: 37,417 in 2004, of which 25,393 are in the Commission (CEC, 2004d, p. 155; see chapter 3). This is modest compared to national and local governments: in 2005 the US federal government had 1,949,900 employees (BLS, 2006). So the idea of the Commission as a vast and unwieldy bureaucracy is completely false. The small size of the Commission is the result of the limited policies for which the EU is responsible, and the way in which these policies are operated. Government policies with large numbers of employees, such as health, remain the responsibility of national governments. National governments and their employees largely operate EU policies. Administration has remained a small and stable proportion of total EU expenditure as a result of the continued limitation of the EU powers and responsibilities.

Concerns over administration also relate to issues about administrative competence and corruption highlighted by the resignation of the Santer Commission in 1999. Three aspects of the EU and its administration are important in this respect. First, the multinational character of the administration makes it difficult to devise suitable codes of conduct, because different countries have different ideas of what is acceptable. Thus, the employment of relatives and friends by governments and officials is normal in some countries but not in others. Second, the small size of the Commission, in relation to its responsibilities, has made it difficult to keep track of expenditure. There have been difficulties with the employment of contract workers, and the supervision of EU programmes is hampered by a shortage of staff. The Commission budget department has had particular problems. The European Court of Auditors has noted some progress but there are still problems in providing assurance of the reliability and legality of much agricultural, structural, internal and external expenditure (European Court of Auditors, 2005, p. 11). Third, the member states have the primary responsibility for monitoring most programmes. The Commission has a rather ambiguous managerial and supervisory role, but generally no powers to carry out investigations in the member states. Administrative reform has been the aim of the Commission but progress has been slow and the problem of monitoring the operation of the policies in the member states remains.

Administrative expenditure is heavily concentrated in Belgium and Luxembourg, but the extent of the benefits this confers on these countries is limited. With other areas of expenditure, it is possible to argue that EU expenditure is largely for activities that would have occurred anyway, and so it is a net addition to GNI. Administrative expenditure either involves the use of resources such as labour, capital and land, or pays for individuals who are citizens of other member states. While Belgium and Luxembourg undoubtedly enjoy multiplier and balance of payments effects, this benefit is far less than the total amount of administrative expenditure in their countries.

19.7 Net contributions to the EU budget

A member state's net contribution (NC) to the budget is the difference between the amount it pays in own resource revenue and the amount it receives from allocated expenditure.[29] The Commission position on NCs has changed: it used to argue that national concerns with NCs are mistaken, and that the budgetary costs and benefits are an inaccurate measure of the costs and benefits of EU membership.[30] While this is true, it is irrelevant; whatever the overall costs and benefits of membership, the EU should be equitably financed. Another frequent observation is that the budget is too small to matter. However, the amounts involved are very large: EU expenditure is greater than the GDP of all twelve new member states except Poland. Unlike national budgets, which are largely transfers from one group within the national economy to another, payments to the EU represent invisible imports and reductions in GNI, and receipts from the EU represent invisible exports and additions to GNI. The Commission now accepts that NCs can be unfair and there needs to be a correction mechanism (CEC, 2004g).

Figure 19.6 plots NCs for 2004 against GNI per head, revealing a weak negative relationship between them. The new member states are paying their full budget contributions, even though their receipts of EU expenditure are relatively low, but as a result of transitional relief they are all net recipients from the budget. They are, however, less generously treated than Portugal and Greece, the poorest EU15 member states, which receive net benefits equal to 2.2 per cent and 2.4 per cent of

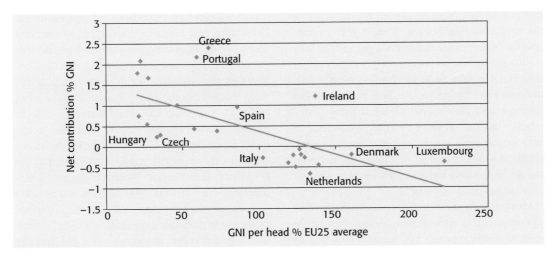

Figure 19.6 Net contributions to the EU budget and GNI per head, 2004. *Sources:* European Court of Auditors (2005), CEC (2006d).

GNI respectively. Ireland, with the fourth-highest GNI per head in the EU, receives net benefits of 1.2 per cent of GNP.[31] Luxembourg, the EU's and the world's richest state, has NC similar to that of the other higher GNI EU15 member states even ignoring its substantial administrative receipts. Seven member states with GNI between 100 and 130 per cent of the EU average have net contributions of between −0.1 per cent and −0.5 per cent of GNP. The budget thus has a rather haphazard impact: overall it is redistributive, but the relationship between NCs and GNI is weak (De la Fuente and Domenesh, 2001).

National governments are very well aware of their NCs, and if they think they are being treated unfairly they will demand that the situation be resolved. The most infamous example of this is the British problem, a recurrent issue from 1973 when the UK joined the EEC until its resolution in 1984, unfortunately with a rebate specific to the UK. The UK correction for budgetary imbalances is calculated as follows: in the current year, the correction is calculated on the basis of the imbalance in the previous year, equal to the percentage share of the UK in VAT and GNI payments minus its share in total allocated expenditure, multiplied first by total allocated expenditure and then by 0.66.[32] The correction is financed by increasing the own resource contributions from other member states,

and not surprisingly this is strongly resented. The UK's position within the EU has also changed substantially: when the rebate was agreed in 1984 the UK was the fourth-poorest of ten member states, today it is the fifth-richest of twenty-five, a point emphasized by the fact that new member states with very low levels of GNI per capita are contributing to the UK rebate. Nevertheless, without the rebate the UK would be the second-largest proportional net contributor to the EU budget.[33]

There has been a hardening of attitudes towards the NCs budget. Two developments have been crucial: the changing situation of Germany and EMU. German unification has put tremendous pressure on the federal government's budget, with a net transfer of 4 per cent of GDP from West to East Germany (CEC, 2002c, p. 2). This burden has been made worse by the related poor performance of the German economy. Germany is, therefore, no longer willing or able to act as the paymaster for Europe; indeed it wants to reduce its NC. The change in German attitudes has been mirrored by the Netherlands, Austria and Sweden calling for reductions in their NCs. Economic circumstances are also a factor for these countries, but for euro area members EMU budgetary restraint is also a problem (see chapter 10). NCs to the EU budget of 0.5 per cent of GNI do not seem very significant compared to government budgets of 30 to 50 per cent of GNI. But these NCs loom much larger in relation to the Stability and Growth Pact's upper limit for public sector deficits of 3 per cent of GDP and the medium-term requirement for the budget to be close to balance or in surplus. With monetary policy determined by the ECB on the basis of the euro area conditions, national fiscal policy remains the one flexible short-term element of macroeconomic policy in national governments' hands. NCs to the budget eat into this national margin for flexibility and so have become a much more salient political issue.

With the current range of revenue resources and expenditure, it is difficult to achieve a fair distribution of budgetary costs and benefits and thus of NCs. Over time the complexity of the revenue system is increasing as more and more adjustments are made to make the system more equitable. Policy reform could achieve a fairer outcome, but to conflate reform and equity could compromise the objectives of reform. In the absence of reform, NCs can be restricted by limiting budgetary expenditure and this is what has happened. A much better solution would be a redistribution mechanism, which would ensure a fair distribution of net contributions (De la Fuente and Domenesh, 2001). Such a system would have the enormous advantage that each member state would feel the effects of new expenditure commitments on its net contribution, and thus budgetary considerations would not bias policymaking.[34]

19.8 The EU budget and EMU[35]

There are two macroeconomic roles for the budget in a monetary union: fiscal policy and transfers between regions. Fiscal policy is the manipulation of the balance between government expenditure and revenue so as to influence aggregate demand in the economy. The small size and requirement for balance mean that the EU budget cannot have a role in fiscal policy. Regions within a monetary union that face asymmetric shocks can no longer use the exchange rate as a shock-absorbing mechanism. With automatic transfers from the central/federal budget, fiscal policy will act as a means of interregional risk sharing by transferring

resources between regions (see chapters 10–12). These transfers perform three types of function (Fatás, 1998): intertemporal stabilization, interregional insurance and interregional redistribution. The first two stabilize regional income and the third reduces inequalities in income levels between regions. Intertemporal stabilization smooths fluctuations in regional income levels due to the stabilization of the national economy by movements in the national public sector deficits: the Keynesian stabilization function. Interregional insurance transfers tax revenue from fast-growing regions to slow-growing ones when economic cycles are imperfectly correlated between regions. Interregional redistribution involves the transfer of resources from more to less prosperous regions, so it is related to levels of rather than changes in income. Such redistribution might be justified in terms of the solidarity of the nation-state, to achieve a fairer individual distribution of income, or to enhance overall economic efficiency. The delineation of these transfers in theory and their separation in reality are another matter; in national monetary unions transfers between regions fulfil all three functions.

Interregional stabilization is not possible using the EU budget, so how important is this stabilization and how much of a problem is its absence? Initial research (Sala-i-Martin and Sachs, 1992), indicated that interregional flows of public finance were important in reducing fluctuations in regional income. Gradually more refined research techniques have whittled away at the estimated effects and more recent research suggests that federal taxes and transfers only reduce regional income fluctuations by 10 per cent (Fatás, 1998; Asdrubali et al., 2002). These estimates of stabilization are for the US, a monetary union comparable in size to EMU. Whether it is a good basis for comparison with EMU could be questioned because of the difference between US states and EU countries. The national economies[36] of EMU remain diversified so their vulnerability to asymmetric shocks and, consequently, the need for interregional stabilization is less. The greater separation of EU nation-states may also enhance the potential for differences in rates of wage and price inflation: an effective alternative adjustment mechanism. By comparison with the US, European national economies lack adjustment mechanisms such as labour mobility and cross-border capital holdings and flows, but are perhaps less vulnerable to asymmetric shocks than US states.

19.9 The EU budget and enlargement

The 2004 enlargement placed large potential demands upon the budget because of three characteristics of the Central and Eastern European countries[37] (CEECs): low income levels, the large total size of their populations and the importance of agriculture (see chapter 26). Since contributions to the budget are roughly related to GNI (see section 19.4), the CEECs only add a small amount to EU revenue from own resources but would add significantly to EU expenditure because of their demands on the structural policy and agricultural budgets.

The Commission proposals for budgetary and policy reform in response to enlargement were contained in *Agenda 2000* (CEC, 1997b), and involved both limiting expenditure in the NMS (no direct agricultural payments and a limit on structural spending), reducing structural expenditure in the EU15 and some growth of expenditure (structural expenditure in the NMS and additional agricultural expenditure). Expenditure in other areas was to be tightly controlled, so that with enlargement the budget would expand by around 11.5 per cent over 1999 expenditure, remaining well within the existing own resources ceiling. This was very stringent given the characteristics of this enlargement; other enlargements had led to substantial expansions in the budget.

The eventual Berlin Agreement in February 1999 cut back the proposed modest increase in expenditure and postponed many difficult decisions (European Council, 1999a). Agricultural reform was scaled back and the size of reductions in structural expenditure in the EU15 reduced. The combination of a lower overall level of expenditure and side payments[38] was sufficient to satisfy those countries demanding a reduction in their NCs. The Berlin Agreement provided only an interim solution because the decision not to make direct payments to the NMS came to be seen as unreasonable; the expansion in the number of potential new members and the requirement for a mid-term review of the CAP meant budget reform remained on the agenda. The Brussels Agreement (European Council, 2002b) finalized the financial arrangements for enlargement. It contained five principal elements. First, there was to be no extra expenditure for enlargement; the Berlin ceiling is to be respected. Second, direct payments are to be extended to new member states at the rate of 25 per cent in 2004, rising to 100 per cent in 2013. Third, there is to be financial stability for the CAP: guaranteed expenditure from 2007 to 2013 cannot exceed the real-terms expenditure in 2006. Overall expenditure that is agricultural market-related and direct payment expenditure during 2007–13 is to be kept below that for 2006 plus 1 per cent per annum. Fourth, this is without prejudice to provisions on the reform of the CAP in the Berlin Agreement and the international commitments of the EU, including the Doha WTO round. Fifth, if forecast cash flow under the budget is less than in 2003 for any new member state, compensation will be offered. This agreement only provided for the initial eighteen months of enlargement when expenditure would be limited by the phasing in of direct payments and the gradual build-up of structural expenditure in the new member states.

This was the starting point for the negotiations on the 2007–13 financial framework – the first to require unanimous agreement among the twenty-five member states. These negotiations needed to reconcile four contradictory demands: first, the need for additional 'enlargement expenditure'; second, the desire for additional expenditure in new priority areas; third, the demands for large NCs to be reduced; fourth, an unwillingness among other EU15 member states to increase their NCs, or to reduce their net benefits and in particular to retain structural spending. The only area of near unanimity was the demand that the UK's rebate should be reduced, a demand the UK was only prepared to accede in conjunction with CAP reform. The Commission's initial proposals were for a modest expansion of expenditure (CEC, 2004e): payment appropriations were to be on average 15 per

Table 19.7 EU financial perspective for 2007–2013

	% change in payment appropriations 2007–13 compared to 2006		% share of expenditure 2007–13
	Commission 2004 proposal	European Council 2005 agreement	
1. Sustainable growth	43.5	14.8	**44.2**
1a. Competitiveness for growth and employment	115.9	18.0	8.6
1b. Cohesion for growth and employment	27.1	14.2	35.6
2. Sustainable management and protection of natural resources	3.3	−4.6	**43.0**
Agriculture – market-related expenditure	−1.6	−3.6	33.9
Other expenditure	20.6	−8.2	9.1
3. Citizenship, freedom, security and justice	91.6	7.0	1.2
4. The EU as a global player	21.7	−35.9	5.7
5. Administration	19.0	10.9	5.8
Appropriations for payments in 2004 prices	*15.6*	*2.7*	*1.0 GDP*

Sources: European Council (2005b), CEC (2004f), European Parliament, Council and Commission, 2006.

cent higher in real terms over the 2007–13 period, compared to 2006. Under the new categorization of expenditure by objective rather than by policy, the greatest proportional growth of expenditure was on citizenship, freedom, security and justice, but in absolute terms the largest expansion was in the sustainable growth category, competitiveness (mainly R&D) and cohesion; also expenditure on external action was to increase substantially. On the revenue side a generalized correction mechanism was proposed which would apply a 66 per cent rebate to any country that exceeded a reasonable net contribution set at 0.35 per cent of GNI. This would have improved the budgetary situation of twenty-three EU countries by 0.3–0.8 per cent of GNI, but Austria's budgetary contribution would have increased by 0.2 per cent of GNI and the UK's by 0.26 per cent (CEC, 2004i, p. 70).

A deal was eventually reached in December 2005 (European Council, 2005b).[39] The outcome followed the familiar pattern of expenditure restriction, limited reform, side payments, the postponement of difficult issues, plus the adjustment of the UK's rebate. The overall growth of the budget was reduced substantially so that instead of the proposed 15.6 per cent increase, real

expenditure on average for 2007–13 is to be only 2.7 per cent higher than in 2006. All categories of expenditure are to be reduced, with the largest cuts in competitiveness, citizenship, and the EU as a global partner (table 19.7). The two largest items of expenditure – agricultural market and cohesion expenditure – fare better, with only marginal cuts in agriculture. The cohesion budget looks tight given the additional expenditure in the NMS.

The demands from the Netherlands, Germany, Sweden and Austria for reductions in their net contributions were partially met by the constraint in overall budgetary expenditure. They also benefited from reductions in VAT contributions, and in the case of the Netherlands and Sweden from reductions in their GNI contribution. The positions of new member states were enhanced by the concentration of structural funds on poorer states and poorer regions. These provisions were partially financed by reductions in the UK's rebate, which remained in full on all expenditure except that relating to the new member states. On this expenditure the UK, except for CAP market expenditure, will contribute a maximum 10.5 billion euros extra over the 2007–13 period and from 2009 it will contribute fully to this expenditure.

There will be a comprehensive reassessment of the financial framework in 2008/9.

19.10 Conclusion

The 2005 agreement follows closely the pattern established in 1999: a low overall growth of expenditure based on the expansion of GNI but not in the EU's percentage share. This, together with gradual decline of agricultural expenditure, permits the growth of expenditure on structural and other priority areas, within tight expenditure constraints. But the EU has again postponed difficult decisions on the fundamental problems of the budget.

The EU budget faces the challenges of equity and the future development of the EU. The problem of equity is vital because member states will block future developments with budgetary implications unless the financing and expenditure system of the EU is fair. Reform of the CAP would help make the budget fairer and would release funds for the expansion of other policies and for expenditure in the new member states. Structural operations can be justified as facilitating convergence and providing a visible EU response in problem regions. Generally, the concentration of funds should be enhanced, but all member states should continue to receive some structural funding; it would be undesirable to create sub-groups of client and donor states within the EU. These changes would make the budget fairer, but with the EU likely to continue with a narrow range of financial resources and expenditure policies, equity in the budget can only be achieved by a generalized redistribution mechanism. This would ensure that net contributions were related to GNI per head in a consistent and equitable manner. Failure to resolve these problems would mean that the EU budget would still be concentrating on dealing with past problems of agriculture and the regions rather than developing the EU of the future, e.g. laying emphasis on R&D and environmental expenditure (Sapir et al., 2004b).

That the EU does not have a budget comparable to existing federations is both unarguable and unsurprising. It is unarguable because of the requirement of balance, its small size, the composition of expenditure and the fact that it is financed largely by national contributions, not its own taxes. It is unsurprising because the EU is very far from a political federation, made up as it is of mature nation-states determined to preserve a significant degree of national sovereignty. Thus the expenditure and revenues of the EU tier of government will continue to develop slowly. The most important areas of federal government activity will remain national because there are few clear advantages and many problems in moving provision to the EU. This is not to suggest that there should be no further EU-level development of policies. The strongest arguments here relate to internal security and CFSP. The likelihood is, therefore, that EU budgetary responsibilities will remain limited, in keeping with its status as a confederation.

NOTES

1 The general budget of the EU excludes the European Development Fund (see section 19.6.4).

2 Moral hazard is the problem that if the government guarantees the financial viability of banks in a crisis, this may encourage greater risk-taking by banks, which in turn could lead to a crisis.

3 Where the proportion of income paid in tax increases as income rises.

4 There is again a moral hazard problem here: if the government provides adequate pensions this reduces the incentive, particularly among the less well-off, to purchase private pensions.

5 In practice many services are the shared responsibilities of different levels of government. This may allow some of the benefits of centralization and decentralization to be achieved. It may also blur responsibilities and be associated with problems of administration.

6 It would be difficult to justify such variation for policies funded from national taxation; the call is usually for equality of provision.

7 Externalities and economies of scale do not necessarily require central government provision; cooperation among local governments may be sufficient, but this can be problematic (Berglöf et al., 2003, p. 9).

8 Comparisons of income are probably made within rather than between countries, even with the euro.

9 For a different view see Berglöf et al. (2003).

10 For a discussion of the EU's stabilization role see section 19.8.

11 Deficits would be carried over as expenditure, but surpluses are normal because planned expenditure (commitment appropriations) is usually underspent, so actual expenditure (payment appropriations) is usually lower.

12 It also guarantees loans.

13 Treaty amending Certain Financial Provisions of the Treaties establishing the European Communities, *OJ* L, 2, 2 January 1971.

14 If the budget is not approved, the EU works with the previous year's budget.

15 The same principles should apply to benefit systems.

16 This is the 'Rotterdam problem', so called, because Rotterdam is the port of entry for many goods that are then sold in other countries, notably Germany.

17 The Netherlands also seemed to be making excessive contributions but this was largely because of the Rotterdam problem.

18 It was reduced to 1 per cent in 1988 and 0.5 per cent in 2002; from 2007 it will be 0.3 per cent. For 2007–13 lower VAT rates apply to Austria, Germany, the Netherlands and Sweden.

19 A sugar substitute made from other agricultural products.

20 For the 2007–13 period the Netherlands and Sweden will benefit from a reduction in their GNI contribution.

21 Shown by the fact that countries are near or on the 45 per cent line indicating that their income relative to the EU average is the same as their contribution.

22 This depends largely on the composition and amount of previous production.

23 Expenditure in the new member states in 2004 was low because of the gradual implementation of direct subsidies.

24 But not in an efficient manner: 20–50 per cent of expenditure (depending upon the measure) ends up as an increase in farm household incomes (OECD, 2003, pp. 54–75).

25 Sixty-two per cent of structural spending payments were for Objective 1 regions in 2004 (European Court of Auditors, 2005, p. 131).

26 Structural expenditure in the new member states was low in 2004 because structural programmes were being developed.

27 A small element of the external action is operational expenditure on joint actions decided under the CFSP.

28 Candidate countries in 2007 are Croatia, Macedonia and Turkey; potential candidates are Albania, Bosnia Herzegovina, Montenegro and Serbia including Kosovo.

29 Not all expenditure can be allocated to individual member states; the categories not allocated are administration for the reasons given (in section 19.6.5), external action and pre-accession aid – 13.3 per cent of expenditure in 2001.

30 There are in addition methodological problems with the measurement of net contributions (CEC, 2004h, annex II).

31 This is due to delayed adjustment to Ireland's improved economic circumstances and substantial CAP benefits.

32 Further adjustments are made for the capping of VAT and the increase in the member states's 'own resource' collection costs from 2001. From 2009 the additional expenditure due to the 2004 enlargement will be eliminated from the calculation.

33 The UK's 2004 net contribution without the rebate would have been 0.57 per cent and the Netherlands 0.65 per cent of GNI.

34 For example, a member state's NC can improve significantly as a result of new expenditure commitments because its benefits may outweigh its small share of the costs.

35 See Ardy (2002b) for a fuller discussion of these issues.

36 It is national economies that are important here because the persistence of large national budgets means that interregional transfers can continue within nation-states, albeit constrained by the requirement of the Stability and Growth Pact.

37 This analysis concentrates on the CEECs, because Cyprus and Malta are so small that their impact on the budget is minor.

38 The increases in the proportion of customs revenues retained to cover the cost of collection from 10 to 25 per cent, various special situations for structural funds and adjustments to the financing of the UK rebate.

39 It was finalized after negotiations with the EP, which squeezed a little more expenditure out of the Council, and some redistribution towards competitiveness, citizenship and JHA with small reductions for external relations and administration.

20

The Common Agricultural Policy

ULRICH KOESTER AND ALI EL-AGRAA

Unlike EFTA, the EU extends its free trade arrangements between member states to agriculture and agricultural products. The term 'agricultural products' is defined as 'the products of the soil, of stock-farming and of fisheries and products of first-stage processing directly related to these products (Article 32.1, Amsterdam Treaty, to which all the articles in this chapter refer), although fisheries has developed into a policy of its own – see chapter 21. Moreover, in 1957, the EEC Treaty dictated that the operation and development of the common market for agricultural products should be accompanied by the establishment of a 'common agricultural policy' among the member states (Article 32.4).

One could ask: why were the common market arrangements extended to agriculture? Or why was agriculture (together with transport) singled out for special treatment? Such questions are to some extent irrelevant. According to the General Agreement on Tariffs and Trade (GATT, now WTO, the World Trade Organization – see chapter 1, section 1.2):

a customs union shall be understood to mean the substitution of a single customs union territory for two or more territories, so that . . . duties and other restrictive regulations of commerce . . . are eliminated with respect to substantially all the trade between the constituent territories of the union (GATT, Article XXIV:8(a); see appendix to chapter 1).

Since agricultural trade constituted a substantial part of the total trade of the founding members, especially in the case of France, it should be quite obvious that excluding agriculture from the EEC arrangements would have been in direct contradiction of this requirement (see next section). Moreover, free agricultural trade would have been to no avail if each member nation continued to

protect agriculture in its own way (see section 20.3), since that would likely have amounted to the replacing of tariffs with non-tariff trade barriers (NTBs) and might also have conflicted with EC competition rules (see chapter 13). In any case, any economic integration arrangement that excluded agriculture had a zero success chance. This is because the Treaty of Rome represented a:

delicate balance of national interests of the contracting parties. In the case of West Germany the prospect of free trade in industrial goods, and free access to the French market in particular, was extremely inviting. In the case of France the relative efficiency of her agriculture . . . as compared with West Germany held out the prospect that in a free Community agricultural market she would make substantial inroads into the West German market . . . Agriculture had therefore to be included (Swann, 1973, p. 82).

The purpose of this chapter is to discuss the need for singling out agriculture as one of the earliest targets for a common policy; to specify the objectives of the Common Agricultural Policy (CAP); to explain the mechanisms of the CAP and their development to date; to make an economic evaluation of its implications; and to assess the performance of the policy in terms of its practical achievements (or lack of them) and in terms of its theoretical viability.

Before tackling these points, it is necessary to give some general background information about agriculture in the EU at the time of the formation of the EC and at a more recent date.

20.1 General background

The changing role of agriculture in the economies of member states can be demonstrated on the basis of some salient facts:

1. At the time of the signing of the treaty many people in the original Six were dependent on farming as their main source of income; indeed, 25 per cent of the total labour force was employed in agriculture – the equivalent percentage for the United Kingdom was less than 5 per cent and for Denmark about 9 per cent. The respective share for the EU15 in 2003, the year before the second last enlargement, was 5.2 per cent.

2. At the inception of the EC, the agricultural labour force was worse off than most people in the rest of the EC: for example, in France about 26 per cent of the labour force was engaged in agriculture, but for the same year the contribution of this sector to French GNP was about 12 per cent.[1] The respective shares in 2003 were 4.4 per cent of the labour force and 2 per cent of GNP. The last figure certainly exaggerates the disparity of agriculturists as many of them have an additional income from off-farm work and from capital invested outside the agricultural sector.

3. A rapid fall in both the agricultural labour force and in the share of agriculture in GNP occurred between 1955 and 1995,[2] and this trend is being maintained, albeit at a slower pace.

4. The structure of the sector has changed significantly over time. Agriculture used to be one of the most labour-intensive sectors in the early days of the EU, but has become one of the most capital-intensive. Consequently, the agricultural sector has become much more heterogeneous over time. Approximately two-thirds of farm holdings were between 1 and 10 hectares (ha, hereafter) in size at the time of the formation of the EC. Nowadays, the structure is much more diversified, partly because of enlargement, but also in the old member states:

   (i)   there is a growing large farm sector which cultivates an increasing share of land (62.5 per cent of land is in the hands of farm operators who cultivated more than 65 ha in 2003);

   (ii) there are farms which use the most recent technology (conventional farms) and others which constrain themselves by adhering to the rules of organic farming (organic farms);

   (iii) a fairly high proportion of farms are run part-time (23 per cent in 2003), but their share in total cultivated area is declining over time.

5. Agriculture in the EU did not use to be well integrated in the overall economy; the share of revenue spent on purchased inputs was less than 40 per cent in the 1960s, but is now well above 50 per cent.

6. The share of income spent on food has declined significantly over time (Engel's law). In the 1960s, it was about 40 per cent, but is now less than 15 per cent in the EU15; it is in excess of 35 per cent in some new member countries.

7. The policymakers reacted to these changes by an ever increasing intensity of regulation. It started with mainly intervention on the markets for temperate-zone products (grain, sugar and milk), expanded to the regulation of Mediterranean products (vegetables and fruits), and ended up with the regulation of farms by setting constraints on decisions made on farms.

8. It is no surprise that EU expenditure on agriculture continued to grow over time; the average rate of change from 1960 to 2003 was 6 per cent.

9. In assessing the impact of policy measures one should also take into consideration that ownership in agriculture has changed. At the inception of the EC, farms were not only small, but most of the farmers owned the land which they cultivated. However, the growth of individual farms has been more through the renting of land than purchase. Thus, many farmers cultivate more rented than owned land. Moreover, the last enlargement has added some agricultural sectors which are mainly based on tenant farming.

20.2 The problems of agriculture

Although economists praise the advantages of a free market economy, the agricultural sector in most countries has been more or less regulated by specific policies for centuries. Something seems to be special about agriculture. In this section we analyse six reasons for this special treatment: food security concerns, agricultural income, efficiency concerns, stability of markets, food safety concerns and environmental concerns.

20.2.1 Food security concerns

It is well known that there are significant fluctuations in food supply at the regional level. If markets were to function perfectly, fluctuations in regional production would cause no concern as long as the world supply was stable. Regional trade and stockpiling could easily stabilize regional food consumption. However, markets are not perfect. Interregional trade may not stabilize consumption, as markets are not perfectly integrated due to high transaction costs. Moreover, specific policies may hinder interregional trade flows. Private stockholders may not hold high enough stocks in order to stabilize consumption on the regional level, making stockpiling a risky investment, as the outcome of future harvests and future prices are not known. Market failure and policy intervention may also lead to food security concerns by other nations. Thus, most countries have food security included in the list of their agricultural policy objectives. Of course, how governments should intervene in order to achieve the objective would depend very much on the size of market failure and on available policy alternatives. The more integrated the markets, the better the flow of information and the lower the transport costs. Regional integration schemes with trading agreements mitigate food security concerns at the regional level. Markets in the EU are more integrated than in insulated countries with protectionist policies. The WTO has also helped to integrate agricultural markets by setting rules for trade. Private stockpiling is more effective in stabilizing food consumption if stockholders are not exposed to unpredictable interventions by governments. As far as the EU is concerned, markets are fairly well integrated regionally, so regional fluctuations in production should not lead to food security concerns. Nevertheless, most countries

pretend that price support policies are also needed to secure food. Price support will certainly increase food self-sufficiency, defined as the percentage ratio of domestic production over domestic consumption. However, it is highly questionable whether a higher degree of self-sufficiency for food due to protectionist policies really contributes to the achievement of food security. Food security is mainly related to income and availability of food. Poor people may not have the income to buy food. High food prices lower their purchasing power, and thus lead to food insecurity for vulnerable households. Moreover, protection leads to a lower overall income in the economy and makes people poorer. Hence, an efficient food security policy should focus on the poor and not just on available supplies on the markets. The latter is a necessary condition to secure food, but it is not sufficient.

20.2.2 Agricultural income

There is a widely held perception that income from farming does not increase as much as non-agricultural income in a growing economy. The argument is based on a closed economy and limited mobility of labour. The relationship can be clarified using a simple model, where demand is assumed to depend on income and prices:

$$q^D = q^D(Y, B, p) \tag{20.1}$$

where q^D = quantity demanded of the agricultural product, Y = income, p = price of the agricultural product, and B = population size.

Supply is assumed to depend on prices and a supply shifter, which stands for the effect of technological change:

$$q^S = q^S(p, a) \tag{20.2}$$

where q^S = quantity supplied of the agricultural product and a = supply shifter due to technical change.

It is assumed that demand and supply are equated by the prevailing price. Hence:

$$q^D = q^S. \tag{20.3}$$

From equations (20.1) and (20.2) one gets:

$$\frac{dq^D}{q^D} = \eta \cdot \frac{dy}{y} + \varepsilon_{q,p}^D \frac{dP}{P} + \frac{dB}{B} \qquad (20.4)$$

and

$$\frac{dq^S}{q^S} = \varepsilon_{q,p}^S \cdot \frac{dP}{P} + \frac{da}{a} \qquad (20.5)$$

where $\varepsilon_{q,p}^D$ = price elasticity of demand, $\varepsilon_{q,p}^S$ = price elasticity of supply, and η = income elasticity of demand.

Equating equations (20.4) and (20.5) and solving for the relative change in P results in

$$\frac{dP}{P} = \frac{1}{\varepsilon_{q,p}^D - \varepsilon_{q,p}^S} \left(\frac{da}{a} - \eta \frac{dy}{y} - \frac{dB}{B} \right). \qquad (20.6)$$

From equation (20.6) one draws certain conclusions. Prices will decline if the value in the bracket is positive. It will be positive if the rate of technical change da/a is larger than the product from the rate of change of per capita income in the economy multiplied by the elasticity of income plus the rate of change in population. Hence, technical change in agriculture is price depressing, but only under certain conditions. If there were no technical change, but high population growth without economic growth in the economy ($dY/Y = 0$), prices would go up as predicted by Malthus. The reality of the last fifty years shows that technical change in agriculture has been large enough to offset the price increasing effects of income and population growth worldwide. Indeed, as the elasticity of income declined, with higher income and population growth somewhat flattened, technological progress in agriculture tended to lower food prices even more.

However, even if there were technological progress, farm prices may not have fallen. For example, if the elasticity of demand were infinite, prices would remain unchanged. This situation may materialize for a small open country[3] such as New Zealand. The shift in the domestic supply curve due to technical change will not alter prices, as the country is a marginal supplier of food products on the world market. However, for the world as a whole the price elasticity is fairly small and therefore prices come under pressure. Yet, even if prices do fall, labour income in agriculture may not decline. If labour input in agriculture were completely determined by opportunity costs, i.e. income which could be earned in alternative occupations, the price elasticity of supply would be high, leading to a lower decline in prices. Hence, price elasticities of supply and demand are crucial for the effects of technical change on agricultural prices and incomes. If sectoral labour markets are not well integrated, labour income in one sector may deviate from that in others, but if they are integrated, differences in labour income will reflect preferences for work, protection of the environment and/or living in the countryside; differences in qualifications; and so on.

The current situation concerning labour market integration certainly differs across countries. It can be shown that labour markets are more integrated in developed market economies where information is available and transaction costs are low. Hence, it was no surprise that Gardner (1992) in his seminal article proved that there was no income disparity in the US, i.e. farmers' total income from farm and non-farm activities was about the same as that of other people in society.

If policymakers nevertheless assume that there is a need to support farm incomes by politically setting prices above market equilibrium, they will affect the number of people engaged in agriculture, but not necessarily their income per work unit. Yet, in spite of this reasoning, policymakers in most countries intervene in order to affect farm incomes.

20.2.3 Efficiency in agriculture

Efficiency concerns the use of factor inputs in the agricultural sector. The sector produces efficiently if the ratio of total output to total input, i.e. total productivity, cannot be increased by an alternative use of factors. The agricultural sector may lack efficiency for at least three reasons:

1. Individual farms do not employ the most efficient technology. Farmers may lack the

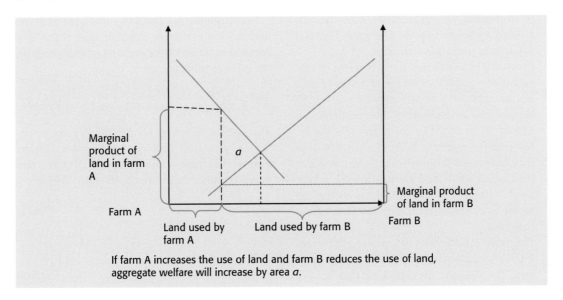

Figure 20.1　The welfare effects of the suboptimal use of land

know-how to find out about the best technology, they may be conservative and may not want to change, or they may not have their own capital or access to credit which allows them to be in the forefront of change. Hence, most governments intervene in order to provide information to farmers, speeding up the use of new technologies.

2. The size of farms is too small to take advantage of economies of scale and economies of size. Individual farmers may like to expand their farms to a more efficient size; however, the growth of some farms has to be accompanied by the shrinking or closing of others, as there is a land constraint in agriculture. In order to improve efficiency, land should move to those farms that generate a higher marginal productivity of land than shrinking or dissolving farms. Optimal use is made of land if its marginal productivity is the same in all uses. The optimum situation will change from time to time as factor prices change in the economy and new technologies can be introduced in agriculture. Consequently, there is a tendency for the marginal productivity of land to differ across farms. The problem can be illustrated by figure 20.1, where it is assumed that in the initial situation the marginal productivity of land

is higher on farm A than on farm B. A transfer of land from farm B to farm A up to the quantity where the marginal value of land is the same on both farms will increase the value of total production. The decline in production on farm B is smaller than the increase in production on farm A. Hence, the total gain in welfare is equal to area a.

The optimal allocation of land will materialize only if land markets function perfectly. However, land markets are property-rights-intensive and the transfer of land may incur high transaction costs. The prospective buyer and seller of land have to find out the likely future returns of the land and the likely interest rates. Hence, there is great uncertainty on both sides of the market. There may even be an outcome where there are no transactions on the market. The suppliers may have a high reservation price for land, possibly because they consider land ownership as a hedge against risk, or because they value land ownership more than the ownership of other assets and hence ask for a high price. The buyer may only be willing to offer a low price because of the uncertainty of future returns. The result can be that there is no intersection of the supply and demand curves since the former lies consistently above the latter. Actually, such a situation seems to prevail in some regional markets in transition countries.

3. Farms might also be inefficient in terms of allocation due to lack of access to credit. Transaction costs for creditors may be quite high because the assessment of the creditworthiness of farms might be costly and the risk for the creditor might be high. Such a situation may arise when farmers are not the owners of the land or when land markets are not active. Lack of credit history contributes to limited access to credit in transition and developing countries.

4. The technical efficiency of farms might be considerably smaller in comparison to other sectors. The reasons are again related to the peculiarities of agricultural production. Agriculture experienced a higher rate of technical change, thus making it difficult for many farmers to produce using old technology. Further, the steady outflow of labour might lead to larger heterogeneity in the quality of the agriculturists, with many farms not achieving their full technical potential. Finally, many restrictions on input use in combination with tax advantages for keeping up agricultural production and selective investment aids might lead to a systematic overuse of factors and thus increased technical inefficiency.

In short, market failure on land, labour markets and markets for rural finance provide rationales for government intervention in order to improve the efficiency of agriculture. Promotion of research and extension as well as measures to increase the mobility of land and labour are most often incorporated in the policy package.

20.2.4 Stability of markets

Agricultural markets tend to be volatile. The basic reasoning has already been offered by Gregory King, an English scientist living from 1648 to 1712. He found that a 1 per cent change in grain production resulted in more than a 1 per cent change in grain prices. This finding says implicitly that the price elasticity of demand for grain is less than 1.

The reasoning can easily be illustrated with the help of some algebra. Assume that there is a demand function where demand only depends on the price of the product:

$$q^D = q^D(p). \tag{20.7}$$

Also assume that supply is completely price inelastic, i.e. a vertical line in the diagram. Further assume that there is no storage and all that is produced has to be consumed in the same period:

$$q^S = \bar{q}^S \tag{20.8}$$

and

$$q^D = q^S. \tag{20.9}$$

Solving this system with respect to the relative change in p results in:

$$\frac{dp}{p} = \frac{1}{\varepsilon_{q,p}} \frac{dq^S}{q^S}. \tag{20.10}$$

According to equation (20.10) the percentage changes in price resulting from a 1 per cent change in supply will be larger, the lower the price elasticity of demand in absolute terms. It is often argued that the price elasticities for agricultural products decline with growing income and, hence, fluctuations in prices may become even more pronounced in a developed economy. However, it has to be kept in mind that the model derived above was based on the assumption that total production in a given period of time had to be consumed in the same period. If one allows for storage, market demand in a specific period will depend on demand for consumption purposes in that period and of demand for storage. The latter takes into account expected prices in future periods and storage costs. Hence, storage leads to an inter-temporal integration of markets. If expectations are correct, price differences between two points in time should not be higher than storage costs and a reasonable profit to cover risk and interest. As storage costs have significantly decreased over time, the inter-temporal price integration should have become stronger.

The impact of interregional trade on the price elasticity of demand points in the same direction. If there were fluctuations in regional production, exporters or importers would step in and link regional prices to those in other regions. Hence, the blessing of a good harvest would be spread to other regions and the curse of a bad harvest would be mitigated by imports from other regions. Thus, the regional price elasticity of demand does not only depend on demand for consumption purposes in the region, but also on prices in other regions and on transport costs. Transport costs have significantly declined over the last fifty years, in particular for shipping. It is cheaper to transport grain from the US Gulf to Rotterdam by ship than from Munich to Hamburg by train or lorry. Hence, an open trading economy would help mitigate fluctuations in regional production. Domestic market policies to stabilize price fluctuations are less needed nowadays than in past centuries.

20.2.5 Food safety concerns

Food safety has become a more important element in agricultural policy for many countries. This development may seem surprising to an outside observer. It is questionable whether food has really become less safe over time: the opposite is more likely. Animals are healthier nowadays than fifty years ago and new technologies in food conservation and preparation have lowered food risk. Nevertheless, there are new developments which have led to food safety concerns. New technologies which are based on biotechnology have created new production processes and new products which are not always safe. Hence, control of the food chain is needed. People are aware that food is not a search good where one knows the quality of the product. Instead, many food products are credence goods. The consumer neither knows the quality of the product nor the production process, so has to trust in its quality. However, trust will only be sustainable if food scandals are prevented. Of course, producers and traders have a genuine interest in creating and preserving trust, but the individual producer or trader cannot control the complete marketing chain. Moreover, new products, such as genetically modified organisms in food and feed products as well as chemical and biological fertilizer and pesticides, have to be tested before they are allowed to enter the market. Hence, it is a genuine task for a government to take care of this type of market failure.

20.2.6 Environmental concerns

In general, concern for the environment has increased in most countries over time. Hence, the impact of agricultural production on the environment has become of higher interest. Some countries, in particular the EU nations, Japan, South Korea, Norway and Switzerland, emphasize the multi-functionality of agriculture. Agriculture produces not only the typical agricultural products like food, feed and renewable primary products, but also by-products. By-products can be 'bads', which are non-marketed goods that lower the population's welfare, or 'goods', which are non-marketed goods that increase welfare. Hence, policies have to be defined to take care of these by-products. Of course, the policy instruments used have to be different from those employed in the past to raise agricultural income.

The arguments presented may justify governmental interference in agricultural markets. As the importance of individual justifications for intervention has been changed over time policies should also have changed. However, the change in policies in most countries is not in line with the changes in their rationale. Policies have pronounced path-dependencies. Policy instruments which have been introduced in the past cannot easily be removed, as any policy change leads to winners and losers. The loss often materializes in the short or medium term, whereas the gain arises in the long term. Take, for example, a reduction in politically set grain prices. Grain producers will immediately see a loss and lobby against it. Consumers may gain if bread prices eventually decline. However, that will take time and the gain for the individual consumer is quite small compared to the loss of the individual grain producer. Hence, it is much easier to organize producers and to lobby against price reduction than to organize consumers. This fact helps to explain why governments in democratic countries are inclined to be more producer-friendly than consumer-friendly. It also explains why policies are as they are and why present policies are often not in line with economic reasoning. They are constrained by the past. What has been decided in the past is relevant for today even if it is not justified on economic grounds. The agricultural policies which were introduced in the 1930s at the time of the depression often determined the main policy instruments of recent times. Changes will mainly occur if there are binding budgets or external constraints such as those of the WTO.

20.3 Objectives of the CAP

Owing to the variety of agricultural support policies that existed in Western Europe at the time of the formation of the EC, it was necessary, for the reasons given at the beginning, especially French insistence, to subject agriculture to equal treatment in all member states. Equal treatment of coal and steel (both necessary inputs for industry and therefore of the same significance as agriculture) was already under way through the ECSC and the importance of agriculture meant that equal treatment here was vital.

The objectives of the CAP are clearly defined in Article 33 of the EU Treaty. They are:

1. To increase agricultural productivity by promoting technical progress and by ensuring the rational development of agricultural production and the optimum utilization of all factors of production, in particular labour.
2. To ensure thereby 'a fair standard of living for the agricultural community, in particular by increasing the individual earnings of persons engaged in agriculture'.
3. To stabilize markets.
4. To ensure the availability of supplies.
5. To ensure that supplies reach consumers at reasonable prices.

The Treaty also specifies that in working out the CAP, and any special methods which this may involve, account shall be taken of:

(i) the particular nature of agricultural activity, which results from agriculture's social structure and from structural and natural disparities between the various agricultural regions;
(ii) the need to effect the appropriate adjustments by degrees;
(iii) the fact that, in the member states, agriculture constitutes a sector closely linked with the economy as a whole.

The Treaty further specifies that in order to attain the objectives set out above a common organization of agricultural markets shall be formed. This organization shall take one of the following forms depending on the product concerned:

(a) common rules as regards competition;
(b) compulsory coordination of the various national marketing organizations; or
(c) a European organization of the market.

Moreover, the common organization so established:

may include all measures required to achieve the objectives set out . . . in particular price controls, subsidies for the production and distribution of the various products, stock-piling and carryover systems and common arrangements for stabilization of imports and exports.

The common organization shall confine itself to pursuing the objectives set out in Article 33 and shall exclude any discrimination between producers and consumers within the Community.

Any common price policy may include all measures required to attain the objectives set out in Article 33, in particular regulation of prices, aids for the production and marketing of the various products, storage and carryover arrangements and common machinery for stabilizing imports or exports.

Finally, in order to enable the common organization to achieve its objectives, 'one or more agricultural guidance and guarantee funds may be set up'.

The remaining articles (34–8) deal with some detailed considerations relating to the objectives and the common organization.

The true objectives of the CAP were established after the Stresa conference in 1958 which was convened in accordance with the Treaty. The objectives were in the spirit of the Treaty:

(i) to increase farm incomes not only by a system of transfers from the non-farm population through a price support policy, but also by the encouragement of rural industrialization to give alternative opportunities to farm labour;

(ii)   to contribute to overall economic growth by allowing specialization within the Community and eliminating artificial market distortions;

(iii) to preserve the family farm and ensure that structural and price policies go hand in hand.

It can be seen, therefore, that the CAP was not preoccupied simply with the implementation of common prices and market supports; it also included a commitment to encourage the structural improvement of farming, particularly when the former measures did not show much success (see the later section on assessment). However, the focus of the CAP so far was on market organizations for individual agricultural commodities. This part is nowadays called the 'first pillar of the CAP'. The so-called 'second pillar of the CAP', its rural development regulations, was only formally created under the *Agenda 2000* reform. Hence, market and price policy is discussed first in detail followed by a section on structural and rural policy.

Before looking into how the EC went about trying to fulfil these aims, it is vital to understand the role played by the EC institutions directly involved with the CAP as well as by those institutions specifically created for the CAP.

20.4 The birth of the CAP and the institutional setting

At the time of its inception, the CAP was supposed to be a major engine of European market integration; there was a widely held hope that positive integration in agriculture would force other sectors to follow the same route. However, such expectations have not materialized; the annual price negotiations for agricultural products made evident the divergence in the national interests of EU member states, with decisions being dominated by compromises between them rather than by EU-wide interests.

Agriculture is a special case in the integration process. As most countries had more or less

strong national agricultural policies in the pre-integration phase, they were not willing to let market forces play freely in an integrated economy. Hence, positive integration was needed, i.e. specific policies for agricultural and food markets were needed at the Community level. In markets for industrial products a major policy decision was made at the beginning of the integration process to dismantle trade barriers without increasing the external level of protection (see chapters 1, 24 and 27). In contrast, agricultural policy has been regulated through fundamental policy decisions made both at the beginning and throughout this period. Consequently, one can assume that agricultural markets in the Union have been more affected by policy decisions than by pure market forces.

It is argued below that the institutional and organizational set-up of the CAP was misconceived from the very beginning. Due to this, market forces have played a minor role relative to political decisions in determining the development of agricultural policy in the Community.

20.4.1 The foundation of the CAP: a crucial policy failure[4]

It is likely that European integration was only possible on a political level because the main countries leading the integration process (France and Germany) finally agreed on some form of CAP. However, that does not imply that without the specifics of the CAP that was then created, European integration would not have happened. If that were the case, there would hardly be any reason to discuss the 'misconception' of the CAP. This hypothesis can be denied, as the Treaty of Rome cannot support it. The Constitution of the European Community – the Treaty – foresaw alternatives for integrating agricultural policy. The Treaty remained vague as to the nature of the common agricultural policy. It could consist of common rules of competition or of coordination of national market organizations or of a 'European' market organization. It was to take nearly three and a half years of argument to settle the basic principles of a common policy after the Treaty was signed. It took another three years, from 1962 to 1964, to agree on one of the key questions – a common level of cereal prices. The second key question – to find a long-term agreement for financing the CAP – was solved after a further one and a half years.

The fact that agreement was reached reflects a strong political commitment in favour of a common Europe by all members. National interests diverged considerably. Possibly owing to Hallstein, the first President of the European Commission, the price agreement was finally settled in 1964. When the Commission first submitted the proposal for the unification of cereal prices to the Council of Agricultural Ministers (Council, hereafter), the Council rejected it and asked for a modified version, which would more closely match individual national interests. Hallstein, a strong personality, resubmitted the original proposal after only half an hour arguing in favour of the unification of Europe. He asked the Council to either endorse the proposal unanimously or accept the resignation of the Commission. This contributed to the sense that a common Europe dominated national interests. Since then, the Commission has never again fought national interests in favour of Community interests so convincingly and so crucially.

It seems justified to investigate how the organizational and institutional setting created in the first years of the CAP has affected the evolution of the policy. The purpose is to draw lessons for the prospective design of the CAP. Moreover, it should be kept in mind that, at the time of designing the policy, the importance of organizations and institutions was less obvious than it is today.

20.4.2 A model of the decision-making process

Prescriptive policy decision models assume that policymakers try to maximize a well-defined objective function taking economic conditions as a given. It would follow that policies change because objectives and/or economic conditions change. This prescriptive decision-making model does not reflect reality in a reasonable way, particularly as it does not take into account that present choices greatly depend on past decisions. In actuality there is a certain degree of path dependency in policies – see figure 20.2. Path dependency explains why economic policies change only gradually over time, ratcheting up their effects, unless significant shocks in the economic environment force massive adjustments (like the Great Depression in the 1930s).

Following this basic idea, the status quo of a given set of policies determines the policy decisions in the next period. This assumption is in contrast to the prescriptive policy approach where policymakers are seen as newly born in each period and not bound by past decisions or conditions on the political market. According to the underlying assumption in this section, the specific economic and political environment at the birth of the CAP affects the evolution of the policy in the following years and also determines the influence of member countries.

20.4.3 The main players in European agricultural policy

Market and price policies, which have been the main determinants of developments of agricultural policy, have been the domain of European decision-makers from the very beginning of the CAP. Hence, it makes sense to base the analysis on the players foremost at the EU level. Moreover, only those players coming into existence with the foundation of the CAP (the Council) or deriving their power in the field of agricultural policy from the existence of the specifics of agricultural policies (the Commission) will be considered; thus nothing will be said about the European Parliament (see chapter 3). Actually, the European Parliament is much less involved in agricultural policy decisions than in any other legislation. Whereas Parliament has to agree on most EU legislation, it has only to be informed, but is allowed to express its opinion, in the field of agriculture. This peculiarity is somewhat surprising, as agriculture still attracts a large share of EU expenditure (in fact, the stalled constitutional treaty foresees an adjusted decision-making mechanism for agricultural issues in the same way as for other sectors).

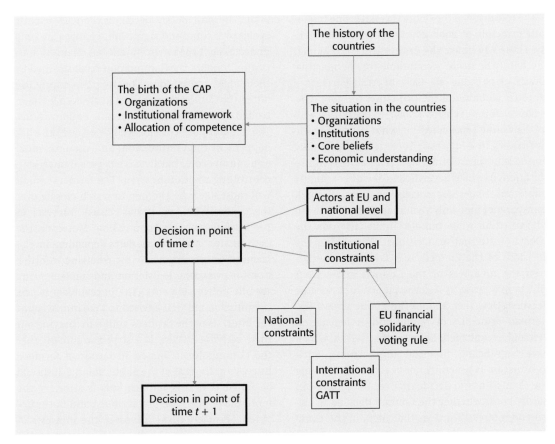

Figure 20.2 The decision-making process: a stylized model

The role of the Council

We begin with the Council of the European Union since it is the ultimate EC legislative body.

It could have been predicted that the legislative machinery at the Community level would lead to policy failure. The ministers in the Council are in most cases more interested in the welfare of the farming population and less in society at large. It is true that the farm minister, like any other minister, has to swear to serve the public interest. However, who can expect that someone will be impartial when his/her main political support comes from a special interest group? Of course, there are always conflicts among interest groups that have to be settled, leading to compromises. But will someone who has strong vested interests be an unbiased arbiter? Hence, it can be concluded that the creation of the main player at the Community level has provoked policy failure.

It might be argued that the Commission, as expected, might balance the 'power' of the Council (see chapter 3). Unfortunately, the development of the CAP proves that the Commission was not in a position to serve the interests of the general public. The specifics of the CAP demand regular legislative decisions by the Council, the most important of which up to 1995 were the annual price decisions. The pressure to come to an agreement in the Council placed significant constraints on the Commission. Proposals had to be submitted which could eventually be accepted by the Council. Hence, the final proposal was generally less a reflection of the interests of society at large and more of a compromise between the divergent interests of farmers or groups of farmers in the Community.

The role given to the Council violates one important principle of good governance:[5] accountability. Those who make the decisions in the Council can hardly be made accountable for the negative effects. First, due to lack of transparency – (another violation of the principles for good governance), it is not clearly known to the public who in the Council has voted for what. Other legislative bodies in democratic societies accept public presence in the meetings as a general rule. Not so the Council, which nevertheless decides on highly important issues for society at large. Second, transparency not only demands information on who voted for what, but also information on the effects of alternative decisions. Concerning the decisions of the Council, it is doubtful whether even the members of the Council know what effects may arise as a consequence of a specific decision. How then should the public know? The German principles of public budget legislation demand a cost-benefit analysis of activities, which have 'significant' financial implications. Such information is generally not available at the time the Council has to decide. Hence, the public can hardly know whether the Council decided in the general interest. Third, as the voters in the country of their origin do not elect the members of the Council, the voters can hardly control them.

Thus, the Council is most likely a partisan body, favouring the interests of the farm lobby: lack of transparency and control allows the Council members to act in favour of interest groups.[6]

The role of the Commission

The Commission is supposed to balance the national interests in the Council (see above and chapter 3). However, the Commission is a bureaucracy, so it is most likely to follow the general behaviour of a bureaucratic organization. According to the findings of the 'new political economy' (Downs, 1957; Buchanan and Tullock, 1962), the individual members pursue their own objectives taking into account the constraints imposed on them. It is generally accepted that bureaucrats prefer policy decisions which lead to more regulations and higher budget expenditure.

Of course, the Commission's bureaucrats are constrained in their behaviour. First, they are bound by past policy decisions. Policies usually evolve over time, and significant changes are only undertaken if the environment has changed drastically.[7] Second, the Commission is constrained by the budget and by some control. Concerning the latter, the Commission is most likely even less controlled than national bureaucratic organizations. The general public is not well informed on what happens in the Commission, and the individual Community voter hardly has a personal interest in controlling the Commission. The farmers' union will most likely be the one to watch closely over the Commission, as it has vested interests in the activities of the Commission. Moreover, the Commission is in some respects dependent on the farmers' union, especially for receiving information for preparing legislation and implementing specific policy elements. The bureaucrats in the Commission are well advised to take into account the interests of the farmers' union in carrying out their activities. There is a strong argument that the Commission is biased in favour of farmers' interests at the cost of the public at large. It should be noted that this built-in bias is stronger the more the policies are protectionist and not transparent. Protectionism increases the interests of the farmers' union to collect information on the activities of the bureaucrats in the Commission. The same holds true for lack of transparency. In addition, the lack of transparency increases the cost of collecting information. This will divert more non-farmers than farmers from collecting information. The lack of transparency is related to government intervention in favour of farmers. Farmers may even have a stronger interest in collecting information on non-transparent policies. Higher collecting costs will likely be compensated by direct benefits accruing from non-transparent policies. There is no such effect for non-farmers. Thus, the presumption is well founded that the Commission is more interested in protection than in liberal policies. It might be true that this presumption holds for any bureaucracy, but it is most likely stronger for the Commission than for national bureaucracies. Costs for collecting information for non-farmers are certainly higher at the EU than at the national level. Hence, the Commission is more prone to neglecting general welfare effects relative to national bureaucracies. Of course, there are some institutionalized controlling organizations set into place, such as the Court of Auditors, the European Court of Justice (ECJ) and, to some extent, the European Parliament. The first two can be quite effective. However, they are only supposed to check whether the activities of the Commission are in line with the law. It is beyond the tasks of the ECJ to investigate whether the Commission or the Council have taken adequately into account the interests of the public at large in carrying out their activities. It is debatable if the Court of Auditors is supposed to accept these duties. It is strongly opposed by the Commission. Anyway, the Court of Auditors has not been very effective in opposing protectionist tendencies in the Commission and the Council.

20.4.4 Institutions affecting the CAP

The evolution of the CAP is not only influenced by the Council and the Commission (players); it is even more dependent on the institutions set in place. According to North, 'institutions are the rules of the game in a society, or more formally, are the humanly devised constraints that shape human interactions' (North, 1990, p. 3). It is obvious that the outcome of the game (the shape and performance of the CAP in our case) not only depends on the organizations, but also on the allocation of competence among the players and the rules they have to follow. It will be shown that the main institutions put into force at the inception of the common market support the protectionist bias of CAP decisions.

The principle of financial solidarity

The principle of solidarity is considered to be one of the three pillars of the common agricultural market organizations (Tracy, 1989, p. 255). Indeed, it makes sense to finance common activities – such as the CAP – in solidarity, i.e. out of a common budget. However, such a financial scheme may create additional divergences in national interests. Indeed, the past and present pattern of financing the Community budget and enjoying the benefits of Community expenditure creates

significant divergences in national interests (Koester, 1977, pp. 328–45). First, the welfare of individual countries is affected differently by increases in common prices for individual products. Second, individual countries may have interests which depart from those of the Community for promoting production growth. Third, countries may be more or less inclined to implement Community policies.[8] It should be noted that integration of countries might generally have distributional implications for individual countries. Such effects just follow from differences in the countries' production and consumption patterns. However, the distributional effects of the financial system of the CAP are policy-made. Any collective that creates institutions increasing the divergence of interests of the individual members weakens the viability of the collective.

The principle of 'preference for agricultural products'

It seemed to make sense to the founders of the agricultural product market organizations to formulate the 'preference for agricultural products' as one of their basic tenets. Domestic users should first of all consume domestically produced products before relying on imported food. In reality, domestic consumers could do this of their own free will, as they do in many countries for specific food items. However, the founders of the common market organizations seemed not to believe in freedom of consumer choice. Instead, external protection has been accepted as the main instrument to achieve the principle of 'preference'. Making foreign supply more expensive does increase consumption of domestic products. Of course, the consumers have a higher preference for buying domestically produced goods, largely because they are forced to do so. Therefore, 'preference for agricultural products' is another way of saying 'external protection of domestic producers'.

The realization of this principle was most important for the evolution of agricultural policy in the Community. First, in connection with the principle of 'financial solidarity', it created additional divergences of interests among the countries as it gave rise to invisible transfers of income among the member countries. Second, the implementation of

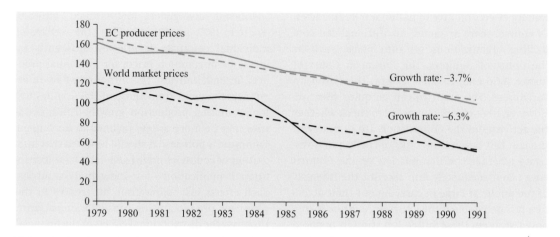

Figure 20.3 Development of EU and world market prices for agricultural products. *Sources:* CEC (1994, p. 17).

this principle created great pressure on the Council and gave it much more political power than existed in other sectors. It was accepted from the inception of the market organizations that the principle of preference for agricultural products would be enforced by a system of variable levies for the main agricultural products. Strangely enough, the Council was allowed to decide annually about the magnitude of preference given to domestic products, and thus on the magnitude of the external rate of protection.

Having discussed the interests of the Council members and the distributional effects of the common financial system, it is understandable that annual decisions on the rate of external protection placed, on the one hand, great pressure on the Council to secure agreement, especially because of the divergent interests of the various countries. On the other hand, the Council had enormous discretionary powers, which could be exerted in favour of farmers. It goes without saying that such a system opens the door for strong lobbying efforts. Hence, it should not be surprising that the Council could hardly resist responding to the interests of the farm lobby. It is true that the overall prices for farm products did fall over time (see figure 20.3), but up to the mid-1990s less than the aggregate level of world market prices; hence, the nominal rate of protection even increased over time in spite of growing surpluses. It should be noted that external rates of protection have even

been increased for products for which there was already a surplus in the Community. External protection could hardly have been justified for securing preference for domestically produced products. Indeed, the principle of 'preference for agricultural products' played hardly any role in the justification of price proposals and price decisions. Much more important was the income objective. This leads to a discussion of the misconceived CAP: the allocation of competence between national member countries and Community organizations.

It was only the negotiations in the Uruguay Round (1986 to 1994) which posed binding constraints on EU price support policy (see below).

20.4.5 The allocation of competence between member countries and the EC

It is well known that the EU is in charge of market and price policy, whereas member countries have more freedom in conducting structural policy, although constrained by EU-set rules. Indeed, such an allocation of competence makes sense. Market and price policies rely heavily on the rate of external protection, and there are good arguments for having a common degree of external protection for all member countries. However, supranationalizing market and price policies can cause problems for the Community if the decision-making body is allowed to set the external rate of protection annually and if the members of the decision-making body, the Council, bias their decisions in favour of farmers. Even if not supported by the Treaty of Rome, market and price policy has been used as a means to achieve the income objective.[9]

It is obvious that national interests diverge significantly on the price changes needed to achieve the national income objective. First, the need to increase national agricultural income is more related to income changes in the national economies and less so to farmers' incomes in other countries. Hence, differing growth rates in overall national income may result in divergent needs for increasing agricultural income. Second, an increase in institutional prices in EU currency leads to divergent increases in actual farm gate prices among member countries (Colman, 1985, pp. 171–87), as the transmission coefficient between institutionalized prices and farm-gate prices varies significantly across countries. Allocating the responsibility for the income objective to the Community and accepting price support as the main instrument to achieving it necessarily enlarges the divergences in national interests with respect to price policy. It could have been expected that price changes would generally be at the cost of those parties that had no voice in the negotiations, i.e. the consumers, taxpayers and foreign trading partners. However, the European policymakers could not externalize the costs of their decision without any constraints, and it is to these we turn next.

The importance of voting rules

Voting rules can be quite important for the behaviour of a collective. The founders of the Community had foreseen in Article 148 of the Treaty that the Council should generally decide by majority rule. Indeed, this seems to correspond with a democratic system where majority votes are normally accepted. However, the majority voting rule is more questionable if voters differ significantly in their preferences and if the individuals are affected to a different extent by the decision of a collective. Accepting majority rule for every decision would give rise to significant divergences in national interest concerning the CAP. Therefore, it is not surprising that two years after the first price decision was made, France demanded that deci-

sions be unanimous in cases which could be considered of vital interest for any single country – hence the 'Luxembourg compromise' (see chapters 2 and 3). Thus, the Council made decisions only by unanimity up to 1982/3. The unanimous voting rule is mainly attractive when there is significant heterogeneity among the voters. This avoids exploitation of a minority. However, it is well known that groups are well advised to apply this rule only for cases which are of the utmost importance, because the 'expected external costs'[10] of such decisions are high. Unfortunately, the design of the CAP implied that policy decisions would have quite different effects on the individual countries. Hence, it might have been impossible to reach an agreement on the individual elements of a proposal presented by the Commission. There has always been at least one loser, possibly the European paymaster, who would have voted against the proposal. However, due to the specifics of the CAP, a mechanism for discretionary decisions was built into the system, and it was only feasible to decide on packages (logrolling). The outcome was certainly a compromise among the Council members and their decisions were generally not in the interests of the Community at large. The move to majority voting in the 1980s has contributed to the ability of the Community to change its agricultural policy. However, the tendency to externalize the costs of the decision is still prevalent.

The voting rules are of the utmost importance if policy changes affect the financial system of the EU. Individual member countries check proposals for changes with respect to national implications. Proposals which may improve the rationale of the policy from an EU perspective would not be likely to be accepted by the Council if some (important) member countries were to lose. Hence, the past reforms of the CAP tried to stabilize the already established pattern of national and regional gainers and losers from the CAP.

20.4.6 Constraints on CAP policymakers

Foreign trade restrictions

From the very beginning, agricultural policymakers had to take into account restrictions imposed by international trade agreements, principally the GATT. The external rate of protection could not be increased for some feed imports. This constraint had significant implications for the other constraints, i.e. budget outlays (CEC, 1988b), which will be discussed below. The growth of expenditure for the market organizations for grain and milk depended directly on the constraints imposed by GATT.

Actually, GATT could have posed a much more binding constraint on CAP policymakers had its Article XVI:3 been taken literally. It states that subsidies to agricultural exports (and other primary commodities) are only allowed provided the exporting country does not capture more than an equitable share of world export trade (see, inter alia, Tangermann, 1991, pp. 50–61). However, a clear definition of the term 'equitable share' was never agreed. After the EC became self-sufficient for individual products one after another, exports increased more than world trade, leading to an increase in the share in world trade.[11]

Foreign trade constraints became more binding after GATT's Uruguay Round (1986–94) was finalized. Until the late 1970s, the EU and the USA had opposing trade interests. The USA, as the main exporter of temperate-zone agricultural products, was from the very beginning interested in high world market prices for them. In contrast, the EU as an importing region preferred low prices. However, in the late 1970s, the EU turned into an exporter of most of these products. Low world market prices led to negative terms of trade effects and boosted export subsidies, which in turn resulted in complaints by trading partners. Therefore, the EU agreed to open a new trade round with the focus on agricultural trade. The outcome of the negotiations was that the EU, like other GATT members, had to accept some significant constraints in its foreign trade regime, the details of which are analysed below.

These restrictions also obliged the EU to change its domestic policies for most agricultural products (see below). Further reforms can be expected after agreement is reached on the ongoing WTO Doha Round. CAP experience indicates that the driving force behind policy changes is neither rational economic considerations nor internal budgetary constraints, but rather external trade restrictions.[12]

One may wonder whether these trade constraints may have guided the CAP in a more welfare-maximizing direction had they been there at the time of CAP's inception. The answer would most likely be in the negative. The constraint has contributed to non-uniform rates of protection, thus increasing the overall welfare loss incurred from securing for farmers the given income level. The EU, and its main trading partner/opponent, the United States, could have enjoyed higher welfare had EU protection rates been higher (Koester and Tangermann, 1990). It is true that the restrictions on the import side for feed and some vegetable oils made protection for grain and milk more costly in economic terms. However, it is doubtful whether this had a more than marginal effect on the decisions of policymakers.

Past experience does support the view that the main driving force of domestic policy changes, the foreign trade constraint – more specifically the pressure of trading partners – has eventually led the CAP to adopt a superior resource allocation policy. The Uruguay Round forces the CAP decision-makers to accept a cut in import tariffs of 36 per cent on average, to reduce the quantity of subsidized exports, to lower the outlays for export subsidies and to reduce domestic support. These imposed changes required great changes in the application of CAP instruments (see below). Some of these changes, such as the move to decoupled direct payments (see below), have certainly improved the allocation of resources. However, the institutional constraint due to the principle of financial solidarity did hinder genuine reform. The birth of the 'second pillar' gave rise to a new set of instruments which stabilized the distributional flows of EU expenditure and led to some new instruments, in particular concerning environmental constraints, which increased the intensity of regulation and conflicted with the objective to improve allocation of resources (see below).

The budget constraint

One of the main domestic constraints faced by agricultural policymakers is the budget. Even if

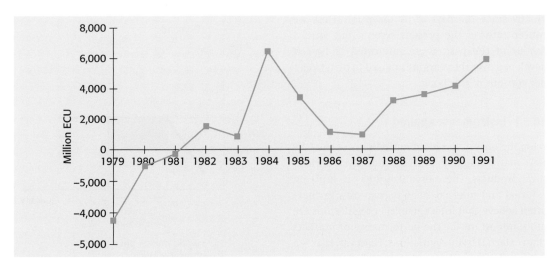

Figure 20.4 The development of the EU trading situation. *Source*: CEC (1994b, p. 15).

governmental expenditure is not an adequate indicator for costs and benefits of any policy activity, expenditure plays an important role. First, most governments are restricted in their total outlays due to limited access to tax revenue. Therefore, the individual expenditure items compete with each other. The Minister of Agriculture has to complete with other government ministers for additional spending. Second, budget outlays are a visible indicator of governmental activity. Increasing expenditure on agriculture seems to convey to the public that the government is intervening more strongly in favour of farmers. Of course, this indicator is not at all adequate for mirroring the total transfer accruing to agriculture. It is well known that European policymakers relied more on invisible than on visible transfers before the CAP reform of 1992.[13] Nevertheless, the general public is more informed on the visible transfers, and hence they constrain policymakers in this respect. It was most likely the budget constraint which led to a more prudent price policy after the EU had passed self-sufficiency for the aggregate of agricultural products at the beginnings of the 1980s (see figure 20.4).

Constraints by non-agricultural pressure groups

Governmental interference in the markets in favour of farmers places both direct and indirect taxes on other sectors of the economy (Koester, 1991, pp. 5–17). Surprisingly, there was, at least in Germany, a tacit agreement between the farmers and the industrialists' unions that agricultural policy be left to the former. The industrialists may have viewed agricultural policy as unimportant, given that they were more focused on the divergence of interests within their own ranks. Some of them profited greatly from the CAP. Hence, they did not agree on a clear line of opposition to the CAP. The attitude of the industrialists' union changed in the 1980s when it became frightened of the trade repercussions caused by aggressive agricultural export subsidies. It was only then that they published a clear statement demanding a less distortive CAP. This supports the view that foreign trade constraints are most likely the main driving force for domestic policy changes.

One may wonder whether the consumers' unions could play a crucial role in constraining agricultural policymakers. There is hardly any evidence supporting the role of these interest groups; generally, they seem not to be well represented in most countries. Not being well staffed, they therefore lack the information and the power to push for policy changes.

20.5 The market organizations of the CAP

The CAP has an extremely complex set of instruments and regulations, which have changed greatly since the days of its inception. Here we concentrate on the present system, but with a flavour of the past; those interested in how it developed over the years are advised to turn to earlier editions of this book.

20.5.1 Instruments applied

From the outset, the main ingredients of the CAP were market organizations for individual agricultural products. These organizations are built on external and internal trade regulations. Farmers often believe that internal market regulations are more important for the performance of markets than external trade regulations. However, that is a fallacy. As the main objective of the market organizations is to provide a higher income for farmers, the main instrument is price support. Domestic prices are higher than import or export prices. A wedge between domestic and world prices can only prevail if there are border measures in place. Hence, external trade regulations are more important for the performance of domestic markets. Consequently, the following presentation starts with an analysis of the external trade regulations.

20.5.2 Import regulations

Variable levies and specific import tariffs

At the time of foundation, the EU was an importer of the main temperate-zone agricultural products. Hence, the market organizations were set up for import situations. Originally the EU had set threshold prices for the main agricultural products (individual grains, sugar, milk, and beef). These prices were set at the annual price negotiations; hence, these prices were politically determined. Under normal conditions, these threshold prices were far above the world market prices (c.i.f. prices, i.e. including cost, insurance and freight). The gap between the two prices was made up by variable levies. Variable levies are comparable to duties levied on imports, but as the levy changes with changing world prices, it becomes completely divorced from world market prices. How it functions is clarified with the help of figure 20.5. Import prices are determined by the c.i.f. world

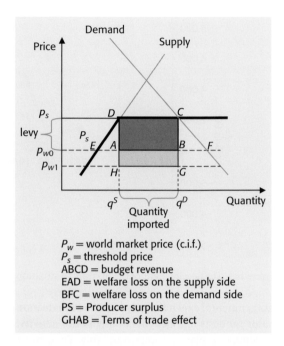

P_w = world market price (c.i.f.)
P_s = threshold price
ABCD = budget revenue
EAD = welfare loss on the supply side
BFC = welfare loss on the demand side
PS = Producer surplus
GHAB = Terms of trade effect

Figure 20.5 The impact of variable levies on domestic prices

price plus the variable levy. The supply curve on the EU market is equal to the domestic supply curve up to the price p_s and at this price it is equal to the world market supply curve plus the levy. If it is assumed that the EU is a relatively small country which has no impact on the world market price, the supply curve faced by the EU deviates and becomes a horizontal line. The EU is assumed to be a price taker on the world market. The variable levy shifts the world supply curve upwards to the level of the threshold price. The threshold price will be the domestic price at the point of entry of the imported product. The EU has set the same threshold prices for a well-defined product for all ports of entry. These prices strongly determine domestic prices at any other location, as regional prices are strongly correlated across different locations. The main difference between local prices and threshold prices are transport costs.

Figure 20.5 shows that the typical market organization at the time of setting up the schemes had positive effects for the budget. The EU could have increased its so-called own reserves by charging variable levies on imports. However, the scheme also had negative welfare effects. Domestic producers received incentives to increase their produced quantity, but incurred higher costs than the EU would have had to pay for imports, resulting in a welfare loss of EAD on the supply side. Domestic consumers would like to have consumed a higher quantity at world market prices, but they are taxed by domestic prices above world market prices. The welfare loss on the demand side is BFC. Thus, the figure shows that the budget effects of a specific policy are not identical to welfare effects.

It might have been that the EU could already exert market power on some markets in the first years of its existence, i.e., the world supply curve on the EU market would have been upward-sloping. Assuming such a case, the setting up of variable levies which reduced the EU demand on world markets led to lower world market prices, generating a positive welfare effect for the EU, a terms of trade effect. The terms of trade effect did generate budget revenue by increasing the levy and at the same time amounted to positive welfare gains offsetting parts of the Harberger triangles. The overall welfare impact, however, was probably negative.

The system of variable levies existed until 1995 when the new WTO rules came into force. WTO agreements required that all non-tariff barriers to trade, such as variable levies, had to be transformed into tariffs, the term employed being 'tariffication'. The tariff equivalents of 1986–8 had to be lowered by 36 per cent on average, but by at least 15 per cent for individual commodities. Hence, tariff rates should not be higher than the new bound-reduced tariff rate. However, as world market prices were very low in the base period, the EU has had no problems in securing the domestic price at the desired level. Anyhow, at the last minute the EU managed to get a special regulation for those grains for which there are intervention prices on the domestic market. According to this regulation the domestic threshold price is set at 155 per cent of the domestic intervention price. The difference between the threshold price and a hypothetical c.i.f. import price (world market price) is charged on imports. The main difference

on the grain market which had to be introduced was the rule concerning the threshold price. It used to be a political price which could be set annually at the discretion of the Council of Ministers. The new rule sets the price in fixed relation to the intervention price and the EU agreed not to increase the intervention price during the term of the agreement (1995/6 to 2001/2). Of course, the EU is free to lower the intervention price, which it did in the year 2000.

The second rule concerned the definition of the relevant world market price. Prior to the agreement, the EU considered the c.i.f. price to be the relevant offer price of foreign countries at the borders of the EU. This practice caused problems, as imports had declined over time, and hence it was difficult to find the representative c.i.f. price. In the Uruguay Round EU trading partners agreed to accept the representative market price in the US as the representative world market price. Adding costs for insurance and freight results in the hypothetical EU c.i.f. price. As long as this price is lower than the EU threshold price and as long as the price gap is smaller than the tariff that the EU could apply according to the agreement, the EU charges the difference between the threshold price and the c.i.f. price. Thus, the old system continued almost unchanged up to 2003. The effect of the regulation is clarified with the help of figure 20.6.

The domestic price is determined for imports in panel (a). Importers can offer at prices p_w plus t, the tariff or levy. The supply curve deviates at price p_d on the domestic market if the importing country is a relatively small country. The country generates revenue equal to $(q^d - q^S) * t$; (the asterisk is used throughout to indicate multiplication). However, the welfare loss for the country is equal to a plus b.

If t is a variable levy, as it used to be for most EU agricultural imports before the Uruguay Round, t varies with the world market price, leaving the domestic price completely divorced ('decoupled' in the jargon) from the world market price. Domestic prices are stable even if world market prices vary. If domestic supply falls short due to a bad harvest, the supply curve shifts to the left, allowing for a greater volume of imports.

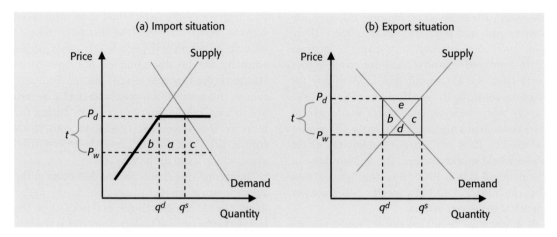

Figure 20.6 The effect of variable levies or fixed tariff rates

In 2002 a further change in the import regulations for medium- and low-quality wheat was introduced. The EU realized that due to high market prices in the US based on a bad harvest, import levies had to be set at zero. At the same time some Eastern European countries, in particular Ukraine and Russia, had excellent harvests and could offer wheat to the EU even below the intervention price. Hence, the EU managed to replace the import regulations for medium- and low-quality wheat and feeding barley by tariff rate quotas (see below on the functioning of these regulations).

If the country is an exporter of the product under consideration, the tariff or levy will not determine the domestic market price directly. However, a country cannot be an exporter with prices above p_w. Foreign supply would enter the market and drive domestic prices downwards to the world market level. Panel (b) shows that part of the tariff may become redundant. The tariff rate could be lowered without resulting in more imports. The country incurs budget expenditure equal to $(q^s - q^d) * (p_d - p_w)$, i.e. $b + d + c + e$. However, the welfare loss is equal to the triangle below the demand and supply curves, $b + d$ and $c + d$. A comparison of panels (a) and (b) clearly shows that the welfare losses of trade policies are not related to budget effects, but only to the price gap between domestic and world market prices and the price elasticities of demand and supply.

Ad valorem tariff rates

There are a few agricultural products where the EU charges only an ad valorem tariff, e.g. potatoes and tropical products, or in addition to other import restrictions. Ad valorem tariff rates are also used to provide specific protection for EU processing industries. Concerning tropical products, the ad valorem tariff is higher for processed products than for raw materials (tariff escalation) providing additional protection for the domestic processing industry. Ad valorem tariff rates have to be preferred to specific tariffs or variable levies if the products under consideration are heterogeneous and one levy for a set of highly differentiated products would lead to undesired distortion in trade flows. Take the case of fruit and vegetables where ad valorem tariff rates are applied. Even a product like cabbage is highly differentiated. If there were one specific tariff for all varieties or one levy, high-quality products would enter the EU markets at a lower percentage charge than low-value products. Hence, domestic producers of high-quality cabbage would be put at a disadvantage compared to producers of lower-quality cabbage. If the EU were to introduce alternative specific tariff rates for individual qualities the administrative burden would be very high. Hence, it is reasonable to apply a variable levies system or specific tariff rates only for fairly homogeneous products.

Tariff rate quotas

Tariff rate quotas are a new element in agricultural trade; they were introduced in the Uruguay Round. WTO member countries have to allow each other minimum access to their markets, amounting to 5 per cent of consumption in the period 1986 to 1988. These imports enter the EU market at a lower tariff rate than is normally applied. In January 2003 such a system was also introduced for some grains (see above).

The effect of this import regulation is clarified with the help of figure 20.6. Panel (a) depicts the situation of an import case. The country charges the tariff t and tariff revenue is $t*(q^d - q^s)$. If the country has to charge a lower tariff rate for within-quota imports, the tariff revenue forgone is equal to $(t - t_q)*q^*$, where q^* stands for the tariff quota. Thus, the country loses revenue and enjoys a lower welfare if the tariff quotas are allocated to foreign exporters. If the quota is auctioned, the loss for the country might be minimal; private traders, whether foreign or domestic, would be willing to pay a price per unit of import quota about equal to the difference between the domestic price and the world market price. The only deviation would arise from transaction costs. Actually, only 12 per cent of tariff quotas are auctioned (Skully, 1999). The EU does not apply an auction system for any tariff quota.

Panel (b), which is more important for EU agricultural markets, shows the export case. It is assumed that the domestic price p_d is lower than the world market price p_w plus the tariff rate t. This is a typical EU situation. The tariff was set at the time when the EU was still an importer. Having matured to an export situation there are no more imports. The actual tariff rate could be lowered (by the difference between $p_w + t$ and p_d) without affecting imports, i.e. part of the tariff is redundant (in the jargon, there is water in the tariff rates). The EU has actually bound tariff rates which are partly redundant, i.e. tariffs can be lowered without giving rise to imports. Allowing tariff quota imports, the EU has to increase subsidies for exports as $p_d > p_w$. These additional subsidies imply a welfare loss for the EU, but only if the tariff quotas are allocated to foreign exporters.

Preferential access

It is widely agreed that the CAP distorts world agricultural markets. Hence, trading partners complained about restricted access to EU markets. The EU response was to offer preferential access to its market. First, trade preferences were granted to some countries which had lost market access to countries which joined the EU (see chapters 24 and 26), for example New Zealand's quota for butter exports to the United Kingdom and the US's quota for maize exports to Spain and Portugal. In 1975 preferential access was granted to some African, Caribbean and Pacific countries (ACP countries) that had former colonial ties to EU member countries. In the 1990s, the EU signed the so-called European Agreements, the Association Agreements, with selected Central and Eastern European countries which granted them import quotas. In 2001, the EU markets were opened completely for imports from some Balkan countries and for most imports from the forty-nine least-developed countries. In the latter case, the only restriction is for imports of bananas, rice and sugar, but only for a transition period. The effects of these agreements can be clarified with the help of figure 20.7. The EU supply curve shifts to the right by the amount of the preferential quota or by the unrestricted imports. The EU either loses tariff revenue or has to spend additional amounts on export restitutions (see below). Hence, the welfare loss for the EU is equal to the price gap between domestic prices and world market prices multiplied by the quantity of preferential imports. The indirect impact of the 'Everything But Arms' (EBA) agreement on the common market organization for specific products may be substantial, as the case of sugar illustrates (see below), because unrestricted imports are deleterious for products with binding production quotas in combination with high external protection.

20.5.3 Export regulations

Until the end of the Uruguay Round in 1994, there were no real constraints on agricultural exports. GATT rules did not allow export subsidies on manufactured products. The US was instrumental in introducing the GATT waiver for agricultural

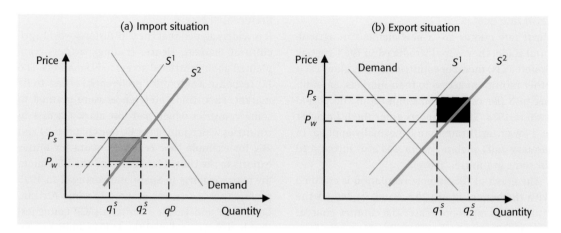

Figure 20.7 The impact of preferential access to EU markets

exports, but GATT set the proviso that they should not be used to capture more than an 'equitable share' of world exports of the product concerned (GATT's Article XVI:3). As it was not clear what the term 'not more than an equitable share' actually meant, countries were free to use export subsidies. This waiver was of the utmost importance for the functioning of EU markets up to 1992. The EU developed from an importing to an exporting region for almost all temperate-zone products, even with the lowering of the rate of nominal protection. In spite of declining real agricultural producer prices, the shift in the supply curve due to technological change was higher than the shift in the demand curve due to income growth. The EU was not forced to reduce prices in order to avoid surpluses at support prices, as the surplus could be dumped on the world markets. The differences between domestic and world market prices were met by the EU budget. The Uruguay Round Agreement posed a significant constraint on EU policymakers. They had to agree to cut the volume of subsidized exports by 21 per cent (based on 1986–90) and the amount of subsidies paid by 36 per cent (same base period). The impact of these constraints can be illustrated with the help of figure 20.8.

Depending on the market situation, either quantity or expenditure constraints could become binding. So far, volume constraints have become binding on some markets. As long as EU prices are above world market prices, domestic supply has to

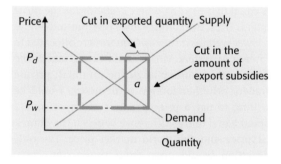

Figure 20.8 The impact of subsidized export constraints

be restricted to domestic demand plus the permitted volume of subsidized exports minus the quantity imported on minimum market access s (this is not in the figure) (tariff rate quotas).

Therefore, EU policymakers were forced to change the market regulations for some commodities; before the agreement was signed, the EU had already instituted drastic cuts in institutional grain prices of 30 per cent (the 1992 McSharry reform, see below) and enlarged the cut by another 15 per cent in 2000 (CEC, 1997a). A further drastic change in market organizations was decided in June 2003, when price cuts for milk and beef were agreed upon, and in 2005 for sugar.

The payment of export subsidies causes more administrative problems than charging imports. If the Commission wants to bridge the gap between domestic prices and competitive export prices it has to know the relevant export price. However, these prices are not quoted on a market, so instead the Commission has to collect information on prices in importing countries and take into account import charges and shipping costs (freight, insurance and harbour costs). This information is difficult to get, in particular for the many differentiated processed agricultural products. Moreover, the Commission has to know how much of the raw material had been used to produce specific processed products. Take the case of pasta. Pasta can be produced on the basis of common wheat and eggs or durum wheat. As the price gap for common wheat is smaller than that for durum wheat, the kind of wheat is important for quantifying the amount of export restitutions, i.e. subsidies. Another case is the export of wheat flour. The Commission has to know how much wheat is needed to produce one unit of wheat flour. The necessary information is not easily available; only the flour mills can provide it, but it is naïve to expect them to report it correctly. This may explain why the EU used to be very competitive on the international wheat flour market, where the EU share was in excess of 60 per cent for many years. The share of the wheat market was no more than 16 per cent in the 1980s.

Problems were even more pronounced on the meat market, as export restitutions differed for different cuts of meat. They were the lowest for offal and high for high-quality meat. Hence, there was a tendency for false declaration; indeed, the European Court of Auditors found most fraud to be in meat exports.

20.5.4 Domestic market regulations

Intervention purchases

Intervention prices are prices at which intervention agencies are obliged to buy in unlimited amounts of a specific product like grain or limited amounts under certain conditions. These prices were introduced in order to stabilize markets. Hence, these prices, which are politically set, were supposed to be below normal market prices at the time when the market organizations were designed and first implemented. Therefore, these

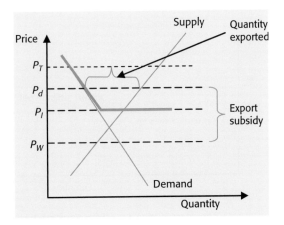

Figure 20.9 The importance of intervention prices

prices are below the import price (p_T) at which international competitors can enter the domestic market. As long as foreign supply was needed to clear the EU grain market at a price related to the threshold price (p_T) (see above) the intervention price was not relevant. Actually, buying in took place only in some regions due to market imperfection as long as the EU was in grain deficit. However, gradually the EU matured to an exporter of grain and the intervention price could become the relevant market price if the EU did not enter the market by paying export subsidies. The situation is shown with the help of figure 20.9. The domestic demand curve becomes completely elastic at the intervention price if private and official demand does not clear the market at prices above the intervention price. The actual market price will be above the intervention price if the government pays export subsidies. These subsidies raise domestic demand. The effect is that the domestic demand curve will be completely elastic at a price (p_I) which is equal to the world price plus the subsidy per unit of export. It should be noted that the effect of an export subsidy on domestic prices does not depend on the quantity exported, but on the subsidy per unit of exports. Even if the EU produces a small surplus on a market, as in the case of pork with a degree of self-sufficiency of about 103, the price effect of the subsidy can be very high. Figure 20.10 clarifies this point. The volume of export is fairly small, but the gap between the domestic and world market prices is fairly high.

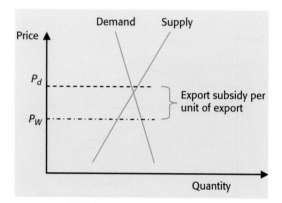

Figure 20.10 The effect of export subsidies on domestic prices

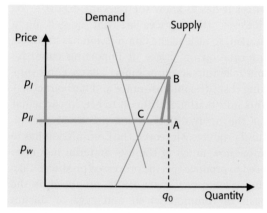

Figure 20.11 Price cuts and direct paymkents: the case of grains

Without any foreign trade regulations, the domestic prices would be at p_W.

Direct payments

Direct payments have become a most important element of market organizations since the McSharry reform. These payments were originally introduced on the grain and oilseeds markets in order to compensate for the cut in institutional prices, attracting the term 'compensatory payments'. The basic idea was to offset the income loss due to the price cut, and to do this as accurately as possible payments were linked to the area cultivated under cereals or oilseeds. Figure 20.11 depicts the effects. Grain intervention prices were reduced by 30 per cent. Policymakers assumed that the income loss would be equal to the area $(p_I - p_{IV}) * q_0$. The actually lost income was lower since it is the negative change in producer surplus (area $p_I p_{II} CB$), hence the overcompensation was area CAB. As the payment was linked to the use of the land (it was paid per hectare of land under grain cultivation), payments were part of the gross margin earned in grain production. Hence, the area under grain production did not decline. The effect of lower prices on yields may show up after a long period of adjustment as a new set of technologies may be needed. So far yields have continued to increase over time. Consequently, total grain production did not decline in spite of the drastic price cut. Due to the direct payments the supply curve became steeper below the former intervention price p_I. The

supply curve may have even shifted to the right as there was overcompensation leading to an increase of profitability in grain production.

In 1999 the Council decided on a further drop in grain prices by 15 per cent (*Agenda 2000*, CEC, 1997a) and to reduce beef prices by 20 per cent and dairy prices by 15 per cent. The latter became effective from 2005/6 onwards. The (falsely) calculated income losses (see the argument above) are supposed to be compensated by half. In the case of beef, payments were per animal, but in the case of dairy products they were initially linked to the reference quantity, i.e. the amount of milk a producer can achieve at high guaranteed prices. Both types of direct premiums have been incorporated in the single farm payment starting from 2005 (see below).

The CAP reform in the 1990s put more pressure on European farms than the previous policy changes. However, the price cuts leading to a reduction in external protection were widely replaced by direct payments. Figure 20.12 clearly shows that in the aggregate for the OECD and in the main member countries the average level of support as measured by producer support estimates (PSE)[14] were fairly stable over time.

The 2003 Council decision introduced a major change in direct payments, the single farm payment scheme. The Commission had proposed simplifying the market and price policy by summing up all the different entitlements of individual

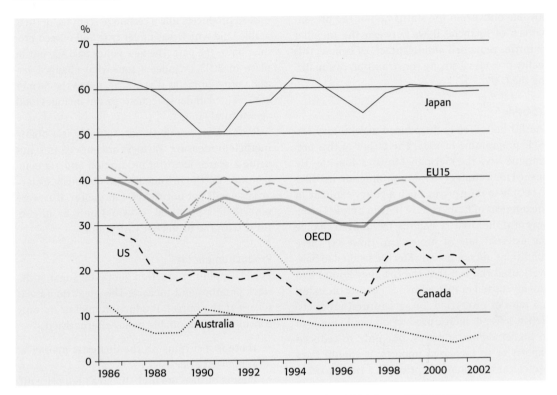

Figure 20.12 Support level in the OECD and selected member countries, % PSE. *Source*: OECD (2003).

farmers by direct payments and introducing one single payment, based on past payments, and completely decoupled from production. Moreover, the proposal foresaw making the entitlement for payments tradeable. The Council was not able to reach such a wide-ranging agreement. However, the principle was accepted, but member countries were allowed to introduce some coupled payments for some period or to introduce coupled payments when there is a serious drop in regional production. Moreover, countries can link payment to area and pay a flat rate at the national level, possibly differentiated with respect to arable or grass land. Furthermore, member states were allowed to introduce limitations on the tradeability of the payment entitlements.

The basic idea behind the change was political. It was argued that payments justified as compensation for price cuts could not last for ever. Hence, another rationale for carrying on with gifts for farmers was needed. Some politicians, supported

by the EU Commission, hoped that the prevailing form of direct payments can be sold to the public, arguing that these are payments for farmers' contributions to a multifunctional agriculture. It was believed that this reasoning would be more convincing if payments were tied to the condition that farmers use 'good agricultural practice' and if some of these payments were directly linked to participation in environmental programmes.

Unfortunately, the new justification for direct payments would have been convincing only if it had been accompanied by a significant change in the national and regional distribution of payments. Such a change had to follow the national and regional needs for a multifunctional agriculture. However, the distribution of payments across nations has not been changed: a change in the gainer and loser situation across the member countries was not acceptable to the Council. Again, this policy decision proves the strong path dependency of the CAP: policy changes seem to be possible only when the status quo of the present pattern of financial flows between the member countries remained almost intact. Of course, this reality provides a strong constraint on rationalizing the CAP.

Set-aside

The EU had already introduced a voluntary set-aside programme in 1988. The father of this programme was the German Minister Kiechle. He pushed for a strategy to lower production in order to be able to raise prices. Such a policy could be in the interests of farmers were they in a closed economy or if the country had the freedom to change the external rate of protection. However, these conditions did not prevail. Kiechle seemed to have overlooked the fact that the Uruguay Round had already started in 1986, aimed at cutting the external rates of protection for agricultural products. Hence, lower domestic production would not lead to higher domestic prices, but only to reduced exports or to increased imports. It should have been clear that domestic prices in a trading economy are determined by world market prices and the external rate of protection.

Anyway, the voluntary set-aside programme was not attractive for most EU member countries (Koester, 1989b). The EU included in the 1992 reform package quasi-compulsory set-aside. Farmers with above a certain size of grain production (90 tonnes) had to set aside a certain percentage of the area under production in order to qualify for the direct payments. The EU included this element in the reform package in order to gain acknowledgement in the GATT Round. Trading partners, in particular the US, were interested in a reduction in EU grain production. It was widely accepted that the EU grain policy depressed world market prices; hence EU production was supposed to be cut. As the EU did not want to lower prices to the world market level and as it wanted to compensate producers for the price cut, it included a production-curtailing measure. The EU rightly expected that the US was not very interested in whether the EU reduced production by liberalization through clear price cuts or through more control measures such as set-aside. Thus, beginning in 1993, the EU instituted a set-aside programme which demands that grain and oilseed producers idle a certain percentage of their arable land which was under crop and oilseed production in the past. The new policy package put in place in 2003 includes a somewhat changed set-aside programme as it is not related to the former area planted under specific crops, but includes total agricultural land.

From an economic stance, set-aside is a highly inefficient measure. Farmers are enticed into not using a scarce factor of production and are compensated for the income loss, so obviously society at large will get not richer, but poorer. If it were nevertheless practised, it would only be to continue with the protective CAP policy.

Production quotas

The EU applies production quotas on sugar, milk, stark potatoes and tobacco. The sugar quota was set up at the outset. Production quotas are only considered a reasonable policy alternative if:

- there is a surplus on the domestic market at supported prices;
- budget outlays are high due to a high price differential between domestic and world market prices and a high exportable surplus;
- domestic production is growing, leading to even higher outlays in the future; and
- there is a bottleneck which allows the produced quantities to be controlled at acceptable financial costs.

The first three conditions prevail on many agricultural markets in the EU, but the bottleneck arises mainly in the selected markets where quotas have been introduced. In the case of sugar, all the sugarbeet has to be processed in factories where the quantities can be checked. As to milk, most of it is nowadays delivered to EU dairies (over 95 per cent), but much less than this in the new EU countries. In Poland it is only about 60 per cent.

The analysis of a quota system will focus on the milk market regime. Quotas were introduced in 1984 because surpluses on the milk market were rising and the price differential between domestic and world market prices was extremely high. The rise in milk production was not expected at the time of the inception of the milk market regime.

In 1967/8 cows were mainly fed on domestically produced fodder. Hence, milk production was constrained by the domestic capacity to produce feed. However, the situation changed quickly due to some specifics of the trading regime for feed imports. In GATT negotiations the EU had agreed to apply low tariffs on imports of feed in exchange for being allowed to introduce the variable levy system for the main temperate-zone products. At that time, feed (soya, tapioca and others) was not imported in sizeable quantities. However, with increased EU grain prices the willingness to pay for imported feed went up. The decline in shipping rates also contributed to booming imports of feed. A mixture of soya meal or cake and tapioca was used as a perfect substitute for grain. Thus, milk production became less dependent on farm-grown fodder and it expanded heavily. Farmers not only increased milk yield from just over 3,000 kg per cow in 1967 to about 5,000 kg per cow in 1983, but also increased herd size, taking advantage of economies of scale in milk production. Hence, it became less feasible to increase the income of milk producers through support prices. The situation is depicted in figure 20.13. At the given milk price, most of the producers milking less than twenty cows did not make a profit since average costs were above the milk price. However, those farmers milking in excess of twenty and less than a hundred cows could make a profit. Hence, there was a huge incentive for increasing herd sizes for milking, almost irrespective of the amount of arable and pastureland used on the farm. Thus, milk production grew much faster than milk consumption, leading to growing exportable surpluses. EU policymakers could have lowered prices long before 1984, as the problem was already visible for many years prior to that. However, they postponed making a decision, as they did not dare to provoke farmers. In 1984, drastic measures were needed to correct the problem: a significant price cut by about 12 per cent was considered as unacceptable, so the introduction of a quota system was seen as a reasonable alternative.

Policymakers and bureaucrats generally prefer a quota system to price cuts. Quotas are attractive as they do not lead to an immediate high-income

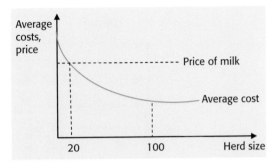

Figure 20.13 Average costs in milk production and milk prices

loss. Bureaucrats may even value highly the new control system that has to be instituted as a consequence: the higher the bureaucratic burden, the better the prospects for job promotion. In contrast, economists generally oppose quota systems because of misallocation of resources. An efficient farmer cannot expand production without gaining additional quotas. If they were tradeable, the farmer would buy them, but the costs of expanding production would increase. Hence, structural change would be held up. Moreover, quota systems contradict the basic idea of a customs union: production cannot move to those regions and enterprises which are the most efficient ones.

Consumption subsidies

EU policymakers use different forms of subsidy. Payments for price reduction as described above are special subsidies. There are others, offered to reduce production costs, such as interest subsidies for investment or for stimulating demand. Let us examine the latter.

Consumption subsidies are most important in the milk market. Some 50 to 90 per cent of the total annual EU demand for skimmed milk powder has been supported in this way over the past twenty years. The figure for butter is 15 to 35 per cent. Hence, without these subsidies, the exportable surplus would be much higher.

The budget effects of the subsidy schemes are difficult to assess. If the alternative was to get rid of the surplus by exporting a higher volume, the answer would be straightforward. If domestic demand for the subsidized product is price

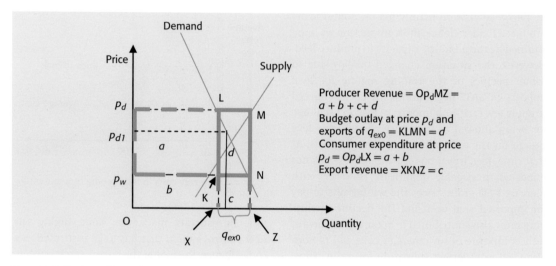

Figure 20.14 Budget effects of EU demand for domestic consumption as compared to export subsidization

inelastic and world market demand for the additional EU exports is completely elastic (small country assumption), budget outlays would be higher with subsidizing EU demand. The comparison is depicted in figure 20.14. Total revenue for producers is financed by consumers, export revenue and budget outlays. The original situation for the domestic market price p_d is shown in the figure. If the government decided to subsidize domestic consumers, the demand curve would shift to the right, increasing the demand at price p_d. This would have the same effect as lowering domestic prices, say from p_d to p_{d1}. However, consumer expenditure at price p_{d1} would be lower than at price p_d if the price elasticity of demand were smaller than 1 (in absolute terms), a condition which definitely holds for EU butter demand. Moreover, if domestic consumers expanded their purchases on the domestic market, the exportable surplus would decline. Hence, revenue from sales to the world market declines. Thus, the area $a + b + c$ would be smaller than in the initial situation. Consequently, budget outlays have to be larger to cover producer revenue.

The assessment of the subsidies on butter and skimmed milk powder would lead to a different result were welfare effects the focus. The marginal willingness to pay at price p_d is larger than the world market price. Reducing consumer prices

through subsidies creates additional welfare. The analysis is presented in figure 20.15.

Reducing domestic prices through subsidies increases demand, the increase in the willingness to pay is equal to the bold-bordered trapezoid, but the loss in revenue is only the rectangle given by the export quantity in the initial situation multiplied by the world market price. Hence, there is an overall welfare gain. Actually the welfare gain would be even higher if domestic consumers were confronted with world market prices by subsidizing the difference between producer and the world market price. This proves once more that budget effects are not related to welfare effects.

20.5.5 The market regimes

Grain market regime

The grain market regime plays a major role in EU agricultural markets. Grain production determines the agricultural income directly, but also indirectly as it affects production costs for pork, poultry, eggs and milk. Moreover, profitability of grain production is crucial for the comparative advantage of the other field crops, including fodder crops, as grain prices are a main determinant of land and lease prices. The grain market organization includes, as do most market

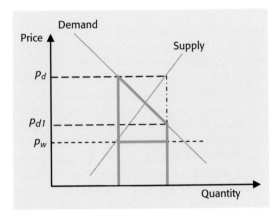

Figure 20.15 Welfare effects of consumer subsidies

organizations, provisions for external trade and for internal market regulations. The external trade regime is more important for domestic price formation, as internal prices can only deviate from import or export parity prices if there are border measures in place, which drive a wedge between the two prices. Like all members of WTO, the EU has lost the ability to change border measures at its discretion since import tariffs for grains have been bound on a fairly high level, making a significant share of the tariff redundant. Hence, some grain and processed grain imports can only enter the EU market on a preferential basis. Therefore, internal policy measures and the regulation of exports determine domestic prices. The latter is the most binding. The EU has, in accordance with the other WTO members, agreed:

(i)   to cut the subsidized export quantities for all agricultural exports, classified with respect to specific groups, from the 1986 to the 1990 level by 21 per cent;
(ii) to reduce the payments of export subsidies by 36 per cent; and
(iii) to allow minimum access of imports of at least 5 per cent of domestic use during 1986–8.

As long as the EU produces an exportable surplus and has to pay export subsidies, i.e. if domestic prices are above export parity prices, the exportable quantity, which can be subsidized, is given by the following equation:

Subsidized exportable surplus =

   Domestic production − domestic use

     − minimum market access − imports due to

   other preferential agreements

Alternatively, domestic production is restricted by the following equation:

Domestic production = Domestic use

    + subsidized exportable surplus − minimum

   market access − imports due to other

   preferential agreements.

In order to comply with the export constraints, the EU has either to cut domestic production at prices above export parity or to lower domestic prices to the level of the export parity price. The EU is willing to accept the second alternative. Grain prices have been reduced in two steps, first by 30 per cent in a 1992 decision and by another 15 per cent as part of the *Agenda 2000* agreement of March 1999. Since 2000, EU prices for some grains have been equal to world market prices and exporters have occasionally been competitive on the world markets without subsidies. However, prices for some types of grain are still somewhat above world market prices and the EU pays export subsidies in order to get rid of the surplus.

Domestic market regulations on the grain market include intervention prices, set-aside obligations with payments of premiums, and direct payments per area cultivated with grains. Intervention prices are minimum prices on the wholesale level for specified qualities of individual grains. They are the same for all grains and for all locations. These prices have become less important over time as the administration has pushed up domestic market prices above the intervention price level. This was done by reducing the intervention prices close to the level of world market prices, by abolishing intervention prices for rye which was the main surplus grain with high protection rates and – if necessary – by paying export subsidies high enough to bridge the remaining gap between domestic and world market prices. The profitability of producing grain was highly determined by direct payment per ha of grain up to the 2003 reform. The new system of direct payments does not affect the profitability of individual products any more, as it is decoupled from production. Hence, the profitability of grain has been reduced significantly since 1992, the beginning of the reform process.

Market regime for oilseeds, sunflower seeds and soya beans

The market regime for oilseeds, sunflower seeds and soya beans has no special border regulation. However, there was an area payment, which had been set equal to that of grains as part of the *Agenda 2000* package. The 2003 reform integrated this type of payment into the single farm payment (SFP) scheme. Hence, the market regime for these products has been completely liberalized.

Market regime for olive oil

The market regime for olive oil used to be highly regulated and highly protective. However, in April 2004, the European Commission adopted reforms of this market regime in line with the main principles of the reform in 2003. The new system became effective in 2006. The main difference from the other market regimes is that only part of the payment (60 per cent) is decoupled and added to the single farm payment. The other part may still remain linked to production, but may be directed to small holdings or marginal areas.

Market regime for sugar

The market regime for sugar used to be one where the *internal* market was intensively regulated. The system survived without any significant changes from its beginning in 1967/8 to 2006. However, a new system was instituted in July 2006. There is still a production quota for sugarbeet, isoglucose and inulin, but the former differentiation between A sugar with the highest prices and B sugar with somewhat reduced prices (about 31 per cent depending on the world market price) has been suspended. Moreover, prices for white sugar and minimum prices paid for beet to producers will be reduced by 36 per cent and 39.5 per cent until 2009/10. The intervention price will be in place only for the transition period, but at a level 20 per cent lower than in the past. The intervention price

will be replaced by a reference price which does not commit the Commission to intervene in the market. A further significant change concerns the so-called C sugar: farmers are allowed to produce beyond the allocated A and B quotas, but the price has to be negotiated with the processing factories. In most cases, the price for C sugar is very much tied to the world market price. Hence, this quantity of sugar is exported without the payment of export subsidies. Starting in 2006, C sugar production is no longer possible; instead, the over-quota production must either be transferred into the next marketing year, or can be used for the production of certain products, e.g. bioethanol. As an additional compensation, sugar factories in the member states can buy up to 1.1 million tonnes additional quota, with country-specific limits, at a price of 730 euros per tonne.

One may wonder why this market regime, having survived all past attempts at reform, has finally been reformed, and drastically. Again, as stated above, the pressure to reform was due to constraints imposed by trading partners. First, the Uruguay Agreement required a change, in particular as C sugar was considered part of subsidized sugar, due to cross-subsidy effects for A and B sugar. Second, sugar imported through preferential agreements and re-exported was also considered as subsidized exports. Hence, the WTO dispute settlement body ruled that the EU had to stop the exports of C sugar and the re-exports of preferential sugar from May 2006 onwards. Third, the EU had agreed on an 'Everything but Arms' initiative with the poorest forty-nine countries: these countries are basically allowed to export all products, except for arms, duty-free to the EU. Even with a transition period for sugar (up to 2009), the implications are quite clear: the EU could not continue to have, in most years, sugar prices three times the world market prices.

Of course, these significant changes in price led to reduced revenues from sugarbeet production. Hence, the new legislation includes compensation of about 64 per cent, which will, however, eventually be included in the single farm payment scheme or in the case of area payment in the flat rate area payment. On the other hand, sugar farmers already received some overcompensation in those countries where the SFP scheme involves area payments because the area for sugarbeet became eligible for SFP payments under the new regime.

Market regimes for fruit and vegetables

The market regimes for fruit and vegetables are less intensively regulated than those for temperate-zone products. The EU avoids direct intervention as most of these products are only storable for short periods at high costs, and in addition price incentives may stimulate production growth significantly (high price elasticity of supply). Nevertheless, producers are protected. Premiums for withdrawal are paid if representative market prices are below set buying-in prices. These premiums can be considered as the lowest market price. Withdrawal is mostly done by producer organizations. The external trading regime includes tariffs, depending on the season, and export subsidies.

Market regime for milk products

The market regime for milk products, like the other main market organizations, relies on external trade regulations and on domestic market measures. The external regime is comparable to that for grains, i.e. it is widely constrained by WTO rules. However, internal measures are specific. First, the domestic price is not stabilized by intervention prices for the raw materials as is the case for grains. Because it is expensive to store liquid milk the farm price for milk is stabilized by intervention prices for butter and skim milk powder; these two products contain the main marketable ingredients of milk fat and protein. By fixing the price for butter and skim milk powder, the farm gate price is significantly determined.

Up to the CAP reform of 2003, milk and sugar products were the most protected in the EU. The quota system for these products did allow high domestic prices without resulting in increases in production. However, the WTO Uruguay Round agreement and the expected outcome of the Doha Round initiated further significant reforms. The 2003 reform implied a significant liberalization by lowering intervention prices for butter and skim milk powder by 25 per cent and 15 per cent respectively over a period of four years for butter and three years for skim milk powder. Moreover, intervention purchases for butter were limited in time and in volume. It is expected that the farm price for milk may drop by as much as one-third from 2003 to 2010. About 60 per cent of the loss in income will be compensated by direct payments. These payments will be incorporated into the single farm payment after a transition period lasting until 2007 when part of the payment will be linked to the quota. Hence, the reform has significant impact on the profitability of milk production. It is likely that small and medium-sized dairy farmers will either expand significantly in order to exploit economies of scale or stop reinvesting, and thus will give up milk production in the medium and long run. Consequently, the quota may become redundant as total milk production in individual countries might fall below the allocated quota.

20.6 Rural development policy

Rural development policy was formally created under the *Agenda 2000* reforms and was termed the 'second pillar of CAP'. Some of the policy instruments have been in place as part of EU structural policy since the 1970s and 80s, but most of them have been introduced in the 1990s.

There are some sound economic arguments for placing stronger emphasis on structural measures than on market and price policy. First, the Union has been enlarged significantly over time and this has widened the heterogeneity between the member countries and between the regions. Therefore, the market and price policy became less effective over time, increasing the demand for specific structural measures. Nevertheless, one may wonder whether the second pillar instruments and, in particular the method of financing, is a true rationalization for the CAP.

The regulation quotes three objectives for rural development policy:

1. improving competitiveness of the agricultural sector,

Table 20.1 Measures under the Rural Development Regulation, by category

Competitiveness of agriculture	Land management and environment	Broader rural development
<ul><li>Investment in farms;</li><li>Support to young farmers;</li><li>Vocational training;</li><li>Early retirement;</li><li>Investment in processing/ marketing;</li><li>Land improvement;</li><li>Re-parcelling;</li><li>Setting up farm relief services;</li><li>Marketing quality products;</li><li>Agricultural water resources management;</li><li>Development and improvement of infrastructure related to agriculture;</li><li>Restoring agricultural production potential.</li></ul>	<ul><li>Compensatory allowances in less favoured areas and areas with environmental restrictions (LFA);</li><li>Agri-environment programmes;</li><li>Afforestation of agricultural land and other forestry measures;</li><li>Environmental protection in connection with agriculture and forestry.</li></ul>	<ul><li>Basic services for the rural economy and population;</li><li>Renovation and development of villages;</li><li>Diversification of agricultural activities;</li><li>Encouragement for tourism and craft activities and financial engineering.</li></ul>

Source: Gay et al. (2005, p. 8).

2. protection of environment and landscape, and
3. improving living standards in rural areas and support of diversification.

In line with the three objectives, specific instruments are also foreseen for the achievement of the individual objectives (see table 20.1).

The list of instruments clearly shows that agriculture is considered the main sector which should be supported when aiming at rural development. Indeed, the preamble of the regulation makes it clear that the focus should be on agriculture or activities closely related to agriculture. Moreover, it is clearly stated that payments to farmers in cases of environmental measures should be calculated on the basis of income forgone, and could surpass income forgone by as much as 20 per cent.

It may be surprising that rural policy focuses mainly on agriculture, when the sector is not dominant in terms of rural GDP and even less so with respect to regional employment. Data for England and for the UK as a whole reveals that agricultural GDP in regional GDP was, respectively, only 1.2 per cent and 1.5 per cent in 1997.[15]

The share of agricultural employment in rural areas was 4 per cent in the UK in 1996, the same as for construction, but much less than for distribution, hotels and restaurants with 24 per cent, and services with 20 per cent.[16] These figures are only averages for one country. Of course, there is a huge variance across countries and regions. However, there is a general trend indicating declining shares for agricultural GDP and employment. Moreover, conventional agriculture has become a highly capital-intensive sector resulting in an even lower agricultural share in regional employment than in regional GDP. Hence, it is obvious that agriculture is hardly the dominant sector in rural areas today in most regions in the EU and is less likely to be so in the future.

The objective of 'enhancing the competitiveness of agriculture' raises major economic concerns. Policy-induced improved competitiveness of a specific sector in a region does not necessarily enhance the competitiveness of that region. The New Bundesländer in Germany proves the opposite: agriculture was highly supported not only by high price support, but also by investment aid.

Table 20.2 Actual and planned performance indicators of supported farms in Schleswig-Holstein in the target year (fourth year after investment)

	Quartiles of labour income in DM/work unit			
	First quartile	Second quartile	Third quartile	Fourth quartile
Number of farms	78	77	77	77
Actual labour income/work unit	12.192	39.571	61.064	109.415
Planned labour income per work unit[1] according to Farm Investment Plan (FIP)	37.606	39.346	40.599	41.563
Earned interest rate	−6.7	−0.5	3.6	9.5
Profit in the target year[2]	23.389	62.273	90.647	122.514
Planned profit according to FIP	74.262	76.422	77.402	81.248
Surplus[3]	−40.641	−12.813	52.181	21.045
Supported investment	262.757	273.156	255.962	264.278
Own means	103.110	88.231	88.004	90.512
Subsidy equivalents	71.827	88.447	73.078	76.363

Notes:
1 Labour income per necessary work unit.
2 Four years after the actual year of support.
3 Profit minus withdrawals for private and other use.

Source: Striewe et al. (1996).

The policy resulted in a highly capital-intensive agricultural sector, but with very high rural unemployment rates. Agriculture would have employed more labour with less investment aid and the region would have been better off without support. It is strange that advocating investment in farms is still considered a reasonable instrument for supporting agricultural competitiveness. There are some evaluations of investment aid which clearly show that the overall effect is not positive or cannot be identified when positive. Table 20.2 provides the findings of one piece of research in Germany. All supported farms were very similar before investment, at the time they had to submit their business plan (farm improvement plan). However, they were very dissimilar four years later, in the so-called target year. Half of the supported farms were not able to generate a positive interest rate, proving that the investment was a failure even from a financial point of view, and it was even more so from an economic point of view, as market prices were much higher than national shadow prices.

The second pillar measures raise the suspicion that policymakers aimed to compensate farmers for their loss in income due to the enforced reduction in support provided by pillar 1 measures. This suspicion is also supported by the created linkage between expenditure for pillar 1 measures and those for pillar 2. Direct payments, introduced to compensate the income losses due to price reductions, will be partly reduced over time and the savings will be incorporated into the second pillar measures. Again, this procedure could be a basis for rationalizing the CAP, but only if it were accompanied by a change in the distribution of funds between countries and regions. Such a change would be necessary since the need for rural development measures varies significantly between countries and regions. Such redistribution is not built into the new scheme. Of course, that would be understandable were the main purpose of the new approach only to stabilize support for agriculture, even if the term had to be changed.

Table 20.3 Most probable implementation by EU25 member states of the policy options approved by the Luxemburg compromise

Member state	Arable crops partial decoupling				Livestock partial decoupling				Reference for the single farm premium				
	25% direct premiums	or 40% durum wheat premiums	0–40% olive and olive oil sector	0% tobacco[3]	50% sheep and goat premium	100% suckler cow + 40% slaughter premium	or 100% slaughter premium	or 75% male beef premium	Individual farm premium	Hybrid model simple	Hybrid model dynamic	Implementation period	Integration of milk reform in SFP
France	X				X	X			X			2006	2006
Belgium + Luxembourg[1]							X (Belgium)		X	X (Lux.)		2005	2006 (Belgium) 2005 (Lux.)
Netherlands					X		X		X			2006	2007
Austria						X			X			2005	2007
Germany				X							X	2005	2005
Finland					X			X			X	2006	2006
Denmark					X			X		X		2005	2005
United Kingdom[2]									X (Wales, Scotland)	X (North.)	X	2005	2005
Ireland									X			2005	2005
Sweden							X			X		2005	2007
Spain	X		X (5 %)	X	X	X			X			2006	2006
Portugal						X			X			2005	2007
Greece	X				X	X			X			2006	2007
Italy				X					X			2005	2006
Rest (EU10)[4]											X	2007–09	–

Notes:

[1] Belgium and Luxembourg are modelled together in Common Agricultural Policy Regional Impact (CAPRI).

[2] Within the United Kingdom. England has chosen a dynamic hybrid model, Wales and Scotland a farm historical premium scheme and Northern Ireland a static hybrid model.

[3] Sixty per cent of tobacco payments are allowed to be coupled until 2010. Afterwards, 100 per cent decoupling must be assumed.

[4] For the EU10 countries no partial decoupling is considered. A flat rate premium is assumed to increase gradually over time until 2013 (in 2012, 90 per cent of the negotiated premium ceiling values are paid to agricultural activities).

Source: Arts. 66 and 68 of Council of the European Union (2003b); Art. 110 Reg. EC/(64/2004; partially based on the compilation made by Massot Marti, quoted in Britz et al. (2006, p. 218).

20.7 The future of the CAP

As already described, there have been specific driving forces behind the evolution of the CAP. These forces are likely to become stronger in the near future. The Commission has already responded to the pressure to reform with the 2003 reform package. However, further changes can be foreseen, due to pressures from outside and within the EU.

First, it is questionable whether the present CAP is able to cope with the present constraints imposed by WTO. It is likely that the price reduction for sugarbeet will prove inadequate and growing preferential imports may enforce further price cuts for sugar.

Second, the ongoing Doha Round will most likely require further adjustments to the CAP. The EU has already agreed to abolish export subsidies up to the year 2013. However, final agreement concerning the gradual timing of the downsizing of export subsidies and other changes has not yet been formally reached. Nevertheless, it can be expected that the Doha Round – if there is eventually a final agreement – will result in a complete abolition of export subsidies. This change will require further reform steps. Take the case of milk: if there are no export subsidies for milk products, yet domestic milk production still surpasses domestic consumption, dairy exporters can only pay world market prices on the domestic market. If intervention prices are above world market prices there would be no exports and the surplus would have to be bought in by intervention agencies. That would certainly not be a sustainable situation. Therefore, it can be predicted that prices of products presently in surplus would either fall to the level of world market prices or to a higher level where domestic production equalled domestic consumption. However, the latter situation would probably prove unsustainable in the long run; it would imply price ratios on domestic markets which are not in line with world market prices. Export products would be implicitly taxed relative to products in self-sufficiency or imported. It would be rational from an economic point of view to move to world market prices for all products. Thus the new regulation, allowing no payments of any export subsidies, might open the door for pressure to liberalize agricultural markets completely.

Third, the 2003 CAP reform did not completely achieve its objective, namely the complete decoupling of payments. The final agreement allows member countries significant leeway in implementing the new system (see table 20.3). There are only few countries which follow the basic idea of the proposal by the Commission. National derogations may be needed in order to allow for differences in national interests due to the homogeneity of the countries. However, the present variation in implementing direct payments conflicts with WTO objectives and also distorts the production pattern within the EU. For example, model calculations show that suckler cow production is declining in Germany due to complete decoupling, but increasing in France due to partial decoupling (Küpker et al. 2006). It is hardly credible that WTO members would allow a continuation of this policy and some member countries may also ask for changes if they realized the distortive effects.

Fourth, further enlargements of the EU are likely (other Balkan countries and Turkey). It is questionable whether some of the new member states as well as the prospective ones have the administrative capacity to apply the CAP in its present form. These fears concern most of the second pillar measures. The European Court of Auditors has stated many times that there are many irregularities and even frauds accompanying the implementation of these measures. Hence, improvement in governance is highly needed. Hopefully a new system will be created which does better than the present one in terms of subsidiarity, transparency and accountability.

20.8 Conclusion

Since the prospects for change have already been discussed, the conclusion should be in the nature of an assessment of the CAP as it has developed over the four decades or so since its inception. Before doing so, however, the reader needs to be reminded that the CAP support system has become rather complicated since it retains the original system for certain products while applying new methods for others and/or building them on top of the old.

Judged in terms of the need at the time of the formation of the EEC for a common policy, the CAP is obviously a success. Also, judged in terms of its own objectives, the policymakers agree that it seems to have had several successes. However, it is questionable whether the CAP has contributed to its own objectives, let alone to its overall goal.

Any assessment of a policy cannot just focus on the development of specific variables, such as productivity or income. Instead, it has to be based on a comparison of 'with' and 'without' the CAP. The situation 'with' is easy to observe, not so the situation 'without', since one has to specify what alternative policy would have been in place (one would need a reference situation or base line: the *anti-monde* discussed in chapter 9). Second, the effects of this alternative policy would have to be analysed. The first point certainly contains a value judgment as there is no consensus on how to specify the alternative policy; if analysts based their assessment on different reference systems, their results would necessarily differ. If, for example, agricultural policymakers claim that there is no alternative to the given policy, they implicitly assess present costs as zero.

Here, it is assumed that the alternative would have been a less protective CAP. What then would have been the effects of the CAP according to the objectives mentioned in the Treaty and stated in section 20.4?

1. *Effect on agricultural productivity.* Assume that there is a production function as mirrored in figure 20.16. Given factor input F_0, production would be q_0, hence the productivity tan α. Reducing prices, the marginal suppliers have to leave the sector, leading to productivity tan β. As tan $\beta >$ tan α, productivity at lower prices would have been higher. As price support reduced migration out of the sector, resulting in the survival of marginal farms, it affected productivity negatively. It should be noted that this reasoning holds even if the productivity increase in EU agriculture had been greater

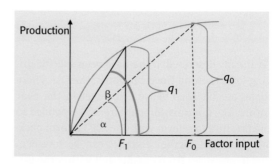

Figure 20.16 The effect of price support on productivity

than in other countries and in excess of that for the industrial sectors.

2. *Effect on agricultural income.* There is no doubt that the total income generated in farming is higher with support prices than without. However, the important question is whether *income per unit of labour* is higher. Economists tend to argue that income per unit will be equal to the opportunity cost in the long run. Price support will increase income in the adjustment period, but after adjustment the income differential will be the same as at lower prices. Indeed, there is some evidence for this argument. Take the German case. Agricultural prices had to be lowered in 1967/8 when the common prices were set. Out-migration increased, and after the adjustment agricultural income was again about 60 per cent of average income, reflecting preferences. Higher prices do not only increase the income of those who are in the sector, they also influence decisions to take up farming. Hence, employment in the agricultural sector depends on the price level. Thus, one has to take into consideration the transfer efficiency of price support. Part of the income lost by those in the non-agricultural sector results in dead-weight losses (negative welfare effects); another part is transferred through the market mechanism to others who were not targeted, in particular landlords who are the main winners of price support.

3. *Effect on the stability of markets.* If the CAP was supposed to stabilize prices, it has been a great success. Intervention prices helped stabilize market prices. However, if the CAP was supposed to stabilize revenue or income, it has

probably failed. A shortfall in production due to a bad harvest might be compensated by higher prices in free markets. Actually, the revenue would be less volatile if the price elasticity of demand were larger than 0.5 in absolute terms. Taking into account the demand for storage and for interregional trade it is likely that the elasticity is larger than 0.5.

4. *The effect on food security.* High support prices help to increase supply under normal conditions. However, food security only becomes a problem under abnormal conditions, such as natural catastrophes, wars or trade conflicts. Even if a country is able to feed its population under normal conditions, it is not at all sure that it will have the capacity to produce enough food in abnormal conditions. Take, for example, the case of milk production. It was stated above that EU farmers partly produce the milk on the basis of imported feed. Moreover, a lot of imported energy is needed in order to supply the market. Had trade ties fallen apart, these requirements would not have been met. Hence, the present production level does not allow one to conclude that food would have been available in emergency situations.

5. *Effect on reasonable consumer prices.* It is quite clear that the CAP was, right from the very beginning, a burden for the European consumer. Thus, the CAP has failed badly in trying to achieve the policy objectives set for it.

Has it done better in attempting to achieve general economic or overall policy objectives? Concerning general economic objectives, the answer is clearly in the negative, given the welfare effects identified in the analysis above. Nevertheless, one has to accept two positive political effects. The first is that the CAP has mitigated the adjustment process, albeit not in the most efficient way. It has been argued that income transfers linked to the personal income situation of farmers would have been more efficient from the viewpoint of economics. Lack of endorsement of this alternative may be due to its political infeasibility: policymakers can only select those alternatives that are acceptable to the electorate. Of course, what the electorate would accept would depend, among others things, on information about the alternatives and their effects. Perhaps economists should have been more forceful in addressing both the population at large and politicians on this alternative, but could their academic performance match farmers' political clout?

It has been shown that there is a strong path-dependency in agricultural policy since the decisions taken at the outset have influenced ensuing development. It is arguable whether policymakers had an alternative at that time. Member countries had to be convinced to give up their national autonomy in agricultural policy and there was only a little political leeway left: it was necessary to incorporate agriculture into the European integration scheme. Policymakers achieved this at the beginning, but the evolution of the policy has not much improved the situation. National markets are not well integrated because of quotas for milk, sugar and tobacco, and also because of EU expenditure constraints, such as limits on direct payments. Nevertheless, the Council decisions of June 2003 create hope for improvement, at least with regard to the main pillar of the CAP.

NOTES

1 A rough indication of the average levels of income for farmers, relative to the incomes of those in other occupations, can be obtained by comparing the share of agriculture in total labour force and national output. Such a comparison indicates that at the time of the inception of the EEC, average agricultural incomes in the three largest countries (France, Germany and Italy) were only about 50 per cent of those in other occupations (Ritson, 1973, p. 96).

2 'Agricultural incomes have risen, but in France, Germany and Italy there is little evidence that the gap in incomes between agriculture and other occupations has diminished' (Ritson, 1973).

3 That is, a country which has no impact on world prices.

4 A policy failure indicates that policy decisions have reduced welfare for society at large.

5 'Governance is defined as the manner in which power is exercised in the management of a country's economic and social resources for development' (World Bank, 1992, p. 1).

6 It should be noted that the Council does not necessarily act in the interests of the majority of farmers.

A minister might possibly act in the 'perceived' interests of farmers or in the interests of some special sections of the farming population.

7 It should be noted that the main features of most countries' protectionist policies have been put in place in periods of crisis for agriculture; see Petit (1985).

8 See, for example, the divergence in national interest for implementing the set-aside programme (Koester, 1989b, pp. 240–8).

9 It should be noted that Article 33 of the Treaty neither mentions that policymakers are supposed to achieve a specific income objective nor states that prices should be set to contribute to the achievement of the income objective.

10 Expected external costs are defined as disadvantages to an individual due to constraints imposed on the individual by collective decisions.

11 This point is discussed in more detail and empirically supported in Koester and Tangermann (1990).

12 Indeed, this observation should not be surprising for students of public choice. Western democracies have strong pressure groups which strongly resist fundamental changes.

13 The invisible transfer, due to producer prices being higher than import or export parity prices, was considerably higher than the visible transfer before the CAP reform; see Ballenger, Dunmore and Lederer (1987).

14 The producer support estimate is a measure used to indicate by how much farm income is increased by governmental interference.

15 DEFRA (2006).

16 DEFRA (2006).

21 The Common Fisheries Policy

BRIAN ARDY AND ALI EL-AGRAA

21.1 Introduction

The Common Fisheries Policy (CFP) illustrates both the potential and the limitations of EU policy. Fisheries are an inherently difficult sector to manage. Issues such as competing views on property rights and tensions between scientists, fishers and conservationists are well known in fishing communities across the world. The crisis in most major fish stocks has heightened tensions in debates over the conservation and management of stocks. Key aspects of the sector such as trade, processing and ownership are becoming increasingly internationalized but this has been a difficult process in a sector where individualism and a strong sense of community runs deep. One of the challenges for fishery regimes is to compete effectively in the global market but at the same time to cushion communities from social costs and economic decline.

There is a logic in an EU fisheries policy: much fishing activity is conducted across and beyond national territorial waters and fish take no notice of national boundaries. Fish such as mackerel, herring and cod often migrate hundreds of miles during their lifecycles. They may spawn in one area, become juveniles in another and reach maturity in a third. About 90 per cent of North Sea cod, for example, spend their first year in waters off the coasts of Denmark, Germany and Holland, but by the time they are three years old and ripe for catching most of them will have migrated to British territorial waters. If successful, the conservation of fish stocks could in the long run be a positive sum game for all the member states in a situation of declining resources. As Shackleton (1983) points out, 'the condition seemed to exist for experts to take a problem and produce a rational assessment of what was the common interest of the Community without vital interests blocking a settlement'.

However, an analysis of the CFP shows how difficult it is to design a policy for the management and regulation of a Common European pond and the 'problem' of the CFP is one that has bedevilled the EU since the inception of the policy in 1970. By the early 2000s, the policy had reached a crisis point, having failed to manage dwindling fish stocks, to respond to wider environmental concerns or to satisfy competing national interests. A number of fish stocks, including North Sea cod, were in a state of collapse despite a significant decline in the fishing fleet. The policy lacked legitimacy because it imposed regulations in a highly diverse sector where there were no strong norms of obligation to a commonly accepted set of rules or institutions. There is a long chain of command from the politicians and scientists in Brussels to the fishers who are operating the policies on the high seas. One of the major problems facing the CFP is that many fishers do not comply with the detailed rules and regulations emanating from Brussels. Opinion is divided about whether the solution to this problem of non-compliance is greater uniformity and centralization or a move towards a more regionalized form of CFP which would bring the institutions closer to the stakeholders. The Commission has acknowledged that one reason for non-compliance may be that the stakeholders do not feel sufficiently involved in the policy-making process. At the same time it has made strenuous efforts to try and ensure more effective methods of compliance across the EU by, for example, establishing Commission inspectors.

This chapter will begin by setting out the background to the development of the CFP. It will go on to outline the main policy objectives and nature of the policymaking process. It will then outline the recent reforms of the CFP. Finally, it assesses the institutional and governance issues associated with delivering a more effective CFP, which will be able to address the challenges of fish stock collapse and wider environmental concerns.

21.2 Background

The fisheries sector[1] of the EU is small in terms of output and employment; even when associated activities are taken into account, the sector accounted for 1 per cent of EU GDP in the early 1970s but less than 0.3 per cent by 2003.[2] EU15 employment in the sector has been in steep decline, decreasing from 1.2 million in 1970 to 369,184 in 2003:[3] 0.2 per cent of total employment. Although fisheries are only a small sector within the EU economy, the activity tends to be concentrated in peripheral regions where there is often little alternative employment. The sector as a whole is in steep decline: EU25 catches declined by 18.3 per cent between 1993 and 2004 (table 21.1). The pain has been unevenly spread depending on the type of catch; the decline of fishing in the new member states, excluding Bulgaria and Romania whose entry is too recent to take into consideration, occurred during the transition process. The four largest producers – Denmark, Spain, the UK and France – account for over half the EU catch.

About 38 per cent of the total volume of EU fisheries production is now by aquaculture. Aquaculture is a growing industry worldwide and to some extent it compensates for the decline of sea fisheries. Even so, the EU as a whole imports more fish than it produces, with only Denmark, Spain, the Netherlands, Ireland, Malta, Estonia, Slovenia and Cyprus having positive trade balances in fishery products in 2003.

The industry and its representatives tend to be highly fragmented. In any one country fishermen are divided amongst types of fishing (long distance or inshore) and structure of ownership (individual, family, conglomerate). Modernization has been

Table 21.1 EU fish catch, 1993 and 2004 (metric tonnes)

	1993 (% of total catch)	2004 (% of total catch)	% change (in total catch)
EU15	88.60	90.22	−16.8
NMS10	11.40	9.78	−29.8
Denmark	20.53	18.36	−26.9
Spain	14.99	14.38	−21.6
UK	11.84	11.03	−23.8
France	8.82	11.27	4.4
Netherlands	6.36	8.79	13.0
Italy	5.48	4.70	−29.9
Poland	5.44	3.23	−51.4
Sweden	4.71	4.55	−21.1
Portugal	4.03	3.72	−24.6
Ireland	3.83	4.72	0.7
Germany	3.48	4.41	3.6
Greece	2.19	1.57	−41.5
Estonia	2.02	1.48	−40.1
Latvia	1.95	2.11	−12.0
Finland	1.86	2.27	0.0
Lithuania	1.61	2.66	35.0
Belgium	0.50	0.45	−25.0
Cyprus	0.14	0.03	−80.0
Hungary	0.11	0.12	−12.5
Czech Republic	0.04	0.08	66.7
Slovenia	0.03	0.02	−50.0
Malta	0.01	0.02	0.0
Slovakia	0.01	0.03	100.0
Luxembourg	0.00	0.00	
Austria	0.00	0.00	
EU25	7,266	5,938	−18.3

Source: Eurostat (2006a, b).

asymmetric across the EU and there is a growing gulf between artisanal fishing and the highly technological deep-sea fleets. As with agriculture, the diversity of the sector adds to the difficulty of constructing an effective common policy. This has been compounded by the political salience of the issue. The dangerous and to some extent romantic nature of the occupation, the strong sense of community and, in recent years, the linking of fishing not only to regional but also in some cases to national identity, has meant that fishing interests often carry disproportionate weight within the EU.

Fisheries were included in the definition of agricultural products in the Treaty of Rome (see chapter 20), and the two industries do have much in common. Both are subject to price instability: in the case of fisheries this is because of the highly specialized human and physical capital in the industry, making its short-term supply highly inelastic, and also because fish has a rather low price elasticity. Both have low-income elasticities for their products and both are prone to random shocks from natural causes over which there is little control. During the 1950s both sectors were made up of large numbers of small self-employed producers. Both policies are set within an international regulatory framework and face the challenges of internationalization, globalization, and increasing environmental and consumer pressure. There are, however, fundamental differences between the two sectors. Agriculture is about managing excess, while fisheries is about managing scarcity. Fisheries interests are much more diffuse and poorly organized at the EU level. Finally, and most importantly, the nature of ownership of resources is much more fiercely contested in fisheries than in agriculture.

The development of the CFP followed a pattern typical of many other policy areas: authority for the policy was vested in the Treaty of Rome, general principles were laid down some years later and the detailed aspects of the policy were negotiated subsequently over many years with successive enlargements and the changing international framework acting as catalysts for policy change. In the early 1960s, fish stocks were relatively evenly spread among the six member states and there was little international regulation of fishing. By the mid-1960s, the French and Italian governments became aware that their industries were becoming increasingly uncompetitive, especially compared to the German fishing fleet, and began to put pressure on the Community to devise structural aid for their fisheries. However, the real drivers for the establishment of the CFP were changes in the international situation and the impending enlargement to include Denmark, Ireland, Norway and the UK.

Historically, states had ownership over narrow territorial waters (typically 3–4 miles) and competed for stocks on the high seas which were deemed to be common property. This practice was workable because stocks were plentiful and 'belonged' to no one until they were caught. The increasing technical capacity of ships in the post-Second World War period and the growing awareness of threats to stocks meant that this regime began to be questioned. During the 1960s, there was an agreement that any vessel could fish anywhere outside a 12-mile coastal limit, which was reserved for the country whose coast bordered this zone or for states which had historically fished there. However, prompted by unilateral action in 1970 by Iceland claiming exclusive fishing rights within 50 miles of its coast, the United Nations decided in 1976 that any state could establish an exclusive economic zone (EEZ) in waters up to 200 nautical miles from its coastline.

This policy (eventually ratified in 1982 under the UN Convention on the Law of the Sea) had dramatic implications for EC countries, most of which had traditionally fished far from their shores in deep-sea waters. The EC responded by setting up its own EEZ in January 1977. Once the decision had been taken by the EC to set up an EEZ, policymakers had to evolve a system for distributing the stock amongst the member states (for further details see Wise, 1996).

The second factor precipitating the development of a CFP was the impending enlargement of the Community to include the fish-rich nations of Denmark, Ireland, Norway and the UK. These countries had large fishing stocks and the existing states were obviously keen to establish the principle of 'equal access' to fish-rich Community waters before enlargement took place. A policy was quickly hatched so that it became part of the *acquis communautaire* which the new states had to accept on joining. In 1970, an agreement established the right to equal conditions of access to fishing grounds and set the guidelines for a common structural policy. It also laid down some provisions for conservation measures and for financial aid for restructuring the industry. While the UK, Denmark and Ireland strenuously opposed the equal access principle, the issue was not high enough up the political agenda for it to jeopardize the long-awaited and much disputed Community membership. In the end, Norway declined to join the Community, partly because it feared the effects of the equal access principle on its fisheries (see chapter 2). The CFP did not fully come into force until 1983, when it was successfully negotiated because of the impending accession of Spain and Portugal. These two countries had larger fleets than any of the existing member states and had also lost much of their long-distance fishing opportunities in the 1970s. However, pressure from the UK, France and Ireland meant that Spain and Portugal were prevented from having equal access to Community waters until 2002.

The current CFP has evolved in response to a number of factors: biological (the condition of stocks), economic (the single market and trade liberalization) and political (the protection of national interests and enlargement) – see Wise (1996). The CFP and its interpretation by the European Court of Justice (ECJ) is guided by two key principles: equal access to fishing grounds within the common pond (with the exception of 6- and 12-mile coastal strips and special derogations such as the North Sea box around Shetland); and relative stability which fixed the rights of member states' access to waters. Relative stability, which is a highly contentious principle within the CFP, and which in fact distorts the principle of equal access, is based on historic fishing patterns and special interests. For example, in 1983 the UK received an additional cod quota to compensate for the losses from the Icelandic stocks which it had traditionally fished.

The ECJ has, over the years, maintained the principle of non-discrimination in fisheries by upholding the right of non-nationals to buy vessels (and hence a proportion of fishing quota) from other member states. Typically Spanish (and in some cases Dutch) owners have bought UK vessels, thus entitling them, for example, to fish hake in Irish waters and land their catches directly in ports in north-west Spain. This practice is highly controversial and states such as the UK and France have retaliated by tightening up on licence regulations. The ECJ has now stipulated that there needs to be an economic link between coastal communities and vessels which have access (through flags of convenience) to national quotas by insisting that a certain percentage of fish caught is landed in the home port. In practice, policing such complex arrangements has proved very difficult. The case of 'quota hoppers' is interesting because it is an example of a free market principle at work within fisheries and shows the tension between supranational rules and national identities (Lequesne, 2000b).

Until the 1990s the main objective of the CFP was to manage catches so as to ensure an equitable access to supplies across member states, rather than to promote the welfare of the marine system, and fisheries were viewed more as an economic good than as a natural resource (McCormick, 2001). Conservation of resources was not an issue until 1983 and it is only since the mid-1990s, under conditions of severe decline in the stocks, that there has been any serious attempt to develop an ecosystem approach to stock management. This shift towards a more precautionary approach to fisheries was also influenced by the changing international agenda and the growing importance of environmental groups.

The search for equity and uniformity at the European level led to a highly complex system of rules and regulations. Superficially, the policy is marked by its centralization, with a reliance on regulations rather than directives (see section 3.4). In practice, however, there is a great deal of diversity and unevenness of implementation and enforcement across the member states.

21.3 Policy objectives

The CFP negotiated in 1983 gave the EU considerable leeway to prescribe detailed sets of rules for four main policy areas: market, structure, conservation and external relations.

Under the *marketing* policy, fisheries are subject to similar principles to agriculture, including common marketing standards, the institution of a price support system and the establishment of producers organizations (POs). The POs play a key role in many states. For example, in the UK, the nineteen POs decide the allocation of quotas and the granting of licences and permits. The marketing policy is commonly viewed as one of the few successful parts of the policy and has been little modified over the years. Until recently, consumer interests have not played a large part in the CFP, but since the mid-1990s there has been growing pressure on the industry to deliver fresh and wholesome fish. This is part of a changing culture within the food industry in general but also reflects the activities of pressure groups in the area. An example of a more environmentally orientated outlook is the initiative between the multinational Unilever and the World Wide Fund for Nature to set up the Marine Stewardship Council. This council supports more responsible fishing by giving certification to processors who restrict their purchases to fish that are being managed sustainably. Although this has been criticized by some as a marketing gimmick, the council has been quite successful in raising the public's awareness in campaigns such as 'dolphin-friendly' tuna.

Structural assistance for fishing was instituted in 1970 to 'promote harmonious and balanced development' of the industry and the 'rational use of marine resources' (Holden, 1994). Until the mid-1980s, the key aim of the structural policy was to invest in the European fleet in order to catch more fish. However, over time the structural policy has become more flexible and more integrated with other aspects of the CFP. A growing awareness of the damage that over-capacity was having on Europe's fish stocks led in 1983 to the introduction of multi-annual guidance programmes (MAGPs), designed to link structural and conservation policy. Increasingly, MAGPs are used to achieve effort limitation and reduction rather than fleet renewal, although they seem to have limited effectiveness in this role (Suris-Regueiro et al., 2003). The targets put forward by the Commission under the MAGPs are vigorously debated, and invariably moderated upwards, by fisheries ministers, who are keen to ensure that the burden of cutback is as small as possible and is fairly distributed amongst the member states. Financial assistance for communities dependent on fisheries is now integrated into a single Financial Instrument for Fisheries Guidance, which forms part of the EU structural funds (see chapters 19 and 22). EU aid for fishing now systematically requires some form of co-funding from the member states. Financial assistance cannot be given if states have failed to meet their decommissioning targets.

The aim of *conservation policy*, which now forms the core of the CFP, is the responsible exploitation of living marine resources on a sustainable basis (Council Regulation nos. 170/80 and 3760/92), taking into account its implications for the marine ecosystem and socioeconomic implications for producers and consumers. There are two main conservation policies: quotas and total allowable catches (TACs); and technical instruments.

The TACs are now used as a means of conserving stocks although they were originally introduced as a means of allocating shares of available resources to the member states. The Commission bases its policy recommendations on information received from the International Council for the Exploration of the Seas (ICES). ICES scientists monitor stocks and their relative health by setting a precautionary level of spawning stock biomass (SSB – total weight of a species capable of reproducing) for each fish type below which stocks should not be allowed to fall, and a precautionary fishing rate above which the EU fleet should not go. Scientific evidence is often fiercely contested by fishermen on the grounds that it is out of date and is not sensitive enough to changing conditions. Fisheries science does depend on highly complex biological and economic modelling. The interrelated lifecycles of many fish (approximately 50 per cent of fish are eaten by other fish or marine predators), the multi-species nature of most stocks, and the complex nature of the ecosystem mean that predicting fish stocks either through scientific data or through experiential knowledge remains fundamentally uncertain.

The advice provided by national teams reporting to ICES is assessed by ICES's Advisory Committee on Fisheries Management (ACFM) and the Commission's Scientific, Economic and Technical Fisheries Committee (STEFC). The Commission then tries to strike a balance between the advice of ICES and what is likely to be politically acceptable when it draws up proposals on quotas and TACs for the December meeting of the Council of Fisheries Ministers. Once the ministers have agreed the TACs, it is the responsibility of the member states to share out the quotas amongst their fishers and to enforce these quotas.

A second element of conservation policy is technical conservation. These measures include: minimum mesh sizes; minimum landing sizes; catch limits; selective gear including square mesh panels and escape hatches for undersized fish; limits on the length of beam and size of drift nets (since 1 January 2003 a ban on drift nets for tuna swordfish has been in place to remove the negative impact on dolphins and other non-target species); tonnage/power regulations; and the closure of fishing grounds for part of the year.

In *external relations* the Commission has the sole power to negotiate and conclude fisheries agreements with non-member states (see chapter 24). These include reciprocal arrangements over fishing rights, access to surplus stock, access to stock in return for financial compensation, and more recently the development of joint enterprises. The EU currently has agreements in place with some thirty countries (for more details see Lesquesne, 2005). The external policy of the EU has become more important with the shrinking of the Community's own resources. It has come under heavy criticism from environmentalists and from the European Parliament (EP) because it has been seen as exporting the EU fisheries problem by exploiting the resources of developing countries. There is little coordination between the external aspect of the CFP and the EU's international development policy (see chapter 25).

21.4 Policy process

Fisheries policymaking is characterized by a multi-level system of governance ranging from the international arena, where a legal framework is set by the international fisheries regime, to the European, national, regional and local levels which are responsible for the implementation and much of the monitoring of policy. At the core of this policymaking process lie the supranational institutions of the EU – the EP, ECJ, the Commission and the Council of Ministers (see chapter 3). The EP only has a consultative role in CFP, but its Fisheries Committee is becoming an increasingly important player in shaping policy and in liaising between fishers and the Commission. The

ECJ has also been active in fisheries policy, with landmark decisions made upholding principles of non-discrimination in the fisheries sector. Historically, the key interests in the fisheries sector have been fishers and industry representatives, but increasingly environmental groups and consumers are entering the policy arena.

The policymaking process for fisheries is as follows. Policy initiatives come from DG Fisheries in the Commission which makes proposals against a background of scientific advice provided by international scientists. The Fisheries DG will typically consult with its advisory committee, regional fisheries interests, and other directorates in the Commission. This policy process is very complicated and can be inaccessible to many fishers who are not part of an established policy community. Proposals from DG Fisheries are typically watered down in the Council of Ministers where states advocate on behalf of their fishermen. Policy within the Fisheries Council is largely decided on the basis of qualified majority voting (QMV; see chapters 3 and 27), leading to a series of trade-offs and bargains between the states.

The final policy emerging from the Council seldom reflects the scientists' advice because of the way this is supplied (Daw and Gray, 2005), bargained and traded through an intense political process (see Ritchie and Zito, 1998; Payne, 2000; Lesquesne, 2005; Holden, 1994). The example of the evolution of a policy to cope with the 2002 stock crisis illustrates this point.

When it came to advising on the TACs for 2003, the ICES and STEFC recommended a moratorium on the cod fishery and on the cod-related fisheries of whiting and haddock. In view of the likely detrimental social and economic impact, the Commission recommended to the Council a substantial reduction in cod and related TACs. The Council, at the December 2002 meeting, set the 2003 TACs for the three stocks at substantially higher levels than the Commission had recommended. The eventual decision (Council regulation (EC) no. 2341/2002 of December 2002) saw a 45 per cent cut in the cod TAC. Haddock was cut by 50 per cent, whiting by 60 per cent and plaice by 5 per cent. The CFP reform and the management of the stock crisis at the end of 2002 were marked by interventions from, among others, the British Prime Minister Tony Blair and the French President Jacques Chirac on behalf of their fishermen.

Once the policy recommendations are made they are passed on to the member states who then share out the nationally allocated quotas. Member states are also responsible for the implementation and monitoring of a large number of technical and conservation measures such as the days-at-sea regulations, tonnage and gear size regulations, minimum landing sizes and vessel capacity. Responsibility for the implementation of policy falls to a variety of national, regional and local agencies across the member states. This complexity of institutional arrangements adds to the unevenness of policy implementation across the EU (Lequesne, 2005, p. 368). One of the key difficulties in the CFP is ensuring that fishers comply with the rules. There are a number of reasons for non-compliance. Firstly, some operators ignore the regulations because adherence may be too costly (especially when profit margins are small), they are too complex to work out, too bureaucratic to comply with, or quite simply too difficult to implement in small craft. Secondly, many regulations have technical inconsistencies. Finally, many rules are simply ignored or flouted.

There are about as many ways of flouting the rules in the CFP as there are rules to keep. Three key problems are the landing of illegal or 'black' fish, discarding fish back into the sea and the misreporting of information. 'Black' fish are landed illegally and are not reported as landings at the designated port, or are landed at other ports in the EU or outside the EU where no record is taken. Landing illegal fish not only depletes the stocks but also undermines the accuracy of stock and TAC predictions, which is a particularly serious problem when stocks are in decline. A second problem is the discarding of fish that are not the right size or species. This is a major problem within the CFP with estimates of 50 per cent for some catches. Discarded fish are a waste and also a major pollutant of the marine environment. Again, discarding is to some extent caused by the rigidity of some CFP rules, such as the requirement for single-species landings in some areas. The final key group of problems are misrecording

or misreporting stock, or misdeclaring species in catches that are legally landed in other respects. All this creates havoc with the science on which the decisions on quota allocations are mainly based.

This discussion of the policy process has shown that effective collective solutions and radical policy change are inhibited by national and political interests and that the policy structure leads to short-term political interests shaping policy. One of the main problems is that while the Commission is trying to effect a medium-term policy, TACs and quotas have historically been negotiated annually. Another problem is that representatives of the fishing industry have little direct role in the decision-making process (Symes, 1995). Finally, procedures and guidelines are misunderstood, ignored, circumvented, falsified or merely flouted (Cann, 1998). One of the responses of the Commission to this problem has been to put forward more controls. This has served to further alienate the fishers.

21.5 Reform of the CFP?

The CFP has in many ways been in a process of reform since 1983 with the Mediterranean enlargement of the EU, when a commitment was given to review the CFP and in particular the principle of relative stability in 2002. The promised reform and re-negotiation of the CFP was to some extent deflected by the emergency measures which had to be put in place to deal with the crisis in stocks, and many commentators were disappointed by the limited changes proposed, particularly given the range of interests consulted during the drawing up of the reforms.

Between 1998 and 2002 there was an unprecedented period of consultation of stakeholders and the industry by the Commission. The consultation began with 350 questionnaires being sent out to representatives and organizations involved in fishing in all EU member states. This survey revealed a great deal of dissatisfaction with the CFP and emphasized problems with the conservation policy, enforcement difficulties and issues of equity. The Commission then organized a number of regional consultations (or road shows) across all the major fisheries regions in the EU, which led to more in-depth discussion of governance and institutional questions. In March 2001, on the basis of these two consultations, the Commission launched a consultative Green Paper on the reform of the CFP, with open invitations for evidence and comment. Over 300 submissions were made from stakeholders ranging across inshore and deep-water fishermen, processors, anglers, environmentalists, the food industry and consumer organizations. Finally, the Commission held a public hearing in Brussels in June 2001, which was attended by 400 delegates from across the EU. This hearing gave particular emphasis to whether the management of the CFP should be regionalized. The polarity of views expressed ranged from an anti-regionalist perspective adopted by the Spanish contingent to a proposal for a full regionalization of decision-making powers put forward by the British, Dutch and Swedish delegates. Other key issues discussed which elicited mixed and polarized responses were the privatization of the CFP (through the introduction of a form of individual transferable quota) and issues of enforcement and compliance.

On the basis of the numerous consultation exercises and the Green Paper, the Commission drew up a reform of the CFP which was put to the Council in December 2002. The final document inevitably represented a compromise between the different views, especially on highly charged issues such as regional management. On the issue of the privatization of quotas, the Commission did seem to have taken note of the majority opinion during the consultation exercise by allowing flexibility at the level of the member state. Many of the traditional areas of the policy such as relative stability and special derogations remain for the time being, although after January 2003 Spanish, Portuguese and Finnish vessels were allowed to fish for unallocated quota in the North Sea.

There were a number of modest changes proposed for the governance and management of the CFP but no radical reform in the 2002 CFP reform package:

1. Central to the reform was a longer-term approach to fisheries management. In particular, proposals were put forward for a multi-annual approach to management. This policy was accompanied by a subtle shift in the roles of the Commission and the Council, with the Commission being responsible for the policy after the agreement in the first year. This does give the Commission a great deal more weight in the process of allocation.

2. There was a renewed and stricter commitment to capacity reduction and control to bring the fleet in line with available resources. The importance of linking effort limitation to catch limitation was reinforced. There is an attempt at greater coherence in the policy, with new regulations being introduced to establish an emergency fund to decommission vessels, in order to help states which need to meet recovery plan targets for reducing fishing outings – only those states that need to reduce their fishing expeditions by 25 per cent or more will be eligible for funding.

3. The reforms also stressed the importance of ecosystem management and the precautionary principle. The objective of the CFP became to 'provide for sustainable exploitation of living aquatic resources and of aquaculture in the context of sustainable development, taking account of the environmental, economic and social aspects in a balanced manner'. Chapter 1, Article 2(1), states that in order to meet the objectives, 'the Community will apply a precautionary approach to fisheries management and will aim at . . . a progressive implementation of an ecosystem based approach to fisheries management'.

4. There was considerable discussion about increasing the role for industry and stake-holders by setting up regional advisory councils (RACs). These councils were to include fishermen and scientists, representatives of other interests such as the aquaculture sector, and environmental and consumer groups who have an interest in the sea area or zone concerned. National and regional authorities from any member state may also participate and the Commission may be represented at the

meetings. The Councils can only advise the Commission on policy and have no policy-making role.

5. Conservation remained the cornerstone of the CFP following the reforms:
   - multi-annual recovery plans for stock outside safe biological limits, initially for North Sea and west of Scotland cod but to be introduced for other stocks;
   - establishing targets for the successful exploitation of stocks;
   - limiting catches and fixing the number and type of fishing vessels authorized to fish;
   - limiting fishing trips;
   - adopting technical measures (fishing gear, catches that may be retained; delimiting zones which can be fished; protection of spawning areas; minimum size of landing);
   - establishing incentives to promote low-impact fisheries;
   - conducting pilot projects on different types of fishing management techniques.

6. The objective of the structural policy remains the achievement of a 'stable and enduring balance between the capacity of fishing fleets and the fishing opportunities available to them in and outside of Community waters'. The previous support system of FIFG will be retained but aid will be concentrated on scrapping fishing vessels. The old system of MAGPs has been replaced by a simpler system which gives more authority to the member states to achieve a balance between fleet capacity and fishing opportunities. Finally, member states were to be able to provide short-term aid to the industry in emergency situations.

7. Fisheries agreements are now called 'fisheries partnership agreements' to denote a new focus in external relations. These will 'allow for the provision of funds for the EU partners to advance fisheries development objectives, for the transfer of technical knowledge and capital to achieve sustainable development'. This policy will (supposedly) make a contribution in developing countries to food security, poverty alleviation and sustainable development.

8. The reforms outlined a whole series of measures designed to improve the enforcement of community policy. New powers have been introduced at community level to penalize states by reducing fishing quotas if there is persistent non-compliance.

There have been a number of other reforms in the area of the environment. In addition to the cuts in TACs, limitations in the number of days at sea have also been introduced for many cod stocks in the North Sea. Fishermen can fish for between nine and twenty-three days per month depending on the type of stock and the gear used, although many fishermen argue that these limitations have little meaning because the TACs are so low that they have already caught them within the first fortnight of the month.

These reforms have failed to resolve the fundamental problem of the CFP: the inability to limit catches to a sustainable level (Daw and Gray, 2005; Gray and Hatchard 2003). Thus, although catches have been reduced (table 21.1), this reduction has left catches in excess of safe biological limits. Overall fishing in EU waters exceeds these limits and the excess has been growing. The situation in relation to particular types of fish is even more serious (table 21.2). The situation in the EU can be contrasted with that of Iceland where national conservation measures have enabled the catch to be sustained.

21.6 Conclusion

The CFP reform has not marked a radical shift in the way the EU organizes fisheries. However, there are signs of change. A new level of governance has been introduced. A more consultative approach is in evidence and there is more coherence in the technical aspects of the policy. The CFP is placing more emphasis on a medium-term strategic management of stocks and the discourse of ecosystem management is becoming more common.

There are fundamental problems still confronting EU fisheries – declining stocks, over-capacity, cumbersome rules and regulations which are

Table 21.2 Fish catches outside 'safe biological limits' (%)

	1994	1995	1996	1997	1998	1999	2000	2001	2002	2003	2004
Demersal[1]	35	30	35	47	50	51	42	61	46	61	62
Pelagic[2]	14	10	9	15	3	4	5	49	4	22	12
Benthic[3]	31	27	40	37	38	31	49	41	36	31	29
Industrial[4]										41	39
Total	13	10	11	14	6	8	10	40	8	22	21

1. Species that live on shallow ocean beds.
2. Species that swim together in shoals in the open ocean.
3. Species that live just above the sea bed.
4. Other species caught for processing.

Source: Eurostat (2006a).

poorly implemented, and competing national interests. Solving these problems will require not only further technical reform and tough conservation methods, but an improved system of governance which has the support of its major stakeholders.

NOTES

1 Fishing, fish processing and aquaculture.
2 Statistics from Eurostat (2006) unless otherwise stated.
3 Of this number 185, 923 are in fishing, the remainder in processing and aquaculture (Salz et al., 2006, p. 17).

22 Regional policy

HARVEY ARMSTRONG

Member states of the European Economic Community are 'anxious to ensure their harmonious development by reducing the differences existing between the various regions and the backwardness of the less favoured regions' (Preamble to the Treaty of Rome, 1958).

In order to promote its overall harmonious development, the Community shall develop and pursue its actions leading to the strengthening of its economic and social cohesion. In particular the Community shall aim at reducing disparities between the various levels of development of the various regions and the backwardness of the least favoured regions or islands, including rural areas (Article 158, Consolidated Version of the Treaty Establishing a European Community, 2002).

These two quotations, forty-four years apart, illustrate the strength of the EU's commitment to regional policy; a commitment which at first sight seems curious. The EU has aspirations to become something approaching a federal system. Regional policy of the type we know in the EU is, however, rarely found in long-established federal countries such as the US, Canada and Australia. Understanding EU regional policy requires an appreciation of the uniqueness of the European situation, with its patchwork of independent nation-states moving step by step towards closer economic, social and political relationships.

This chapter examines EU regional policy at an important moment in the step-by-step process of European integration. The accession of ten new member states (NMS10) in 2004, and a further two in 2007, has significantly widened regional economic disparities in the EU and in doing so has forced the Union to bring in radical changes in regional policy from 2007 onwards.

This chapter begins with an examination of the case for having an EU regional policy running alongside the regional policies operated by each of the member state governments. This is followed by an overview of the ways in which economic integration can affect regional disparities. Attention will subsequently be concentrated on the EU regional policy which emerged from 1989 onwards in the aftermath of the single market. This policy was strengthened and reformed after the 1992 Treaty on European Union and again in 1999. The regional policy in place during the current 2000–2006 budgetary period (spending on which will continue until 2008) is nevertheless in large part that which was created in the great reforms of 1989. Finally, the key issues which confront EU regional policy in the immediate future will be examined. In particular, the EU's regional policy response to eastern enlargement in the form of a reformed policy for 2007–13 (see table 19.7) will be considered.

22.1 The case for an EU regional policy

Regional policy has always been controversial. It is undeniably interventionist. Those who distrust the competence of governments fear that regional policy penalizes successful businesses in prosperous regions while simultaneously encouraging unsuitable economic activities in the depressed regions. To those who hold this opinion, regional disparities are the inevitable outcome of the market system – something to be tolerated until market forces such as labour migration, capital investment and expanding trade combine to automatically revitalize low-wage depressed regions. Supporters of regional policy are much more sceptical of the ability of market forces to solve long-standing regional problems.

Even if one accepts the view that there is a case for government intervention in the form of a regional policy, this does not in itself constitute a case for an EU regional policy. The crucial question from an EU point of view is why a separate EU regional policy is required *in addition to* those of the individual member states. Those of the individual member states have continued alongside EU regional policy over the years since 1975 (when the European Regional Development Fund was established – see section 22.3.1). There is no suggestion that they should be laid aside in favour of a single EU regional policy.

Several distinct arguments can be advanced in support of a regional policy operated at EU level. Each argument will be considered in turn.

22.1.1 The 'vested interest' argument

The nation-states of Europe are becoming increasingly integrated economies. Rapidly expanding trade links, together with much freer capital mobility and more slowly growing cross-border labour migration, are being stimulated by EU initiatives such as the single market (see chapter 7) and monetary union (see chapters 10, 11 and 12). Increasingly, the economic well-being of citizens of one member state depends on the prosperity of the economies of other members. The presence of disadvantaged regions experiencing low incomes and high unemployment is in the interests of no one. Put another way, the citizens of one member state have a *vested interest* in ensuring that the regional problems in *other* member states are reduced. An EU regional policy can therefore be justified as a mechanism which allows one member state to become involved in policies which stimulate economic activity in the regions of other member states.

Why do citizens in a prosperous member state such as Germany have a vested interest in helping to solve regional problems in, say, Greece or Poland? Because the solution of regional problems elsewhere generates benefits which spill across member state boundaries. The most important of these is naked economic self-interest – the presence of less-prosperous regions reduces buying power and hence serves to impoverish all. Other spillover benefits include the desire to see greater equity across the EU and a wish to preserve local cultures and languages.

22.1.2 The 'financial targeting' argument

The second main argument in support of an EU regional policy is concerned with the effectiveness with which regional policy is operated in Europe. Regional policies are expensive to operate and resources must be found from public sector budgets. The disadvantaged regions of the EU are not evenly distributed among the member states of the EU. Some member states carry such a burden of disadvantaged regions that they constitute depressed regions in their own right. This has traditionally been the case with some of the member states in the Mediterranean south of the EU (e.g. Greece). Enlargement of the EU in 2004 to incorporate the significantly poorer NMS10 countries (the Czech Republic, Cyprus, Estonia, Hungary, Latvia, Lithuania, Malta, Poland, Slovakia and Slovenia) and Bulgaria and Romania in 2007 (NMS12) has greatly expanded the number of member states of this type.

Given the inevitable pressure on public sector budgets, it is not surprising to find that it is precisely those member states with the most severe burden of regional problems which have the greatest difficulty in financing an active regional policy. Leaving regional policy wholly to the member states is not therefore effective from an EU perspective. Member states such as the UK and Germany, with fewer regional problems, have been best able to afford an active regional policy. Those with the most severe regional problems such as Greece and Poland face chronic budget difficulties and find it hard to fund their domestic regional policies adequately.

The difficulties faced by member states in ensuring that the most disadvantaged EU regions receive the greatest volume of assistance represent a powerful case for an EU regional policy. Member states on their own are simply unable to target regional policy funds on the most disadvantaged regions. Only the EU, it can be argued, is capable of drawing resources from more prosperous parts of the EU and ensuring that they are allocated to the most heavily disadvantaged regions.

22.1.3 The coordination argument

The third argument which can be made in support of an EU regional policy concerns the advantages of a coordinated approach. The EU has immense potential to improve the effectiveness of regional policy by acting as a supranational coordinating body. Regional development initiatives within the member states are offered by a bewildering array of organizations. As well as the member state governments, typically also involved are regional governments, local governments, non-elected development agencies and, increasingly, private sector organizations, community and voluntary organizations as well as an array of joint venture schemes between private and governmental bodies.

Lack of coordination can be very wasteful. Firms seeking assistance in the disadvantaged regions may be bewildered and deterred by the complexity of the types of help on offer. Different regions may compete, using regional policy subsidies as a weapon, for one another's firms or for the inward investment projects of US and other foreign firms (a process known in the EU as 'competitive bidding'). In addition, valuable development opportunities (e.g. cross-border transport links – see chapter 16) may not be properly implemented as a result of coordination failures. The coordination agenda for an EU regional policy is clearly a wide one.

22.1.4 The 'effects of integration' argument

This is the most controversial of the arguments advanced in support of an EU regional policy. EU involvement in regional policy, it is argued, is necessary to overcome the adverse regional impacts of the integration process. This argument rests upon two suppositions. The first is that economic integration, if left to its own devices, tends to cause a worsening ('divergence') of regional disparities. The second is that it is the EU, rather than the member states, that is best placed to tackle the regional problems which develop as integration proceeds. Both suppositions have been the subject of fierce debate. The effect of integration on regional disparities is an issue of immense

importance and will be considered further in section 22.2.

22.1.5 The 'effects of other EU policies' argument

A further argument frequently advanced in support of EU regional policy is that it is needed to help mitigate the adverse regional effects of other EU policies. A number of EU policies are known to have particularly severe effects on the disadvantaged regions. VAT, for example, a major source of EU revenues, has long been known to be a regionally regressive tax (CEC, 1979c; van den Noord, 2000; and chapter 15). Other EU policies also have their own distinctive patterns of regional effects (CEC, 1996d; CEC, 2001c; CEC, 2003g). The adverse regional effects of the EU agricultural price guarantee policy – a major item in the EU budget – have been a source of particular concern. The traditional concentration of EU Common Agricultural Policy (CAP) help on products such as cereals, milk, oilseed and beef (products of the more prosperous northern EU farming regions) has meant that despite repeated reforms of the CAP, more prosperous northern regions continued to benefit most throughout the 1980s and 1990s (CEC, 2000d). More recent evidence has shown that a succession of reforms since the McSharry reforms of 1992 have slowly ameliorated the adverse regional impacts of the common agriculture policy (see chapter 20), but that its regional impacts remain far from favourable (CEC, 1996d; CEC, 2003g).

The ideal solution, of course, to the problem of policies with adverse regional impacts such as the CAP would be to alter the nature of the policies themselves. Reforming an EU policy at source is, however, only possible to a limited degree and there are usually dangers to the integrity of the policy itself if it is pushed too far in a 'pro-regional' direction. The EU, therefore, has adopted a twofold approach as part of its regional policy effort. First, regular research studies are made of major EU policies to identify, and where possible rectify, policies with adverse regional effects. Second, EU regional policy initiatives are designed, wherever sensible, to mitigate the adverse regional effects of other EU policies.

22.1.6 The 'further integration' argument

This argument centres upon the incomplete nature of the EU integration process. An EU regional policy, it is argued, is necessary to ensure that the benefits of integration are more fairly spread. Only if this is done will all member states be willing to countenance further steps towards full integration. This argument too is a controversial one. Even if one concedes that economic and political union is an acceptable goal, there is little hard evidence that *regional* disparities prevent *member states* from agreeing to further integration. The argument remains, however, a persuasive one. Indeed, it can be argued that this 'further integration' argument may well have been key in ensuring that regional policy is to both continue and be allocated additional funding after 2007 despite recent very strong criticism of the effectiveness of EU regional policy to date (Sapir et al., 2003a).

The list of arguments in favour of a separate EU regional policy is a long one. The case is a strong one too. It should be noted, however, that there is no logical case here for a *complete* transfer of regional policy powers from member states to the EU. Indeed, the EU's own commitment to 'subsidiarity' – the maximum devolution of powers – requires that member states, regional and local governments and other partner organizations all have a role (see chapters 2 and 3). The vast majority of modern types of regional policy initiatives (e.g. advice to firms, training policies) also require an active local input to be effective. The remoteness of Brussels from many of the problem regions, the lack of specialist local knowledge and experience at the centre, and the virtue of allowing variety and experimentation in regional policy all suggest that partnership and not dominance is the appropriate EU role.

22.2 The effects of integration on EU regional disparities

The implications of economic integration for EU regional disparities are still imperfectly understood. The economic processes at work are extremely complex and long-lasting. The regional effects even of the creation of the original customs union have not yet been fully experienced, and the regional implications of the single market process are still really only in their early stages, even though the legislation for it was largely completed by 1992. Add to these the regional ramifications of the 1996 enlargement (which saw the accession of Austria, Finland and Sweden), together with the geographical effects of monetary union in 2002 and the accession of the NMS12 in 2004/7 and one can see just how complex the effects of economic integration are. Each of these steps in the process of economic integration has its own very distinctive 'regional footprint' and each has set in train effects which will take decades fully to emerge. Nor will the system have time to draw breath in the decade ahead. Monetary union remains an incomplete process and further future extensions of the euro area, combined with new accessions thereafter, perhaps Croatia and Turkey, will trigger yet more complex 'regional footprint' effects right across the EU.

An examination of the existing pattern of regional disparities in the EU reveals an array of problems which are formidable by comparison with those in other parts of the world such as the US. Figure 22.1 shows regional GDP per capita in 2003 for the then fifteen member states (EU15) as well as for regions in Croatia and the twelve new states which acceded by 2007. The EU already had wide regional disparities prior to the eastern enlargement of 2004. The GDP per capita disparities within EU15 were more than twice as great as those found in the US. Prior to eastern enlargement, for the EU15 countries which then comprised the EU, GDP per capita in the richest 10 per cent of regions was around 2.6 times greater than that in the poorest 10 per cent. Following eastern enlargement, for the EU27 countries this ratio has risen to around 5:1, revealing a dramatic widening of regional disparities. Just how stark are the additional challenges being posed for EU regional policy by the new accessions is clearly revealed in figure 22.1. GDP per capita data for 2003 shows that the region of EU27 with the highest GDP per capita, inner London, was almost thirteen times

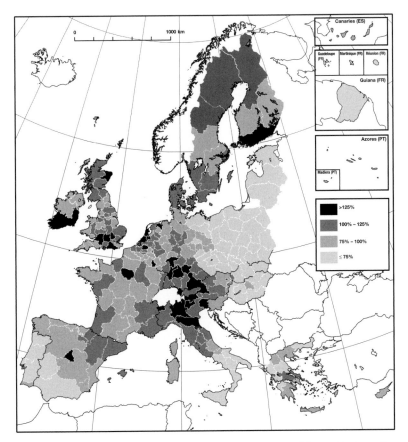

Figure 22.1 Regional gross domestic product per head, at purchasing power parities, 2003. *Source:* Eurostat (2006c, map 1), © EuroGeographics Association for the administrative boundaries.

more prosperous than the poorest, north-east Romania (Eurostat 2006c).

Figure 22.2 shows the extent of EU regional disparities using another popular indicator, the regional unemployment rate. The picture here is much less clear than the core–periphery pattern revealed in figure 22.1 for GDP per capita. Nevertheless, figure 22.2 reveals just how severe the regional unemployment rate disparities are in EU25. In 2004, regional unemployment rates ranged from a mere 2.4 per cent in Dorset and Somerset (the region with the lowest EU25 unemployment rate) up to a massive 24.9 per cent in the region of Dolnośląskie in Poland (the region with the highest EU25 unemployment rate).

The regional problems confronting the EU are extremely diverse as well as being severe. EU regional policy in the past has variously recognized

a whole array of different types of regions with distinctive problems. These have included 'lagging regions' (regions whose GDP per capita is below 75 per cent of the EU average and whose regional problems are the most severe in the EU), declining manufacturing areas, certain rural regions, fishing communities, mining and steel regions, inner city areas, low population sub-Arctic regions in Sweden and Finland, island economies and the remote 'outermost regions' (i.e. the Azores, the Canary Islands, French Guyana, Guadeloupe, Madeira, Martinique and Réunion). In other words, EU regional policy has always clearly recognized just how diverse are the *types* of regional problem faced as well as how *severe* a challenge they represent.

Despite the great variety of EU regional problems, the overwhelming impression that one obtains from statistics such as those presented in

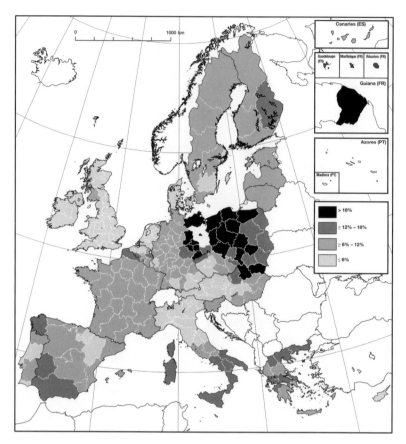

Figure 22.2 Regional unemployment rates (males plus females), 2004. *Source:* Eurostat (2005b, map 1), © EuroGraphics Association for the administrative boundaries.

figures 22.1 and 22.2 is that there appears to be something of a 'core–periphery' pattern to EU regional disparities. A high proportion of the more prosperous regions lie at the geographical centre of the EU, whereas disadvantaged regions tend to be grouped around the periphery. Within the existing EU27 the most disadvantaged regions tend to be particularly (but by no means wholly) in the Mediterranean south and among the new member states of Central and Eastern Europe. Prior to 1995 the core–periphery pattern was even more pronounced than it appears now because Ireland (both Northern Ireland and the Republic), as well as parts of northern and western Britain, were also highly disadvantaged. As figure 22.1 shows, however, extremely rapid growth of both GDP and employment in Ireland (and to a lesser extent in western Britain) in the 1990s has

transformed these areas, so that the underdevelopment of the EU's 'western periphery' is much less pronounced than it once was. The traditionally prosperous core of the EU stretches from central England to northern Italy. There is evidence of the more recent emergence of a growth belt from northern Italy through the south of France and into northern Spain and, as we have seen, across western Britain into eastern Ireland. This does not, however, alter the overall conclusion that a 'core–periphery' situation prevails in the EU.

The 'core–periphery' nature of EU regional problems has existed for many years. It is the outcome of economic processes predating the existence of the EU, and others that have come into existence as a result of the EU. Economic integration is a process which is progressing continuously on a worldwide scale. Improvements in transport infrastructure and transport technology have gradually reduced freight cost barriers to trade. So too have the general improvements in production technology, which have had the effect of reducing the transport inputs required to assemble materials and distribute the output of manufacturing industry. Moreover, in the post-war period there has been a consensus in favour of freer trade which has led to successive international steps (e.g. WTO agreements and the policies of the IMF and the World Bank aimed at developing countries) designed to reduce the barriers to trade (see chapters 24 and 25). The member states of the EU have participated in these worldwide processes of integration, and the pattern of intra-EU regional disparities which we observe today has been affected by them.

In addition to the broad integration processes common to all countries, the EU has acted to trigger its own distinctive 'accelerated' integration. The current maps of regional disparities (such as figures 22.1 and 22.2) have been affected by these too. The regional effects of the single market process have not yet been fully experienced, partly because the complete single market has yet to be implemented, and partly because the effects are extremely long-term in nature. The effects of the convergence process leading up to monetary union in 2002 were felt in the 1990s (e.g. via pressures on member state budgets), but the longer-term regional impacts of monetary union itself are yet to be experienced. Moreover, existing regional disparities continue to be affected by the creation of the EU customs union in 1958, and by the successive widening of the customs union to include new member states in 1973 (Denmark, the UK and the Republic of Ireland), 1981 (Greece), 1986 (Spain and Portugal), 1991 (East Germany), 1996 (Austria, Finland and Sweden) and 2004/7 (the NMS12).

No two rounds of economic integration ever have an identical effect on regional disparities. Each round in the integration process can be thought of as having two groups of effects: a unique regional imprint or pattern of effects, combined with a 'core–periphery' effect in common with other rounds. The creation of the original customs union, for example, involved the removal of tariffs which had previously provided

most protection to *manufacturing* industries. The most severe effects of this act of integration were therefore experienced in regions most heavily dependent on manufacturing industries. The creation of a single market between 1989 and 1992 involved the removal of an array of non-tariff barriers. In this round of integration both manufacturing and service industries were affected. It is thought that a distinctive group of some forty manufacturing sectors were most affected by the single market, along with certain types of services such as banking and finance (CEC, 1988a; Quévit, 1995; Begg, 1995). Some regions are clearly more at risk than others, giving rise to a distinctive regional imprint. Monetary union has plunged most EU15 regions into a larger single currency area than before and has stripped the member states of exchange rate and monetary policy powers frequently brought to bear in the past to help disadvantaged regions. Monetary union too is therefore likely eventually to impinge more on some regions than on others (Ardy et al., 2002).

While it is obvious that each round in the integration process has its own distinctive regional impact, why integration in the EU should exhibit systematic core–periphery effects as well is less clear. Evidence to date suggests that integration tends to trigger two sets of countervailing forces, one set tending to cause regional *convergence* while the other tends to bring about regional *divergence*. The existing core–periphery pattern of regional disparities suggests that at least in some periods in the past the divergence forces must have predominated.

In more recent years there seems to have been something of a rough balance between divergence and convergence forces. Which set of forces will predominate in the years to come is an issue of major importance to the EU. Interestingly, the most recent evidence available suggests that whilst at the present time there seems to be a rough balance between the forces of regional convergence and divergence within the EU, the picture is actually rather more complex than this. The period since 1995 has witnessed a situation in which economic disparities (e.g. in GDP per capita) *between countries* have narrowed. However, this has been accompanied by a widening of regional disparities *within some member states*, leading to an overall situation of only a very slow decline in regional disparities (CEC, 2005a; Cambridge Econometrics/Ecorys-NEI, 2004). The widening of regional disparities within member states is most dramatically seen in the NMS12 where the regions containing the capital cities (e.g. Prague, Bratislava, Budapest, etc.) have gained rapidly at the expense of more peripheral regions, but countries within the EU15 such as the UK have also seen within-country disparities widen since 1995. Why this pattern of simultaneous convergence and divergence is happening within the EU is not well understood, but is clearly of profound importance for the task which EU regional policy must face.

The forces tending to bring about *convergence* of regional disparities within the EU are predominantly a series of automatic equilibrating processes which occur whenever a system of freely functioning markets is in operation. Free trade in goods and services will, it is argued, lead to regions specializing in the production and export of goods and services in which they have a comparative advantage. Under traditional trade theory such as the Heckscher–Ohlin model, all regions benefit from this process and regional differences in wage rates and capital rentals are also eliminated (Armstrong and Taylor, 2000). The convergence effects of freer trade are reinforced by the effects of freer factor mobility. Where wage rates differ significantly between regions, there is an incentive for labour to migrate from low-wage to high-wage regions, a process which reduces regional wage inequalities. Capital investment, meanwhile, is attracted to the disadvantaged regions by the low wages and excellent labour supply available there. This too reduces regional inequalities. The combination of freer trade and large-scale factor mobility offers real hope for the convergence of regional disparities in the EU, and these processes lie at the heart of modern neoclassical 'conditional convergence' theories of regional growth which predict convergence of regional disparities (Sala-i-Martin, 1996). It is thought, however, that these processes operate only very slowly and that decades will be required before their full effects are felt. Moreover, there

are forces leading to divergence of regional disparities. It is to these that we now turn.

At the heart of the economic integration process set in motion by the EU has been a desire to achieve free trade and the free movement of labour and capital. In order to enjoy the benefits of integration (Emerson et al., 1988; CEC, 1988a), it is essential that a major restructuring of industry should occur. The various allocation and accumulation effects generating economic gains from integration require regions to switch production and concentrate on those goods and services for which there is a comparative advantage (Baldwin et al., 1997). The greater the integration envisaged, the greater the potential benefits, but the greater too are the restructuring implications. Painful though the restructuring process is for those involved, in principle it should be experienced by all regions. The crucial question, therefore, is why integration in the EU seems to be associated with systematic core–periphery effects. A series of different divergence forces are thought to accompany the integration process:

1. *Economies of scale.* These represent a potent source of benefit from integration. The concentration of production at larger plants can lead to great efficiency gains. Firms seeking to exploit economies of scale are likely to be attracted to regions at the geographical core of the EU. Input assembly costs are lower, and access to the whole EU market is much easier from central locations. Moreover, the core regions are already the most prosperous regions and therefore represent the strongest markets.

2. *Localization and agglomeration economies.* Localization economies arise when firms in the same industry locate close to one another (e.g. because of access to labour with appropriate skills, information flows, ability to subcontract work, etc.). Agglomeration economies occur when firms from many different industries locate close to one another (e.g. because of transport facilities, financial facilities, etc.). These 'external economies of scale' effects tend to strongly favour the core regions of the EU. Firms are drawn towards existing successful

agglomerations of economic activity. The core regions of the EU contain almost all of the main financial, industrial and capital cities and are a potent magnet for new activity. The traditional 'Marshallian' localization and agglomeration economies have been incorporated in a variety of new theories which predict industrial clustering and hence a concentration of economic activity in those regions which are fortunate to have been able to develop successful industrial clusters. Theories such as post-Fordism have stressed the advantages of clustered small firms in new industrial districts such as those in the 'Third Italy' within the traditional geographical 'core' of the EU (Dunford, 2000; Bagella and Becchetti, 2000). Porter's work has also highlighted the interacting sets of forces which can generate industrial clustering and the geographical concentration of economic activity (Porter, 1990), as have social capital theories of regional growth (Putnam, 1993). Within mainstream economics, new economic geography models of regional growth and some versions of endogenous growth theory also predict clustering and hence the possibility of divergent growth (Midelfart-Knarvik et al., 2000).

3. *Intra-industry trade and dominant market positions.* Modern trade theory is increasingly sceptical of the ability of all regions to share equally in the growth associated with freer trade. There is evidence that intra-industry trade in similar products has shown the most rapid growth among the more prosperous core regions and member states of the EU (Neven, 1990 and chapters 6 and 24). Regions in the Mediterranean south of the EU have fallen behind in participation in this important and fast-growing type of trade. Intra-industry trade is important because of the fast pace of expansion of this type of trade, particularly the horizontal exchange of almost identical products. By contrast, the new member states in Central and Eastern Europe do appear to be engaging in an increasing amount of intra-industry trade, but of the less lucrative vertical intra-industry trade category, supplying Western Europe with semi-processed inputs. Similarly,

much trade in manufactured goods in the EU is now dominated by large multinational enterprises. These firms are already concentrated in the core regions of the EU and it is thought that they may exploit their ability to dominate markets in ways which disadvantage peripheral regions. Opening up peripheral regions to competition from large multinational firms could have serious effects for the smaller and less powerful firms more frequently found there.

4. *Lack of competitiveness in peripheral regions.* Research commissioned over the years by the EU (IFO, 1990; CEC, 1999c; Cambridge Econometrics/Ecorys-NEI, 2004) has provided powerful evidence that many firms in the EU's peripheral regions face severe problems in meeting the competitive challenges posed by integration. The lack of competitiveness is based on a combination of factors largely outside the control of the firms themselves. These include poor location, weak infrastructure facilities (e.g. transport, telecommunications), low-skill labour forces, and local tax and financial sector problems.

5. *Selective labour migration.* The peripheral regions are also weakened, as integration proceeds, by the loss of migrants. The freeing of labour mobility stimulates migration from peripheral to core regions. Migration is highly selective. It is the young, the skilled and the economically active who migrate. Their loss is a severe blow to peripheral regions seeking to compete in an integrated EU. The surge in migrants from some of the main NMS10 countries which acceded to the EU in 2004 towards those members of EU15 willing to accept them (e.g. the UK) is a worrying example of this type of process at work.

6. *The loss of macro-policy powers in peripheral member states.* This is a particular problem at the present time because of monetary union. Those member states which have joined the euro have lost control of their exchange rates as well as other aspects of their monetary policy such as interest rates. Full monetary union has meant the complete loss of powers to try to protect a weak local economy by way of currency

devaluation. Euro members have lost the power to use monetary policy to stimulate a weak local economy (see chapter 10). Even fiscal policy is being increasingly constrained under monetary union because of the Stability and Growth Pact (SGP; see chapters 11 and 12) and constraints on member state public sector budgets within the euro area. Peripheral member states face a future of very limited macro-policy powers. This will restrict their ability to protect their local economies.

The divergence forces set out above seem convincing and strong. There has been considerable discussion of the possibility that the divergence forces may interact and reinforce one another in such a way that *cumulative causation* occurs. This is where the loss of firms and a continuous outflow of migrants so weakens a peripheral economy that it can no longer attract new economic activities and hence goes into a downward spiral of decline. This is by no means a theoretical possibility. A number of rural regions of the EU (e.g. the west of Ireland, parts of southern Italy) have historically experienced depopulation on a large scale.

Evidence from federal countries with a long history of being fully economically integrated, notably the US, suggests that in the long term integration is associated with convergence of regional disparities rather than divergence (Sala-i-Martin, 1996). This evidence implies that the convergence forces at work eventually come to predominate over the divergence forces. The ensuing balance of forces results in a process of convergence which is slow (2 per cent per annum in the US), but is also sustained over a long period.

The evidence for convergence among EU regions is much more contested, partly because good statistics do not exist for the long periods of time necessary to check whether or not convergence is occurring. The balance of the evidence that is available suggests that cumulative causation has not occurred in the EU. Most researchers have found that prior to the mid-1970s regional disparities in the EU had experienced quite a long period of narrowing. This was followed by a period of widening disparities in the late 1970s and early 1980s. As noted earlier, the EU's regional

disparities, at least as far as GDP per capita figures are concerned, seem to have stabilized in the later 1990s and have begun very slowly narrowing again (Armstrong, 1995a, 1995b; CEC, 1999c, 2001d, 2003c, 2005a). However, this evidence remains rather controversial, for some analysts have also found evidence for *divergence* among EU regions, at least for certain periods of time (Dunford, 1996; Magrini, 1999). Moreover, as also noted earlier, recent years have seen convergence between member states being accompanied by divergence between regions within many member states. What can be said, however, is that the spells of overall regional divergence which have been observed tend to have been apparently short-lived. Economic integration does appear, on the whole, to be associated with a narrowing of regional disparities, although currently at a painfully slow rate.

22.3 Current and future EU regional policy

22.3.1 The origins of modern EU regional policy: the reforms of 1989, 1994 and 1999

EU regional policy traces its origins to the decision in 1975 to create a European Regional Development Fund (ERDF). The policy subsequently underwent minor reform in 1979 and 1984 (Armstrong, 1978, 1985), followed by a major reform in 1989 (CEC, 1989a). The 1989 reform was specifically designed to accompany the introduction of the single market and integrated a number of previously separate EU funding mechanisms, renaming them the 'structural funds'. The EU's structural funds comprise the ERDF, together with the European Social Fund (ESF), the Guidance Section of the European Agricultural Guidance and Guarantee Fund (EAGGF) and, since 1994, a Financial Instrument for Fisheries Guidance (FIFG) – see chapter 19. The Cohesion Fund, also created in 1994, acts in many ways like one of the structural funds although it is not in fact strictly one of them.

EU regional policy continues to this day to be operated in its essential characteristics on the basis of the reform to the structural funds introduced in 1989. The reformed policy provided the basis for further reforms in 1994 (designed to accompany steps towards monetary union – CEC, 1996d) and 1999 (designed to prepare the way for CEEC enlargement – CEC, 2000c). A further round of major reforms is now under way, to be implemented during the budget period 2007–13. Whilst this new set of reforms has again left the 1989 system largely intact, the need to try to cope with the challenges posed by eastern enlargement has meant that this latest reform has had to be a far-reaching one (CEC, 2006a, 2006d, 2006l, 2006m, 2006n).

22.3.2 EU regional policy since 2000

EU regional policy during the 2000–6 budget period and for the successor period 2007–13 is being operated in all of its essential characteristics on the basis of the major reform to the structural funds of 1989. In order to ensure that funding is as precisely targeted as possible (the principle of *concentration*), since 1989 the structural funds have been given the task of attaining specific *priority objectives*. At one time there were no fewer than seven priority objectives. By the 2000–6 budget period these had been cut back to just three. There will again be just three priority objectives for the 2007–13 budget period, although these are not the same as in 2000–6, as table 22.1 shows.

Superficially, objective 1 (called the 'lagging regions' objective in 2000–6 and the 'convergence' objective in 2007–13) will change very little between the two budget periods. This objective is focused on the most disadvantaged regions in the EU (i.e. those whose GDP per capita – at purchasing power parities – is under 75 per cent of the EU average) and is designed to help them to catch up with the rest of the EU. This objective is by far the most generously funded of the three (commanding some 70 per cent of total funding in 2000–6 – 137.06 billion euros at 1999 prices, and over 80 per cent in 2007–13) and with less stringent requirements than for the other objectives in terms of percentages of investment costs met and national matching funding targets.

Since the EU sets the criterion for eligibility for objective 1 regions (i.e. under 75 per cent of the

average GDP per capita), the map of eligible regions is effectively set by Brussels, not by the member states. Figure 22.3 shows the eligible regions during 2004–6 (this is an amended map following the accession of the NMS10).[1] As can be seen from figure 22.3, within the pre-2004 EU15 countries the objective 1 regions are concentrated in the southern Mediterranean and in parts of Ireland and the UK. It should be noted that the other EU15 regions with objective 1 status in 2000–6 (namely parts of northern Sweden and Finland, and many of the outermost regions – shown in the inset boxes on figure 22.3) are there by special dispensation since many of these regions had by 2000 exceeded the 75 per cent of EU average GDP per capita criterion for eligibility. They were retained as objective 1 regions in recognition of their special geographical 'handicaps' (low population densities in Scandinavia and remoteness from EU markets for the outermost regions). As also can be seen from figure 22.3, the accession of ten new member states in 2004 brought in a huge swathe of regions in Central and Eastern Europe which automatically became eligible for objective 1 status. Indeed, only small enclaves within the NMS10 (e.g. Prague, Bratislava) were *not* automatically eligible for objective 1 assistance.

Figure 22.4 shows the map of eligible areas for objective 1 for 2007–13. Comparison of figure 22.3 with figure 22.4 shows that a dramatic change will occur after 2007. Very large areas in the old EU15 will lose eligibility for the lucrative objective 1 funding, particularly in Sweden, Finland, the UK, Ireland, Spain, Italy and Greece. From 2007 onwards, the map of eligible objective 1 regions will be dominated by Central and Eastern European countries. Indeed, if anything figure 22.4 understates the 'shift eastwards' of EU regional policy, since every single region within Bulgaria and Romania, which acceded in 2007, is also eligible for objective 1.

The reason for this dramatic change in the map of eligible objective 1 regions lies in the very low income levels of the NMS12 countries. Most are still struggling to recover from the collapse in their economic performance in the 1990s when the Communist system came to an end. Since the

Table 22.1 Priority objectives for the 2000–2006 and 2007–2013 structural funds

2000–2006 budget period		2007–2013 budget period	
Priority objective	*Funds*	*Priority objective*	*Funds*
1. *Lagging regions* To promote the development and structural adjustment of the regions whose development is lagging behind	ERDF ESF EAGGF (Gu) FIFG	1. *Convergence* To speed up the real convergence of the least developed regions and member states	ERDF ESF CF
2. *Conversion* Supporting the economic and social conversion of areas facing structural difficulties	ERDF ESF	2. *Regional competitiveness and employment* Strengthening regions' competitiveness and attractiveness, as well as employment through innovation, the knowledge society and investment in human resources	ERDF ESF
3. *Adaptation and modernization* Adapting and modernizing policies and systems of education, training and employment	ESF	3. *European territorial cooperation* To strengthen cross-border cooperation through joint local and regional initiatives – cross-border, transnational and interregional cooperation	ERDF
Community initiatives (CIs) *Interreg*: Cross-frontier, transnational and interregional cooperation	ERDF	*Community initiatives (CIs)* None	
Leader: Restructuring of rural areas	EAGGF (Gu)		
Equal: Discrimination and labour market gender inequalities	ESF		
Urban: Disadvantaged urban neighbourhoods	ERDF		

Notes:

1. ERDF = European Regional Development Fund, ESF = European Social Fund, EAGGF (Gu) = Guidance Section of European Agricultural Guarantee and Guidance Fund, FIFG = Financial Instrument for Fisheries Guidance, CF = Cohesion Fund.

2. The Community Initiatives are special programmes focused on specific types of regional problems with a pan-European character, financed from the structural funds and much more controlled from Brussels than the main regional programmes.

2000–6 map of eligible areas is based on a region's GDP per capita relative to the *EU15 average*, whereas the 2007–13 map is based on the *EU25 average*, and since the new member states are significantly poorer than the EU15 countries, the result has been a very large fall in regions within EU15 countries which are eligible.

The EU is committed to softening the blow for regions losing their eligibility between 2000–6 and 2007–13. Some limited transitional assistance is being continued after 2007 for so-called 'phasing out' (or 'statistical effect') regions. These are shown on figure 22.4 and represent those regions which *would have* been eligible had

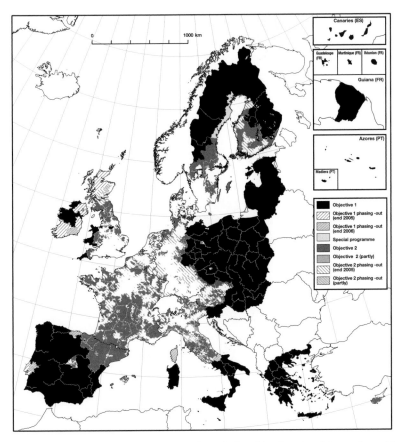

Figure 22.3 Structural funds (2000–6): eligible regions under priority objectives 1 and 2, together with regions eligible for transitional assistance. *Source:* European Commission, **website: http://ec.europa.eu/regional_policy/sources/graph/cartes_en.htm**, © MEGRIN for the administrative boundaries, regional and national data.

the EU15 average GDP per capita figure been used but which are too prosperous when an EU25 average is used. The provision of transitional funding after 2007 will soften the blow, but this cannot disguise the severe shock to many EU15 regions which have long enjoyed objective 1 status but which are scheduled to lose this after 2007. It is the inevitable outcome of the decision to admit so many relatively poor Central and Eastern European countries in 2004/7 and the need somehow to free up regional policy resources to help them integrate successfully with the rest of the EU. The 'switch east' in objective 1 funding is the single most important change between 2000–6 and 2017–13 since objective 1 has been allocated

81.54 per cent of all of the structural funds in 2007–13.

Turning to objective 2, as table 22.1 has shown, the 2007–13 objective 2 has a very different name ('regional competitiveness and employment') to its 2000–6 counterpart ('conversion of regions facing structural difficulties'). Comparing figure 22.3 with figure 22.4 also suggests a massive change in eligible areas, since the map of eligible objective 2 areas in 2000–6 is a complex patchwork of almost exclusively EU15 regions, whereas the 2007–13 objective 2 areas comprise all regions other than objective 1 (i.e. effectively a 'non-regional' objective). The change in the map of eligible areas for objective 2 is actually a little misleading. This is because in 2000–6, unlike the

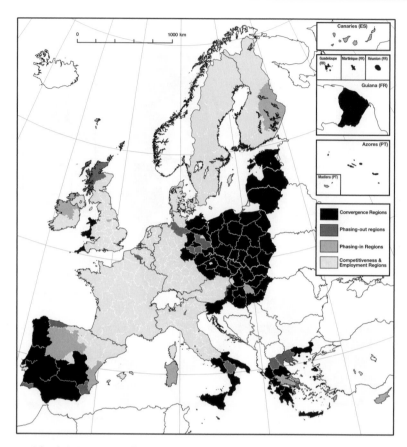

Figure 22.4 Structural funds (2007–13): eligible regions under priority objectives 1 and 2, together with 'phasing-in' and 'phasing-out' regions. *Source:* European Commission, **website: http://ec.europa.eu/regional_policy/sources/ graph/carstes_en.htm,** © MEGRIN for the administrative boundaries, regional and national data.

objective 1 regions (which were designated by the Commission), the objective 2 regions (see figure 22.3) were designated by each member state, but within guidelines established by the Commission. These guidelines actually allowed something of a rag-bag of objective 2 regions to be designated: mainly regions suffering from industrial (i.e. manufacturing) decline, certain disadvantaged rural areas, certain urban areas suffering severe economic, social and environmental problems, and fishing communities in decline. The member states took advantage of the latitude granted to them in designating objective 2 regions in 2000–6, resulting in 18.2 per cent of the EU15 population eventually falling into the map of objective 2 eligible areas shown in figure 22.3. It is inevitable that the member states

during the 2007–13 period will again focus the objective 2 funding on similar sorts of regions facing structural difficulties, and hence the detailed map of objective 2 eligible areas for 2007–13 is not yet available. Indeed, an even wider rag-bag of areas might end up being assisted under objective 2 since the Commission has recently been devoting considerable attention to the problems faced by regions suffering 'geographical handicaps' (especially islands, mountainous regions and very remote regions). Moreover, as with objective 1, the 2007–13 programmes allow for limited transitional funding for regions which would have lost objective 1 status and dropped to objective 1 irrespective of the change in the objective 2 eligibility rule (so-called 'phasing-in' regions – see figure 22.4).

The real difference between objective 2 during 2000–6 and objective 2 during 2007–13 lies in the strategic thrust anticipated for the programmes funded. The 2007–13 structural funds are to be much more strictly focused on Lisbon Agenda objectives (see chapter 14). In other words, EU regional policy is to be harnessed to the attainment of pan-EU goals rather than more limited regional goals. This is why the new objective 2 is called the 'regional competitiveness and employment' objective. The objectives set by the Lisbon Council of 2000 (endorsed and expanded in successive summits afterwards) were a response to the need to restore EU competitiveness in international markets and the growing jobs crisis in the EU, particularly for young persons. There is now a determination to bend EU regional policy to make a greater contribution to the more strictly *economic* Lisbon Agenda of jobs and competitiveness. This can be seen in both the name of the new objective 2 and also in its focus on policies to stimulate innovation, the knowledge society, entrepreneurship, the protection of the environment and the enhancement of workers' skills. This commitment to economic aims and the Lisbon Agenda ranges more widely than just the regulations for the 2007–13 objective 2, in two ways:

- The 2007–13 objective 1 programmes too are expected to be more focused on attaining Lisbon Agenda goals, and will be closely scrutinized by the Commission to ensure that this occurs.
- The Commission has produced a new set of strategic guidelines (CEC, 2006o) for the EU as a whole and tailored to each of its twenty-seven member states, which place great emphasis on the need for regional programmes in 2007–13 to ensure that they energetically seek to enhance jobs and competitiveness.

Returning to table 22.1 and figure 22.3, it can be seen that 'supporting the adaptation and modernization of policies and systems of education, training and employment' (objective 3) regions are not identified on figure 22.3. This is because objective 3 during 2000–6 was designed to be implemented *outside* of the objective 1 regions and therefore was effectively a 'non-regional' objective, although in practice it has been the disadvantaged regions which have benefited the most from it. The 2000–6 objective 3 will be subsumed within the new 2007–13 objective 2 and is therefore destined to disappear completely as a separate objective.

It is not only objective 3 that is disappearing in 2007. In addition to the main programmes operated through each of the 2000–6 priority objectives, a small portion (5.35 per cent) of the structural funds have been held back for spending on four Community Initiatives (CIs). The CIs have a history stretching back to 1979 and represent programmes of assistance targeted on specific problems of a wide nature and which are thought best tackled through a pan-EU initiative. These too are to disappear completely after 2007.

Finally, as table 22.1 shows, there is to be a completely new objective 3 for the structural funds during 2007–13: European territorial cohesion. This in fact builds upon the work of one of the 2000–6 CIs (Interreg.). It provides a small pot of money (only 2.5 per cent of the 2007–13 regional policy budget) to stimulate cross-border and transnational economic development initiatives. Some 181.7 million people live in the EU's border regions, and the breaking down of the former Iron Curtain has also left a legacy of poor cross-border links within the newly expanded EU.

As noted earlier, the EU has always deliberately concentrated the bulk of its financial assistance on the very poorest areas: in practice the objective 1 regions. During the budget period 2000–6 the allocations, by objective, have been as follows (all at 1999 prices):

Objective 1	137.06 billion euros
Objective 2	22.45 billion euros
Objective 3 (non-regional)	24.05 billion euros
Community initiatives (CIs)	10.44 billion euros

As can be seen, objective 1 dominates the structural funds (commanding some 70 per cent of the total allocations), while objectives 2 and 3 were allocated only 11.5 per cent and 12.3 per cent respectively of the full 2000–6 budget. This concentration process is to be continued, and

Table 22.2 Regional policy in 2007–2013: indicative allocations (€ million, 2004 prices)

Country	Convergence	Regional competitiveness and employment	Territorial cohesion objective	Total
Austria	159	914	228	1,301
Belgium	579	1,268	173	2,019
Bulgaria	5,888	0	159	6,047
Cyprus	194	363	25	581
Czech Rep.	22,979	373	346	23,697
Denmark	0	453	92	545
Estonia	3,011	0	47	3,058
Germany	14,324	8,370	756	23,450
Greece	17,447	584	186	18,217
Finland	0	1,426	107	1,532
France	2,838	9,123	775	12,736
Hungary	20,243	1,865	344	22,452
Ireland	0	681	134	815
Italy	19,255	5,640	752	25,647
Latvia	4,010	0	80	4,090
Lithuania	5,999	0	97	6,097
Luxembourg	0	45	13	58
Malta	747	0	14	761
Netherlands	0	1,477	220	1,696
Poland	59,048	0	650	59,698
Portugal	18,216	843	88	19,147
Romania	16,912	0	404	17,317
Slovakia	9,664	399	202	10,264
Slovenia	3,646	0	93	3,739
Spain	23,411	7,628	497	31,536
Sweden	0	1,446	236	1,682
UK	2,594	6,232	642	9,468
Total	251,162	49,127	7,750	308,041

Notes:
1. Total figures include €392m unallocated.
2. 'Convergence' objective column includes Cohesion Fund (€61,558m) and 'phasing-out' funding (€12,521m).
3. 'Regional competitiveness and employment' column includes 'phasing-in' funding (€10,385m).

Source: CEC (2006l).

indeed strengthened, during 2007–13. Table 22.2 sets out the indicative allocations for funding in 2007–13 ('indicative' since the actual expenditures will depend on how the member states and regions actually spend the money in the years ahead).

Table 22.2 illustrates both the dominance of objective 1 funding (81.54 per cent of the total 2007–13 budget) and also just how much money is being targeted on the NMS12 (157,801 million euros or 51.22 per cent of the total budget), despite the presence of transitional funding within EU15 countries and despite the arrival of Bulgaria and Romania in 2007. Transition funding is only a small amount of the total, comprising some 12,521 million euros (4.06 per cent of the budget) for the 'phasing-out' regions and 10,385 million euros (3.37 per cent of the budget) for the 'phasing-in' regions – the safety net for the (mostly) EU15 regions losing eligibility as a result of eastern enlargement is therefore not a very big one.

22.3.3 Strategic planning, programming, partnership and additionality

As well as the commitment to concentration of assistance and much closer coordination of the activities of the EU's financial instruments, the regional policy which has emerged in the aftermath of the 1989 reforms places great emphasis on four further principles. They are the use of a system of multi-annual programmes of assistance, the need for a close partnership between all of those involved in regional policy, a commitment to subsidiarity (the retention at EU level of the minimum necessary powers; see chapter 2), and a desire that EU money should be a genuine supplement to regional policy spending by the member states (additionality). None of these principles was entirely new to the 1989 reform package, but the 1989 reforms represented the first comprehensive attempt to create a regional policy 'delivery system' that would allow the principles to be achieved. These four great principles continue to underpin EU regional policy and will continue to do so in 2007–13.

22.4 Some key issues for the future

EU regional policy has shown itself to be capable of evolution and change over the years since its introduction in 1975. Some of the key issues that EU regional policy must confront in the immediate future are legacies of the past (e.g. additionality and the underfunding of the policy). Others, such as the response of the policy to monetary union and eastern enlargement, are much newer issues. Each will be considered in turn.

22.4.1 The challenge of eastern enlargement

The EU has always found it necessary to make changes to its regional policy whenever new accessions have occurred. In most cases this has taken the form of an increase in the budget for regional policy and a re-designation of the map of the assisted areas, but without the fundamental principles of the policy itself being disturbed. At first sight, the 2007–13 reforms appear to be simply another new episode in this process of accommodating new member states. Unfortunately, the eastern enlargement of 2004 has proved much more difficult to deal with and the resulting decisions for the 2007–13 period leave a lot to be desired. As figures 22.1 and 22.2 have shown, the NMS have much lower GDP per capita levels than most of Western Europe and also, by and large, higher unemployment rates. The problems posed by eastern enlargement have not been fully resolved by the 2007–13 reforms. On the contrary, a series of issues remain. Each will be considered in turn.

Institutional capacity and corruption

Many of the NMS12, despite rapid progress in some countries, remain within a painful period of adjustment and transition from their former Communist economic, legal and political systems towards a more Western model. This fact alone is of major importance for regional policy because it means that the institutional and governance structures in some of the acceding states make it difficult for them to effectively absorb preaccession and structural funds money directed at them. The first wave of ten countries (generally the more prosperous ones) poses enormous challenges for an EU which has been shaken by the cost and difficulty of integrating the first of the former Communist states, East Germany. Nor is it just a question of effectively absorbing the structural funds coming their way. Many of the new member states lack regional tier governments and are frequently highly centralized, having limited administrative capacity in the more peripheral regions. Moreover, closely associated with institutional and legal capacity problems is the issue of corruption. Corruption is, of course, by no means confined to Central and Eastern European states. The EU has, however, struggled to prevent fraud in EU15 regional policy programmes and the challenge in some of the NMS is an even greater one.

The underfunding of regional policy

The EU budget is dominated by two items: the CAP and the structural funds. Between them they command the majority of the full EU budget (see chapter 19). The economic decline in many of the Central and Eastern European states which followed the collapse of Communism in the early 1990s, together with the decision to encourage them to seek early accession, triggered an enormous debate on how the challenge to adequately fund EU regional policy in both the NMS and EU15 countries could be met. This challenge is even more severe as several of the NMS are major agricultural producers and hence eligible for very large CAP assistance as well as the structural funds.

Preliminary estimates during the 1990s of the likely additional burdens on the EU budget as a result of eastern enlargement raised the alarming prospect that, under the then existing CAP and structural funds eligibility rules, the EU was most unlikely to be able to cope (Baldwin et al., 1997). As far as regional policy was concerned, the budget challenge was essentially one of where to find the additional funds to meet the costs of an accession situation in which virtually all of the new member states would automatically qualify for objective 1 status. The result was a compromise:

1. *Cuts to regional policy in EU15 countries.* Eligibility and spending (in real terms) in the more prosperous EU15 countries in order to free up funds for a 'shift east' in funding has been the inevitable outcome. This process was actually begun during the 2000–6 budget period. The structural funds in EU15 were cut from 32,045 million euros in 2000 to 29,170 million euros in 2006. Many EU15 regions found themselves losing structural funds eligibility or being downgraded in 2000 (these are shown as the 'transitional funding' regions on figure 22.3). Overall, the population of EU15 countries eligible for either objective 1 or 2 fell in 2000 from 50.6 per cent of the population to 40.4 per cent, with the bulk of the cuts falling on objective 2 regions. As we have seen in the previous section, this process has been taken further in the 2007–13 reforms, although once again transitional funding arrangements are being used to

soften the blow. The elimination of the CIs in 2007 will also hit EU15 regions. No one knows what the effects of the cutbacks in EU15 disadvantaged regions will be, or whether it will be possible for the affected regions to somehow maintain continuity for programmes not yet completed (e.g. by accessing member state funding). There are real dangers of premature withdrawal of funding in this situation.

2. *Finding more money for the overall structural funds budget.* An obvious solution to the budget challenges posed by eastern enlargement would be to raise the overall size of the budget. The EU remains, however, severely constrained in its ability to do this by: (a) the reluctance of its member states to grant the EU extra tax powers or member state contributions, and (b) a decision taken by the Council of Ministers in 2002 to fix CAP spending in the EU15 at its planned 2006 level through until 2013 (in nominal terms) *prior to* a deal being made on what the structural funds budget would be for 2007–13. This effectively removed at a stroke the most obvious single source for extra regional policy money – a radically reformed and reduced CAP. Despite these constraints, some extra money has been found for the 2007–13 regional policy budget, as table 22.2 has shown. This has been found by setting the overall EU budget at 1.048 per cent of the combined GNI of the EU, and by relying on economic growth over the period through until 2013 to generate higher tax yields. The result is by no means enough.

3. *Reducing the entitlement of the new member states.* Finally, the new member states have not been given the kind of entitlement to structural funds money that they would have been entitled to prior to 2000. The Commission has justified this by arguing that the new member states would simply not have been able to effectively absorb the kinds of funding per capita enjoyed by, say, Portugal and Greece prior to 2000. Whilst there may be some truth in this argument, it also remains a fact that they are not being offered what an early generation of acceding countries were able to rely upon. The risk here, of course, is that the new member states may find that it takes them a lot longer

to catch up with the rest of the EU than would otherwise have been the case.

The regional impact of enlargement

Eastern enlargement poses a further challenge to the structural funds. As has been noted earlier, each act of economic integration tends to produce a set of broad core–periphery effects within the EU, and also a distinctive geographical pattern of losing and gaining regions. Eastern enlargement is also thought likely to have its own distinctive set of regional impacts within the EU15 member states. Estimates of these impacts remain rough and ready, but it is thought that it is the new entrants themselves that will gain most, while the EU15 countries will enjoy an expansion of perhaps one-quarter of 1 per cent on their combined GDP. However, within the EU15 countries it is likely that it will be the relatively prosperous regions of the north of the EU (especially in Germany, France and the UK) that will gain the most from eastern enlargement, particularly in Germany (Baldwin et al., 1997). The structural funds within the existing EU15 countries will therefore have to cope not only with budget cuts and restricted eligible areas, but also with a new set of strains on the existing regional disparities.

The structural funds remain small, commanding less than half of 1 per cent of the combined GDP of EU member states. The experience of Britain in the 1960s, when the UK government operated a regional policy with better funding (relative to GDP) than the current EU regional policy and still failed to eliminate relatively narrow regional disparities, suggests that EU regional policy is still significantly under-funded. The fact that regional disparities even just within the existing EU15 member states remain stubbornly persistent and narrowed in the 1990s at only the slowest of paces gives added credence to those who argue that regional policy is seriously under-funded.

22.4.2 EU regional policy and monetary union

The attainment of monetary union for the majority of EU15 member states in 2002 has important implications for EU regional policy which have yet to be confronted. EMU is effectively a further step in the long process of economic integration. Like, for example, the customs union and the single market, EMU is certainly resulting in a distinctive regional imprint, combined with some general core–periphery effects. Moreover, all regions are experiencing structural change as the full implications of EMU work their way through the economic system. That this would occur has been known for many years (CEC, 1990a; Emerson et al., 1991).

Precisely what the regional impacts of EMU will be remains a controversial issue and one made more uncertain by the fact that some member states such as the UK have not yet decided when (if ever) they will join the eurozone. The Stability and Growth Pact (SGP) continues to bring pressure to bear on member states' budgets, and hence on their ability to ameliorate regional problems by way of public spending in disadvantaged regions. In the longer term it remains very unclear whether monetary union will lead to convergence or divergence in regional disparities. By accelerating the process of economic integration, monetary union should enhance the convergence forces at the heart of the neoclassical growth model. However, 'the theoretical and empirical evidence suggests that convergence can occur, but it is not inevitable' (Ardy et al., 2002, p. 17). Those who take a less sanguine view of the regional impact of monetary union point to the loss of exchange rate and monetary policy powers which have been used in the past by some member states to protect their weaker regions. The eurozone is also some distance from being an optimum currency area (see chapters 10 and 11). The inadequate nature of labour and capital mobility levels within the EU, together with the absence of the kinds of inter-state and interpersonal fiscal transfer mechanisms which exist in genuine federal states (and which cushion economic changes with adverse regional effects), remains a serious worry.

22.4.3 Attaining the Lisbon Agenda objectives

The 2007–13 structural fund reforms place great emphasis on refocusing EU regional policy on 'hard' economic objectives, particularly the enhancement of competitiveness in international markets. This is an enormous challenge. By definition, regional policy must spend its resources in some of the most deprived parts of the EU. Even within the relatively more prosperous parts of EU15 countries it has not in the past proved easy to ensure that the structural funds are well spent. This is, after all, one of the reasons why the regional disparities are proving so stubborn to eliminate. The 1990s saw what can best be described as 'mission creep' in structural funds programmes, with many types of projects having rather 'softer' environmental, social inclusion and anti-discriminatory objectives being funded. How difficult will it be for disadvantaged regions to find sufficient suitable projects which can meet the harsher requirements of the Lisbon Agenda?

22.4.4 Additionality and subsidiarity

Despite the successive reforms of the structural funds, it is clear that additionality remains a serious problem for EU regional policy. Member states faced with domestic public sector budget problems will always be tempted to cut their local regional policy efforts as EU regional policy is expanded. Similar comments apply to subsidiarity, where some member states remain reluctant to release powers to regional and local partners. This remains the case in the UK despite the creation of elected regional governments in Scotland, Wales and Northern Ireland. English regions still do not have elected assemblies.

22.4.5 The final division of policy powers

Perhaps the most fundamental issue that continues to face EU regional policy in the new millennium, as it did in the 1990s, is the division of regional policy responsibilities among the different tiers of government involved. The commitment to subsidiarity is useful, but does not answer the crucial question of what the final assignment of regional policy powers is to be. This is particularly important in an era of multi-level governance in which the powers of the member states appear to be waning. What is to be the final role for the member states? What is to be the role of the EU and the regional governments? Until this is decided, the EU will continue to find itself in a series of conflicts with the other partners in the regional policy effort.

NOTE

1 The 'phasing-out' regions identified on figure 22.3 represent regions which in the 1994–9 budget period had enjoyed objective 1 or 2 status but whose pace of economic development had been such that by 2000 they were no longer eligible. The EU has a system of allowing temporary 'phasing-out' assistance on a diminishing basis to prevent a sudden withdrawal of funding.

Social policies: the employment dimension

BRIAN ARDY AND ALI EL-AGRAA[1]

23.1 Introduction

By the time of the Treaty of Nice, the EU had acquired a broad responsibility in the social field, which can be found in issues concerning employment, industrial health, industrial social costs, labour mobility and the role of social spending in social affairs. In particular, a more integrated approach to social issues, combining employment, social protection and economic and budgetary policy, is arguably in the making.

In the early EC years, broader issues of social welfare seemed of little relevance but the subsequent growth of its social competences has been notable. There are a number of reasons for this. Social affairs now form a large component of national public policy which, in turn, has to be fitted into a European framework and more problems have a transnational element. Community policies have also matured and as they reached into detailed areas of life, such as in the equal opportunities policy, they become more visible. Consequently, many people and organizations now recognize that their interests may be as well served by lobbying in Brussels as in national capitals. The history of the EU also shows that the Commission, normally backed up by the European Parliament, has always believed it should play an active and positive role in social affairs and, particularly during the 1980s, it stepped up the social momentum as part of the drive to strengthen the political legitimacy of the EC in the move towards European union. It is hardly surprising that the Commission has clashed with national governments which still wish to claim credit with their citizens for their work to improve the conditions of life. Differences

of opinion have surfaced, notably over the 'social dimension' of the single market. Here the biggest single issue has been whether the Community needs a common framework of employment law and certain rules relating to working conditions in order that the single market may work effectively. Subsequently, the argument from Brussels has been that the EU must become 'closer to its citizens', a view that encourages an ever more important social role. The result of these pressures is that social policy now covers a wide range of individual policies with no less than five Commissioners and their directorates having direct responsibilities for the items under the umbrella of social policies.

The legal foundations for social policies are to be found in the Treaties of Rome (EEC), Paris (ECSC) and Rome (Euratom) as modified by subsequent developments. The Single European Act (SEA) brought changes, which were deemed necessary because of the move to the 'internal market' (see chapter 7), while the Maastricht and Amsterdam Treaties both widened responsibilities and sharpened up existing ones. Some Treaty provisions are clear-cut but others are of a very general nature and do not require legislation so much as political programmes, with the result that at any moment there is a wide variety of social activities that demand a different degree of commitment from member states. A consequence of this is the growing overlap of interest with that of national authorities which leads to both cooperation and conflict. Although national governments remain primarily in charge in matters such as mainstream education, personal healthcare, the value of social security benefits and housing provision, and national sources of finance are overwhelmingly important, it is routine for ministers to attend specialist Council meetings to agree both Community policy initiatives and joint activities in these matters. It is important, however, to retain a sense of perspective. Community interest is often marginal to the main body of work carried out nationally since it derives in the first instance from economic objectives, and the current emphasis upon subsidiarity suggests this division is intended to remain. An example is in education, where the EU accepts that member states are primarily responsible for fulfilling educational needs, but sees a role for a 'European dimension' through supporting language teaching, mobility of staff and students and cooperation between educational establishments in different member states.

Political rights having been covered in the TEU, discussion moved on to human and social rights. The commitment in Article 6 (EU) is to respect the European Convention on Human Rights and Fundamental Freedoms, and the possibility of suspension of membership in the case of violation has been added to the treaty. The question is still raised whether the EU should formally subscribe to it. The European Court of Justice (ECJ) has studied the question more than once, concluding that to do so would require a full-scale treaty revision (Opinion 2/94, 28.3.96). There are further references to the importance of human rights in the treaties, including their significance for the common foreign and security policy. It is also usual to find that contractual ties with third countries make 'respect for democratic and human rights' an essential part of the text and the Commission is being particularly watchful in the case of aspiring Union entrants and the recipients of development aid.

Putting aside for now the European Employment Strategy, the 1990s were mainly years of consolidation, if not of relative stagnation in European social matters. The European Council in Lisbon (23–4 March 2000), followed by the Nice Council (7–10 December 2000) marked a new beginning. A new strategic goal was set for the Union for the next decade: 'to become the most competitive and dynamic knowledge-based economy in the world, capable of sustainable economic growth with more and better jobs and greater social cohesion' (see chapter 14). Implementing this strategy was to be achieved by improving the existing processes. More integration of social domains separated until then (for instance employment and social protection) and of economic and social policies was expected from this method. The ultimate goal was to modernize the European social model by investing in people and combating social exclusion.

23.2 The Treaty of Rome

Although the Treaty of Rome was relatively weak on the social side it was strong enough to allow much development. First, it had general objectives of a broadly social character, such as a high level of employment and social protection and a raised standard of living. Second, it contained recognition by the member states of the need to improve living and working conditions and expectation that social policies would gradually align under the impact of the new system. There was agreement to collaborate in specific fields such as labour legislation, working conditions, vocational training, social security, industrial health and welfare and trade union and collective bargaining matters. Here the Commission was given the responsibility of promoting collaboration. In this way, scope for joint action was left open should the evolution of the EC require it, but common policies were not considered inevitable. Third, the question of the effect of social costs on competition was raised in 1957. The sensitivity of French industry on this point led directly to the principle of equal pay for men and women. This has proved the basis for some significant policy developments. Fourth, the belief that labour should not be ineffectively utilized led to the setting up of the European Social Fund (ESF), the aim of which was to help both occupational and geographical mobility. In addition, the treaty included an agreement to establish the common principles of vocational training.

The fifth item of great social significance was the adoption of the principle of the free movement of wage earners, along with rules to give it practical effect and to ensure the equal treatment of such migrants with indigenous workers (see chapter 8). It was agreed, also, that rules would be necessary to allow the free establishment of the self-employed and for services to be provided across frontiers. The free movement policy, together with its supporting policies of employment exchange collaboration, maintenance of social security rights and protection of equal working rights for migrants, was a major EC success although it owed much to the buoyant economic conditions of the time. Subsequent attempts to move the policy into the much more difficult area of social integration and social equality, and to evolve a policy towards migrants from outside, have been far harder to accomplish.

23.3 The Single European Act and the Social Charter

The prime social aim of the SEA (see chapter 2) was to develop the provisions made necessary by the internal market, although there were disagreements as to what these were. It also began the process of widening the concept of social policy. It made an important statement of principle in its preamble affirming the fundamental civil, political and social rights of citizens, drawing on the work of the Council of Europe for this. By doing so, it strengthened the EC's moral base and thus the hands of those who wished to see the EC play a more positive social role. A special section of the SEA supplemented the Rome Treaty. It agreed to pay special attention to better health and safety standards at work and to harmonizing standards while maintaining existing high ones. This reflected the fear that firms would be tempted to cut standards as they entered a more competitive situation. Minimum standards were to be introduced gradually by directives and passed by qualified majority voting (QMV; see chapters 3 and 28) in the Council of Ministers. At the same time, a cautious note was sounded by stressing that the conditions in member states must be taken into account and the needs of small businesses considered. A dialogue between management and labour at the EC level, which might in turn lead to formal agreements between the two sides of industry, was to be set up.

Certain reservations about the use of QMV continued. In the social field, unanimity was still required for free movement rules, the rights and interests of employed persons and for the passing of directives that would require alteration in the methods of training for, and practice in, some professions. The treaty referred to the need for the Commission to use high standards when regulating health, safety and environmental issues and when dealing with consumer protection.

Underlying these legislative provisions were considerable uncertainties. Some member states feared that, by having EC standards imposed upon them, their goods would become uncompetitive; others feared pressure to lower their standards to meet competition from members with lower labour costs. Denmark added a special declaration to the SEA designed to ensure it could continue with its own high standards. The UK was anxious to prevent the imposition of labour regulation that would damage the upsurge of small businesses and thought the social dialogue provisions would encourage the revitalization of trade union power which the Conservative government had been attacking at home. No solutions were found to these conflicts of interest but the SEA, by introducing clauses to satisfy everyone, made future conflict inevitable. This soon began to occur.

The SEA gave a boost to the development of social policy. New initiatives to encourage language teaching, student exchanges and better vocational training and to establish health and safety norms soon began to appear and were broadly acceptable to member governments. However, the Commission was less successful in mobilizing support for proposals relating to working conditions. The opposition was led by the UK whose government disliked such formal controls over business and was suspicious of the opportunity offered by some of the proposals for the growth of trade union power. The UK government also objected to what it deemed a misuse of Treaty powers in that directives were being proposed under cover of the implementation of the single market when they were not really necessary for that purpose. Consequently, they could be passed by QMV. The matter received great publicity when the Commission produced a Charter on the

Fundamental Social Rights for Workers (the Social Charter) setting out the proposed actions thought necessary in consequence of the single market. There were forty-seven initiatives in all, many of them non-controversial and some already agreed, but others moved on to contested ground. In December 1989, the Social Charter was accepted by all governments other than the British and it became, not a legally binding document, but a statement of proposed action which the Commission subsequently used as a document to organize its work.

The ECJ is now formally empowered to ensure the respect of fundamental rights and freedoms by the European institutions. In 2000 the Charter of Fundamental Rights was jointly proclaimed by the Council, the European Parliament and the Commission. This Charter used the previous Social Charter as one of its sources, but has been enlarged to include civil, political, economic, social and societal rights. Its preamble emphasizes the foundation of Europe on the universal values of human dignity, freedom, equality and solidarity. The Convention for the Future of Europe recommended (in July 2003) that this Charter should become part of the European institution; it is indeed included in the stalled Constitution, adopted in June 2004 (see chapters 2 and 28).

23.4 The development of social policy

Given the rather incoherent guidance of the early years, it is not surprising that the development of EU social policy was patchy. The first decade saw major steps taken to implement the policy on labour movement, a formal adoption of the equal pay policy, a narrow exploitation of the ESF and considerable study of, and research into, labour questions, but there was a sense of social policy hanging fire. However, a new impetus could be detected by the end of the 1960s when hopes in Western Europe were high for social improvements, and the EC benefited from this optimism. Widespread unease existed over the problems of the disadvantaged, social inequalities and the increasing distance between the citizen and the services run by big bureaucracies originally developed to help the ordinary man and woman. There was a certain vacuum in social policy which enabled the EC to establish a role. The Hague conference in December 1969 agreed that the EC needed to go further in the pursuit of common economic and political goals in which a 'concerted social policy' would have a part. This line was continued by the Paris summit of 1972 which asserted the importance member states attached to vigorous action in the social field. Specifically, it referred to the need to widen participation in decision-making, and action to lessen inequalities and to improve the quality of life. The political momentum thus established led to the first social action programme (SAP). Its hopes were, however, quickly dashed by the onset of recession and the burden of large-scale unemployment, and it was this that began to dominate social concerns as the EC experienced structural changes in employment patterns, including a rapid growth in part-time and shift work, together with formidable problems of long-term and youth unemployment. A major preoccupation for the EC became the need to analyse unemployment issues, encourage cooperative action by member states and support programmes to help to overcome specific problems such as lack of training.

By the 1980s, a new momentum in the EC can be discerned, in which social policy had an important role. In 1981, the newly elected French socialist government had proposed a programme for a 'social space' for the EC, and the following year the European Parliament called for a reform of the treaties and the achievement of a European union which would require a new policy for society. The entry of Greece, Portugal and Spain added another dimension by turning attention away from the urban problems of the more developed north to the importance of devoting resources to the characteristic problems of agricultural inefficiency, disguised unemployment in rural areas and lack of training for industrial work. The later entry of Austria, Sweden and Finland maintained the interest in social policy and brought the strong Scandinavian welfare tradition into the counsels of the EU.

The urge to establish the single market and the insistence that this must be accompanied by some steps towards cementing European unity drove the Community towards a fresh consideration of citizens' rights. The European Council accepted two reports from the ad hoc Adonnino committee in 1985 which included a host of recommendations for building 'the people's Europe'. Some were new; others asked for current policies to be pursued more rigorously. Although some were implemented, others ran into difficulties.

23.5 The Treaty of Union and its perspectives

Subsequent to the passing of the SEA, controversy in social matters revolved round questions raised by the single market and, in particular, over possible extensions of the European employment law. The Maastricht negotiations led to a totally unexpected result. Amended Articles 2 and 3 reiterated the social goals of the Treaty of Rome but in a broader, often more explicit form. They then included respect for the environment, a high level of employment and social protection and the raising of the standard of living and the quality of life. Subsequent objectives included free movement of people, measures concerning the entry of people, a continuation of the ESF and the policy of cohesion, a contribution to a high level of health protection, to education and training and to the flowering of culture, as well as to consumer protection and to measures in the sphere of tourism.

Most importantly, the treaty established the legal concept of Union citizenship 'to strengthen the protection of the rights and interests of the nationals of the member states'. Citizens were given the right to move and reside freely, to vote and stand as candidates in municipal and European parliamentary elections in all member states on the same terms as nationals (each right being subject to certain limitations). Citizens, when outside the Community, received the right to diplomatic protection from the services of any member state. They may now petition both the European Parliament and the European Ombudsman. Directives were in place to give effect to these political rights and the Ombudsman has been appointed.

The novelty was that eleven (later fourteen) of the then fifteen member states, excluding the UK, signed an attached protocol and agreement, popularly known as the Social Chapter (now fully incorporated in the treaties, see below). This affirmed their wish to continue with the Social Charter and clarified the goals. Article 1 of the agreement included 'the promotion of employment, improved living and working conditions, proper social protection, dialogue between management and labour, the development of human resources with a view to lasting high employment and the combating of exclusion'. The agreement made explicit that the Community is competent to act in the fields of the working environment, working conditions, equality of men and women concerning opportunities and treatment at work, the social integration of excluded groups and with regard to the information and consultation of workers. It established the right of the Council to pass directives on minimum standards by the use of QMV for matters of health and safety, working conditions, information and consultation, equality at work and the integration of those outside the labour market. The Council may also act, by unanimity, on social security and protection, protection of redundant workers, the defence and representation of workers' and employers' interests, employment conditions for third-country nationals, financing of measures for employment and job creation (but not the use of the ESF, which is in the main treaty). Pay, the right of association and the right to strike and impose lockouts are specifically excluded, while states may continue to provide specific advantages for women in order to equalize their working opportunities.

The agreement introduced a decision-making role for management and unions – what has been called the European Social Dialogue. Its incorporation was formally asked for at the Maastricht Intergovernmental Conference by the European social actors (UNICE, ECPE, ETUC). First, member states may delegate to the social partners the task of implementing directives relating to the above goals. Second, the Commission must consult them before submitting any formal social policy proposals. And, third, the agreement recognized that the social partners may be in a position to agree on actions themselves. In addition, they could agree to ask for the formal structures to implement agreements they have reached. Some analysts saw the clauses relating to the social dialogue and the role of the social partners as very significant, arguing that they signalled a new way of applying doctrines of partnership, consultation and openness and of implementing the principle of subsidiarity. The protocol was concerned with the use of the Community's institutions by the signatories to the agreement. In 1996, the Commission argued that the social dialogue could well be promoted at the sectoral level, leaving the European discussions to concentrate on strategic priorities. The more broadly these were defined, the stronger became the case for admitting representatives of voluntary organizations, the churches and local authorities to membership.

The effect of the agreement on social policy was tiresome rather than significant since it was always the intention to get all members to agree if at all possible and only to use the agreement as a last resort. British employers' and union organizations were represented through the European umbrella organizations, so Britain's voice was not entirely excluded. However, it was just as well that the then new Labour government announced in 1997 that it was ready to accept the agreement which thus became incorporated into the legal structure with the Amsterdam Treaty.

The Union treaty also brought changes regarding the entry of migrants. Most member states were under pressure from nationals of third countries then present and, in consequence, immigration and asylum policies were being re-examined. The Council of Ministers obtained the duty to determine the third countries whose nationals must be in possession of a visa, at first by unanimity, but from January 1996 by QMV. Emergency arrangements may be made to deal with a sudden inflow of people. Migratory movements also affected the Community role in ensuring cooperation in the fields of justice and home affairs (see chapter 2).

All in all, the Union treaty gave the EU more standing in social affairs, tidied up existing policies and made explicit where the Union had arrived in the execution of its work. This, in itself, helped to avoid future arguments about the legal

basis of proposals. The more significant developments in the 1990s are to be found in the broadened objectives and enhanced role of the social partners, and the launching of the European employment strategy, developments which have been consolidated through the Treaty of Amsterdam and implemented by the following European Councils. The unpopularity of the European project that surfaced during the ratification of the Maastricht Treaty heightened the belief that the EU must not only do more for the general public but be seen to be doing so. The temptation for governments to negotiate strategic compromises between national interests by themselves (and thus to do without the Commission) accelerated the search for a new 'softer' European method. An open method of coordination was set up in Lisbon (2000) and incorporated into the Treaty of Nice. It intended to develop a more integrated approach to social policies, through the coordination of national policies and under the umbrella of the Broad Economic Policy Guidelines (see chapters 11 and 12). Experimenting first with employment affairs, it is intended to extend to many other fields such as social exclusion, pension and welfare reforms, and so on.

In the previous editions, this chapter then turned to examine individual policies in more detail, reflecting the fact that achieving a high level of employment and modernizing the European social model were the major preoccupations of the time. This remains desirable, but one would require a whole book to deal adequately with the EU social model. Here, we have decided to concentrate on employment and unemployment not only because they have become the major issue in this area, but also because their importance impinges on most of the chapters in the book.

23.6 Employment policy

It was inevitable that employment policy would develop at the EU level, because of its political importance, the problem of unemployment and the growing transfer of economic policymaking to the EU. It was, however, difficult because of the wide range of policies that impinge upon employment, the political sensitivity of these policies and the very substantial variation in the nature of these policies across the EU. This meant a uniform policy was not possible, that decision-making powers had to remain with the member states, and that policies could differ across them. Thus the European Employment Strategy (EES) was born, further refining the open method of coordination (OMC) as a new system of EU governance.

The rest of this chapter examines the way in which this policy has been developed. There follows a consideration of the economic theory and evidence relating to employment performance on which the EES is based. Then the nature of the OMC is analysed in general and in relation to the EES. Next the employment performance of the EU particularly in relation to the EES targets is discussed. The final assessment considers the relationship between the EES and the employment performance of the EU.

23.7 The development of the European Employment Strategy

A very wide range of government measures affect employment and these measures vary substantially between member states. They are in turn bound up with national traditions and institutions. This has made it difficult for the EU to develop an employment policy. This is illustrated by the breadth of the areas such a policy would have to encompass:

1. *Taxation:* income taxes affect choices over whether to work, how much to work, where to work and what work to do. Other taxes can have similar effects. Income taxes have a negative substitution effect on work by making leisure cheaper, and a positive income effect making workers poorer, and so encouraging them to work more. Income tax and social security contributions combine to determine the overall tax on labour. Implicit tax rates[2] on labour in the EU25 average 35.6 per cent, but there is a wide variation between 23.1 per cent in Cyprus and 45.7 per cent in Sweden.[3]

2. *Social security:* affects choices over whether to work and how much to work, and interacts with the tax system, to give rise to unemployment traps (very high rates of tax on moving from unemployment to employment). It is not only the levels of benefit that are important but their duration, the qualifications for receiving them and the way the system is administered.

3. *Education and training:* are important in determining the quality of the workforce, its skills and adaptability, and thus its employability. With the increasing rate of structural change in the economy, the emphasis is on lifelong learning so that workers are able to use new technology and to move into new occupations. The quality of education and training systems varies a great deal across the EU (OECD, 2006b).

4. *Employment protection:* legal rights of workers, particularly with regard to dismissal/redundancy and types of employment – fixed-term versus permanent, part-time versus full-time. The EU has a wide range of employment protection from very limited protection in the UK, Ireland and the new member states (NMS) to high levels of protection in Sweden, Germany and Italy.

5. *Employment services:* the provision of advice, information and incentives to encourage unemployed workers to find new jobs. These services can be supplied by public or private employment agencies. They will be important in determining the efficiency with which the unemployed are matched with vacancies.

6. *Industrial relations:* the system by which workers and employers reach agreement over wages and other conditions of employment. Collective bargaining between trade unions and employers is the norm, but this can take place at the plant, company, industry or even to a certain extent the national level (Ireland and the Netherlands have national agreements to determine overall wage increases). So there is a spectrum ranging from the very decentralized in the UK and in the NMS to centralized systems in many other EU countries.

7. *Minimum wages:* legislative to set minimum wages. Some EU countries do not have minimum wages (e.g. Italy[4]) and even where they do

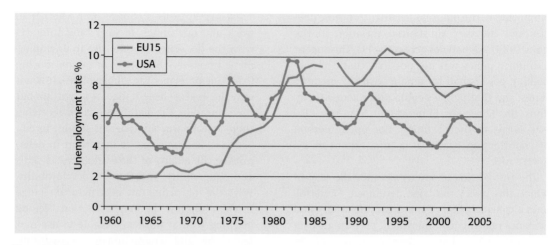

Figure 23.1 Unemployment EU15 and US, 1960–2005. *Note:* The discontinuity in the EU15 series is due to a change in the statistical series used. *Source:* CEC (2006d), OECD (2006a).

exist, their level in relation to average wages varies a great deal from less than 33 per cent in Portugal and Spain to nearly 60 per cent in France.

8. *Active labour market measures:* are policies to try to influence employment directly, e.g. employment subsidies, work experience, training, etc. Active measures try to increase the possibility of employment while passive measures just provide the unemployed with financial support. Sweden has invested heavily in such measures, while they are much less important in other countries such as Greece and Spain.

Given the sensitivity of the issue, it is not surprising that in the heady high-growth-low-unemployment era of the 1950s employment was not a central issue for the EEC Treaty. However, a high level of employment is one of the major aims of the common economic policy in Article 104 of the Treaty. Employment was referred to in Article 118 in connection with European collaboration in the field of social policy, but employment policy played only a subordinate role compared to the – mainly neoliberally inspired – economic integration of this period. Community activities were, therefore, limited to the coordination of national social policies including measures concerning the free movement of workers (Arts. 48–51), the Euro-

pean Social Fund (Arts. 123–7) and vocational training measures (Art. 128).

In the 1960s low unemployment was the norm and so employment was not a European issue, but this all came to end with the oil crises of the 1970s. Growth slowed, employment fell and unemployment increased. In the early post-war period US unemployment had been higher than European unemployment, but after 1974 European unemployment rose faster, and while US unemployment fell from the early 1980s Europe's remained high (figure 23.1).[5]

The EU response to the oil shocks was nationalistic: governments tried to solve their own problems with macroeconomic expansion and the new protectionism. There were some EU action programmes on social policy but coordination of national employment policies remained limited. With EU unemployment high and generally poor economic performance in the 1970s and early 1980s the single market was developed (see chapter 7). It was hoped that this would raise EU economic performance, creating jobs and reducing unemployment (Emerson et al., 1988). These hopes were not fulfilled and unemployment rose even higher in the early 1990s.

The continuation of weak employment performance in 1980s meant the fight against unemployment was becoming a major objective of the EU, and employment policy shifted from being a facet of social policy to an important aspect of economic policy. Given concerns over public support for the EC, it had to be seen to be tackling the major economic problem of the time. The aim of a high level of employment was – for the first time – integrated into the legal framework of the EC with Article 2 of the Maastricht Treaty in 1992. This development was supported by the 1993 Delors White Paper on growth, competitiveness and employment (CEC, 1993b) and the 1994 European Council summit in Essen resulting in a shift of approach from employment protection towards employment promotion. The summit also introduced a multilateral monitoring mechanism for employment, and the emphasis of policy was shifted from employment protection towards employment promotion (Ferrera et al., 2000, pp. 77–8). Five priorities were identified, which later became central to the EES: improving employment opportunities; increasing the employment intensity of growth; developing active labour market policies; adopting measures to entice the long-term unemployed back to work; and reducing non-wage labour costs.

This 'Essen Strategy' was integrated as Title VIII (Arts. 125–30) of the 1997 Amsterdam Treaty to promote broader convergence between the member states' employment policies by involving a wide range of political and social actors, while at the same time national labour market systems were to be respected. The integration of the title into the TEU was in order to foster the development of an EU employment strategy particularly promoting 'skilled, trained and adaptable workforce and labour markets responsive to economic change with a view to achieving the objectives defined in Article 2 of the Treaty on European Union and in Article 2 of this Treaty' (Art. 125). The same year, a special European Council on employment took place in Luxembourg to put into operation the new coordination mechanism. Hence the employment chapter became effective before the official ratification of the treaty by the member states, the 'Essen Strategy' became the Luxembourg process and the EES was launched. The Lisbon European Council added the non-binding target of an employment rate of 70 per cent by the year 2010 (European Council, 2000c).

The Stockholm European Council further set additional targets of a 60 per cent female employment rate and a 50 per cent employment rate for older people (55–64 years) (European Council, 2001).

23.8 Employment performance: economic theory and evidence

The rising long-term trend in European unemployment and its associated low level of employment have been subject to extensive economic research. Of particular interest has been the disparity in measured performance between the US and the EU, and the very substantial differences between European countries. This section surveys this research in order to identify the way in which economic systems and institutions may be modified to promote higher employment.

The labour market in advanced economies is subject to constant change, with a myriad of factors altering demand and supply conditions. Some firms and sectors are shedding workers, while others are hiring new workers. This process determines the overall volume of job creation,[6] which will in turn depend upon levels of and changes in wage rates, the structure of wages[7] and productivity. Given the complexity of this process, there will always be frictional, structural and regional unemployment. Beyond this, unemployment will be determined by real demand and in the long term unemployment will tend towards a level consistent with stable inflation – the natural rate of unemployment (see below). Unless wages are flexible, wage rates may not adjust to ensure that supply and demand are reconciled at a reasonably high level of employment/low level of unemployment. The functioning of the labour market and its institutions will influence the extent of this unemployment by determining the efficiency with which the unemployed and vacancies are matched, and the flexibility of wages.

Economic theory suggests that unemployment can be viewed in two extreme ways. First, frictionless equilibrium: in this case labour markets adjust rapidly to shocks (productivity, oil prices, or interest rates) and the market is generally near to its long-term equilibrium with regard to unemployment (the natural rate of unemployment, NRU; NAIRU rather – see chapter 10). Thus the actual employment rate approximates to the long-term equilibrium rate – the rate at which trade unions, employers and workers have no tendency to change their behaviour, provided the exogenous variables which they face do not change. Second, prolonged adjustment: in this case the response of the labour market to external shocks is sluggish because of the costs and difficulty of adjustment. In such a labour market unemployment can differ substantially from the long-term equilibrium rate for prolonged periods. In this case Keynesian remedies of expanding demand could have long-term effects on employment. With these as the polar cases, most economists believe that actual labour market behaviour contains elements of both extremes. The positioning on the spectrum between these extremes will have a strong effect on the explanations for unemployment and the policy prescriptions for its reduction.

Besides differences in the dynamics with which equilibrium is approached, the concept of equilibrium can be viewed in stock or flow terms. Stock approaches consider the relationship between the employment from firms (aggregate demand for labour) and the available workforce (aggregate supply of labour).[8] Flow approaches consider the relationships between people entering and leaving unemployment over a period of time. So the stock approaches emphasize the total number of unemployed and the flow approaches the turnover of the unemployed and the length of unemployment.

23.8.1 Labour market flexibility

The EES can be regarded as building on the OECD jobs strategy (OECD, 1994, 1997) and is concerned with raising labour market efficiency, based on the frictionless equilibrium models of the market. Here the labour market, and in particular the real wage, will respond to shocks to establish the NRU. The actual unemployment rate lies close to the long-term equilibrium and the upward trend in European unemployment is, therefore, the result of exogenous changes that affect the efficiency of

the market in creating employment and reducing unemployment (Layard et al., 1991; Morgan and Mourougane, 2001). The dynamics of the process are seen to have little effect on the NRU (Nickell, 1997; Blanchard and Wolfers, 2000; Daveri and Tabellini, 2000). Rising unemployment is in this view the result of changes in structural factors affecting the NRU.

The stock of workers and the flow into the market will largely be determined by demographics,[9] with younger workers and women returnees entering the labour market and older workers retiring or becoming inactive. An efficient labour market would find work for the available workforce, so an increase in younger people with their higher employment rate could lead to an increase in employment and a decrease in the unemployment rate. Shimer (1998) suggests that 70 per cent of the fall in US unemployment since 1979 could be attributed to demographics. But others believe that the workforce is endogenous to employment opportunities because of variations in the participation rate and immigration (Garibaldi and Mauro, 2002, p. 84).

The prospects of those entering the workforce and of the unemployed finding jobs depend upon how well they match the requirements of employers' vacancies in terms of the geographical location of employment, education, skills and experience. They will also depend upon the ability of labour market institutions to match the unemployed to the available vacancies.

The willingness of workers to accept jobs will vary with the generosity and availability of benefits compared with the real wage on offer. There are four aspects of the benefit system that could influence equilibrium unemployment: the level of benefits; the duration of benefits; the coverage of the system; and the strictness of its operation. These factors will affect the workers' reservation wage – the wage required to entice an unemployed worker back into employment. The level and duration of benefits do seem to be positively related to the NRU (OECD, 2006c, pp. 58–61). Bassanini and Duval (2006) estimate that reducing the gross replacement rate[10] by 10 per cent would decrease the unemployment rate of men aged 25–54 years by 1.2 per cent and increase their employment rate by 1.7 per cent. Generosity of benefits seems particularly to affect the employment rates of young, old and female workers, and to increase the duration of unemployment. However, these disincentive effects can largely be offset by sanctions for failure to undertake job search or to accept reasonable offers of employment (de Koning et al., 2004). But changing the rules is not enough; enforcement is crucial (Grubb, 2000). Given the large increase in numbers on non-employment benefits in the 1980s and 1990s which has still to be reversed (OECD, 2006c, p. 76), it is important that these activation approaches are extended to non-employment benefits. Otherwise the unemployed can easily end up on these other benefits, nullifying the reforms to unemployment benefit.

Social security contributions and indirect taxes drive a wedge between the wage cost to an employer and the real wage of the employee. The effect of this wedge on the supply and demand for labour depends upon their sensitivity to price changes. The effect on labour supply is ambiguous, because the income effect of taxation encourages work effort, and the substitution effect discourages it. The actual effects are difficult to measure because of the differing circumstances of workers and potential workers and the complexity of the tax and benefit systems. The effect is greatest where the increase in tax is combined with benefit withdrawal to create unemployment traps: increases in the financial returns of low-wage workers lead to higher levels of employment (OECD, 2005d, ch. 3). The effect seems to be greatest on entry to/exit from the market, rather than on the number of hours worked, and to affect partners in couples with only one worker and lone parents (Carone and Salomäki, 2001).

OECD countries exhibit a large increase in the size of the wedge from the 1960s to the 1990s, so this is an obvious candidate to explain the secular rise in unemployment. The effect on unemployment, however, depends crucially upon the extent to which employees can pass part of this increase onto employers (Pissarides, 1990; Nickell and Layard, 1999). Most empirical studies find that the tax wedge is positively related to unemployment and negatively to employment and thus accounts for a substantial proportion of the secular rise in unemployment (e.g. Daveri and Tabellini, 2000; Bassanini and Duval, 2006).

The number of vacancies available could also be affected by employment protection legislation (EPL). The legal protection of workers will tend to make employers more reluctant to hire workers because it is more difficult to reduce employment. EPL, however, also discourages employers from making workers redundant during a recession. So its effects on unemployment are ambiguous, at least in the short term. The evidence on the effects of employment protection legislation on unemployment is inconclusive (Elmeskov et al., 1998; Nickell et al., 2002; Bassanini and Duval, 2006). Part of the problem here may lie in the difficulty of accurately measuring changes in the severity of EPL, because the devil is in the detail of the legislation and its implementation (Bover et al., 2000). While EPL protects existing jobs, it concentrates labour turnover and job insecurity on groups such as young people, women and the long-term unemployed (Bertola et al., 2002); partial reform compounds these problems (Blanchard and Landier, 2002)

Wages levels will also be affected by the strength of trade unions and their ability to bargain for higher wages. This strength cannot be measured directly, so proxies have to be used. Density measures the proportion of workers in trade unions. Coverage is the proportion of workers whose wages are determined as a result of collective bargaining agreements between trade unions and employers. Generally studies have not found significant relationship between union density and coverage and unemployment (OECD, 2006c, p. 84). This may in part be because unions' effect on wages may be offset by coordination[11] of wage bargaining (Nickell et al., 2005, Nickell and Layard, 1999; Booth et al., 2000) which is more likely to occur when unions are strong.

Labour market adjustment can take place via the physical movement of workers – migration. Migration seems to be an important method of adjustment in the US but not in Europe. Interregional migration is much more sensitive to changes in wage differentials in the US than in Europe (Eichengreen, 1993; Obstfeld and Peri,

1998b). Migration from the NMS to the EU15 has been higher (CEC, 2006r, pp. 79–84) and this may have been a factor moderating wage growth in the Ireland and the UK, but its impact has been marginal for most EU15 countries. For the NMS it does moderate unemployment but at the expense of the loss of young, enterprising and educated workers, although as the migration may be temporary this effect could ameliorate over time (Diez Guardia and Pichelmann, 2006, p. 7). Extra-EU immigration is also significant for some countries, such as Spain, allowing faster employment growth.

Active labour market policies (ALMP) seek to increase the likelihood of the unemployed obtaining a job and encompass a wide range of policies including training, work experience, employment subsidies, help with job applications, etc. Macro-econometric studies find that increased spending on ALMP reduces unemployment (Scarpetta, 1996; Nickell, 1997; Elmeskov et al., 1998), but there are some statistical problems with these studies. A recent state-of-the-art study indicates that only spending on labour market training reduces unemployment and that this expenditure can be used to offset the effects of higher unemployment benefit levels (Bassanini and Duval, 2006). Studies using micro data show that the efficiency of different types of measure varies: with job search assistance is generally effective, but employment subsidies are not (Robinson, 2000; Martin and Grubb, 2001; Kluve, 2006).

One important difference between the original OECD (1994) job strategy and the reassessment (OECD, 2006d, pp. 18–19) is the recognition that market flexibility is not the only way to improve employment performance. Market flexibility, decentralized wage bargaining, low benefits, low taxation and weak employment protection do raise employment but with widening income inequality. Flexi-security is an alternative consisting of coordinated collective bargaining, generous welfare benefits, higher levels of employment protection, and activation of the unemployed through benefit administration and active labour market policies. This achieves high employment and low-income inequality, but with high levels of public expenditure. Success-

ful policies are shaped by and have to respond to the institutional environment of each country. While the EES allows national variation, it is shaped around a common prescription, which may not always be appropriate for the heterogeneous group of countries to which it is applied (Seferiades, 2003).

23.8.2 Persistence and unemployment

Alternative explanations stress the importance of lags and persistence mechanisms in the labour market's process of adjustment to shocks. One of the more developed examples is the chain reaction theory of unemployment which views unemployment as part of a prolonged adjustment process (Henry et al., 2000; Karanassou et al., 2002). Rising European unemployment is the result of the interplay between labour market shocks and the slow process of adjustment to these shocks. Each shock has a chain reaction impact upon unemployment, which extends over a considerable period of time. The long-run equilibrium is the NRU, but actual unemployment can differ substantially from this rate, because of its long adjustment. The fundamental difference between these models is, therefore, the speed of the adjustment process.

These differences are important for two reasons. First, the emphasis on policies designed to reduce unemployment will be different according to the view taken of its determination. If it is believed that the rise in European unemployment is the result of an increase in long-run equilibrium unemployment, then the emphasis will be on factors that influence this equilibrium. Thus the measures taken to reduce it would, for example, concentrate on the amount and duration of unemployment benefits, the wedge, the power of trade unions, etc. In contrast, if persistence is believed to be the problem, then the concentration should be on reducing employment protection and on active labour market policies and training. The effects of policies may be different according to the theoretical perspective. Thus, from the point of view of the NRU, employment protection legislation has an ambiguous effect discouraging hiring and firing. In terms of persistence, reducing firing costs lessens job inertia and contributes to the reduction in unemployment. Second, the German experience of the shock of unification will have had a much longer-lasting effect on unemployment according to the persistence hypothesis.

23.8.3 The macro economy and unemployment

The approach of the jobs strategy and the EES has been criticized as ignoring the other essential component of employment policy – that of macro-economic management to achieve full employment. The macroeconomic policy mechanisms within the EU are geared towards economic stability, particularly price stability, not full employment. Thus the EES views employment and unemployment as strictly labour market problems (Schettkat, 2001) and problems for the unemployed themselves (Serrano Pascual, 2003). The basis for the contention that instability of the macro economy, as measured by the stability of the unemployment rate, was positively related to the NRU[12] (OECD, 1999b, p. 44) has been questioned. The estimated relationship is only significant if Finland and Sweden are included, the two economies where the estimates are most questionable (Casey, 2004, p. 344).

23.9 The European Employment Strategy

23.9.1 The Legal Basis of the EES

Confusingly, employment policy can derive from two separate parts of the Treaty (CEC, 2002o): Title VIII Employment Articles 125–30, and Title XI Social Policy, Education, Vocational Training and Youth, Chapter 1, Social Provisions Articles 136–45. The employment title clearly establishes that the development of a coordinated strategy for employment shall be based on the open method of coordination (OMC; see section 23.9.2 below). The harmonization of laws and regulations is specifically excluded (Article 129). The social provisions chapter is concerned with workers' rights, widely defined (Article 137):

a. working environment, workers' health and safety
b. working conditions
c. social security and social protection
d. redundancy rights
e. information and consultation of workers
f. collective representation of workers and employers
g. employment of third-country nationals
h. social inclusion in the labour market
i. equality between men and women in the labour market
j. combating social exclusion
k. modernization of social protection.

Workers' rights can be improved by coordination under the open method (Article 137.2a) but also for rights a–i by directives, which define minimum requirements for gradual implementation (Article 137.2b). The decision procedure directive relating to a, b, e, h and i is Article 251, calling for co-decision with the Council acting on a qualified majority. For c, d, f and g the Council must act unanimously on a proposal from the Commission after consulting the European Parliament and the various committees. The most sensitive areas of employment policy, therefore, require the unanimous agreement of member states before EC law can be introduced. There is, of course, some ambiguity over the delineation between these areas: the Work Time Directive was introduced as a health and safety measure, which the UK government contested, but the ECJ confirmed that this was the correct basis for this law.[13] The introduction of the employment title has made clear that the sensitive areas of employment policy will be coordinated under the OMC despite the existence of a Treaty base for legislation under the traditional community methods.

23.9.2 The open method of coordination

The OMC is a new method of policy coordination, which is being applied to new areas of EU policy. To understand this method it is necessary to contrast it with the traditional or classical community method – the coordination of policy by harmonized legislation. The classical method has the following characteristics:

- *Supranational:* Laws agreed on a Commission proposal by co-decision between the Council (qualified majority vote; QMV – see chapter 3) and the European Parliament (EP).
- *Uniform:* EC laws provide the basis of the policy, which is applied in the same way across the EU.
- *Enforcement by penalties and incentives:* Member states have to introduce and implement the legislation. Failure to do this could ultimately lead to fines. Where expenditure is involved, compliance with the rules is required to receive funding.
- *Oversight:* The Commission is responsible for the operation of the policy, typically delegated to member states. Periodic review occurs on the basis of Commission reports, which are considered by the Council and the European Parliament.

The OMC has somewhat different characteristics:

- *Intergovernmental:* Guidelines, not laws, based on a joint report by the Commission and the Council, with the Council making the decision by qualified majority after consulting the European Parliament.
- *Subsidiarity:* The guidelines contain targets and suggest areas where action is needed but policies are entirely at the discretion of each member state.
- *Enforcement by recommendation, peer pressure and benchmarking:* Recommendations can be addressed to member states but there are no penalties for non-compliance and no financial incentives. But there is peer pressure from other member states, possible adverse publicity for failure to achieve benchmarks, and learning from the successes and failures of other countries.
- *Oversight:* This is provided by the Council and to a limited extent the EP on the basis of reports by the Commission and the Council.

Thus the OMC is a flexible, de-centralized instrument of policy coordination leaving the implementation of measures defined by the EU broadly to the member states. The method operates through persuasion, peer pressure ('naming, blaming and shaming'), mutual socialization,

epistemic convergence, public accountability and experimental learning, and includes elements of flexibility, subsidiarity, multi-level and policy integration, inclusion and participation, deliberation and knowledge-sharing (CEC, 2002m). The 'OMC represents a new form of regulation, that is softer than the classical legalistic approach, but is more than a simple non-binding recommendation or a political declaration' (De La Porte and Pochet, 2002, p. 12). It can be defined as a new form of soft coordination within the framework of EU decision-making and intergovernmental cooperation procedure incorporating supranational elements. By issuing guidelines, the OMC develops a relatively clearly defined EU policy in areas which have traditionally been out of the EU remit. Thus, even if the OMC has no binding forces (one of its main weaknesses), it contributes to the development of common views and ideas when it comes to problem-solving in the EU.

23.9.3 The EES process

The EES is part of the annual general economic policy coordination process in the Broad Economic Policy Guidelines, which reviews and coordinates macroeconomic policy and economic reform (see chapter 12). The Employment Guidelines (EGs) is the document that the EES contributes to this process. The EG specify the objectives and policies to be pursued by member states to achieve the overall employment targets. The EGs are accompanied by Employment Recommendations (ERs) which identify the particular employment problems of each member state and indicate what actions are necessary to tackle these problems. The EGs and ERs are adopted by the Council on a Commission proposal, acting by a qualified majority, after consulting the EP, the Economic and Social Committee, the Committee of the Regions and the Employment Committee (see chapter 3).

The EGs, and more particularly the ERs, are derived from the Joint Employment Report (JER) prepared by the Commission and the Council. The JER provides an overview of the employment situation and an assessment of the progress made by the member states in the implementation of the Employment Guidelines in the previous year. The remaining challenges for the member states are also highlighted. The JER contains both an analysis of progress across the EU under the major agreed objectives and guidelines, and a brief country-by-country review. Key common indicators underpin the analysis and are summarized in the annexes. The analysis in the JER in turn draws upon the reports on the member states; the National Action Programmes (NAPs). The NAPs describe national performance against EES targets and indicators under the various headings, the measures taken and proposals for further action. They are drawn up by national governments in conjunction with lower tiers of government and in consultation with the social partners. This annual cycle can be characterized as a permanent monitoring and review process through the JER, the recommendations to the member states and peer review of policies. This cycle is accompanied by a multi-annual (medium-term/five-year) evaluation of the EES, in which the national and the overall progress of EU employment policy is assessed and reviewed.

EES objectives have shown considerable stability. Until the 2003 reforms they were grouped around four pillars: employability, entrepreneurship, adaptability and equal opportunities. The employability and equal opportunities pillars contained specific employment objectives. The entrepreneurship and adaptability pillars were concerned with improving employment performance by enhancing the business environment and the operation of businesses. Under the employability pillar, five objectives have been promoted since 1998 (Council of the EU, 1997b); the 1999 Employment Guidelines (Council of the EU, 1999b) added one more and the 2001 guidelines (Council of the EU, 2001) another two. This means that in 2002 (Council of the EU, 2002b) the employability pillar had eight aims:

1. reducing youth unemployment;
2. prevention of long-term unemployment;
3. more employment-friendly tax and benefit systems to reduce poverty traps and provide incentives for the unemployed/inactive to seek employment;
4. developing skills in the context of lifelong learning: thus the education and training system is to equip individuals to enter employment and be able to adapt to changes in the employment needs of the economy;
5. combating discrimination and promoting social inclusion by access to employment: this reflects the growing interest in social inclusion and relates to disadvantaged groups generally, particularly the disabled and ethnic minorities;
6. developing policies for active ageing: this relates to the need to raise the employment rate of older workers, as well as to the need to encourage a more active retirement, with hopefully fewer demands on health and social welfare services among the elderly;
7. active policies to develop job matching: some unemployment is the result not of a lack of jobs, but of the inability to match the unemployed with the available jobs (vacancies). Thus employment rates can be raised and unemployment rates reduced if the matching efficiency of the labour market is improved;
8. to prevent and to combat emerging bottlenecks: with structural change a fact of life in production and employment, it is important that the labour force has the skills, training and mobility required for the jobs that are available.

The second pillar, entrepreneurship and job creation, aimed to create and support new businesses, new sources of employment and certain sectors of the economy, particularly services. These aims relate to the general improvement of the economic environment, and therefore the employment performance of the economy.

The third pillar was adaptability: modernizing work organizations is concerned with the reconciliation of contractual/working arrangements with the needs of a more competitive and knowledge-intensive economy, or in other words flexibility with job security. Thus although there are minimum standards of employment protection, employment security is seen more in terms of functional flexibility, achieved through high-quality training and lifelong learning. Thus this pillar is concerned with improving employment performance and the quality of work.

The fourth pillar, equal opportunities between men and women, was related directly to the 60 per cent employment rate target for women. Although the target is set in terms of the employment rate of women, it can also be seen as a means of reducing female unemployment or inactivity, the increased employment implying increased female participation. Participation is to be raised by policies to reconcile work and family life, such as childcare and parental leave. The quality of female employment is also important and this is to be assessed primarily in terms of the pay gap between men and women. Thus this becomes an additional objective of employment policy.

With the interim evaluation of the EES (CEC, 2002p), the EGs were revised for the period 2003 to 2010. The Commission identified four major issues for EES reform: first, the need to set clear objectives in response to the policy challenges; second, the need to simplify the policy guidelines without undermining their effectiveness; third, the need to improve governance and partnership in the execution of the strategy; and fourth, the need to ensure greater consistency and complementarity with respect to other relevant EU processes, notably the BEPG.

Based on these priorities and on the decision of the 2002 Barcelona European Council, the synchronization of the Luxembourg process with the BEPG and the Internal Market Strategy (IMS) was proposed by the Commission in September 2002 in order to reinforce the implementation of the Lisbon targets and to put more emphasis on the medium-term aspect of the EES. The 'Employment package will thus benefit from being more directly related to the overall policy approach . . . [and from improving] the complementarity and mutually supportive character of the two sets of instruments' (CEC, 2002n, p. 21). The Commission now presents the implementation and evaluation of the BEPG, the EES and the IMS at the same time each year in January, and after the Spring European Council Summit in April, the guidelines on economic and employment policy. This synchronization strengthens policy coordination in the socioeconomic area.

The current EES splits the employment package. The first part, the *Joint Employment Report*, is presented by the Commission, as part of the *implementation package* in January each year before the Spring European Summit. The second part, the Commission's proposals for EGs and the recommendations, is submitted after the Spring Summit as part of the *guidelines package* together with the BEPG in April. The Council adopts the guidelines in June after the European Council meeting and the NAPs are submitted in October, completing the annual cycle.

The objectives of the guidelines are to be consistent with and complementary to the BEPGs, to better respond to the demands of an enlarged EU. Instead of the rather ambiguous pillars of the old policy there are now three clearer overarching objectives. The EGs and the BEPGs will only be fully reviewed and amended every three years. In the intervening years they are only changed if necessary. Nevertheless, annual proposals for guidelines are kept as required by the treaty. The objectives and policies of the new EES were defined in Council of the EU (2003c); there are three overarching and interrelated objectives of the new EES:

1. full employment
2. improving quality and productivity at work
3. strengthening social cohesion and inclusion.

In 2003 these were to be achieved by ten guidelines, but the 2005 EGs (Council of the EU, 2005a) specified eight guidelines for the 2005–8 period:

i.   Implement employment policies aimed at achieving full employment, improving quality and productivity at work, and strengthening social and territorial cohesion. This overall guideline aimed to raise employment rates by modernizing social protection systems, by improving the adaptability of workers and enterprises, and by investment in human capital.
ii. Promote a lifecycle approach to work. This requires increasing employment of young people, increasing female participation and reducing gender gaps, improving work–life balance, active ageing (increasing participation of older workers), and modernizing social protection systems to make them sustainable and enticing participation.

iii. Ensure inclusive labour markets, enhance work attractiveness, and make work pay for job-seekers, particularly disadvantaged people and the inactive.

iv. Improve the matching of labour market needs, modernize employment services, reduce barriers to mobility, manage migration and ensure skills meet labour market needs.

v. Promote flexibility combined with employment security and reduced labour market segmentation, having due regard to the role of the social partners. This required reviewing employment legislation, reducing undeclared work, better management of change, innovative and adaptable work organizations, and support for transitions in occupational status.

vi. Ensure employment-friendly labour cost developments and wage-setting mechanisms, the right framework for wage bargaining and reduction of the tax burden on the low-paid.

vii. Expand and improve investment in human capital by inclusive education and training policies, by reducing early school leavers, and by lifelong learning strategies open to all.

viii. Adapt education and training systems in response to new competence requirements: improving the attractiveness, openness and quality of education and training, broadening the supply of education and training opportunities, easing access to education and training, and developing competences for future skill requirements.

It is arguable how much of a change this represents. In practice the EGs have not changed very much from year to year. Full NAPs will only be required every three years and intermediate reports concentrate on new policy developments and focus on the implementation. In reality the NAPs already concentrate on new policy developments and implementation, so the extent to which this reform has reduced the work involved in the process is questionable. The clearer objectives may, however, help the policy become more effective.

23.9.4 The EES and employment policy

The EES is designed to improve EU employment performance by encouraging member states to redesign their national employment policies, incorporating successful features from other countries. This process is supposed to occur as a result of policy learning, peer review, benchmarking and naming and shaming. While the EES could be criticized for its lack of sanctions, this was inevitable in such a sensitive policy area, and in any case the effectiveness of such sanctions could be questioned in view of their failure in the coordination of economic policy (see chapter 12). However, the effectiveness of the policy can be questioned: it is difficult to establish an impact on national policy, and there does not seem to be a clear institutional pathway through which national policy is influenced (Watt, 2000). Naming and shaming is unlikely to be effective because of the low public profile of the policy, with very little debate in national parliaments or reporting in the press. Interviews with policymakers in the UK and Germany suggested that the effect of the strategy on national policymaking was very limited (Ardy and Umbach, 2004). The policies introduced were based on national preferences and priorities, although the EES may have had some impact on agenda setting. Similarly the impact of the peer review process has been minor (Casey and Gold, 2005). The involvement of the social partners in the process was also rather perfunctory and the process was predominantly in the hands of an expert elite. One of the more significant attempts at reform, the Hartz reforms in Germany, do not seem to reflect the EES (Watt, 2003), although Kemmerling and Bruttel (2006) find evidence of some policy diffusion. The effect of the EES is also reduced by the extent to which member states can water down Commission proposals so that the restraints on national policy are substantially reduced (Watt, 2004, pp. 131–3). It may be that the effect of the strategy is more subtle, in the long term influencing the views of this elite and thus gradually influencing policy.

National employment policies have moved in the way the EES intended. The duration of unemployment benefits has been reduced and conditions tightened, but their generosity has not been decreased. These changes are shared with the rest of the OECD, and some EU15 countries have not implemented changes (OECD, 2006c, p. 58). Similar developments can be found for labour taxation, including social security contributions and active labour market policies (ALMP), although the record is more patchy for the latter (OECD, 2006c, pp. 89, 70). There are, however, concerns over the extent to which declared intentions carry through to policy; spending on ALMP has not increased despite falling 'passive' labour market expenditure (ETUI, 2003, p. 19). What all this seems to indicate is that governments have implemented EES policies where this fitted in with their own priorities (Zeitlin, 2005), but whether it will be effective in shaping national employment policies in the long term is an open question.

23.10 The EES and EU employment performance

The fundamental problem in assessing the effect of any policy is to identify what would have happened in its absence, i.e. the *anti-monde* (see chapter 9). In the case of the EES this problem is complicated still further, as argued above, by the weak link between the EES and national employment policy. However, there has been a general drift towards the employment policies contained in the EES. This section considers whether this shift has been accompanied by improved employment performance, without ascribing causation.

There is a very wide range of possible measures of employment performance and these different measures may rate countries' performance differently. These measures are also subject to ambiguities, which may distort their value. For example, the EU has adopted employment rates as the measure of employment performance partly because government policies distorted measured unemployment. The measures of performance considered here are employment and unemployment rates, and the relationship between economic growth and employment. The EU incorporates a wide range of performance on these and other employment indicators – one reason why it was

thought that the policy learning process incorporated in the EES would be productive in this area.

23.10.1 Employment rates in the EU

The employment rate (ER) is the number of employed and self-employed divided by the total population of working age. This is probably the most reliable measure of employment performance; it avoids problems associated with targeting unemployment such as the use of measures to manipulate the figures, examples of which are early retirement and the misuse of benefits (see section 23.5.3). There are still some problems with ERs which may be distorted by an increase in part-time work.[14] ERs also overemphasize the benefits of paid employment and undervalue the social activities of the economically inactive, such as childcare. The EU wants to increase the employment rate to improve the sustainability of welfare policy by reducing the dependency ratio – those not employed as a proportion of those employed.

ERs are also sensitive to cyclical factors, rising in booms and falling in recessions, so in analysing trends it is important to separate the cyclical from the long-term trends. This separation is complicated by the possibility that factors such as labour market reforms may also permit higher rates of economic growth.

As can be seen from figure 23.2, employment rates have risen in most of the EU15, with the exception of Austria and Germany where they have stagnated. Average ERs rose from 59.8 per cent in 1994 to 60.7 per cent in 1997 and 65.2 per cent in 2005.[15] Only four EU countries meet the EES target of a 70 per cent overall ER: Denmark, the Netherlands, Sweden and the UK. Austria, Finland, Ireland and Portugal are close to the target, with Ireland and Finland showing impressive employment growth. Germany, Luxembourg, Spain, France, Belgium and Greece have ERs in the 60–65 per cent range. Spain has shown a particularly impressive increase in employment. Italy is the only EU15 country with an ER below 60 per cent (at 57.6 per cent in 2005); however, even this laggard has experienced a recent improvement in employment.

The process of transition, and in particular structural change, in the Central and Eastern

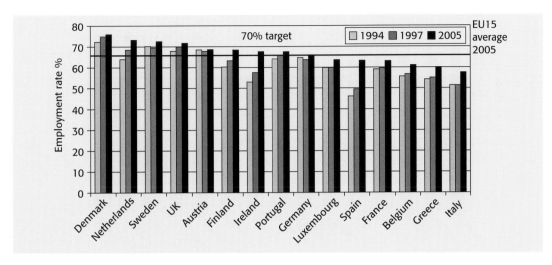

Figure 23.2 EU15 total employment rates, 1994–2005. *Source*: Eurostat (2006d).

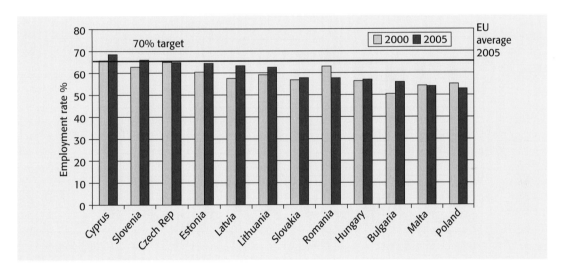

Figure 23.3 New member states total employment rates, 2000–5. *Source*: Eurostat (2006d).

European countries (CEECs) led to a substantial reduction in ERs (figure 23.3). In most of these countries the trough of employment associated with transition has passed and ER rates are rising again, due to the countries' comparatively rapid rates of economic growth: unweighted average ERs rose from 59.8 per cent in 2000 to 60.4 per cent in 2005. Cyprus and Slovenia have growing employment and their rate is near the 70 per cent target. The Czech Republic, with stable employment, and Estonia, Latvia and Lithuania, with growing employment, all have ERs of between 60

and 65 per cent. Slovakia, Hungary and Bulgaria have relatively low but improving ERs, in Malta ERs are stable and in Romania and Poland they are declining. Both Romania and Poland have large agricultural sectors the contraction of which is likely to exacerbate the employment situation for a considerable period.

Total ERs hide large differences between different categories of workers such as female and older workers, for which the EES has set targets. Female ERs are increasing in all EU15 countries (figure 23.4): the average rate increased from 49.3 per cent

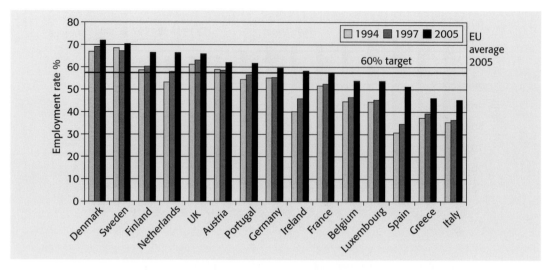

Figure 23.4 EU15 female employment rates, 1994–2005. *Source*: Eurostat (2006d).

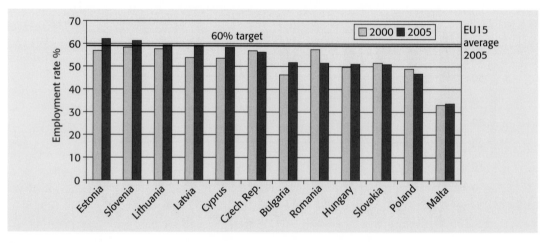

Figure 23.5 New member states female employment rates, 2000–4. *Source*: Eurostat (2006d).

in 1994 to 57.4 per cent in 2005. The fastest growth of female employment is not surprisingly occurring in the countries with the fastest overall employment growth, Spain and Ireland. But even countries with static overall ERs like Austria and Germany saw rising female ERs, with male rates decreasing. The differences between countries remain substantial, with Danish and Swedish ERs exceeding 70 per cent; Finland, Austria, the UK and Portugal also meet the 60 per cent target. Germany, Ireland and France have female ERs at the target, and Belgium, Luxembourg and Spain's

ERs are in the 51–4 per cent range. Greece and Italy have much lower rates at 46.1 per cent and 45.3 per cent respectively.

Female ERs, like overall ERs, are lower in the NMS, with an unweighted average of 53.5 per cent in 2005 (figure 23.5). These moderate rates of employment growth reflect the employment situation and, unlike the EU15, some NMS (Romania, Slovakia and Poland) have falling female employment. By contrast, Estonia and Slovenia meet the EU target and Lithuania, Latvia and Cyprus are close to the target. The Czech Republic, Bulgaria,

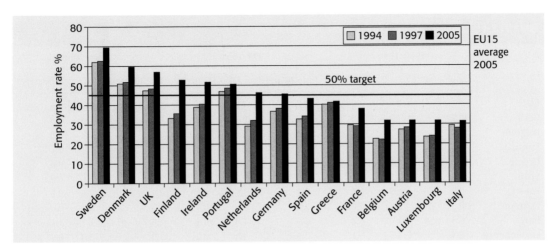

Figure 23.6 EU15 employment rates of older workers, 1994–2005. *Source*: Eurostat (2006d).

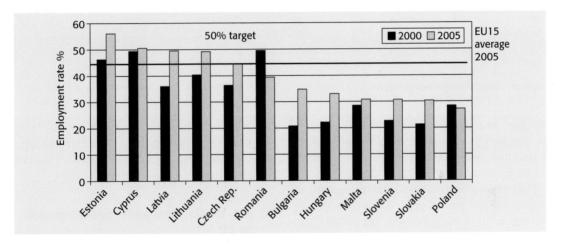

Figure 23.7 New member states employment rates of older workers, 2000–4. *Source*: Eurostat (2006d).

Romania, Hungary and Slovenia also have female ERs above 50 per cent. Poland has a rate of 46.8 per cent and Malta's rate is very low at 33.7 per cent.

There are very wide differences in the employment rates of older workers[16] in the EU15 (figure 23.6), ranging from 69.4 per cent in Sweden to 31.4 per cent in Italy; these differences are the result of a combination of factors, such as variation in statutory retirement age, generosity of pensions, the extent to which retirement is used instead of unemployment and the overall employment situation. Across the EU15 the ERs of older workers is improving; Sweden, Denmark, the UK, Finland, Ireland and Portugal already meet the 50 per cent

target. The Netherlands, Germany, Spain and Greece have rates of between 41 and 46 per cent, while France, Belgium, Luxembourg and Italy have rates of between 31 and 38 per cent.

In the NMS the ERs of older workers are low (figure 23.7), reflecting the lower overall levels of employment but also the difficulties older workers face adjusting to a rapidly changing economy. However, the ERs of older workers are now rising in ten of these countries, although not in Romania and Poland. Only Estonia and Cyprus meet the 50 per cent target, but Latvia and Lithuania are very close. The Czech Republic has a rate of 44.5 per cent, and Romania, Bulgaria,

Table 23.1 EU15 employment and GDP growth, 1980–2005

	1980–1989			1990–1997			1998–2005		
	Employment	GDP	Elasticity	Employment	GDP	Elasticity	Employment	GDP	Elasticity
EU15		2.3		0.2	1.9	0.1	1.2	2.2	0.6
Germany	0.9	1.9	0.5	0.2	2.4	0.1	0.4	1.4	0.3
Belgium		2.2		0.3	2.0	0.1	1.0	2.0	0.5
Denmark	0.4	1.4	0.3	0.1	2.3	0.0	0.4	1.9	0.2
Greece	1.1	0.8	1.4	0.4	1.5	0.3	1.2	4.2	0.3
Spain	0.4	2.7	0.2	1.0	2.2	0.4	3.5	3.8	0.9
France	0.2	2.5	0.1	0.1	1.6	0.1	1.1	2.4	0.5
Ireland	−0.5	3.1	−0.2	2.8	6.4	0.4	4.3	6.8	0.6
Italy	0.6	2.6	0.2	−0.1	1.4	−0.1	1.5	1.3	1.2
Luxembourg	0.5	4.6	0.1	0.9	4.1	0.2	1.9	5.0	0.4
Netherlands	1.1	2.0	0.5	1.9	2.7	0.7	1.0	2.0	0.5
Austria	0.1	2.0	0.1	0.5	2.5	0.2	0.6	2.2	0.3
Portugal	0.0	3.4	0.0	0.3	2.6	0.1	1.0	2.0	0.5
Finland	0.9	3.6	0.2	−1.7	0.7	−2.5	1.4	3.1	0.5
Sweden	0.8	2.3	0.3	−1.5	1.0	−1.4	1.0	3.0	0.3
UK	0.6	2.4	0.3	−0.1	1.9	0.0	1.0	2.8	0.4
EU15 − (B+G)	0.5	2.4	0.2	0.2	1.8	0.1	1.5	2.5	0.6

Source: CEC (2006d), own calculations.

Hungary, Malta, Slovenia and Slovakia have rates in the 30–9 per cent range. Older workers in Poland have an ER of only 27.2 per cent, reflecting the difficult overall employment situation.

The picture which emerges from this analysis of employment is one of general improvement in relation to all three EES targets. Within this generally improving situation there is considerable variation in performance in relation to both the targets and the general development of employment. The employment situation in the NMS is considerably worse than in the EU15 but with the pace of transition slowing and with the benefit of relatively rapid economic growth, the employment situation is improving. The countries in the EU15 performing well on these benchmarks are Denmark, Sweden, the UK, Denmark, the Netherlands and Finland, with Ireland on present trends to join them soon. Weak performers are Belgium, Greece and Italy, with Germany living on its past performance with recent poor employment growth. In the NMS the performances of Estonia, Cyprus, Latvia, Lithuania and the Czech Republic are comparatively good. Malta has fairly

weak performance but Romania's deteriorating employment situation is a cause for concern. Poland has both very weak performance on the benchmarks and a deteriorating situation.

23.10.2 Employment and economic growth in the EU

The improvement in EU employment since 1997 may be due to the EES or it may be the result of other factors affecting employment, most notably higher economic growth. As can be seen from table 23.1, the average growth rate of EU15 GDP was higher over the period 1998–2005 (2.2 per cent) than it had been during 1990–7 (1.9 per cent), but lower than in the decade before that (2.3 per cent); hence some of the improvements in employment are as a result of this higher growth. The growth of employment and GDP is analysed for the member states and for EU15 minus Belgium and Germany – EU15 minus (B+G). Belgium is excluded because data is not available for the whole period. The substantial upheaval in Germany caused by unification means that it is atypical and trends over this period are difficult to assess.[17] For this EU15 minus (B+G) grouping it can be seen that GDP growth averaged 2.4 per cent in the 1980s but employment increased only 0.5 per cent, giving an employment GDP elasticity of 0.2 per cent.[18] The growth in 1998–2005 was almost the same (2.5 per cent) but employment increased by 1.5 per cent, an elasticity of 0.6. The period 1990–7 was one of slow growth, only 1.8 per cent per year, and employment only increased by 0.2 per cent, an elasticity of 0.1 per cent. This is a very crude assessment because the relationship is probably not linear: there is likely to be a threshold level of GDP growth below which employment will contract, which may account for the very poor performance during 1990–7. But it is apparent that the improved recent performance is not just the result of increased GDP growth.

The improved employment intensity of growth is not all good news, however, because of its relationship with productivity. Employment will be equal to the increase in GDP minus the increase in productivity. For example if GDP growth is 2 per cent and labour productivity growth is 2 per cent, then the existing employed workers can produce all of this increase in output and employment growth will be zero. Employment can be increased by raising the growth rate or by decreasing productivity growth. The increased employment intensity of EU growth means that the growth of labour productivity in the EU has slowed, which implies more but not better jobs. This suggests an inconsistency in a strategy trying to improve the employment intensity of growth while raising productivity. Lower labour productivity growth may reflect factors that are perhaps less damning than this implies; to an extent it is the result of fewer hours worked (see chapter 14). EU unemployment has fallen most heavily on workers with lower skills and lower productivity: employment of these lower-skilled workers, while obviously desirable in its own right, would tend to lower overall productivity growth.

23.10.3 Unemployment in the EU

The unemployment rate is the number of unemployed divided by the labour force (the number in employment and self-employment plus the unemployed). In the past measurement of the unemployed was ambiguous but now ILO standardized unemployment is the generally accepted measure: the number of people not in employment who are looking for work, measured by surveys. The other side of the ratio, the labour force, remains problematic; the labour force equals the population of working age minus the inactive (those not in employment or looking for work). The inactive is not a stable group. It is affected by the proportion of women who work, which is increasing over time; the increasing numbers of full-time students; early retirement; and other factors. Despite falling unemployment in the UK there are over two million economically inactive people who want jobs (Barham, 2002).[19] Two significant groups of working age are inactive rather than unemployed as a result of government measures: excessive numbers on incapacity benefit, and those on government training and employment schemes. Incapacity benefit is more important: in the UK it has become an alternative unemployment benefit system, with long-term benefits at higher levels than the UK unemployment benefit Job Seeker's Allowance (JSA) – see Beatty et al. (2002, pp. 10–17). In 2005 1.4 million people were unemployed but more than 1.5 million were claiming invalidity benefit. In all probability at least half of these claimants would be willing to work if jobs were available (Ardy and Umbach, 2004; Beatty et al., 2002), increasing the overall unemployment rate from 4.7 per cent to 7.2 per cent. This problem of hidden unemployment distorting the figures is not confined to the UK. For example, in Sweden recorded unemployment was relatively low at 6.3 per cent in 2004, but total unemployment, including hidden unemployment, is estimated to be much higher at 15 per cent (Bengttson et al., 2006). Hence, comparisons of unemployment need to be made carefully.

EU15 unemployment in 2005 ranged from 4.3 per cent in Ireland to 9.8 per cent in Greece (figure 23.8). Some countries have been very successful in reducing unemployment: Ireland, the UK, Denmark, and more recently Finland and Spain. But there are also countries where unemployment has risen: Austria, Luxembourg and Portugal, which have relatively

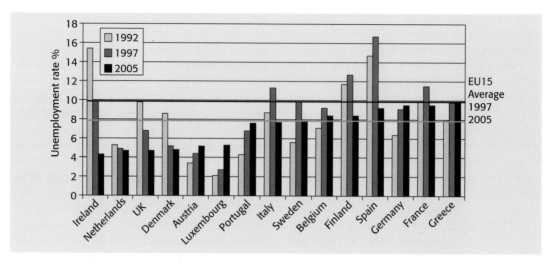

Figure 23.8 EU15 unemployment rates, 1992–2005. *Source*: CEC (2006n).

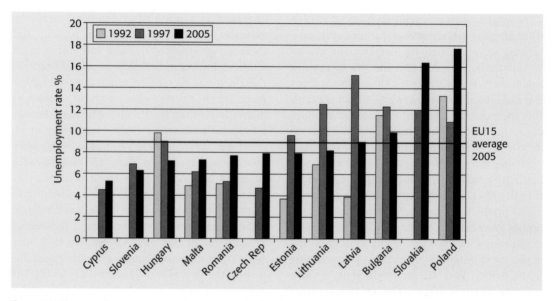

Figure 23.9 New member states unemployment, 1992–2005. *Source*: CEC (2006n).

low unemployment, and Germany and Greece which have high unemployment.

The NMS had an even wider range of unemployment rates in 2005: 5.3 per cent in Cyprus and 17.7 per cent in Poland. Unemployment in most of the NMS is below the EU15 average, but in Latvia, Bulgaria, Slovakia and Poland it is above it (figure 23.9). Latvia, Lithuania and Bulgaria have achieved recent large reductions in, but unemploy-

ment is rising in Cyprus, Malta, Romania, the Czech Republic, Slovakia and Poland. Unemployment remains a very significant problem for Slovakia and Poland.

The incidence of unemployment varies among different groups within society, with younger and older workers being particularly vulnerable, and the EES targets reductions in the unemployment rates of these groups. Young people are particularly

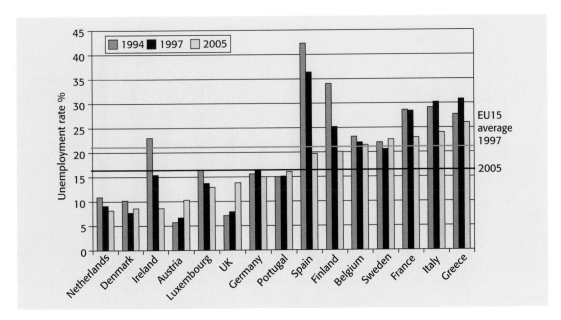

Figure 23.10 EU youth unemployment rates, 1994–2005. *Source*: Eurostat (2006d).

vulnerable to unemployment, because they have the potentially problematic transition from education to employment. In addition they are at a disadvantage in the labour market because of their lack of experience and an employment record, especially in countries where the overall unemployment rate is high. Thus, in 1994 Spain's youth unemployment rate peaked at 42.3 per cent (figure 23.10).

Youth unemployment remains high in the EU but has been falling in most EU15 countries, especially in Ireland, Spain and Finland, but it has risen in Austria, Luxembourg, Portugal and Sweden. The difference between the rate of youth and overall unemployment has also narrowed, but still remains substantial. Although generally low rates of overall unemployment are associated with low rates of youth unemployment and vice versa, there are some exceptions. Germany has above average overall unemployment but below average youth unemployment; Sweden has the opposite.

Similarly, youth unemployment is a problem for the NMS, eight of which have rates near the EU15 average and four (Bulgaria, Slovakia, Romania and Poland) significantly above (figure 23.11). Again the high youth unemployment is associated with high overall unemployment. Youth unemployment has

fallen significantly in Lithuania, Bulgaria, Latvia, Estonia and Slovakia but it has been rising in Hungary, Romania, Cyprus, Poland and the Czech Republic.

The accuracy of the youth unemployment rate as a measure of the youth employment situation is, however, questionable. The central problem is that a substantial and increasing proportion of the 15–24 age group is in full-time education and they may be employed, unemployed or inactive. The unemployment rate compares the total of 15–24-year-olds who are unemployed with the sum of the employed and the unemployed. Hence youth unemployment rates are sensitive to the number of young people in full-time education, and the proportion of this group that works. Thus comparisons of youth unemployment rates across countries will be distorted by variations in these proportions.[20]

Most unemployment is for relatively short periods, but some people remain unemployed for lengthy periods. Long-term unemployment is not only dispiriting for the unemployed, it also affects the employability of those involved, who can drift into economic inactivity. Long-term unemployment is sensitive to the overall level of unemployment because when unemployment rises, the period of

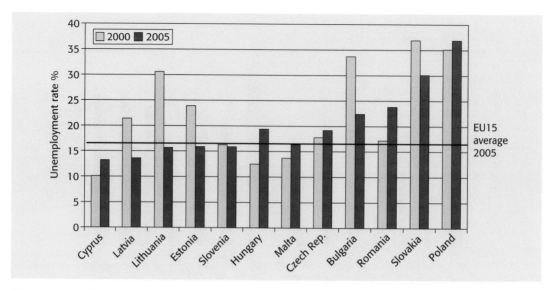

Figure 23.11 New member states youth unemployment rates, 2000–5. *Source*: Eurostat (2006d).

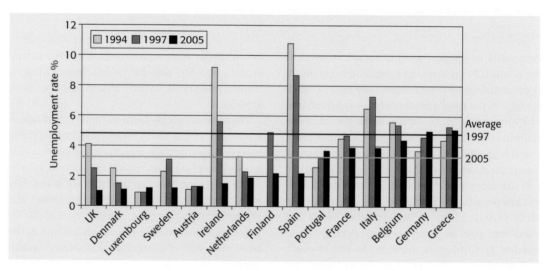

Figure 23.12 EU15 long-term unemployment, 1994–2005. *Source*: Eurostat (2006d).

job search lengthens. Also employers can be more selective. So for vulnerable groups, such as those without formal educational qualifications, long-term unemployment increases (Dickens et al., 2001a). Undoubtedly, cyclical factors have contributed to the fall in long-term unemployment in the EU.

Long-term unemployment is measured by the proportion of the labour force that has been looking for work for more than a year. In the EU15 such unemployment has fallen dramatically; the average has dropped from 5.0 per cent in 1994 to 3.3 per cent in 2005, with particularly large falls in Spain and Ireland (figure 23.12). However, Portugal, Germany and Greece have seen increasing levels of long-term unemployment. Care is needed in interpreting these statistics because they are sensitive to government measures to cope with unemployment – the problem of hidden unemployment, already discussed.

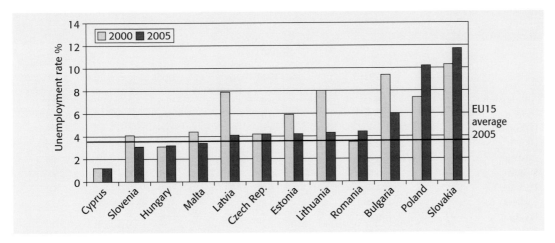

Figure 23.13 New member states long-term unemployment, 2000–5. *Source*: Eurostat (2006d).

The high overall level of unemployment in the NMS is associated with structural change in these economies; therefore they also have high levels of long-term unemployment (figure 23.13). Only Cyprus, Slovenia, Hungary and Malta have long-term unemployment rates below the EU15 average and Poland and Slovakia have particularly high rates. However, in most countries long-term unemployment is either falling or stable, the exceptions being Romania, Poland and Slovakia.

23.10.4 The natural rate of unemployment

The measures of labour market performance considered so far are partial; one possible measure of overall performance is the natural rate of unemployment (NRU, NAIRU or NAWRU).[21] This is the level of (structural) unemployment, reconcilable with a constant rate of inflation. This derives from the expectations-augmented Phillips curve (see section 10.3.2) in monopolistic product and labour markets (Layard et al., 1991). According to this view structural unemployment represents an equilibrium in the sense that, once established, workers and employers have no incentive to change real wages. The NRU equilibrium occurs when expectations are met with wages rising in line with prices after taking into account the growth of productivity. Structural unemployment will not necessarily be constant. Over time if structural factors in the economy change, then it will change (McMorrow

and Roeger, 2000). It could be argued that the NAIRU follows the actual employment rate because of persistence effects (Gordon, 1998) or that there might be a multiplicity of NAIRU (Akerlof et al., 2000; De Vincenti, 2001). If the NRU is a little more than the existing unemployment rate, then its utility in explaining differences in unemployment is clearly diminished. Obviously, care is need in interpreting the concept of the NRU and in its estimation (Staiger et al., 1997).

Bearing in mind these qualifications, it can be seen (table 23.2) that during 1991–2005 there has been only a marginal improvement in the EU15 NAIRU, but this apparent stability conceals large variations in performance between countries, from 3.5 per cent in the Netherlands to 9.7 per cent in Greece. There have been reductions in the NAIRU in nine member states, particularly spectacularly in Ireland; this reinforces the general impression of improving EU15 labour market performance. France's NAWRU has remained relatively stable but in Sweden, Portugal, Austria and Germany it is estimated to have increased, albeit by relatively small amounts.

There is even greater variability in the NMS, with the NAIRU varying between 4.9 per cent in Slovenia and 18.1 per cent in Lithuania. In most of these countries the NAIRU is increasing – significantly in the case of Lithuania, Cyprus, Hungary, the Czech Republic and Poland. In Malta, Estonia and Slovakia the NAIRU is decreasing – by

Table 23.2 Non-accelerating wage rate of unemployment, 1991–2005

	NAWRU %			% change
	1991	1997	2005	1991–2005
Netherlands	6.1	4.5	3.5	−2.6
Ireland	15.0	9.4	3.8	−11.2
Denmark	6.4	5.8	4.2	−2.2
UK	8.4	6.7	4.7	−3.7
Austria	3.4	3.9	4.9	1.5
Sweden	3.9	7.1	5.1	1.2
Portugal	5.4	5.2	6.7	1.3
Finland	8.0	12.8	7.4	−0.6
Belgium	8.4	8.1	7.5	−0.9
Italy	9.3	10.1	8.1	−1.2
Germany	6.7	7.5	8.7	2.0
Spain	15.1	14.3	9.3	−5.8
France	*9.2*	*10.3*	*9.4*	*0.2*
Greece	7.4	9.1	9.7	2.3
EU15	**8.4**	**8.6**	**7.5**	**−0.9**
Slovenia		4.3	4.9	0.6
Estonia		8.3	5.9	−2.4
Slovakia		6.5	6.0	−0.5
Latvia		6.0	7.4	1.4
Cyprus		2.4	7.5	5.1
Hungary		4.0	8.7	4.7
Malta		14.7	9.6	−5.1
Czech Republic		6.7	10.0	3.3
Poland		12.3	15.1	2.8
Lithuania		9.5	18.1	8.6

Source: CEC (2006d).

quite large amounts in the case of Malta and Estonia.

23.11 Conclusion

There is little doubt that employment policy in EU member states has changed since the introduction of the EES and that this has been associated with an improvement in employment performance. What is less clear is the association between these changes. Similar change in employment policy (OECD, 2006c) and employment performance has occurred across the whole of the OECD (OECD, 2006d) so the independent influence of the EES is difficult to identify. The OMC used

by the EES seems to work in a similar way to the OECD job strategy by influencing the conventional wisdom on employment policy, so its added impact seems to stem from the more intensive nature of the interaction between the EU and national governments and administrations. The increasing acknowledgement of the importance of the interaction between different aspects of employment policy and the national institutional setting means that the national differentiation of the common policy has become more important. So the continued success of the EES depends not only upon its ability to identify desirable employment policy reform but to appropriately differentiate between member states – not an easy task.

NOTES

1 This chapter was contributed by Doreen Collins in the first six editions, but she was joined by Robert Salais in the last. Their departure is not meant to detract from their excellent contribution, only to reflect the fact that a proper treatment of the subject would require a whole book in its own right and that employment has become not only the dominant issue in this area, but impinges on practically all the policies covered in this book. Our acknowledgement of their contribution is clearly reflected in how much we have relied on them in sections 23.1–5.

2 The ITR is the total tax revenue as a proportion of the value of the activity being taxed; for labour it is total income tax and social security as a proportion of income. The ITR is a measure of the tax burden on the particular economic activity.

3 The lowest rates in the EU15 are in the UK (24.8 per cent) and Ireland (26.3 per cent).

4 But there may be other institutional arrangements to set effective wage floors.

5 Although since the mid-1990s there has been a reduction in EU15 unemployment.

6 Or destruction.

7 Problems could arise, for example, if low wages were too high to generate sufficient employment for the low skilled.

8 Or more usually the wage curve that reconciles the demands of trade unions with those of employers. Since both have market power, wages are determined by a bargaining process.

9 Since according to these models, unemployment is near to its natural rate.

10 The level of unemployment benefits as a percentage of earnings.

11 Coordination can be achieved by centralized bargaining or by institutional features as in Germany.

12 So stabilizing the macro economy will lead to a reduction in the NRU.

13 This was at a time when the social protocol, including what is now Article 137, did not apply to the UK. What did apply was QMV for health and safety measures but unanimity for measures relating to the rights and interests of employed persons (Article 95). Now social policy applies to the UK, as working time is clearly QMV under Article 137 a or b.

14 Eurostat figures include everyone who has had at least one hour's paid work in the week of the survey.

15 Statistics are from Eurostat (2006d) unless otherwise stated.

16 Aged 55–64 years.

17 There are also problems with Finland and Sweden which suffered severe recessions in the 1990s.

18 For every 1 per cent GDP increases, employment increases by 0.2 per cent.

19 Thirty-one per cent of inactive men and 26 per cent of inactive women of working age wanted a job in 2001.

20 A further complication concerns differences in the amount of work undertaken in the informal economy.

21 Or the non-accelerating inflation rate of unemployment or the non-accelerating wage rate of unemployment (NAWRU), which are equivalent.

Part VI   EU external relations

Part VI of the book deals with the external relations of the EU. Chapter 24 covers EU trade relations with its major partners within the context of the Common Commercial Policy run by the EU Commission on behalf of all EU member nations. Chapter 25 tackles EU relations with the developing world in terms of trade, aid and preferential trading arrangements.

24 EU external trade policy

MARIUS BRÜLHART AND ALAN MATTHEWS[1]

The external trade policy of the EU involves nearly one-fifth of world trade. Hence an understanding of the principles and practice of the Union's trade policy, the Common Commercial Policy (CCP), is of vital importance to any student of the global trade environment. Ongoing research on the CCP has addressed both broad themes and detailed aspects of the Union's trade policy (Gavin, 2001; Memedovic et al., 1999; OECD, 2000b; Messerlin, 2001; Meunier, 2005). The *Trade Policy Review of the EU*, the biennial publication by the World Trade Organization (WTO), provides insight into how trade specialists view the EU and, no less importantly, how the EU sees its own role. A number of features of the EU's CCP make it particularly worthy of study.[2]

First, while commercial policy originally focused on tariffs and other border measures as they affected trade in goods, the scope of the policy today is much more diverse. Policies affecting trade in services and the conditions influencing foreign investment have become increasingly important. As tariffs were reduced in successive rounds of multilateral trade negotiations to near insignificance, other policy areas which fall under the general heading of regulatory issues have become increasingly relevant to international trade: intellectual property, technical standards and regulations, competition policy, labour standards and environmental policy, to mention the most prominent. Many of these regulatory issues reach deep into the heart of domestic policy concerns, with the result that trade policy has become increasingly politicized and controversial in recent years.

Second, EU commercial policy has developed a highly complex set of trade relations with third countries, reflecting in part the way the granting of trade preferences was virtually the sole instrument of EU foreign policy in the past. The resulting hierarchy of preferential trading schemes has been determined by a mixture of trade, strategic and foreign policy concerns in which the conflicting interests of member states, as well as hard bargaining between the Union institutions and the member states, have played an important role. The 1990s saw a significant extension of EU regionalism. Following the launch of the Doha Round of multilateral trade talks in 2001, the EU announced a moratorium on further expansion of its regional trade arrangements, but this has not prevented continuing negotiations on creating such arrangements with a number of its trading partners.

Third, EU commercial policy is shaped by the Union's obligations (and reciprocal rights) under the WTO, which came into being in 1995. The purpose of the WTO is to establish and monitor the rules for trade policymaking in its members and to encourage the liberalization of trade through successive rounds of trade negotiations to reduce tariffs and other barriers to trade in goods and services. One of its core principles is that of most-favoured nation (MFN) treatment, which means that members undertake not to discriminate in their treatment of imports originating in different members (see chapter 1). The EU played a major role in the Uruguay Round Agreement conducted under the auspices of the General Agreement on Tariffs and Trade (GATT) which established the WTO. It was among the strongest proponents of the further comprehensive round of trade negotiations which was initiated in Doha, Qatar in November 2001. The suspension of the Doha Round in 2006, however, has revived the tension between the EU's commitment to multilateral trade liberalization through the WTO and its ongoing concern with regional and bilateral agreements outside that organization.

This chapter investigates these themes in five separate sections. The first describes the pattern of trade between the EU and the outside world. The second presents an overview of the principles and policy instruments of the CCP. The third considers EU trade policy specifically towards its main trading partners. The fourth contains an analysis of trade policy issues which are coming to the forefront in ongoing trade negotiations. The concluding section considers the future development of the CCP.

24.1 EU trade and specialization patterns

24.1.1 The structure of EU trade

The EU constitutes the largest trading bloc in the world. Excluding intra-EU trade, exports from the Union accounted for 18.1 per cent of world merchandise exports in 2004. The shares of the United States and Japan were 12.3 per cent and 8.5 per cent respectively (table 24.1; see chapter 5 for a historical perspective).

External trade has tended to grow about twice as fast as GDP in most parts of the world and the EU is no exception. Over the period 1995–2005, EU25 trade volumes increased by more than 6 per cent annually in real terms, compared with 2.3 per cent GDP growth. A useful aggregate measure of trade dependence is the ratio of exports plus imports of goods and services to GDP. For the EU25 this stood at 26.1 per cent in 2004, a level similar to the figures for the US (25.1 per cent) and Japan (27.0 per cent).

About 46 per cent of extra-EU trade is directed towards developed countries. Within the developed countries group, the United States is the largest trading partner, followed by Switzerland and Japan (table 24.2). If intra-EU trade is added to extra-EU trade with developed countries, we find that more than four-fifths of the Union's trade is with countries of broadly similar income levels. This is a familiar empirical phenomenon worldwide, but it runs counter to the expectation that trade flows should be greatest between countries

Table 24.1 The EU in world merchandise trade, 2004

Exports from	Value	
	($bn)	%
European Union (excluding intra-EU trade)	1203	18.1
United States	819	12.3
Japan	566	8.5
Other	4054	61.1
Total world (excluding intra-EU trade)	6642	100.0

Source: WTO (2006, table I.6).

that are most different in economic structure. It has given rise to new approaches to the theoretical modelling of the causes of trade (Krugman, 1994).

Developing countries account for 43 per cent of extra-EU trade but for only 14 per cent of total EU trade. Most developing countries rely far more on the EU as an export market than the EU does on them. For example, in 2004, 22 per cent of India's exports went to the EU, but only 1.8 per cent of EU exports went to India, and India's exports accounted for only 1.7 per cent of total EU imports. African countries in general are even more dependent on the EU market. The asymmetry in bargaining positions is modified somewhat by the strategic importance of some developing-country primary-product exports, oil being an obvious case in point. The most dynamic element in EU–developing country trade, though, has been the growth in manufactured goods trade with south-east Asian countries. This repeats the general pattern: as countries become more industrialized (i.e. more similar) they trade more with one another.

The commodity structure of EU trade varies greatly by geographical area (table 24.3). Trade with developed countries consists predominantly of trade in manufactured goods. In 2004, these goods accounted for 88 per cent of the Union's exports to developed countries and 81 per cent of its imports from them. Trade with developing countries has a different composition. Primary products figure more prominently in their exports

Table 24.2 EU merchandise trade by area, 2004

	Imports		Exports	
	$bn	%	$bn	%
Developed countries[a]	529.7	14.0	625.2	16.8
of which:				
United States	195.0	5.1	288.5	7.8
Switzerland	77.6	2.0	93.2	2.5
Japan	91.7	2.4	52.6	1.4
Developing countries[b]	601.3	15.9	461.2	12.4
Commonwealth of Independent States	112.4	3.0	80.8	2.2
Other	37.2	1.0	36.6	1.0
Extra-EU	1280.6	33.8	1203.8	32.4
Intra-EU	2510.4	66.2	2510.4	67.6
Total EU	3791.0	100.0	3714.2	100.0

Notes:

[a] Europe, North America and Japan.

[b] Africa, South and Central America, Middle East and Asia (excluding Japan).

Source: Computed from WTO (2006, tables A12 and A18).

Table 24.3 Commodity composition of EU trade with major trading groups, 2004 (% shares)

	Manufactures		Agricultural products		Fuels and other products	
	Exports	Imports	Exports	Imports	Exports	Imports
Developed countries[a]	87.5	81.2	6.5	5.9	6.0	12.9
Developing countries[b]	88.8	67.3	6.5	11.7	4.7	21.0
Commonwealth of Independent States	88.6	19.4	9.6	4.7	1.8	75.9

[a] Europe (excluding intra-EU trade), North America and Japan.

[b] South and Central America, Africa, Middle East and Asia (except Japan).

Source: Computed from WTO (2006, tables A18 and A22).

to the EU. Agricultural products comprise 12 per cent of the total, and fuels and other products a further 21 per cent. However, the share of manufactured goods in total imports from the developing countries has grown dramatically in recent decades (up from 18 per cent in 1980 to 67 per cent in 2004).

The EU's extra-EU merchandise trade is traditionally close to balance. A small deficit was recorded in 2004, corresponding to 0.6 per cent of EU GDP. So far, the Union's trade balance has not rated much comment; this contrasts with the debates surrounding the United States deficit (6.1 per cent of GDP) and the Japanese surplus (2.4 per cent of GDP). Nevertheless, some bilateral trade imbalances have been perceived as troublesome, in particular the persistent deficit with Japan. The trade balance's economic importance derives from its being both a lead indicator and the largest component in the balance of payments on current account. This balance includes services trade and other current transactions. Trade in commercial services, comprising travel, transport, royalties and business services corresponds to some 26 per cent of the EU's total trade with third countries.

In trying to work out the effect of a customs union such as the EU on partner and third countries, customs union theory focuses on the share of intra-union versus extra-union trade. The growth of intra-union trade could be due to either trade creation (a good thing) or trade diversion (a bad thing). As a general rule, the greater the absolute growth of extra-union trade, the less the danger of trade diversion. In the EU's case, two facts stand out. First, the share of intra-EU trade in total trade has risen markedly from 42 per cent in 1961 to 67 per cent in 2004. As integration among EU members outpaced liberalization with the rest of the world, this relative expansion of intra-EU trade is in line with the predictions of theory (see chapter 6). Second, the increase in the intra-EU trade share was accompanied by a rapid absolute growth of extra-EU trade. This indicates a preponderance of trade creation over trade diversion. Further analysis suggests that, with the important exception of agricultural trade, the rise in intra-EU trade has not been at the expense of non-EU countries (Sapir, 1996).

24.1.2 Intra-industry v. inter-industry trade

Much academic interest has focused on the composition of international exchanges in terms of intra- and inter-industry trade. Intra-industry trade (IIT) refers to the mutual exchange of similar goods between countries. This type of trade runs against the predictions of neoclassical trade theory, according to which countries would export one set of products – those in which they have a comparative advantage – while importing an entirely different set of products – those for which the comparative advantage is held by other countries. IIT is based not on country-specific advantages, but on determinants such as consumers' taste for variety, increasing returns in production and the inter-

national dispersion of various stages in the production process of advanced industrial goods. IIT therefore typically dominates trade among diversified high-income economies.

Trade within the EU exhibits generally high shares of IIT. Brülhart and Elliott (1998) have shown that, on average, the share of IIT trade among EU countries rose from 48 to 64 per cent over the 1961–92 period. Given that the definition of an 'industry' in that study is very narrow (the five-digit level of the Standard Industrial Trade Classification, which distinguishes more than 2,000 'industries'), this is strong evidence that intra-EU trade is driven by forces other than the type of comparative advantage once emphasized in the textbooks.

According to computations by the OECD (2000b) for the 1970–98 period, the IIT share of extra-EU trade has also been growing continuously. Countries with the largest and most diversified industrial bases (Germany, France and the United Kingdom) typically have the highest levels of IIT with third countries. Greece, Portugal and most of the 2004 and 2007 accession countries have lower IIT levels – their extra-EU trade relations are still largely inter-industry. The proportion of IIT in the EU's trade with developed countries such as the United States is high, as one would expect, and with developing countries it is low. IIT with Japan, however, is surprisingly low, a fact often interpreted as a symptom of the impenetrability of the Japanese market to manufactured exports from the West. Low IIT levels could imply that further trade liberalization with these countries might involve substantial structural adjustment costs for both parties (see Brülhart, 1998). This may explain in part the insistence on a certain minimum level of economic development being achieved by applicant countries before accession to full membership of the Union was agreed.

24.1.3 External trade and economic specialization: high-tech industries and low-skilled workers

Changes in the EU's trade structure and trade policy regime have stimulated corresponding

Table 24.4 Extra-EU trade in selected technology-intensive products, 1980 and 2004 ($ billion)

	Year	Exports	Imports	Trade balance	Change in balance 1980–2004
Chemicals	1980	35.7	17.2	+18.5	
	2004	190.9	109.3	+133.6	+115.1
Machinery and transport equipment	1980	115.9	58.0	+57.9	
	2004	541.3	438.8	+102.5	+44.6
Electrical machinery	1980	11.9	5.7	+6.2	
	2004	57.6	55.2	+2.6	–3.6
Office and telecom equipment	1980	11.3	17.2	–5.9	
	2004	100.6	180.5	–79.9	–74.0
Automotive products	1980	27.5	8.2	+19.3	
	2004	125.9	52.5	+73.4	+54.1

Source: Computed from WTO (2006, table A18).

changes in the pattern of specialization of member states. The share of agricultural employment in total EU15 employment has fallen from 12 per cent in 1970 to 4 per cent in 2004 (see chapter 20). There has been a sustained expansion of the services sector, and a fall in the share of manufacturing jobs from 33 per cent to 19 per cent in the same time period. Some industrial sectors were particularly hard hit. For example, since 1984, EU15 employment has shrunk significantly in iron and steel (down 50 per cent or 257,000 jobs by 2004) and in clothing and textiles (down 33 per cent or 1,510,000 jobs by 2004).

Of course, specialization pressures induced by external trade are not the only forces that shaped the observed changes in the EU's production structure. Even if the EU had existed in autarky, changes in technology, incomes, tastes and demography would have led to structural adjustment. For this reason, it is difficult to isolate and quantify the impact of external trade liberalization on observed specialization trends. However, some insights into the processes at work have been yielded by recent empirical analysis. We concentrate here on two sectors for which the role of extra-EU trade has been subject to particularly intensive debate and substantial research: high-technology industries and low-skill intensive industries. Both have been identified as losers in the EU's trade liberalization; the former due to the

presumed insufficient R&D efforts in the EU, the latter due to the inexorable law of comparative advantage.

Trade performance in high-tech products has been a source of concern to the EU for many years. The concern focuses on Europe's perceived poor performance in high-tech sectors relative to the US and East Asian 'Tiger' economies, most importantly Japan. One way of measuring this is by the technology balance of payments, i.e. the difference between exports of technology (such as international licensing contracts and technical assistance) and imports (such as purchases of foreign patents, know-how and R&D). According to OECD estimates for 2001, the EU15 had a deficit in technology of $4.6 billion in contrast with an American surplus of $22.3 billion and a Japanese surplus of $5.7 billion. Another type of indicator examines patterns in high-tech merchandise trade, such as the share of high-tech exports in total manufacturing exports, which, according to World Bank statistics for 2003, shows the EU (20 per cent) falling well behind Japan (27 per cent) and the United States (29 per cent). Other trade statistics provide less conclusive results. Table 24.4 shows that the EU has negative trade balances in some key high-tech sectors such as office and telecom equipment but enjoys a surplus in others such as machinery and cars. Indeed, according to the OECD (2002c), over the 1994–2000 period the

EU has increased its share of the world export market in four of the five highly technology-intensive sectors analysed (aerospace, electronic goods, computers and precision instruments) and lost market share in only one (pharmaceuticals). It would therefore be wrong to claim that Europe is generally falling behind in terms of competitiveness in high-tech sectors.

The problem of high-tech industries relates to the strategic positioning of the EU economy. Low-skill intensive industries give rise to a different type of concern. In the latter case, it is generally accepted that the EU will lose market share to third countries. What is at issue is the pace of change and its effects on the incomes of low-skilled workers, particularly against the backdrop of the EU's high unemployment (see chapters 5 and 23). Some argue that the law of comparative advantage has been working to the detriment of European blue-collar workers and, in an unholy combination with institutional labour-market rigidities, has fuelled unemployment.

Trade economists have conducted numerous analyses with the aim of isolating trade-related determinants of structural change. Two concepts of structural change have been used: changes in wage differentials across industries and changes in unemployment rates. The starting hypothesis is that the liberalization of trade vis-à-vis unskilled labour-abundant developing countries has depressed demand for unskilled labour in industrialized countries. Trade liberalization therefore either (a) contributes to the widening gap between skilled and unskilled wages, as in the United States and the UK, or (b) contributes to rising unemployment of unskilled workers, where union power and restrictive labour-market legislation impede United States-style flexibility of wages. In the EU case, attention primarily focuses on whether increased imports from low-wage countries have exacerbated the unemployment problem.

Most available studies cover the United States or the entire OECD, rather than just the EU, and a number of different methodologies are used. Some studies estimate average factor contents of imports and exports, and infer net effects on domestic factor demands. Other studies regress changes in factor demands over various determinants including import penetration. A majority of analyses find that trade liberalization accounts for some of the fall in demand for blue-collar workers in developed countries. However, the contribution of trade to the rise in the skill premium is at most 20 per cent; by far the bigger culprit is trade-independent technological change (Slaughter, 1999).

A contrary conclusion was reached by Wood (1994, 1995) who argued that import penetration from the developing countries is a major cause of falling demand for low-skilled workers in the OECD. He refined the standard factor-content analysis and found empirical evidence that manufactured imports of OECD countries tend to have higher low-skill contents than similar goods produced locally, and that imports thereby crowd out low-skill jobs in developed countries. Furthermore, he detected a tendency for OECD industry to engage in 'defensive innovation', substituting capital for low-skilled labour in order to survive competition from low-wage exporters, and he pointed to the (often ignored) surge in service exports from those countries. He concluded that demand for unskilled labour relative to skilled labour in OECD countries in 1990 fell by about 20 per cent compared to what it would have been had prohibitive barriers been imposed on trade with the developing countries. Neven and Wyplosz (1999) also found evidence of defensive innovation by EU industries in response to competition from developing countries, but the magnitude of their estimated employment and wage effects is very small.

The nature of the trade–employment link is likely to remain a controversial topic for some time. As the EU reduces its external trade barriers under WTO commitments, and as the exporting capacity of developing countries increases, the pressures for trade-induced specialization will also intensify. Underlying the empirical debate about the significance of trade liberalization for EU market adjustment there is a strong *normative* consensus against a return to protectionism. Even though trade liberalization is acknowledged to produce losers, winners are still in the majority. The policy response suggested by economic theory is not to re-impose trade barriers to non-EU imports, but to deregulate EU markets while providing social 'safety nets', to subsidize employment of low-skill workers (in the short term), and to invest in education (in the long term).

24.2 The Common Commercial Policy (CCP)

24.2.1 EU trade decision-making procedures

The key provisions of the CCP are contained in Articles 131–4 (ex Articles 110–16) of the Treaty of Rome.[3] Article 131 contains the well-known aspiration:

By establishing a customs union between themselves member states aim to contribute, in the common interest, to the harmonious development of world trade, the progressive abolition of restrictions on international trade and the lowering of customs barriers.

The cornerstone of the CCP is Article 133. It sets out the important rule that:

the CCP shall be based on uniform principles, particularly in regard to changes in tariff rates, the conclusion of tariff and trade agreements, the achievement of uniformity in measures towards the liberalisation of export policy and in measures to protect trade such as those to be taken in the case of dumping or subsidies.

Article 133 defines CCP coverage only with an illustrative list – mostly tariffs, anti-dumping or anti-subsidy measures, and trade agreements. Trade in goods, including agriculture, falls unambiguously within the Community's competence. Decision-making concerning trade in goods under Article 133 functions on the basis of qualified majority voting (QMV) in the Council (see chapter 3). Subject to the Council's approval, the Commission is empowered to conduct negotiations in consultation with a special committee appointed by the Council for this purpose, the Article 133 Committee, and within the framework of such negotiating directives as the Council may issue to it. For example, the Commission negotiates on behalf of the member states in the WTO. In the cut and thrust of negotiations, the Commission may sometimes interpret its mandate in a way with

which some member states may disagree, and this has been a source of tension in the past.

Multilateral trade agreements increasingly cover a wider range of topics including services, intellectual property rights, e-commerce and investment where the Community's competence to negotiate and implement trade policies is much less clear. In 1994, the European Court of Justice (ECJ) was asked to rule on the division of competences with respect to services and intellectual property rights. The Court ruled that the Community had exclusive competence with respect to cross-border trade in services but that member states retained joint competence with the Community for trade issues involving commercial presence and factor movements. As a result, the WTO Agreement was signed by representatives of both the EU Council and the member states. In 1997, the Amsterdam Treaty modified Article 133 to grant powers to the Community to negotiate agreements on services and intellectual property, but only on the basis of unanimity. The Nice Treaty in 2001 further tilted the balance towards exclusive competence by extending majority voting to these areas (with certain exceptions such as agreements that relate to trade in cultural and audiovisual services, education, social and human health services as well as transport services, which remain outside the scope of Article 133). But other areas of growing significance, such as investment issues or the traditionally contentious area of export policy, remain under the unanimity rule. Unanimity also continues to prevail in the limited instances where it is required for internal decisions, such as taxation matters (see chapters 3 and 14) – this is called the principle of 'parallelism'. The absence of QMV in these areas could make the conclusion of future trade negotiations cumbersome where the outcome is presented as a 'single undertaking' because, de facto, unanimity is required for the entire agenda (OECD, 2000b).

24.2.2 Instruments of the CCP

The principles of the CCP are put into effect by means of trade policy instruments and trade agreements. First, we survey the principal

Table 24.5 Import-weighted average applied MFN tariff rates in selected countries, 2004 (2003 for EU25), %

ISIC code	Industry	EU25	US	Japan
1	Agriculture, forestry, fishing	14.2	4.5	2.4
2	Mining and quarrying	0.1	0.0	0.0
3	Manufacturing	7.0	3.1	2.5
31	Food, beverages and tobacco	22.4	8.2	8.3
32	Textiles and apparel	10.2	10.6	9.6
33	Wood and wood products	6.2	1.3	2.9
34	Paper and paper products	6.3	0.1	0.0
35	Chemicals, petroleum products	5.7	3.3	1.7
36	Non-metallic mineral products	7.5	4.4	1.1
37	Basic metal industries	6.7	1.0	0.6
38	Fabricated metal products	7.6	2.6	0.8
39	Other manufacturing	5.6	1.8	0.2
	Total all products	6.7	2.7	2.0

Note: The tariff averages in this table are calculated by weighting tariff rates on individual goods by the relative importance of the value of each good in each country's imports.
ISIC = International Standard Industrial Classification.

Source: UNCTAD (2006).

instruments of EU trade policy, while trade agreements with non-EU countries are discussed in section 24.2.3.

Tariffs

The most visible element of EU trade policy is the common external tariff (CET). More than 10,000 individual products are distinguished at the eight-digit level of the combined nomenclature (CN) which lists the duty rates applicable to each product. The structure of the EU's tariff schedule is compared to those of the US and Japan in table 24.5. These are applied tariff rates, weighted by the volume of imports of the affected goods.[4] In all three countries, higher tariffs are imposed on imports of agricultural products, food, textiles and clothing. The import-weighted average tariff rate was 6.7 per cent in the EU compared to 2.7 per cent in the US and 2.0 per cent in Japan. The revenues from import duties flow into the general EU budget, after a 20 per cent deduction retained to cover the costs of customs administration by the importing country (see chapter 19).

Tariff averages mask substantial variation of tariff levels across individual products. For example, following the Information Technology Agreement signed in 1997, the EU phased out remaining tariffs on most computer and telecom-related goods. At the other extreme, 'sensitive' imports such as trucks, cars, clothing and footwear continue to attract high tariffs, in excess of 10 per cent *ad valorem*. The peaks are even more pronounced in the agricultural sector. MFN tariffs on meat, dairy products and cereals were 28 per cent, 38 per cent and 39 per cent respectively in 2004, with individual tariffs exceeding 200 per cent in the case of some dairy products.

Non-tariff barriers

In addition to tariffs, the EU has made significant use of various non-tariff measures to limit imports, although their importance has diminished considerably since the late 1980s, as WTO rules have enforced a stricter discipline in their use. Non-tariff barriers (NTBs; see chapters 6 and 7) include quantitative restrictions, price controls and regulatory barriers. Specific examples include import quotas, voluntary export restraints, discretionary licensing, anti-dumping duties or prohibitions for health or safety reasons.

Quantitative restrictions on imports are generally not permitted under WTO rules. Quotas were imposed on imports of clothing and textiles under successive Multifibre Agreements (MFAs) and regulated by the WTO Agreement on Textiles and Clothing since 1995. Under this Agreement, the EU eliminated these quotas by 2005 in a phased fashion. Quotas on banana imports designed to protect the market for ACP banana exporters were removed from 2006. Quotas remain in place for imports from non-WTO countries such as textile-related and other basic manufactures from former Soviet Union countries.

As visible trade barriers are dismantled, other ways of restricting imports in 'sensitive' sectors are resorted to. Frequent recourse to anti-dumping measures is an example of such practice. Dumping is defined as the selling in export markets below some 'normal' price. The 'normal' price of a good is commonly defined as the price prevailing in the exporter's home market. Such divergences could arise if firms exported products at very low prices in order to capture markets abroad and to eliminate competition. The imposition of anti-dumping measures is permitted under WTO rules, if dumping 'causes or threatens material injury to an established industry . . . or materially retards the establishment of a domestic industry'. Complex pricing policies and adjustment for indirect cost factors leave a degree of arbitrariness in the calculation of dumping margins and 'material injury'. WTO rules also permit countries to take countervailing action against exports which have benefited from subsidies in the exporting country provided such exports cause or threaten to cause material injury to a domestic industry. Safeguard clauses under WTO provisions allow signatories to take special measures against import surges or particularly low import prices which cause material injury to domestic industries.

The EU has had frequent resort to anti-dumping measures. In 2001, the EU had the second-largest number of product categories with measures in force after the United States. Over the period 1991 to 2003, the number of EU anti-dumping measures in force fluctuated between 101 and 175 and shows an increasing trend over time (WTO, 2004). Anti-dumping actions take one of two forms: (a) anti-dumping duties equivalent to the dumping margin or (b) undertakings by exporting countries not to sell to the EU below an agreed price. The most affected product categories are iron and steel products, consumer electronics and chemicals. The EU rarely applies countervailing duties and, in almost all cases, the investigations concern products which are also subject to an anti-dumping investigation.

Regulatory barriers

Products imported into the EU must comply with relevant regulations, where they exist, to meet health, safety and environmental objectives. Technical regulations are mandatory rules laid down by the EU or the member states, while standards are non-mandatory rules approved by a recognized body such as a standards institute which provide an assurance of quality to consumers. Compliance is established by means of conformity assessment procedures. Regulations may lay down product characteristics or their related process and production methods, or they may deal with the terminology, symbols, packaging and labelling requirements applying to a product or production method. Examples include noise and emission limits for machinery, or labelling requirements such as health warnings on tobacco products or the energy consumption levels of household appliances. Such regulations raise the cost of exporting where a manufacturer has to meet a different set of standards or pay for the cost of demonstrating compliance with the importing country's rules.

The EU's use of regulations and standards must comply with its obligations under the WTO Agreement on Technical Barriers to Trade (TBT Agreement) and, for food safety and animal and plant health measures, the WTO Agreement on the Application of Sanitary and Phytosanitary Measures (SPS Agreement). These obligations generally require the EU to use international standards where they exist unless they can be shown to be inappropriate, to avoid discrimination against imported products and to avoid creating unnecessary obstacles to international trade. Between 1995 and 2003 the EU or its member states notified between 76 and 437 new regulations annually

under the TBT Agreement, while additional measures were notified to the SPS Committee (WTO,
2004). Some of the more important trade disputes
involving the EU have occurred around the use of
regulatory import barriers such as its ban on
the import of hormone-treated beef, maximum
aflatoxin levels in cereals, dried fruit and nuts, and
its labelling requirements for genetically modified
foods.

Trade rules for services

Extra-EU services trade received a multilateral legal
base through the General Agreement on Trade in
Services (GATS), which was negotiated during the
Uruguay Round. The scope of this agreement
encompasses both the right to do business across
countries and also the right to establish local subsidiaries, since it also applies to services provided
by foreign affiliates of multinational firms. GATS
extends the non-discrimination MFN rule to all service sectors, although members can derogate from
this for particular sectors listed in the annex to the
agreement by each signatory (the 'negative list').
National treatment (i.e. treatment equivalent to
that given to domestic suppliers of a service) is
granted to foreign suppliers, but only in the sectors
where a member makes an offer to do this by listing it in its schedule of commitments (the 'positive
list').

As a result of these qualifications, the GATS provides limited coverage of service sectors, but it
contains provisions for continued negotiations.
Like other developed countries, the EU is an
enthusiastic proponent of freer trade in services.
Such is invariably the case for sectors in which
countries enjoy a decided comparative advantage.
Where such an advantage is less clear, e.g. in the
case of audiovisual services, where Europe is a
major net importer from the US, free trade is seen
as posing a threat to European cultural identity.
As already noted, an agreement was reached on
telecommunications in 1997, according to which
sixty-nine WTO members granted each other (and
most other WTO countries) national treatment in
all forms of telecommunication services, thus covering over 90 per cent of global telecommunications. Negotiations on financial and professional
services were also completed successfully, but

proposals for maritime transport were blocked by
the US.

The treatment of public services in the GATS
has proved controversial. Whatever the merits of
the debate on whether the privatization or deregulation of public services might lead to an
improvement or a deterioration in their quality,
most people would agree that this is an issue
which should be discussed and decided by citizens
rather than through the technocratic processes
of multilateral agreements. Fears have been
expressed that the GATS could require EU governments to open up the provision of public services
to competition. However, the EU has included supplementary specifications in its horizontal commitments which allow subsidies to the public
sector and the granting of exclusive rights to
public utilities. Even in public service sectors
where the EU and its member states have made
market access commitments (such as private education and hospital services), they retain the right
to regulate these activities with a view to achieving legitimate public objectives.

24.2.3 Regional trade agreements

The EU has developed an elaborate web of preferential trade agreements (see chapter 1). Initially,
these were mainly with neighbouring countries
and former colonies, but they now extend to
transcontinental agreements without these geographical or historical rationales such as those
with Latin American countries. WTO rules allow
the formation of regional trade agreements (RTAs)
as long as trade barriers on average do not rise
after integration, tariffs and NTBs are eliminated
within the area on 'substantially all' intra-
regional trade, and the project is notified to the
WTO in time for it to determine whether these
conditions are satisfied (see chapter 5, especially
the appendix on WTO's Article XXIV).

The EU's penchant for regional trade agreements is apparent from table 24.6. The most
favourable treatment is given to those countries
that either fall into the least developed category,
or are members of the Cotonou (formerly the
Lomé) Agreement, or have completed bilateral
trade agreements with the EU. Next come the

Table 24.6 The EU's network of preferential trade agreements, 2005

Type of trade regime	Name of agreement	Countries involved
(a) Single market (b) Customs Union (c) Free Trade Area	European Economic Area (EEA)	Iceland, Liechtenstein, Norway Turkey, Andorra, San Marino Switzerland, Israel, South Africa, Mexico, Chile, Faroe Islands
	Euro-Med Association Agreements	Algeria, Egypt, Israel, Jordan, Lebanon, Morocco, Palestinian Authority, Syria, Tunisia
(d) Partnership and co-operation agreements (MFN treatment)		Russia plus members of CIS
(e) Non-reciprocal contractual preferences	First-generation Mediterranean agreements	
	Lomé/Cotonou	African, Caribbean, Pacific countries
(f) Non-reciprocal autonomous preferences	Generalized System of Preferences (GSP)	Other developing countries plus members of CIS and western Balkan countries
(g) Purely MFN treatment		Australia, Canada, Japan, New Zealand, Taiwan, Hong Kong, Singapore, United States, South Korea

Notes:
1. The Euro-Med Association Agreements are scheduled to establish a free trade area by 2010.
2. The WTO waiver that covers preferential aspects of the Cotonou Agreement expires in 2008. The EU's Economic Partnership Agreements will then replace the trade chapters of the Cotonou Agreement.

middle-income and poor countries that benefit only from non-contractual discretionary preferences offered by the EU under the terms of its Generalized System of Preferences (GSP). At the bottom of the hierarchy are countries which are members of the WTO but not of the GSP which receive the ironically named MFN treatment. Until 1998, there were just five countries in this category (Australia, Canada, Japan, New Zealand and the United States) but they have since been joined by Hong Kong, South Korea, Singapore and Taiwan after their graduation from the GSP.

However, the geographical coverage exaggerates the relative importance of trade links with preferred partners in value terms. The shares of extra-EU imports from MFN countries, from countries covered by reciprocal trade agreements and from countries benefiting from unilateral concessions are each about one-third (OECD, 2000b). In fact, the share of imports entering under MFN terms may be

as high as 70 per cent given the importance of non-dutiable imports and administrative rules which restrict the use of the preference schemes by the beneficiary countries. An example of the latter are rules of origin (ROO) which determine whether a product has undergone sufficient processing to qualify as originating from a preference-receiving country. By making the rules more restrictive, the EU can disqualify many exports from receiving preferential treatment (see Cadot et al., 2005). The EU's Pan-Euro system, introduced in 1997, ensures that the same ROO apply to all preferential agreements signed by the EU, which helps lessen the degree of complexity of preferential regimes under the CCP (Estevadeordal and Suominen, 2005).

As world trade becomes more liberalized, the preferential value of RTAs will diminish. In the long term, it is very likely that all WTO members will enjoy relative freedom of access to Europe's market. EU products might, however, suffer from discrimination created by other RTAs. To avert this danger the EU is seeking conformity across the board to WTO rules. As a result, its own RTAs are becoming less discriminatory, more insistent on reciprocity from the partner country and more broadly focused than in the past. They address regulatory issues, right of establishment, foreign investment, competition policy, financial aid and technical cooperation as well as standard tariffs and import barriers per se. Thus, opposition to RTAs on the grounds that they breach the non-discrimination principle of GATT has diminished considerably over the years. The suspension of negotiations at WTO level in 2006, however, raises the spectre of at least a temporary increase in the relative importance of discriminatory trade liberalization.

24.2.4 Estimated welfare effects of the CCP

The EU is generally perceived as having a relatively open and liberal trade policy. This perception is supported by its role as the world's single largest importer; its relatively low tariff levels on manufactured goods; its extensive network of preferential access agreements; and the stance it has taken in pushing for further multilateral trade liberalization through the WTO. Messerlin (2001) paints a more sceptical picture by taking into account the tariff peaks in agriculture and the role of anti-dumping duties. He calculates that the average tariff-equivalent extra-EU trade barrier across agricultural and industrial sectors amounted to roughly 14 per cent in 1990 and 12 per cent in 2000. Using different data and estimation methods, Bouët (2002) reports an average tariff equivalent for 1999 of 9 per cent for the EU. Bouët's estimate is somewhat lower than Messerlin's for three main reasons: he uses applied tariffs rather than bound ones, he takes account of anti-dumping duties only on those trade partners to whom they legally applied, and he takes account of the preferential access granted by the EU under regional and bilateral agreements.

Messerlin (2001) estimates that the total cost to the EU of its remaining external trade barriers in 2000 amounted to around 7 per cent of GDP – roughly equivalent to the national income of Spain. Again, Bouët (2002) arrives at a lower estimate, valuing the net welfare loss from the CCP at around 2.5 per cent of EU GDP. Here, the difference is due mainly to the fact that Messerlin's estimate includes not only the traditional dead-weight loss from trade restrictions, but also the tariff revenue and producer rents, which he assumed to be largely squandered. Bouët, on the other hand, follows the standard theoretical approach strictly and considers only the dead-weight loss. Neither Bouët's estimates nor Messerlin's incorporate the effect of indirect trade barriers such as EU-specific technical regulations and product standards; nor do they incorporate the effects of continuing protection in service sectors. On the other hand, their estimates make the standard assumption in calculations of this kind of full employment, an assumption whose validity may be questioned in the EU at this time.

It is no surprise, therefore, that the estimated benefits from liberalization of the CCP are also significant. Economists of the GATT (1994), for example, projected EU income in 2005 to be higher by $164 billion in 1990 prices as a result of the Uruguay Round. When compared to an estimated total world gain of $510 billion, this implies that the EU obtained fully one-third of the global gains. For an 'ambitious' deal concluding the currently frozen Doha Round, Decreux and Fontagné (2006) predict a total world gain of $126 billion in 2020, of which $33 billion would accrue to the EU. Clearly the EU is a major beneficiary of the trend towards global non-discriminatory trade liberalization.

24.3 Trade relations with the main partners

24.3.1 Developing countries

In spite of their relative economic weakness, developing countries are a key trade partner for the EU (table 24.4). The present pattern of trade agreements owes as much to history and proximity to the EU as to economic rationale. These trade arrangements are discussed in detail in chapter

25 and only a very brief summary is provided here. The Mediterranean countries, for instance, are bound to the EU by many ties. Fear of excessive immigration from these areas has given the EU an added incentive to assist their economic development through strong trade preferences. Following the 1995 Barcelona Declaration, the EU and eleven Mediterranean countries agreed to form a Euro-Med free trade area by the year 2010. Also contained in this programme are pledges to abolish obstacles to trade in goods and services on a reciprocal basis. Bilateral FTAs incorporating these principles have already been signed with several Mediterranean countries (see chapter 1).

Prior to the Barcelona programme, the Lomé Convention was the EU's most preferential agreement with developing countries. Signed in 1975, and renewed at regular intervals thereafter, it gave a group of African, Caribbean, and Pacific (ACP) countries free access to EU markets for manufactures and a substantial range of primary goods. The Lomé accords encompassed more than tariff reductions. They included commodity protocols which provided preferential prices to ACP exports of bananas, sugar and beef, as well as providing for the relaxation of NTBs, more flexible application of safeguard clauses and rules of origin, and exemption from MFA restrictions. Trade preferences were supplemented by special aid and technical cooperation arrangements.

In spite of this preferential access, the ACP countries' export performance in the EU market has been disappointing. Their market share of EU imports declined from 5.1 per cent in 1970 to 1.5 per cent in 2004 (UNCTAD, 2004). The EU therefore proposed the negotiation of regional economic partnership agreements (REPAs) with groups of the ACPs, establishing free trade areas in place of the non-reciprocal access these countries enjoyed before. This move was also prompted by the criticisms made of the discriminatory nature of the EU's non-reciprocal preferences in the WTO bananas case. It became clear that getting the necessary waiver from WTO rules for these preferences was going to be more difficult in the future. The Cotonou Agreement, which replaced the Lomé Convention in 2000, envisages the negotiation of REPAs over the period 2002–8 eventually

leading to duty-free access for most EU exports to ACP countries as well as for most ACP exports to the EU.

For most non-ACP developing countries the GSP dictates the degree of preferential access for their exports to the EU. Initiated in 1971 by UNCTAD, the purpose of the GSP was to help developing countries to industrialize through exports to the developed world. The GSP provides substantially weaker trade preferences than the Lomé Convention or the Cotonou Agreement. However, under the 'Everything But Arms' initiative adopted in February 2001, the EU has granted duty-free and quota-free access for all products from the fifty least-developed countries under its GSP, with the exception of arms (preferences for Myanmar are currently suspended on human rights grounds). These special arrangements for least-developed countries will be maintained for an unlimited period of time and are not subject to the periodic renewal of the standard GSP scheme.

The EU's multiplicity of agreements and special arrangements with developing countries is undergoing considerable re-assessment. This issue is examined in greater depth in chapter 25 but some general comments can be made here. First, as global trade liberalization gathers steam and trade barriers crumble, the practical usefulness of trade preferences has diminished. Preference erosion is likely to accelerate markedly over the next decade. This will pose special problems for the ACP countries that have enjoyed for many years advantageous access to the EU market. Second, attention is likely to focus more on issues such as the right of establishment in services markets, attraction of foreign investment, rights to tender for public sector contracts in partner countries, and competition law. We will hear less about trade preferences and more about development programmes. Third, developing countries will have to provide reciprocity in future RTAs if they are to be acceptable under WTO rules. This means they will have to reduce their own import barriers as well. For some there will be a serious loss of government revenues as a result and some (small) danger of trade diversion. While some developing country governments tend to see the reduction in tariffs as a 'concession', trade theory suggests the opposite conclusion. Properly managed, the liberalization of imports can bring considerable benefits to their economies.

24.3.2 The United States

The United States is the EU's largest trade partner, accounting for 20 per cent of combined extra-EU imports and exports (see table 24.2). Although EU trade with industrial countries is in principle governed by the rules of the WTO, this has not prevented controversy arising on many specific issues.

EU economic relations with the United States have been based on strong political and cultural ties as well as common economic interests. Yet, at times, it appears as if the two partners are locked into a state of perpetual crisis. In the past, trade wars have threatened to erupt because of disputes over issues as diverse as steel, hormone-treated beef, aircraft noise, subsidies to Airbus, genetically modified crops and bananas. The EU has complained about unilateralism in United States trade legislation, 'Buy American' restrictions, discriminatory taxes, public procurement and restrictions on non-nationals in the services industries. Some European grievances were vindicated in September 1999, when a WTO panel confirmed that US export subsidies granted through 'foreign sales corporations' and covering approximately $250 billion worth of US exports were in violation of WTO rules and had to be abolished by October 2000. After much foot-dragging, and following the imposition of retaliatory tariffs by the EU on US imports, the US finally repealed the legislation in late 2004. The EU launched further WTO proceedings against the US in 2002 for an increase in American protection levels against steel imports. For its part, the United States feared a protectionist 'fortress Europe' arising from the single market programme and continues to accuse the EU of unfairly subsidizing high-tech sectors such as aviation. The most acute and enduring cause of friction, however, has been trade in agricultural products, particularly the EU's refusal to allow imports of hormone-treated beef and its moratorium on approving genetically modified crops for sale.

Although full-scale trade wars have threatened to break out on many occasions, the strong mutuality of interests between the United States and the EU has, on each occasion thus far, saved them from the brink. Trade relations are characterized by constant levels of minor friction rather than a deep divergence of interests. Indeed, the contentious sectors in transatlantic trade are commonly estimated to account for a mere 1–2 per cent of total trade. There is even talk of eliminating all trade barriers, thereby creating a 'new transatlantic marketplace' of some 700 million affluent consumers. A Transatlantic Free Trade Agreement could yield welfare gains in the range of 1–2 per cent of GDP for Europe and 1.6–2.8 per cent for the United States (Boyd, 1998).

24.3.3 Japan

Trade policy towards Japan has been marked by resistance to what is perceived as excessively rapid import penetration in a narrow range of product markets. It is also marked by internal disunity within the EU. Some member states, such as the United Kingdom and Ireland, have become important hosts to Japanese investment. Naturally, these member states have tended to view sales by Japanese firms more benignly than those with a small presence of Japanese-owned production facilities. Also, countries whose domestic industries compete directly with Japanese goods tend to take a tougher line in the trade policy debate than those for which Japanese sales compete only with other imports. Thus the high share of Japanese passenger car imports in Ireland (43 per cent) and Denmark (34 per cent) aroused little concern, whereas Italy and France were highly resistant to any easing on restraints on Japanese imports despite having much lower import shares (5 per cent and 4 per cent respectively in the mid-1990s).

The EU's persistent trade deficit with Japan has been a bone of contention. It has been attributed to the combined effects of the strong competitive performance of Japanese firms, to Japan's high savings rate and, controversially, to Japan's reluctance to open its market to EU exporters. In 2004, 7.2 per cent of total extra-EU imports came from Japan, while the Japanese market absorbed only

4.4 per cent of EU exports. This trade imbalance is made particularly contentious because Japanese exports tend to be highly focused on a small number of sectors (automobiles, consumer electronics).

On the basis of explicit barriers to trade, the Japanese market appears relatively open. In the Uruguay Round Japan has committed itself to a trade-weighted tariff average on industrial goods of 1.7 per cent. This is the second-lowest average of all countries (surpassed only by Switzerland). However, there are important implicit barriers to imports. First, access to the Japanese market is restricted by regulatory obstacles such as the arbitrary specification of technical standards for electrical appliances and conditions for participation in the financial services market. Japanese non-acceptance of international standards as well as European certification procedures hamper trade in areas such as the agro-food sector, pharmaceuticals and construction. Second, the existence of tightly connected business groups ('keiretsu'), built upon interconnected manufacturers and distributors, makes it particularly difficult for European firms to sell to Japan.

The EU has exerted pressure on Japan to liberalize access to its market, albeit using a less confrontational strategy than the United States. Consultation is the keyword in EU trade diplomacy with Japan. Annual summit meetings have been held between the Japanese Prime Minister, the President of the European Council and the President of the Commission since 1991, and a permanent dialogue was established in 1993 between METI, the Japanese ministry for economics, trade and industry, and the corresponding Commission directorate. A 'Regulatory Reform Dialogue' has been maintained since 1995 to reduce the thicket of regulations that hampers trade and foreign investment. In addition, export-enhancing schemes such as assistance for marketing in Japan and special visit and study programmes have been initiated to facilitate access to the Japanese market for European business.

Concern over Japanese import penetration has quietened down in recent years. One reason is that the Japanese economy has proved to be weaker and more vulnerable than was believed a decade ago. Another is that despite the deficit with Japan, the EU enjoys a large overall trade surplus. Hence, to object too strenuously to Japan's surplus might give ammunition to countries which had a deficit with the EU! Third, following the major reforms of its financial sector in the late 1990s, access to Japan's market has become easier for European investors. More European companies now have a stake in good relations with Japan. Fourth, EU manufacturing companies have raised productivity by copying Japanese techniques. 'Just in time' techniques are now commonplace. Fifth, as Europeans have gained in confidence, they are more ready to acknowledge that failure to obtain market share in Japan could partly be due to their poor knowledge of the Japanese market. One piece of evidence on this is what has been called the 'knowledge deficit': the population of Japan is one-third of the EU but there are five times more Japanese people living in Europe than Europeans in Japan. Finally, Japanese companies are becoming more open and more prepared to engage in cooperative ventures than in the past. The Nissan–Renault merger is an exemplar of this kind of cooperation. Clearly, the EU strategy of encouraging exports to Japan and promoting investment between the two countries is superior to protectionism. One must remember that the EU consumer has gained enormously both from access to Japanese goods and from the efficiency improvements forced on European industry by exposure to Japanese competition.

24.4 Trade policy in a globalizing world

On 14 November 2001 the members of the WTO concluded the Fourth Ministerial Conference with a decision to launch a new WTO round – the Doha Development Agenda – comprising both further trade liberalization and new rule-making, underpinned by commitments to provide more effective special and differential treatment to developing countries. The negotiations, initially scheduled to last three years, were suspended in July 2006 without agreement having been reached. The EU had four stated objectives at the time of the launch of the Doha Round: (i) to further liberalize access to markets for goods and particularly services; (ii) to strengthen coverage in the areas of investment, competition, transparency in government procurement, intellectual property and trade facilitation; (iii) to ensure that more assistance is provided to developing countries to help with their integration into the global economy; (iv) to get the WTO to focus more on issues of public concern such as the environment, animal welfare and food safety, ensuring that trade rules are compatible with the wider interests of society as a whole. A more implicit objective, but which nonetheless carries much weight in the actual negotiating process, is the EU's desire to shape WTO rules on agricultural trade to enable it to maintain support for the European model of agriculture (see chapter 20). This section examines some of the issues at stake in this comprehensive agenda.

24.4.1 Trade and intellectual property rights

Intellectual property is an increasingly important part of international trade. Most of the value of new medicines and other high-technology products lies in the research, innovation, design and testing involved. People who purchase CDs, videos, books or computer programmes are paying for the creativity and information they contain, not for the materials used to make them. Considerable value can be added even to low-technology goods such as clothing or shoes through design and the use of brand names. These 'knowledge goods', ranging from computer programmes to pop songs, and 'reputation goods' such as trademarks or appellations of origin, account for an unquantifiable but undeniably growing share of the value embodied in traded products. The nature of trade policy with respect to such knowledge and reputation goods differs radically from policy aimed at liberalizing merchandise trade, since the main concern is not to abolish obstacles to imports (as countries are generally keen to attract knowledge goods), but to safeguard owners' property rights. Negotiations on intellectual property rights therefore do not consist of bargaining on abolition of barriers, but on agreements to set up minimum standards of ownership protection.

From a theoretical viewpoint, the enforcement of intellectual property rights is a double-edged sword (see Primo Braga, 1995). In the short run, protecting owners of knowledge goods (e.g. through patents) violates the rule that public goods, whose marginal usage cost is zero, should be free. Static efficiency considerations therefore advocate a lax implementation of such property rights, to allow maximum dissemination. In the long run, however, the generation of additional knowledge goods is costly: resources have to be invested in research and development, and this will only occur if a future pecuniary return on such an investment can be safely anticipated. A zero price of knowledge goods is therefore socially sub-optimal in a dynamic sense, because it discourages innovation.

Property rights on reputation goods also have their advantages and drawbacks in equity terms. Trademark protection on one hand increases the monopoly power of owners, and thereby restricts competition, but on the other hand it can increase consumer welfare by allowing product differentiation and facilitating product information.

Both sides of the theoretical argument have been advanced in multilateral negotiations on intellectual property rights. Since developed countries, including the EU, tend to be the owners and exporters of intellectual property, while developing countries are net importers, the former generally argue in favour of stricter property-right enforcement than the latter. This was particularly evident during the Uruguay Round. These negotiations culminated in the Agreement on Trade-Related Aspects of Intellectual Property Rights (the TRIPS Agreement), which, alongside the GATT and GATS, forms one of the three pillars of the WTO. TRIPS negotiations were championed mainly by the United States and the EU against much initial opposition from developing countries. Divisions surfaced again when it appeared that TRIPS protection would prevent developing countries from gaining access to generic drugs as part of their public health programmes. At Doha in November 2001, WTO ministers issued a declaration emphasizing that the TRIPS Agreement should not prevent member states from protecting public health. They confirmed the right of countries to grant compulsory licences (authorization, under certain conditions, to produce a drug or medicine without the consent of the patent holder) and to resort to parallel imports (where drugs produced by the patent holder in another country can be imported without their approval) where appropriate. A further waiver was agreed in 2003 to allow countries producing under a compulsory licence to export to eligible importing countries. This was particularly important for the least-developed countries which do not have the indigenous pharmaceutical manufacturing capability to produce their own generic drugs.

Under the TRIPS accord, signatories have to establish minimum standards of intellectual property right protection, implement procedures to enforce these rights and extend the traditional GATT principles of national treatment and MFN practice to intellectual property. It was agreed that twenty-year patent protection should be available for all inventions, whether of products or processes, in almost all fields of technology. Copyright on literary works (including computer programmes), sound recordings and films is made available for at least fifty years. Under the agreed transition period, most countries had to take on full TRIPS obligations by 2000, while the least-developed countries were allowed to postpone application of most provisions until 2006 with the possibility of a further extension.

24.4.2 Trade and competition policy

The relationship between trade and competition policy was first raised by the US, which for many years, like the EU, claimed that Japanese corporate groups undermined market access for foreign suppliers by buying largely from each other and maintaining closed distribution chains. More recently, the EU has made the running, arguing that anti-competitive practices by businesses can have a significant impact on access to markets. It has sought rules that would require countries to introduce a national competition policy and to enforce it. It has also highlighted the need for more international cooperation to deal with questions such as international cartels and multijurisdictional mergers. This market access agenda

is not necessarily shared by developing countries who have been more concerned about possible anti-competitive behaviour by large multinational companies at their expense. They are also unhappy at the prospect of undertaking additional commitments in an area where they have limited capacity and foresee limited gains. Reaching agreement is also made more difficult, as in the case of intellectual property rights, by theoretical disagreements as to what appropriate competition policy should be.

The EU succeeded in getting a WTO working group on the interaction between trade and competition policy established at the WTO ministerial meeting in Singapore in December 1996. This group discusses the relevance of fundamental WTO principles of non-discrimination and transparency for competition policy. There is no question of trying to harmonize domestic competition laws, but even reaching agreement on a more general framework is proving difficult. The Doha Declaration had set the objective of establishing a multilateral framework on competition policies, but this topic was dropped from the remit of WTO negotiations in 2004. The question being of evident concern to the EU, it is certain to appear again sooner or later on the international policy agenda.

24.4.3 Trade and the environment

Environmental policy moved to a prominent position on the trade agenda during the 1990s (see chapter 18). Up to then, virtually the only environmental concern to affect trade policy was the protection of endangered species. With the rise of ecological awareness and transfrontier pollution problems such as ozone depletion, acid rain and global warming, trade policy came to be seen as a significant element in a country's overall environmental policy.

The main trade policy issue in this debate relates to the use of import restrictions on goods whose production creates negative transborder environmental externalities. Economic theory suggests that in such circumstances the most efficient remedy is to apply direct environmental policy at the source of the externality (e.g. through pollution taxes, eco-subsidies or regulation; see chapter 17). However, environmental policies are often difficult to enforce, so this first-best option may not be feasible. In that case, import restrictions may be the only practicable policy tool. The main drawback of import restrictions against polluting countries is that they provide protection to domestic producers of the importable good, and ecological arguments are therefore vulnerable to abuse by domestic protectionist lobbies. For this reason, trade measures should be temporary and accompanied by efforts to implement environmental policies in the polluting countries.

Even if the externalities are dealt with by environmental policies adopted at the source, new problems can still emerge. Environmental policies affect the competitiveness of open economies. Thus, countries with lax environmental legislation are blamed for 'ecological dumping', and import-competing industries in countries with stringent laws may lobby for protection to ensure a 'level playing field'. As before, the first-best way of ensuring a level playing field is by achieving some degree of coordination in environmental policies across countries. This does not necessarily mean that all countries must adopt exactly the same environmental regime, but it provides a powerful rationale for seeking agreement on environmental policies on a multilateral basis. Even if an agreed way of eradicating 'ecological dumping' could be found, it remains questionable if trade restrictions are the most appropriate remedy. Restricting imports can be counterproductive as it promotes the domestic activities which the environmental policy is attempting to restrain.

On another tack, some environmentalists argue that the rising volume of international trade in itself is causing serious damage to the environment. Oil leakage from tankers and pollution from increased road haulage are classical examples. They recommend a reduction in trade if necessary by protection as a solution. The standard economic response would be that trade restrictions are inefficient and that policy should instead be aimed at the source of the problem (e.g. taxation of oil shipments and on the use of polluting fuels by lorries). One could agree with this while pointing out that such correct policy action

may not be politically feasible. Witness, for example, the way in which the European Commission's proposals for a carbon tax have been resisted by business interests (see chapter 18).

We conclude that trade policy is certainly not the best, and can often be an inappropriate, instrument to protect the environment. International dialogue and agreed domestic policy measures are a more efficient alternative. The main platform for such negotiations is the WTO Committee on Trade and Environment, which was established in 1995. Discussions in this committee have so far been a mere stocktaking exercise, and its reports have rarely contained specific proposals. The EU, like everybody else, supports the case for multilateral environmental agreements, but the difficulty lies in getting countries to agree.

24.4.4 Trade and labour standards

The social dimension to increased international trade has received increasing attention given the concern that trade and investment flows should benefit people at large and not just international business. This has led to calls for a 'social clause' in WTO rules which would allow trade barriers to be invoked against imports from countries deemed to violate minimum labour standards. Human rights and moral advocates of a social clause see it as a way of promoting and enforcing core labour standards and helping to eradicate exploitative working practices. The difficulty is that trade sanctions will do little for the bulk of the labour force in developing countries which is employed in the informal sector, and could even have the opposite of the desired impact. A less well-founded argument is that lower labour standards, especially in developing countries, give them an 'unfair' competitive advantage which will either lead to 'social dumping' (the ability to sell goods abroad more cheaply analogous to 'ecological dumping'), or to the erosion of existing social standards in developed countries (the 'race to the bottom' argument) as footloose firms threaten to uproot to take advantage of laxer standards elsewhere. This version of the pauper labour argument is no less a fallacy for being restated in modern guise. Focusing only on labour costs ignores the substantially higher productivity of labour in developed countries. Developed countries are perfectly able to compete in the sectors where they have a comparative advantage.

The 1995 World Summit on Social Development in Copenhagen identified four core labour standards for the first time, and these were later confirmed by the 1998 International Labour Organization (ILO) Declaration on Fundamental Principles and Rights at Work. The four core standards are freedom of association and collective bargaining, the prevention of child labour, the elimination of forced labour, and the outlawing of discrimination. The EU is strongly committed to the protection of core labour rights, but the debate is about the appropriate role for the WTO in this task. The ILO enforcement mechanism, being limited to ratified conventions, is rather weak. Hence the attraction of using the WTO with its rules-based system and binding dispute settlement mechanism as the means to ensure compliance.

In the first WTO ministerial conference in Singapore in December 1996, the EU was among those which suggested that a WTO working party be created to look into the links between international trade and working conditions. The proposal was fiercely resisted by the developing countries which saw it as a guise for protectionism and a cover for more restrictive trade measures. The final declaration confirmed that the ILO was the competent body to 'set and deal' with labour standards. At the Seattle ministerial conference in 1999, the United States returned to the working party proposal while making clear that its ultimate objective was to incorporate core labour standards into all trade agreements and make them subject to trade sanctions. This was a major reason for the failure of the Seattle conference. Labour standards therefore do not feature on the agenda of the Doha Round negotiations.

The EU has opposed sanctions as a way of enforcing core labour standards, but it continues to insist on the necessity of showing that trade liberalization does not lead to a deterioration in working conditions. It has proposed strengthened mechanisms within the ILO to promote respect for core labour standards, a review mechanism

between the WTO and the ILO, as part of which a trade angle would be linked to the reviews conducted by the ILO, and support for private sector and voluntary schemes (such as codes of conduct and ethical labelling schemes) (CEC, 2001a; CEC, 2006p). It has also used social incentives under its GSP scheme to promote core labour standards by providing additional trade preferences for countries which comply with these standards and allowing for the withdrawal of preferences where beneficiary countries practise any form of slavery or forced labour.

24.5 Conclusions

An 'open' market is an elusive goal. Despite much liberalization, the EU continues to maintain strong defences against sensitive imports. Even under an optimistically liberal scenario, it will be some time before Australia and New Zealand will be able to sell agricultural produce or India textile and clothing products into the EU market without let or hindrance. However, this chapter concludes that the direction of change has leaned, and will continue to lean, towards easier access. The fortress Europe, which some had feared would be erected around the single market, has happily not materialized.

The scope for further negative integration, in the sense of reduction of tariff and non-tariff trade barriers, is approaching exhaustion, but in its place there will be greater emphasis on positive integration (see chapter 6). That means requiring governments to adapt domestic policies and institutions so as to ensure that the scope for expanded trade is not frustrated by differences in regulation, market institutions, technical standards and taxes. Linkage between trade issues and other policy areas once considered exclusively in the national domain will grow in importance over time.

Regionalism is still a strong focus of EU trade policy but its future direction is unclear. A recent Commission Communication noted that current regional trade agreements were largely driven by the EU's neighbourhood and development policies, but served its trade interests, particularly in Asia, less well. Using market potential and the level of protection against EU export interests as criteria, it identified ASEAN, Korea, Mercosur, India, Russia and the Gulf Cooperation Council as potential new preferential trade partners (CEC, 2006q). Some worry that this pursuit of regionalism, with its discriminatory stance against third countries, might be at the expense of the stability of the multilateral trading system. Whether regionalism is a 'building block' or a 'stumbling block' for an open multilateral system is a hotly debated topic among economists. Some argue that it risks prompting the construction of rival free trade areas centred on the Americas and Asia with the prospect that trade disputes between these rival blocs could shake the foundations of the multilateral system. The more positive view is that the EU's regional trade arrangements can act as a laboratory for rule-making in some of the more contentious trade policy areas, as arguably was the case with the internal market programme, and that experience shows that the EU has pursued a policy of 'open' regionalism which is compatible with its multilateral obligations.

The precise form of the EU's future external policy will depend on several factors. First, the increasing heterogeneity among EU members is likely to increase the difficulty of reaching consensus on trade policy. This will strengthen the hand of those who call for the transfer of exclusive competence in all aspects of trade policymaking to the Union, but member states will fight hard to retain as much leverage and influence as they can.

Second, the maintenance of strong economic growth remains crucial. Enthusiasm for integration gathers momentum when an economy is doing well. To some extent European integration and external liberalization are fair weather phenomena. It is also true that the process of liberalization itself tends to improve the weather! A prime concern at present is the EU's high rate of unemployment (see chapter 23). Free trade and unemployment are uneasy, even incompatible, bedfellows. The welfare gains from increased imports do not impress the unemployed. It is remarkable how effective the Commission has been in forwarding its trade liberalization agenda. One reason may be that many EU coun-

tries have a significant balance of payments surplus; when exports exceed imports, it becomes difficult to blame unemployment on excessive imports.

Third, public support and understanding of the benefits of an open trade policy can never be taken for granted. Public opinion finds it difficult to accept that trade rules might be used to require the EU to import food it deems unhealthy, or products which might damage its environment, or that other trade rules might prevent action being taken to promote animal welfare or improved working conditions. What makes these issues difficult to handle in a WTO context is that, although they are open to abuse for protectionist purposes, they are largely driven by consumer rather than producer concerns. The EU has proposed strengthening the 'precautionary principle' in WTO rules which would allow countries to invoke protection even where scientific opinion is divided on the likelihood of a threat to health or the environment. These concerns also explain why the EU has addressed the linkages between trade and the environment and trade and labour standards, despite the opposition from many trade partners. The EU has also highlighted the need for trade policy to contribute to sustainable development. Sustainability impact assessments are now conducted on its WTO proposals and on bilateral trade initiatives. Governments and business leaders must ensure that trade policymaking remains transparent and accessible if public confidence in the process is to be maintained.

Finally, it is important to reiterate that the stakes in the debate on EU trade policy are high, particularly at a time of considerable uncertainty in the world economy and growing international tension. Estimates were given earlier (see section 24.2.4) of the cost to the EU of its remaining protectionist barriers, but these would pale into insignificance if there were a breakdown in the multilateral system and protectionist barriers began to increase again. The danger that the resurgence of regionalism might lead to a world of competing trade blocs would be much more real if confidence in the multilateral trading system were damaged. The willingness of developing countries to pursue more open trade strategies would undoubtedly be undermined if it were felt that the industrialized countries, including the EU, no longer had the stomach for free trade. Balancing the conflicting interests of domestic lobbies, not least agriculture, as well as of the member states is an enormous challenge. EU trade policy will continue to fascinate, and to shape our futures, in the years ahead.

NOTES

1 The authors are grateful to Dermot McAleese for his permission to build on his chapter in earlier editions of this book and for his helpful comments on this chapter, and to Hansueli Bacher for valuable research assistance.

2 Responsibility for trade in goods and increasingly ser- vices and the trade-related aspects of regulatory mea- sures rests with the European Communities (EC) rather than the European Union (EU) – see chapters 2 and 3. For ease of exposition, however, we refer to the 'EU's' Common Commercial Policy throughout this chapter.

3 The observant reader will note that there are now only four trade articles in the Treaty where previously there were seven. The remaining three were repealed.

4 Note that weighting the tariff rates on individual goods by the value of imports of those goods implies a downward bias in the estimation of the average trade-impeding effect of tariffs, because the value of imports will naturally be lower in goods that are sub- ject to high tariffs. The tariff averages reported here should therefore be interpreted as lower-bound approximations.

25 The EU and the developing world

ALAN MATTHEWS

The EU's economic size and its role in world trade mean that it is a key player in structuring the global economic environment for developing countries (DCs) through its aid and trade policies. EU member states are the largest trading partner of DCs, providing 18 per cent of their imports and taking 18 per cent of their exports. The EU and its member states provide some 52 per cent of total official development assistance (ODA) worldwide. It also has a significant indirect influence through its active participation in international organizations that manage the world economic system. The Union's development cooperation policy is comprehensive in its approach, including trade arrangements, development assistance and political dialogue. A number of useful studies have analysed the different elements of the EU's relations with developing countries and help us to better understand the dynamics behind these relationships (Arts and Dickson, 2004; Cosgrove-Sacks and Scapucci, 1999; Stokke and Hoebink, 2005; Van Dijck and Faber, 2000; Van Reisen, 2000). Important and even radical changes are currently taking place in the EU's development policy. The purpose of this chapter is to highlight these changes and to discuss their longer-term significance.

Four themes can be highlighted at the outset. First, the economic environment in which the EU's relations with DCs are played out is changing rapidly. The most striking feature of economic growth over the past three decades has been the growing differentiation in economic performance (table 25.1). Overall differences in GNI per capita between developed countries and DCs remain large – in 2005, average income per capita was $35,131 in the industrialized countries but only $1,746 in the low- and middle-income DCs. However, for some DC regions the gap has been narrowing rapidly. This is particularly the case for the group of Asian 'newly industrializing economies' (Hong Kong, Singapore, South Korea and Taiwan) and the East Asia and Pacific region (dominated by China). During the 1990s, income per head in these country groups had an annual growth rate of 4.0 per cent and 6.3 per cent respectively, compared to just 1.8 per cent in the OECD countries.

The economic performance of Latin America and the Caribbean has been less strong. Following average 3.3 per cent annual growth in the 1970s, the region was devastated by the debt crisis in the 1980s which led to a 'lost decade' for development in which living standards declined. Recovery in the 1990s was weak and has been further undermined by falls in economic activity in the early years of this decade as capital flows into the region dropped sharply, reflecting investors' fears of the financial fragility of the region in the aftermath of Argentina's default on its foreign debt in 2001, the biggest default in history. However, its performance has still been stronger than that of either the Middle East and North Africa or Sub-Saharan Africa. In the latter, average living standards have contracted steadily for two decades as a result of a combination of natural disasters, slumping commodity prices, economic mismanagement, civil strife and, most recently, the AIDS epidemic. World Bank forecasts for the period to 2015 project that these differences will persist, with yearly per capita growth rates of 5.3 per cent in East Asia and 4.2 per cent in South Asia contrasting with 2.6 per cent in the Middle East and North African region and 1.6 per cent in Sub-Saharan Africa (table 25.1). As will be seen in this chapter, the latter are the two regions on which EU development policies have a particular focus. Thus, EU

Table 25.1 Growth of real per capita GDP by region, 1971–2015

	GNI per capita 2005 (current dollars)	Growth per cent				
		1971–80	1981–90	1991–2000	Forecast 2001–6	Forecast 2006–15
World	6,987	1.8	1.3	1.2	2.1	2.1
High-income countries	35,131	2.6	2.5	1.8	1.6	2.4
Industrial countries	n.a.	2.6	2.5	1.8	1.6	2.4
Asian NIEs	n.a.	7.2	3.5	4.0	2.0	3.5
Low- and middle-income countries	1,746	2.6	0.7	1.5	3.7	3.5
East Asia and Pacific	1,727	4.6	5.8	6.3	6.4	5.3
South Asia	684	0.7	3.3	3.2	4.5	4.2
Latin America and the Caribbean	4,008	3.3	−0.9	1.6	1.2	2.3
Europe and Central Asia	4,113	2.5	0.9	−1.8	5.0	3.5
Middle East and North Africa	2,241	3.6	−1.1	1.0	2.5	2.6
Sub-Saharan Africa	745	0.5	−1.1	−0.5	1.8	1.6

Source: World Bank (2003, 2006b) for growth data and World Bank (2006c) for GNI per capita.

development policy is required to address an increasingly disparate group of DCs, where the appropriate mixture of policy instruments is going to vary depending on the circumstances of the particular country or country grouping being considered.

Second, many of the old foundations of past EU relationships with developing countries are being swept away. These relationships were based on a mixture of trade preferences and development aid to promote trade and development in the weaker DCs, while restrictive trade measures (high protection against agricultural imports, quotas on the imports of textiles and clothing, and anti-dumping duties on the import of particularly competitive manufactured goods) and the absence of financial aid characterized EU relations with the more advanced DCs. Many DCs pursued inward-looking development strategies and were little interested in attracting private foreign investment. The liberalization of world trade and capital movements in recent years is gradually transforming these relationships.

Trade preference schemes are weakening for two separate reasons. The first is economic: trade liberalization under the auspices of GATT/WTO is reducing the value of trade preferences and the EU has been searching for new models of cooper-

ation. The second is legal: the EU's network of discriminatory preference schemes runs counter to GATT/WTO rules on regional trade arrangements (see chapter 1), but for years the EU was able to persuade other WTO members to condone them. In the mid-1990s, it decided it would no longer seek to make an exception of these arrangements and instead would enter into WTO-compatible trade arrangements with its developing country partners. These are required to be free trade areas covering substantially all trade between the contracting parties (see Article XXIV, appendix to chapter 1). Thus the EU has been actively pursuing regional trade agreements with many DCs, seeking to convert its selective preferential agreements into free trade ones.

Third, EU development cooperation policy is evolving rapidly. Private capital flows have come to dwarf the role of development aid as a source of investment capital in DCs. In the face of growing dissatisfaction with the outcome of aid programmes and growing 'aid fatigue', the search has been on to define new roles for aid and to see where it can be used most effectively. The EU has undertaken a comprehensive re-evaluation of its development cooperation policy objectives which has placed poverty alleviation at the centre. It has been an enthusiastic supporter of the Millennium

Development Goals (MDGs) launched at the UN Millennium Development Summit in 2000, which include the goal of reducing global poverty by 50 per cent from its 1990 level by 2015. At the same time, development cooperation is also required to come to terms with the changed world after 11 September 2001. There is now a closer link between security and development policy, as emphasized in the 2003 EU Security Strategy which defined security as the 'first condition for development'. The higher salience of South–North 'contagion effects' arising from issues such as terrorism, migration, disease and pollution may lead to aid being driven more by the security concerns of the donor rather than by the development interests of the recipient in the future.

Fourth, EU development cooperation policy has been characterized by a strong regional emphasis with particular groups of partner countries such as the African, Caribbean and Pacific (ACP) states, Asia and Latin America (ALA) countries, the Mediterranean countries and, more recently, PHARE and TACIS countries (these are the countries of Central and Eastern Europe and the Former Soviet Union, respectively; see section 25.2.2). The most long-lived and comprehensive of these regional arrangements has been the relationship with the ACP countries, originally under successive Lomé Conventions and now under the Cotonou Agreement. The Lomé Convention, first signed in 1975, was hailed at the time as a model for a new type of development partnership between industrialized countries and DCs. Its innovations of partnership, deep trade preferences and long-term contractual aid commitments were certainly novel at the time. However, the EU's geographical priorities have been rapidly changing in the 1990s following the end of the Cold War and reflecting the changing importance of different DC regions in international trade. Priority is now given under the European Neighbourhood Policy to the stability and development of neighbouring countries and to aid for countries in crisis in the regions nearest to the EU. The ACP countries are no longer as central to EU development cooperation policy as was once the case. On the other hand, the EU in 2005 launched its Africa Strategy which re-emphasized its commitment to support for

African countries which remain among the poorest and least-developed in the world (Council of the EU, 2005b). Not surprisingly, these shifts and realignments have generated considerable controversy and debate. There is a continuing tension between those who stress the regional approach based on recognition of historical and strategic linkages with former European colonies and neighbouring countries, and those who argue for a more global approach concerned predominantly with poverty reduction.

This chapter explores the way the EU interacts with the DCs through both its trade and its development cooperation policies. Section 25.1 concentrates on the trade arrangements intended to benefit DCs and Section 25.2 on the development cooperation or financial aid arrangements. Section 25.3 concludes by highlighting some of the main issues in the current debates on the EU's relations with the developing world.

25.1 Trade policy

Trade is a key mechanism for development. At the multilateral level, trade policy can contribute to ensuring a fair and equitable trading system which facilitates the integration of DCs into the international trading regime at their own pace. At the EU level, trade policy can facilitate access to EU markets by lowering trade barriers through multilateral liberalization and preferential schemes. EU trade policy can also influence the DCs' own trade policies through economic and trade cooperation agreements and by encouraging regional arrangements between them.

The EU's trade policy towards developing countries originally took the form of autonomous non-reciprocal preferential arrangements. These were of two kinds: the Generalized System of Preferences (GSP) available to all DCs and special preferential schemes for particular groups of countries. The two most important special schemes were the trade preferences under the Lomé Convention (now the Cotonou Agreement since 2000) with ACP countries and those with the Community's neighbours in the southern and eastern Mediterranean. Non-reciprocity meant that DCs were not required to offer similar preferential access to their markets in return for the access privileges they are granted to the EU market. The schemes differed according to the products covered, their contractual basis and the size of the concessions offered. Together, they formed a hierarchy of preferences with the ACP signatories to the Lomé Convention in the most preferred category, the Mediterranean countries in an intermediate category and most ALA countries in the least preferred category with GSP preferences only.

This trade policy has become even more diverse since the mid-1990s. In 2001, the EU decided to admit all products from countries on the UN list of least-developed countries (LDCs) duty- and quota-free (though duty-free imports of bananas, rice and sugar remained subject to quotas for a further transition period). At the same time, the EU initiated moves to convert its special preferential schemes with the Mediterranean and ACP countries into reciprocal free trade areas (FTAs), while it has also forged FTAs with some distant trading partners, notably South Africa, Chile and Mexico, and negotiations with Mercosur on an FTA have been ongoing since 2000. What explains these different strategies, and what does the future hold for the EU's trade relations with developing countries? We seek to provide answers to these questions in this section.

25.1.1 The Generalized System of Preferences

Preferences contradict the most favoured nation (MFN) principle of the WTO, but a provision known as the enabling clause which granted a waiver for autonomous tariff preferences to DCs was adopted in 1971 for a ten-year period and renewed as part of the final outcome of the Tokyo Round of GATT negotiations in 1979 for an indefinite period. This legitimizes the grant of general non-reciprocal preferences to DCs, and further allows deeper preferences in favour of LDCs. The EU introduced its GSP scheme in 1971. It covered all DC-manufactured exports but only some agricultural and food products. GSP products are divided into sensitive and non-sensitive categories. Originally, non-sensitive products were offered duty-free access while the preferences for sensitive products were characterized by quotas and ceilings, thus limiting the quantities involved.

In the 1995 revision of its GSP scheme, the EU did away with quotas and replaced them with tariff preferences that varied according to the sensitivity of the products. A further simplification took place in 2001. Under the general GSP scheme available to all DCs (including China), the EU granted duty-free access on non-sensitive products and partial tariff preferences on sensitive products. The usual tariff preference on sensitive products was a flat 3.5 percentage points (replaced for textiles and clothing by a 20 per cent preference margin which, on a tariff of 15 per cent, for example, would yield a preference of 3 percentage points). For many exporters, these relatively small margins are not worth the extra paperwork involved in applying for GSP status.

Additional preferences were available under social, environmental and drug trafficking clauses (the 'super GSP'). For products receiving the flat rate preference of 3.5 percentage points under the general arrangements, the extra preference was 5 percentage points. In the case of textiles and clothing, an additional 20 per cent preference was available under these arrangements. The additional incentives under the social clause were available to countries complying with so-called 'core labour standards' (see chapter 24), while those under the environmental clause were available to countries complying with international standards on forest management. The incentives to encourage countries to fight drug production and trafficking were initially introduced in the form of duty-free access for certain products originating in the Andean Community but were subsequently extended to some other Latin and Central American countries, and later to Pakistan. This latter extension prompted India to bring a case under WTO rules alleging that there was no basis in the enabling clause for a preference donor to discriminate *between* developing countries (apart from the possibility for more generous preferences to LDCs as a whole). In ruling on India's complaint, the WTO Appellate Body ruled that the term 'non-discriminatory' required that identical tariff treatment should be available to all similarly situated GSP beneficiaries (but not necessarily to all GSP beneficiaries, as India had argued), but still found in favour of India's complaint on the grounds that the EU's GSP drug arrangement failed to meet this criterion.

Partly in response to this ruling, the new EU GSP scheme introduced on 1 January 2006 reduces the number of GSP arrangements from five to three. Preferential margins under the general arrangement for all GSP beneficiary countries are maintained although the product coverage is extended, mostly in the agricultural and fishery sectors. In addition, a GSP Plus arrangement is introduced for poorer and more vulnerable economies. This extends duty-free access to all sensitive products provided that beneficiary countries can show that they comply with a range of conditions on human and labour rights, environmental protection, the fight against drugs and good governance. However, the arrangement is limited to lower-income economies, land-locked countries, small island nations and those countries which can demonstrate that their economies are poorly diversified. This open-ended list based on published criteria ensures that the new EU scheme complies with the WTO ruling to give equal treatment to all similarly situated GSP beneficiaries. The third arrangement maintains the 'Everything But Arms' (EBA; see chapters 22 and 24) scheme of duty-free and quota-free access for all imports from LDCs. Apart from arms and ammunitions, which are permanently excluded products, the extension of the scheme to bananas was delayed until January 2006, for rice until July 2009 and for sugar until September 2009. The essential value of the EBA arrangement is that it extends duty-free access to those agricultural products which are otherwise excluded from the GSP. While seen as the 'jewel in the crown' of the EU trade relationships with DCs, its overall importance should not be exaggerated. The immediate impact of the EBA has been negligible, largely because the LDCs currently export so little in the product categories which were liberalized.

The EU scheme has always provided for the 'graduation' of more competitive suppliers. This is defended by the EU on the grounds that it is intended to ensure that the preferences are targeted on those countries which genuinely need them, but it also reduces the competitive pressures on EU domestic firms. Based on certain criteria, a country may be excluded from the GSP altogether or graduated from certain products. Under the 1995 scheme, the criteria applied for exclusion were a complex combination of income level, a development index and an export specialization index. Under the 2006 scheme, these have been replaced with a single simpler criterion: the country's share of the EU market expressed as a share of exports from all GSP countries. The threshold has initially been set at 15 per cent, with a 12.5 per cent limit for textiles and clothing.

The EU GSP is intended to stimulate exports from DCs in three ways. First, trade is generated as improved market access makes imported goods more attractive relative to domestically produced alternatives; this is trade creation (see chapter 6). Second, to the extent that DCs and industrial countries are exporting similar products, preferential tariff reductions may help to switch trade to the DC supplier; this is trade diversion (see chapter 6). From the point of view of DCs, both effects are additive and positive. Third, the GSP may have a longer-term effect to the extent that it enhances the attraction of the preference-receiving country as a location for inward foreign direct investment (FDI) seeking to export to the EU.

Generally, analysts have had difficulty in finding a positive effect of GSP trade preferences on exports apart from the rent transfer accompanying duty-free entry of goods (rents arise because DC exporters can benefit from the remaining tariff protection to the EU market against third countries, though this depends on the bargaining power of exporting firms in the DCs vis-à-vis the importing firms in the EU). Critics point to a number of flaws with GSP schemes. Non-reciprocal preferences such as those offered by the GSP lie outside the purview of WTO rules and thus can be unilaterally modified or cancelled by donor countries at any time. This uncertainty is likely to discourage investment in beneficiary countries to take advantage of these preferences, which is meant to be one of their primary rationales. The EU scheme has offered minimal concessions on sensitive products (more than half of the total) which are often those in which the DCs have a comparative advantage. Because there is a cost to firms in learning about and making use of preferences, it is often not worth their while to apply for preferential treatment. In the case of textile and clothing imports, quotas were maintained on all significant suppliers under the Multi-Fibre Arrangement until it was dismantled at the end of 2005 (see chapter 24). Tariff preferences on agricultural products have been very limited, mainly because of the difficulty in reconciling preferential access with the protection provided by the CAP (see chapter 20), but also even in the case of tropical products which the EU does not produce itself, in order to protect the margin of preference provided to more preferred ACP and Mediterranean suppliers. The value of preferences is also reduced by restrictive rules of origin. Rules of origin are necessary to determine if a particular product originates in a preference-receiving country; if drawn too tightly, such rules may make it difficult for firms from the exporting country to claim originating status and thus benefit from the margin of preferential access provided.

25.1.2 Relations with the ACP states

The relationship with the ACP states began in 1957, at the inception of the European Community, with the Yaoundé Conventions. This was followed by a series of five-year Lomé Conventions starting in 1975 following the accession of the UK to the EU. Since 2000 relations with ACP countries have been governed by the Cotonou Agreement which was signed in 2000 and came into force in 2003. This introduced significant changes in philosophy and instruments compared to the Lomé Conventions. As noted earlier, the Lomé Conventions were based on a partnership model, deep trade preferences and contractual financial commitments. This section concentrates on the trade preferences provided, while the aid element is examined in Section 25.2.3.

Under the conventions the EU offered duty- and quota-free access to exports from ACP countries, although again a major exception was exports covered by the CAP. However, more preferential treatment than to other countries was extended for CAP products. In addition, four commodity protocols annexed to the Lomé Convention provided preferential access for a specified quantity of exports from a selected group of traditional ACP suppliers of bananas, rum, sugar and beef. This trade regime was extended under the Cotonou Agreement until the end of 2007.

Despite the fact that the ACP states were at the top of the EU's hierarchy of preferences, with the most favourable conditions of access to the EU market, they have become increasingly marginalized as EU trade partners over time; the share of ACP exports to the EU market has fallen by more than a half, from 8 per cent in 1975 to 2.8 per cent in 2004. Furthermore, in 2004, 50 per cent of total ACP exports came from only four products: oil (26 per cent), diamonds (11 per cent), cocoa (9 per cent) and wood (4 per cent). This data is often used to argue that trade preferences have not worked, and indeed there is some support for this, but it is not the whole story. The importance of the trade preferences granted is often overstated. On average, 50 to 60 per cent of ACP exports to the EU never received any preferences because they were non-dutiable, irrespective of source. Another 5 to 10 per cent of ACP exports to the EU fell under the special import regulations of the CAP. Ultimately, only about 35 to 45 per cent of ACP exports received preferences. These were mainly tropical beverages, for which demand is quite price inelastic and where demand is reaching saturation in the EU. Further, the margin of preference enjoyed by ACP states fell as the EU's MFN tariffs were cut under successive GATT negotiations for products such as coffee, cocoa and vegetable oils.

Trade preferences require a supply capacity to make them effective, and arguably economic mismanagement and supply-side difficulties also limited ACP exports. But even with good economic management, ACP countries have been specialized in commodities with poor market prospects, and where the deterioration in export prices has had a devastating effect on development efforts. It can be argued that trade preferences failed to promote the necessary diversification. On the other hand, where progress in diversification was made, the products to benefit, such as textiles, fisheries and horticultural products, were those which enjoyed a substantial margin of preference over the EU's MFN and GSP tariffs. On balance, however, ACP trade preferences have not been seen as a success, and this was one of the factors leading to their revision in the Cotonou Agreement in 2000.

In 1996 the Commission published a Green Paper to promote discussion on the post-Lomé relationship with ACP states. Central to this discussion was the nature of future trade relationships in the context of WTO rules. Because the EU's special preferences for ACP countries are clearly discriminatory in the context of the WTO enabling clause discussed in the previous section, the EU had to seek a waiver from the WTO to permit it to offer this more favourable market access. This waiver came under sustained attack during the 'banana dispute' in the WTO, and the EU indicated right from the start of the post-Lomé negotiations that it was not willing to seek further waivers to defend its trade regime with the ACP. It therefore sought new WTO-compatible trade arrangements in the form of reciprocal FTAs with ACP states.

This shift was implemented in the Cotonou Agreement. In future, trade relations with ACP countries will be based on reciprocal free trade agreements which will take the form of Economic Partnership Agreements (EPAs). EPAs will cover not only trade in goods and agricultural products but also services, and will also in addition address tariffs, non-tariff and technical barriers to trade such as competition policy, protection of intellectual property rights, sanitary and phytosanitary measures, standardization and certification, trade and labour standards, trade and environment, food security, public procurement, etc.

The Cotonou Agreement lays out the basic principles and objectives of the new economic and trade cooperation between the ACP and the EU, but does not itself encompass a full-fledged trade regime. Negotiations started in 2002 and the new agreements are to be completed by 2008. A further transitional period for the implementation of the agreements can run up to twelve years. A waiver was granted to maintain the current ACP–EU trade regime until the end of 2007 at the fourth WTO Ministerial Conference in Doha in November 2001.

The other novel aspect of EPAs is that the Commission is negotiating not with individual ACP countries but with six regional groups. These are West Africa, Central Africa, Eastern and Southern Africa, Southern African Development Community, the Caribbean and the Pacific. EPAs are thus intended to consolidate regional integration initiatives within the ACP. However, the task is complicated by the overlapping membership and fragmented nature of African regional groupings (see chapter 1). Many NGOs are critical of what they see as undue pressure being put on weak economies to open their markets for both goods and services to EU imports and to agree to rules on investment which they have previously rejected in the ongoing Doha Round of multilateral trade negotiations. They are concerned at the implications of the loss of tariff revenue for the ability of ACP economies to maintain minimum levels of government expenditure (Oxfam, 2006). The Commission's view is that EPAs are a way to help ACP countries to break out of their situation of economic dependency by helping them to build productive capacity and regional markets. It argues that the ACP countries will have a long transition period over which to lower their tariffs and will continue to be able to protect their sensitive sectors even in a WTO-compatible FTA. It also points to its significant commitment to provide funding to help ACP countries to meet the challenges of preparing for free trade with the EU.

If, at the end of the negotiations, there are some countries which do not want to join in an EPA, alternative possibilities will be considered 'in order to provide these countries with a new framework for trade which is equivalent to their existing situation and in conformity with WTO rules'. ACP LDCs already benefit from the almost free access to the EU market through the EBA arrangement under the GSP. For non-LDC countries, the most likely option is the standard GSP arrangement or the new GSP Plus.

One long-run consequence may be the fragmentation of the ACP which could be divided into a number of different groups, each with different access conditions to the EU market. These could include the LDCs availing themselves of EBA conditions, low- and middle-income countries negotiating EPAs (divided in turn into separate regional groupings) and low- and middle-income countries that do not want an EPA and which might be offered GSP status. Whether the ACP states will be able to maintain a unified negotiating position under this new trade framework is an open question.

25.3.3 Relations with the Mediterranean and the Middle East

Formal relations with the countries of the south and east Mediterranean go back to the Treaty of Rome which enabled France to keep, through a special protocol, its special relationships with its former colonies, Morocco and Tunisia (Algeria was still an integral part of France at the time). The 1973 war between Israel and its Arab neighbours, followed by the oil embargo, led to renewed efforts for improved cooperation. The first common EU policy was the Global Mediterranean Policy (1973–92) which involved all the non-EU Mediterranean countries except Libya and Albania. Bilateral cooperation agreements were signed covering not just trade preferences but also aid through financial protocols. The southern EU enlargement to include Spain, Portugal and Greece in the mid-1980s reduced the benefits of trade preferences particularly to the Maghreb countries (below) given the similar export patterns of the two groups of countries. The new political climate in the early 1990s following the 1991 Gulf War and the fall of the Berlin Wall led to a renewed Mediterranean policy (1992–6). This increased the amount of development aid and extended trade preferences, as well as extending cooperation to issues such as human rights, the environment and the promotion of democracy.

In the mid-1990s, under pressure particularly from Spain, there was an attempt to breathe new life into the Euro-Mediterranean relationship through the Barcelona process or Euro-Mediterranean Partnership. This was launched by the Barcelona Declaration issued following a conference of the fifteen EU member states and twelve Mediterranean countries in November 1995. The twelve Mediterranean partners are Morocco, Algeria, Tunisia (Maghreb); Egypt, Israel, Jordan, the Palestinian Authority, Lebanon, Syria (Mashrek); Turkey, Cyprus and Malta. Cyprus and Malta became EU members in May 2004. Turkey has had a customs union agreement with the EU since 1996 and has been a candidate country since 1999. Libya has observer status at certain meetings. Thus currently the Euro-Mediterranean Partnership associates nine countries with the EU.

The main aims of the Barcelona Declaration are:

*   establishment of an area of peace and stability based on fundamental principles including respect for human rights and democracy (political and security partnership);
*   creation of an area of shared prosperity through the progressive establishment of free trade between the EU and its partners and among the partners themselves in order to create a Euro-Mediterranean FTA by 2010, accompanied by EU financial support for structural reform in the partners and to help cope with the social and economic consequences of this reform process (economic and financial partnership);
*   implementation of mutual understanding among peoples and the development of an active civil society (social and cultural partnership).

The FTA is implemented through bilateral Association Agreements between the EU and the nine Mediterranean countries. These replaced the earlier cooperation agreements concluded in the 1970s which provided for non-reciprocal preferences. By 2006, Association Agreements had been signed between all Mediterranean partners and the EU with the exception of Syria. All Association Agreements provide for trade liberalization of manufactured goods, with free access for Mediterranean exports and gradual tariff dismantling over a transitional period for EU exports. For agriculture, asymmetric reciprocal preferences are granted by the parties. The agreements also include provisions relating to intellectual property, services, technical rules and standards, public procurement, competition rules, state aid and monopolies. In these areas, the partner countries are expected to approximate their laws to those of the EU in order to facilitate trade.

As well as bilateral trade liberalization, the Mediterranean partners are committed to implementing regional free trade among themselves, but only limited progress has been made to date. In May 2001, four members of the Barcelona process (Morocco, Tunisia, Egypt and Jordan) signed the Agadir Declaration under which they aim to establish an FTA among themselves. Turkey must accede to all the EU's preferential agreements under its CU agreement with the EU, though so far these are limited to Morocco and Tunisia. So, in practice, the partnership resembles more a hub-and-spoke arrangement in which the EU has negotiated Association Agreements with the North African and Middle Eastern states. As a result, the EU–Mediterranean Partnership has not yet fulfilled the high hopes held out at the time of the Barcelona Declaration. In the political background is the Arab–Israeli conflict and the Middle East peace process. The Madrid Peace Conference and the breakthrough at Oslo were major factors in making the Barcelona process possible. Conversely, the cessation of the peace process has slowed down progress towards the objectives set out in the Barcelona Declaration.

25.1.4 Relations with Asia and Latin America

The remarkable growth of the East Asian economies in the 1980s and the first half of the 1990s was reflected in a significant expansion of trade and investment flows between the EU and developing Asia. The EU–ASEAN Cooperation Agreement signed in 1980 was the cornerstone of EU Asia policy for many years. ASEAN initially emphasized economic and development cooperation and did not intend the creation of an FTA (see chapter 1 on this and membership). The 1992 decision to create the ASEAN Free Trade Area by 2003 reignited EU interest in the region. In 1994, the Commission produced its first overall Asia Strategy paper (CEC, 1994c) which was updated in 2001 (CEC, 2001b). In 1996, at the initiative of Singapore's Prime Minister, a series of Asia–Europe meetings (ASEM) were introduced which

now provide the framework for political dialogue. The Asian partners include many of the ASEAN countries as well as China, Japan and South Korea. Following pressure from EU exporters, a Trans-regional EU–ASEAN Trade Initiative was launched in 2003 to promote regulatory cooperation between the EU and ASEAN on topics such as sanitary, phytosanitary and technical barriers to trade. The EU has expressed interest in building on this initiative to create a fully fledged EU–ASEAN FTA.

As was the case for Asia, EU Latin American policy was almost non-existent in the early years of the Union. The EU's attention was focused on Africa and no member state had a particular interest in Latin America. In the early 1970s, political contacts were maintained through meetings with the group of Latin American ambassadors in Brussels and in 1971 Latin American countries became beneficiaries of the EU's GSP. Relations remained limited in the 1980s, partly because of the debt crisis which meant that European investors lost interest in the region, and partly because of differences over the Falkland War between the UK and Argentina, which led to the suspension of the Brussels dialogue.

Since the mid-1980s, however, cooperation has been intensifying. The EU membership of Spain and Portugal in 1986, with their traditional links with Latin and Central America, provided the impetus for this. At the same time, however, Latin American countries were throwing off the old import-substitution model of economic development and beginning to open up their markets under the influence of the Washington consensus. The EU share of Latin American imports had been falling, which provided another reason for forging closer links. Formal institutional ties have been established since 1990 with the Rio Group, which now comprises all of Latin America as well as representatives from the Caribbean. Ministerial meetings have been held annually between the EU and the Rio Group since 1987. Political dialogue with the Central American countries began just a little earlier in 1984 with the San José Dialogue. Political relations with Mercosur (see chapter 1) were institutionalized by a cooperation agreement in 1995, while political dialogue with the

Andean Pact countries was institutionalized in the Rome Declaration in 1996. Regular bi-annual summits are now held between EU, Latin American and Caribbean heads of state to develop a strategic partnership between the two regions. Conflict resolution, democratization and human rights, social progress and the reduction of inequality and the environment are among the themes emphasized in these dialogues.

Political dialogue with ALA countries has been accompanied by attempts to forge closer trade relations and by increasing flows of EU development assistance. Trade relations have been based on the GSP since 1971. During the 1970s, the Commission promoted trade agreements with a number of ALA countries but their substantive significance was small. They generally confirmed MFN reciprocal recognition while sometimes granting quotas under more favourable access terms for some ALA exports. As noted above, the Andean Pact and some Central American countries received more favourable GSP preferences in order to help them in the fight against illegal drugs. On the other hand, ALA countries have been the most frequent targets of EU anti-dumping actions (see chapter 24), for instance in the textiles and clothing sector for which GSP preferences are already very restricted and where quantitative restrictions on imports applied until the end of the MFA in 2005.

The 1990s saw a new phase in trade relations with Latin America with the initiation of discussions on association agreements with Mexico (which entered into force in 2000) and Chile (concluded in 2002). These initiatives were undertaken to minimize the consequences of trade diversion arising from similar US agreements with these countries. Negotiations on an FTA with Mercosur were initiated in 2000, also in response to the US initiative to launch a free trade area for the Americas. The negotiations collapsed in 2004 with both sides unhappy with the extent of the market-opening offers from the other side, although discussions continue at a technical level. Negotiations on political and cooperation agreements are planned with Central America and the Andean Community to create the conditions for future arrangements similar to those with Mexico and Chile.

25.1.5 Evaluation of EU trade policy towards developing countries

The major thrust of EU trade policy towards developing countries is a move away from the autonomous preference-based and regionally discriminatory trade arrangements of the past to a more horizontal but differentiated policy emphasizing reciprocal free trade arrangements with low- and middle-income DCs and the duty- and quota-free access now offered to all LDCs under the EBA scheme. This shift has been driven partly by a realization that it would become increasingly difficult to gain WTO waivers for regionally discriminatory non-reciprocal preferential trade arrangements in the future, and partly by dissatisfaction on the part of the EU with the outcome of the previous non-reciprocal preferences. Also, the reduction in EU tariff barriers in successive rounds of trade liberalization has steadily reduced the advantages of preferential treatment. The EU argues that free trade agreements will have positive outcomes for the partner countries, through encouraging a more efficient allocation of resources and greater competition, and by creating a more attractive location for FDI. However, some potential drawbacks should be noted.

For the ACP and Mediterranean partners, entering into a free trade agreement is an asymmetric liberalization process. For manufacturing products, these countries already enjoyed duty-free access to the EU market (though in the case of the Mediterranean countries ceilings operated for sensitive products such as textiles and clothing), so the main impact is the unilateral removal of trade barriers on EU exports entering partner country markets. While consumers and producers who will now have the possibility of importing cheaper intermediate products will benefit, many firms, particularly small and medium-sized enterprises, may be forced to close with a consequent rise in unemployment. Also, the continued barriers to agricultural trade in the agreements, which is the sector where many of the partner countries have their comparative advantage, make adaptation to the required structural changes more difficult. Some fear that a consequence of this asymmetric liberalization may be trade diversion in favour of EU exports, that is, the substitution of EU imports for cheaper products currently being supplied by third countries. This would add to the economic costs of these agreements for EU partners (for estimates of the impact on the Euro-Med partners, see the studies cited in McQueen, 2002).

Proponents of these agreements therefore emphasize the likelihood of dynamic gains, particularly that the contractual nature of these agreements will lower uncertainty by locking in trade liberalization policies in the partner countries, thus helping to attract greater FDI flows. Also potentially important are the provisions to tackle non-tariff trade barriers (NTBs), thus lowering the transaction cost of trade and reducing the impact of regulatory trade barriers. For the ACP countries, a further issue which needs to be addressed is the reduction in tariff revenues as duties on EU imports are eliminated. This could curtail government spending at the same time as increased support for industrial restructuring and assistance to cushion the costs of transitional unemployment is required, unless other means to broaden the tax base are found.

The EU announced a self-imposed moratorium on new FTA initiatives prior to the 1999 Seattle WTO Ministerial Council in order to focus EU efforts on promoting the new WTO multilateral trade round. Following the suspension of the Doha Round negotiations in July 2005, the EU indicated a revision of this position in its 'Global Europe' document the following year (CEC, 2006u). This document noted that the EU's current FTAs serve its neighbourhood and development interests well, but its trade interests less well. The content of existing agreements is too limited, in that they fail to address regulatory and 'behind the border' trade barriers (see chapter 24). The EU does not have agreements with the world's most dynamic markets, particularly in Asia, while many of these priority markets are negotiating FTAs with its competitors (such as ASEAN members with Japan or Korea with the US), threatening the EU with a loss of market share. The document therefore announced the EU's interest in concluding a range of further FTAs, particularly with countries with significant market potential and where existing barriers to EU exports were high. Based on these criteria, the document highlights agreements with ASEAN, Korea, Mercosur, India, Russia and the Gulf Cooperation Council as of direct interest to the EU. While at the same time restating its commitment to a successful conclusion of the Doha Round multilateral negotiations, the document clearly signals that the EU is 'open for business' when it comes to concluding a range of FTAs with developing countries in the future.

25.2 Development cooperation

This section examines the EU's development cooperation programme, referring to the provision of development aid. Development assistance is a shared competence between the EU and the member states. We will refer to EU aid as external assistance managed by the European Commission unless it is otherwise clear from the context that aid provided by the member states is also included. Net disbursements of ODA (see box 25.1) by EU member states in 2005, including EU aid, were $55.7 billion, more than half of the total aid provided by the members of the OECD's Development Assistance Committee (DAC). Of this, the EU programme amounted to $9.6 billion (7.5 billion euros), or just under 20 per cent of the total. In addition, the EU provides Official Aid (OA, see box 25.1) to countries such as the more advanced Balkan countries as well as Belarus, Russia and Ukraine among the New Independent States of the former Soviet Union (see table 25.2).

EU development assistance policy evolved in a haphazard fashion without clear objectives or justification for many years. Its modest start was when eighteen African countries, mainly ex-colonies of France and Belgium, were associated with the EU under the Yaoundé Convention (1965). UK accession to the EU raised the question of the treatment of its ex-colonies in Africa, the Caribbean and the Pacific. This led to the Lomé Convention in 1975 which over the next quarter-century determined the use of the European

Box 25.1 Understanding EU aid

Total EU external assistance can be broken down by category of assistance, by source of financing, by political responsibility, and by method of management.

Categories of external assistance

There are two categories of external assistance. Official development aid (ODA) is defined by the OECD Development Assistance Committee (DAC) as grants or loans to DCs provided by the official sector on concessional financial terms, with the promotion of economic development and welfare as the main objective. Official aid consists of flows on aid-like terms but to countries which are not considered as DCs by the OECD DAC. We refer to ODA as aid, and the combined total as external assistance.

Sources of financing

The Union's external assistance programme has two distinct sources of funding: funds allocated through the EU budget and contributions by member states outside the EU budget to the European Development Fund (EDF). Decisions on budget funds are made with the involvement of the European Council, the European Parliament and the Commission (co-decision procedure; see chapter 3). The final decision is made by the Parliament, but within the limits/ceilings agreed in the financial perspective. EDF funds are contributed by member states on a voluntary basis according to a specific distribution key, and decision-making power rests with the Council of Ministers without any legal basis for the involvement of the Parliament and the Commission, although

these funds are managed by the Commission on behalf of the member states. EDF funds are allocated solely to ACP countries and overseas countries and territories (OCTs), while aid via the EU budget is provided mainly to non-ACP countries. Budgetized assistance is allocated according to either a geographical or a thematic approach under specific budget headings.

Political responsibility

Responsibility for EU external assistance is divided among three Directorates General (see chapter 3) in the Barroso Commission which took office in 2004. DG Development provides policy guidance on development policy and is responsible for aid to ACP states and for the Humanitarian Aid Office (ECHO). DG Enlargement provides pre-accession assistance for candidate countries and potential future members in the western Balkans. DG External Relations is responsible for remaining external assistance mainly to Asian, Latin American and Mediterranean countries and is also responsible for EuropeAid.

Management of assistance

EuropeAid was set up in 2001 to implement the disbursement of EU external assistance regardless which DG has political responsibility. It implements all EU aid projects with the exception of pre-accession financing instruments, humanitarian assistance, macro-financial assistance, Community Foreign and Security Policy, and the rapid reaction facility. ECHO is in charge of humanitarian assistance, while the other programmes are administered by their respective DGs.

Development Fund (EDF) for both groups of countries. In the following year, aid resources were made available to other DCs for the first time, and in 1977 cooperation agreements were signed with neighbouring countries in the southern Mediterranean. Bilateral arrangements were subsequently made with countries in Asia and Latin America, and in the 1990s countries in Eastern Europe and central Asia gained their own

regional programmes. The historical legacy of this evolution was a diffuse array of policies, budgets, administrative procedures and aid instruments. This section describes the EU ODA programme and some of the recent changes in its management, designed to make it a more efficient and effective instrument in contributing to the sustainable economic and social development of DCs.

Table 25.2 EU external assistance, 2001–2005, € billion

	2001	2002	2003	2004	2005
Total EU development assistance	7.7	7.9	8.7	10.3	10.7
Of which: ODA	5.9	5.9	6.0	6.9	7.5
OA	1.8	2.0	2.7	3.3	3.2
Financed by: EDF	2.1	1.9	2.4	2.5	2.5
Budget	5.6	6.0	6.3	7.7	8.2
Managed by EuropeAid	5.4	5.3	5.6	6.2	6.4
Of which: ODA	5.0	4.9	5.2	5.9	6.1
OA	0.4	0.4	0.4	0.4	0.3
Managed by other DGs	2.3	2.6	3.1	4.0	4.3
Of which: ODA	0.9	1.0	0.8	1.0	1.4
OA	1.4	1.6	2.3	3.0	3.0

Note: See Box 25.1 for categories.

Source: CEC (2002r, 2003j, 2006w).

25.2.1 EU development co-operation principles

As noted, before the Treaty of Maastricht in 1992, EU development cooperation policies had evolved piecemeal and in a fragmented fashion. The main innovation of this Treaty was to establish policy objectives for EU development cooperation and to set out how it should relate to the policies of member states. Three policy objectives are stated in Article 177:

Community policy in the sphere of development co-operation, which shall be complementary to the policies pursued by the Member States, shall foster:

– the sustainable economic and social development of the developing countries, and more particularly the most disadvantaged among them,
– the smooth and gradual integration of the developing countries into the world economy,
– the campaign against poverty in the developing countries.

The Article further states that Community policy in this area shall contribute 'to the general objective of developing and consolidating democracy and the rule of law, and to that of respecting human rights and fundamental freedoms'. The emphasis on the complementary nature of Community policy implies that development aid is an area of shared competence where the EU operates in parallel with the member states (in contrast to trade policy which is broadly the prerogative of the Union level alone; see chapters 2, 3 and 24).

Article 178 establishes the important principle of policy coherence, in that it requires that 'the Community shall take account of the objectives referred to in Article 177 in the policies that it implements which are likely to affect developing countries'. Article 179 sets out that decision-making should be based on qualified majority voting using the co-decision procedure (see figure 3.1). However, decisions on the EDF, an extra-budgetary arrangement designed to provide financial support to the ACP countries, are explicitly excluded from this provision and continue to be taken on the basis of unanimity.

The relationship between the EU aid programme and those of the member states is addressed in Article 180 which states:

The Community and the Member States shall coordinate their policies on development co-operation and shall consult each other on their aid programmes, including in international organisations and during international conferences. They may undertake joint action. Member States shall contribute if necessary to the implementation of Community aid programmes.

The significance of this Article is that it gives the EU the legal responsibility to coordinate its own development cooperation policy with the policies of the member states. As noted by the OECD, this makes the EU 'a unique donor in that it plays a dual role in development, as a bilateral donor providing direct support to countries, and as a co-ordinating framework for EU Member States' (OECD, 2002a, p. 21).

In summary, these provisions in the Maastricht Treaty define three principles on which development cooperation policy should be based:

- *complementarity* between the development policies of the member states and the Commission;
- *coordination* between member states and the Commission in the operation of these policies;
- *coherence* of all Union policies so that they take development objectives into account.

A fourth principle was added by the Amsterdam Treaty in 1997:

- *consistency* of all external actions of the Union in the context of all external relations, including security, economic and development policies.

While the strategic focus on poverty reduction as the main development policy objective in the Treaty was welcome, this needed to be refined and made more specific for operational purposes. The diversity of the different programmes and projects supported by the EU threatened to overwhelm the institutional capacity of the Commission, both in Brussels and in the field, to manage these programmes. A more selective prioritization of what the EU should try to do was clearly desirable. The first attempt to set out these priorities was the Statement on the European Community's Development Policy in November 2000 (Council of the EU, 2000). This statement identified six priority areas for EU action based on where the EU could demonstrate value added and comparative advantage as compared to other donors. These were macroeconomic policies and the promotion of equitable access to social services; food security and sustainable rural development; transport; trade and development; regional integration and cooperation; and institutional capacity-building particularly for good governance and the rule of law. In addition, four cross-cutting issues were identified, namely, human rights, gender equality,

protection of the environment and conflict prevention. Humanitarian assistance was seen as an additional activity but not as a priority area for long-term development assistance (OECD, 2002a).

The 2000 statement has since been superseded by the European Consensus on Development which was jointly adopted by the Commission, the member states meeting within the Council and the European Parliament in December 2005 (Council of the EU, 2005c). Unlike the 2000 statement, the Consensus on Development sets out, for the first time, the common vision that guides the actions both of the Commission and the member states in development cooperation. It takes into account the commitments made by the EU at various international conferences in the preceding five years as part of its support for the MDGs, as well as advances made in development best practice to ensure more effective aid. Unlike the earlier statement, the consensus document was preceded by a wide public consultation process which gives it much greater legitimacy. The consensus is divided into two parts: the EU common vision on development is the subject of Part 1, whereas Part II, entitled *The European Community Development Policy*, sets out the policy guiding the implementation of this vision for the EU aid programme under the responsibility of the Commission. The key elements of the common vision are the joint commitment to poverty eradication, to ownership of development strategies by partner countries, to delivering more and better aid, and to promoting policy coherence for development. It identifies the particular role and comparative advantage of the EU aid programme relative to the member states, and highlights eight areas for Community action: trade and regional integration; the environment and sustainable management of natural resources; infrastructure, communications and transport; rural development, agriculture and food security; governance, democracy, human rights and support for economic and institutional reforms; conflict prevention and fragile states; human development; and social cohesion and employment. While this may seem a comprehensive list of development activities, the commitment to complementarity and greater coordination between the Commission programme and those of the member states is intended to ensure more effective aid delivery in the field.

25.2.2 Aid volumes and trends

In the 1990s, the volume of EU aid grew at an average annual rate of 5.3 per cent. The growth was largely in terms of budgetized aid (see box 25.1), as disbursements through the EDF remained static in real terms and even dipped in the mid-1990s (OECD, 2002a). During this period, the volume of aid provided by member states declined, so that by 2000 the EU programme accounted for around 20 per cent of total EU ODA. This proportion was as high as 50 per cent for Italy but only around 5–10 per cent for those countries, such as Denmark, the Netherlands and Sweden, that exceed the UN target contribution of 0.7 per cent of GNI. Since 2000, total EU ODA has increased sharply from $25.3 billion in 2000 to $55.7 billion in 2005 (including an exceptionally high figure for debt relief of $14.7 billion in 2005) in response to the commitments made at the UN Millennium Summit. Although EU aid administered by the Commission also increased in this period, from $4.9 to $9.6 billion, it now makes up a somewhat smaller proportion of total EU aid than at the beginning of the decade.

In response to the challenge of meeting the MDGs, the Commission encouraged member states to increase their ODA contributions at the European Council meeting in Barcelona in March 2002. In 2002 the combined EU members had a weighted average ratio of ODA to gross national income (GNI) of 0.32 per cent. The Commission target at the Barcelona Council meeting was to raise the average amount of ODA to 0.39 per cent of GNI by 2006, with a minimum country target of 0.33 per cent. More ambitious targets were set in 2005 and reconfirmed in the European Consensus, when the EU adopted a timetable for member states to reach the 0.7 per cent of GNI target set by the United Nations by 2015, with an intermediate collective target of 0.56 per cent by 2010. These commitments should see total EU aid (Commission plus member states) double to over 66 billion euros in 2010. Through this effort, based on DAC calculations, the EU will provide 78 per cent of the expected additional global ODA by 2010. The European Consensus states that at least half of this increase in aid will be allocated to Africa. In 2005, total EU aid was equivalent to 0.44 per cent of EU GNI, which included a significant amount for debt relief in that year, While this suggests that the EU as a whole is on track to meet its 2006 Barcelona target, Greece, Italy, Portugal and Spain will need to increase their ODA if the individual country target is to be met (CEC, 2005f).

A feature of the EU development assistance cooperation is the importance of geographical programmes. During the 2000–6 Financial Perspective, these were: the Pre-Accession programme for East European Countries (PHARE); the technical assistance programme for Eastern Europe and Central Asia (TACIS); community assistance for reconstruction, development and stabilization in the Balkans (CARDS); external assistance to Asia and Latin America (ALA); support to the Mediterranean and Middle East countries (MEDA); and the European Development Fund for ACP countries (EDF). Each of these programmes had its own management committee made up of the Commission and member states. There were a further fifteen thematic programmes dealing with issues such food security, poverty diseases, reproductive health, environment, NGOs, etc. Finally, the EU is the largest funding agency for emergency and distress assistance, much of which is channelled through ECHO, the EU's Humanitarian Aid Office.

Managing the EU aid programme on the basis of such a mixed and complex set of instruments in an efficient and coordinated way was becoming an increasingly difficult task. A simpler framework has been agreed for the 2007–13 Financial Perspective (see figure 25.1). The new framework comprises six instruments only, four of them new (the instruments for humanitarian aid and macro financial assistance continue without modification). In addition, the number of thematic programmes has been rationalized from fifteen to seven. The relative importance of the various instruments in the new framework of EU external action is shown in table 25.3, which underlines the growing attention paid by the EU to its immediate neighbours and to security issues.

Table 25.3 Overview of expenditure within heading 'EU as a global partner', in the 2007–2013 Financial Perspective (billion euros at 2004 prices)

	2006	2007	2008	2009	2010	2011	2012	2013	Total	Change 2006/13 %
Instrument for pre-accession	1,121	1,193	1,290	1,353	1,452	1,565	1,660	1,700	10,213	52
European neighbourhood and partnership instrument	1,274	1,390	1,400	1,437	1,470	1,530	1,640	1,720	10,587	35
Development cooperation instrument	1,862	2,000	2,060	2,116	2,167	2,190	2,246	2,324	15,103	25
Instrument for stability	531	232	268	338	363	400	430	500	2,531	−6
Common foreign and security policy	99	150	185	220	250	285	310	340	1,740	245
Provisioning of loan guarantee fund	220	188	185	181	178	174	171	167	1,244	−24
Emergency aid reserve	221									−100
Other	894	1,046	1,081	1,094	1,129	1,196	1,222	1,278	8,046	43
Total for the EU as a global partner	6,222	6,199	6,469	6,739	7,009	7,339	7,679	8,029	49,463	29

Source: CEC (2006x).

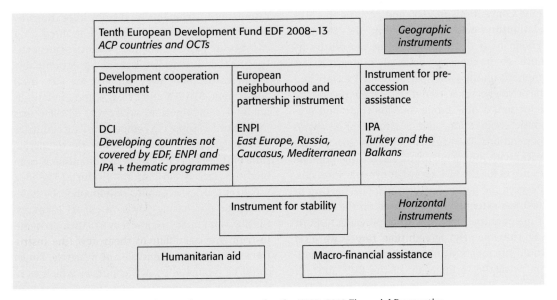

Figure 25.1 EU development assistance instruments under the 2007–2013 Financial Perspective

Moreover, the EU has responded to the criticism that its aid programme was not sufficiently poverty-focused. For example, the OECD (2002a) peer review of the EU aid programme highlighted the declining share of the poorest nations in EU aid disbursements, arising from the change in the geographical priorities for EU aid. Since the reform of external assistance in 2000, the share of low-income countries has grown from 32 per cent of disbursements in 2000 to 46 per cent in 2005, and the share of LDCs from 22 per cent to 33 per cent (CEC, 2005g). Another indicator is the pattern of aid allocation by sector, where the EU programme was criticized for the low proportion spent on social sector spending. However, by 2005 the share of EU aid devoted to the social sector amounted to 45 per cent, compared to 16 per cent for economic infrastructure, 16 per cent for budget support, 10 per cent for emergency aid and just 6 per cent for production activities, with a further 6 per cent spent on multi-sectoral and cross-cutting issues. Indeed, one might now query if the balance has not swung too much against support for the production sectors, and in particular agricultural and rural development, given the dependence of most poor people on food production for their livelihoods.

25.2.3 The Cotonou Agreement and the European Development Fund

As noted, the Cotonou Agreement succeeded the Lomé Conventions in 2000 and governs the EU's relationships with the ACP countries. The new agreement is distinguished from the old by its more comprehensive political dimension, its emphasis on the participation of civil society and the private sector, a strengthened focus on poverty reduction, a new framework for trade and economic cooperation, and a reform of financial cooperation. The Agreement lasts for twenty years, with financial protocols setting out the resources for the EDF agreed at five-year intervals. However, the period for the ninth EDF starting in 2000 was extended to 2007 based on the transfer of uncommitted balances from previous EDFs. It was subsequently agreed that the tenth EDF would run for six years from 2008 to 2013 to coincide with the termination of the EU's 2007–13 Financial Perspective. The first revision of the Cotonou Agreement was concluded in early 2005. It strengthens the political dimension and cooperation in the area of security as well as making minor adjustments in the management of EDF funds. Although it was intended to include the amount to be allocated to the tenth EDF as part of

this revision, this was not settled until the end of 2005 as part of the overall negotiations on the EU's Financial Perspective for the 2007–13 period.

The aid component of the agreement is divided into programmable and non-programmable allocations. The programmable ones are extended to individual ACP countries and regions through National and Regional Indicative Programmes. They are given every five years on the basis of a formula reflecting objective criteria based on demographic, geographic and macroeconomic conditions (GNP per capita, external debt, etc.). One of the innovations in the Cotonou Agreement was a shift to including performance indicators as well as needs in the allocation of EU aid resources. The main instruments for programming grants are the country and regional strategy papers. These papers set out general guidelines for using the aid as well as an indicative operational programme setting out how the money will be spent. A regular programme of review of these papers provides the means whereby performance measures are taken into account in future allocations of EDF funds.

Non-programmable funds are generally quick-disbursing instruments, and prior allocations by country are not defined. They are granted on a case-by-case basis to whichever countries meet the specified conditions. The main non-programmable resources of Lomé were support for structural adjustment, STABEX and SYSMIN, and humanitarian and rehabilitation assistance. STABEX was introduced in Lomé I to compensate ACP countries for the shortfall in export earnings due to fluctuations in the prices or supply of non-mineral commodities, largely agricultural products. The idea was to encourage economic development by stabilizing the purchasing power of export earnings. STABEX was joined in Lomé II by SYSMIN, a scheme to help alleviate fluctuations in revenue arising from the production and sale of minerals. Funds could be requested by ACP countries which were dependent on mineral exports for a substantial part of their export earnings, and if there were problems in the production of minerals, or development projects were threatened by a substantial fall in export earnings.

Under the Cotonou Agreement, STABEX and SYSMIN have been ended, although a new system

Table 25.4 EDF global commitments by programming and financial instrument, € million

	EDF6 1985–90	EDF7 1990–5	EDF8 1995–2000	EDF9[1] 2000–7	All (%)
Programmable aid	5,285	7,751	8,276	8,493	77%
Of which:					
Non-budget support (projects)	5,224	6,125	6,174	6,061	61%
Budget support	61	1,626	2,101	2,432	16%
Non-programmable aid	2,130	3,031	3,040	722	23%
Of which:					
Venture capital	544	839	1,157	–	7%
HIPC and Global Fund	–	40	1,060	630	4%
STABEX, FLEX	1,451	1,703	708	92	10%
SYSMIN	134	449	114	–	2%
Total	7,415	10,782	11,316	9,215	100%

Note: [1] Not all allocated money under EDF9 has yet been committed.

Source: CEC (2006y).

has been introduced to mitigate the losses caused by shortfalls in export earnings. The balance between programmable and non-programmable resources in recent EDFs is shown in table 25.4. There is a clear trend away from non-programmable resources towards programmable resources, and in particular towards budget support rather than project grants. This is in line with the EU's commitment to improve the effectiveness of aid by aligning it more closely with recipient countries' own priorities and procedures.

The volume of EDF resources was not increased significantly under the Cotonou Agreement. The Financial Protocol for the ninth EDF amounts to 15.2 billion euros, compared to 14.625 billion euros for the eighth EDF. In addition, the remaining funds from previous EDFs (amounting to 2.9 billion euros in 2003) have been transferred to EDF9 and are used in accordance with the new conditions. Although an increase in nominal terms, it represents a reduction in real terms and even more so in per caput real terms. The amount allocated to the tenth EDF to begin in 2008 and covering a period of six years was eventually agreed at 22.68 billion euros in December 2005. Budgetization of the EDF, as proposed by the Commission, was once again rejected by the member states and the EDF will continue as an extra-budgetary fund. The agreed amount was intended to ensure that the funds available would be maintained at least at the same level as the ninth EDF, taking into account the effects of inflation, growth within the EU and enlargement to ten new member states in 2004. A further small adjustment is being made now that Bulgaria and Romania have joined the EU. However, many of the committed resources only reach the ACP countries many years after they have been allocated. The slow disbursement of EU aid was just one of the factors which led to a radical overhaul of the management of the EU aid programme at the end of the 1990s.

25.2.4 Management of EU development assistance

Despite the growth in the volume of EU ODA, its management and effectiveness was severely criticized in a number of reports at the end of the 1990s. Particular attention was drawn to the following weaknesses:

- The complexity of the development cooperation system, which before the 1999 reform of the Commission under Commission President Prodi (see chapter 3), involved five Commissioners and four Directorates General in addition to ECHO.

- The splintered framework of aid management, based around geographical programmes, meant that there was no coherent vision of aid priorities and little consistency in the weights given to the different aid elements in each geographical programme. There was a proliferation of ad hoc programmes, each with its own budget line, regulations and procedures which made the overall programme very inflexible.
- Too much emphasis was placed on monitoring procedures and inputs and too little on evaluating outputs and results. Projects and programmes rarely had performance indicators and almost no evaluations had been undertaken prior to the 1990s to document what had been achieved.
- The decision-making process was very centralized with little authority delegated to field offices. Approval of policies, regional and country strategies, individual projects and contracting was centralized in Brussels.
- Staffing had not kept pace with the growth in disbursements, leading to a great reliance on external consultants for the design and implementation of projects and programmes.

A particular concern was the large and growing problem of disbursing funds which had been committed. While in 1990 outstanding commitments stood at three times annual disbursements for the EU, by 2000 this had grown to a multiple of four for EU budget funds and to a multiple of six for EDF funds (OECD, 2002a). Court of Auditors' reports noted that as much as half of the annual budget would be committed in a rushed manner in the last month of the year. There may be good external reasons for the difficulties in drawing down funds, including the low absorption capacity of recipient country administrations, especially in ACP countries, and restrictions arising from the abuse of human rights or the breakdown of the rule of law. However, internal problems, such as inadequate staff numbers to administer the programme and the large number of different budget lines and instruments, created inefficiencies and inflexibilities. Reform of the EU's aid management system was desperately needed.

The reform process was initiated when the new Commission took charge in 1999 with a restructuring of the external relations (RELEX) services. The overall objective of the reform was to speed up implementation of external assistance and to improve the quality of aid delivery. The configuration of political responsibilities introduced then was broadly maintained when the Barroso Commission took office in 2004 (see box 25.1). The number of budget lines will have been reduced from over thirty to just six when the 2007–13 Financial Perspective comes into force. The idea of a single External Relations Council to ensure greater consistency in the EU's external actions was introduced in 2002, thus abolishing the Development Council, although some development NGOs regard this as a retrograde step, fearing that development will become subordinate to foreign policy within the RELEX family.

In January 2001, EuropeAid was created to strengthen the implementation of EU development programmes worldwide and to bring consistency to programme management. EuropeAid's mission is to implement the external aid instruments of the Commission which are funded by the EU budget and the EDF. It does not deal with pre-accession aid programmes (PHARE, ISPA and SAPARD; see chapters 22 and 26), humanitarian activities or macro-financial assistance. It has undertaken a series of reforms to improve the efficiency and effectiveness of EU aid, including strengthening the project evaluation process and devolving project and programme management to Commission delegations in the field (CEC, 2005h). Since 2001, the Commission has published an annual report on EU development policy and the implementation of external assistance which provides greater transparency on this area of activity. More recently, the focus has shifted to implementation of the international agenda to improve the coordination and harmonization of aid procedures. The EU signed the Rome Declaration on Aid Harmonization in 2003 and the Paris Declaration on Aid Effectiveness in 2005 which commit it to specific targets to improve aid delivery by 2010.

25.2.5 Strategic issues in the EU development cooperation programme

Coordination with bilateral programmes

Coordination in aid policies and programmes between the EU and member states is a legal obligation under the Maastricht Treaty, but is proving hard to achieve in practice. Policy coordination at the most basic level might include the exchange of information between donors on their current and future activities, on their experiences with project management and on their evaluation and monitoring results. At a more intensive level, it could involve agreement on development objectives or on aid strategies for individual country recipients. The extent of coordination has been very limited in the past. In the European Consensus on Development, the EU and member states are committed to working towards joint multi-annual programming based on partner countries' national development strategies and their own budget processes. They also propose to make greater use of common implementation mechanisms including shared analysis, joint donor-wide missions, and the use of co-financing arrangements. Cox et al. (1997) caution that coordination at country level may often be more efficiently undertaken by multilateral agencies such as the World Bank or UNDP who can also bring non-EU donors into the picture. For example, the EU increasingly aligns its development strategies at field level with the World Bank-inspired Poverty Reduction Strategy Papers for the poorest countries involved in the highly indebted poor countries (HIPC) initiative.

Complementarity

Complementarity between the EU and member state aid programmes was another principle announced in the Maastricht Treaty, but no guidance was provided as to how this might be interpreted. One interpretation is that it should lead to a division of labour between donors, whether on geographical, sectoral, functional or thematic lines (Cox et al., 1997). Specific aid activities would be assigned to individual donors, based on their comparative advantage, proven competence in the area, etc. Possible advantages would be the creation of economies of scale and concentration of expertise in particular agencies, a reduction in unnecessary duplication of programming, and minimizing the administrative burdens on recipient countries of having to deal with multiple donors with different objectives, reporting requirements and administrative procedures even in the same sector. But the difficulties are also obvious. Donors would have to agree on the reallocation of tasks, and Cox et al. argue that there is little evidence on the balance of costs and benefits either for donors or recipients. They see little advantage in trying to achieve country rationalization but recommend that the EU might try to encourage greater sectoral specialization among member state donors at country level. The sectoral priorities set out for EU aid in the 2005 consensus statement can be seen as reflecting the principles of complementarity in action, although the list is so comprehensive that one wonders whether it is intended to limit the scope of the EU aid programme in the future. The Commission has begun to produce a Donor Atlas which presents information on each EU donor's strategic frameworks and activities, and which is intended to trigger further discussions on donor complementarity.

Coherence

Policy coherence was the third important principle established in the Maastricht Treaty. Coherence is the need to ensure that the objectives and impacts of different EU policies and agreements do not contradict or undermine each other. The OECD (2002a) report on EU aid policy highlighted some areas where the EU faces challenges in this regard. For example, while adopting a less protectionist trade policy would benefit most developing countries, LDCs which already have duty-free access to the EU market under the EBA scheme, or ACP countries which currently benefit from commodity protocols under the Cotonou Agreement, may lose out. EU agricultural policy has frequently been attacked for its adverse effects on developing world agriculture. Agriculture is usually the sector where the least liberal concessions are offered by the EU in its free trade agreements. EU-subsidized farm exports have undermined local markets to the detriment of local producers in a number of documented instances, including beef exports to coastal West Africa in the late 1980s, dairy exports to Tanzania, Brazil and Jamaica, and canned fruit and vegetable exports to South Africa. The purchase by the EU of fishing rights in the coastal waters of ACP countries to support the EU's fishing industry (see chapter 21) may have a detrimental effect on local artisanal fisheries and accelerate the decline in fish stocks. To address such problems, the EU includes a section on policy coherence in each of its country strategy papers which is intended to get the right 'policy mix' for each country. In 2005, the EU identified a total of twelve policy areas that had great potential to contribute to the MDG objectives. It made a 'policy coherence for development' commitment with respect to each of them, in order to improve coherence with the EU's development policy objectives. Whether this will be sufficient to overcome the sometimes entrenched opposition of EU producer lobbies remains to be seen.

Conditionality

Policy conditionality has been a further contentious issue in EU development cooperation policy, not least in its relations with the ACP states. In the original formulation of the Lomé partnership model, the intention was that ACP governments would identify their own priorities and jointly manage project implementation. With the growing emphasis on structural adjustment lending and policy conditionality by the Bretton Woods institutions and diminishing confidence in governance structures in many ACP states, the EU began to take a more interventionist approach. The dilemma, of course, is that a greater role for the EU in policy formulation may lead to a loss of local 'ownership'. Implementation of conditionality has also been a problem where different donors insist on different and possibly even contradictory policy conditions, thus overwhelming the local administration.

Another important change which has increased conditionality has been the growing concern with human rights and good governance, which, as we have seen, was enshrined as an objective of the EU's development policy in the Maastricht Treaty. All EU trade and cooperation agreements now include provisions for political dialogue, with the EU making clear that sanctions will be imposed if human rights are breached or the rule of law overturned. Again, the most contentious debates have taken place with the ACP states. In the negotiations on the Cotonou Agreement, the EU pushed strongly for the concept of good governance as a central part of the political dialogue, with a view particularly to targeting corruption in the administration of recipient countries. The ACP states saw this as an intrusion on their national sovereignty and were reluctant to agree to what they saw as an open-ended extension of conditionality. In the end, the final compromise put into the Cotonou Agreement designates good governance as a fundamental element which could, in certain circumstances, trigger non-execution of contracted aid flows. The strengthened political dialogue included in the first revision of the Cotonou Agreement in 2005 should ensure that recourse to punitive measures is only taken as a last resort.

25.3 Conclusions

From an aid relationship with its ex-colonies, the EU has evolved a complex set of relationships with the DCs embracing trade preferences, development assistance and political dialogue. This chapter has summarized the main features of these relationships and how they are changing over time. For reasons of space, not all aspects of these relationships could be covered. The chapter concentrated on trade arrangements and development assistance, and nothing was said, for example, about EU humanitarian aid or food aid. Both trade and development cooperation policy have been areas of dynamic policy development in recent years. Three themes in particular stand out as shaping the EU's relations with developing countries over the next decade.

First, the forging of FTA agreements with DCs brings the EU into uncharted territory. These agreements not only require reciprocal tariff concessions from the EU's partners, but are also much more comprehensive in their scope than anything the EU has negotiated with its DC partners until now. In some cases, these negotiations have not been easy. In the case of the trade and cooperation agreement with South Africa, for example, the EU took a hard negotiating line and the final agreement has been criticized for being less than generous to South Africa. The key unresolved problem for the EU in such negotiations concerns the status of trade in agricultural products protected by the CAP, which is very often an area where the DC partner has a comparative advantage. An agreement with Mercosur, for example, is hard to envisage unless the EU is more forthcoming on agricultural trade concessions. For the DC partners, offering concessions on services and approximating regulatory provisions with EU laws will be major economic and administrative challenges. Although the potential gains are large, they are also uncertain.

Second, the changing status of the ACP countries in the EU's development policy priorities is clearly evident. The success of this grouping in maintaining a negotiating unity, when it is bound together more by historic links to the EU than by common interests, has been remarkable. But it does look like an increasingly fragile unity. The EU insistence on negotiating regional EPAs will fragment ACP countries into regional groupings, leaving EDF funding and political dialogue as the only unique parts of the EU–ACP relationship. This is not to argue that Africa, in particular, will not remain a central concern for EU development cooperation policy, but this will be justified more by the latter's poverty alleviation mandate than by historical sentiment. The EU's Africa Strategy is an important marker in this regard, as it treats North Africa and Sub-Saharan Africa as a unity and points to the African Union as its interlocutor on the African continent. The strategy is presented as a 'partnership for security and development', indicative of the significant focus the EU wishes to give to security matters in Africa. Separate strategies for the Caribbean and the Pacific are in preparation which may further undermine the relevance of the ACP group.

Third, despite the European Consensus on Development, there remains ambiguity about the role which the EU aid programme should play relative to the member states. Is cooperation between national, bilateral agencies in the context of the Paris Declaration sufficient, or should member states channel a larger share of a growing aid budget through Brussels? Apart from any general unwillingness of member states to cede further authority to the EU, there has been an often justified view that the quality of the EU aid programme has not matched the standards of national programmes. However, there has been a generally recognized improvement in EU aid policy since the substantial reforms in 2000. The effectiveness of EU aid has been enhanced since the creation of EuropeAid as a single implementing agency; the simplification of the legal basis for development assistance in the new Financial Perspective; the decentralization of management authority to delegations in the field; and the commitment to harmonization and alignment in line with the Paris Declaration. It is problematic, however, whether the EU aid programme will be rewarded for this improved performance. The total budget for external action in the new Financial Perspective, as well as the size of the tenth EDF up to 2013, are now fixed. The increases agreed, in the context of the overall EU commitment to reach the UN target of 0.7 per cent of GNI by 2015, imply a sharp fall in the relative size of the EU programme. In the absence of any revision of the Financial Perspective, or the creation of some special-purpose instrument which would channel more bilateral aid resources through the Commission, the weight of the EU aid programme will gradually diminish over the next decade.

Part VII The enlargement, success and future of the EU

26 Enlargement
27 Has the EU been successful?
28 The future of the EU

Part VII of the book is concerned with the enlargement, success and future of the EU, and devotes a chapter to each of the three topics. It is therefore in the nature of an overall evaluation of the success or otherwise of the EU and its future prospects; hence it serves as a conclusion for the book. In case anyone wonders how enlargement fits into this general picture, one would say that, from the EU perspective, enlargement is part of its mission and vision and from the applicants' point of view it is a reflection of their confidence that the EU is where their future lies. As the EU becomes more mature, involves more member states and encompasses more aspects of public policy, it will face a complex set of decisions about how it should organize itself for the greatest benefit. Economic analysis has a lot to contribute to that set of decisions as the three chapters explore from different directions. In the more immediate future, however, the EU is trying to rethink the blueprint established for it by the Convention on the Future of Europe after the proposed 'Constitution' was rejected by referendums in France and the Netherlands. While it has aspirations to set out the next fifty years for the EU, the vision does not have the depth and foresight that the Treaty of Rome had for the first five decades. Thus this part is more the opening of a debate about the future than a conclusion.

26 Enlargement

DAVID MAYES

The enlargement of the EU and its more effective operation as a larger unit are the key issues of the current policy agenda. The EU admitted ten new members in May 2004 (Cyprus, the Czech Republic, Estonia, Hungary, Latvia, Lithuania, Malta, Poland, Slovakia and Slovenia), and Bulgaria and Romania at the beginning of 2007, after some difficult debate on whether they really meet the entry criteria. Furthermore the process will continue during the present decade. Entry negotiations with Turkey and Croatia began in October 2005 and other Balkan countries may soon add their names to the list. The Republic of Macedonia (the former Yugoslav Republic of Macedonia in EU terminology to ease Greek sensitivity) became a candidate country in December 2005 but negotiations are yet to begin.

The change in the nature of the EU has been considerable. It is not so much that these first steps have added over 100 million more people to the EU (with over 100 million more to come when the others join) compared to the previous 380 million inhabitants but that the number of member states is doubling from fifteen to around thirty. The number of faces round the table has the potential to impede the operation of many of the components of the EU if traditional formats are not changed. In the initial stages the economic impact of enlargement in absolute terms is very small – the first group of new members added less than 10 per cent to EU GDP – but this share is increasing as they are growing more rapidly. The potential effect is, however, much greater, as the structure of activity could change markedly if the new members continue to converge so fast to the levels prevailing among the existing members.

Enlargement is now almost entirely a matter of looking eastwards. Although the last but one round of enlargement ended up with rather fewer countries than expected, as only Austria, Finland and Sweden of the EFTA countries joined on 1 January 1995, there are no immediate plans to explore closer relationships with the remainder – Switzerland, Liechtenstein, Norway and Iceland. Of these, only Switzerland is not in the European Economic Area (EEA), which effectively brings them into the 'internal market', with the exception of agriculture and fishing (see chapter 2).

Initially it appeared as if the enlargement process might be a little more spread out. The next steps were spelled out in the Amsterdam summit and in *Agenda 2000*, which was published in 1997 by the Commission (CEC, 1997b). In particular the appendices to *Agenda 2000* set out the Commission's opinion on the applications from the ten Central and Eastern European countries (CEECs; see above). The way forward for negotiation over membership was then opened for the Czech Republic, Estonia, Hungary, Poland and Slovenia – in addition to Cyprus, which was agreed on earlier. The others on the list were for later consideration, as indeed was Turkey.

However, the picture changed steadily thereafter. There was a considerable outcry from the second group of countries and the Luxembourg Council in 1997 went out of its way to emphasize that all the applicant countries were to be included in the enlargement process from the start, although more active negotiations were to be confined to the first six. However, in 1999, the new Prodi Commission suggested that all the applicants should be actively considered for membership and admitted when 'ready'. This procedure was approved at the Helsinki Council in December, and Malta, which had renewed its application after a change in government, was added to the list, making twelve countries that could join to swell the EU to twenty-seven members. A further surprise in 1999 was the ending of the Greek outright opposition to Turkish membership, so that discussions could advance.

When the EFTA countries were being considered for membership, there was no real question as to whether they met the appropriate criteria, with the exception of the issue of political neutrality. The question was merely whether they were willing to accept the conditions of joining, and in the case of Norway and Switzerland the answer was negative. The negotiation process was very one-sided (see chapter 9 in Mayes (1997b) by Brewin for an exposition). Subsequently, due to real concerns over whether the Union could cope with the particular applicants, it became necessary to spell out the criteria for membership much more explicitly. Turkey obviously provides the greatest problem because of its size, agricultural nature and the relatively low level of GDP per head. Thus, it is now possible to explore the full political economy of the process of enlargement much more clearly. Furthermore, as the extent of enlargement has progressed, the EU has reached the point that it has to make changes in its administrative structure and finances if it is not to find the system becoming increasingly unworkable and the cost unacceptable. The last two budget negotiations have seen the budget diverge below the permitted EU GDP limits, as the larger net contributors seek to limit their exposure to prevailing levels (see chapter 19).

Tackling the issue of administrative and political gridlock is being addressed in a number of stages. The 2000 intergovernmental conference (IGC) started the process with extensive changes to the system and coverage of qualified majority voting and the composition of the European Parliament to incorporate all the applicant countries. This was incorporated into the Nice Treaty that came into force in 2003 (see chapter 2). The Nice Treaty also provided an option for the European Central Bank (ECB) and Commission to make proposals on voting in the Governing Council of the ECB. The ECB opted for a system of rotating votes for groups of national central bank governors that will come into effect when the number of euro area members exceeds fifteen; there are thirteen members as of 2007, with the three Baltic states eager to join, which would trigger the change if they succeeded.

The next step is a more thorough overhaul of the structure of the system following the suggestions of the Convention on the Future of Europe embodied in the new 'Constitution' (see chapters 2, 3 and 28). The remit was much wider than simply trying to make sure that the existing system could cope with enlargement and involved the drawing up of a constitutional blueprint on which the longer-term union could be based. These recommendations, or something like them, could have sweeping implications for the role of the Commission vis-à-vis the Council and indeed for the democratic legitimacy of the enterprise (Collignon, 2003). The proposals the Convention made are controversial: sufficiently so that, arguably, they led to rejection in 2005 by referendums in France and the Netherlands. Although most of the countries that do not require referendums have actually ratified the constitutional treaty, the process is stalled till the member states can think of a way of making the proposals more popular. The form of the proposals represents another step on the path of integration in a detailed treaty rather than an enduring 'constitution' despite the use of the word. They were the subject of an intergovernmental conference in 2004 that drew up the new treaty. Unlike previous discussions, the Convention was a novel attempt to involve a wide range of the interested parties from government and parliaments at all levels and from the social partners. It was all the more disappointing for the framers that it should be rejected in referenda in two core countries, given the relative success in ratifying previous treaties. It is not clear what the final outcome will be, as some governments see the proposals as not looking far enough into the future of closer integration, while others want to see some powers returned to the national level.

Our aim in this chapter is, however, limited. Chapter 28 deals with the main questions of the future development of the EU. We concern ourselves with four specific issues:

1. how the process of enlargement has developed over the last two decades;
2. how the widening of the EU on the present occasion has been agreed, and the criteria used in choosing whether states are ready for membership;
3. the problems that the increase in size and dispersion of economic behaviour and institutions bring – particularly for the budget, labour mobility, running the system and adapting to economic and monetary union (EMU);
4. the problems that delay or exclusion may hold for those countries not in the first set of twelve new members.

These form the next four sections of this chapter. We end on a more speculative note, largely because some of the more major decisions on the future of the EU are still to be taken.

26.1 The process of enlargement

Even from its earliest stages the European Community hoped to embrace the whole of 'Europe':

The high contracting parties, determined to lay the foundations for an ever-closer union among the peoples of Europe, resolved to ensure the economic and social progress of their countries by common action to eliminate the barriers which divide Europe . . . and calling upon the other peoples of Europe who share their ideal to join in their efforts (Preamble to the Treaty of Rome).

However, it took sixteen years from its foundation in 1957 before the Community was first expanded in 1973, with the addition of the United Kingdom, Denmark and the Irish Republic. The delay was not because others did not want to join. The UK applied unsuccessfully in both 1963 and 1967, but it was not until the beginning of the 1970s that a set of terms could be found that were acceptable both to the UK and to all the existing members.

This problem of achieving a balance between what the applicants would like and what the existing members would be prepared to concede would be inevitable under such circumstances. The expansions to include Greece in 1981 and

Portugal and Spain in 1986 were not without their difficulties, but the problems of the applicants were dealt with by having extended periods of transition in sensitive areas and by having explicit arrangements to assist in the structural development of disadvantaged regions, which in the case of Portugal meant the whole country. Even at that stage, it was clear that the process of enlargement presented problems for the Common Agricultural Policy (CAP; see chapter 20), which was (and still is to a lesser extent) the major area of expenditure in the EU (see chapter 19). Since the structure of the CAP was aimed largely at northern European temperate products, it did not offer an easy balance of gain for the applicants, and new explicit expenditures were necessary to offset this (through the structural funds).

The fourth enlargement in 1990 offered no such problems as no new treaty was required. When the former DDR joined the Federal Republic of Germany, no constitutional change was required since the eastern *Länder* were viewed as in effect being temporarily under a different administration. The questions to be resolved related to assistance with structural change and the timing of the transition periods for applying Community law. The speed of change during that period meant that there was little time to consider any wider implications. The EC was in the middle of the main phase of implementing the completion of the internal market following the Single European Act of 1986 (SEA; see chapter 2) and was considering the steps to be taken towards EMU and forming the EEA.

Until the collapse of the former Soviet Union (FSU) and the regime changes in Central Europe, the remainder of EFTA – following the exit of the UK, Denmark and the Irish Republic – faced various constraints in joining the EC or indeed in developing closer relations with it. Despite negotiating entry along with the UK, Denmark and the Irish Republic, Norway had rejected membership in a referendum, and hence there was difficulty in mobilizing political enthusiasm for membership. Iceland is not only very small in population, even compared with Luxembourg, but has also been relatively slow in participating in European integration and has an economy of a very different character, until quite recently dominated by fishing. However, the dramatic changes over the last decade and the extensive investment in Europe mean that attitudes are changing. Austria, Finland, Sweden and Switzerland all had concepts of neutrality built into their policy or constitutions. In the last two cases it was largely a matter of independent choice, whereas in the former it was a consequence of the construction of Europe after the Second World War. These states were therefore either unwilling or unable to contemplate membership while the Cold War continued. Liechtenstein followed a path very similar to that of Switzerland. The changes further east led to a major reappraisal. Finland in particular was very keen to find means of strengthening itself with respect to its eastern neighbour, first because the collapse of trade with the FSU contributed to a drastic cut in Finnish GDP, and second because of the political instability. Finland only gained full independence from Russia in 1917 and was forced into losing territory at the end of the Second World War.

However, economic motivation was appearing in addition to the political attractions. As it became clear that the completion of the SEA would mean a substantial step towards closer economic integration for the EC, there was an incentive, both for the EC and for EFTA, to try to deepen their relationship. Unless the EFTA countries adopted the conditions of the single market there was a danger that they could gain a substantial cost advantage through their free trade agreements with the EC. Hence the EC had a clear incentive to form a closer agreement. By the same token, if the EFTA countries wanted equal access for services, a new agreement was required. This led to the formation of the EEA in parallel with the Treaty on European Union in 1993.

Whereas the free trade agreements between the EFTA countries and the EC had all been bilateral, the EEA agreement was a single document which applied to all of the countries – or rather almost all, as Switzerland rejected membership of the EEA in a referendum in December 1992. (Liechtenstein has broken ranks with Switzerland and joined the EEA.)

One might have expected the EEA to be a very good compromise for the EFTA countries as it brought the gains of access to the single market without broaching the sensitive subject of agriculture and without the need to participate in the bureaucratic mechanisms of the EU. The Cohesion Fund which was set up to provide a transfer from the better-off parts of the EEA to the relatively disadvantaged regions was a relatively small price for the EFTA countries to pay (see chapters 19 and 22). However, two facets of the process encouraged a different view. First, the EU was simultaneously taking another step towards integration with EMU, which might again place the EFTA countries at a disadvantage. Second, the negotiation of the EEA had not been a very happy experience for the EFTA countries (see Brewin, in Mayes, 1997b). The process had been very one-sided, with the EC only being prepared to discuss variations in the timetable for transferring the relevant parts of the *acquis communautaire* into the EFTA countries' domestic law. At the last moment the European Court added to the rather one-sided nature by insisting that jurisdiction over the agreement could not be shared as originally negotiated.

Thus the EFTA countries found themselves having not just to accept most of the EEA terms as a fait accompli but having relatively little opportunity to influence the development of future legislation. They thus had many of the responsibilities of the EU members but without the same rights. It was not even a matter of accepting the status quo. The EU was moving on. The Maastricht Treaty made it clear that deepening was to come before further widening of the EU. There would therefore be further steps which could put the EFTA countries at a disadvantage. Furthermore, there was even the danger that some of the Central European countries, such as Hungary, Poland, the Czech Republic and Slovakia, might overtake them in the process of achieving membership, as the focus of interest, in Germany in particular, had clearly moved towards the east.

From the EU side, membership by the well-off EFTA countries was likely to provide few problems and could result in clear benefits in terms of increased resources to deal with the concerns of structural change. They were likely to be net contributors to the EU budget, not net recipients, and if they were to accept all the existing *acquis communautaire* there was very little downside. The market would be widened and the usual range of efficiency and dynamic gains would be available. There was therefore no need to draw up detailed rules or justifications to determine which countries were to be admitted to membership. At the same time, the CEECs were undergoing such trauma in their transition to market economies that they were clearly not in a position to cope with membership; nor indeed could the EU have coped readily had they joined.

The process of enlargement was therefore divided rapidly into two streams, without outright negotiations for membership being undertaken with the four EFTA applicants, but a range of other agreements for a slower pace of integration being concluded with the CEECs. The Visegrad countries, Hungary, Poland, the Czech Republic and Slovakia, were given the fastest initial track, with separate Europe agreements in 1993–4. Free trade agreements were concluded with the Baltic states of Estonia, Lithuania and Latvia in 1994 and new Partnership and Cooperation Agreements with Russia and Ukraine in the same year. The negotiations were shorter than for any of the previous enlargements, lasting only some thirteen months, and Austria, Finland and Sweden joined in January 1995 after the referendum in Norway rejected membership, just 38,000 votes swinging the result. It is interesting to note that there was no overwhelming public enthusiasm in any of these applicants – in contrast to many of the CEECs – implying that the popular view did not coincide with either the idea of clear economic benefits or that of obvious political imperatives.

The negotiations themselves, which followed those on the Maastricht Treaty with a gap of only a few months,[1] were relatively straightforward, with agriculture, fisheries, energy and regional problems being the main stumbling blocks. A five-year phase-in period was agreed for the most difficult parts of the CAP, while a new Objective 6 on low population density regions was included for the structural funds to accommodate the Nordic countries' particular regional problems

(see chapter 22). Voting within the enlarged Council caused some debate among the existing members and it is interesting to note that the member states only agreed to let the total budget for agriculture expand by 74 per cent of the rise merited by the increase in EU GDP, a prelude to the more difficult negotiations then envisaged.[2]

The negotiations for the recent enlargements to EU25/27 were more difficult for two main reasons. The first is the EU concern that the changes they feel necessary are actually being implemented in practice – not just legislated – and that the applicants have the administrative capacity to make the changes. Not only have the applicants got to make more sweeping changes even to get to the same starting point as previous applicants but the *acquis communautaire* itself has grown substantially in size. Conversely, the applicants themselves had worries over adjustment in sensitive areas, such as agriculture, inefficient industries from the previous regime, the social dimension requirements in terms of working conditions, etc. On previous occasions the EU negotiated quite long transition periods but this time round it was preferred to postpone admission, as happened with Romania and Bulgaria, rather than have run-in periods greater than five to seven years even in the most sensitive area of labour mobility.

Further expansion is likely to be piecemeal. Croatia may be able to conclude an agreement in the reasonably near future but progress for other Balkan applicants and particularly Turkey will probably be slow. Ukraine has also been looking towards the EU in recent years but there, as in Turkey, sheer size presents problems for the existing members. Beyond that point the EU would have to start rethinking its definitions, and such discussions are not currently on the table. Even admitting Bulgaria and Romania, which was agreed in September 2006, appeared to be hanging in the balance.

Many of the applicants may wish to move rapidly to membership of EMU as well, especially if their currencies could be fragile or if, like Estonia, they have a currency board based on the euro. However, this was not on the table. Joining EMU requires separate consideration by the ECB and the

Commission, which prepare convergence reports, and a decision by the Council in the light of them. Only Sweden and Greece were considered in the reports for 2000, Greece being admitted as a result. Sweden was considered again in 2002. The first group of new members could only be considered in 2006 after a two-year period conforming to the exchange rate fluctuation requirements of ERM II (see chapter 11), with the prospect of membership in 2007. Only Lithuania and Slovenia applied, with Slovenia being successful.

26.2 Deciding on a wider membership

Deciding upon admitting other applicants on this occasion was a much more difficult task than in the case of the EFTA countries, as in the short run admitting any of them would have involved net costs for the existing members. It was therefore necessary to have some criteria which would help to keep the costs and difficulties within manageable bounds. In effect these were that the applicants should be economically and politically ready, in the sense that they could meaningfully adopt the principles of the Treaty on European Union and adapt their economies within a reasonably short timetable to the full rigours of the EU market. The Copenhagen Council in June 1993 adopted three key principles to express this by stating that membership requires that the candidate country:

- has achieved stability of institutions guaranteeing democracy, the rule of law, human rights and respect for and protection of minorities;
- has a functioning market economy as well as the capacity to cope with competitive pressure and market forces within the Union;
- has the ability to take on the obligations of membership, including adherence to the aims of political, economic and monetary union.[3]

Agenda 2000 (CEC, 1997b) took a step forward by assessing all the ten CEECs in a single comparative framework. It was thus possible to see not only the assessment of where the five countries first selected for negotiation lay, but where others would lie in the future. The individual country assessments were each around 120 pages in length. As negotiations progressed so updates were published, ending with the conclusion of the negotiations. Thus the process was concluded for the first twelve countries but they are continuing for Croatia and Turkey.

The assessments evolved from a simple listing of the measures that have been adopted into a view of how they actually operate in practice. However, they do not represent an attempt to assess the costs and benefits to either the applicants or the existing member states. While this could have been done along the lines of, say, the *European Economy* (1996) evaluation of the internal market, the outcomes would depend upon which and how many of the applicants joined at any one time. Therefore, it was probably wise to neglect the cost–benefit approach and stick to assessment of a group of indicators. One consequence, of course, is that the assessment was relatively imprecise. Jovanovic (2002) discusses what might enter the list but raises the important issue that the balance and timing of the costs of change and the reaping of benefits may be rather different on this occasion from previous enlargements. This arises simply because of the increased size of both the *acquis communautaire* and the economic gap between the starting point for the new members and the level of the old member states. It is therefore important for both parties to ask the question whether the development process is better advanced by extensive assistance from the EU or through actual membership. Membership imposes additional costs both literally in terms of having to make budgetary contributions and practically in terms of the extent and pace of the adjustment of economic and administrative behaviour and institutions. Subsequent applicants have had to face exactly the same decision and despite some discontent in the new member states, particularly since they joined, it seems likely that the remaining Balkan states will be keen to press ahead rapidly. (With apparent declining enthusiasm for enlargement among the existing members it may seem good sense to press ahead in case the door shuts, even temporarily.)

All of the countries involved in the accession process, whether or not deemed ready for negotiation of membership were therefore treated together under common budget headings in Part 3 of *Agenda 2000*. Bulgaria, Latvia, Lithuania, Romania and Slovakia, which were initially excluded from the fast track, were promised not just a further report by the end of 1998 but assistance with making the changes.

Criteria beyond simple income per head were taken into account in making the judgments about readiness for membership.[4] Slovakia, which had the third highest GDP per head in 1995 (after Slovenia and the Czech Republic), was not included in the first-round list, primarily because of lack of progress under the first, political, condition. Estonia, on the other hand, which had the second lowest GDP per head, was included because it had made good progress on all three fronts. With a GDP per head around a third of that prevailing in Portugal and Greece and less than a quarter of the EU average, Estonia's adjustment process would clearly be very extensive. One question mark was therefore over the speed. The process could have been long, but it could also have been short, aided in part by its close links with Finland. Estonia was also the smallest applicant at that stage with a population of only 1.5 million.[5] Table 26.1 sets out the information on the general structure of the economies that applied at the time.[6] Immediately noticeable from the table is the contrast between incomes per head at current exchange rates and at purchasing power parity (PPP). This effective undervaluation of the exchange rate is a feature of the adjustment process to which we return later.

Once it is decided that an applicant meets the Copenhagen criteria, the negotiations themselves then become a matter of running through the thirty-one chapters of the *acquis communautaire*. In the case of the most recent applicants it has not been necessary to agree derogations or transitional arrangements, with the clear exceptions of the environment, employment and social policy, taxation, agriculture, and freedom of movement of persons. (There have also been issues in the fields of competition, transport, fishing and energy.)

Not surprisingly, some of the recommendations over the pace of accession were controversial and some of the states relegated to the second round might have been the greatest potential gainers from membership. By 1999 the position had changed somewhat. The lead group was making steady but not necessarily uniform progress towards meeting the conditions for membership, while some of the following group made rapid advances.

The process of enlargement has been able to progress steadily thus far with few awkward discussions over where the word 'European' reaches its technical or, more likely, political limits. The decision that Turkey counted as a European country had long been made, for instance.[7] However, from an economic point of view there is no particularly good reason why boundaries should be drawn on the basis of centuries-old decisions by geographers as to where the continents should be thought to start and end. The Russian Federation spans the Urals and, although there are various divisions in the Federation, particularly in the south, there are strong economic links across the Urals. The economic resources in Siberia are such that European Russia attaches a very strong importance to the region and drawing that particular division would make little sense to them. The Far Eastern zone is already being drawn into the Asian economy and its development will probably be strongly influenced by the other parts of Asia and the Pacific (Bollard and Mayes, 1991).

Similarly, if we look southwards, in Roman times it made more sense to think of the Mediterranean as a region – a region based on sea rather than landmass. Travel was easier by boat than by land and there was considerable economic interdependence across the region. The same line of argument can be advanced for the Baltic. As we have noted, the links between Finland and Estonia are one of the reasons why Estonia moved to a position suitable for membership rather more quickly than many other Central European countries. Similarly, Swedish banks play an important role in the development of the banking system in all of the Baltic states.

Most current definitions of 'Europe' therefore tend to depend on a combination of economic, political, cultural and geographic links and divisions.[8] However, it is only the eastwards definition that appears to have given the EU much

Table 26.1 Basic data for applicant CEECs and EU member states, 1998

	Area (1000 km²)	Population (millions)	Population density (inhabitants/ km²)	GDP at current market prices			GDP at purchasing power standard			Agriculture (% of employment)
				(billion ECU)	(ECU per head)	(ECU per head as % of EU average)	(billion ECU at PPP rates)	(ECU per head at PPP rates)	(ECU per heads as % of EU average)	
Hungary	93	10.1	109	41.9	4,149	21	98	9,703	49	7.9
Poland	313	38.7	124	140.7	3,636	18	281.1	7,264	36	20.7
Romania	238	22.5	95	33.9	1,507	8	123	5,467	27	39
Slovakia	49	5.4	110	18.1	3,352	17	49.9	9,241	46	8.6
Latvia	65	2.5	38	5.7	2,280	11	13.5	5,400	27	18.3
Estonia	45	1.5	33	4.6	3,067	15	10.7	7,133	36	9.9
Lithuania	65	3.7	57	9.6	2,595	13	22.9	6,189	31	23.8[a]
Bulgaria	111	8.3	75	11	1,325	7	38.2	4,602	23	23.2[b]
Czech Republic	79	10.3	130	50.1	4,864	24	125.2	12,155	61	5.8
Slovenia	20	2	100	17.4	8,700	44	27.2	13,600	68	12.7
CE10	1,078	105	97	337	3,547	18	796.7	7,588	38	
As % of EU15	33	28	84	5	18		11	38		
Belgium	31	10.2	329	223.7	21,920	110	229.9	22,538	113	2.3
Denmark	43	5.3	123	155.8	28,472	143	123.4	23,277	117	3.7
Germany	357	82.1	230	1,921.8	23,282	117	1,779.4	21,686	109	3.2
Greece	132	10.6	80	108.6	10,233	52	143	13,569	68	20.3
Spain	506	39.4	78	520.2	12,899	65	633.3	16,088	81	8.4
France	544	58.8	108	1,297.4	21,661	109	1,214.4	20,640	104	4.5
Ireland	70	3.7	53	75.8	20,479	103	79.4	21,384	107	10.4
Italy	301	57.6	191	1,058.7	17,837	90	1,160.4	19,774	99	6.8
Luxembourg	3	0.4	133	16.4	36,428	183	14.8	34,660	174	2.5
Netherlands	42	15.7	374	349.7	21,448	108	329.8	21,009	106	3.7
Austria	84	8.1	96	188.4	23,493	118	179.6	22,224	112	6.8
Portugal	92	9.9	108	97.6	9,615	48	142.3	14,293	72	13.7
Finland	338	5.2	15	114.8	21,621	109	102.6	19,882	100	7.1
Sweden	450	8.9	20	212	22,884	115	171.3	19,343	97	2.8
United Kingdom	244	59.2	243	1,252.8	20,599	104	1,171.0	19,765	99	1.9
EU15	3,236	375	116	7,472.6	19,868	100	7,486.8	19,906	100	5

Sources: [a] 1996; [b] 1994; Eurostat (various years) *Eurostat Yearbook: The Statistical Guide to Europe*, Luxembourg.

of a problem. Expansion westwards could have included Greenland had its inhabitants decided differently. In any case, non-European parts of France and Spain already form part of the EU. Turkey poses a problem because of its size. It is more than half as large as all the CEECs consid-ered in *Agenda 2000* and similar in size to the twelve new members taken together. GDP per head is in the same league as that of the members of the CEECs that were not in the first round of new members (see table 26.3). Furthermore, the very agrarian nature of Turkey, with around half of the population still working in that sector, could pose major budgetary strains on the EU unless the basis of expenditure is altered still further. This is a feature also shared by Bulgaria and Romania. Calculations made by the UK Foreign and Commonwealth Office in 1992 suggested that Turkey would have been a recipient on the then rules of some 12 billion ECU a year, which would have been equivalent to 15 per cent of its GDP and 5 per cent of the total EU budget (House of Lords, 1992). The calculations by the Commission in *Agenda 2000* for all the potential applicants and the likely cost for those which become members is an order of magnitude smaller, reaching only 19 billion ECU per year in 1997 prices by 2006. Turkey is still likely to remain on a slow path to membership even though Greek objections to the principle of Turkish membership have been withdrawn.[9] Questions over adherence to the non-economic Copenhagen criteria remain.

The EU has, however, shown itself willing to tackle some of the hard political questions in enlargement by agreeing to the accession negotiations with Cyprus without the prior requirement of a political solution to Cyprus's continuing divisions. This still presents several problems, not least the lack of recognition of a legal authority for the Turkish-speaking north. It was hoped that the accession negotiations would themselves help to resolve some of the dispute. However, the end of the negotiation process was reached with the issue still unresolved. Proposals by the UN to end the division were hotly debated and despite the Turkish Cypriot majority agreeing, the reunification proposals were rejected by the Greek Cypriot majority and only they entered the EU. Clearly the Greeks and the Greek Cypriots now hold very strong bargaining cards, as enlargement has to be agreed unanimously and not by qualified majority.

The issue of Malta becoming a member was removed from the agenda for a while when Malta withdrew its application in early 1997. However, with an income per head similar to Spain and Portugal and 75 per cent of its trade being with the EU, it was no surprise that reactivation of the application led to successful negotiations with Malta and its inclusion in the first group of new

members.[10] While the fiscal and organizational issues highlighted in *Agenda 2000* have to be addressed, difficult questions such as the position of Russia[11] can be put on one side for the time being as Russia advances up the ladder of closer association.[12]

26.3 Coping with a larger Union

There are four major economic facets related to enlargement that are worth exploring at this juncture:

1. the budgetary cost particularly related to encouraging structural adjustment and to implementing the CAP;
2. the impact on labour mobility;
3. the manageability of economic institutions;
4. the problem of achieving convergence in the context of EMU.

26.3.1 Budgetary costs

Somewhat surprisingly, CEC (2000a) suggested that the EU would be able to absorb the budgetary consequences of enlargement reasonably readily and budgets were set out on an annual basis up to 2006 (see chapter 19). For example, the Commission concluded (CEC, 2000a, vol. I, p. 74): 'Maintaining the current agricultural guideline would not pose any difficulty in covering identified agricultural expenditure needs.' Initially, this seems to be at variance with calculations about the impact of full membership by all ten countries on the EAGGF Guarantee section of 11 billion ECU per year by 2005 (CEC, 2000a, vol. II, p. 42). However, staggering membership and phasing in the introduction of the full CAP and positing structural changes in the applicant countries enables this sum to be massively reduced.

The actual agreement turned out to be somewhat different from that planned but the principle still applies. The total disbursements came nowhere near challenging the EU budgetary limits. Agricultural costs, including rural development, run at less than half the level of the structural measures. The 2007–13 budget has also now

Table 26.2 Financial Framework, 2007–2013

Programme area	2007	2008	2009	2010	2011	2012	2013	Total 2007–2013
1 Sustainable growth	51,267	52,415	53,616	54,294	55,368	56,876	58,303	382,139
1a Competitiveness for growth and employment	8,404	9,097	9,754	10,434	11,295	12,153	12,961	74,098
1b Cohesion for growth and employment	42,863	43,318	43,862	43,860	44,073	44,723	54,342	308,041
2 Preservation and management of natural resources	54,985	54,322	53,666	53,035	52,400	51,775	51,161	371,344
of which: market related expenditure and direct payments	43,120	42,697	42,279	41,864	41,453	41,047	40,645	293,105
3 Citizenship, freedom, security and justice	1,199	1,258	1,380	1,503	1,645	1,797	1,988	10,770
3a Freedom, security and justice	600	690	790	910	1,050	1,200	1,390	6,630
3b Citizenship	599	568	590	593	595	597	598	4,140
4 EU as a global player	6,199	6,469	6,739	7,009	7,339	7,679	8,029	49,463
5 Administration	6,633	6,818	6,973	7,111	7,255	7,400	7,610	49,800
6 Compensation	419	191	190					800
Total commitment appropriations	120,702	121,473	122,564	122,952	124,007	125,527	127,091	864,316
as a percentage of GNI	1.1	1.08	1.07	1.04	1.03	1.02	1.01	1.048
Total payment appropriations	116,650	119,620	111,990	118,280	115,860	119,410	118,970	820,780
as a percentage of GNI	1.06	1.06	0.97	1	0.96	0.97	0.94	1
Margin available	0.18	0.18	0.27	0.24	0.28	0.27	0.3	0.24
Own resources ceiling as a percentage of GNI	1.24	1.24	1.24	1.24	1.24	1.24	1.24	1.24

Source: OJ C 139, 14 June 2006.

been agreed (table 26.2), extending the time horizon even further and emphasizing the steady move away from agriculture towards cohesion and the unwillingness to expand the budget as Bulgaria and Romania join.

Even the structural measures are of an order of magnitude smaller than can be accommodated without breaking through the current 'own resources' ceiling for EU expenditure of 1.24 per cent of EU GDP (see chapter 19). According to the calculations, the percentage will fall from around 1.1 per cent at the beginning to 1 per cent by 2013. These conclusions are, of course, based on a variety of assumptions and would be violated if, for example, economic growth were slower than assumed. The new member states are absorbing around 30 per cent of the structural funds at the beginning of the period and the eligibility of regions in the existing member states falls as they approach average income levels. Even the topic of the UK rebate has been addressed and that will be reduced as agricultural spending falls. The additional expenditure on enlargement was a little over 15 per cent of the EU15 budget by 2006 or 0.16 per cent of EU GDP. Expenditure on the EU15 was to be the same in 2006 as in 2000, having peaked in 2003. Thus although the issues are slowly being addressed, the large bulk of expenditure as well as revenue remains in the EU15 (or EU12 for that matter).

26.3.2 The movement of labour

It is likely that wider enlargement will impose more substantial strains than those posed by the enlargements of 1981 and 1986, simply because of the extent of the income differentials. In the first place, it is possible that the nature of the integration will exploit inter-industry rather than intra-industry trade as has been the case until now. There may be a tendency to concentrate more labour-intensive and lower value-added activities in the CEECs. In these circumstances, differentials between the various parts of the EU may not converge quite as fast as they otherwise would have done. The impact may be relatively complex if the development involves relocating existing activities from elsewhere in the EU. The existing member states are already experiencing high unemployment, and relocation of labour-intensive activities will only serve to exacerbate the employment difficulties of change even if total real incomes rise at the higher rates hoped for in the Lisbon Council's strategy in 2000 (see chapters 14 and 23). Member states such as Ireland, which have developed rapidly on the back of relatively mobile foreign direct investment (FDI), may find that this production moves, now that their wage levels are no longer low by EU standards and are much higher than the levels in the twelve new members.

The example of the continuing difficulties of integrating East Germany is not a good one. For a start it occurred over a decade earlier, before any prior adjustment could take place. Second, it was decided, against the advice of the Bundesbank, to offer a very high rate of exchange for the Ostmark, thereby bringing wage levels much more rapidly into line than productivity would indicate reasonable.

An alternative scenario is that the extent of the differentials results in a degree of labour mobility that has hitherto not been too much of a concern for the EU. Substantial unemployment differentials have persisted in Europe (Mayes et al., 1993, and chapter 23), not just between member states but also within them. The economic incentives to move are not as effective as they are in the US, for example, where the population is much more mobile. In part this is a function of history. A large proportion of families in the USA do not have roots in the same location going back more than a short period. In Europe, on the other hand, many families have lived in the same place for centuries and therefore have much stronger ties.

With very large income differentials, the incentive to move, even if only for part of the working life, may be sufficiently strong to overcome the inertia that has prevailed in Western Europe. It is noticeable in Finland, for example, where urbanization has been largely fairly recent, that many city dwellers still have family homes in the country or have built cottages there so as to be able to return.[13] Mobility from east to west to work may therefore be substantial by comparison with the past.

However, just these same concerns were expressed when Greece, Portugal and Spain were about to join the EC (see Chassard in Mayes et al., 2001). In practice not only was there no substantial inflow from the new members, but neither was there any obvious worsening of working conditions through some form of social dumping and cut-throat competition leading to a general decline in standards. Nevertheless, the agreement that was negotiated reflected these concerns. With the exception of Cyprus and Malta (where the income differential and populations are small) there was to be a two-year period during which the existing member states could apply safeguards to protect themselves from some of the consequences of rapid migration. (Austria and Germany could apply flanking measures to protect themselves from the impact of cross-border provision of some services.) This transition period should end after five years but could last as long as seven. The new members could reciprocate and apply similar barriers. Indeed Malta has gone further than this and negotiated an option for a seven-year safeguard. Not all countries have chosen to apply these safeguards, particularly the UK and Ireland, and others, including Finland, have chosen not to apply many of the barriers they could after the expiry of the initial two years as the pressure turned out to be less than feared.

Table 26.3 Structural indicators in the new member states, 2005

	Unemployment (%)	Participation (%)	Debt/ GDP ratio	Deficit/ GDP (%)	Price level (%) of EU	Inflation (%)	GDP growth (real %)	Current balance (%)
Bulgaria	9.9	75.3	29.9	3.1	31	5.0	5.5	−11.8
Cyprus	5.3	72.4	70.3	−2.4	83	2.0	3.8	−5.7
Czech Rep.	7.9	70.4	30.5	−2.6	46	1.6	6.0	−2.3
Estonia	7.9	70.1	4.8	1.6	47	4.1	9.8	−10.6
Hungary	7.2	61.3	58.4	−6.1	46	3.5	4.1	−7.4
Latvia	8.9	68.7	11.9	0.2	54	6.9	10.2	−12.4
Lithuania	8.3	68.4	18.7	−0.5	48	2.7	7.5	−7
Malta	7.3	58.1	74.7	−3.3		2.5	2.5	−12.9
Poland	17.7	64.4	42.5	−2.5	54	2.2	3.3	−1.5
Romania	7.7		15.2	−0.4	39	9.1	4.1	−8.7
Slovakia	16.3	68.9	34.5	−2.9	41	2.8	6.0	−8.5
Slovenia	6.5	70.7	29.1	−1.8	67	2.5	3.9	−1.1

Source: European Economy (2006).

With this run-in period, average income differentials could have closed by more than ten percentage points by the time the borders are as open as between the existing member states. However, it is not the average that is the appropriate measure, but the extent to which the more disadvantaged can anticipate improving their position by moving. This unfortunately could still be very considerable even in 2011. Unemployment rates in some of the accession countries are high and participation rates low (see table 26.3).

There are two obvious offsetting features to the fear of labour migration. The first is the extent to which capital moves in the opposite direction. As discussed in chapter 8, FDI movements have up till now been relatively small compared to what one might have expected, especially after allowing for privatization and the acquisition of financial institutions. Again one might look to the example of Ireland where well over a decade of incentives was needed before the achievement of the very rapid take-off (see Hodson in Mayes et al., 2001). The second is the development of social and other infrastructure, assisted by the structural and cohesion funds. The inflow will be of the order of 1 per cent of GDP but as a proportion of spending in the relevant area the contribution could be as much as a third. The effect will be non-trivial over a decade.

26.3.3 The manageability of economic institutions

The Commission has already recognized its own need to restructure as the EU continues with a set of institutions designed for a Community of six. As of 2007, it has twenty-seven members. Almost all of the new members use at least one language that is new to the EU. They want their stake in the running of the Union. Despite suggestions to the contrary, the expansion to fifteen member states occurred without major changes except the splitting up of portfolios. The Santer Commission proposed to restructure its own procedures, with decentralization, rationalization and simplicity as the three watchwords. It suggested that it should concentrate on the core functions and hive off the others to executive agencies which can be nearer the customers. It recommended that the number of commissioners be reduced to one per member state and that the Council needs to reconsider its voting rules. Although progress has been slower than hoped, the changes are now occurring. The Prodi Commission that came in during 1999 introduced a range of changes, reorganizing the portfolios and the structures of the directorates general. In many respects this was a response to the need to give a new face to the

Commission following the forced resignation of the Santer administration, rather than just an attempt to create a body that could cope with enlargement. The intergovernmental conference (IGC; see chapter 3) and the subsequent Nice Treaty succeeded in making further changes to the structure of operation of the Commission, Council, Parliament and their interaction (see chapter 3). Nevertheless, the complexity continued to grow and the changes were closer to 'more of the same' than a wholesale reform. As mentioned, the Commission changed to having one member per country but considering having fewer members than countries remained for the future and any such change will have to be agreed by unanimity. Qualified majority voting (QMV; see chapter 3) was extended a little and the formulae changed in favour of the larger countries. Further changes were incorporated in the 'Constitution' and hence the next step in improving the operational efficiency of the system is already agreed but not ratified. In the meantime the institutions have to be able to operate and cope with the increased numbers. It has been suggested that a structure where it is difficult to introduce change might actually be appropriate, given that the EU is reaching maturity, but this does not reflect everybody's agenda.

The structure of the ECB sets a precedent whereby it is possible to operate at the highest level without one person drawn from each member state (see chapters 3 and 12). The Executive Board has only six members. However, the Governing Council, the primary decision-making body, has one member from each participating country. Thus as of 2007 it has nineteen members, and both the Commission and the Council president are also able to attend (and speak but not vote). There will always be a reluctance to give up either any existing powers or a seat at the table. Other institutions such as the World Bank and the IMF had to handle this problem a long time ago to prevent administrative complexities getting out of hand, but experience in such organizations is not a particularly optimistic indicator of the likelihood of a very successful reorganization. The need for rationalization, of course, applies not just to the Commission, but also to all

of the institutions. The Governing Council of the ECB made a first attempt at a solution under the provisions of the Nice Treaty by proposing that although all members should continue to be present and have the right to speak, only a sub-set should have the vote at any one time (ECB, 2003). They proposed that the Executive Board members should have the vote all the time, whereas the National Central Bank governors should be placed in one of three groups according to a criterion that gives a five-sixths weight to GDP and one-sixth to the balance sheet of monetary institutions. The process will start when the number of member countries exceeds fifteen, i.e. two more than at present, as that was the number possible at the time of the Maastricht Treaty. Initially there will be two groups, the first having the five largest members and the second the rest. Once there are twenty-two member countries the second group will be divided in two, with half the total number of governors being in the second group and the remainder in the third. The three groups will have four, eight and three voting rights respectively, which the members of each group will exercise in rotation. Thus with twenty-seven member states, to take the ECB's own example, the governors in each group will have voting frequencies of 80 per cent, 57 per cent and 38 per cent, respectively.

This arrangement is complex and, while it has been agreed by the Council, there is time for it to be changed before it comes into operation. The net effect is that, with the exception of Poland, all the new members find themselves in the group with the lowest voting frequency and the existing members do not. It will be a very long time before GDP and financial development improves enough to give the new members rights that bear any relation to the size of their population. The Commission picked up this point in its response to the Council on the proposal, suggesting that an equal balance between GDP and population would reflect precedent elsewhere. It also pointed out that from the point of view of monetary policy decision-making, having twenty-one voting members is rather large (CEC, 2003b). This is already contentious. The Finnish parliament, for example, objected to the ending of the principle of one country one vote for monetary policy. Since monetary policy is aimed at the euro area as a whole, and the members are all on the Governing Council in a personal capacity and not as representatives of their respective member states, one might have thought that this would be the easiest area to agree a reduction in numbers. Clearly wider agreement over ECOFIN and the other bodies involved in the management of EMU is going to be a hard battle.

26.4 Coping without enlargement

One question which is not well addressed in the existing literature is how the aspiring applicant countries could cope without membership of the EU. Indeed, there might be benefits from staying out. It is not clear that Bulgaria and Romania have suffered from a three-year delay. The reason that the question is largely ignored is simply that these countries, Russia and Croatia excepted, have found it very difficult to attract inward investment, whether from private sources or through governmental or intergovernmental agencies. Such investment usually requires considerable conditionality either explicitly or implicitly. The requirements for loans and project finance at the governmental or related level tend to include elements concerning fiscal and monetary prudence, the creation of market mechanisms, frameworks for property rights, etc. In the case of funds from the EU, the necessary framework is much more explicit and comprehensive. Furthermore, that framework does not usually conflict with what is required by other public sector lenders or donors. There is therefore an incentive to adopt the framework irrespective of other considerations because it offers the fastest and most substantial route to achieving satisfactory structural change.

The private sector inflow, on the other hand, has a wide variety of motives (Nam and Reuter, 1992). While these will normally include an adequate infrastructure framework and some certainty about being able to enjoy the return on the investment, the same requirements for market openness may not be present, as the investor may well wish to gain from exploiting a monopoly position. In some respects, a less open and integrated market may appeal to the investor because it offers a greater certainty of maintaining cost advantages and privileged market access.

It might appear a rather short-sighted approach to permit such distortions to emerge, but the starting point is not an open market. The attraction of inward investment can be greater where there is the opportunity to buy existing incumbent firms with monopolies or near monopolies. This has been revealed very clearly in the case of New Zealand (Mayes, 1996), where inward investment over the years 1989–95 exceeded that of the whole of the Czech Republic, Hungary, Poland and Slovakia combined, despite the fact that their combined population was about twenty times larger. The domestic resources of the host countries possessed neither the financial capital necessary to make the investments to become internationally competitive nor the access to the necessary technological expertise and market contacts to make such investments successful.

As a result New Zealand has achieved a very rapid turnaround in just a decade, moving more swiftly into recovery than the CEECs, and experiencing a much smaller loss of GDP in the process. Of course, the circumstances are not directly comparable as the extent of distortions and lack of competitiveness were far greater in Europe. Nevertheless, there could be advantages in allowing the transformation of existing enterprises in a process of more measured transition (Mayes, 1997a) as the social costs need to be balanced against the rate of exploitation of the economic gains. Achieving this balance between 'cohesion' and competition has been a key feature governing the use of the structural funds inside the EU. There is a limit to which regional divergences are politically acceptable. Beyond that limit, people would vote against the process of change even though the longer-run outcome from it is clearly better, because they find the short-run costs too high.

The EU's approach as expounded in *Agenda 2000* seeks to address this point both by assistance to the countries not yet accepted for membership and by the transitional aid for those ready for membership. The irony in this arrangement is, however, that the further advanced in the process of integration a country is, the greater assistance it receives from the EU. If, however, one were to take a view on the extent of need, then those furthest from being able to cope with membership might be thought to be those with the greatest need for assistance in the process of transformation. In part, this is a question of absorptive capacity (as the economy progresses so it is able to cope with more projects and faster structural change), but it is also a question of incentives. If less conditionality were to be attached to EU help, then the degree of transformation of the recipient economies might be lower.

Altering the process of adjustment to full membership of the EU, particularly by delaying the point at which labour mobility can be freer, may also affect the structure of the applicant economies. As discussed in Baldwin et al. (1995), it is not immediately clear which way a less-integrated economy might develop. It will be less attractive to investors as a base for production for the whole market if there are barriers to export, but then it will need a wider range of production itself because of the same barriers. As there is a minimum time needed to establish viable firms with a higher value added product, there may be some attraction in a more measured pace of change. However, the history of 'infant industries' and related arguments for slower transition is very mixed, with considerable success stories to point to in Asia and the Pacific region and much more disastrous experiences in much of the rest of the world. It is thus not clear whether there are any clear steps, other than the process of rapid opening towards the EU model, that would diminish the risk of getting locked into a rather unattractive form of inter-industry specialization.

Phinnemore (1999) poses the question of whether the aspiring applicants to the EU might not be better advised to stop one step further back in the process and settle for association agreements as longer-term arrangements. Under such agreements it is possible for the applicants to get a wide range of benefits from trade and investment if they adopt the *acquis communautaire* and yet avoid agreements on politically difficult subjects like fishing and agriculture. The EEA is the principal example. Iceland, Liechtenstein and Norway seem satisfied with the balance. However, in many respects this involves giving up more powers than if they were full members, as they do not have any say in any new EU legislation that falls in the areas covered by their agreements. In the case of the current applicants, they all have rather more to gain from membership than the EEA members, which had no aspirations under the structural funds. They would have been net contributors rather than beneficiaries.

26.5 Concluding remarks

One cannot help but be impressed with the rate of change in the EU over the last fifteen years and with the changes proposed for the coming few years: the enlargement to include Spain and Portugal, the Single European Act, the Maastricht Treaty, the EEA, the agreements and programmes with Central and Eastern Europe, the enlargement to include Austria, Finland and Sweden, completion of Stage 3 of EMU with the founding of the ECB and the issuing of the euro, and a further enlargement with twelve new members. One might have expected that something or other would have collapsed along the way, particularly given some of the political difficulties with agreeing the Maastricht Treaty.

Furthermore, this major expansion of programmes has been accompanied by a substantial budgetary expansion, but not one on the scale envisaged earlier when the MacDougall Report (CEC, 1977a), for example, looked at what would be the minimum size for a budget with a more federal feel to it (see chapter 19). For more than two decades it has been thought that the CAP would have to change markedly, but while it has indeed changed it is still a dominant area of expenditure. It is merely that the structural funds have added a second major category. The Union has been able to cope financially with the existing ceilings, and looks set to do so until 2013.

One must ask whether there is a stage at which the process will have to change its character. The rejection of the 'Constitution' at least gives pause for thought. Taking a purely 'European' definition of the Union, the limits to size are beginning to come within the horizon for thought if not for actual long-term planning. Beyond Stage 3 of EMU the process of closer integration in other areas of economic, political and social affairs appears to be relatively slow (by comparison at least). However, it remains to be seen how much the member states find that, for example, existing fiscal diversity is sustainable under monetary union. The temptation is always to think that the next stage in enlargement or indeed in 'deepening' the Union will be the one that triggers a more major change in the character of the institutions and the nature of the common policies and expenditures. To some extent such a change is likely over the next few years with the new enlargement maturing, but reluctance to change thus far suggests that the member states may prefer to accept the complexities and consequent inefficiencies for rather longer.

Any conclusion on this subject in this edition of the book is likely to be overtaken by events, as many of the necessary decisions may be taken soon, some within months. One might be forgiven for looking at history in a different sense and noting that grand international undertakings have a penchant for overreaching themselves, but the experience is not universal and some such arrangements can last for centuries – millennia in Asia.

NOTES

1 The Commission produced its favourable 'Opinions' on each of the applicants rapidly. (Norway's entry to the negotiations was officially delayed until April 1993 to allow the Opinions to be completed, although it had been involved in aspects of the negotiations earlier.)

2 Further negotiations over the CAP in June 2003 still only made limited progress, not reducing the overall level of expenditure and only partly decoupling payments from production. The subject is by no means ended and will be heavily debated by the new members.

3 The 'EFTA' group negotiations were already in progress at the time.

4 The accuracy of these GDP per head comparisons is, of course, limited but they are not so wrong as to invalidate the qualitative argument.

5 But with a land area bigger than Belgium, the Netherlands or Denmark. Malta and Cyprus are considerably smaller in size but with a relatively high income per head and hence likely to have more limited problems of adjustment. As a result, they were also part of the first group of countries to be admitted.

6 The rapid growth rates in the applicant countries quickly outdated the original assessment and by the time of the decision not only was the gap with the existing members noticeably smaller but the distinction between the two groups of applicants, Bulgaria and Romania excepted, was not so obvious.

7 The 1964 Ankara Association Agreement with Turkey made clear that it was in principle eligible for membership. The question was merely when it would be ready. *Agenda 2000* makes it clear that Turkey will be judged on the same criteria as any other applicant. Turkey is receiving assistance from the EU to help it with the transition.

8 Sometimes the arguments over the appropriate boundary have been put in terms of the limits of the former Austro-Hungarian Empire, sometimes the extent of Christianity and sometimes the limits of Catholicism (Crouch and Marquand, 1992).

9 Now that the Greek-speaking part of Cyprus has joined the EU, there is the added complication of how they will view the membership of Turkey and of the Turkish-speaking part of the island.

10 The referendum on membership was a close call. Public and political opinions in Malta are still divided over the issue, as the history of making and withdrawing the application indicates.

11 Interestingly enough the Italian Presidency of the Council for the second half of 2003 suggested reopening the issue of the inclusion of Russia.

12 In Mayes (1993), I described the EU as having a series of concentric circles of closer affiliation for countries depending upon their geographic nearness. Since 1995 the EU has had a common border with Russia. With the 2004 and 2007 expansions the boundary has moved outwards and Belarus, Ukraine and Moldova now have common borders with the EU. The 'nearness' will thus continue to increase in geographic terms.

13 In part, this may be a special feature of the slow development of forests, where important proportions of rural family wealth can lie. It may take three generations to be able to reap the benefit from planting.

27 Has the EU been successful?

ALI EL-AGRAA

Has the EU been successful is a question that is often being asked. Taken at face value, however, the question is meaningless. As we have seen, the ultimate objective of those who founded the EU was to bring about the political unity of Europe. If the question is meant to solicit an answer on how the EU fares today within that ideal, then even when the entire membership has adopted the euro, as well as the stalled constitutional treaty, the EU would still not have reached the finishing line, so in this sense it has not been successful. Some would even go further, claiming that it may never do so, since there are both national governments and various sections of the EU population who do not share the dream.

However, as discussed in chapters 2 and 26, the EU neither started with the whole of Europe nor does it presently completely engulf it. Also, the EU has reached its present total membership of twenty-seven in stages, through five enlargements (1973, 1986, 1995, 2004, 2007) and an accession (1981), all but one roughly a decade apart, each one bringing with it new problems, slowing down if not altogether frustrating the progress that had been achieved before, thus complicating future development. This was compounded by the tumultuous changes in the world economy for which the EU could not be held responsible (see below), at the very least not entirely so. Thus the very fact that the EU is still here, has been able to introduce all the developments that have been discussed in this book, and has more nations waiting to join the club, are clear signs that it has been very successful indeed, i.e. not only surviving against all odds but also remaining attractive to others are true accomplishments.

It would therefore be more sensible to concretize the question by asking whether the EU has been able to achieve the goals it set out for itself in every major treaty and in specific policy areas. With regard to the latter, an adequate answer would require a complete and exhaustive enumeration of all the conclusions reached in almost all the chapters in this book, but that would be unnecessary, due to duplication, and unwarranted, given space limitations (for a comprehensive panorama, see Tsoukalis, 2005, and Gillingham, 2003). As to the former, one can provide general answers by considering the aims set for the 1958–69 transition period in the 1957 EEC Treaty of Rome, those concerning the first enlargement and EMU adopted in the Hague summit of 1969, and those concerning the introduction of the euro in the Maastricht/Amsterdam treaties and the latest enlargements. The chapter deals with precisely these selections, but instead of simply enumerating aims and setting them against achievements or otherwise, they are presented in terms of the general context of the development of the EU, as in chapter 2.

27.1 The aims set for 1969

Between 1958 and 1969, the EEC transition period, the original six member nations were preoccupied with the construction of the 'community' envisaged in the 1957 Treaty of Rome for the EEC. There is no need to evaluate the ECSC (Treaty of Paris, 1951) because all but those dead set against any kind of European integration would concede its success and acknowledge it as the basis for the drive behind the creation of the EEC. As to Euratom (Treaty of Rome, 1957), it should be plain that it then involved only France. Therefore, if the question were about the EEC success at the end of

1969, then it would be about whether the EEC was able to meet the targets it set itself in the treaty (see chapter 2, p. 31).

As mentioned in chapters 1 and 2, two of the major aims were the creation of the customs union and the common market, and on these the answer is straightforward. The basic elements of the customs union (i.e. the removal of the internal tariffs, the elimination of import quota restrictions and the creation of the common external tariffs (CETs)) were established a year and a half ahead of schedule (tables 27.1 and 27.2 provide their evolution). As to the common market elements, initial steps were undertaken and measures proposed to tackle the many non-tariff barriers (NTBs) to the free movement of goods, services and factors of production. However, laying down the rules for mobility was no guarantee of its taking place, especially in the case of labour since Europeans had a strong tendency to stay close to their birthplace and still largely do (see chapter 8). Given this proviso, one can say that by 1969 a recognizably common market existed.

Recall that the aims also included the creation of common policies. Because of French demands, sometimes bordering on threats, the CAP was almost fully operational by 1969. However, as Button clearly shows (chapter 16), the common transport policy was slow to evolve; but transport was not just an industry, it was and is largely a provider of services and publicly owned, thus not easy to tackle (witness the havoc created by privatization in some EU nations, especially the UK). Moreover, as demonstrated in chapters 2 and 23, the European Social Fund (ESF) and the European Investment Bank (EIB) were duly established and were fully operational at an early stage, with the EIB given a treble-A rating: the highest award. Furthermore, as Brülhart and Matthews argue (chapter 24), steps were taken to create a Common Commercial Policy (CCP), and, as Matthews clearly shows (chapter 25), the original six undertook appropriate trade and aid arrangements in respect of their colonial and increasingly ex-colonial dependencies. Also, a rudimentary system of macroeconomic policy coordination was devised (chapter 11). Thus, there was complete success in the case of the customs union, and

Table 27.1 EC intra-area tariff reductions (%)

Reduction date	Reduction based on the 1/1/1957 level	Cumulative reduction
1 January 1959	10	10
1 July 1960	10	20
1 January 1961	10	30
1 January 1962	10	40
1 July 1962	10	50
1 July 1963	10	60
1 January 1965	10	70
1 January 1966	10	80
1 July 1967	5	85
1 July 1968	15	100

variable and steady success with regard to the common market aspects, although, given their nature, that was hardly surprising.

27.2 The aims set for the period from 1969 to the early 1980s

When the transition period came to an end in 1969, it would have been possible for the original six to state that their mission had been accomplished, given that their 'official' remit was for only economic unity. That would be utter nonsense, given the 1955 Benelux declaration for economic integration paving the way for political unity (chapter 2), but let us ignore that for the moment. There were several reasons, however, why it was neither possible nor appropriate for the EU to stop there, and these relate to the variable success just mentioned and to practical considerations. First, the creation of common policies in such fields as agriculture and competition required an administration to operate them. That was because decisions regarding agricultural prices had to be taken on a seasonal or annual basis and markets had to be continuously manipulated in order that those prices should be received by farmers. And the activities of businessmen and governments had to be continuously monitored in order that factors that would otherwise prevent, restrict or distort competitive trade would be eliminated. Second, as we have just seen,

Table 27.2 The establishment of the CET (%)

	Industrial products		Agricultural products	
Adjustment date	Adjustment	Cumulative adjustment	Adjustment	Cumulative adjustment
1 January 1961	30	30		
1 January 1962			30	30
1 July 1963	30	60		
1 January 1966			30	60
1 July 1968	40	1,000	40	100

although substantial progress had been made in achieving the aims covered in the previous section, when the transition period was approaching its end it had to be admitted that substantial policy gaps still remained to be filled before it could be claimed that a truly common market existed.

Nevertheless, with memories of the Second World War still fresh in people's minds, and plans for immediate political unity thus having been shelved, it would have been possible for the member nations to state that, subject to the need to operate existing policies and to fill obvious policy gaps, no further economic integration or institutional development should be attempted. In fact the EU decided quite the contrary: new areas of economic policy were opened up and old ones were substantially changed.

In 1969, during the Hague summit, the original six decided that the EU should progressively transform itself into an EMU. Although important measures were subsequently introduced in order to achieve the EMU, the goal of reaching this aim eventually failed (chapter 11). This was, however, due to the global economic difficulties of the early 1970s, the Nixon and oil shocks, and to the first enlargement of the EU which brought in three countries (Denmark, Ireland and the UK) with different economic structures and problems. Nevertheless, the idea did not go away, since in the late 1970s a more modest scheme for a monetary stability zone was successfully introduced – the EMS (chapter 11). Moreover (but this overlaps with the next section), in 1989 the member nations endorsed the Delors Report, committing themselves to achieving an EMU with a single currency, the euro, in three stages. As we have seen (chapter 11), the first began on 1 July 1990, the second in 1994 and the third in 1999 for the eleven member nations which passed the strict conditions specified for this purpose and which had no 'opt-outs', with Greece joining later in 2002 and Slovenia in 2007. With the demise of the 1970 EMU being mainly due to the two major world shocks, one could be perfectly justified in claiming that the EEC was not to blame for missing its EMU target then.

The EMU proposal was only one of a succession of new policy initiatives during 1969–72. Indeed, this period can be described as one of great activity. First, in 1970, the original six reached a common position on the development of a Common Fisheries Policy (CFP) (chapter 21), although total commitment was not to be achieved until 1983. Second, at the Paris summit of 1973, agreement was reached on the development of new policies in relation to both industry and science and research (chapter 14). Third, the summit also envisaged a more active role for the EEC in the area of regional policy, and decided that a European Regional Development Fund (ERDF) was to be established to channel EEC resources into the development of the backward regions (chapter 22). Fourth, the summit also called for a new initiative in the field of social policy (chapter 23). Fifth, later in the 1970s, the relationship between the EU and its ex-colonial dependencies was significantly reshaped in the form of the 'Lomé Convention' (now renamed the Cotonou Agreement; see chapters 24 and 25). Finally, there was the series of institutional developments, discussed in chapters 2 and 3, especially the summit meetings and their formalization into the European Council, arguably bringing the EC somewhat closer to the people.

It is obvious from all these developments that the EEC needed financial resources not only to pay for the day-to-day running of the EEC but also to feed the various funds that were established: the ESF, ERDF and, vitally, the European Agricultural Guidance and Guarantee Fund (EAGGF). As revealed in chapter 19, in 1970 the EEC took the important step of agreeing to introduce a system that would provide the EEC, and specifically the general budget, with its own resources, thus relieving it of the uncertainty of annual decisions regarding its finances as well as endorsing its political autonomy. Another step of great importance was the decision that the European Parliament should be elected directly by the people, not by the national parliaments or chosen by governments. In addition, the EEC decided to grant the European Parliament significant powers over the general budget; as we saw in chapters 3 and 19, this proved to be a very significant development also in terms of vetting the finances. Finally, but by no means least, was the development of the political cooperation mechanism. It is important not to forget that dedicated Europeans had always hoped that the habit of cooperation in the economic field would spill over into the political arena, especially into foreign policy matters. That has indeed happened: the political cooperation that we see today can be said to date from the Hague summit of 1969 and was formally inaugurated in 1970.

Although there have been a series of institutional developments, the relationship between the member nations has undergone a significant change. When the member nations signed the Treaty of Rome, they opted for a Council of Ministers which could take decisions on the basis of a supranational majority voting system. However, the insistence of the French led to the 'Luxembourg compromise', extending veto powers to member nations on issues which directly affect them. In addition, and especially after 1969, the centre of gravity of decision-making within the EEC became the European Council by offering

blueprints on which the Commission bases and formulates its proposals for legislation.

The method of operation of the European Council is cast in the traditional intergovernmental mould. As Swann (1988) argues, the development of inter-governmentalism might have been expected to slow down the pace of progress within the EU: the unanimity principle would always force the EU to adopt the lowest common denominator and that might mean little or even no change whatever. However, that was certainly not the case in the early 1970s: as we have seen, a number of new initiatives were launched and in the main those initiatives were designed to further the process of integration. Thus, despite the setback in terms of no progress with democratic decision-making, the EEC continued to be successful.

Inter-governmentalism was still strong in the 1980s, but the performance of the inter-governmental EC of the early 1980s was markedly less dynamic than that of the early 1970s. A good deal of activity within the EU then centred around quarrels over matters such as the reform of the CAP and the general budget, especially the UK's 'unfair' contribution to it. However, settling such vital issues could hardly be deemed lack of success, since the clearing of problems is a prerequisite for further progress.

To this list of achievements one should add another, but also state a negative one. On the negative side is that despite developments in foreign policy cooperation, and even when the Maastricht and Amsterdam treaties are fully implemented, the EU will continue to lack two essential attributes of a state. These are responsibility for external affairs and defence. Thus, in spite of the serious discussions being conducted recently on these issues, as is argued in chapter 2, the EU has a great gap in its competences, but its weight makes it highly significant in world economics and thus in world politics. The positive side is that the significant achievements of the EU during the post-1969 period made it very attractive. This attraction is demonstrated by:

1. its first round of enlargement to include Denmark, Ireland and the United Kingdom in 1973;

Table 27.3 1972 New members' intra-area tariff reductions (%)

Reduction date	Reduction based on the 1/1/1972 level	Cumulative reduction
1 April 1973	20	20
1 January 1974	20	40
1 January 1975	20	60
1 January 1976	20	80
1 July 1977	20	100

Table 27.4 1972 New members' adjustment to the CET (%), for products which differed by more than 15% from the CET

Adjustment date	Adjustment based on the 1/1/1957 level	Cumulative adjustment
1 January 1974	40	40
1 January 1975	20	60
1 January 1976	20	80
1 July 1977	20	100

2. the adhesion of Greece in 1981;
3. its second round of enlargement to include Portugal and Spain in 1986;
4. its third round of enlargement to include Austria, Finland and Sweden in 1995;
5. its fourth round of enlargement, admitting ten new members in 2004 (Cyprus, the Czech Republic, Estonia, Hungary, Latvia, Lithuania, Malta, Poland, Slovenia, and Slovakia);
6. its latest enlargement, admitting Bulgaria and Romania in 2007.

Of course, the last three items go beyond the period under consideration, but they do focus the picture. Returning to the successes, one concrete point concerns whether the countries involved in the first three items have been able to negotiate their transition periods successfully or otherwise. Tables 27.3 and 27.4 give the timetable for the adjustments in the CETs and the dismantling of the internal tariffs for the three countries involved in the first enlargement: Denmark, Ireland and the United Kingdom. The tables do not cover all groups of commodities. For example, tariffs on coal imports were abolished from the day of accession, and tariffs on certain groups of commodities given in Annex III of the Treaty of Accession were abolished on 1 January 1974. In the case of the CETs, those tariffs that differed by less than 15 per cent were adjusted on 1 January 1974. Import quota restrictions were also abolished from the date of accession. Measures having equivalent effects to the import quota restrictions were eliminated by the deadline of 1 January 1975. None of the three new member nations had any difficulties in achieving these changes.

In the case of Greece's adhesion, a five-year period was agreed for the progressive dismantling of residual customs duties on Greek imports of products originating in the EU and for the progressive alignment of Greek tariffs to the CET. Customs duties on Greek imports from the EU were to be reduced in six stages commencing on 1 January 1981, with a reduction of 10 percentage points followed by a further reduction of the same number of percentage points on 1 January 1982 and four annual reductions of 20 percentage points so that all customs duties on Greek intra-EU trade were to have been removed by 1 January 1986. Alignment of the CET was to follow the same timetable.

Quantitative restrictions between Greece and the EC were to be abolished on adhesion, with the exception of fourteen products for which Greece was authorized to maintain transitional quotas. These quotas were to be progressively increased during the five-year transitional period and to be completely eliminated by 31 December 1985. As a general rule, the minimum rate of increase for such quotas was 25 per cent at the beginning of each year for quotas expressed in value terms, and 20 per cent at the beginning of each year for quotas expressed in volume terms. Measures having equivalent effect to quantitative restrictions were to be eliminated upon adhesion, except for the Greek system of cash payments and import deposits which were to be phased out over three years (see *Bulletin of the European Communities*, no. 5, 1969, for these and further details).

In the case of Portugal and Spain, a ten-year transitional period was agreed. For Portugal, this was divided into two equal (five-year) stages for the majority of products and a basic seven-year period for others, although some measures would apply for the full ten years. For Spain there were some variations, but the essentials were basically the same.

It can be categorically stated that Greece, Portugal and Spain navigated their transition periods successfully. With regard to the three members joining in 1995, there was practically no transition period since they were members of EFTA, and, as we have seen, EFTA and the EU have had free trade between them in manufactured products for a very long time and continue to do so through the EEA arrangement, with Switzerland enjoying the privilege without membership. Indeed, the only derogation from immediate implementation of all EU legislation was a four-year transitional period during which the new members could maintain their higher than EU health, safety and environmental standards. It is too soon to discuss the latest enlargements, but their transitions are fully set out in chapter 26.

So far there has been one withdrawal. The position of Greenland was renegotiated in 1984, but it remains associated under the rules of 'Overseas countries and territories'. A special agreement regulates mutual fishing interests. So Greenland's withdrawal cannot be recorded as a failure.

Of course, one should point out that, in contrast to this rosy picture, a number of non-tariff barriers remained. However, as we have seen (chapters 2 and 7), the aim of the 'internal market' is to abolish these either directly or indirectly via the harmonization of technical specifications, hence to promote the right environment for getting rid of them. All these non-tariff barriers are fully set out in chapter 7, but here, in advance of the next section, it suffices to say that the necessary legislation has been almost fully adopted and that the internal market, although falling short of expectations, has nonetheless been fairly successful.

Thus the totality of all these developments over the period from 1969 to the early 1980s (and beyond) clearly indicates complete success in some areas, qualified success in others and very little progress when it comes to a common defence policy and a unified foreign policy stance. However, the overall picture is clearly one of success. This is of course not meant to distract from the demerits of the policies adopted or steps taken; these are stated in the relevant chapters.

27.3 The aims set for the period from the mid-1980s to the present

Without a shadow of doubt, the stars in this period are the 1987 SEA, which now regulates all the activities of the EU; the Maastricht Treaty, as per the Amsterdam Treaty of June 1997, when fully implemented, with the euro being adopted by more than the twelve of the then fifteen member states; the Nice Treaty, when all the ten to fifteen nations have actually joined. As shown in chapters 2 and 7, the SEA contained policy development based upon the intention of having a true single market in place by the end of 1992, with free movement of capital, labour, services and goods rather than the patchy arrangements of the past. As mentioned above, the necessary legislation enabling these has been almost fully adopted and the internal market, although falling short of expectations, has nonetheless been fairly successful.

The SEA also introduced, or strengthened, other policy fields. These included: responsibility towards the environment; the encouragement of further action to promote health and safety at work; technological R&D; work to strengthen economic and social cohesion so that weaker members can participate fully in the freer market; and cooperation in economic and monetary policy. In addition, the SEA brought foreign policy cooperation into consideration and provided it with a more effective support than hitherto, including its own secretariat, housed in the Council building in Brussels.

Institutionally, as we have seen, it was agreed that the European Council would take decisions by QMV in relation to the internal market, research, cohesion and improved working conditions and that, in such cases, the European Parliament should share in decision-making. These developments were followed later by agreement regarding the control of expenditure on the CAP (which, as we have seen in chapters 19 and 20, has been a source of heated argument for a number of years) and, most importantly, a fundamental change in the EU general budget (chapter 19).

Before turning to the second star, the Maastricht Treaty, recall that a three-stage timetable for EMU started on 1 July 1990 with the launching of the first phase of intensified economic cooperation, during which all the member states were to submit their currencies to the exchange rate mechanism (ERM) of the EMS (chapter 11). The main target of this activity was the UK whose currency was not subject to the ERM discipline; the UK joined in 1991 (the decision was announced at the Madrid summit in June 1989, while Margaret Thatcher was still in office) but withdrew in 1992 when the UK could not maintain the ERM parity for the pound. During the second stage, which started in 1994, the EU created the European Monetary Institute (EMI) to prepare the way for the European Central Bank which started operating on 1 January 1997. As we have seen, the Treaty allows Denmark and the UK to opt out of the final stage when the EU currency rates were to be permanently and irrevocably fixed and a single currency (the euro) floated. They exercised their option, as did Sweden (for different reasons), but Denmark and Sweden will continue conducting referendums on this issue and the UK may do so (below).

Although the stipulated earlier (1997) floating of the single currency had to be waived and only eleven member nations adopted the euro on 1 January 1999, one can hardly be justified in claiming that the EU has not been successful recently. Apart from the achievements just mentioned, Greece adopted the euro in 2002 (although there are accusations of cooked accounts for the purpose) Slovenia joined in 2007 and the European Central Bank has been successful in its operations. Also, the British Labour government opted for participation in the 'Social Chapter' and decided to run a referendum on euro membership, if and when the UK passed the Chancellor of the Exchequer Gordon Brown's tests, although on 9 June 2003 Brown declared that the tests had not been passed (chapter 11). Sweden had a referendum on the euro in September 2003 which proved unsuccessful. Moreover, membership of NATO has been extended to the Eastern European nations with the endorsement of Russia, which signed an agreement to that

effect in May 1997. Finally, serious discussion is being conducted regarding the creation of a European army for the defence of Europe, especially in the light of the debates leading to the Iraq war and enlargement being on schedule.

One should of course ask: what about the Constitutional fiasco? Is not the rejection by referenda in France and the Netherlands a clear indication of failure? The answer is simple. Those rejections have not stopped the majority of member states (eighteen out of the twenty-seven) from ratifying the constitution. It is therefore not dead but rather stalled, given the experience with the Maastricht and Nice treaties. Moreover, many analysts would agree that the rejections in France and the Netherlands, two of the founding members of the EU, were based on disaffection from their domestic governments. All this is tantamount to saying that the constitution cannot be evaluated in the same way as all the items considered here; discussion of it relates to the future and is therefore left to the next chapter.

27.4 Conclusion

The main conclusion is that when one considers the major phases through which the EU has developed, each with its own aims and aspirations, one would find that the EU has been very successful indeed. This success has been not only in terms of achieving *negative* integration (see chapter 1), but also in adopting a host of *positive* integration measures and largely succeeding in meeting them. Moreover, when the Maastricht, Amsterdam and Nice treaties have become a full reality and the twelve nations involved in the last two enlargements have successfully settled down, the EU will be much closer to a complete economic union, and will have gone beyond that in certain respects and cover practically the whole of Europe. One could also argue that the developments that have taken place are on the whole an evolution consistent with the aspirations of the founding fathers. Whether the EU is edging closer towards realizing their dream of a United States of Europe is a matter for the future of the EU and is the subject of the final chapter.

28 The future of the EU
ALI EL-AGRAA

This chapter is devoted to a very brief response to the often-asked question regarding where the European Union is heading in the future. There are at least two reasons for this brevity. The first is that the book is already very long. The second is that the answer is heavily dependent on what happens to the Constitution, which has been shelved, but not buried, since its rejection by referendums in France and Denmark. It is not buried because since then it has been ratified by eighteen of the twenty-seven member nations (see section 2.2.6, especially table 2.2 page 40). Moreover, the experience with the ratification of the treaties of Maastricht (at first Denmark rejected it) and Nice (Ireland did the same) reinforce this expectation.

To offer a meaningful answer to the question, one needs to take into consideration the views of all those concerned who play influential roles in the drive behind European integration. Thus one must not only seek the vision of the founding fathers, and of the recent and present EU political leaders, but also look into the contents of the Constitution. The purpose of this chapter is to do precisely that.

28.1 The vision of the founding fathers

As fully documented in chapter 2, the founding fathers dreamed of the creation of a United States of Europe. This was because they believed that there was no other means of putting an end to the continent's woeful history of conflict, bloodshed and suffering, i.e. they saw unity as the only way to the achievement of eternal peace in a continent with a long history of deep divisions and devastating wars. This call for unity was later reinforced

through the need for a common defence against Soviet expansionism, orchestrated under the umbrella of the Warsaw Pact, which threatened the survival of democracy in Western Europe: hence the widening of the 1947 Brussels Treaty Organization to form NATO in 1948, under the auspices of the United States.

The switch of emphasis to economic integration came to the fore later on, but in a reinforcing manner. There were two facets to it. First, with war wounds fresh in people's minds during the early 1950s, it was felt that political integration was out of the question then. That is why, when calling for the creation of the European Economic Community, the Benelux countries reasoned that experience gained through working together in the economic field would pave the way for political unification later on: experience clearly shown by the success of the European Coal and Steel Community, which commenced operations in 1952 and lasted for fifty years. Second, Europe then, and now, stood no chance of survival against, let alone of being on a par with, the United States and Japan in terms of economic excellence and influence in world affairs without being united on both fronts. Thus, with economic unity being only a means to an end, until a single European nation became the reality, the energies of those dedicated to the dream of the founding fathers were still devoted to finding ways of realizing it.

However, there are those who question the wisdom, in the modern age, of creating one nation for either the purpose of peace or for economic prosperity. With regard to peace, they argue that the ethnic-based struggles in Eastern Europe and the splitting of Czechoslovakia and Yugoslavia show that separation may be a more stable equilibrium, especially with Russia now being relatively weak and focusing on economic reform and industrial rebuilding (see, inter alia, Feldstein, 1997, pp. 24–6). They can appeal to reality to reinforce their argument by claiming that today there are not many of the founding fathers around and vehemently asserting that their dream is not shared by the new generation of Europeans. Add to this the obsession with national sovereignty and the call for political unity goes out of the window. However, those who hold or endorse these views have the responsibility to provide a convincing argument as to why they believe that these newly separate independent nations would have been truly peaceful indefinitely had they stayed out of the EU; after all, they joined in the belief that unity was their only guarantee against retrograde steps regarding both their independence and democracy. In other words, it is difficult to take seriously arguments which project from the 'limited experience' of the 1980s/90s, even if it were representative, into the indefinite future, not to mention the depressing implication that only those of the same ethnic background can achieve true unity.

As to the benefit of size for economic excellence, some argue that the experience of smaller nations such as Switzerland, Singapore and New Zealand is ample proof that size does not matter. That may be so, but successful individual small nations have no chance whatsoever of exerting any influence globally; hence their fortunes are heavily dependent on what happens on the international stage.

There is therefore no need to dwell on this issue, not only because it is entirely up to the reader to decide which side represents her/his inclination, but also, importantly, because the political vision of the founding fathers relates to the indefinite future, the road to which is inevitably far from smooth. It is of the essence, however, to learn what the present EU leaders think the EU future will entail, since one wants to know if their vision contradicts or lends support to, if not coincides with, that of the founding fathers. This is in spite of the fact that supportive policies adopted in the immediate future may not become the permanent reality since they may be negated later on by governments of opposing colours, but here we are concerned with projecting from present and past experience.

28.2 The vision of contemporary politicians

Turning to the vision of contemporary political leaders, one needs to know their views regarding whether the opening up of the EU internal market and the full implementation of the Maastricht, Amsterdam and Nice treaties are ends in themselves or merely staging posts on the way to greater economic and political union. To concentrate attention and liven up the debate, I shall consider interchanges between the leaders of the main driving forces behind EU integration: France, Germany and the European Commission, and the largest reluctant partner, Britain. Due to space limitations, I shall concentrate on two examples of interchange, one between them before the adoption of the euro, the other recent and ongoing, since these should enlighten us about general trends as well as show us if Britain is still out on a limb (see Young (1998) for excellent documentation and analysis).

28.2.1 The vision of political leaders: the 1980s and 1990s

The first example relates to the interchanges that took place between then British Prime Minister Margaret Thatcher (now Baroness Thatcher), the President of the Commission during the late 1980s, Jacques Delors, and Germany's Chancellor Helmut Kohl. During the summer of 1988, Delors predicted that 'in ten years' time 80 per cent of economic, and perhaps social and tax legislation would be of Community origin'. In early September of the same year, he followed this with a speech to the UK's Trade Union Congress (TUC) in which he spoke strongly of the 'social dimension' of the internal market, and called for a 'platform of guaranteed social rights', including the proposal that every worker should be covered by a collective agreement with his or her employer: a proposal that is close to the hearts of most British trade unionists.

Later, during the same month (on 20 September), Thatcher – speaking in Bruges, appropriately – at the College of Europe, responded in very strong terms: 'We have not rolled back the frontiers of the state in Britain only to see them re-imposed at a European level, with a European superstate exercising a new dominance from Brussels.' Subsequently, she repeated similar phrases regarding the 'nightmare of an EC government' on many occasions. She did this in Luxembourg and Madrid, alongside Lake Maggiore in Italy during a summit meeting, and before the Conservative Party Conference in Brighton in the UK. Nor did she confine her attacks to broad policy issues. She also attacked every single practical measure by which her fellow EU leaders sought to achieve progress within the EU. She told a somewhat bemused Italian Prime Minister (Ciriaco De Mita) at Lake Maggiore, 'I neither want nor expect to see a European central bank or a European currency in my lifetime or . . . for a long time afterwards.' A few years later, Thatcher declared that she regretted having endorsed the EMU of the Maastricht Treaty during the Madrid Summit of June 1989, and backed William Hague for the leadership of the Conservative Party to succeed her immediate replacement (John Major) simply because Hague had vehemently announced that qualification for membership in his shadow cabinet would require unwavering commitment to ensuring that the euro would have no place in Britain. Hague's choice of Michael Portillo as Shadow Chancellor soon after the latter's return to politics was consistent with that stance since Portillo was, and continues to be, a vehement opponent of the UK adopting the euro, and actually believes in its imminent demise on the grounds that no single European currency has ever succeeded, without any reference to dissimilarities with past experiences!

The first rebuttals of Thatcher's vehement utterances came not from the 'socialist' leaders of the other EC member nations at the time, such as President François Mitterrand of France, Prime Minister Felipe Gonzalez of Spain or Prime Minister Andreas Papandreou of Greece. They sensibly kept their feelings to themselves and left it to the more right-wing prime ministers, Germany's Chancellor Helmut Kohl, Italy's Ciriaco De Mita,

Holland's Ruud Lubbers and Belgium's Wilfred Martens, to respond to her. The most outspoken was Chancellor Kohl, hitherto Thatcher's closest ally. He declared flatly in Brussels in November 1988 that:

1. All internal frontiers within the EC must disappear by 1992.
2. Tax harmonization is indispensable.
3. A European police force is the answer to crime and terrorism.
4. By pooling sovereignty, the EC states will gain and not lose.
5. The EC must have (in alliance with the United States) a common defence policy, leading to a European army.

He did not mention Thatcher by name, but every point he emphasized was one on which she was on record as taking the opposite view.

It should be stressed that Thatcher's stance on these matters suggested that she believed that the EU was predominantly a zero sum game: every increase in the EU sovereignty was at the expense of that of the member nations, especially the UK's. However, most of the other EU leaders had fewer illusions about what the medium-sized member countries of the EU could achieve by themselves: very little indeed. They reckoned that by 'pooling sovereignty' they would increase the range of possibilities for the EU as a whole and thus indirectly for their own countries as well. Hence, Kohl's carefully considered remarks on this subject should have been much appreciated, particularly since Germany was not one of the smaller EU nations; indeed, not only is it the largest country in the EU in terms of both population and GDP, but one of the main drivers behind European unification.

In short, it could be claimed that the other EC leaders saw Thatcher following the example of Charles de Gaulle, whose anti-EC policies in the 1960s held back the development of the EC, ironically including the admission of the UK (see chapter 2). The comparison may have been one which Thatcher herself found flattering; would she have realized, however, that de Gaulle's intransigence eventually did much to undermine French influence for a long time both within the EC and outside it? Yet, despite all this, one should not forget what de Gaulle stood for; in 1967, he said: 'if a united Europe is to be built by itself and for itself without being subjected to an economic, monetary or political system that is foreign to it, if Europe is to counterbalance the immense power of the United States, then the ties and rules that hold the community together must be strengthened, not weakened'.

Although Thatcher was in a minority of one within the EC, she put herself in that position entirely by her own doing – her isolation was self-inflicted. She had been in that situation before, when she fought her long and hard battle to reduce the UK's contribution to the EC general budget, which then attracted much grudging admiration from the leaders of the other member nations. Although they objected to her tactics, they recognized that she was protecting a vital British interest and was seeking to remedy an evident injustice. However, their sympathy for the position she adopted in the late 1980s (and continues to espouse today) was non-existent. She was thought to be acting out of sheer perversity, or at least out of nationalism of the narrowest possible kind.

So what is the message behind this interchange in terms of the vision of the EU leaders in the 1980s regarding the future of the EU? Before responding to this question, it is pertinent to ask another: why the jump from Thatcher to Hague, i.e. has Major been left out because his position towards the EU resembled that of Thatcher and Hague? The answer is that although Major did not follow closely in Thatcher's footsteps within this context, his government's downfall was partly due to a deep division within the Conservatives over the role of Britain within the EU: a division made starkly clear by the two candidates who contested the final vote for his replacement – Kenneth Clarke, a committed pro-European, and William Hague, who, as we have seen, was a devout anti-European. One can therefore claim a consistent British government attitude towards EU integration over the Thatcher period and its immediate aftermath.

Thus the answer is that, during the period under consideration, Germany and the President of the Commission, as well as the silent majority of EU nations, saw the EU as evolving beyond the commitments entered into then. In short, they envisaged the EU becoming more than an economic and monetary union with a common currency and coordinated policies on foreign affairs, defence and justice and home security. Britain took a different view and was supported by Denmark, her closest ally since well before the creation of EFTA in 1960, after it became clear that Britain could not go along with what the original Six aspired to (see above and chapter 2). However, since Britain had always seen a different role for itself from that envisaged by the 'continent', one can claim that the countries most involved with EU integration acted in a manner which suggested that the future would bring about deeper integration. Although this was not expressed in the form of concrete political unity, what is pertinent is that their vision for the next steps to be taken for further EU integration was consistent with the dream of the founding fathers.

28.2.2 The vision of the present political leaders

We now turn to the second example of interchange by considering what the present EU leaders think of how the future should be shaped for the EU. By 'present' is meant both those immediately following the above as well as the current leaders.

The 'immediate' leaders

With regard to the former group, without a shadow of doubt the debate was opened by Joschka Fischer, the German Foreign Minister, on 12 May 2000, in a speech delivered at Humboldt University. He began by asking his audience to allow him to 'cast aside . . . the mantle of . . . Minister' and to speak, deceptively, in a purely personal capacity. He said that 'in the coming decade, we will have to enlarge the EU to the east and south-east, and this will, in the end, mean a doubling in the number of members. And at the same time, if we are to be able to meet this historic challenge and integrate the new member states without substantially denting the EU's capacity for action, we must put into place the last brick in the building of European integration, namely political integration' (translated into English in Joerges et al., 2000). He added that this 'finalité politique' would be preceded by the formation of a 'centre of gravity' within the Union: an 'avant garde', the driving force for the completion of political integration. With regard to the institutional arrangement, he asked for 'a constitutional treaty centred around basic human and civil rights; shared sovereignty and a clear definition of competences between European and nation-state levels of governance; a division of powers among the European institutions, including full parliamentarization and a European Parliament with two chambers, a European government and, possibly, a directly elected president, with broadly administrative powers'. With this 'division of sovereignty' between the EU institutions and the nation-states, he thus distanced himself from a European superstate transcending and replacing the national democracies.

The speech attracted a great deal of criticism and generated open hostility in some quarters where the word federation is not in the dictionary of European integration. Also, scholarly reactions have come from all and sundry, ranging from criticism of Fischer's logical inconsistency in wanting a federation where the member states remain sovereign, to the fact that he had not worked out the path to be taken to the ultimate objective. With regard to inconsistency, Leben (in Joerges et al., 2000, p. 101) argues that classical constitutional theory recognizes only confederate and federal states and hence wonders if there can be a third type: 'a federation but not a federal state, as . . . Fischer's speech seems to suggest?' However, our concern here is with what political leaders think, so let us turn to them: those interested in purely academic discussion should turn to the excellent collection in Joerges et al. (2000).

A year later, on 30 April 2001, German Chancellor Gerhard Schröder added to Fischer's framework in the publication for the November congress for his Social Democrat party. He called for the restructuring of the EU institutions, including the building of the European Commission into a strong executive, the transformation of the Council of the European Union into a chamber of European states, and the drafting of a constitution for the EU. Singling out the weaknesses of the common agricultural and regional policies, he laid stress on greater transparency by insisting that the member states should themselves assume responsibility for the tasks that they can carry out more effectively than through a central administration, which is consistent with the subsidiarity principle, incorporated in the Amsterdam Treaty.

On 27 June 2000, French President Jacques Chirac, in a speech delivered to the German Parliament in Berlin, called for the formation of an 'inner core of EU members' willing to push more rapidly towards further integration, thus echoing Fischer's appeal for a centre of gravity, which some would rather call a two-speed Europe (see chapter 2). Also, he endorsed the idea of a future constitution for the EU. Some analysts saw this as support for Germany's call for EU federalism; others as politically calculated rhetoric lacking in substance. He stressed, however, that neither France nor Germany envisaged the creation of a 'European super-state which would take the place of our nation states', i.e. he was advocating 'not a United States of Europe, but a Europe of united states'.

On 28 May 2001, Lionel Jospin, while still French Premier, spelled out his vision for the EU as a 'federation of nation states', but rejected the German views of federalism and distanced himself from President Jacques Chirac's idea of a 'pioneer group' to forge ahead with integration. Noting that 'federation' might appear to be a simple and coherent word, but that it was subject to several interpretations (see above), he went on to reject any model based on the German federal system. He added that 'if federation means a gradual, controlled process of sharing competences, or transferring competences to the union level, then this refers to the federation of nation states coined by [ex-EU Commission President] Jacques Delors and is a concept which I fully support'. Being a dedicated socialist, he reinforced his previous suggestions that the EU should enhance its social legislation with the adoption of a social treaty, the firming up of tax harmonization, and a tighter legal framework to enshrine the role of public services in the EU.

Of the EU member nations considered here, this leaves the present British government: present, since Tony Blair has been at the British helm for a decade. The leader of the reformed Labour Party (some argue it is the old Conservative Party in pleasant disguise) is warm towards the EU, hence out of step with Baroness Thatcher, not the other EU leaders. Since assuming office in 1997 he has been very sympathetic towards the EU. In a speech in Ghent (near Bruges where Thatcher delivered hers) on 23 February 2000, he said that he believed that, by winning the argument for economic reform in Europe, he could mould the EU agenda and in doing so simultaneously defuse much of the resentment Britons felt towards the EU. In short, he wants the UK to act from within the EU to the betterment of the EU itself and to make it attractive to Britons, adding that British ties with the US have been undermined by the failure of the UK to play an active role within the EU. Later, he committed his government to the adoption of the euro, provided that Britain passed his Chancellor's five (now six) tests (the 'Brown' tests) and that UK citizens endorsed adoption in a referendum afterwards. However, he remains adamant that he does not see the EU going beyond the economic field and that the alliance with the US will be strengthened; the events leading to the 2003 US–British (and alliances) war with Iraq clearly demonstrated that.

On 6 October 2000, in his speech to the Polish Stock Exchange in Warsaw, Blair elaborated on his arguments and came up with his proposals for EU political reform, which, given its date, were obviously his response to Fischer and submission to the Convention of the Future of Europe. First, he wanted the European Council to set the agenda, which is what it actually does (see chapter 3), but with the President of the Commission playing a part in drawing up the agenda, the Commission continuing as the guardian of the treaties, and the Council having term presidencies with greater continuity. Second, he did not want to see a single document called the EU Constitution, opting for continuation of the present system of treaties, laws and precedents, i.e. to retain the British style of an unwritten constitution, and to decide on what is to be done and not done at the EU level: thus be more specific about subsidiarity. Third, he wanted to have a second chamber for the European Parliament whose most important function would be to review the EU's work. Fourth, he wanted to streamline the Commission, since with enlargement it would have thirty members and would become unworkable, but he indicated that there was no need to discuss this then. In short, he wanted to see the EU as a 'superpower, but not a superstate . . . an economic powerhouse through the completion of the world's biggest single market, the extension of competition, an adaptable and well educated workforce, the support for businesses large and small'. Thus he reiterated what Chancellor Gordon Brown said on 27 June 2000, all of which amounted to saying 'no thank you' to Fischer, though the overall tone of the government is one of positive commitment to a slightly strengthened EU.

One should add that against this positive but limited change in the British government's attitude towards the EU, the then leader of the Conservative Party, Iain Duncan Smith, held views consistent with Thatcher's. However, the Conservative Party is not united in this respect, since it has a significant faction with very positive views on EU integration. This remains the present position with both the party and its leader, David Cameron, who, in his first conference speech as leader of the Conservative Party on 4 October 2006, uttered not a single word on the EU, but later reiterated that he left Europe to Hague, now Shadow Minister for Europe. Since we have already stated Hague's position, there is no need to repeat it; hence the position of the Conservatives remains as stated above.

To complete the picture, one must consider the position of the then President of the European Commission, Romano Prodi, who was the Italian Prime Minister during 1996–8 and resumed that position in 2006, but in a very fragile coalition. He expressed his opinions on many occasions, but no more clearly than in a speech delivered to the French National Assembly on 12 March 2003. He asked: 'What Europe do we want? What common projects are we aiming for? Just a "supermarket" or a political area that allows us to defend convictions on the world stage?' His response can be briefly captured from his statement that the Commission highlights 'the need for a Union that can "exercise the responsibilities of a world power"', that current disagreements between EU leaders about the war in Iraq 'will eventually help defend the idea on which European integration was founded' and 'when a political Union emerges, it will reap the benefit' of this approach.

Thus not only were practically all the major players still envisaging the EU going beyond its commitments then, but also evolving into some sort of a closer political union. The debate on whether this should be 'United States of Europe' or a 'Europe of united states' does not undermine this, since, to reiterate, a federation can take different forms. Hence the vision of most of the former major EU political leaders was consistent with the substance of the dream of the founding fathers.

Before turning to the current leaders, even more comment on federation is warranted. According to constitutional theorists, federalism fulfils two major functions. The first is a vertical separation of powers by assigning separate responsibilities to two government levels; the components and the federation are usually geographically defined, 'although "societal federalism" considers non-territorial units as components of a federation' (Börzel and Risse, 2000). The second is the integration of heterogeneous societies, but without destroying their cultural and/or political autonomy (Börzel and Risse, 2000). Implicit in both functions is that the components and the federation have autonomous decision powers which they can exercise independently; thus sovereignty is shared or divided, rather than being exclusively located at one level. Even without the legitimate monopoly of coercive force, the EU has acquired some fundamental federal qualities. As witnessed by this book, it possesses sovereignty rights in a wide variety of policy sectors. These range from exclusive jurisdiction in the area of EMU to far-reaching regulatory competences in sectors such as consumer protection, energy, the environment, health/social security and transport. Also, the EU is 'increasingly penetrating even the core of traditional state responsibilities such as internal security (Schengen, Europol) and, albeit to a lesser extent, foreign and security policy' (Börzel and Risse, 2000). In most policy areas, EU law is not only superior to national law; it can also deploy direct effect giving citizens the right to litigate against their states for violating the EU laws conferred on them (see chapter 4). This is part of a second development, which has been addressed more recently. The EU is transforming itself into a political community

within a defined territory and with its own citizens, who are granted (some) fundamental rights by the European Treaties and the jurisdiction of the European Court of Justice ... With the Treaties of Maastricht and Amsterdam, however, the single market has been embedded in a political union with emerging external boundaries [Article 11 of the Union treaty refers to the protection of the integrity of the Union and its external boundaries] and proper citizenship' (Börzel and Risse, 2000).

Not only has the EU developed into a political community with comprehensive regulatory powers and a proper mechanism of territorially defined exclusion and inclusion (EU citizenship), it also shares most features of what defines a federation. First, the EU is a system of governance which has at least two orders of government, each existing in its own right and exercising direct influence on the people. Second, the EU treaties allocate jurisdiction and resources to these two main orders of government. Third, there are provisions for 'shared government' in areas where the jurisdiction of the EU and member states overlap. Fourth, EU law enjoys supremacy over national law: it is the law of the land (see chapter 4). Fifth, the composition and procedures of EU institutions are based not solely on principles of majority representation, but guarantee the representation of 'minority' views. Sixth, the European Court of Justice serves as an arbitrator to adjudicate on conflicts between EU institutions and the member states. Finally, the EU has a directly elected parliament (Börzel and Risse, 2000).

The EU only lacks two significant features of a federation. One is that the member states remain the 'masters' of the treaties, i.e. they have the exclusive power to amend or change the constitutive treaties of the EU. The other is that the EU has no real 'tax and spend' capacity, i.e. it has no fiscal federalism. 'Otherwise, the EU today looks like a federal system [see chapter 19], it works in a similar manner to a federal system, so why not call it an emerging federation?' (Börzel and Risse, 2000). In short, one wonders why the word federalism frightens some EU nations and citizens so much.

One obvious reaction to the position of these political leaders would be that their statements summarized above should not be taken seriously since they were meant merely to set the scene for the Convention for the Future of Europe (see chapter 2). In other words, given past experience, these positions would have to be greatly watered down if consensus was to materialize, and consensus would be needed on the occasion since a positive decision would require unanimity. This was especially so when it was being claimed that the Convention was to be a historic moment for the EU, just as the Philadelphia convention was for America, since it would give the EU a single legal personality and provide all its institutions with a constitutional basis for their powers as well as transfer sovereignties over internal affairs (immigration, cross-border crime, drug trafficking) to EU institutions. One should add, however, that Peter Hain, British Prime Minster Tony Blair's representative on the Convention, took to insisting that it would be much less important than the Maastricht Treaty.

It is therefore pertinent to add something on the draft constitution, submitted on 6 February 2003, to find out what light it sheds on the matter, and follow this by considering the final draft, adopted in the Thessaloniki Greek summit on 20 June 2003, and signed in Brussels in the intergovernmental conference in June 2004 (see section 2.2.6), since doing so will help shed light on the above-mentioned 'watering down' during negotiations.

Consider the first articles of the 2003 draft constitution, largely attributed to Valéry Giscard d'Estaing, chairman of the Convention and former French President, and his twelve-member 'inner praesidium' (easily accessible from the EU website at http://european-convention.eu.int). It envisaged a major role for the EU in the economy, foreign policy and even space exploration. Sixteen of its forty-six articles dealt with EU aims, values and powers. Article 1, on establishing an entity for the EU, stated that it should be: 'A Union of European States which, while retaining their national identities, closely coordinate their policies at the European level, and *administer certain common competences on a federal basis*' (italics added). Article 3, on EU objectives, calls for, inter alia, the 'development of a common foreign and security policy, and a common defence policy, to defend and promote the Union's values in the wider world'. Indeed, 'the tone of the document is more federalist than expected', and in particular the 'Commission was pleased with the clause to allow national governments and the European Parliament to give the EU more powers' (*Financial Times*, 7 February 2003), if needed for the attainment of the objectives set by the Constitution.

These were labelled surprising proposals, given that the Convention had been entrusted with proposing a framework and structures for the EU which were geared to changes in the world situation, the needs of EU citizens and the future development of the union. In other words, the Convention was largely meant to simplify and restructure the EU basic treaties (Giuliano Amato, one of the two vice-chairmen of the Convention and ex-Prime Minister of Italy, Project Syndicate/Institute for Human Science, 2002). No wonder Britain immediately labelled the draft 'unacceptable', claiming it went further than expected towards creating a federal Europe (*Financial Times*, 7 February 2003). However, Amato responded in the same article by arguing that the 'institutional structure . . . should also reflect and help develop Europe's broader aspirations. Europe must be more than a vehicle of economic integration.' What was even more interesting was that Giscard d'Estaing, the Convention's chairman, proposed the streamlining of the EU foreign policy apparatus by the creation of a single post of EU Foreign Minister (to replace the two roles then held by Javier Solana, EU foreign policy chief, which he still holds, and Christopher Patten, EU Commissioner in charge of external relations) as well as scrapping the rotating six-month presidency of the European Council (*Financial Times*, 16 April 2003).

That was the draft, but how does it compare with the final draft, signed in June 2004? In this book we have tried our best to avoid duplication, but for easy comparison it may be justified to repeat here the skeleton of the Constitution given in section 2.2.6:

(a) It sets out a single simplified EU treaty.

(b) It creates a post of president of the EU Council, serving up to five years instead of six-monthly rotation.

(c) It creates a post of EU Foreign Minister, who will head a newly created EU diplomatic service.

(d) It gives greater scope for defence cooperation among member states, including procurement.

(e) It gives new powers to the EP over legislation and the annual EU budget.

(f) It enables national parliaments to ensure EU law does not encroach on member states' rights.

(g) It abolishes the national veto in some areas, including immigration and asylum policy.

(h) It retains the national veto in tax, defence and foreign policy, and over financing the EU budget.

(i) It introduces a new 'double majority' voting system for the EU Council of Ministers, requiring at least fifteen member nations to make a decision, comprising 65 per cent of the EU population.

(j) It introduces a mechanism for those member nations wishing to leave the EU.

(k) It increases the power of the 'eurogroup' (the countries that have adopted the euro) to decide own policies.

(l) It incorporates an EU Charter of Fundamental Rights, including the right to strike, with legal provision limiting its application in national courts.

(m) It reduces the size of the EU Commission starting in 2014, with commissioners sent from only two-thirds of member states on a rotation basis.

(n) It raises the minimum number of seats in the EP for small member states from four to six, and sets out a limit of ninety-six for the big members.

It should therefore be apparent that the changes to the first draft have been minimal. Thus, it would seem that the pre-Convention utterances were not mere political gesturing, especially when one takes into consideration that eighteen of the twenty-seven member countries have actually ratified the Constitution, with more about to follow, and the only two to reject it were not the governments concerned (see above), but were the opinions of citizens who were basically expressing disappointment with their own governments.

The current leaders

Turning to the current leaders, the only changes in this context have been in Germany, with Angela Merkel becoming Chancellor on 22 November 2005, and in the Commission, with its president, José Manuel Barroso, ex-Prime Minister of Portugal, assuming office in 2004. As mentioned, Romano Prodi returned to Italy's premiership on 17 May 2006 and since he has uttered nothing to contradict his stance on Europe, we need not dwell on him. We do, however, need to consider Blair to check for consistency on the part of the UK.

In his speech to the European Parliament on 23 June 2005, Blair said that the EU 'is a union of values, of solidarity between nations and people, of not just a common market in which we trade but a common political space in which we live as citizens'. He added that 'I believe in Europe as a political project. I believe in Europe with a strong and caring social dimension.' And he rejected the 'division between the Europe necessary to succeed economically and social Europe' and stressed that 'Political Europe and economic Europe do not live in separate rooms.' Critics would, of course, immediately respond by stating that his programme for the UK presidency of the EU, for which this was the preamble, was far removed from what he had stated, but that would be churlish since we are concerned here with his vision for Europe.

As to Chancellor Merkel, she has stated that the Constitution must be revived, stressing that clearing the EU institutional mess must be a priority over economic reform. In his presentation to the European Parliament on 26 September 2006 of the Commission's positive assessment of the fitness of Bulgaria and Romania to join the club on 1 January 2007, Barroso said 'it is time for a pause', adding that it would be unwise to expand the EU further 'before it upgraded its creaking institutions, through the ratification of parts of the Constitution'. Thus both are agreed on the need to do more, but have not yet stated categorically what the EU's future should be, which is natural, given that they have not yet been at the helm long enough to utter anything with confidence.

28.3 Conclusion

Thus the majority of European political leaders who really matter envisage a long-term future for the EU which is not limited to what it has achieved to date. Those who share the dream of the founding fathers would stress that this is tantamount to being on the road leading to the creation of a United States of Europe. They would, however, differ with regard to how soon they will arrive there and what precise form they want it to take. To put it differently, economics may seem to have been the ultimate objective, but in the light of utterances by European leaders, it remains only a vehicle to some other end.

References

Throughout this book reference is made to numerous Communications by the Commission of the European Communities (CEC) or European Commission to the Council. The official system adopted by the EU for these is quite clear: for example, COM (88) 491 means Communication number 491, issued in 1988. To avoid cluttering the main text, they are not referred to as such, but rather by their entry under the CEC as below. Note that EU publications are still issued under CEC, not CEU.

Reference is also frequently made to the Treaties of the European Communities. Some of these are published by Her Majesty's Stationery Office (HMSO), now The Stationery Office (TSO), in the United Kingdom, but the most comprehensive set is issued by Sweet and Maxwell, which is listed here. Also listed is the Commission's comprehensive guide to the Maastricht Treaty (CEC, 1999d) and there is a comparative text by Euroconfidential of Belgium titled *The Rome, Maastricht and Amsterdam Treaties*. Note that, in order to save space, CEC publications issued by the Office of Official Publications in Brussels do not have Brussels stated at the end, nor do those published in both Brussels and Luxembourg, but those issued only in Luxembourg do.

Throughout the book, *EU Bulletin* is used to refer to the Commission of the European Communities' *Bulletin of the European Communities*, now *Union* (various issues), and *OJ C, OJ L* or *OJ CL* (where L stands for legal) refer to the Commission's *Official Journal of the European Communities/Union*. Again, the EC/EU's own system of referencing is clear.

Abbott, K., Keohane, R., Moravcsik, M., Slaughter, A.-M. and Snidal, D. (2000) 'The concept of legalization', *International Organization*, vol. 53, issue 3.

Acs, Z., Audretsch, D. and Feldman, M. (1994) 'R&D spillovers and recipient firm size', *Review of Economics and Statistics*, vol. 100, no. 2.

Adedeji, A. (2002) 'History and prospects for regional integration in Africa', paper presented on 5 March at the African Development Forum III, held in Addis Ababa, Ethiopia.

Adelman, M. A. (1969) 'Comment on the "H" concentration measure as a numbers equivalent', *Review of Economics and Statistics*, vol. 51.

Agha, A. and Houghton, J. (1996) 'Designing VAT systems: some efficiency considerations', *Review of Economics and Statistics*, vol. 78.

Aiginger, K. and Pfaffermayr, M. (2000) 'The Single Market and geographic concentration in Europe', presented at the EARIE Conference, Lausanne on 11 December.

Aitken, N. D. (1973) 'The effects of the EEC and EFTA on European trade: a temporal cross-section analysis', *American Economic Review*, vol. 68.

Akerlof, G, Dickens, A., Perry, W. and George, L. (2000) 'Near rational wage price setting and long-run Phillips curve', *Brookings Papers on Economic Activity*, vol. 30, no. 1.

Allen, C., Gasiorek, M. and Smith, A. (1998) 'The competition effects of the Single Market in Europe', *Economic Policy*, 27.

Allen, P. R. (1983) 'Cyclical imbalance in a monetary union', *Journal of Common Market Studies*, vol. 21, no. 2.

Allen, P. R. and Kenen, P. (1980) *Asset Markets, Exchange Rates and Economic Integration*, Cambridge University Press, Cambridge.

Alston, P. and Weiler, J. (1999) 'An "ever closer union" in need of a human rights policy: the EU and human rights', *European Journal of International Law*, vol. 9.

Alter, K. (1996) 'The European Court's political power', *West European Politics*, vol. 19.

(1998a) 'Who are the "masters of the treaty"?: European governments and the European ECJ', *International Organization*, vol. 52.

(1998b) 'Explaining national court acceptance of European Court jurisprudence: a critical evaluation of theories of legal integration', in A.-M. Slaughter, A. Stone Sweet and J. Weiler (eds.), *The European Courts and National Courts: Doctrine and Jurisprudence*, Hart, Oxford.

(2000) 'The European Union's legal system and domestic policy: spillover and backlash', *International Organization*, vol. 53.

(2001) *Establishing the Supremacy of European Law: The Making of an International Rule of Law in Europe*, Oxford University Press, Oxford.

Alter, K. and Meunier-Aitsahalia, S. (1994) 'Judicial politics in the European Community: European integration and the pathbreaking Cassis de Dijon decision', *Comparative Political Studies*, vol. 26.

Alter, K. and Vargas, K. (2000) 'Explaining variation in the use of European litigation strategies: EC Law and UK gender equality policy', *Comparative Political Studies*, vol. 36.

Alter, K., Dehousse, R. and Vanberg, G. (2002) 'Law, political science and EU legal studies: an interdisciplinary project', *European Union Politics*, vol. 3.

Amiti, M. (1998) 'New trade theories and industrial location in the EU: a survey of evidence', *Oxford Review of Economic Policy*, vol. 4, no. 2.

Anderson, M. and Liefferink, D. (eds) (1997) *European Environmental Policy – The Pioneers*, Manchester University Press, Manchester.

Ardy, B. (1988) 'The national incidence of the European Community budget', *Journal of Common Market Studies*, vol. 26, no. 4.

(2002a) 'The EU budget and EU citizens', in S. Hatt and F. Gardner (eds.), *Economics, Policies and People: A European Perspective*, Macmillan, Basingstoke.

(2002b) 'The UK, the EU budget and EMU', in Ali M. El-Agraa (ed.), *The Euro and Britain: Implications of Moving into the EMU*, Pearson Education, Harlow.

Ardy, B. and Umbach, G. (2004) 'Employment policies in Germany and the UK: the impact of Europeanisation', Anglo German Foundation for the Study of Industrial Society, London and Berlin, www.agf.org.uk.

Ardy, B., Begg, I., Schelkle, W. and Torres, F. (2002) *EMU and its Impact on Cohesion: Policy Challenges*, European Institute, South Bank University, London.

Argyris, N. (1993) 'Regulatory reform in the electricity sector: an analysis of the Commission's Internal Market proposals', *Oxford Review of Economic Policy*, vol. 19, no. 1.

Armstrong, H. W. (1978) 'European Economic Community regional policy: a survey and critique', *Regional Studies*, vol. 12, no. 5.

(1985) 'The reform of European Community regional policy', *Journal of Common Market Studies*, vol. 23.

(1995a) *Growth Disparities and Convergence Clubs in Regional GDP in Western Europe, USA and Australia*, Report for DG16, European Commission, Brussels.

(1995b) 'Convergence among regions of the European Union', *Papers in Regional Science*, vol. 40.

Armstrong, H. W. and Taylor, J. (2000) *Regional Economics and Policy*, 3rd edn, Blackwell, Oxford.

Armstrong, K. (1998) 'Legal integration: theorising the legal dimension of European integration', *Journal of Common Market Studies*, vol. 36.

Armstrong, K. and Bulmer, S. (1998) *The Governance of the Single European Market*, Manchester University Press, Manchester.

Arndt, H. W. and Garnaut, R. (1979) 'ASEAN and the industrialisation of East Asia', *Journal of Common Market Studies*, vol. 17, no. 3.

Arndt, S. W. (1968) 'On discriminatory versus non-preferential tariff policies', *Economic Journal*, vol. 78.

(1969) 'Customs unions and the theory of tariffs', *American Economic Review*, vol. 59.

Arnold, F. (1994) *Economic Analysis of Environmental Policy and Regulation*, Wiley, New York.

Arnull, A. (1990) 'Does the ECJ have inherent jurisdiction?', *Common Market Law Review*, vol. 27.

(1991) 'What shall we do on Sunday?', *European Law Review*, vol. 16.

(1996) 'The European ECJ and judicial objectivity: A reply to Professor Hartley', *Law Quarterly Review*, vol. 112.

Arts, K. and Dickson. A. (eds.) (2004) *EU Development Cooperation: From Model to Symbol*, Manchester University Press, Manchester.

Asdrubali, P., Sorensen, B. and Yosha, O. (2002) 'Channels of interstate risk sharing: United States 1963–1990', *Quarterly Journal of Economics*, vol. 111.

Audretsch, D. and Thurik, R. (2001) 'Linking entrepreneurship to growth', *STI Working Papers 2001/2*, OECD, Paris.

Audretsch, D., Baumol, W. and Burke, A. (2001) 'Competition policy in dynamic markets', *International Journal of Industrial Organization*, vol. 19, no. 5.

Australian Society of CPAs (1998) 'Tax reform in New Zealand – the shape of things to come in Australia', *Discussion Paper*, May, cited in Cnossen (2002).

BAE Systems (2000) 'Updating and development of economic and fares data regarding the European air travel industry', *2000 Annual Report*, BAE Systems, Chorley.

Bagella, M. and Becchetti, L. (2000) *The Comparative Advantage of Industrial Districts: Theoretical and Empirical Analysis*, Physica-Verlag, Heidelberg.

Bailey, S. J. (2002) *Public Sector Economics: Theory and Practice*, 2nd edn, Palgrave, Basingstoke.

Balassa, B. (1961) *The Theory of Economic Integration*, Allen and Unwin, London.

(1967) 'Trade creation and trade diversion in the European Common Market', *Economic Journal*, vol. 77.

(1974) 'Trade creation and trade diversion in the European Common Market: an appraisal of the evidence', *Manchester School*, vol. 42.

(1975) *European Economic Integration*, North-Holland, Amsterdam.

Baldwin, R. (1989) 'The growth effect of 1992', *Economic Policy*, no. 9.

(1994) *Towards an Integrated Europe*, CEPR, London.

Baldwin, R. and Krugman, P. A. (2004) 'Agglomeration, integration and tax harmonization', *European Economic Review*, vol. 48, no. 1.

Baldwin, R., Haaparanta, P. and Kiander, J. (1995) *Expanding Membership of the European Union*, Cambridge University Press, Cambridge.

Baldwin, R., François, J. F. and Portes, R. (1997) 'The costs and benefits of Eastern enlargement: the impact on the European Union and Central Europe', *Economic Policy: A European Forum*, vol. 24.

Baldwin, R. E. (1971) *Non-tariff Distortions of International Trade*, Allen and Unwin, London.

Ballenger, N., Dunmore, J. and Lederer, T. (1987) 'Trade liberalization in world farm markets', *Agriculture Information Bulletin*, vol. 516, May.

Bangermann, M. (1994) 'Information technology in Europe: the EC Commission's view', in *European Information Technology Observatory*, EITO, Frankfurt am Main, p. 12.

Barents, R. (1982) 'New developments in measures having equivalent effect: a reappraisal', *Common Market Law Review*, vol. 19.

Barham, C. (2002) 'Economic inactivity and the labour market', *Labour Market Trends*, February.

Barnard, C. (1995) 'A European litigation strategy: the case of the Equal Opportunities Commission', in J. Shaw and G. More (eds.), *New Legal Dynamics of the EU*, Clarendon Press, Oxford.

Barnard, C. and Sharpston, E. (1997) 'The changing face of Article 177 references', *Common Market Law Review*, vol. 34.

Barrell, R. (2002) 'The UK and EMU: choosing the regime', *National Institute Economic Review*, no. 180, April.

Barrell, R. and Pain, N. (1993) 'Trade restraints and Japanese direct investment flows', mimeo, National Institute of Economic and Social Research, London.

Barry, A. (1993) 'The European community and European government: harmonization, mobility and space', *Economy and Society*, vol. 22.

Bassanini, A. and Duval, R. (2006) 'Employment patterns in OECD countries: reassessing the role of policies and institutions', OECD Economics Department Working Paper, no. 486, Paris.

Baumol, W. J. and Oates, J. E. (1988) *The Theory of Environmental Policy*, 2nd edn., Cambridge University Press, Cambridge.

Bayoumi, T. and Eichengreen, B. (1995) 'Is regionalism simply a diversion? Evidence from the evolution of the EC and EFTA', Discussion Paper no. 1294, Centre for Economic Policy Research, London.

(1996) 'Operationalising the theory of optimum currency areas', Discussion Paper no. 1484, Centre for Economic Policy Research, London.

Beatty, C., Fothergill, S., Gore, T. and Green, A. (2002) 'The real level of unemployment 2002', Centre for Regional Economic and Social Research, Sheffield Hallam University.

Begg, I. (1995) 'The impact on regions of competition of the EC Single Market in financial services', in S. Hardy, M. Hart, L. Albrechts and A. Katos (eds.), *An Enlarged Europe: Regions in Competition?*, Jessica Kingsley, London.

Begg, I. and Grimwade, N. (1998) *Paying for Europe*, Sheffield Academic Press, Sheffield.

Bellamy, R. and Warleigh, A. (1998) 'From an ethics of participation to an ethics of participation: citizenship and the future of the EU', *Millennium*, vol. 27.

Bengtsson, K., Ekström, C. and Farrell, D. (2006) 'Sweden's growth paradox', *The McKinsey Quarterly*, Economic Studies Country Reports, http://www.mckinseyquarterly.com/home.aspx.

Benvenisti, E. (1993) 'Judicial misgivings regarding the application of international law: an analysis of attitudes of international courts', *European Journal of International Law*, vol. 4.

Berglas, E. (1983) 'The case for unilateral tariff reactions: foreign tariffs reconsidered', *American Economic Review*, vol. 73.

Berglöf, E., Eichengreen, B., Roland, G., Tabellin, G. and Wyplosz, C. (2003) *Built to Last: A Political Architecture for Europe*, CEPR, London.

Bergman, D., Brunekreet, G., Doyle, C., von der Fehr, N.-H. M., Newbery, D. M., Pollitt, M. and Regilbeau, P. (1970) *A Future for European Agriculture*, Atlantic Institute, Paris.

Bergmann, L., Brunekreeft, G., Doyle, C., von der Fehr, N.-H. M., Newbery, D. M., Pollitt, M. and Regilbeau, P. (1999) *A European Market for Electricity?*, CEPR, London; and SNS, Stockholm.

Bergstrand, J. D. (1985) 'The gravity equation in international trade: some microeconomic foundations and empirical evidence', *Review of Economics and Statistics*, vol. 67, no. 3.

Bertola, G., Blau, F. and Kahn, L. (2002) 'Labor market institutions and demographic employment patterns', NBER Working Paper no. 9043, Cambridge, Mass.

Bhagwati, J. N. (1969) *Trade, Tariffs and Growth*, Weidenfeld and Nicolson, London.

(1971) 'Customs unions and welfare improvement', *Economic Journal*, vol. 81.

Bishop, S. and Walker, M. (2002) *The Economics of EC Competition Law*, Sweet and Maxwell, London.

Bishop, W. (1981) 'Price discrimination under Article 86: political economy in the European Court', *Modern Law Review*, vol. 44.

Björksten, N. (1999) 'How important are differences between euro area economies?', *Bulletin*, Bank of Finland, Helsinki.

Blanchard, O. and Landier, A. (2002) 'The perverse effect of partial labour market reform: fixed-term contracts in France', *Economic Journal*, vol. 112, no. 480.

Blanchard, O. and Wolfers, J. (2000) 'The role of shocks and institutions in the rise of European unemployment', *Economic Journal*, vol. 110, March.

Blandford, D. (2002) 'Multifunctional agriculture and domestic/international policy choice', *The Estey Centre Journal of International Law and Trade Policy*, vol. 3, no. 1.

Blaszczyk, B. (2005) 'Lisbon Strategy: a tool for economic and social reforms in the enlarged European Union', *Studies and Analysis*, no. 310, CASE (Centre for Social and Economic Research), Warsaw, www.case.com.pl/upload/publikacja_plik/8442581_sa310.pdf.

Blom-Hansen, J. and Christensen, J. G. (2004) *Den Europaeiske Forbindelse*, Magtudredningen, Aarhus.

BLS (2003) 'Federal executive branch employment', Bureau of Labour Statistics, USA, www.bls.gov/oes/2001/oesi3_901.htm#b00-0000.

(2006) 'Employees by major industry sector', US Department of Labour, http://www.bls.gov/ces/home.htm.

Bode, E., Krieger-Boden, C. and Lammers, K. (1994) *Cross-border Activities, Taxation and the European Single Market*, Institut für Weltwirtschaft, Kiel, cited in Cnossen (2002).

Boehmer-Christiansen, S. and Skea, J. (1990) *Acid Politics: Environmental and Energy Policies in Britain and Germany*, Pinter, Washington D.C.

Boeri, T. (2005) 'Lost in translation', *Intereconomics*, March/April.

Bollard, A. E. and Mayes, D. G. (1991) 'Regionalism and the Pacific Rim', *Journal of Common Market Studies*, vol. 30.

Boone, J., Sadrieh, A. and van Ours, J. C. (2004) 'Experiments on unemployment benefit sanctions and job search behaviour', CEPR Discussion Paper, no. 4298, London.

Booth, A., Burda, M., Calmfors, L., Checchi, D., Naylor, R. and Visser, J. (2000) 'What do unions do in Europe', a report for the Fondazione Rodolfo DeBendetti, Milan, http://www.frdb.org/english/Labour/report1_17giugno00.pdf.

Börzel, T. A. and Risse, T. (2000) 'Who is afraid of European federation? How to constitutionalise a multi-level governance system', in C. Joerges, Y. Mény and J. H. H. Weiler (eds.) (2000).

Bottasso, A. and Sembenelli, A. (2001) 'Market power, productivity and the EU Single Market program: evidence from a panel of Italian firms', *European Economic Review*, vol. 45.

Bouët, A. (2002) 'Commentaire sur l'article "Niveau et coût du protectionnisme européen" de Patrick A. Messerlin', *Économie Internationale*, vols. 89–90.

Bovenberg, A. L. (1994) 'Designation and origin based taxation under international capital mobility', *International Tax and Public Finance*, vol. 1, no. 3.

Bovenberg, A. L. and Cnossen, S. (1997) *Public Economics and the Environment in an Imperfect World*, Kluwer, Dordrecht.

Bovens, M. A. P. and Yesilkagit, K. (2005) 'De invloed van Europese richtlijnen op de Nederlandse wetgever', *Nederlands Juristenblad*, issue 10 (11 March).

Bover, O., García-Perea, P. and Portugal, P. (2000) 'Iberian labour markets: why Spain and Portugal are OECD outliers', *Economic Policy*, vol. 31, October.

Boyd, G. (ed.) (1998) *The Struggle for World Markets: Competition and Cooperation Between NAFTA and the European Union*, Edward Elgar, Cheltenham.

Brander, J. and Spencer, B. (1983) 'International R&D rivalry and industrial strategy', *Review of Economic Studies*, vol. 50.

Braunerhjelm, P., Faini, R., Norman, R., Ruane, F. and Seabright, P. (2000) 'Integration and the regions of Europe: how the right policies can prevent polarization', *Monitoring Integration*, vol. 10, CEPR, London.

Brenton, P. (2003) 'Integrating the Least Developed Countries into the world trading system: the current impact of EU preferences under Everything But Arms', World Bank Policy Research Working Paper 3018, World Bank, Washington D.C.

Brenton, P. and Winters, L. A. (1992) 'Bilateral trade elasticities for exploring the effects of 1992', in L. A.

Winters (ed.), *Trade Flows and Trade Policy After 1992*, Cambridge University Press, Cambridge.

Bretschger, L. and Hettich, F. (2002) 'Globalization, capital mobility and tax competition: theory and evidence for OECD countries', *European Journal of Political Economy*, vol. 18, no. 4.

Bright, C. (1995) 'Deregulation of EC competition policy: rethinking Article 85(1)', *1994 Annual Proceedings of Fordham Corporate Law Institute*, vol. 21.

British Petroleum (2006) *BP Statistical Review of World Energy*, http://www.bp.com/liveassets/bp_internet/globalbp/globalbp_uk_english/reports_and_publications/statistical_energy_review_2006/STAGING/local_assets/downloads/pdf/statistical_review_of_world_energy_full_report_2006.pdf.

Brittan, L. (1992) *European Competition Policy: Keeping the Playing Field Level*, Brassey's Inc., Washington D.C.

Britz, W., Heckelei, T. and Péres, I. (2006) 'Effects of decoupling of land use', *German Journal of Agricultural Economics*, vol. 55 (Agrawirtschaft, Jahrgang 55).

Brooks, M. R. and Button, K. J. (1992) 'Shipping within the framework of a single European market', *Transport Review*, vol. 12.

Brown, A. J. (1961) 'Economic separatism versus a common market in developing countries', *Yorkshire Bulletin of Economic and Social Research*, vol. 13.

Brülhart, M. (1998) 'Marginal intra-industry trade and trade-induced adjustment: a survey', in M. Brülhart and R. C. Hine, *Intra-Industry Trade and Adjustment: The European Experience*, Macmillan, London.

Buchanan, J. M. and Tullock, G. (1962) *The Calculus of Consent*, University of Michigan Press, Ann Arbor.

Buckley, P. J. and Casson, M. (1976) *The Future of the Multinational Enterprise*, Macmillan, Basingstoke.

Buigues, P.-A., Ilzkovitz, F. and Lebrun, J. F. (1990) 'The impact of the internal market by industrial sector: the challenge for the member states', *The European Economy/Social Europe*, Office of Official Publications of the European Commission, Luxembourg.

Buiter, W. H. (2000) 'Optimal currency areas: why does the exchange rate regime matter? With an application to UK membership in EMU', *Scottish Journal of Political Economy*, vol. 47. no. 3, August.

Buiter, W. H., Corsetti, G. and Roubini, N. (1993) 'Excessive deficits: sense and nonsense in the Treaty of Maastricht', *Economic Policy*, vol. 16.

Bureau of Economic Analysis (2006) *Gross State Product*, http://www.bea.gov/bea/regional/gsp.htm.

Burley, A.-M. and Mattli, W. (1993) 'Europe before the court: A political theory of legal integration', *International Organization*, vol. 47.

Buti, M., Eijffinger, S. and Franco, D. (2002) 'Revisiting the Stability and Growth Pact: grand design or internal adjustment?', mimeo, November, Centre for Economic Research, University of Tilburg, Netherlands.

Button, K. J. (1984) *Road Haulage Licensing and EC Transport Policy*, Gower, Aldershot.

(1990) 'Infrastructure plans for Europe', in J. Gillund and G. Tornqvist (eds.), *European Networks*, Centre for Regional Science (CERUM), UMEA University, Stockholm.

(1992) 'The liberalization of transport services', in D. Swann (ed.), *1992 and Beyond*, Routledge, London.

(1993) 'East–west European transport: an overview', in D. Banister and J. Berechman (eds.), *Transportation in a Unified Europe: Policies Challenges*, Elsevier, Amsterdam.

(1998) 'The good, the bad and the forgettable – or lessons the US can learn from European transport policy', *Journal of Transport Geography*, vol. 6.

Button, K. J. and Gillingwater, D. (1986) *Future Transport Policy*, Croom Helm, London.

Button, K. J. and Keeler, T. (1993) 'The regulation of transport markets', *Economic Journal*, vol. 103.

Button, K. J. and Swann, D. (1992) 'Transatlantic lessons in aviation deregulation: EEC and US experiences', *Antitrust Bulletin*, vol. 37.

Button, K. J., Hayes, K. and Stough, R. (1998) *Flying into the Future: Air Transport Policy in the European Union*, Edward Elgar, Cheltenham.

Byé, M. (1950) 'Unions douanières et données nationales', *Économie Appliquée*, vol. 3. Reprinted (1953) in translation as 'Customs unions and national interests', *International Economic Papers*, no. 3.

Bygrä, S., Hansen, C. Y., Rystad, K. and Søltoft, S. (1987) *Danish–German Border Shopping and its Price Sensitivity*, Institut for Graenseregionfroskning, Aabenraa, cited in Cnossen (2002).

Bzdera, A. (1992) 'The ECJ of the European Community and the politics of institutional reform', *West European Politics*, vol. 15.

Cadot, O., Estevadeordal, A., Suwa-Eisenmann, A. and Verdier, T. (2005) *The Origin of Goods: Rules of Origin in Regional Trade Agreements*, Oxford University Press, Oxford.

Callon, M. (1986) 'Some elements of a sociology of translation: domestication of the scallops and fishermen of St. Brieuc Bay', in J. Law (ed.), *Power: Action and Belief: A New Sociology of Knowledge*, Routledge, London.

(1998) 'Introduction: the embeddedness of economic markets in economics', in M. Callon (ed.), *The Laws of the Markets*, Blackwell, Oxford.

Calmfors, L. et al. (1997) *EMU – A Swedish Perspective Report of the Calmfors Commission*, Kluwer, Dordrecht.

Calmfors, L. and Corsetti, G. (2002) 'A better plan for loosening the Pact', *Financial Times*, 26 November.

Cambridge Econometrics and Ecorys-NEI (2004) *A Study on the Factors of Regional Competitiveness*, Report for the European Commission, DG Regional Policy, Brussels.

Cann, C. (1998) 'Introduction to fisheries management viewpoint', in T. S. Gray (ed.), *The Policies of Fishing*, Macmillan, Basingstoke.

Cappelletti, M. (1987) 'Is the European ECJ "running wild"?', *European Law Review*, vol. 12.

Carone, G. and Salomäki, A. (2001) 'Reforms in tax-benefit systems in order to increase employment incentives in the EU', Economic Paper no. 160, European Commission DG for Economic and Financial Affairs.

Casey, B. (2004) 'The OECD Jobs Strategy and the European Employment Strategy: two views of the labour market and the welfare state', *European Journal of Industrial Relations*, vol. 10, no. 2.

Casey, B. and Gold, M. (2005) 'Peer review of labour market policies in the European Union: what can countries really learn from one another?', *Journal of European Public Policy*, vol. 12, no. 1.

Casey, P. (2005) *After the Financial Services Action Plan: A Repeat of the post-1992 Blues?*, Brussels: Centre for European Policy Studies: Commentaries, 17 June, http://www.ceps.be/Article.php?article_id=468.

Cathie, J. (2001) *European Food Aid Policy*, Ashgate, Aldershot.

Cecchini, P. (1988) *The European Challenge 1992: The Benefits of a Single Market*, Gower, Aldershot.

CEPII/EU Commission (1997) Volume 2 on 'Impact on trade and investment', *The Single Market Review*, Office of the Official Publications of the European Communities, Luxembourg, and Kogan Page, London.

CEPR/European Commission (1997) Volume 3 on 'Impact on trade and investment', *The Single Market Review*, Office of the Official Publications of the European Communities, Luxembourg and Kogan Page, London.

Chalmers, D. (1993) 'Free movement of goods within the European Community: an unhealthy addiction to Scotch whisky?', *International and Comparative Law Quarterly*, vol. 42.

(1997a) 'Judicial preferences and the community legal order', *Modern Law Review*, vol. 60.

(1997b) 'Community trade mark courts: the renaissance of an epistemic community?', in J. Lonbay and A. Biondi (eds.), *Remedies for Breach of EC Law*, John Wiley, Chichester.

(1998) 'Bureaucratic Europe: from regulating communities to securitising unions', Council of European Studies, Baltimore, Md.

(1999) 'Accounting for "Europe" ', *Oxford Journal of Legal Studies*, vol. 19.

(2000a) 'Postnationalism and the quest for constitutional substitutes', *Journal of Law and Society*, vol. 27.

(2000b) 'The positioning of EU judicial politics within the United Kingdom', *Western European Politics*, vol. 23, no. 4.

Chandler, A. (1990) *Scale and Scope: The Dynamics of Industrial Capitalism*, Harvard University Press, Cambridge, Mass.

Chlomoudis, C. I. and Pallis, A. A. (2002) *European Union Port Policy: The Movement Towards a Long-term Strategy*, Edward Elgar, Cheltenham.

Choi, J.-Y. and Yu, E. S. H. (1984) 'Customs unions under increasing returns to scale', *Economica*, vol. 51.

Christiansen, T. (1997) 'Reconstructing European space: from territorial politics to multilevel governance', in K. Jørgensen (ed.), *Reflective Approaches to European Governance*, Macmillan, Basingstoke.

Cnossen, S. (1987) 'Tax structure developments', in S. Cnossen (ed.), *Tax Coordination in the European Community*, Kluwer, Deventer.

(1999) 'What rate structure of Australia's VAT?', *Tax Notes International*, 24 May.

(2001) 'Tax policy in the European Union', *FinanzArchiv*, vol. 58, no. 4, tables 8 and 9.

(2002) *Tax Policy in the European Union: A Review of Issues and Options*, electronic documents, University of Maastricht, METEOR, www.edocs.unimaas.nl/.

Cnossen, S. and Bovenberg, L. (1997) 'Company tax harmonisation in the European Union: some further thoughts on the Ruding Committee Report', in M. Blejer and T. Ter-Minassian (eds.), *Macroeconomic Dimensions of Public Finance: Essays in Honour of Vito Tanzi*, Routledge, London.

Cnossen, S. and Smart, M. (2005) 'Taxation of tobacco', in S. Cnossen (ed.), *Theory and Practice of Excise Taxation*, Oxford University Press, Oxford.

Coase, R. (1937) 'The nature of the firm', *Economica*, vol. 16.

(1960) 'The problem of social costs', *Journal of Law and Economics*, vol. 3, October.

Cobham, D. (1996) 'Causes and effects of the European monetary crises of 1992–93', *Journal of Common Market Studies*, vol. 34.

Cockfield, Lord (1994) *The European Union: Creating the Single Market*, Wiley Chancery Law, London.

Codognet, M.-K., Glachant, J.-M., Lévêque, F. and Plagnet, M.-A. (2002) *Mergers and Acquisitions in the European Electricity Sector: Cases and Patterns*, CERNA, Centre d'économie industrielle, École Nationale Supérieure des Mines de Paris, Paris.

Coleman, D. (1985) 'Imperfect transmission of policy prices', *European Review of Agricultural Economics*, vol. 12.

Collignon, S. (2003) *The European Republic*, Kogan Page, London.

Comité intergouvernemental créé par la conférence de Messina (1956) *Rapport des chefs de délégation aux Ministres des Affaires Étrangères*, Brussels.

Commission of the European Communities (various issues) *Bulletin of the European Communities/Union (EU Bulletin)*.

(various years) *Social Report*.

(various issues and items) *Official Journal of the European Communities*.

(three times a year) *Social Europe*. Also, supplements.

(annual) *Report on Social Developments*.

(annual) *Employment in Europe*.

(1957) *First General Report on the Activity of the Communities*.

(1961) *Memorandum on the General Lines of a Common Transport Policy*.

(1963) *Report of the Fiscal and Financial Committee* (the Neumark Report).

(1968a) 'Premières orientations pour une politique énergétique communautaire', in *Communication de la Commission présentée au Conseil le 18 Décembre 1968*.

(1968b) *First Guidelines Towards a EC Energy Policy*.

(1970a) 'Report to the Council and the Commission on the realisation by stages of economic and monetary union in the Community', *EU Bulletin*, Supplement no. 11 (the Werner Report).

(1970b) *Corporation Tax and Income Tax in the European Communities* (the van den Tempel Report).

(1970c) *Industrial Policy in the Community*.

(1972) *First Report on Competition Policy*.

(1975) *Social Harmonization – Inland Waterways*, COM (75) 465 final.

(1976) *Fifth Report on Competition – EEC*.

(1977a) *Report of the Study Group on the Role of Public Finance in European Integration*, 2 vols. (the MacDougall Report).

(1977b) *Twenty-Five Years of the Common Market in Coal: 1953–1978*.

(1979a) *Eighth Report on Competition Policy*.

(1979b) *Social Harmonization – Inland Waterways*, COM (79) 363 final.

(1979c) *Report of Committee of Inquiry on Public Finance in the Community* (the MacDougall Report).

(1983) *Thirteenth Report on Competition Policy*.

(1984a) *Civil Aviation Memorandum No. 2: Progress towards the Development of a Community Air Transport Policy*, COM (84) 72.

(1984b) *Review of Member States' Energy Policies*, COM (84) 88.

(1985a) *Completing the Internal Market* (White Paper from the EC Commission to the EC Council), COM (85) 310.

(1985b) *Fourteenth Report on Competition Policy*.

(1985c) *Progress Towards a Common Transport Policy, Maritime Transport*, COM (85) 90 final.

(1987a) *Sixteenth Report on Competition Policy*.

(1987b) *European Environmental Policy*, Economic and Social Committee and Consultative Assembly.

(1987c) 'The Single European Act', *OJ L* 169, 29 June.

(1988a) *Research on the Cost of Non-Europe: Basic Findings*, 16 vols. (the Cecchini Report).

(1988b) *Disharmonies in US and EC Agricultural Policy Measures*.

(1988c) *Commission Review of Member States' Energy Policies*, COM (84) 88 final, 29.

(1988d) *The Main Findings of the Commission's Review of Member States' Energy Policies: The 1995 Community Energy Objectives*, COM (88) 174 final, vol. I, 3.

(1988e) *The Internal Energy Market*, Commission Working Document.

(1989a) *Guide to the Reform of the Community's Structural Funds*.

(1989b) *Council Resolution on Trans-European Networks*, COM (89) 643 final.

(1989c) *Communication from the Commission to the Council on Energy and the Environment*, COM (89) 369 final.

(1990a) 'One market, one money: an evaluation of the potential benefits and costs of forming an economic and monetary union', *European Economy*.

(1990b) *Second Survey of State Aids*.

(1991a) *Twentieth Report on Competition Policy*.

(1991b) *Opening up the Internal Market*.

(1991c) *Amended Proposal for a Council Regulation (EEC) Establishing a Community Ship Register and Providing for the Flying of the Flag by Sea-going Vessels* (presented by the Commission pursuant to article 149(3) of the EEC Treaty, COM (91) 54/I final.

(1991d) *Commission Proposal for a Council Directive Concerning Common Rules for the Internal Market in Electricity*, COM(91) 548 final.

(1992a) *Transport and the Environment – Towards Sustainable Mobility*, COM (92) 80.

(1992b) *The Future Development of the Common Transport Policy: A Global Approach to the Construction of a Community Framework for Sustainable Mobility*, COM (92) 494 final.

(1992c) *A Community Strategy to Limit Carbon Dioxide Emissions and to Improve Energy Efficiency*, COM (92) 246 final.

(1993a) 'Stable money: sound finances', *European Economy*, no. 53.

(1993b) 'Growth, competitiveness, employment: the challenges and ways forward into the 21st century', *White Paper*, COM (93) 700.

(1994a) *The European Report on Science and Technology Indicators*, DG XII.

(1994b) 'EC agricultural policy for the 21st century', *European Economy*, Reports and Studies no. 4.

(1994c) *Towards a New Asia Strategy*, COM (94) 314 final.

(1995a) *Citizens Network*, COM (95) 601.

(1995b) *High Speed Europe*.

(1995c) *An Energy Policy for the European Union – White Paper of the European Commission*, COM (95) 682.

(1995d) *White Paper – Teaching and Learning: Towards the Learning Society*, COM (95) 590 final.

(1996a) *Energy for the Future. Renewable Sources of Energy – Green Paper for a Community Strategy*, COM (96) 576.

(1996b) *Report from the Commission on the Application of the Community Rules on Aid to the Coal Industry in 1994*, COM (96) 575.

(1996c) *Services of General Interest in Europe*, COM (96) 443.

(1996d) *First Report on Economic and Social Cohesion*.

(1996e) *First Cohesion Report*, COM (96) final.

(1996f) 'The 1996 single market review', *Commission Staff Working Paper*, SEC (96) 2378.

(1996g) 'Green paper on relations between the European Union and the ACP countries on the eve of the 21st century', CEU/DG VIII.

(1996h) *XXVth Report on Competition Policy 1995*.

(1996i) *Impact of the Third Package of Air Transport Liberalization Measures*, COM (96) 514.

(1996j) *The First Action Plan for Innovation in Europe*, COM (96) 589.

(1996k) *European Environmental Legislation*, vols. 1–7, CEU DG XI.

(1996l) 'Community framework for state aid for research and development', *OJ C* 405, pp. 5–14.

(1996m) *Proposal for a Council Decision Concerning the Organization of Cooperation around Agreed Community Energy Objectives*, COM (96) 431 final.

(1997a) *Fifth Survey on State Aid in the European Union in the Manufacturing and Certain Other Sectors*, COM (97) 170.

(1997b) *Agenda 2000: For A Stronger and Wider Union*.

(1997c) *XXVIth Report on Competition Policy 1996*.

(1997d) *Green Paper on Sea-ports and Maritime Infrastructure*, COM (97) 678 final.

(1997e) 'Notice on the definition of the relevant market for the purposes of Community competition law', *OJ C* 372.

(1997f) 'Notice on agreements of minor importance', *OJ C* 372.

(1997g) *The Single Market Review*, 39 vols., Luxembourg and Kogan Page, London.

(1997h) *Action Plan for the Single Market* CSE (97) 1 final, 4 June.

(1998a) *Proposed Regulations and Explanatory Memorandum Covering the Reform of the Structural Funds 2000–2006*, DG XVI.

(1998b) *Communication from the Commission to the Council and the European Parliament on Implementation and Impact of Directive 91/440/EEC on the Development of Community Railways and Access Rights for Rail Freight*, COM (98) 202 final.

(1998c) 'Financing the European Union: Commission Report on the operation of the Own Resources system', DG Budget, www.europa.eu.int/comm/budget/agenda2000reports_en.htm.

(1998d) *Risk Capital: A Key to Job Creation in the European Union*, SEC (1998) 552.

(1999e) 'Convergence report 1998', *European Economy*, no. 65.

(1999a) *Sixteenth Annual Report on the Application of Community Law 1998*, COM (99) 301 final.

(1999b) *Mutual Recognition in the Context of the Follow-Up to the Action Plan for the Single Market*, COM (99).

(1999c) *Sixth Periodic Report on the Social and Economic Situation in the Regions in the Community*, Luxembourg.

(1999d) *The Amsterdam Treaty: A Comprehensive Guide*.

(1999e) 'Regulation 2790/1999 on the application of Article 81(3) of the Treaty to categories of vertical agreements and concerted practices', *OJ L* 336.

(1999f) 'White Paper on modernisation of the rules implementing Articles 85 and 86 of the EC Treaty', *OJ C* 132.

(1999g) *Institutional Implications of Enlargement*.

(1999h) *White Paper on Food Safety*.

(1999i) 'Community guidelines on state aid for rescuing and restructuring firms in difficulty', *OJ C* 288.

(1999j) 'Financial services: implementing the strategy for financial markets: action plan', COM (1999) 232.

(2000a) *Agenda 2000 – Setting the Scene for Reform*, 2 vols., www.europa.eu.int/comm/agriculture/publi/review 98/08_09_ en.pdf.

(2000b) *Working Party on the Future of the European Court System*, Luxembourg.

(2000c) *Structural Actions 2000–2006: Commentary and Regulations*.

(2000d) *The Community Budget: The Facts in Figures*, SEC (2000) 1200, Luxembourg.

(2000e) *Second Progress Report on Economic and Social Cohesion: Unity, Solidarity, Diversity for Europe, its People and its Territory*.

(2000f) 'Guidelines on vertical restraints', *OJ C* 291.

(2000g) 'The application of Article 81(3) of the Treaty to categories of specialisation agreements', Regulation no. 2658/2000 of 29 November 2000, *OJ L* 304, 05.12.2000, p. 3.

(2000h) 'The application of Article 81(3) of the Treaty to categories of research and development agreements', Regulation no. 2658/2000 of 29 November 2000, *OJ L* 304, 05.12.2000, p. 7.

(2000i) *The European Community's Development Policy*, COM (2000) 212, 26 April 2000.

(2000j) 'The European Community's development policy', Statement by the Council and Commission, 10 November.

(2001a) 'Promoting core labour standards and improving social governance in the context of globalisation', COM (2001) 416.

(2001b) 'Europe and Asia: a strategic framework for enhanced partnerships', COM (2001) 496 final.

(2001c) *Spatial Impacts of Community Policies and Costs of Non-coordination*, Study for DG-Regional Policy.

(2001d) *Electricity Liberalization Indicators in Europe*.

(2001e) *European Transport Policy for 2010: Time to Decide*, White Paper.

(2001f) *Reinforcing Quality Services in Seaports: A Key for European Transport Policy*, COM (2001) 35.

(2001g) *Company Taxation and the Internal Market*, COM (2001) 582 final.

(2001h) *Green Paper Towards a European Strategy for Security of Energy Supply*. These are two documents, one of which is technical.

(2001i) *XXXth Report on Competition Policy 2000*.

(2001j) *European Economy*, Supplement A, Economic Trends, no. 12.

(2001k) 'Commission notice on agreements of minor importance which do not appreciably restrict competition under Article 81(1) of the Treaty establishing the European Community (de minimis)', *OJ C* 368, 22.12.2001.

(2001l) 'Commission notice on the applicability of Article 81 to horizontal co-operation agreements', *OJ C* 3, 06.01.2001, p. 2.

(2002a) 'Communication from the Commission to the Council and European Parliament', ECFIN/581/02-EN rev. 3, 21 November.

(2002b) 'Evaluation of the 2002 pre-accession economic programmes of candidate countries', Enlargement Papers no. 14, DG ECFIN.

(2002c) *First Progress Report on Economic and Social Cohesion*, COM (2002) 46 final.

(2002d) *31st Report on Competition Policy 2001*, Luxembourg.

(2002e) 'Tableau de bord des aides d'état', COM (2002) 242 final.

(2002f) *Towards a European Research Area, Science, Technology and Innovation: Key Figures 2002*, Luxembourg.

(2002g) 'The EU Economy 2002 Review', Statistical Annexe, *European Economy*, no. 6, www.europa.eu.int/comm/economy_finance/index_en.htm.

(2002h) *Financial Report 2001*, DG Budget, www.europa.eu.int/comm/budget/index_en.htm.

(2002i) *Excise Duty Tables*, REF 1.015, August, DG Taxation and Customs Union, www.europa.eu.int/comm/taxation_customs/index_en.htm.

(2002j) *VAT Rates Applied in the Member States of the EU*, DOC/2908/2002-EN, Situation at 1st May, DG Taxation and Customs Union, www.europa.eu.int/comm/taxation_customs/index_en.htm.

(2002k) *Activities of the EU in 2000 in the Tax Field*, DOC (2003) 2101, 27 January, DG Taxation and Customs Union, www.europa.eu.int/comm/taxation_customs/index_en.htm.

(2002l) 'Commission notice on immunity from fines and reduction fines in cartel cases', *OJ C* 45, 19.02.2002, pp. 3–5.

(2002m) 'Co-ordination of economic policies in the EU: a presentation of key features of the main procedures', DG Economic and Financial Affairs: Euro-Papers no. 45, July.

(2002n) 'Communication from the Commission on streamlining the annual economic and employment policy co-ordination cycles', COM (2002) 487.

(2002o) 'Consolidated version of the treaty establishing the European Community', *OJ C*, 325, 24.12.2002, pp. 33–184.

(2002p) 'Taking stock of five years of the European Employment Strategy', COM (2002) 416.

(2002q) 'The internal market – 10 years without internal frontiers', Commission working document, http://ec.europa.eu/internal_market/10years/docs/workingdoc/workingdoc_en.pdf.

(2002r) *Annual Report 2002 on EC Development Policy and the Implementation of External Assistance in 2001*, COM (2002) 490.

(2003a) 'Evolution of the performance of network industries providing services of general interest', working paper by Frederik Bolkestein, Perdo Solbes Mira and David Byrne.

(2003b) 'Commission opinion on the ECB recommendation on and amendments to Article 10.2 of the statute of the ESCB'.

(2003c) *Second Progress Report on Economic and Social Cohesion*, COM (2003) 34 final.

(2003d) *Eurobarometer*, no. 5, Public Opinion Analysis, www.europa.eu.int/comm/public_opinion/.

(2003e) 'Proposal for a Council regulation on the control of concentrations between undertakings', *OJ L* 20, 28.01.2003, pp. 4–57.

(2003f) 'Establishing common rules for direct support schemes under the common agricultural policy and establishing certain support schemes for farmers and amending Regulations (EEC) no. 2019/93, (EC) no. 1452/2001, (EC) no. 1453/2001, (EC) no. 1454/2001, (EC) 1868/94, (EC) no. 1251/1999, (EC) no. 1254/1999, (EC) no. 1673/2000, (EEC) no. 2358/71 and (EC) no. 2529/20', http://eur-lex.europa.eu/LexUriServ/site/en/consleg/2003/R/02003R1782-20060101-en.pd.

(2003g) *Analysis of the Impact of Community Policies on Economic and Social Cohesion*, report by Labor Asociados to the European Commission DG Regional Policy.

(2003h) 'Programme for the promotion of short-sea shipping: proposal for a Directive of the European Parliament and the Council on Intermodal Units', COM (2003) 155 final.

(2003i) 'Internal market strategy: priorities for 2003–2006', COM (2003) 238.

(2003j) *Annual Report 2003 on EC Development Policy and the Implementation of External Assistance in 2002*, COM (2003) 527.

(2004a) 'Commission Regulation 773/2004/EC of 7 April 2004 relating to the conduct of proceedings by the Commission pursuant to Articles 81 and 82 of the EC Treaty', *OJ L* 123.

(2004b) 'Guidelines on the assessment of horizontal mergers under the Council Regulation on the control of concentrations between undertakings', *OJ C* 31.

(2004c) 'Commission Notice on the co-operation between the Commission and the courts of the EU Member States in the application of Articles 81 and 82 EC', *OJ C* 101.

(2004d) *Financial Report 2004*, Luxembourg.

(2004e) 'Building our common future – policy challenges and budgetary means of the enlarged Union 2007–2013', COM (2004) 101 final.

(2004f) 'Financial perspectives 2007–2013', COM (2004) 487 final.

(2004g) 'Financing the EU: Commission report on the operation of the own resources system', COM (2004) 505 final, vol. I, report.

(2004h) 'Financing the EU: Commission report on the operation of the own resources system', COM (2004) 505 final, vol. II, Technical annexe.

(2004i) 'Proposal for a system of the ECs' own resources', COM (2004) 501 final.

(2004j) 'Proposal for a Directive of the European Parliament and the Council on evaluating port security', COM (2004) 76 final.

(2004k) 'Proposal for a directive on services in the internal market', COM (2004) 2.

(2005a) *Third Progress Report on Cohesion: Towards a New Partnership for Growth, Jobs and Cohesion*, Communication from the Commission COM (2005) 192 final.

(2005b) 'Second implementation report of the Internal Market Strategy 2003–2006', COM (2005) 11.

(2005c) *White Paper on Financial Services 2005–10*.

(2005d) *Eurobarometer*, vol. 64, first results.

(2005e) *Eurobarometer*, vol. 63.

(2005f) 'Proposal for a decision concerning the seventh framework programme of the European Community for research, technological development and demonstration activities (2007 to 2013)', COM (2005) 119.

(2005g) 'Working together for growth and jobs: a new start for the Lisbon Strategy', COM (2005) 24.

(2005h) 'Qualitative assessment of the reform of external assistance', Commission staff working document, SEC (2005) 963.

(2005i) *Green Paper on Energy Efficiency or Doing More with Less*, COM (2005) 265 final, Luxembourg, http://ec.europa.eu/energy/efficiency/index_en.htm.

(2005j) *Report on Progress in Creating the Internal Gas and Electricity Market*, COM (2005) 568 final.

(2005k), 'Mergers and acquisitions', DG ECOFIN, note no. 2, June.

(2006a) 'Directive of the European Parliament and of the Council on services in the Internal Market', COM (2006) 160.

(2006b) 'Transposition of Financial Services Action Plan Directives, http://ec.europa.eu/internal_market/finances/actionplan/index_en.htm#transposition.

(2006c) 'Single Market in Financial Services Progress Report 2004–5', SEC (2006) 17.

(2006d) 'Annual macroeconomic database AMECO', DG Economic and Financial Affairs, http://ec.europa.eu/economy_finance/indicators/annual_macro_economic_database/ameco_en.htm.

(2006e) 'Internal market scoreboard', June 2006, no. 15, DG Internal Market, http://ec.europa.eu/internal_market/score/index_en.htm.

(2006f) 'VAT rates applied in the member states of the European Community', DOC/1803/2006, DG Taxation.

(2006g) 'Excise duty tables part III, manufactured tobacco', Ref 1.022, DG Taxation and Customs Union, January.

(2006h) 'Excise duty tables part I, alcoholic beverages', Ref 1.022, DG Taxation and Customs Union, January.

(2006i) 'Implementing the Community Lisbon Programme: progress to date and the next steps towards a Common Consolidated Corporate Tax Base (CCCTB), COM (2006) 157.

(2006j) 'Excise duty tables part II, energy products and electricity', Ref 1.022, January.

(2006k) *Structures of the Taxation Systems in the European Union 1995–2004*, DG Taxation, Doc. TAXUD E4/2006/DOC/3201.

(2006l) *A Reformed Cohesion Policy for a Changing Europe: Regions, Cities and Border Areas for Growth and Jobs*, Inforegio Factsheet.

(2006m) *Regions and Cities for Growth and Jobs: An Overview of Regulations 2007–13 on Cohesion and Regional Policy*, Inforegio Factsheet.

(2006n) *The Growth and Jobs Strategy and the Reform of European Cohesion Policy: Fourth Progress Report on Cohesion*, Communication from the Commission COM (2006) 281.

(2006o) *The Community Strategic Guidelines on Cohesion 2007–2013*, Commission Communication COM (2006) 386.

(2006p) *Promoting Decent Work for All*, COM (2006) 249.

(2006q) 'Global Europe: competing in the world', DG External Trade.

(2006r) 'Enlargement, two years after: an economic evaluation, *European Economy. Occasional Papers*, no. 24.

(2006s) 'Keep Europe moving – sustainable mobility for our continent', mid-term review of the European Commissions's 2001 Transport White Paper, COM (2006) 314 final.

(2006t) 'State aid scoreboard: statistical tables', DG Competition.

(2006u) 'Global Europe: competing in the world', DG Trade.

(2006v) *Green Paper: A European Strategy for Sustainable, Competitive and Secure Energy*, COM (2006) 105 final, downloaded 22 October 2006 from URL http://ec.europa.eu/energy/green-paper-energy/doc/2006_03_08_gp_document_en.pdf.

(2006w) *Annual Report 2006 on EC Development Policy and the Implementation of External Assistance in 2005, Annex*, SEC (2006) 808.

(2006x) *A Financial Perspective for Europe's Future*, http://ec.europa.eu/financial_perspective/world/index_en.htm.

(2006y) *Annual Report of the Financial Management of the 6th–9th European Development Funds (SDFs) in 2005*, SEC (2006) 977.

Conant, L. (2001) 'Europeanization and the courts: variable patterns of adaptation among national judiciaries', in J. Caparaso, M. Cowles and T. Risse (eds.), *Transforming Europe: Europeanization and Domestic Structural Change*, Cornell University Press, Ithaca, N.Y.

(2002) *Justice Contained: Law and Politics in the European Union*, Cornell University Press, Ithaca, N.Y.

Cooper, C. A. and Massell, B. F. (1965a) 'A new look at customs union theory', *Economic Journal*, vol. 75.

(1965b) 'Towards a general theory of customs unions in developing countries', *Journal of Political Economy*, vol. 73.

Copenhagen Economics (2005a) 'Economic assessment of the barriers to an internal market for services', *Copenhagen Economics*, http://www.copenhageneconomics.com/publications/trade4.pdf.

Corden, W. M. (1972a) 'Economies of scale and customs union theory', *Journal of Political Economy*, vol. 80.

(1972b) 'Monetary integration', *Essays in International Finance*, no. 93, Princeton University, Princeton, N.J.

(1977) *Inflation, Exchange Rates and the World Economy*, Oxford University Press, Oxford.

Cosgrove-Sacks, C. and Scappuci, G. (1999) *The European Union and Developing Countries: The Challenges of Globalisation*, Macmillan, Basingstoke.

Council of the European Communities (various years) *Review of the Council's Work*.

(1962) 'First regulation implementing Articles 85 and 86 of the Treaty', Regulation No. 17, *OJ L* 013, 21.02.1962, pp. 0204–0211.

(1977) Sixth Council Directive 77/388/EEC of 17 May 1977, on the harmonization of the laws of the Member States relating to turnover taxes – Common system of value added tax: uniform basis assessment, *OJ L* 145, pp. 1–40.

(1989a) 'Regulation 4064/89 on the control of concentrations between undertakings', *OJ L* 395.

(1989b) *European Energy Charter*, COM (91) 36 final.

(1992a) 'Council Directive 92/77/EEC of 19 October 1992 supplementing the common system of value added tax and amending Directive 77/388/EEC (approximation of VAT rates)', *OJ L* 316, 31/10/1992, pp. 1–4.

(1992b) 'Council Directive 92/79/EEC of 19 October 1992 on the approximation of taxes on cigarettes', *OJ L* 316, 31/10/1992, pp. 8–9.

(1992c) 'Council Directive 92/84/EEC of 19 October 1992 on the approximation of the rates of excise duty on alcohol and alcoholic beverages', *OJ L* 316, 31/10/1992, pp. 29–31.

Council of the EU (1995a) 'Council Directive 95/59/EC of 27 November 1995 on taxes other than turnover taxes which affect the consumption of manufactured tobacco', *OJ L* 291, 06/12/1995, pp. 40–5.

(1995b) 'Council directive concerning indirect taxes on the raising of capital', consolidated text, *OJ L* 2, pp. 1–8, 1 January.

(1997a) 'Regulation 1310/97 amending Regulation 4064/89 on the control of concentrations between undertakings', *OJ L* 40.

(1997b) 'Council resolution of 15 December 1997 on the 1998 Employment Guidelines', *OJ C* 30, 28/01/1998.

(1997c) 'Directive 96/71/EC of the European Parliament and of the Council of 16 December 1996 concerning the posting of workers in the framework of the provision of services', *OJ L*, 18, pp. 1–6.

(1998) 'Regulation 994/98 on the application of Articles 92 and 93 of the Treaty to certain categories of horizontal state aid', *OJ L* 142.

(1999a), 'Regulation 659/1999 laying down detailed rules for the application of Article 93 of the EC Treaty', *OJ L* 83.

(1999b) 'Council resolution of 22 February 1999 on the 1999 Employment Guidelines', *OJ C* 69, 12/03/1999.

(2000) *The European Community's Development Policy Statement by the Council and the Commission*, 10 November.

(2001) 'Council decision of 19 January 2001 on the 2001 Employment Guidelines', *OJ L* 22, 24/01/2001.

(2002a) 'Council Directive 2002/10/EC of 12 February 2002 amending Directives 92/79/EEC, 92/80/EEC and 95/59/EC as regards the structure and rates of excise duty applied on manufactured tobacco', *OJ L* 046, 16/02/2002, pp. 26–8.

(2002b) 'Council decision of 18 February 2002 on the 2002 Employment Guidelines', *OJ L* 60, 01/03/2002.

(2003a) 'Council Directive 2003/48/EC of 3 June 2003 on taxation of savings income in the form of interest payments', *OJ L* 157, 26/06/2003 pp. 38–48.

(2003b) 'The implementation of the rules on competition laid down in Articles 81 and 82 of the Treaty', Regulation No 1/2003 of 16 December 2002, *OJ L* 1, 04.01.2003, pp. 1–25.

(2003c) 'Council decision of 22 July 2003 on the guidelines for the employment policies of the member states', *OJ L* 197, 05/08/2003.

(2004) 'Council Regulation (EC) no. 139/2004 of 20 January 2004 on the control of concentrations between undertakings (the EC Merger Regulation)', *OJ L* 124.

(2005a) 'Council decision of 12 July 2005 on the guidelines for the employment policies of the member states', *OJ L* 205, 06/08/2005.

(2005b) *The EU and Africa: Towards a Strategic Partnership*.

(2005c) 'Joint statement by the Council and the representatives of the Member States meeting within the Council, the European Parliament and the Commission', in *The European Consensus on Development*, 14820/05.

(2005d) 'Council Regulation (EC) no. 1777/2005 of 17 October 2005 laying down implementing measures for Directive 77/388/EEC on the common system of value added tax', *OJ L* 288.

Court of First Instance (2002) *Statistics of the Judicial Activity of the Court of First Instance*, Luxembourg.

Cox, A. and Chapman, J. (2000) *The European Community Extend Cooperation Programmes*, European Commission.

Cox, A., Healey, J. and Koning, A. (1997) *How European Aid Works*, Overseas Development Institute, London.

Craig, P. (1997) 'Democracy and rule-making within the EC: an empirical and normative assessment', *European Law Journal*, vol. 3.

(2001) 'The jurisprudence of the Community courts reconsidered', in G. de Búrca and J. Weiler, *The European Court of Justice*, Hart, Oxford.

Crawford, J.-A. and Florentino, R. V. (2006) 'The changing landscape of regional trade agreements', Discussion Paper no. 8, World Trade Organization, Geneva.

Crouch, C. and Marquand, D. (1992) *Towards Greater Europe: A Continent without an Iron Curtain*, Basil Blackwell, Oxford.

Cruickshank, A. and Walker, W. (1981) 'Energy research development and demonstration policy in the European Communities', *Journal of Common Market Studies*, vol. 20, no. 1.

Culem, C. G. (1988) 'The locational determinants of direct investment among industrialised countries', *European Economic Review*, vol. 32.

Curzon Price, V. (1974) *The Essentials of Economic Integration*, Macmillan, Basingstoke.

Cuthbertson, K., Hall, G. H. and Taylor, M. P. (1980) 'Modelling and forecasting the capital account of the balance of payments: a critique of the "Reduced

Form Approach"', National Institute Discussion Paper no. 37.

Daintith, T. and Hancher, K. (eds.) (1986) *Energy Strategy in Europe: The Legal Framework*, de Gruyter, New York.

Dam, K. W. (1970) *The GATT: Law and International Economic Organization*, University of Chicago Press, Chicago.

Dashwood, A. and Johnston, A. (eds.) (2001) *The Future of the European Judicial System*, Hart, Oxford.

Daveri, F. (2004) 'Why is there a productivity problem in the EU?', CEPS Working Document no. 205, Brussels, Centre for European Policy Studies, Brussels.

Daveri, F. and Tabellini, G. (2000) 'Unemployment, growth and taxation in industrial countries', *Economic Policy*, vol. 30.

Daw, T. and Gray, T. (2005) 'Fisheries science and sustainability in international policy: a study of failure in the European Union's Common Fisheries Policy', *Marine Policy*, vol. 29, no. 3.

De Búrca, G. (1992) 'Giving effect to European Community directives', *Modern Law Review*, vol. 55.

De Grauwe, P. (1975) 'Conditions for monetary integration: a geometric interpretation', *Weltwirtschaftliches Archiv*, vol. 111.

(2005) *Economics of Monetary Union*, Oxford University Press, Oxford.

De Koning, J., Layard, R., Nickell, S. and Westergaard-Nielsen, N. (2004) *Policies for Full Employment*, Department of Work and Pensions, London, http://www.dwp.gov.uk/publications/dwp/2004/pol_full_emp/layard_report.pdf.

De la Fuente, A. and Domenesh, R. (2001) 'The redistributive effects of the EU budget', *Journal of Common Market Studies*, vol. 39, no. 2.

De la Mare, T. (1999) 'Article 177 in social and political perspective', in P. Craig and R. Dehousse, *The European Court of Justice*, Macmillan, Basingstoke.

De La Porte, C. and Pochet, P. (2002) 'Introduction', in C. De La Porte and P. Pochet (eds.), *Building Social Europe through the Open Method of Co-ordination*, Peter Lang, Brussels.

De Vincenti, C. (2001) 'Customer markets, inflation and unemployment in a dynamic model with a range of equilibria', *Metroeconomica*, vol. 2, no. 1.

De Vos, R. (2006) 'European Green Paper', *Refocus*, May/June.

Deaton, A. S. and Muellbauer, J. (1980) 'An almost ideal demand system', *American Economic Review*, vol. 70.

Decressin, J. and Fatás, A. (1995) 'Regional labour market dynamics in Europe', *European Economic Review*, vol. 39.

Decreux, Y. and Fontagné, L. (2006) 'A quantitative assessment of the outcome of the Doha Development Agenda'. CEPII Working Paper no. 2006-10, Paris.

DEFRA (2002) *Directing the Flow: Priorities for Future Water Policy*, UK Department for the Environment, Food and Rural Affairs, November.

(2006) 'Rural economy and employment', http://www.defra.gov.uk/erdp/docs/national/section5/employment.htm.

Dehousse, R. (1998) *The European Court of Justice*, Macmillan, Basingstoke.

Dehousse, R. and Weiler, J. (1990) 'The legal dimension', in W. Wallace (ed.), *The Dynamics of European Integration*, RIIA, London.

Deloitte (2006), 'Country snapshots', http://www.deloitte.com/dtt/section_node/0,2332,sid%253D11410,00.html.

Denis, C., McMorrow, K. and Röger, W. (2004) 'An analysis of EU and US productivity developments (a total economy and industry level perspective)', *European Economy: Economic Papers*, no. 208.

Denis, C., McMorrow, K., Röger, W. and Veugelers, R. (2005) 'The Lisbon Strategy and the EU's structural productivity problem', *European Economy: Economic Papers*, no. 221.

Denison, E. F. (1974) *Accounting for United States Economic Growth 1929–1969*, Brookings Institution, Washington D.C.

Devereux, M. P. and Griffith, R. (2001) 'Summary of the "Devereux and Griffith" economic model and measures of effective tax rates', Annex A of CEC (2001g).

Devereux, M. P., Griffith, R. and Klemm, A. (2002) 'Corporate income tax reforms and international tax competition', *Economic Policy*, vol. 17, issue 35.

Devroe, W. (1997) 'Privatization and Community law: neutrality versus policy', *Common Market Law Review*, vol. 34.

Dezalay, Y. (1992) *Marchands de droit. La réstructuration de l'ordre juridique international par les multinationaux du droit*, Fayard, Paris.

Dickens, R., Wadsworth, J. and Gregg, P. (2001) 'What happens to the employment prospects of disadvantaged workers as the labour market tightens', in R. Dickens, J. Wadsworth et al. (eds.), *The State of Working Britain: Update 2001*, LSE Centre for Economic Performance, London.

Diez Guardia, N. and Pichelmann, K. (2006) 'Labour migration patterns in Europe: recent trends, future challenges', *Economic Papers*, no. 256, CEU, DG Economic and Financial Affairs, Brussels.

Domenesh, R., Maudes, A. and Varela, J. (2001) 'Fiscal flows in Europe: the redistributive effects of the EU budget', *Weltwirtschaftliches Archiv*, vol. 136, no. 4.

Dosser, D. (1973) *British Taxation and the Common Market*, Knight, London.

Downs, A. (1957) *An Economic Theory of Democracy*, Harper, New York.

Doyle, C. and Siner, M. (1999) 'Introduction: Europe's network industries: towards competition', in Lars Bergmann et al., *A European Market for Electricity?*, CEPR, London; SNS, Stockholm.

Dunford, M. (1996) 'Disparities in employment, productivity and output in the EU: the roles of labour market governance and welfare regimes', *Regional Studies*, vol. 30.

—— (2000) 'Catching up or falling behind? Economic performance and regional trajectories in the new Europe', *Economic Geography*, vol. 76, no. 2.

Dunning, J. H. (1977) 'Trade, location of economic activity and the MNE: a search for an eclectic approach', in B. Ohlin et al. (eds.), *The International Allocation of Economic Activity*, Macmillan, Basingstoke.

ECA *see* European Court of Auditors.

ECB (2001) *The Monetary Policy of the ECB*, Frankfurt, August.

—— (2003) 'Recommendation on an amendment to Article 10.2 of the Statute of the ECB', Frankfurt, 3 February.

—— (2006) *Convergence Report 2006*, Frankfurt, May.

The Economist (2006) 'VAT fraud and trade: costly carousel', 1 June.

EFTA Secretariat (1969) *The Effects of the EFTA on the Economies of Member States*, Geneva.

—— (1972) *The Trade Effects of the EFTA and the EEC 1959–1967*, Geneva.

Ehlermann, C.-D. (1995) 'State aids under European Community competition law', *1994 Annual Proceedings of the Fordham Corporate Law Institute*, vol. 21.

—— (ed.) (2003) *European Competition Law Annual 2001: Effective Private Enforcement of EC Antitrust Law*, Hart, Oxford.

Eichengreen, B. (1993) 'Labor markets and European Monetary Unification', in P. Masson and M. Taylor (eds.), *Policy Issues in the Operation of Currency Unions*, Cambridge University Press, Cambridge.

El-Agraa, A. M. (1979a) 'Common markets in developing countries', in J. K. Bowers (ed.), *Inflation, Development and Integration: Essays in Honour of A. J. Brown*, Leeds University Press, Leeds.

—— (1979b) 'On tariff bargaining', *Bulletin of Economic Research*, vol. 31.

—— (1979c) 'On optimum tariffs, retaliation and international cooperation', *Bulletin of Economic Research*, vol. 31.

—— (1981) 'Tariff bargaining: a correction', *Bulletin of Economic Research*, vol. 33.

—— (ed.) (1983a) *Britain within the European Community: The Way Forward*, Macmillan, Basingstoke.

—— (1983b) *The Theory of International Trade*, Croom Helm, Beckenham.

—— (1984a) 'Is membership of the EEC a disaster for the UK?', *Applied Economics*, vol. 17, no. 1.

—— (1984b) *Trade Theory and Policy: Some Topical Issues*, Macmillan, Basingstoke.

—— (1988a) *Japan's Trade Frictions: Realities or Misconceptions?*, Macmillan and St Martin's, New York.

—— (ed.) (1988b) *International Economic Integration*, 2nd edn, Macmillan and St Martin's, New York.

—— (1989a) *The Theory and Measurement of International Economic Integration*, Macmillan and St Martin's, New York.

—— (1989b) *International Trade*, Macmillan and St Martin's, New York.

—— (1997) *Economic Integration Worldwide*, Macmillan and St Martin's, New York.

—— (1999) *Regional Integration: Experience, Theory and Measurement*, Macmillan, London; Barnes and Noble, New York.

—— (2002a) 'The UTR versus CU formation analysis and Article XXIV', *Applied Economics Letters*, no. 9.

—— (ed.) (2002b) *The Euro and Britain: Implications of Moving into the EMU*, Pearson Education, Harlow.

—— (2003) 'The enigma of African integration', *Journal of Economic Integration*, vol. 19, no. 1. A simpler version can be found in 'La integración regional en Africa: un intendo de análisis' (Understanding African integration), *Tiempo De Paz*, vol. 67, November 2002.

El-Agraa, A. M. and Hu, Y.-S. (1984) 'National versus supranational interests and the problem of establishing an effective EU energy policy', *Journal of Common Market Studies*, vol. 22.

El-Agraa, A. M. and Jones, A. J. (1981) *The Theory of Customs Unions*, Philip Allan, Oxford.

—— (2000a) 'UTR vs CU formation: the missing CET', *Journal of Economic Integration*, vol. 15, no. 2.

—— (2000b) 'On "CU can dominate UTR"', *Applied Economics Letters*, no. 7.

Eleftheriadis, P. (1998) 'Begging the constitutional question', *Journal of Common Market Studies*, vol. 36.

Elmeskov, J., Martin, J. and Scarpetta, S. (1998) 'Key lessons for labour market reforms: evidence from

OECD countries' experiences', *Swedish Economic Policy Review*, vol. 1.

Emerson, M. (1988) 'The economics of 1992', *European Economy*, no. 35.

Emerson, M., Anjean, M., Catinat, M., Goybet, P. and Jacquemin, A. (1988) *The Economics of 1992: The EC Commission's Assessment of the Economic Effects of Completing the Internal Market*, Oxford University Press, Oxford.

Emerson, M., Gros, D., Italianer, A., Pisani-Ferry, J. and Reichenbach, H. (1991) *One Market, One Money: An Evaluation of the Potential Benefits and Costs of Forming an Economic and Monetary Union*, Oxford University Press, Oxford.

EMI (1998) *Convergence Report*, Frankfurt, March.

Erdmenger, J. and Stasinopoulos, D. (1988) 'The shipping policy of the European Community', *Journal of Transport Economics and Policy*, vol. 22.

Estevadeordal, A. and Suominen, K. (2005) 'Mapping and measuring rules of origin around the world', in O. Cadot et al. (eds.), *The Origin of Goods*, Oxford University Press, Oxford.

ETUI (2003) 'Economic and employment outlook', report by the ETUI to the ETUC Executive Committee (unpublished, cited by Watt, 2004).

Eureka (2006) Eureka Projects in Figures, http://www.eureka.be/inaction/portfolio.do.

European Council (1988) 'Brussels European Council', *Bulletin of the European Communities*, no. 2.

(1992a) *Run-up to 2000: Declaration of the Council of 18 November*, Collection of Council Statements on Development Cooperation, vol. I, 05/92.

(1992b) 'Edinburgh European Council', *Bulletin of the European Union*, no. 7.

(1997) 'Special Luxembourg European Council on Employment', *Bulletin of the European Union*, no. 11.

(1998) 'Cardiff European Council', *Bulletin of the European Union*, no. 6.

(1999a) 'Special Berlin Council 24–25 March, Conclusions of the Presidency', *Bulletin of the European Union*, no. 3.

(1999b) 'Cologne European Council', *Bulletin of the European Union*, no. 6.

(2000a) 'Presidency conclusions: Lisbon European Council 23 and 24 March 2000', *Bulletin of the European Union*, no. 3.

(2000b) 'Council Decision of 29 September 2000 on the system of the European Communities Own Resources', *OJ L* 253, 7 October.

(2000c) 'Lisbon European Council', *Bulletin of the European Union*, no. 3, I.5–I.17.

(2001) 'Presidency conclusions: Stockholm European Council 23 and 24 March 2001', *Bulletin of the European Union*, no. 3.

(2002a) *Presidency Conclusions: Copenhagen European Council*, 12–13 December.

(2002b) 'Brussels European Council, 15–16 December', *Bulletin of the European Union*, no. 12.

(2003) 'Financial perspective 2000–2006 (tables) – EU 25 in 1999 and 2004 prices', *OJ L* 147, 14 June.

(2005a) 'Brussels European Council, 20–21 March', *Bulletin of the European Union*, no. 3.

(2005b) 'Financial Perspective, 2007-13, CADREFIN 238', 15915/05.

European Court of Auditors (various) 'Annual report concerning the financial year', *OJ*, www.eca.eu.int/EN/reports_opinions.htm.

(1995) 'Court of Auditors: annual report concerning 2004', *OJ C* 340, 12 November.

(2001) 'Annual report concerning the financial year 2000', *OJ C* 359, 15 December, www.eca.eu.int/EN/reports_opinions.htm.

(2002) 'Annual report concerning the financial year 2001', *OJ C* 295, 28 November, www.eca.eu.int/EN/reports_opinions.htm.

(2004) 'Court of Auditors: annual reports concerning 2003', *OJ C* 293, 30 November.

(2005) 'Court of Auditors: annual reports concerning 2004', *OJ C* 301, 30 November.

European Court of Justice (1983) 'Commission of the European Communities v. United Kingdom of Great Britain and Northern Ireland. Tax agreements applying to wine'. *Case 170/78 European Court Reports*, p. 02265.

(1996) *Notes for Guidance on References by National Courts*, Proceedings of the Court 34/96, Luxembourg.

(2002) *Statistics of the Judicial Activity of the Court of Justice*, Luxembourg.

(2005) *Annual Report of the Court of Justice*, OOPEC, Luxembourg.

European Economy (1996) 'Economic evaluation of the internal market', *Reports and Studies*, no. 4.

European Environmental Agency (2005) *Market Based Instruments for Environmental Policy in Europe*. Technical report no. 8/2005.

European Financial Services Round table (2003), 'Message to the European Council: the single market for financial services – breaking the gridlock', EFSRT, Brussels, www. efr.be/members/upload/publications/41955 singlemarket. pdg.

European Parliament (2001a) 'Task Force, Statistical Annex, November, Enlargement', www.europarl.eu.int./enlargement_new/statistics/default_en.htm.

(2001b) 'Tax coordination in the EU – the latest position', Working Paper, ECON 128, DG Research, www4.europa.eu.int/estudies/internet/workingpapers/econ/pdf/128_2n.pdf.

European Parliament, Council and Commission (2006) 'Inter-institutional agreement between the European Parliament, the Council and the Commission on budgetary discipline and sound financial management', *OJ C* 139, pp. 1–17.

European Research Group (1997) *The Legal Agenda for a Free Europe*, The Group, London.

European Union (1997) 'Treaty of Amsterdam', *OJ C* 340.

Eurostat (annual) *Basic Statistics of the Community*, Luxembourg.

(annual) *Statistical Review*, Luxembourg.

(2001) *European Union Foreign Direct Investment Yearbook 2001*, Luxembourg.

(2005a), *Structures of the Taxation Systems in the European Union*, Luxembourg.

(2005b), *Regional Unemployment in the European Union and Candidate Countries*, Statistics in Focus: Economy and Finance, no. 3/2005, Luxembourg.

(2006a), *Facts and Figures on the CFP: Basic Data on the Common Fisheries Policy*, Luxembourg.

(2006b) *Fisheries Statistics Online*, Luxembourg.

(2006c), *Regional GDP in the EU, the Accession Countries and Croatia in 2003*, Statistics in Focus: Economy and Finance, no. 17/2006, Luxembourg.

(2006d) 'New Cronos database', accessed via Economic and Social Data Services, www.esds.ac.uk.

(2006e) 'Economy and finance', in Government Statistics, online.

Fatás, A. (1998) 'Does EMU need a fiscal federation?', *Economic Policy*, vol. 26, April.

Feldstein, M. B. (1997) 'The political economy of the European Economic and Monetary Union: political sources of an economic liability', *Journal of Economic Perspectives*, vol. 11.

(2002) 'The role of discretionary policy in a low interest rate environment', NBER Working Paper 9203.

Ferrera, M., Hemerijck, A. and Rhodes, M. (2000) *The Future of Social Europe: Recasting Work and Welfare in the New Economy*, Celta Editora, Oeiras.

Fielder, N. (1997) *Western European Integration in the 1980s: The Origins of the Single Market*, Peter Lang, Bern.

Finon, D. and Surrey, J. (1996) 'Does energy policy have a future in the European Union?', in F. McGowan, *European Energy Policy in a Changing Environment*, Physica-Verlag, Heidelberg.

Fischer, P. A. (1999) *On the Economics of Immobility*, Verlag Paul Haupt, Bern.

Fitzgerald, J., Johnston, J. and Williams, J. (1988) 'An analysis of cross-border shopping', Paper no. 137, Economic and Social Research Institute, Dublin.

Fitzpatrick, P. (1997) 'New Europe and old stories: mythology and legality in the EU', in P. Fitzpatrick and J. Bergeron (eds.), *Europe's Other: European Law between Modernity and Postmodernity*, Ashgate, Aldershot.

Flam, H. (1998) 'Discussion', *Economic Policy*, vol. 27.

Fleming, J. M. (1971) 'On exchange rate unification', *Economic Journal*, vol. 81.

Forrester, I. and Norall, C. (1984) 'The laicization of Community: self-help and the rule of reason: how competition law is and could be applied', *Common Market Law Review*, vol. 22.

Frankel, J. A. (1997) *Regional Trading Blocs in the World Trading System*, Institute for International Economics, Washington D.C.

Frankel, J. A. and Rose, A. K. (2002) 'An estimate of the effect of common currencies on trade and income', *Quarterly Journal of Economics*, vol. 117, no. 2.

Frey, B. S. and Stutzer, A. (2006) 'Environmental morale and motivation', Working paper no. 288, Institute for Empirical Research in Economics, University of Zurich.

Friedman, M. (1975) *Unemployment versus Inflation? An Evaluation of the Philips Curve*, Institute of International Affairs, London.

Frohberg, K. and Weber, G. (2001) 'Ein Ausblick in die Zeit nach vollzogener Ost-Erweiterung', Institut für Agrarentwicklung in Mittel- und Osteuropa, Halle, July, cited in Swinnen (2002).

Fujita, M. and Thisse, J.-F. (1996) 'Economics of agglomeration', *Journal of the Japanese and International Economies*, vol. 10.

Gardner, B. L. (1992) 'Changing economic perspectives on the farm problem', *Journal of Economic Literature*, vol. 30, no. 1.

Garibaldi, P. and Mauro, P. (2002) 'Anatomy of employment growth', *Economic Policy*, vol.17, no. 34.

Garrett, G. (1992) 'International cooperation and institutional choice: the European Community's internal market', *International Organization*, vol. 46.

(1995a) 'The politics of legal integration', *International Organization*, vol. 49, no. 4.

(1995b) 'Capital mobility, trade and the domestic politics of economic policy', *International Organization*, vol. 49, no. 4.

Garrett, G. and Tsebelis, G. (1999) 'The institutional foundations of supranationalism', www.sscnet.ucla.edu/polisci/faculty/tsebelis/workpaper.html.

Garrett, G. and Weingast, B. (1993) 'Ideas, interests and institutions: constructing the European internal market', in J. Goldstein and R. Keohane (eds.), *Ideas and Foreign Policy*, Cornell University Press, Ithaca, N.Y.

Garrett, G., Keleman, R. and Schulz, H. (1998) 'The European ECJ, national governments and legal integration in the EU', *International Organization*, vol. 52.

GATT (1994) *Market Access for Goods and Services: Overview of the Results*, Geneva.

Gavin, B. (2001) *The European Union and Globalisation*, Edward Elgar, London.

Gay, S. H., Osterburg, B., Baldock, D. and Zdanowicz, A. (2005) 'Recent evolution of the EU Common Agricultural Policy (CAP): state of play and environmental potential', specific targeted research project, no. SSPE-CT-2004-503604, Impact of Environmental Agreements on the CAP document number: MEACAP WP6, p. 8.

Geddes, A. (1995) 'Immigrant and ethnic minorities and the EU's "democratic deficit"', *Journal of Common Market Studies*, vol. 33.

Gehrels, F. (1956–7) 'Customs unions from a single country viewpoint', *Review of Economic Studies*, vol. 24.

Gerber, D. J. (1998) *Law and Competition in Twentieth Century Europe: Protecting Prometheus*, Clarendon Press, Oxford.

Geroski, P. and Jacquemin, A. (1989) 'Industrial change, barriers to mobility and European industrial policy', in A. Jacquemin and A. Sapir (eds.), *The European Internal Market: Trade and Competition*, Oxford University Press, Oxford.

Giannetti, M., Guiso, L., Jappelli, T., Padula, M. and Pagano, M. (2002) 'Financial market integration, corporate financing and economic growth', European Commission Economic Paper no. 179, Brussels.

Gibson, J. and Caldeira, G. (1995) 'The legitimacy of transnational legal institutions: compliance, support and the European Court of Justice', *American Journal of Political Science*, vol. 39, no. 2.

(1998) 'Changes in the legitimacy of the European ECJ: a post-Maastricht analysis', *British Journal of Political Science*, vol. 28.

Gill, S. and Law, D. (1988) *The Global Political Economy: Perspectives, Problems and Policies*, Johns Hopkins University Press, Baltimore, Md.

Gillingham, J. (2003) *European Integration, 1950–2003: Superstate or New Market Economy?*, Cambridge University Press, Cambridge.

Glachant, J.-M. (1998) 'England's wholesale electricity market: could this hybrid institutional arrangement be transposed to the European Union?', *Utilities Policy*, vol. 7.

Golub, J. (1996a) 'The politics of judicial discretion: rethinking the interaction between national courts and the ECJ', *West European Politics*, vol. 19.

(1996b) 'Sovereignty and subsidiarity in EU environmental policy', European University Institute Working Paper, RSC no. 96/2.

Goolsbee, A. (1998) 'Does government R&D policy mainly benefit scientists and engineers?' *American Economic Review*, vol. 88, no. 2.

Gordon, R. (1998) 'Foundations of the Goldilocks economy: supply shocks and the time-varying NAIRU', *Brookings Papers on Economic Activity*, vol. 29, no. 2.

(2004) 'Why was Europe left at the station when America's productivity locomotive departed?', CEPR Discussion Paper 4416, Centre for Economic Policy Research, London.

Gormley, L. (1994) 'Reasoning renounced? The remarkable judgment in Reck and Mithouard', *European Business Law Review*, vol. 63.

Gorter, J. and de Mooij, R. (2001) *Capital Income Taxation in Europe: Trends and Trade-Offs*, SDU Utigevers, The Hague.

Goyder, D. (2003) *EC Competition Law*, Oxford University Press, Oxford.

Granovetter, M. (1985) 'Economic action and social structure: the problem of embeddedness', *American Journal of Sociology*, vol. 91.

Gray, T. and Hatchard, J. (2003) 'The reform of the Common Fisheries Policy's system of governance – rhetoric or reality?' *Marine Policy*, vol. 27, no. 6.

Green, R. J. (2001) 'Markets for electricity in Europe', *Oxford Review of Economic Policy*, vol. 17, no. 3.

(2006) 'Electricity liberalization in Europe – how competitive will it be?', *Energy Policy*, vol. 34, no. 16.

Green, R. J. and Newbery, D. M. (1992) 'Competition in the British electricity spot market', *Journal of Political Economy*, vol. 100, no. 5.

Greenaway, D. and Hine, R. (1991) 'Intra-industry specialisation, trade expansion and adjustment in the European economic space', *Journal of Common Market Studies*, vol. 29. no. 6.

Gros, D. (1996) *A Reconsideration of the Optimum Currency Approach: The Role of External Shocks and Labour Mobility*, Centre for Economic Policy studies, Brussels.

(2005) 'Perspectives for the Lisbon Strategy: how to increase the competitiveness of the European economy?' CEPS Working Document, no. 224, Centre for European Policy Studies, Brussels.

(2006) 'EU services trade: where is the single market in services?', Brussels: Centre for European Policy Studies, Commentaries, 13 February, http://www.ceps.be/Article.php?article_id=511.

Gross, L. (1984) 'States as organs of international law and the problem of autointerpretation', in L. Gross (ed.), *Essays on International Law and Organisation*, Martinus Nijhoff, Amsterdam.

Grossman, G. M. and Helpman, E. (1991) 'Trade, knowledge spillovers and growth', *European Economic Review*, vol. 35.

Grossman, G. M. and Hossi-Hansberg, E. (2006) 'Trading tasks: a simple theory of offshoring', unpublished paper, Princeton University.

Grubb, D. (2000), 'Eligibility criteria for unemployment benefits', *OECD Economic Studies*, vol. 31, no. 4.

Grubel, H. G. and Lloyd, P. (1975) *Intra-industry Trade: The Theory and Measurement of International Trade in Differentiated Products*, Macmillan, Basingstoke.

Grubert, H. (2001), 'Tax planning by companies and tax competition by governments: is there evidence of changes in behavior?', in J. R. Hines Jr. (ed.), *International Taxation and Multinational Activity*, University of Chicago Press, Chicago.

Gullstrand, J. and Johansson, H. (2005) 'The disciplinary effect of the single market on Swedish firms', *Open Economies Review*, vol. 16, no. 4.

Guruswamy, I. D., Papps, I. and Storey, D. (1983) 'The development and impact of an EC directive: the control of discharges of mercury to the aquatic environment', *Journal of Common Market Studies*, vol. 22, no. 1.

Guzzetti, L. (1995) *A Brief History of European Union Research Policy*, Commission of the European Communities, DG XII (Science, Research, Development).

Gwartney, J., Holcombe, R. and Lawson, R. (2006) 'Institutions and the impact of investment on growth', *Kyklos*, vol. 59, no. 2.

Haas, E. B. (1958 and 1968) *The Uniting of Europe*, Stevens, London.

Haberler, G. (1964) 'Integration and growth in the world economy in historical perspective', *American Economic Review*, vol. 54.

Habermas, J. (1996) *Between Facts and Norms*, Polity Press, Cambridge.

Haigh, N. (1989) *EEC Environmental Policy and Britain*, 2nd edn, Longman, Harlow.

Hancher, L. (1997) 'Slow and not so sure: Europe's long march to electricity market liberalization,' *Electricity Journal*, vol. 10, no. 9.

Hancher, L., Ottervanger, T. and Slot, P.-J. (1999) *EC State Aids*, Sweet and Maxwell, London.

Harding, C. (1992) 'Who goes to court in Europe? An analysis of litigation against the European Community', *European Law Review*, vol. 17.

Harlow, C. (1996) 'Francovich and the disobedient state', *European Law Journal*, vol. 2.

Hartley, T. (1996) 'The European Court, judicial objectivity and the constitution of the EU', *Law Quarterly Review*, vol. 112.

(1999) *Constitutional Problems of the EU*, Hart, Oxford.

Hayek, F. A. (1945) 'The use of knowledge in sociey', *American Economic Review*, vol. 35, no. 4.

Hazlewood, A. (1967) *African Integration and Disintegration*, Oxford University Press, Oxford.

(1975) *Economic Integration: The East African Experience*, Heinemann, London.

Hedemann-Robinson, M. (1996) 'Third country nationals, EU citizenship, and free movement of persons: a time for bridges rather than divisions', *Yearbook of European Law*, vol. 16.

Heitger, B. and Stehn, J. (1990) 'Japanese direct investment in the EC: response to the internal market 1993?', *Journal of Common Market Studies*, vol. 29.

Helm, D. R. (ed.) (2005) *Climate Change Policy*, Oxford University Press, Oxford.

Helm, D. R. and McGowan, F. (1989) 'Electricity supply in Europe: lessons for the UK', in D. R. Helm, J. A. Kay and D. J. Thompson (eds.), *The Market for Energy*, Oxford University Press, Oxford.

Helm, D. R., Kay, J. A. and Thompson, D. J. (eds.) (1989) *The Market for Energy*, Oxford University Press, Oxford.

Hemming, R. and Kay, J. A. (1981) 'The United Kingdom', in H. Aaron (ed.), *The Value Added Tax: Lessons from Europe*, Brookings Institution, Washington D.C.

Henrekson, M., Torstensson, J. and Torstensson, R. (1996) 'Growth effects of European integration', Discussion Paper no 1465, Centre for Economic Policy Research, London.

Henrichsmeyer, W. and Witzke, H.-P. (1994) *Agrarpolitik*, Band 2, Bewertung Willensbildung, UTB für Wissenschaft, Eugen Ulmer Verlag, Stuttgart.

Henry, S., Karanassou, M. and Snower, D. J. (2000) 'Adjustment dynamics and the natural rate', *Oxford Economic Papers*, vol. 52.

Hervey, T. (1995) 'Migrant workers and their families in the EU: the pervasive market ideology of Community law', in J. Shaw and G. More (eds.), *New Legal Dynamics of EU*, Clarendon Press, Oxford.

Hildebrand, D. (2002) *The Role of Economic Analysis in the EC Competition Rules*, Kluwer Law International, The Hague.

Hill, C. (1997) *Convergence, Divergence and Dialectics: National Foreign Policies and the CFSP*, RSC 97/66, EUI, Florence.

Hodson, D. and Maher, I. (2004), 'Soft law and sanctions: economic policy coordination and the reform of the

Stability and Growth Pact', *Journal of European Economic Policy*, vol. 11, no. 5.

Hoekman, B. and Konan, D. (1999) *Deep Integration, Non-discrimination and Euro–Mediterranean Free Trade*, Development Research Group, World Bank, Washington D.C.

Hofheinz, P. and Mitchener, B. (2002) 'EU states agree to open energy markets by 2004', *Wall Street Journal Europe*, 18 March.

Holden, M. (1994) *The Common Fisheries Policy*, Fishing Book News, Oxford.

House of Lords (1992) *Enlargement of the Community*, Select Committee on the European Communities, Session 1991–1992, 10th Report, HL55, HMSO, London.

Huizinga, H. (1994) 'International interest withholding taxation: prospects for a common European policy', *International Tax and Public Finance*, vol. 1, no. 3.

IFO (1990) *An Empirical Assessment of the Factors Shaping Regional Competitiveness in Problem Regions*, study carried out for the EC Commission.

Inklaar, R. M., O'Mahony, M. and Timmer, M. (2003) 'ICT and Europe's productivity performance: industry level growth accounting comparisons with the United States', Groningen Growth and Development Centre, Research Memorandum GD-68.

Institute for European Environmental Policies (2003) 'Environmental integration and the CAP', a report to the European Commission, europa.eu.int/comm/agriculture/envir/report/ieep_en.htm.

International Energy Agency (2001) *Oil Supply Security: The Emergency Response Potential of IEA Countries in 2002*, Paris.

(2002) *Energy Balances of OECD Countries, 1999–2000*, Paris.

(2006) *Energy Balances of OECD Countries 2003–2004*, Paris.

International Monetary Fund (2001) *Government Financial Statistical Yearbook 2001*, Washington D.C.

(2004) *Government Finance Statistics Yearbook, 2004*, Washington D.C.

Jacqué, J.-P. and Weiler, J. (1990) 'On the road to EU – a new judicial architecture: an agenda for the intergovernmental conference', *Common Market Law Review*, vol. 27.

Jamasb, T. and Pollitt, M. (2005) 'Electricity market reform in the European Union: review of progress toward liberalization and integration', *Energy Journal*, vol. 26, no. 3.

Jeppesen, T. (2002) *Environmental Regulation in a Federal System: Framing Environmental Policy in the EU*, Edward Elgar, Cheltenham.

Joerges, C. (1996) 'Taking the law seriously: on political science and the role of law in the integration process', *European Law Journal*, vol. 2.

Joerges, C., Mény, Y. and Weiler, J. (eds.) (2000) *What Kind of Constitution for What Kind of Polity? Responses to Joschka Fischer*, Robert Schuman Centre for Advanced Studies, European University Institute and Harvard Law School, www.iue.it/RSC/symposium.

Johansson, B. K. Å. et al. (2002) *Stabilisation Policy in the Monetary Union – A Summary of the Report*, Commission on Stabilisation Policy for Full Employment in the Event of Sweden Joining the Monetary Union, Stockholm.

Johnson, H. G. (1965a) 'Optimal trade intervention in the presence of domestic distortions', in R. E. Baldwin (ed.), *Trade, Growth and the Balance of Payments*, Rand McNally, Chicago.

(1965b) 'An economic theory of protectionism, tariff bargaining and the formation of customs unions', *Journal of Political Economy*, vol. 73.

(1973) 'Problems of European Monetary Union', in M. B. Krauss (ed.), *The Economics of Integration*, Allen and Unwin, London.

(1974) 'Trade diverting customs unions: a comment', *Economic Journal*, vol. 81.

Johnston, A. (1999) 'The EC Energy Law 1999: reciprocity and the gas and electricity directives', *CEPMLP Internet Journal*, vol. 4, no. 9, www.dundee.ac.uk/cepmlp/journal/htm1/article4-9.html.

(2001) 'Judicial reform and the Treaty of Nice', *Common Market Law Review*, vol. 38.

Jones, A. J. (1979) 'The theory of economic integration', in J. K. Bowers (ed.), *Inflation Development and Integration: Essays in Honour of A. J. Brown*, Leeds University Press, Leeds.

(1980) 'Domestic distortions and customs union theory', *Bulletin of Economic Research*, vol. 32.

(1983) 'Withdrawal from a customs union: a macroeconomic analysis', in El-Agraa (1983a), chapter 5.

Jones, C. and Gonzalez-Diaz, F. E. (1992) *The EEC Merger Control Regulation*, Sweet and Maxwell, London.

Jordan, A. (1999) 'European water standards: locked in or watered down?', *Journal of Common Market Studies*, vol. 37.

(2005) *Environmental Policy in the EU: Actors, Institutions and Processes*, 2nd edn, Earthscan, London.

Jovanovic, M. (2002) 'Eastern enlargement of the EU: topsy turvy endgame or permanent disillusion', mimeo, UN Economic Commission for Europe, November.

Karanassou, M., Sala, H. and Snower, D. J. (2002) 'Unemployment in the European Union: a dynamic reappraisal', Discussion Paper no. 531, IZA, Bonn, Germany, www.iza.org.

Kay, J. A. and King, M. A. (1996) *The British Tax System*, Oxford University Press, Oxford.

Keller, W. (2002) 'Geographic localization of international technology diffusion', *American Economic Review*, vol. 92, no. 1.

Kemmerling, A. and Bruttel, O. (2006) ' "New politics" in German labour market policy? The implications of the recent Hartz reforms for the German welfare state', *West European Politics*, vol. 29, no. 1.

Kemp, A. G. and Stephen, L. (2001) 'Prospects for gas supply and demand and their implications with special reference to the UK', *Oxford Review of Economic Policy*, vol. 17, no. 3.

Kenen, P. (1969) 'The theory of optimum currency areas: an eclectic view', in R. A. Mundell and A. K. Swoboda, *Monetary Problems of the International Economy*, MIT Press, Cambridge, Mass.

Kenny, S. (1998) 'The members of the ECJ of the European Communities', *Columbia Journal of European Law*, vol. 5.

Klemperer, P. D. and Meyer, M. A. (1989) 'Supply function equilibria in oligopoly under uncertainty', *Econometrica*, vol. 57, no. 6.

Kluve J. (2006) 'The effectiveness of European active labour market policy', IZA Discussion Paper no. 2018, Bonn.

Knight, F. H. (1921) *Risk, Uncertainty and Profit*, Houghton Mifflin, New York.

Koester, U. (1977) 'The redistributive effects of the EC Common Agricultural Policy', *European Review of Agricultural Economics*, vol. 4, no. 4.

(1989a) *International Agricultural Trade Consortium*, Washington D.C.

(1989b) 'Financial implications of the EC set-aside programme', *Journal of Agricultural Economics*, vol. 40, no. 2.

(1991) 'Economy-wide costs of farm support policies in major industrialized countries', in K. Burger, M. N. de Groot, J. Post and V. Zachariasse (eds.), *Agricultural Economics and Policy: International Challenges for the Nineties*, Elsevier, Amsterdam.

(2004) *Grundzüge der landwirtschaftlichen Marktlehre*, 3rd edn, Vahlen Verlag, Munich.

Koester, U. and Kirschke, D. (1985), 'Die hausgemachte Krise in der Agrarpolitik', *Wirtschaftsdienst*, vol. 65, no. 7.

Koester, U. and Tangermann, S. (1990) 'The European Community', in F. Sanderson (ed.), *Agricultural Protectionism in the Industrialized World*, *Resources for the Future*, Washington D.C.

Kok, H., Lejour, A. and Montizaan, R. (2004) 'The free movement of services within the EU', CPB, Netherlands Bureau for Economic Analysis, CPB Document 69, http://www.cpb.nl/eng/pub/cpbreeksen/document/.

Kok, W. (2004) *Facing the Challenge: The Lisbon Strategy for Growth and Employment*', report of the High Level Group chaired by Wim Kok, OOPEC, Luxembourg.

Komninos, M. (2002) 'New prospects for private enforcement of EC competition law: Courage v. Crehan and the Community right to damages', *Common Market Law Review*, vol. 39.

Korah, V. (1997) *An Introductory Guide to EEC Competition Law and Practice*, 4th edn, Oxford University Press, Oxford.

(1998) 'The future of vertical agreements under EC competition law', *European Competition Law Review*, vol. 19.

(2000) *An Introduction to EC Competition Law*, 7th edn, Hart, Oxford.

Korah, V. and Sullivan, D. (2002) *Distribution Agreements under the EC Competition Rules*, Hart, Oxford.

Kramer, L. (2003) *EC Environmental Law*, 5th edn, Sweet and Maxwell, London.

Krauss, M. B. (1972) 'Recent developments in customs union theory: an interpretative survey', *Journal of Economic Literature*, vol. 10.

Kreinin, M. E. (1972) 'Effects of the EEC on imports of manufactures', *Economic Journal*, vol. 82.

(1973) 'The static effects of EEC enlargement on trade flows', *Southern Economic Journal*, vol. 39.

(1979a) *International Economics: A Policy Approach*, Harcourt Brace Jovanovich, Orlando, Fla (also subsequent editions).

(1979b) 'Effects of European integration on trade flows in manufacturers', Seminar Paper no. 125, Institute for International Economic Studies, University of Stockholm, Sweden.

Krueger, A. O. (1974) 'The political economy of the rent-seeking society', *American Economic Review*, vol. 64.

Krugman, P. A. (1979) 'Increasing returns, monopolistic competition and international trade', *Journal of International Economics*, vol. 9.

(1990) 'Policy problems of a monetary union', in P. de Grauwe and L. Papademos (eds.), *The European Monetary System in the 1990s*, Longman, Harlow.

(1991) *Geography and Trade*. MIT Press, Cambridge, Mass.

(1994) *Re-Thinking International Trade*. MIT Press, Cambridge, Mass.

Krugman, P. A. and Venables, A. J. (1990) 'Integration and competitiveness of peripheral industry', in C. Bliss and J. Braga de Macedo (eds.), *Unity with Diversity in the European Community*, Cambridge University Press, Cambridge.

—— (1996) 'Integration, specialization, adjustment', *European Economic Review*, vol. 40.

Kumm, M. (1999) 'Who is the final arbiter of constitutionality in Europe?: three conceptions of the relationship between the German Federal Constitutional Court and the European ECJ', *Common Market Law Review*, vol. 36.

Küpker, B., Hüttel, S., Kleinhans, W. and Offermann, F. (2006) 'Assessing impacts of CAP reform in France and Germany', *German Journal of Agriculture Economics*, vol. 55 (Agrarwirtschaft, Jahrgang 55).

Ladeur, K.-H. (1997) 'Towards a legal theory of supranationality – the viability of the network concept', *European Law Journal*, vol. 3.

Laffan, B. (1997) *The Finances of the European Union*, Macmillan, Basingstoke.

Lamfalussy, A. (1963) 'Intra-European trade and the competitive position of the EEC', *Manchester Statistical Society Transactions*, March.

—— (2001) *Final Report of the Committee of Wise Men on the Regulation of European Securities Markets*, CEU, Brussels.

Landler, M. (2006) 'Europe's image clashes with reliance on coal', *New York Times*, internet edn, 20 June.

Latour, B. (1993) *We Have Never Been Modern*, Harvester Wheatsheaf, London.

Layard, R., Nickell, S. and Jackman, R. (1991) *Unemployment: Macroeconomic Performance and the Labour Market*, Oxford University Press, Oxford.

Lee, J.-W. and Swagel, P. (1997) 'Trade barriers and trade flows across countries and industries', *Review of Economics and Statistics*, vol. 79, no. 2.

Lehtinen, T. (2003) 'The coordination of European development cooperation in the field: myth and reality', ECDPM Discussion Paper 43, ECDPM, Maastricht.

Lesquesne, C. (2000a) 'The Common Fisheries Policy', in H. Wallace and W. Wallace (eds.), *Policy Making in the EU*, Oxford University Press, Oxford.

—— (2000b) 'Quota hopping: the Common Fisheries Policy between states and markets', *Journal of Common Market Studies*, vol. 38, no. 5.

—— (2005) 'Fisheries Policy', in H. Wallace, W. Wallace and M. Pollack, *Policy Making in the European Union*, Oxford University Press, Oxford.

Lindberg, L. N. and Scheingold, S. A. (1970) *Europe's Would-be Policy Patterns of Change in the European Community*, Prentice Hall, London.

Lindner, J. (2006) *Conflict and Change in EU Budgetary Politics*, Routledge, London.

Linnemann, H. (1966) *An Econometric Study of International Trade Flows*, North-Holland, Amsterdam.

Lipgens, W. (1982) *A History of European Integration*, vol. I: *1945–47: The Formation of the European Unity Movement*, Clarendon Press, Oxford.

Lipsey, R. G. (1960) 'The theory of customs unions: a general survey', *Economic Journal*, vol. 70.

Lockwood, B., de Meza, B. and Myles, G. (1994) 'When are destination and origin regimes equivalent?', *International Tax and Public Finance*, vol. 1.

London Economics (2002) *Quantification of the Macroeconomic Impact of Integration of EU Financial Market*, London Economics for DG Internal Market, http://ec.europa.eu/internal_market/securities/docs/studies/report-londonecon_en.zip.

Loveman, G. and Sengenberger, W. (1991) 'The re-emergence of small-scale production: an international comparison', *Small Business Economics*, vol. 3, no. 1.

Lucarelli, B. (1999) *The Origins and Evolution of the Single Market in Europe*, Aldershot, Ashgate.

Lucas, N. J. D. (1977) *Energy and the European Communities*, Europa Publications for the David Davies Memorial Institute of International Studies, London.

Lucas, R. E. (1988) 'On the mechanics of economic development', *Journal of Monetary Economics*, vol. 22.

Ludlow, P. (1982) *The Making of the European Monetary System: A Case Study of the Politics of the European Community*, Butterworths, London.

MacCormick, N. (1993) 'Beyond the sovereign state', *Modern Law Review*, vol. 56.

—— (1996) 'Liberalism, nationalism and the post-sovereign state', in R. Bellamy and D. Castiglione (eds.), *Constitutionalism in Transformation: European and Theoretical Perspectives*, Blackwell, Oxford.

—— (1999) *Questioning Sovereignty*, Oxford University Press, Oxford.

MacDougall Report (1977) *see* Commission of the European Communities (1977a).

McCormick, J. (2001) *Environmental Politics in the EU*, Palgrave, Basingstoke.

McGowan, F. (1993) *The Struggle for Power in Europe*, RIIA, London.

Machlup, F. (1977) *A History of Thought on Economic Integration*, Macmillan, Basingstoke.

McKinnon, R. I. (1963) 'Optimum currency areas', *American Economic Review*, vol. 53.

McMahon, J. (1998) *The Development Cooperation Policy of the EC*, Kluwer Law International, Dordrecht.

McManus, J. G. (1972) 'The theory of the international firm', in G. Paquet (ed.), *The Multinational Firm and the National State*, Collier Macmillan, New York.

McMorrow, K. and Roeger, W. (2000) 'Time-varying Nairu/Nawru estimates for the EU's member states', Economic Papers 145, European Commission, DG ECFIN.

McQueen, M. (2002) 'The EU's free trade agreements with developing countries: a case of wishful thinking?', The World Economy, vol. 25, no. 9.

Magrini, S. (1999) 'The evolution of income disparities among the regions of the European Union', Regional Science and Urban Economics, vol. 29.

Maher, I. (1995) 'Legislative review by the EC Commission: Revision without radicalism', in J. Shaw and G. More (eds.), New Legal Dynamics of EU, Oxford University Press, Oxford.

Majone, G. (1994) 'The rise of regulatory policy making in Europe and the United States', Journal of Public Policy, vol. 11, no. 1.

(1998) 'Europe's democracy deficit: the question of standards', European Law Journal, vol. 4.

Mancini, G. (1998) 'Europe: the case for statehood', European Law Journal, vol. 4.

Marer, P. and Montias, J. M. (1988) 'The Council for Mutual Economic Assistance', in A. M. El-Agraa (ed.), International Economic Integration, Macmillan and St Martin's, New York.

Marin, A. (1979) 'Pollution control: economists' views', Three Banks Review, no. 121.

Marques-Mendes, A. J. (1986) 'The contribution of the European Community to economic growth', Journal of Common Market Studies, vol. 24, no. 4.

Marshall, A. (1920) Principles of Economics, Macmillan, Basingstoke.

Martin, J. and Grubb, D. (2001) 'What works and for whom: a review of OECD countries' experiences with active labour market policies?', Swedish Economic Policy Review, vol. 8, no. 2.

Martin, S. (2001) Industrial Organization: A European Perspective, Oxford University Press, Oxford.

Martin, S. and Scott, J. T. (2000) 'The nature of innovation market failure and the design of public support for private innovation', Research Policy, vol. 29, nos. 4–5.

Mathä, T. (2006) 'The euro and price differences in a cross-border area', Journal of Common Market Studies, vol. 44, no. 3.

Mattli, W. and Slaughter, A.-M. (1998) 'Revisiting the European ECJ', International Organization, vol. 52.

Mayes, D. G. (1978) 'The effects of economic integration on trade', Journal of Common Market Studies, vol. 17, no. 1.

(1983) 'EC trade effects and factor mobility', in El-Agraa (1983a), chapter 6.

(1988) Chapter 3, in A. Bollard and M. A. Thompson (eds.), Trans-Tasman Trade and Investment, Institute for Policy Studies, Wellington, New Zealand.

(1993) The External Implications of European Integration, Harvester Wheatsheaf, London.

(1996) 'The role of foreign direct investment in structural change: the lessons from the New Zealand experience', in G. Csaki, G. Foti and D. G. Mayes (eds.), Foreign Direct Investment and Transition: The Case of the Viseg.rad Countries, Trends in World Economy, no. 78, Institute for World Economics, Budapest.

(1997a) 'Competition and cohesion: lessons from New Zealand', in M. Fritsch and H. Hansen (eds.), Rules of Competition and East-West Integration, Kluwer, Dordrecht.

(1997b) The Evolution of the Single European Market, Edward Elgar, Cheltenham.

(1997c) 'The New Zealand experiment: using economic theory to drive policy', Policy Options, vol. 18, no. 7.

(1997d) 'The problems of the quantitative estimation of integration effects', in A. M. El-Agraa (ed.), Economic Integration Worldwide, Macmillan and St Martins, New York.

(2004) 'Finland the Nordic insider', Cooperation and Conflict, vol. 39, no. 2.

Mayes, D. G. and Begg, I. with Levitt, M. and Shipman, A. (1992) A New Strategy for Economic and Social Cohesion after 1992, European Parliament, Luxembourg.

Mayes, D. G. and Suvanto, A. (2002) 'Beyond the fringe: Finland and the choice of currency', Journal of Public Policy, vol. 22, no. 2.

Mayes, D. G. and Virén, M. (2000) 'The exchange rate and monetary conditions in the euro area', Weltwirtschaftliches Archiv, vol. 136, no. 2.

(2002a) 'Macroeconomic factors, policies and the development of social exclusion', in R. Muffels, P. Tsakloglou and D. G. Mayes (eds.), Social Exclusion in European Welfare States, Edward Elgar, Cheltenham.

(2002b) 'Policy coordination and economic adjustment in EMU: will it work?', in Ali M. El-Agraa (ed.), The Euro and Britain: Implications of Moving into the EMU, Pearson Education, Harlow.

(2002c) 'Asymmetry and the problem of aggregation in the euro area', Empirica, vol. 29.

(2002d) 'The exchange rate and monetary conditions in the euro area', Empirica, vol. 29.

Mayes, D. G., Hager, W., Knight, A. and Streeck, W. (1993) Public Interest and Market Pressures: Problems Posed by Europe 1992, Macmillan, London.

Mayes, D. G., Bergman, J. and Salais, R. (2001) Social Exclusion and European Policy, Edward Elgar, Cheltenham.

Meade, J. E. (1980) *The Theory of International Trade Policy*, Oxford University Press, Oxford.

Meade, J. E., Liesner, H. H. and Wells, S. J. (1962) *Case Studies in European Economic Union: The Mechanics of Integration*, Oxford University Press, Oxford.

Mehta, K. and Peeperkorn, L. (1999) 'The economics of competition', in J. Faull and A. Nikpay (eds.), *The EC Law of Competition*, Clarendon Press, Oxford.

Meij, J. (2000) 'Architects or judges? Some comments in relation to the current debate', *Common Market Law Review*, vol. 37.

Mélitz, J. (2001) 'Geography, trade and currency union', Discussion Paper no. 2987, CEPR, London.

Mélitz, J. and Zumer, F. (1998) 'Regional redistribution and stabilization by the center in Canada, France, the United Kingdom and the United States: new estimates based on panel data econometrics', Discussion Paper no. 1892, CEPR, London.

Memedovic, O., Kuyvenhoven, A. and Molle, W. (eds.) (1999) *Multilateralism and Regionalism in the Post-Uruguay Round Era: What Role for the EU?*, Kluwer, Boston.

Merrills, J. (1998) *International Dispute Settlement*, Cambridge University Press, Cambridge.

Messerlin, P. A. (2001) *Measuring the Costs of Protection in Europe*, Institute for International Economics, Washington D.C.

Meunier, S. (2005) *Trading Voices: The European Union in International Commercial Negotiations*. Princeton University Press, Princeton, N.J.

Midelfart-Knarvik, K. H., Overman, H. G., Redding, S. J. and Venables, A. J. (2000) 'The location of European industry', Economic Paper 14, DG for Economic and Financial Affairs, Commission of the European Communities.

Mintz, J. M. (2002) 'European company tax reform: prospects for the future', *CESifo Forum*, 3/1, www.cesifo.de/.

Molle, W. and Morsink, R. (1991) 'Direct investment and European integration', *European Economy*, special issue.

Monti, M. (1996) *The Single Market and Tomorrow's Europe: A Progress Report from the European Commission*, Office for Official Publications of the European Communities, Luxembourg; Kogan Page, London.

Morgan, J. and Mourougane, A. (2001) 'What can changes in structural factors tell us about unemployment in Europe?', ECB Working Paper no. 81, October, www.ecb.org.

Motta, M. (2004) *Competition Policy: Theory and Practice*, Cambridge University Press, Cambridge.

Moser, S. and Pesaresi, N. (2002) 'State guarantees to German public banks: a new step in the enforce-ment of state aid discipline to financial services in the Community', *Competition Policy Newsletter*, no. 2, June, pp. 1–11.

Munby, D. L. (1962) 'Fallacies of the Community's transport policy', *Journal of Transport Economics and Policy*, vol. 1.

Mundell, R. A. (1961) 'A theory of optimum currency areas', *American Economic Review*, vol. 51.

(1964) 'Tariff preferences and the terms of trade', *Manchester School*, vol. 32.

(1973a) 'A plan for a European currency', in H. G. Johnson and A. K. Swoboda (eds.), *The Economics of Common Currencies*, Allen and Unwin, London.

(1973b) 'Uncommon arguments for common currencies', in H. G. Johnson and A. K. Swoboda (eds.), *The Economics of Common Currencies*, Allen and Unwin, London.

Musgrave, R. A. (1959) *The Theory of Public Finance*, McGraw-Hill, New York.

Nam, C. and Reuter, J. (1992) *The Effect of 1992 and Associated Legislation on the Less Favoured Regions of the Community*, Office for Official Publications of the European Communities, Luxembourg.

Neill, Sir P. (1996) *The European ECJ: A Case Study in Judicial Activism*, European Policy Forum/Frankfurter Institut, London/Frankfurt.

Neumayer, E. (2001) 'Improvement without convergence: pressure on the environment in EU countries', *Journal of Common Market Studies*, vol. 39, no. 5.

Neven, D. J. (1990) 'Gains and losses from 1992', *Economic Policy*, April.

Neven, D. J. and Wyplosz, C. (1999) 'Relative prices, trade and restructuring in European industry', in M. Dewatripont, A. Sapir and K. Sekkat (eds.), *Trade and Jobs in Europe: Much Ado About Nothing?*, Oxford University Press, Oxford.

Neven, D. J., Nuttal, R. and Seabright, P. (1993a) *Competition and Merger Policy in the EC*, CEPR, London.

(1993b) *Merger in Daylight*, CEPR, London.

Neven, D. J., Papandropoulos, P. and Seabright, P. (1998) *Trawling for Minnows: European Competition Policy and Agreements Between Firms*, CEPR, London.

Newbery, D. M. (1999a) *Privatization, Restructuring, and Regulation of Network Industries*, MIT Press, Cambridge, Mass.

(1999b) 'The UK experience: privatization with market power', in Lars Bergmann, B. Bergman, G. Brunekreeft et al., *A European Market for Electricity?* CEPR, London; and SNS, Stockholm, pp. 89–115.

(2001) 'Economic reform in Europe: integrating and

liberalizing the market for services', *Utilities Policy*, vol. 10.

Nicodème, G. (2001) 'Comparing effective corporation tax rates: comparisons and results', Economic Paper no. 153, EU Commission, DG Economic and Financial Affairs.

Nicholl, W. (1994) 'The battles of the European budget', *Policy Studies*, vol. 7, July.

Nickell, S. (1997) 'Unemployment and labor market rigidities: Europe versus North America, *Journal of Economic Perspectives*, vol. 11, no. 3.

Nickell S. and Layard R. (1999) 'Labour market institutions and economic performance', in O. Ahsenfelter and D. Card (eds.), *Handbook of Labour Economics*, vol. III, North Holland, Amsterdam.

Nickell, S., Nunziata, L., Ochel, W. and Quintini, G. (2002) 'The Beveridge Curve, unemployment and wages in the OECD from the 1960s to the 1990s', LSE Centre for Economic Performance, http://cep.lse.ac.uk/pubs/download/dp0502.pdf.

Nickell, S., Nunziata, L. and Ochel, W. (2005) 'Unemployment in the OECD since the 1960s: what do we know?', *Economic Journal*, vol. 115, no. 500.

Nicoletti, G., Scarpetta, S. and Boylaud, O. (2000) 'Summary indicators of product market regulation with an extension of employment protection legislation', Working Paper no. 226, OECD, Paris.

North, D. C. (1990) *Institutions, Institutional Change and Economic Performance*, Cambridge University Press, Cambridge.

Notaro, G. (2002) 'European integration and productivity: exploring the gains of the Single Market', London Eonomics, London.

Oates, W. E. (ed.) (1977) *The Political Economy of Fiscal Federalism*, Lexington Books, Toronto.

(1999) 'An essay in fiscal federalism', *Journal of Economic Literature*, vol. 37, no. 3.

Obstfeld, M. and Peri, G. (1998a) 'Regional non-adjustment and fiscal policy', *Economic Policy*, vol. 26, April.

(1998b) 'Asymmetric shocks: regional non-adjustment and fiscal policy', *Economic Policy*, vol. 28.

Odudu, O. (2006), *The Boundaries of EC Competition Law – The Scope of Article 81*, Oxford University Press, Oxford.

OECD (various years) *Economic Survey of Europe*, OECD, Paris.

(various issues) *Geographical Distribution of Financial Flows to Aid Recipients*, OECD, Paris.

(1988a) *The Newly Industrialising Countries: Challenges and Opportunity for OECD Industries*, OECD, Paris.

(1988b) *Taxing Consumption*, OECD, Paris.

(1994) *The OECD Jobs Study*, OECD, Paris.

(1997) *Implementing the OECD Jobs Strategy*, OECD, Paris.

(1999a) *SOPEMI: Trends in International Migration: Annual Report 1999. Continuous Reporting System on Migration*, OECD, Paris.

(1999b) *Implementing the OECD Jobs Strategy: Assessing Performance and Policy*, OECD, Paris.

(2000) *The European Union's Trade Policies and their Economic Effects*, OECD, Paris.

(2001) *Multifunctionality: Towards an Analytical Framework*, OECD, Paris.

(2002a) *European Community Development Cooperation Review Series*, OECD, Paris.

(2002b) *Revenue Statistics 1965–2001*, OECD, Paris.

(2002c) *Main Science and Technology Indicators*, OECD, Paris.

(2003) *Agricultural Policies in OECD Countries: Monitoring and Evaluation*, OECD, Paris.

(2005a) *OECD/EEA Database on Instruments Used for Environmental Policy and Natural Resources Management*, OECD, Paris, http://www2.oecd.org/ecoinst/queries/index.htm.

(2005b) 'The benefits of liberalising product markets and reducing barriers to international trade and investment in the OECD', Economics Department Working Papers no. 463, OECD, Paris.

(2005c) 'The EU's Single Market: at your service?', Economics Department Working Papers no. 449, OECD, Paris.

(2005d) *Employment Outlook*, OECD, Paris.

(2005e) *Main Science and Technology Indicators*, database accessed via Economic and Social Data Services, www.esds.ac.uk.

(2006a) *Main Economic Indicators*, annual database, accessed via Economic and Social Data Services, www.esds.ac.uk.

(2006b) *Education at a Glance: 2006 Indicators*, OECD, Paris.

(2006c) *Employment Outlook: Boosting Jobs and Income*, OECD, Paris.

(2006d) *Boosting Jobs and Income: Policy Lessons from Reassessing the OECD Jobs Strategy*, OECD, Paris.

(2006e) *Labour Productivity Database*, http://www.oecd.org/topicstatsportal/0,2647,en_2825_30453906_1_1_1_1,00.html.

(2006f) *OECD Economic Outlook*, 79, OECD: Paris.

O'Keeffe, D. (1998) 'Is the spirit of Article 177 under attack? Preliminary references and admissibility', *European Law Review*, vol. 23.

Olson, M. (1982) *The Rise and Decline of Nations: Economic Growth, Stagnation and Social Rigidities*, Yale University Press, New Haven, Conn.

Oort, C. J. and Maaskant, R. H. (1976) *Study of Possible Solutions for Allocating the Deficit which may Occur in a System of Charging for the Use of Infrastructure Aiming at Budgetary Equilibrium*, EEC.

OPEC (2005) *Annual Statistical Bulletin*, Geneva.

Owen, N. (1983) *Economies of Scale, Competitiveness and Trade Patterns within the European Community*, Oxford University Press, Oxford.

Owens, S. and Hope, C. (1989) 'Energy and the environment – the challenge of integrating European policies', *Energy Policy*, vol. 17.

Oxfam (2006) *Unequal Partners: How EU-ACP Economic Partnership Agreements Could Harm the Development Prospects of Many of the World's Poorest Countries*, Oxfam International, London.

Padoa-Schioppa, T., Emerson, M., King, M. et al. (1987) *Efficiency, Stability and Equity: A Strategy for the Evolution of the Economic System of the European Community*, Oxford University Press, Oxford.

Page, E. (1998) 'The impact of European Legislation on British public policy making: a research note', *Public Administration*, vol. 76.

Palmer, M. and Lambert, J. (1968) *European Unity*, Allen and Unwin, London.

Panagariya, A. (2002) 'EU preferential trade arrangements and developing countries', *The World Economy*, vol. 25, no. 10.

Paxton, J. (1976) *The Developing Common Market*, Macmillan, Basingstoke.

Payne, D. C. (2000) 'Policy making in nested institutions: explaining the conservation failures of the EU's Common Fisheries Policy', *Journal of Common Market Studies*, vol. 38, no. 2.

Pearson, M. and Smith, S. (1991) *The European Carbon Tax*, Institute for Fiscal Studies, London.

Peeperkorn, L. (1998) 'The economics of verticals', *EC Competition Policy Newsletter*, vol. 2.

Pelkmans, J. (2001) 'Making network markets competitive', *Oxford Review of Economic Policy*, vol. 17.

Pelkmans, J. and Winters, L. A. (1988) *Europe's Domestic Market*, Routledge, London.

Perman, R., Ma, Y., McGilvray, J. and Common, M. (2003) *Natural Resource and Environmental Economics*, 3rd edn, Pearson Education, Harlow.

Peterson, J. and Sharp, M. (1998) *Technology Policy in the European Union*, St Martin's Press, New York.

Petit, M. (1985) 'Determinants of agricultural policies in the United States and the European Community', International Food Policy Research Report 51, Washington D.C.

Phelps, E. S. (1968) 'Money–wage dynamics and labour market equilibrium', *Journal of Political Economy*, vol. 76.

Phillips, A. W. (1958) 'The relation between unemployment and the rate of change of money wages in the United Kingdom', *Economica*, vol. 25.

Phinnemore, D. (1999) *Association: Stepping Stone or Alternative to EU Membership?*, Sheffield Academic Press, Sheffield.

Phlips, L. (1993) 'Basing point pricing, competition, and market integration', in H. Ohta and J.-F. Thisse (eds.), *Does Economic Space Matter? Essays in Honour of Melvin L. Greenhut*, Macmillan, Basingstoke.

(1995) *Competition Policy: A Game Theoretical Perspective*, Cambridge University Press, Cambridge.

Pisani-Ferry, J. (2002) 'Fiscal discipline and policy coordination in the eurozone: assessment and proposals', mimeo, Commission of the European Communities.

Pissarides, C. (1990) *Equilibrium Unemployment Theory*, Basil Blackwell, Oxford.

Plötner, J. (1998) 'Report on France', in A.-M. Slaughter, A. Stone Sweet and J. Weiler (eds.), *The European Courts and National Courts: Doctrine and Jurisprudence*, Hart, Oxford.

Political and Economic Planning (PEP) (1962) *Atlantic Tariffs and Trade*, Allen and Unwin, London.

(1963) 'An energy policy for the EEC', *Planning*, vol. 29.

Pollack, M. (1997) 'Delegation, agency, and agenda-setting in the European Community', *International Organization*, vol. 51.

Pollard, P. (2003) 'A look inside two central banks: the European Central Bank and the Federal Reserve', *Federal Reserve Bank of St Louis Review*, January/February.

Porter, M. (1990) *The Competitive Advantage of Nations*, Macmillan, Basingstoke.

Posner, R. (1976) *Antitrust Law: An Economic Perspective*, University of Chicago Press, Chicago.

Press, A. and Taylor, C. (1990) *Europe and the Environment*, The Industrial Society, London.

Prest, A. R. (1979) 'Fiscal policy', in P. Coffey (ed.), *Economic Policies of the Common Market*, Macmillan, Basingstoke.

Prewo, W. E. (1974a) 'A multinational interindustry gravity model for the European Common Market', PhD dissertation, Johns Hopkins University, Baltimore, Md.

(1974b) 'Integration effects in the EEC', *European Economic Review*, vol. 5.

Primo Braga, C. A. (1995) 'Trade-related intellectual property issues: the Uruguay Round agreement and its economies implications', in W. Martin and L. A. Winters (eds.), *The Uruguay Round and the Developing Economies*, World Bank Discussion Papers no. 307, Washington D.C.

Public Accounts Committee (2002) *Tobacco Smuggling*, 3rd report, Session 2002–2003, HC 143, Stationery Office, www.parliament.the-stationery-office.co.uk/pa/cmcmpubacc.htm.

Putnam, R. D. (1993) *Making Democracy Work: Civic Traditions in Modern Italy*, Princeton University Press, Princeton, N.J.

Quigley, C. and Collins, A. M. (2004), *EC State Aid Law and Policy*, Hart, Oxford.

Quévit, M. (1995) 'The regional impact of the internal market: a comparative analysis of traditional industrial regions and lagging regions', in S. Hardy, M. Hart, L. Albrechts and A. Katos (eds.), *An Enlarged Europe: Regions in Competition?*, Jessica Kingsley, London.

Raisman Committee (1961) *East Africa: Report of the Economic and Fiscal Commission*, Cmnd 1279, Colonial Office.

Rameu, F. (2002) 'Judicial cooperation in the European courts: testing three models of judicial behaviour', *Global Jurist Frontiers*, vol. 2, issue 1.

Rasmussen, H. (1986) *On Law and Policy in the European ECJ*, Martinus Nijhoff, Dordrecht.

(1998) *European ECJ*, GadJura, Copenhagen.

(2000) 'Remedying the crumbling EC judicial system', *Common Market Law Review*, vol. 37.

Rawlings, R. (1993) 'The Eurolaw game: some deductions from a saga', *Journal of Law and Society*, vol. 20.

Rehg, W. (1996) 'Translator's introduction', in J. Habermas, *Between Facts and Norms*, Polity Press, Cambridge.

Reich, N. (1997) 'A European constitution for citizens: reflections on the rethinking of union and community law', *European Law Journal*, vol. 3.

Resnick, S. A. and Truman, E. M. (1974) 'An empirical examination of bilateral trade in Western Europe', *Journal of International Economics*, vol. 3.

Ritchie, E. and Zito, A. R. (1998) 'The CFP: a policy disaster', in P. Gray and P. Hart (eds.), *Public Policy Disasters in Western Europe*, Routledge, London.

Ritson, C. (1973) 'The Common Agricultural Policy', in *The European Economic Community: Economics and Agriculture*, Open University Press, Milton Keynes.

Robinson, P. (2000) 'Active labour-market policies: a case of evidence based policy-making?', *Oxford Review of Economic Policy*, vol. 16, no. 1.

Robson, P. (1980 and 1985) *The Economics of International Integration*, Allen and Unwin, London.

(1983) *Integration, Development and Equity: Economic Integration in West Africa*, Allen and Unwin, London.

(1997) 'Integration in Sub-Saharan Africa', in Ali M. El-Agraa (ed.), *Economic Integration Worldwide*, Macmillan and St Martin's Press, New York.

Rodger, B. (1999) 'The Commission's white paper on modernisation of the rules implementing articles 81 and 82 of the EC Treaty', *European Law Review*, vol. 24.

Romer, P. M. (1986) 'Increasing returns and longrun growth', *Journal of Political Economy*, vol. 94.

(1990) 'Endogenous technological change', *Journal of Political Economy*, vol 98, no. 5.2.

(1994) 'New goods, old theory and the welfare of trade restrictions', *Journal of Development Economics*, vol. 43.

Rose, A. K. (1999) 'One money, one market: estimating the effect of common currencies on trade', Working Paper no. 7432, National Bureau of Economic Research, Cambridge, Mass.

Russell, C. S. (2001) *Applying Economics to the Environment*, Oxford University Press, Oxford.

Ruttan, V. W. (1998) 'The new growth theory and development economics: a survey', *Journal of Development Studies*, vol. 35.

Sachs, J. D. and Shatz, H. J. (1994) 'Trade and jobs in U.S. manufacturing', *Brookings Papers on Economic Activity*, vol. 1.

Sala-i-Martin, X. (1996) 'Regional cohesion: evidence and theories of regional growth and convergence', *European Economic Review*, vol. 40.

Sala-i-Martin, X. and Sachs, J. D. (1992) 'Fiscal federalism and optimum currency areas: evidence from Europe and the United States', in M. Canzoneri, V. Grilli and P. Masson, *Establishing a Central Bank: Issues in Europe and Lessons from the US*, Cambridge University Press, Cambridge.

Salz, P., Buisman, E., Smit, J. and de Vos, B. (2006) 'Employment in the fisheries sector: current situation', Final Report (FISH/2004/4), LEI BV, Framian BV, - http://ec.europa.eu/fisheries/publications/statistics_en.htm.

Sand, I.-J. (1998) 'Understanding new forms of governance: mutually interdependent, reflexive, destabilised and competing institutions', *European Law Journal*, vol. 4.

Sandford, C. T., Godwin, M. T. and Hardwick, P. J. (1989) *Administrative and Compliance Costs*, Fiscal Publications, Bath.

Sapir, A. (1995) 'Europe's single market: the long march to 1992', Discussion Paper, CEPR, London.

(1996) 'The effects of Europe's internal market programme on production and trade: a first assessment', *Weltwirtschaftliches Archiv*, vol. 132.

(1998) 'The political economy of EC regionalism', *European Economic Review*, vol. 42.

Sapir, A., Aghion, P., Bertola, G. et al. (2003a) *An Agenda for a Growing Europe: Making the EU Economic System*

Deliver, report of an Independent High-Level Study Group Established on the Initiative of the President of the European Commission, Brussels.

(2003b) *An Agenda for a Growing Europe: The Sapir Report*, Oxford University Press, Oxford.

Scaperlanda, A. and Balough, R. S. (1983) 'Determinants of US direct investment in the EEC revisited', *European Economic Review*, vol. 21.

Scarpetta, S. (1996) 'Assessing the role of labour market policies and institutional settings on unemployment: a cross country study', *OECD Economic Studies*, vol. 26.

Schepel, H. (1997) 'Legal pluralism in Europe', in P. Fitzpatrick and J. Bergeron (eds.), *Europe's Other: European Law between Modernity and Postmodernity*, Ashgate, Aldershot.

Schepel, H. and Wesseling, R. (1997) 'The legal community: judges, lawyers, officials and clerks in the writing of Europe', *European Law Journal*, vol. 3.

Scherer, F. M. and Ross, D. (1990) *Industrial Market Structure and Economic Performance*, Houghton Mifflin, New York.

Schettkat, R. (2001) 'Structural revolution: the interaction of product and labor markets', *Intereconomics*, vol. 36, January/February.

Schiff, M. and Winters, L. A. (1998) 'Regional integration as diplomacy', *World Bank Economic Review*, vol. 12, no. 2.

Schilling, T. (1996) 'The autonomy of the community legal order – through the looking glass', *Harvard Journal of International Law*, vol. 37.

Schmalensee, R., Joskow, P. L., Ellerman, A. D., Montero, J. P. and Bailey, E. M. (1998) 'An interim evaluation of sulphur dioxide emissions trading', *Journal of Economic Perspectives*, vol. 12, no. 3.

Schreiber, K. (1991) 'The new approach to technical harmonization and standards', in L. Hurwitz and C. Lesquesne, *The State of the European Community: Politics, Institutions, and Debates in the Transition Years*, Lynne Rienner, Boulder, Colo.

Schüler, M. and Heinemann, F. (2002) 'How integrated are the European retail financial markets? A cointegration analysis', Zentrum für Europäische Wirtschaftsforschung GmbH, ZEW Discussion Paper no. 02-22, ftp://ftp.zew.de/pub/zew-docs/dp/dp0222.pdf.

Schumpeter, J. (1934) *The Theory of Economic Development: An Inquiry into Profits, Capital, Interest, and the Business Cycle*, Harvard University Press, Cambridge, Mass.

Scitovsky, T. (1954) 'Two concepts of external economies', *Journal of Political Economy*, vol. 62.

(1958) *Economic Theory and Western European Integration*, Allen and Unwin, London.

Scott, J. T. (1998) 'Law, legitimacy and EC governance: prospects for "Partnership"', *Journal of Common Market Studies*, vol. 36.

Scully, R. (1997) 'The European Parliament and the co-decision procedure: a reassessment', *Journal of Legislative Studies*, vol. 3.

Seferiades, S. (2003) 'The European Employment Strategy against a Greek benchmark: a critique', *European Journal of Industrial Relations*, vol. 9, no. 2.

Serrano Pascual, A. (2003) 'A contribution to evaluation of the European Employment Strategy: what lessons from the first five years of implementation of the EES?', in E. Gabaglio and R. Hoffmann (eds.), *European Trade Union Yearbook 2002*, ETUI, Brussels.

Servan-Schreiber, J.-J. (1967) *Le défi américain*, Denoöl, Paris.

Shackleton, M. (1983) 'Fishing for a policy? The CFP of the Community', in H. and W. Wallace, *Policy Making in the European Community*, Wiley, Chichester.

Shapiro, M. (1996) 'Codification of administrative law: the US and the EU', *European Law Journal*, vol. 2.

Shaw, J. (1996) 'EU legal studies in crisis? Towards a new dynamic', *Oxford Journal of Legal Studies*, vol. 16.

(1999) 'Postnational constitutionalism in the EU', *Journal of European Public Policy*, vol. 7.

Shaw, J. and Wiener, A. (1999) 'The paradox of the "European Polity"', Harvard Jean Monnet Working Paper no. 10/99.

Shibata, H. (1967) 'The theory of economic unions', in C. S. Shoup (ed.), *Fiscal Harmonisation in Common Markets*, vols. I–II, Columbia University Press, New York.

Shimer, R. (1998) 'Why is the US unemployment rate so much lower?', in B. Bernanke and J. Rotemberg (eds.), *NBER Macroeconomics Annual 1998*, Washington D.C.

Silvis, H., van Rijswijck, C. and de Kleijn, A. (2001) 'EU agricultural expenditure for various accession scenarios', Report 6.01.04, Agricultural Research Institute, The Hague, cited in Swinnen (2002).

Sinn, H.-W. (1991) 'Taxation and the cost of capital: the "old" view, the "new" and another "view"', in D. F. Bradford, *Tax Policy in the Economy*, vol. V, MIT Press, Cambridge, Mass.

Siotis, G. (2003) 'Competitive pressure and economic integration: an illustration from Spain, 1983–1996', *International Journal of Industrial Organization*, vol. 21.

Skully, D. W. (1999) 'The economics of TRQ administration', IATRC Working Paper no. 99–6.

Slaughter, A. J. (1999) 'Globalisation and wages', Centre for Research on Globalisation and Labour Markets, research paper 99/5, Leverhulme Trust, London.

Slaughter, A.-M. (1995) 'International law in a world of liberal states', *European Journal of International Law*, vol. 6.

Slaughter, A.-M., Stone Sweet, A. and Weiler, J. (1998) 'Prologue', in A.-M. Slaughter, A. Stone Sweet and J. Weiler (eds.), *The European Courts and National Courts: Doctrine and Jurisprudence*, Hart, Oxford.

Smith, A. J. (1977) 'The Council of Mutual Economic Assistance in 1977: new economic power, new political perspectives and some old and new problems', in US Congress Joint Economic Committee, *East European Economics Post-Helsinki*.

Snyder, F. (1999a) *Global Economic Networks and Global Legal Pluralism*, EUI Working Paper Law, vol. VI, Badia Fiesolana, San Domenico.

(1999b) 'Governing economic globalisation: global legal pluralism and European Law', *European Law Journal*, vol. 5.

Sodupe, K. and Benito, E. (2001) 'Pan-European energy cooperation: opportunities, limitations and security of supply to the EU', *Journal of Common Market Studies*, vol. 39, no. 1.

Solow, R. M. (1957) 'Technical change and the aggregate production function', *Review of Economics and Statistics*, vol. 39.

(1987) 'We'd better watch out', *New York Times*, 12 July, Book Review 36.

Sørensen, P. (1998) 'Discussion', *Economic Policy*, vol. 27.

Staiger, D., Stock, J. and Watson, M. (1997) 'The NAIRU, unemployment and monetary policy', *Journal of Economic Perspectives*, vol. 11, no. 1.

Stavins, R. N. (1998) 'What can we learn from the Grand Policy Experiment?' *Journal of Economic Perspectives*, vol. 12, no. 3.

Stein, E. (1981) 'Lawyers, judges and the making of a transnational constitution', *American Journal of International Law*, vol. 75, no. 1.

Stewart, K. and Web, M. (2006) 'International competition in corporate taxation: evidence from OECD time series', *Economic Policy*, January.

Stiglitz, J. (1997) 'Reflections on the natural rate hypothesis', *Journal of Economic Perspectives*, vol. 11, no. 1.

Stokke, O. and Hoebink, P. (2005) *Perspectives on European Development Cooperation*, Routledge, London.

Stone Sweet, A. and Brunell, T. (1997) 'The European Court and national courts: a statistical analysis of preliminary references 1961–1995', *Journal of European Public Policy*, vol. 5.

(1998) 'Constructing a supranational constitution: dispute resolution and governance in the European Community', *American Political Science Review*, vol. 92.

Stone Sweet, A. and Caporaso, J. (1998) 'From free trade to supranational polity: the European Court and integration', in W. Sandholtz and A. Stone Sweet (eds.), *European Integration and Supranational Governance*, Oxford University Press, Oxford.

Strasser, S. (1995) 'The development of a strategy of docket control for the European ECJ and the question of preliminary references', Harvard Jean Monnet Working Paper, vol. III.

Streit, M. (1991) *Theorie der Wirtschaftspolitik*, WiSo-Texte, 4th edn, Werner-Verlag, Dusseldorf.

Striewe, L., Loy, J.-P. and Koester, U. (1996) 'Analyse und Beurteilung der einzelbetrieblichen Investitionsförderung in Schleswig-Holstein', *Agrarwirtschaft*, vol. 45, no. 12.

Stroux, S. (2004), *US and EC Oligopoly Control*, Kluwer Law International, The Hague.

Sundelius, B. and Wiklund, C. (1979) 'The Nordic Community: the ugly duckling of regional cooperation', *Journal of Common Market Studies*, vol. 18, no. 1.

Suris-Regueiro, J. C., Varela-Lafuente, M. M. and Iglesias-Malvido, C. (2003) 'Effectiveness of the structural fisheries policy in the European Union', *Marine Policy*, vol. 27, no. 6.

Swank, D. (1998) 'Funding the welfare state: globalization and the taxation of business in advanced capitalist economies', *Political Studies*, vol. 46, no. 4.

Swann, D. (1973) *The Economics of the Common Market*, Penguin, London.

(1988) *The Economics of the Common Market*, 4th edn, Penguin, London.

Sweet and Maxwell (regularly updated) *European Community Treaties*.

Symes, D. (1995) 'The European pond: who actually manages fisheries?', *Ocean and Coastal Management*, vol. 27, no. 1.

Szyszczak, E. (1996) 'Making Europe more relevant to its citizens: effective judicial process', *European Law Review*, vol. 21.

Tangermann, S. (1991) 'Agriculture in "international trade negotiations"', in K. Burger, M. de Groat, J. Post and V. Zachariasse (eds.), *Agricultural Economics and Policy: International Challenges for the Nineties*, Elsevier, Amsterdam.

Tani, M. (2002) 'Have Europeans become more mobile? A note on regional evolutions in the EU: 1988–1997', School of Economics and Management, University of New South Wales at the Australian Defence Force Academy.

Temple, J. (1998) 'Community antitrust law and national

regulatory procedures', *1997 Annual Proceedings of Fordham Corporate Law Institute*, vol. 24.

(2004) 'National measures restricting competition, and national authorities under Article 10 EC', *European Law Review*, vol. 29.

Temple Lang, J. (1999) 'The new growth evidence', *Journal of Economic Literature*; vol. 37, no. 1.

Teubner, G. (1997) 'Breaking frames: the global interplay of legal and social systems', *American Journal of Comparative Law*, vol. 45.

(1998) 'Legal irritants: good faith in British law or how unifying law ends up in new divergences', *Modern Law Review*, vol. 61.

Thirlwall, A. P. (1979) 'The balance of payments constraint as an explanation of international growth rate differences', *Banca Nazionale del Lavoro Quarterly Review*, March.

(1982) 'The Harrod trade multiplier and the importance of export-led growth', *Pakistan Journal of Applied Economics*, vol. 1, Summer.

Thornton, D. L. (2002) 'Monetary policy transparency: transparent about what?', Federal Reserve Bank of St Louis Working Paper 2002-028A, November.

Tinbergen, J. (1952) *On the Theory of Economic Policy*, North-Holland, Amsterdam.

(1953) *Report on Problems Raised by the Different Turnover Tax Systems Applied within the Common Market* (the Tinbergen Report), High Authority of European Coal and Steel Community.

(1954) *International Economic Integration*, Elsevier, Amsterdam.

(1962) *Shaping the World Economy: Suggestions for an International Economic Policy*, Twentieth Century Fund, New York.

Tracy, M. (1989) *Government and Agriculture in Western Europe 1880–1988*, Harvester Wheatsheaf, New York.

Tridimas, T. (1996) 'The ECJ and judicial activism', *European Law Review*, vol. 19.

Trubek, D., Dezalay, Y., Buchanan, R. and Davis, J. R. (1994) 'Global restructuring and the law: studies of the internationalization of legal fields and the creation of transnational arenas', *Case Western Reserve Law Review*, vol. 44.

Truman, E. M. (1969) 'The European Economic Community: trade creation and trade diversion', *Yale Economic Essays*, Spring.

(1975) 'The effects of European economic integration on the production and trade of manufactured products', in B. Balassa (ed.), *European Economic Integration*, North-Holland, Amsterdam.

Tsebelis, G. (1994) 'The power of the EP as a conditional agenda-setter', *American Political Science Review*, vol. 88.

Tsebelis, G. and Garrett, G. (1997) 'Agenda setting, vetoes and the EU's co-decision procedure', *Journal of Legislative Studies*, vol. 3.

(2000) 'Legislative politics in the European Union', *European Union Politics*, vol. 1.

Tsebelis, G. and Kreppel, A. (1998) 'The history of conditional agenda-setting in European institutions', *European Journal of Political Research*, vol. 33.

Tsoukalis, L. (2005) *What Kind of Europe?*, Oxford University Press, Oxford.

Tullock, G. (1967) 'The welfare costs of tariffs, monopolies and theft', *Western Economic Journal*, vol. 5.

UK Civil Aviation Authority (1993) *Airline Competition in the Single European Market*, CAP 623, CAA.

UK Treasury (2003) *UK Membership of the Single Currency: An Assessment of the Five Economic Tests*. http://assessment.treasury.gov.uk.

UNCTAD (2002) *Participation of the African, Caribbean and Pacific Group of States in International Trade*, UNCTAD/DITC/TNCD/Misc., 22 August, Geneva.

(2004) *Handbook of International Trade Statistics 2003*, New York.

(2006) *TRAINS Database*, Geneva.

Ungerer, H., Evans, D. and Nyberg, P. (1986) 'The European Monetary System – recent developments', *Occasional Papers*, no. 48, IMF.

United Kingdom Government (1996) *Memorandum by the British Government to the 1996 Intergovernmental Conference on the European ECJ*, Foreign and Commonwealth Office, London.

Urrutia, B. (2006) 'The EU regulatory activities in the shipping sector: a historical perspective', *Maritime Economics and Policy*, vol. 8.

US Bureau of Economic Analysis (2003) *Regional Accounts Data*, www.census.gov/.

US Census Bureau (2003) *State Population Estimates*, www.bea.gov/bea/regional/data.htm.

(2006) *Annual Population Estimates*, http://www.census.gov/.

US Department of Energy, Energy Office Administration (1997) *Electricity Reform Abroad and US Investment*, September.

Valbonesi, P. (1998) 'Privatization and EU competition policy: the case of the Italian energy sector', in Stephen Martin (ed.), *Competition Policies in Europe*, Elsevier Science, Amsterdam.

van den Noord, P. (2000) *The Size and Role of Automatic Stabilisers in the 1990s and Beyond*, Economics Department Report no. 230, OECD, Paris.

van der Linde, J. G. and Lefeber, R. (1988) 'IEA captures

the development of European Community energy law', *Journal of World Trade*, vol. 22.

van Dijck, P. and Faber, G. (eds.) (2000) *The External Economic Dimension of the European Union*, Kluwer Law International, Dordrecht.

van Reisen, M. (2000) *European Union Global Player: The North-South Policy of the European Union*, International Books, Dublin.

Vanek, J. (1965) *General Equilibrium of International Discrimination: The Case of Customs Unions*, Harvard University Press, Cambridge, Mass.

Vanhalewyn, E. (1999) 'Trends and patterns in state aids', *European Economy Report and Studies: State Aid and the Single Market*, no. 3.

Venables, A. J. (2003) 'Winners and losers from regional integration arrangements', *Economic Journal*, vol. 113.

Verdoorn, P. J. and Schwartz, A. N. R. (1972) 'Two alternative estimates of the effects of EEC and EFTA on the pattern of trade', *European Economic Review*, vol. 3.

Vernon, R. (1966) 'International investment and international trade in the product cycle', *Quarterly Journal of Economics*, vol. 80.

Verwaal, E. and Cnossen, S. (2002) 'Europe's new border taxes', *Journal of Common Market Studies*, vol. 40, no. 2.

Viegas, J. M. and Blum, U. (1993) 'High speed railways in Europe', in D. Banister and J. Berechman (eds.), *Transport in a Unified Europe*, Elsevier, Oxford.

Viner, J. (1950) *The Customs Union Issue*, Carnegie Endowment for International Peace, New York.

Volcansek, M. (1986) *Judicial Politics in Europe*, Peter Lang, Frankfurt.

von Geusau, F. A. (1975) 'In search of a policy', in F. A. von Geusau (ed.), *Energy Strategy in the European Communities*, Sijthoff, Leiden.

Von Hagen, J. and Mundschenk, S. (2002) 'Fiscal and monetary policy co-ordination in EMU', Oesterreichische National Bank Working Paper 70, August.

Von Thünen, J. H. (1826) *Der isolierte Staat in Beziehung auf Landwirtschaft und Nationbalökonomie*, Perthes.

Vos, E. (1998) *Institutional Frameworks of Community Health and Safety Regulation: Committees, Agencies and Private Bodies*, Hart, Oxford.

Waddams Price, C. (1997) 'Competition and regulation in the UK gas industry', *Oxford Review of Economic Policy*, vol. 13, no. 1.

Wallace, L. (2006), 'Ahead of his time: Laura Wallace interviews economist Robert Mundell', *Finance and Development*, September, International Monetary Fund, Washington, D.C.

Wallace, W. (ed.) (1990) *The Dynamics of European Integration*, Pinter, London.

Walters, A. A. (1963) 'A note on economies of scale', *Review of Economics and Statistics*, November.

Wang, Z. and Winters, L. A. (1991) 'The trading potential of Eastern Europe', CEPR Discussion Paper no. 610, CEPR, London.

Wanlin, A. (2006) *The Lisbon Scorecard VI: Will Europe's Economy Rise Again?*, Centre for European Reform, London.

Ward, I. (1996) *A Critical Introduction to European Law*, Butterworths, London.

Watt, A. (2000) 'What has become of employment policy? Explaining the ineffectiveness of employment policy in the European Union', *Basler Schriften zur europäischen Integration*, vols. 47/48.

—— (2003) 'The report of the Hartz Commission in the context of the European Employment Strategy', unpublished manuscript (cited by Watt, 2004).

—— (2004) 'Reform of the European Employment Strategy after five years: a change of course or merely of presentation?', *European Journal of Industrial Relations*, vol. 10, no. 2.

WB-BML (Wissenschaftlicher Beirat beim Bundesministerium für Ernährung, Landwirtschaft und Forsten) (1998) *Integration der Landwirtschaft der Europäischen Union in die Weltagrarwirtschaft*, Angewandte Wissenswchaft, Heft 476, Bonn, www.verbraucherministerium.de/forschung/wissbeirat/gutachten/itegration_der_landwirtschaft_d,htm.

Weale, A., Pridham, G., Cini, M. et al. (2000) *Environmental Governance in Europe: An Ever Closer Union?*, Oxford University Press, Oxford.

Weatherill, S. and Beaumont, P. (1999) *EU Law*, 3rd edn, Penguin, Harmondsworth.

Weck-Hannemann, H. and Frey, B. S. (1997) 'Are economic instruments as good as economists believe? Some new considerations', in Bovenberg and Cnossen (1997).

Weiler, J. (1993) 'Journey to an unknown destination: a retrospective and prospective of the European ECJ in the arena of political integration', *Journal of Common Market Studies*, vol. 31.

—— (1994) 'A quiet revolution: the European ECJ and its interlocutors', *Comparative Political Studies*, vol. 26.

—— (1997a) 'To be a European citizen: Eros and civilisation', *Journal of European Public Policy*, vol. 4.

—— (1997b) 'The EU belongs to its citizens: three immodest proposals', *European Law Review*, vol. 22.

—— (2001) 'Epilogue: the judicial Après Nice', in G. de Búrca and J. Weiler, *The European Court of Justice*, Hart, Oxford.

Weiler, J. and Haltern, U. (1998) 'Constitutional or international? The foundations of the community legal order and the question of judicial Kompetenz-Kompetenz', in A.-M. Slaughter, A. Stone Sweet and J. Weiler (eds.), *The European Courts and National Courts: Doctrine and Jurisprudence*, Hart, Oxford.

Weise, C. (2002) 'How to finance Eastern enlargement of the EU: the need to reform EU policies and the consequences for the net contributor balance', Working Paper no. 14, October, European Network of Economic Policy Research Institutes, www.enepri.org.

Weiss, L. W. (1971) *Case Studies in American Industry*, 2nd edn, Wiley, New York.

Wesseling, R. (2000) *The Modernisation of EC Antitrust Policy*, Hart, Oxford.

  (2005), 'The rule of reason and competition law: various rules, various reasons', in A. A. A. Schrauwen (ed.), *Rule of Reason – Rethinking Another Classic of European Legal Doctrine*, Europa Law Publishing, Groningen.

Wessels, W. (1997) 'An ever closer fusion? A dynamic macropolitical view on integration processes', *Journal of Common Market Studies*, vol. 37.

Whitwill, M. (2000) 'European deregulation: one year on', The Uranium Institute 25th Annual Symposium, London, 30 August–1 September.

Wilhelmsson, T. (1995) 'Integration as disintegration of national law', in H. Zahle and H. Petersen (eds.), *Legal Polycentricity: Consequences of Pluralism in Law*, Dartmouth, Aldershot.

Wilkinson, D. (1997) 'Towards sustainability in the EU? Steps within the European Commission towards integrating the environment into other EU policy sectors', *Environmental Politics*, vol. 6.

Williamson, J. and Bottrill, A. (1971) 'The impact of customs unions on trade in manufactures', *Oxford Economic Papers*, vol. 25, no. 3.

Wils, W. (1999) 'Notification, clearance and exemption in EC competition law: an economic analysis', *European Law Review*, vol. 24.

  (2000), 'The undertaking as subject of EC competition law and the imputation of infringements to natural and legal persons', *European Law Review*, vol. 25.

  (2003), *Optimal Enforcement of EC Competition Laws: A Study in Law and Economics*, Kluwer Law International, The Hague.

Winters, L. A. (1984) 'British imports of manufactures and the Common Market', *Oxford Economic Papers*, vol. 36.

  (1985) 'Separability and the specification of foreign trade functions', *European Economic Review*, vol. 27.

  (2000) 'EU's preferential trade agreements: objectives and outcomes', in P. van Dijck and G. Faber (eds.), *The External Economic Dimension of the European Union*, Kluwer Law International, Dordrecht.

Wise, M. (1984), *The Common Fisheries Policy of the European Community*, Methuen, London.

  (1996) 'Regional concepts in the development of the CFP', in K. Crean and D. Symes (eds.), *Fisheries Management in Crisis*, Blackwell Science, Oxford.

Wolf, M. (1983) 'The European Community's trade policy', in R. Jenkins (ed.), *Britain in the EEC*, Macmillan, Basingstoke.

Wolfram, C. D. (1999) 'Measuring market power in the British electricity spot market', *American Economic Review*, vol. 89, no. 4.

Wonnacott, G. P. and Wonnacott, R. J. (1981) 'Is unilateral tariff reduction preferable to a customs union? The curious case of the missing foreign tariffs', *American Economic Review*, vol. 71.

Wood, A. (1994) *North–South Trade, Employment, and Inequality*, Oxford University Press, Oxford.

  (1995) 'How trade hurt unskilled workers', *Journal of Economic Perspectives*, vol. 9.

Wooders, M., Zissimos, B. and Dhillon, A. (2001) 'Tax competition reconsidered', Warwick Economics Research Paper no. 622, University of Warwick.

World Bank (1992) *Governance and Development*, World Bank, Washington D.C.

  (2003) *Global Economic Prospects of Developing Countries*, World Bank, Washington D.C.

  (2006a) *World Development Indicators Database*, accessed via Economic and Social Data Services International, http://www.esds.ac.uk/international/.

  (2006b) *Global Economic Prospects of Developing Countries*, World Bank, Washington D.C.

  (2006c) *World Development Indicators Database*, http://siteresources.worldbank.org/DATASTATISTICS/Resources/GNIPC.pdf.

World Trade Organization (WTO) (2002) *Trade Policy Review: European Union 2001*, vols. I and II, Geneva.

  (2004) *Trade Policy Review: European Union 2004*, vols. I and II, Geneva.

  (2006) *International Trade Statistics Database*, http://www.wto.org/english/res_e/statis_e/statis_e.htm.

Yarrow, G. (1991) 'Vertical supply arrangements: issues and applications in the energy industries', *Oxford Review of Economic Policy*, vol. 7, no. 2.

Young, H. (1998) *This Blessed Plot: Britain and Europe from Churchill to Blair*, Macmillan, Basingstoke.

Zeitlin, J. (2005) 'The open method of co-ordination in action: theoretical promise, empirical realities, reform strategy', in J. Zeitlin and P. Pochet (eds.) (2005).

Zeitlin, J. and Pochet, P. (2005) *The Open Method of Co-ordination in Action: The European Employment and Social Inclusion Strategies*, Peter Lang, Brussels.

Ziltener, P. (2004) 'The economic effects of the European Single Market project: projections, simulations – and the reality', *Review of International Political Economy*, vol. 11, no. 5.

Zürn, M. and Wolf, D. (1999) 'European law and international regimes: the features of law beyond the nation state', *European Law Journal*, vol. 5.

Author index

Subject index

Page numbers in *italics* indicate tables or figures